A MYSTIC WAY

Nicholas Hagger is a philosopher, cultural historian, poet and former lecturer in Islam and Japan. He presented the tradition of the metaphysical Fire or Light in *The Fire and the Stones,* and its challenge to reductionist science and philosophy in his recent book *The Universe and the Light.*

By the same author

The Fire and the Stones
Selected Poems
The Universe and the Light
A White Radiance
Awakening to the Light

A Mystic Way

A Spiritual Autobiography

NICHOLAS HAGGER

ELEMENT

Shaftesbury, Dorset ● Rockport, Massachusetts
Brisbane, Queensland

© Nicholas Hagger 1994

Published in Great Britain in 1994 by
Element Books Ltd
Longmead, Shaftesbury, Dorset

Published in the USA in 1994 by
Element, Inc.
42 Broadway, Rockport, MA 01966

Published in Australia in 1994 by
Element Books Ltd
for Jacaranda Wiley Ltd
33 Park Road, Milton, Brisbane, 4064

Cover design by Max Fairbrother
Design by Alison Goldsmith
Typeset by Wendy Murdoch
Printed and bound in Great Britain by
Biddles Ltd, Guildford & King's Lynn

British Library Cataloguing in Publication
data available

Library of Congress Cataloging in Publication
data available

ISBN 1-85230-478-2

CONTENTS

"I woke to find myself in a dark wood,
Where the right road was wholly lost and gone."
                    Dante, *Inferno*

"Young man everywhere, profit from the fact that
nobody knows you."
                    Rilke, *Malte Laurids Brigge*

"The friends that have it I do wrong
When ever I remake a song,
Should know what issue is at stake:
It is myself that I remake."
                    W. B. Yeats

"Each hour shortens life."
                    Sundial at St Austell's parish church

"Redeem the time."
                    T. S. Eliot

"Better build schools for boys than build and sell
gibbets for men."
                    Ragged School song, 1840-1850

NOTE

The construction of this Autobiography presents a succession of events in accordance with the view of time and memory stated in p159 and pp776-77, that the present is endlessly added cumulatively to the past so that new layers are endlessly added to previous layers. The theme of the Light and the Mystic Way is thus presented within a philosophical context of a creative process, Being within Becoming.

Later on I have regarded my *Diaries* entries as events, and similarly each new entry modifies or qualifies the layering of the past. *Diaries* entries written at the time retain the freshness and accuracy of an event on the day it happened, and to some extent avoid imposing a present construct on past experience. Using my *Diaries* entries as a source catches the cumulative process of my thinking as each thought emerges from my life, and the cumulative effect of the Light on me as I progress up the Mystic Way to the summit where all paths meet.

PART ONE

THE PURGATIVE WAY

EARLY INFLUENCES: CHILDHOOD AND SCHOOLDAYS
1939 – 1954

As I gaze on the green fields I lay in as a child and see them in my mind's eye filled with golden buttercups, and walk to the house by St. Michael's Mount where I ran as a child and which I return to some school holidays, I am filled with a sense of a pattern. My beginning is very much present in my life now, and there seems an inevitability about my progress from an ordinary boy to the man I am. Listening to the drone of bees in the summer forsythia in my childhood garden which is full of the echoes of little people I knew, I have a sense that we are bees of the invisible, to use Rilke's words. I set out from my hive in the morning and found a Way I always instinctively knew was there. The Way has led me through Nature and the central idea of civilisations to an understanding of the universe. Mine was a seeking generation, and I sought the meaning of life. Gazing at a frog in my lily pond, aware of the mud and the glorious flower in the sun, I feel the pattern also has a mysterious meaning.

My parents were musical; my mother, Norah Broadley, was a violinist who gave recitals in East Grinstead and London between 1932 and 1938 ("East Grinstead violinist's triumph" is one headline), and my father, Cyril Hagger, was a member of the Royal Choral Society and sang as a tenor for the Fleet Street Choir. On one occasion he sang the Messiah at the Royal Albert Hall. They met on a train at Paddington station, which I was to visit so many times. My mother came from an affluent family that had left Yorkshire and settled in Sussex. It was an East Grinstead Methodist family, the Broadleys, who lived at Lonsdale House, Lingfield Road and, after 1925, at Daledene in Lewes Road. In 1910, her father owned one of the first two cars in East Grinstead. My father came from a poorer Church of England family in New Barnet. He had polio when he was 14, and for the rest of his relatively short life he had a game leg and walked with a limp. He worked in local government. He started his career in 1925 with East Barnet Urban District Council and in 1931 was appointed accountancy assistant to Mitcham Borough Council. In the 1930s he went to church in Streatham. My parents married at East Grinstead in August 1937, and the local paper reported: "There was a pretty wedding at the Methodist Church, East Grinstead, on Saturday....The ceremony created considerable interest for the bride and her family are widely known and highly esteemed in the district."

On my mother's Broadley side, the family really went back to the Rev. Benjamin Broadley, my great-grandfather, who was a typical 19th century itinerant Methodist Minister and who was a naval chaplain in India and Malta and served in different parts of the UK. He was a champion of Lord's

Day Observance. From him I inherited a restless desire to see different parts of the world and to quest for truth. He was father to two boys, John and George, who together set up a tailor's business in Bromley in the 1890s, and certainly before 1897, when George stood on Victoria station, liked the sound of the name East Grinstead, and on an intuitive hunch, without knowing anything about the place, took the train out there and founded the East Grinstead branch of the business. From him I inherited a good business sense. George had two sons and three daughters, one of whom was my mother.

George's wife was a Harding, and that side of the family included a Mr Harding who wrote on weather for the *Times* – from him came my instinctive connection with the *Times* – and who lived in Tulse Hill and then at 65 Holmewood Gardens, near Christchurch Road, Streatham, where my grandmother lived until George allowed his in-laws to live in a spare house he had, 2 Bakewell Road, Eastbourne. The Harding side of the family also included my great-great-grandmother Mrs. Burton who owned a school in Croydon. She had her 100th birthday party in 1912 and my mother was the youngest guest and was therefore given a Queen Anne table which had been split prior to that occasion when "Uncle Frank" played leapfrog over it and fell on the middle.

My father's side of the family is less well defined, but goes back to the 17th century, when there were graveyards of Haggers, Lords of the Manor on the Essex-Hertfordshire-Cambridge border. (The Hagars were Lords of the Manor in Bourn, Cambridgeshire in the 17th and 18th centuries, and there are Haggers in Great Chesterfield churchyard.) There were Quaker Haggers, and I once found a Quaker burial-ground of Haggers in that region. The name Hagger is either Old Norse (in which "hagr" meant "fit or ready") or Old English (in which "haeg-gar" meant a "hedge-warrior"), and in Middle English the name was related to "hacgard" and the Yorkshire "hagar" or "wild, untamed man". I cannot claim to have the characteristics of an exceptionally fit, wild and untamed hedge-warrior, but my father's father had worked in Canada sawing trees, and from my father's side I inherited the Old Viking sense of adventuring ("plundering") abroad, the Quaker Inner Light, an instinctive relationship to trees and my father's singing, a down-to-earth, practical sense and an instinctive Nonconformism. I know little about my father's mother's family.

Put the Broadleys, Hardings and Haggers together, and you get a picture of Nonconformism, foreign travel, business, writing, schools, love of forests and music – all of which have come out in me at different times and in different forms. (The music has come out in me as poetry.) These are my roots; my trunk and branches are my own.

I was born in London in 1939, just before the Second World War when the British Empire was still at its height and intact. I was born in the London Hospital, where my mother's sister (Margaret Broadley) had been a nurse since 1923 and later became Assistant Matron. A London Hospital receipt has survived recording that my father paid £5.10s towards the cost of maintaining my mother in hospital for a week in May 1939. I was two weeks late and had a mop of hair. The Princess Royal visited the London Hospital when I was three days old and I was presented and apparently gripped the Royal finger and was paid a flattering Royal compliment. A nursing friend of my aunt's, Kathleen Husband, gave me a duck when I was three months old, and her daughter was most put out that I did not say "Thank you" for it.

A friend of my grandmother's was the artist Gwen Broad, whose paintings of her native Cornwall and etchings of her farm, Hill Place (which dates from 1296) still adorn my home. (She came from near St. Austell, and her husband Nanscawen drove her into town three times and was then asked his intentions. On their marriage Gwen's mother sold the St. Austell house and bought Hill Place in East Grinstead.) On 2nd July 1939 she wrote to me the following prophetic letter which now hangs on the wall outside my study: "To Dear Little Nicholas, With every good wish for a life filled with love and usefulness. Your Dawn has commenced in sunshine, may the eventide have just sufficient clouds to make a glorious sunset! With love from Your Mother and Father's friend, Gwen M. Broad."

The Second World War soon broke out. Looking at black and white films of the Nuremberg rallies of Hitler strutting like a puppet before thousands of helmets, and of Chamberlain who all but outwitted him (according to Goebbels' diaries), I am amazed that I came into that world that has passed away, taking with it the trilby hats and cloth caps worn by the crowds in London streets. I incarnated at a very perilous time.

My mother should have been extremely well off. Her father's tailors and outfitters business in East Grinstead, Hayward's Heath and Hove (after temporary shops in Horsham and Eastbourne) was supposed to look after her mother and her two brothers and two sisters. (Other branches in Folkestone and Bromley were run by his brother's family.) Unfortunately the business was cornered by one of the brothers, George, and his wife. The other brother, Tom, had died in 1918 – he had overstated his age to join the RFC and was pilot of a Bristol Fighter that went down over enemy lines in France on 15th September, shortly before the Armistice - and my mother's father had died in November 1926. He had cancer and was given a lead cure, and the lead poison killed him. My mother's widowed mother inherited the family business. Her husband's will left everything to her on condition that George had the Hove business and his three daughters were provided for from the East Grinstead business, but she was persuaded to part with most of it to George and his wife Lucy. According to Perkins Copeland's Profit and Loss accounts for East Grinstead (not Hayward's Heath and Hove, which my grandmother had no share in) for the year ending 20th February 1949 (which are somehow now in my possession), my grandmother retained a quarter share of East Grinstead, George had a half share, and Lucy had a quarter share. George paid for his three quarters over 21 years (between 1931 and 1952) at £250 per year capital and 7% interest. (In 1949 my grandmother made a net profit of just over £623 on her quarter share and received just over £55 in interest on capital, against a net profit of £1,870 made by George and Lucy, who also had Hayward's Heath and Hove in their entirety. For this they paid £5,250 over 21 years.) Soon after the outbreak of the Second World War my grandmother was persuaded to translate what she had saved from the accrued annual earnings of her quarter share (all that remained for her daughters) into $3^1/2\%$ War Loan. (In July 1940 she bought £725 $3^1/2\%$ War Loan at $96^3/16$ for £698 1s 9d.) Unfortunately, War Loan eventually slumped and my grandmother lost most of it. George and Lucy blamed my grandmother's unwise investment, whereas my mother and her two sisters privately considered it sharp practice to wrest control of what was intended for all of them.

My parents lived at a house they bought, 20 Fairview Road, Norbury to be near my father's work at Mitcham Town Hall. In those early days they dabbled in property. It will help an understanding of the financial background of our family in the 1940s if I am precise about their properties. My mother had four: Pentire, Blackwell Road, East Grinstead, which she bought in 1936 and sold in 1941; 15 and 17 Moat Road, East Grinstead, which she had from 1937 to 1948; and eventually 2 Bakewell Road, Eastbourne, the house where her mother's parents, the Hardings, lived, which was not sold until 1968. My father also had four properties: 52 and 54 Westfield Road, Cheam, which he bought in 1938; Goscar, 284 Croydon Road, Caterham, Surrey, which he bought in November 1939 and sold in 1944; and 53 Queensborough Terrace, W2, which he acquired at some point and sold in 1949.

After a spell from May to September 1939 at 20 Fairview Road, Norbury, which my father subsequently let for most of 1941 and 1942, and another spell from December 1939 to May 1940 at Goscar, 284 Croydon Road, Caterham; Caterham was bombed on a Sunday in May 1940 while we were living there and as it was obvious that London was going to be bombed I was evacuated: my mother took me to live with my grandmother in the safety of East Grinstead, where we had lived briefly from September to December 1939. (During this time my father lived in digs at 32 Tooting Bec Gardens, Streatham.) My grandmother had left Daledene in 1935 for St. Anton in Maypole Road. The house was named after a holiday in St. Anton, Austria in 1934, and it has since been pulled down to make way for a post office. There are photographs of me sitting on the lawn at 11 months and standing with a tennis ball in one hand. I remember that magical house well. There were toy soldiers (Canadian Mounties and Scottish bagpipers) and coloured matches on the mantelpiece in the front room, and a clock that chimed each quarter and struck each hour. There was a gong that boomed for meal times, and a maid with a cap, Lily, brought me my food. My grandmother was generally called "Ga-ga" after my babyish attempt to say "Grannie". The garden had a crazy paving path with trees on either side that made a covered arbour walk. There was an old scooter with yellow stripes which when I was older I tried to ride down one of the paths to Percy, the gardener who worked in a mysterious shed. It was filled with magical things including a round wheel which spun round, faster and faster. I can still hear the rhythmic pulse of Percy's knifegrinder.

In 1941 my mother took me away from this Paradise to Beecholme in Cranston Road, a nearby semi with one front room. An envelope "On His Majesty's Service" addressed to my father and postmarked February 1942 has survived, and my brother Robert was born prematurely in March 1942. I can recall standing at the gate and looking at the cellar window just above the earth, and wondered because my mother told me there were frogs in the cellar. I can recall standing in the front room window seeing my father go to work to the left, above a hedge, and raise his stick. On the back lawn there was a pine tree of enormous height. Finding it again many years later I was disappointed to note that it was little taller than me. Sometimes my aunt Argie (so called after my babyish attempt to say "Margaret") took me for a walk down the Lewes Road towards Ashhurst Wood to a wood off Imberhorn Lane that was full of primroses. It was off on the right, and as there was a public right of way the gate had "Shut This Gate" written on it, and my aunt called it "Shut This Gate Wood", and I ran knee deep into the primroses and was blissfully happy.

In and around East Grinstead the war made little impact, but in November 1942 my father began a new job in Essex, as chief accountant in the treasurer's department of the Chigwell Urban District Council. My father lived in digs to be near his work from November 1942 to March 1943, when we all moved to a rented semi-detached, 52 Brooklyn Avenue, Loughton in Essex, and I soon became aware of our vulnerability. My first memory there is of sitting in my high chair looking at a large map of Europe on the wall. It was filled with pins with different coloured heads which marked the fronts of battles whose progress my father followed on the "wireless". The wireless stood on the nearby bureau (or desk with a flap). I can remember playing ships by sitting in my high chair and rocking it, and my giantess of a mother leaving the sink and coming from the kitchen with a round bowl with rabbits round the edge. Very often a flypaper hung from the ceiling. I can remember sitting in my pram outside the Post Office in the High Road. In East Grinstead I smiled at everybody, but now I knew nobody, and according to my mother I once asked, walking out of the gate with my brother Robert in his pram, "Could we meet someone to smile at?" Some time after, I sat on the stairs – to this day I can see a particular tread – and once there was a tremendous crash and the windows blew in and I was excited. We were in the corridor of German bombers.

Air raids were frightening. My father would come and sit by my bed and tell me an on-going story about "Peter and his dog". I loved these stories, and was always pleased when there was an air raid because I could hear the next instalment of the story. My mother's idea of a bedtime story was different. She wrote *The Rainbow Children* in which my brother and I were the main characters, and climbed up a rainbow and spoke to Thor on his thundercloud. My feeling for Old Norse saga began at this time. Otherwise we had Beatrix Potter read to us. My favourites were *Peter Rabbit* and *Jeremy Fisher* – I loved the reference to the butterfly sandwich and the trout's dive.

In May 1943 my parents sent me to school at Essex House at 258 High Road under the Misses Huntleys, who were missionaries. I remember little of my time with them in the Methodist church hall.

One late evening in March 1944 my father said he would take me for a walk to the Post Office. We shut the front door and went down the path to the front gate when the police station siren went and there was a white flash and for a long instant everything was lit up as bright as day. Then there was a rattle, a clatter and a crash as the glass fell out of the windows. My father turned back from the gate and without saying anything hurriedly limped back to the front door, and I jumped excitedly and said "A bomb, a bomb." And indeed, a string of German stick bombs had fallen in the Forest and around Loughton. Six stick bombs fell on the cricket field less than 200 yards away.

At the end of the spring term 1944 when in reading I was "beginning to recognise and match words" according to my report, I was taken away and in April 1944 began across the road in Oaklands School, which was at 363 High Road on the corner of Trap's Hill in a Regency house that has since been pulled down (and which was across the road from the cricket field). Oaklands had been opened by Miss Lord in 1937. She later told me that she opened the school with one pupil who was made to troop in and out of the school all day to give the impression that there were many pupils.

Miss Lord had been trained at the Froebel Institute, along with her colleagues Miss Reid and Miss Root, and she had then taught at Oaklands School, Blackheath for 15 years, before coming out to Loughton. She had stayed at Miss Butler's at 86 Spring Grove, a friend of her aunt's who later provided the funding for her to start her own Oaklands School. Froebel's ideas permeated the new school: closeness to Nature, discovery through observation, and approaching the spiritual unity of the universe. The Oaklands uniform was fittingly green with a badge of an oak tree, as it still is.

I remember the green gate and standing upstairs in assembly near the Nature table, which had an aquarium and tadpoles, and singing "We plough the fields and scatter" very loudly. All around me sang lustily and with great enthusiasm. We also sang the school hymn, which included the lines: "After the sun the rain,/After the rain the sun,/This is the way of life/Till the work be done." At the back there was a garden with a lawn and a high Georgian brick wall, and at break the teachers sat and drank tea on the small veranda adjoining the house while we played on the lawn. When the police station siren sounded an air raid warning, we were put in the Morrison shelter in the back garden, a rusty iron contraption like a zoo cage. One of the teachers put a rug on the grass, and we lay on our fronts with a book and peered through the mesh at the sky, looking for planes and puffs of smoke and parachutes floating down. I remember a boy called Robin Fowler lying next to be and showing me a brown Japanese bank note with a herd of cattle on the back. I swapped it for a sweet and still have it. I can remember walking home to Brooklyn Avenue in the company of Robin Fowler and his mother. On one occasion my shoelace came undone, and Mrs. Fowler did it up for me as I was unable to tie my own laces.

One night in Brooklyn Avenue I could not sleep. There was a kind of knocking under my bed. It was probably the iron springs in the bed, but the knocking was terrifying and I dared not move. I lay awake for most of the night. The next day at school I confided in a friend who said "I was under your bed all last night, I was doing the knocking," and I believed him.

In June 1944 the first V-1s (doodlebugs) landed in our part of Britain, and the more terrible V-2 rockets were first used in September 1944. At school we sang at break: "Music while you work,/Hitler is a twerp,/Like his army/He's all gone barmy,/Music while you work."

CHILDHOOD AND SCHOOLDAYS

In August 1944 we went to Ilfracombe for a holiday, to escape the V-1s. The South Coast was prohibited (because of D-Day and its aftermath), and the beach toll was 1d per person. The weather was rotten, and the wind blew coffee as it left the thermos. I can see the grey beach and the sea in a rocky bay and my father in a striped one-piece bathing costume that went over his shoulders and nearly came down to his knees lying in the water where the sea gently washed onto the shore.

I believe it was in our bedroom at Ilfracombe, which I can see clearly, curtains and cot and all, that I read *The Naughty Ninepins* on my own, one of my favourite childhood books. It was about little Tony who was given two wooden dollies, Bluebell and Buttercup, who came alive when no one was looking and caused havoc, for which the cat was unjustly blamed. Tea-time was referred to as "pleasant tea-time". I still have the book, and it has been a favourite of all my children.

In September 1944 Oaklands School moved from Trap's Hill to its present site in Albion Hill. I moved with the school and remember the sea of buttercups in the main field, where the oak tree badge found its counterpart in a huge oak that was reputed to be 800 years old. We sat underneath the tree and smoked acorn pipes and I remember the crunch of brown acorns underfoot, and the horse in the second field. I lay in the buttercups and one of the girls said "Do you like butter?" and held a buttercup under my chin. "If there's a reflection, you do," she said. "Yes, you do." In the idyllic bushes round that ever-green field there were nooks and crannies, and each one was a camp. Different boys set up army headquarters there and one was a concentration camp. I was captured one day and guarded all break, a broken branch blocking my escape, the sentries mercilessly forbidding me to rejoin my friends and play. Occasionally we cut ourselves, and took our bleeding fingers to the study where they would be coated in yellow-brown iodine, which stung appallingly. There was a thunderstorm one day, and I remember some of the children my age chanting as their coats were put on, "It's raining, it's pouring, the old man's snoring."

That autumn we used to sit and have tea on the lawn at the back of the house in Brooklyn Avenue. There were greengages in the garden, with those strange, green lantern-like fruits. In some black and white photos my father is lying beside me on the grass on a rug. At the end of the garden there was a stream and in the next garden Freddy Durrant used to mow his lawn. He was the local shoe shop owner (Durrants, opposite Lopping Hall) and my brother Robert used to go and peer through the fence and call "Dumma, dumma Bobby 'lower" (i.e. "Durrant, Durrant, pick Bobby a flower"). It must have been that autumn that a neighbour and Methodist church worthy Mrs. Lash (whom I called "Mrs. Eyelash") came to early supper, and I crawled under the table and tied her shoelaces together, to the great amusement of my brother Robert and to the outraged indignation of my parents, who did not realise what had happened until she stood up at the end of the meal and collapsed back on her chair. Sometimes Robert and I played cricket on the sloping concrete that led from the gate to the garage, by the side door. I used to order Robert to play, and once when he rebelled and I raised my voice, a policeman passed and I said "My brother won't

9

play with me" and he went and found Robert and made him bat.

In the winter of 1944 my father's parents came to stay. It was a foggy time, and my grandfather went for a walk. He had white hair and a white moustache and looked like Lloyd George; he had lost a finger in a Canadian sawmill, and he did not return. I was sent to look for him, and I found him in the fog. He had fallen over under a lamp-post further down Brooklyn Avenue towards the High Road and had cut his head, and I led him home and helped my mother to bandage him. Later we took him back to his flat in Station Road, New Barnet. It had a black fire-escape at the back, and I remember an old-fashioned room with old-fashioned Victorian-Edwardian furniture.

It was about this time that I was invited to tea at some of the large local houses, at the house of Justin Lindy, son of the architect, off Golding's Hill and at Ripley Grange, the house of Pelham Clark (whose ex-wife I now employ).

In April 1945 I had twin sisters, who died at the age of five and six weeks. My father had me into his study to break the news and asked if I would help him tell my brother, and I felt important as I helped explain Katharine and Mary had died.

In the early summer of 1945 Churchill toured his constituency. He began at Woodford and came to Loughton and spoke from King's Green in front of the war memorial with Mrs. Churchill at his side. The Prime Minister congratulated his constituents on surviving rockets and flying bombs, and said that if he was called away during the Election (a reference to Potsdam) Mrs. Churchill would take his place. I was taken by Mr and Mrs. Allwood, the Methodist Minister and his wife, and pictures survive which show the edge of my head very close to Churchill.

I do not remember the end of the War. I can remember bulletins on the radio, and I suppose I heard about the end of hostilities from one of those. I did not attend the Victory celebrations in London, and there was no television to see them.

After the end of the war, in July 1945, we moved for a fifth time to the WVS (Women's Voluntary Service) and ARP (Air Raid Protection) house nearby, Journey's End, which was one of the two original 1870 houses in Station Road. We rented it from the Maitlands, the owners of Loughton Hall and donors of Lopping Hall, which the family gave to the people of Loughton following an infringement of their lopping rights. I carried a model of a grey battleship round to the new home, which had cut telephone wires sticking out of the skirting in every room, and bare floorboards. Somehow I had had my sixth birthday party in the garden of the new house at the end of May. (I believe it was known that we would be renting, and we were able to use the garden.) It was a hot, sunny day, and there was a long table covered with a white tablecloth on the lawn near redcurrant bushes, and I had over 20 guests. Robin Fowler gave me a book on birds. I said "I've got this already", and my mother said "No you haven't." "I have, Aunt Flo gave it to me," I persisted with the compulsive truthfulness and honesty of a child. Someone had spilt damsons on the white tablecloth and my mother was rubbing salt on the stain. (I can see the scene so clearly I can almost reach out and help rub salt on the stain.) She stopped. "No you haven't" she said, kneeing me into submissive silence, and I thought how unfairly untruthful the adult world was. To this day I have two copies of *More About British Wild Birds by* Eric Pochin, one inscribed by my Aunt Flo.

That summer I drew six-spot burnets, kingfishers, a dragonfly, several newts and a frog.

We settled into Journey's End very quickly. Journey's End *was* a green gabled house and I shared the large bedroom at the back with my brother. We slept in single beds, and there was a gas fire. I can remember being ill about this time. The gas fire glowed and my mother brought me arrowroot, a creamy concoction in a bowl, and I spooned into my mouth sitting awkwardly up in bed. Between the beds there was a black wooden cupboard with a door with a loose metallic catch, and I used to click it open and shut after lights out. Our bedroom door was always left open so that the landing light fell across the entrance to our room, and my brother and I would talk until my parents called "That's enough" or "Good night". Often while I waited to go to sleep there would be a musical event from the dining room. My father would play the piano and sing in his quavering tenor voice, "And fairies are flying", or (from Elgar's *Dream of Gerontius*) "And Gently I Dip Thee Into The Lake". Sometimes my mother practised the violin, and I often heard Vivaldi's or Mendelssohn's violin concerto drifting beautifully and richly up the stairs. Occasionally there was a musical evening and we would hear the voices of guests downstairs in the hall.

Christmas was a magical time. Holly with red berries appeared above the mirror over the nursery fireplace, mistletoe hung from the lampshade in the centre of the room, and paper chains made of linked ovals of paper ran diagonally from corner to corner of the nursery, meeting in the middle. On Christmas Day my brother Robert and I found presents stacked round two farmhouse chairs (chairs with spindles in their back) in the nursery. They were wrapped in paper with holly and red berries and glitter like snow. To our great wonder a cardboard prop-up of a 1920s Father Christmas holding a small Christmas tree appeared on the breakfast table each Christmas, and the Christmas cake had half a dozen small china Edwardian bandsmen on it, one beating a drum.

In the evenings my father would sometimes stand on the red and black tiles of the Journey's End kitchen floor and fill my hot-water bottle, while my boyish eyes watched wonderingly at his indifference to a possible splash-back that might scald his skin on the back of his hairy hand or fingers.

We walked or took the red double-decker bus to school in the morning after a cooked breakfast of fried bread and bacon or eggs in the nursery. We passed the Council Offices where my father worked. I could see the front door from my bedroom window. The bus stopped at the Crown, where there was a shelter. Sometimes as we waited we would swing on the bar at the back of the shelter, and when we were older we turned somersaults over it. We got off the bus at Albion Hill, crossed the road and ran up the hill to school.

A MYSTIC WAY

In those days Oaklands was covered in ivy, at least at the back. There were two large acacia trees near the front door. We took off our green caps, green blazers and satchels and hung them on one of the pegs by the window nearest the gate. I can remember Mabel Reid, the co-owner and a teacher supervising us. At break we ran in the main field or climbed and swung in the jungle gym, a wooden structure which stood below the study window. It was considered extremely big to reach the top. I can still see Ann Fisher (later Mrs. Holland, a member of the Oaklands staff for many years) running in the vicinity of the grass tennis court near the jungle gym, a shock of fair hair.

Being musical, my parents wanted me to be musical, and I was given piano lessons, much to my chagrin at break. This meant that I could not play with my little friends. While they were hunting for conkers and crouching over worms or any flying thing that had lost a wing and were discovering the joys of the hedgerow, I was sitting with Kathleen Goldie (who was soon to die of TB) learning "All Cows Eat Grass" and "Every Good Boy Deserves Fun". I can see her finger pointing at the music in the gloom of what is now Oaklands computer room while outside were sounds of play. I hated it, and my musical progress (or rather, lack of progress) was a great disappointment to my parents.

However, I had some facility with words – I loved reading and was taught to write in a Marion Richardson hand – and a very strong sense of rhythm, and I have no doubt that my parents' musical abilities came out in me as poetry. My life long interest in poetry was stimulated by poems about Nature and long chunks of Longfellow's *Hiawatha*, whose rhythms I loved. I knew very early on that Tennyson had lived at High Beach and written "Ring out wild bells" about Waltham Abbey, and that the poet Clare had lived at Lippitts Hill Lodge near the Owl. We copied out Christina Rossetti's "Who has seen the wind?", Kenneth Grahame's "All along the backwater" and Blake's "The sun does arise" and "Little lamb who made thee?" (for both of which I got a star). In the course of the summer term 1946 I was writing faultless sentences in ink. At this time we were encouraged to observe Nature. We were taken for regular Nature walks to look for jays and magpies, and between January and October 1946 I kept a very full bird diary, drawing each bird and recording where I had seen it, on our rubbish dump or our garden fence. We did a lot of drawing which also sharpened my observation. We drew scenes from Hiawatha with tents and Red Indian feathers, and the British might at the end of the war provided another source of art. Much of my art work that has survived includes drawings of planes and ships. I drew trains with "LNER" on the side of the engine, and Elizabeth Clay, who was in my class, always said afterwards that she knew I was clever because I knew what LNER stood for and she did not. In my drawings the Union flag and the Nazi swastika were given much prominence, along with reports on the doings of the House of Windsor. I did a project, "Countries of Europe".

I walked home for lunch as did my father. Sometimes I put a penny (1d) in the red pillar box slot machine opposite Albion Hill and stuck the red stamp that came out on the side of my cheek, a brief a craze in 1945/6. I arrived home before my father, and sometimes I would go down to the

CHILDHOOD AND SCHOOLDAYS

Charringtons office at the end of Station Road and wait for him to come hopping and limping alongside his stick at 1 o'clock, sometimes with a pipe in the corner of his mouth, and always smiling under his balding head. I ran alongside him, telling him my news, and then we would all sit at the Nursery table and have lunch, which my mother brought up the steps from the kitchen. The kitchen had an original red and black tile floor that went back to around 1870.

After lunch we went back to school, and it would sometimes be Games. Mabel Reid took rounders. She wore an eyeshield and bowled underarm on the main field, near the oak tree of the school badge. Once, wearing short trousers and probably aged 6, I took the red double-decker bus (no. 20) and stood on the platform with my football boots round my neck, and rang the bell once as the bus sped towards the Request stop by the Crescent. The driver ignore the ring and sped on, and I panicked and jumped and hit the ground and slithered in the direction of the bus, and the football boots clattered on the High Road, and I lay crying with badly grazed knees and elbows opposite Albion Hill, down which a lady came to my assistance. I can see her advancing now; her hair was done up in a grey bun and I can see exactly what she was wearing. "The bus didn't stop," I blubbed. It was feared I had fractured my skull, but I had not. (A week later Christopher Imms, a boy who lived two doors down from us in Station Road, jumped off the bus at the same spot and in similar circumstances, and fractured *his* skull.)

In the evenings we had supper at the nursery table, all taking part in the conversation, and my father often had bread, dripping and cheese. In the winter we all sat round the coal fire, holding out our hands to the glowing coals and feeling the warmth on our cheeks. Then we would take it in turns to go to the bathroom, where there was a pink tin of Chemico for cleaning the enamel basin and bath.

At the end of the year some pupils who had been awarded a lot of stars were given a Gold Star Prize. This was given in assembly and was generally a book on Nature, such as *The Seashore I Know*. Such was the importance attached to such an honour that the first time I was awarded a Gold Star Prize I ran down Station Road and my mother heard me shouting "I've got a Gold Star Prize".

That summer, I believe it was, I danced at St. Mary's church fête. Oaklands danced on the Vicarage lawn, an event which happened every year from around 1946 until 1991.

On Sundays my mother made us put on our Sunday clothes and we all walked to the Methodist church, a 1905 Gothic building. We sat in the long wooden pews which had long carpet-like seating and a tray and holder at the end for any wet umbrellas. There was children's church, and the children sat at the front and filed out to the hall. I spent many hours sitting in a pew and looking at the round clock with Roman figures. Time seemed to pass incredibly slowly in church, no matter whether the Minister spoke or the choir sang or we had an interminable prayer.

Once children's church put on a short play in the hall. It was based on the song "Soldier, Soldier Will You Marry Me/With Your Musket, Fife and Drum", and revelling in the magic of the words and the music, I played the soldier. I was dressed up and stood on the stage before a packed audience under a flimsy wire which had curtains at either end. There was a chest, and the girl kept opening it and removing a garment, which I had to put on. I remember I wandered off before I had finished my part, and I was firmly pushed back on stage. I did not want to continue, I did not like the audience beneath me in the darkened hall. Another time I sang "Fairest isle, all isles excelling" (i.e. Britain) "cradled mid the glassy sea" for a children's church Eistedffod. I also sang Shakespeare's beautiful lyric "When daisies pied, and violets blue".

Home, schooland the Methodist church – these were the three influences that shaped me in those early post-war years. And there were the annual holidays. In August 1945 we went to Bognor. We stayed with a Mrs. Bolt at 26 Glamis Street. One sunny morning I went out with my father to buy a paper. Outside the newsagents I saw on a hoarding news that America had dropped an A-bomb on Hiroshima, and had a profound sense from my father's reaction that the world had changed and nothing would be the same.

There is one influence I have not mentioned: Epping Forest, which surrounds Loughton. It was never far away. Loughton was in a three-sided crater, and from Buckhurst Hill at one end to the cricketfield at the foot of Church Hill at the other end, there was deep forest on the eastern side. From the upstairs of Oaklands School or the wooden seat at the top of the sloping cricket ground, Loughton seemed to be a clearing in the Forest as it was in the 19th century. To the west there were fields and the valley of the River Roding where there were kingfishers. Many times we walked up Station Road, crossed over into Forest Road and saw the Forest at the end, humped and brooding, dark and sulky in winter and gloriously green and cheerful in the summer.

My aunt Argie still describes the "lure of the Forest" for us. She would take us for walks when she visited us from the London Hospital, and would cross us over the High Road into Forest Road, and then we were compelled to run as if attracted, drawn, pulled by a force like the sea, as if in the grip of something elemental which controlled our blood.

My brother and I used to walk to the Stubbles in Nursery Road. This was an open clearing of heath land surrounded by scrub and Forest. Here we could kick a ball, but as there were many wild flowers and brambles butterflies were plentiful and I spent hours with my net, catching azure blues and peacocks and small tortoiseshells and Red Admirals, studying them in the captivity of my jar. Then we watched the dragonflies skim and hover round the pond. There was gorse, and there were many berries, and there was a stream we used to follow, jumping over it and jumping back. Sometimes we fished in the stream at the top of Forest Road, catching sticklebacks and minnows with home-made nets made from a cane, a round piece of wire and sewn-together flour bags. Again, we compared what we had in our jars. One Good Friday we strayed into the soft clay bog on the other side of Forest Road and came home with our sandals caked with clay.

The school took whole classes into the Forest. Sometimes Mabel Reid would take us to Strawberry Hill where there are two ponds. We fished in the inner of the two ponds, opposite a fallen beech, and found dragonfly larvae and caddis, newts and tadpoles, and brought them back for the school Nature table. We drew Canadian pond weed and water violets, and all the seeds of the Forest flowers and trees, and fungi, observing every detail with minute precision. On these Nature walks we listened to bird songs and learned to identify the willow warbler and wren, and sometimes heard the nightingale. Sometimes we walked to the bottom of the school grounds and round to the old Pollards estate house which has since been demolished. There was a Roman-style mosaic and many daffodils in spring. On the way back we would cross Warren Hill to the woods and Mabel Reid would stop us, "Shh, an owl," and we would all listen intently for what was being presented as a dramatic and significant event. Knowing my interest in Nature, my parents bought at auction a specimen cabinet of butterflies and moths and two old glass cases of birds' eggs.

Further afield there were traces of history in the Forest. There were Mesolithic pillow mounds at High Beach, and the low walls of Ambresbury Banks in Epping where Boadicea defeated Suetonius Paulinus's London garrison of Romans between 59 and 61AD according to one view. There was also the Iron Age fort, also by tradition associated with Boadicea, at Loughton camp, across the road and down a path from Strawberry Hill. Mabel Reid took us. We took the path down into a dip and up again, scuffling leaves, and cut into the Forest and arrived at earthen walls in a beech wood. There was a hollow tree, which had been struck by lightning, that we climbed in. At one point the camp sloped away and you could imagine the Romans storming up the slope. We re-enacted such battles with sticks and often lay dead in the thick yellow-brown brittle beech leaves of the previous autumn, which formed a carpet on the Forest floor. I believe it was contact with Loughton camp that first stirred my sense of history and life-long interest in the Romans. In History we drew an ancient English camp and village, a Roman house and amphitheatre, Caesar and a Roman soldier, Hadrian's Wall and Augustine "the preacher from Rome".

The Forest shaped my early consciousness. It was never far away. The Journey's End garden was full of spiders and stag beetles, and hedgehogs sometimes ran across the lawn. There was an apple tree and two pear trees, one in the middle of the lawn, and in the summer there were always windfalls and these attracted wasps. I helped store the apples and pears in one of the three cellars. There was a fence of trailing honeysuckle which was full of bees. There were roses and Michaelmas daisies and lime-trees at the front. I found a lime hawk moth on one of the leaves. I helped in the garden, picked the gooseberries and redcurrants, the peas and runner beans. I dug the beds, careful not to spear any earthworms or to tread on snails which lived on the pail. There was ivy up the fence by the clothes post. We had a bird table. I put out the bacon rind and sat in the window with my bird diary and Observer's book of birds, noting the birds that came. I soon had all the Observer's books, and when I got a Gold Star prize at school it was always a Nature book I received: *The Countryside I Know, The Hedgerow I Know, Birds' Eggs*. At school there were oaks in the two fields, and there were always sticks on the grass and hawthorn blossom (or may) and then berries. There were foxes' lairs and badgers' sets and rabbit holes. There were squirrels. I quickly became a woodlander, alert to the changing colour of leaves, knowing the different kinds of tree and their fruit, knowing about wild flowers and of course Forest ponds, knowing the haunts and habitats of birds, butterflies, moths and flowers.

When my father talked about people he knew at the table, the very names suggested Nature and the Forest: there were Gale and Willingale (two of my father's colleagues), and Digweed (the undertaker). My father would talk to my mother at lunch time in a code of initials, to shield the confidential events of the morning from us boys. "W," he would say. "Willingale," I would say.

I grew with the seasons, I lived in the rhythm of the days and the months. There were glorious summer mornings when the sky over the Council Offices was a brilliant blue, there were still evenings of almost unbearable beauty when the family sat out in deck chairs, watching the gnats dance and listening to the black birds' piping and chatting while we played on rugs. In the winter there was snow on the back fence and the birds pecked at every crumb on the bird table. When I went to sleep the shadows of the branches of the pear tree on the lawn were projected onto my bedroom wall by a streetlight, and when the wind blew the shadows moved. As a result I have always needed to live near trees.

Loughton itself was a shaping force. Epping Forest is in the Clay Country. Originally the Loughton population lived off the Forest and the land as woodsmen, pollarders, gravel men (who took gravel from the pits that are now the Forest ponds) grooms, nursery growers, farmers and a few professional families. The railway brought commuters into the area and a dormer town of prefabs went up in Debden in the post-war years to re-house the bombed out from the East End, but despite an influx into the area, the village remained traditional. It stretched between the cricketfield at one end, and the Oaklands fields at the other end, and there was a row of alternate pink cherry and white almond trees opposite Gould's clock. There were four churches along the High Road (C of E, Methodist, Baptist, Catholic) and four pubs but Loughton in those days was very much a village in which everyone knew everyone. For at least ten years after the war the same well-known figures said "Good morning" to you in the High Road: J. W. Faulkner, the Town Clerk, my father's boss; Mark Liell in his bowler hat, the solicitor and JP; and William (later Sir William) Addison, the author of books on Epping Forest who kept the bookshop opposite the Royal Standard, where I bought my Observer's books with birthday and Christmas book tokens. Addison always had time for me and gave me his full attention, although he must have had his current book on his mind, and he widened my reading, urging me to buy Observer's books I would not otherwise have bought. I was sent shopping for my mother in the holidays. I got potatoes from the open-air White Shop, opposite St. Mary's. It was kept by Gladys, who looked like a witch. She wore a faintly Dutch pointed head-dress and her grimy face always had a cheerful smile. She wore mittens that left her fingers free to pick up her vegetables and weigh them on her brass-coloured scales before shooting them into the wicker basket I carried.

CHILDHOOD AND SCHOOLDAYS

Food was of course rationed, and I remember walking with my mother to the Food Office at the High Road end of High Beach Road and queuing with my ration book and having my coupons cut. Sometimes we went shopping, to Williams the grocers and Dewhursts. Williams gave out plastic discount tokens with 1d or 6d or 1/- written on them, or whatever the amount was. My mother collected these and handed them back in at the little cashier's window. There was a metallic slicer for bacon, and sometimes cheese. Dewhursts had sawdust on the floor. Loughton House Stores near the police station delivered what we ordered to our house. The drapers sold rolls of linen and had an overhead change provider on a wire, and I used to love watching it fly backwards and forwards, once with the note a customer proffered (a reddish brown 10/- note or green-blue £1) rolled round, and then back with the change. Occasionally we went to Durrants' shoe shop where we were greeted by our next door neighbour ("Dumma", as my brother called him). There were rows of chairs and sloping foot rests with rubber pimples on them, and there were waist high viewers for your feet. You tried on a new pair of shoes and then put a foot into the viewer and saw the skeleton of your toes inside the outline of the shoe, as in a green sea.

Loughton was full of characters. Holy Grey was a balding man with enormous eyebrows who cycled round Loughton, kneeling and praying at all the crossroads. He had a saddlebag of small copies of the *New Testament*, which he had brought from Addisons bookshop out of his earnings as a labourer in W and C French and he would give these away. I saw him come out of Addisons with some books, and the following Sunday I saw him praying at the junction of Brook Road and Alderton Hill. Cars slowed down and passed him carefully, no one hooted him. My brother and I were kicking a stone to each other and Holy Grey got on his bike and ponderously cycled over and dismounted and said "Yer can't play football on Sundays." He gave me a copy of the *New Testament*. "Here, read this. It will teach you about God."

Another character was Dafty (as he was universally known). He was a semi-tramp with a vacant smile who lived in the High Road, and Mrs. Dafty pushed a box on wheels in which sat five very small children. Dafty sometimes worked as a road sweeper, but they all seemed very poor and very grimy. Nevertheless they all looked happy, even Mrs. Dafty was permanently smiling.

In Woodford there was a sad lady, nicknamed the Duchess, who stood in a shop doorway near the Castle dressed in long out-of-date clothes. It was rumoured that her son had been killed in the War, and she could not accept his death. She went every day to the station to meet him and then stood all day in the shop doorway.

Such characters I looked at with the wonder of a young boy. To me such eccentricity was normal, just as it had been natural and normal to be bombed by the Luftwaffe.

The Methodist Minister was a vivid character. The Rev. Gordon Brigg had been an RAF padre and every Sunday he told the children a story. He had a very definite manner in the pulpit, nodding his head (which had a broken nose) and thrusting it forward pugilistically, pausing at the same

17

time to emphasise his last word. "There was a boy called William Stickers," he said one day, and he described how Stickers stole and hoped to get away with it, and began to see posters all over town: "Bill Stickers will be prosecuted." In the end he confessed. The adults all laughed as he developed this story. Another time he told a story about a boy who left home for a holiday and sent a telegram back to his parents: SOS, LSD, JPB (the boy's initials). I grasped that stories contain truths and lodge in the memory in a way that other teachings do not.

At the Methodist church each Sunday were a number of vivid characters. There was Mr Bedwell, the incredibly thin doorman who arrived by bike and sat by the hymn books in the back pew. There was old man Occamore who inched his way in on two sticks, his legs bent outwards and away from each other, with a bald head. He looked at least 90. There was his bald son Ebenezer Occamore who played the organ. And there were a surgeon and an accountant who between them took children's church, and a bald headmaster who read the notices from the front, standing gravely between the pulpit and the communion table. And there was Mr Yelland, who took the collection; he was always in a suit and wore glasses that concealed a colossally magnified eye and he was very quiet and I never knew what job he did. And there were many others, including Lionel Murray, who as Len Murray became Secretary-General of the TUC and later Lord Epping Forest.

I sat with my mother in the pews until children's church, and I observed all their physical abnormalities and peculiarities of behaviour and mannerisms, and I am sure I developed an eye for significant detail during those interminably boring Sunday mornings when I had to be on my best behaviour and felt artificial in church. Had Chaucer been a Methodist in Loughton in the 1940s, I am sure he would have included some of those characters in his *Prologue*.

The two years I spent at "the new Oaklands" I was very happy. I loved the structured learning within a context of Nature: writing and reading, then running out to play in the field or on the lawn, surrounded by the Forest, the birds and berries of the seasons. I related well to my teacher; the Headmistress, Miss Lord, was a remote but pleasant figure, sitting in the "study" which always had an open door. Photographs taken at the time show all pupils in the school, without any teachers, standing in tiered rows with the ivied back of Oaklands behind them, and the jungle gym nearby. I appear as a serious little boy with straight hair and an intent look while others smiled around me.

My work progressed, and my parents had me lined up for Chigwell School which was then a direct grant grammar school. It had been founded in 1629 – the main building in front quad was Caroline and dated from the time of the Metaphysical poets – and its most famous pupil was William Penn, the Quaker, who later founded Pennsylvania. There are three letters from the Headmaster, Dr James (who soon afterwards went to Harrow), dated March 1946 and signed in his tiny hand, recommending me for entry

CHILDHOOD AND SCHOOLDAYS

(via the Essex County Council Scholarship Exam) in September 1947.

In March 1946 my little sister Janet was born. She had a hole in her heart and when she came home she was permanently flushed and in discomfort, often in pain. She cried a lot, and when she went to sleep we all had to be very quiet because if she woke she would be awake for several hours.

I kept in touch with the London Hospital where my aunt Argie worked. In 1946 Queen Mary visited. I saw her arrive, wearing maroon and a round maroon hat and marvelled as she briefly sold garden produce at a stall. In the summer of 1947 my brother and I spent a week staying with my aunt at her flat in Newark Street. We went by green line and the driver put us off at Bow instead of Whitechapel. My aunt was told this when she met the green line and we were not on it. She was beside herself with anxiety and told the London Hospital's head porter who went out and found us and brought us back into matron's office. On the Sunday we went to the Tower church. Being Methodist, my brother and I had not seen choirboys before. I had told my brother the story of the murder of the little princes which I had heard at school, and my brother said of the choirboys, "Here come the little princes."

At Oaklands we were taught to be collectors of things. The summer term of 1946 I began collecting butterflies. I was given a butterfly net, a killing jar of ammonia and a tin of relaxing fluid to make it easier to mount them. With hindsight it was a cruel thing to do, and I did not catch very many; but I loved to study them after I had caught them.

For my birthday my parents gave me a 12-drawer specimen cabinet, which they found in a local auction. It was filled with butterflies, moths and beetles, and included a death's head moth. They also found two cases of birds' eggs which had probably been assembled at the turn of the century, judging by the antiquity of the lettering in the labelling. There was a guillemot's egg and a razorbill's and many other eggs. I still have the eggs, but sadly the collection of butterflies, moths and beetles decayed.

Soon it was the seashore that fascinated me. In August my brother and I returned to Bognor and again stayed at 26 Glamis Street without our parents (as my mother was pregnant). My grandmother and my aunt Argie came with us. My letters to my parents reveal that we went on a motorboat and saw Punch and Judy on the pier. I found some shells and caught 26 crabs at Aldwick and lots of shrimps. I found "a emty (sic) shell of a whelk" (an image that recurred in Japan and found its way into my poem *The Silence*). I went to Felpham (where Blake lived) and to Folkestone, where "I saw France but only the cliffs and forests" through a telescope, but new places were no substitute for the rock-pools.

About this time I started collecting stamps and coins. I saw an advertisement for free stamps in the *Children's Newspaper*, which was delivered each week. I sent for stamps on approval and received mint specimens of mysterious shapes: triangular and diamond shaped stamps. My father bought me an album, and I swapped stamps at school. I also began to collect coins. I was friendly with Gwen Thomas, the daughter of Mr Thomas, the local bank manager at Barclays, High Road, Loughton and one day Mr Thomas had me to tea. After tea he took me into the foreign currency room in the bank where there was a mound of foreign coins, about knee high to me as I was then. Mr Thomas said I could take as many as I could hold in two hands. I climbed onto the trodden-down sandcastle of coins and plunged in my hands, lifted them, spilling coins and carried my handfuls to a strip of bare floor. Gently I opened my hands. Out fell magical coins: African coins with holes in them, Indian coins shaped like diamonds, Arab coins with serrated edges, coins with marvellous crowned heads and mysterious currency units – rupees and piastres and mills.

One day as I walked home from Oaklands I watched a mechanical excavator digging up the plot of waste land on the corner of the Crescent and the High Road. I saw something gleam, and bent and picked up a small copper coin. Part of it was corroded, but after soaking the coin clearly showed a balding man with SC on the back, and I later had the head identified as Caracalla's. From this I conclude that there was a Roman or Roman-British settlement in the vicinity of Oaklands School in the 3rd century AD.

My discovery of historical coins got me into trouble. I used to walk home with a boy called Michael Rogers who lived in Ollards Grove, and not long after my visit to the bank I had tea in his house and admired a Charles I golden guinea which his brother had. Somehow, between them, Michael and his brother gave it to me. I had to announce the gift to my parents and at Michael's suggestion said I found it in the honeysuckle on the roof of next door's cycle shed. It was a beautiful coin, a golden guinea with a perfect face, and I used to gaze at it and wonder at that head being cut off with an axe. Unfortunately Michael's father, a Reverend, contacted my father and asked for it back, and I had to surrender a face I had fallen in love with, a face that stood out from the coin and was more real to me than any picture of Charles I.

My mother had a work-basket with real Chinese coins sewn on the top. Each one had a square hole and Chinese ideograms round it, and on one side were the four gates of a Buddhist stupa, a symbol of heaven which incorporated Yin and Yang. I cut these coins off one at a time, and wondered at the far away places they had come from, not realising that the central hole probably symbolised eternity.

Soon I was also collecting cigarette cards. I discovered my love for these in hospital. That winter I was not well. I had a bad cough and only the white spots on my lungs later confirmed that I had latent TB. In January I had acute earache. My mother kept me in bed in the warm but one night my earache got worse and worse so I was almost screaming with pain, and in early February I was rushed to the London Hospital in an ambulance. The bell rang non-stop like a fire alarm. I had suspected meningitis and mastoid inflammation, and responded to a new drug, penicillin. Later a hearing expert proved on an audiometer that I suffer sensory neural loss between the outer ear and the brain in the middle of my right ear, and concluded that the screaming pain I felt in the ambulance was in fact meningitis, caused by my tubercular chest infection. This infection was eating away part of the bone towards the brain, as a result of which I now have some nerve deafness. The penicillin stopped it. If it hadn't I would have died, and he said it was quite clear that the penicillin saved my life.

In the end I had my tonsils out. I convalesced in Buxton Ward under an ear-nose-and-throat specialist. Buxton Ward was a children's ward, and there were boxes of cigarette cards, complete sets of sea fish and fresh water fish and of course birds. My favourite set was of small creatures such as harvest mice and newts. There was something exact about the illustrations, nothing sketchy. I marvelled at a card of a flying fish with wings. In the ward I did jigsaw puzzles and looked at the images on the cigarette cards, and when I came out and returned to school, I found that besides having stamps and coins in their pockets, some of the Oaklands pupils had some of the cigarette cards I had seen in hospital and were willing to swap. I particularly tried to collect cards showing pond life, including newts.

I remember my father saying good night to me about this time, leaning over me as I lay in bed and touched his nose, which in those days seemed enormous. He crouched by my bed in the upstairs front room nearest Lopping Hall and told me the Americans would send a rocket to the moon, and I was amazed. About this time I attempted my first *Biggles* book and feared that the villain, Erich von Stalhein, was on the landing, and my father laughed, an abandoned chuckle that somehow allayed my fear. Soon afterwards we played football on the Stubbles, and, swinging his good leg, my father kicked the ball high over my head, and as goalie between two posts marked by clothes, I was unable to save it. When we returned home we talked in his bedroom, and were very close. Suddenly he said: "You won't want to know me when you're older. Its natural, all children think like that. I'll be the old codger." And I said, "I'll always be close to you." It was inconceivable that I might one day disagree with him.

The entrance exam for Chigwell School took place on a warm Saturday afternoon in a New Hall. It was supervised by the legendary Arnold Fellows, a giant of a man with a shock of white hair. Cowed, we sat in rows facing top field: I was about fourth from the front and slightly to the left of the centre. There were two essays. One was "The London Clapham Omnibus", a reference to the fact that there is a memorial slab to George Shillibeer, its inventor, in Chigwell parish church. I did not know that an omnibus was a bus, so I did the other essay: "Newts". I wrote at length and with great enthusiasm about the newts I had observed in the Oaklands nature table aquarium with their frog spawn-like spots on their bodies: the great crested newt with its speckled yellow-orange underbelly and ridged dragon-like back; the palmate newt; and the common or smooth newt. I wrote about their little, barely webbed hands and feet, and how they resembled lizards. I got into Chigwell.

In early April my father took my brother and me to see a memorable Amateur Cup Final at Wembley. It was Bromley v Romford. Bromley won 1-0 through a headed goal by Brown before a crowd of 100,000. I can see Arthur Caiger walking briskly out to lead the Community Hymn singing, which included "Abide with Me". My father preferred amateur to professional football because he found it more enjoyable (though less skilful), which is why he watched Barnet when he visited his father at weekends.

That summer term was my last at Oaklands. My most vivid memory is

21

of sitting in Mabel Reid's class in the old Nursery at Oaklands (the large upstairs classroom) when suddenly in walked a boy in St Aubyn's uniform without a word, John O'Donald. He stood at the front of our class, and Mabel Reid said with her hands on his shoulders, "Now I want you to see how smart he is." I watched from my seat near the back while John O'Donald stood, smiling and preening himself. A girl called Marion Jordan with wire in her teeth and plaits sometimes walked home with me, and once we found a semi-derelict building we had no right to be in, and she crouched down in the centre of the floor.

Soon I began collecting autographs. The summer of 1947 was baking. There was a water shortage and the water cart stopped outside Journey's End, and we ran out and we filled jugs with water and carried them back into the home. I can remember my brother Robert running in the garden wearing the airman's helmet that hung in the cellar along with the tin helmet, which I sometimes wore as we refought the war in our imagination. In August, perhaps to escape this water shortage, we stayed with my cousin in Folkestone, and my father came down for a day and took me by bus to Canterbury to see Denis Compton. In 1947 Compton scored 18 centuries and 3,816 runs, and on this summer's day, with Middlesex batting in sunshine and the sun dazzling from car windscreens, Compton came in number 4 and made a century (106), brushing back his tousled hair and dancing down the wicket to hit the leg-spinner Dougy Wright back over his head. "There he goes again" my father said as Compton charged down the wicket to get to the pitch of the ball, risking being stumped. When he reached 100 he put his bat up and tossed his head and mopped his brow, and in my memory that moment became an image outside time, a (to me) permanent vignette of dashingly spontaneous bravado and cheek. I did not get his autograph on this occasion, but I grasped that contact with such gods who generated the applause and who were on cigarette cards was an admirable aim in itself, and I asked to be given an autograph album so that I could set about contacting such people.

About this time – perhaps it was in the course of the summer term – my father had Journey's End painted, and sitting on the Council Offices wall reading *Beano* and *Dandy*, Michael Rogers said accusingly rather than enviously, "Your father must be rich, if you're having the house painted," and I felt guilty. "My father's not rich," I hastened to assure him. Having a rich father seemed a terrible thing to have.

From 1947 until the 1960s my father supplemented his salary by letting a property, 6 Warrington Gardens, London W9 (now demolished), which he leased from the Church Commissioners. (I suspect the lease was paid for out of the sale of my mother's Moat Road houses.) This property comprised a number of single rooms which were occupied by overseas visitors. My father used to go up to London and collect rents, especially on a Friday evening. In due course he installed our domestic help, Mrs. Skilton, and her husband as managers, and his Friday trips involved sitting with them. Both he and Mr Skilton would sit by the fire and smoke their pipes and discuss the week, and my father would return on the tube with his takings. This arrangement continued throughout our school careers, and enabled my father to educate his children and give us a higher standard of living than we would otherwise have had.

I went to Chigwell by steam train on a misty day in September 1947. My mother came with me. She put her bicycle in the guard's van and then pushed her bicycle from Chigwell station to the School, with my bulky kitbag on the handlebars. At the age of eight, I was the youngest boy in the School, and having found the changing-room, deposited my kitbag (which said "N.O.Hagger", causing a boy to comment, " I shall call you 'Yes Hagger'") I was transferred to the wrong place. The chapel had been damaged in the war, and morning prayers for the senior school took place in New Hall under the new chaplain Mr Davenport. Somehow, I was taken to join them, and found myself with boys several years older than myself. No one noticed that I was in the wrong place, and I, expecting everything to be strange, did not realise anything was amiss. The chaplain recited Church of England prayers, and being Methodist I did not know the responses and there was much kneeling down and standing up again which were strange to me. Consequently I was caught standing when I should be kneeling and vice versa. So horrendous was my lostness that now I go out of my way to make sure new boys and girls in my care feel at home and are in the right place on their first day.

Eventually I found my way to Hainault House, a Victorian house that stood on the edge of the 50 acre site, and to Miss Crabtree's class. There I took my place in a class of between 20 and 30 confident-looking young boys, all more of my own size, and applied myself to the work Miss Crabtree asked us to do. At break the muddy ground nearby became a marble pitch, with gulleys in the earth that filled with water when it rained. "Anyone play me marleys," Dickie (Hitler) Leng bellowed, striding through the throng of marble-players who held bags of one-ers and glarnies. On all sides I heard strange contracts being made: "You lay, four cannons, no more, nothing in the game, keeps."

September was conker time, and also new to me were the conkers on strings. Boys skewered holes through conkers, so the white inside corkscrewed out, and threaded them on boot laces so they rested on a tied knot. "Bags froggy wallop," I heard (the first hit described in terms of the French Napoleonic wars), and while one boy held out his conker on a string, another took aim, raised his conker to shoulder-height and hit downwards. When he split the other's conker, the value of his own was increased by the value of the one he had split. "Mine's an eighty-sixer," I heard.

At break we walked down to the Tuck Shop and I bought a sticky bun with chocolate on the top for 2d. Older boys inspected me like entomologists inspecting an insect and pronounced, "You're a new bug" (new boy). I walked back, and standing at the top of Lower Field a boy called Mattick approached me near a boy called Seagull and imitated one of the masters whose nickname was Whistle and said "Treat-o". I did not know what he meant, and did not realise he was asking for a piece of my bun.

I began then to realise that one had to be streetwise to survive the hurly-burly of break and lunchtime in the presence of older boys. I quickly grasped that it was advisable not to mention if it was your birthday, as twenty boys upended a boy in glasses so he lay on his back and forty hands gave him the bumps, one for each year of his life, throwing him four feet into the air and pulling him down, shouting out "one-two-three...", lurching and reversing his stomach through sickening G-forces. This lesson (of the need for streetwisdom) was brought home to me when last thing Miss Crabtree wanted to know who in the class had the glue. It was a seemingly harmless question, and at Oaklands such questions were commonplace and were not attended by thoughts of punishment. We were encouraged to be open, honest and sincere, and so I replied with Oaklands helpfulness: "Strictly, Miss." In fact I got the boy's name wrong, but Miss Crabtree was able to work out where the glue was and retrieve it with a "You must return it when you have finished with it." After school I learned how different things were at Chigwell from what they were at Oaklands, how the Chigwell code involved concealing things from teachers whereas the Oaklands one was based on helping them. "You're a sneak," one of the boys (who was particularly good at bullying) said to me as I packed my satchel to walk back past the church to the station. "You sneaked on Strickland. You're a sneak." I sensed that he had influence and put my arms through my satchel straps and edged for the door. "You're a sneak. Come on everybody, chase the sneak."

I ran for it, and they ran after me calling "Sneak, sneak." I ran past the church and down the hill and only paused when I heard the footsteps recede. Out of breath I found a boy called Coleman beside me, and together we walked to the station, caught the steam train to Woodford and another to Loughton.

That first day began with my feeling an outsider and ended with what at Eton would have been called "Shelley-baiting", as I was chased into solitude by most of those I had hoped would be my new friends. My illusions had shattered, and I was now in a school whose rough-and-tumble vied with *Tom Brown's School Days*. Gone were the cosy days in which pupils and staff shared Nature walks and looked on each other as friends. In their place were days in which pupils and staff were at war, and pupils cribbed and cheated and pulled the wool over Miss Crabtree's eyes, and woe to anyone who did not subscribe to this conflict between boys and the Establishment.

The porch doorway to the oldest part of Chigwell School has a stone cross on a steeply sloping roof, and over the door a stone shield bears a mitre and underneath the date AD 1629.

Chigwell School was founded in 1629 by Archbishop Harsnett, a baker's boy from Colchester who rose to become Archbishop of York, and on the way, after he became vicar of Chigwell in 1597, wrote a book (*Declaration of Egregious Popish Impostures*) about one of the key spiritual issues of the day, whether Catholic priests were in fact able to cast out devils, which Shakespeare read (he used it for *King Lear*, taking some of Edgar's fiends from it) and which Milton used for *L'Allegro*. As Archbishop of York,

CHILDHOOD AND SCHOOLDAYS

Harsnett was deemed to be on the side of York in the earlier Wars of the Roses, and so we all wore white roses on Speech Day. The first half of the 17th century was a time of intellectual ferment as independent-minded Protestants continued and cemented the break from Rome and then decided whether they were Royalist or Puritan as the Civil War loomed. It was the time of the Metaphysical poets Donne and Marvell and the Church of England poet-divines such as Herbert and Traherne who defined their Protestantism in verse. There was a pioneering spirit abroad as new causes were espoused. Symptomatic of this spirit was William Penn. After living in Puritan Essex and attending C of E Chigwell from 1650 to 1654, Penn adopted a new religion, Quakerism, had four spells in prison and eventually went to the New World and founded Pennsylvania as a refuge for Quakers.

I have come to feel my roots lie in this time when science had not gone materialistic and Donne opposed the new sceptical philosophy, when there was still Unity of Being and sensibility; I have come to think that I have given philosophical expression to Penn's Inner Light. Chigwell stood for a strong spiritual tradition, independence of thought, character-building, and a pioneering spirit: both Harsnett and Penn founded institutions (a school, a state) and I see my own founding (a school, a movement) as being within their tradition. Chigwell also stood for finding one's own way to the top, hard work, and with its 48 acres of playing fields a sense of team spirit, an ethos that was summed up in the school song, which was written by a Chigwell vicar, the Rev. T. Marsden, between 1885 and 1892 and which was sung at certain ceremonial events:

> Which is the way to be happy?
> Not only the long-living day,
> To keep sound in your mind and your body,
> And hard at your work and your play.
>
> Find a way or make a way!
> Brave old Harsnett's son!
> The upward way, the onward way,
> The way the founder's gone.

My unpropitious start was not typical of my first year at Chigwell School. I learned the new rules quickly and my report for the Easter term, 1948 showed that although I was still the youngest boy in the school I came first in everything in JS (Junior School) except French, in which I came 3rd. I was thus 1st in English, Maths, History, Scripture and Geography. Nature Study/Science was ungraded but by the summer term I had come 1st in that too, and was awarded the form prize for the year. This I received a year later at the first Speech Day under the new regime of the new Headmaster, D. H. Thompson, in July 1949, from Henry Willink, Master of Magdalene College, Cambridge: a book (rebound in ribbed binding by the school) on butterflies.

The work clearly suited me. Miss Crabtree set the sort of homework I loved doing, and in Maths I took to my Housemaster Arnold Fellows ("AF"), who dominated the classroom in a shirt and braces and who worked on a system of incentives: a pile of sixpences on the master's desk, one of which if you answered correctly he flicked for you to catch. I do not think I was unduly competitive; I just completed whatever task I was set, whether it was classwork or homework, as thoroughly and as quickly as I could. My form position was a satisfactory response to those who had persecuted me on my first day, and the relative effortlessness with which I achieved it, and my adoption of marbles and football, enabled me to survive without further bullying and showed that I had adapted Oaklands' methods to the changed circumstances of Chigwell.

The winter of 1947 was very severe. The train chuffed through snowdrifts ten feet high, and there was a fuel shortage. One day Miss Crabtree told us about basic fuel and a boy called out "basic fool" and we all laughed. One after another we were called out by an irate Miss Crabtree to explain why we had laughed and each in turn said "Basic fool".

Although it was freezing outside, there were no concessions on Games Days, and prefects (including Bernard Williams, later a philosopher) insisted we wore no vests underneath our football shirts, and braved the cold. We poor wretches of 8 shivered in the subzero temperatures, our fingers numb and making only half-hearted kicks at the football when it came our way, and then we were prey for the Reverend Whitford ("Whistle") to say in his peculiar nasal voice, "You're playing like little girls today" and make an example of one or two of us, smacking us hard behind our legs so that in addition to being numb with cold we had red slap marks that stung. At the end of Games we sometimes had a "call-over", to check that we were all present. We all stood in forms in alphabetical order, and we all had a number. If the boy in front of us was absent we called his name and then our number. The whole operation evoked the regimentation of the war.

Perhaps because of this exposure to the cold, I was never completely well, and always had a latent snuffle. But I trudged to and fro between Chigwell station and the school in the freezing conditions without being seriously ill and even survived the unheated carpentry shop, where, virtually in the open air, we tried to saw mortice and tenant joints with our frozen fingers. ("Where's the bevil?" Lister, the "carp" teacher, would ask with unfailing regularity.)

The discipline was strict, and beside the incentive of the pile of sixpences was the cane. AF called himself "the Cruel Master" and caned anybody who ate in the street or had his hands in his pockets or did not wear a cap or did badly in class, and I can still see a boy called Ellis being marched out of assembly – and sometimes our classroom – and hear the crack of the cane from AF's study door and see Ellis returning, pale and chastened while the class sat deathly silent, heads down to work. In the spring AF caned a boy called Kevin O'Leary, and that afternoon my mother took him and me for a picnic on the Stubbles. We went down to look at the stream and I asked him "Did it hurt?" and was fascinated as he gave me an account of the suffering that was inflicted, which seemed of the order of executions, an instance of man's cruelty to man.

In March my little sister Janet died, aged 18 months. She never recovered from the hole in her heart. We had to tiptoe past her pram in the hall, for if we inadvertently woke her she might cry for two hours because she would be in pain. Sometimes I rocked her to sleep by jogging the pram arm gently up and down. She was always uncomfortable with a red little face, and death was a merciful release.

Soon afterwards one break I watched a boy swinging on a low branch on the edge of Lower Field at school. He jumped off and the end of the branch sprang back up and gashed me above my right eye, splitting the skin, and I still have the scar.

It must have been about then that we began playing cricket in the garden. In our imagination I was England and my brother was Australia. I cannot overemphasise the extent to which cricket nourished my imagination. When I snicked the ball past the rose-bed to the swing, in my mind I was at the Oval leg-glancing Lindwall to the boundary; I was actually there, in that great expanse of green, and the Council Offices at square leg was the gasometer. When I reached 50, I put my bat up like Compton, and when he was caught on a flowerbed I became another England batsman. On washing day we had to bowl through or round the washing, which was clothes-pegged to a line held up by a forked stick 6 feet long.

Sometimes we hit the ball next door into Dr Mautner's garden and had to retrieve it by crawling through a hole (a missing paling) in the fence and hunting in an overgrown orchard. The fruit trees there had sticky bands round the bark of their trunks to discourage ants, and milk-bottle tops on their twigs, which tinkled in the breeze, to discourage birds.

In the summer of 1948 we hired a car and went to the coast. On the way back we passed Kennington Oval during the final Test against Australia, and I saw the news hoardings outside, "England all out 48." Len Hutton had made 30. I can still see the scene outside the Oval that disastrous day with great clarity; I could now draw the exact number of people outside the ground, where they all stood or went about their business, reacting to or oblivious of the catastrophe that had been England's innings.

In September I spent a week away from my parents with my aunt and grandmother at the Lawns Hotel, Hove. We had a room on the second floor and I worked the lift. A gong sounded for meal times. My uncle George, who had commandeered my grandfather's business, drove us to the Devil's Dyke, from which I saw the Isle of Wight, and there was Punch and Judy by the pier. I sailed a yacht with a pale green hull and white sails in the concrete pool of a local park with my two cousins, Richard and John.

In September Grange Court opened as a war memorial to Old Chigwellians who fell in the world wars, with AF as Housemaster. A large, rambling Georgian building, it had a wide central passage and staircase, at the foot of which AF had his study. We had assembly in the passage, which was my form 2 classroom. Outside at the back were steps and a large lawned area where we played "King-he" at break. At the beginning of the game there was only one "he", and he threw a tennis ball at everyone playing. You were allowed to fist it away, but if it hit you then you turned "he" and tried to get the others. Break would end with the "hes" jumping for a high ball to catch it and the "non-hes" jumping to fist the ball away, very often with a handkerchief wound round their knuckles. At the end of break AF would appear, shrugging his shoulders and tossing his head (because, legend had it, he was involuntarily afraid of a snake falling down his neck) and he would cup his hands and shout: "Hoi, all in." Such was this giant's effortless authority that immediately the game would stop and everyone would call "All in, ally-ally-all in" and race for the classroom.

AF was a giant of a character. He was enormously larger than life. He wore braces, often without a jacket – he demonstrated swanking by putting his thumbs under his braces and opening out his fingers and turning his nose disdainfully into the air – and he exuded an air of pleasantness, saying loudly "Boodgye" instead of "Goodbye" in a deliberately comic Spoonerism. On a spring morning he would close his eyes as if going into a rapture and chant ,"When the air feels soft and balmy, I feel soft and barmy too." He was rumoured never to sleep but to sit in his study and work all night. Sometimes he appeared for a service in Chigwell parish church in his pyjamas, saying he had not had time to dress, and he would then wear a cassock over his pyjamas. His attitude to life was to think things out for himself. He drove a Morris 12 – AVW 124 – and the running boards on either side went up and down as the car moved. The village policeman stopped him in the High Road and said "They're very dangerous, sir" (meaning "Get them fixed"). "Ah, yes, I see," said AF, and lifted the running boards off and put them in the back of the car where Claud Salmon was sitting, so that it looked as if Claud Salmon was going skiing. Problem solved with a radical solution. AF's voice was very loud and could be heard for miles from the Top Field cricket pitch where he coached the Under 12s. Dr Pratt, who lived in the house Alan Sugar now occupies down Roding Lane next to the school grounds, asked Thompson, the Head, if "Fellows could keep his voice down as my wife likes to have a rest after lunch".

AF now taught me English. He taught parsing by telling stories about the Great Detective and Mrs. Clutterbuck, his housekeeper. He wrote sentences about the Great Detective's exploits on the board, and drew boxes round them, and we had to parse them in our books. Again, the pile of sixpences was put at the front, and anyone "on Satis" who got a Non-Satis in any subject would be marched out and whacked with his cane. ("Zonc" AF would say as the crack rang out.) Designating the report system "Satis" emphasised the Latin influence on the school, which also came out in free auctions: when a boy wanted to give something away between lessons he would call out "Quis?" (who?) and all would shout "Ego", and the boy judged the first to call would have the possession. In woodwork we all made a block of wood shaped like a book, and when we took out a book from the library we put the wood in its place with the name of the book and our details written on the back. Then, anyone who wanted a book with the subject of the one we had, could ask us to return it.

At school there was a poetry recital prize. I recited in the Swallow library a poem called *Yellowhammer*, which was in a Christmas present I had had from the Town Clerk, J. W. Faulkner: *The Junior Weekender's Book*. It contained the line "a little bit of bread and no cheese". I believe I won.

I now began to know what it was to have less good teachers. The Maths

28

master, a moustached man called Smith, could not keep order and set hundreds of sums as punishments, which merely demeaned his standing (and subject) in our eyes. Sammy Goldsmith, the Geography teacher, wheezed and coughed and cleared his throat between each sentence because he was badly gassed in the war. Neither were effective teachers and my work suffered in their areas. I knew they were no good, but could do nothing. My father had a scathing contempt for teachers. "They're all Labour," he would say.

Between February and May 1949 my father bought Journey's End from the Maitlands for £600, and we immediately had the builders in.

In the summer of 1949 AF began to teach us Latin. We had to sing the nominative, vocative, accusative, genitive, dative and ablative of "nauta" to the tune of "Life on the Ocean Wave": "Nauta, nauta, nautam, nautae, nautae, nauta; nautae, nautae, nautas, nautarum, nautis, nautis." AF conducted us like Sir Malcolm Sargent. Sometimes he made us chant the Siamese national anthem: "Oh, wa, ta, na Siam" (or "Oh, what an arse I am"). He had a tremendous dramatic sense. Once he had a paper bag he did not want, and he blew it up into a ball and banged it with his hand, so that we all jumped.

AF also taught us cricket. In the nets he would stick a penknife in the ground on the good length spot and bowl his slow offbreaks at it, and as often as not knock the penknife back. In our practice games if a boy played a bad shot he would bend him over and whack him with his bat. Although I was still too young for the Under 12 team, one of the team was absent and I was picked to play one match against Forest School, away. AF had personally demonstrated the cross-batted pull shot, swivelling with bent knees and gently hitting the ball with a cross bat. I batted number 11 because I was much younger than the rest, and on receiving a short ball did the exact movements that AF had taught us, and scored 4 on the short boundary at square leg. AF was umpiring in the vicinity and he called out "Good shot", the only time I have heard an umpire intervene loudly in a partisan way in a cricket match. (When one boy was bowled he called, "Camel, should have played forward.")

It must have been this year that our class sang as a choir at the summer concert: "He is my goose,/By train he came,/And Henry is his funny name"; and "Cricklewood girls, don't you want to go to Somerset,/Somerset girls don't you want to go to town,/Somerset girls don't you want to go to Cricklewood" etc. We also sang: "Beechwood fires burn bright and clear,/Bright and clear, bright and clear,/Beechwood fires burn bright and clear,/If the logs are left a year." It was either this year or next year that our class sang *Prince Igor*: "Sing we, praises, to our, glorious, Kha-an."

It would have been at this time that I went to tea with David Gordon in Chigwell Rise and played in his back garden where there were beehives. A large bumble-bee dive-bombed me; I saw it coming when it was still a long way off and made evasive swatting gestures with my hands, but it got through my defences and stung me on my right cheek, and as my face throbbed with pain and swelled up it was no consolation that the bee had sacrificed its life by leaving its sting in me, and was lying dead on the grass. It seemed impossible that all was One when creatures could do that to humans.

The Speech Day I belatedly collected my prize stands out in my mind for the church service in the morning. It was held in the C of E Chigwell parish church. Most boys wore suits and boaters (or "bashers") and white roses as the school's founder had been Archbishop of York and was therefore deemed to have been a Yorkist in the much earlier Wars of the Roses. We all sat in pews. I was next to a boy called Richard Fradd, and when the vicar called "Let us pray", we all knelt on our hassocks. Fradd got out his marbles and positioned two on the floor and flicked one so that it chinked in a cannon in the middle of a prayer while we shook with mirth. He flicked again, missed and the marble rolled under the pew in front. Fradd dived quietly after it to retrieve it and reappeared, triumphantly holding it before the end of the prayer.

I record this episode for two reasons. First, I now employ Richard Fradd's wife, and frequently hear news about his as a result of his market gardening. And secondly because it exemplifies the irreligiousness of our attitude to religion. It would have been virtually impossible to predict my current attitudes from those unpromisingly distracted beginnings when my soul was dormant.

Looking back, I have the impression that my soul remained unawakened for the next four years, yet there were stirrings as I passed through adolescence, amid the routine of cycling to school, cricket, football, marbles, cycling home, homework and reading adventure stories in bed every night and at the weekend. I had a growing interest in the ancient Romans and Greeks, and in archaeology.

As to the archaeology, our dentist in those days was Howard Carter's brother. He had a surgery in the High Road, and to get me relaxed before he drilled my teeth he would tell me stories about his brother's find of Tutankhamun's tomb in November 1922. He would say, "And then, my brother turned the corner and saw ....Open wide." And after another bout of drilling: "....A wonderful gold mask from the 14th century BC." He told me about the curse attached to the tomb, how "To whomsoever shall disturb these remains death shall come on winged wings", and I was spellbound. I relate my life-long interest in ancient Egypt to Dr Carter's stories.

At home there was a new baby. My younger brother Jonathan was born in February 1949, and my other brother and I were consequently packed off to stay with my cousin at 4 Julian Road, Folkestone in the spring and summer of 1950. I had stayed in the house before, and had travelled from it to see Denis Compton. I can remember ITMA on the radio in those days and a toy cupboard with a curtain. A few years ago I found myself in the area and called, and strangers showed me in and to my distress that back room where we had our tea under the high mantelpiece had been irrevocably changed. The garden still had a brick construction wicket-high in the lawn, and walls on either side where we played cricket boisterously, sometimes hitting the ball into the jungle of high runner beans on one side or into the better kept garden on the other side. Part of the fun of those days was then climbing over and retrieving the ball.

CHILDHOOD AND SCHOOLDAYS

In the mornings we used to run round Kingsnorth Gardens and play cricket and football, and once we were taken to Canterbury to see Kent play cricket against the West Indies, who had Ramadhin and Valentine playing for them, and then onto the Cathedral. Sometimes we visited an old lady across the road, Miss Mapleton, who was looked after by her companion, Caroline. We also took the bus to church where the preacher was a Mr Baker, and in the bus on the way back I made up ribald rhymes about him, which my Aunt Flo found funny and joined in, contributing some lines of her own. We regularly took the bus to the sandy beach and above the concrete arches beneath the promenade there were entertainers, and there, raking his glowing potash, squatted Rex D'Alston, a prophet with long hair. A small crowd gathered round him in a semi-circle and he stared at his ash and poked it with a divining twig and said "God is dead" and my Aunt Flo tried to move us on. But I hung back , fascinated. A board of press-cuttings had pictures of how he had cycled blindfold through Folkestone and found a watch that had been hidden by the Mayor. This man had strange powers, and I always lingered, and sometimes, having come to recognise me, he addressed me, raking his potash, and I had an obscure feeling that he was a kind of John the Baptist who was preparing the way for something I would do. Then one day he wasn't there any more, and I asked after him for a while and then stopped thinking about him.

It must have been during this holiday that I stood with my brother Rob and cousin Richard near the pier and watched a man sell household goods to a crowd. He and his assistant had a lot of clocks in suitcases. "'Ere," he called , "a bargain," holding up an old-fashioned alarm clock on legs, "half a crown." He tapped the back several times with his finger. "'Ere," he shouted, looking at me, "is that ticking?" I knew he was doing it with his finger, but his finger *was* making a ticking noise, and I began to say, "If by ticking you mean 'Can I hear a sound....'" Theatrically – for this was street (or promenade) theatre – he interrupted me. "Is it ticking, yes or no?" "If ticking means – " "Yes or no?" "Yes," I said. "You're a bigger liar than I am," the man said, and everyone laughed.

It would have been during this holiday that my brother, my cousin and I were taken to visit Aunt Lucy above the Hove shop. Lucy gave us lunch out of our purloined inheritance, and Richard did not like the ham. The first floor window was open, and when the grown-ups were not looking he threw his piece of ham out of the window. We looked to see where it had landed, and to our consternation and mirth realised it had fallen on a lady's hat, and that the lady was walking down the road oblivious to what had happened. That, at least, is how we all remember it.

We also visited my grandmother in East Grinstead and went to see Aunt Maud, my grandmother's sister, who lived nearby in Crescent Road with her companion, a bespectacled Miss Walter, and a small dog "Cheekah", which ran at us and snapped at our ankles. Aunt Maud wore her grey hair in a cottage loaf bun. The house was like a Victorian junkshop, and there was a stuffed crocodile and an armadillo shell, which Rob and I went to. Aunt Maud said we could have them one day, but a few years later her mind went and she invited the baker in to help himself to what he wanted, and he went off with my choice, the crocodile. My brother did receive the armadillo.

31

A MYSTIC WAY

There were Channel swimmers by the open-air swimming pool and in the summer we watched them train every day. The most successful ones were Egyptians like Mari Hassan Hamad; the British hope was Eileen Fenton, who had been attacked in training by a 6 foot shark which had been killed and was on display. The British trainer was an enormous man called Sam Rocket. The Channel swimmers did interminable numbers of lengths, crawling relentlessly forward in goggles and turning with a great splash, while some sat in the sun and signed autographs. They stayed in the guest houses in Marine Crescent opposite, which had their countries' flags hanging out from under the roof on sloping flagpoles. The race that year seemed to be two ways, from Dover to Cap Nez Gris and back. Covered in oil they waded ashore in France and then turned round and swam back through the night with only a small boat to keep them company, and I have the impression that Mari Hassan Hamad won.

My Aunt Flo had been divorced and would shortly remarry, and my new Uncle Reg was about and he joined in the fun, chasing us round the garden and hiding from us. He was a taciturn man, but he was good at frightening us. When we went home my cousin Richard came to stay with us and we were happy.

Back in Loughton my brother Rob and I would sometimes go and watch the cricket, either at Loughton cricket ground or the other side of the railway line, where there was a field with a small wooden grandstand. It was quite safe in those days for two young boys to wander on their own. Sometimes there was a fair on that field, and I recall the ghost train there and queuing to see Toey Tailor, an armless man who did incredible things with his toes, including playing the piano and lighting cigarettes.

My brother Rob and I continued to spend many hours playing cricket in the garden. There was a concrete strip at the back of Journey's End, and a shed, which was the wicketkeeper. We stood the swing seat on its side as stumps and bowled from an upturned pail by the back door, and played Test Matches. I would be England and bat first, as I was the elder, and Rob would be Australia and not get a bat until I had been each player in turn. Denis Compton always played carefully and scored a lot of runs. There were clear rules. It was 4 to the fence round the garden and out if the ball landed on any flowerbed without bouncing or went into next-door's garden. The matches lasted all day with regular interruptions, and any batsman who reached 50 put his bat up to acknowledge the applause of the crowd, which in our imaginations was real. Our minds and ears were actually deafened by the appreciative roar.

We still attended the Methodist church every Sunday and went to Fellowship in the afternoon, and in October I had to copy out Bunyan's hymn "He who would valiant be" and enter a church handwriting competition. I had an immaculate, somewhat babyish hand, and I collected 1st prize. The following spring I was not well and had a spell in the London Hospital; the trouble was again of an ear-nose-and-throat nature and I had my sinuses washed out. In the summer I was captain of the Under 12s at cricket, and for the next three or four years I was captain of the Under 12, Under 13œ, Under 15 and Under 16 at both cricket and football, and I had a say in who was in the team, greeted the opposing captain, tossed the coin and made the decision as to whether to bat or to field at cricket, or whether to choose end or kick-off at football.

Each summer the Headmaster's XI played the school at cricket, and we would see the players he had invited walking slowly in the hot sun down towards the 1st XI pitch, and there were rich pickings to be had for those who dared to ask for autographs: John Strachey, the Labour Minister; the actor Trevor Howard; and one of our childhood idols, Alan Lavers, the hard-hitting Essex all-rounder from the 1930s and 1940s.

Around this time John Dutchman joined the Chigwell staff and took us for Geography. He played amateur football for Corinthian Casuals and Pegasus, and later England, and we were overjoyed at having a "star" teach us and I tried extremely hard in Geography. When Pegasus got to Wembley for the amateur cup final of 1951 he gave us free tickets and we cheered as Pegasus won 2-1. In May 1951 the Festival of Britain opened on the South Bank in London. Looking back now and seeing it captured on black and white film, I feel it all seems very dreary, but then it was immensely exciting. My family went and spent a tiring day walking round and looking at all the exhibits. We thrilled at the curved "Dome of Discovery" and the seemingly unsupported Skylon, an aluminium exclamation mark, and marvelled at the Royal Festival Hall, and were indignant that a cup of coffee should cost 9d. It seemed that Britain had a wonderful future. I entered a church competition entitled 'A Visit to London in AD 2000' and recorded that I went to Lord's "to see England v The Rest of the United States of Europe". I had no doubt at the age of 12 that Churchill's Zurich speech of 1946 would result in a United States of Europe.

The General Election campaign of October 1951 brought Winston Churchill to Loughton. He spoke in the hall of Loughton High School for Girls (now Roding School) and I stood on the steps as his car arrived and stepped out and stopped him as, bent over his stick, he came up. I held out my autograph album, and he signed: W. Churchill. I felt contact with him and sensed that he would recur in my life in some form.

Every year around then we went to the Schoolboys' Exhibition at Olympia, and I would spend time among the stamps and coins, and I always sought out the author: Anthony Buckeridge one year; Enid Blyton another; and Capt. W. E. Johns. They signed autographs and smiled, unlike the footballers from Spurs or Arsenal who came in fives and looked ill at ease and signed their name in illegible, loopy or backward-sloping writing.

I read an enormous amount at this time. There was a penny library in the High Road near Lopping Hall, with books very often on shelves that were on wheels and parked on the pavement. I read all the Biggles books, and so vivid was my imagination that I was still sure Erich von Stalhein, the villain, was on the landing after lights-out. (I have been delighted by the recent proposal identifying the slim, delicate-featured Biggles with my imperial Outsider-hero T. E. Lawrence, who was admitted into the RAF by the recruiting officer, author of the Biggles books W. E. Johns in 1922, although I am still convinced that Biggles was Squadron-Leader Bigglesworth, who was still alive in a Home Counties nursing home aged 93 in 1993.) At the time I did not know the word "agent" and announced to the family that I had borrowed *Biggles, Secret Aggent*, pronounced with a 'g' rather than a 'j'. I read Rider Haggard's African adventure stories, Conan Doyle's Professor Challenger and Sherlock Holmes stories and some Agatha Christie, and of course Just William, Billy Bunter and Jennings. We often listened to Children's Hour on the radio, and my favourite was Norman and Henry Bones. It was a joy to wake up on a Sunday morning and stay in bed, reading a hundred pages or more before getting up to eat my mother's sausage pie with marmite.

We had our family meals round the nursery table. There was a high tea about 6, which was always something cooked – welsh rarebit was one plate my mother used to put in front of us – and supper was later. At the weekends and in the holidays we had breakfast, lunch, tea and supper round the table, my mother sitting at one end and my father at the other, and we all discussed the things we had done and the issues of the day. As a result I had opinions on current affairs and the church sermon, and sometimes enjoyed the cut-and-thrust of debate. To this day I remain convinced that talking at the table is an excellent way of bringing up children to think for themselves, express their opinions clearly and communicate effectively.

At school we still played marbles, and it must have been about this time that I won the only twenty-fourer in the school. It was owned by the King of Marbles, little John Hinman who managed to flick the massive piece of glass without a foul fob. It was a muddy day, and the gulleys on the marble pitch behind the Tuck Shop were filled with water; and a huge crowd gathered to watch at the end of lunch time. I played a twelver into Hinman's twenty-fourer I won the first game, and we completed the four cannons in the second and decisive game and sank the twelver. Neither of us would flick the twenty-fourer two yards to the gulley, two yards of corridor between shoes and bent heads. Both of us moved the huge marble with our foot, a form of saying "Pass". Then the bell went for afternoon lessons. "You've got to go," I told Hinman. He bent and flicked. Two dozen boys held their breath as the marble gathered pace but then slowed down in the mud and came to rest on the edge of the gulley. It was like a golfer narrowly missing a long putt. Quickly I flicked the twenty-fourer into the gulley and dipped my hand in the muddy water to retrieve it and ran across Top Field to class, the owner of the only twenty-fourer in the school. I held it for just 24 hours. Hinman challenged me to a rematch and I lost it the next lunch time. (Doug Sweet now owns Hinman's twenty-fourer, having won it 24 times.)

Every morning I cycled to school, and in the summer I took "the Roding route" via Avondale Drive and across the playing fields to the River Roding. I pushed my bicycle across a humped-backed bridge, looking for fish in the narrow river below, and then cycled along the towpath to the opening of a narrow path that led behind the playing fields of Buckhurst Hill Boys School and alongside Chigwell RAF base, and came out at the bend of Roding Lane. I then cycled up under the overhanging trees to school. When I returned home the evening sun would pour down through the trees, and as I freewheeled down Roding Lane the mottled light-shadow effect of the sun through the leaves was sometimes so intense that I had to close my eyes to avoid having a migraine.

In February 1952 King George VI died and Queen Elizabeth I acceded to the throne. Each break we drank free milk from bottles in a crate in the lobby – the gulping of milk always made my eyes ache for a minute or two – and it was in the lobby, with its old etching of William Penn among the American Indians in what became Pennsylvania that the Rev. Whitford ("Whistle") excitedly told a group of us about the lying-in-state and funeral, and the coming coronation. (In the science lab he demonstrated God's care by whacking anyone who crossed him with a bunsen burner tube or cable.)

In March 1952 my sister Frances was born. She was a twin, but her brother died. There were now four children who survived in our family, six having died (there having been a miscarriage between me and my brother Robert) and the years had made my parents resigned but resilient, even defiant. My father never went to church now. He would garden on a Sunday and come in and say, "I've been looking at the worms, trying to understand how life works." He still worked at the Council Offices and limped home for lunch, but he had become more sombre. My mother remained religious and had a framed floriate inscription: "Nothing but infinite pity is sufficient for the infinite pathos of human life." That word "infinite" was an influence on my childhood, as was Kipling's *If* – which was on the wall: "If you can keep your head when all about you /Are losing theirs...." ?

About this time I broke my right index finger in closing the large partition that separated BS1 and BS2. Several of us tugged at the huge wooden folds, which suddenly opened, snapping my finger in the straightening hinge and cocking up the bottom end of my nail. I can recall looking calmly at my finger. It was a sickening sight – enough to make me feel faint – but it was numb and I felt no pain immediately.

The only social life I had was at the Methodist church. After church on Sunday my brother and I visited my grandmother, who had moved from East Grinstead to 20 Brook Road, Loughton, opposite the library. She lived there with my aunt Argie and we told them about our week, and sometimes we walked there with the daughters of a local family. Sometimes my grandmother had her neighbours in and I joined them for a game of pit. Occasionally there was a fellowship party at the house of our class leader, and we would play Murder in the Dark, and again I would shyly hold conversations with girls. Once there was a fellowship outing to *The Boy Friend* and Hugh Gaitskell was sitting in the seat in front of me. He turned round and asked if I was enjoying it. One Christmas at this time Oaklands had a dance for some of the former pupils. There was an MC and a live band, the boys were in black tie and the girls sat on chairs all round the main hall. There was a Paul Jones. I politely danced with some of my former classmates until about 9.30 p.m., and then suddenly had an overpowering urge to escape the charade of "wall-flowers" and be alone. So I quietly slipped out and walked home. My mother greeted me with: "Why are you so early? Go back. You must go back." I was sent back. I slipped back into the Oaklands hall without comment and stayed to the end, but I did not enjoy the evening. My adolescent shyness with girls meant that I was not completely sure what to say.

Little by little I was becoming fascinated with the past. The more Latin I did the more mysterious the Romans seemed, and my reading included Lloyd Douglas's *The Robe*. I now read historical novels. My coin collecting gathered pace. Electrification had replaced steam, and in the holidays I travelled up to London on the tube on my own, and (having read about them) I discovered B. A. Seaby's in Margaret Street behind Oxford Street (as it was then). I climbed the stairs and often about this time spent an afternoon rummaging in the reject boxes which contained coins with minor blemishes. I would give my finds to old Mr Seaby, a grey-haired man of about 75 who spoke with a guttural accent. He was very patient, and he would peer at each coin through his eye-magnifier and say "Vitellius" or "Vespasian" or "Augustus" or "Drusus" or "Hadrian". Each reject Roman coin was 6d, and for two years I spent my pocket money in collecting coins (which I still have) of each Roman Emperor, and slowly included Greek coins. I loved to handle portraits of Julius Caesar, especially when I was reading Tacitus's *Caesar at Alexandria*, and the magic of handling coins of Greek battlegrounds such as Plataea entranced me. I fell in love with a silver drachma from Euboea with a female (goddess's?) head, hair rolled, on it. It was from Chalcis, 369-336 BC, and priced at 10/6d, and I spent some birthday money on it, and when I proudly showed my mother, she said in horror: "You didn't, you spent 10/6d for *that*?"

Soon I knew more about the 1st century AD and the 5th century BC in Athens than I did about the 20th century in Britain. Ancient coins have an individual beauty about them, like poems; and my collection of coins was to me then what a collection of my poems is to me now.

At school I had developed a love of English Literature. We read several Shakespeare plays and I acted in *Julius Caesar*: I was a messenger and took part in the crowd shortly after returning from hospital. I was very much a minor player, but I loved the language of Shakespeare and knew whole chunks of the play by heart – a far more rewarding way of spending two months than on some more modern plays with arid language. In class we read Coleridge's *Ancient Mariner* and again I was drunk with the language. I liked Donne as well. I had somehow developed a love of literature, but there was little time to indulge it; the endless round of lessons, matches and homework left little time for bedtime reading, though I did go to the public library each week and choose books. It was the only outing during the weekday evenings, and without television (which was not yet widespread) every evening was spent in reading, of some sort, with occasional radio listening, especially to the promenade concerts in the summer and to the Sunday evening classic, which might be *Oliver Twist* or the *Forsyte Saga*. Listening to drama stimulated my imagination, and Nancy pleading "No, not the club, Bill" brought Dickens visually to the mind's eye in a way that television never can.

My reality at this time was in school. I can see myself sitting in BS1 (now the library) under the bust of Archbishop Harsnett, the founder, during Latin, scholarship boards on high, with Mr Stott and then young Mr Owens, who set us too much homework. In 1952 we had our annual holiday in a hotel in Paignton. My brother and I discovered that a deckchair attendant on the sands was a Torquay United Footballer, Hugh Brown. My brother and I got his autograph.

I remember little of this time as I progressed from the Under 13¹/₂ to the Under 15, and was old enough to make the long tube journey to watch

Chelsea (our hero was Roy Bentley) and to spend a day at Lord's or the Oval, taking a bottle of Tizer to swig, which we made last all day. Each Easter there was a tennis tournament at the Connaught Club, Chingford. My brother Robert and I would cycle there and spend the morning fielding balls from the practice serves of Tony Mottram and other Wimbledon stars. In the afternoons we watched the matches, going from court to court until we found one that gripped us. In the summers at school there was a fair amount of bullying of an arm-twisting nature. A boy called Bastin was particularly sadistic, and my father taught me how to elbow sharply backwards and wind an attacker from behind, advice I put into practice on my tormentor Bastin with satisfying results. (He doubled up in agony and left me alone after that.) On a winter Saturday afternoon about 5 o'clock I would walk to Loughton station, very often through fog or smog (particularly in 1953 when the fog was a sulphurous yellow against the old street gas lamps), where the newsvendors called "*Star, News* or *Standard*" and "Paper late", and I would buy an *Evening Standard* so that my father could read the football reports.

Each winter I had some friends to a Christmas party, and we played charades in the Nursery. I can see "Curly" Wood act out "robust", first of all rowing a boat, then putting lumps under his sweater, and finally winding a scarf round his neck, wearing gloves and nursing a hot-water bottle as a contrast to the robust man beside him who wore no protection against the cold.

I vividly remember the morning of 28th January 1953, when, in chapel at school, while singing *Light's abode, celestial Salem*, several of us looked at our watches and observed the exact moment that Derek Bentley was hanged for a murder he did not commit. Apparently Bentley lived in the same road as I did in Norbury, and according to my mother there were occasions (which I was too small to remember)when he spoke to me. Now, in his Dark Night, I felt a special connection and was mentally executed alongside him that January morning.

At the end of March, after spending ten days in bed with flu and pharyngitis, I played a messenger in the three nights of Mr Davenport's production of *Julius Caesar*. I had to rush up some steps to the stage and declaim four lines, and then rush out again. I now think of Eliot's *Prufrock*: "No! I am not Prince Hamlet, nor was meant to be;/Am an attendant lord." I was also in the crowd, and reacted to Antony's funeral speech and attacked Cinna the poet.

A local worthy, Col. Sir Stuart Mallinson, threw the grounds of his White House open to the public once or twice a year, and every April he invited a cricket professional to teach local schoolboys. In April 1953 it was Laurie Fishlock, the Surrey opener, and I was somehow chosen for coaching, and won a comment which Sir Stuart wrote to my parents in his own hand, "Shows promise with bat and ball." A year later I made 38 not out for Chigwell at St. Dunstans, and to my delight Fishlock was umpiring at the other end (for St. Dunstans).

The Coronation of Queen Elizabeth I took place on 2nd June 1953. Everyone found someone with a television and watched it. We went to a family connected with the Methodist church and saw the frail girl surrounded by deferential old men in robes pronounced Queen in a ceremony that suggested to me the fragility of British power.

Some time later, the team which successfully conquered Mount Everest on the eve of the Coronation showed a film and gave a lecture at the Royal Festival Hall. Sir John Hunt and Sir Edmund Hillary did most of the talking. I was there, and afterwards I got their autographs. Hillary was a hero of physical endurance, who had braved freezing temperatures and dizzying drops to stand on the roof of the world. His courage made him briefly another kind of hero for us to admire.

In August 1953 we had our holiday at a cottage in Bembridge in the Isle of Wight. My father had just bought a black Austin 70, a spacious, wide car which had a box fitted on the accelerator so his game leg could reach it, and I can recall a very steep hill where we got stuck and a stranger took the wheel and drove us to the top of the gradient. I laboriously read Edmund Burke (who my father sometimes spoke of, along with Dostoevsky) when the family sat in armchairs in the evening, everyone occupied with something. ("Dig and delve," my father used to say, "go to the library and find things out for yourself.")

The best heroes remained cricket heroes. As soon as we returned from Bembridge, on Monday August 17th my brother and I went to see England play Australia on the second day of the critical Oval Test when England won the Ashes back for the first time since 1934. We got up at 4.30 a.m. and caught the first tube to the Oval, and queued from about 6 and got in. It was a hot day, and we saw England's first innings, which was dominated by Hutton, who scored 82. Each shot was momentous, we hung on every ball. Life was simple. It was a straightforward contest between the terrifyingly fast Lindwall and the heroic Hutton who pushed and nudged England's score towards an unspoken total that would win back the Ashes.

That year, it must have been, the Head Boy was an American, Fletcher Hodges. He was more mature that any other boy in the school – he was about 21 – and he came from Kentucky, near the Sewanny river. He had definite ideas about punishing boys. He was allowed to cane , and he caned a boy called Ayton so hard in his games clothes that he split Ayton's shorts to ribbons and as Ayton crawled to matron he left a trail of blood in the passage and up the wooden stairs. This was soon common knowledge in the school.

By and large I escaped the cane – except for three occasions. The first time I was caned (in June 1953) was because I had been put in imposition school (i.e. an hour's detention taken by a master after school), and the Under 15 "manager", "Charlie" Venn (who had been to Worcester College, Oxford, where I was to go) wanted me to go to his cricket net. He did a deal with the master who had put me in "impot", and upstairs in Church House he bent me over and gave me three nonchalant strokes, which stung and spread, and then promptly invited me to tea that afternoon, and played halma. I did not fully realise at the time that he was queer. Twenty years later he was told off by the Head for laziness and he committed suicide in that same room.

The second time I was caned was with four other boys by a master called Claud Salmon. I can't remember why, but I know the other boys told me to put an exercise book inside my trousers, which I did, and that poor blind "Claud" did not detect what I had done because I stuck my elbow out and took the three slashes on my arm. That afternoon I was batting for the Under 15 in a match and a boy fielding at slip (from another school) said, "Hey, you've got three stripes on your arm," and I said, "Yes, I've been made a sergeant." Claud Salmon is dead now.

These two episodes did not really affect me, unlike the third time I was caned. Some exeats I went to see Chelsea play football, very often with a boy called Porter. One exeat I had somehow got across a foppish prefect called Wells, a tousle-headed, bespectacled, unco-ordinated, budding priest who had played the ridiculous Cinna the poet in *Julius Caesar*. He had put me in Labour Squad, which normally meant hoeing weeds round the school, and very often in the Head's garden after afternoon classes were finished. (As in Zen, which later set me to hoe weeds in a temple garden, there was an element of weeding your own soul.) But as there was no Labour Squad during an exeat he made me change in and out of games clothes three times, and when I said I had an arrangement to meet Porter, who would be waiting for me on Woodford station, and to go to see Chelsea, he told me with malicious glee that I would be changing in and out of games clothes another twenty times. It was unjust and an abuse of power, but the system afforded no remedies; on an exeat there was no one to appeal to. I told him that for a would-be priest he lacked compassion, I called him a bully and a sadist, said "You're a slob, Wells," and went. I met Porter at Woodford, and we watched Chelsea play.

On the Monday, the Head Boy, who was then nicknamed Robbo (to rhyme with Yobbo) asked to see me, and told me in his yobspeak, "I'm goin' ter whack you 'cos yer cheeked Wells and didn't do what he said." Vainly I protested that Wells's punishment was unreasonable. Immediately all prefects took up positions military-style at either end of the passage outside the PR (Prefects Room) door and at different ends of the PR, I had to bend over a leather armchair, and Robbo ran at me three times and three times there was a tremendous crack and three stinging numbing pains and wheals marked my buttocks. When I emerged, trying to put a look of scorn and scathing contempt on my flushed face, the atmosphere was as if an execution had taken place. Crowds of curious boys had gathered and were held at a distance by prefects who had cordoned off the PR. When I was among them they surrounded me asking for the details: "How many?" "Did it hurt?" "Robbo's a yob." "Wells is a twit – and a slob." "It's not fair." For the rest of that day I was a hero. I do not know what became of Robbo; nothing much, for he never kept in touch with Chigwell afterwards. The effect of this episode led me to question and despise authority, which had shown it was unable to deal with its own abuse of power save by terrorist means analogous to capital punishment. And I have to record that the violence in no way changed my opinion of Wells.

It must have been about this time that the Pyramid Club swindle took place. Older boys persuaded younger boys to hand over sixpences and shillings and promised a never-ending profit for all, urging perpetual investment. In fact the Pyramid Club greatly rewarded the few organisers at the top while everyone else lost their money. The racket was stopped, but it taught us about life and Old Chigwellians still laugh about it, and I flatter myself that I can now spot a "Pyramid Club swindle" before I invest in it.

My mother had Continental au pairs to help with the four children. I can remember Michèle Maurel and Huguette (who were French), Lilian (who was Swiss) and Marty (who was German), and in September 1953 I went to France to stay with Michèle's family. I spent a couple of days in Paris, and remember sipping an ice cold coca cola late at night on the dark Champs Elysées, and then we went to their holiday home in the Calvados district of Normandy for a week. It was at a village called Le Home sur la Mère, near Cabourg, not far from the D-Day beaches. The house was almost on the beach, which was generally deserted, especially in the evenings, and there was half a mile of sand at low tide. To swim I had to wade miles before the water came up to my waist. It was hot but I played tennis a lot on the family's tennis court, and at supper our six course meal always began with the carrying in of an enormous tureen. On two evenings this was filled with sorrel, the reddish wild plant. Cooked, it looked like beans and I hated the taste, although I had to eat it. I borrowed a bicycle and cycled around the surrounding countryside, and went shrimping, and I spoke French all the time and became a Francophile, particularly relishing the lassitude after lunch when the family sat in deck chairs and did nothing until their digestive process was finished. The family drove me to Ouistreham, which had associations with the war, and to Caen, so I could see where Montgomery was bogged down after D-Day.

On Sunday 18th October 1953, when I was 14, Field Marshal Montgomery visited the school. About a dozen boys were approached to meet him after chapel, and I was one of these. In the course of the previous week "Gobi" Stott, who took us for Latin in BS1 (sitting under the bust of Archbishop Harsnett) and who later researched his *History of Chigwell School* in India, had set us Latin proses (translations from English into Latin) in which Caesar had to be rendered "Montegomerius". Monty sat on a wooden seat in mufti with his back to the chapel, looking across Top Field, while we gathered, and then we walked to New Hall. I remember Monty standing and addressing us in New Hall, with his back to the stage as we sat in a semi-circle. A thin, dartingly alive man with a pointed nose, he told us we were the nation's future leaders, and that as a commander of two million men in the last war he believed it was a commander's first duty to gain the trust and confidence of his men and demand integrity, courage and enthusiasm from them. "If you can win their hearts," he said, "then there is nothing you cannot do," and he told us the story of El Alamein and said, "And I went through the Germans at El Alamein," and he paused for effect and made a sawing movement with his right hand, "like a knife going through butter." (Many years later, wanting to know whether his victory at El Alamein could be attributed to the intelligence of Ultra rather than his own skill, I wrote to him on the strength of this occasion, and his housekeeper wrote back on Monty's behalf saying that I was welcome to visit him. Unfortunately he died just before I could make my visit.)

About this time my mother employed a local girl, Pam Humphreys (now Pam Giblett) to come in after school and bath the children and help with the washing-up. My brother Robert had entered an eisteddfod, and she asked, hands in the kitchen sink, "Did you get a good crit?" (She meant "criticism"). She was to write articles about me in the local newspaper.

In the spring and summer holidays of 1953 I had begun to write a novel. It was influenced by the radio programme *Journey into Space* and was first of all about a journey to the moon, and later to a planet called Holacanthus. It had a realistic beginning, and I researched details regarding the universe in the local library, where our next door neighbour Miss Attwood worked. She found me books and kept them for me, and I went in and spent hours reading them and taking notes. I filled several exercise books, and announced to my startled parents that one day I would be a writer. Having lived through the economic conditions of the 1930s, my parents wanted me to pass my exams and get a secure job. My father wanted me to do Law and go into a company like Shell, and then perhaps to go into politics. To my parents, writing was on a par with their music: to be done as a hobby, not as a living. Alarmed, they persuaded me to write to Capt. W. E. Johns, author of the Biggles books, on the strength of a chat I had had with him at the Schoolboys' Exhibition and ask his advice. In February 1954, well into my 'O' level year, he wrote back from Park House, Hampton Court: "I think you should get your exams over before you try writing a story. You can't do both at once." I took his advice. But my first juvenilia put me in touch with the universe, and began my thinking about the universe which continues to this day.

'O' level year was my third year of learning Greek, and we did Euripides' *Alcestis*, chunks of which I learned in the Greek. The History master, Oldfield, had advised us to buy G. O. Sayles's *The Medieval Foundations of England*, and my father gave me this book, inscribing it "for Christmas 1953". At the time I found it very turgid, but although I did not realise it then, it contained my spiritual foundations. The rest of the year was one of endless homeworks in Latin and Greek, History, French, Maths and English Language and Literature (trigonometry and gobbets), interrupted only by cricket and football matches and cross-country running in the spring term.

I remember our English master, Davenport, taking us for English in BS1, and reading out our latest essays for stylistic faults. "'I myself', " he read, and he interjected "that's Shillito – " and to this day I could not write "I myself". Then he said: "Haig's essay is vague. You know the advertisement which is in all the tube stations: 'Don't be vague, ask for Haig.' That's what Haig needs to remember, Don't be vague." And again, to this day I cannot come across an example of vagueness without thinking of that situation.

I ran in the Bean Cup and remember running through ploughed fields and frozen hoof-holes, five miles up hill and down dale past senior boys who wore headphones and talked into bulky ex-army walkie-talkies, occasionally walking hugging an acute stitch below the heart and then entering the gate to the last field between Vicarage Lane and the High Road and sprinting down a long narrow path lined with spectators to the tape where a master stood with a clipboard – and then collapsing onto the long grass, having come 11th on no training.

Billy Graham, the American Fundamentalist evangelist and friend of Eisenhower, made a crusade to Haringey between February and May 1954, and a party went from the Methodist church. At the end Billy Graham called "Come up, come up and be saved." As hundreds streamed towards the stage I knew I had to get up. Something had stirred in my soul. I did not know why, I just knew that the moment was significant. I went down to the front and was later seen by a helper, who was disappointed to know I already belonged to a church. Later I was seen by the Methodist Minister, Mr Grant, who thought me susceptible to the music without understanding that I had a fundamental craving for the eternal which this situation had somehow triggered.

'O' level was remarkable for an experience I had before I took the Greek Set Books paper on July 21st. I was not confident in my translations of Euripides *Alcestis* and Thucydides book 4, and the night before the exam I dreamt I saw the paper. I woke with the four passages still in my mind and hastily found them in the books and prepared them, and when I went into the exam and turned the paper it was as I had seen. All four passages were there. When I recounted this to my aunt Argie she told me she had had a similar experience when she took her London Matriculation in 1921. She had dreamt that she had seen the first two or three questions of her History paper, and had discussed them with a friend over breakfast and the questions were just as she had seen. My experience left me with a sense that the mind has powers we have barely begun to understand.

With 'O' level over, I returned to my writing. We had our annual holiday at Westgate, in a hotel on the front between Margate and Herne Bay. Several days were very wet, and the rain lashed in from the sea. There were high windows in the room my brother Robert and I shared, and I sat and wrote as the rain beat on the roof and lashed the windows, and I felt as peace as if I had contacted a future self. I believe it was here that my parents sat on the beach with the Salters, and I dug sandcastles with William, who later sent me a letter that included a brilliant drawing of "the latest fashion". We also visited Frinton in 1954, and it was at Walton-on-the-Naze that I bought an ice cream from a balding, bespectacled man standing in an ice cream booth on the beach, and someone said "That's Edgar Sanders, he was let out from behind the Iron Curtain. He was in the papers, arrested for spying." I went and got his autograph: E. Sanders. It was only recently that I found out what he did. He had been arrested in Hungary in 1949 for espionage and imprisoned in March 1952, when there was talk of his being exchanged for a Chinese woman, Lee Ming, until Churchill vetoed the exchange. Sanders was unconditionally released on 17th August 1953.

Later my brother and I stayed with my cousin Richard, who had moved from Folkestone to Merrow near Guildford. He lived at 31 Holford Road near the Downs. We often ran up to stretch of the Downs which formed a Golf Course at the end of the road. The first tee overlooked a kind of valley. There was rough down to the bottom and then a sloping fairway up to the green, and we spent hours playing there and walking to Newlands Corner, a local beauty spot. One early morning my uncle Reg took us out on the Downs to look for mushrooms. It was extremely misty and we found a lot of mushrooms, and there were a lot of rabbits. We came into breakfast hungry and cooked some of the mushrooms we had picked, and life was good.

CHILDHOOD AND SCHOOLDAYS

It was in the rough under the first tee that I had my first mystical experience. It was really a kind of pantheistic experience. It would have been in the summer of 1954, I suppose, on an immensely hot day. I had broken away from the others and I collapsed into the rough and lay among wild flowers and sedge under the blue sky and suddenly realised that everything around me was alive. There were azure blues and meadow browns in the rough all round me, and time stopped and I had a tremendous sense of the unity of the universe, which I can recall to this day, and which I have never forgotten.

Interpreting that experience now, I believe I saw Nature through my soul that day. Lying in the rough, I was still, I gazed with the eye of an embryonic poet and sensed a reality beyond the everyday mundane things. The universe was a place of great beauty, and it was thrillingly alive, full of crawling, flying things. I was taken back to a time I was surprised by frosty stars after having tea at Michael Rogers' house, 24 Ollards Grove, Loughton (where Mark Liell and Mabel Reid had previously lived), and awareness of physical beauty entered my life as if that day was – if not an awakening – then an early stirring of something within me. If I had to choose one moment to relive on my death bed, I would be quite content to let the timelessness in the rough typify my ideal relationship with the universe.

2.

UP TO OXFORD: AWAKENING TO DESTINY
1954 – 1958

Soon afterwards I went to Stratford-upon-Avon for a few days and saw *Othello*. I went alone and, being somewhat shy, welcomed my own company. I stayed with a friend of my mother's who went to work, and I had to stay out all day. I visited Shakespeare's birthplace and Ann Hathaway's cottage and spent many hours sitting near the Avon. I had passed my 'O' levels and had got 89% for English Literature, which consisted of Chaucer's *Prologue* and *Macbeth* (which I virtually knew by heart), and I was hoping to study English Literature for 'A' level. But in June I had collected the form prize for the year, and the Headmaster, Mr Thompson, wanted me for his classical sixth, and my wish to read the poets – which I knew within myself I had to – was overruled.

Wanting me to do Law, my father had persuaded me to have James's *Introduction to English Law* as my prize. He talked of getting me articled to London solicitors, and the next two years of 'A' level immersed me in Latin, Greek and Ancient History, which I loved. I had a very good classical education. We sat in the library (now called the Swallow Room) at a long table under the dome in chairs with mitres on their backs, seated on frayed blue cushions whose scrapes each time we moved echoed up into the dome. We read a lot of Plato, and thought about his invisible reality or being, "to on", which made me want to be a philosopher, and we sometimes had classes in the room adjoining the Tuck Shop, over the door of which a notice in Greek read "phrontisterion", "thinking-shop", and another notice in Greek "meden agan", "nothing too much", a saying attributed to Solon which held up the Aristotelian mean. (These exhortations and examples have since been removed, which is a great pity.) In the library we read some of the *New Testament* in Greek. We read the epic poets Homer and Virgil, and the poetic dramatists Aeschylus, Sophocles (*Oedipus Tyrannus*) and Euripides. The poets Ovid, Horace and Catullus I had already encountered, and the materialist philosophers Democritus and Lucretius. We read Tacitus and Thucydides, two wonderful historians who made me want to be a historian, and we covered the history of Greece to just after the Peloponnesian war and the history of Rome to the end of the Republic, and I began thinking about military and political systems, reactionaries and revolutionaries, the causes of wars and the conflicts between Rome and Carthage, Athens and Sparta. I related these conflicts to the First and Second World Wars and to the British Empire under Churchill (who was Prime Minister until April 1955). Soon I had gone back into prehistory and was making my own maps of sites in Minoan Crete. We were all taken to hear a live lecture in London by Michael Ventris on the Minoan script Linear B. I read the Greek myths and spent weekends making charts of all the Greek gods and of the Roman emperors, and the idea took hold that I should become an archaeologist, and write about ancient civilisations.

For pleasure I read Robert Graves and first became half-aware that I possessed strange powers. Standing in the dining-hall I described how much I was enjoying *I, Claudius* and *Claudius the God*. The glass tumblers for our water were by our laid places, and one suddenly exploded, disintegrating into tiny pieces, and a boy opposite me said very excitedly to me, "It was your voice that did that. Voices can penetrate glass if they resonate in the right way."

It must have been in the summer of 1955 – although it may have been the previous year – when I was given an original Tutankhamun figurine and effigies of various Egyptian gods. One of the Chigwell Latin and Greek masters was George Harvey Webb ("Spider" Webb), and in his slow and deliberate voice he used to tell us to carry a book with us wherever we went: "You can read all Latin and Greek literature in the original on the top of buses." ("If you do not stop this persistent ragging about," he used to say when we were younger, "I shall have to resort to the old expedient of keeping you in after school.") He never prepared his lessons and heard our prepared translations unseen but he always knew the meanings of the most difficult words. He was an eccentric of great ability who carried a book by Wilamovitz, a textual scholar in Greek, in his pocket, and he enlivened treble Latin on Wednesday mornings by discussing French Existentialism and some of his exploits. He claimed to have done everything conceivable, including walking into Buckingham Palace in German uniform during the war to test the security of the system. He reached the first floor before he was challenged, or was it the King's bedroom? He also claimed at different times to have been a monk in Armenia and a Romanian spy, and got our imaginations going, made us think of unlikely careers in monasteries or espionage. A few years previously he had married a millionairess ice dancer and had got through £2 million. The fortune was finally exhausted because he bought a boat from George Dawson. He had to attend a staff meeting and sent a 6th former to the auction, who bought the wrong boat. He then lived in a caravan in the school grounds. Soon afterwards he left Chigwell to play the fiddle in Brendan Behan's *The Hostage* at Joan Littlewood's Stratford theatre for £10 a week. (I had a drink with him and Joan Littlewood after the performance I saw.) Later he taught at Harry H. Corbett's E15 Acting School.

He kept the bookloft and rooting round for classical texts I came across a glass case of Egyptian figurines, and said "Sir, do you want these?" "No," he said, "they have Tutankhamun's curse on them. They came from Tutankhamun's tomb. When I was in Egypt in 1922 I took them from Howard Carter when he wasn't looking" (I recalled how Howard Carter's dentist brother had told me stories about Tutankhamun) "and they have brought me nothing but ill luck. If you are not superstitious you can have them." And saying "Oh, thank you sir" I ran with them down the stairs and across the school to the cycle shed and put them in my saddlebag and later cycled home with them. What I had was a perfect wooden shawabti of Tutankhamun, two wooden effigies of gods (one Horus) and many small figures of gods with animal heads and a figure of Osiris. Some years later I

45

took Tutankhamun to the British Museum and the expert there pronounced it genuine but said the crucial lettering had rubbed off the bitumen at the back. Now, I made lists of all the Egyptian pharaohs as well.

Between 1953 and 1956 Loughton became more urbanised, and from our garden, at weekends when I was cutting the lime-tree branches and twiglets with the long-arm – Journey's End had a screen of lime-trees in front of it – groups of Teddy boys would walk past with their spivvy hair styles and drainpipe trousers, making their way from the station to the cinema in the High Road, and increasingly their loud cat-calls disturbed the weekend silence.

In the summer holidays we spent hot golden afternoons lying in our bathing costumes on a rug on the lawn under the pear tree. Sometimes the tin bath tub with handles would be filled with water and little Frances would splash in it. Once I remember Frances sitting in the kitchen drain in her bathing costume, playing with a live wasp. There were always windfalls on the grass, and therefore wasps, and sometimes the tin bath was used to collect apples and pears, which were stored without touching on the shelves in the cellars, which were dark and forbidding and full of exciting things.

That summer I made my debut as a club cricketer. I joined Buckhurst Hill Cricket Club in June 1955. I was proposed by a neighbour, B. D. Rhodes and seconded by Alan Lavers, the ex-Essex cricketer who was 1st XI captain. Soon afterwards I was invited to play for Alan Lavers' XI against Loughton on the Thursday of Loughton's cricket week. There was a huge crowd, with people sitting five deep all round the ground as happened frequently in those pre-television days, and Loughton batted first on a sweltering day and made over 200. We went in just before tea and almost immediately were 4 for 2. I batted no. 4. A fast bowler called John Holmear charged in down the slope and I hit him for a boundary, and there was applause all round the ground. He charged in again, the ball whistled towards me, and trying to deflect it to leg I spooned a catch which, diving, he took brilliantly to thunderous applause. I was out. Alan Lavers later typically saved the day with a hard-hitting 73 not out, batting in the later stages of his innings with Mr Macy, husband of one of my sometime employees. Later we socialised with the other side, and the captains walked round with jugs of beer. Alan Lavers said firmly, "Nicholas, you should have a shandy." It was my first taste of shandy. I played two or three games for the 3rd XI after that, and then played no more cricket that season.

My adolescent shyness had grown into a (pre-poetic) sensitivity, and I was now most at my ease when I lived in the past. In the summer of 1955 we went via Stonehenge to Exeter, where we stayed at the Great Western Hotel, and then had our annual holiday near St. Michael's Mount, staying at a house called Trevarthian, which has since been turned into flats. My brother and I slept in the large book-lined room that opened onto the veranda and looked onto a lawn with small palm trees; it was a library, and for my bedtime reading I found a book on Marshal Voroshilov and the Communist Revolution. I hired a bicycle, and went off into the narrow Cornish lanes and found a megalithic chamber tomb in a deserted field. I parked my bike, climbed a stile, found the entrance and entered the tomb and suddenly my archaeological interests had extended to British prehistory, and I cycled round the Cornish lanes with an ordnance survey map looking for every stone circle or ancient monument I could find, and tried to imagine the people who built them. My parents would sit on the beach opposite St. Michael's Mount, and I would appear at lunchtime for our picnic and at suppertime for our evening meal, but otherwise I roamed through Nature and steeped myself in the past.

That winter I tried to take my youngest brother Jonathan to see Bolton (his favourite team) play at Fulham, but the match was fogged off. We arrived before this was known and I can now see, standing behind a goal, the fog closing in on the centre circle so we could not see the other end. To compensate for his disappointment I took him to the British Museum and showed him some of the treasures of past civilisations. The British Museum was a typical place for me to go at that time.

Soon I was writing letters to the Archaeological Correspondent of the *Times* about Troy (he replied at length) and to the British School at Athens, who invited me to hear Sinclair Hood on the excavations at Knossos, with Sir Mortimer Wheeler in the chair. From the audience Leonard Cottrell asked a question and made a comment and I wondered at being so close to the author of *The Bull of Minos*. Through the Council for British Archaeology I subscribed to the Calendar of Excavations and was invited to join a dig at Chester.

And so in April 1956 I took the train from Euston to Chester and stayed in a hotel in Chester's Bridge Street and joined an excavation in its second week. Two narrow trenches were already dug, and I was given a trowel and a brush and, squatting uncomfortably in the bottom of each trench in turn between bits of Roman brick, probed and prised and gouged and found a lot of Roman tiles and several Roman nails. Soon the other volunteers were asked to start a third trench, and I worked with them while they ran into a belt of glass in a medieval robbers' trench (an area where medieval robbers had destroyed Roman remains and left their own coloured glass). The digging was beginning to pall, and was, quite frankly, becoming boring, and I was already disenchanted when the Curator of the Grosvenor Museum slipped while clambering between trenches and knocked down half of two Roman buttresses I had dug out. Then, in the course of taking photographs, the experts pronounced that I had been squatting in a cloaca – a Roman sewer – and that the tiles and nails had been thrown down there deliberately to get rid of them. The idea that I had been excavating a sewer did not appeal, and I rapidly lost interest in the dig – and in becoming an archaeologist.

The next day I was "unwell" and spent the morning by the River Dee. The weather was glorious, the sun shone, there was a blue sky and the weir frothed while I lay on the bank. In the afternoon I took a bus to Llangollen through beautiful moorland scenery. I came home early and (my interest in the USSR having been stirred by the book on the Voroshilov I had found in Cornwall) went straight from Euston to Downing Street where I saw the new leaders of the Soviet Union, Bulganin and Krushchev, arrive for a meeting with Eden, who had just taken over from Churchill as Prime Minister. By the time I observed the round, ebullient, balding Krushchev and the gravely bearded, white-haired Bulganin outside no. 10 I had somehow ceased to consider archaeology as a career and had taken up a new interest in politics.

This new interest was semi-dormant during the summer term as I worked hard revising for my 'A' level exams. In February my brother Robert, after months of unquenchable thirst when he would run to the kitchen tap and drink two or three glasses of cold water, was diagnosed a diabetic, and after being stabilised and put on insulin he was learning to cope with a diet that involved weighing portions of food on a small set of scales. My parents had lost six children and this was a further blow, and my father in particular became more melancholy and stoical. My one relief was cricket. I played for the school 1st eleven, under the captaincy of Alan Hurd (who later played for Essex and for the Gentlemen of England against Australia). I had some good innings: 48 against Eltham, which I cannot remember at all; and 42 against the Headmaster's XI. I remember this knock as it was a brilliant day with a blue sky, and Alan Lavers, who had seconded me for Buckhurst Hill, was bowling. Sometimes when I went out to bat I just felt I would do badly, and I did. Sometimes I went out knowing I would do well, and I did. And this was on one of those days I felt confident. I thrashed Lavers to the boundary twice in an over, and after the second four he stood arms akimbo in the middle of the pitch and said, "Nicholas, you can't do that, that was a good length ball." I said, "I've done it, and watch out or I'll do it again." But my best innings of the season was by far and away the 27 I scored at Bancroft's on their dismal, drizzly Visitation Day. Bancroft's made 109 and I opened the batting for Chigwell, and I could not put a foot wrong, I felt almost godlike. Wickets fell the other end, and we were 65-6 at the close. Each run of my 27 was middled and struck firmly, and I could have had double that score but for brilliant fielding.

To this day I believe cricket is an excellent training for life. It teaches one to approach problems with the right temperament, to block several situations and then to progress when there is a loose delivery. It is extremely satisfying when no opportunity to score is lost, as I found that afternoon at Bancroft's.

My new interest in politics coincided with Suez. On 26th July 1956 Nasser seized the Suez Canal, and throughout the coming months it seemed I might be called up for impending military action.

It is easy to think of fighting when you are in uniform. Every Monday for two or three years I had taken part in the Combined Cadet Force, wearing itchy khaki, belt and gaiters and parading with a rifle, and had risen to be a Lance-Corporal. The company commander in those days was Colin Murrant, who later married Alan Lavers' daughter – who is now an employee of mine. I found the CCF fairly boring, and can recall classroom sessions on how to strip a bren gun, lessons brilliantly caught by Henry Reed in his poem *Lessons of the War* which begins "Today we have naming of parts." I was in Signals, and for Cert A had to learn about the handset (Don Mark V). The annual corps camp that August was at Castlemartin, near Pembroke in South Wales. I remember it was extremely wet to begin with, and we walked on, and slept on, duckboards. We were on a hill and the water poured underneath our duckboards as we tried to sleep, oozing up between the wooden slats and soaking us. We walked to the NAAFI tent for our breakfast and collected a packed lunch and then we went out into the countryside and fought a never-ending war, occasionally ducking along hedgerows, moving in on the enemy (the other side), and firing blanks at them but usually digging ourselves in and making as little contact with the enemy as the British troops made with the Germans in the Great War. At one point we dug ourselves in near an orchard where there were a lot of crabapple trees and windfalls, and we balanced crabapples on the end of our rifles and fired them in the air and they rose in a parabola and rained around Capt. Taylor, the officer in charge of us, who took a dim view of our bored antics.

I soon tired of these war games, and the first sunny day I reported for my sandwiches and then gave my platoon the slip and went absent without leave. Doubling up, I ran along a hedgerow, my rifle in one hand and my packed lunch in the other, and dodged the cross-fire between both sides and at the end of a valley ran up a hill to safety and eventually, as I had intended, I came out on top of cliffs about 200 feet high, where I was safe from all sniper fire, and saw the sparkling blue sea beneath me, and Stack Rocks. I tore off my tie and my itchy shirt, tugged off my boots and gaiters and my khaki trousers and collapsed in my pants on the springy turf and spent an idyllic day sunbathing, gazing across the Rocks beneath me at the sea, and eating my sandwiches. I felt at one with Nature, and it was only towards sundown that I reluctantly put my itchy clothes back on and threaded my way back through the closing stages of the battle to my platoon, in time to march home.

A fortnight later I was back in Wales as our annual holiday was at Llandudno. We stayed at the Hydro Hotel, and each evening, after the excursions – when my brother and I walked up and down Snowdon, where "it rained once and a mist blew up once", and we all drove to Conway Castle and across the Menai Bridge to Anglesey – I would sit in the Hotel's glass veranda and make maps and drawings of Roman ruins and take cuttings about Suez from the paper and stick them in a book of press clippings. I had a complete record of the Suez crisis, and I used to say, "If I'm going to be drafted, I want to know what I'm dying for." I felt I was moving in my uncle Tom's footsteps, and that just as he had joined the RFC and been killed so it was possible that I would be called up to fight against Nasser.

While in Llandudno I heard that I had passed my 3 'A' levels. I had done sufficiently well to have a County Major Scholarship if I passed the entrance exam into a university (the system then).

My growing interest in politics led me to write to our MP, John Biggs-Davison, to ask for a ticket to one of the Suez debates, and Biggs-Davison (a free right wing spirit who was to become known as a Suez rebel) replied and later sent me a Strangers' Gallery ticket for the debate on September 12th, when Eden unveiled a three-power plan for a Suez Users' Association. It was the beginning of the collusion which led to the Suez debacle, and Nasser swiftly described it as a provocation. I was completely absorbed. I can still see Eden, tall, grey and elegant, standing at the despatch box, speaking (it seemed) for approaching an hour to a packed House, and Gaitskell replying, and later I went into the corridor and found groups of MPs debating heatedly. I interjected in one group and found myself the focal point of attention. "If you kick someone's ankle often enough they will retaliate," I said. "That's not a fair parallel," snapped a grey-haired Labour MP. And I was attacked and defended by people speaking at the same time, heatedly shouting each other down, and I came away feeling involved, a participant, I had made contact with our leaders.

From Loughton Methodist church pulpit, the Minister, a dour, severe northerner, Mr Grant, who had a parting down the middle and spectacles, preached sermon after sermon on the wickedness of the Government's Suez policy. His sermons were more political than religious, and, angry at his one-sidedness, I wrote a letter saying so and refuting his position, and sent it to the local paper, *The Gazette*, under the pseudonym Tiberius. The letter was printed very prominently, my parents were mildly horrified – my father said "It's always a mistake to rush into print" – and poor Mr Grant suffered what almost amounted to a nervous breakdown and left the district soon afterwards.

At the end of October Israel marched on Egypt, and in early November Anglo-French forces bombarded Suez. Soon afterwards the Chigwell Debating Society had a debate on Suez. The Chigwell Debating Society is reputed to have had a higher standard than the Oxford Union in the 1940s and early 1950s, when budding Professors like John Boardman and Bernard Williams took part. It still had a high standard, and I proposed the motion for the Government, and John Ezard (later of the *Guardian*) spoke against the Government. The debate was held in the library, which was packed, and I mustered the most support (including support from the Head Boy, David Senton) and won. I cycled home with John Ezard afterwards, and so began a life-long friendship, despite our conflicting political attitudes.

Following the failure of the Hungarian Uprising in November 1956 a party of Hungarian refugees was brought to Grange Farm, next to Chigwell School, for temporary accommodation, and I remember standing with other boys and watching as one Hungarian, a young man in his 20s dressed in shabby clothes, put his hand in his pocket and held out a handful of Hungarian coins for us to have, as they were no longer any good to him. I took one.

About this time my father got me on the count for local and general elections. The count took place in a polling booth hall, and I was generally paired with Mr Digweed, the undertaker, and we sat and made piles of crosses while the candidates toured with rosettes, anxiously comparing the height of our piles.

To make my newly diabetic brother's lot more pleasant my parents acquired a black and white television in the autumn of 1956. The family watched it in the dark while I worked upstairs in my room, and I went downstairs and joined them about 10.30 p.m. Most of the programmes were police files like *Dragnet* and game shows hosted by the likes of Michael Miles, and there were Tommy Trinder and Jerry Desmonde at the Palladium, and the adverts had jingles such as "Omo adds brightness". But once all the Angry Young Men were interviewed together down a long table, including Colin Wilson, Stuart Holroyd and Ken Tynan.

A boy at school, Pagan (now the Rev. Keith Pagan) was extremely interested in the activities of Sir Oswald Mosley and his Union Party which anticipated a United States of Europe. He was fascinated by our British mini-Hitler, and when he found out that Mosley was to speak in Trafalgar Square he persuaded several of us to go and hear him. Mosley's supporters wore black shirts in the 1930s, but now they wore white shirts and beat drums, and we stood under Mosley who wore a suit and addressed us from a plinth on a policy which is now the policy of the Conservative government (i.e. support for the Maastricht treaty).

That winter every weekend my brother and I repaired to the sitting-room on our own and at 7.30 we listened to Victor Sylvester's ballroom dancing (generally a selection of waltzes and foxtrots) and I did enormous family trees on scrolls of all the Roman Emperors and all the Greek gods and heroes, and made several maps and drawings of Mycenae and of Minoan sites in Crete. In the course of these evenings I found a mistake in Robert Graves's *Greek Myths*, a reference to Diomedes at the time of the Trojan War and again several hundred years later. I showed it to Webb outside the Chigwell Staff Room one break, thinking I had misunderstood, and he roared with laughter. "He makes it up," he said, "he's bound to make mistakes." My faith in books was severely shaken by this episode, and after that I was wary, wondering if the author had got it right, and accepted nothing uncritically.

In December I went up to Oxford and took the entrance exam in classics for a cluster of colleges that included Worcester College with a view to reading Law (at my father's wish). The one consolation was that I might go into politics. We had papers morning and afternoon, with interviews some evenings, for four days. There were 100 of us, sitting for 4 places, and many were from schools like Eton and looked very confident and sophisticated, and I thought I had no chance. We sat in a dingy room with high windows, and in the general paper there was a question on the political parties, which I answered with my new-found enthusiasm. On the Friday evening there was a viva voce with the Provost and several dons. The Provost was Sir John Masterman, a gaunt, gentle, slow, deliberate, elderly Edwardian with brushed back hair and 1910 cricket fields in his face, and I was asked my hobbies. "Collecting Roman and Greek coins," I said. "Oh," said the Senior Tutor, A. N. Bryan-Brown, who was Public Orator and made speeches in Latin on official occasions, a tall, balding man with wispy grey hair round his ears, "and what do you know about the coins of Corinth?" Some years earlier I had actually swapped – my recollection is that it was for a sweet and a biscuit, his that it was for a fossil, an ammonite – a coin from Corinth which David Hoppit (later property correspondent of the *Daily Telegraph*) owned, and I described how it had a horse on the back. "It can't" said Bryan-Brown. "Well," I said, "it has – I've got it." And there was attentive (and admiring) amusement from the other side of the table. (Around 1989 Hoppit had me to dinner and said: "I had a coin from Corinth which I stupidly swapped. I want it back." I said: "It was a lovely sweet, and nothing can undo the sacrifice I made by not eating it, not even the possession of your coin – which incidentally got me into Oxford.") I am sure that the Corinthian coin was a detail by which they remembered me, and which made me stand out after the event from the other 100 young men.

Having heard that I had got into Oxford, but would have to wait a year and a half before going up, my father was anxious that I should commence legal articles, and it was arranged that I would leave school at Easter. I could not wait to leave school, which had suddenly palled. During the spring term of 1957 I felt unmotivated. The Oxford comment on my Latin prose was "patches of purple", which Thompson read out under the dome, and everyone laughed. I knew my classics would never be more than patches of purple prose, and having achieved my goal I lost all inclination to improve on my performance. I wanted freedom. We post-Oxford entrance classicists were encouraged to attend lessons in English Literature, and during those last few weeks I read Donne and Coleridge, and suddenly, with stunning abruptness, the enthusiasm I had had for Literature over two years previously returned. I remember sitting on a garden seat in Lower Field one gloriously sunny morning in March as my school days were drawing to a close. For pleasure I was reading the *Faber Book of Modern Verse*, and reading Hopkins' *Wreck of the Deutschland* I thrilled to the language and took my eye off the book in the warm sun and knew that I was going to be a poet.

I slipped away from Chigwell just as I had slipped away from the war games at corps camp. I withdrew without anyone noticing I had gone. Soon afterwards I went to Italy, a holiday I had planned for a long time. I youth-hostelled with David Hoppit, who wore shorts and an enormous rucksack. I had planned where to go. We went to Rome and saw all the ruins and the catacombs and the Sistine Chapel, and went to Horace's villa at Licenza in the Sabine Hills about 22 miles NE of Rome and I found his "fons Bandusiae" or spring nearby and dipped my hands in the limpidly clear stream and sipped the water and imagined Maecenas giving him this estate in the mid-30s BC. Then we went to Naples and visited Pompeii and Herculaneum and climbed Mt Vesuvius. (On the way down, striding and skidding down through the powdery ash, I fell off. I flew through the air and landed on my arms, grazing my elbows.) We went to Sorrento and Capri. Then we got a pilgrims' ticket to Sicily. This was especially cheap and required us to visit the weeping madonna in Syracuse as pilgrims. On the way to Sicily we got off at Paestum to see the Greek temple, and I was desperately ill. We were on our own and had to wait at least a day until my retching had stopped. In Syracuse we stared with repelled curiosity at the wax-like face of the statue of the Virgin Mary which was reputed to have shed actual tears, and then got our pilgrims' ticket stamped by a man who sat at a table near the cathedral door. We had a wonderful time in Catania, and went to the Blue Grotto and saw Etna erupt the day after we went up it. Lorenzo, the warden of the Catania Youth Hostel, swam with us – I got sea urchins' spikes in the soles of my feet – and then he took us out in a small rowing boat, and I remember him at dusk, singing on the silky, silver-blue water, "Santa Nucia" as Etna spurted red behind his balding head. We returned to Rome, where David Hoppit saw a group of girls from a convent school standing outside a cathedral, and went and talked to them, and met the lady who is now his wife. (His coin changed my life, and my itinerary changed his life.)

I was steeped in Roman and Greek ruins, but it was the literary echoes that fascinated me most: the Spanish steps and the house where Keats lived, and Keats' tomb near Ostia with its sad inscription about his own transience: "Here lies one whose name was writ in water." While in Sicily I spent a whole afternoon sitting by the sea, watching the waves come in and repeating Keats's "It keeps eternal whisperings around", I looked at the blue Mediterranean and sensed the ghosts of Shelley and Byron.

When I got back to Essex, my father put me in Mark Liell's office in Attwater and Liell for a week to see if I liked the Law. I spent a week observing the work Mark Liell did and found it boring, I read Chester Wilmot's *Struggle for Europe* in every available moment while Mark Liell sat hunched over his desk, his back towards me. At one point he asked what I was reading, and I showed him. He said, "Not bad." I did not enthuse about the Law, but more importantly, from my father's point of view I did not say it was impossible, and in the course of May and June Articles were arranged with a London firm.

I had to fill in time before beginning in the Law, and I took a job near Loughton bus garage, making motorcycle sidecars for a couple of months. It earned me 3/- an hour, and I was with a small firm of about ten working class people in a corrugated hangar. I hated it, I had nothing in common with any of the people there, although they were mostly very decent towards me. From 8 a.m. to 5 p.m. I sawed struts of wood and riveted them together and passed them on to an older man called Joe who hammered metal round them. That June was baking and the heat on the corrugated iron roof was unbearable. The whole set-up was my idea of hell. At morning break, lunch break and tea breaks I read a few snatches of Keats and Shelley, but it was hard to be alone and Music While You Work was on the radio all day.

The one thing that kept me going was cricket. I played for Buckhurst Hill 1st eleven under Alan Lavers. Our opening game was at Westcliff, who had Harold Crabtree and Colin Griffiths, two county bowlers. I had a dream debut. Buckhurst Hill batted first, and out of our 121-7 I scored 40, the highest score, sharing a partnership with Alan Lavers. Westcliff beat us by 6 wickets, but my place was guaranteed throughout that season. Buckhurst Hill now wanted me to play cricket on Sundays. I agreed, and came into conflict with my mother, who as the granddaughter of a Methodist Minister had been brought up with strict Lord's Day Observance, which meant following the Puritan Sunday and abstaining (among other things) from organised games. Although she begged me not to play, I answered her objections and went ahead. My season ended during cricket week in August, when, watched by Alan Hurd on the boundary, Tony Durley (an Essex player) and I had a long partnership of over a 100, he scoring 85 and I scoring 31, which nearly saved the game for Buckhurst Hill. But not all my innings were that glorious. Generally after my innings was over I would sit in the pavilion, half-looking at the cricket, and read Keats, Shelley and Byron, and Alan Lavers once or twice suggested that I should not be reading poetry but should be concentrating on my team-mates' performance at the wicket. (Later I read with delight that J. M. Brearley, captain of

England, read Tolstoy on one occasion after an early dismissal, apparently without being told off. My boundary reading was of course putting my Chigwell classics master Webb's advice into practice, that I should carry a book in my pocket at all times.)

It was a tremendous relief to leave the motorcycle sidecar factory at the end of June. I started my articles with Gregory, Rowcliffe and Co. at 1 Bedford Row, London WC1, travelling by tube. I received no pay; on the contrary, my father had to pay 200 guineas a year so that I could be a free office boy for the firm, as it were. The Georgian building in Bedford Row was grimy in those days, with windows that had never been cleaned. There were six partners, and I was articled to Francis Brickdale but spent my time with Peter Pierrepont (who died in 1989). I sat at a desk and he dictated letters and called "Miss Watts" to bring his secretary running from the next room, and flicked rubber bands about his office and was irreverent about the Law. He had a domed head and spectacles and a pleasing smile. Opposite me sat a Mr Marsh, who wore spectacles and had stick-out teeth. He said nothing all day, burying himself in immensely lengthy tax computations, but when tea arrived he would say, "Ah, tea, delicious tea," always the same words. Elsewhere the office was full of creatures from another age: deaf old Dorrit could have been Dickensian, and there were two other old men in the Ledger Department, and Bob the fetal office boy (who got paid) had a twisted grin. The Law I did was incredibly tedious. It was wills and marriage settlements and estates. It was all to do with tidying up after death. Clients would ring up, some of them Lords, and sometimes I would take messages. Sometimes I was an errand boy to counsel. The way of life of the clients had nothing to do with the Literature I was discovering: John Osborne and Samuel Beckett, Hemingway and Milton. I hated it. I toyed with writing a play: I began one called *Syme in his Window* and another called *Pachomius*, which was about a flood that wiped out a community of desert mystics. (The idea came from nowhere, and I half-wonder now if it was a far memory.) I still read. And when I came home by tube, reading Hemingway or Milton, and went to my room, I felt discontented, trapped in a subject I did not want to do.

During the evenings and the weekends of the summer of 1957 I learned to drive on my aunt Argie's Mayflower. My aunt and my mother took it in turns to accompany me as I drove up Tycehurst Hill and down Spareleaze Hill. Eventually in September I took my test on my father's A70. The test was in Brentwood. To acclimatise me my Aunt had driven me all round Brentwood but I had to drive myself there. The A70 was a powerful car and I was slightly late. I drove at 70 mph, and during my test found it very hard to keep below 30 mph "If you exceed the speed limit once more," the examiner said, "I will fail you." I then turned a corner very slowly as a cyclist went straight on and swerved to avoid me and fell off. The examiner reckoned it was the cyclist's fault and I passed.

One late summer evening, when there was a glorious sunset that washed through the windows and bathed the floor, I was making my usual weekly visit to Loughton library, which was then in Brook Road, in a building since demolished. Suddenly, standing between shelves, I saw my own shadow and I had a glimpse of my future, of the person I might become, a giant out in the future, to whose wisdom I had to ascend, and with whom I would be united if I created myself, or recreated myself, along Existentialist lines. It was a moment in which I was aware of my destiny, of what I had to work towards and will into being, and it left a profound effect on me.

One evening, waiting at Chancery Lane station for a tube, I saw a poster: PHILOSOPHY. It advertised a course of lectures at the London School of Economic Science in the Haymarket. I was moved to take the telephone number, and I spoke to them the next day and enrolled. It was a course of 12 lectures in practical philosophy or wisdom, in what is now known to be the Advaita system (Non-dualism, founded by Sankara): the Indian road to enlightenment. The same lecture was repeated every night of the week, very often with a different lecturer, and from the outset there was a strong emphasis on practical or experiential wisdom and the *Upanisads*, and the whole ethos was semi-Gurdjieffian. Much was made of the need for greater awareness and attention, and we were set exercises to heighten our awareness during the coming week.

About the second week I went to the Haymarket coffee-bar to kill time before the lecture began, and on the table in front of me saw a printed card about a forthcoming visit Colin Wilson was making to the Fleet Street coffee-bar, where he used to be a washer-up. I had read about *The Outsider*, and now *Religion and the Rebel* was about to come out. I went alone to hear him one evening after work. There were probably 50 standing in a small area, and there was a leather chair on which he stood. Young, wearing thin spectacles and a polo-necked sweater, he was so assured, so inwardly confident, not nervous at all. He had read everything and he could not have been much older than 25. After his message about how our civilisation was in spiritual decay, someone asked him, "What's your view of how life began?" He replied, "I see it as breaking through like a leak in a dam." "Isn't that naive?" "Well, if it's naive then Shaw and T. E. Hulme and Bergson held that view and so they're naive." And then he was onto the next question, riding the criticism with considerable aplomb.

I was most impressed. Here was a new kind of god. This was better than Denis Compton or Roy Bentley, this was a real life Shelley, and I knew that one day I would know him, and stay with him, and be as assured about the universe as he was. He was outside all disciplines, he was a role model: a writer who reflected on the meaning of life. He declared, "I think of myself as a genius," and he made the idea of genius accessible, and attainable in the present rather than a quality to be found only in the dead.

That evening my awakening was complete, and my inner growth was now continuous. The next day I went to Holborn library at lunch time and Loughton library in the evening and I borrowed books by a number of the authors Colin Wilson had mentioned. The practical philosophy lectures took on added importance, and soon my bedroom was filled with books. I was now reading *The Outsider* and many of the books referred to in it. One Saturday afternoon John Ezard called to see if I would go for a walk in the Forest. He was shown up to my bedroom, and he surveyed the books on the counterpaned bed and said, "Do you realise you've got the best books of

A MYSTIC WAY

Western civilisation here?" There were about 20 books, including Dante, Shakespeare, Kierkegaard, Dostoevsky, Blake, Hesse, Goethe, Camus, Sartre and Eliot; the *Bhagavadgita*, the *Upanisads* and the Bible. We walked in the Forest and discussed our reading, and he threw in new books I had not come across, such as Yeats and O'Neill. I took Eliot's *Selected Poems* with me on the tube and read it until the cover nearly fell off, and then I went to Loughton library and found books on what the poems meant and I read them. On one of my visits to the library my father accompanied me, hopping and limping along Brook Road with his brown-orange stick, and I remember explaining on the way home that I had chosen Joad's *God and Evil* because "the most important thing in life is to know why we're here".

That autumn and winter, my room at the firm of solicitors became a kind of reading room. I was moved down to the Trust Department next to Mr Rowcliffe's front-facing room ("the holy of holies") where the completely bald, moustached senior partner sat motionless at a leather desk, a cigarette between his lips with an inch of drooping ash which trembled each time he gave a quiet cough and signed letters until his incredibly poised and elegant secretary, Miss Watts, announced that his taxi had arrived. In my large room at the back I sat at a desk near three managing clerks. I was in front of Mr Sidney Davis, who dictated letters fluently, hand-clicking a dictaphone. A blotchy, red-headed drunkard called Smith was opposite me, and Janes, who played truant to play minor counties cricket for Buckinghamshire or Bedfordshire, sat behind Smith. (Janes got away with it until he made 141 not out and was banner headlines on the back page of the *Evening News*, which Mr Rowcliffe read. Janes was called in and given a very severe warning.) Much of my time was spent in dipping into the books I had found. From Holborn library I found William James's *The Varieties of Religious Experience* and Pascal. From Loughton library, Tolstoy and Mann. At a time when English Literature was turning provincial I had opened fully to the Continental influences, and had little time for the Law. In the train home I read T E. Hulme and Bergson. In the long winter evenings, sitting in front of the gas fire in my bedroom, I read the four main novels by Dostoevsky: *Crime and Punishment, The Brothers Karamazov, The Possessed* and *The Idiot*; and I lived Raskolnikov, Ivan, Stavrogin, Kirilov and Mishkyn.

One Saturday afternoon shortly before Christmas John Ezard took me to see a matinée of a pantomime in Ilford with Ken Campbell, who had just won a school essay prize for an essay on O'Neill. The play was knockabout, but afterwards we went back with the director and main actor, a man called Jimmy who lived in a converted signal box. We sat on the floor near various levers which had survived the conversion, and I remember Jimmy saying that according to F. C. Lucas the three key concepts of criticism were taste, discrimination and judgement. (Campbell has since become an actor and director.) Shortly afterwards the three of us went up to London and found the Partisan coffee-bar and played chess there on the chequered tables. Just to sit in the Partisan was to make an Angry statement, and to appear an Angry Young Man.

One afternoon Ezard called on me and we walked to the nearby house of

Alex Comfort, whom he knew, and I met the lean, bespectacled poet who extended a withered arm and hand, which I shook. We sat with his son, a short-trousered boy, and watched *Quatermass* on black-and-white television, during which his wife appeared. Later Comfort left home and later still wrote *The Joy of Sex*.

The lunchtimes when I did not go to Holborn library I went to Lincoln's Inn Fields and listened to the speakers at the mini-Speakers' Corner there. Sometimes Allen and Drabble, two of the three other articled clerks in my firm, would walk by. They wore pin-stripes and bowler hats, unlike me, and looked down their noses at me for listening to the arguments from the soap boxes and for sometimes joining in.

That winter I met up with a Jewish boy who was also going to study Law at Worcester College, Alan Magnus. He was in articles in Fleet Street, and some lunchtimes he would invite me to the Fleet Street Jazz Club to hear Kenny Ball. He jived superbly and he taught me to jive and took me to Chris Barber's and Cy Laurie's. (Cy Laurie's revivalist Club was in Windmill Street, near Piccadilly, and I twirled under his clarinet to my favourite number, "You made me love you", not realising that one day we would live near each other.) Some evenings we went to a coffeebar in Soho, the Macabre, and I many times sat drinking coffee to the background music of *Magic Moments* and *Diana*.

In Loughton there was nothing to do in the evenings save read or walk with John Ezard, and (in view of my contact with John Biggs-Davison) I was persuaded to join the Young Conservatives who met every Friday evening at the Hideaway café in the parade of shops that extended from the site of the old Oaklands. The Chairman wore a bow tie, and each week there was a speaker – one day it was the young Peter Walker, who stood and spoke impressively without notes – and we would ask questions. One day I spoke particularly emphatically, praising the Angry Young Men for their questioning of Society, and the speaker said, "Well, there's an angry young man," and everyone laughed. There were plenty of girls (mostly secretaries), and regular dances and social events between the meetings, and there was a general concern to carry forward the cause by canvassing or delivering leaflets. Soon I had revived a magazine called *Right Wheel* and written a long article on nuclear weapons. In February 1958 this came to the attention of Biggs-Davison, who in March sent me a note saying that the editorial was "extremely well-written" and who wrote to me in May, "You have done well to grasp the nettle of nuclear weapons." I looked up to a young man called Derek Dowley who was incredibly handsome, a local James Dean, and who had a different glamorous girl friend each week and casually announced that he had finished with each in turn when they were virtually swooning for his attentions.

That winter I studied the Trust Accounts and Book-keeping part of the Law Society's Solicitors Intermediate exams. It was hard, gruelling work, which I did not enjoy. I took a Gibson and Weldon correspondence course, which was based on Rowland's *Trust Accounts and* Carter's *Book-keeping for Solicitors*. I took the exam in March and passed. Work at the firm of solicitors was now even more boring, and the following typed communication, which has somehow survived, still makes me cringe:

57

A MYSTIC WAY

"Mr Hagger, Estate of the late Lady Baker. Will you please prepare a Corrective Affidavit showing back tax and sur-tax and penalties as agreed with the Inland Revenue, £5,000. P.W.P. 22/4/58." I cringe now as I cringed at the time for, what did it mean? Why was the Affidavit necessary, let alone important? I was just not interested in penalties agreed with the Inland Revenue. I had the ability and the skill to keep Trust accounts and books, but quite simply there were more urgent things to think about than a late lady's tax problems and Corrective Affidavits.

One night as I travelled home the tube stuck in a tunnel and there was an eerie silence and a voice spoke my name. I realised I was standing near Hughes, who used to sit next to me in the Chigwell School Latin class in the library under the dome. He was holding Sartre's essay *Existentialism is a Humanism*, which he showed me. "It's about freedom," he said. "I'm in an office I hate, and I wish I could be free." When I got home I went straight to Loughton library. The book was not in stock but I ordered it, and when it came I read it two or three times, and mulled over the free choice which might shape the person I wanted myself to become.

The Methodist Minister who had been appointed to replace Mr Grant was spending the first year of his tenure in the US, and his stand-in from autumn 1957 was an American called Ralph Bickford, a swarthy, simian, bespectacled small man who was in England for just a year. One morning in church he lent over the pulpit and told the children, "You know, I don't believe in Hell." I was asked to take him to a football match. It must have been in the spring of 1958 that I took him to watch Leyton Orient. We stood behind one of the goals about half way up the hill and leaned on an iron crash barrier, and saw the blond star Tommy Johnstone (who always wore a white wristband) score. I explained the rules, and at half time we talked about the church. On the way home he told me in a sombre, almost despairing voice that church services had become mechanical for him, that he was going through the motions and had lost his faith. He told me he had been diagnosed as a diabetic and that he would start treatment in America. Some months after he left it was announced that he had died of undiagnosed diabetes. I was sure he had chosen to do nothing out of metaphysical despair, and this encounter turned me further away from the Church.

Several times in 1958 I went to the Royal Court Theatre, and sat in the cheapest seats at the top and saw plays that were part of the 1956 theatre movement. In the interval George Devine, white-haired and bow-tied, would be about, and afterwards we went next door to the pub. There, after John Osborne's *Epitaph for George Dillon* I met Robert Stephens, and there too I encountered Patrick Magee, an actor in Beckett's *Waiting for Godot* who told me things about the meaning of the play. "Beckett writes in French," he said, "and to understand 'Godot' you need to be aware of the words 'godailler' ('puckered, wrinkled') and 'godiche' ('clumsy, oafish'). Godot suggests God as a wrinkled oaf. Beckett told me a story: 'Two thieves were crucified next to Christ. That both were damned do not presume, that both were saved do not despair.'" It was scepticism, but I was then concerned to find a purpose to life, and these sentiments had resonance.

My reading had gone on apace: Shaw, James, Rilke, Nietzsche, Kafka,

58

D. H. Lawrence, Turgenev and Joyce. I now kept a pocket book and headed pages "plays", "novels" and "poetry", and listed authors and works as fast as I read them. I now needed to discuss these books. In May, as something of a Sartrean free choice, I wrote to Colin Wilson, asking to meet him. He replied from Old Walls, Bodrugan Farm, Mevagissey in Cornwall, saying he could not meet me until September. I wrote back in June, sending him a long letter, reminding him that he claimed to stand for religious existentialism and asking him for further information about the purpose of life. Colin Wilson wrote back in June referring me to Stuart Holroyd, the author of *Emergence from Chaos,* a fellow Angry Young Man, giving me his phone number, and I met Stuart Holroyd outside the Dominion theatre, Tottenham Court Road. He was a small, quiet, intensely serious young man in a checked shirt with the top button done up and no tie, and a jacket. He had an Existentialist bent, and said of a particular girl I mentioned, "I took her on a train." I talked at great length with him in a Soho coffee-bar. I had read *Declaration*, and I discussed the Angry Young Men with him, and I remember another meeting when we had dinner at the Star Bar in Soho, a small Indian restaurant, and went on to see Eliot's *The Elder Statesman.* (I remember saying "We don't want anything to do with any system, the individual alone is important" and Holroyd asked me to repeat this.) Holroyd invited me to join the Sparticans.

At the end of June I attended a meeting of the Sparticans. About 30 young left-wing men and women sat angrily in a circle in a room in London, and although Colin Wilson was not there, Bill Hopkins and Stuart Holroyd had a lot to say about what needed to be done to change society. I came away with George Hay, who on the tube handed me a leaflet saying "Spartica is a map for the lost" and the next day he wrote me a letter telling me that full membership was 5/- a month, payable to Greta Detloff, the Treasurer, and as there was no HQ or source of revenue, could I run off some membership forms on the Young Conservatives' duplicator?

That summer of 1958 I was torn between left wing and right wing influences, between the revolutionary Angry Sparticans who looked to Colin Wilson and the socialising Young Conservatives who looked to John Biggs-Davison; and from this time on I have always given expression to these two apparently conflicting sides of my nature: the religious existentialism I then associated with Colin Wilson and the right wing Establishment I then associated with the independent and well-read Suez rebel, Biggs-Davison.

But I was still stuck with the Law. I plucked up courage to spend a couple of evenings with Miss Watts, on one of which we saw *The Bridge on the River Kwai* and I missed the last train home and had to sleep on the sofa of the flat she shared with a girl friend in Fulham. But she was too involved as Mr Rowcliffe's secretary to pay much attention to my misgivings about office life. At the end of July to my intense relief I finished my year in the firm of solicitors. Brickdale took me out to lunch and gave me a book on Greece, and I was temporarily free. That summer I came to grasp that I could exercise my freedom more.

A MYSTIC WAY

In August I went to Greece. John Ezard, saying goodbye enjoined me: "Come back an artist." I travelled with Alan Magnus, and we went with a party from Chigwell School, going with them for three days on the train through Yugoslavia to Athens where we left them and went off on our own, Youth Hostelling with sleeping-bags and a primus stove for six weeks, during which we grew beards. We spent three days visiting the ruins of Athens and going to Thermopylae, Delphi, Thebes, Sunium (I sat at Sunium where Byron sat) and Marathon. We went up Mt Parnassus but it was too hot to go up Mt Helicon. It was unbearably hot – there was a heat wave from the Sahara and it was 130°F in the shade – and a siesta was obligatory. I wrote: "The sun clings to each part of the body like a vice, and the breeze is like a draft from an oven. I am less allergic to the heat than Alan who finds it very hard going." We set off round the Peloponnese and went to Eleusis and then Daphnae, where in the groves adjoining the monastery there was a wine festival and we were allowed to wander among the trees and to sample any one of 36 different Greek wines as many times as we liked. After a Dionysian evening we had no difficulty in falling asleep. We went on to Megara, Corinth, Patras, Olympia, Pilos and Sphacteria (where I walked up the path Cleon took), Kalamai, Tripolis, Argos, Nauplion, Epidaurus (where we slept on the stage of the theatre and tested the amazing acoustics at dawn, listening to each other's whispers), Tiryns and Mycenae – sheer paradise for one who knew the history of those places – and on hillsides all round the Peloponnese we saw the huge letters OXI ("ochi"), "no" to Macmillan's plan for Cyprus. I wrote: "Greece is a land of dust, stones, dry grass and (in Corinth) flies." And: "Every day is the same, blazing hot. The country is a land of dust, flies, rocks and shrubs (waste land in fact) ....Eliot must have written 'What are the roots that clutch, what branches grow/Out of this stony rubbish' and 'the cricket no relief' in Greece. The cricket chirps all day and all night – like the ticking of a clock we are used to it." I noted that the retsina was "disgusting" and the beer "always flat". We had a bath in Tripolis for 2/6d.

At the end of August we took a boat from Peiraeus to Crete. We sat on deck with black-clad women and goats and sheep, and many were sick. In Crete we berthed at Iraklion and encountered a Cretan who led us to a museum not far from the sea. It was fully furnished and it turned out to be the house of Kazantzakis (the author of *Zorba the Greek* who once attended Bergson's lectures and who had died the previous October), and I can remember standing in Kazantzakis's study near his chair, and going out onto his veranda and standing in his garden and looking towards the sea. It was as if destiny were pointing a way. While in Crete I visited the Minoan palace at Knossos and Phaestos, a flat stone base of a palace surrounded by mountains. There was a visitors' book in a guest house nearby and, repelled by some of the other tourists with their trappings of wealth, I wrote, "Being is more important than having."

After three days in Crete we took a boat to Rhodes, and having seen the island, including Lindos. We took a caique to Turkey, intending to make our way to Istanbul. The caique was actually running arms and we put in on a deserted shore and the nearest bank was two days away at Izmir, so we turned round and came straight back with the caique. There was a tremendous storm and the boat was swamped by huge waves and we had to bail out. (I later wrote a story based on this experience.) After our return to Rhodes we took a coach to the Valley of the Butterflies, where our guide threw a stone at a tree, disturbing thousands of camouflaged butterflies that slept on the bark, so that the air was filled with a swarm of red wings.

We went onto Mykonos via Cos and Patmos. We were rowed ashore, and found a small, white, old house for 2/6d a night. Donkeys brayed outside and we breakfasted on the front on bread, butter and honey. The sea was a very deep blue-indigo and very choppy, and we took a small boat across to the island of Delos, the old Athenian treasury.

Back in Athens we met up with the party from Chigwell and returned with them on the train. At Belgrade station I left the train with one of the school party, Ian Will. We left our passports and luggage on the train and went to a station café and fell into conversation about Tito with a Yugoslav student. I looked up and saw our train retreating down the platform, green flags crossed at the back and the usual guarding soldier with a rifle on the observation platform below them. I let out a yell – in a flash I realised the danger of being without money or a passport in a Communist country – and set off in pursuit with Will running behind me. The guard levelled his gun at me, and Mr Croft, the master in charge appeared on the observation platform with Alan Magnus and several of the party who, despite the armed soldier, began shouting encouragement. I ran the race of my life, and as I reached the end of the platform pulled level with the end of the train. "I can make it," I shouted back at Will, "what should I do?" "Jump," he shouted, "you go on." "Jump," shouted Mr Croft and Alan Magnus and the boys, "jump." I jumped and caught the handle and landed on the bottom step up to the observation platform at the very moment the train accelerated and as I turned back, Will was already fifty yards back, a forlorn figure in shirt and shorts, without passport or money. Will was arrested and spent a week in a Yugoslav prison. There was an international incident, his case was front page news and his father had to send him money and a new train ticket to get home. Will turned up at Worcester College, Oxford a year after me.

Somehow that jump became symbolic of an existential choice. I had jumped, I had acted, I had changed my future. If I had not jumped, I would have been in a worse situation. I soon grasped that there was a lesson to apply in my own life.

In October I went up to Oxford, the first member in my family this century to go to university. I lived in a downstairs bedsit, which had an electricity meter, at 20 Worcester Place, a small terraced turn-of-the-century house with steps up to the front door, round the corner from the College, along with Alan Magnus and four other undergraduates and a grumbling landlady who lived in the basement. I found that Magnus and I had a joint tutorial together, with our tutor A. B. Brown, an urbane, owlish man with spectacles who smoked cigars.

From the outside, the entrance to Worcester College (so-called because it was founded in 1714 by a Worcestershire man, Sir Thomas Cookes) was railings and a blackened facade and clock, but beyond the porters' lodge and cloisters there was a very imposing lawn, on one side of which was an 18th century terrace with staircase accommodation and on the other side of which was the older medieval part known as the cottages, where De Quincey had rooms. The cottages were part of Gloucester Hall, which was founded by Benedictine monks in 1283 and which stood on the site of what was later to become the College. I saw the Worcester College tradition as being predominantly 18th century – social-rationalist, elegant and Augustan – on a medieval base that included 14th century mysticism. In the late 1950s many of the undergraduates wore cavalry twill and ties and sweaters – not jeans – and gowns were worn to Hall and tutorials.

We went into College for meals in Hall and for tutorials, at which Magnus and I read our essays in turn. The first essay I read had a literary style and Magnus's was a string of points, and Brown said, "From the point of view of what the Law requires, Hagger should be more like Magnus, and Magnus should be more like Hagger."

But I did not want to jettison my literary feel, that was the trouble, and poring over the cases of Criminal Law, Roman Law, and the History of the English Judicial System, I kept thinking of the books I might be reading – books about the meaning of life and the purpose of the universe, about individuals rather than systems, subjects more interesting than offences against property and possession such as the law of larceny as applied to windfalls and R v Cunningham (1957); the various rights in Justinian's code; and the hundred and assize courts and "nisi prius" jurisdiction. I was asked to play football for the College and attended various societies, including the Union debates, at one of which , after much agonising, I voted against unilateral nuclear disarmament and defeated the motion 291 to 290 by my free choice. But I still had a lot of time alone, and especially around tea-time I would sit on my bed in my room and ponder, sometimes playing my record-player, and the conviction grew that just as I had jumped from the platform onto the train so I should jump from the Law into a more congenial subject.

I now saw Oxford as a faintly depressing place: a modern city filled with gloomy and decaying colleges and blackened stone, and an emptiness filled with the braying upper class accents and undergraduates in cavalry twill, monied young men from privileged homes with snobbish attitudes. Within this Oxford was another, of a few undergraduates eager to read all European literature and to relate all knowledge, interested outside their subject, yearning to become "intellectuals", valuing knowledge for its own sake and talking with intellectual passion. Perhaps this second Oxford disappeared in the course of the 1980s as a Thatcherite emphasis on the market made undergraduates very aware of unemployment and concentrate on getting good jobs.

Very early on I saw a long-haired young man in a suede jacket and instantly recognised him and confronted him, "Haven't I seen you in the pub next to the Royal Court?" "Yes," he said, "I've been living very near Sloane Square." Ricky Herbert and I became close friends, along with an older mature student, Kingsley Shorter. They both read Modern Languages, and soon we were meeting for coffee at the Playhouse up the road or going back to Ricky's room in College, and I was hearing about Huysmans'

AWAKENING TO DESTINY

A Rebors ("Against Nature") and Stendhal's *Le Rouge et le Noire*, and discussing the pre-existentialist outlooks of Des Esseintes and Julien Sorel. How real our literary heroes were to us. They had the force of vivid living people we knew. I very swiftly declared myself an Existentialist and developed a philosophy of the free act which (like jumping for the train in Belgrade) could affect one's life. "You're free," I used to urge them, "you can go over to that girl and ask her out tonight, even though she's a total stranger. Only social convention, your own nature (your fear of embarrassment) and habit hold you back."

As a result of conversations such as these (which generally took place over coffee) I was thought of as an Existentialist, and was identified with the free act. And I was given opportunities to put my own thinking into practice at the parties and jiving sessions I attended in the Union cellars. I met several girls, as did Alan Magnus, whereas Ricky and Kingsley and some of the others tended to hold back as spectators. Ricky's hero was Dostoevsky's Underground Man, and he used to speak very amusingly of his view of life "from under the floorboards". As my discussions with Ricky and Kingsley, and sometimes with Kingsley's friend Perry Anderson, who was reading Russian Literature and spoke excitedly about Bazarov in Turgenev's *Fathers and Sons,* widened to include German and Russian, as well as French, literature, the idea began to grow that I, who stood for the free act, was absurdly bound by the Law, and that I should break free from the Law by exercising my freedom.

Incongruously (as incongruously as being an Angry Young Man and a Young Conservative at the same time) at this time I played several games of football for the College. We wore chocolate and pink and played in the College grounds beyond the lake. Our captain was Brian Bond, a historian who sent me cards in the vacations. One of our players, Doughy Rowe, a squat tousle-haired bull of a man, was killed in a car crash soon afterwards. There was some support from the touchline when we played, and Brian Bond, our centre half, used to call out from behind me (I was inside left) "Come on Woggins" (meaning Worcester College), and when occasionally I scored, "Oh well played."

Upstairs at 20 Worcester Place lived David Pitman, the younger brother of Robert Pitman of the *Sunday Express*, who was the husband of Pat Pitman, a collaborator of a book on murder with Colin Wilson. He was reading Milton's *Paradise Lost* and Anglo-Saxon grammar, and he told me about his tutor, the very young Christopher Ricks, and slowly my old desire to do English Literature at 'A' level resurfaced. The writers ahead in the English course had all looked at life and made their definitive statements about it – Donne, Coleridge and Tennyson – and I wanted to absorb their wisdom in preparation for a task I felt would take me abroad, and for a destiny linked with poetry which I instinctively knew was ahead for me. Deep down I knew that to be a poet I had to study the poetic tradition, although writing poems in the future would never earn me a living.

When I returned to Loughton for the Christmas vacation I raised the matter with my parents. They felt I should continue with the Law, that a BA solicitor would have the world at his feet and could go into politics like Biggs-Davison or go into Shell. But in the evenings I drank in the local

Holly Bush with John Ezard, who was reading English at Cambridge, and our conversations revolved around different authors and their interpretation of life, and I knew within that I had to change to English Literature. Sometimes we went up to London and visited the bookshops in Charing Cross Road; Foyles was a particularly favourite haunt of ours, and there we obtained all William Golding's books, including *Free Fall*.

In the spring I changed my room for a room in the Riding Stables just opposite the College. This was possible because a Tanganyikan, Pitakabisa (who was later to give me a visa for Tanzania), had had to leave, and the vacant room coincided with a time my landlady was being exceptionally difficult. I piled all my belongings into a supermarket trolley and pushed them round the corner to my new room.

After agonising about my choice I eventually raised the prospect of a change with both Brown (my Law tutor), who said I would do very well if I stayed with the Law, and Christopher Ricks (the English tutor) who lived next door to the Riding Stables. He had me to his house and questioned me, his vigorous eyes searchingly bright under his young bulbous forehead. He asked what I thought of Pasternak's *Dr Zhivago* and when I said "It's in the grand Dostoevskian tradition" he said, "I would have thought it's in the grand Tolstoyan tradition." I explained I was thinking of *The Devils* (or *The Possessed*). We discussed Colin Wilson, and he said "I shall die without having read Colin Wilson's latest book. It's regrettable, but there we are." Ricks had a great ability to use irony to state a position. Ricks said, "Your motives for changing would be mine if I were in the same position."

At the end of February I wrote to my parents, saying that Brown and Ricks would be happy for me to switch if the County , Gregory Rowcliffe and they were happy. I expected deferment from National Service, which it had been announced was to end in 1962. I wrote, "I have in the next two weeks to make a decision which you may consider wrong." I then waited for a reply.

The reply came in early March, an envelope in the Worcester College H pigeon-hole in my father's handwriting. I found it before breakfast and took it down past the cottages to the College lake, sat on a stone seat near the arched gate and opened it, my destiny as a poet at stake. It was a glorious sunny morning and no one was about; I was completely alone. My father's letter was dated 1.3.59 and I read: "Dear Nicholas, I have read your letter, and from what you say it does appear that you are almost persuaded to make the change in studies you contemplated in the vac and over which we had so much discussion. There is really very little for me to say for a decision of this nature must be personal to you....What it really means is that you have found the Law dull and unsatisfying."

It was a four page letter but as soon as I grasped that I was being given his consent, a sense of freedom and tremendous exhilaration welled up in me, I felt a tremendous elation, and as I looked up at the lake, with trees reflected in it and a trace of cloud from a higher world still, everything blended and I had a profound feeling that I was the lake and the lake was in me, I seemed to grow in stature, I felt I had always existed, I was filled with a great power, I felt I had rejected a future as a lawyer and could now progress towards my future as a poet and the power filled me with a conviction, a certainty, that this would happen. The power was in the universe, and later, having returned to my room without going into the Hall for breakfast, I wondered at the power of my mind which could suddenly become the universe.

My free act had put me in charge of my destiny, I was in direct contact with my soul, and instinctively knew within that I had been faithful to a call from my future direction, a call I dimly heard but could not decipher.

In the Easter vacation (in early April) I went to Paris on my own. I found a room in the Latin Quarter, near St. Germain des Prés. It cost me 12/6d a night, and I ate well at a self-service restaurant nearby. I spent many hours sitting in the park of the Isle St. Louis in the middle of the Seine, reading Milton's *Paradise Lost* in its entirety and revelling in each Homeric simile and poring over *King Lear* and other Elizabethan plays, on which there was to be a "collection" (exam) on the first day of the new term. I visited the Louvre and Michèle Maurel's Paris flat, and I went to the cinema some afternoons and saw Dostoevsky's *Idiot* in French. I also visited Sartre at the Rue Napoleon, briefly. I had done my research and found out the address of his apartment. I rang the upstairs doorbell, and the great man himself came to the door, fairly formally dressed, the familiar squint behind his spectacles, and on the landing I had a short conversation with him in French, explaining that I would like to discuss freedom with him, and M. Roquentin from *La Nausée* and certain points from *Existentialism is a Humanism*. His reply in French seemed courteous enough, but it was couched in language I did not fully understand and explained he was about to leave for an engagement. I withdrew, overjoyed at having had contact with one of my literary gods.

Back in Oxford, I did my collection on *King Lear* in the hall and did better than any of my year "without having read any English" as Christopher Ricks put it. I had my first tutorial with Ricks. It was a hot day and we left his room and went into the gardens and sat on a wooden seat in front of the 15th century building. He asked me what literature I liked. I said, "Mystical literature, for example Blake and Wordsworth." He said, "I shall teach you to like social satire." (He stood for the 18th century College tradition, I instinctively stood for the medieval tradition.) I was open to the new influence, but in retrospect that first exchange summed up our different approaches. For the next two years he spoke warmly of the verbal, social approach of the Augustans and social satirists, whereas I looked forward to the more mystical approach. And although in due course I was glad to read Dryden and Pope, my taste did not change in any way; rather it deepened.

I embarked on doing English in two years instead of three (or five counting the two years of 'A' level I had missed). I worked hard on Shakespeare and his contemporaries, and enjoyed reading Marlowe and Middleton (to whom Ricks brought a fresh, verbal approach, seeing certain key words as being ambiguous so that Beatrice and De Flores understand different meanings and misunderstand each other). I struggled with the Anglo-Saxon passages, having missed the groundwork the others had done while I was doing Law. I had to learn Anglo-Saxon as thoroughly as I had learned Latin – there were tests on Anglo-Saxon grammar – and I failed to see the point of mastering such a dead language merely to comment on *Beowulf*, and I resented the time I was expected to devote to such a futile pursuit when there were such interesting books to read and discuss. Some lunchtimes and most early evenings I went with Ricky and Kingsley to the Randolph, a hotel at the top of Beaumont Street, where the "Randolph Set" met. Of the characters who drank there Ian Flintoff, the Shakespearean actor (and later Labour supporter) virtually lived there. He was always there from opening time to closing time and he was always accompanied by newspaper men, including Rex someone from the *Daily Express*. There were always half a dozen men and women there, some on the fringe of films, and it made a good Oxford base for us Bohemians.

We were actually semi-Beatniks. We dressed daringly and were sometimes joined by Michael Horovitz and David Sladen, two avant-gardist Beatnik-followers. Horovitz published *New Departures*, a very avant-garde magazine, and at his parties in Hinksey marijuana was passed round and Horovitz would himself write a poem. I saw him write one poem influenced by Ginsberg's *Howl* that was 375 lines long (many lines comprising only one word) in about four minutes, a practice I did not consider poetry, not even avant-garde poetry, but rather stream of consciousness – or spontaneous self-expression. On another occasion he held a poetry event, I believe in a room at the Oxford Playhouse. About 40 sat cross-legged on a carpeted floor, and various poets recited from memory. Near the end Horovitz asked publicly whether I had a poem to recite, and though I declined I now wonder whether Providence was giving me a nudge through him.

There were several parties and I got drunk several times, and lived by excess in my spare time as if testing for myself by the breach of it Aristotle's "meden agan" ("nothing too much") which was inscribed over the door of the Greek room by the Tuck Shop at Chigwell. I was drunk with excess of freedom. Ricky used to take a relatively harmless stimulant, Preludin, which was passed round to heighten consciousness. For a few weeks that summer term I led an abandoned life in the evenings, living for the moment, taking pleasure in alcohol, reeling back drunk to the Riding Stables, revelling in my new-won freedom. One night I returned depressed and drunkenly experimented with hanging myself. I rigged up a noose and stood on a chair, and suddenly, quite distinctly – I can still see him – my grandfather appeared in the corner of my Riding Stables room and lifted a hand as if to stop me. The next day I heard he had died about the time I saw him. Yet in spite of my excesses I was disciplined enough to get my work done – I worked every morning – and when there was a commem at the College I hired a dinner jacket and took part. I remember Woodrow Wyatt arriving in bow tie and with immaculately groomed black hair, and two or three of the tutors lying drunk in the corner of a marquee about 4 in the morning. And I attended a number of meetings, including a large gathering in the Randolph for Arnold Wesker, who when asked "What is socialism?" replied "Brotherhood" to tumultuous applause.

About this time I was invited to the Old Chigwellians' sherry party in the Merton rooms of Richard Wallace, and I was delighted to see AF standing by the mantelpiece. He told me he would be retiring in 1960 and would live in Barnes. "I've never had a house," he said, "I've always lived in the school or Grange Court." He asked me what I would do, and without hesitation I said I would be a writer, to which, without hesitation, he (the author of *The Wayfarer's Companion*) replied: "Whatever you write, send it to me. I may not understand it, but I will proofread it for you and make sure it's in accurate English." I never took him up on this generous offer. In 1965 he married a French woman and died eight years later, and it was affectionately suggested by more than one Old Chigwellian that the French woman had worn him out. His widow locked up his house in Barnes and strangely it remained intact for getting on for 20 years until in the early 1990s representatives of Chigwell School combed through AF's records and books.

That summer term I saw quite a bit of Lady Rosemary Fitzgerald, the Earl of Kildare's daughter, along with a waif who was arrested and put in Holloway jail for fraud. Back in Loughton in the vacation I found out that the family had switched their allegiance from Methodism to C of E to fit in with the Chigwell School chapel, leaving my aunt Argie to continue holding up her parents' Methodist banner.

In early August I walked up to Oaklands one evening, slipped through the High Road gate, and sat in the summer hut (where the Garden Room now is), overlooking the main field. It was as if a guardian angel, having steered me away from Law to English, was bringing me face to face with a future task and destiny, showing me what was ahead. It grew dark, and I sat on, pondering my childhood and what the future held as a mist rose and blotted out the stars.

3.

LOOKING ABROAD: MARRIAGE AND SCEPTICISM
1958 – 1963

Almost immediately afterwards I left England to hitchhike round Spain and had my first concentrated tussle with metaphysical attitudes.

I travelled to Paris with Fred Young, a stocky crew-cut young man who later worked for a tabloid with great success who wore a black shirt and dark glasses and modelled himself on Marcek in *Ashes and Diamonds*, even moving his glass backwards and forwards in a Paris bar like Marcek, causing the drink being poured to be spilled. With us came John Ezard, who was then somewhat vague and unco-ordinated and shambolic, a complete contrast to Fred Young's precision and panache. We travelled to Paris and at 6.30 p.m. got a lift with a French international footballer to the Spanish Costa Brava. He drove his fast car all night, and somewhere near the Pyrenees got out at dawn and gazed at hills and a valley and sighed, "Une très jolie vue."

Somehow John Ezard and I were separated from Fred Young. We went to Barcelona whereas Fred got a lift to south Spain. We went to a bar in the Ramblas which at lunchtime was full of whores and American servicemen, and we got talking to a girl called Anastasia, who said she did not like what she was doing and that we should watch out as the girls slipped pills into the men's drinks. We chatted to a serviceman called Spinney, who said memorably of God, "You don't have to tell me, I know there's a man up there." We saw a bull fight, the cruelty of which John found obscene, and then spent three days hitching to Valencia. At Cambrils (outside Tarragona) we slept by the sea and were awoken by seven black-coated figures holding hands and wearing black capes and hats, who performed a totendanse (dance of death) on the sea shore. In Valencia we slept on a traffic roundabout, and then pushed on to Malaga to catch the Fiesta, and encountered Fred Young standing beside a road. In Malaga we all slept on the beach, and the rats were as large as cats. At dawn, waking in my sleeping-bag, I saw them slinking low against the skyline, and then scurrying off into the shadows. Soon we pushed onto Coin, a mountain village about 40 kms outside Malaga, to catch the Fiesta there, and found the main street lit with fairy lights and thronged with people and dancers to thumping Spanish music. There were many stalls and fair-booths, and there was much to drink.

We met an American who gave us a card saying Angus Ward. "I'm Angus Ward," he said. "I'll put you up." He gave us directions and said he'd meet us at his house. From locals we found out that Senor Ward was an ex-American Ambassador who lived high up on the hill in great security. We set off into the dark and climbed away from the sounds of the Fiesta, and up in the mountains came to his dark walled enclosure and rang the gate buzzer. Senor Ward came to the gate, wearing shorts. He was between 50 and 60 and slightly balding. It was not the man who had given us the card. He took the card and said he did not know the man who had sent us. "I'm afraid you've been the victim of a trick. All I can suggest is that you sleep on the hillside here. It's warm, you'll be all right." We were very tired and we lay our sleeping bags on the turf above the lights of Coin and lay back and the stars were incredibly bright, they were moving and squirming and squirting (as I said in a story I wrote of this title) "like a tray of live winkles". The whole universe was alive, and I saw hundreds of shooting stars before I fell asleep. It was the end of the dog days when there is always a crowd of shooting stars, but to me the experience had a mystical force, reinforcing the idea that the universe was vital rather than mechanistic.

From Coin we returned to Malaga, which was hot and stank after the mountain air, and another bull fight at which Chicuelo II was slightly gored. Ernest Hemingway was present, sitting one row from the front in a maroon shirt, silver-bearded, and someone told us that he was to be found in the evenings at the Miramar Hotel. We went on to the bar there, passing Danny Kaye who was singing into a microphone near a band in the humid grounds outside, and sure enough Hemingway was standing in the air-conditioned cool with a drink in his hand and a few people who were waiting to approach him while he listened intently to a couple of men, watching with deep, sensitive eyes. John Ezard and I joined the small group with our drinks, and when there was an opportunity I told Hemingway that I wanted to be a writer – he nodded barely perceptibly – and that we had been to the bull fight. He gave me his full attention and, very gently, drawled, "There's a mano a mano at the end of the week. Ordonez and Dominguin. You must see that. It'll be the best bull fight of the year." I did not know that he had been following the rivalry between the no 1 and no 2 bullfighters all summer and was writing about it. Ken Tynan was sitting drinking Scotch about ten feet away, and he too, (he later told us) was in Malaga for the mano a mano.

I stood beside Hemingway, this big gentle man, recalling the Nick Adams short stories and Lt Henry and Krebs and his other heroes, and the collapse of values after the First World War, which he had so memorably reflected, my mind too full of individual questions about his work to ask any one question beyond the others, and a man joined us and said, pushing in on our conversation, "Tell me, Mr Hemingway, don't you feel the bulls of today aren't as big as they were some years ago?" Hemingway gazed at him with his sensitive eyes and slowly took 300 pesetas from his pocket and slapped the three notes into the man's hand and said, "Go and buy yourself a book on bull-fighting, you stupid bastard." I was taken aback, for the man who had been so gentle to us had suddenly turned aggressive, and while I adjusted to my surprise a woman came up and said flattering things about his work, to which Hemingway quietly said, "C—r." I gathered that Hemingway belonged to everybody; he was a public institution, and everyone went and spoke to him and he reacted with sympathetic understanding or honest irritation depending on the person, holding up a mirror to their own nature as perhaps all great men do. We turned away from Hemingway, the contact slight but real as it was enough to get the measure of the man and relate the man to his stories (as in the case of my conversation with Sartre). And those few minutes made a lasting impression so that when I heard, sitting in a tiny pub at the end of Smarts Lane, Loughton one lunch time, that Hemingway had shot himself after hypertension was diagnosed (actually depression and anxiety requiring electric shock treatment), I felt genuinely sad, as though a friend had died.

We queued for tickets to the mano a mano before the sun got up the next morning, and went that same evening, a Friday, as the cool began to set in after the day's heat. We sat in the second row back (the same as Hemingway who was further round the ring). The long rivalry all summer between Ordonez and Dominguin had boiled up into a climax, as the no 1 and no 2 bullfighters outdid each other in daring. My recollection is that Luis Dominguin went first, then Antonio Ordonez, each killing his large but weakened bull by standing up to its half-hearted charge and plunging the sword into the bull's neck. Then Dominguin had his second bull. It was a huge bull and Dominguin looked magnificent in his bullfighter's clothes, proud, erect and apparently fearless. The bull was lively and charged and thudded into the wooden barricade just below us, behind which Ordonez, who was acting as matador, ran and hid. Then Dominguin did a series of stunning passes, not moving his feet at all and bending, quite still, holding out his sword and cape to the bull, suggesting complete mastery. It was thrilling to watch and at each pass the crowd roared "Olé" and there was deafening applause at the end. Haughtily, almost contemptuously, Dominguin threw down his sword and cape, turned his back on the bull and knelt down just beneath us and facing us, his hands in the air, all caution thrown aside in a breathtaking display of courage.

The bull charged, and tossed him and he flew through the air. The bull charged again and gored him in his side, rolling him over. The crowd screamed, matadors (including Ordonez) ran out and flapped their capes to distract the bull, turning it round and round on itself. But slowly, incredibly, Dominguin got up, blood oozing through his tunic, and waved the matadors away. His white face was twisted with pain, but he recovered his hat, sword and cape, and just as still and poised as before, executed a whole series of brilliant passes to more "Olés" and thunderous applause, and then completed a perfect kill, plunging his sword over the bull's horns and turning his back dismissively as the bull moved its head from side to side and it sank to its knees. Then proudly, stiffly, his pale face still twisted in agony, he walked to the side of the ring below us, unaided – and collapsed, the side of his tunic stained red. The crowd was on its feet roaring, and as I stood on my seat I saw Hemingway waving his arms. This mano a mano would be the climax of his book. Dominguin was put on a stretcher and taken to hospital where his recovery was slow.

The rest of the evening was an anti-climax. Ordonez had watched the events from behind the wooden barricade. He looked pale, now confirmed as no. 1 by the elimination of his challenger. The next bull was a tiny bull, it seemed little larger than a pig, and Ordonez did the bare minimum before dispatching it. Ordonez had won the mano a mano but Dominguin had the glory.

LOOKING ABROAD

We had taken to sleeping on the beach at Torremolinos, 14 kms away from Malaga. We hitchhiked out from Malaga at night and hitchhiked back in for the evenings. Late that next afternoon we stood beside the road, and a huge car (I believe it was a Rolls Royce) slowed down. In the front sat Lord Hercy Belville, an Oxford undergraduate of great wealth, whom I had met several times in the Randolph Hotel. In the back sat Ordonez. Lord Belville waved and drove on. (Not long after he was very badly injured in a car crash.)

From the hot dry south of Spain we hitchhiked north to San Sebastian through dusty, central Spain, and by the side of the road I read the Penguin anthology of the Metaphysical poets (selected by Helen Gardner). I can see myself squatting in an arid hilly landscape, the road stretching in each direction and no trees, reading Donne, Marvell, Herbert and some of the more minor Metaphysical poets, and discussing with John Ezard the metaphysical world view, and how the perspective of these poets differed from that of the secular poets today. I associated the poets with Eliot's religious outlook and their questioning of worldly values with the questioning of the heroes of Sartre and Hemingway, who nevertheless remained very worldly. In retrospect I can see that I was groping towards a vision of an invisible reality which Coleridge and Shelley knew, although I scarcely realised this at the time.

The next year deepened my knowledge of poetry and writers, and these in turn nourished my soul. Back in England I had work to do for collections. My parents were in Exmouth and then Le Touquet (from which they returned early as my father had phlebitis), and I worked on Old and Middle English texts, including *Beowulf* and *Gawain and the Green Knight*, begrudging the time spent on answering questions about these dead languages, and on Chaucer, Spenser, Skelton, the Silver poets of the Renaissance, the 17th century poets, Restoration drama and a first look at the Augustans.

That autumn I lived in College in the 18th century terrace, in a sitting-room with Regency-striped curtains overlooking the gardens at the back, room 9 on staircase 5. I had a small bedroom off it with a bowl for a jug of water which the scout (servant) brought in each morning. I was woken by my scout, Harris, and spent the mornings at lectures or in the Bodleian library or Radcliffe Camera, where I often looked at the spiral staircase, and the afternoons working in my room, leaving the evening free for going out or, when one of my weekly essays approached, going into the College library and drawing together all the books I had read to write my essay. The tutorial in Literature was one to one. I would go to Ricks's book-lined room in the cottages, sit and read my essay through. He would then make verbal comments which I noted down and we discussed issues arising from his response to what I had written (which was always favourable). Sometimes we discussed his latest book review for the *Sunday Times*. Then he would set me my next essay and rattle off from memory a reading list of about 20 books or journals, while I scribbled them all down. He carried all the PMLA (Publication of the Modern Languages Association) and RES (Review of

English Studies) references in his head, and was never wrong. The English language, Old English and Middle English classes involved groups of 6 to 12 of us, although there were tutorials which we attended in pairs. We had Tittensaw for Old English, a pallid, slow, dreamy young man who looked 17 and was in complete contrast to Ricks, who was a live wire, always fidgeting and never still and poised to strike with a rapidly delivered and highly articulate view which I found very stimulating. I can remember being paired with David Oxley, who became a leading figure in Rugby League. (He used to disappear at weekends to play in Rugby League, and the College never knew this, he told me some years later.)

Many of the texts we studied were uncongenial, and I wondered at the wisdom of making us learn Anglo-Saxon and Middle English, two dead languages, just to be able to translate for exam purposes chunks of Old English and Middle English literature of questionable interest (some bits even more boring than the Law) when there were such delights to be encountered in the 20th century. But I gritted my teeth and stuck it out, and I always got something from any poet we read. Spenser's *Fairie Queene* left me cold, but I loved his *Prothalamion* and *Epithalamion*. Wyatt and Surrey seemed forbidding but I loved looking for evidence of Wyatt's affair with Ann Boleyn and relating his sonnets to the events which led to his execution. Donne's *Aire and Angels* and Marvell's *Garden* I also loved. Through my reading of 17th century literature I first encountered the mysterious Light which was in every minor poet of the time, but which never seemed to be mentioned in modern critical books or 20th century authors, except for fleeting references in Eliot. During my second year in College I took to working at night in the College library. I climbed the spiral staircase opposite the porter's lodge, and sometimes I stayed up all night, writing an essay. I would go to bed at dawn with a profound satisfaction, and go to sleep listening to the birds singing, and would wake two hours later in time for my tutorial.

I was still a prophet of freedom and had not yet interiorised my concept and connected it to the realisation of the Light. I sometimes saw an Italian lady about this time (a married woman from Cremona called Mina who was studying English in Oxford) and looked into the Gloucester Arms for Ricky on the way home. And it must have been in this term that, as we left the Gloucester Arms and went for a walk one evening, I urged Ricky to define himself in terms of one definitive, Raskolnikovian act and establish his freedom for all time in a symbolic gesture. Ricky had read Goncharov's *Oblomov* , which is about a man who takes to his bed and asks why he should be interested in current affairs or anything. I played Stolz to his Oblomov and urged him to put aside his false attitude. We were crossing a bridge over the canal that runs near Worcester College – it must have been Hythe Bridge – at the time, and I said to Ricky, in the middle of my philosophical harangue, "For example, there is nothing to prevent you from standing on the side of this bridge and jumping into the water to prove that you are free. To choose to do something in breach of habit as an 'act gratuit' and reject all Oblomovian sloth – that is a demonstration of freedom." It was dark, and to my astonishment without a word Ricky did as I said. Still wearing his suede jacket, he got up on the iron top of the bridge

72

and casually disappeared. I bent over and heard a terrific splash at least 20 feet below and saw white froth and foam in the moonlit dark. Then there was silence "Ricky?" I called. Then there was a sploosh and, rising like a river-god from the stagnant water, Ricky waded dripping moonlight to an iron ladder which was mounted on the sheer stone wall, and climbed up it and stood, dripping from head to toe and said, "I'm free." "Bravo," I congratulated him. "You've demonstrated your freedom in a way that will never be forgotten." One or two passers-by stopped and looked at us oddly with a mixture of curiosity and suspicion. We headed for the college, and Ricky squelched his way, still dripping, through the lodge. Evans, the porter, called "Good night sir" to us, and Ricky called casually "Good night Evans", as Evans stared in disbelief at the apparition that went by. News of what Ricky had done soon spread. My reputation as the philosopher of freedom was enhanced, and soon John Gretton wanted to put on Camus' *Caligula* at the Playhouse with me playing the lead, but the College Buskins decided to do *Two Gentlemen of Verona* instead.

I believe it was this term as well that I ran into a young and bearded Peter O'Toole in the Gloucester Arms. He was sitting with his chauffeur, waiting for his wife Sian Phillips to finish her performance at the Playhouse. He told me how he was currently playing Shylock at Stratford and we discussed his interpretation of the part, and he said he had a bottle of vodka; could he come back to my room to drink it? This was in O'Toole's drunken period before *Lawrence of Arabia*, and I took him back to my room and the chauffeur produced not one but two bottles of vodka and I produced a copy of *The Merchant of Venice* and for the next three hours we had an increasingly drunken interpretation of just about every line of the play, O'Toole stressing feeling, I stressing the academic side with some historical nuances that he was not aware of. Suddenly I looked at my watch and saw that it was midnight, long after the theatre had finished and long after the College gates were closed. By now O'Toole was declaiming great chunks of Shylock's part and I had to get him and his chauffeur to climb out of the grounds without being caught. I got him down to the bottom of the staircase and he broke away from me and I found him wanting to pee in the Law library. I got him to the washroom toilets on our staircase, and then propelled him into the gardens at the back, emphasising the need for silence. As we approached the rear gate there was a noise and we retreated into bushes. Someone ran at the 9 ft high gate from outside, fingers and then a bespectacled head appeared over the top in the dark, an ankle swung onto the top of the gate and a man jumped down our side in the dark wearing a dinner jacket and black tie. "'How like a fawning publican he looks!/I hate him for he is a Christian,'" bellowed O'Toole in his Shylock voice, and, terrified, Mr Campbell, the history tutor, rushed off towards the terrace. Then the chauffeur and I had the job of getting a completely drunk O'Toole over the 9 ft gate. We stood him against the gate, took a leg each and heaved upwards. Still quoting Shylock, O'Toole was bent double over the gate. We took a foot each and heaved up again. For a few seconds O'Toole lay on top of the gate, declaiming Shylock at the top of his voice. Then he disappeared. We heaved ourselves up to look over and saw O'Toole lying on the pavement the other side. He picked himself up and wandered in a zig-zag direction still reciting Shylock, while I gave the chauffeur a bunk-up and then hauled myself up to see the chauffeur running after O'Toole in the direction of the Playhouse.

In November I met a girl called Margot. She had black hair and dressed like a Chelsea witch, and she appeared in Oxford and claimed to be an undergraduate. I saw her for perhaps three weeks, and then she was arrested and put in Holloway for obtaining money by false pretences. The whole squalid episode amused Ricky and displeased Mina.

Christmas approached, or as Ricky memorably put it, "Christmas has come round again, bringing its annual burden of good cheer." Back in Loughton, I worked for the post office, delivering Christmas mail to Tycehurst Hill and Spareleaze Hill. I read the 18th century Augustans: the excessively rationalistic Johnson, Swift, Dryden and Pope and "social satire", a theme I pursued through the next term.

On Christmas Eve I drank with John Ezard in the Holly Bush. There were decorations and paper hats; there was a party atmosphere and a lot of raucous laughter. I sat in the corner of the pub feeling more and more disgusted at the mindless materialism and ignorance of the meaning of Christmas, and just before midnight (for there was a licensing extension) I told John Ezard I was free and that I would address everybody on the subject. This would be an Existentialist choice. I stood up and rapped the table with my beer glass and called for silence and gave all a short lecture on how it would be better to close the churches as they were obviously not interested in the true meaning of Christmas. I just had time to get my message across. "Out," shouted the landlord, and he lifted the flap on the counter and advanced towards us and took me by the arm, and we were unceremoniously bundled out of the pub onto the street, where I announced that we were "outside" society.

In January I went down to Cornwall for a few days. I visited Colin Wilson, who had written *The Age of Defeat*, which was discussed among the undergraduates. How I came to arrive at Tetherdown, Gorran Haven I have no recollection. I cannot just have turned up. Did I write to him from Oxford? Perhaps, I don't think I rang. Anyway, there, living on the edge of a cliff with a view over the sea, was the young bespectacled, eager man who had spoken so fluently and confidently in the Fleet Street coffee-bar, and now I was able to hold forth about some of the writers I was studying. He was very welcoming for someone who was public property. We discussed the writers he was writing about, and the Beats and metaphysics, and because (I seem to recall) his parents were living upstairs, Colin rang D. S. Savage, the literary critic (author of *The Withered Branch*) who lived in Mevagissey. I was put up at the Lawns Hotel, a guest house which Savage kept. A grave, Russian-looking man with greased dark hair and a well-groomed beard, Savage despised Colin Wilson's popularity – he was particularly scathing about *Ritual in the Dark* – and I gathered I was something of an ambassador between the two households. Savage reverentially produced a suitcase and showed me the unpublished essays of the deceased Catholic E. F. F. Hill, which he was trying to publish.

Colin Wilson met me at the Ship, Mevagissey (which has since been burned down). He bought all the fishermen a drink and when he was there all eyes were upon him. He drove me back to Tetherdown, and I remember walking outside in the dark, he denying that he was a Fascist (as someone had suggested); and telling me how he had enjoyed hitchhiking in France, reading Plato and not really minding if he never got a lift. He was extremely open about experiences he had had in the spirit of an Existentialist philosopher, and always sought to relate particular experiences he shared to a general truth, a trait I liked and admired. I remember him describing an intimate experience he had had. It was refreshing that such experiences could be shared objectively for the Existentialist conclusions that could be drawn. Such conversations suggested that *all* experience is the currency of philosophy, that nothing should be held back, that the philosopher had a total commitment to understanding experience. I warmed to him, and felt uncomfortable each night I went back to Savage's and heard Savage's withering comments about his lack of talent as a novelist. During the days, when I was not sitting with Colin Wilson, I visited the sea and on one occasion took a bus and found Old Walls, the house to which he had fled at the beginning of his Outsider's exile in Cornwall. I returned to Oxford with my Outsider's credentials reinforced.

I had swung back to poetry and back at Oxford began writing poems; or rather, I felt the urge to write poems and was discontented with what came out. That term I heard a creased-faced W. H. Auden give a recital of his poems from memory – he completely dried in the middle of *The Willow-wren and the Stare* – and I also heard Theodore Roethke give a reading of his poems. And Christopher Ricks, an Empsonian, invited the poet William Empson, author of *Some Versions of Pastoral* and *Seven Types of Ambiguity*, to chat to us, which he did, bespectacled and bearded, though I suspect Ricks got more out of the occasion than we undergraduates did.

That spring I attended some lectures on Yeats given by J. I. M. Stewart (alias Michael Innes), even though they were outside my course, and, coming out of Schools where the lectures took place one Tuesday morning about 11.15, and standing in the High Street where Auden often wandered after giving a lecture as Professor of Poetry at that time, I had a strong glimpse into the future. In my mind's eye I saw a small harbour where I knew I would one day live. I wondered if it was in Ireland, for it was a rural harbour, but I knew I would write poetry there.

In March I visited Cambridge with Peter Wollen, one of the Randolph Set, and sat with John Ezard in his rooms at St. Catherine's. A quiet man was present, Ian McKellen.

That Easter John Ezard and I resumed our walks in Epping Forest. We used to meet on the open Forest land near the stream off Staples Road, and on one occasion when I was there first I heard a hidden voice (John's) comically chanting from the woods some words of Huysmans' *A Rebors* ("Against Nature"): "'It all comes down to syphilis in the end,' said Des Esseintes."

I had heard from my father about a graveyard of Haggers who were Quakers and Lords of the Manor in the 17th century and lived on the Essex-Cambridgeshire border near Royston. One day I took the A70 and picked up John and we drove to Audley End. We followed a signpost to Royston and followed several hunches until, on a corner, in a place I have not since been

A MYSTIC WAY

able to find (but which may have been at Bourn), I came across a church with a churchyard. Walking among the graves and peering at the tombstones I saw a number were Haggers, and I was sure that this was the churchyard my father had referred to.

One night John and I left the Holly Bush and walked up to Strawberry Hill when it was misty, and John quoted Coleridge's *Christabel,* "Is the night chilly and dark?/The night is chilly but not dark." In the afternoons we followed the stream off Staples Road into the Forest and discussed Arthur Miller and Tennessee Williams, and on one occasion Ezard quoted Coleridge's *Dejection: an Ode*: "'I see, not feel how beautiful they are.'" "I'm numb within," he would say, "I've lost the power to respond to Nature with feeling." Shortly afterwards I heard he was in hospital. And our walks came to an end.

In the mornings that Easter I read Defoe, Richardson and Fielding, and wrote an essay on the 18th century novel. It was a fine spring and I spent a lot of time sitting in the Journey's End garden, sometimes on the wooden garden seat near the ivy and sometimes in a deck-chair near the pear-tree on the lawn. I also had to read the Romantic poets, and returned to Wordsworth, Coleridge, Keats, Shelley and Byron, seeing them with more mature and critical eyes. And I spent as much time reading Kingsley Shorter's copy of Rilke's *Duino Elegies* and comparing French and German Romanticism with the British Romantic poets. At this time I met an Austrian girl in London, Inge, and took her to a theatre, and I remember getting her impressions of Rilke.

In the summer of 1960 a young man called Graham Wallis appeared in College. He had no money and no possessions except for his filthy clothes, and for a couple of weeks he slept in people's rooms (mainly Ricky's). He was on drugs and professed to know some of the American Beats and the conversation revolved round the experience of beatitude. He borrowed my copy of Dostoevsky's *Idiot* and when I got it back the white parts of the cover had turned grubby brown. Then one hot summer's day he got too daring and sunbathed on the main lawn. There was a sprinkler on, and peeling off some of his clothes he had a public wash and shower, which, judging from the state of my *Idiot*, was long overdue. He was challenged by a porter and apprehended, removed from the College and banned from re-entry. A couple of years later he died. I wrote a very short story, *A Barbiturate for a Bad Liver,* about his death.

Wallis's visit had consequences as some of the undergraduates, including Ricky, became more Beatified. A coloured young man with an impeccably upper class accent used to arrive with marijuana and smoke it in the room next to mine. (The undergraduate whose room it was, the ultra-leftist heir to an eminent banking family, got drunk on election night and loudly lamented the Conservative victory up and down our staircase, waving a bundle of share certificates.) Kingsley was not drawn in. He had returned to Subud and used to disappear "to sit in a draughty drill hall and wait for an experience of the Absolute" as he put it, with his own inimitable wit. As Kingsley progressed deeper into mysticism and most of our other contemporaries professed left wing political journalism – Perry Anderson would found the *New Left Review*, and the Union Secretary and Treasurer

76

Peter Jay and Paul Foot would both become left-inclined journalists – Ricky was increasingly drawn towards the Beatnik drug culture. I knew it was not right, and said so, and I watched with sadness as he pursued a fascination that would result in opium addiction; the way of De Quincey, who first experienced opium while an undergraduate at Worcester College in 1804 and who later wrote *Confessions of an English Opium-Eater*.

My parents came up for my 21st birthday, and stayed at the Mitre. They came and looked at my room on staircase 5, at the back, and I remember telling my father by the mantelpiece: "I'd be happy if in a hundred years' time someone took down my work from that shelf and learned how to live from it." With some birthday money I bought a portable typewriter and set about teaching myself to type in anticipation of becoming a writer. Stuart Holroyd had told me that it was important to take a typing course, and I booked myself into a local typing school and was taught touch-typing to music. Sometimes, late at night, Ricky, stoned, would wander into the washroom at the bottom of our staircase and say with glassy eyes, "If you become a famous writer, will you give me a hand-out?" Once he said, "You look like an *Old Testament* prophet with intense eyes." Other times he would say, echoing *Ecclesiastes*, "There's nothing new under the sun," and with put-on Oblomovian tiredness, "It's all futile anyway, so why bother to write anything? Give up and take weed like me." He had a very attractive girl friend called Anne, who was a nursing sister and looked like Bridget Bardot, and I knew there were psychological complications in this relationship as Ricky took to running himself down in public, announcing to crowded rooms, "Do you realise there is a half-man here?" It was extremely funny and it enhanced his popularity, and he succeeded in getting people to laugh with him rather than at him by this comic ploy, but the actual pain behind the humour drove him to seek further escape in Beatnik drugs, and intensified his retirement into a drug-dream.

I was now an Angry Existentialist and had eliminated all traces of the Young Conservative. I even reluctantly allowed myself to become College CND representative despite having voted against unilateral nuclear disarmament a year earlier. I justified my change of outlook on the grounds that I was questioning my values and assumptions. We were above all a questioning, thoughtful generation who looked behind and rejected the received social truths and sought to know the meaning of life through intense mystical or existential vision. It was this aimed-for vision which linked my way of looking to that of the youthful Colin Wilson, Stuart Holroyd, Kingsley and Ricky (who looked for meaning in heroin and LSD), and the John Ezard of our Forest walks. We were a seeking generation, a generation of seekers.

In the summer term H. J. Blackham, author of *Six Existentialist Thinkers* (which I had read) visited the College and gave an open-air talk one evening in the Provost's courtyard. I can see him standing and addressing us about Kierkegaard, Heidegger, Jaspers, Marcel, Sartre and Camus, and I went and had a talk with him afterwards, very much the resident College Existentialist. It would have been this term, too, that I heard F. R. Leavis in a vast hall. He arrived late, looking like a tramp wearing an army shoulder-bag which he put on the stage and rummaged in for his notes. Then he stood at the lectern and spoke to us with a rapid, rambling delivery and all I can remember was his praise of D. H. Lawrence's letters which "were dashed off in great haste".

At Oxford I spent much of my time reading outside my subject. I found it stimulating being in contact with students of philosophy, history and Continental and Russian literature, and as each mentioned Dante, Goethe and Turgenev I attempted to track down the work they referred to so that I could see the insight I had heard in context. Much of Oxford was a time of exploration and discovery – more outside English Literature than within it. Instinctively I had already grasped that breadth was as important as depth.

I still went to the Randolph in the evenings and had got to know some of the girls very well. There I met the actor who played the intense piper in the Polish film *Kanal*, Vladek Sheybal. One night Peter Wollen announced that he had been invited to a party at Cliveden, Lord Astor's house, and would I go with him on the back of his scooter? Peter Wollen was a bit vague – he had got Milton and Spenser muddled up and I was not confident that he would find the way – but incredibly just after dusk we drove through the great wrought-iron gates of Cliveden and were soon standing on the raised terrace with stone buttresses, sipping champagne with a couple of hundred "beautiful young people". There was swimming in the swimming-pool, where a year later (on 9th July 1961 according to Ivanov's memoirs, *The Naked Spy*), Profumo was to encounter a naked Christine Keeler, and about 5 in the morning I had quite a long talk with Bill Astor as he came to refill my glass. (Later I met Lady Astor who had had a Light experience before the Profumo Affair burst upon public attention in 1962/3.)

I played four times for the College at cricket and made a good score each time. Increasingly cricket seemed a waste of a day, and the fourth occasion I went into bat after attending a long sherry party with the Chaplain and made 50, hitting the ball hard and middling it with a certainty I never had when sober. Shortly afterwards, on 25th June 1960 I played my last game of cricket. I went back to Chigwell School for Speech Day to see my brother Robert collect the Knightley Chapel Reading Prize, and walked down to the 1st XI pitch to watch the School – captained by my brother Robert – play the Headmaster's XI. The Headmaster's XI were one short and Robert asked me to play. Flannels were found, and I fielded at mid-off as the School batted first and my brother Robert was bowled by David Horton for 11. The Headmaster's XI then batted, having to score approaching 200, and we were soon in trouble. I batted no 3, and although completely sober this time, hit everything I could hard and high, not caring if I were out, and I just could not get out. "Nick, get out," Robert would say between the overs, "you're playing to make the numbers up, not to stop the School winning." I tried to oblige, but my high hits kept missing the fielders and I ended (I believe) on 62 not out, and the Headmaster's XI had drawn. Several of my former teachers, including Mr Davenport, came and congratulated me, and I thought that if I were to stop playing cricket it should be at such a high point. I never donned flannels again.

I had met an English lady schoolteacher, Mary, who had finished a year's course at Oxford and who was going to teach in Ankara for a year. I had spent some golden days full of sun and summer with her at the beginning of the vacation, and we were full of idyllic countryside and fresh air. As I was holidaying in Greece I had arranged to travel out with her and leave her in Greece. When a neurotic heiress on the fringe of the Randolph Set, Jill Bradbury, who was reading English and who lived in remoter Essex, heard I was going, she insisted on flying out to Greece to join me, so we could return together. She had had me to Ludham Hall, Braintree to stay, and I had been up the tower and walked across the estate to the Blackwater and collected eggs from the hens, and I could see there was a temptingly comfortable set-up if I could bring myself to co-exist with Jill.

I raised money for the trip by working very part-time for a small debt-collecting agency which was run by a College scout (servant). An ex-jewel-thief with a national notoriety, he had been in prison and had escaped twice through impossibly narrow openings and was nicknamed Rubberbones. Having served his sentence and become a College scout, he had been invited by the Provost to address a conference of prison governors. From the platform he had told his former prison governors what was wrong with their prisons, and – sweet revenge! – after setting up a debt-collection agency he had actually had to collect a debt from his main prison governor. A thin, lean man, he rode about on a motorbike, and I sat behind him on the pillion and rang doorbells and tried to collect debts from various impecunious and elderly dons who reluctantly shuffled away from their manuscripts to wheedle articulate excuses at the front door. I made enough commission to make my trip a possibility.

I supplemented this money by selling programmes at the Soho Fair. I heard about this from Herbie Butterfield, one of the Randolph Set. I contacted the organiser, reported to a house in Noel Street on July 9th, paid 1/- per programme and then stood on various Soho street corners selling each for 1/6d. Several of the Randolph Set were doing it, and we met up in the Helvetia or one of the other Soho pubs at regular intervals to compare notes. Every 20 programmes we sold left us with 10/- , some of which went in the pubs, but I managed to save enough for Greece. I remember Bernard Kops, and on another day John Osborne, walking by.

I took a boat to Belgium and hitched to Amsterdam and met Mary and we travelled by train via Yugoslavia. We went to Athens and saw the Acropolis in a fierce heat and then got straight out to the Greek islands. We got to Spetsai, and were invited to spend five (free) days on a yacht in Spetsai harbour by a Greek local who seemed to like us. Every morning we went ashore, and every day the "krik-krak" (fast motor launch with a low back) went across to the island of Spetsopoula, where the billionaire Stavros Niarchos lived, and I sent a message via the driver of the boat asking if we could visit Spetsopoula, and I can see the "krik-krak" returning and the driver leaping out yelling "Niarchos Niarchos" and waving a letter – which merely regretted that he would be unable to receive us as he had only recently arrived.

We went on to Porto Cheli, a very small place, and while swimming met a rich Athenian couple who had a summer residence on the hill there. In the evenings we all ate in the only seaside café. We always had yoghurt for pudding and drank a carafe of retsina. One evening the Greeks all stood and formed themselves in an unsteady line and a man with a domed head and parchment white face arrived in a fisherman's clothes and paraded up and down the line, inspecting them. "Grivas," a waiter said to me, "Colonel Grivas." It was indeed the Greek leader of EOKA who had lived underground in Cyprus while fighting there. He had just successfully brought self-determination to Cyprus (EOKA) – the first elections of the new Cyprus had taken place in July – but he had not been successful in establishing Greek rule in Cyprus (Enosis). After the inspection he sat at the next table and I sent a message over via the waiter, "Can I please interview you for a British newspaper?" The answer came back, "He say no, he don't like Macmillan." I sent a return message saying "I'm not part of the British government, I will interview you sympathetically about Enosis." This was too much for Grivas. He stood up and everyone else jumped to their feet and lined up again, and after a brief inspection he left. I tried to follow him but he had simply vanished without trace.

I left Mary in the care of the Greek family – a year later she told me she started a relationship with the husband – and waiving goodbye left for Athens and met Jill who had just come off a plane.

The next part of the holiday was a total disaster. I had virtually run out of money, and Jill wanted everything 5-star. We got out of Athens as soon as we could and went to Euboea, to which I felt drawn because of the silver drachma I had found in Seaby's and bought some years back. In Calchis Jill booked in at the most expensive hotel while I slept on the beach. We travelled around as best we could, but she complained that Greece was ugly and that I was content to eat in ugly places (as opposed to the very expensive places she wanted to eat in). From Calchis we took a boat to Sciathos to see Rupert Brooke's tomb. In the course of climbing up to it I encountered a grave that had collapsed inwards and saw the skeleton lying on its back, looking at the blue sky, surrounded by pines and whirring cicadas in the heat. I wrote a few poems, feeling a common bond with Brooke, and then we took a boat to the mainland and hitchhiked and took a bus into Yugoslavia. Once or twice Jill used the sleeping-bag she had bought and kept me company sleeping under the stars, but she could not sleep and talked all night, keeping me awake and I just wanted to escape. (She was like the neurotic woman in Eliot's *Waste Land*, who said "My nerves are bad tonight..../Speak to me....Speak.") I had now run out of money and she would not lend me any, although she had hundreds of pounds of travellers cheques. In Skopje I changed my last £10 into Yugoslav currency and had just enough to buy a bus ticket to Dubrovnik. and a boat ticket to Rijeka in Croatia, after which my return train ticket could be used. I managed to get Jill on to the boat and as we steamed from Dubrovnik via Split to Rijeka she behaved unreasonably, sitting in a German's bagged deck-chair and complaining when she was shouted at. I can remember passing along the beautiful wooded Dalmatian coastline, but being too concerned to avoid Jill and various irate passengers really to enjoy it.

Somehow we got home. I believe Jill went by plane from Venice and I took the train. What I do know is that I was relieved to have escaped her, and that nothing would induce me to settle with her in Ludham Hall, as she would have driven me mad. Two months later I had a note from her: "I have been reading this morning and suddenly it struck me how absolutely despicably I acted by you and with you. I feel I ought almost to ask you to forgive me or at any rate to blot it out of your memory."

Back in Loughton I saw something of a girl called Polly, whom I had met earlier that year. I read the Victorian novelists and poets for a collection and went for solitary walks in the Forest and watched the dry leaves turn and begin to fall, and I thought about wrinkled human beings. As I faced my third year and the pressures of finding a job I felt faintly depressed, and I returned to Oxford in inner turmoil to the digs I had found, a first floor room a bus ride down Walton Street. It was in a tiny two up, two down terraced house and I was on top of the landlady and her husband, a most uncongenial couple who went to bed at 10 and expected me to do the same and not creep up the stairs in the dark. I stood it for a fortnight – during which Inge came and Jill Bradbury visited me and we went to a pub round the corner (the Walton Arms) and Iris Murdoch came in and had a chat (Jill knew her) – and then found a room at 57 Southmoor Road, a house with an absentee landlord. I had a first floor room at the back, overlooking a garden at the end of which ran a canal and beyond which I could see Port Meadow.

The absentee landlord appeared once a week to collect rent, which was £2.10s. My parents visited soon afterwards, and my father was shocked. He said, "It's no better than a condemned house." I lived next door to two girls – two secretaries – and here came other girls I knew for tea, including Jill Bradbury, who picked up my Tutankhamun figurine from the mantelpiece and dropped it, chipping a piece off the foot. Here, because there was no landlady, one of my friends brought a French girl called Dominique, who slept on my floor. Here the next day came John Ezard, and we all went for a walk in Port Meadow, along the tow-path by the brimming river towards Binsey Green, and I remember John speaking of "Resistentialism", and explaining to Dominique, "Res (les choses) sont contre nous." On the way back we passed a number of swans, and the river looked high and arctic with the flat fields and Oxford behind it.

It must have been in November that the former President of the Oxford Union, Jo Trattner, turned up in the girls' room next door. He wore an overcoat and a scarf, and I went for a walk with him and he told me how as President of the Union he had dealt with a protest against Macmillan (the Prime Minister was a guest speaker) and earned unpopularity. We walked to Jericho, a working class district in Oxford's suburbs, and had a drink in a pub with sawdust on the floor, the Jericho Arms. He came by several times after that and we walked the streets or went to Port Meadow.

Sometimes I read a Victorian novel a day, and although the examination course ended in 1860 I longed to study Blake, Hardy, Yeats and Lawrence, and pleaded with Christopher Ricks to be allowed to write essays which would help me when I was a writer. He said firmly, "Only when, and if, you've completed the course," but the creative urge was strong and I wrote several poems. I read Jung and recorded my dreams in a notebook that was permanently beside my bed – for two years I had had recurrent dreams of being executed as a soldier – and I had an overpowering urge to write. I knew poems would never bring me enough to live off. Abruptly I began writing a play. It was conceived as a poetic drama, but the more I wrote the more realistic it became. It was a piece of juvenilia, but it had great feeling in it. It took a chunk out of each week's work but it got me into the habit of writing.

I had become very friendly with the two girls next door and had noticed one of them kissing her boy-friend under the gaslamp as I came home. They encouraged me to look in on them for coffee, and early one evening I found one of them by herself, wearing black, and began a relationship with her which lasted the rest of my time at Oxford. Caroline was a very young, beautiful blonde who did not look unlike Marilyn Monroe. She was full of feeling: when she was happy she brimmed with confidence, and when she was not happy she was withdrawn and vulnerable. Some evenings she felt depressed and she would go and sit by the canal and cry alone, and she did not want to be disturbed. I could hear her through my open window, crying quietly in the twilight by the canal, and I wondered what the mind that was doing the crying was enduring. Sometimes we went for a walk across the railway bridge into Port Meadow and looked at the wild horses and walked to the bridge over the river and crossed over to the tow-path. Even in early winter it was a lovely walk on a Sunday afternoon and we would come home just before dark and have tea. I would toast sliced bread against my gasfire.

That Christmas I returned home. I again worked for the post office. I delivered Christmas parcels from a large removal lorry with a tail held by chains, and we arranged parcels in order and delivered to Spareleaze Hill and Tycehurst Hill and other parts of Loughton. I had a few free days and I went up to the British Museum and worked in the Library. I used to sit between the Greco-Roman-style columns on the front steps at lunch time, and at closing time I always stopped and looked at the autographed manuscripts of writers on my way out to the steps.

One night in the new year I went out and returned home late to discover I had left my key behind and that the house was in darkness. I went round the back and found a ladder that just reached to my brother Robert's window ledge and climbed and tapped on his small window. He sat up in bed and opened the window outwards and said, "Colin Wilson rang. He wants you to go down to Cornwall to write an article, he will pay your fares." And so it was that, after chatting to Colin Wilson the next day on the phone, I took a train from Paddington to St. Austell and rang him from a nearby call box and waited for his car. He drove me back to Tetherdown and we drank goblets of wine.

I spent getting on for a week with him in Cornwall. During the day I camped on the sofa while Colin sat in his chair by the permanent log fire with his electric typewriter on an arm which he pulled across or pushed aside. At night I walked to the chalet in his garden and slept in one of the two rooms there. The window looked across the cliffs to the sea, and each morning I woke early and walked down to Gorran Haven and had coffee and bought a paper because Colin did not surface until getting on for 11.

LOOKING ABROAD

We wrote the article on the first day. *The Sunday Despatch* were paying £100 for an article about drug-taking at Oxford, and I provided some vivid details from what I had seen on the Beatnik fringe at Oxford. (The article caused a storm of controversy, and questions were asked about it in the House of Lords) After that we settled into a daily rhythm. I worked on the sofa, he worked in his chair and inundated me with chapters to read and extracts of his work. On one occasion the baker came to the door and he showed the baker how far he had got. In those days Colin Wilson was lean, vigorous and mentally energetic, and virtually every sentence he spoke contained another writer's name. I told him about my encounters with Sartre and Hemingway, and the Metaphysical and Romantic poets, and he was very definite as to how one should live as an Existentialist. He described his early struggle to read books while doing odd jobs – he would have Shaw open while wheeling barrowloads of cement and read a page between wheeling loads – and told me about Continental writers such as Wedekind and Durenmatt who were on the fringe of my consciousness. Those were exciting days; it is impossible to communicate the sense of intellectual excitement that being in Colin Wilson's company generated at that time, when the tiniest everyday event was related to an overall Existentialist philosophy and knowledge was related to living in a way that no Oxford tutor related it. And there was a directness and openness about his conversation which cut across all taboos and seemed liberating: "I sit here and work," he said, "and Joy brings everything. Just call 'Pepper' or 'Salt' or 'Sex' and it will appear."

Towards the end of my stay I wandered down to Gorran Haven harbour and stood on the wall and looked at the sea and felt an exile like the Old English Wanderer and Seafarer. Mary had written urging me to teach in Ankara for a year. Suddenly I made a decision. I knew I had to live abroad. I did not know where, I had to get away from England and work out my own "existence philosophy" through fresh and strange impressions. I had to live *outside* my own civilisation and discover myself as a writer, find out what kind of writer I was to be. The prospect of living alone in an unknown place filled me with a certain dread, but one of my favourite Old English texts was from *Beowulf* –"wyrd oft nereth unfaegne eorl thonne his ellen deah", "fate often preserves the undoomed warrior when his courage is strong" – and I prided myself on being undoomed and on having courage. I was sure I would survive and that my quest would be successful. On my return we went to the Rising Sun, Portmellon, where there was a watersplash in those days as the tide sometimes covered the road, and where I told Colin Wilson of my resolve. I told him: "I shall become a wanderer, an exile, for ten years."

I had been invited to take part in a Brains Trust of young people who were ex-pupils at Oaklands School (which I now own). An arrangement to catch the right train was made, but somehow we all overslept. Colin Wilson drove me at breakneck speed to St. Austell, and we arrived to see the London train pulling out of the station. Without hesitation, and with a promptness typical of the excellent host that he was, he set off for Plymouth to race the train. "I don't like to be beaten," he said. He drove incredibly fast, but when we reached Plymouth again the train had just gone. So there was nothing for it but for me to wait for the next train. I said goodbye to Colin, who went off to buy books in Plymouth, and settled down to wait. By the time I arrived at Oaklands School, Loughton, the Brains Trust was in progress. I took my place at the speakers' table, late, explaining I had been delayed in Cornwall, and answered questions. My mother asked, "What is the ideal age to get married?" and I replied without hesitation: "About thirty. Because by then you'll have done what you want to do."

I put my determination to go abroad into practice by sitting the Civil Service's Method 2 exam, which was an entry to the Senior branch of the Foreign Service. News of my encounter with Grivas and how I had tried to interview him had spread. I had been invited to sherry with the College Provost, Sir John Masterman, the previous November, and I believe it was he who suggested I should sit the exam with a view to going into the Foreign Office. I went to London for it and sat the papers, which contained literary questions I enjoyed answering and unpalatable, turgid questions about "expenditure on public roads in Great Britain" and involving charts of vehicle licences. I had to sit in a group of would-be Ambassadors and discuss Sarrault and the nouveau roman, among other topics. Having debunked the nouveau roman with Colin Wilson I could hardly contain myself at the bland dinner-table passionless approach of others in the group who were simply not concerned with the merits of the works, but were only concerned to name-drop. Colin Wilson would not have stood for this. The Angry Young Man and the Young Conservative in me had co-existed uneasily, but the Existentialist writer in me simply could not co-exist with these smooth diplomats. There and then I decided the Foreign Office was not the place for me.

What overseas careers other than the Foreign Office remained for one determined to live abroad in the early 1960s? From the 1880s to the 1940s bright young men (like Biggs-Davison) had gone out into the British Empire as administrators, to India or Africa, and had taken responsibility and pioneered and faced strange terrain and learned about themselves. Some (like my uncle Tom) went out to one of the world wars and faced extreme situations before an enemy. But the Empire was no more; when I was a boy it had been given away, and following the advent of nuclear weapons world wars were (thank goodness) no longer possible. The only post-1940s equivalent for a would-be writer was to throw oneself into the Cold War, to join the tussle for the Middle East, Africa or South East Asia between the Soviet Russians and the Americans and their local agents, following in the imperial footsteps of sometime writer-spies such as Defoe, T. E. Lawrence (my hero), Kipling, Somerset Maugham, John Buchan, Compton MacKenzie, Graham Greene and Malcolm Muggeridge. Or else one could go abroad and lecture to overseas students like Robert Graves and John Heath-Stubbs (in Alexandria) or William Empson and Edmund Blunden (in Japan). A host of writers had lived as expatriates at universities in exotic places, and the British Council had acted as an agency and set up contract appointments at universities in foreign countries for Lawrence Durrell (whose *Alexandrian Quartet* was much discussed at that time) and for Anthony Burgess (who wrote a Malaysian trilogy). In the early 1960s the British had not withdrawn east of Suez and it maintained a world-wide operation for overseas lecturers on a far grander scale than happens today. To teach in an exciting place was like crossing the frontier of Western civilisation and teaching the "barbarians" rather than doing battle with them; it was like leaving Rome for the extreme conditions of barbarian life.

For some months I had developed an increasing interest in the East. Ricky had always been interested in Buddhist and Hindu thought, and Kingsley's interest in Eastern thinking had grown. I remember one particular discussion we had in the Randolph about this time in which Ricky asserted that there were no accidents and that there was "no self". I knew within that I had to go to Japan, and to that end I contacted the British Council and had an interview in London in March. The British Council acted as an agency and set up contract appointments at universities in foreign countries.

By Easter I had finished the English course, and I had in fact written essays on Blake and Yeats (Michael Horovitz lent me his essay on Blake), and ahead was the drudgery of revising Old and Middle English and I was ready to leave. Quite simply, I had had enough of work I didn't want to do and I wanted to concentrate on what I did want to do, as I used to tell my associates at that time: the All Souls don Alasdair Clayre; an Old Chigwellian and young research student Stephen Medcalf, who came to tea from time to time; and a ginger-haired undergraduate called Noel, who wrote poems – he showed me one about Oxford at night in which the moon "slid behind Tom Tower" – and who became private tutor to one of the Rothschild family on leaving. A number of girls also made regular visits, including Jenny Terrell, Naseem Khan (who became a journalist), Geraldine James (who began work at the Royal Shakespeare Theatre, Stratford in July) and Jill Bradbury, who still kept inviting me to Ludham Hall, and when I refused persuaded Ricky to go instead.

I now wanted to write a play about Cromwell called *The Holy Brotherhood*, and I wrote to the History tutor Mr Campbell (the one Peter O'Toole had frightened) and received a letter back pointing me in the direction of what to research. I did not know that the Illuminati were known as the World or Universal Brotherhood, and that I would need the concept of the Brotherhood in over 30 years' time.

It soon became apparent that it would be hard to go to Japan immediately as there were no vacancies there for September. The British Council advised me to consider going elsewhere for a year. The need to obtain a job of some sort was looming and I found snippets of poems just coming of their own accord, often at the most inconvenient times. I yearned to have the freedom to write. I remember going to hear Alain Robbe-Grillet, a French avant-gardist novelist who described objects in great detail, and saying to Alasdair Clayre on the way out that my problem was to find a job that would allow me to write. I wanted to get settled.

I had met Herbie Butterfield, who was also reading English, at the Randolph. He had an engaging blink and at the house where he was living he told me he had read over 90% of his vast library of books. I told him that I would one day write a great novel, great in length as well as in stature, and he said "If it's long, no one will read it." (Kingsley had been present and had said, "You'll be happier if you recognise that like me you're a consumer not a producer of culture.") It must have been just after the gruelling and long drawn-out Final examinations, during which I had a tummy bug and a deeper than usual aversion to Old and Middle English grammar and which I could not wait to get out of the way, that I went down to London one late afternoon and ran into Herbie in a crowded London street. Unusually for him he was in a dark suit, and he told me he had just been interviewed by the British Council for a job at Baghdad University, that he had got it but had decided he was not going to go as he would stay with his girl friend. "You can go in my place if you like," he said.

Baghdad was then known as a dangerous place (as it is today). The ruler was the revolutionary Kaseem who opposed the British over Kuwait. But Baghdad was also a very romantic and historical place. I was terrified at the thought of becoming a lecturer and exposing my nervousness, but if being a lecturer gave me some time to write, then I would force myself to do what I dreaded – existentially choose to act against my own nature. There and then I went to the British Council's headquarters at 65 Davies Street and I registered my interest in going to Baghdad. Being already on the British Council's books, I was interviewed very soon afterwards by Arthur Plowman, the Head of Department in Baghdad, an elderly man with a face like a skull and dreamy eyes and a lifetime's service in the British Empire, and at the beginning of July I was asked to have a medical. Soon, in early July, I heard that I would be going to Iraq at the end of September.

Was it luck or was it Providential, that meeting with Herbie Butterfield? Was Ricky right to assert that there are "no accidents", that everything that happens is by Providential design? I felt elated, for all that year I had wanted to escape England, and the escape had just happened.

The question then became: what would I do about Caroline? I had a discussion with her, and she felt deeply about me and wanted to join me in Baghdad and find a job there. But as soon as she tried there were obstacles: visa complications, objections from her parents – she was 19 – and lack of work. It rapidly became clear that the only way she could accompany me and live with me in a Moslem country would be as my wife. Back in Loughton I thought about this next step very carefully as I wandered through Epping Forest, examining my feelings for her, and I reckoned that I had a stark existential choice: either marry and live with her for the few years ahead that I could foresee, or say goodbye now. Mary returned from Ankara, looking glamorous and sunburnt, and said when I met her, "You don't need to marry her." However, eating my words in the Oaklands hall that the ideal time to marry was 30 (my better judgement), I asked Caroline to marry me. I was 21 and she 19.

Now I rejected Christianity. Over the last two years I had had occasionally discussions with Geoffrey Ainger, the Methodist Minister who had replaced the American who had succeeded Mr Grant, about Camus and Ivan Karamazov. He had lent me his thesis on Camus. In early September I visited him and told him that I would like excommunication. He told me it was impossible: "I admire your integrity, your perception. I'd feel betrayed if you accepted God's word before you were sure. Knowing God is like being undermined." I asked: "What would you say to Ivan Karamazov?" He said: "I'd say 'Come to church', just that, 'Come to church.'" But, I tried to say, church is full of insincere bourgeois who have not thought deeply, not of outsiders who see too deep and too much, that's not an answer. (Two or three years later I heard he had left the Church and his wife and become a rent-collector.)

After introductions to each other's families and many organisational arrangements Caroline and I were married on 16th September 1961 at St. Clement Danes in the Strand, the church whose bells say "Oranges and Lemons", and the reception took place in Dulwich. John Ezard said, "Caroline will never be bored with Nicholas." We honeymooned in and around Arundel and visited villages like Pulborough, going no farther as our priority was to get ourselves off to Iraq.

I will not describe those days in detail as my purpose is not to dwell on social organisation but to explain how an ordinary background could lead to the metaphysical attitudes I now have. My wife's parents lived in a large house in Alleyn Park, West Dulwich. They were retired (he was an ex-RAF Group-Captain – and I left Caroline there while I attended a British Council course at Midhurst in Sussex. It was at Dunford House, which was associated with Richard Cobden who was behind the repeal of the Corn Laws in 1846 and who stood for free trade, and over 20 of us were lectured by various double-barrelled ex-imperialists and ex-colonials on what we might expect in the countries we were about to live in. The main event of each day took place on the croquet lawn in the evening, where a permanently dazed-looking, dark-haired comedian among us, Logan-Reid, (with whom I shared a room), put his foot on his ball and ruthlessly hit any ball near his into a ditch. Soon afterwards I attended a conference for language teachers in London – Naseem Khan was there on her way to Finland – at which a much-moustached, silver-haired F. C. Billows introduced the direct method of teaching language by speaking at us in Turkish. (Later, I went out to an adjoining room and found him fast asleep on his back on the carpeted floor.)

I returned to Dulwich and packed for Baghdad. The University of Baghdad had supplied air tickets and the British Council a clothing allowance of £100 to buy tropical clothing, but otherwise I had no money. I had lived off my grant, which had now stopped, and my father gave me £180 in national savings certificates, which he had saved for me from the time I was a boy. I cashed these and the balance in my Post Office Book and left for Baghdad with £8 in the world, and a few wedding presents. Our baggage was limited, and we were prepared to live out of the contents of three suitcases for getting on for a year. I was desperate for my first salary payment.

We flew Iraqi Airlines. It was my first flight, and I had my first contact with happy-go-lucky Arabs when the pilot invited me into the cockpit high above clouds and cheerfully allowed me to take the control column and steer the plane. In the course of doing this I tilted the plane down and up, and when I returned to the passenger section, looking sheepish, nearly everyone was bent over a paper bag, so bad was the turbulence I had caused.

A MYSTIC WAY

In Baghdad we were met by the Representative of the British Council, Ross-Thomas, a sandy-haired, balding man whose paintings of Iraqi landscapes hung over mantelpieces all round Baghdad. The airport was full of noise, a crowd of Arabs had just cut the throat of a sheep and were dipping their hands in the blood and putting handprints on a nearby wall to ward off the Evil Eye. A radio played that whirly-twirly Arab music we were to hear so often. We were driven to the Hotel Sindibad, where dinner was served at 10 p.m. (Eating at 10 p.m. has since become a lifelong habit.)

The next morning I reported to the University, driving in a taxi through hot, messy, sprawling, dusty, noisy streets that were full of soldiers, and passing desert sand and palms and barefooted Arabs, sheep and goats. I returned salutes and said "Salaam a lecum" to various officials and to the staff farrash (servant). My salary was virtually the same as the level my father's had reached after 40 years. Back at the Hotel Sindibad I reviewed the options as to where to live. In a heat of 120 degrees we visited an unfurnished mustama (villa), an empty building with thick stone walls and floors, but the rent was £400 a year, excluding servant, food, fridge and furniture, and with £8 and a salary of £112 a month, I could not see how we could afford it for the nine months of my contract. Consequently we moved into the virtually empty, spacious and well-furnished YWCA by the airport, which was run by a Lebanese woman called Sophie, where we had the large double front room, a watchman (Hachim) and a servant (one-eyed Yelda) who cooked our meals. We had the use of the sitting-room downstairs, where slim lizards lived on the mosquito netting of the windows and licked any flies that came too near, darting out a tongue and pulling the fly in before you could blink, and of the table-tennis table and library; and rent and food together were something like £36 a month for the two of us. Almost immediately Caroline got a job at the kindergarten next door, and we settled into the routine of rising early , at 6 a.m., having a siesta from 2 to 4, and going to bed around 11.

As soon as we had moved in, I took an antiquated bus to Rashid Street and a group taxi from the main square, Bab Sherji, which I shared with various sheep and goats and women wearing black abbayas and negotiated an advance on my salary and met my students, all of whom seemed older than me, in the College cafeteria, where they announced, "We are very pleased to know you, we will now have a party." Almost immediately they arranged to take me to Ctesiphon, the Persian winter capital, for a picnic. We sat under the famous arched ruin there, the ruin of the palace of the Sasanian king Shapur I.

The YWCA was out in the sand desert, and it was so hot that we had to sleep with the windows open. Minute sandflies crawled through the fine mesh of the mosquito netting and I was bitten all over, and was soon delirious with a temperature that fluctuated upwards from 104. I was in bed, with a high fever and malarial-type sweats and shiverings, and could not keep gibberish out of my head and kept seeing confused and hideous pictures. My aunt Argie had written to an Iraqi doctor whose wife had been a nurse at the London Hospital, and I first met him when he visited me. "How are you?" he asked. "I've got a temperature of 107," I replied in a lucid moment. "You can't, you would be dead," he said, taking my temperature. Then he said "Oh," for it was indeed 107.

Baghdad, city of Arabian nights where so much history happened. I had so many new impressions. Now we were settled in, I warmed to it, and soon established a routine. The muezzin's first call from a nearby mosque was at 5.30 a.m. Every morning at 6.45 a.m. I had a lift to the College of Education on a minibus. We drove from Mansoor under wonderful dawn skies through some of the 15 million palm trees alongside the misty, shimmering Tigris and across the bridge to Waziryah, and periodically the driver would spot a friend and slow down and shout through the window, "Schlon saher, schlon ek?" ("How are you?") A jocular reply was "Nejleh gaher," "I have a filthy cough and horrid cold". My first lecture was at 8. Lectures were informal and chatty and book-related, and took place in antiquated, dark classrooms with a raised mullah's dais. The students were little younger than I was and were quite lively. Whatever I tried to teach them, they had a lot to say. When I had free time between lectures and wanted to escaped the long staff room where Arthur Plowman sat and we all had tables round the walls, I went to the nearby resource centre, the Centre for English Studies, and worked in the small garden. Sometimes the bushes were full of locusts, and I often prepared lectures and marked books with a\ dozen locusts over four inches long crawling round my writing hand and many more crawling on my back. I returned home at 1 p.m., travelling to Bab Sherji past mosques with golden domes and blue and yellow minarets and then walking along "Smallpox Alley" (I called it), a narrow medieval Turkish street with an open sewer down the middle, and braving the line of begging abbayaed women near the bus stop, took the 20 bus to the YWCA. One-eyed Yelda, a Christian Chaldean who spoke Aramaic, the language of Christ, had lunch waiting for us. Once he stopped me treading on a scorpion which sat in the middle of the kitchen floor. Lunch generally consisted of egg-plant. Then we had our siesta under the ceiling fan which looked like an aeroplane propeller, winding towels around our middles to avoid catching a chill, and then we rose and either I sat and worked or wrote until dinner, or else we went out, sometimes to Dr Shubber's house for dinner with his family, sometimes with an Iraqi friend like Sabih the banker, who took us to eat mazgoof (fish) by the Tigris. When we stayed in I would work at my desk in the corner of the room until Caroline persuaded me to abandon my work. "I adore you," she used to say, "I wouldn't mind if you killed me, if you wanted to." (Saying this was her way of surrendering her whole being to me.) In those Baghdad evenings we were very happy.

We were invited to the 38th anniversary of the Turkish Republic at the Turkish Embassy. We were drinking long whisky and sodas and shelling and munching "fistak" (pistachio) nuts in the grounds at the back when soldiers suddenly began jumping up and down on the settees, which stood in the open air, doing a security check. Then Gen. Kaseem, the man who had the revolution in 1958 and murdered the royal family, made his entrance and walked among us, surrounded by his guards. Suddenly a band struck up the anthem and I saw people running in different directions.

A MYSTIC WAY

Kaseem, bare-headed and wearing khaki, stood at the salute about a yard from me while I stood to attention. For a minute we stood side by side, he looking at me out of the corner of his eyes, and when the anthem was finished Ross-Thomas approached and said, "I say, you're brave. Don't you realise that he's a target at the salute? There might be snipers on the rooftops beyond those palms. When Kaseem takes the salute, you get as far away from him as you can."

Being out in the desert, we always had scenes beneath our windows that could have come from the Bible. There was a sarifa (mud-hut) settlement near us, and there were always sheep, goats and camels, including one-humped dromedaries, and fodder-laden donkeys being driven along the sandy tracks by shepherds in long robes or bare-footed boys in striped night-shirts (jellabas). There were parrots and other vivid birds, one of which Yelda called a "baba ra". One day I heard a shriek from Caroline and rushed downstairs and found Yelda standing over a small whimpering puppy with a knife. "Yelda's cut its ears off," she sobbed. "Sir," he said, puzzled, still holding the ears, "we always do this or bugs get into ears and kill it. This help the dog." In the evenings groups of pye-dogs prowled below our windows. Once when it was very hot we risked the sandflies to sleep on the flat roof. We wheeled our beds out and lay and watched the crescent moon on its back over rows of silent palms that ringed the airport and incredibly bright stars. At the weekends we took a taxi to the souk (market) – the taxi-driver always asked for "rubba dinar" (a quarter of a dinar or 250 fils) – and we looked at the carpet sellers and brass coffee-pot sellers and revelled in the intimate atmosphere in which artefacts of beauty were bargained for over small cups of "chai" ("tea"). I now knew that a young blonde woman in Baghdad causes a perpetual sensation, and the Dutch Cultural Attaché asked Caroline to model some clothes at a department store. I discovered what marriage was like when she returned from her first modelling rehearsal to say she had been offered a lovely three-piece suit (which she had with her) at the bargain price of £65. In vain I protested that we had to pay £36 rent and live off the rest of the £112 for a month, and repay the advance on my first month's salary. She pleaded, her salary would buy our food. The suit became an issue, and, aware that I had uprooted her from her own country, I gave in, knowing it was economic madness.

In November the rains came. Baghdad had always been full of hazards; for example, manhole covers suddenly went missing at bus-stops, so if we were not careful we could fall 50 feet down into the open sewers while getting off a bus. Now the electric system was alive, and it was safer to ring door-bells with a pencil in case we got a shock. All the roads turned thick with mud, and Arabs hitched their night-shirts and tip-toed through the streets, while the boys treated the coming of water after the baking summer as we regard snow, and joyfully rolled in the puddles. The sarifa (mud-hut) families were incredibly welcoming, and it must have been about this time that I was invited in to take tea with twenty mud-hut dwellers, and learned that their weekly income was 4/2d: two bottles of leben (yoghurt) sent to market.

I noticed and remembered all the visual details with a poet's eye, but I wrote no poems. Now that the pressure was on me to support a family, I thought of writing as mass-communication, and in those days that meant writing a novel, although few novels earned very much. After I had finished my work for my lectures I spent many evenings sitting at my desk making notes for a novel that was never written, until Caroline implored me, "Come to bed, darling." Those evenings set up a writing discipline that was to help me for the rest of my life.

Almost immediately Caroline had appendicitis and was operated on by Dr Shubber. She had a private room in the hospital, and when I went to visit her I passed through wards where families of a dozen or more squatted round the beds, brewing tea.

We had Christmas lunch at Dr Shubber's, where we were given a plate decorated with a bearded, winged bull which still hangs on my wall, and soon afterwards we flew to Basra. In the air above Ur I received the words "Life Cycle" and scribbled down headings for a work on a whole life and its cycle. This was an embryonic version of my vision of civilisations which eventually became *The Fire and the Stones*. We took a boat up the Shatt al-Arab towards Abadan. As we progressed up the brown river we passed through idyllic scenery: peasants burning peat among jungle palms on the banks on either side, signs of peace and tranquillity. For several hours we were transported into a pre-industrial age, and the visit left a lasting impression.

Soon afterwards an Iraqi friend drove us to a lake beyond the Euphrates in very fertile ground, and we visited Gourna, where the Tigris and Euphrates meet, the site of Paradise. Dug-out boats were drawn up on the shore, and we saw the Tree of Knowledge (or the forbidden fruit), at which Abraham is supposed to have prayed. Nearby we saw Lazarus's tomb, which is claimed by both Christians and Moslems.

At the mid-year break in January we took a group taxi across the desert via Rutba to Bethlehem. Thence we travelled to Jericho, the Dead Sea – we walked to the caves where the Dead Sea Scrolls were found at Qumran and saw some jars being carried out – and then to Bethany, where we saw the site of Martha's and Mary's house, and the River Jordan. We went onto Jerusalem, where we visited the Mount of Olives where Jesus lived; Gethsemane, the grotto where Jesus was arrested; Calvary (a church has been built over the original rock); and the Garden Tomb. In the Via Dolorosa I bought a silver Russian Orthodox cross. We went onto Amman, Damascus and then Beirut, before returning by desert bus, bumping over red-brown sand and stones with no path and only a compass as guide. I pondered on Christianity and felt nothing divine happened in the Garden Tomb. I had a profound sense that I had visited these places for a reason that would be revealed in the future.

When we returned, from our room we saw a plane crash on the runway next to the YWCA. It could not get its wheels down, and it circled several times, using up fuel, while crowds gathered all round the perimeter fence as the news spread, and watched at the plane came in low, skidded, slewed sideways amid a cloud of red dust, and came to a standstill. All round the airport Arabs climbed over the fence and rushed towards the aircraft, cheering and ululating with joy, and I felt a bond with the invisible human beings whose lives had been at risk, and was thankful that they were safe.

I had had three months of new impressions and sensations, but I was also assimilating and reflecting. Since November I had begun to synthesise all the knowledge I had acquired in all subjects, including the sciences and philosophy, working at a table in a corner of our room in the YWCA. I felt wonderfully alive. Visually I had absorbed much of the Middle East, and I had also digested my experience. I had seen much that was visually interesting and may vivid things – the streets were full of many nationalities such as Lurs carrying furniture on their backs or peacock-worshipping Yezzidis – but I had not met any Sufis, and the Islamic culture I had experienced was pretty decayed and superficial. I found the Arabs generally lacked depth and were more decayed than westerners. Although I was glad I had come to look I did not intend to remain here like Ross-Thomas and become an expert on the differing customs of each region. I knew I had to move on, and I handed my resignation into Arthur Plowman from July.

I now felt slightly discontented, for I was aware that the immediate vivid social and political impressions were in some way an obstacle to the long-term philosophical reality I should be finding. Reading Camus's *Rebel* while travelling between Baghdad, Jerusalem and Damascus and synthesising my knowledge in all disciplines were a way of expressing the sense that I ought to be understanding my experience.

The bizarre outer distractions of Baghdad were very soon in evidence at the start of the new term in February. Almost immediately it was Ramadan, the Moslem month of fasting. I had one notorious class 3B, who had followed a lady lecturer home and threatened to beat her up unless they all passed the coming examination, and who had rioted when I caught two of them blatantly cheating during my examination. (They had risen up like a pack of cards when I confiscated the papers of the two cheats, and I stood my ground while reinforcements arrived.) Arthur Plowman ranted at the staff and said that all 3B should fail, and when three of us failed 15 of them he changed his mind and gently said they should all pass. The 15 included one young lady, Semira, who wore an abbaya to College but who sang in a night-club every evening and whose passably accurate English compositions were about the men she went home with. When Arthur realised he had passed Semira, he seized her script and wrote "Failed" across the top. We protested that Semira was good enough to pass. Then word spread that the University was making it harder to pass, and so the students went on strike.

I had a few days' holiday and eventually lectures resumed. I was told that there was a spy of Kaseem's in every class. I had to teach Tennyson's *Ulysses*, which begins "It little profits that an idle king", and any mention of any king was totally banned by the revolutionary government of "the honest and faithful Leader, Brigadier-General Abdul Karim Kaseem" (the words with which the *Iraqi Times* began every front page story). Nevertheless I threw off ideas in lectures – there may not have been freedom of speech in Iraq, but there was freedom of speech in my class – and several times I mentioned Existentialism. A group of 40 year old students told me, "We discuss you every evening in the hostel, and we say we must talk with Mr Hagger on thees (sic) subject of Existentialism."

I relocated my reason for being in Iraq when we went to Babylon with a grey-haired small lecturer called Groos. On the way we saw some storks on top of an old caravanserai (or camel night-house). They had just arrived from Africa and we had seen storks perching on telegraph poles and minarets, and we stopped and climbed onto the roof of the caravanserai. I had been reading with 3B the *Rubaiyat of Omar Khayyam* in the 1859 edition of Edward Fitzgerald's translation, and I quoted from the roof, thinking of Kaseem as the Sultan:

> "Think, in this batter'd Caravanserai
> Whose Doorways are alternate Night and Day,
> How Sultan after Sultan with his Pomp
> Abode his Hour or two and went his way."

(I loved Omar Khayyam who perfectly evoked my feelings about Baghdad.)

Babylon was low sand-coloured walls, some with bulls and griffons on them, with the palm-lined Euphrates nearby. We wandered round and picked up some slabs with cuneiform on them. I was arrested and was made to surrender them as "government property". We went on to Nimrod, the ziggurat or high place which was the original site of the Tower of Babel. I found more slabs there, and poked in the totally unexcavated town nearby and found a coin. As in the case of my visit to Jerusalem and the other ancient places in the Middle East, I sensed that I had come to Iraq to absorb past civilisations for some project that lay ahead in the future. I felt that I was locating my destiny.

Back in Baghdad Caroline rode every day in the desert. An Iraqi had said we could exercise his grey stallion, and I borrowed another stallion and we rode bare-backed into the desert several times. Caroline started a new morning job – I forget how she came to be asked – working in the Embassy Commercial Office which was hidden above a bank. She was given a lift into work by a Major who was Military Attaché, and on the way they observed the new Army equipment which the "brave Iraqi Army" had taken delivery of. On one occasion they found a new Russian truck of unknown use, and as it was parked near the YWCA I went to have a look at it and was nearly arrested by the Army. We had a good view of the road from the YWCA and often saw troops marching by, all out of step. We took to counting the tanks that went by each morning, which Caroline relayed to the Military Attaché on his way to work.

One day, I arrived at the University campus and found myself in the middle of a fight between Communist students and Nationalist students. About 30 students including some from 3B, scythed and kicked, and I shouted "Stop this", and to my amazement they all ran off. Then I saw the Army arrive with Sten guns, and I ran off so that I would not have to denounce any of the students I had seen.

Journeying to and fro between the University, I often passed the Ministry of Defence. It had railings around it and on high, on a small pillar behind the railings, was a bullet-ridden car in which "the honest and faithful

Leader" (zahim) had survived one of the 28th assassination attempts against him since he took power three years previously. He had crawled from the bullet-riddled car screaming, "I am immortal," and in speeches afterwards he ranted, "They can shoot me from the right and they can shoot me from the left, but they will never kill me, I am immortal." And the postage stamps hailed him as the Great and Glorious, Honest and Faithful, Bright and Shining Leader whose Immortal Revolution of July 14th, 1958 shall outlive history, who has given freedom to all Iraqis and who shall be ranked as a prophet". The Leader's picture was in every street and in every shop, and I did not have to talk to the students to know that he had become a tyrant. I could feel the opposition growing. Everywhere were the poor who had not benefited from the Revolution. They leered and squinted with the eye disease trachoma; they had scars and boils and faces pocked with smallpox. They blew their noses into the gutter and hitched up their robes and squatted to defecate in full view of everybody. They lived a poor, basic and somewhat ugly existence, and the brave Army did nothing for them except cane-beat them or rifle-butt club them into line when the Leader came past.

In Iraq I sympathised greatly with the poor. Every day I passed lines of abbayaed women who held their hands out and looked pleadingly with trachomatous eyes and implored from pocked faces "Filous", and I often put 10 fils in each hand. I was left wing to the extent that I was on the side of the poor and the downtrodden and against the system that oppressed them, over which Kaseem presided as a figurehead. At the same time I sensed that they were all victims of a particular stage the Arab civilisation had reached, and I was not on the side of Communism at all, and was if anything right wing in accepting their plight with the same resignation that a doctor like Dr Shubber accepted it, and tried to ameliorate it.

There was a spell of great tension over Kuwait when I could almost cut the atmosphere in Bab Sherji and when I was watchful in case I was attacked as I walked between buses, but generally we endured an internal military dictatorship that was wary of the Kurds who were 500 miles away, and very wary of the students and of any freedom of expression they might direct at the regime.

Ramadan finished and it was the Id, the feast after the fast. I could feel it in the atmosphere, things were boiling up. At the end of March there was another skirmish between the Communists and the Nationalists, and a boy was knifed through the heart and killed outside the Dean's door on a Sunday, and eight others were taken to hospital and placed on the danger list. Later one of my best students, a fair-haired girl called Kawtha, approached me in some distress. "They are saying I killed the student," she said. "Please say I was in your class." I looked at my register. She had been absent that Sunday. "Did you kill him?" I asked. "No," she said. I did not know whether to believe her but I gave her the alibi she wanted.

Soon after there was a demonstration at the nearby Institute, where I did some part-time teaching. The students called "Ya-yescot" ("hip hip-boo") until the Army arrived, and they fled, being chased by portly Army men.

Then one day I arrived at the College to see a long queue of students. They were waiting to approach a table at which (I found out) sat the Chief of Secret Police, Yusef Abood, in the open air. Near him was a large Black

94

Maria with open doors. Each student went either to the left – into the College or to the right – into the Black Maria and thence to prison. "The College has been closed," one of the students told me, "every student must re-register, and perhaps must go to prison. The old Dean has gone to prison. Our new Dean is the Chief of Secret Police."

When College resumed the next day, I discovered that half 3B were missing. When I called the register from the mullah's platform there was a silence against every other name, and the reliable Jalal said, "They're in prison, sir." I resolved to visit them, and obtained directions to the prison from the Administration and turned up at the prison gates on a baking day. The prison was ringed with a timber-framed barbed wire fence and gates, and a soldier in uniform let me in, and I wandered across the sand to a number of waist-high zoo cages with bars. I bent and peered within each. Each was enclosed on three sides and open on the fourth, barred side. The first three contained strangers, the fourth contained many of 3B. Several students were sitting on the sand, their knees drawn up under their chins, holding the bars in their fists. "Sir," they greeted me, "God save you sir, thank you for coming sir, kefalek, how are you, are you fine?" One of them said, "I'm sorry my homework will not be in but as you can see there are no facilities for writing in this prison."

Soon afterwards the new Dean called a meeting requesting "support for new disciplinary measures on knifing students". About a hundred people sat in a long room that had the atmosphere of a trial, and the new Dean, a simian man who shelled nuts as he gabbled in Arabic spoke at length beside a whirring fan. An interpreter sat next to me and summarised briefly in English for us British lecturers. The new Dean exonerated the students and blamed the lecturers "for not disciplining students who knife students". He looked at me as he said this. Then he said strongly: "I ask you to vote that a committee be established to hang the old Dean of the College and the President of the University for inefficiency and crimes against the people." And he began to trump up accusations. Arthur Plowman sat as if shell-shocked, totally paralysed, a look of horror on his face, and I leaned forward and whispered, "I can't possibly stay, we all need to walk out together." And so we did. We all stood and walked out, the entire English Department, most of them not understanding what was being said.

One day when we were out the Army arrived and according to Yelda went to our phone and unscrewed the mouthpiece and put in a steel band. When I returned I unscrewed the phone and removed the band. But a few days later, apparently, the Army called again and installed a new one.

During April I used to travel back from the University with an immaculately dressed student of mine who was twice my age, Yaseen. He wore Western clothes and a red fez. We sat in the bus together and talked. One day he said, "Sir, can I please pass the examination. I live in a sarifa (mud-hut), I have four wives and sixteen children, and if I fail I must repay three years' grant of over £600, and my family will not eat. I know my English is very poor, but you are a kind man. Please to remember my wives and children when you mark my paper." And as I made sympathetic and detached noises he added, "Oh, I do part-time in the Ministry of Defence. I know the Secret Police are watching you. I have seen your file. If you will help me I will help you. I will tell you about the Secret Police information on you."

Being honest and valuing Western standards I did not compromise my judgement; I reserved my right to bring an open mind to his exam paper. He nevertheless went ahead with his side of the bargain, and each day we travelled he had new information to give me about the difficulties I was in with the Secret Police. The case was very simple. I had been observed talking with Communists, and I had given Kawtha of 3B, a well-known Communist agitator, an alibi. There were deliberations that I might be arrested, and Yaseen promised to tell me if a decision was taken to arrest me.

I was waiting to leave Iraq now. At the YWCA I spent part of the heat of the day reading in the cool of the library. There were many novels by Graham Greene, and I read them all under a ceiling fan which rotated like a propeller blade. I had plans to buy a cheap cottage in Cornwall and my father had found a place in Falmouth and another at Coverack, on which he sent me details. The British Council wondered whether we would be interested in going to Bangkok or Laos. With a sense of my task in life I wrote to my parents that I would like to work in Japan, and in "India, Africa, South America, Mexico and Russia for short periods". Then in May it was confirmed that Caroline was pregnant, and that the baby would be due in December, which made me focus on England.

To leave Iraq in Kaseem's day you had to visit every Ministry and get a clearance stamp. Only after you had accumulated a dozen stamps could you get an exit visa. To leave by June 6th you therefore had to start Ministry-visiting in mid-May. I had written part of a story called *The Mad Dictator* about Kaseem, but this was interrupted by long visits to the Ministries, the worst of which was the Ministry for Electricity, which had no record of the YWCA electricity and therefore could not give me a clearance stamp. I was making so little progress by the end of May that we despaired of getting out before July, and then Yaseen told me, "The Secret Police are delaying your exit. They are creating difficulties for you because of Kawtha. I will write something and put it on your file, that will help you. But you should telephone the Dean, Dr Yusef Abood."

I did as Yaseen said. I gave Yaseen time to write something for my file. Then I rang Abood at the College, not at the Headquarters of the Secret Police. I explained that I was meeting resistance at the Ministries. Abood said, "Hold on," and there was a delay. Then he said, "Let's get things shifting, then." And suddenly clearance stamps were produced in minutes. I made more progress in the next two days than I had in the previous two weeks.

About this time there was an open air end of year gathering for the College to say goodbye to an elderly lady teacher. It took place after dark under floodlights, and, seemingly oblivious to the fact that the College was now a branch of the Secret Police, Arthur Plowman spoke very emotionally before hundreds of students. He ended, his voice breaking, "Well done, thou good and faithful servant," and it was clear that he was in tears and might suddenly swoon.

The last time I left the University I travelled to Bab Sherji with Yaseen.

He wore his usual red fez. The examinations were now over. I had marked his paper. He had easily passed on merit. I suffered no crisis of conscience. I told Yaseen that he had passed. "God save you, Mr Hagger," he said, "my wives and children will say 'God save you'. We will drink tea to you in our sarifa (mud-hut) tonight. My four wives will be very grateful to you."

The Iraqi Airlines plane took off from the runway nearest the YWCA. The plane banked, and beyond the wing I could see the YWCA beneath me, in a waste land of sand surrounded by thousands of palms. I thought I could see Yelda, our servant, sweeping the flat roof. I looked back on the nine months I had been there. They had been picaresque and full of incident, and half 3B would end up as butchers in some future tyrant's security machine. I had visited many ancient places, which I was meant to do, and I had disciplined myself into sitting at a desk in great extremes of temperature and attempting to write. There had been some purgation in the harsh desert conditions. But I had somehow remained stuck in the outer world. Instinctively, I knew I needed a development within which had not yet taken place.

On landing in England we were met by Caroline's father who drove us home to Dulwich. We had an upstairs room in the great house at 46A Alleyn Park, which was due for demolition in a year and half's time. It was a relief to be out of the Baghdad heat and away from its crazy politics. I had been able to save enough to live on for a year, and for the first month we savoured being back in England, and took a holiday in Jersey which my grandmother paid for. We flew to St. Helier and stayed on a cliff near Gorey. I can remember sitting on the beach below our hotel reading Conrad's *Under Western Eyes*, and climbing up the cliff with my heavily pregnant wife. We toured the island, enjoying the green of Jersey after the yellow desert and appreciating the simple orderliness of the people after the raucous Arabs. In September at my father's request I gave a talk at the end of a Rotary Club lunch at the Bald Faced Stag, Buckhurst Hill, about my experiences in Iraq.

While I was in Iraq my family had transferred their allegiance from the Methodist Church of my mother to the Church of England, my father's Church, so that my brothers, who were used to daily Church of England services in the school chapel, and sister could sing in the choir at St. Mary's. With the creeping ecumenism since the war, the distinction between churches had increasingly broken down, and there were interdenominational services which included both congregations, so the move from nonconformism to Establishment was less fundamental than it might once have been.

Now that I was in England with a lump sum in the bank, the pressure was on me to write something that might earn a living for my family. Consequently I thought of a novel, not poems which I knew could never keep us.

In Iraq I had become interested in the conflict between mechanism and inner growth. Now I reread Grey Walter's *Living Brain* and contrasted the materialist's view that mind is brain function with Jung's focus on mandalas, symbols of a centre beyond the personality or ego, symbols of the self. The contrast was an objectivisation of my own inner life, and I found external images for it. I visited the Upjohn brain in London, a vast octopus of jumping lights which simulated the physiological basis of thinking. (Today Maurice Edelman has provided a far more subtle visual aid with his Darwin III and IV perceptual machines, which are computers in which group of neurons form perceptions.) I also bought a book on Tibetan mandalas at a small bookshop near the British Museum and incorporated the wisdom of India, China and Japan. Out of this tussle came a dialectic between a mechanist and a believer in the soul which I wrote as a Dostoevskian novel throughout the autumn.

I was divided between believing that death is the end for mind, and the view of the poets that there is a soul which survives death, and the novel, *Mandalas*, seemed the best vehicle for working out this self-division. My antipathy for Christianity meant that the materialist's view had the upper hand, and it seemed that Christians who believed in the soul had quite simply not understood that all mind could be reduced to electrical activity in the brain. I absorbed the view of science.

At that time we lived on the brink of the abyss in more than one way. The climax of the Cuban crisis on Saturday 27th October 1962, when the world held its breath expecting a nuclear attack from the Soviet Union, found me in the Charing Cross Road near Foyles. It was nearly deserted, and I can recall the tension in the air. All was quiet. Then there was a loud bang, and I saw men duck and put their hands over their heads and, expecting a nuclear strike, people ran out of the shops. In fact it was a car which had backfired loudly at the junction of Charing Cross Road and Oxford Street, level with what is now Centre Point. But our minds were attuned to Moscow and the prospect of sudden annihilation. More than any generation in history we lived on the verge of extinction that month, and our outlook was nihilistic. We could be exterminated at any time, life had no meaning, therefore live for the moment and hope to experience existential joy.

In the afternoons I went for a walk, often to Dulwich Park, or dug weeds in the vegetable garden at the house, and in the evenings I walked down to the pub at the end of the road, the Alleyn's Head, and drank with some of the Dulwich College teachers and discussed their subjects. Otherwise I lived in a room near the railway line, wrestling with my inner conflict, while rats scratched under the floorboards – the two dogs and cat sometimes caught one of them – and periodically an electric train rushed through, drowning all sound. As the trains ran through the night we all took sleeping pills so as not to be woken.

My wife's pregnancy advanced and one evening in December she gave birth at home. She had not wanted to have the child in hospital, and the midwife arrived as soon as the contractions began. I listened through the door: "One more push." And then the doctor announced that I had a daughter. It was a cold, icy night, and I walked with the doctor to the Alleyn's Head afterwards and bought him a pint of beer.

The winter of early 1963 was extremely cold. There was a family party at Journey's End on Boxing Day, and I sat in the dining-room bay window as it began to snow and watched my father rise and make a speech. The snow that fell on Boxing Day lay on the ground until March. The effect was Arctic. There were some wonderful snowscapes, my wife and I cared for little Nadia and I disappeared at intervals to carry forward the novel, which was progressively running into difficulties as the conflict within myself shifted. Watching the new baby, I could not believe in the mechanism and materialism that had seemed so plausible in the autumn, I moved back towards a view of humans as comprising feelings and a soul. My own inner growth undermined the dialectic of my own novel, in which science confronted religion, and it increasingly looked like a skin a snake had sloughed off. I was more interested in the present snake than in its out of date skin.

Novels – indeed all works of art – are models of reality. Authors, painters and composers say "Life has patterns like this". I had embarked on a view of reality I had outgrown. Equally, novels – indeed all works of art – mirror the extent of the creator's inner growth. By the spring I had moved beyond the inner state I had known in the autumn. Artists who have outgrown their works look back on them with embarrassment, and now I had started to grow in the deep snow of early 1963, I would not be satisfied with any art I produced until my growth was complete. I recognised this, although I did not know that I would continue to grow, and outgrow my own work, for the next 25 years. I knew I had set myself the long-term task of becoming a serious writer about the meaning of life and our Age, like T. S. Eliot, and that I must not become an entertainer who sold books to make a living. Meanwhile, the money I had saved in Iraq was almost spent.

In February there was a revolution in Iraq. Arif, a former schoolfriend of Kaseem's, personally lead the assault on the Ministry of Defence, where Kaseem defended himself with a pistol to the end. According to information I was later given he fought to the last round and then came out at the salute and said to Arif, "I saved your life now you save mine." He was arrested by Arif, driven to a television station and together with a hated judge and another man, shot on live television. An Arab then cut off his head and swung it to and fro in front of the television camera for all to see. The television station then played Mickey Mouse cartoons. So ended the life of a tyrant who had butchered the Royal Family and dragged their bodies through the streets behind a lorry in 1958. He had died as he had lived, by the gun, and he was not after all immortal. Yusef Abood was put in prison, and Arthur Plowman and a number of the foreign lecturers were ordered to leave.

In April my father had a brain haemorrhage and was on the danger list in Whipps Cross Hospital. Two days later I visited him. He gave me a limp handshake and seemed in an emotionless dream, he did not understand what I said. The next day he had four fits with convulsions and lay in a cot, thinking he was at a banquet. In early May he had two heart attacks, and a week later a third one, and then a fourth. I visited him. He told me he had felt a crippling pain as the clot moved from his leg to his heart, and that he had struggled for breath.

Occasionally in the evenings I used to attend poetry readings given by the Dulwich Group of poets. They were held at the Crown and Greyhound. I bought a beer and then sat upstairs in the room where readings were held. I can remember hearing George MacBeth and Edwin Brock. Howard Sergeant sometimes chaired meetings, and I remember talking with B. S. Johnson (who died soon afterwards), a conversation which carried on while we had a pee, during which he said: "I am concerned to push the technical experiments in the novel to their utmost." (He was in the tradition of Sterne's *Tristram Shandy* and Joyce. One of his novels came loose in a box and the reader could change the order of the pages as he felt fit.)

At the end of May I contacted the British Council to go abroad again. I had always known that I had to go to Japan to absorb the wisdom of the East; and it was Japan I applied for.

Desperate for money – down to my last £8 – and wanting to study growing things, I took a temporary job as an LCC labourer on 5/- an hour in Dulwich Park. On the first day I hoed sorrel and ground elder round the famous Dulwich rhododendrons with an ex-naval rating, John Armstrong. It was a hot summer and I worked from 8 until 5. Sometimes Caroline brought Nadia down in the pram to see me in the afternoon. It was hard, backbreaking work – sometimes I had to dig a long trench with a fork in a great heat – but the discipline did me good. It was mindless work – I was committing a kind of "mind-suicide" like T. E. Lawrence in the RAF – and I only half grasped that I had embarked on a purging of myself, a purgation of my lower ego and its senses. It was like being in a monastery, and tilling fields all day. In the evenings, worn out, I attempted to write and managed part of *Confessions of a Rationalist* which represented the current stage of my inner growth, a move against the rational, social ego. I also wrote a story called *The Riddle of the Great Pyramid*, which was about the apparent purposelessness of the toil that built the Great Pyramid. It was comparing my own backbreaking efforts with those of the slaves who built the Great Pyramid.

But while I toiled on in the summer heat of June and July, I observed details about rhododendrons, which revert to type, and azaleas. I learned about their habits and those of begonias, bellis daisies and polyanthus. I studied the activities of seeds of germinations and sproutings, and moved further away from mechanism. Voltaire's Candide discovered that the secret of happiness was to "cultivate one's garden", a practical philosophy that ignored speculation, and in terms of my inner growth I found my time in Dulwich Park very rewarding.

In early June Ricky visited me with the news that Graham Wallis had died. Ricky was teaching English as a foreign language in London, and he was still fascinated by drugs. He wanted to try opium and I tried to dissuade him.

At the end of June I was moved out of the Park to local schools, where I cut the grass together with an illiterate rascal called Gordon who pretended to read the newspaper every tea-break, sometimes holding it upside down, and who was paranoid about our Superintendent, Marshall, who he thought was constantly spying on us. As if Providence were giving me a nudge, I surveyed school life at Rosedale School, at Langbourne Junior off Bowen Drive and especially at Kingsdale School. From the grounds I watched the pupils race about in their playground at lunchtime. I was outside the school activities, an outsider, and felt at peace.

In the middle of July I had an interview with the British Council for a post in Japan, and at the end of July I was interviewed by a Japanese. I did not learn that I had got the job until the second week of September. During the wait I had another visit from Ricky, and my father had another stroke which left him unconscious for five hours. I visited him the next day in Whipps Cross Hospital. He was dazed.

It had begun to get chilly outside, and Gordon was becoming more difficult to work with – everything I said was relayed to Marshall in an attempt to ingratiate himself – and so I changed jobs and took a job in the Kingswood library, processing books and stamping dates. The day I started I heard that I was going to Japan to lecture at two universities who would share me from November. I was overjoyed, Caroline more resigned. Nadia was now nearly one and was healthy, and it was time to earn some proper money.

A week after I started at the library my father had a third stroke and was unconscious from 8 a.m. to 4 p.m. He was too ill to be moved to hospital. He lingered on at home for another month and his breathing became more laboured. Every fifth breath was difficult. I visited him on October 8th and he insisted we drank Guinness from our silver tankards, he sitting up in bed. I poured his bottle into his tankard and handed it to him. He took one sip and went into a choking convulsion and wept "This is the end," and when I tried to reassure him: "No, this is the end." Downstairs the television tube went, and the picture shrank to the size of a postage stamp.

Two days later he slipped into a coma and five days later he died. I went to the house and found the family drinking port, relieved. I went up to my father's room and stood and my mother came and said "There's nothing terrible in death" and she pulled back the sheet and left me alone with him. I gazed a long time at his still face and closed eyes that had, out of the best intentions, opposed my destiny, and I thought of his heroic struggle and suffering. He had had polio at 14, and had seen six of his ten children die. Within the last seven months he had endured 2 brain haemorrhages, 4 convulsive fits, 4 heart attacks, and 4 strokes. He had been a stoic of massive proportions, and I was glad I had made my peace with him over the final ritual Guinness. I was filled with a sense of the ultimate futility of his long struggle, but through my nihilism and despair I had a strong feeling, or conviction, that mechanism was wrong, that there is a soul and that his soul had fled to another world.

The funeral took place three days later in St. Mary's church, Loughton. The coffin was carried in and placed on a raised trestle table at the front. The church was full, and I saw Thompson, the Chigwell Head, standing at the back. After the service we drove through the Forest in Austin Princesses to Parndon Wood Crematorium and passed men who stood to attention and crossed themselves or took off their hats.

The librarian, who was called Fowler, had a beard. One day he said of my impending visit to Japan, "You're a thinker *and* a man of action," and he added: "If you're going to be a poet you will write about eternity." I was then too filled with nihilism and despair – despite my acknowledgement of the necessity of the immortal soul – to recognise the aptness of his comment.

One day a man with dark hair and spectacles came into the library and the librarian, Fowler, introduced me. It was W. B. Emery, the Egyptologist. Later I encountered him walking in Alleyn Road and stopped him and had a chat about my *Riddle of the Great Pyramid*. I asked him what he thought the riddle was, and was pleased he did not know. His frank admission confirmed to me that there was a riddle, an instance of how we attract people we need through what we are doing. Many years later, when I researched the Egyptian bull-cult in 1981, I found that Emery had discovered the Sarapeum-like labyrinth among the 1st dynasty tombs: the first evidence for the bull-cult.

As I got myself off to Tokyo, in between reading Crébillion fils, I reflected that all the strands in my life had come together. We had to vacate the Dulwich house in the course of November so that it could be demolished and smaller houses built on the land. I finished the library job. I bought a maisonette in Loughton (9 Crescent View) on mortgage for £2,750 and prepared to let it while I was away. My father had died. And I was starting a new job in Tokyo. I was given a clothing allowance of £100 by the British Council, but otherwise I had just £5 to my name.

The day before I left England I visited Epping Forest and walked to the Strawberry Hill pond up Robin Hood Lane. I stood by the fallen tree and gazed for a long time at the island. I was still bruised from my father's death. Suddenly I became immensely aware, of trees, mallards, water boatmen, everything, and it was inconceivable that the whole scheme should be to no end. Everything had purpose. I intuitively sensed a principle in the universe which could not be reduced to science, a principle I thought of as "the Life-Intelligence". It had a purpose which could be deduced from its forms, of which we are one, and from the plan, but the purpose was removed from our understanding, so we would never know its ends. That experience by the Strawberry Hill pond ranked with the experience by the Worcester College lake. Both were mystical experiences, glimpses of a reality beyond that of our everyday consciousness.

I had stayed in England 17 months between leaving Iraq and leaving for Japan. In that time I had seen my daughter born in the British climate and on the British Welfare State; and I had seen my father through his death. It was right to be in England for this time but my destiny called, and the East for which I had yearned, and I knew I would now make progress towards a metaphysical vision.

4.

JAPAN AND REMAKING: BIRTH OF A METAPHYSICAL POET
1963 – 1967

We flew to Japan first class. It was a long flight, and when we arrived in Tokyo I stepped out of the plane, crumpled and travelworn, holding my eleven-month old daughter in a blue blanket and clutching a yellow teddy bear. I was puzzled to see a line of four Japanese in tails near a huge limousine. "There must have been a VIP on the plane," I said to Caroline, and then I realised they were greeting me. They were all august Professors. As one of them shook my hand my daughter was sick on his arm. One of the Professors scraped and fawned, "Your appearance will, I am sure, be acceptable to the students, Professor Hagger."

It was only slowly that it dawned on me that I was a full Professor, "an invited foreign Professor". We were driven through the concrete sprawl and slagheap that was Tokyo to the International House, and told there was no urgency to prepare anything. I made visits to my two main universities, which were ferroconcrete, glassy modern buildings in different parts of Tokyo, and the next day we were driven to a furnished wooden bungalow at 108 Kohinata Suido-cho, Bunkyo-ku. It had a front garden with small palms and a small back garden with a veranda and a wall over which we had a good view of Tokyo. There was bamboo and all the windows had mosquito nets. It had a maid's room off the kitchen. The kitchen was infested with cockroaches, which scuttled in the cutlery drawer. It had a television. The bathroom had a deep and spacious erotic bath; it had a ledge for sitting on, and there was room for two to bath up to the neck in hot water. Here, I understood, my predecessor used to hold his classes at the end of his life. "His scholarship," I was told, "was not – er – to be esteemed."

My main university, Tokyo University of Education, was where Empson had come in 1931, as a Professor. He had been sent home in 1934 for swimming naked and riding home naked in a taxi. It was only when I had met the students in some of the gloomy, dingy classrooms there and had talked to the staff and walked with some of the younger lecturers, who earned little more than £30 a month, that I was told by my assistant that I was the first Invited Foreign Professor since William Empson. The post had been advertised and James Kirkup had applied from Kuala Lumpur along with four others. I had read Kirkup's book about his time at Sendai immediately before leaving England. The university had decided on Kirkup, but no one would take the responsibility of rejecting the other four applicants and so the British Council had been consulted, the intention being that they would appoint Kirkup. The British Council and Kirkup had quarrelled, and, understanding "professor" as "lecturer", the British Council had advertised the post as such and had found me. The Japanese had concluded that I was better than Kirkup. Hence the welcoming party at the airport. With hindsight, I believe they wanted someone who was too young to remember what the Japanese had done during the war. Now, at 24, I had what Nietzsche and Rupert Brooke both had at a similar youthful age, a Chair. In a matter of 10 weeks I had gone from park labourer to successor to William Empson, the rational poet admired by the Movement poets, and replacement for the poet James Kirkup.

At least 10 days went by before I gave my first lecture. During this time we moved into the bungalow and were invited to lunch by the British Council Representative E. W. F. Tomlin, technically my boss and author of *Great Philosophers of the East* and *Great Philosophers of the West*, both of which I had read. Tomlin was that rarity these days, a metaphysical philosopher. Although he represented Britain along with A. J. Ayer at philosophy conferences, he had written *The Approach to Metaphysics*, and, influenced by his long friendship with T. S. Eliot (his last book was entitled *T. S. Eliot, A Friendship*), his conversation was always against the logical positivist and linguistic analyst school of thought. He was then dome-headed and looked disconcertingly like Profumo. He lived alone with his maid and was always formally dressed and proper and correct. He sat at the end of a long, wide dining table and we talked about Kierkegaard and metabiology. Soon afterwards I learned in the corridor of my main university, from an assistant, that President Kennedy had been murdered.

I went into Tokyo University of Education on a Monday and Friday morning. I made the 12 minute walk through a residential area under a pall of black smoke from a distant chimney and came out by Myogadani station. The students proved to be very varied. I had different groups. They ranged from a group of Ph.D. students to students with hesitant English, and I taught English literature and language, emphasising the 20th century. They very quickly took to someone of their own age, and very soon my lectures were very well attended. On a Tuesday I went to Keio University on the subway (as the tube is called in Tokyo), and had two classes, from 1 p.m. to 3 p.m. with 180 and, after green tea, from 3.15 p.m. to 5.15 p.m. with 160. There was no microphone, and none was needed. They all did exactly as I wanted. The boys all wore black students' uniforms, and when I said, "Take up your pens," 180 hands immediately reached out, and when I said "Write" 180 heads would go down. At Keio I taught classes in modern English Literature, emphasising poetry.

I soon found travelling about Tokyo a wearying experience. The streets and subway were always crowded, there were always queues of fuming cars and taxis, and I had to fight my way through walls of people. I was far taller than the Japanese, and, even more than in Iraq, felt different. There were not many Westerners about. The traditional Japanese streets with open rice-paper doors and paper lanterns were charming and inviting, but wherever any foreigner (gaijin) went there was hesitant alertness and suppressed tension and (perhaps in consequence) a desire to giggle. Modern Tokyo was garish and gaudy, vulgar and in bad taste – the Ginza, for example, was a riot of tasteless neon and much of the architecture was undistinguished modern ferroconcrete – but traditional Japan still had the old samurai values and could be found in Noh, Kabuki, ikebana (flower-arranging), the haiku and Zen and its many wooden houses. And although the modern Japanese wore a suit, his mind was still traditional and he was ruled by an old feudal code of loyalty, and by "on" (obligation) and "giri" (honour). He lived in semi-contractual relationships and did his utmost to avoid incurring obligations (for example, by bringing a present every time he visited a home) and his good name and preservation of his face were of vital importance. The modern Japan repelled me, the traditional attracted me for its aesthetic values. I soon realised that there is a sensitivity in the Japanese spirit that is very quick to appreciate beauty, and in due course I warmed to the annual spring appreciation of the cherry blossom and the annual autumn sadness ("mono-no-aware"). I was quick to understand the Japanese and how they thought, and knew (as many foreigners did not) how to avoid making demands of them that made them anxious, ill at ease and resentful.

I had chunks of the week free. There were two other English lecturers at Tokyo University of Education, Dr Blyth, the expert and author of books on Zen Buddhism, who was ill; and Brian Buchanan, a balding bespectacled lecturer who always wore a brown suit and shared a room with me and who had been in Japan for many years. Although Scottish by birth, he had lived in Ireland, and as Mrs. Patrick Campbell had been his godmother he knew Maud Gonne, Yeats's obsession, and Synge, and he had met many writers and political activists in Dublin: he had been dandled on Shaw's knee and he had met MacBride, who was shot by the British during the Easter 1916 uprising.

Buchanan had a house at Nobe, a fishing village by the Pacific, and we soon got out of Tokyo and spent a weekend with him. The village consisted of thirty thatched houses by a long and completely deserted sandy beach, surrounded by horseshoe valleys where local peasants planted paddy fields of rice. At night the air was filled with the sawing of cicadas and the croak of frogs. We sat on the tatami matting with the rice-paper doors open, looking at the moon while exotic flying beetles flew in, attracted by our light, and crashed to the floor. We drank saké and talked literature and history until it was time to totter for a last stroll by the dark moonlit water before returning to our futons, the fold-out bedding that lies on a Japanese matting floor. Buchanan nicknamed me "Shelley" because he said I facially resembled the Romantic poet who was his specialist subject.

Now at last I pushed aside considerations of having to make money out of my writing, whose themes were essentially uncommercial, and let the themes speak for themselves. I found myself increasingly drawn to poetry and slowly realised I was a poet rather than a novelist, a perception I "forgot" from time to time and had to relearn.

The Japanese gardens at the International House and at Chinzanso near the bungalow made a great impression on me. We set off for Chinzanso by walking down a steep bouldered incline that reminded me of Cyclopean Mycenae, to Edogawa bridge. There was a Zen influence I loved, and I particularly liked the stone lanterns with a light, suggesting the Buddha's enlightenment, which shone in the evenings, and the symbolic fireflies that were released from time to time. In those early days I wrote *The Expatriate*, a poem about an expatriate in such a garden (I had had the idea for the poem in the International House garden), and also a sonnet, *The Pilgrim*. In early December I met an American poet who had nearly finished a spell teaching at Tokyo University of Education, Tom Fitzsimmons, a large grey-haired man who had blown out from pemphigus, which he described to me as "an allergy against yourself" and which required cortisone treatment, a brooding spirit of raw brilliance. I took to meeting him in Tokyo and we spent several evenings drinking and discussing literature.

At Keio I emphasised friendly vigour. The students liked my lack of formality. The Professor in charge of me there said approvingly, "You have boiled up the students." There was an abstract statue in the grounds called Nothing – it had a hole in it which symbolised eternity, and Stephen Spender had liked it on a visit – and after I had referred to this in a lecture several of the students asked to meet me in a nearby restaurant "for a metaphysical discussion", which was "chaired" by Shinsuke Ando, the young don who looked after me.

Just before Christmas Ando took me to meet Keio's Professor Emeritus and Japan's most famous poet, Junzaburo Nishiwaki, author of *January in Kyoto* which came out a year after Eliot's *The Waste Land* and had a similar effect on Japanese poetry. It could be said that Nishiwaki was then the T. S. Eliot of Japan. I arrived at his home soon after 3 p.m. for what should have been a half-hour's visit. I was still with him at midnight. Very soon whisky was produced, and the silky-haired bespectacled septuagenarian began speaking of the Nobel Prize, saying that if he were given it he would accept it for Japan's sake. He then startled me by saying: "I want to kiss hands with Mr Hagger and toast his figure, his face, his hair, his knowledge and his mind. He is the greatest Englishman, a real scholar. I am seldom wrong in my intuition, but one day you will be the greatest man in England – and not only England, all of Europe. One day you will get the Nobel Prize. But never forget. Make the public come to you on your terms. Impose your will on the public. As Wordsworth said, teach the public the taste by which you are relished." Ando had begun to interject, "As Professor Nishiwaki is unexpectedly drunk ..." but now he said, "Professor Nishiwaki is not a sycophant." I still think of Nishiwaki's "intuition" as a call to a destiny I am still very far from realising – the destiny of a Goethe, Jung or Eliot – but to whose spirit I must remain faithful and committed.

I had kept a sporadic journal from my first day at Oxford. In 1963 I had begun to make regular short entries in a desk diary and now that I had the leisure in Japan I began to write fuller entries. Throughout my time in Japan I wrote a page a day in a red Collins Royal 52 diary, and I have written daily entries since, although not at such full length.

On Christmas Eve we had our first earthquake. It was as if a tube had gone under the bungalow; for ten seconds the floor shook and walls creaked and the windows rattled and the glass in the bookcase rang out. It got worse and just when I thought the ceiling was coming down, and stood up as it were to hold it up, the rattling stopped. There were regular such earthquakes during my time in Japan.

We now had a maid, Emiko. On Christmas Day leaving our daughter, we attended a lunch party for all the British lecturers in Japan at Tomlin's. Tomlin had gone to some pains to recreate an English Christmas here, the other side of the world, and there were paper hats and mottoes. There was a mishap with the Christmas pudding and Tomlin told off his kitchen staff for not lighting the brandy. It was impossible to talk philosophy in this social situation. But after a visit to Nobe's booming sea and a 25 course meal at Professor Narita's on New Year's Day, which made me sick, I invited Tomlin on his own, and we discussed the history of science, brain physiology and the Absolute – he was a great defender of the Absolute – and he attacked Humanism and Existentialism and scoffed at Kingsley Amis, "one of my lecturers and now regarded as the father of English Literature, what are things coming to?" I was disappointed that he regarded himself (like Eliot) as a Christian, for it somehow lowered his philosopher's standing to mix the Absolute with such doctrinal issues as the Virgin birth and the Resurrection. I served him sashimi (raw fish with horseradish) and I remember him blinking and saying gravely, at his most formal, holding chopsticks, "Oh, er, an enormous lump of horseradish has just come down my nose."

I was in turmoil. Tomlin insisted that the purpose of life was to attain the Absolute, that "not having a metaphysic is committing mental suicide". My thoughts turned to oneness and unity – to reality – and I was aware of the limitations of scientific materialism and mechanism. In my anguish I quoted Whitehead: "Scientists who spend their life with the purpose of proving that it is purposeless constitute an interesting subject of study." I pondered eternity and wrote down as many quotations as I could find on eternity. My diary entries – and I continued keeping a daily diary but in more detail than in England – contrasted the mechanist and metaphysical approaches to reality.

In the first months of 1964 my influences were metaphysical Tomlin and anti-Absolute Fitzsimmons who affirmed the physical basis of everything. I was torn within between the approaches they represented, and I tried to rewrite my novel by dwelling on the conflict between a pro-metaphysical priest and a mechanistic scientist. I was on the side of the priest, on the side of growth; but against Christianity. I had met one of the fringe members of the Oxford Randolph set, Adrian Hohler, who had turned up two roads away from me. He was with the British Embassy and was to learn Japanese for two and a half years. He said, "Tomlin's theories are more preposterous than mechanism."

In April it grew hotter and I had a troublesome ear infection. The British novelist Anthony Powell visited Japan, and I had a short chat with him at the Japan-British Society one evening. He was stockier than I had expected and spoke with an Oxford accent. He told me, "Novelists fall into two types: those who produce and reduce, and those who produce and add." He belonged to the second type, he said, and his day's work was expanding 30 words into 90 and then into 300. Just over a week later I met Edmund Blunden, the Great War poet and author of *Report on Experience* which begins "I have been young and now am not too old". He had known Buchanan for many years, and now Buchanan held a small lunch in a Japanese restaurant for Blunden, Alec Hardy (his ward) and me. I sat cross-legged on the tatami matting next to Blunden, a hook-nosed beady-eyed, quietly-spoken, modest man whose hair stood on end. He had been badly gassed in the First World War, and had several asthmatic attacks during lunch, in the course of one of which I clapped him on the back several times. We discussed different poets and Epping Forest, including the Owl, the pub near High Beach, where we arranged to meet. (The meeting never took place. A date was fixed when I was back from Japan in 1966 but he cancelled it at the last minute as he was unwell. During the lunchtime we were to meet a murderer called Roberts, who was on the run and living rough in the Forest, burst into the Owl and robbed all the guests at knifepoint.)

On Wednesdays I now went to Tokyo University and lectured on English poetry in the afternoons to a group of between 30 and 40, and on Thursdays (at Tomlin's insistence) I now went to the Bank of Japan for three hours and had conversation classes with the Vice-Governor, Tadashi Sasaki, and an Executive Director, and corrected the English of turgidly written letters and speeches.

There was a holiday on May 5th, "koi-nobori", when carp streamers flew from flagpoles. In May I met Fitzsimmons and discussed a film we wanted to make, on the self-creation and self-unification of a dying man who sees all his opposites reconciled. I am sure this idea shaped my impending poetic development, and the theme of self-unification now became central to my thinking.

I now entered a new period in which I was preoccupied with remaking myself and cleansing my consciousness. I now opened myself more fully to the Buddhist enlightenment, images of which abounded in Japan.

One of the largest was at Kamakura, which we visited at the end of May, the 13th century bronze Dai-butsu or Big Buddha, sitting serene and aloof in a grove, in the vision of enlightenment. I became poetically alive and wrote *The Oceanographer at Night* about the need for stability. I thought deeply about the decline of Western civilisation in relation to its spiritual vacuum and discussed this with a Tokyo University lecturer, Tony Rainer. I had agreed to rent half a house in Nobe that Adrian had shared with an Embassy colleague. We went down to view it, and as we slid open paper doors gigantic spiders fell plop onto the tatami matting. Down in Nobe the next weekend the sweltering night was full of jungle sounds – croaking frogs, whooping birds, hooting owls and of course cicadas – and I walked in the horseshoe valleys among brightly coloured spiders and brilliant butterflies and soaring shrikes, and a red, black and yellow mountain adder slid out of a hedge and confronted me. Later I used to go out with a forked stick in Nobe and sometimes encountered four or five snakes of differing colours, which I pinned briefly and then released. I walked to a Shinto temple under a huge hill and gazed at the boat that represented eternity.

In June Fitzsimmons left to return to Michigan and I attended the Tokyo University of Education farewell party for him in a Ginza restaurant. Fitzsimmons spoke of the Zen archery he was doing, and seeing my interest in Zen, Professor Irie promised to introduce me to a colleague and phonetic namesake, Professor Haga, who had written a best-selling book on Zen that made him a Japanese authority. I had briefly met my colleague Dr R. H. Blyth in a corridor at the university – he was coming out of his room and locking the door, and he smiled wanly and rather puckishly through his last illness (he would die in October) and shook my hand – and now I was duly introduced to Haga and in mid-July I met him and one of my graduate students at the university and we took the train to Ichikawa City and made our way to a meditation centre ("dojo"), a large room with polished boards and open sides near an overgrown garden with washing on a line. Haga smoked a cigarette and fanned himself during the introduction. I was the only non-Japanese. There were several rows of shaven seekers and we meditated cross-legged in the lotus position, which I found acutely uncomfortable. There was group chanting and a bell rang, and then there was a long silence in which I was instructed to count my breaths up to a hundred. I found this unhelpful. I knew of course that Zen was anti-rational and I wanted to know what enlightenment ("satori") involved. No one told me what the Buddha saw, and I might see, while meditating behind half-closed eyes. I was merely instructed to sit and count my breaths, the first step. The onus was on me to find my way from there, and in case any of us lost our attentive consciousness, or worse still, nodded off, a hefty man in a yukata lurked among our cross-legged rows with a wide stick, like a teacher's blackboard ruler, which he wealded formally on any meditator he adjudged to need it. Having spotted inattentiveness or bodily interference, he bowed, whacked the insufficiently aware seeker on the back so there was a loud crack, and then bowed again in respect for his soul. (During the eating of rice with chopsticks from a bowl held in the hand, anyone who spilt a grain of rice was also beaten because rice has Buddha-nature just as we do.)

Eventually there was a lecture. The Master sat in a prominent position and we sat in rows. Speaking in Japanese, the Master set us a koan (parable, puzzle). It was translated for me in whispers by Haga and my graduate student who sat on either side of me. A man was hanging onto the top of a tree with his teeth and his Master came by underneath and asked him, "What is the truth of the teachings of Zen?" He must reply because it is impolite not to reply to your Master. We were instructed to reflect on it, and if we had not found the answer by the time we went to bed then we should sit up and meditate instead of going to sleep, and we should die in bed if necessary.

There was one more meditation, while a flying beetle and a huge moth zoomed and flitted around our heads, and then we slept in futons on the tatami matting floor of a nearby room. We were awoken early the next morning for another meditation, in the course of which, one by one, the seekers had to go to the Master and give their explanation for the koan. It was all very orderly. While we meditated, one rose and glided into the Master's room, there was a murmur of an answer, and then, crack! He returned, beaten, and resumed his cross-legged lotus position and the next took his place. Again there was a murmur and a crack. Without exception, everyone was beaten. Haga whispered "Would you like to go?" The hefty man was near me, holding his stick like an executioner holding a samurai sword, and I shook my head. But on the train on the way home (for this meditation concluded my visit) he asked me why I thought they had all been beaten, and I said: "They made the mistake of speaking. The answer the Master wanted to hear was a silence. He who knows does not speak and he

109

who speaks does not know." (This last sentence was a quotation from the *Tao te ching*.) To which Haga said: "You are right. You have understood. Zen takes you beyond language to a place of silence where you can know satori or enlightenment."

I had mastered the first stage, and now I was ready for satori. Ten days later I went to Kogenji temple with the graduate student Mr Munekata. We passed tombs and a statue of the Buddha, and the Master was bald and bespectacled and in a yukata. I meditated in a great heat among rows of silent cross-legged Japanese and then slept, and meditated again just before dawn with the rice-paper doors open to the night and the whirring cicadas. The meditation lasted an hour and a half, and through my half-closed eyes, sitting like a Buddha, I now and again glimpsed the progress of the dawn in the polished floor. I went very deep and got below the level of time and differences and becoming to a timeless being in myself which could have existed forever, and I did not want the meditation to end and afterwards felt very peaceful and inwardly whole. I saw how the Buddha might have reached a state in which his bodily aura was enlightened from within.

In July and August we made more visits to Nobe where the sun was fierce and there were brilliant butterflies and dragonflies, hawks and snakes in the paddy fields, and I bathed in water bubbling at 110°F. I visited Hakone, outside Tokyo in the mountains, to give a course, and bathed in sulphur, and we all went to Nikko and saw the Toshogu shrine, the Kegon Fall, Lake Chizuka and the nearby pine forest. And at the beginning of September I visited the Shinto shrine at Karuizawa with Ando. All through the hot summer I suffered from minor physical ailments which reflected the change in climate and diet: tropical ear, pyorrhoea in my gums, tooth decay, sunburn and corns.

At Keio Ando wanted my course to include European Literature, and when I suggested teaching it within the context of Colin Wilson's *Outsider*, to my surprise he enthusiastically agreed. I accordingly ordered 160 hardback copies which eventually arrived in boxes. (Years later Colin Wilson told me, "Someone ordered vast quantities of the hardback of *The Outsider* in Japan." I was able to own up.)

In September the Olympic Games took place in Tokyo. Planes flew overhead and described the Olympic rings in the sky, and many foreigners descended on Japan. I read Eliot's *Four Quartets* for my class at Tokyo University. My creative work had become a prose trilogy which explored a metaphysical theme, but with hindsight I can see I still had not made the inner development that would enable me to demonstrate the metaphysical theme. I was still torn between mechanism and the life force, between the healthy vision of Kazantzakis's *Zorba the Greek* and the more religious vision of Eliot, Hulme and the Buddha. Now my inner need for purgation, to purify myself within, expressed itself in terms of cigarettes. I had begun to smoke intermittently before Oxford, in the excruciating boredom of the solicitor's office and had carried on in varying degrees for seven years, and after a visit to Dr Morton about my internal wheezing I now resolved to beat the habit. For five days I fought the craving for nicotine, sweating out my self-denial, and then Adrian, Tony and I climbed Mt Fuji. We took a bus to the 5th stage and then climbed towards the crater to within a thousand feet of the top – to a height of 9,000 feet – before we had to turn round to catch the last bus back. The clear mountain air among the snowy crags cleansed my senses, and when the sun slid behind the crater and there was a sudden chill we encountered a bald Mexican singing. He craned back his head and held up a sow's bladder from which a jet of saké poured a yard long into his throat, and in that moment I felt that existence was essentially good.

I was purging myself. I had given up smoking, but was not yet ready to give up drinking, although I knew I would in due course. I was teaching Modernism in Literature, and down in Nobe pondered the conflict between rural and city values. The British Council gave a reception for the London Symphony Orchestra during which I met Sir Arthur Bliss, who had white hair and a white moustache and shook my hand unintroduced and gazed at me with his blue eyes (a meeting which certainly coloured my later poem, *The Conductor*), and then I went to give a lecture in Hiroshima. I travelled overnight on the sleeper train and spent a wretched night on a bunk above a steel ladder – there was no seat beneath – being jogged and jolted under a bright centre light that would not turn off, and I arrived without sleep or breakfast to address 300 girl students on Eliot in a vast hall. I was greeted by the most beautiful American nun, Sister Frances. She would have been stunning in any worldly situation, and the contrast between her looks and her wimple was acute. She chatted to me both before and after my one and a half hour lecture, and there was such a spiritual simplicity and beauty and purity in her face and eyes that I was quite smitten, and the encounter later found its way into *The Silence*.

I went into Hiroshima after the lecture and stood in the Peace Memorial Park and gazed at the tangled iron of the A bomb dome (the pre-1945 Industrial Exposition Hall) and reflected on the horror of the 20th century and the inhumanity of war, yet the strange necessity of this symbolic atomic destruction which had ended a war that seemed unendable as the Japanese would never surrender without a command from their Emperor, and I saw the dropping of the A bomb as fitting into a complex pattern rather as Arjuna came to regard war after his troubled discussions with Krishna in the *Bhagavadgita*.

I was becoming increasingly sure that I could relate the concerns of our Age to a historical pattern and towards the end of November I bought all 10 volumes of Toynbee's *A Study of History* at Kinokuniyas bookshop in Tokyo. So began my long study of the rise and fall of civilisations in Gibbon, Spengler and Toynbee which would eventually result in *The Fire and the Stones*. The next day, stirring to my historical theme, I wrote a poem *And Scholars will Ask* , and a week later a companion poem, *Odi et Amo*.

I was now feeling a new joy at being alive. Down in Nobe I revelled in the bamboo under a blue sky, at gentians and corn violets in the horseshoe valleys and at the circling shrikes above. Later I stood on the deserted Pacific beach in a great wind which flapped my trousers like sails and tore through my hair as the sea thudded in and my *Diaries* record: "I felt at one with everything and ran and danced in the wind (for I was alone) and laughed and chased my shadow for joy at being alive."

A MYSTIC WAY

I also recorded on 10th December that I had been undergoing "a development that is obscure even to myself in its extent". I wrote that I was going through a "momentous time", "a spiritual conflict" in which I acknowledged a new "spiritual or self-realisational depth" in myself. I did not like to acknowledge that the spirit actually existed, and delved into Toynbee on higher religions. Satori was slow in coming, but I recorded on 30th December that in the year since I left England I had become "progressively more pro-religious and anti-scientific", and that there had been an "increase in spiritual penetration" and a "heightened awareness of social trends".

My inner development was accelerated by the arrival in Tokyo in December of Frank Tuohy, the 44 year old author of *The Ice Saints* and a master of the short story form. He was Professor at Waseda, the main rival private university to Keio. I first met him at the British Council scholarship interviews, which we both supervised, and found him prosaic and abrupt, not realising that shyness made him put on an aggressive monosyllabic mask as a defence.

Just before Christmas, however, we took Tuohy on a packed train to Nobe. We had to stand and there was a sensitivity, a gentleness about him now which was altogether different from the front he had put on at the British Council. We walked in the sun and drank a large bottle of whisky and talked about writing, and he began sharing his observations which, although I pulled against them because they were unmetaphysical and sceptical, made me reconsider my own artistic attitudes and therefore stimulated a development in my own art, particularly poetry. The next morning we walked to the Shinto shrine that had Russio-Japanese etchings, and talked about novelists and poets and life and social attitudes and writing techniques.

Tuohy used to go for walks with Wittgenstein and used to say he was the only living witness to Wittgenstein's last period. He reflected Wittgenstein's view that man is a social being and that all philosophical problems are a question of language. Tuohy was a Wittgensteinian. Now Wittgenstein is regarded as being as significant as Socrates or Spinoza. I always questioned the Wittgensteinian primacy Tuohy gave to language. Reality is not contained in language, and man contacts it in his more solitary moments. Reality is not exclusively social. There was thus a constant tussle between Tuohy and me. The tension consisted in my keeping quiet at the two fundamental assumptions Tuohy made in his conversation – that reality is social and all philosophical problems evaporate when you focus on the language in which they are expressed – and sometimes I could not keep quiet and then I was in open conflict with Tuohy, who was often waiting for the conflict to appear.

At Christmas Tomlin had a Christmas party with turkey, crackers, carols and folk-music, and Tuohy was privately scathing. A conflict clearly developed between metaphysical Tomlin and sceptical Tuohy, who both embodied different polarities of my inner experience.

In early January I went to Kyoto and Nara on my own. I took the bullet train and sped over a sleeping city at dawn and watched the sun rise behind misty mountains and shine on curly-tiled roofs. That first day in Kyoto I visited the Ryoanji Stone Garden – a 15th century Zen garden with raked stones and rocks that had a deep and almost impenetrable meaning – but I did not comment on it in my *Diaries*; it was merely mentioned among golden and silver pavilions and castles. I spent the night in a ryokkan (inn) and next morning went to Nara and visited the Tempyo shrines in the park or forest. Death-stones lined the steps up to the shrines. It was freezing, and sitting in an open-air restaurant I wrote a poem about how all culture is dominated by death.

I was choosing myself as a poet. Towards the end of January we visited Nobe, and the sea jumped with diamond explosions in the sun and, as I walked I was aware of a "fire in my head". I was reading Pound's *Cantos* and reflecting on the pattern in my own life and how this might be caught in a series of states of mind. On 26th January I had the idea of writing a series of a hundred poems that revealed a pattern. And two days later I began writing an early draft of what was to become *The Silence*, a long poem in the tradition of Wordsworth's *The Prelude*, and am now amazed that out of such unpromising and hesitant beginnings emerged a work that dominated the rest of the year, and longer, and which I still regard as my masterpiece. Two days later still I recorded that I must be prepared to choose myself as a poet.

This development had happened within a month of my first meeting with Tuohy in Nobe, and looking back I can see that it had a certain amount to do with my relationship with Tuohy. At the end of January, for example, I see I had tea with Tuohy and that we discussed among other things: resonance, what makes a poetic line poetic, the relationship between the familiar and the strange, and other poetic subjects. (My 1965 *Diaries* record these conversations in some detail.) On the other hand, I was already groping towards being a poet before Tuohy arrived, and it may be that he merely accelerated the process within me.

I continued to write through February and March. Adrian left Tokyo – Tony took over Adrian's share of the rent for the Nobe house – and my grandmother died in Loughton after a fall at the age of 90. I went to see a Noh play. Bandy-legged musicians beat drums and whooped and I caught the theme "Life is but a dream", but there was no overt hint of what enlightenment meant. In my poetry I observed the dying away of the man of ideas and the birth of the poet within me as I read and pondered and wrote. On April 25th I first got the name "Freeman" for the hero of *The Silence*. The name floated in from the beyond and had a similar feel to "Everyman". It was a fine day, and I went on to Nobe and revelled in the croaking frogs. On my next visit on 2nd May I poked among the rock-pools and watched a starfish and observed a sea-slug spinning a yellow thread of eggs. Later I went up into the paddy fields and found some wild orchids of different shapes and colours, and newts with scarlet bellies swam between the planted rice.

In May it grew hot. I continued my researches into Modernism while carrying forward my own poems. I identified with Robert Graves's Modernist gropings in broken images:

A MYSTIC WAY

"He is quick, thinking in clear images;
I am slow, thinking in broken images.
He becomes dull, trusting to his clear images;
I become sharp, mistrusting my broken images."

On one visit to Nobe I read Pound's *Mauberley* on the train. It made a great impression on me. I was able to read Camus, Kafka, Hesse and T. E. Lawrence for a class on European Literature. I also based some lectures on Frank Kermode's *Romantic Image*. The Chinese exploded an atomic bomb, and soon afterwards we had a storm that was 120 times as radioactive as usual according to local American radio. I went to dinner with Tuohy that same sweltering night and met Leon Stover, an American anthropologist who was to come up with a new theory on Stonehenge. The oppressive heat in Tokyo made us appreciate the relative cool of Nobe, and during these visits I went snake-hunting with a forked stick and remember catching a snake that puffed itself up and changed colour into a brilliant red pattern. Another time I remember a centipede five inches long, with legs like rose-thorns, crawled in the dust by our front steps, and a local pronounced it deadly.

I had been told that I had been appointed tutor to a member of the Imperial family. At first it seemed I would be tutor to the Crown Prince (the present Emperor) but then it turned out that I would be tutor to his younger brother, Prince Hitachi. An Imperial chauffeur-driven car collected me and drove me to his small palace, chamberlains lurked in doorways and I met His Imperial Highness, who was then a grave, quiet, bespectacled, uncertain man of around 28 with immaculately smarmed down hair. A Japanese who was also teaching him acted as go-between that first visit, but a week later I had a class with the Prince on my own, and met his beautiful wife, Princess Haneko, and soon I was going three afternoons a week for between two to three hours. Officially I taught him English, but it soon transpired that he did not know what to discuss with foreign Ambassadors during the many evening dinners he had to attend. He did not know what to discuss with the Egyptian Ambassador, and when I mentioned the Sphinx and the Pyramids he looked blank, so we agreed to do a course on world history, starting in 3,000 BC and coming down to the present. This was the ground I later covered in my Grand Unified Theory of world history, *The Fire and the Stones*. Soon each time we had our class in the teaching room up the palace stairs, the door would open and a chamberlain would come in with ten books on a silver tray and say, "Please write ten questions for the Romanian (or whatever) Ambassador." Soon, through His Highness, I was asking the Soviet Ambassador about the disputed territory of Wallachia and the British Ambassadress about her bugbear John Osborne. In due course we read an English poem each session, one by Keats or Shelley, for example. The Prince read aloud in a stirring voice and then sat back, unwilling to look any deeper into the poem's meaning.

The Prince was very formal. There was a television programme two evenings a week about the doings of the Imperial family, and at first I found his behaviour with me little different from the formal behaviour he showed on film. Little by little he opened up. Once he told me about his terror when

114

the Americans entered Tokyo at the end of the Second World War. When aged about 8, he was hidden under a bed and from under the bedcover he saw army boots reach the top of the stairs and approach. He expected to be bayoneted but a kakhi arm reached underneath and yanked him out. He had been very sheltered. He had never heard of income tax and I had to explain to him how it worked. He said, "It is not fair." I said, "We non-royals live under an unfair system." There seemed to be little freedom of speech in the palace, but as in my classes in Iraq there was full freedom of speech in my classes with him, and I said exactly what I thought; presenting it in a slightly deferential way, referring to "Your Highness".

University classes ended for three months, but classes with the Prince and the Bank of Japan continued through the hot summer. I believe it was at this time that I went to the Bank of Japan to read Anthony Sampson's *Anatomy of Britain* with the Vice-Governor, Tadashi Sasaki, a fairly corpulent, smiling man in his late 50s with immaculately groomed hair, and found him standing at the telephone. He gestured to me to sit down and put one hand over the mouthpiece and said, laughing: "It is Lord Cromer, Governor of the Bank of England. He wants a loan from the Bank of Japan. Shall I give it?" I knew of Harold Wilson's financial crises, and that the British economy constantly needed an injection of funds at that time. I nodded and said, "Yes, please." He nodded and returned to his conversation and the loan was granted.

I regularly dined with Tuohy, usually at our house but sometimes at his house or at a restaurant. (Once we made a disgraceful semi-drunken scene outside the Rosier after being charged for large beers instead of small beers. We lobbied passers-by until a police car arrived to arrest us. We were allowed to proceed when it was established we were Professors.) Caroline and I spent much of the summer in Nobe. One weekend there was a great wind that flapped my black shirt and sand trousers and there were white-crested waves. Another weekend it was very wet and I drank in Nobe with Buchanan and Blunden's ward, Alec Hardy. I was reading a lot of psychology and was steeped in Freud, who saw the artist as a neurotic, and Rank, who rebelled against him and emphasised the creative will of the artist, and Jung, who also went his own way and emphasised creativity. Among the cicadas and flying beetles of those hot Nobe evenings I confronted and rejected Freud.

At the end of July Tuohy and I spent a night at a Zen Buddhist temple in Kitakamakura: Engakuji. In the course of the walk from the station we stopped at Tokeiji temple to visit the tombs of my late colleague R. H. Blyth and Daisetsu Suzuki. I had been hoping that Master Asahina would meet us, but instead we found a young shaven Zen priest who promptly forbad us to wear socks, knowing that the mosquitoes were bad there and that they bit the feet of foreigners while they sat still in the lotus position. "You must achieve satori in spite of the mosquitoes," he told us. "You must overcome the mosquitoes, pass beyond them, be one with them." We meditated in silence among whining mosquitoes, the only two foreigners among rows of Japanese, and as usual there was chanting and the spells of silence were haunted by a huge man with a vicious-looking stick to beat the unawake. Tuohy meditated immediately on my right, and, detecting shifting limbs, I came out of my inner trance and looked out through half-closed eyes and saw a deadly centipede like the one I had seen at Nobe, with fat red legs, crawling slowly towards us. Tuohy's breathing became noisier, and the man with the stick approached and prodded him in the back. Tuohy collapsed in a terrified heap on the floor, causing a disturbance, but pulled himself upright when the man with the stick prowled round to the front, detecting an opportunity to administer a beating, and together we sat totally still, watching the centipede approach. Just when it seemed it would touch the knees below my bare upturned feet it veered off to my left, but I could not relax and return to the inner vision now that my survival instincts were aroused.

The experience of the centipede was a turning point for Tuohy. We tried to sleep nearby, but tossed and turned, imagining centipedes lurking in the corners of the room along with the usual cockroaches. Tuohy was always one to dwell on the awfulness of situations in his writing, and I remember him groaning aloud, "Three hours and then labouring? Oh God." We did not sleep a wink and before dawn we were marched round the temple and its garden in a long line, and then Tuohy and I were set to sweep the path near the latrines, which stank. Tuohy muttered as he went through the motions and made half-hearted sweeping movements, and I pointed out that what we were doing was symbolic of inner purification: "We are cleaning the path to the foulness in our soul, we are working on the cleansing of ourselves." To which Tuohy retorted, "I'd rather be me, unclean, than have to do this."

Soon afterwards we meditated again, and almost immediately I went very deep, and soon the only reality was a profound silence, across which unreal sounds intruded, our lungs moved and cicadas scraped, and I knew among the dawn shadows that all was a unity. I had left the outer world of existence, with its emphasis on different phenomena, and had reached an awareness of being, in which all differences were really not different, like the pebbles in the Ryoanji Stone Garden.

In early August I went to Gora to address a conference and stayed among the sulphur-springs there. In the hot evening, feeling that Freud was an obstruction across my path, I sat outside and read Ira Progoff's *The Death and Rebirth of Psychology*, and warmed to Rank's rejection of Freud, and I wrote the first draft of the passage which includes the line "I cannot live by Freud", which is now in *The Silence*. On the way home I travelled with a Japanese who spoke English with a stammer, and suddenly, intuitively, I knew I could cure it. I made him take three deep breaths, and some faith transference happened, and the stammer went.

When I got back to Tokyo I was invited to dinner with the Prince and Princess at the palace. The three of us went for a walk in the grounds, going out through billowing lace-curtains. We headed past a lotus pool towards a pine-wood, and ducking under pine boughs and admiring a blue-tailed magpie while a chamberlain kept behind us at a discreet distance with a camera, to make conversation I pointed out some nesting boxes high up in the pine-trees and asked, "Are those nesting boxes for birds?" "No," the Prince replied "They are my ancestors." It is a shamanistic Shinto belief that the souls of Imperial ancestors became "kami" or "divine spirits" on their death and dwelt in trees, and the living erect nesting boxes as homes for them.

We then went back indoors and dinner was served in a small room. Four ladies-in-waiting stood along one wall, listening to everything we said, and I conversed in English with the two of them, and found the Princess full of vitality. She often seemed to forget her position and spoke jokingly in excellent English, and then remembered her position and deferred to the Prince, who, being anyway rather monosyllabic, sometimes looked left out of the conversation. I kept trying to bring him in. The next day I went to Nobe and drank with Buchanan and Penson, and Penson mentioned the most important book in his life, Ralph Waldo Trine's *In Tune with the Infinite*, which, he said, his father always kept by his bedside and which he found in a jumble sale in the 1930s and had been by his bedside for over 30 years. I found my grandmother's copy in 1966 and it has been by my bedside ever since.

In mid-August we went to Kyoto as the guests of the Bank of Japan. We took the afternoon New Tokaido train on a sweltering day and were met in an air-conditioned car and driven to an air-conditioned room in an inn, and next morning we visited Nara and saw the Todaiji Big Buddha. After lunch at the Kyoto Hotel we visited the thousand statues at Sanjusangendo temple, which I brought into *The Silence* as Freeman's "thousand selves". The next morning I made my second visit to the Ryoanji Stone Garden, which now adorns the back cover of my *Selected Poems*, and saw the simple pebbles and rocks as revealing that all existence is one underlying unity (being), and that the border or frame round it is quite arbitrary as it is infinite and boundless.

Soon after this I underwent another development. Tomlin had asked a few British and Japanese Professors, including Tuohy and me, to write 5,000 word essays on Eliot, who had died in January 1965. (In his last book, *T. S. Eliot, A Friendship*, Tomlin later recorded that I visited him after hearing of Eliot's death.) At Nobe soon afterwards I began my article, which involved thinking deeply about Modernism, and on 15th August noted in my *Diaries*, "I have been undergoing some kind of a centre-shift" and that "I can feel the irrational all round my reason; it is a fact, something I can be aware of half a dozen times a day". I was still hunting for a poetic image of the relationship between reason and the irrational ten days later – I eventually found it in the concept of a marriage of a man, woman and child like Nadia – and in early September I lunched with Tuohy and discussed the image and symbol in some detail, while still writing my essay.

A further development began on 11th September 1965. I had worked on my essay all day and could not sleep. I closed my eyes and a succession of images rose: scrivenings in a foreign language – Arabic or Hebrew – in yellow and blue; a puddle and an orb of fire within it; corn stalks with many ears of corn; a whirlpool. Then it seemed I was going down a well, and saw the orb of the sky getting smaller as I descended. Two days later, on September 13th, I had more images behind closed eyes, also late at night. A series of gold heads went slowly by as if on a conveyor belt: some Egyptian, some Negroid, some Babylonian. Then there were exquisite diamonds in green and mauve which lasted 30 seconds. When I got off to sleep I dreamt I was on the second floor of a Turkish Byzantine café and there was an earthquake and I rushed down the stairs and out into the courtyard through falling masonry to find everything in ruins, all foundations crumbled. Then I was in a morgue among many corpses, which suddenly sat up and came to life, jingling their bones.

I did not finish my essay until the end of September, and had then written almost no poetry for six weeks. The essay was a vindication of the method I was groping for in *The Silence*, abbreviated narrative in an emotionally linked sequence of images, and although I was tired from the heat and the effort of the reading and research, I felt I had justified my poetic method. Now I had time to walk to the Cathedral and gaze at symbols which trap the eternal. I was still sleeping very badly, and on October 6th, still awake at dawn, I thought I understood the Absolute in terms of the Stone Garden: at the underlying level of unity there is no difference between the particular forms of existence, and the Absolute manifests itself through unity.

My development reached a climax in mid-October. On October 8th I went to a Tutankhamun exhibition, and saw the gold mask which had arrived in Japan from Egypt. It corresponded to one of the Egyptian gold heads I had seen in mid-September. The next day we went to Nobe. The trees were full of autumnal tints, the sky was blue, the rice had been harvested from the paddy fields, which were full of stumps, and dry rice hung like straw from poles. The sea had a typhoon swell. On October 10th, back in Tokyo, I wrote the passage about the Stone Garden in *The Silence*. Later that same evening I went for a drink with Tuohy, who invited me to go to China with him the following spring, and write some articles. Later that night I dreamt Tuohy told me, "Your energy is outgoing in one direction like a stream or unimpeded shoot." In the late evening of October 11th I went to the bathroom from our dark bedroom and, turning on the light, was flooded with golden light behind my closed eyes. The pattern was of rings, each linked into a golden net.

The next few days I worked very intensely on sections of *The Silence*, in the course of which I fulfilled my teaching commitments and attended a farewell reception at the palace of Prince and Princess Hitachi, who were making a State visit to Britain at the expense of the British Government. I had been involved in planning this visit and had given advice on how to address the various people the Prince might expect to meet, and now 40 formally dressed very old Japanese men lined the wall and the Prince went round bowing, and shook hands with me, the only foreigner, while the Princess walked behind carrying a nosegay. Then there was a collective chant of "banzai" ("victory"). I spent much of October 16th searching for an image for my centre, which became the image of a child between a husband and wife (Nadia's role in my marriage) and writing the "poet of the self" passage and on Sunday October 17th I was so tired in the afternoon that I slept.

I seemed to sink down within myself, and when I awoke at 4.30 p.m. and went to my study and looked out of the bungalow window I seemed to be a floor below my thoughts. I sat down and thought about the centre of myself in relation to the cosmos, and as my *Diaries* record: "Sainthood suddenly came within my grasp – I understood Tao, that just as my self-centre unites me, so Tao could unite life and death and all cosmic opposites and pluralities, so that all men are brothers." The next morning, October 18th, a Monday, I stayed at home, and as my *Diaries* record: "All morning I have been filled with a round white light: I cannot see it, except occasionally when I glimpse it and am dazzled, but I know it is there. It is like a white sun. This is, I suppose, what Christians refer to as the soul – the centre of the self. And the mystical experience is given meaning by the relation between the centre and the sun, so that everything is one." I observed that it was not the universe that had changed, but my self and my perception of it "so that it now seems more harmonious". I observed that it "would be easy to follow a path of sainthood".

Looking back I can see that these brief gleams in 1965 represented my first illuminative life, a first glimpse of satori or enlightenment following a shift from my rational, social ego to a new centre within my self, my soul. I had no doubt that the development was a consequence of my long process of self-discovery as I wrote *The Silence* and that I had glimpsed a Light within my soul. On October 31st I connected the experience with a passage I found on "luminous phenomena, photisms" in William James's *The Varieties of Religious Experience* in which James quotes Charles Finney's *Memoirs* (1876): "A light perfectly ineffable shone in my soul....This light seemed like the brightness of the sun in every direction. It was too intense for the eyes....I think I knew something then, by actual experience, of that light that prostrated Paul on the way to Damascus." This quotation is in a chapter on "conversion", and James shows that conversion cures and unifies the sick soul and divided self and takes it to potential sainthood.

It is in the nature of the Mystic Way that nothing is simple, that as soon as progress is made there is immediate regress. I suspect that the Light I glimpsed in my soul was too dazzling for me to see again without damage to myself, that I had to transmute myself within like an alchemist to be able to withstand the divine vision. I sensed this at the time, for I recorded in my *Diaries* on 18th October that this white sun might explode with energy, causing me to go completely insane. Anyhow, almost immediately I backtracked, not wanting to believe that this sun was eternal, wanting to be one with my fellow men who had not seen this Light. I swung back from the metaphysical vision of *The Secret of the Golden Flower* to a materialistic, humanist view of suffering humanity, safe in the view of darkness after exposing my being to the Absolute.

Two days after the experience Tuohy, Caroline and I visited a Jewish trader in Tokyo and I bought two strings of baroque pearls. Baroque pearls are misshapen pearls, and they found their way into the dedication of *The Silence*, the pearls symbolising images. I was groping towards a new Baroque art, and had received the lines:

> "I heard a cry from the old Professor's darkened room,
> 'The Age of Analysis is dead!'
> Books lined with dust, a buzzing fly....

A MYSTIC WAY

> While naked on the petalled lawn,
> A new Baroque age is born."

Peter Jenkins, the *Guardian* columnist, visited Japan and wanted to see Tuohy, who asked me to explain the Japanese code of behaviour to him, which I did at some length. I read Nietzsche, Rilke and Dostoevsky for my teaching and continued *The Silence* and felt anew that (as I put in my *Diaries*) "life just is and that all the meanings are rational impositions", a point Tuohy reinforced during a drunken dinner with us, at the end of which he fell on the floor and crawled on his hands and knees. His writing, he said, was "all cod", and "security and a warm fire are the most important things" while Nietzsche, Blake, Rilke and Dostoevsky had "nothing important to say". I now distinguished a "social-rationalist" tradition of writers that included Kingsley Amis, Larkin and Tuohy, and an "individualist" tradition in which man develops and discovers his soul, which included William James, Rilke, Eliot, Colin Wilson and me. In other words I had now come down on the side of the irrational against reason, but in my movement back to humanism I was still trying to have it both ways. I was emotionally on the side of those who saw an invisible Reality behind the world – the poets Blake, Watkins, Barker and Gascoyne – but I refused to accept that the phenomenal world was as unreal as Noh drama and Buddhism maintained. On December 3rd I stated the idea for another long poem, which was to become *Old Man in a Circle* and in the course of late November and December I reread the salient bits from the four major novels by Dostoevsky and from the major works of Camus for my class of postgraduate students.

My renewed outer, social vision expressed itself in *The Silence* as renewed attention to the decaying social background of European civilisation. I related this to Toynbee and the *Old Testament* prophets. At the same time as I increasingly edited my poems together, like a film editor, to make one continuous narrative, I increasingly took a unitive view. American radio carried daily reports about the new American involvement in Vietnam, which had been stepped up in June. Prince and Princess Hitachi, whose State visit to Britain was already in the past, invited us both to dinner and we ate a six course meal by candlelight on a long wooden table while the four kimonoed ladies-in-waiting lurked in the shadows by a screen, and while Caroline chatted fluently to the Princess I exhausted all the safe, acceptable subjects (like riding and dogs) with the Prince. (I knew from experience that anything political or personal I introduced simply evaporated.) On Christmas Day we walked to the Cathedral, which made me think again about the social aspects of Christianity, and on Boxing Day Tuohy came to dinner and we discussed the decay of Britain at great length, a social theme, Tuohy putting the welfare of human beings above the health of the civilisation.

Perhaps it was Tuohy's influence, but the New Year, 1966, saw a continued increase in my social perspective as I deliberately strengthened the context of my metaphysical vision.

In January I slept badly, and was sometimes unable to write. In *The Silence* I was showing a healthy man opposing a sick society whose religion is dead and who creates a substitute for that religion by rediscovering spiritual vitality or vital energy in his art. I was still fascinated by history. In the afternoons I sometimes walked to the Cathedral with my daughter and gazed at the table bathed in white light, and on the way home my daughter played hide and seek with he full moon: "Bo, I see you moon." In Nobe with Buchanan, I read Blake and Vernon Watkins and wondered if the phenomenal concealed the real as they maintained, or whether the phenomenal alone exists as Nietzsche and Rilke maintained. At night, after drinking saké and walking under brilliant stars, I lay awake in silence, unable to sleep, and imagined myself dying and then dead and being nothing, and felt a cold terror under the stars. I was sure there was nothing real – no spiritual reality – behind the phenomenal. Later I wrote in my *Diaries* of "the vertical vision", and contrasted vertical growth with horizontal ease and Establishment decay.

I wrote on, expressing the vertical vision as a shoot breaking a crown. I read T. H. Hulme, and prepared for the visit Tuohy and I were to make to China. The exit and re-entry visas were a problem as no one travelled to China at that time – Mao had sealed his country off from the West and imprisoned the Reuter correspondent – but I rang someone who came to Buchanan's Christmas parties, Emé Yamashita, who was in charge of the China problem and a former private secretary to Prime Minister Sato, and he referred me to an official in the Foreign Ministry, whom Tuohy and I visited. We took a bottle of whisky with us to give him an obligation ("on") and our bribe stood on his desk for a few minutes while we talked, and then he transferred it onto the floor. We were given our re-entry visas.

Throughout February I read books on China. We were to write newspaper articles for AP, the *New York Times* and the *Sunday Telegraph*, and in a month I became an authority on Communist China. I codified my reading in a pocket book which I could carry around with me. All this time I had a premonition that something would happen, and on 13th February recorded in my *Diaries*: "Put my papers in order in case of the unlikely event of my being killed in an air-crash in China."

I flew to Hong Kong on March 3rd in a Canadian Pacific DC8. It was a terrible flight; there was a lot of air turbulence and we went through a storm. The plane was only half full, and at one point the Captain came and stood by the seat in front of me, a slightly hook-nosed balding man in a white shirt with epaulettes, and he chatted to two air hostesses who were Asian, one Chinese and one Japanese. I met Tuohy and spent two nights in Kowloon. We took the ferry across to Hong Kong where we encountered Princess Margaret, who was making a royal visit. The following day as we stood on Kowloon platform to go to China, Tuohy handed me a newspaper without comment, and I read on the front page that my Canadian Pacific plane had crashed at Tokyo airport on its return, killing between 60 and 70 people including the crew and the two air hostesses. The hook-nosed captain and the Chinese and Japanese air hostesses were pictured on the front page. I stood quietly, awed by my precognition, seeing the three of them standing together and chatting within 24 hours of their death, waiting for their extinction, condemned without realising it, and again I felt at one with my fellow man. Were we not all standing before a wall, every moment of our lives, and unaware that execution was about to happen?

In China I felt acutely close to my fellow man. The train took Tuohy and me through paddy fields and blue hills to Canton, where we were met by a guide (who was surprised we were not Japanese) and driven in an old Humber Hawk to our hotel through streets crowded with blue clad pedestrians and cyclists – there were very few cars – and past posters of American soldiers being strangled by Chinese. Canton was a hot, southern town – everyone was on the streets, in the open air – and we jostled through crowds to a primitive department store and then visited the Communist opera *The East is Red*, which recounted the Liberation, the fall of the capitalists and the victory of the proletariat who rushed about the stage carrying red flags and were greeted with thunderous applause. Any mention of Chairman Mao was applauded, and I slowly began to grasp that my Chinese fellow man had been conditioned to behave in accordance with a political myth.

This realisation increased the next day when we were taken to a People's Commune towards Fushan and toured the small whitewashed farm outhouses of the peasants, which were more primitive than the Roman ruins as Herculaneum. Everywhere we went we were applauded and whoever we spoke to told us they were saving for daily needs. There was a deceptive spontaneity in the happy faces, as if the conditioned reflex had in China become spontaneous. We walked on the foreigners' island near the Pearl River and the next day we visited a teachers' training college which was later the Red Guards' centre for South China, and we were mobbed by students with joyous faces. It was exhilarating to be with them – Tuohy found the same and said that the faces "defied analysis" – but their joy reminded me of the propaganda joy in *The East is Red*, and although I was wary, I believed that China had thrown up a new joyous man, like the being in Blake's *Glad Day*, a joyous man who had lost his freedom and was compulsively joyful. We visited the Pearl River to see the sampans and some rehousing and we went to a boat primary school to see how happy the pioneer children were, and the guide asked "Have you any criticism?" and spoke of the benefits of self-criticism, which both Tuohy and I sensed was a contributing factor in the reconditioning of the Chinese people.

We flew to Hangchow where our guide was Mr Wi. Hangchow had a quiet, majestic beauty and serenity. There was a stillness after the bustle of Canton, a great lake and distant mountains. But the conditioning was still there. We visited a middle school where we found propaganda being taught: British working conditions have apparently not changed since Dickens and in America blacks are whipped for smoking in the street. After lunch by the lake we visited a tea commune where joyous four year olds did a tea dance and then came to us to shake hands and ask "How are you uncle?" ("Susu nin ha?"): tiny children who had been conditioned to be spontaneous with perfect manners.

We took a freezing train to Shanghai, and again we received a joyous welcome from more children and from the workers in a workers' community and tool and thresher factories. Then we visited the Ma Lo commune and the peasants showed us how they occupied the former landlord's house. They took us to a kind of stable (the former pigsty) and a man in a padded blue boiler suit sat up from the straw. They brought him out, and the peasants gathered round him in a wide circle and our guide explained: "He is the former landlord. You see, we have kept him alive." The landlord stood impassively, his hands limply by his sides, while the peasants all grinned joyously, and in that moment I felt very sorry for the former landlord. I knew that my fellow man included lepers and social pariahs like this landlord, and impulsively (and probably dangerously) I strode into the centre of the large circle and shook hands with him and gazed sympathetically into his submissive eyes. I knew that the way of Christ was better than this way, which regarded a human being as expendable and remouldable material.

Our two Shanghai guides were more hardline than our Canton and Hangchow guides, and I gathered from one of them that all was not well in China when I quoted Mao's famous saying in support of free speech "Let a hundred flowers bloom and a hundred schools of thought contend" and was corrected: "No, let a hundred flowers bloom through weeding out the past." The peasants who had surrounded the former landlord had weeded him out and were now blooming, that was what the guide wanted me to know. And next morning we were taken to meet Mr Liu, son of the former match king of Shanghai, who lived under house arrest. His millions had been impounded by the State but he was allowed to enjoy the benefit of some of the interest from his fortune. He had been at Cambridge and greeted us in a suit, a man in his 50s who spoke fluent English, and served us tea, coffee, biscuits and iced cake and in the course of being grateful to Chairman Mao for being allowed to live as he did, he said: "I have had to unlearn my capitalist ways, I have been remoulded. These Americans call it brainwashing, which is the process of seeing things in their right perspectives. It takes a long time and patience." It could have been a Westerner speaking, but then, almost in mid-sentence the reconditioned, remoulded mechanism took over, and like a gramophone record repeating he cut in: "Thanks to Chairman Mao I have my life, my interest and a chance to understand Communism, thanks to Chairman Mao I can take part in the new China from this house." I was nauseated at the way Mr Liu had been treated as material to be remoulded.

We went on to visit the children's district palace and watched tiny children follow an assault course based on the Long March and queue to knock down a life-size cardboard cut-out of President Johnson, and three year olds sang us "Embroidering the Portrait of Chairman Mao" and I knew the Party propagandists had put the smiles on their innocent faces, just as they had conditioned 800 young pioneers in blue shirts and red scarves to smile and applaud us. All the Chinese who smiled at us smiled with conditioned gratitude, and bearing in mind that millions were starving in the 1940s, could I really say that well-fed remoulded minds were less good than unremoulded starving children? It was the dilemma of Dostoevsky's Grand Inquisitor, who fed the poor and gave them happiness in place of their Christian freedom which included hunger and unhappiness.

A MYSTIC WAY

The next day in Shanghai we began to realise that there was a new movement to suppress criticism. At Futan University we were told that intellectuals who despise labour had been influenced by capitalists, landlords and bourgeois teachers, and so all intellectuals must be encouraged to love labour by working in the countryside. The final Communist vision was of a breaking down of barriers between peasants, workers and intellectuals, between country and town, and between manual and mental labour. No one said that the Cultural Revolution – a new remoulding – had begun, but we had indirectly been told of its beginning.

We went to Nanking by train. Our position had worsened. In Shanghai my locked luggage at the hotel had been torn and opened during our visit to Mr Liu, and a letter of introduction written by Emé Yamashita, in case I needed it, had been opened, read and returned to a different place in my luggage. We had been questioned about photographs we had taken of junks and nuclear shelters. In Nanking our guide was hostile and suspicious, watchfully silent as we visited a department store, Nanking University and the Ming tombs. Yet again we were applauded by 400 children, and I saw that the intellectuals were being suffocated so that the Party could be sure of the children in the future, and that China was a society conditioned to guarantee the survival of the Communist Party.

We made the long train journey to Peking, where we were met by our guide Mr Tsu and driven to the Hsin Chiao Hotel. Peking in March was brown mud and dust, and we visited the Great Wall. I noticed the people were more dour in the north, more grim and less joyous, and recorded on March 15th, intuitively and prophetically sensing the first beginnings of the Cultural Revolution: "The trouble with China is that the struggle's over and is moving into the boredom of establishment, but Mao cannot afford to admit this; and so there have to be trumped up struggles today: 'the class struggle is not over', and the struggle of the militia to defend the revolution against its mythical enemy." These words were immediately vindicated when we visited Peking University the next day.

We arrived expecting to see thousands of students, but the huge campus with its beautiful curly-tiled buildings and carved stone bridges was virtually deserted. We were taken to see a second year class, where ten students read slogans about Chairman Mao from the blackboard, and when I asked to see a 3rd or 4th year class I was told by a Professor, "They are in the countryside." I probed and was told by a clearly frightened Professor Chao in the US house: "They went in August and will be back sometime soon. It's socialist re-education." Over lunch Tuohy and I discussed the situation and agreed that the 3rd and 4th year were being punitively remoulded in Sinkiang. After lunch we visited a students' dormitory and a 5th year student acted as spokesman for the dozen students there. He said: "The 3rd and 4th year are sent individually to Sinkiang, and live, eat and work with the peasants, who supervise them. They have no books. History and philosophy are being remoulded to get rid of bourgeois ideology, and have been moved permanently to the countryside." I asked the 5th year student, "Why aren't you in Sinkiang?" He replied, "Because I've got a medical certificate." "In other words," I said, "attendance in the countryside is compulsory unless there is a reason for exemption?" Mr Tsu tried to intervene, but I insisted and the student agreed. As soon as Tuohy and I were able to confer we agreed that we had uncovered a purge. Indeed we had. This was the first evidence the West had of the Cultural Revolution.

That evening Mr Tsu took us to a film about the creation of a commune. I told Mr Tsu that I wished to return to Peking University for a discussion with the Vice-President: "I am not satisfied with the explanation we have received. There were no students. I want to hear where the students are." Mr Tsu said we could not return to Peking University and tried to convince us we had misunderstood the 5th year student, but all next day, which was icy, I kept up my demands while we visited the Forbidden City and a prison, where counter-revolutionaries impassively made gloves. In the evening Tuohy did not come with us to see a play about a Viet Cong hero, who had a joyous expression on his face as he was executed by the Americans, but I persevered, and in the interval I told Mr Tsu how my students were imprisoned in Baghdad. He suddenly relented and said "I will arrange for you to see the Vice-President at Peking University."

The next day I woke to a duststorm. We visited the Temple of Heaven, and lunched with a British diplomat called Donald in an old-style Peking house and discussed our suspicions about the coming purge. The following day Mr Tsu took us to meet Professor Hwang, the Vice-President at Peking University, and other nameless young Communist observers. Mr Tsu said, "No notes to be taken." Under their noses I took a complete transcript of the hour-long interview, in which it was made clear that the students in the countryside were following a Party line, not a University line, and that their courses had been interrupted. In addition to Sinkiang some students were in Szechwan and some in Hopei. The students were clearly being indoctrinated, remoulded and purged. For the rest of the day I skirmished with Mr Tsu. Over lunch I said that the British concessions were given back voluntarily in 1945 and not seized by Mao in 1949, that Mao had lied. "You cannot trust Mao's history books," I told him. In the afternoon we visited the Garden of Delight in Harmony with its green lake, and in the evening we ate Peking duck in an old Peking street and I told Mr Tsu how the Party ruled in Orwell's *1984* and asked him: "If the Party told you that Chairman Mao has been wrong, would you believe it?" He answered: "Impossible." "Would you betray your father to Chairman Mao?" I asked. "Of course," Mr Tsu said. "My father merely begat me, whereas Chairman Mao saved me."

In my skirmishes with Mr Tsu I was on the side of Western freedom of thought, the right to vote out a country's leaders, the truth of history, and the individual criterion of the truth. I was on the side of Western Christendom and not Communist materialism. The next day we went to the Peking children's palace, and children and pioneers joyously fired machine guns at cardboard GIs and waved flags, and I felt like Christ looking with great sadness at this miserable remoulding. Children should not be regarded as material for remoulding. After lunch we went to the church. The main doors were barred, old men sat and camped outside. One small door was open and we went in. An old woman knelt in prayer, and there were 14 framed pictures of the suffering servant. Again I identified with Christ. Later we visited two museums, one covering the period from the beginnings of man to 1926, and the second one covering from 1926 to the present. At this second museum rows of Red Army men were being indoctrinated sitting on the floor. Later we walked in People's Square, and I reaffirmed Christ's values against the shallow, rootless, happy, conditioned, unfree world of this quarter of the world's population. I reaffirmed the individual against the collective, and felt very sad for my fellow Chinese human being.

From Peking we flew back to Hangchow, and then back to hotter Canton, whence we took the train back to Hong Kong. At Kowloon station fifteen porters dived for our luggage and, like newsvendors and barmen, expected tips. I was back in freedom and sanity, but Hong Kong seemed a trivial place beside the weighty thoughts China had given rise to. We flew on to Tokyo, and improbably Caroline and Nadia were at Tokyo airport to meet me. I had many newspaper articles to write, and there was much to digest.

China had changed me. I had rejected materialistic Communism but now I thought more deeply about our decaying European social structure which in some ways was as wanting as China's. In the course of opposing the remoulding and reconditioning of a quarter of the world's population, I had a yardstick which I now applied to the West. The experience of my three weeks in China had questioned all Western attitudes, and I knew this rethinking could only be good for my poetry.

I returned from China with a universal "law of unreality": that the more society suffers from unreal living (which I equated with the social ego), the more it is in decay. Hong Kong was in decay, and so was Britain – I saw this with great clarity. China was in decay too, but in a different way. As I worked on the newspaper articles I mulled over a complementary law, that vitality poured into institutions from the central self (spiritual striving) arrests, indeed reverses, decay.

I spent several days sitting with Tuohy, pooling ideas and taking his dictation of drafts for our articles. He frequently digressed to talk about style, and told me, for example, how sentences connect and how form is physiological, and he banned all adverbs and relative pronouns. I found much of this advice very helpful. Working with Tuohy, I felt as Pound must have felt working for Yeats, or Beckett for Joyce. Learning the art of good writing is to some extent an oral tradition, and an apprentice bard has to attach himself to a Homer and learn the technical tricks. Tuohy was the only Homer available in Japan. He was moody while we worked together, and once told me that for him writing was like sitting on his pot as a child.

We left all reference to our discovery of the Cultural Revolution out of the articles and sent a cable to *Newsweek*, in New York offering them the world scoop on the Peking University purge for $2,000. They replied rejecting this opportunity and asking for the article we had agreed to write. During the following weeks we offered our scoop to various "experts". Edward Crankshaw, for one, wrote back saying flatly that he did not believe our story, that if it were true there would be a purge as significant as Stalin's purges in the USSR of the 1930s. In August 1966 the Cultural Revolution broke as a news story and our scoop ended up as a retrospective account in *Encounter* of December 1966. My share was £50.

Our articles duly appeared, in the *New York Times*, in the *Sunday Telegraph*, in a series in *AP* and of course in *Newsweek*. The China trip paid for itself and there was a small profit. Soon I was able to get back to *The Silence*, which I edited, revised and typed up. It was on 28th April that the title came to me: *The Silence*. The combination of China and reviewing my poem turned me further away from metaphysical reality, and I recorded on 2nd May, "I am anti-Absolute." I was interested in expressing the decay of our civilisation, and I was very interested in an article in *Time Magazine* about post-imperial swinging Britain, which came out in May. When my poem was finished it was nearly 1,450 lines long. I showed it to Tuohy. He praised much of the technical side but wanted it to be social-rationalist discourse rather than image, and obey the linguistic principles of Wittgenstein, and he applied Movement criteria to it; and so I eventually showed it to Tomlin, who as a friend of Eliot immediately understood my early post-Modernist aims and outlook. "Mr F. T." of the dedication began as Frank Tuohy and turned into Frederick Tomlin, reflecting the tension between the two polarities in my being.

For much of May and June I pondered on eternity, on how stillness took me into the silence of eternity and the Zen reality, and I felt that inner vitality and growth can be found in a healthy culture. I had left the decayed West and had come to the healthy East to find this drive in myself, which in *The Silence* I called a drive to my Shadow. I was aware that I had become semi-Eastern during my time in the East and that I had had to leave the West to discover this vitality within myself, of which the East is aware.

In Britain the Labour Party had won a General Election, and I wanted to visit Britain to catch the new post-imperial atmosphere. I had arranged for all three of us to return home for a visit of ten weeks in June, travelling the cheapest route on money largely advanced by the Bank of Japan. The day before I left I wondered if history has a pattern and wrote: "I would like to believe in Britain's freedom to emerge ...but deep down feel there is a decline ahead, a decline into a USE (United States of Europe)." I saw Britannia as a dying whore and knew I would write a poem on the theme.

We travelled from Tokyo to Nakhodka on a Russian boat. It was festooned with coloured streamers as we left, and we ploughed through sun and then mist while Russians played chess on the back deck and in the evenings did Cossack dancing, sitting on their haunches and shooting out each leg in turn and raising their arms and whirling in a thrilling abandon. We passed Hokkaido and on the third day arrived in Nakhodka, a trafficless town whence we took a seemingly pre-1917 train to Khabarovsk. After a glimpse of a snowless Siberia we flew in a deafening turbo-prop Aeroflot plane that throbbed and rattled like a wartime bomber, and nine hours later we were in Moscow and drove to the Hotel Minsk in Gorky Street, which had an open lift.

We now began to get to know Russian life. Everything suddenly became a battle. Catching the waiter's eye, obtaining Nadia's bedding, buying appleade, booking an Intourist tour – all took hours. Nevertheless I managed to get us on a tour of the Kremlin for noon the next day. We walked round the Archangel Cathedral and as I looked at the early 16th century icons and murals of Grand Dukes on pillars I glimpsed a new poetic form, a poem on Communism in pictures which would combine my impressions of China and my impressions of the USSR. I began this immediately. It became *Archangel*. We went on to Red Square and visited Lenin's tomb and saw Lenin's pale face under a brilliant light.

That evening we caught a train to Brest, Warsaw and Berlin, which we approached through the dark ruins and dimly lit streets of the eastern side and suddenly encountered the blaze of West Berlin. I wrote the first 150 lines of *Archangel*, and two days later we had crossed Flanders and arrived in London at Victoria Station and were met by Caroline's parents, who drove us to 55 High Beech Road, Loughton, a house my brother Robert had bought, which we were renting so as not to disturb the tenants in our flat. I arrived a practising poet who had a vision of Reality to integrate in the decaying European and Communist civilisations.

In Loughton I caught up with my family, including my widowed mother, and gloried in English things: in red pillar boxes, the whine of a milk float and white-flannelled cricketers on Loughton cricket field, which I visited with my brother Robert. After China and Russia, and assumptions of imprisonment and execution, this was a quaint, stable, secure, little life. I walked in the Forest to the two ponds off Earl's Path, and gazed at the pale water lilies, the water irises and the sodden leaves under the beeches. I re-entered the little life of shopping, doctors' surgeries and television news. No one wanted to know too much about the Far East, and I was content to renew my roots in the West.

I was acutely conscious that I had Britain for ten weeks and would then be separated from it again. I was an Outsider, but I drank in every impression, gazed at every detail in the buildings as I had done in Iraq, saw everything my family took for granted with fresh eyes. I drove out into the Essex villages and marvelled at the steeples that dominated the flat countryside, gazed at the green leaves, greedy for each English detail. I went up to London to sell some China photos and stopped at every statue and went into every church or Cathedral and marvelled at the wealth of our cultural heritage, comparing each holy place with the bare Cathedral in Tokyo. I went again to a lunch near Trafalgar Square, and, walking down Whitehall towards Downing Street, saw Big Ben peep over trees and Nelson raise his arm. I retraced my childhood, discussing situations I remembered with my mother and going back to Chigwell School for Speech Day, where I observed the gouged bricks and decayed noticeboard and spoke to some of my former teachers. The Head, Thompson, was off hand: "Where are you back from?" I told him a little about China and how misunderstood it was, to which, gazing into the distance, he replied, "Oh, that's nice isn't it."

I quickly made an upstairs room at the back of my brother's house my study and spent whole mornings writing *Archangel*. Some evenings we dined with my mother in the Journey's End nursery, and some evenings I went out with my younger brother Jonathan to the Holly Bush or Royal Standard, or further afield to the Owl. I visited Waltham Abbey. I broke off from *Archangel* and started on *Blighty*, in which Britain – as Britannia – is a decaying whore. I regarded myself that summer as the chronicler of Britain's decay, as the poet of decay.

I met a number of people from my past. In July I met John Ezard, who was working for the *Oxford Mail*. He had predicted that I would move away from the West and towards the East, and that on my return we would be out of shouting distance, and we talked across the distance between us, he saying he was no longer interested in ideas, theories or the universe while I looked for a life beyond bourgeois "normality" and confessed to opening myself to Eastern wisdom. I had tea with my former Oaklands teacher Mabel Reid, who had just retired and was living in Elm Cottage near the school. I lunched with my Aunt Lucy who in the late 1920s had stolen my mother's fortune, and I disturbed her enough with my forecasts of decline and decay to give her a sleepless night worrying about her business and a crash in shares. (I had brought this theme into *The Silence*, in the passage about Mrs. Hall.) I went to Dulwich (Caroline's parents had moved from their demolished house to 177 South Croxted Road) and strolled in the Park, gazing at the ducks, widgeon and quails on the small lake and feeling for the park labourers, and I visited the library and chatted to the warden.

The warden told me a story, and that night I had the idea of writing 100 stories, prose-poems that would focus on intense experiences that shaped people's lives. On 15th July I wrote *Limey*, which was based on the warden's story. Although I had attempted short stories at Oxford and after, this was the first of 500 stories in my prose-poem style. Each evening I now went to the Standard for a nightcap and I took my writing with me and did my corrections, sitting in the corner, just as Sartre had done in the Café Bonaparte in Paris.

I had gone up to London and visited the Banqueting House, and seen the window through which Charles I had stepped before his execution on a platform outside, and I resolved to write a poem on Cromwell, which I began to draft. Another day I went to the Tower, and another day I took Caroline to the Cheshire Cheese and visited the Rhymers' Club cellar. We also went to hideous Harlow and charming Sawbridgeworth, to which some of the older Loughton families, including Mark Liell's, had moved to escape the creeping urbanisation of once rural Loughton, and I steeped myself in the past and saw myself as being in a tradition of Protestant Reformism, that is, Puritanism: reforming doctrine into the experience of the silence and eternity. Both in my poetry and during these visits I deliberated on the conflict between spiritual reform and political revolution. I was still writing *Archangel*, and finished it on July 23rd. My haloed Archangel Michael in the Russian icon I had seen embodied the Russian Byzantine tradition and prophetically looked forward to a time when Communism had collapsed. After writing the last line I went for two glorious walks in brilliant sunshine, one of them to the Stubbles and the Witches' Copse. Two days later I walked to the Iron Age fort, Loughton camp, and saw the pollarded trees as brain nerves, a recurrent image from when I was writing *Mandalas*.

We spent a week in Bognor with my mother, younger brother and sister. We travelled through East Grinstead and visited the 13th century Hill Place and "Aunt Gwen", the artist Gwen Broad who wrote to me soon after I was born. She was slightly scrawny and severe-looking, with red-rimmed devout eyes. We visited Broadley Brothers (the East Grinstead branch of the family business) and I returned to St. Anton, my grandmother's house in East Grinstead, and found the arbour over the winding path, and beyond it the tool-shed. I visited Beecholme, where I found to my dismay that the pine had been cut down, and Daledene. On our arrival at Bognor, we gathered in the television room of the Marlborough Hotel where we were staying and watched the World Cup soccer final, England v West Germany, and cheered when Geoff Hurst (later an Oaklands parent) scored the only hat-trick a British player has achieved in a World Cup final in the 20th century. At Bognor I spent much of each day reading about Cromwell on the beach and in the evenings we drove out to surrounding villages, including Felpham, where I saw Blake's house. One day we were visited by my Aunt Lucy, and I "innocently" asked her questions about how she acquired the family business in 1926, while her son Tom prowled around trying to change the subject.

We went to Chichester. I wanted to get the feel of the UK as a whole and connect myself to literary places of special interest to Japanese, and alone I made a quick tour of Scotland and Ireland. I flew to Edinburgh and walked among the black-grey buildings and the crumbling closes along Royal Mile, and visited Holyrood Castle and Knox's House. I took the train to Glasgow and flew to Belfast and toured the drab terraces and gaudy 1890s pubs, and the next day went to Dublin and toured the city in a taxi driven by one of the 1916 rebels, who took me inside Kilmainham prison and showed me the yard where the Easter 1916 martyrs were shot by the British. Then I visited all the places connected with Joyce's *Ulysses*, and the next day took a train to Gort and visited Coole Park where Yeats's friend Lady Gregory lived, and thought of the many-sided Major Robert Gregory who died young. Then I went on to Sligo to visit Yeats's grave in Drumcliffe churchyard under Ben Bulben.

I returned by air in time for a promenade concert at the Royal Albert Hall, which Sir Malcolm Sargent conducted, and the idea for *The Conductor* came to me (see my *Diaries* for 12th August). The next day I sped up to Huntingdonshire and visited Cromwell's house in Ely and then Little Gidding, made famous in Eliot's *Four Quartets*, and Ferrar's tomb.

With only a week of my holiday left I felt an extrovert tourist. I had lost contact with the silence, I was living an outer life rather than the inner life I had found in Japan. I went to church at St. Mary's, Loughton. My brother Robert was a churchwarden and handed me two books. There were two hymns by George Herbert, but I found the service a communal drama that bore little relation to the silence. Jill Bradbury came, and she, Caroline and I drove to Lippitt's Hill, where the poet John Clare was a mental patient, and walked in the Forest near High Beach. Jill had grown her hair well down over her shoulders, and she wore trousers and walked across the leaves in bare feet. She talked about her past, saying she had lost herself at Oxford and had become "a neurotic bore". I warmed to Jill, not realising that she would commit suicide in September (something I did not discover until early 1971). Two days later I met Ricky at Notting Hill Gate. He had a

130

limp, having been knocked down by a bolting horse, and he told me Jill had been in a mental hospital in Northampton in 1964, the sister mental hospital to Lippitt's Hill. Ricky asked "How is your inner life going?" This was a question no one else I knew would ask so directly, except perhaps John Ezard, and I told him about the silence and the white light, and Ricky became very excited and spoke of the death of the ego. I said "The Oxford nihilism was a prelude to inner unity", and Ricky agreed. I said "Unreal living is a prelude to real living", and again he agreed. We moved to Chelsea and drank four and half pints and discussed the new Reformation and agreed that one day we would bring it into being. I returned home to Journey's End at 12.30 a.m. to find the family waiting for me, and I was elated as I had renewed contact with my inner spring.

I met John Ezard in the Royal Standard and told him about my meeting with Ricky. He reiterated: "Ricky must have developed the same way as you. I have abandoned all ideas and no longer need to interpret experiences. We have no common language. You are living at a deeper level than when you left England."

My last day in England I felt a great sadness. I went up to the Forest to say goodbye. It was very peaceful, and I wished I could be buried between the two ponds. In the Journey's End garden, under the nursery window, Nadia blew a string of soapy bubbles through a wire ring, and watching them float and explode I thought it was an image for our ephemeral universe. I went to the Owl and later had a final drink with my brother Jonathan in the Standard. Caroline was tearful when I got home. She wanted to stay in England and not return to exile. I felt the same. And next morning, on the train at Liverpool Street I felt tears coming as I leaned out of the window to say goodbye. I was not sure whether my feeling was for my family, the Forest or England, or all three, but I knew it was attributable to an impending separation from something. I now felt I belonged to England. Being an exile had taught me to value it and love it. England was decayed, but I had rediscovered my roots in the past. And crossing the Channel I felt a nomad, I was insecure, and for the next 24 hours both Caroline and I had wet eyes several times.

My feelings had purified and intensified. My purgation was continuing almost unnoticed, I was living through my new centre.

We returned to Japan the same way that we had come, via Moscow, where we stayed in the fortress-like Hotel Ukraina. The next day I was able to visit Semyonovsky Square, where Dostoevsky awaited execution, and the Dostoevsky Museum, which had a picture of Stariez Amvrosec, thought to be the original for Father Zossima in *The Brothers Karamazov*. In the afternoon I went to the Revolution Museum and unsuccessfully tried to see their portrait of Kalyaeev, one of Camus's "Justes" who assassinated a Grand Duke and then asked for death. We flew back to Khabarovsk where I saw the funeral that formed the basis of my short story *A Spade Fresh With Mud*, and then took the train to Nakhodka and the boat to Japan. During the voyage it got hotter, and I worked on Cromwell and pondered opening a school for self-realisation, which eventually happened (briefly) in 1992. I correctly identified this course as an escape from art.

Back in Japan for one more year, I resumed my former way of life. I revised a couple of poems, *The Oceanographer* and *Twilight,* and made some revisions to *The Silence*, and immediately sensed the oneness of the earth and the universe, from which selfhood separates. I thought again of the death of the ego, the Buddhist dying away from self, which I had partially undergone. I found Tuohy more social-rationalist than ever, and we went down to Nobe with Buchanan and talked about the decay of Britain against booming Pacific rollers and tinkling autumn crickets.

Sartre and Simone de Beauvoir came to Japan and spoke at Keio University. Earlier I had lectured on M. Roquentin's response to the Negro singer in *La Nausée*, and I sat in a hall among 2,000 Japanese while de Beauvoir harangued us on feminism for an hour in French. Then Sartre, dressed in a navy suit and looking more tall and respectable than the man I met in 1959, took over and sat sideways on before the microphones and spoke barely audibly about how being an intellectual meant opposing the Americans in Vietnam and the French in Algeria, and on how women and intellectuals are the victims of the structure of their society. There was nothing about *La Nausée* and nothing about the philosophy of Existentialism, the two subjects I wanted to hear.

A week later Jon Halliday came to dinner. He had been in the Oxford Randolph Set, and was now a Marxist teaching at Reading University, and during his visit to Japan he was staying with Adrian. He wore rimless glasses and embodied Sartre's view that an intellectual opposes the Americans. We discussed China and he did not want to hear any criticism of Mao, and dismissed the 20 million who may have been killed by the Communists as a mere "culture pattern". He brought me up to date with the various doings of the Randolph Set, who all seemed to have gone into teaching, magazines or psychiatry.

I continued to read world history with the Prince and was reading Whitehead and phenomenology with my postgraduate class. I now realised that I felt more settled within myself, now that I had completed the self-discovery reflected in *The Silence* and was living from a new centre. I was sleeping better and was less introspective. In October I began my longish poem on Cromwell, and wrote *An Inner Home* about Epping Forest, drawing on my recent visit to Waltham Abbey and expressing my sense of inner growth, which I measured against the enduring Forest. I wrote *The Conductor*, which was about uniting the way of action and the way of contemplation. At the very moment I finished the first draft of this poem the post came, bringing a letter from my older Oxford friend Kingsley, who was now a Russian interpreter with the United Nations and who was now preaching the philosophy of freedom and way of action I had preached at Oxford. "I see now," he wrote, "that you were perhaps fighting for your life at a time when most of us didn't even know there was a war on." I had been down the way of action, and since coming to Japan had embarked on a way of contemplation, and was now concerned to combine the two in a great self-unification. I felt I was ahead of Kingsley, and had left him behind.

A few days later for the first time I dipped into Evelyn Underhill's *Mysticism* and read about the Way of Contemplation, and "a gradual handing over of the reins from the surface intelligence to the deeper mind" until "individual activity is sunk in the great life of all". That was exactly what had happened to me while I was writing *The Silence*. And as I recorded in my *Diaries* on 24th October, "the main thing about that poem was that I did it all for myself, without any aid or guidance, and so I did not know where I was going. I was travelling along a completely unknown road without the slightest idea of what was at the end."

My awareness of the All was extended by discussions on the Will of Heaven I had at the end of October and in early November with one of my pupils at the Bank of Japan, an Executive Director, Mr Fukuchi. He explained that Zoroastrianism had left an impact on China in Yin and Yang, which are united within the Tao whereas Ahriman and Ahura Mazda had no equivalent unity in ancient Persia, and he told me that the first mention of Yin and Yang in China was c1143/2BC in the *I Ching*, on whose 64 hexagrams he was an authority. Originally, he said, a hexagram was arrived at by heating a tortoise-shell until it cracked, but now it was done through laying 50 bamboo sticks on a table. His hobby was to use the sticks, and next week he brought them to our class and told my fortune. He placed one stick on the table (to signify God) and held the remaining 49 over his head, and then divided them into two (heaven and earth) and went on subdividing each group until he was left with hexagram 46, "Shang", whose variation is hexagram 32, "Hang". "Shang" means "earth-wind" (bottom and top) and "ascent, advancing upwards blindly", "great progress and success". Mr Fukuchi said: "That is the Will of Heaven for you. This must be one of the best hexagrams in the *I Ching*."

As part of my ascent or "advancing upwards blindly" to a union between action and contemplation I began writing the 100 stories or prose-poems I had glimpsed in England, in which I contemplated images of action. All through November and December I wrote one or two stories a day. From time to time I went down to Nobe and drank with Buchanan, and I attended a reception for Prince Hitachi's birthday and learned that Princess Haneko had seen me walking, deep in composition (and contemplation) wearing old clothes near Edogawa bashi (bridge), news of which had dominated the Imperial dinner table that night. In my *Diaries* I wrote increasingly philosophical reflections on the unveiling of Being, on Heidegger, Sartre, Julian Huxley and the dialectic in Dostoevsky, and I still wondered whether history has a pattern in relation to centuries (rather than decades). I clashed several times with Tuohy on the problem of pain, he insisting that no one cares for the suffering of humanity as opposed to the suffering of individuals we know, preferring positivist feeling to my contemplative sense of all mankind, the human All.

Writing prose as opposed to poetry made me feel I was living less deeply, and I recorded this impression on 7th December: "I feel I am losing touch with my inner life .... As long as I am writing stories about other people, this trend will continue: action at the expense of contemplation. I live more deeply in poetry than I do in prose. In prose I am perceptive, in poetry I am all-intuitive. Perhaps I shall finish my stories and then plunge back into meditative poetry." Just before Christmas I started my next long poem, which became *Old Man in a Circle*, and reflected in my *Diaries*, "I have been off poetry too long .... for me, the writing of poetry is a spiritual act." And on 31st December: "I have completed my rebuilding of myself and escaped the tyranny of theories" for "the role of the Artist in society".

My role in Japanese society was illustrated on December 14th when I received a telephone call from Prince Hitachi complaining about an article in the *Times*, written by Fred Emery (the *Times* correspondent in Tokyo), criticising Sato, the Prime Minister. (Fred had invited me to a couple of his parties and we had spent part of one hot Tokyo evening discussing Bancroft's School, where he had been, a neighbour of my own Chigwell School.) The Prince hummed and hahed and expressed the Government's displeasure at the article, would I communicate this to Emery? I rang Fred Emery, who immediately said: "What a splendid response." I rang the Prince back to say I would bring the *Times* article with me to the next class, and that we would read it. I reflected that the Japanese Prime Minister had protested to the *Times* by getting the Prince to use me as a go-between. I felt I was becoming an insider, and longed to return to England.

In January I decided to leave Japan on October 18th. The decision caused me some soul-searching because Professor Narita had invited me to stay on with a Chair "for life", but Caroline still hankered for Britain, as I did, and Nadia's convent school was to close in July, and there was not another satisfactory school in Tokyo It made sense for us to return to the flat in Loughton and for Nadia to attend Oaklands School. I told Professor Irie at my main university. Two days later he said: "We shall be sorry to see you go. We want your successor to be exactly the same as yourself. We want someone like yourself in every respect."

Those last nine months I lived at a lower intensity than in 1966, but at a higher level of thought. It was as if I were thinking through my new centre now, and I felt more detached, even when we spent a day huddling over an oil stove at Nobe as the fall-out from Mao's fifth nuclear explosion came down as rain. For the first six months of 1967 I wrote a story – sometimes two – each day, and intermittently I worked on *Old Man in a Circle*. At the same time I read a lot of history, including Toynbee. I briefly taught Colin Wilson's *Religion and the Rebel* at my main university, and my *Diaries* are filled with observations about the decline of Western civilisation and the future of Britain: expressions of higher thought.

The book on Eliot to which I had contributed had been launched at Sophia House, and the British Ambassador arrived and met us contributors, who included Tomlin, Tuohy and Professor Nishiwaki. (Two Jesuit priests, Father Peter Milward and Father William Johnston, were also present.) Tomlin had read my poems and he told me he found them very exciting, but the only really deep feeling I experienced at this time was on 1st February, when, sitting in my study at home, for two hours I felt a great sorrow from the bottom of my being (perhaps connected with my decision to resign) – somewhere between my throat and my stomach, and probably in my heart – and at the same time I felt I loved everything so deeply I wanted to cry. I wrote in my *Diaries*: "I am existing in the depths of my being, I am pure feeling, and the feeling is love ....I am alive in my depths ...and I feel as if I am going to burst into tears because everything is good. My wife is clattering knives. That is good. Everything is good: the rattling window, the chord on the piano, the condensation on my window. I have seen to the very bottom of my being, and there is no abyss. Just a profound sadness and a great exaltation."

There was a heavy fall of snow, which hung on the fruit trees like blossom, and there was a slow thaw. The annual British Council conference took place, and Tuohy gave a couple of talks which had an almost Johnsonian authority – one on "Desirable English and Available English" – to which one lecturer remarked "Blunt but true", a phrase that summed up Tuohy's genius. I saw Tuohy a couple of times after that, and in mid-March he came to a last dinner in which he was very gentle towards my poetry, and next morning we visited him just before he left Tokyo to return to England. He was in a suit and waistcoat, and his hair was brushed very neatly and he looked immensely sad and spent a long time saying goodbye at the window of our taxi. He stood limply and his eyes were slightly red. Then he turned messily and walked back up his path and I felt tears coming and reflected that before his arrival I was like Michelangelo's Adam, awaiting creation, and that his touch was the touch of God.

Tokyo was not the same after Tuohy had gone. Harry Guest had arrived to take up a teaching post, dressed exceptionally informally and with long matted hair, but I saw little of him. I took my family down to Nobe. Once it was wet and there were drops of rain under every bud, and the plum blossom was out. Another time the paddies were full of croaking and some frogs sounded like castanets, and the next morning I slid open the window and lay in my futon and watched birds flit in the glorious air. I had of course informed the British Council that I was leaving Japan. They briefly offered me a job in Libya, which appealed because of the Mediterranean location and proximity to Egypt, but in May they informed me that the post had been filled, and I was reconciled to spending a year in England.

I thought about England a lot, and soon began a play, *The Noddies*, about my experience as a park labourer in Dulwich Park. This was written between 6th and 23rd May while I reacted to de Gaulle's rejection of Britain's application to join the EEC, and while I read more Toynbee for my postgraduate class. About this time Kenneth Rexroth, the American poet, visited Japan and a colleague of mine at my main university, the Californian Ruth Witt-Diamant, invited us to meet him. He was an elderly, grey-haired slightly dandified man, who had little to say about poetry – he listened to me but did not contribute much – and the only remark of his that I can remember was of Caroline: "You remind me of an Austrian tart I once knew. That's intended as a compliment, she was the most beautiful woman I've seen." (Tuohy had once said something similar of Caroline: "She has real beauty and elegance, she's the most beautiful woman I've met.")

In June we listened to American radio for news of Israel's progress in the 7-day war. I returned to *The Eternicide*, but interrupted my rethinking on that novel on July 17th when in Nobe I had the idea for the poem that became *Fire-Void*, sub-titled "A Rubbish Dump at Nobe, Japan: An Investigation of Nature and History, Pattern and Meaning". A fortnight earlier I had been teaching Spengler's *Decline of the West*.

135

A MYSTIC WAY

That summer there were two freak natural events. At the end of July there was a vicious storm, the most vicious I have ever experienced. The rain lashed down, trees bent, and the lightning – at first like lights being turned on and off almost continuously – suddenly turned to bolts which echoed down and fell all round our bungalow. At least six just missed us. I went to the French windows and looked up and saw a jagged fork leaping down, coming straight at me . Instinctively I turned and gathered Nadia into my arms, still watching the descending fork over my shoulder, and it cut away at the last minute and struck some scaffolding just beyond our garden wall, about ten yards from where I stood, and there was a round ghostly glow. I am sure it was the little understood phenomenon known as ball lightning. With a sinking stomach and very shaken, I continued telling Nadia a story about Nobe, and another bolt landed next door and knocked down a concrete clothes line and burnt all the washing. Then there was an awesome quiet and suddenly the cicadas began singing and all was cool and our cat crept out from under the settee and everything was back to normal.

In August we were nearly drowned by a tidal wave. I had awoken in Nobe to a brilliant dawn but the sea was full of rollers that crashed and foamed in. I composed a poem, *The Sea is like an Eiderdown,* in my head, and then Caroline and I took Nadia in for a swim with her rubber ring. Suddenly an enormous roller crashed down on us as we were just out of our depth. I saw it coming and grabbed Nadia, and as she clutched my little left finger my bloodstone ring washed off and was lost. Later a huge roller appeared about 100 yards out, at least four foot above the sea. It was racing in – there must have been an earthquake as it was a tidal wave – and I tried to flee it, holding Nadia by her arm. But it came in too quickly and in the end I turned and faced it. It crashed down on us and we were buried in boiling foam. I had held onto Nadia, and when we surfaced I saw another wave just as large bearing down on us. I held Nadia high above my head, took a deep breath and the full force of the wave hit my back and knocked me onto my side. But I held onto her and stood up and waded hard for the beach. The two tidal waves had gone right up over the top of the beach, a tremendous distance, and we were extremely lucky no one was drowned.

At the end of August I briefly revised *The Silence*, and the next month I prepared to leave Japan. There was a round of visits to the tax office and farewell gatherings. The Bank of Japan gathering was in a sushi bar called the Edinburgh, and I was served wriggling prawns out of a tank, which I had to gulp down, heads and all, trying not to vomit. The Keio gathering was at a restaurant in Kyobashi, which had a saké vat and we could taste the wood in the saké. Then we were served a live sole that squinted dolefully through its two eyes while we picked the flesh from its back with chopsticks. Then it gulped a couple of breaths, wriggled its bare spine and fins and flipped its tail, and with a reproachful, hurt squint it died. Tokyo University of Education held a perfunctory stand-up function at the Mikasa Khaikan, and Tomlin had us for a brief drink at the Sanbancho Hotel.

I made a last visit to the Prince's palace. On my way there the air-conditioned car slowed and Princess Haneko was alongside my window, walking with a shopping bag. "You see, Professor Hagger," she said, "I have been shopping as you suggested." I had encouraged her to go out into society and be normal. "Good," I said approvingly. Prince Hitachi seemed very sad to see me go.

We made a final visit to Nobe and I stood near threshers and gazed at the tubs of grain and the pile of chaff. And we visited the Dalai Lama's exhibition of mandalas in a Ueno department store. There were about 100 17th century mandalas on moth-eaten silk showing the seven stages of satori, and as I gazed at the symbolism a lone Japanese shouted to no one in particular. I asked for a translation, and was told: "He says they are Chairman Mao's property, not the Dalai Lama's, and that they should not be shown in Tokyo but should be in Tibet."

I went to the Hong Kong and Shanghai bank to collect a currency licence, and I got into conversation with the cashier. "Have you seen everything you wanted to during your stay in Japan?" he asked. "Yes," I said, "except that I haven't met a kamikaze." To my surprise he invited me to a small room nearby and ordered tea and said to me, "I was a kamikaze." And he told me about a raid which 378 made on Okinawa on 31st March 1945. Only three had returned alive, of which he was one. They were supposed to fly low over the US ships three times and crash the third time. But there was low cloud. He had not crashed his plane. He had flown around in shame and lost face, and had met up with the other two pilots. They all agreed that they should return home, and to their astonishment they were greeted as heroes. There is now a national monument to them, which he visited every March 31st.

The same day I took Caroline to the airport and put her and Nadia on a plane for London. Buchanan and Professor Irie came to say goodbye. After they had gone I returned to spend a night in International House, where four years earlier I had had the idea for *The Expatriate*. I left Japan the next day.

I spent three weeks returning home on my own through the Far East. My main university paid my first class air fare in cash and I flew second class and was able to stop off at 14 different cities, the hotel bills being covered by the difference between the 1st and 2nd class fares. The tour provided an excellent review of civilisations, and shaped the historical view that eventually became *The Fire and the Stones*. The full details are in my *Diaries*.

My first stop was in Manila, where I absorbed the Spanish colonial background and visited places connected with the Japanese occupation and the US liberation, and walked in Quiapo square and saw a Philippino lying on his back, being tied to a cross with ropes as part of a religious devotion. In the evenings I sensed the danger and decay of the place.

Next I widened my knowledge of Chinese influence. I flew onto Hong Kong and found a black market "money exchanger" and encountered a crowd near the Peninsular, crouching near a "Danger" sign. I joined them and was told there was a bomb in a red can, which I could see in the middle of the road 50 yards away. The bomb disposal squad packed sandbags round it and shot it up with a pistol, and there was a report like a thunderflash. Round the corner there was another bomb, and we had a repeat performance, and I felt elated at the bright yellow blast. I visited

A MYSTIC WAY

Macao by hydrofoil and walked on the Portuguese waterfront and noted
Maoist slogans and dress, and was the only passenger on the return journey
past distant Chinese mountains in a causeway of setting sunlight. I toured
Hong Kong, visiting all the historical sites, and then flew on to Singapore,
which was humid, visited the sites and went to Jahore across the causeway
the Japanese used for their invasion during the Second World War. On the
way back I passed some fire-walkers. Yogis in yellow with bare, ash-
marked feet stood near a fire that was already ashes. The fire-walking had
happened.

Next I looked at the South East Asian civilisation in Indo-China. I flew
on to Saigon. The Vietnam war was being fought and our plane was shelled
as we came in, and we had to climb steeply, during which our bodies were
exposed to the pressure of many Gs. We then approached the airport from a
different direction, virtually nosediving onto the runway. Saigon was a war-
time city with girls camped in the des Nations hotel corridors, and there
were currency dealers everywhere, one of whom cheated me by giving me
only a fifth of my money by doubling back a wad of notes and then using
immensely quick sleight of hand. I had a drink at the Continental (on whose
veranda Greene sat while visiting South Vietnam for *The Quiet American*),
and that night from the hotel roof I saw the distant flash of a bomb across
the river and flares and heard the distant thump of guns.

The next day, acting from inner compulsion to seek out danger, I went to
Bien Hoa in an American army bus with anti-grenade mesh over the
windows. I just got in, wearing mufti, and travelled with several uniformed
GIs. We drove along an insecure road that was frequently mined and
ambushed, over the river and through palms and swamp land, past rural
villages of corrugated hovels and melon-stalls until we came to several
American bases enclosed in barbed wire and sandbags, where sat dozens of
transport planes. Here was later fought the decisive battle of the war. I
looked, aware that there would be a future significance, and returned to
Cholon, the Chinese suburb of Saigon, where I got off the bus intending to
wander in Chinatown. But a storm loomed with thunder and a GI waved me
in to the base without checking my security, and I found myself sheltering
from the rain with uniformed GIs who invited me to take a beer from the
fridge. Then a wall-mounted phone rang. "Answer it," a GI called, and an
American General asked "Have you got the address of the Annopolis
Trenching Billet? It's on the board in front of you." I looked and gave him
the address and hung up, my contribution to the day's war done. Then a
guard whistled and said "Your bus is here", and I went out and sat on
another bus which took me into Central Saigon. My foray into the
countryside round Saigon convinced me that the Americans had an almost
impossible task in winning the war, and that each base was permanently
under siege. They were so lax about security it would have been easy for
enemy sympathisers to infiltrate them, just as I had done in my capacity as
tourist.

I flew on to Angkor via Pnom Penh and visited the stunning Khmer ruins
in the jungle, which closed round them in the 13th century, and studied the
Buddhist and Hindu statues, including several of a detached Siva with an
erect lingam. The Khmer Rouge were in the surrounding jungle but were

yet to take Cambodia over. I returned to Pnom Penh, a pleasant French town on the rivers Sap and Mekong, and Prince Sihanouk, the Leader, passed, sitting beside the President of Mauretania. I stayed at Le Royal and travelled round Pnom Penh by cyclo-pousse or trishaw, pedalled by a boy. Later that night he took me into an opium den (I left without smoking opium). Next morning we encountered Sihanouk again, and he parked his trishaw and joined the throng that lined the kerb and jumped up and down, cheering loudly and clapping his hands over his head. Then he got back on his trishaw as though nothing had happened. Earlier I had asked "Do you like the US better than the Viet Cong?" and he had said "I no say, I too small. If I say policeman handcuff me and take me to prison." I have sometimes wondered how he fared under Pol Pot. Did he survive the killing fields by leaping up and down and cheering and clapping, the "small" man's way of surviving a tyranny?

I had the idea of going to North Vietnam to write some newspaper articles, and the next morning I visited the Viet Cong Embassy. I was told to clear off by an old woman and was bundled out of the gate by an old man and a fearsome young tough. I kept ringing the bell at the gate and the old woman reappeared with a form which included the heading "motif" and eventually she returned all smiles and I was shown into a room with a glass case, a picture of Ho and a replica of Tran at the stake awaiting execution, and in came a mild Mr Van, a smiling man with a parting down the middle and a blue shirt. He wrote down my details, including my visit to China, and said he would refer them to HQ, and on the way out the three chucker-outers saluted me. Nothing ever came of my approach.

I left rural Cambodia and flew to industrial, built-up Bangkok. Early the next morning I visited the Floating Market with its brown-green water, hovels on stilts and sampans laden with fruit, and after that visited the royal palace and marvelled at the images on the temples.

Then I flew on to the Indian civilisation, to Calcutta, and drove in from the airport through paddy fields and palms, passing bare-footed stragglers and squatters in the road, and that evening, as firecrackers celebrated the coming of the goddess as a sacred cow, walked round town, stepping over and round the hopeless homeless lying on the streets, limply propped against trees or lying on steps, their penises often showing. My first impression of India in Calcutta was of pink and dirty stucco and balconies, honking horns and rickshaw drivers, and everywhere crowds of people, and many poor. I saw them at dawn as I drove to the airport, sleeping in the open air, no bedding, no cover, just sleeping where they happened to be as if self-preservation no longer mattered.

I flew on to Katmandu past Everest, which was bright white on a range against blue, and walked in the medieval town's fresh mountain air among hens and sheep under a square tower with the face of a curly-eyed Buddha on it and I was accosted by a Tibetan refugee who took me off to a barn-like house where we climbed to the first floor and sat on sacks of oats and he unrolled mandalas on straw. I bought one for $8. Soon after I encountered an ex-gurkha and bought a thanka of Yamantaka, conqueror of death (one of the fierce protective deities whose worship was introduced by Padmasambhava in the 8th century) for $30, and later went up to the first floor of another barn and bought a 400 year old cosmic clock mandala for $21. That night once again there were fireworks for the goddess – the festival was a day later in Katmandhu than in Calcutta – and I was told that the fireworks were to wake people up to the cow.

I flew on to Delhi and visited the old Red Fort and the Moghul palace with its Persian couplet saying ecstatically "If there is a paradise on earth, it is this, it is this, it is this" and I thought about the place of the Moghul time in the whole of the Indian civilisation.

My next stop was Istanbul where I visited the Byzantine and Ottoman ruins, which I was later to place in the Byzantine-Russian and Arab civilisations respectively. I visited the Sultan's palace and hareem, Hagia Sophia, the church Justinian built, and finally Mehmet's Topkapi palace.

After that I looked at the Austro-Hungarian empire. I stopped at Budapest and visited both sides of the Danube, and then went to Vienna in pursuit of the Habsburgs and visited the church which contains their tombs and the Summer and Winter palaces. Finally I went to Paris and stayed in St. Germain des Prés among the Maoists and drank in Sartre's Café Bonaparte and visited the British Council to see if there might be work teaching English as a foreign language.

As a result of my time away from the European civilisation I had got to know the Arab, Japanese, Chinese, Byzantine-Russian, S. E. Asian and Indian civilisations, and numerous empires within those civilisations. I had not left England in 1963 to study world history – I was driven by a desire to absorb the wisdom of the East – but I returned in 1967 with a better grounding in world history than I could possibly have expected. It seemed to have happened by accident, but in view of the fact that this knowledge was crucial to *The Fire and the Stones*, may it not have been the result of Providence rather than accident?

As I landed at Heathrow, where Caroline and Nadia were waiting for me, I felt I had achieved an enormous amount during my four years in Japan. I was now a poet, I had located a new centre in myself, I was stable and growing, and I had improved my knowledge of European society and world history.

PART TWO

THE ILLUMINATIVE WAY

5.

LIBYA: DARK NIGHT AND WAY OF LOSS
1967 – 1970

Back in decaying England (the kingdom or purlieu of the social ego) I lost contact with my inner development and poetry. The next four years I lived in the outer world and progressively encountered difficulties in my everyday life. Looking back I can see that I entered a Dark Night of Sense, in which I was detached from sensual attachments and the life of my ego in what I came to see was a Way of Loss – a loss of the life of the ego in favour of the new centre I was now learning to live through. I underwent a subterranean purification of my inner being while outwardly all that I had been attached to went wrong.

We lived in the maisonette I had bought, 9 Crescent View, Loughton. Crescent View is a terrace of brick flats with a sloping lawn, and our flat was two-bedroomed on the ground floor with another lawn by the back door. Two very old ladies lived in two of the other three flats, and here I settled to rewrite *The Eternicide*. Nadia started at my old school, Oaklands, in nearby Albion Hill, just across the High Road. The following Saturday there were fireworks in the school field before several hundred people and the parents served food in the hard tennis court, and I met Miss Lord, my Headmistress, dragging a box of crisps behind her. In the afternoons I always went for a walk, sometimes to look at the cows in the field at the end of Albion Hill, which meant walking past Oaklands and Mabel Reid's cottage – I took Nadia in for tea one afternoon and sympathised with Mabel Reid's near-blindness – and sometimes in the Forest, where I scuffled through copper beech leaves. We frequently visited my mother at Journey's End, and sometimes went to Dulwich to see Caroline's parents, and twice a week I went to London to give English lessons to Japanese, once to traders in offices on the corner of Park Lane and Oxford Street, and once at the Bank of Japan near St. Paul's. We were living off what I had saved in Japan, and it now seems a very basic existence: we had no car, which meant walking everywhere, and we had no central heating which meant keeping warm with paraffin heaters.

In the evenings I often met my younger brother Jonathan, who was training to be an accountant. He had been on audits when he had done nothing but tick, and it fell to me to encourage him to persevere with his ticking. We discussed Harold Wilson's devaluation. I met John Ezard a couple of times in the Standard. He was about to start with the *Guardian* in London, and told me: "I've got to the top of a profession I entered by accident. I went to the *Gazette* office to apply for a post as library assistant, and was offered a job as local reporter, and have gone on from there." We discussed the younger generation, and he professed to be uninterested in the meaning of life: "My attitude is Wittgensteinan and Cambridge." At the end

143

of November I met Tuohy in Soho, and drank with him at the Yorkminster and lunched with him in an Italian restaurant round the corner.

In December it snowed heavily. I went for a walk in the Forest and the tree trunks had snow on them, and the hoof marks were frozen and the leaves were crunchy, and there was a golden sun. The ponds had ice and snow on them, the air was cold, and I had ruddy cheeks and took great strides and revelled in the sounds my feet made, the smack, crunch and crack of my progress, and I rejoiced as the frosty tiles of cottages showed through trees. The snow lay on the ground over Christmas until mid-January, when there was a thaw and Nadia's snowman dwindled. I took Nadia up to see the cows and we told the cows the thaw would continue. The next weekend we went for a walk with Mabel Reid, and Miss Lord, Nadia's Headmistress, drove by and stopped for a chat.

At Oaklands we had met Paddy Manning, whose daughter was in Nadia's class, and she had invited us to a cocktail party in her house off Baldwin's Hill. We attended a wine and cheese at Oaklands, when both Miss Lord and Miss Reid received presentations from the Parents Association, to mark the school's 30th anniversary, and at an Open Evening I talked near the piano and then looked round the school with the Mannings. John Manning criticised a wall display which said "I love little pussy, his coat is so warm". "It's not 'pussy', it's 'cat'," he said. "It needs someone to come in and modernise Oaklands." Neither of us was aware then that one day I would be doing the modernising.

Nadia was very settled at school, full of who had fallen over and the doings of the other children, and I was aware that we would soon have to go abroad again as our money was slowly running out. It grieved me to see her so settled and to know she would have to be uprooted. I was struggling with my novel, and all round me there seemed to be confusion. (Confusion is an aspect of the onset on a Dark Night.) Mrs. Smith, one of the old ladies in our block, kept hallucinating. She imagined a "busman" was sitting menacingly in her room. She died in March. My mother had a dinner for Christine Janes, née Truman, the tennis player, which I attended. We spent a couple of days in Tuohy's cottage, Tumbler's Bottom, Kilmersdon, Somerset, a stone slate-coloured building. Tuohy was not there and I absorbed the Somerset village life and visited Bath and Weston-Super-Mare, returning home via Avebury and Silbury Hill, whose mound I recognised as a ziggurat built to the moon-god. Soon afterwards I attended a "Free Greece" demonstration in Trafalgar Square to observe the new political consciousness at first hand.

Spring turned to summer. The pear blossom in the Journey's End garden was like melting snow, everywhere leaves were tender and green. Daisies lay like breadcrumbs on the grass, and in the Forest ponds wriggling tadpoles clustered round weed like thorns. I gave a lecture on Japan in a huge house overlooking Epping Forest. We made a couple of visits to Caroline's brother in Kimbolton, Huntingdonshire, and I absorbed the British village life including beagles, and then we all stayed with Tuohy in Somerset.

At the end of June the British Council wrote and offered me a lectureship in Tripoli, Libya, where I had nearly gone the previous year. I had to go as our money was running out. I would be able to save enough to pay off the mortgage on 9 Crescent View. Caroline did not like Essex places or Essex people – she found them cold and unhistorical, false and lacking in taste – but she was reluctant to go and to uproot Nadia.

I had finished my novel and was now interested in the 1968 student revolution, and in the anarcho-syndicalism and Maoist revolutionary outlook that had swept into Britain from France, and I was already planning my next novel, which became *The Age of Cartoon*, about revolution in Britain and the demand for justice. Following my talk I had been invited to a gathering at Holmhurst in Manor Road, Loughton. Holmhurst became Beechwood in that novel. Biggs-Davison was present, and he invited me to the Commons on July 11th and we had a drink on the terrace and discussed the student revolution and publications such as *Black Dwarf* which I had been reading. He told me, "I was talking to an ex-Head of MI6, he says this student business is almost over." I was fascinated at the mentality that rejects the System, a variation on the outsider theme, and presented the Maoist revolutionary's point of view from my knowledge of China, and my approach to the Viet Cong in Pnom Penh. Ten days later (accompanied by Caroline's older brother) I attended the anti-American, anti-Vietnam demonstration which marched on the American Embassy in Grosvenor Square. I went purely as an observer, to have a look. Huge numbers of students jumped up and down, shouting "Ho, ho, Ho Chi Minh", and a group wearing Chinese clothes shouted out "What shall we have for breakfast? Let's eat the American Ambassador for breakfast." The square was enclosed by cordons of police and there were police horses. Once in the Square the demonstrators burst through the cordons into the gardens and fought with the police. The mounted police exercised crowd control, and the demonstrators rejoined the march and moved out to Park Lane. The violence spilled over into Park Lane, and there was stone-throwing outside the Hilton Hotel and I heard cries of "Fascists" and "To the palace", and glimpsed a time when the House of Windsor would be overthrown. Afterwards Caroline's brother and I found a Joe Lyons near Marble Arch and discussed the afternoon's entertainment over apple strudels.

I had devoted little thought to poetry, although I had written a lyric or two and had thought about Old Norse saga. In early August I had the idea for a poetic epic, a vast work for which I made preliminary notes. In early September, while pondering *The Silence*, I came up with the idea for a sonata as a poetic form, and in early October I had the idea for a poem to be based on Rodin's Gate of Hell. I identified my art as a Baroque art.

That summer I somehow lost my way. I became sidetracked into my Japanese pupils, having classes with one of them, a girl called Junko, in the Lord Raglan, near St. Paul's, and taking another to meet Len Murray of Loughton Methodist church, who was no. 2 at the TUC. I was diverted into the student revolution. I digressed into TV drama: I wrote *The Busman*, a TV script about the death of Mrs. Smith, our neighbour. In September I twice drove round the villages of the Essex-Suffolk border and Constable country. I would have loved to have lived in one of them and not gone abroad, but like Masaccio's Adam I once again became an exile from Paradise. I left for Libya having forgotten what I was looking for, having lost the clear view of my direction that I had discovered in Japan, I found my relationships with my mother and solicitor brother had become strained. Caroline now doubted what we were doing. It is typical of a Dark Night that what has before seemed clear is now confused, as all the personality's worldly attachments and desires break down. In the Crescent View bathroom were two mirrors, and as I stood between them, naked after bathing, I saw in one mirror: image behind image of myself receding ever further. I was lost in multiplicity.

My preoccupation with the outer world increased in Libya, where, as in Iraq, I was bombarded by new impressions. I had bought a car – a green Volkswagen – and we drove it to Libya. We crossed France, stopping at Versailles and Fontainbleu and spent a night in Avignon, and visited the Palace of the Popes the next morning. Buchanan had been a guide there in the 1920s, and he had told me about the pornographic bedroom the Pope used, which was now under lock and key. I tried to see this, but was flatly told it did not exist. We went on to Marseilles and took a boat for Tunis, and lying awake on a bunk in the creaking, throbbing cabin I briefly glimpsed my true path: "I am the author of *The Silence,* and don't even think of that, for most of the time....I am the author of *The Silence*, my life is a quest for the meaning of life." We slept in Tunis, a white town with blue shutters and Arabs with red skull caps. Early next morning we drove to the ruins of Carthage, and I stood for a long time by green water under an orange sun and thought of Hannibal, Scipio and St. Augustine.

We drove through Tunisia, past a Roman amphitheatre and through a duststorm to Tripoli, a yellow Italian town spread across sand interspersed with palm trees, ugly modern buildings and petrol stations, alongside a silver sea. We spent a night in the depressing National Hotel, all marble floors and surly servants and greasy food, and next morning I visited the university and met my New Zealand Head of Department, a severe-looking elderly man with spectacles, and the grim Dean, who spoke no English, and various university officials at the Faculty of Teacher Training.

Then I went with one of the suited Arabs who had hung around the National bar to meet our future landlord, a young, handsome ex-Army man of an old Turkish Ottoman family, the Ben Nagys, who took us to a flat in Colina Verdi. It was down a sandy lane opposite the Ben Ashur mosque, and faced a greengrocers. The flat was on the ground floor, had a bulging Turkish balcony with a gold-coloured rail, and had a small garden with an orange tree and a grapevine, under which I parked the Volkswagen. Inside there were two bedrooms, and all the floors were marble. We took it and here we unpacked the Bulgarian furniture the university provided, and assembled it ourselves.

As we had not got straight our landlord, whom we called Ben, gave us a candlelit dinner in his vast villa in Giorgimpopoli, which was served by his servant Ahmad. Ben spoke immaculate English and there we met his two brothers and learned that he had been no. 3 in the Army. He had resigned because his best friend had been assassinated in Benghazi on the orders of the Army Chief. Ben was rumoured to be next on the list as he had been in

Egypt during Nasser's revolution and in Iraq during Kaseem's revolution, and was regarded as a dangerous potential revolutionary. Now he had his own property company.

Libya in November 1968 was still ruled by King Idris and his pro-Western Ministers who sold plots of the country to oil-prospecting companies. It consisted of a few towns, mostly near the coast, and vast stretches of desert. There was a large Western community who manned the schools and university, hospitals and many companies. We soon found our way around Tripoli, down Shara Adrian Pelt to Castle Square and the Old City with its narrow arched streets and peeping women in white barracans, and back up Istiqlal Street to the King's Palace.

Almost immediately Ben drove us to Sabratha, a Roman town by the sea not unlike Carthage, and I gazed at the Temple of Isis and Apuleius's basilica. On the way home we talked revolution, and Ben said a coup would have to be planned very carefully, when both the King and the Crown Prince were in one of the two main cities. Soon afterwards Ben invited us again to his villa for mafroum (mincemeat in potato), and we met Shukri Ganm, a young partly Turkish oil executive who spoke faultless English and greeted me with "Four people at your College are now in the Foreign Office". The next night Ben gave a party and invited us. Ten single girls – teachers, nurses and UN secretaries – drank whisky with Army and Police Colonels and a moustached, mournful newspaper magnate, Chatter. Some of the girls came and told me how Libyans propositioned them in the street with obscene details of their sexual vigour and prowess, and how they said "La, la" ("No, no"), and how they would never again go to a party at which the Minister for Petroleum was present. Ben told me that Chatter was in partnership with the Minister for Information, and Chatter suggested I wrote some articles for his English language paper, *The Daily News* – under a pseudonym because of my university contract.

We lunched with the British Council Representative, a squat man called Keight who looked like Lawrence Durrell, and the next day Ben took us in his large car past the white beaches of Homs to Leptis Magna, Libya's other Roman town with acres of streets and white ruins by a deep blue sea. Here, standing on mosaics among fallen torsos and sun-god heads, I felt at one with Roman – and Mediterranean – man. I responded to the North African universe Camus had described further along the coast in Algeria, and on the way back, seeing a scarlet-robed Bedouin standing on red-brown earth, a tiny figure against a vast sky, I had a sense that God was everywhere. I warmed to the wide open spaces and was concerned at the poverty of the Bedouins and Arabs we passed, and again on the way home I discussed revolution with Ben. He agreed he had a responsibility to act for all the people "when the time is right, and if I choose the wrong time I may ruin it for others". He told me, "I would rather be a peasant. An intellectual worries about society, about justice – you suffer, you suffer."

By now my everyday life had acquired a pattern. I woke to cocks crowing and a prayer from the mosque at the end of our lane. In the mornings I left our flat in Colina Verdi and drove along sandy lanes and pitted roads to the university. There were a dozen Western lecturers (mostly British) in our small staff room, and I taught classes in English Language or

Literature to groups of about 20 Arabs, some very rich and some very poor. I returned home for lunch. Nadia had been at school, and in the afternoon I walked with her and Caroline along the sandy, cactus-lined lanes. Here I taught Nadia to ride her bicycle, running along behind her and letting go. There was always a group of Arabs sitting outside one-eyed Mohammed's greengrocers, and our gaffir (gardener cum odd job man), Milud, snoozed out his siesta in the shade of our wall. Sometimes we went for a picnic among pines near the blue sea down the Homs Road, sometimes with another British Council or teacher's family. We were sometimes visited by Ben and Shukri, and in the evenings I wrote my novel or went out to an Arab dinner at Ben's, where he had always invited plenty of single girls. As the weeks went by Caroline became more and more pro-Libyan and distant from me. Sometimes I lay awake and thought, and the night air was filled with hooting owls.

Ramadan came, and went. The end of Ramadan was signalled by a blast from the castle cannon. There was chanting and excited howling on the mosque's loudspeaker, and there were yellow lamps among the palms, under brilliant white stars. The Feast had come. We went to the 24th December Independence Day parade and watched columns of soldiers and armoured cars approach the Crown Prince in Castle Square while the Libyan airforce and American thunderjets from the Wheelus air base roared overhead in what looked like a dress rehearsal for the coming coup. On Christmas Day we went to my Head of Department's house where all the Western lecturers gathered for games, and brandy was lit in a blue flame so we could all take hot snap dragons (raisins) from it.

Caroline had grown away from me. During Ramadan she had taken to disappearing on long shopping trips on her own in the afternoons, and she withdrew from me in the evenings into tense silences. She would not discuss her change of outlook, and was irritable and critical. She did not want to be touched. Nadia, who was just 6, was very affectionate ("I want to marry you, and if I can't marry you I want to stay with you"), but Caroline urged me to go to the Elizabethan Club on my own, and she was happier sitting with her thoughts. In January (a time of powercuts and candlelight) I had a long discussion with Caroline about our marriage and she concluded she wanted to stay married "but try leaving me alone for a bit". She was much calmer and much gentler now, but I was very much on my own. In vain I tried to arrest this trend, which compounded my inner confusion and sense that I had lost my way.

The period from February to August 1970 was dominated by Ben's Ministers' coup. The conversations about revolutions I had had with Ben on the way back from Sabratha and Leptis had converted him – not that he needed much converting – and his plans for revolution now mirrored the revolutionary outlook of the hero in my novel, *The Age of Cartoon*, and my writing and my life were now proceeding in outer tandem.

I knew there was a coup afoot in early February. Ben visited us and said several of his ring had met on his farm and that he was going to Cairo with someone "to secure our exits". I asked who the President would be, and Ben enigmatically said: "He will be the one who smiles the most." He added: "You'll be the first to know when it happens, we'll make you British Ambassador." Nothing much happened until late March, when, after a blue storm over the Sahara, wind whirling and rain lashing, we were invited to Ben's for dinner with the usual single girls, and Ben and Shukri quarrelled over who was to blame for the corruption in Libya. Ben said it was the King, "that stupid old man", while Shukri said it was the Prime Minister (who was Ben's tenant). They shouted at each other across the table, striking increasingly dismissive and warlike postures, and, eyes smouldering, Shukri strode out into the night. With hindsight I realised that this passionate quarrel was really about whether there should be a coup against the King (Ben's view) or whether the King should merely dismiss the Prime Minister (Shukri's view).

At the beginning of April my financial state was parlous: the Italian store, Guido's, gave us credit, and each month we were unable to pay off what we owed. I knew Shukri was close to Chatter, the newspaper magnate, and I visited him and asked him to fix me up with a job with Chatter. He did, on condition that my articles appeared under a pseudonym. I visited the office of *The Daily News* near Castle Square, and for the next four months I wrote two pages in Tripoli's only English Language paper. It came out weekly, on a Sunday, and I wrote the two centre pages about Libya. I had just written a poem called *Barbary Shores*, and so I chose as my pseudonym "the Barbary Gipsy". A headline proclaimed "Round and About with the Barbary Gipsy". Each Friday, the Moslem day of rest, I set out with a camera and took some photos of a Tripoli ruin or a Libyan tourist attraction such as Sabratha, Leptis, Gourna or Souk El Juma'h (a camel market), and I wrote the text each Saturday and delivered my copy to Chatter's no 2, Ansari, in the office near Castle Square. Ansari edited my copy; almost immediately he was accused in an unsigned letter to the Prime Minister of being an Egyptian spy but no action was taken as the letter was unsigned. On Sunday the paper would come out, King Idris was my earliest reader, and expatriates would ask me "Have you read this week's Barbary Gipsy?" "No," I'd say, and they would tell me what I had written while I concealed my smirk and feigned novel interest.

In early April Ben began hosting parties for a ring of Libyan Ministers who wanted a pro-Western coup. I did not know it, but the King had apparently told his Ministers he was getting too old to govern and that he proposed to abdicate, and a coup was forming around the Minister for Petroleum, who it was understood would not be the President. Ben gave several parties for the Minister for Petroleum, a large pale-eyed, softly-spoken, shambling man, and for other Ministers, including the Minister of State for Prime Minister's Affairs (a rotund smiling man with greased black hair) and the Minister for Youth, a thin man. The parties began about 10.30 p.m., the Ministers wore suits and drank whisky, and there were half a dozen Yugoslav nurses or secretaries. There was a lot of banter and laughter and dancing to Western pop music, and the parties ended about 2.30 a.m., usually when the Minister for Petroleum abandoned his previous restraint and pushed a Yugoslav girl into the fountain. On one occasion he was pushed into the fountain himself, to general merriment. On another occasion he fell off a saddle chair on to the floor and was too heavy to move. The Minister of State for Prime Minister's Affairs stood by, muttering: "He is quite all right, very bad chair, Khalifa get up."

When I first talked revolution with Ben, it was out of concern for the poor, not to line the pockets of these exploiters. From the outset I saw these parties for what they were, and wrote in my *Diaries* of "the Profumo-type follies of a newly independent, dying pre-populist state" and of "the Farouk extravaganza". I wrote: "I join the damp orgies of the ruling class, but I sympathise with the poor." I had contempt for the luxurious follies and corruption of what I knew was a pre-revolutionary, dying order, but the Ministers openly talked about how, when the time came, they would not recognise Britain unless I was appointed British Ambassador and I received their banter with amused detachment and was a fascinated observer of the decayed rites of their too publicly run coup.

In April Angus Wilson, the novelist, visited Tripoli, and for the newspaper I met him at the Libya Palace Hotel. He was a squat, ruddy-faced man with white hair who gushed impressions. We sat and had a drink in the bar with his secretary Tony, with whom he constantly bickered: "Get us a second drink. Have they come? You said the Spanish weren't here, but they were." He asked me many questions, to some of which I replied cautiously, knowing his sexual leanings, and he remarked: "This is a very philistine place. It's newly experienced wealth – from oil – like the Tudors or else it's puritanism, the tension here." That was the tension between the Ministers' follies and the coming revolution.

Next day Angus Wilson gave a lecture at the University, speaking without notes about the writer and society, leaping from idea to idea with great fluency, and later we went to the waterfront so I could take his picture for the newspaper. He posed, leaning on the balustrade, crossing his legs, and as we walked back we discussed how one image can give rise to a novel, and I asked him about Tuohy's view that a writer should have a distinctive voice. He stopped and said very simply: "You'd be well advised not to follow Tuohy's advice. He's very insecure, I know as he wrote me several letters. A writer should *not* have an identifiable voice. He should not approach experience with a preconceived ready-made notion of it, and to do so is to reveal one's insecurity, to hide under the identity of an individual voice. I can't read Greene because I know what it's going to be like, because of his individual, recognisable voice." Like Sartre and Hemingway, Angus Wilson was public property and belonged to everybody, but for twenty minutes he had focused completely on me, and when I left him I was glad I had ignored Tuohy's Wittgensteinian advice regarding *The Silence*, and resolved to continue to be open to experience, to continue my quest to understand the universe without judging it in terms of preconceived pessimistic, social-rationalist ideas. I wrote a letter to Tuohy, reflecting my conversation with Angus Wilson and challenging the Tuohyian view of voice.

It was getting hot and we spent afternoons sunbathing on our roof, and once in a friend's garden, sitting under a mulberry tree near pomegranates in red-orange bloom. There were pink oleanders outside our bedroom window and the bougainvillaea was out in the Castle. For the newspaper I covered an American singer at the Uaddan night-club, which included interviewing her before and after her show, and I went to the Casino for a Barbary Gipsy article. We went swimming at a white beach at km 13 down the Homs Road.

There were more parties for Ministers in the course of May, and potential chiefs of police, immigration and customs were present, along with other second-ranking officials. At the last of them, shortly after Ben had visited Tunis, there was a disturbance in Ben's front garden where Ben's servant had discovered the current young police chief, who had climbed the gate to spy on the gathering through a window. Several of the party rushed out into the dark garden and there was a lot of shouting before the intruder was expelled. Afterwards Ben said to me at the bar where the Ministers sat, "He wanted to find out who is here, he tried to breach our security. We will have to be more careful from now on."

The next party was at the Minister of Health's farm at the beginning of June. We met the Minister for Petroleum at the house of the Minister of State for Prime Minister's Affairs, and Ben's two brothers arrived with four Yugoslav girls. Ben said to me in front of the two Ministers, "I want you to come to Djerba with me, when do you finish at the University? We will be there for a few days. I shall go off and leave you." It was clear that he would be meeting someone in Djerba, and that he wanted to use us as cover. We all drove out to the Minister for Health's farm. The Minister for Health wore a red fez, and we sat on his terrace near a fountain in the hot dark, drinking whisky with trees below us and all round, and crickets fluting under a huge moon. There were a peacock and a gazelle in a cage nearby, and there was sporadic dancing to Western music and we ate juicy chops with our fingers, and when the Minister for Petroleum pushed one of the Yugoslav girls (called Maeda 1) in the fountain and was himself splashed it was time to go home. As I went to the bathroom I passed the Minister of Health's bedroom. The door was open, and I saw a holster and revolver slung round his bed top, and saw deep into the insecurity of being a Minister in an Arab country. A week later the Minister of Health was sacked.

Soon after, there was another party at the King's farm. This must have been the twentieth party involving Ministers I had been to. The food was served by the King's personal servant. I can recall a large room with basket seats hanging from the wooden ceiling, and an upstairs. There were some 20 or 30 guests, and the fact that the King's place was being used suggested to all that the King was looking with favour on Ben's enterprise. For the first time there was mention of Dr Omar Muntasser, the Libyan Ambassador to London and son of the first Libyan Prime Minister, and I was asked to interview him for the newspaper when I returned to London for a holiday in the summer. Ben said he was going to London "to see my doctor", with a laugh, and it seemed that Muntasser was going to be the new President, probably because Muntasser's family could hold the provinces together and prevent a break-away like Biafra. Shortly afterwards I saw the King driving in the back of a black car away from his palace, an old impassive, white-haired man in a white barracan gliding by me. It was hard to imagine that he had been an anti-Italian freedom-fighter.

A MYSTIC WAY

In early July after the University exams and end of term we left Nadia with a friend and Ben drove Caroline and me to Djerba, an island off Tunisia. This was the island of Homer's Lotos-Eaters, and it now comprised a local souk and low hotels along the white beaches where modern fun-lovers ate their escapist lotus. We stayed at the Tanit Hotel by a beach, and at the night-club by the sands that first evening Ben exercised his "horria" ("freedom"). He was like a whirlwind, picking up several single girls until he opted for a young French girl with green eyes and tumbling hair called Jacqueline, whom he asked me to persuade on his behalf as his "lawyer". Jokingly I made out a case for Ben, which she rebutted in skilful and hilarious English and Ben got nowhere. To me Jacqueline said, "I mean no disrespect to your friend but I cannot. With you, yes, but not your friend." Next morning he called out when she appeared, "Did you dream of me?" She said "A cauchemar" ("a nightmare"). Ben went out and sunbathed by the pool as the heat got up. The other side of the pool two Italian girls appeared in cloche hats and bikinis, and Ben yelled "Hey, thé" and they veered in obedient unison and joined us for tea while Ben giggled and again handed the task of persuading them to me.

I was watching Ben carefully and waiting for him to leave us for his contact. Ben now began talking about business ventures involving hotels and that afternoon he left us with Jacqueline sunbathing on the white hot beach and cooling ourselves in the waves ("dans les vagues") and went missing. There was no warning, I was suddenly aware that he was not around. Later when he returned he said he had driven to the Hotel Ulysses to consider buying part of a hotel as a business venture. Later he told me he had met Saad eddin Bushwerib, an Army commander who lived in the block of flats behind ours in Tripoli.

We were away four days and returned to Tripoli on the fifth day. A fortnight later (having paid off Guido's bill through my journalism), and having spent a night at the Libya Palace Hotel where I saw the American landing on the moon (sitting in the foyer with thirty cheering Arabs), we flew back to England for five weeks' leave, and stayed at the Dulwich house where Caroline's parents now lived, 177 South Croxted Road. We visited Loughton, which I found more urbanised and proletarianised, and then went to Oxford and Stratford-upon-Avon, where we stayed at the Falcon, and met Buchanan, who was at Alveston Manor, and then went on to stay with Tuohy at Kilmersdon in Somerset. We had lunch with him and then sat in the cloverfield in front of Tumbler's Bottom, and visited the church at Mells where Sassoon is buried, and we had a long conversation about voice and agreed that writers fall into two camps: those who explore and include, who have no voice; and those who interpret in terms of their own vision and exclude – shut out – who have a voice. I wrote in my *Diaries*: "Not having a voice is a sign of exploration and truthful reporting about the universe."

In West Dulwich I finished my novel on revolution, *The Age of Cartoon*, and wrote newspaper articles about the new London. I visited the new in-places like Le Kilt, the Round House, the Arts Lab, the Seed restaurant and Carnaby Street, and caught swinging London in terms of merrie dandies whose clothes were Mannerist: slightly elongated. I went to a Pentameters

152

poetry reading at the Freemasons Arms, Belsize Park and heard a poetaster, John Horder, then the *Times* poetry correspondent, read some of his 60 lavatorial variations, and lamented the collapse of standards and the evident link between the majority of the poets and homosexuality. I went to the Colony Room, an out of hours drinking club frequented by Dylan Thomas of which I was a member, and renewed my acquaintance with Muriel Belcher, the legendary hostess of the Colony, and drank champagne with the artist Francis Bacon, who I remember freely announced to all who were listening: "I like it up the arse." The next time I went to the Colony I was with Caroline. Muriel said, "Caroline is very nice and you are very lucky to have such an attractive wife."

I had rung Dr Muntasser and I went to Phillimore Gardens and interviewed him for the newspaper. I was doing a special feature on Libyan-British relations in which I put similar questions to both Goronwy Roberts, Minister of State at the Foreign Office, and to Dr Muntasser and compared their answers. My piece appeared on August 24th with a photo of Dr Muntasser, and it was translated into Arabic and carried in all the Libyan Arabic papers. I found Dr Muntasser tall, elegant, very correctly spoken and with considerable charisma. He invited Caroline and me back for a drink with his wife on August 22nd, and as I left the Libyan Embassy that evening he shook my hand and said, "I will be seeing you very soon in Tripoli."

I sensed that the coup was imminent. I was depressed to leave England, especially Epping Forest – we had a final walk and caught minnows and waterbeetle in the two ponds on Strawberry Hill, and then drove to Baldwin's Hill and visited the Blackweir pond with the grating and found the Lost Pond which Epstein used to visit every day – but was conscious I could pay off my mortgage from my last year in Libya, and was excited about the coming revolution. We flew to Libya and were met by the chauffeur of the Minister of State for Prime Minister's Affairs, Beshir al-Muntasser, who gave us dinner that same evening. I told him about my meeting with Dr Muntasser. Beshir invited us again to dinner on August 30th, and Saad eddin Bushwerib's name was raised. "September 5th it will happen," Beshir said.

On September 1st 1969 I was awoken at 5 by shots and dogs barked. There were more shots at 6.30. It was my first day back at the University, and I set off for work in my green Volkswagen. I found I was driving through deserted streets. Every shop was closed and there were no traffic policemen. Thinking there was a strike against Israel, I carried on, but when I reached the University the gates were closed. Puzzled, I sat in my car and looked at my pocket diary to check that I had come back on the right day. Then I heard shooting further up the road and realised something exceptional had happened. I turned the car and headed for home. Now on every street corner there were single soldiers in plimsolls. (They had worn plimsolls to creep into Tripoli at dawn.) Each soldier raised his rifle and fired into the air, then slowly and casually reloaded. They were firing live rounds, I could hear them echoing. I sat well down in the front seat and drove past the first soldier holding my breath, then the next soldier. Mine was the only car on the streets. I jumped all the traffic-lights. At one point I saw I was driving towards an armoured car, and, as if it were Field Day at Chigwell School, I immediately turned off the road and rejoined it further down, having bypassed the armoured car. I passed several more armed soldiers before I returned to our flat in Colina Verdi.

A neighbour came to the door and said, "There's been a coup." Her husband was turned back at bayonet point. "It's Army," she said, "the police are resisting." For the next couple of hours there were many single shots like firecrackers and distant gunfire, shots in twos or threes. There seemed to be a battle for the telecommunications centre down the road, and shooting was reported around the King's palace. Caroline, Nadia and I sat in our hall, where there were no windows and we were safe from stray bullets, and listened to the radio. The local radio station was playing Western music and Ben's favourite piece came on. Periodically a voice said in English, "Citizens, you have waited a long time for this Liberation." Then came the dramatic statement from the BBC Overseas news: "There has been a coup d'état in Libya and sources say that the new leader is Saad eddin Bushwerib, an Army officer." Mohammed, the one-eyed skull-capped greengrocer across our sandy lane had the same story: "This very bad. King very good man. This Saad eddin Bushwerib and Ben Nagy. Ben Nagy will be number 2."

For a while I was sure that Ben's coup had worked. I could not understand why they had brought the date forward from September 5th to September 1st, but ten months' plotting seemed to have succeeded. With amused detachment I could look forward to occupying the British Embassy as Ambassador.

What had in fact happened was that the left wing nationalist Gaddafi and his fellow junior officers had found out about Ben's Ministers' pro-Western coup, perhaps from the policeman, Ali, who had tried to gatecrash Ben's party, or perhaps through Egyptian or Soviet sources. Any one of the Yugoslav girls could have informed the KGB who could have informed Gaddafi. The translation into Arabic of my interview with Goronwy Roberts and Dr Muntasser had precipitated Gaddafi's action. With hindsight it is clear that the publication of my interview with Dr Muntasser triggered the coup, for it suggested that Muntasser was a successor to the King thus forcing Gaddafi (and those behind him) to act. Gaddafi had struck four days early while the King was on holiday in Turkey, but had cunningly let the media believe it was Saad eddin's and Ben's coup to install Muntasser, in order to secure American and British acceptance of the coup. Gaddafi had in fact used the Arabic version of my newspaper article about Muntasser. Saad eddin was in Rome when the BBC announcement was made. A representative of the Libyan Embassy in Italy found him drinking coffee in a café and told him he was the new leader, and for a few hours he believed he was, concluding that Ben had struck early. The King's wealthy adviser, Omar Shalhi, visited the British Foreign Secretary to request British intervention, and, again believing Saad eddin was in charge and the coup was pro-Western, Britain did not respond to Shalhi's request.

With hindsight it seems that Gaddafi was encouraged to seize power by the New World Order group who work for a world government. In 1972 he would expropriate Bunker Hunt's oil and equipment holdings, and the silence of the Western governments and the oil companies would give OPEC the confidence to raise oil prices in 1973, to the main benefit of Western oil companies such as Esso and Shell in which the Rockefeller-Rothschild alliance has a great stake. He would train terrorists to destabilise nation-state-based Western governments.

For us in Tripoli the next two days were filled with shooting. There was a curfew. It was announced on the radio that anyone who broke it would be shot. A Czech neighbour broke curfew to bring us bread. There was a lot of tension, a lot of waiting for news. It was announced on the radio that anyone found in possession of arms would be shot. Nadia overheard me telling Caroline this and on her own initiative she found her toy revolver and hid it in one of her Wellington boots. On the third day curfew was lifted between 11 and 2 to allow us to buy food. I drove to Guido's store past groups of armed soldiers. Guido's was packed and six armed men shouted "No beer, no whisky, no wine, no alcohol", and Guido himself was saying to his customers, "You heard the Army, no alcohol." I said to Caroline, "That's unlike Ben and the Ministers." We drove home and curfew began again and on the next news we learned that all the Ministers were under arrest. Beshir, the Minister of State for Prime Minister's Affairs, was quoted as saying, "We did our best but the problems were too great." A friend of Ben's came and said that Ben and his brothers had disappeared; they were being hunted by the Army. The country was sealed off. All Westerners were effectively hostages.

It was now clear that the coup was not Ben's, but we did not know whose it was; only that there was an anonymous Revolutionary Command Council (RCC). I drove into an anti-Shalhi demonstration in Castle Square and saw a dummy representing Shalhi hanging from a gallows on a lorry. Two days later I went into my newspaper office and found Chatter there. He said: "I'm expecting the Army to come and close us down. Get out on the streets and write your impressions of the Revolution. Praise the Revolution as much as you can." I went out into the streets and walked among chanting, shouting demonstrators in Castle Square, and described the banners and the tanks decorated with palms, the lorries driving around with 30 to 40 young men and children in the back waving palm-fronds and beating tom-tom like on the metal sides, as at a wedding. I thought of Tolstoy's question in *War and Peace*, "What is the force that moves nations, Napoleon or the common soldier?"

In the course of the next week I wrote my last article for *The Daily News*: a reflective piece on the stages of revolutions, and on what was wrong with the American, French, Russian and Chinese old regimes that created a pre-revolutionary situation. (This thinking resurfaced in *The Fire and the Stones*.) In due course at a reception the new British Ambassador came to the door to greet me – did he know I was nearly in his shoes? – and he let me know that he had read the article. He discussed it with me at some length.

The British did not intervene, to our relief. Each day we awaited a British invasion and a bloodbath with some dread. Then my mother wrote and said Biggs-Davison had mentioned me in Parliament. She enclosed a letter from him asking for my reaction to the Revolution: did I think the British should have restored King Idris? I wrote back distinguishing the historical and political position from the terror of the British who would be caught in the middle of a counter-revolution. There was a terror abroad in the streets, and our foreboding put us all in an abnormal state of mind. We were all subjected to an unspoken mental stress. We were not confined as hostages are confined but Tripoli had become a kind of open prison and each time we crossed it we felt the stress of hostages in relation to their guards. I cannot emphasise enough that this stress affected us all during the next few months.

From about September 15th everything grew worse. The Libyan press was closed down. All staff of *The Daily News* were sacked. I was told the news when I went into the office. A flustered Chatter sat limply at his desk. He said goodbye and left, and Ansari told me, "There may be hangings, there can be no pity under socialism." He also said that Chatter's machinery was owned by the Minister of Information, who had been paying our salaries as *The Daily News* never made a penny, and there was corruption to be rooted out. Soon after Gaddafi was on television saying, "I would like to say that some journalists will be imprisoned, some will be punished and some will be executed."

A couple of afternoons later there was a knock on my front door and a plainclothes Libyan and an armed soldier motioned me to accompany them. Reassuring Caroline as best I could, I went with them. They drove me to a radio station that was surrounded by armoured cars. I was led into a chaotic corridor where uniformed men rushed about and there was a lot of shouting. What if they knew of my role in Ben's coup? I was taken into a room where an immaculately groomed man sat in uniform with all my articles in a pile in front of him, including the article with Dr Muntasser's picture. Muntasser had apparently been kidnapped in London and escorted back to Tripoli under guard, and it was probable that the RCC had questioned him about my association with him. The man said in English: "I am the military censor and we know about your activities and how you visited Muntasser. You wrote these articles in breach of your University contract. You committed a crime against the people of Libya. Do you admit that you wrote these?" Standing by my guard, I said, "I do." Outside I could hear a lot of noise and I half expected to be led out and put in front of a wall. I was frightened but aware of my freedom. "You supported the King," the censor continued. "I didn't," I said. "The King was our earliest reader, and in my article *The Old British Consulate and the Baker*, for example, I criticised the working conditions of bakers under the King's regime. I describe them as waist deep in a pit sunk in a shop. I opposed the King." With my help the censor found the article and read the paragraph I indicated. He deliberated. Then he looked at me. "You are right," he said, "this criticised the King. We are not happy about your activities and your visit to Muntasser. You must not write any more articles or do any work other than your University work or you will be shot, and you will be watched by our Security from now on." He nodded to my guard. I left the room tense, wondering if I was being taken out to be shot. I was still unsure of how much they knew about my work for

Ben's coup. At the gates of the fortified radio station I began to feel relieved and exhilarated. There was no firing squad and I was driven back to my flat. A few days afterwards I heard that the military censor was dismissed for being found in bed with a Western woman.

Caroline greeted me with undisguised relief. She had been greatly worried for herself and Nadia, and the episode greatly affected her sense of security in Libya. From then on two men in a fawn Volkswagen sat outside our flat watching my movements. When I left they followed my car. They travelled to the University with me, and when I went to the bank (when the banks re-opened) they came in with me. They were pleasant enough. I smiled and said "Hello" to them and they smiled and said "Hello" back, and they loitered discreetly about a yard away from my elbow. For a while I was virtually under house arrest. The fawn Volkswagen preyed on Caroline's mind.

I had been plunged into a Dark Night. Curfew kept us off the streets at night. There was no television, and little radio. We were thrown back on ourselves. The Libyan Revolution was puritanical, and it was difficult to find alcohol. For a while Guido supplied black Bavarian beer for L£2.50; it came in boxes packed round with vegetables, and I carried it out under the soldiers' noses to my car. But sometimes there was no beer, and I was forced to detach myself from any craving for alcohol I had. Caroline remained aloof. Each day I went to the University. The Vice-Dean was arrested. On one occasion I had a class of 120 students dressed in military uniform all with loaded rifles propped against their desks, and I taught them a Hemingway story about gentleness. Each day there were decrees from the Revolutionary Command Council on the theme of the slogan "Freedom, Unity, Socialism" (i.e. freedom from the West, unity with Arabs, left wing policies), and drawings of hangings appeared on many walls throughout Tripoli. I had to take my driving licence and identity card to Castle Square to get them stamped "Republic" and I was shouted at by a soldier. One day all Western lettering was banned. All street signs were scrubbed out and I had to paint out the Western numbers on my car's number plates. The message was clear: Libya was now outside Western civilisation, across the frontier, among the "barbarians".

For three weeks I lived like one of the Egyptian Desert Fathers. True, I had a flat rather than a hut on my strip of the Sahara desert, but with basic food and no alcohol and a tense and fearful wife who wanted to be left alone, a fawn Volkswagen outside our gate and no recognisably English lettering anywhere, I was in a state of deprivation of all sensual comforts. Some afternoons I sunbathed on our flat roof for an hour, sometimes with the local radio. The hit song of the moment was, "What are the dreams of the everyday housewife?" The silence of those long desert evenings under curfew was broken only by the occasional drone of an Army lorry and a howling pye-dog.

On September 23rd I wrote: "I want more isolation, I don't want to get near other people. I am against contemporary materialism....I am against hedonism....I must be in revolt against materialist hedonism because it is too unspiritual."

But suddenly everything changed. I had taken to chatting with the gloomy Czech who lived down our sandy lane, and all of a sudden other people (principally Americans) insisted on getting near me, American alcohol became plentiful, and the fawn Volkswagen suddenly disappeared. An American oil couple we had met at an oil party called four months later, out of the blue, in early July, and now invited us to an early supper which ended in time for us to get home before the beginning of curfew. The wife was a dark-haired Louisiana belle and former beauty queen called Cat, and she made brandy Alexanders which looked like chocolate ice creams and which we took onto the roof of their huge Giorgimpopoli villa, and, overlooking the insane asylum in the evening sun, their triplets playing happily, her husband (who was from Dallas) offered to teach me a computer language and make me an analyst-programmer on $1,000 a month. There was some summer lightning on the horizon and Chopin billowed out of the window, and Cat looked so vivacious. I accepted the computer books and struggled to learn PL/1, which made as little as sense as the Law: did people really feel these mathematical symbols were important, did they really pay $1,000 a month to operate this meaninglessness? I believe it was soon after this that we all went down on the beach near the Crown Prince's palace to see the Phoenician ruins and she lay spreadeagled on the cliff in a red trouser suit, her black hair tumbling round her shoulders, as if she lay face down on a double bed.

Into this situation came a friend of Caroline's, Daphne, an upper class English divorcée now living on Malta with her parents. She stayed with us. Her American fiancé, who was also in oil, had broken off their engagement in the summer. She had brought furniture out to Tripoli to marry him, and she was suing him for breach of promise so as to recover the cost of transporting the furniture. She came for the court case. I was uneasy about the morality of her claim – breach of promise is not a modern concept – and my Czech friend referred with a giggle to an impending "battle of the imperialists". We took Daphne to meet him and his wife. We all drank lashings of cognac and whisky. We crept home drunk after curfew, pursued by baying wolf-dogs. We took Daphne to her court. The courtroom turned out to be covered in dustsheets, and so we took her to sunbathe by the Uaddan pool, where we spent several lunchtimes, and to Ben Othman's villa, and we took her up to the American oil couple's villa, where a Spanish psychiatrist with a goatbeard held forth. He in turn invited us all to a party at his house the next night, where there was another American oil couple (the wife was half Irish, half German Jewess). There was also an Irish oil man, who struck up a friendship with Daphne. The talk was very free, and entertaining a house guest quickly became synonymous with alcoholic hedonism. I heard that the beautiful Louisiana belle had been raped by her father when she was five and was an emotional cripple as a result, and that the psychiatrist was something of an existentialist who created situations in which he could observe his guests in detachment. "I am a voyeur," he told me. There were many see-through blouses and everyone seemed to be on the verge of an affair with everyone else.

Daphne's court case was heard soon afterwards. Her lawyer, a

DARK NIGHT AND WAY OF LOSS

Palestinian called Akram, had tried to persuade me to be a witness and perjure myself, by saying that I had heard her American fiancé say he would marry Daphne. He was very hurt when I refused to say this. In the event the case was held in Arabic, the doorkeeper shouting names in Arabic. The American stood with a man on crutches, Daphne gave her evidence. She won, damages would be assessed at a car and between £1,000 and £2,000 and we repaired to the Café del Postes near the Bank of North Africa to celebrate Daphne's victory. Then Daphne announced that she had broken off with her fiancé because he bored her, which made me feel very uneasy, and she then went out to dinner with her Irish admirer.

The next day I took Daphne to BEA to book her ticket back to Malta. There was a crowd outside the Ministry of Foreign Affairs and I saw the new British Ambassador arrive to present his credentials. On the way back I saw a large crowd outside the same building and suddenly there was a roar and Gaddafi, the leader of the revolution, appeared and waved, a young man with a straight back and sides haircut in a peaked cap. The crowd waved their hands and chanted "Ga-ddafi" and so great was the enthusiasm that he was unable to get into his landrover.

Soon the new British Ambassador, Donald Maitland (later Heath's Chief Press Secretary) attended a gathering for all the lecturers and teachers. I was the first to speak to him, and he asked me if I'd ask a question after his speech. When his speech had finished he said "Any questions?" and I asked: "What impression have you formed of the new Libyan leader, whom the BBC have wrongly called Col. Gaffadi." Maitland replied that the RCC were a group of nationalists who were now putting Libya first.

The drinking accelerated. It was now a kind of rebellion against the Puritanical regime and its coup. We all visited Cat's, and the next day the Irish-German Jewess gave a party where we drank Pimms and gin. We did not know that the Irishman had been having a long affair with the Jewess. He told her he wanted to marry Daphne, and he stalked out of the party, slamming the door, and Daphne followed, tipping gin into the punch, while the Jewess sat in the bathroom and snivelled. She showed me a book by an author she knew in Lahore and said, "They're doubles, I want him to play this author's role, that's the trouble." Later we all got very drunk and I passed out in the guest room and woke to hear Cat whispering in my ear....Later we walked home after curfew, risking a bullet. Her last evening Daphne spent with her Irish admirer, and stayed out until 6.30 a.m., returning to say a brief goodbye.

Daphne had gone but a chain of events had been set in motion. Does not this narration consist of sequences or chains of events? According to Whitehead an event is a nexus of actual occasions at a given time and place. According to Geoffrey Read, a Leibnizian philosopher I know who has refined Whitehead's ideas of process, time is a succession of events, and past events are not obliterated but added to by present events, with the result that the past always persists in the present, so that the first events in a chain are added to by present events and co-exist with them. Like superstrings in physics, events cluster together, one after another, in chains. The chains of a lifetime are tangled, mixed up together like a bowl of spaghetti: or like the

159

tent-shaped net of a computer spirograph representing an oil field which I saw on Cat's husband's office wall when I collected my computer books.

It is still painful to record the chain of events which led to the collapse of my marriage and which was a central part of my Dark Night. I want to skate over this part of my story but I must face it as the events were important to my development. I should probably have paid more attention when I told Caroline after Daphne's departure "You are very mature" and she said: "Detached, bored, not mature."

We were in an existentialist situation: we had not chosen the Revolution, we had to make choices within its context although we were not responsible for the events it created. Obsessed with a desire to see the man who had brought about the changes in Libya that were affecting my life, I went to a rally in Castle Square. A huge Nazi-style eagle (similar to the eagle in the ruins of Hitler's Chancellery) spread its wings over the platform. (Like the National Socialist Hitler, who was anti-British, anti-American and anti-Jew, the nationalist-socialist Gaddafi wanted to turf out the British and American bases and obliterate Israel, which was why his revolution was code-named "Palestine".) A great drape hung from the Castle; it showed Gaddafi trampling Shalhi underfoot. Hundreds of Arabs under banners chanted slogans led by a black-suited man on the platform. I was virtually the only foreigner present while Arabs swarmed over stationary tanks and hung onto ladders propped against palm trees. The music blared out "Allah akbar", and there was a roar, and down the steps, hatless, came Gaddafi, surrounded by joyous soldiers. There was a confused pause, and suddenly guns fired into the air, ships boomed their guns and jets whistled overhead. Then Gaddafi started speaking, inconclusively, haltingly – and now there was a continuous hubbub and everyone began to walk away. I felt he had no presence, he did not come across then as a charismatic leader.

Soon afterwards Col. Gaddafi came to the University. He held an open-air meeting in the front car park which was filled with seated students. He sat at a table, wearing a white shirt and without a hat, with four RCC men in red berets holding machine-guns, and spoke haltingly in Arabic. The student next to me said in English, "This man is too simple to be our Leader."

The Spanish psychiatrist brought the Irish-German Jewess round to visit me and saw art in unacceptable psychiatric terms ("The artist is a neurotic") while a butterfly fluttered in the room and died on our dried flowers. The next day the two of them held a party and invited Cat and her husband, and us. We drank Canadian Club and the Spaniard again belittled art: "It's not real, why is it so important to you? You are involved in it, to us it is like a beer can. Like cooking." The next day we went to an American party at which the Wheelus Base commander was present, a giant negro who wore a crown on a chain round his neck ("I've had enough of this b—y revolution, I want to be pro-King"), and I met the Base psychiatrist who agreed with me about the Spaniard: "He's too eager to recruit patients, an artist is not a neurotic." I returned discontented and lay awake, listening to barking dogs, aware that (as I put in my *Diaries*) "I am and always have been a poet, whose mission should be the image....My memories must be created into something new, into a record of our time." I again pondered the epic I knew I must write.

A couple of days later the Spaniard came round with "sad news". The Irish-German Jewess and her American husband had been accused of being CIA agents and had been given 48 hours to leave Libya. We went round to their house and found a room full of people drinking bourbon. The expelled couple were making the best of a bad job, overtly keeping their spirits up with tears not far away. We left as a storm began with forked lightning blasting down. Two days later there was an all day goodbye packing party at the expelled couple's house. A dozen expatriates drank bourbon and rum punch and I was introduced to "Cliff, the Head of the CIA in Tripoli", who questioned me about my activities. He did not seem to have any idea who was in the RCC. I told him, "The only way to reverse this expulsion is to go to the Dean at the University, he has a connection with the RCC (Revolutionary Command Council)." Cat and her husband were there (her husband talked with Cliff), and Cat and the Irish-German Jewess sat side by side on the same poof until again a storm rumbled, and we walked home with the muezzin calling.

Two days later the Spaniard invited us to another party and the Irish-German Jewess and her husband were sitting in the corner. "Am I dreaming?" I asked. "You were right," the husband said, "the Dean did know someone in the RCC." From this episode I was sure that Gaddafi was a genuine Arab nationalist and heir to Nasser who had come to the attention of the world government lobby, and that he was not installed by the CIA, whose Libyan Head had little idea of who was running Libya – in fact, less idea than I had.

The reversal of the expulsion left me with a reputation for knowing what was going on inside the Libyan Revolution, and I now found myself the target of extreme American interest. At the beginning of November Cat had a party in her Giorgimpopoli villa. There was a log fire, Cat wore a pink dress that exposed the rounds of her breasts – I was already half in love with her – and her oil company husband disappeared with Caroline, and Cat found them on the roof together, and Caroline shut herself in a room and cried while Cat and I talked on the front steps. There were other Americans present, and I sensed that I was being walled round by them, but I was so confident of being able to control the situation that I did not leave. We slept that night in a guest double bed – Nadia was staying with a friend – and I remember the blue sky over yellow battlements the next morning, and Cat in her "robe" brightly pouring coffee.

When we got home Caroline cried and said, "You're my only security, everything's crumbling, I ought to go, for your sake," and "I regret these incidents that have spoilt our marriage. Why won't people leave me alone?" We drove to the Homs Road beach and I said: "Marriage is cohabitation between two strangers who share common experience." The Mediterranean came in, wave upon long ribbony wave, we walked below the rocky sea-cliffs and I bent and picked up two green corroded Libyan coins near some sea-lavender and said: "Like our marriage, us. We've gone green and corroded." And Caroline began crying behind her dark glasses and a pearly tear rolled down her chin and she said "I've messed things up, I've messed up our marriage." But later still, she became blank and self-justificatory, and when our cat messed on Nadia's bed she burst into tears and asked to be left alone.

Intuitively I half-sensed a disaster was coming, but I did not sever contact with Cat and her husband, believing Caroline was too dependent on me to flee to anyone else, not realising how desperately she wanted to escape Libya. Cat and I were getting closer – Cat had turned to me – and I wrote in my *Diaries*, "I must be a poet about my life....I am a parer-down, creating out of my own skin and pain." We should not have gone, but we spent an evening at Cat's, talking until 3 a.m. in front of the olivewood log fire (the logs were green and steamed), sipping vodkas and rums, enjoying the warm atmosphere despite the cold revolution outside, and I said I was prepared to choose poverty and leisure against satiety and possessions, to keep the senses alive. I was already embarking on self-stripping. We stayed the night. A few days later the poinsettias were out round our balcony, and I wrote in my *Diaries* that "I react with instinctive holistic joy in spite of my reason". Cat went to Italy with a friend, and Caroline and I went up to spend an evening with her husband and the triplets and there was a great peace in the room. I thought he looked like Norman Wisdom. We went again when Cat was back, and again the family sat round the fire, drinking cognac.

At the end of November I had a profound sense that my marriage was crumbling. I hankered for a new view of man within a new view of our civilisation, I yearned for a sense of something being important, but every time I met the Spaniard he said: "Nothing is important: art is not important to society, but it fulfils a need in you." I was in crisis, I was in conflict. We now went out in the afternoons with Cat and her husband. We went to the palace where Mussolini stayed when he visited his troops in 1940, and to the silk-walled Crown Prince's palace, which the RCC had opened to the public to reveal the luxury in which the ex-regime lived, and I felt I was neglecting my art and had abandoned myself to events.

The end came abruptly. On December 4th Caroline was ironing her kimono on the ironing board. I told her Cat had asked to talk to me. She stopped and said, "I know what she wants to talk to you about." She said Cat's husband had "asked me to marry him" and she had "promised".

I was winded. I could not believe what I had heard. It was all arranged. They were going to live in London in Portman Square. She would have Nadia. They might eventually go to America. I began to argue but it was a fait accompli. I went out and got into the car. I drove to Cat's and found her alone and told her. She did not seem to be surprised. The Spaniard had got wind of what was afoot and had said something to her. She looked at me, her beauty queen hair tumbling round her shoulders, and said, "Bring Caroline up here and we'll sort things out."

I cannot exaggerate the despair I felt as I returned home. I was confused. Did I want to reverse the turn of events? Half of me said "Good riddance", but there was Nadia to consider. I could not bear the thought of being separated from her. Caroline had put a hot-water bottle in my bed and we lay in silence, back to back, each thinking about the future. It was our last night together. My *Diaries* simply record: "Break-up of my marriage. A bleak day." My Dark Night was upon me in earnest.

The Mystic Way demands a detachment from the ego's sensuality. Sometimes, if the withdrawal of attachment is too slow in coming, life sweeps away the object of the attachment to allow self-stripping to take place, a paring down, a remaking of oneself. In this sense, suffering can be a divine gift for it affords the possibility of a change that would not otherwise happen. And events that at the time seemed disastrous may later appear as a blessing.

The next day Caroline, Nadia and I went up to Cat's villa and the four of us had a meeting while the children played outside. Cat's husband reaffirmed that he would be living with Caroline, who reaffirmed that she wished to end her marriage to me. I was filled with an overpowering brinkmanship, the feeling that to throw them together would bring her back, that to push her away would bring her to her senses – that to push away was to keep. After an hour Cat stood up and said to me "Come on", and we left together. We went back to my flat, and I broke down and cried for half an hour, and I remember Cat held me and whispered to me, "You'll be a great writer one day after this suffering, it'll deepen you and your work." Instinctively I knew she was right, and that I was an oyster enduring a piece of grit in its most sensitive part which would eventually produce a pearl, but at the time the pearl seemed a long way away.

I was taking each day at a time, not thinking in terms of months or years. For the next nine days, which were a holiday for the Feast, we lived in my flat. Cat cooked steaks and served them on paper serviettes in the American way and we ate by candlelight and drank white wine and reviewed our lives and our future need to grow. We talked a lot and, thrown together, made love until she had multiple orgasms, as if unblocking something that had always been blocked could compensate for our emotional misery.

Very early on Cat asked to visit the Spaniard. We arrived to find him packing, and an air rifle stood in a corner. "It is for sale," the Spaniard said, "£5." It was a capital offence to possess a firearm under the Libyan Revolution, but I bought it. "If the RCC find it," the Spaniard said, pocketing the £5, "you will be shot." He then had a private talk with Cat in the kitchen and suggested she went to Madrid immediately. Twice after that he came round, bringing valium, and insisted on seeing Cat alone to urge her to leave me, and on his last visit he offered to leave his wife to live with her.

Cat now resolved to return to her children. She tied a leopard scarf round her throat and said " I must go back." It was Nadia's birthday, and Nadia came. Cat cooked her lunch and I gave her a nurse's uniform and we took Nadia back and had an unsatisfactory meeting with her husband, who refused to give her any maintenance if she went to Madrid. Cat returned to me for one last night, and the next day she moved back to her villa. Her husband moved out to stay with the Irishman. Caroline moved out with Nadia to a colleague's leaving me alone with the air rifle, which I picked up several times a day and cocked. Life is most intense within the context of death.

The Feast was finished but there was a strike at the University. The New Zealand Head of Department had been dismissed by the RCC, and classes were suspended, pending a new timetable. I visited Nadia and had unsatisfactory discussions with Caroline. In the evenings I went up to Cat's villa and had dinner with her in front of the hissing logfire. Then one day the Morality Police arrived at the Irishman's and asked questions, and, fearing deportation, Cat's husband moved back to his own villa. He arrived while I was there, menacing and quarrelsome, and suddenly Cat shrieked and crashed down her hand on a sideboard and said "I'm emotionally in pieces, I want to go back to the States with my children, and then go to Madrid." She and her husband talked quietly in the bedroom, and reached agreement that she could go with her children in four days' time and have her maintenance, provided she did not have any contact with me.

Christmas was approaching. I was totally alone in my emotional desert. Cat did not want me to endanger her maintenance, and my colleague did not want me to visit Caroline and Nadia, who would soon be returning to England. I did, however, go round and see Nadia on that Christmas morning, and had the agonising task of explaining to Nadia that she would be going home to England. I broke down, and was unexpectedly invited to stay to Christmas lunch, after which I went to see Nasser ride in a jeep with Gaddafi and Numeiri of Sudan while hundreds of Arabs ran along Adrian Pelt chanting "Na-sser, Na-sser."

I saw Cat a couple of times more before she went to the States. Now she had her ticket and her maintenance she was relaxed again. I said goodbye to her with great sadness, and then I focused on Nadia. I took her to a beach, and when it was time for her to leave Libya I drove her to the airport while Caroline drove with Cat's husband. I waved goodbye to the plane near a pushed-aside boarding staircase which led nowhere. Then I drove back to my empty flat and cried.

On 1st January Col. Gaddafi again visited the University. The classes were lined up to greet his jeep. Fascinated by a man whose actions had had demonstrable effects within my life, rather as Pierre in *War and Peace* was fascinated by Napoleon, I stood with my class near my Czech friend who was near his. The jeep stopped right by me. Four RCC men with red berets and machine guns jumped out, and Col. Gaddafi got out. He then wore a short back and sides Sandhurst haircut and a peaked Hitler-style military hat with the crossed swords of the Libyan Revolution's emblem on the front. There was a roar, and my students surged forward and surrounded Gaddafi and began kissing him. The four RCC men lost control of the situation, and Gaddafi kept his arms by his sides like a tailor's dummy and closed his eyes and seemed to wince each time he was kissed. He was thrown up against my left shoulder and for a few timeless moments which I can still recall I had Gaddafi's head resting on my shoulder, his eyes closed. In those few unreal moments I felt incredibly free, as if I had somehow tamed my Napoleon. His Hitler hat was digging into my shoulder, and as if making a statement about the Libyan Revolution I shrugged and the hat went rolling off. My Czech friend saw and after Gaddafi had gone he whispered to me, tee-heeing, "I saw you knock off the dictator's hat." We discussed the situation. "That was very strange," he said, "Gaddafi does not like being touched." Gaddafi spoke in the University hall, sitting at a table, and there was opposition and he was howled down by the students at one point.

I was in a mess. There was a heaviness behind my lungs, I was full of wants and attachments, I was drawn to outside situations that were unworthy of me. I went to work in the mornings but from lunchtimes on I spent great tracts of time alone in the flat, sunbathing, washing, ironing, cleaning, occasionally listening to the BBC Overseas service, walking past Nadia's empty room, spending the evenings in, sweating out my misery as if it were an appalling cold. I was frequently in tears. American radio still often played "What are the dreams of the everyday housewife?" and "Love-child". A hit song that seemed to be played all the time, "Honey, Come Back", always opened me up.

Cat's husband came to collect Nadia's remaining toys, which he was taking to London. He said, "I feel I'm going to pieces. It's a bad situation, I mean, you wanting Nadia." Two weeks later, after his return from London, I went to the Giorgimpopoli villa and after a lot of evasion he said: "I don't think Caroline and I are going to make it. I want to be with my children." I was relieved. He hadn't told Caroline yet, but "I did tell her 'If anything happens to us, don't go back to you.'" I was indignant. He was going back to London and would tell her then. While he spoke an American girl came to the door, and he later admitted that he had slept with her the night before he went to London.

The February vacation was upon me. I was not sure whether deep down I wanted Caroline back. It was pointless going to London before Caroline had heard directly from him that the relationship was over – she would not believe me – so I went to Egypt.

Egypt was then being attacked by the Israelis. I arrived in Cairo the day 70 Egyptian civilians were killed in an air-raid on a factory in the outskirts. Cairo was prepared for war. During the day distant guns thumped, at night there was blackout: all windows and car headlights were painted blue, and there were no streetlights. People loomed and faded in an eerie silence and occasionally a searchlight swept the sky and an ack-ack gun opened from a rooftop. There were sandbags on the Nile bridges and round the Ministries. I moved into a small hotel overlooking the Nile. The other guests were a few elderly Europeans. I had a room with a balcony and I sat in the spring sun and watched the curved white sails of the boats drift like dorsal fins along the silver-green river and the eaglets soar overhead. At night I went down into the noisy streets and wandered among the shops and honking horns, taxi-drivers, guides and touts, and ate a solitary meal and drank Stella beer.

I visited all the ruins: the Pyramids, Memphis and the necropolis at Saqqara. I flew down to Luxor and nearly got my head taken off by a low-diving Israeli Phantom. I crossed the Nile to the City of the Dead and steeped myself in tombs and sarcophagi, funeral processions and headless wicked souls and texts from *The Book of the Dead*. As the small motorboat chugged back across the Nile to Luxor it seemed I was crossing back to life, and later, riding in a gharry to a temple alongside the Nile, watching the horse canter under the whip past a woman milking a goat and the fluttering papyrus at the cabman's feet which would be the horse's fodder, and the scrawny old hag in black he stopped and spoke to – his wife – I renewed my contact with Nature and simple living and yearned for a permanent wife. Back in alienated Cairo I dined alone at the hotel, and was overtaken by tears and went to my room and looked at the drifting silver-blue and orange river in the setting February sun, and knew I had to get away to Alexandria.

A sad fat man in a tarboosh fell on me at Alexandria station and, with much puffing, waylaid me to a cheap hotel off Nebi Daniel. I took a room overlooking the sweep of the bay. All the other guests were Russian sailors, who never left their rooms. Zagloul Square was packed. Socialism and war-blackout had toned down the Mediterranean sensuality Durrell wrote about, and I spent the evenings drinking in the gloomy emptiness of the blacked-out Cecil Hotel. I went to El Alamein on the desert bus and was arrested for wandering too near a Sam 3 Russian missile site. I was driven to a barbed wire encampment and interrogated by a Captain for two hours before being released.

I flew back to Tripoli. From the aircraft I gazed down at the desert, and imagined a man standing with his feet on the sand, his head under the stars, and no civilisation or materialistic possessions to clutter him. This was the human condition: man at one with Nature, whereas city living shut out this relationship with Nature. I saw Western civilisation as a distraction, a theme I was to develop in later poems. I saw that the way back to a real relationship with Nature was therefore a stripping of illusions, a turning away from clutter and distractions, a paring down, a Way of Loss; and that what would be left after this further purgation would be what was real. On the plane I resolved to leave Tripoli and go straight out into the Sahara desert, withdraw from civilisation like the Desert Fathers.

There was still a week left of the vacation, and my Czech friend had already said that he could arrange for me to go into the Sahara with the Czech Road Company, which had begun building a 310 km road from Nalut to Ghadames. He arranged for me to start at dawn two days later, and I travelled by lorry. Only a few kilometres of the road had been asphalted, and by noon we were past Nalut, heading into a great sea of sand along a bumpy track made by the lorries that supplied six camps. Here, in corrugated sheds in the middle of a stony waste, lived the roadmakers for stretches of a year or more. They sat in their primitive mess and slept in their flimsy hardboard bedrooms. I stopped for lunch at camp 2 and spent the first night in camp 3, where I now had a wooden bed in a room with three Czechs.

There was no lorry the next day, so after an austere breakfast I walked over the nearest sandhill and stood utterly alone in a great buff sandsea under a huge blue sky. Now I was the man in the desert I had imagined in the plane. The spring weather was not too hot, and I spent the whole day wandering alone in the desert. I was amazed that it was alive. There were white flowers, small moths, flies, birds and small slithering trails from scorpions and snakes. Part of the desert was actually in flower, and all the while there was a great blinding mirror of a sun and my black shadow.

DARK NIGHT AND WAY OF LOSS

That night after supper I heard jackals whining. I went outside and glimpsed one. I followed it out into the desert until I could no longer hear the camp generator. Then I stopped and looked at the great frosty stars. They were like lights on a Christmas tree.

The next day there was a lorry, and we bumped into the Red Stony Desert under a vast sky and made camp 5 for lunch. I was still 40 kms from Ghadames, the underground town whose streets were dark tunnels, and no transport was scheduled to go there. I spent the night in camp 5 sharing a room with a Czech engineer, and the next morning set off to walk to Ghadames. The Czech engineer caught me up in a jeep, and said "I have a day off, I will drive you to Ghadames." It was just as well, for I would have got lost. There was not even a track, and we passed the grave of an Arab who had tried to walk: a body-length rectangle of stones on the sand. Soon afterwards we broke an axle. We crawled slowly on and passed camp 6 and two hours later saw the oasis of Ghadames: a strip of palms beyond sandhills the shape of gravemounds. It took a long time to approach. We drove across the concrete runway which was the airfield, and passed the necropolis, hundreds of stone graves on a hill. Boys ran alongside us, and Tuareg in headdress that showed one eye stared in curiosity. The jeep stopped before the only hotel, a low white front near mud walls and palms.

And then I saw the spring, Ain El Faras. It was a square walled-in pool about 30 yards across. The water was beautifully clear and there were green underwater plants. Small white sulphur bubbles wobbled up. There were six worn, polished steps and the water sparkled and rippled sunlight. I went down and dipped in my hand. The water was warm. This spring was 4,500 years old, and was made at the same time as the Great Pyramid. I booked in at the hotel, said goodbye to the Czech engineer, who returned to camp 5 to repair the broken axle, and spent the whole afternoon sitting by the spring. The Tuareg left me alone, and I felt happy. I had recognised and found somewhere in myself that corresponded to the spring, conduits from which made by the Romans carried water to the underground baths in the tomb-city where old men still wore togas and took them off to wash. I had found a spring of creativity and forgiveness. Everyone was sinful and weak, and everyone was entitled to come to this spring which to me that afternoon represented God, whose divine bubbles wobbled to the surface.

The next day I walked in the underground tunnels, peeping into underground homes and seeing men in togas living as their forefathers lived 2,000 years ago. And I bought some pieces of Saharan rock called Rose of the Desert, a crystalline rock that is only found near Ghadames and which is shaped into a rose by the desert wind. By the time I took off from the concrete runway in a small plane and flew back to Tripoli I had stripped myself of the clutter of Western civilisation and located a spring of love in my heart. I thought I wanted Caroline back.

Again I want to skate over the next stressful semi-tearful weeks in Tripoli; how Cat's husband rang Caroline, drunk and incoherent, and ended their relationship, how Caroline wrote saying she felt "shaky and rather frightened", how I rang her from the Libya Palace Hotel and we had an achingly close conversation, how I wrote to her extending forgiveness and she wrote back asking for a year's separation "until I can prove to myself that I can be responsible and cope with my emotions and life generally". In a second letter she wrote that she had met Daphne for lunch and that Daphne had invited her to Malta in April: "How do you feel about our meeting in Malta – if you can come over for a day or two? I agree that we should meet. I think we'd talk far better if we were both on foreign ground. I still feel the same about separating for a year." I did not want a separation now, and although no exit visas were being granted to Libyan government employees like me, I managed to persuade the University to give me four days off "to attend an important meeting in London". In another letter Caroline reiterated the case for separation, saying she did not want to be "merely a pretty flower in your buttonhole". I sent her the money for her air ticket to Malta.

I left Tripoli on a Saturday during the celebrations for Evacuation Day, which was in honour of the British withdrawal from the Tobruk and El Adm bases. The flight was delayed and I sat for four hours where I had watched Caroline leave and thought: events gather round places like flotsam round a breakwater or on a beach. The sea comes in and washes an event away and then brings a similar event back to the same breakwater and beach. I had the feeling that there is a pattern beneath events that is as powerful as the tides. We wobbled over the brown crags of Malta and landed at Luqa where Daphne and Caroline waited for me. Caroline was depressed, shaky and tearful.

Daphne drove us up to the north of the island, past stone walls and isolated castles, red poppies and yellow daisies, to a seaside village of modern flats in St. Paul's Bay, and to the glassy Crystal Inn. Here I would stay, going round to Daphne's parents for meals, and in a small white room with a narrow bed and a high window Caroline and I met alone. I told her I was there to talk about the future, not the past, and that I wanted us to get back together. She told me "We must separate", but did not give a reason. We had to break off to walk to Daphne's parents for lunch, struggling against a great wind by a rough sea, and we then returned. I need to skate over how after a quarter of an hour she announced she did not want to talk again until 10 p.m., how she and Daphne were going out that night to dinner with two RAF men they had met the night before and she would come to me at 10, and how I spent a miserable drizzling evening alone, walking in darkness between the four clusters of lights that lit that otherwise black part of the coast, killing time. She did not turn up. At the end of the evening I stood in the dark by the sea, which dashed in on dark, larval rocks, stinging my cheeks, and before that foaming, boiling surf and that black crinkled sea the anger and indignation I felt deep down came to the surface, and a separation took place between the warmth I knew I wanted and the woman who had given it to me until now. I did not go to sleep until 2.

The next morning was sunny with a blue sky, and the sea was a rough indigo. It was windy and I walked past red poppies and small blue irises to Daphne's parents' house, but it was a Sunday and all the curtains were drawn. I hung around on the waterfront and when I returned there were signs of life and I found Daphne and Caroline having breakfast. I said she had not come the previous evening. Caroline said, No, they had gone back to the Officers' Mess at Luqa and had not got in until 2. I said simply that the arrangement was not that of a woman who wants to get back to her husband, and went back to my room. She followed and asked if I would be leaving Malta and said that Daphne's boy friend was to take us on a tour of the island that afternoon. Thinking of Nadia, I agreed to join the tour.

The tour took us round all the bays from Sliema to Cospicua. Daphne's boy friend flew Canberras to photograph the Russian fleet. He was a quiet young Scot, and there was little opportunity to talk until I returned to my hotel, where there was a celebration in progress, and we talked in my room against distant drunken singing. Caroline said, "It's better if you find someone else." That evening Daphne and her boy friend and I went to the Roundabout, and Daphne went and spoke to a bald-headed man sitting at the bar. Caroline could not take her eyes off him. I did not then know it would be her next husband, and that Daphne was encouraging our separation.

The next morning Caroline called for me wearing an RFC badge and Daphne drove us to a place in St. Paul's Bay that juts out into the sea, where we had drinks. Caroline was aggressive, and Daphne said, "This is a complete breakdown." On the beach outside the restaurant there were some dghajsas, local boats with eyes painted on the prows, some with elaborate eyelashes. We drove to Valetta and ate at the British, whose balcony overlooks the Grand Harbour and Fort St. Angelo and later we walked in Valetta. I stayed and visited the church of the Knights, St. John's Co-Cathedral, and took the bus back to St. Paul's Bay. I had another session with Caroline in which she said she was no longer emotionally involved with me. She left, and I sat on, sobbing quietly on my bed as dusk fell.

That evening Daphne, Caroline and I had dinner in the waterfront restaurant. I tried to feign high spirits. There were musicians present, the ladies were asked to choose songs. Daphne chose *Yesterday*, Caroline *Luglio* ("July"). Afterwards we drove to Mdina, the medieval capital which is known as the Silent City because there is never anybody on the streets. As a result of our midnight walk Caroline's mood changed, and during a drive north until we could see Gozo the next morning, my last on Malta, she began to be forward-looking. The change of heart began when, looking at the island where St. Paul was shipwrecked, I quoted, "And ah for a man to arise in me that the man I am may cease to be." I wrongly attributed the quotation to Paul instead of Tennyson in *Maud* (a wrong attribution that was to become significant later). I said, "It sums up how I feel now, not shipwrecked, but emotionally wrecked." Caroline said she wanted to write the quotation down, and asked me to bring some casserole dishes in July as "we'll need them". Daphne said quietly to me, "I should think you'll get back together." But Caroline's change of mood was short-lived, and after a final walk in Golden Bay that afternoon she picked flowers on a low cliff and wistfully told me to find a woman to look after me in Tripoli. At the airport I told her she rotated between three moods – aggressive, depressed, elated – and that she was like the three whirling disks in a fruit machine: "If you don't get the orange on each, you get nothing."

I flew back to Libya, and lived alone and heard nothing for two weeks.

Then I received two letters by the same post, one softly asking for a divorce and the other saying she had been to see a solicitor. By the next post I received a letter from Daphne saying that after I left she had seen little of Caroline as she was out with David, the bald-headed man I had seen at the Roundabout. I communicated my knowledge of the situation to Caroline and received an angry letter saying we should communicate through solicitors from now on. I heard nothing from her for six weeks.

My Way of Loss was agonising. I was still attached to Caroline, and I had to become detached as the sensual attachments of my ego continued to be purged. If she had died, I could have adjusted. But she was there, I could feel her like an amputated foot, and it was still possible that there might be a reversal of her position. I had not yet emptied myself of hope, and my attachment was a torment. I had companions in Tripoli, a couple of nurses mainly who nursed me emotionally in their separate ways, and I allowed myself to be distracted, as when an Italian took me out to lunch and tried to recruit me into the Mafia. The fawn Volkswagen returned and now sat outside my gate again for large parts of the day.

Then there were two more letters from Caroline, both pressing for a divorce, and I began to court danger. It was as if I were trying to destroy the part of my ego that still hankered after Caroline. I wandered into parts of Tripoli where I might be arrested, and openly bought wine at Guido's, carrying boxes of a dozen bottles out to my car blatantly and driving round the foreign community supplying it with wine. Amid worsening xenophobia – the Libyan leaders were Robin Hooding the American oil companies and were preparing to expel 25,000 Italians – the RCC had set up a new department within the Ministry of Interior "to watch the foreigners", and the system of fawn Volkswagens was now reinforced by a team of Arabs in maroon skull-caps who hung around the street corners, but I carried on quite openly, refusing to limit my freedom.

One hot night I was drinking Caroline out of my memory at the villa of the couple she had spent Christmas with, and a Chinese nurse, when some time after 2.30 a.m. the gatebell rang. I answered it while the others hid the wineglasses. A tarbooshed Arab pointed to my car and showed me a card saying "Ministry of Interior, Security Forces" and behind him a lean vigorous Arab of about 30 in an enormous car called in English: "I want you to get in. You come for questioning." I asked him who he was. "I am not permitted to disclose my identity. I am connected with the Revolutionary Command Council. The man from the Ministry of Interior is here at my instructions, so you must comply. I know you are with some friends, they will come too." The husband staggered to the gates in shorts; he was very drunk. "You will all come with me for questioning," the Arab said. He wore a Western suit. "I will give you a beer. I have the supply we confiscated from Guido's on the first day of the Revolution." There was no alternative but for the four of us to get in the back of his wide car and he drove us to a villa in a nearby sandy lane where four Arabs stood in Western shirts, and he sat us round a circular table near dozens of crates of Oea beer which looked as though they had been there since the coup. "I am not permitted to disclose my identity," he repeated. "You may call me Mohammed. Now my questioning. We have had this evolution – not revolution – to restore the dignity of Libya. What is your opinion of it?" With don't-care abandon I spoke out: "You want me to speak the truth? There's no freedom for the Libyans, it's a police state. And it's intolerant to prohibit drink." Whereupon the husband whose villa we had been in swayed and fell off his chair with a crash on to the floor.

There was a long silence. Then Mohammed leapt to his feet. "You have been drinking. I know you" (he pointed at me) "got twenty litres of wine from Guido's four days ago." (This was true.) "I have had your flat searched, and I know you have a gun, which is a capital offence. I know you have been writing against Libya both in newspapers before the Revolution and now. I know you are a spy. Don't argue. The others I will deal with later, but I am going to have you executed. I will arrange it now." He strode out to a telephone and started dialling, and I remember thinking how white he looked: he had curly fair hair and blue eyes.

We all looked at each other. The husband picked himself up off the floor and crawled back on to his chair. The Chinese girl ran after Mohammed apologising hysterically, only to meet a shout of abuse. She returned sobbing uncontrollably. I went out and tried to reason with Mohammed, who was gabbling fanatically in Arabic on the phone. "No," Mohammed said, ringing off, "if I decide you'll be executed, you will be. I will telephone the British Ambassador now." Clearly the Arab he had spoken to had told him he must report news of my execution to the British Ambassador. He hunted in a book and found a number and dialled. It was now nearly 4 a.m. and (luckily for me) there was no reply. Mohammed slammed down the receiver and said with terrifying finality, "I am going to execute you myself." He strode into the next room. At the door the Chinese girl said in panic, "He's got a gun." Mohammed returned brandishing a revolver in his right hand. "It's a Luger," he said. He sat back in his chair and pointed it at me. Everyone else sat very still.

I did not feel afraid. I knew it was important to talk and keep talking, for that was my only chance to control the situation. "It'll leak out and it'll be bad publicity for Libya," I said. I carried on talking, saying the first thing that came into my head. I was aware that at any moment Mohammed could squeeze the trigger, but I had no feeling of wanting to resist. I felt a tremendous peace, as though I had surrendered to the situation. I felt serene, and honestly did not care if I was shot. I thought of the words carved in Greek over T. E. Lawrence's lintel in his house at Clouds Hill, Dorset, "Ou phrontis", "I don't care" (words attributed by Herodotus to Hippocleides, the champion dancer who having failed to complete a dance before the King of Sicyon and having forfeited the prize of a bride, spoke them when told "You have danced away your bride"). I thought of a quotation from *Luke*: "Whosoever will save his life shall lose it." As I carried on talking I was aware that I had stopped saving my life in the sense of clinging to it, being attached to it, and I felt glad that Caroline and Nadia were safe. "Whosoever will lose his life for my sake, the same shall save it." In some way I felt that by surrendering my life it would somehow be given back to me. "You believe in the sword," I said. "I represent the word. You believe power's

171

down the barrel of a gun, I believe it is in the nib of a fountain pen." I expected this to push him over the brink and that he would pull the trigger but he did not, and at 5 a.m. Mohammed suddenly said, "All right, you are free. You can go, all of you. But I warn you, I'm going to have you watched."

Later I found out that my tormentor was one of the most dangerous men in Libya, Mohammed Barassi. He was a Baathist – Baathists believe in execution – and he was in charge of presenting the RCC on the media and in charge of the department for watching foreigners in the Ministry of Interior. Some time afterwards he became Libyan Ambassador to the UN. After a coup all laws are suspended and remade, and as one of those doing the suspending and remaking he actually did have the power to execute me, I was later told.

We were driven back to the villa where we had been arrested, and I drove home. Something had happened to me, and I felt I had let go of something, including Caroline. I felt I had undergone a kind of death. For an hour I had lived through a new self that was not upset. I had known a thrilling intensity.

From them on I had four men watching me. In addition to the two in the fawn Volkswagen I had a man who sat permanently in my garden and another man who came and rang my doorbell and asked me in French how I was getting on with selling my furniture and leaving Libya. He told me in French his job was to "regarder l'étrangers".

My desire to find this new self again drove me to look for further dangerous situations. These happened after hot boring mornings invigilating and tedious afternoons marking scripts. I went to a show in honour of the leaders who were attending the Arab Summit and was badly jostled by the crowd. I also attended a big rally in a sports stadium and stood ten feet from the "Royal Box". After an hour's military music Col. Gaddafi arrived in a jeep and made a long speech. All round me were skull-capped, barracaned Libyan workers, and I was seized by two plainclothesmen. "You have a gun in your pocket," one said, patting me. He plunged his hand in my pocket and removed: my dark glasses. I submitted to incidents like this as if to a Zen priest's stick, mortifying my old self and remaking it, preparing for the act of surrender that lay ahead.

My conversations with my Czech friend had ranged widely over life and women. When we drank together he turned gloomily philosophical and on one occasion said memorably: "The way to retain your faculties to a very old age is to have sex until your eighties. Adenauer once said, 'When squirt stops,'" (he pointed to his loins and then to his head) "'this stops.' Brain continues when squirt continues." Our discussions had shown him to be very disillusioned with Breznev's post-Dubcek Czechoslovakia, and I helped him defect to Britain. He did not have the money for his wife and himself to travel to London and I found someone who arranged to give him a loan. I had to give him a wad of notes. Because I was watched it was too dangerous for me to go to his home, so I arranged to meet him in a supermarket (not Guido's). So far as I recollect it was called the International and faced the sea. I was followed while I collected the money and then I drove to the supermarket. He was waiting for me with a supermarket trolley, and my followers came in with me and stood at either end of the aisle as if they knew what was going on. The nearest I could get to the Czech was the other side of a five-foot high rack of provisions. I loitered, pretending to examine my next purchase. Through a chink in the tins I could see the Czech doing the same the other side. I could see where his trolley was. I glanced at both my minders, and saw they were both looking sideways, distracted by other things. I quickly opened my shirt, where I had hidden the wad of notes, gripped the notes and lobbed them over the rack. Through my spy-hole I saw they had landed in the trolley. The Czech had seen too, and he immediately pushed his trolley towards the check-out, pocketing the wad. I had taken an appalling risk but I did not care and I felt exhilarated that my aim had been true.

Soon afterwards, sitting alone at home one hot night (June 19th) with my radio tuned to the BBC Overseas Service, I heard the stunning news that Edward Heath had won the General Election and would be British Prime Minister.

In my last three weeks I struggled round a dozen Ministries, collecting all the signatures I needed to allow myself, my car, my goods and my money to leave Libya. As in the case of Iraq the most bureaucratic office of the lot was the Electricity Office, which passed me and repassed me between its numerous departments. All the while I was followed by my four men, two of whom came everywhere with me.

The day before I was due to leave there was an attempt to arrest me. When I returned home my ghaffir pointed at the grapevine and at five bunches of grapes which lay in the dust. One-eyed Mohammed came across and said, "He say you stole these grapes. For sure, I see you last night, ten o'clock. These police take you to prison." Two armed, uniformed policemen then stepped out and motioned me to go with them. Thinking quickly I edged nearer my car and kept them talking, saying they were my grapes to pick. "No, they Libyan grapes, they belong Revolution for sure." I said I had to get something from my car. I had taken my key from my pocket, and I quickly opened the door, jumped in, started the engine and roared out. The two policemen jumped aside and I was away and heading for Giorgimpopoli. I stopped by the sea and thought and drove to the flat of the Biafran Jerry Okoro, the Tripoli correspondent of the London *Times*, whom I had got to know. (He had taken me to a large meeting at the Uaddan which was attended by the US Ambassador, and he had invited me to a small party at which I met a cartoonist for the main Libyan paper who said to me: "You have the deepest and saddest eyes I have ever seen.")

I spent the rest of the day with him. In particular we discussed how the British Ambassador to Libya, Donald (later Sir Donald) Maitland, had just been made Edward Heath's Chief Press Secretary. I wrote him a letter of congratulations. I returned to my lane in the evening. I drove past my flat at high speed, but there was no sign of any armed policemen and the greengrocer had closed. I went back and reversed my car in under the Revolution's grapevine. I had already cleared my flat: piles of possessions lay by the back door. In a few moments I threw all my belongings into the car. I threw the clothes in loose. Then I drove off at break-neck speed and spent the night at Okoro's, sleeping under the stars on a huge veranda.

The next morning I left Tripoli. I crossed the Tunisian border at 5. One of the Libyan guards drove two nails into one of my rear tyres, and I came to a halt in the Tunisian desert at dusk. I had to change a wheel. A camelcade of nomads approached and watched menacingly, eyeing my possessions which I had to unpack to get at the spare wheel. I outstared them and completed the change with a show of slow don't-care indifference.

6.

LONDON: DETACHMENT, PURGATION AND ILLUMINATION
1970 – 1972

I have dwelt on Libya at some length because it began the drastic purgation and remaking of myself which was to lead to illumination. I have no doubt that I was traumatised to some degree by the events of Libya. I had not been a hostage in the sense of being confined in a small dark room, but I had been kept under virtual house arrest in an open prison with no possibility of leaving Libya until my contract expired, and I could not consider going abroad again and being at the mercy of more young revolutionaries and potential executioners and again being separated from Nadia. I knew I would change my career. At the same time I still yearned to have Caroline back; although I knew it was impossible I hoped against hope for a miracle, a change of heart on her part, and I felt a fissure across my being which frequently had me in tears. My purgation was still very embryonic and I was not succeeding in holding myself together.

This was apparent during the long drive back. I drove all day and ate alone in Medenine, where I spent the night. I went on to Gabes and spent the next night in Hammamet, where I stayed three days. By day I lay on the windy beach and thought, 'The sun is shining, the sea is blue, the hills are beautiful, but ... I am unhappy.' Hell is unhappiness, and the natural beauty mocked my emotional terrain, which was a region in Hell, and although I met a German woman, Lilly, Caroline was everywhere and I felt fissured in my being. I wrote a poem which was to be the first to be written of my sequence *The Gates of Hell*. I went on to mountainous and beautiful Algeria in the footsteps of Camus and stopped at Souk Ahras and spent a night at Constantine and then went on to Algiers and Oran, where I felt broken up inside sitting alone in a restaurant and wrote another poem. I crossed Morocco to Tangier, and then over to Spain. I spent three days in Marbella, staying at the Melia Don Pepe, where I met an English aristocrat, Monica, and then I drove up the coast, via Barcelona to the Italian Riviera and Rapallo.

I had written to Ezra Pound from Libya, having spent part of June thinking about the epic I knew I would one day write, and which is still ahead of me: a long poetic work in the tradition of Homer, Virgil, Dante, Milton and Pound which I have been planning on and off for 25 years. An American poet, Pound was arguably the originator of the Modernist movement in 20th century English Literature. At 24 he was secretary to the 48 year old Yeats and turned him into a Modernist poet, and he cut out half of Eliot's *Waste Land*; he had also been writing his own 20th century epic *The Cantos* for 57 years, and had helped Joyce and Hemingway. In 1970 Pound was 85 and was known to be largely silent following his incarceration for 12 years without trial at St. Elizabeth's Hospital for his "treason" in broadcasting that, among other things, the US government was controlled by Jewish bankers, and (it has since transpired) he had come to reject much of his life's work, believing he had been "wrong". (He did not know that the domination of the world by bankers was to increase in the 1970s, 1980s and 1990s.)

On 16th July I found a hotel and then drove to Sant' Ambrogio and asked directions from passers-by and was told to go to a "casa rossa" (red house) on top of a mountain. I arrived about 7 and knocked at the back door and Pound appeared, bearded, in his slippers. He turned away and went back in, and his companion Olga Rudge came up the garden. Yes, she said, she had got my letter (which was simply addressed Ezra Pound, Rapallo) and it would be convenient to see him immediately. I followed her in and was shown into a large room with many books, some sculptures, a circular table with papers on it, and a sofa. Pound sat apart beside a window in great silence. He had a serene face and troubled eyes. I spoke about my knowledge of Japan and China, including the Cultural Revolution – he had got Yeats to look at Japanese Noh plays, hence Yeats's own plays, and he had got the idea for his own *Cantos* from China through Fenollosa in 1913 – and I spoke about my interest in developing his innovations and my plans to write a poetic epic, and said: "You've been writing the *Cantos* for 57 years, so you're the best person to ask about a method which is going to involve me in many years of work. You compressed 26 lines into two: 'The apparition of these faces in the crowd;/Petals on a wet black bough.' Is it possible to compress at length over twelve books?" He listened to me for 15 minutes in complete silence – he was like the Delphic Oracle, you asked a question and listened to the silence which revealed your own heart – and then he merely said, "Wait until Antonio comes, he'll answer these questions better than I can. Or ask Desmond O'Grady or Graves," and later, as I persisted: "It's worth trying." I continued to persist, saying the epic can sum up the culture of the last 30 years in twelve books, and Pound asked suddenly: "Have you had twelve experiences that sum up the culture of the last thirty years?" I said, "Yes. For example, my experience of China."

At that point Olga Rudge, a violinist brought up in Italy, his mistress and mother of his child, returned with coffee. She was younger than he was, in her 70s I judged, and she was rather rude: "If you put everything on a postcard, then he'll take you seriously." To which Pound said: "T. E. Hulme said to me, in 1915, 'Everything a writer has to say can be put on half a side of a postcard, and all the rest is application and elaboration.' Have you got the application and elaboration?" Then in came an Italian neighbour and writer, who introduced himself as "Pescatore, like a fish" with his mistress and an Italian boy, and suddenly the room was filled with talk. Pound did not say a word. He sat in silence in the open window, a full moon over his shoulder, very sad and apart, blinking constantly, and I noticed a sculpted head carved by Gaudier-Brzeska and saw a copy of Yeats's *Mythologies*. I spoke about my visits to China and Russia and talked about my travels, and about 9 Pescatore turned to me and said, "You know, I've been visiting Mr Pound for ten years, but I've never heard his voice." He stood up to go, and I stood up to go with him, thinking I wouldn't get much more out of Pound.

But as the neighbours trooped out with Olga Rudge and I lingered to say goodbye to the Oracle, unexpectedly Pound stood up and grabbed my arm and pointed to the chair in front of him and said: "Here sit down, sit down, you don't have to go yet do you? I've been thinking and listening to you. You've been around a lot, I think you can do what you want to do: put the culture and the Age into twelve poems." Inspired, I sat down on the chair at the circular table and told him I knew I could. He said "Your long preamble about myself wasn't necessary" – he did not seem to want to acknowledge his technical innovations – and when I said I could *see* the pattern ahead, "I can *see* the poem," he said: "If you can see it, then you've already done it. Seeing it's half the battle." We talked on. On the circular table, upside down as I looked, was his handwritten text of the latest canto – I could read "a place of skulls" – and as we discussed the technical side of writing an epic he said: "It doesn't matter where you begin. It's like making a table, it doesn't matter which leg you put on first so long as the table stands up at the end." Olga Rudge kept intruding, saying "Ezra, it's time for your orange juice", which she put in front of him, and later, "Ezra, it's time you went to bed." To which he said flatly, "Leave us alone, woman." (I'm sure I heard the "woman" at the end of his muttered sentence.) I asked him about many details in his study, including the statue by Gaudier-Brzeska. When eventually, just before midnight, I stood up to take my leave, he stood up too, and we stood together. I was surprised he was so tall. I told him, "When I am 70 I will have a reputation like yours" – he looked at me queerly – "and I will think of this evening. I believe two eras in English Literature are spanning each other, although this will not be apparent until the next century." He extended a hand and shook me warmly by the hand – there was nothing feeble about his handshake – and he held onto my hand and looked intently into my eyes like a healer transmitting an energy and brightening my aura, like a poet passing on a seed from a tradition he has grown, and in what I took to be an endorsement of what I had just said he repeated: "If you can see it, you've already done it." Then he lapsed into oracular silence and returned to his chair and sat as silent as the future, the full moon over his shoulder, and I left while Olga Rudge scolded him (and by implication me) for staying up so late. I thought it sad that Modernism and all his questionings should have ended in a silence.

I returned to my hotel after midnight transported into another world, in touch again with my destiny, aware that I would write my poems, in Paradise rather than in Hell, full of purpose and meaning, far removed from Caroline and everyday living and the littleness of Libya. I wrote my *Diaries* entry into the small hours and the next day I drove to Geneva and thence to Annemasse, and stayed with Jacqueline, the girl we had met on Djerba, at the small hotel her parents kept, Les Pleiades. She gave me a room with an enormous double bed. The following day we drove into the mountains so that we had a spectacular view of a snow-covered Mont Blanc above Lake Leman, and having seen that Pound was my Shadow, that he embodied a future self, as we sat in my car I spoke of the mountain as the measure of man and told her my future task, which, to quote my *Diaries*, was: "To search through everything, through literature, art, philosophy, every culture, every country, different people, until in the end I have a total knowledge about what man is, i.e. in terms of himself. Then I shall hope to know what he is in terms of Nature and his society and context. This distinction is very important. Man between his birth and death – vertically, waiting in the desert; and man measured horizontally in relation to Nature and his society and other people. My huge 40 year task must do both of these." Two days later I wrote in a similar vein: "My destiny... is my huge work, my series of poems that will take 40 years to finish and that will be as long as *Paradise Lost*. It will be Tchaikovsky and Brahms in poetry, a great symphony of suffering and joy. I need tranquillity; and joy."

My visit to Pound buoyed me up, but my return to England was dismal. I drove all night and arrived on a cross-channel ferry on a wet Sunday morning. I drove to London and unsuccessfully looked for a room off the Brompton Road. (I saw a card in a window and went to 13 Egerton Gardens, where I was shown an upstairs room with no view and walls covered in silver foil. Providentially I had been directed to the house where I was to meet Margaret, but the right room was not yet ready.) I rang Caroline but she was "not in". It rained and rained and in the end I drove out to Loughton and spent the night at my mother's. I got through to Caroline about 10. She said, "I don't see any point in seeing you, there's nothing to discuss. But if you insist...." She added: "I haven't told you this because he only proposed recently. But I'm definitely marrying David when he gets his divorce in 18 months' time. I have told Nadia that you will not be living with her any more." That night I cried myself to sleep in my old room. I had swung from complete exhilaration in my destiny to total despair. I awoke in tears the next morning, the sun hot on my cheeks.

I met Caroline in London. I saw her golden hair up Sloane Avenue and immediately felt how a part of me it was, although now apart from me. We sat in the King's Arms, Sloane Square (the Royal Court theatre pub). I had a gentle talk with her and she pleaded for a divorce. I drove back to Loughton and kept dissolving into tears. It felt as though I would never get over the situation, my tears were as uncontrollable eight months after the event as they had been the previous December. I visited a solicitor to discuss divorce proceedings. His name was appropriately Payne.

I had my reunion with Nadia outside the Dulwich Crown and Greyhound. Nadia got out of the red MG Caroline had borrowed and, still wearing her school uniform, ran to me and held my hand and then went shy. We all had lunch in the Crown and Greyhound garden and Nadia remained within earshot and talked intelligently, almost too politely. She chattered a lot and was outgoing. I drove her to Essex and was appalled to hear her ask why I had chosen not to live with her any more, and I had to explain that it was Mummy's choice, not mine. "But can't you still come and live with Mummy?" she asked, "I'm sure it'll be all right if I ask her." We spent a week at my mother's and I took her swimming in the local pool, walking in the Forest or to the Tower. I always put her to bed and kissed her good night. I took her back to the Crown and Greyhound where Caroline was waiting, and she went to Yorkshire for a fortnight.

Then I drove her to Sandgate where my mother was spending a fortnight. We were on the front and at high tide the sea flung great fountains of spray on the promenade, and sometimes the road was awash. At low tide we went down onto the shingle and paddled near the rocks and she found a green crab. One dawn I took her to the harbour and showed her the fish market where plaice and skate were being auctioned while the fishermen stood smoking near their nets. Another morning I took her to the Amusement Arcade and she went on a roundabout that whizzed round too fast and she clung onto a painted horse, a look of happy terror on her face while I stood feeling an unbearable tension, a sickening lurch in my stomach that a parent feels when a child is in danger. At bedtime the sea crashed outside her window, and there was a long drag of pebbles and I would whisper "I love you" and she murmured back "I love *you*".

Soon afterwards Caroline went to Malta for two weeks to be near her future husband. Nadia stayed in Essex. I took her shopping and to visit her old school friends, revelling in the freedom to lead a normal life after the privations of Libya. We looked for conkers. Caroline stayed on an extra week in Malta, and on the first afternoon of the September term I drove to Nadia's school and took her for a walk in the Park. After that, as autumn turned through golden-reds to yellows, and apples fell in the Essex garden, I took her for a weekend in Essex every fortnight. We collected leaves and holly with red berries and observed the wood mushrooms and red toadstools and puffballs that grew in the beech woods. In the evenings I put her to bed and slipped out for a drink in the Owl or Turpin's Cave (a very old house where Dick Turpin was reputed to have hidden) and when I returned I always checked that her covers were over her. Sometimes I picked her up from school and drove her to the Park and we fed the squirrels. I protected her, helped her, and was a permanent presence in relation to which she could feel secure.

During this time I hardly saw Caroline for two months. I could not face living at my flat in Loughton, and I had found a double room with two beds that overlooked some gardens near the Brompton Oratory. It was on the first floor of 13 Egerton Gardens SW3, and it had long French windows and a balcony opposite a plane tree. It let in the morning sun, and the rent was £10.50 a week. I brought two suitcases of clothes and personal papers and nothing else so that I could simplify my life and finish my paring down. Here I established a routine. After a gloomy breakfast with wrecked people in the basement, I sat at my desk and wrote *Chains*, a novel on Libya, and occasional poems, and gazed out at a huge plane tree and a white Georgian terrace. Sometimes I put on the radio, sometimes I boiled coffee on the hotplate. I lunched in South Ken (sometimes at Dino's, a haunt at one time of T. S. Eliot's) or the King's Road or in one of the Knightsbridge pubs and I sometimes walked round one of the Museums, most usually the Victoria and Albert. Then I worked until evening when I went out and drank beer and ate at a small inexpensive restaurant like the Chelsea Kitchen.

The Spanish psychiatrist had told me I would be more independent: "You will have a narrower range of feelings: you will suffer less but you will enjoy less. You will have relationships you like but do not need." Such a shift is consistent with a shift from the ego to a new centre, and I already found I did not need the women I met. This suited me because I did not want to get involved until I had chosen my course and found out which way my future was going. I fled involvement with one by consorting with several: there was Jennifer, Zoe, Mary, Monica, Florence, Susan, Ruthie, Eleanor, Angela and others – there was safety in numbers. I was still in Hell for I lived in the past and was merely passing the present. I lunched with Tuohy in a Greek restaurant near his London base. He was going to live in Somerset, alone, and he suggested I wrote some articles on Libya. He told me: "Writers should marry peasants or other writers."

I duly contacted the national newspapers and was asked to write articles on Libya for the *Times* and *Sunday Telegraph*, which I did. The *Times* article was commissioned by Brian MacArthur, whom I visited at John Ezard's suggestion. We had a drink together; he was no 2 to the Features Editor, Charlie Douglas-Home, and I remember the huge bags he had under his eyes from the strain of his work. My *Times* article spoke of the Libyan Revolution as an "armed sit-in on the throne" by a group of 28 year olds, and my *Sunday Telegraph* article predicted that Gaddafi would be in power for 40 years, nearly 25 of which have already passed. Brian MacArthur said there would be freelance work when the *Times* article had appeared.

I soon got in with the London poets. I met John Ezard, who told me: "Men and books have things to give you, not women." John Ezard took me to a party at Bernard Stone's bookshop, Turrets, off Kensington Church Street, and the next day he arranged for me to meet blind, grey-haired John Heath-Stubbs. He lived in a shabby room in Sutherland Place, with a faded patterned carpet. He insisted on pouring my tea with the independence of the blind, and I can still recall the tea missing the cup and cascading onto the table and the floor. He said of Pound: "You don't have to have been anywhere to write about culture, you must go in your imagination, not physically." He added, "Pound isn't discursive enough, his images don't communicate," a traditional writer's swipe at a compressed Modernist, as I pointed out. He gave me a flimsy copy of his *Artorius*, the beginning of an epic. After tea we walked around the corner to the pub, he talking all the while and groping with his white stick, and we sat and discussed mythology in poetry while he peered in my direction and groped for his beer.

There was always a meeting of poets (or in some cases, poetasters). Several young poets listened to what I had to say, and I declared a Poetry Revolution which would restore grand themes, seriousness and prophecy after a Movement-dominated time of triviality and smallness. This would be like the 1798 or 1912 literary revolutions, both of which were effected by two men (Wordsworth and Coleridge, Eliot and Pound) and would move away from the social themes of Larkin to the deepest meanings and the meaning of life. I said a poet is a man with a whole vision, not a dreamer in private. The Revolution would get in touch with common people again: metre, diction and rhythm must be close to the rhythms of common speech, and within this "common touch" I emphasised incantation in poetry to differ from the Movement's argument. I spoke with conviction for I believed in myself. I resolved to write 100 poems by writing a poem a day. Daphne and the Irish-German Jewess both appeared, separately, in Chelsea, but I was so involved with the poets I barely had time to see them. I began revising

DETACHMENT, PURGATION AND ILLUMINATION

The Silence. I went to a poetry reading organised by Leonie Scott-Matthews at the Freemason's Arms, Hampstead.

I went with John Ezard to a party at Heath-Stubbs's and talked about the Poetry Revolution with the young Bernard Saint, a precocious teenager who had lived with George Barker, Heath-Stubbs and others since he was 16. He had a lean face and wore a black velvet jacket. Towards midnight he read a poem by Vernon Watkins about midnight (his *Ballad of the Mari Lwyd* which contains the lines "Midnight. Midnight. Midnight. Midnight./Hark at the hands of the clock"); after which everyone got very drunk, including Eddie Linden, who chased all and sundry round every room. I recoiled from the homosexual milieu of this all-male poetry world, and I spent the next day with Bernard Saint at his rooms in Balham, where he lived with his older BBC wife, Jeanne. He told me he was a Nature poet, that in terms of the sun man is not a city being, that the city is irrelevant. "I am in my Blue period," he said, "my primary colours are fields and the sun." He said: "I go into an ecstatic trance, a reverie and write a poetry of high dream and celebration. The images come out in an order and rhythm that must not be disturbed. Anything else is stilted or, like the Movement poets, very weak." I told him he was writing a poetry of sutras, that he chanted, and he agreed. But he disagreed when I said that like Keats he was writing of "joys" and that he had to progress to "the agonies, the strife/Of human hearts".

The next day, 17th August, I met him and his wife at the Chelsea Markham, and we argued about the long poem. We then met Heath-Stubbs and walked with him to the Pavistock; blind Heath-Stubbs tap-tapping the road with his stick. "Pop music," Heath-Stubbs told me, "is inferior to poetry in the same way that Victorian ballads were inferior to the *Lyrical Ballads*." Bernard's wife Jeanne became bored, and we all went to Maxim's and drank ouzo and retsina and watched a Greek dance. In the course of the evening Bernard Saint said, "The way to have a Poetry Revolution is to produce brilliant poetry that dazzles, as Pound did." Soon after I spent a couple of nights staying with the Saints, and sat on the sofa while Bernard sat at a table and typed up a poem he had just written, which contained the line "My folk were water gypsies". Bernard took me to meet Martin Green and we had a literary conversation. Later still I met the Saints in a Knightsbridge pub and Bernard suddenly said, "Look, that man's blessed with a rainbow and doesn't know it," and I looked and saw a rainbow thrown by the pub's stained glass on his knee.

Bernard Saint seemed to everybody at the time to be the new Rimbaud, the brilliant 19 year old who had absorbed technical knowledge from George Barker, John Heath-Stubbs and others, and who would take the poetry citadel by storm. "I've developed beyond George Barker and he doesn't know it," Bernard told me. In fact he produced one slim volume and then returned to the Bristol area to teach. The poets I met at this time included Peter Shingleton, John Blackwood, John Horder (an anal man who still went on about his lavatorial poems), Maurice Carpenter, Leonie Scott-Matthews (who visited me from time to time), Bill Butler, (who told me that for him, "writing a poem is like a tree putting out leaves and MacBeth and Lucie-Smith f—d it all up by turning it into movements") and Asa Benveniste, a dark-haired printer who ran Trigram, a small press that he was keen to sell to me, and which I did go through the motions of endeavouring to buy. I planned to publish an anthology of poets who were implementing the Poetry Revolution. All these poets formed a kind of sub-culture who met every lunchtime or evening at a pub, very often the Elephant in Kensington, which was near Turret's bookshop. Bernard Stone put on wine evenings where the drink was free and poets like Dannie Abse, Michael Hamburger and Edward Lucie-Smith could be met.

I was discontented with myself. I was living in chaos, lurching from one meeting with marginal people to another, and pub lunches sometimes left me drunk by 4.15, and there was always a girl in the evenings. ("If you pick up a lot of rubbish," John Ezard told me, "some of it will stink.") In the course of August I had written *The Flight*, but I was aware that I had not finished enough poems of my own to run a Poetry Revolution at this time – I was still revising *The Silence* – and that I was still groping towards the metaphysical vision which would distinguish my Poetry Revolution from the Movement. I longed to withdraw from the time-wasting social round to write and pare myself down. I knew that I was not an instant poet who came across best at a poetry reading, but rather a literary poet with a perspective that went beyond the reason and encompassed an Eastern Mystic Way.

I now had work freelancing for the *Times*. The World Council of Churches had just given a lot of money to African liberation movements, and Charlie Douglas-Home asked me to contact the African representative of each movement and write a piece. I rang them all up and met them, sometimes in the Way In at the top of Harrods, and I now had no time to meet the poets. Politics had replaced poetry, and I thought about the wretched of the earth. My investigations led to my being given a confidential document from the WCC's Programme to Combat Racism, detailing exactly what the sums of money were to be spent on. It filled three whole columns on the centre page one Saturday, and I felt hard done-by because the rest of my research was not used. There was reaction from the Archbishop of Canterbury and others, and I was soon set my next "homework" to research and write an article on.

In early October I was missing Caroline more than ever. I wrote in my *Diaries* rather self-dramatically, "I have suffered a loss as great as Tennyson when he lost Hallam." Caroline was completely out of reach: I saw her sun-flaxen blonde hair when I returned Nadia on a Friday afternoon, but she had returned from Malta with David, who had a month's leave and had moved into the Dulwich house. One morning Caroline told me over the phone she would be taking Nadia up north to live near David in a year's time. She said: "David needs to get to know Nadia better so I don't want you to see her at weekends now, and I want you to start divorce proceedings immediately."

The strain of the situation was tearing me apart. I was crumbling away inside. To get outside myself I went to see Chelsea play Manchester City on Saturday October 10th, but the whole match I was face to face with a choice. After the match I drove to Essex. It was misty and my mood darkened with the evening. When I arrived at my mother's I sat alone in the dining-room, feeling engulfed by the situation, helpless, knowing that a breakdown was looming unless I brought Caroline to a final choice. In that room, with a statue of Beethoven in a picture over the piano and a ha'pen'y ship toasting fork in the fireplace, I knew that I was attached to Caroline and Nadia, that my attachment was causing me to suffer without a solution, and that I must choose to push them away. I wandered out into the garden, and my agony is captured in my poem *Journey's End*.

That night I drove past the mesolithic pillow mounds at High Beach and walked down the Forest lane to Turpin's Cave and drank too much before the log fire. The grotesque publican, massive as an oak with two fingers missing, shuffled into the back room and returned carrying a pint of bitter near his gigantic pot belly while I sat with my feet in the hearth, feeling the glow of the fire on my cheeks and gazing at the knobbly locals who laughed happily round drinks in groups. I awoke early and from 5 a.m. to 10 lay alone, thinking. It was exactly six months after my meeting with Caroline on Malta, and the situation had dragged on and could not be allowed to continue. A resolve came into my despair. Either I was married to Caroline or I wasn't. It had to be all or nothing. That morning I telephoned the Dulwich house. Caroline's mother answered. As usual Caroline was "out". "Tell Caroline," I said, "either she presents herself in the Crown and Greyhound at 7.15 or every undertaking I've made in the past is invalid." "Oh all right," she snapped.

Caroline came to the Crown and Greyhound with David. She looked matronly, with her hair up, wearing a thick coat. He was stolid in a sports jacket, balding and sandy-haired, the man I had seen at the Malta Roundabout. He sat in silence. I told Caroline that this was our last chance and that I was making a final attempt at a reconciliation. I said we'd have separate holidays, meet in Italy for three days and then live together for a trial period of three months, which we could do legally without prejudicing our chances of divorce. She looked down and said, "No, definitely not." In that case, I said, there will have to be a divorce, and I left the pub and stood on the kerb. Through the coloured glass I could see them sitting together at the crowded bar. They were talking together and Caroline looked into his eyes. They were happy and wanted to be happy. Only I stood in their way. I simply had to choose to lose Nadia, to surrender her to her mother and let her go north. For her sake I must stop being attached to Caroline.

There is no greater Hell than to choose to lose someone who you care about more than your own life, to choose quite freely to push them away. My Way of Loss had become a Way of Renunciation. Standing on the kerb I accepted the situation behind the coloured glass, and, acknowledging I could not have tried harder or done any more to stay married for Nadia's sake, walked away from the trauma of Libya, put it behind me, and began a permanent move into the new centre within myself where there were no attachments.

My Way of Detachment reversed my Way of Involvement. Having clutched I now pushed away. I sat in my room and wrote my reflections and in the evenings I escaped into girls. Almost immediately there was a party at Turrets Bookshop. It was given by the poet George MacBeth, and after discussing the long poem with Michael Hamburger I somehow came away with MacBeth and two girls. MacBeth then had a drooping moustache. I drove them to a restaurant (the Chelsea Kitchen in the King's Road) – MacBeth said nothing memorable whatsoever and was purely interested in talking to the girls – and then I drove them to a discotheque, Le Kilt in Soho. I remember MacBeth skip-danced up Dean Street. I drove them all home and never saw MacBeth again.

My article on the World Council of Churches had been deemed a success, and my editors pushed me in the direction of the African liberation movements. At their request I visited the London representatives of SWAPO (Peter Katjavivi) and UNITA (Jorge Sangumba) and of other liberation movements, and found the *Times* Diary were always willing to publish any story I had about their on-going drive for the freedom of Namibia, Angola, Zimbabwe, Mozambique and the rest. Three fellows from the *Times* Diary invited me to a very civilised lunch in a private room in the Black Friar, the pub near Blackfriar's Bridge, which was round the corner from where the *Times* was then housed in Printing House Square, and I remember Nick Ashford and two others chatting to me as the four of us stood before the fireplace with drinks. Jorge Sangumba of UNITA invited me to a party, and spoke with great loyalty and devotion about Jonas Savimbi's "state within a state" in Angola. (I last ran into Jorge in February 1974 in Foyles, when he was Foreign Secretary of UNITA, and we had a chat. Sometime afterwards he was hacked to death in Angola in mysterious circumstances – it was alleged in the press that Savimbi's henchmen were implicated – and his body burned.)

My journalism now began to cause the sort of problems I associated with Libya. I returned to Egerton Gardens one day to find the door to my room damaged and my room wrecked. My bed was rucked up and there were papers everywhere. Nothing was stolen, someone had gone through my work with a very heavy hand. It could have been anyone I was writing about – Libyans, South Africans, Russians, Chinese – but John Ezard said, "Good old Special Branch." I said, "No, this crowd haven't any finesse, they use brute force. These were foreigners." But I had no evidence.

Now that I had pushed Caroline away, my sense of destiny returned and I realised I had caught the disease of the Age: my ascetic soul had been entrammelled in the permissive Age of Want, and it was only now that I began to extricate myself from its clutches. I saw various girls, including some to whose names I cannot now put faces, and was not involved with any of them. I had two regulars, Angela and Susan, and the rest came without effort on my part: I met them while eating in the Chelsea Kitchen or having a drink in the Markham or the Admiral Codrington or attending poets' parties: actresses and poetesses and secretaries and journalists. I was only attached to Nadia. I bought her a watch and a bicycle, I took her to *Scrooge*, I drove through thick fog to visit her on her birthday and at Christmas I drove her to Essex and we went for walks and looked at the snow on fences and boughs and the snow sparkling on frozen grass and starlings shuffling on white roofs. Once, after returning Nadia, I had a drink with Caroline and she told me: "I stopped loving you early on, I don't know why. I just did. I came to look on you as a friend."

My green Volkswagen, nicknamed "Saturnalia", still had its Libyan number plates. I had found that if I parked it on a double yellow line in the most policed thoroughfare and went into a department store, all that happened was that the police put a note under the wipers saying "Dear visitor, the laws in this country do not permit car-drivers to park their vehicles on yellow lines" and so on. For several months I had the freedom of London and parked at will in Oxford Street, Kensington High Street, Charing Cross Road. Then one day after an act of Arab terrorism as I drove Angela there was a screaming of police sirens and I was stopped and hauled out of my car and questioned as to why I had Arabic number plates. I explained I had returned from Libya and had not yet had them changed. I was told that I must in future use English number plates. The game was finally up.

In January 1971 I took a teaching job. I was enjoying my freelance journalism and really wanted something to supplement my income, something that would leave me free to write my articles in the late afternoons and early evenings, but also something that would act as a discipline without eroding my newspaper time. In instinctive mortification I said I was not interested in working in higher education or in a secondary school, which would involve a full-time commitment for which I was not yet ready, and I agreed to go to an ESN (educationally subnormal) school and teach backward boys in Deptford, where the commitment ended at 3.30. I thought of the job in terms of T. E. Lawrence's "mind-suicide" in the RAF, wishing to escape thoughts of Caroline that caused me pain and seeking to still my mind of sensual attachment to allow my soul to grow.

The school, Riverway School, was near the Thames in Blackwall Lane at the Blackwall Tunnel end of Greenwich, and here I found myself taking the top class of 15-16 year olds, many of whom had been expelled from their normal schools for violent and maladjusted behaviour. I also patrolled a playground where 150 tearaways rushed about between river mists. They were poor and ragged, underprivileged and disadvantaged orphans, thieves and village idiots. No one understood why I had taken a university Professor's skills to "the dregs of society", but to me it made perfect sense: mixing with the poor and the downtrodden has always been an essential part of Purgation – St. Francis of Assisi gave up wealth to mix with beggars – and it allowed me to get beyond words and relocate the silence in myself, pare away my academicism and, like Blake, immerse myself in latter-day chimney-sweeps and little boys lost. "Blessed are the poor in spirit": I soon found a happiness in caring for my charges, taking them for football and on outings, healing their deprived and damaged lives with such caring love as I could give them. I earned £136 a month, less £51 deductions, and had to live on £85 and the rent I received from 9 Crescent View.

I gave the Head, a shock-haired Welshman called Mr Macho who also lived in London, a lift to and from school each morning. The staff were a blunt, dour, proletarian crowd whose hearts were in the right place, and who sat around discussing minutiae in the small staff room at break and lunch time. In the late afternoons I did my newspaper work. I spoke much less to Caroline, ringing her merely to make arrangements to collect Nadia, and I found she came towards me, calling me "darling" and coming out to be introduced when I called for Nadia with a new girl, Paula.

A MYSTIC WAY

The divorce took place in April at the Law Courts. It was a sunny day, I was on my own. I parked on a double-yellow line, not caring, and waited outside court 44. Payne's managing clerk said to me, "I've studied all the documents, and I can tell you, the reason your marriage failed was your wife's withdrawals." I answered questions in the witness box while Caroline sat with David at the back of the court. After the nisi was granted I acknowledged Caroline's sad smile with a depressed wink, then went out and sat in Lincoln's Inn Fields for the rest of the afternoon, listening to sounds from the land of the living – a motor mower, a plane – and feeling too limp, exhausted and drained to cry out the tears that kept threatening to turn me inside out. Caroline had custody of Nadia, I had access.

The next three weeks I continued seeing Paula. It was an unhappy and wretched relationship. She had just moved to a flat in Highgate. When I was with her she could be very loving ("when you're soft you look very beautiful" she used to say), but she made no bones about there being someone else, an older man she had seen for years who often stood her up, and she always told me when she would be "busy" with him. She was sometimes warm and inviting, sometimes cold and indifferent, and she told me a string of stories whose truth or falsehood I could never establish: she worked for a branch of the secret services, she was having an abortion, she was dying of lung cancer. It was not the stable relationship I needed – she used to say "You're too decent for me, you're giving me a conscience, I've never had a conscience" – and I spent many evenings on my own "in the Devil's Chelsea", as I spoke of it. I wrote in my *Diaries*: "I am seeking God the hard way, in the Devil's Chelsea." Again: "I am the monk manqué of the medieval *Carmina Burana* who sings his rollicking Don't Care songs in the tavern and cheerfully complains of the wheel of Fortune ('quicquid enim florui/felix et beatus/tunc asumo corrui,/gloria privatus'). With one difference: I am genuinely tortured by my body." Like the Desert Fathers I struggled to overcome the temptation of my body, and there was much to tempt me in the King's Road that summer.

During this time my newspaper work attracted the attention of foreign surveillance squads, and often when I went out on my own teams of Palestinians, Africans or Chinese would come and drink near me and follow me out, a throwback to the fawn Volkswagens of Libya but in the centre of London. I took all this in my stride: I became adept at giving my tails the slip, sauntering to a corner and sprinting round the next corner so that they could not see where I had gone, or if (as sometimes happened) there was car surveillance, jumping the traffic lights as they changed from orange to red. On one occasion, when I was returning home feeling broken up having parked my car in the dark outside 13 Egerton Gardens, a team of swarthy Palestinian-looking men got out of a Volkswagen and tried to intercept me before I opened my front door. I thought one of them held a gun. I opened my front door and slammed it in their faces and ran upstairs to my room and lay on the floor with the lights off, peering under the long curtain that hung above the bottom of the French windows. Through the bars of my balcony I saw them loiter in the dark by the Gardens for a good half hour, and I expected an imminent attack, either through the front door and up the stairs or shots from across the street, before they drove off. That summer as I pursued my Purgation among the Devil's spies, the streets sometimes became a nightmare.

Living alone, I found much relief in taking the backward boys out. One day a week I had a coach at my disposal. Mr Macho had told me I would have a "scale 2" (promotion to a higher rate of pay) with responsibility for outings from September, and he had asked me to take the coach driver's test. The first I knew of it was when he said one day: "I want you to be able to drive the coach. You've got your test in fifteen minutes' time, you'd better learn how to switch on the ignition." The examiner was already sitting in the seat beside the driver's, and with no practice at all I climbed into the driving seat and drove the examiner round Greenwich, knocking over a bollard with my tail as I turned right from Blackwall Lane into Trafalgar Road. Incredibly I passed, and was certificated to drive the coach myself. I put my class in it and took them somewhere. We went to the Serpentine on two or three occasions, and the boys went out in the boats. Sometimes Paula, sometimes John Ezard rendezvous-ed with me on these outings. John Ezard interviewed me on tape for an article he was writing. I remember on one occasion walking with a group near Trafalgar Square and turning round to find one of my party was missing. Then I saw him calling "Standard, Standard" at an unattended news-stand. He was selling the pile of evening papers, giving the right change and pocketing the rest like an experienced market trader, although officially he was too backward to be in a normal school. By and large I civilised and socialised my class on these outings, got them to behave like normal souls although occasionally there were ferocious conversations in which one accused another of being a "wally" or a "div" or a "lake" (Deptfordese for "backward" on account of the association of "river" in "Riverway" with "lake") and the one accused would come to me, hurt, and say, looking mad, "Sir, I'm not a wally, am I?"

Into this waste came my Oxford friend Ricky. I walked to the Markham one evening and saw him sitting over a beer alone. It transpired he was living in South London square, and we took to meeting up once or twice a week in "the whorehouse" as I called the Markham, and talking philosophy as we ate at the Chelsea Kitchen where the wooden tables were like tables in a monastery and satisfied my craving for simplicity, and he would join me in bewailing the futile sensuality to which we seemed to be doomed.

From time to time that nightmarish summer I wondered if there would be deliverance from my Dark Night. I did not expect the deliverance to appear within the house, 13 Egerton Gardens. The occupants of the other single rooms were bizarre: next to me was an ex-Miss UK, now a whore who used the room occasionally for elderly clients whom she beat with a cane; below me was a Black Magic witch or rather warlock, and his white-faced blonde wife, who told me he had been crucified upside down on Hampstead Heath; and there was also a security guard at Harvey Nichols; and an elderly aristocratic lady fond of showing documents to prove she was "a cousin of the Queen", which on inspection turned out to be doctors' prescriptions. All these gathered in the basement for breakfast which was served by the landlady who also ran the telephone system, and was not averse to giving incoming callers a piece of her mind for disturbing her. "This isn't an office you know," she shrieked at Charlie Douglas-Home, the

Times' Features Editor, when he tried to reach me urgently, and when he said "I'm sorry, I didn't know," she added "Well you know now," and put the phone down on him. Into this extraordinary collection of people one morning appeared Margaret Riley, a painter, potter and (I was to find out) mystic probably in her early 50s who had left her millionaire husband and was living in a room on my floor, at the back, while she pondered what to do next. It was a palace of art, her room; every available inch was taken up with stacked and leaning canvases of her peaceful and symbolic landscapes, she had brought her life's paintings with her. And her door was permanently ajar.

"Good news," the old lady said that morning, "Jimmy's in charge now. Mrs. Wilson's out. She was drinking three bottles of Scotch a day on money she took out of our rents." And in the course of celebrating our liberation from the tyranny of Mrs. Wilson's tongue Margaret and I began talking about art. She was Austrian, from Vienna, and she took to looking into my room for short chats. In our talks she told me she looked back to the Austro-Hungarian Empire and that she had had a love affair with a Hungarian General at the time of the Hungarian Uprising of 1956. The Hungarian General had been executed by the Russians in a railway yard. Margaret urged me to withdraw from all the extraneous people in my life and when I told her about my idea that events are chains she said, "I will make you a pot of chains at the Pottery." A few days later she took me to the Chelsea Pottery where there were several wheels and pairs of hands kneading red clay and shelves of pots awaiting firing in the kiln. She was about to fire a pyramid without a top, and she showed me, without explaining. A few days later she brought it to my room in a white plastic bag and gave it to me.

It was a clay pot shaped like a pyramid. It had a red clay base and comprised 15 narrowing triangles, one above the other. Each triangle was made of a round tubular-shaped excrescence which she had rolled like plasticine in the palm of her hands. "You see," she said, "the self, made of chains. Smash one side and what's inside gets out, it's all one." The Way In was the Way Out, I saw; smash the "I" and get inside yourself, and you're at one with the trees and the sky. The wanting "I" must die. And I noticed the paring down, the search for simplicity: the triangles got smaller and smaller as they approached the open top of the pyramid. Chains of events, works of art – they got sparer as they were accumulated and pared down.

Later, gazing at the pyramid of chains I saw that there were two ways of living. The Way of Involvement included chains of cause and effect, a mesh of accident in which the inner self was separated from the world, and the "I" selfishly faced outside and indulged itself, doing what it wanted and shutting out the flow. The opposite Way of Detachment involved a flow and a purpose, it was free from chains of events, and there was a unity between the inner "I" and the world outside just as there was a unity between the air in my pot and the air outside, and the "I" had the self-discipline to release the people it had been attached to and to love selflessly, as it should, and experience eternity as a timeless flow; and the real self, the heart, which was part of the one, centred in God. I saw that the distance between the two ways was the difference between false values and true values.

In June I felt purposive again. I was not a "still pond" (Paula) but a flowing stream, a stream that appears still on the surface but which is flowing in one direction underneath as in my poem on "the Waltham stream". Each day Margaret kneaded and shaped my soul like the clay she used to make a beehive. My Sisyphean endurance of my situation seemed over. Margaret said: "Something tremendously important is happening inside you. I can see it and you don't understand it. Ponder it while I am away. You are seeing the truth." Pondering, I felt like a Zen seeker who had found a spiritual teacher in an unexpected place and was progressing along the path to enlightenment.

On July 7th Ricky's friend Bertie gave a dinner for Claire Toynbee. For some reason Ricky never turned up. I took Irene, a separated (she told me) married woman I had met who was a look-alike for Bridget Bardot, and had waist-length hair. We all met in the Churchill. Bertie had washed his hair with three eggs and whisky. We ate at a small restaurant nearby, and I was able to ask Claire about her grandfather, Arnold Toynbee, the author of *A Study of History*. Claire left early, and Bertie behaved outrageously and threw his shoes in the Thames and we all went back to his London house and drank wine in his small back garden, where Ricky now arrived.

Margaret went to Vienna for a holiday and sent me a card of a church seen through an arch with an elaborate iron gate top across its middle. I spent some evenings with Ricky during which we picked up a couple of girls I saw again (one of whom, Maureen, had a flat in the Edgware Road) and on another occasion I danced half one night with a laughing Indian squaw, Minehaha (an American actress in *Hair*) at the Pheasantry. It must have been about this time that I met Nancy, a South African liberal with long dark hair. I discussed "wu wei" with Ricky (action being non-action) and Goethe. "You're like Faust," Ricky told me, "always seeking beyond the horizon, ...like Tennyson's Ulysses 'far beyond the paths of all the western stars'." Ricky took me into a church near Kensington High Road and read aloud psalm 22 from the Bible on the lectern: "'My God my God, why hast thou forsaken me?...O my God, I cry in the daytime but thou hearest not....But I am a worm, and no man.'" I wrote in my *Diaries*: "I want to reject the King's Road for 10 years of art – for the search and quest of Baudelaire and Faust. The Flight has ended; I want to resume my Search....What am I searching for? My identity?" I told Ricky that there would be "a Poetry of Search" and that we might be "the Beardsley and Dowson of the 70s".

School broke up and Caroline took Nadia to Scarborough for much of the summer holidays. I visited Nadia's school fête before she went – she was dressed as an Elizabethan page boy and I bought posies from her – and later we visited the toucan that lived in the Dulwich Park aviary. On July 26th in the Markham I met an American psychic in her 30s called Michele. She approached me and said, "I am a psychic, I see things. I just want you to know that I've seen your face on the cover of *Time Magazine*. You're going to be involved in some sort of a revolution, and you will be famous. I knew your father was dead as soon as I met you. And I knew you'd be famous." She told me, "You will be approached by a man with an offer. I see £5,000. I can see you waving a yellow piece of paper. By the end of the next twelve months you will consequently have moved out to a big house.

You will be engaged and married within a year and a half. In due course you will do no teaching and you will have a lot of money. You are going to buy a big house. I can see it, but there's sadness on the way, a death. You will be fomenting revolution and will be in *Time Magazine*. Famous. You'll have a long long life and die very old. You'll have a little illness with your lungs, for example pneumonia, bronchitis." She explained she could pick horses to win races for other people but she couldn't do it for herself. "You've got something in your room right now," she said, "some writing you've done. You've no idea how famous that's going to be once you've had the revolution you're going to be involved in."

Margaret returned from Vienna and told me I had been mixing with the wrong people. She immediately set out a Negative Way. "Stop talking, work." "Don't tell me about it." "Be now here, not beyond." "Don't force it, let it come spontaneously, from underneath." "Don't explain." Again and again as we spent time together in the evenings she gave expression to an instinctive Taoism. "Don't give it a name, don't say it....Don't act, it will happen spontaneously....Don't cut the evening up. Don't chase. If you do no work today, it doesn't matter. The bees can't make honey all the time, I can't push my flowers to grow." In short, I came to feel that the way forward was the way back, a Negative Way in which apparent regress was in fact progress. Wu wei.

I spent many evenings with Margaret, both in our rooms and visiting Knightsbridge pubs or eating in Lubas, Yeoman's Row or the Clareville Street bistro, and I completed my purification. I wrote in my *Diaries* for August 8th: "I have found a direction, rediscovered my identity as an artist, returned to the Eastern Tao below the will." I dismantled the superfluous, unnecessary things I was still involved with – unnecessary drinks for example – and I now began to discard, declutter the remainder of my unnecessary words and ideas. I saw that there is a flow and that time cuts up; that the feelings are ruined by time. I realised I had a river of days flowing through me. It flowed in one direction, not hearing the people shouting from the bank, detached from everything, unaware of the girls sunbathing on the shore. I had been like a river with tributaries going off at the sides, and now all my energies were going in one direction.

I was now practising automatically a catechism of "don'ts" which I listed as follows:

Don't say it, it will kill the feelings.
Don't put it into words, silence is better.
Don't read, sit still and feel.
Don't compare, it exists by itself, it is unique.
Don't act, it will happen spontaneously.
Don't struggle, it will happen unconsciously, you cannot push the flowers to grow.
Don't try, never control events.
Don't work if you don't feel like it, you *will* feel like it.
Don't get upset if it turns out badly, it doesn't matter.
Don't chase it, it will come to you.
Don't run, be still; let go.
Don't go towards anybody, wait.

Don't expect quick results, a tree grows 365 days for a crop that lasts four.

Don't accept unnecessary invitations, they are messy.

Don't waste energy, keep it inside you as a force.

Don't let people trample on the garden of your soul, protect your flowers.

Don't let people tread mud all over your carpet and disturb your peace.

Don't let others tell you about their mess, you are the one who has to sweep it away, you are not a dustman.

Don't do bitty things, do one thing and one only.

Don't be dependent on riches, live among them but be able to walk away from them.

I now realised what Cat had meant when she said: "To grow you have to be alone to eliminate your needs." What remained was the timeless flow underneath, the flow that continues quietly and unobserved from day to day, which schedules and timetables chop up, which the world of "I" shuts out, depriving the being of inner unity. Slowly I found myself preferring silence or classical music to speech. Slowly, like a blind man, I *felt* the world round me, rather than saw it. Slowly I started to live through my heart and soul, and became the mouthpiece of my unconscious depths. I had discovered the art of living which a wanting generation had lost, and I saw it was my role to point the way. I saw another meaning in my pyramid of chains. The triangular tubes showed empty triangles like my triangle with Paula and my triangles with Caroline. They were all empty, there was nothing inside them. And yet at a deeper level, they had shut in my inner being and had prevented me from getting access to myself. I saw that I had to undergo a profound shift in my way of looking at the universe, and of seeing myself.

Margaret said to me: "You are like a man 20 years older. In ten years you have crammed 20 or 30 years of experience. You must stop now. No more going towards....Be still. Sit still. Watch. Don't go towards anybody. You will see the difference. You broke with Caroline because you had the silence of your poem and she did not. You'd have both gone on having affairs, you'd have destroyed yourselves. She was very capable but there was a limit, you had to go forward – or down. You had the silence in Japan, that is your strength." I saw now that the Way Up and the Way Down were different for me, and yet the Way Down had led to the Way Up and in that sense they were one and the same Way. "The chains shut in your flow. You can't shut it in. But there is no top now." Then she added: "You are like a flower, that flower on my veranda. It was beautiful but when I came back from Vienna it was nearly dead. So I nipped off these parts and discarded them and now it is growing again. I have not wasted my time with you. You are quick to understand. You will have few words now. If there is a flow I get angry when unimportant things interfere, when things from outside spoil the flow."

I now saw that it was right that I had pushed Caroline away, that perhaps Providence had wanted me to do this all along so that I could be reunited with my deeper self. I saw that there was my flow and the Great Flow, and that my flow was part of the Great Flow. To express it in terms of the Stone Garden, my stone was one of the stones in the Stone Garden. I had to surrender to my instincts, let go, not analyse or control. Margaret said to me: "The flow....That music out there says 'The answer is the flowing wind'. You should not want, that is not the real self. Don't want, and then you will feel the flow." Of my visit to Ezra Pound she said: "He understood, he showed you by example. Why should he speak to boring people, why should he? You talked about the silence, he replied by example. He knew you were not ready for it, so he said what he could." Then she spoke of her pottery: "It happens, it just turns out....It is in the firing. The beehive got lost. Your lid got lost. I knew I should leave the pyramid open, for that was my message to you."

Margaret was giving me the precise instructions of a spiritual teacher, and in the Zen tradition I had not found my teacher in a temple or church but hidden in a bizarre house near the Devil's Chelsea. "You must be master of everything," she told me, "not its slave. You must find the centre of yourself, your heart. Do not ask why or when or where, it cuts the flow. Don't compare, and then you will live through your heart." Pondering these words, I realised that I must see my depths not as something still but as a moving flow, and I wrote in my *Diaries*: "I have so far seen the ground of my being/the silence/God/the Sahara pool as something still....I now see it as a flow/as the bottom of a river/as Tao – a way. As something moving. God is a process – the flow."

On August 8th I took Margaret to Essex to see the Strawberry Hill pond with its fallen beech tree. Heather grew on the patch of open grass. Margaret said, "This is your heart, you're silent here." We had a drink in the Owl and then returned to Kensington to eat in the bistro. I felt well, my hands were relaxed, I had let go. I wrote in my *Diaries*: "I have turned round for the Way Back..., the Way of Discarding....A momentous day..., the consequences will reverberate like Saturday's thunder for months to come, possibly years. I am whole again, myself, other people don't matter." Margaret said: "You have sought from people – women, writers. Forget them and stop wanting. Don't want." I wrote in my *Diaries*: "I am in touch with the ground of my being. I can be still." "I show the flow in my skies," Margaret said. "Three things are important: head, heart, ground." Looking at her paintings, I thought they belonged with the visionary landscapes of Palmer, Blake and van Gogh, just as my poems belonged with the work of the Metaphysical poets. "I will never be influenced by anybody," she told me. "I will go by how I feel."

I was aware that I was locating a new energy within myself. I wrote in my *Diaries*: "Move...and you are aware of stillness beneath you. Be still...and you are aware of movement beneath you....See the underlying flow." Margaret put her hand on my head and said "You've got it there, you can do it," and not knowing yet what I had to do I thought of Ezra Pound's "If you can see it you can do it". I pondered my soul and wrote: "My soul is suffering from malnutrition."

Now the natural world took on a more vivid, intensified hue. I went to Worthing for five days. I took Nadia to Sompting Abbots, a neo-Gothic school where she was holidaying with children of her own age, and I stayed nearby in the Anchorage on the front. On the beach I found pebbles shaped by the flow of the tides, and saw the flow in each pebble and some pines

192

bent by the flowing wind. I watched the hotel flowers bent double in the wind, red and yellow roses, red roses nodding their heads and yellow roses shaking theirs under grey clouds whirled by a high tide wind which flapped the red flag. I met a girl, Valerie, an abandoned wife who was all legs and mini-skirt and long hair, who expected no talk and was content to be at my side because she was mine. I took Nadia up on the Downs and we picked a bunch of poppies in a wheatfield. I spent an idyllic afternoon with Valerie on the edge of the Downs, feeling at one with the grass and the earth and the trees and the beetles and the flies and the sky. I was sorry to leave the simplified life of Worthing: its silence at meals, the birds, sea, sky, pebbles, flowers, Downs and rural local settings.

Back in London I processed piles of Portuguese war communiqués I had been sent for an article. Margaret advised me to postpone my poetry revolution: "If they're weak, knock them aside with your work." I thought I felt my volcano, which had been dormant for four years, rumbling poetry and suggesting a coming eruption, I knew that I would soon be writing poems each day again. I felt whole and very creative, I knew that ahead of me was a poetry of vision.

I took Nadia to Essex for a few days, and spent an hour watching the destruction of a wasps' nest in a grill in the Journey's End brick wall. A man puffed white chemical from a canister and the wasp guards sent out radar signals and a dozen wasps came flying to the grill and went into the nest, only to emerge with chemical on their wings, to become sleepy and die.

In London again, still analysing Portuguese war communiqués, I took more tuition from Margaret. She spoke of the pyramid in terms of the work ahead of me: "You have a solid base out of experience. You have 15 works to go before you get to the top." On another occasion she pointed out that the pyramid shape, besides being a tomb, is a triangle, and that she was also thinking of sexual triangles behind sexual triangles: "It is also about containing and releasing – God cannot be contained by chains. A pyramid of chains that is waiting to be smashed." She insisted on not knowing about Dylan Thomas: "I don't want to know, don't tell me about Dylan Thomas. He is on the bank. He is not my river, my existence. It doesn't matter what others have written or thought." I again felt a poetry eruption ahead and she told me: "You are so lucky, you don't know how lucky you are. You are alive." A few days later we looked in at the Brompton Oratory and she pointed out the eternal light in the basket and asked me to light a candle, and as I placed it in the candleholder she said, "God is Light." I knew I had finished with physical beauty. I wanted spiritual beauty now.

Margaret now underwent a change. She took to sitting in solitude in her room, with her door closed, and went to bed early "to be fresh for work." She did not visit me in the mornings any more, and she took to having conversations with a priest at the Brompton Oratory. I did not immediately realise that she was returning to her Viennese Catholic faith and that she now spent much of the day in mystic prayer. I found that I too was going early to bed. "Detachment puts something into the eyes that others want," Margaret had said, and I found myself embodying a detachment from the King's Road, whose permissiveness only brings Hell. One evening

193

A MYSTIC WAY

Margaret cooked me sausages and said: "You have learnt more in the past two months than in the last five years. Don't talk about the past now, be forward-looking. Never try to keep people or control events, they disappear as soon as you do." But after that she said more and more: "Leave me alone, I want solitude and silence."

I went out to Essex again with Nadia and we flew her kite and caught purple and maroon grasshoppers on the Stubbles and Nadia caught a brown frog which she carried home in cupped hands. She also put some acorns she had found in a medicine jar so we could watch them sprout roots. I took Nadia to Paddy Manning's house in Moreton and fished a dead tench out of the pond and helped fell seven elms that had the beetle that caused Dutch elm disease. I hewed the wood with an axe and burnt the branches in the field ("If it's no good," Margaret said later when I told her, "cut it down.") I walked on my mother's lawn and thrilled at the mystery of a pear. I wrote in my *Diaries*: "Earth, roots, sap, flow, buds, sun, water, air, sun, and – hanging supreme, still in the twilight – a pear! For me to eat!" I looked on Nadia as a miniature rose, some of whose blooms were fresh, others dead; and I was a gardener with a watering can.

In early September I returned to Worthing for a weekend to stay with Valerie and I saw with a new intensity. On the Friday, in the sun, the sea was like shoals of fish, leaping and tossing. I thrilled to trees bent in the wind, and to the flow of the wind in the sea. There was a tortoiseshell on the pebbles. We went up on the Downs and there were forget-me-knots on the chalk. Night fell over a cornfield, and the moon was round, like a balloon over the corn. The moon had a strange white glow around it, and I noticed it was the same with the horizon the next day. There was a whiteness between the sea and the sky I had not seen before, and I felt ecstatically peaceful.

On the Saturday morning I read Evelyn Underhill's *Mysticism* (which I had happily packed) in my Worthing room and read of the Dark Night as "this last and drastic purgation of the spirit". I reviewed my mystic life and felt that after a first glimpse of Light in Japan I had plunged into an exhaustion which had lead to the mess of Libya, from which I was only now emerging. I wrote in my *Diaries*, there in my Worthing room: "I am on the journey and I am not sure how far I have gone, how far I have got to go....Something is happening to my perception: the glow that unites the moon and the corn....The white that unites sky and sea – yet it is hardly there....something is happening to my way of *seeing*, and I do not understand." Later I wrote of "this mystic glow around beautiful everything, this strange white light round the sea, the sky". The experience found its way into my poem *Flow: Moon and Sea*.

On the Sunday morning I woke and lay with my eyes closed and was surprised by two visions: one of a cross with a white light behind it, and one of a small figure of the Virgin Mary. I thought nothing more of these. We drove to Brighton and lay on the pebbles in the hot sun and later went up to the Devil's Dyke, which I had visited as a child, and wandered among the brambles on the golf links. I returned to London and mentioned some of this to Margaret, who said enigmatically, "God is always the same." The next day the autumn term began at school and I had little time to contemplate this experience until next weekend. One evening during the week Margaret said, "You're like a beautiful garden that is overgrown," and I thought of how Tuohy and I were symbolically set to hoe weeds in the Zen temple in Japan.

I was on the verge of the two most intense months of my life. I was whole, alive, fresh, and had had a glimpse of what was to come. A spring in my clear consciousness was about to wobble visions up, like the bubbles in the spring of Ain el Faras at Ghadames.

I now come to the momentous day, Friday 10th September 1971, the equivalent for me of what Monday 23rd November 1654 meant to Pascal, who wrote down his experience and sewed the parchment into his doublet and *wore* it until he died, so important was his illumination to him.

The day began unpromisingly as an ordinary school day, the last day of the first week of the autumn term. I returned home and wrote a letter to my solicitor agreeing to the divorce nisi being made absolute (the final surrender) and posted it. I washed two shirts, a pair of pants and a pair of socks in the bathroom and hung them up to dry, and had a bath. I shaved. Margaret came into my room and sat on the bed nearest the French windows. I picked up Underhill's *Mysticism* and opened the book at random and sat on my bed so that she was next to me on my left. I read aloud a passage about the philosopher's stone, how it turns metal into gold. Then about 5.30 there was a knock on the door and I went to the wall phone on the landing and found myself speaking to John Ezard. He had met Margaret the previous evening – Margaret had asked me to introduce him as she was having a problem with her husband and needed a journalist's view on it – and John's comment (ever-sceptical) had been: "I don't think she's a mystic, I think she's wearing mysticism as a hat." He repeated this view now. I did not disagree, I received his words without expressing an attitude, and retired to my room and carried on reading to Margaret. I read passages on different mystics: St. Teresa, Mme Guyon. There was more on the philosopher's stone and mention of the Light.

I felt a quickening within me. Margaret said, "It's a Flowing Light, it flows upwards. Just sit and feel the peace." We sat side by side and looked at the plane tree for about half an hour. Then she said quietly, "Lie down." I lay down. She said, "Shut your eyes." I shut out the world, and waited, watching within. At her direction I gave my breathing to the twilight until I fell into a trance. And from behind my closed eyes, looking *into* my closed eyes I saw white light, flowing upwards: a tree, white against the black inside me, a bare winter tree of white fire, flowing, rippling as if in water. I put my hands over my eyes, I wanted nothing outside to spoil the brightness of what I saw within, and then, as it were, a spring opened within me like the spring in the Sahara, and for a good hour and a half the visions wobbled up inside me like the wobbling bubbles in Ain el Faras. I remembered the first two most clearly: a centre of light shining down from a great height, and then a white flower, like a dahlia or a chrysanthemum, with very detailed, breathtakingly beautiful cells. This was my first glimpse of the celebrated Golden Flower, the centre and source of my being.

There were too many visions for me to remember one quarter of what I saw. But almost immediately a sun broke through my inner dark and hung in the "sky" with a dazzling whiteness. Then I saw a fountain of light and then all was dark and I saw stars, then strange patterns, old paintings I had never seen before, old gods and saints. When I came out of it, I was refreshed. I felt turned inside out and wobbly at the knees, as if I had made passionate love.

Having been born a Catholic, Margaret went off to pray. Alone, I fell on my knees in the dark. I screwed up my eyes to shut out the outer world, and there was a white point, a small circle of light that went deep up into the heavens. I said aloud, "I surrender", and the light moved and changed until it became a celestial curtain blown in the wind, like the aurora borealis.

Then I felt limp, exhausted. I had to stop. Blissfully happy I went and drank in the Bunch of Grapes. I just wanted to forget. I was filled with an afterglow, and my fingers were moist.

In the interests of faithfulness as to what I experienced, I now quote from my *Diaries* entry, which was written at 8.20 p.m.:

"It came in me: a tree, white against black inside me, a bare winter tree of white fire, flowing, rippling as if in water....And more. A centre of light shining down as if from a great height, rays coming down like rocket blasts or fireworks. Then a white flower like a chrysanthemum (detailed cells). And so much more....A sun breaking through cloud (a moon?) Stars. And a fountain of white light. Patterns like my mandala. And I was behind my chest – in my *heart* – lying down, breathing slowly and deeply with half closed eyes, near sleep as at Worthing when I had two visions, in Valerie's sister's room, but this was what I tried to find in the temple. When I sat up I felt as if I'd made love, I felt refreshed, turned inside out, and wobbly at the knees. I asked to be alone. Margaret had seen a bishop with a crozier ('God' she said) and a painting with 'God sitting on a throne'. She went to pray. I wanted to write this....It was dark, my window was open. The clock ticked, distant traffic roared. I fell on my knees in the dark, hands clasped and there was a white point, then a circle of light that went deep deep up into the heavens. I said 'I surrender' and the light moved and changed till I felt exhausted – but again, as after love. I want to push it away now, forget about it and have a drink in the Bunch of Grapes. I feel relaxed. After all my seeking, I have found my heart, my centre, my soul, I have found my white light. I feel exhausted but blissfully happy. Full of love. It is as if I had made love in my chest, my knees. And now, I do not feel alone. There is an aura around me.

"'Prayer'....I now have something to commune with. A round blob, sometimes like a jellyfish, sometimes like a celestial curtain blown in a wind – the aurora borealis in the *Marvels of the Universe*. That is what I now have found. Feel too limp and exhausted to write any more. Or to communicate my weary jubilation."

Almost immediately afterwards I began to interpret: "Me and my Flowing Light. Nothing else. Everyone has it. The saints are ordinary people who have well kept gardens – there is nothing 'heroic' about them. They are no more forward than me. I was like a child that does not know it can walk until it has been told it can...until it has been taught. I am like a little boy – worn out by such little effort. Though as I grow....I am quite drunk with it. So wobbly on my knees. Drunk with love. Can't take any more now. Too tired. At great peace. At such peace that if I were pastor Bonhoeffer, I could die with tranquillity."

The next day I closed my eyes, buried my eyes in the crook of my arm, and it happened again. I saw a beautiful dome made of light, like a spider's web, and then a sumptuous yellow and purple tomb. Then, like an old gold death mask, on a primitive shield, the magnificent face of God. When I finished I felt shaky again, like a child taking its first tottering steps.

Almost immediately I made another attempt to define what had happened in my *Diaries*: "At peace. Feel turned inside out still, infinitely relaxed, totally un-nervous. Want to pass on what I have discovered to Caroline and Nadia – for *their* good. I have been loved by a great light. I still feel as if I have made love. This is enlightenment. Satori. Illumination."

And again: "Fingers wet after vision: inside a cave, which became a beautiful dome seen from inside in spider's web like, filigree light. Also, earlier, a sumptuous tomb (yellow and purple here). An old primitive OE (Old English) shield with a face, looming up – the face of God, like an old gold death mask....All this after Margaret returned from confession at the Brompton Oratory and we talked about the Way and read the three temptations (don't ask for proof, don't want) and discussed the poor in spirit. Margaret: 'If people throw stones at me – revile me – I give them bread....I have fallen from the pinnacle of the temple, I shouldn't be up there....The Catholic Church is the only one for me.' Now feel shaky again, like a child that has taken tottering steps."

I had enough strength to walk to the Brompton Oratory. Its Italianate baroque splendour always uplifted me, and I later found it appalling that the KGB would use St. Patrick's Chapel as a dead-letter box. For some time I stood in the aisle. At length, for the first time for years I went into the pews and knelt and gave myself to the silence. I concentrated on the point of white light between my closed eyes, and observed the eternal light in the basket, the light which is never put out and from which all candles are lit. And I felt an immense peace.

That night I lay again for an hour and half. I saw a silver egg which I thought was the philosopher's stone; a round mirror; a shadowy Christ on a cross; a flaming devil in white light; a saint with a halo round his head. The visions poured up: a yellow rose; black thorns against squirming, moving white lines; a child that looked foetal; a high death-mask, like an Eastern god, with a high crown. And then, with breathtaking clarity, Christ: a man with dark brown hair, a crown of thorns, and a reddy-brown robe worn round his shoulders and gathered by a pin under his chin. It was a direct frontal view, the vision gazed straight at me.

Then there were more patterns, like frost on glass. And all the time there were hints of a white flower and suns and shafts of light. My arm was across my eyes to black out the dusk, and every so often I had to stop and rest. Then I saw a starless night, with an outline of something at the top, as though I were looking up at the universe from the bottom of a round pit. Through this a point of white light always broke, and as it got larger, everything started again. In the end I saw a long white-hot line like the trunk of a tree, down the centre of my being, and I again knelt and said "I surrender." And, as if in answer the point of light swelled into a vivid moon.

And again I need to record what I wrote in my *Diaries*: "Shaky moist fingers, cold feeling on forehead after spending 6.30 p.m.-8 p.m. lying on my bed with Margaret having visions. An egg, in silver, empty inside – I thought it was the Philosopher's Stone: a round mirror: Christ on the cross – shadowy, and a flaming devil or demon in paisley blotches of white light: a saint with a halo round his head in full length facing to the right: and then – how can I remember out of the abundance of them – a yellow rose; black thorns against squirming, moving white lines; a child – a foetus; a death-mask, like the Buddha, with a high crown, probably in gold though it looked white of course; and, with breathtaking clarity, Christ – I think in effigy: with a crown of thorns, brown – dark – brown hair and a Roman robe gathered at a pin under the chin (he looked straight at me) and worn round the shoulders; then....what? Patterns? Like frost on glass. And a primitive shield. All the time there were hints of a white flower and suns, and shafts of light fell towards me. Sometimes after a rest (for my arm was across my eyes to black out the dusk outside and it ached every so often and I had to rest) I saw a starless night, I was looking up into an empty universe...very aware of distance and space. Then it would all begin again, starting from a point of white light which got larger, then broke, like a moon through clouds, scattering spider's webs of shapes. The long white-hot line like the trunk of a tree in the centre. After Margaret went to her room I fell on my knees and covered my eyes with my palms and said again, 'I surrender', and the still point came up and broke through the night into a vivid moon, as if in answer. Then worn out and wobbly on my knees, I knew it was time to stop. I have found my heart, the centre of myself. *Practice*, knowledge is not enough, there must be practice."

After that I had several evenings of visions. I saw the Flower a number of times. I saw the philosopher's stone – an egg in the heavens above a tree. I saw prison gates, and, gathering in a majestic splendour among the stars and floating down, nearer and nearer and nearer, looking slightly to the right, full of experience-frowns and bearded like a Greek sculpture or a Rodin, the magnificent aged face of God. I saw the sky as van Gogh painted it, and a recurring vision was of a river of Flowing Light. This made me say: "Time is the cutting up of eternity, which can be known through the Silence." Yet when it came to evaluating what had happened to me, I was reluctant to give it any metaphysical significance. I preferred to think, 'I've made direct contact with my imagination.' I regarded my visions as being no more metaphysical than the opium vision Coleridge had of Xanadu.

I fell asleep on the Saturday night exhausted. Once again in the interest of faithfulness to the visions I experienced when I awoke the next morning, I quote from my *Diaries* for 12th September: "This morning more visions: a red flower and, after streaks of white, then red light across the centre of my being – the great cable of my soul: prison gates with arrows, in black; an egg in the heavens above a tree, an egg which turned into the Philosopher's Stone; and again, gathering in majestic splendour among stars and then floating down nearer and nearer, the magnificent aged face of God, looking slightly to the right, all experience-frowns and bushy moustached and bearded, like a great Rodin or Greek sculpture. And so much more, I have temporarily forgotten. Now do not feel so weak on my knees. I am learning to walk. How long will this period of illumination last?" On that Sunday, "both my clocks stopped within a quarter of an hour of each other." Looking back, I am sure the intensity of the energy that flooded in stopped the clocks.

And again, still from 12th September: "Before lunch. Lay on my bed, hands over my eyes. More visions. In colour against stars, paintings in blues and yellows and reds and browns. The face of God again, as an old master. Again, as a Russian icon. Earlier, a white wheel. I emerge from these contacts with my imagination and soul fresh and whole in my centre....Still the images come. A tree, wide trunk, a white light behind it....earlier red lights – red for my throbbing passion....And more: the night sky and star seen through a crown of black thorns. A yellow mountain range sloping down and a blob of a moon. And hundreds of van Gogh rings round the stars – all in white. Perhaps I should become a painter of these visions. Also, life spreading like roots or nerves round blobs – in thin and white map contours."

And again at 3.30: "Vision: a golden star (two triangles?) on a blue wall, golden rays pouring out of it. Then a silver star in the heavens, white round it, turning into an amoeba? a jellyfish? An iced-cake ceiling melting into a sky and whirling stars"

At Dino's, a waitress had caught my eye and smiled. She was from Columbia. I spent the next two hours out with her and then: "Back to visions: Tudor suns, bamboo leaves, wrought iron gateways." The next day was a Monday, and I spent most of it at school. My *Diaries* record of the evening: "Vision: Tudor rose." And the following day: "Visions abating."

I now understood that in my soul I had an inner television, and I understood how man lived life before the 1880s, before electricity when there were dark nights and no external television and merely inner prayer to keep one feeling at peace. And I did feel at peace. I had the Mystic Peace. I was not in Hell now. I sat, utterly still, and gazing at the plane tree outside my window brought an ecstatic serenity. I felt at one with my surroundings, I was a stranger to nothing. I had found that joy and love of everything which is the highest meaning and the justification of suffering. "Stop looking and you will find," Margaret had told me, meaning I would find my heart. I had found.

It was now apparent that something had happened on September 10th. At the very same moment that I made the breakthrough into a life of imaginary vision, Margaret felt a call back to the Church – at the very same time. Now she spoke more and more of the Church, telling me it was the centre which stopped one from "pulling people to pieces", and she urged me to speak to a priest. But I knew I wouldn't. I was not interested in relating my experience to any doctrinal belief. Margaret told me: "Your task is to teach the younger generation, be a prophet to the younger generation. They will take it from you. Then you can say: 'I did it the hard way – at my school.'" I knew that I had a role in relation to the younger generation, but I felt it would be as an artist now, not as a priest. "No more mountains for you," Margaret said. "You've climbed the last one."

There was a lull for a few days while Caroline, Paula and others crowded back from the outer world, and then on 24th September I brought Margaret some dahlias and thrilled at how like my golden flower they were. Later that day I had more visions: "The flowers in my soul. Streaks of white light inside me. The picture book of my imagination – leafing through it like an old scrapbook of strange patterns."

I still thought of having located my imagination rather than an external metaphysical reality, and I wrote in my *Diaries* on 25th September: "After the suffering, the gain that justifies the suffering, the meaning....I have found the source of my being, the fountain of my imagination, the spiked dahlia of the golden (white) flower." And again: "The meaning of life – the highest meaning – is to be found in joy, to get which you have to suffer. A stern message to the young....to find the joy, and live, you must suffer." I meant that you must suffer at a deep level, at the deep level of losing everything, for it gives you meaning; not at the level of shallowness when there is no accompanying meaning, only futility.

But I was groping towards God. I saw we are on the threshold of a new epoch, that a European rebirth was in the air, one that restored the soul after a time of doubt, that a new view of man and of the universe was ahead and consequently a new philosophy. It would be based on the mystic six: self-stripping, not-wanting (or detachment), discarding (or purifying), growing, flowing and peace. Perceptivism was the word I used, for man must change his perception so that he perceives the unity of the universe. The philosophy would recover the inner life our age has lost. I now knew deep down that I had found the source of my being, the fountain of my imagination, the "God in myself".

Margaret put a completely Christian interpretation on what had happened to me. "Visions such as yours only happen to someone with a calling," she said at the beginning of October. "The spirit needs solitude to grow in the heart." And she announced that she was preparing to leave 13 Egerton Gardens, so that I would have the best conditions of solitude in which to grow.

The Illuminative Way is tidal. The beyond approaches and for a while covers the sand and shingle of the social ego like a tide, but after the tide has receded the sand and shingle are there again, and the ego is apt to explain the encroachment in terms that do not threaten it. So it was that my rational, social ego, when faced with interpreting my visions and the Light in my *Diaries*, immediately saw it in terms that were familiar to itself: the imagination. That explanation enabled me to assimilate what had happened, adjust to it, but looking back now I believe my interpretation was only partially correct. For although, yes, the visions were from my imagination, my imagination itself was part of the tidal flow of the Light from the beyond, which was always behind the white crests and surf of the visions. Beyond all the visions was the Light. Or to change the image and see it in terms of the Ghadames spring, the visions were the bubbles but the Light was the underground spring from which they wobbled to the surface of my gazing mind.

It was only as time went by that I realised that I had been through a conversion, a "turning around". Eventually I would see that the events of September 10th appeared to "turn me around" from a materialistic outlook to a metaphysical outlook, but in fact those events were themselves part of a process, much of which was subterranean, unconscious, so that when the events of September 10th happened they seemed to my rational, social ego to be of the order of an accident that had happened to me rather than the culmination of something I had been seeking, something for which I had been trying – which, when seen historically in this account, is how they must appear. Would the breakthrough have happened if I had not undergone the trauma in desert Libya? I doubt it.

I now entered a confused time of gains and fallow consolidation. In fact there were more tangled confusions than I can list. At the time I had little understanding of why, but as things turned out the more I accepted that I was losing Nadia, the more I became aware of the underlying law of the universe.

I was waiting for Nadia to move to Lincolnshire with her mother. In October I began looking for a flat I could buy on mortgage to escape the house of rooms where I was living. I looked in Islington and Chelsea, and recoiled from dark squares where I knew I would feel depressed when Nadia had gone north and Margaret had left. I saw less of Margaret, but she still gave me advice on the Negative Way: "Don't be overgrown, snip off the overgrown parts of yourself with secateurs." "Be dignified, like the moon, the moon is dignified." I spent a weekend in Worthing with Valerie, and gazed at the berries and the hips and haws while I lay with her under a drifting sky.

In my *Diaries* I wrote about "holism..., the need to be whole....Discard and you have yourself, whole. Don't want, and others will not touch you. Then you grow as a whole. The mysticism is a consequence of growing into a whole." I took Nadia to Essex for a weekend and among the Forest ponds let the whole world into my soul, felt it through my heart. "What's the toadstool feeling?" I asked her. "'I'm peaceful in the shade.' What are the bullheads feeling? 'I'm happy under my bank.' What is that leaf feeling? 'I'm so tired I can't hold on any longer.' What are the fallen conkers feeling? 'We're snug under these dead leaves and full of flowing lines.'"

And suddenly I felt with the shattering force of a discovery, the law of Nature: the law of the seed. I drew a diagram in my *Diaries* and labelled it "one law of life", and I put the diagram on the blackboard for my class the next day and explained it to my backward boys: "The earth, the air, the sun and the rain are all there to help the seed grow. The wind blows the seed to the earth, the sea makes rain and waters it, the sun warms it. Everything has its place in the Great Plan. Animals, birds, fish, men hunt each other, eat fruit, plants, vegetables to help their seed to grow. Trees, flowers and humans flower to be fertilised, so that their seed can grow. There is never an accident: no man has five heads or seven legs, the corn never ripens in December, the trees never go bare in the summer." It was one law we cannot see: "You can't see the moon by day, but you can by night." It was one law we cannot touch: "You cannot touch the wind." I was so struck by my insight that I took my boys to the Natural History museum and spent an hour showing them diagrams of how a flash of lightning hit the sea and made the first living cell.

My insight was a breakthrough. It took me right outside myself, I saw from the point of view of the whole. Now I saw it was useless to ask *why* anything happened, *why* one hazel nut grew and others did not. Why did the wind blow this sycamore wing here and that one there? There was no why, it just had to be accepted. And human life followed the same law. Things happened in the course of the working of a law, and a girl going north had to be accepted like prematurely fallen blossom. I wrote in my *Diaries*: "Why, why – do not ask why. The moon pulls the sea, the sea tides help water the shore and make plants grow, they left behind the earliest forms of life....Seaweeds put down shoots on wet ground, the sun made them grow, sea animals put seed in wombs, then ate the plants, the fruit....Everything has its place in the Great Plan, the great mystery, and technology merely hides the Mystery, cities hide it. The wind (air) fertilises and blows the poplar seed and the sycamores to the ground (the earth), the sea (water) makes clouds and rain waters the earth so that the seed grows, and the sun (fire) warms it up. The whole plan and Mystery involves: growth. The elements are there to help the seed grow....Hence the family urge – feeling for the mate and the child....So what is God? The Unknowable, the Mystery, the Law of the Seed."

Then I made an enormous acceptance. Looking out at the autumnal gardens from my room, I felt an immense law rolling through all Nature and human life. It moved imperceptibly slowly, "at the level of eternity", a "long splendid flow of generations upon generations", the law of God. Families succeeded one after another, each with its sufferings, through bud and flower and fruit, now revelled-in and now forgotten. There were accidents and separations, but these were only at the level of time. Underneath the process was as inexorable as the seasons. And, sitting opposite my plane tree, I felt for a short while that everything was for the best. Did not the falling of the blossom herald in the fruit? I felt that the events would happen regardless, so I should surrender to the Great Flow. I should not fight to get Nadia back, I should not control events, I should not choose, *not try*. I was not sure whether I believed in the goodness of the Great Flow, but I wrote: "There is nothing more I can do, so I shall do nothing and accept my suffering and wear it silently and have faith in what happens. I shall trust in the Great Purpose. I will surrender Nadia to the Great Flow."

I had accepted everything. I felt instinctively that at the level of flow there are no accidents; events are only perceived as events at the level of the ego. In fact, I felt, we are all seeds – we all contain a white sun – and some grow in good earth and some fall by the wayside onto stony ground, and there is no why as to what the great rolling law of God ordains. "Don't ask why," Margaret had said, "accept." I spent a long time staring at *John* 12.24: "Verily, verily, I say unto you, Except a corn of wheat fall into the ground and die, it abideth alone: but if it die, it bringeth forth much fruit." I saw from the point of view of the whole, as God sees things, and in my *Diaries* I wrote down "Unitism" as the philosophy that would catch this. Somehow I had unzipped my real self which was connected to, and inseparable from, the whole.

DETACHMENT, PURGATION AND ILLUMINATION

On October 18th I had a vision of a very bright diamond with an egg in it. I recorded the event in my *Diaries* at 6.30 a.m.

I had accepted Nadia's departure, but suddenly it was postponed. Over the telephone Caroline told me things had not worked out and they would not now be going until April. I was overjoyed and redoubled my efforts to find a flat with two bedrooms, so that Nadia could come and stay.

I took the backward boys swimming at Greenwich Baths, and there, while I got them out of the water and changed and lined up, I met a young teacher who patrolled the swimmers from the school that had the next slot, All Saints church school, Blackheath, Ann. The day I heard that Nadia was staying I had a drink with Ann. She was a young girl of 21 and shared a house in Greenwich with other girls. Her room was on the ground floor. She was a spirited girl, and I took her back to Egerton Gardens, where she met Margaret. I did not know that she would become my second wife. It was as if Providence had accepted my most recent surrender of Nadia and had given her back *and* a new wife for good measure.

Suddenly, abruptly, I now lost my sense of a Great Flow. Exhausted by my repeated gains, I was plunged back into darkness. My entry in my *Diaries* for October 25th states "Vision – saw the Flower again yesterday" but I had few visions now and did little writing, I was lost in the outer world of my teaching and journalism.

Margaret gave me another pot. We had been in the Bunch of Grapes, where I found myself sitting next to Bernadette Devlin, a young pro-IRA revolutionary MP with steely eyes who did not look round but shut out, unseeing. The pot was a small urn of tubular rings with four snails on the outside, clinging like limpets. "The snails make it look ugly, it is more perfect without them," Margaret said. "They are four people who need to be flicked off." Soon afterwards she told me, "God is One and never changes. I paint God's world. I don't need people."

My journalism had taken a strange turn. On 24th September 1971 Heath, the British Prime Minister had expelled 90 Soviet diplomats – 105 Russians in all – after a KGB defector gave secret information on spying in Britain. One of my journalistic contacts who had a line to the KGB through the World Council of Churches, whose information had always been right, told me that Philby, who was now a KGB General, would retaliate by naming a dozen British subjects as spies, and that I would be one of them – presumably as a result of the help I had given my Czech friend that enabled him to defect from Libya. I was warned that the world's press would descend on me. It was a bizarre possibility, but my whole situation was bizarre at this time – with the Light on the one hand and surveillance squads in the streets on the other hand – and for two days I held my breath. The announcement was duly made and mentioned two or three British names, but no mention was made of me. I regarded the situation as a false alarm, although privately I now spoke of "the long arm of Kim Philby".

I had written a feature for the *Times* on the Portuguese war communiqués. I remember how I heard news of it. I was driving my class in the grey coach one Thursday and became stuck in traffic on the Embankment. There was a phone box nearby. I shouted to the ESN boys to behave, nipped out and rang Charlie Douglas-Home. He said: "It's very good, it has a lot of information that's new. But you draw conclusions. Never draw conclusions, Nicholas. Never apologise and never draw conclusions." He then told me how busy he'd been and what meetings he'd been in and what he'd said to the Editor, and I felt he was sharing something personal with me which increased my loyalty to him. After I rang off I returned to the coach and resumed my control of 20 ESN teenagers. For some reason the article was never printed.

I went to a rally in Westminster Central Hall for Amilcar Cabral, the anti-Portuguese liberation movement leader who had fought in the jungles of Guinea and who was to be assassinated in 1972. At this time a Portuguese graduate who spoke seven languages strangely took over as breakfast cook and chambermaid at 13 Egerton Gardens. She had spectacles and Margaret nicknamed her "Pussycat". Within a week Margaret fell ill and feared she was being poisoned. Soon afterwards it was my turn. I suddenly felt very ill. For a couple of days one weekend I was delirious. I was persistently sick, had a very high temperature and a doctor who called – I was too ill to attend surgery – told me: "You have food-poisoning." The question was, was someone trying to poison me? I slowly got better. Then my room was broken into again, and papers scattered everywhere, and I discussed this with a journalistic contact who speculated that it might be action from the Portuguese. Paula was still ringing me regularly, although I was no longer seeing her, and my contact warned, "Her interest in you may exceed the personal." Everything suddenly seemed suspicious. I ran into Ricky again in the Markham and we spent an evening with a Persian Zoroastrian girl called Vieta.

In the middle of November Ann spent a weekend with me and during the week I visited some of the Greenwich pubs with her, the Waterman's Arms and the Prospect of Whitby. Increasingly at this time the streets were becoming a nightmare again. Wherever I went alone, to a Chelsea pub or the Chelsea Kitchen, there were surveillance squads (for example of six Arabs) who came and drank beside me or ex-war correspondents and Russian experts who opened conversations with me. I longed to escape the drifting picaresque existence among human flotsam one meets when living in a bedsit, and I renewed my efforts to find a flat. I took Ann to Essex one Saturday afternoon and returned to find that all the tenants at 13 Egerton Gardens had been given a month's notice.

Even as I read the letter, Margaret moved out. A taxi came and waited throbbing outside the front door, the driver stacked it with her paintings and a few belongings, and she knocked to say Goodbye and gave me a painting, *Via d'amore*, of Manarola in Italy: a black rock with a sea and a sky, a red church at the top and a splurge of sunlight on a cliff half way down to mark the "path of love". She returned with some plants and thrust them in my arms and said, "It ends in growth." She would not say where she was going, repeating: "Visions such as yours only happen to someone with a calling. The spirit needs solitude to grow in the heart. When you need it, you will find it." From my French windows I saw her drive off in her Aladdin's cave of a taxi.

The next day I lunched at Dino's with Ann. That night I had visions again, and my *Diaries* record: "Visions again. Diamond. Fire. Then a whole succession, including vertebrae (of an old fish) and a constant golden glow, the size of a large sun. Diamonds. Laurel wreath." I wonder whether the laurel wreath was telling me something about the poems I had ahead of me.

In fact I did not leave 13 Egerton Gardens until the following April – the notice was generally ignored – and the next few months were ones of cumulative interpretation. Yet again, as if life was trying to teach me a lesson I had not fully learned, the more I let go of Nadia the stronger grew my sense, and understanding, of God.

The second anniversary of the day I split from Caroline caught me off guard as I drove round Westminster Square and saw the flags out for an Arab State visit. I sent Caroline a card with a poem by Ezra Pound on Venice inside and went to the Brompton Oratory and felt acutely depressed. I woke early the next morning and wrote in my *Diaries*: "Every morning I wake up to a clean sheet and forget my past gains....The Church is necessary....It is the memory of the saintly part of the self – otherwise you only remember by accident." The next day I wrote: "God is always the same, and so is the Church. To see oneself as changing from day to day is to see the necessity for something that is always the same....I backslide from what is real and change."

I took Ann to the Colony Room, the afternoon drinking club in Soho, and I encountered Peter Jenkins the journalist sitting on a stool at the bar, and reminded him of how we had met in Japan. I met Ricky another couple of times and told him I intended to unite all my opposites: deed and reason, sensuality and mysticism, "the four faces of my being". I told him: "There is a sea of cause and effect, but if one makes the move and detaches oneself one becomes an island and it washes by." To which Ricky replied: "You are very near the Kingdom of Heaven."

A week before Christmas I took Nadia to a Christingle service at All Saints, Blackheath, near the school where Ann taught. A christingle is a lighted candle in an orange with a band of red "blood" round it, and the Dean of Southwark gave a sermon on the Light of the World. He told the children, "You are all candles, waiting to be lit inside by the Holy Spirit," and each child was given one to take away. I found the service strangely moving, and I wrote afterwards: "It requires immense effort to keep the Inner Light there amid the world of action."

I spent that evening with Tuohy in Soho. We went to the Swiss Tavern and then the Greyhound; then to an Italian restaurant in Greek Street; and finally to the Wellington. Tuohy talked about the US, blacks and Portugal, and said of my liberation movements: "Revolutionary governments are always underequipped with information about human beings, so I've changed sides." We discussed the breakdown of the West and Tuohy dated it to 1870 or 1880 because: "Men stopped writing novels because they were good at them and became self-conscious (Proust, Joyce). The mechanical side of the West went on developing, but not the arts. And men started to collect antique furniture – things became imitation." We discussed mysticism and he said: "I am too much of an Existentialist to be a mystic, I believe in choices." To which I said, "So you are trapped in your persona, in the 'I, I, I', the outer world." When I began to tell him about my experience of 10th September he changed the subject, and suggested we moved, not wanting to know about experience that threatened his way of seeing the world in social terms.

I had a depressing Christmas. Nadia spent the following week in Essex with my mother and I took Ann and spent a couple of nights there. We fed the mallards and geese on Connaught Waters and went to Queen Elizabeth's hunting-lodge and visited the church in the Forest. I took Nadia to dancing classes and attended the final dance, smiling at her erect, stiff-legged waltz. On January 3rd I recorded in my *Diaries*: "Visions. Bleary eyes from inward-looking. A lot of patterns. Snowflakes. Saints, Pope's head, monk, altar, Cathedral – floating through window, wheels in the night, white light – began and stopped."

January 1972 was a bad time emotionally. I had a lot to do with Caroline who was making arrangements to take Nadia to Lincolnshire in April. I often went to sleep in pain, and often thought of Coleridge's lines in *The Ancient Mariner*: "Each night at an uncertain hour/This agony returns." A pop song "I want to go back there again" seemed to be everywhere, and when I heard it I invariably felt broken up inside. Then I spent weekends with Ann and it all got better. One Saturday night we parked in the Forest and when I next looked out of the car window the Forest was white with snow.

In early February in Greenwich I understood the intensity of my despair as I felt the call back to be a poet. I wrote in my *Diaries*: "I am above all a Romantic poet – an isolated artist carrying on in a philistine and alien society, using image and organic form, interested in such romantic causes as liberation movements, wanting to change the world. Yet at the same time, killing my soul in a studied suicide of politics and women. These must be discarded....Action – for me it is what abstract metaphysics were to Coleridge. An escape....'We Poets in our youth begin in gladness;/But thereof come in the end despondency and madness.' Because poets feel more intensely, they feel the gladness and the despair more than others. I will not be beaten by the despair, the disillusion; I will continue to reflect the natural world....Sing everyday life – and Nature."

Biggs-Davison rang and invited me to the launch of his book *Africa: Hope Deferred*, which took place in a room in the Palace of Westminster. He sat at the end of a long table and talked about it. He insisted I sat next to him on his right, and Adrian Berry of the *Daily Telegraph* sat next to me. Biggs-Davison asked me if I would cover the book for the *Times* Diary. His book was pro-Portuguese, pro-Rhodesian and pro-South African and would be considered extremely right wing by the anti-Portuguese, anti-Rhodesian and anti-South African liberation movement leaders I normally wrote about. I saw Biggs-Davison, who was universally proclaimed the "best read" MP, as out of date. I could see the future – I had felt the wind of change and knew that the Portuguese and Rhodesian and South African whites would lose to the black liberation movements, I saw the transition which Biggs-Davison did not address, preferring to believe it was not taking place. I wrote a piece, sent him a copy, and was relieved that it was never published.

Soon afterwards I spent another evening with Tuohy, meeting him at

2 Aubrey Road in a relative's sitting-room, eating at Costa's and because of a miners' power-cut returning for two final drinks to the house, where I met his relative Lady Flavia and heard about her boy-friend Colin MacCabe, a Structuralist who had written on semiology. At this encounter with Tuohy I reaffirmed my identity as a Romantic poet and Existentialist who is interested in "dynamic growing" ("the upward thrust of the sap") and "rooted growth", rather than analysis in terms of any social theory or class.

I began a further development – a further undermining of my "I" – during the February half term. I spent a weekend with Nadia. I took her up the Monument and felt giddy as I always do with heights, and to the zoo, and on the Sunday we went for a walk in Epping Forest. In my *Diaries* I wrote: "The buds were nearly out: hawthorn and beech. The great tit sang 'see-saw' from near its nest. A squirrel sat still on a branch. I stood on a mossy knoll and looked at the lacy pattern of twigs against a white sky, and later, scuffling through last year's leaves, I felt the scales unfold from around my heart, I burst into happy bud." The account went into my poem, *February Budding, Half Term*, with very little change. The next evening I took Ann to the Chelsea Kitchen. She happened to remark that at school she was illustrating the Creation as it is described in *Genesis*. I said: "Light and darkness come out of a Void." And suddenly I glimpsed deep into reality. Thoughts came up from underneath me, "like bubbles from the Void at the bottom of the Sahara spring", and I told her with absolute confidence that God is a Void. For half an hour I explained to her that to approach God, "you must be negative, you must discard the world of time, of timetables and journalism and money-earners. You must empty yourself of it. Then you get back to the Void underneath. You are filled with a level of living which is eternal, for it has been going on for centuries." So, I said, an emptying is a filling, and the more emptying, the more filling: a loss is a gain, and the more loss, the more gain. "But both time and eternity are parts of the same unity, like the top and bottom of a river, or as light and darkness are parts of the same Void." I repeated that "time is the cutting up of eternity".

Afterwards we went for a final drink in the Southwark George, and the thoughts went on pouring up from the depths of my being. I believed in a great deep presence of a Void that can be known by losing the sense of time, by a deepening in the living. I believed that the artist should be a mere shaper, like the brick walls round the Ain el Faras, for the God in himself, that his function was to rediscover truths which his time-bound Age had forgotten. Above all, I said, "I-I-I is at the level of time, 'I' am not important to eternity but an echo under a silent railway bridge." I insisted that therefore the really important pastimes, from the point of view of eternity, were "leisure and ruminating and sitting in the Brompton Oratory and walking in Epping Forest and writing poetry." I quote from my *Diaries* on February 29th 1972: "I saw that eternity and time are part of a unity which is a Void, in its negative and positive aspects, and that to approach God you must be negative, i.e. get back to the Void and the flow, to the 'something there'. By discarding the positive phenomena the mystic can become one with the Void....Do I believe in God? Yes. In a great, deep presence of a Void that can be known by losing the sense of time – not self-consciously with studied meditation, but by a deepening in the living....My soul thirsts for real things, not for the cheap and vulgar. I am a religious soul bound to a body of fire."

I was confronted with belief in God, and wrote: "So I believe in God, I have got there at last, though I have known it all along. It is the Silence I found in Japan, the spring in the desert I found in the Sahara, the visions I found through the distractions of Egerton Gardens. There is a richness and a deepening, a purpose that can be known and felt, but about which there are no facts. God is a Void that can be felt beneath the bustle of temporal phenomena and events: God is a flow through the temporal phenomena and events. God *is*, at the level of Being, whereas the temporal phenomena and events are at the level of Becoming." I ended: "The artist as an instrument for the God in himself, which is shown as an example to the people, i.e. the artist as hero, rediscovering truths which his time-bound Age has forgotten." I urged myself to get back to poetry as soon as possible, and wrote that "my development as a writer is from the level of time to the level of the eternal".

In early March the *Times* (in the person of Louis Heren) sent me to Frankfurt to cover a World Council of Churches sponsored symposium on the Cunene River scheme, Angola, for the foreign news page. I was away from a Wednesday to a Saturday. I flew to Frankfurt and caught a bus near the Messe to where I was staying in a pine forest at Arnoldsheim in the Taunus mountains. The conference was a longish walk through a German village and bracing mountain air, where 40 or 50 African liberation movement leaders, Communists and organisers met, expenses including air fares paid by the World Council of Churches, and unwillingly stood in prayer before the serious business of opposing Portugal's dam and exposing what it would do to the guerrilla war they were supporting. There was an initial attempt to exclude me on the grounds that the proceedings should not be reported, but I kept myself to myself, nursing my vision of God and the importance of the eternal while writing about the liberation struggles of time and the need for political change, and fighting off 30 different groups which all wanted me to give them publicity in my article. I made my article a scrupulously accurate summary of what was said at the conference, and later heard it was praised by all factions for its fairness after it had appeared. I have often since thought that there was something Providential in my having to consider the World Council of Churches a day after the entry in my *Diaries* on believing in God.

When I returned to London I wrote in my *Diaries*: "God is an itness that can be known through silence (eternity), not noise (time). So the condition of approaching God is quiet: the Brompton Oratory, which, though it is too cluttered, is a symbol of quietness and of the candle-light of the soul (Christingle)." It seemed I had achieved a sudden unification of myself: "I cannot live wholly in eternity, I cannot live wholly in time – I have to have a foot in both creeds. Hence I am Saint and Devil, hence I need a central woman but like girls and pubs – a wife and the Markham are a part of the same unity....So when Caroline got mixed up in time she ceased to mean, she ceased to be eternal. My journal – this *Diary* and dustbin – is the level of eternity contemplating the level of time but also being attracted to time.

As a writer I get my material from time but depth from eternity." Again on March 7th: "How I found God in the Devil's Markham. The search for Caroline ended as a finding of God....I must be an instrument of God's will: purposive, direct. When I am aware of the God in me, I have immense purpose, a river of will in me compared with which I am nothing. I can feel it in me now. With it, I can do anything. My strength. I have understood, God is my strength. The force in me....There is a force flowing through me, like water through a pipe. I could do anything in this mood, absolutely anything. 'I' am completely whole – beside it I am nothing....God is not out there, God is a force that comes through you, that unites you with the flow of everything: an immensely creative force through which everything is possible." Again: "It is the experience that I go for – the experience of gaining the eternal and growing for I am an Existentialist. God is a force in me that helps my growth....The fungus must be knocked off the old way of looking at God. An Existentialist redefinition." And again: "Last night, I believed in God. If you imagine God, it's outside, if you *experience* God it's inside – the ideal for an Existentialist who only trusts what he can see and touch. I've journeyed far beyond Colin Wilson – he's got lost. The watersplash, where the tide washes over the road at Portmellon. I told him I would wander for ten years and I wandered from the idea of God into foreign countries but returned....The force is greater than me and 'I' is small....The only way to find God is within the Devil's Chelsea, like electricity it is + and -, through loss. My search for God in our time (God by itself is not enough, there must be time). So (I) lost the world but gained God as a compensation (in the spirit of *John, ch12*)."

I had visited and made an offer for the top flat at 33 Stanhope Gardens, SW7 and I now heard that a building society had offered the money for the 17½ year lease: £5,000, the exact figure that Michele the psychic had forecast the previous July 26th, and I would be moving in in April, within the 12 month period as she had forecast. It was uncanny, but the estate agent's leaflet was yellow, a colour she had forecast. Then one evening on the radio I heard Viscountess Astor's account of illumination at the age of 28: "I believe we are all on a journey to God, whether we know it or not....At 28 I was like an 18 year old, gay and dizzy, then in despair....Then a brilliant Light enveloped me. Everything was a unity. I understood the mystery. God is not remote, he awaits us....There is a power within each one of us that will transform our life, like a lamp switched on." I did not then know I would meet her, and learn that she was already illumined when the Profumo Affair took place at Cliveden in 1963.

All night I lay awake near Blackheath, thinking about God, and the next day I showed a film at school about " the hermit crabs and starfish between the tides, and – wonder upon wonder! – the self-planting of the corn of wheat which falls to the ground and actually winds itself downwards into the earth and dies". Straightaway I sent one of my boys to the local library to check the quotation I was reminded of, from *John* 12.24: "Verily, verily I say unto you, Except a corn of wheat fall into the ground and die, it abideth alone: but if it die, it bringeth forth much fruit." I felt I had died into the ground of eternity and was now ready to grow again.

Now I began to express my feelings of selflessness. I spent a weekend in

Essex with Nadia and Ann. We visited the Church of the Holy Innocents, which is in the heart of the Forest, and I gave myself to the peace of the ferny graveyard. I suddenly told Ann: "Eternity is not having anything dumped on you from the world of time, no handfuls of earth thrown on your spring....Instead you live in blissfully undisturbed communion with the white Inner Light. So, in this life, it is more blessed to give than to receive, because receiving is having things dumped on you from the world of time. Happiness is in giving...." Later I spoke of love as being "at the level of eternity, it has nothing to do with timetables, it is always there. Hence the love of God."

The next evening I was driving back to my room with Ann. I stopped to walk among the crocuses of St. James's Park and heard the call of my destiny from way beyond myself: "A huge work that would be a vast fulfilment of myself as an artist, a capturing of the eternal world clothed in time." "I vowed," I wrote, "to make a daily rendez-vous with It – God, the Flow, call It what you will – and if It comes I will be happy and write, and if It doesn't I will do other things and hope for next time...." This I would do as a giving of my own experience of the union between eternity and time.

My *Diaries* record: "Today I heard the call of my destiny, among the crocuses of St. James's Park: I was driving along Birdcage Walk towards the Palace and stopped at Ann's request for a stroll. Behind me I felt the call of my future: to clear the way for my long work – which will be like *Paradise Lost* and *Pilgrim's Progress*, a vast fulfilment of myself as an artist. I must write every day – or try to write. Writing and religion are very similar. You must make an appointment with It – a rendezvous – and if It comes you are happy. If not you do other things and hope that next time...." Again: "My 'confusion' of art and religion – at a deep, deep level. Freeman must rechoose himself as an artist, i.e. as a poet of 'the eternal level clothed in time'. He should not become a priest and worship, he is creating himself as an *artist*....Eternity and time – 'when the ruffled surface calmed I saw the clouded ground'. That is the union between eternity and time I dream of."

I now had insight into my past: "I got lost in 1966 and experienced darkness from the end of *The Silence* (mid 1966) until my disquiet at the end of 1969. In those three years, though I had been on the threshold of eternity, I wrote *The Eternicide* – a great error deifying the world of time, totally retrogressive and backsliding – and *The Age of Cartoon* about politics. Also the stories, which got me lost. Could they be my Dark Night, those three years, and could it be that my marriage break-up was necessary to me to take me through to find unitive life?" And again: "My lost years, 1966-1969. I was so tempted, everything went to pieces – *that* was what caused my marriage to break up? When the Dark Night ends, affirmation takes the place of negation....Vaughan: 'I saw Eternity the other night/Like a great Ring of pure and endless light,/All calm as it was bright.'"

This vision helped me through that Easter, which I spent with Nadia in Essex. She knew most of the situation – she had seen her new school and the furnished flat in the grounds of Harrington Hall where she would soon be living with Caroline and David. She knew that Caroline was remarrying on Easter Saturday, and, being "a happy little extrovert" she had accepted it.

She knew that she would miss her Daddy, though, and she said when I tucked her up the first night: "I wish you could still live with me." I reassured her: she would be spending part of her holidays in my flat. And, taking her swimming and to her friends, catching frogspawn with her and holding her hand all round Chingford Easter Monday fair and gazing up as she sickeningly whirled round at terrifying speed in a flying chair, I felt a peaceful resignation I never dreamed I would feel.

On Easter Monday (April 3rd) I saw the Light again. My *Diaries* record: "The Flowing Light again, as I lay with my hands over my eyes. A golden head of Christ and, separately, twice, a crown of thorns, also in golden light. And I am *still* against going to church."

From bud-dust, the trees were in blossom, and I had severed myself from my relationship with Nadia. It was not that I had discarded her or that I did not want her. The question of wanting did not arise, for what *I* wanted, I now felt, was irrelevant to the situation in Lincolnshire. I loved her for herself, not for what *I* got out of it. My love considered only what was good for her, it focused on her, as a Kew gardener focuses his care on a miniature rose, and I was sure she would be happy. My love for her was now the selfless love which can only truly be known through loss, the love which is the highest meaning of love, and it was almost as though I had to lose Nadia to know it.

On April 6th I had more visions. "While combing through this *Diary* – noting the frequency of my mentions of God – I closed my eyes and saw a brown Roman effigy of God. From an old master (I could see the paint cracks) it looked massively solid, eyes closed. Then a white sun, not very bright, and disappearing when I 'looked' at it, but re-emerging when I looked to one side. Then two stars. I must practise early every day....'Prayer', in the sense of inner contemplation and union....Did it again, in broad daylight still, and saw a white ageless face."

When at last Nadia and I got into my car and waved goodbye to my family, and she burst into tears, I said very softly, "You'll see them all again, don't worry. You'll go to your new home and you'll think of us, yes, but we'll still be here. We'll come and see you and your new friends, and think, you won't just have a hamster now, you'll have peacocks in your garden."

So my parting from Nadia was not agonised. I told her animal stories during the journey. I gave her a brief kiss at the gate, squeezed her hand, made a joke, then drove up to London and busied myself with visiting the electricity and gas offices concerning the imminent purchase of my flat. Later I phoned Caroline. She said she had in fact married David.

After that I met Ann, who had been in Cornwall. She gave me a bunch of spring violets. She said they might help me forget Nadia. Standing in my window, looking out at the plane tree, I held the bunch against a sky like a purple bruise and murmured some lines from Tennyson: "'And my regret/Becomes an April violet/And buds and blossoms with the rest.'"

7.

RAPTURES AND CONTEMPLATION
1972 – 1974

I have dwelt on adversity to offer encouragement. Despair can be the precondition of hope. It can be the dismantling of the part of oneself that was the obstacle or barrier to hope. As in a symphony, pain is conquered by joy but remains there, contained in the end. For the pioneering spirit, a new state of consciousness is always possible, even though it is hard-won. There *can* be a triumphant ending, in which the human spirit makes conquests. That is the theme of the rest of my story.

I was now increasingly strengthened by my new found faith in life. The very next day I was seized by God, or "rapt". I felt the divine presence steal up suddenly from below and fill my soul, slow my breathing, lock my body rigid as a fakir's. I was sitting writing in my *Diaries* with Ann, and I went and lay down on my bed and closed my eyes, impervious to the sensations of my body. Totally absorbed in the presence around me, I surrendered the deepest crevices of my soul and was given more visions: of beautiful golden furniture, of temple columns, of a brown statue head, of the celestial curtain, and then, marvellously, of the diamond in luminous blue light. This was the first time I had seen the colour blue in my secret journeys, and it stood out in my memory afterwards, even though it blended into the Golden Flower and was followed by perhaps half an hour of light flashing up into my inner night like a dawn.

When the presence had withdrawn, I wrote in my *Diaries:* "Visions again. So many I can't remember them....There were gold items of furniture (e.g. table leg) and a lot of old masters and temple columns, one old brown statue head, a celestial curtain, the diamond in blue light, and a yellow flower. A lot of light breaking, like a dawn turning into morning or like the sun coming out." Later that evening I reflected in my *Diaries*: "God is a way of life. It is the level of Flow that runs through my life and all life, which unites me to all life: the eternal level. The river (cf spring) united with the sea in the estuary. (This *Diary* is a kind of newspaper of the eternal, a newspaper that contains little on the Presiding power behind the news.) So God is feeling my river of days being a part of the sea of cause and effect – separate from it through 'don'ts' but basically a part of it, the Great Flow. It is felt in acts of union through the Heart and through the Spirit – not the inner sun but the force in man that does not give up. I believe in the Mind, the Heart, the Soul (which sees the inner sun) and the Spirit, which is the force that says 'don't' – don't give up. Definition: the spirit is the force that says 'don't'....Holy Spirit – the eternal level. So the Spirit is the force which speaks from the eternal level and resists the temptations of time."

Four days later on April 12th, I wrote in my *Diaries*: "I believe in the

212

Holy Ghost and Spirit – it comes into me like sap into a tree and gives me faith to solve the next problem, the God in me....I believe in the force and in the teachings of Christ and in the necessity of the Church as a reminder, but I do not believe in the doctrine (divinity of Christ) or the Church (I did not go over Easter, and the Church has as much to do with my force as 33 Stanhope Gardens... – ditto the Pope and the Archbishop of Canterbury)....The divine will tells me that the Church does not represent God, and I have faith in it: there must be a reform in the Church before it can represent the force – that is what It is telling me. So I am in the tradition of Luther and Protestant reform? But – my dilemma – I have accepted so much, can I not accept the Church? Can I not die away from my pride and 'I' into the Church? Am I not feeling 'I want...,I want the Church to be uncorrupt'? If I leave 'I want' out of it, can I not accept the Church?...Just as hem lines change, the Church's presentation changes through decades, though the force is eternal....God...is changeless,...the Church...is changeable....My existentialism: I acknowledge the Force that is God as an experience, and I acknowledge the teaching of Christ as an experience also....Only the pure in heart can see God....The Father, the Son and the Holy Ghost....I know about the Holy Ghost. Is the Son the 'time' part of me – the Reflection – which must die, and is the Father the eternal part of me – the Shadow?...I am on a strange Way of Christ. Kempis 1972 style."

For about a week I had prepared for my move to 33 Stanhope Gardens. I had collected my possessions and books together in Essex and had cleaned and hoovered my new flat, washed the skirting and swept the stairs. On my last night in my room in 13 Egerton Gardens I stared at the ceiling for a long time, trying to decipher the pattern that I had always referred to as chains, and I said aloud: "It's a diamond....No, a Maltese cross. My monastic cell with a Maltese cross on the ceiling, hidden by chains."

I moved into my new flat and spent the first afternoon projecting my vision onto the walls. Being at the top of the house, the flat had a red ladder on the wall above the stairs that led up from the flat's front door, to comply with local authority fire regulations. Over one end I hung my Tibetan thanka of "the Devil" (a blue ape-like god – Yamantaka, conqueror of death – clutching several women) and at the other end high up near the skylight, I hung another treasure, my Tibetan mandala 400 years old, a round orb in gold work that suggested the halo of the Inner Light. Next to this I hung a photograph of a sun halo from the outer world. I was obsessed by circles, and I covered my bedroom walls with pictures of rose-windows, and with views into the deepest orbs of domes.

At twilight I ate peacefully at the dining-table and looked across Chelsea at the lights in dusky windows. Quietly I felt God enfold me. I sat rigid for a while, then stood up and left Ann, went through to my bedroom and lay on my bed in the dark and murmured with my hands over my eyes, "Oh God, I've surrendered Nadia, you've taken Nadia, come into me," and soon I was breathing slowly and deeply, possessed, in union. After perhaps a quarter of an hour my breathing became heavy and reached a kind of sighing climax. Feeling thirsty, I put out a hand for the pewter beer mug I had been drinking from, and God began to slip away. As my body recovered its sensation I felt satisfied behind my lungs. I felt as though a voice had said, "Your loss of

Nadia is not in vain, I will give you greatness," and my eyes were so nearly filled with tears that I could not go through to Ann for several minutes.

I recorded this experience in my *Diaries*: "I am aglow with the mystic Fire....Now I feel full of mystic fire....God came into me and I had to be alone. I turned out the light and lay on the bed and said to myself 'Oh God, I've surrendered Nadia – you've taken Nadia – come into me.' And now I feel full of this power, this strengthening inside my lungs....God came into me. I was totally relaxed breathing deeply, feeling union – *it* possessing *me* – *he*? Then, feeling temporarily thirsty, I reached for my beer, and almost in reproof he started slipping away....God said to me: 'Your loss of Nadia is not in vain.' And my eyes filled with tears, which I could hardly hide from Ann in the sitting-room." Two days later, on 19th April, I wrote in my *Diaries*: "I feel like St. Paul – after reading passages from St. Augustine and St. Gregory in Dom Cuthbert Butler's *Western Mysticism*. Both speak of the inner Light as the aim of mysticism, as God, as Being which is unchangeable, and here I am; I have it – have had it what? Some twenty times since September? No wonder Margaret went off and prayed, no wonder the priest said he had never come across it before. Here I am, having had the experience they write about but have not had....Here I am totally unknown....The drop back into the workaday world. 'Not the height but the drop is terrible'!...Contemplative and active lives. I am like St. Augustine. Go back to him, re-read his 'Light'. I am a latter-day Augustine. 'Rapture' is being snatched up."

After that quite abruptly, I stopped going out. I never went to the Markham or felt the need for variety in women, I even drank less beer. Instead I sat in my window at my leather-covered, antique desk and looked down at the new plane tree beneath me, behind which, like a heart, was hidden a pure white magnolia. I drank gunpowder tea and pottered among my old papers and possessions, rooting myself and paring them down, and I was again snatched by God, this time while finishing a Saturday lunch beside Ann on April 22nd. Looking out over Chelsea, and feeling the peace rising up around me and enfolding me, I put down my spoon, pushed back my chair and sat cross-legged, hands clasped. Soon I was breathing deeply and sinking into a trance that made me rigid, so that I felt no discomfort in what would ordinarily have been an uncomfortable position, and as I sank deeper I saw a wonderful pale blue light that blended with a dazzling white light like a diamond shining in the sun. I sighed in ecstasy as if I were climaxing. Stiffly I walked through to my bedroom and lay on the bed and the light came and went again, only more faintly this time. I came slowly out of my trance. For the rest of that day I felt very creative, very alive, full of intimations of inner power.

I recorded this experience in my *Diaries*: "The second time this week I have been 'rapt' – snatched by God. Again I was sitting at my sitting-room table, looking down on the world beneath me, and again I felt an immense well-being come over me. Everything was good, I felt contented – at peace. Happiness was the wrong word, though I felt happy too. Then I felt it coming up from underneath and filling me, and soon – even though Ann was sitting there – I was breathing deeply and sinking into a kind of trance. I closed my eyes and could not move – sat absurdly cross-legged and hands clasped, in discomfort I did not feel – and as I sank deeper – glory! Inside as at a sexual coming, there was a glorious light blue light that blended with a dazzling white light of much greater circumference than I have ever seen before – almost like a diamond shining in the sun. It was not with me for long, but I went and lay down on my bed and the light came and went, faintly, again, and then I came slowly out of the trance. I had not felt my body at all, for about 45 minutes, and now I finished my pudding: raspberry fool. As the sensation of my body flowed back into me, it filled my penis, and I had an urge to make love....This must have been between 2 and 3.15. Now it is nearly 8....I feel very creative, very alive, full of distant intimations of the power. At peace. Today has been a day of extremes: sending a telex message to Brussels through the GPO, then looking on the face of God – for that is without doubt what happened at lunch this afternoon."

I had another visitation a few days later, on April 28th, which somehow taught me the meaning of divine love. It followed two days of sadness. After a long silence from Lincolnshire Caroline had written to cancel a long-standing arrangement that I would spend a whole weekend with Nadia. Instead I would just have a Saturday afternoon. As if to help me through my sorrow, the presence revealed itself again on the Friday evening, and I was already in a trance when Ann arrived. Realising what was up, she sat in a sensitive quietness while my breathing slowed and my fingers locked so that I again could not hold a spoon without difficulty. I closed my eyes and wandered into my bedroom and actually got into bed. The white light came up with blue tints, and I had the distinct, ecstatic feeling that I was about to witness the appearance of God illuminated, and I felt an ecstasy grow in me. I began to catch my breath and the white light grew brighter and bigger and brighter. Suddenly, there was a round halo before my closed eyes, like a hoop of light, exactly the same as the sun-halo I had pinned near my Tibetan mandala. I gave a gasp and fell away, feeling I had made love, glassy-eyed, peaceful, happy, no longer rigid, my penis swelling. I said afterwards: "The love of God is a physical thing, I didn't know what it meant until this minute." It was then shortly after 10 p.m.

Again I recorded the experience in my *Diaries*: "God came again – a third time over my meal. I sank into a trance and was at the centre of the world outside – above and below the traffic sounds, at the centre. I slowly sank into Him. My breathing got slower, I could hardly move my spoon, my eyes closed. Ann had just arrived and noticed I did not want to be touched. She sat in sensitive quietness. I came through to this bedroom and got into bed and the white light came up with blue tints. God illumined was about to come into me...It came back, a force of love. God is Love. I felt the ecstasy grow in me, then my breath caught as the white light grew brighter and suddenly, there was a round halo inside me, a thin halo like the picture I'm putting over my mandala – a sun-halo – and I had 'made love'. I fell away, turned over, no longer rigid, and now I feel as if I have made love: glassy-eyed, peaceful and happy....I know: God is Love. The love of God is a physical thing."

The next day I had my Saturday afternoon with Nadia. I drove to Horncastle Market Square and received Nadia from Caroline and David, who was in RAF uniform. I drove her to her new school and had a chance meeting with the Head, who walked me round even though it was a Saturday. I lingered in her classroom and then took her to lunch at the Magpie. Nadia chattered happily about her new life: about how her flat was in Lady Maitland's grounds, how she played with Lady Maitland's 12 grandchildren when they were home and helped Mr Knight the gardener plant the seedlings. Sometimes she walked up the road to a neighbouring farm for eggs, and saw hares and pheasants. Once she had woken out of a nightmare at 3 a.m. with the wind moaning and the window clattering, and "you weren't there", but otherwise nothing had been wrong. She seemed very natural, and after lunch we drove to Skegness and found a fair on the front, and she rode on a merry-go-round horse and then went on the big wheel. I got into the float with her and for five minutes gripped the belt of her raincoat in sick tension while we soared up to sixty feet and down again. Afterwards we walked over a dune to the deserted yellow sand. The sea was a quarter of a mile away, under a squally sky, and Nadia ran off until she was a mite crouching over some oyster shells. It began to drizzle and I watched how she was utterly involved in the present.

I was supposed to return her to Horncastle Market Square, but I knew that Harrington Hall, in whose grounds Nadia was living, was the Hall and garden where Tennyson had set *Maud*, which contained the lines I had wrongly attributed to St. Paul on Malta and which Caroline had wanted to write down: "And ah for a man to arise in me,/That the man I am may cease to be!" I also knew that by one of those strange coincidences which makes me see a Providential pattern in the sequence of events that contains my story, the Maitlands who lived at Harrington Hall were the Maitlands, formerly of Loughton Hall, who had sold Journey's End to my father. Now Sir John and Lady Maitland, they had let a garden flat to Caroline, her new husband and Nadia. My curiosity got the better of me, and, having stopped at a garage which gave us directions, we were soon on a winding lane in deep countryside. Then Nadia gave a shout: "Look, here's where I walk for eggs, I live just down there." And, looking across hedges and green fields, I saw the Hall's massive and splendidly ancient grey facade, with its umpteen windows and a line of cars in the great drive. Nadia directed me through great iron gates to the flat over the garage, and she was immediately out of the car and knee deep in the bank of daffodils, "finding leaves to weave into a Palm Sunday cross". I stood among the daffodils and quoted:

> "Come into the garden, Maud,
> For the black bat, night, has flown,
> Come into the garden, Maud,
> I am here at the gate alone."

And at that moment Caroline and David appeared in the drive. They were setting off to meet me in Horncastle, and were evidently taken aback that I had discovered their hiding-place. We all stood and talked briefly in light rain. Then way back at the Hall the front door opened and three tiny figures emerged by the parked cars. Caroline said, "You'll have to move, you're blocking the drive." I went over to the daffodil bank and kissed Nadia, who was totally absorbed in the leaves. Then I got back into the car. From up the drive Lady Maitland's cortège hissed on the gravel. Abruptly I reversed out of the gates.

The four visions of 8th, 17th, 22nd and 28th April became poems: *Visions: Raid on the Gold Mine*; *The Furnace*; *Vision: Snatched by God, A Blue Light;* and *Vision: Love like a Grid*. I was becoming strong enough to bear this new, difficult phase of my recovery. I was on the mend. In Essex Argie remarked to Ann while picking rhubarb, "Nick has looked so much better since he got his flat."

I now found an increasing sense of meaning. In May I took Ann out to Essex again. The woods were full of chestnut candles and bluebells, and I rejoiced in the may. I felt I had unified myself and wrote in my *Diaries*: "I am me, like a great tree I have several branches, all of which are me. My sap can put out leaves in poetry, journalism, novels, politics, teaching, religion, etc. I am like the great plane tree outside my window, and Nadia is the magnolia white and pure, hidden behind it. Or, I am like the chestnut tree, full of candles, each one an illumination." In London I planted a window-box of red geraniums, and on May 7th wrote: "Soon God will come into me. I can feel the presence of the force near at hand." The next day I thrilled to a blackbird singing in the trees in Stanhope Gardens.

Soon afterwards I took the boys to Southwark Cathedral and gazed at the saints behind the altar, which included St. Augustine of Hippo; the tombs of John Gower and Lancelot Andrewes; and the 15th century bosses on the ceiling which showed the medieval faces of Gluttony and Lying. I wrote in my *Diaries*: "The Church stands for real things: it connects me with past generations that have sought real things....It is there, like a supermarket for one who wants food – like a bad supermarket, but the only one available for what I want. The Silence, the Illumination, the only other place I can see pictures of these and be reminded of them is the National Gallery. It is a memory, a reminder. If I were in the East, I would go to the Zen temple. I am in the West, so accept what the Church can give....The Church has lost its health. The deep spiritual vision that colours the sides of a church has largely been lost....I accept the ideal of the Church – what it should be, and what it once was and what it should get back to – but I do not accept the reality, the meaningless service, etc. So when I visit the Church...it is the ideal I think of – the presence of Silence and Illumination – and not of the reality of what it is doing in the world of time."

A few days later I heard a sermon on *John 4.14:* "The water that I shall give him will be an inner spring always welling up for eternal life." The preacher said: "The churches are centres that are supposed to hold spiritual water which is an inner spring to the soul of men." But I knew this was an error, for we hold it in ourselves, and the churches merely encourage it. I bewailed the emptiness at the heart of our generation. On 15th May I wrote: "The Church...is the world of eternity, the house of selflessness, outside which you leave behind 'I, I, I', in which you are clean – the world of eternity – and not the world of time. It is the place where you don't ask why, you accept. It is always the same in essentials (*I* change) so it should not be changed – for the service links me to the line of the ages. The spring should not be in I and I alone, for the 'law of God' is larger than I – the fact that it came up in *me* means it has come up in thousands of others, so it must be seen from the point of view of the Great Flow. All life. The Church is the place set aside to commemorate the working from the point of view of the Whole. Don't see from the point of view of one seed/I but from the point of view of the Whole. Detachment, not involvement....To go to church is to see from the point of view of the Whole, i.e. feel the congregation (as the Whole) over against 'I'....The spring is in the soul of everyone – see from the point of view of the Whole. The Church is only as good as the people in it, so restore the spring in everyone's soul through the Church ('a well' – the sense of a collective spring)."

I was in a spiritual crisis. I had thought myself into a feverish state of mind and I had made myself ill. I wrote: "I have great swollen glands and a sore throat." I had dark melancholic thoughts and a nightmare about Nadia. On May 17th I had some sort of attack in Cliveden Place, near Sloane Square. I was driving back from school with Ann and felt ill. I couldn't breathe and felt peculiar. I felt myself blacking out. There was a singing in my ears, everything rippled away into remoteness, there was a twisting pain in my heart and pressure on my skull which I connected with my spine. I stopped the car and got out, and, thinking I was about to die, walked about. I was shaking and felt breathless. I drove to a doctor, and a second attack began as I waited in the waiting room. I was trembling and shaking and gasping. A doctor laid me on an examination bed and examined me. He said: "It's not a heart attack but exhaustion, strain. It's a warning, a finger from Heaven. You've been doing too much." I immediately grasped that my four April visions had left me with psychological wear-and-tear. The doctor prescribed equanil. The next day there were more heart pains, and I visited my own doctor. He wanted to know what was causing my "overtiredness and overstrain", and he sent me for a check-up at St. Stephen's Hospital, which confirmed the diagnosis of the first doctor.

The Mystic Way is full of instances of the swing back from Light to Darkness through exhaustion. My attacks had done something to my nerves, and I started to shake abominably. My hand shook. Two days later I still felt shaky.

At the end of May I spent five days in Brussels attending a conference on the African liberation movements. It was a relatively high level conference with many governmental ministers and leaders of movements, and of course Church leaders such as Bishop Colin Winter, and I had a lot of interviewing to do for my articles. It was good for me to be able to recuperate in the outer world and to have a respite from further raptures which would have increased my inner exhaustion. I found the time very therapeutic, it was an escape from inner tension. I teamed up with the BBC representative, Michael Popham, who left a trail of hilarity. In the lift he told a particularly funny story about Lord Caradon (then UK Representative to the UN) and the lift stopped in mid-story, and in walked Lord Caradon. We both went to interview the Action Commission and found one man snoozing and no one else there. We were the court jesters. Everyone wanted to be interviewed, and Popham was permanently in the corridors, sound equipment hugely bulky on his back, earphones over his ears, holding a microphone under some important man's nose, his eyes meeting mine in irreverent, unspoken attitudes. He had them queuing to be recorded, and as fast as he finished with one I took over with my reporter's pad. Among my dozens of interviewees I remember interviewing Krishna Menon of India; the Secretary-General of the OAU; and by special appointment at the Hotel Metropole, the Foreign Minister of Tanzania, John Malecela, who invited me to go to Tanzania in the autumn and write articles, if the *Times* would be interested in sending me.

That summer I was involved with the Rhodesians, the various factions of the ANC, ZAPU and ZANU who were seeking to take over the emerging Zimbabwe. I met Bishop Muzorewa at a drinks party given by a Lord, and got to know his deputy, the Rev. Canaan Banana, who invited me back to his bedsit and sat on the edge of his bed in his socks and told me how the ANC would take over Zimbabwe. There was a deputation of four Zimbabweans to the Foreign Office, and as they had no transport they asked me to collect them, which I did, from outside the British Foreign Secretary's door. I drove them away in my green Volkswagen "Saturnalia".

At the beginning of June I took Ann up to Lincolnshire. We put up at the George, Horncastle and took Nadia out. Later that evening we were invited to Harrington Hall, and I had the new experience of sitting opposite Caroline among her old rugs, books and pictures. The next day, we drove round Tennyson country and visited the Old Rectory, Tennyson's birthplace. We all had a drink in a pub with a garden, where Nadia played, and then we all went for a walk in some woods that were full of sunshine and bluebells. Caroline and David walked ahead, sometimes holding hands, and we walked behind with Nadia, listening to the flowing call of the cuckoo. I was not attached, I felt free of the past.

The next week I took my ESN boys to All Hallows, which is on the Thames estuary. A new teacher, Jean, who had a prominent chest and a high mini-skirt and long dark hair, came with me, and (as in the school playground) wherever she went the boys swarmed round her like bees round a honeypot. The boys caught crabs and tried to pull their legs off. I spent a long time looking out to where the river becomes the sea.

In June I heard from the permanent people in my life. I had a card from Tuohy in Australia: a Flemish tapestry of a unicorn being killed by hunters. I knew he saw the unicorn as representing the artist; fabled to live for 1,000 years and the noblest of animals, it had the softness of Christ. I met Ricky, who said to me in the Denmark: "Your 'eternal side' is very Wordsworthian – 'a dim and undetermined sense/Of unknown modes of being' and 'A spirit that rolls through all things'." As usual he talked about Goethe's Faust's "solution by action". I saw John Ezard, who urged me to get my poems published, to which I countered from Pound's *Mauberley*:

> "The age demanded an image
> Of its accelerated grimace....
> Not, not certainly, the obscure reveries
> Of the inward gaze."

I was saying that the Age is wrong for my work, that (to paraphrase Hamlet) the time is out of joint. I said we were living in a time in which the soul has collapsed, and the Age demands meaninglessness such as Francis Bacon gave it, not images of soulful meaning which the true artist produces, saying that "there are more things in heaven and earth, Horatio,/Than are dreamt of in your philosophy" – and is then hunted and killed for his pains like the unicorn.

In early July Nadia came. I took her down into the Gardens beneath my window and we went for a walk round the white magnolia. I sat opposite her on the see-saw and pushed her on the swing, and she ran boisterously and hid behind a rose bush. I heard about her school and she reminisced about Libya. When I returned her to Dulwich, Caroline came to the gate in a maroon velvety dress, nursing a swollen belly. She tried to hide her pregnancy. I said nothing.

The next day I met Ricky and I approached meaning. I recorded our discussion in my *Diaries*: "By the Socratic method, I got him to agree that in Nishiwaki's words, $(+ A) + (-A) = O$. He wanted the negative Beckett way and the positive Faustian way substituted in the first side of the equation, but after careful questioning finally conceded that it was: the World of Time (Beckett and Faust representing different aspects) + the World of Eternity = the Whole, i.e. that time and eternity are in an indivisible unity, a synthesis. Cf Blake, 'Eternity is in love with the productions of time.' So it is not pain *versus* joy, but pain *plus* joy – so Colin Wilson is to that extent wrong. Ditto Sartre (Being *versus* Nothingness). There is life, and so there must be death – for without death there could not be life. One cannot find a meaning in the world of language (which is time), the world of eternity has no language. The Whole is therefore indescribable, and one should not explain to Faust. Everything is opposites, cf Pascal. So Beckett is wrong, for there is neither the pessimistic nor the simple Christian optimistic, but both together – this life is important....Life is a unity formed of a dialectic that is eternal."

I went back to my flat and pondered my insight. My lost family, and my inner peace – the two were contradictory. Pondering on my mixed feelings, I felt again that life is an eternal dialectic between misery and joy, despair and hope, the world of time and the world of eternity. There would be a thousand agonies ahead, but there would also be perhaps fifty joys, and the opposites could not be understood in terms of each other. They had to be seen as parts of a greater whole. Or, as Nishiwaki had told me in a shabby restaurant with sawdust on the floor, $(+ A) + (- A) = 0$. "Zero,...Great Nothing."

Immediately, I was trembling on the verge of a great insight. Life's mysteries suddenly fell away. There was plus *and* minus, time *and* eternity, life *and* death: they were necessary to each other, there could not be one without the other. But it was the whole unity that gave the meaning. I looked out at the Gardens, and my reasoning gave way to existential perception. Then I saw a postcard that Nadia had left on the bed, of the Zen Ryoanji Stone Garden. (She had brought it with her, and years later it appeared on the back of my *Selected Poems*.) It showed pebbles round three rocks, and I already knew that it could be interpreted as earth or clouds and mountains; or as sea or sand and rocks. All stones were parts of one stone, and in the same way, all existence came down to a unity that was infinite. I looked back at the Gardens. The foliage of the great plane-trees obscured the white magnolia, and I felt a hint of a similarity. All the many trees and plants and crawling things in the earth came down to a unity.

Suddenly everything was blindingly clear. The Gardens were like a *spring*, a spring of leaves and seeds, a teeming, abundant, never-ending flow of opposites that went on gushing from nowhere, like the bubbles that wobbled up for thousands of years from the Saharan spring. All life was a spring from a void, a spring of water, of seeds, of creatures, of people, of words.

In an instant, I grasped the meaning of life for the first time. Seizing my pen I wrote in frenzied haste: "If I look at a Chinese character it has significance. If I understand Chinese, it has meaning. If I look at the Stone Garden, it has significance. If I understand the idea of unity, it has meaning. So it is of life. If I look at the world it has significance. If I feel the flow in it, it has meaning. Wordsworth sees the ideogram and describes it, but does not give us its meaning. He doesn't know it, he guesses at it....Tao, the Void, produced the One which produced multiplicity. The Void, negative and fertile, is the spring." Significance was a two-way relationship; meaning had a third dimension concealed within it. To see the world truly, the ego and the reason must both die. Now I knew: all images have meaning, all images teem from the Great Meaning, the One which is also a Great Nothing, a fertile Void.

Then I felt very deeply that the miseries and joys were all reconciled in the Great Spring that flowed through everything and which would gush opposites and contradictions for thousands of years to come. I realised that to that fountain of abundance there was no difference between Caroline and myself, between Caroline's unborn child and Nadia. I felt I should rejoice as much as grieve at Caroline's pregnancy. One person was miserable, another joyful, there could not be one without the other. So, being parts of the same, misery and joy were ultimately the same. In my own life I would still feel a thousand griefs, but I was sure there would continue to be joys. But now I felt the griefs would not have the same hold over me, I would be free of them. And as for my raptures, I felt they would be unions with the One, I would know what was going on now. I felt I would live in the peace which passeth all understanding, largely beyond emotions. I felt that a part of me belonged to the whole. And though I had no idea what might happen to me when I died, I believed so instinctively in the importance of the Great Spring that I did not think it impossible that my "eternal self" might survive in it, in some form. That, however, was mere speculation. What mattered immediately was that I had escaped the chains of emotion and self, I could fulfil my destiny. I felt I could go no further in my inner life for the time being. I had found.

I symbolised what I had found in Ann's birthday present. I gave her an onyx marble egg from Italy, which was like the Chinese Taoist eggs I had seen in Peking. The egg was an image of the One with many opposite lines and colours, wavy lines of the sea, the furrowed earth, clouds and contours, and somewhere, it contained the fleck of a seed, an egg, a mountain top.

The egg symbolised the universe, reality, a heart, though only he who has eyes to see could see it. The egg reflected the world from its centre. It united time and eternity, now and forever.

The school holidays began. In July Nadia came and I took her to the museums and she played in the Gardens. I drove her back to Peterborough and handed her over at the Great Northern Hotel.

My trip to Tanzania was scheduled for September, and I went to the Tanzanian High Commission to obtain a visa and met a coal black Tanzanian in an immaculate suit who turned out to be Pitakabisa, whose room I took over at Worcester College in early 1959. We talked about old times, and he took me to a restaurant in Jermyn Street.

In August I took the train to Cornwall and spent three days with Ann and her mother, who lived in a bungalow on the outskirts of St. Austell, a mile and a half from Charlestown. Ann's late father's car was still in the garage, and the first evening she drove me to Charlestown, a 1790s village which was still a working harbour with a dock and china clay shoots. We went on to Portmellon and we drank at the Rising Sun by the watersplash, where I told Colin Wilson in January 1961: "I shall become a wanderer for ten years." It was like a homecoming, I felt I had returned. We drove to the end of Colin Wilson's lane, where there was a forbidding notice: "No Visitors Unless by Appointment." We came back via Porthpean, where the stars were very bright and we identified the Pole Star and the Plough. The next day we spent roasting in the sun on Charlestown beach under the Harbourmaster's House, and watching crabs like armoured tanks in a large rock pool. We went on to Carlyon Bay where waves boomed in the caves beneath and gulls shrieked round the gorse points. We lay on the cliff tops where bees hummed in the wild flowers and the sea sparkled. In the evening we went to Fowey and walked through the tiny streets and took the ferry to Polruan, a village you might find on the French Riviera, set on a hill. It grew dark as we returned, and the sea was black and silver.

When I got back to London, Nadia came to stay again and I felt ill and recorded in my *Diaries*: "Giddy, as though I am about to faint. Overwork....ever since I had these experiences of God my psychic life has been brittle, liable to break at any time, so that I can no longer push myself as far as I used to. Now I have to recognise limits....1972 is above all the year of ill health for me. When I found, when I ended my search, when my health began to suffer after all the demands I have made on my nervous system."

I took Nadia to Worthing again so she could stay at Sompting Abbots. I again stayed at the Anchorage, which now had a swimming-pool. I visited the rose garden in Sompting church, and saw each rose as a living rooted person. I took Nadia back to Peterborough.

Back in London I wrote in my *Diaries*: "God is a Way of Life behind the level of Flow that runs through all life, which unites me to all life."

At the beginning of September I suddenly and impulsively decided to stop drinking alcohol. I wrote in my *Diaries*: "Something inside me tells me to stop drinking, to go on to soft drinks. It will leave me mentally fresh for the great work ahead; lengthen my evening – help me to work in the evenings; rid me of a dependency, like cigarettes – mark another chain broken and help me to freedom from craving; prevent me from becoming ill....Drink occasionally. But not regularly. The purposive life....Drinking... is a left over from marital strains and break-up....Have a revolution against yourself." I implemented this decision and actually did stop drinking alcohol. This decision was a further consequence of my illumination and four April visions, and marked a further purgation, a further cleansing of the spirit and detachment of it from the senses.

I had had a telex from Tanzania to say I must be in Dar es Salaam by September 14th. The Welsh Head, Mr Macho, had left Riverway, and I now had the embarrassing task of visiting the new Head at his house in SE9 and explaining that I needed to be released from school for two to three weeks at the beginning of the new academic year. The new Head, Mr Wright, turned out to be a shambling, stooping man of between 50 and 60 in spectacles. He encouraged me to go to Tanzania.

About this time as I drove my green Volkswagen in the Cromwell Road I passed the right wing MP Biggs-Davison walking slowly. I stopped and wound the window down and called to him "Want a lift?" He said he was going to the Brompton Oratory, where he prayed while living in Hereford Square. I told him I was going to have a look at Tanzania. As I put him down outside the Oratory he asked rather disparagingly, "Are you taking this car to Tanzania?"

I left for Tanzania on September 10th, having bought suitably tropical clothes. Pitakabisa came to the airport to see me off, and I flew through the night non-stop to Nairobi, coming down in an orange dawn. We flew on to Mombasa past Mount Kilimanjaro, a black blancmange with icing on the top. Mombasa was sticky and an orange bird sang from a giant tree. We flew on over beautiful Indian Ocean islands and arrived at Dar es Salaam, where I was met and driven to the Twiga Hotel in Independence Avenue.

Dar es Salaam (which means "haven of peace") is really an arched yellow and white village on the coast with a lot of trees (coconut and mango) and its outskirts merge with the surrounding bush and contain encampments and little markets in rural settings. My chauffeur drove me around and the first day (after a lot of waiting about) I interviewed the Foreign Minister at length. He wore a round-necked, collarless, short-sleeved top. I grasped that Tanzania was virtually bankrupt and tried to get money out of all comers while being intensely proud and independent, and having got the Chinese to build the Tanzam railway, was trying to winkle further money out of the West; hence their invitation to me. I was then taken to the Gymkhana, an ex-colonial club on the sea. I spent a couple of days touring the bush in a TANU landrover, visiting ujamaas (literally "families"), co-operative or collective farms run on socialist principles which looked like glorified allotments. Here Africans planted crops and shared them out according to the work they put in. They were mainly fields of head-high sisal and maize. I spoke with local TANU officials and saw how the Party controlled the villages. We visited clearings with thatched huts, at one of which the local witch-doctor came and greeted me, shaking his bones. We then flew up to Tanga, which is on the Tanzanian-Kenyan border, and I did the same there. I was looked after by an African official who took me out drinking in the evening.

Back in Dar I interviewed leaders of liberation movements based there: representatives of the OAU, ANC, PAC, FROLIZI, FRELIMO, MPLA, PAIGC and Sam Nujoma of SWAPO. Most memorably, I went for an hour-long walk with the two Rhodesian leaders of ZANU and ZAPU, Herbert Chitepo and Jason Moyo who together formed the Patriotic Front that had been responsible for several explosions and deaths inside Rhodesia. I walked in the middle with the bespectacled Chitepo on one side and the tall, lean Moyo on the other side and asked them whether they did not feel responsible for the deaths they had caused and what it was like living on the run. I found them both highly articulate and polite. Both were murdered not long afterwards, Chitepo when his landrover blew up.

I flew to Zanzibar with a party of Scandinavian journalists, and we were driven through palms straight to the headquarters of the Afro-Shirazi Party (ASP) for a meeting with Aboud Jumbe, Zanzibar's President. We were seated on either side of a long table. I was nearest the chair at the end, in which, under a picture of the former leader Karume, Jumbe sat in a white shirt and throat scarf, with four armed guards in berets behind him (the format Gaddafi had used) and officers in peaked caps, and after a halting but rational account of how he had taken over following the murder of Sheikh Karume at the ASP headquarters he invited questions. I had my tape-recorder on the table in front of me, and I asked the first question: "Who killed Karume?" There was a stunned silence. Jumbe said "Er, um, um, I don't know," and gave a lengthy but vague reply. After Jumbe had left tea was served and the Attorney-General approached me, a young man of about 40. "I was educated at Oxford," he said. "You were very brave. Your question is one that no one in Zanzibar would dare to ask. It is rumoured that Jumbe himself killed Karume." And I realised that it was as if I had asked Macbeth who killed Duncan. Later we went for a complete tour of the island, looking at the clove harvest and cigarette, shoe and sugar factories, and lingering in the slave market where in past centuries Africans were sold as slaves, and where I freely interviewed on tape anybody who would stop and talk. We returned to our Hotel to eat and I left my equipment in my room, and when I returned I found all my tapes had been wiped.

Back in Dar I was taken with the Scandinavian journalists to meet President Nyerere in a house on the outskirts. It had a view of the sea across gardens, and we sat on the veranda in the open air. Nyerere talked to us gravely and impressively, against a background of wild animal sounds and a screaming peacock. Relevant Ministers sat alongside him, and he condemned President Amin of Uganda, whose planes had attacked a border town in Tanzania. Then he asked "Any questions?" I asked, "Can I go to the Chinese railway and see the new section between Mlimba and Makumbako?" Nyerere said, "Er, um, er, I don't know," and conferred with his Ministers. Later that afternoon I was rung up by the Ministry of Information and asked if I wanted to go and see the village Amin's planes had bombed, but I said: "I'd rather go and see the Chinese railway." The next day I was told, "You can go this afternoon but you must travel by landrover with an Australian television crew." And so it was that I met a silver-haired John Temple and his two Australian colleagues and set off with them and a driver for Iringa, where we spent the night at an inn near blue jacaranda trees.

The single-track 1,150 mile long Tanzam railway from Dar es Salaam harbour to Kapiri Mposhi was central to the Tanzanian economy. China was lending money for it, and repayment would be spread over 30 years from 1983. The second phase covered the 98 miles between Mlimba and Makumbako, where the difficulties included broken escarpments in the low plains of the Kilombero valley and mountains as high as 6,000 feet, and the railway had to cross precipitous ravines and quagmires and go through 18 tunnels, one half a mile long. Mountain springs poured through some tunnel roofs.

We arrived at Lugema base camp around midday, and had a Chinese lunch washed down with a lot of beer. I gathered there was a more relaxed attitude to drinking than I had found during my visit to China in 1966. We visited the Great Ruaha bridge which was built in 89 days, and watched a crane hoist wooden sleepers to a posse of bustling men. We then went to Uchindile bridge, at one end of which the Chinese had moved a mountain. Two hundred African and Chinese workers swarmed over the base of the mountain like flies on a great Pyramid, cementing concrete slabs on the sloping earthwork walls with great urgency. Wherever I walked the Chinese took great pride in telling me they had conquered the environment. They had a kind of ant-mentality: they were proud to be part of a collective effort, to be tiny scurrying ants on a dwarfing mountainside.

We spent that night in a mud hut in a Chinese camp at Mkera, near Mlimba. We ate and drank beer with the Chinese, and then all night I tossed and turned on a wooden board with enormous mosquito nets draped all round – I was taking anti-malaria tablets – and when I dropped off I dreamt that Caroline and Nadia had returned to me. I woke to the cold reality of a bush dawn and the Chinese doing exercises near the ablutions, which were a stagnant shallow lake with a great fetid stench.

That morning we walked through tunnel 13, which still leaked a ton of spring water a day at the exit, squashing against the wall as the train trundled through. Stepping from sleeper to sleeper we trudged a mile between two mountains past several groups of Africans working flat out, and inspected the highest bridge, no 25, which balanced on two columns, 150 feet high. We found track-laying in progress near Irangi. Most of the stone-laying had been done, and the tracks were laid at a rate of about two miles a day. A great tracklaying machine suspended a length of railway line against the hot sun and lowered it towards the causeway of stones. A Chinese in a blue suit and a yellow coolie hat blew a whistle and waved a flag and 30 African workmen prised it into place with levers and others flicked nuts on bolts. Then with a hoot and a roar the tracklaying machine edged forward and hoisted another length of line from its back and ran it along a girder so it hung in mid-air.

We spent that night in Iringa, and next morning picked up the Assistant Superintendent of the local police as an escort and the six of us – our driver, the three Australians, me and the policeman – all headed off in the landrover to a local National Park: the Mikumi National Park. In the course of the day we saw lion, elephant, hippopotamus, leopard, cheetah, giraffe, zebra, impala, wildebeest and warthog.

It was extremely hot, and as the day progressed it was clear that our policeman was ill. He actually suffered from malaria, and halfway through our tour he retired to the back of the landrover and lay down, feverish and shivering and sweating. We stopped in an open part of the bush near two trees which threw little pools of shade, in one of which two yards away lay a huge lion with a great mane. At that moment the malarial policeman sat up and shouted "Tsetse, tsetse", pointing at the ceiling of the landrover. And there, yellowish brown, wings folded back, upside down, sat a tsetse fly, known a century ago as the white man's grave. I froze. As if in some awful Zen koan I had a choice: to leave the landrover and be eaten by a lion, or stay in and catch sleeping sickness from the bloodsucking bite of the tsetse fly. I chose to stay in, reckoning that sleeping sickness is preferable to being mauled. For a quarter of an hour we stayed still, loathing to disturb the tsetse fly by starting our engine, and eventually the driver and policeman swatted and squashed the fly just above my head and we could then move on.

Back in Dar again, I was bored. The Minister of Information gave a dinner and sat next to me, questioning me about all I had done and the people I had met. I spent a day or two waiting around to meet the Foreign Minister, Malecela, again. He was away on a trip and I was driven to the airport to meet him and we had a chat in a waiting-room about what I had seen. We agreed my visit had come to an end, and I flew out the next day. I had to kill several hours in Nairobi, and left the airport with a journalist who spoke to me. It turned out to be Murray Sayle, whose articles I had read. We shared a taxi and went round Nairobi together, stopping at various bars he knew and looking at the government buildings.

I was weary when I got back to London, but I felt I had "seen" Africa very clearly. Essentially Tanzania's policy was "Africa first". Tanzania wanted freedom, independence and self-reliance, but needed aid, arms and the railway. Tanzania was afraid of becoming too dependent on China and wanted to turn away from China to the West. In my articles for the *Times* Features page and the *Guardian* I was able to present this view with some clarity, and it was taken up at high level: Sir Alec Douglas-Home, the British Foreign Secretary, visited Dar and offered some British money, and Edward Heath, the Prime Minister, was set to go, but cancelled at the last minute. I had made possible an increase in British influence in Eastern Africa.

Tanzania marked a turning-point for me. The ESN school was now an anti-climax, and I was bored. At the same time I felt I had escaped from feeling into action – the temptation that destroyed some of the Romantic poets and their successors, notably Byron and Rimbaud – and that I should now wind down my journalism and return to contemplation and poetry.

This feeling took a couple of months to implement as I wrote my articles and discharged the aftermath of Tanzania and paid some outstanding bills.

This was still continuing on October 25th, when I appeared on the BBC World Service's live African Morning Show, and was interviewed by Pete Myers on the Tanzam railway. (Incredibly, Mike Popham from Brussels was providing sound effects for the interview before mine, making goon-like plopping noises and all but playing a comb and lavatory paper.) The following day I expressed my desire to withdraw from action to Beryl, a beautiful blonde with eyes as deep as pools who was at a Tanzanian gathering, and later I attended a party at 328A King's Road with the editor of *Africa Confidential*, Godfrey Morrison, and as we sat in a corner together he asked me for my opinion on the other dozen people there. Without thinking I went through all of them, pointing out who was having a relationship with who and what their activities were. At the end I said, "That leaves Mitsy and her Yugoslav lover over there." I had no evidence, but afterwards Godfrey Morrison said quietly, "You were right in every case," and again it seemed that following my illumination I had been given the power to look at a situation and see its underlying realities clearly; a kind of infused wisdom and knowledge which had come with the Light, and which I was to be aware of more in the future.

My heart was pushing through my work like a bloom through excessive foliage. I was now closer to Ann. In early October I found Epstein's Lost Pond again, which I associated with rediscovering my art in the dark wood of external events. Frank Tuohy came up for an evening and we discussed women and the possibility that I might re-marry. Caroline had given birth to a son while I was in Tanzania, and arrangements to see Nadia were now more fraught than usual. (It was suggested I had not been to Tanzania at all, but was making the whole trip up.) And then, on November 6th, I began writing poems again. I wrote in my *Diaries*: "Have started lyric poems....For the first time, now three years later, my grief has become sufficiently distant for me to ritualise it, to contemplate it without crying, merely feeling sad....I have found a subject. Write the fair copies in the green manuscript book in the order in which they are written, and type up the perfected copies....Write something every day....Get up at 6.30." And on 7th November: "Up at 6.30 a.m. today." The green manuscript book Caroline had bought me for my birthday in Libya at my request just before our marriage had broken up, and I thought my poems would be my equivalent to Tennyson's *In Memoriam*. They became *The Gates of Hell*, a title I based on Rodin's portal with three shades on top.

On November 10th I wrote in my *Diaries*: "This last week, from Monday to Friday (today) I have been up at 6.30 a.m. every day, and have consequently written 5 poems out of 100, and have done 5 stories....Now, the loneliness of being an artist. No drinking – I have given up alcohol. Clean senses. Feelings in the moment." A few days later I wrote: "100 pictures...of the same man, in different situations and from different angles. You get a picture of the whole." Shortly afterwards I spent a day with Nadia in Lincolnshire, and Caroline had her new baby with her as she handed Nadia over. On November 19th I had written 14 poems and 37 stories.

Towards the end of November I went to Brighton to help Tuohy entertain four Japanese. They left at 11 and we talked until 3, and after breakfast went for a long walk across the sea cliff, pursued by a strange

Chinese. We discussed how scenes in a novel should be a series of ever higher mountain peaks and bridges, and how you focus close up for tragedy and with distance for comedy. I insisted that philosophy must be rooted in experience. "If I were finding out why leaves die," I said in Sussex Square Gardens, "I would collect 1,000 leaves and catalogue them. So it is in my stories, I am collecting 1,000 people and presenting the evidence." He agreed, and also agreed with my assumptions in my poems, that personal feeling is a better central idea than "Pound's tour of his library or Heath-Stubbs's mythology in *Artorius*"; and that the line of personal feeling in poetry runs from Catullus through Shakespeare's *Sonnets* to Tennyson's *In Memoriam* and Hardy, with Herbert and Hopkins substituting God for a friend as the object of feeling. I said, pointing at a tree, that there is a trunk beneath the writer's branches – his novels, stories, poems, dramatic verse, essays and prose writings – and he quoted Browning to suggest that others know what the trunk is whereas the artist himself does not know.

I was groping towards a new view of man. I wrote in my *Diaries*: "Before Plato, body and spirit were united, but since then they have divided...: and by Rilke's 4th elegy the external world is a blur within the inner mind of the hero. Classicism: harmony with objects. Romanticism: troubled inner self. My work shows Romantic influence, e.g. inner world, imagination as opposed to reason, the value of the individual. If I am to innovate...it must be to root philosophy in experience, i.e. to devise a way of showing a new view of man. Man alone, as opposed to man in society....What is my subject? The result of my stories is to show that man is a unity of mind-body, that divisions have been a mistake. Also, the unity of the world, of Spirit-Nature....The view of man I show, then, is a post-Christian view...in a time of disintegration. Drives of growth....The nude standing in his bath." And on November 25th: "So: it is man's possibilities, i.e. the end of 1,000 stories....We are measured in terms of our possibilities....The existing views of man are dead, man must live by realising his possibilities: 'self' or God?...So my 1,000 stories illustrate man's possibilities, and the poems show a man winning through to his possibilities, which is Existentialism within – and Romanticism that goes forward and does not remain statically within. So if I stand in the nude...I can measure my nude body by (1) the soul, (2) the intellect, (3) the feelings, (4) the imagination, (5) sex (i.e. penis), (6) society – other people, (7) all mankind. But above all, by what I am capable of, what is to become of man, or what is man to become....Heureka! Show a situation, and show him transcending it to bring in his possibilities. That is my trunk: possibilities....My possibilities, not in relation to what I want but in relation to what I can grow....This idea after a night's drinking with Tuohy. My central idea, my trunk."

I was developing a theory of art which lay behind my very short stories and poems. In my *Diaries* I wrote: "Art stages: soul-world muddled up (archaic); classical Age of maturity, i.e. harmony, form as conceived by intellect and observation of world in balance, static; academic and mannerist styles, i.e. world of its own – sickness of styles; then Baroque, uneasiness and longing for freedom, full of rhythm, organic not intellectual: human passion and grief and pain, love and death, all ages of man: plant-like basis. The imagination drinks deeply of its forms, the cosmos itself seems to be throbbing in the soul (my stories). Mannerism – inability of artists to define themselves, upheaval of values....So I stand for a new Baroque Romanticism (from self to world), man measured by his possibilities, no alienation from the outer world – the mannerism of Modernism (Baudelaire, Proust, Picasso, Rilke, Joyce, Eliot, Kafka, Mann, Sartre, Camus, Brecht) – but rather the self glorying in the outer world, full of possibilities within the unity, i.e. the individual. So Tuohy comes from a different tradition altogether, the outer world-Classicism. Possibilities: 'The view which regards man as a well, a reservoir full of possibilities, I call the Romantic' (T. E. Hulme), cf Sartre. Future possibilities – at the end of *The Silence*. So begin with an act of revolt against the whole tradition of philosophy and thought, in the bathroom mirror. Where does it lead?...Two views: freedom and his old nature. A man with two natures." And again: "How to measure man: by his shadow, by what is ahead of him. That is the liberation of man." And again: "Modern man sees man as an animal and not a creature of God. He is arrogant. He measures by himself, believes man can order everything, whereas in fact he has gone astray. Is in chaos without divine help. The end of man is to glorify God."

This intense thinking about my art resulted in another illumination: "December 3rd-4th. A sleepless night after my fever, tossing and turning, seeing the white light again breaking through the universe – a white sun, dim in its centre, so that the light was evenly distributed." It was the third anniversary of my separation from Caroline and, as in Tanzania, I had a nightmare (as I now thought of it) in which Caroline was in love with me again and returned to me with Nadia.

On December 9th I took Ann to the Denmark and in conversation with her I "poured out thoughts about the will, defending it – the deep will....The will is all. You must aspire to mount Everest – it is Everest or nothing. Do not be content with Matterhorns or Snowdons or china clay hills – the lesser television works....The will is all – its greatness. You can be a dustman or a docker in order to achieve a standard in your spare time, and if you do, the Club will welcome you. But otherwise, if you become a docker just to have it easy – you are weak." Again: "One day...I...will prove that my way of will is right, the deep drive beneath the self, that I stand for. The self says I want to stay in bed, I want to go out for a drink now, and the will says 'Get up' or 'not yet'." And on December 10th: "You have to keep the spring flowing. Get up at 6.30 and write and the spring is flowing for the rest of the day. Otherwise the spring is buried like the one in Coleridge's Xanadu caves." I wrote, "So far, 52 stories 35 poems."

A couple of days later, as I drove back from school after a fire drill I passed John Ezard in Deptford. He was waiting for a bus, leaning on a crutch, and I gave him a lift to the *Guardian* office. He told me he was Night News Editor now. I told him I had seen Tuohy, and Ezard said: "His obsession with technique ends in silence. He has nothing to say. *The Ice Saints* was heading that way." Soon afterwards I listed ideas for 12 essays on the soul of the West. I knew I had something to say.

At the end of term there was a party for the ESN boys. Jelly and ice cream were served in the lower hall, and stout Mr Wardlow surveyed the

Dickensian scene like the Beadle in *Oliver Twist*. Later Ann asked me to accompany her to a carol service in Sloane Square. I went reluctantly and found a pitifully small gathering opposite the tube station with almost as many box-rattlers as passers-by, and lo! Ricky came by and seized my right arm. It was another "accidental" encounter. I detached myself and we found somewhere to sit and discussed the eternal level. He agreed that "we should be for the source of the spring in whatever religion it occurs", but pointed out that there is no language for the eternal level and so it has to be conveyed in parables.

After that meeting my thoughts turned to death. On December 21st I wrote "I would not mind dying in my present mood" and: "Have I any confidence...that anyone will read these words? Ever? If I die will they not surely be burned, along with the hand that writes them, and my other *Diaries*? Who else would bother with my suffering and self-understanding after my death, when no one has bothered during my life? Least of all those who have loved me....Encouragement. I have given so much encouragement to others, and no one has given me any, ever." And about 10.45 I was filled with a deep sense of vastation. I wrote afterwards: "This has been like being in the middle of an ocean, drowning, no land near – for death is certain and all is a distraction from it. But I experienced this utterly and totally – it sapped the will and left me unable to sit up straight. This was the vastation experience, I see now, that Tolstoy and William James had; Nietzsche's hour of Great Contempt. Now I can begin the fight back. After being utterly devastated and laid waste – as an experience. It was an attack – an attack of metaphysical giddiness as it were. Nothing was secure, nothing had value. All the works of man were as nothing. All were basically meaningless. It was horrible. Still, I am in good company: Jouffroy, Tolstoy and Nietzsche. Nadia's future struggles and loves were as nothing – that was horrible. Whereas now (1 a.m.) peace has returned. The attack must have come on around 10.45....The breakdown of everything being its theme." I record this experience to show that illumination does not immediately make one immune from sudden loss of meaning. Rather it brings one face to face with death and the denial of meaning in a way that can prepare the spirit for a triumphant overcoming of meaninglessness and confirm its sense of meaning.

I had Nadia for Christmas. I took her to see *Peter Pan*, which is about a little boy who did not want to grow up and who lived in a wood with the lost children, and I took her to Essex for Christmas Day and we went out to Paddy Manning's at Moreton for a gathering of local people. There was more ill-temper when I handed Nadia back to Caroline in Peterborough – at one point she withdrew to her car in dudgeon at something I had said – and I returned home to South Kensington with the vastation experience not far away.

The next day I had another "accidental" encounter. This one was with Ben from Libya in Bute Street. He was walking with his older brother, and I crossed the road and laid a hand on his arm and said: "Col. Nagy, you are under arrest, I have instructions from Col. Gaddafi." He turned, and for five seconds there was horror in his eyes as he believed he was being arrested. Then he let out a large peeling laugh and took me to his flat in Roland

House, Old Brompton Road and told me how he was investing in hotels in London. He said his younger brother had married the daughter of the Minister for Petroleum and now had a steel industry, while the Minister for Petroleum now had an international business in Rome. The Minister of State for Prime Minister's Affairs now worked in an oil company.

A couple of days later I had a drink with the two brothers, and Ben said: "Caroline was looking for financial and political grandeur. She was looking for something – what she was looking for from me I don't know. I am weak when it comes to beautiful women. Her personality was too strong, she wasn't your type. Don't trust women with your secrets. She was ambitious. You did the right thing, you would always have been restless while she was there."

A few days later I spent an evening with Ben. We ate at the Chelsea Kitchen, which Ben dominated, chatting up a Russian waitress so that everyone heard, and he then took me to the 007 bar at the Hilton Hotel, where we sat and talked. "Caroline was always looking," he said. "You treated her kindly and well and politely and with respect, and so she thought she would find others who would treat her more kindly and well and politely, and with greater respect. She was always ready for a party. We gave her a good time because she was a friend, and she expected it all the time, and that couldn't be."

The vastation experience came again on January 12th 1973: "Lay in bed....A creeping paralysis of the will, a feeling of the total futility of everything. The struggles of parents end in old age and silence, engagements and young love end in this loneliness in Kensington, nothing was secure or permanent. I felt a great sadness round the cheerfulness, and nothing cheered me up – not Radio Luxembourg, not even a reference on BBC 2 to my Tanzanian trip ("the Tanzam railway is reported to be ahead of schedule"). It was a total vastation, a complete laying-waste of my sense of a future, of its worthwhileness. The smallness of 'I'....I felt after it had gone that my habitual nature (Reflection) had dominated the Shadow, and its goals and growth, temporarily. I don't know if it is true, but this is the second time I have felt this recently, and I hope it is the last." Those on the Mystic Way later learned to regard the vastation experience as a gift, for it teaches what I felt: the smallness of the rational, social ego which has to be transcended.

Ben came round urging me to get out and about, offering me his philosophy: "You are still young and presentable. You will not always be....You will not have these years again....You can get a body anywhere. Go up to them in the street and say 'Hello, what work do you do? Where are you going?' Or go to a Wimpy or coffeebar and sit near them. Find girls at museums and restaurants. In bars they are spoiled. Look, at least one hour each day." But he did not understand: as an artist I was doing well getting up at 6.30 a.m., not drinking, and writing. By January 19th I had written 72 stories.

Now I had stopped writing poems I turned towards philosophy. I was thinking about authentic living. I wrote in my *Diaries* on January 23rd:

231

"What is my Existentialism but a journey up the mystic ladder, allowing the deeper self to take over from the shallow self?" Inauthentic living "includes all English philosophy – which is trivial and dull" and involved "experiences at the bottom of the ladder". Again: "Belief in the individual....through moments the individual can appreciate a metaphysical reality – authentic Being lived out in their own lives... – and can therefore advance further up the ladder to the unitive life....The inauthentic keeps men from Being, and in moments of intensity the inauthentic disappears, and Being is revealed as it really is. The inauthentic is therefore a barrier in our awareness, which prevents us from seeing pure Being." Out of this insight came a focus on perception: "Percipere est esse...: to perceive is to be. It means there is fundamentally no division between perceiver and perceived, because both form part of a unity: Being." By "to perceive is to be" I meant that the way we perceive can take us to Being as opposed to Becoming, and I recorded that this was very different from the immaterialist Berkeley's "Existence is percipe or percipere" (that phenomenal objects only have existence when they are perceived).

The question then arose, what is "Being"? I groped towards it the next day: "To Ann in car. To perceive is to see – to perceive truly. So everything is a question of consciousness. Being is there to be seen all the time, and if you see the One you must be a part of it, like a fleck on a marble egg. This brings peace – it is the art of living. The Kama Sutra of the spirit. The negative anxiety is finished – horror, dread. These are what you feel at the outset, on the bottom rung of the ladder....All Being is one, and images – in which different aspects of multiplicity correspond – approach the One....You begin with the individual and his 'I, I, I', and when he penetrates through his habits and murky consciousness to the part of himself which is a part of pure Being then he sees from the point of view of the whole." I approached a union on January 29th, when Ann returned from a religious course. I told her, according to my *Diaries*: "The purpose of teaching religion is the purpose of religion, which is to shift from the world of 'I' to the ground of our Being – the eternal world which is the ground of Being. That shift takes place inside you existentially, and parables teach you how to go through that shift. That is religion. Each and all. Each being rests on the ground of All Being. The truth is that All Being is One Being....What is right is what accords with Being, which we can all partake of, authentically, and what is wrong is inauthentic. For the first time in my life I can glimpse the Absolute. I write of inauthenticity and discover Being. I am emerging from the Dark Night of the Soul into the unitive life. My process is over – my shift." And the next day: "The unitive life sensing pure Being, uniting mysticism and Existentialism. Is there still illumination? Perhaps not? In it Being and Becoming are reconciled, within one nature, and one is agent and patient. The aim of life is to go through all the hardships of the journey and come through into *instinctively* knowing that all is pure Being."

I now felt I had achieved the unitive life. My *Diaries* show increasing optimism and confidence: "I am almost at the top rung of the ladder. In my Dark Night I purged my selfhood further – I gave up drinking, at least in the sense of being dependent on drink. I am emerging with a strong sense of Unity, feeling a giant....Soon I shall rest and work. I am a Puritan. I believe in purifying the senses. I like sensual frolics on the bed, but they too must be pure. I must from today, January 29th 1973 become a patient for this great pure Being which lives through me. I have a new self and a fresh life. I have remade myself – my self has been remade....With my new unitive life is coming a confidence, an opinion. I speak my opinion now, but it is not 'me' that speaks it, but the Being that occupies me."

Tuohy came to my flat and we then went to the Elephantand I told him about my ponderings on Being. He said, "You're absolutely right, but I'm trying to be a writer." I tried to explain that there was no division between metaphysical perception and being a writer, that a great writer had to have something to say, that a great writer has great subject matter, that inner developments relating to Being took one closer to becoming a great writer rather than farther away. But he took the conversation back to people we both knew and arrangements, and then left to keep his dinner appointment in Gordon Square.

The next evening, at 12.30 a.m. on February 2nd, the vastation experience returned: "a creeping depression, a paralysis of the will. Everything seems hopeless. Suffering. Sorrow. Some die, others don't, as in *War and Peace* and the seeds of trees....A sadness. A vastation creeping up? Summer evenings, window open, all quiet at dusk, music from a prom is playing somewhere – sadness. Chestnut leaves. Sad." I realised that the basis of the vastation was that it was a view of the ephemeral world of the ego from the point of view of the soul: "We're living through the time of the dead-in-soul. We are bored. We do not feel....The soul is an organ that has gone numb....God offers to restore our soul – so we feel deeply again."

I was aware that I was reflecting our deepest drives: "I must come to terms with my religious temperament. It has dogged me all my writing life, turning *The Silence* into a mystical work, twisting *Chains* into a near-Buddhist tract....I mirror our deepest drives, I am a describer of our deepest life. The authentic life in contact with Being." On February 7th I wrote: "There is authentic Being and inauthentic products by inauthentic people (hideous lights, gimmicky novels)."

My unitive vision was now beginning to see the unity between disciplines: "The end of philosophy is religion – so philosophy and religion are part of a whole. And poetry, that is part of a whole too. I am a holist, as I keep saying. You start off with philosophy (expressed through stories) and end with religion (expressed through poetry). Prose – the search; poetry – the finding." And again: "Humanism deals with man's social self, Romanticism with man's aspiring self. The idea of 'beyond one's present reach' is very important to Romanticism."

I was looking towards Europe, and I suddenly decided to write an essay making a British Existentialism possible. My *Diaries* (February 12th) reflect my growing European identity: "What my essay will say will be: we have lost our inner direction as individuals, and so society's problems reflect the outer 'I' – an I, I, I, an 'I' want – of sectarian groups. The solution ultimately is to return within the human spirit to growth and improvement and betterment, i.e. to an Existentialism ....We must grow a European identity...that will renew the growth in the soul of the West. It is parallel to European Christianity....I am...an Existentialist who is using art to help him in his philosophical investigations that will result in religious, mystical communion." And again: "Existentialism unites the many-sidedness, it's the trunk that unites my branches. In my life I act out my philosophy, my beliefs, my attitudes."

I now opposed materialism. I reacted to an article which took a materialist view of the brain; it held that all our thoughts and feelings originate in the electrical activity of the brain, and rejected any non-material mind or soul. In my *Diaries* I wrote: "So what of Being? The whole point is we can open new 'neuromuscular pathways' in our brain to peaceful contemplation, i.e. by discarding some circuits or pathways and setting others in motion. The secret of harmonious living is to let the 'I' die (stop the neuromuscular pathways connected with self-assertion) and bring to birth the more serene parts of the brain, which feel the unity of the world. This is the authentic part of the self which is in touch with the way the world really is – it sees truly, i.e. it lives from a different part of the brain from the other, more primitive 'self'. So a man can change by vacating one part of his brain for another – yes! Like a nomad changing his abode in the desert. The objection to religion is the after life. That is where Existentialism comes in: it is about this life, and about living authentically and experiencing Being ('the world of eternity'). The secret is in our brains. Thus, the Cerebral Revolution. So, all of us can open the hidden pathways." I focused on my anti-materialist role: "My role is to understand the problems of the Age, not to entertain....If the novel is Gainsborough's social view, my analysis of conflicts is Picasso, and I must not be judged by Gainsborough's standards." And again I looked towards Europe which "can stand for a philosophical force as well as a moral force – a union of mature civilised human beings and not of grasping businessmen".

I went to the Geological Museum to see an exhibition on the age of the earth, and in my *Diaries* I saw the origin of the earth in perspective: "Reduce geological time to 12 hours and say that the earth is formed at noon. At 3.39 p.m. the first living cells appeared, and homo 'sapiens' has been on earth 9 seconds. Our historical period is a split second. So time is unreal! Into this fits the electrical basis of behaviour and personality – neuromuscular pathways – and evolution from the primitive to pure thought by the learning of new pathways." Later still I wrote: "I have been shedding my skin. I have a new skin underneath my old one." Under the old materialist skin was a new metaphysical one.

Between February 15th and 27th I wrote an article *Why I am an Existentialist*. This focused on Perceptivism, my theory of perception, and besides restating the Existentialist tradition in deliberately personal terms that connected with my own living – my needs and desires – I also stated a need for a new European philosophy: "My argument is that Europe needs a philosophical attitude and that Christianity or Existentialism are the only alternatives; that we should create a British form of Existentialism....I am an Existentialist because the old definitions are no good for me, I need a new definition for myself and the new definition must be about the whole of a man...and Perceptivism....Why Europe needs an Existentialism that is Perceptivist. The old definitions are no good for Europe, she needs a new definition and that must be about the whole of man. There must be a revolt in European taste and art....Stick to Existentialism and not Christianity....A new religion is about to be formed." Later this Perceptivism and new religion would evolve into Universalism. I sent my essay to H. J. Blackham, who had visited my Oxford college and in due course he replied taking my view seriously and asking: "Is not your Existentialism nearer to Jaspers than to Heidegger or Sartre?"

I was still writing stories and was approaching 100. On March 12th I thought about my stories in relation to Perceptivism, and became aware of their metaphysical nature, how they brought out that what I perceived belonged to Being: "My stories are moments that are metaphysical, not psychological. All moments belong to a unity, like all flecks on a marble egg, and so the two moments when I visited the Portmellon watersplash belong to a unity, and are more important than moments this afternoon, i.e. they are now out of time, as images, and are therefore by definition in eternity and remembered for ever. So time is unreal and unimportant, it applies only to the 'self of time'. In a moment of intensity we see the world as it really is – we perceive truly and experience our oneness with the perceived, e.g. with the watersplash, we both belong to a greater whole. This experience of Being (i.e. of what we perceive belonging to a unity with us) means we are escaping the chains of time and are seeing something which, though changing (the tide), is a manifestation of something that is always there, something to which it and we belong. Therefore such a moment tells us about our shared belongingness to Being with what we perceive, and is always valid – hence the image....When we perceive truly and experience Being (i.e. our belongingness to Being we share with what we perceive) we are out of time and in eternity, like a marble egg. The way we perceive determines whether we are bound by the chains of time (inauthentically) or whether we escape time for eternity. So I affirm a metaphysical reality, which is the unchanging unity within which all changing Becoming is all moments, plus and minus, high tide and low."

Two days later I wrote to Tuohy: "In the last few months my conviction has been growing that we are on the verge of a new period – it's as if we were living in 1788 and the whole of the Romantic movement were ahead – and I feel that from now my work must develop this new thing." In the same vein I told a woodcutter in the local pub that "Johnson has no right to put down Coleridge", and I wrote scathingly of Larkin: "Larkin sitting in his buses, never had any experience and would have wetted his pants in Tanzania....Wavell got out *Other Men's Flowers*, an anthology. Larkin is a gigantic weed that has been mistaken for a flower. So the business of the new poet is to make a catalogue of those which are flowers and those which are deceptive weeds."

I had been to Lincolnshire at half term – I drove up in a secondhand blue MGBGT I had bought, having sold the Volkswagen, and met Nadia in Horncastle and drove her to Skegness – and I drove up again in March. I was now drinking much less – in instinctive further self-purification, for example, I had no alcohol for a week at the beginning of April – and I collected Nadia from Horncastle and had her to stay. I took her to Essex. My mother had been to East Grinstead and had returned with some of Gwen Broad's paintings, and she offered me *Dusk at the* (sic) *Land's End*, a moody view of a tin mine chimney on cliffs seen from the evening of life, a Tennysonian glance at impending death. She also gave me *Kynance Cove* in which rocks flow like the clouds and create a Zenish unity. Both these paintings now hang in my house. I did some revisions to *The Silence*. I wrote on April 20th "No alcohol for a week" and made plans to get fit to transform myself "from an alcohol-dominated person sowing wild oats into a major, conscientious artist." When Ben rang I told him: "No more drinking. Lemonade only." It came to my attention that I was considered "very eligible" with my flats and car.

On Easter Sunday I went to Cornwall. Ann met me at St. Austell station and I stopped at a call box and rang Colin Wilson, who had had my essay. He was chummy: "Hello Nick, good to hear your voice again." He invited me for Tuesday evening. Easter Monday was wet and we drove round all the bays between Mevagissey and Carlyon, including the tiny china clay port of Charlestown (the local harbour) and I spent a lot of time thinking about perception. It was as if the prospect of returning to Colin Wilson's presence heightened my consciousness, and I felt there was a spectrum of learning-perception and I distinguished 9 modes of perception: passive blur, scanning, selection of detail, range-finding, seeing the whole situation at a glance or comprehending, future perception or ambition, feeling-perception as in feeling the gorse or Nature, meditating-perception (feeling the sap rising in the tree) and unity-perception (feeling the unity of the universe). I visited Colin Wilson with my ideas sorted out.

Ann drove me to Gorran and up the narrow lane of Tetherdown. We arrived at 5 and Colin peered round the door, now moustached, and said, as though it was 12 minutes since he had last seen me and not 12 years, "Nick, go and find Joy behind the greenhouse and ask her where my underpants are will you?" The search for Joy and his pants took an hour. We then sat in the familiar room before the log fire and drank goblets of wine and I showed him my stories – he looked at a few and said they were a good form – and then we discussed phenomenology. He said, "Your Existentialism is too personal." I soon realised we had progressed down different roads. He was on the side of the reason and against poetry and mysticism ("I would belong to a society to suppress poetry and mysticism" he said, conveniently forgetting how much he had written about them, "poetry is waiting passively for meaning whereas good thinking can solve the problem in half the time") and he insisted that to deny one's egotism for the Mystic Way was wrong: "When you have inner being the ego becomes like a wet suit of clothes. You don't want it, so it's a mistake to try and discard it." He darted up and returned with Husserl's *Ideas*, and said, "Husserl makes mysticism unnecessary, you can intentionalise meaning by inner being," an echo of the Colin Wilson I knew in 1961, but he was now less eager and more disillusioned. I was to use the method of Husserl in *The Fire and the Stones*. He said that he had not made a lot of money out of writing: "*The Occult* made £20,000 and saved this house – I owed income tax for years back – but now I have to pay the income tax on the £20,000." He sat with his wife and three children before the log fire and said: "I wanted *The God of the Labyrinth* to be the dirtiest book I had ever written. It's a masterpiece. My hero has 14 sexual experiences one after the other, and my publisher said that was unbelievable and made it 12." We drank several stem-glassfuls of wine, which fumed in the head, and after supper, which was eaten on our knees, his daughter pointed out that his socks had holes in them. He tore them off and threw them on the log fire. Ann felt he was showing off. As if to underline the gulf between us, he gave me a signed copy of his book on Shaw. Because of the difference between us it was to be nearly 18 years before I visited him again.

I was sad that Colin Wilson and I had pulled away from each other. We were proceeding in the same direction – we were not going in opposite directions – but we were on diverging roads. He was the H. G. Wells of our time while I was in the footsteps of T. S. Eliot. I think I disturbed him with my illumination and Light as he had not had the experience and had therefore left it out of his work.

The next morning I took Ann to see D. S. Savage. He had moved from Lawn House in Mevagissey to Suffolk and back to a stone house across the road in Church Street, Mevagissey. He still had Russian black hair and a beard, and he told me he was writing essays on Orwell and Greene, which would be more popular than the book he had done on *The Great Gatsby*. His wife Connie nodded supportingly. He lamented the change of taste and the decline of the man of letters. We returned in the evening. There were a couple of lady academics there, and Savage said: "Truth is self-revelation and subjective." I said it was a pity he had not been at Colin Wilson's the previous night as Colin had said that meaning (truth) came down to perceiving flowers more clearly and thinking from inner being, whereas I had said it was feeling-perception and unity-perception. "He took the scientist's point of view, I took the mystic's," I said. "I was surprised. He was pro-Ramakrishna at the end of *The Outsider*." Savage said, taking my side: "But he misunderstood Ramakrishna and saw him in terms of Vitalism." He looked at my stories and read one or two, frowning, and said they looked a good form. "Because they are so short and have arresting titles, they make you read them. You're onto something here." One of the lady academics asked, "But are they stories?" Savage said: "Yes, they're stories."

The next day we drove to Trenarren and walked to the Black Head past A. L. Rowse's house. Ann picked some flowers which she later pressed. The next day I worked again on *The Silence* in the train going back to London, and I wrote the Trenarren passages into the beginning and the end, little realising that in 15 years' time I would own a house on the Charlestown front that would look out to Trenarren; the house and harbour I had glimpsed ahead of me when I was at Oxford.

On April 30th I had a long and unpleasant phone call from Caroline's new husband. Apparently Nadia had asked him, "If you die in a plane, will I be with my Daddy again?" and this had not gone down well. He accused me of being an unsuitable father to Nadia because of my journalism, and said that from now on I must apply to the Court if I wanted to see Nadia. He had applied to have the Court withdraw my access and interpose itself between Nadia and me, and I thought of Shelley's poem *To the Lord Chancellor*: "Thy country's curse is on thee, darkest crest/Of that foul, knotted, many-headed worm...."

On May 5th, cup final day, I thought intensely about Being. I wrote in my *Diaries*: "Immediacy is important (to perceive truly is to Be) but also...meaning-perception is important, i.e. detachment and perceiving meaning from past to future." I took another look at my 9 modes of perception: "Separate (1) the modes of perception of the world (Becoming-contingency) from (2) the modes of meaning-perception when detached from the world....Thus, depending on the mode of perception used, I can grasp the world as either meaningful Being...or meaningless Becoming....So there is Outer Being, which I can merge myself into, and Inner Being and will. 'Finding myself' comes down to finding one's inner being. So it is not 'the centre of one's contradictions', that is the goal, but the inner will within the contradictions, the chime within the clock. Inner will or Being is the 'visitation' from the world of eternity....I must redefine Being. Outer Being is clear – true perception of the unity of the universe – but what is inner Being? Being filled from underneath by Being that is different from normal everyday consciousness. How does this relate to outer Being?" On the same day I was reading my grandmother's copy of Trine's *In Tune with the Infinite*, the book I first heard of in Japan, which she had dated 1924 and which had come to me after her death. I noted: "'Helled' meant 'separated from', 'heaven' meant 'harmony'. So when we are in 'I, I, I' we are walled from' or 'helled' from the peace, which is the harmony. Hell and heaven are not places, therefore, but states of mind. And to be helled is to be shut off or separated from 'that Spirit of Infinite Life and Power that is behind all'."

On 6th May poems began coming again for a couple of weeks. I wrote the finished versions in the green manuscript book. On the same day I recorded that I had bought some vitamins and was going to start exercises to get my weight down from 14 stone. Now 20 years later, I still do the Canadian 5BX exercises, which were devised for Canadian air force flying crew. You start with one toe-touch, one lying on the floor and sitting up, one butterfly stroke, one double press-up and a few runs-on-the-spot, and build up to 28 toe-touches, 28 sit-ups, 39 butterfly strokes, 19 double press-ups and 500 runs-on-the-spot, all in 11 minutes – and my weight is now still just over 14 stone.

I had known for some time that I should leave the backward boys. I was not doing so much journalism now, and I was in a better frame of mind to take on more responsibility. By and large the backward boys were devoted with occasional semi-violent flare-ups, during one of which I had a chair thrown at me, but though I could have stayed I knew it was time to move on to something better paid. I recognised that it would not be easy to jump back from ESN to academic work in one bound. I wrote 11 letters for jobs I did not want, none of which appealed, and I found myself being interviewed at two of the places. One offered a Scale 3, the second one, Henry Thornton on Clapham Common (Thornton was one of the Clapham sect that included Wilberforce and Macaulay) offered me a Scale 4(£250 p.a. more) for No 2 in the English Department, which had a staff of 10. I visited Henry Thornton to have a look and liked the Head of English, a quiet elderly-looking man, Jim Doolan, who was very well-read in the classics. He asked me what I thought of Eliot, Yeats and Pound, and I explained that I had visited Pound and was offered the job from September. Later he told me, "You said something significant, that you had been to see Ezra Pound, that's why you got the job."

Now that I would no longer be driving between Kensington and Greenwich, Ann sought to move from All Saints, Blackheath and was soon offered a job at another Church of England Primary school, St. James Norland, Holland Park, for September 1973. This would mean that our lives would be lived between Holland Park and Clapham, without any time being spent on toing and froing between London and Greenwich.

Now, I decided, my journalism had come to an end. I had Nadia for half term and then lunched with Tuohy in the Denmark before he left to teach in America. He seemed depressed. He told me he had done some stories but they were "a failure", and his Somerset novel had died on him: "What was wrong was the structure – insufficient plot. Too little happens in Somerset." He said that Somerset society was "the nobs and the yobs and nothing between".

I was still taking my backward boys out each week. One week we went to a British railway station to see the signalbox. After having the levers explained, I was told that the way we had come in was now closed and that the only way back was across the railway lines. "Just walk down to that crossing point and cross where the lines are shallower," the signalbox supervisor said. So I duly trooped my class down to the crossing point and stopped to look both ways for trains – and a railway worker came up and said, "You do know that the highest line is live, don't you?" "No," I said. "Well it is," he said. "You're dead if you touch that one." I asked if there wasn't another way back, but incredibly there wasn't, so I lined the class up and told each boy to jump over the live rail. They all did so successfully. The last one, "wally" Burke, a small unco-ordinated boy with a mad gleam in his eyes and tousled hair, mumbled with rolling pupils, "Sir, I'm not going to be able to jump over that line." "You're going to jump it," I told him. He walked slowly up to the line and stood, his toes an inch away from it. "Jump it, step over it without touching it," I commanded. "I can't, sir." "JUMP," I yelled, and in terror, with both feet together, hands by his sides and palms out like a penguin, he made a little flopping movement and landed with both feet together an inch the other side of the line. "I jumped it sir," he mumbled. In the distance I could see an electric train hurtling towards us. "Run, " I shouted. And he ran. I followed, leaping the live rail and getting clear of the path of the train. Now that I had marshalled them successfully across the live track the full enormity of my predicament hit me. Several of the boys were brain-damaged, it was amazing that no one had trodden on the line.

Another outing was to St. Nicholas's Hospital to see if any of them wanted to work in the kitchens or boiler house or on the porters' trolleys. The Head Porter, a giant, asked us if we wanted to see the mortuary. "See some stiffs? Cor yes," one of the more streetwise boys said, "I'm not squeamish." We went into a room with a scrubbed stone floor and wired glass. The mortician was beady-eyed with rimless spectacles. He said, "The dead bodies are in these fridges." He opened one to disclose three trays. He pulled out a tray to reveal a man of 70 with a cut on his head and open eyes. He was in his own clothes with no winding sheet. "Touch him," said the giant, but no one dared, the boys had gone very quiet. "He's just asleep, see? Died yesterday and fell, see? He's looking at you," he said, and he closed the man's eyes. Then he pulled out a woman of 55, her skull bound in a bandage. Then he pulled out a woman of 70 with a waxish face. Finally, he opened another fridge door and pulled out a much younger woman. "She was alive this morning," he said. The boy who had boasted he wasn't squeamish went out to be sick, while "wally" Burke asked mad questions, his eyes darting from side to side: "Was she alive this morning, sir? Did she have breakfast this morning, sir? Is she dead, sir? Yes, but is she dead?" I left feeling faintly sick and, still smelling the smell of death, I felt it was all the more important to enjoy life now, today. I thought of all the moments that man in the drawer was missing. To be alive was not to be dead in that drawer. I revelled in being alive.

A week later I took the boys to Windsor. "I don't want to see the Queen," Derek La Rivière said, "what's she ever done for us? She doesn't earn her money." "Wally" Burke was frightened of the changing of the guard: six soldiers in red with busbies and bayonets. I talked to a Royal chauffeur and Burke came in on the conversation and asked: "Will the Queen be coming?" "The whole family," the chauffeur said. "Yes, but will the Queen?" Burke asked, and the chauffeur looked at me as if to say 'What nut are you with?' At 1.45 the Queen and the entire Royal Family left from the back gates (Long Walk) in a fleet of black cars. They came out of the gates and drove slowly along the road across the Park, which was lined with waving people. They were on their way to Ascot, and the Duke of Edinburgh was in a top hat, the Queen in green, looking strangely white and pale and unreal. The other members of the Royal Family smiled and waved like puppets. On the way back London was full of large company buildings like Siemens and Honeywell, and I had a clear image of our country: of capitalist companies under a puppet monarchy, represented in Parliament and local government, the existing order kept intact by the police.

It must have been on one of the outings at this time that I looked in on St. Paul's Cathedral with my ESN boys. A section was roped off and a poetry reading was in progress. Someone was standing before a seated audience, wearing a sweater and jeans. He blew into a party tooter, one of those curled up things that expand and toot simultaneously before retracting. "Sir, what's he doing?" asked "wally" Burke. With a shock I realised it was my old Oxford acquaintance Michael Horovitz. So far as I recollect he declaimed between toots: "The Committee of St. Paul's Cathedral's Restoration Fund were blown away on a puff of wind." He tooted again. "Sir, who was blown away?" asked "wally" Burke. "Sir, why's he blowing on that thing? Sir, how were they blown away? Was it the wind? And why's he blowing that thing?" I found it impossible to justify Horovitz's statement to Burke's ESN mind, and I simply said, "It's a bit of fun." "Sir, is he mad, sir?" asked "wally" Burke, and I did not reply. But I felt a call to return to poetry.

School broke up and I left Riverway. At the end of July I went to Worthing and noted in my *Diaries*: "I have not had illumination and picture visions for some months." I recorded: "I am still restless, waiting to discharge the burden of what I have to say in my writing." Tuohy sent me a card from New York of a unicorn chained to a post and surrounded by a fence: the artist, unfree, on display as if in a zoo.

Back in LondonI "looked again....Saw imaginary pictures – saw my imagination: Greek temples, an African mask, and the light nearly breaking and then not breaking. Afterwards read St. Augustine's view of light, and...St. John of the Cross: the secret stair and, more interestingly, the bride longing for the bridegroom and finding the union of mountains and streams in her secret looking. This is a pre-industrial, pre-TV, pre-film skill, to tap one's own imagination. Blake, van Gogh, Yeats, Dylan Thomas and C. Day Lewis have done it. I am a visionary and a mystic. The two are different. The visionary sees his imagination; the mystic feels the oneness of the outer world – having been helped to feel it by the oneness of the Light. I shall restore knowledge of the Light." Later the same day I wrote a poem, *Sunbathing*.

In mid-August Margaret Riley rang and told me she had been living in St. Ives, where she had had a new mystical period. The next day she came to stay and she told me about it. I wrote in my *Diaries*: "A vision she had of Jesus Christ (wearing white, dark hair) in the dark last October – so close she could touch him. 'It all comes from the heart. You discard from the heart, and the heart flows up when it is peaceful and becomes light in the head.' 'When I pray I feel at peace and go deep so I am not aware of my body, and I *see* whoever I'm thinking of – God, Jesus, Mary.' I: 'I can see St. John of the Cross now, a white-haired man with a beard looking to the right, eyes down. And I see a sinister, hooded man near him. Mary is in blue and from a distance.' Margaret: 'It is the heart that starts everything: love. If you are humble you are at peace.' 'Prayer is not speaking to anyone – don't talk.' The light only comes when the heart is at peace, and visions I have thought day-dreams have turned out to be visions. When I (first) knew Margaret she had entered, or was entering, her Dark Night of the Soul – in fact,...the confusion in that house (was) her Dark Night....All this after I queried 'burning *heart*' in St. John of the Cross's secret stair poem. Introversion and quiet – 'You close your door.' The light is 'the spiritual light'. The feeling of love when you have discarded from the heart, and if you live in London it is harder to feel. 'The burning love is not there/It is somewhere in the air.'"

Margaret stayed the night, sleeping in Nadia's bed, and next morning we had a long talk over breakfast. She said she would find a base near Shoreham. Then: "She brought through a small figurine in white Windsor and Newton clay, done in St. Ives. A tall triangle, only the third side surprisingly reveals a side-on figure of the Virgin Mary – her vision. Margaret: 'It's about angles. Most people look along the line and see nothing, whereas if they change their way of looking and peep round the corner, there is this vision....Also I have no triangles anymore. Then it was me and Father Paul protecting the simplicity of the vision. Now my pieces are two-sided, not three....I love simplicity in art....Probably this will not mean anything to most people, they will not understand it. It has to be a little mysterious....Life should be simple. The heart discarding mess and flowing up to the head....' This work, which I have called *Vision*, is a work of puzzling genius at first. But once you understand it, you understand how to change your way of looking. 'Doing that made me feel so happy, so peaceful.' 'I've no angles any more.'"

Margaret gave me some directions: "No one owns me, and I own nobody." "Compare yourself with nobody." "Be yourself. Development is not reaching out for other people. Those who have lost their way are looking, searching, instead of staying and being themselves." "Overcome the conflicts – the heart feels all in One." "The heart is the fountain of all things."

I went for a walk with Margaret in Stanhope Gardens. It was very hot, and we discussed the new European movement in the arts, which I would embody. I drew up the following manifesto for this movement:

"1. There needs to be a new direction in all the European arts, which are stagnating.
2. This stagnation is caused by the fact that the values of the West and in the arts are wrong (body/head). The soul of the West needs to be purified, along with its perception.
3. All the clutter that has gathered like fungus on the soul of the West should be knocked off, and works of art should again come from the heart, which is the spring of peace, from which follows the illumination and visions of the mystical life.
4. The real world should therefore flood back into the arts, fresh and alive. This will be a Baroque period in relation to the cycle of art periods. Subject matter will have primacy, an end to abstraction and the "technique first" attitude.
5. Man is a colossus in chains. When he has escaped his chains he will be seen as he is and as he can become, with all his possibilities – free, at peace, at unity with the universe, living by reality and truth and the meaning of life.
6. Art should therefore concentrate on these positive qualities. It should show examples of them, and if it shows someone who has lost his way, it should make it clear why he has lost his way.
7. Therefore the heart should dominate, not the head: there should be no rules except those which the heart demands. Paintings should not be worked out first, and from each work there must be a feeling, otherwise it will be a dud. The enemy is rationalism, which asks questions, asks why: the reason is an obstacle to feeling peace."

After she had read this manifesto Margaret said: "Silence is peace, there is no thought behind it at all, it is just *it*, like sleep, you don't say I'm going to sleep now." I recorded: "So man should be defined by his heart, not his head. You only get tranquillity through the heart – by discarding. So the ideal of the new age of Contentment is the free, peaceful man: the Colossus of mysticism free from his chains."

I now moved back to shorter poems. I commented in my *Diaries*: "The long poem idea came from the idea of *searching*, which is now seen to be an enemy of peace. Now my aim is to write from the heart, to communicate peace, and this can be done in shorter poems. But stop rhymes. From now, no rules. Free verse. Let the heart control." I had arrived at a new aesthetic for my poetry, which was to take me away from the rigid metrical forms of the Movement for a few years.

I asked Margaret (I quote from my *Diaries*): "What does she think of an image (like the Portmellon watersplash) being a revelation of Being, i.e. at a metaphysical level, not at the level of memory. Answer: it is an image that has touched the heart, a place felt with the heart. These moments are precious. 'Keep it to yourself, you cannot share it, others will not see it as you have.' I said perhaps it was an example of a metaphysical reality – of the One? 'God's world is there for all to enjoy. That joy is natural.'" I *wrote* "The poems I write should be short ones linked together" and Margaret said again: "Compare yourself with nobody, our movement with none other."

I was now acutely aware of a conflict between the reason and the heart. My *Diaries* show I asked Margaret: "What is this metaphysical reality?" "I don't know, I don't think about it," she replied. "You are asking what is the *reason*." I recorded: "So I was trapped again in my own reason. My reason is a mantrap on the estate of peace." I wrote: "My stories are from the heart....On creating from the heart. There are two ways, the sudden impulsive desire to do a story, or the contemplation at peace, 'emotion recollected in tranquillity'. Margaret: 'I cannot just paint that tree out there, I see something and then walk around for a few days and then it comes up and I paint it.' So with my stories. Something happens and I walk round and then it comes up and I write it. The heart is like a spring." She also said: "You enter a church with your heart, not your head." I wrote: "The head must surrender to the heart – the selfish part (head) to the selfless, generous part (heart). The head and the heart....What Caroline said about feelings once: 'I give you feelings (i.e. heart); without them your writing would be arid.'"

Margaret was now full of the European movement I had proposed. She arranged an exhibition in Vienna and I wrote: "The revolution of Perceptivism really began when I met Pound at Rapallo and then announced the idea at various poets' parties and wrote letters to Tuohy and Ezard. Then at Egerton Gardens I met Margaret Riley, who has brought in the painters. Margaret: 'We cannot announce a new development now, as we have not shown anything. We will show it and then they will see for themselves. And there will be our manifesto.'" Margaret said: "You should aim for Europe as a market....You will write for yourself out of your heart – but Europe will be a good audience. It is so at peace, and there is unity. You should come to Vienna....Small beginnings – think humbly – come in slowly, silently." The mention of Vienna made me think of the Vienna Circle, which we were opposing, and even in those days I saw she had been sent to me with the knowledge of the Austro-Hungarian Empire – she knew the Habsburgs – to counteract and neutralise the wrong view of the Vienna Circle.

"Love is from the heart," I wrote. "Image for heart and spirit: a flower growing out of leaves (of heart) – a sunflower....Reread *The Wayward Head and the Heart* (Constant)....Margaret: "The heart of the tree is in the roots. The trunk is the centre from there and it goes upwards, you paint it

upwards.' God is the ground of one's being – so the ground is in the heart."
Again, she said on stillness and movement: 'The heart can feel movement.
If the heart is not still, if it is doing it, it is not letting go, it cannot absorb
those trees." And again: "The heart of the dahlia is in the roots. And if the
roots are deep, it is strong. The deeper the roots the stronger." I wrote:
"Before my break-up I was head, with Caroline as my heart. Now I have
discarded the head and *am* my own heart. That is the painful way of loss."

Margaret spoke of my work, and I wrote in my *Diaries*: "Margaret:
'Never be afraid of failure, each work you do makes the next one easier.' So
the first 50 paintings may be no good, but the last 30 may be works of
genius. 'Your stories are flowing now. You do them quickly.'"

Margaret saw mysticism in terms of the heart. I wrote: "Margaret on
mysticism. It makes you see the beauty of virtue and the ugliness of vice,
e.g. the beauty of humility and the ugliness of self-importance. And also
appreciate the beauty of things you see as opposed to the dirt and squalor
and foul breath and stale beer that Tuohy, who has lost his faith, writes
about....Other countries have mysticism, but it does not come from the heart
(e.g. the Golden Flower) and is not connected with Providence, i.e. the
heart's giving is connected to a web. 'It is linked to the Catholic
faith....Toynbee and Huxley (*The Perennial Philosophy*) are searching,
which is bad, whereas they should just sit still and discard knowledge."
Margaret was ready for more work: "Last May I was confused. I did not
know whether to take a religious direction, go into an organisation in the
Church, but then I saw the European venture was right. You told me so two
years ago: I was not ready. I am reaching the end of a religious period and
now there will be a period of work....Tuohy keeps his sorrow to himself.
His lost Catholicism. He does not speak of his unhappiness. He is restless,
he has lost his peace, and he will not go and ask for help to a priest."

On Sunday Margaret went to confession and I wrote: "Margaret at peace
after confession. 'Your Austrian temperament is held in check in England.
It blends with the self-discipline of your mysticism.'" There was football on
television. She commented: "These empty stars – outlines and no faces." In
reply to something I said she observed: "Brian Patten is lost, he does not
know, he is writing about himself and his wound and his self-pity." I
commented: "The movement we are contemplating should be one of men
who know the truth and the way." I added: "It was necessary for me to
suffer so that I could lose my head and gain my heart, from which all
meaning is perceived. The justification of suffering is in this: that it gains
the heart....Suffering takes you from a heart involved with one person and
not mankind to a heart that is free from the chains of one person, that is
more truly itself, and which can more easily feel for all mankind – brotherly
love....Suffering came into my life and grew new places in my heart, and
now I feel the universe more directly. Except a corn of wheat (the head) fall
into the ground (of humanity) and die, it abideth alone (it stays the head).
But if it die, it bringeth forth much fruit = the heart. Art shows how to live
to people, and is more important than knowledge (university subjects) or
business....Perceptivist, because meaning is perceived through the heart,
after suffering and escape from the head."

Margaret spoke of joy and I recorded: "Father Paul to Margaret: 'Stars, flowers and children are showers from heaven....' Margaret: 'I see *spiritual* stars as gifts alive and teeming for man, stars like a shower, from God.'...Margaret's Elizabeth: 'Why all these wars when God created everything?' 'That is why – don't ask why.' Ivan Karamazov's trouble, you don't feel the meaning with your heart. Margaret's joy. Her flowers and irises (girl among irises). Her feeling of charity for people is going to come out. 'I paint inner beauty, I see the inner beauty like charity, not the physical beauty....You must always keep something to yourself. Joy and sorrow.' Like the places felt through the heart." I wrote: "Art (that is great) = heart."

Of Margaret's religious life my *Diaries* record: "Her call back to the Church came the same day as my call back to the self I had lost – 10th September 1971. Margaret: 'It was Providence. But I had to get away from that place. It was suffocating me. I had to get away from Egerton Gardens.' 'No possessions (materially), the possession is here (in the heart).' 'You become strong through self-denial and self-discipline. The victory of giving (something you wanted for yourself).' 'It's not important if something breaks up, or if you lose somebody, for if it's lost, it was never worth it in the first place.'"

Eventually Margaret left. My *Diaries* record: "Margaret left this morning, nearly leaving behind her sketch book and her *Vision*. This morning at breakfast she commented on the dahlias. Ann had thrown out the dead ones and left the young buds: 'With a little care these buds can develop into a better one than that good one.' Outside at the taxi rank: 'I am going to build another beehive, but one everyone can enjoy....I am a bee flying back to the beehive....The ploughman is at peace, he ploughs straight ahead, he has his direction, he doesn't look to left or right. Or over his shoulder. And when he reaches the end he returns. And there are seeds." She left me with a list of people who had an ugly heart: "I wouldn't like to meet Colin Wilson," she said, meaning that she did not approve of his heart. I wrote: "Margaret and the feeling vision of inner peace. Head and heart....My poetry must flow free. Drop rhyme."

After Margaret had gone I returned to my writing. I recorded: "Felt tired after writing three mystic poems and a story. Then wrote and got the title for (after typing): *A Smell of Leaves and Summer*. This is the title for the 4th hundred stories. (The second at present unwritten.) This is a creative time for me." There were just over two weeks left of the summer holidays. They did not have the significance of the five days Margaret stayed with me, and I prepared for my new job on Clapham Common with something of a heavy heart.

I found Henry Thornton in September 1973 glassy, hectic and crowded. The playground behind the facade was always full of manic games of football, and walking from the staff room across it to the English area involved running a gauntlet of flying footballs and shrieking teenage boys, many of whom were West Indian. The first few days I was rushed off my feet. As Second-in-Command of the English Department under an elderly Head of Department whose great joy was reading Chaucer in the original, I found I was in effect running the Department. There was no syllabus because Jim Doolan did not believe in syllabuses, and the Head of the school asked me to write one. I had to sort through the stock room, which did not seem to have been touched since Henry Thornton was a Grammar School – the old Honours boards from that time were stored up one end – and I had to have meetings with the ten young teachers to co-ordinate what they were doing into a progression. Jim Doolan had told them, "You're an English teacher, teach."

The staff were very well-mannered, pleasant, urbane and well-spoken, and there was a great contrast between the civilised atmosphere in the huge staff room, where over 100 sat in comfortable chairs amid plenty of space, reading papers, and the chaotic rushing about in the playground outside and the confused and noisy congestion in the corridors, which resembled Victoria station at rush-hour. The Head of the school sat in his study all day, coping with paper-work, and discipline was left to his two Deputies. Soon after I arrived I encountered one of them, an ex-RSM of massive bulk, Mr Nicholls, in the playground in a quieter moment. (He had brought the quiet with him.) "How do you keep order in this place?" I asked him. "I'll show you," he said, and he bellowed: "Boy." About 200 yards away a coloured boy of about 11 cringed and turned and scampered up to us. "You keep a cane up your sleeve," Nicholls told me, with all the authority of the Beadle in *Oliver Twist*, "and when you need it, you produce it." He shook down from the right hand sleeve of his threadbare suit a small cane. "Boy," he commanded, "put your hand out." Cowering and with his bottom lip out, the coloured boy sulkily extended his right hand. Swish. The coloured boy ran off, flicking his fingers. No one else was around. "What was that for?" I asked, scarcely believing what I had seen. "Oh, that wasn't *for* anything," Nicholls said, "that's how I keep order in this place."

The senior staff, like the Head of the school and Jim Doolan, went gravely to and fro, an oasis of untroubled calm in the general chaos, while one of the Heads of House, a small balding Welshman, Mr Daniels, patrolled my corridors waving a large cane, which proved effective in persuading the tear-aways to line up. "You need a stick, Mr Hagger," Mr Daniels said with mock-seriousness at the beginning of one of my classes, and he presented me with a cane, which I theatrically put in my cupboard and locked away. I never used it, but when the high tide of chaos rose to threatening proportions outside my classroom I appeared holding it, and the general rushing about suddenly stopped.

I do not know how we got some of the boys to stay in their desks all lesson, let alone do the work we wanted them to do. I took 1st and 2nd years, 4th, 5th, 6th and 7th years. There was an enormous range of ability, and some 15 year olds could hardly write their name. I struggled on with *Macbeth* and *Brighton Rock*, and the dunces would say "Oh sir, can't we play cards today?" and when I had insisted on written work, they handed in wretched work with a pleading "Sir, do you think you could give me an A?" Some just pushed their papers on the floor and stared out of the window. When they did this in other classes, the boys were sent to me and I had them sitting near the front as a punishment. "Sir, what's the use of teaching us?" one class of dim-wits used to ask me. "We're not going to do anything that needs what we learn at this dump of a school." They had a point.

RAPTURES AND CONTEMPLATION

I enjoyed the 6th and 7th year lessons most, the 'A' level classes. A dozen intelligent boys gathered and sat down both sides of a long table in the calm of the long shelf-lined 'A' level room, which had been an extensive 'A' level library in the Grammar School days. Somehow these boys had survived the frenetic rushing about of the younger boys and had come through with some semblance of literary criticism, although in their essays they needed to "tighten up" as Jim Doolan put it. They appeared genuinely interested in the Metaphysical poets, which I had to read with them. I had first found out about the Light from the Metaphysical poets of the 17th century, and I greatly enjoyed combing their poems for references to it. In the calm atmosphere of this long room we had our Departmental meetings. As there was no pre-existing structure whatsoever, except for a list of staff names, the classes they were taking, and the exam set books, we had to start from scratch. Everything was new and Jim Doolan presided over our deliberations at the end of the table, white-haired and horn-rimmed, with a disdainful, detached, sometimes scathing expression on his face.

As the term progressed he and I talked, and he made no attempt to disguise his criticisms of the comprehensive system and of its uncaring attitude in lumping together the more able and the less able on one site. "The more able suffer because of the hooligans," he used to say to me, "and the less able feel inferior because of the more able. It doesn't work. And the meetings are all a waste of time. Yesterday they spent an hour discussing a one-way system to get the children to proceed in an orderly fashion in the corridors, without mentioning once that they rush about as if they're on a football pitch." His criticisms had not gone down well at the top, and when there was a vacancy for Senior Teacher the previous term (a post rightfully Jim's by seniority) the post had been given to a young Head of Science who had been a pupil at the school under Jim and who pretended at public meetings that all was well with the place. Bitterly hurt at the snub, Jim Doolan withdrew even more, from my first day telling me to run the Department as best I could. From the outset I was courted as if I were Head of Department by the English staff and the Head of the school.

One week the discipline problem paralysed the school. An ex-commando, "Tug" Wilson, who had lost fingers at Arromanches, took a party of 5th years to a matinée. In Sloane Square a coloured boy proved difficult. (Sloane Square – again successive events gathered round a place like successive tides round a breakwater.) "Tug" Wilson had given the boy some money and told him to go home. The boy had hit "Tug" Wilson with a right hook and had knocked him out. For some while the ex-war hero lay unconscious in the gutter. The boy was suspended for a couple of days and then allowed back into school, where he boasted that any other master who crossed him would get the same treatment. Appalled that he had not been expelled, the staff held a meeting and threatened to go on strike unless the boy was expelled. There was much talk of the Head not doing enough about discipline. In the end a compromise was reached. I believe the boy stayed in school but was not taught.

A MYSTIC WAY

At first Henry Thornton had returned me to the outer world, but teaching Marvell's *The Definition of Love* and *Dialogue of Soul and Body* took me back to poetry. In early October Margaret arrived uninvited and stayed a night and I showed her Marvell's *Garden*. She said, "If you met Marvell you would talk for a long time, you are on the same level." On 7th October I wrote in my *Diaries*: "Get back to poetry after 5 months" and on October 11th : "I have reached a time of momentous decision. Ever since I started ordering my photos, the thought has been occurring to me: I am a poet, not a novelist. I write of the moment – in poems and short stories; not of patterns and sympathy for characters and trivialities. I should be doing what I told Pound I would do, i.e. become a Milton. Do *Life Cycle*, which I glimpsed above Iraq. I have known this in the past, but my journalism took me off on a different root – *Age of Cartoon* and *Chains*, politics and Libya....I neglected my true way. I had it between 1965-6. *The Eternicide* 1967: that was when I went wrong. Away from God. I lost my way. And now I am finding it again, I must face up to the fact that I have had a false start, like Shaw. (His 5 novels.) I am a poet, not a novelist, just as Shaw was a dramatist and not a novelist. My major work – which I described to Pound – is ahead. Images....Jim on Eliot knowing his method is right because it was used in the Elizabethans, i.e. taking his strength from the past." And again: "The problem is to decide where my destiny lies. I know I have destiny, I know it is to do with my writing. I believe now it is to do with poetry. All my prose work apart from my stories, which are prose-poems, is now a preparation for a new onslaught into poetry. Something original each day....Now I am 34, and I am going to turn myself into a great poet. The conditions are right. I have found my voice....Sing in poetry. I must make poetry come across and give it a new philosophical dignity. The line: think. Old Norse. Vers libre." And again after October 20th: "Buy Catullus and *Piers Plowman*. Get back to poems....Get on to long poems. Do the remaining 9 poems to fulfil what I said to Ezra Pound."

Under the influence of Marvell, I returned to poetry from 10th October 1973 and wrote many poems for the next six months. At half term I went to Lincolnshire and Scarborough to visit the school Nadia might go to, and returned via Nun Appleton House, the site of Marvell's *Garden*. The House had been rebuilt since 1650, and I visited it without appointment. Despite notices warning that I was on private land I was not challenged. Only a piano-tuner seemed to be in and he invited me into the house. I was able to wander freely in the grounds. I wrote bits of what became *A Metaphysical in Marvell's Garden*, sitting by the pool, and I finished this on October 28th. Soon afterwards I wrote "I am entering a new phase in my poetry. A new fusion of image and thought, a new freedom. I am a poet. My feeling is like a lump on my heart (cf the wound and the bow). It is only discharged by poetry. It is not an illness but a labour pain of a pregnant woman: cured only by delivery."

In November I renewed my choice of myself as a poet. I was reading Donne with the 7th year. I loved *Twicknam Garden*. On November 2nd I wrote: "I am a poet. Poetry is about the real world, novels are about an imagined one. I am interested in the real one. Now. (I used to be interested in an imagined one. That is the difference.) Also: poems are about feelings, whereas novels describe (imaginary) events. Tell the story of Freeman's break-up in poems....The best poetry gives you something to dig out, and the satisfaction is in getting there. That is how my poetry is similar to that of the Metaphysicals. I am in the metaphysical vein....I love the physical things." And again: "I must say what I have to say as briefly as possible, without the trappings. I feel a nausea with the idea of character-creation: it is inessential. I am undergoing an upheaval, a development. I am finding myself. I am developing away from prose to poetry. Away from the inessential to the essential....Greatness or nothing. My voice that told me to give up alcohol tells me to concentrate on poetry....I have 10...long poems. No 3 is *The Gates of Hell*....*The Gates of Hell* will flow out of earlier poems....My *Paradise Lost*, my *Life Cycle*....Poetry is the essence: the novel is perfume. And my mind is a poetic mind. I can embody my Age in my poetry....My belated self-discovery. From now on, I must not forget this. I swear: that as from 2nd November 1973, I will be a poet, a whole poet, and nothing but a poet. So help me God. This night...I have made a decision from inside. I proclaim 1967-1972 my 'lost years' – when I was lost to poetry, save for the occasional poem. My Dark Night of the Soul. Five 'lost years' of objectivity and confusion. When I was lost – lost my way among novels." And on November 3rd: "My lost years are over. The voice of my destiny has spoken. I am to be a Milton, I must write a modern *Paradise Lost*. I am to be a Bunyan, I have already written my *Pilgrim's Progress* – and Despair is not an outside person but a state of mind in Freeman's head in my version. I am to be a Goethe, I must write a verse drama about a modern Faust cum Peer Gynt who searches and travels and who finally discovers the meaning of life. I must embody in verse the new Age ahead. From now I will grow in stature and soul. The lost years are over....From now I will live by the spring of my Muse, of my genius: pure." And again: "The last of my long poems will be full of grandeur. The death of a hero. Grand and heroic. First the 'angry years'...; then the 'growing years'; then the 'lost years'; and now, to come in, the 'grand years'."

My talks with Jim Doolan were of great value. I noted that he had "revived the poet in me. With him I can discuss Donne in the staff room as I could not at Riverway." The next day he told me: "The longer I live, the more I am convinced that great poetry comes from the heart. You have to suffer. I've written but it's superficial, not a cry like a man in agony – Marvell or Donne." He also observed "Marvell had to leave Nun Appleton because of Fairfax's daughter – after *The Definition of Love* what else can you do?" and "Shakespeare was going through a hell of a time when he wrote *Lear*". I observed: "I had a choice between suffering and happiness, and I chose to be a poet." The next day, on 9th November I wrote 4 poems.

On December 16th I wrote: "Reading Ovid and Catullus until 1 a.m. as I could not sleep. The Ovidian couplet: dactylic hexameter plus pentameter with disyllabic ending. Or Alexandrine plus pentameter or two pentameters (the first with a feminine ending)....Go into Latin poetry. Make it a hobby. Catullus and Ovid. A third long poem about the modern equivalent of Gallus – called *The Loves* or equivalent." And on December 18th: "Write a group of poems which are dramatic monologues, which together form 100. Do them in the new flat (the Poem Factory or

A MYSTIC WAY

Workshop). Communicate the times. The Roman vision: a time of promiscuity and decay, like ours. Catch the life and times of today in 100 linked poems in the Catullan or Ovidian manner." This was the idea for my sequence of poems *The Gates of Hell*, which looked back to Catullus and Ovid.

In December I found a flat off the Gloucester Road. It comprised the top two floors and roof garden of 10 Brechin Place, and there was a "cabin" where Nadia could sleep. To buy it would mean selling both 33 Stanhope Gardens and 9 Crescent View. Four days later I met the wife of the owner in the street. She said her husband was not keen to sell and she was trying to talk him round. "Perhaps it would help if you came along and saw him," she said. I recorded in my *Diaries*: "I have a certain feeling of Providence about the new venture. Ever since Pat Farley made an appointment for me to see the place when I hadn't asked to. Que sera sera. Whatever will happen will happen....I have no doubts about the rightness of Brechin Place. An inner voice directs me to do it and therefore I will." I visited the owner and he accepted my offer. The day I broke up from school I met his wife in the street again. On Christmas Eve I sold 9 Crescent View to my tenant there for a good price.

That Christmas I spent totally alone. I pondered on standards: "Margaret Riley, Tuohy, Ricky Herbert -- all are against the will and affirm Original Sin. They are all against Revolution....Why do my friends all have reactionary attitudes? And those writers I most admire – Yeats, Eliot, Golding, Horace – they are all against Revolution....It is the inner life not the outer man I am interested in. I am a Conservative. I understand the need for change, but I support the preservation of standards. I stand for standards. And change will destroy those standards, so it must be resisted, though I can understand the feelings of the changers....I am inspired by Christianity though I am not a believer....I am on the side of tradition against change; on the side of grammar schools against comprehensives; on the side of the well-wrought urn, against self-expression. The New Man is a man who is a perfect continuation of the Christian tradition. Yesterday I visited the Victoria and Albert Museum and looked at the plastercast of Michelangelo's David. A giant – who embodies, like Augustus to the Romans, the best in the British Christian tradition."

I wrote amid "creeping loneliness": "The emptiness of the streets, radio and TV programmes I don't want to hear; unable to settle. Just feel restless with loneliness. People far away: Paddy over the phone, telling me she had a card from Caroline. And still, the sad feeling on my heart the whole day....I must remarry. To settle this problem of loneliness once and for all. Remarry for negative reasons – the right deed for the wrong reasons." I read Catullus and noted: "'The calm of mind, all passion spent.' Catullus's only hope with Lesbia was complete renunciation." "My feelings have nearly died," I wrote. "When alone I think of my little (i.e. Nadia) with a quiet detachment. A grief now too deep for tears – a grief that is part of my body. Four years. Just a sorrow." After Christmas I fetched Nadia and had a gentle talk with Caroline in the Sleaford Black Bull for three quarters of an hour. "You should get married," she said quietly.

At the end of the year I looked back on a year of reordering and renewing myself. I had left behind Riverway, my Volkswagen, my African journalism and 9 Crescent View, and would soon leave behind 33 Stanhope Gardens. I had given up alcohol for 9 months, done 5 months of exercises, got rid of my paunch and rebuilt myself with vitamins. I had finished with novels and had finished 100 stories, and was looking towards poems.

I reread the Latin elegiac poets of between c60BC and c20BC, and noted their heroines: Catullus's Lesbia; Gallus's Lycoris; Tibullus's Delia; Propertius's Cynthia; Ovid's Corinna. I wrote: "Ladies began to lead an independent life; traditional ideals of marriage lost their meaning, men and women alike sought love outside marriage....Love-elegies. (Dactylic hexameter-pentameter.)...Later the Christians took the elegy over. Nuns worshipping Christ. Eros became Agape. In his *Odes* Horace adapted Greek metres to the Latin language, e.g. Alcaics, Sapphics, Asclepiads....If Pope can begin an Augustan period, why can't I revive the elegy? Augustus in tranquillising the world, tranquillised letters. A poetry of peace attained." I wrote: "Track down: why was Queen Anne's reign called 'The Augustan' age? Find Goldsmith's essay, find what Augustan qualities Pope took. For sure, it was not the elegiac. Write an elegy in stresses: hexameter and then pentameter. In short, adapt the heroic couplet. Go back to Horace's source in Alcaics etc, but do them in terms of stress. Think: the couplet gives the 'rise and fall of the jet of water' (Ovid) but should it rhyme? Think: blank verse. What about ON (Old Norse) narrative poetry? Tell a story through a sequence of elegies? A golden age can take place now. Our time is very near to that of the Roman Augustan period....The new Golden Age." I also made notes for a heroic epic but was all set to embark on a poetic experiment: elegies in a free form.

In early 1974 I was creative. On January 7th I had the idea for a poem, *The Night-Sea Crossing* and made notes for it during the next few weeks. It "must above all else," I wrote, "be about how to live perfectly". On January 11th I also had the idea for another collection of stories to be called *A Roman in Barbary*.

On 18th January I wrote of the Light: "The Light comes as naturally as the flower blooms or the wind blows – it comes to rich and poor alike, king and peasant, master and servant. All are heirs to it. Peace is being at one with God. We have no contact with yesterday save that it made today. Ditto, tomorrow depends on how we live today. Commit problems to the mystic silence....I must set aside more time for prayer and reflection and silence. I must end each day in quiet and love." I was still reading Trine's *In Tune with the Infinite*, and I noted the law of prosperity and success, and wrote: "Margaret saw that all greatness comes from within-out. That I had to solve my problems within before they could be solved without." Again: "Trine: all lives come from the source of life and of all laws; therefore our mind-power is connected with a source; therefore we attract strong mind-power to us when we have strong thoughts, and weak mind-power when we have weak thoughts. Prayer. So like attracts like, and success is in the thought. God is a Spirit of Infinite Life and Power. The real self is oneness with the life of God, i.e. God is a sum total and source – a spring....The pot of Margaret's – the self. One side has to be smashed to open up the self to the infinite life, i.e. let in the divine inflow."

I reviewed my life "peddling information: teaching, journalism, etc." and wrote that I must *expect* success. I wrote: "Motto for Hell: 'In each creature, the spark of the Divine.' And I thought: the artist communicates the presence of God. 'An inner spiritual sense through which man is opened to the direct revelation and knowledge of God.'...'The divine spark.' In everyone. It will remain a spark unless it is lit. Yet also there is a sluice-gate that keeps out the tide – like a dam across a river. Or again it is like the wall of Margaret's pot, keeping the inside from joining with the air outside. Self....Spark: a fire. I saw a great fire in a grate. Njinsky: 'God is fire in the head.' From now I will 'ponder' night and morning, i.e. lie in bed in the dark and look for the Divine illumination. Night-Sea Crossing – a crossing of the night-sea of the mind. From now, I must journey in the mind. Be a mental traveller."

8

NIGHT OF UNKNOWING: HEAD OF ENGLISH AND REMARRIAGE
1974 – 1977

The next few months proved to be very successful, both professionally and personally. At the end of January I was sent to Stoke D'Abernon on an ILEA course on how to run a Department. We stayed in a country house by the River Mole, and on the first night John Welch, the Chief English Inspector, talked to us and told us "Everyone here has made it", and I thought: This isn't making it, I haven't even begun. I later wrote: "I thought, 'You mediocrities'. For they *were* mediocre, they had all stopped. How low their ambitions were if *this* was 'making it'. Whereas my ambition reaches to the stars. Yeats: 'And hid his face amid a crowd of stars.'" On the Saturday night I went for a walk by the weir and the church, and when I returned there was a commotion. The Chief English Inspector was being carried to his room, drunk. On the Sunday morning I wrote five poems: "My five poems, before and after breakfast in the sun. Now I feel refreshed. I could be a Head of Department without too much difficulty. One grows into new robes. This weekend, borrowed robes." Over the weekend I compared the Augustinian and Pelagian views of education: "Traditionally, education has had the Augustinian point of view: we have original sin and must strive to become perfect, to reach a standard, we accept the culture of the past. The Pelagian point of view asserts that we are perfect, therefore everything is self-expression, therefore standards are rejected and they are as they are, and we must be revolutionaries. Discipline versus rejection of the law:...I came down very definitely on the side of Original Sin and against the perfection of Romanticism....Romanticism grows out of Pelagianism. Or perhaps I have romantic *and* classical streaks to my nature? I am a traditionalist, I am anti-liberal." On my return I wrote a poem about this conflict.

I saw the Light again. On 27th January I wrote: "Wrote six poems and saw a wonderful blue light. Very limpid." And the next day: "Saw a sunflower in my secret journeying." I was obsessed by a tapestry of Burne-Jones, and noted on 29th January, anticipating the title of a collection of poems, "The Heart of the Rose, or: The Pilgrim in the Garden." Soon afterwards I recorded that I had finished writing my poems on Stoke D'Abernon. I also wrote: "Consider setting out my reflective poems as elegies or odes....The difference between the Classical ode and the Romantic ode – both of which were forms of address. Horace wrote to people, like Catullus, whereas Keats addressed things, birds, etc. (like Shelley). I will be Classical....To belong to the English poetic tradition I should try elegies and odes and the other verse forms that the poets tried – not the dribbling non-metre, not rhymed free verse of the poetasters....I have revived the elegy and the ode. I am in a Classical period now – the mature man. Not the youthful Romantic in his twenties....I have turned the elegy into a form of struggle through to a victory, a joy, after a tussle, an argument. Through me speaks an Infinite depth." Soon afterwards I recorded: "1st, 2nd, 3rd, 4th elegies and titles. I have ten elegies altogether. They express an attitude....All should be rooted in specific days between the autumn of 1973 and the summer of 1974. These elegies have just 'come', of their own accord." And again: "'A weekend elegist.' This weekend I have done the 4th, last weekend the 2nd and 3rd. For an introductory note on the elegy. It is not associated with grief in Roman times – the couplet. Marlowe began the heroic couplet. Dryden and Pope, using the classical model. *Annus Mirabilis* and Gray, untypical offshoots. Regular or irregular paragraphing. Rilke. How it is an ideal form for reflection (Coleridge). Claim Marvell's *Garden* as an elegy. The heroic couplet. A provisional title for the elegies: *Pilgrim in the Garden*. From the Burne-Jones tapestry, the Heart of the Rose, a copy of which I sent Jonathan on his birthday."

In the first week of February I sold 33 Stanhope Gardens and was all set to convert my two flats into the larger flat in 10 Brechin Place. On February 6th there was snow and I stayed away from school and thought about the future, and the prospect that my new flat should coincide with a new marriage. I looked within and recorded: "The Tudor images I saw in my looking last night." I pondered on the Infinite Intelligence, and wrote a 5th elegy. On February 16th I visited Nadia with Ann and we took her to Tattershall Castle, where I drafted another elegy. I recorded in my *Diaries*: "Thoughts on the journey to Lincolnshire yesterday. To find God you have to go through the Devil. Man is primarily a spiritual rather than a social being, so God is a more important force than the KGB. To be a great writer you have to write of man in suffering, his triumph over sorrow, the meaning of God and life – the themes of the great symphonies of Tchaikovsky and Brahms. But you don't know these things at 20, they mature slowly in you like good wine in bottles. When good wine has matured however, it lasts so much better than plonk. Today the Devil wears a mask: the permissive society." On the way back I had a long discussion with Ann. As I expressed it in my *Diaries*: "On the journey, discussed weddings with Ann. Finally decided that we should be married quickly, with just her mother and my mother being told." It seemed a natural step to take in view of the property changes, and one that ought to be got out of the way quickly; one that would bring peace and sincerity of heart.

Incredibly, the wedding took place that Thursday with just our mothers present. There was time to go to Oxford for a day. I bought Ann a ring. Thursday was wet. We all wore carnations. We were married at the Register Office at 46 Cheniston Gardens, W8. We lunched at the Hilton, and then Ann and I drove to Hastings – I looked forward to seeing the sea again as I had begun to write *The Night-Sea Crossing* – and stayed at the Royal Victoria Hotel (room 82 on the 4th floor). Queen Victoria's name was in the visiting book for 1875. Outside there was a wrinkled sea, sand, rocks and the cry of gulls. I had with me *Thought Forces* by Prentice Mulford, and I reflected its view in my *Diaries*: "If you want the new, you must not cling to the old, like a bird clinging to its old plumage, a tree to its old fruit."

Our honeymoon was spent touring the South. We saw Hastings Castle and caves, Battle Abbey, Beachy Head, Bognor, Felpham (where I saw Blake's house again), Arundel, Dunford House in Midhurst (which I had not seen since the course I attended in 1961 and which represented, like Oxford, a time before Caroline) Merrow Downs, and Shere church, with its 14th century anchoress's cell. I wrote 8 poems. It was hot, and I returned bronzed by the sun and, flushed with my new status, immediately applied for a job which offered a post of Head of English and Senior Teacher, two rungs up the ladder.

On March 18th I was interviewed at Garratt Green School in Wandsworth. The Acting Head of Department was not a candidate, but the Second-of-Department was ahead of me, a fellow approaching 60, Bob Leach. He told me the Governors had asked him "Why do you want the job?" And he had replied with disarming honesty: "Because it's on my railway line, it's easy to get here." I was grilled by 15 Governors for 50 minutes and offered the job from September. Within 9 months I had progressed from Scale 2 to Scale 6, Head of English and Senior Teacher, a meteoric rise up the teaching ladder.

I told Caroline I was married and was a Head of English. She said, "You married out of spite." But how wrong she was. She told me she and her husband were going abroad, to live in Germany. Nadia had been accepted by Hunmanby Hall, near Scarborough, and we would pay half the fees each. On Malta she had said to me, "You can't get a permanent home in London and a job and stay in England." But now she was unable to stay in England, and I had a place and a better job than her husband had. The wheel of fortune had truly turned remarkably quickly.

We moved out of Stanhope Gardens on March 20th and stayed in Essex until we moved into 10 Brechin Place on April 4th. The pear and apple trees began to blossom and rabbits ran round the lawn. I took the tube from Loughton to Clapham and went up to the Forest each evening on my return. There were many practical arrangements as we moved in to begin our new married life, but I managed to write some poems. Caroline rang to say she would be going to Brugen in May, and that I would have to look after Nadia until she started at Hunmanby Hall in September. My mother offered to have Nadia at Loughton, which meant that she could attend Oaklands for the summer term and be with her former classmates from before we went to Libya – a better arrangement than for her to attend a school in central London. She would come up to us for weekends in Kensington.

We moved into Brechin Place on the 4th anniversary of Malta. It had thick piled carpets, brocade curtains with tassels, expensive wallpaper, a bathroom with many mirrors, and a bedroom with soft lights behind a pelmet over the bed. I had to put up shelves for my books, and my mother provided Jack Skilton, who had looked after 6 Warrington Gardens for my father, and he spent a whole day doing carpentry and electrical work, and would not hear of being paid. "Your father would have wanted me to do it," he said. Outside Harrods I ran into Ben and told him my news. "I really envy you for getting married," he said. "Wish me luck – I want a bride." That night I unpacked my life's writing and surveyed it. I wrote in my *Diaries*: "I understand Kafka ordering all his work to be burnt as he died. I look back over all I have written and find little value in it. There is more value in living and living to the full, and that I have done, in my several careers. Writing is a marginal note, and those who make it absolute are marginal people....I have stories and poems in me, but I do not really care what happens to them." I also observed: "Ezard's sensibility has been eroded by journalism – as has mine by the political world. In a declining time there must be a gulf between the man of sensibility and the corrupt world."

I settled into married life. It was a joy to return to stability and tranquillity after the disturbed years of my bedsit. I still wrote. In mid-April I was on the 8th elegy. I wrote: "Should all my elegies be in heroic couplets and not alternating rhymed? Except the first and the last? Will it make for monotony as opposed to a style? A fusing of thought, feeling, place, symbol, my own life – and old forms. That is what *The Pilgrim in the Garden* stands for. In the Garden of Eden. A fixed rhyme appeals to my new thinking: the tranquillity of order, discipline. Against revolutionary freedom. Traditional poetry. Strict. Be against the rubbish of the present."

We collected Nadia from Peterborough and drove her down and she stayed with us. I changed my MGBGT for a Lotus Elan S4, which I found in *Exchange and Mart*: a royal blue and white and gold racer with a bonnet that sloped to the ground. I had central heating installed in the flat. It was increasingly apparent that Ann was pregnant, and the prospect of a new baby accorded with our new home. With so much happening, I felt I was neglecting my poetry. Between 22nd and 24th April I recorded in my *Diaries*: "I have poured vital energy out into the outer world: getting a new flat, a new wife, a new job, a new car – changing my surroundings. Now I must call a halt. This whirlwind approach must stop and I must 'change my writing'. Here I feel dissatisfied....The great inner vision I had has broken down, albeit temporarily....I have lost the habit of reading. I must delve into books again – read Horace's *Satires* to begin....I am going through a classical phase. What unites me with Marvell and Horace, not to mention Pope, is the form we are trying: the elegy, the ode, the satire. Just as what unites Mahler to Beethoven or Mozart is the symphony. Each symphony – each satire is different, but each one extends the form. Poetry is an eternal thing. And the self should be kept out of it. 'The death of the self' has classical possibilities. Bought Horace's *Satires* and his literary criticism. Horace's advice in the *Art of Poetry*: 'Choose a subject within your powers.'" Again: "Bought Juvenal's satires. Do a series of satires next. Cf Horace's satires. *The Night-Sea Crossing* – make this into a short allegory à la Rolle – a mystical poem about an aspiring soul in a permissive time?"

We – Ann, Nadia and I – drove to Packfords Hotel, where we were staying, and then joined some of the family at the Roebuck, Buckhurst Hill in anticipation of my younger brother Jonathan's wedding. We dined looking out on Scotch pines and a sunset while cows horned round the cars. The next day I put on morning dress and a top hat and drove with Nadia to St. Mary's church, Loughton, in an Austin Princess, white streamers flicking on the bonnet. Jonathan's bride came down the aisle in white. Later we threw confetti and I talked with Miss Lord, Headmistress of Oaklands, who said "We're very glad to have Nadia back at Oaklands." The reception was at Theydon Bois Golf Club (which now advertises my schools in its annual diaries). I spoke with Roger Lineker, my Maths teacher at Chigwell.

I was still writing stories, and had the idea for doing a series of "portraits": "Portraits for the *Times*? Do portraits or sketches of British types – who are also individuals – like a cartoonist, i.e. be topical. Make a point about them. Later: have made a list of some 100 characters from 'Our Town', on the lines of Spy or Chaucer or Steele – a Hogarth in words, a portrait of a community. It must be a series of satires, a criticism of our nationalistic time with its humanistic, Rousseau-istic fallacies, its restlessness and lack of happiness and peace. A portrait of our permissive times, a satire from the basis of Horace and Juvenal. Vivid sketches à la *Prologue*, individualised types. The aim, to show London, i.e. London people. Each portrait to be used topically, i.e. when the teachers demonstrate and hit the headlines, a portrait appears like a cartoon but catching the truth about one of them....Vices: greed, adultery, unfairness, ambition, gluttony, etc. – judge the characters in terms of their vices and with irony." I was very interested in satire: "'Satire' comes from 'satura' or medley, or from 'lanx satura' or dish full of first fruits (offered to the gods). According to the OED, a satire is a poem or prose composition in which 'prevailing vices or follies are held up to ridicule'. (*The Rape of the Lock* is quoted.) So in my stories or satires I am ridiculing certain vices or follies of our times, i.e. these people are suffering from vices of these permissive, materialistic, spiritually enervated times. My standard, by which I judge their vices and follies is therefore one of enlightened human nature: men not enslaved to sex, money and power, and the Conservative view of individual life lived up to a standard, i.e. (judge) people without standards. ('Today everything is possible – everyone writes', etc.) My view of human nature must be that it needs a great effort of will for it to approach perfection. My stamp in all these stories must be: look, this man is ridiculous because of his vices (sex) and his follies (money) – this is how our society expects us to live. Social criticism in this sense, on moral grounds. Like Pope. In an Age of Loss of Faith. These characters must be revealed by their folly or vice – hence the portrait. So exclude all about me, or any about events." I discussed satire with Jim Doolan, who said: "Swift stood for commonsense – the territory of his belief is small." I added: "Departures from commonsense are his excesses. The golden mean of moderation and commonsense, not put in yourself but into the portrait you paint."

In May I became very interested in Classicism: "Classicism is simply, impersonality – in the sense that I concentrate on the object of my attention and leave myself out of it. I paint the person as he is, without investing the situation with any of my hopes and fears....If man is the measure of everything...then what of the universe? What of mysticism? What of the Light in the mind? Of God? Cannot Classicism be – is *not* classicism – reconciled with subordination to divine standards?...Turn against Romantic excess, yet have a Baroque sense of life with a classical attitude."... I also felt acutely conscious of my imperfections as a writer: "My buried life – my lost life....I am making the best of an appalling job. I am overworked here in England and have lost my energy to be a writer – at least currently. Still, if I am destined to be a classical....I must discipline myself. I must get up early in the morning to compensate for these worldly goods which come too easily: power, money, material prosperity – things which sap the soul. My soul is in danger. I must rescue it. My soul is tired. Let it sleep awhile."

I felt creative again: "Do 12 poems called *The Months*. (Starlit night, harvest, Christmas.)" I was still fascinated by satire and planned to write a satirical story in which everyone shrank, so that "size was now an indication of inner moral stature". This became *The Fountain*, which I wrote in May. I noted that in the 1960s "I stood for the spread of English throughout the world and now I stood for the maintaining of English in our decaying society", and I continued my elegies, which reflected this idea. At the end of May I recorded: "I am starting a search for a new kind of poetry – a new development of a traditional form. A new line. In realisation of this I intend to write one poem of every kind – developing each as much as possible, fusing subject and technique." I wrote out ideas for an epic on the unification of Europe, which I saw ahead ("Europe...united under a modern Augustus").

I was also aware that a shift had taken place in Western culture from the left brain to the right brain, from the excessive rational approach of the 1950s to a more creative and imaginative view, a shift from the classical/Christian conception based on discipline to Wordsworth's "a motion and a spirit.../That rolls through all things". Noting that the 12 million neurons in the brain look like a map of London, I wrote: "We need a study of consciousness....Right use of the brain – intense meaning. So: purify the brain and the senses....In the Augustan Age both hemispheres of the brain were developed to the full – the critical/creative Dr Johnson." I recorded that there had been "a loss of two-sidedness: analysis and imagination". Indeed, it seemed that my own life reflected this "shift in our culture". My upbringing was in the classical/Christian tradition and I had shifted to an awareness of the metaphysical beyond.

In June I devised an accent metre: "Since the 16th and 17th centuries exhausted blank verse, and the 18th century the heroic couplet, I must use a 20th century line for my epic; and it can only be accent metre – after Hopkins and Eliot – i.e. 4 stresses (meaning) or accents (natural stress of the word) in mixed metres with no rhyme. This will be the basic line....Jim Doolan: 'You will uncover it in your writing. The subject comes first.' Great themes, great lines....In the elegies, use a Modernist accent metre, i.e. modernise the traditional form." Of my coming epic I wrote: "I see that my whole life has been a preparation for this: for this I read Homer and Virgil at school and English at Oxford (Milton in the holidays having given up Law). For this I went to the Middle East and Japan – Hiroshima and to El Alamein. Now it is all to come together." I wrote *Blind Churchill to the Night*, "some 90 odd lines exploring the accent metre I am developing for my epic". I talked with Jim Doolan and wrote: "the accent metre is saved from being the first thing that comes into my head (the fírst thíng that cómes into my héad) by devices, e.g. alliteration, internal rhyme. There must also be ' a ghost of a regular form behind the arras of free verse'. So I must strive for a line that is sometimes blank verse, sometimes stress-verse, i.e. metrical stress rather than accent. Hopkins objected to 'the ármy of unálterable láw', i.e. it must be scannable, but you shouldn't say it as 'the armee of unalteraybe law'. A blank verse line in which there are 4 stresses and devices....So my epic should not be written in metre or in free verse, but in metrical stress, i.e. you can do it one way and it scans, you can do it another way and it stresses." I felt a profound sense of my future. "You are a poet," I wrote, "and you have it in you to become a very great poet." And: "I do not need to go abroad again. I have seen enough of the world and its ways. From now on, I will travel in my imagination and explore inner space." And I again wrote: "Become a 'mental traveller'."

I had not forgotten the Light, and wrote: "The barriers that cloud perception – spiritual perception – are self-righteousness, avarice, lust, anger, gluttony, envy, inertia, and they must all be burnt away by the divine fire. I am guilty of some of these. Yet not very often. 'The Pearl of great price.' The Cloud of Unknowing pierced with light....My 'perceptivism' – spiritual perception....See the heart as the 'inpouring of life as light'. Do not keep consciousness on the surface...and see the heart as a fount of living spirit, of life-force." A few days later Margaret paid a brief visit on her way to Vienna and enjoined me: "The Church represents the laws of living. You must look at that light and not be blinded....See through the heart and the spirit." After she had gone I pondered Church reform: "Have the old philosophies failed or have we failed them? The perceptivism I spoke of – it is there in the old ideas of *The Silence*....An institution exists to guard the idea of the Heart and the Silence – the Church. Now that European Christianity may unite, perhaps a Christian Reformation can be launched which will strip the Church of its inauthenticity and make it authentic again."

In early July I was off work with a painful knee, which was diagnosed as "housemaid's knee" or "muscular rheumatism", and between July 4th and 16th I wrote the final version of *The Night-Sea Crossing*, which saw life and death as being reconciled within a greater whole and overcome by eternity, and which employed sonata form. I had considered how musical form might work in poetry, and this was a symphonic poem. I wrote in my *Diaries*: "Both life and death are reconciled in the idea of eternity as a fountain, that reduces all to dust and goes on reusing the same in new forms. God, the divine. So Tao contains life *and* death." The next day I wrote: "The lower elements of consciousness imprisoned in a house of flesh and dominated by the external senses must be transformed. The inner spiritual man must be released by the crucifixion of the old man on the Cross of denial....It is the soul that undergoes suffering in uniting with the lower elements of consciousness – its crowning work is to lift up and transform all the lower elements of consciousness....The reason for all suffering is so that the soul can unite with the lower elements of consciousness and lift them up, i.e. the birth of the inner spiritual man who believes 'the infinite Intelligence illumines and directs me'....'The Heavenly Fires of the Heart.'"

Soon afterwards I arrived at a new "stress metre" line: "Was substituting today in room 14, with an awful class, and was pondering my first elegy and the tension between scansion and stress, and suddenly it hit me – I had a system of primary and secondary stress. In white-hot heat I scribbled out some pencilled notes on a scrap of paper about library books, and put it to Jim who opposed it: 'Overtechnical', 'The natural voice'. But I wasn't quite there! I found it in Hopkins, the ⊓, and then I realised I had a system of primary stress – a 4 stress line. All that remained was to check the rules of primary/secondary stress in word-combinations from my days of teaching English as a Foreign Language. It was in the file I made up, my Prosody Notes. So there we are. I have my line. 4 stresses, 4 primary stresses. I used to sit on a garden seat on Lower Field at Chigwell and read Hopkins in the *Faber Book of Modern Verse*. I did not know that he held an insight for me." (Again I see a submerged pattern in my life.)

I again contemplated: "My mental and moral chaos. After my initial consciousness of God in 1966, a chaos invaded me and I could not cope adequately with things around me....Now I am a different person with a new centre of consciousness....I have got my soul back. I must commit it to the Light." On July 14th I wrote: "All day, filled with a sense that 'the Divine Wisdom guides me, the Infinite Intelligence has selected me to achieve high consciousness in poetry'."

As the end of term approached Jim Doolan felt sad that I was going. "We're a dying breed," he told me. The day before we broke up he asked what he should do. I said, "If the tide of mindlessness and ignorance is coming in, you should get up and move your deck-chair higher up the beach." He said: "Yes, but where? Where can I get a job at 56? I can't go anywhere where I'd lose my pension. I'm trapped." The next day he presented me with a copy of *The Tempest*, and said: "Further to our conversation yesterday, I find myself going back to *The Tempest* more and more."

I felt genuinely sad to leave Henry Thornton. The reason I had been there was to talk poetry with Jim Doolan. I was moving further up the beach to a girls school with the post of Senior Teacher and reduced teaching commitment Jim had been denied, and I was sorry to leave him exposed to the tidal waves set off by the tempest of inner city comprehensive education.

The summer holidays of 1974 were dominated by my growing interest in mysticism, by my poetry and, one way or another, by Tuohy and Margaret. The first day of the holidays Tuohy came to a salad lunch at 10 Brechin Place on his way to Brighton. I explained my stress metre, tracing it back to Coleridge's *Christabel*, which has 4 stresses in a line, and he spoke of Yeats as the best poet of cadence after Shelley. He said: "People legislate for their own systems – that's what Hopkins did. You do it first, then make the rules afterwards." He said that Milton was the turning point in the elegy, and insisted that poets need a disciplined form to work against. I debunked the ungrand themes of the rational Movement, quoting Roy Campbell:

> "You praise the firm restraint with which they write;
> I'm with you there, of course,
> They use the snaffle and the curb all right,
> But where's the bloody horse?"

I was still looking for the Light, but the daily grind of Henry Thornton had denied me a peaceful, tranquil heart and soul, without which the Light cannot be seen. I wrote: "I have been a month in darkness – perhaps more. Though nightly I have looked for the Light. I am still in purgation. Yet what more can I give up? I have surrendered alcohol and so much. Is it Nadia again? Will I swing into Light in August, when Nadia is in Germany? Is my spiritual life doomed to be a see-saw? Darkness when I have Nadia near me, and Light when I have lost her, and she is out of reach? Is this the meaning of divine Love? If so, it is a cruel, absolutist Love. All or nothing. Yield all or receive nothing. I feel the Fire of Love in my heart, but see no Light when I press my hands over my closed eyes." But I also wrote at the end: "The Fire of Love and Light burns up our sins, cleans out our soul. Sixties – years of sin. Seventies – years of inner cleanliness." And I related the Fire or Light to the universe: "Cosmic rays which bombard us 20 times a second – the energy and force of life, which renews the soul, makes the plant grow, gives vigour to the world, and is the quickening force in the soul of man. A power that pours out through the entire universe, way beyond our sense. It is love. The cohesive power of the entire universe is love; all things are composed of energy, which is light, which is spirit." And again: "A theory. Cosmic rays stream onto earth from the loving heart of the universe. They enter our body at 20 times per second. By being 'I' (Reflection) we can resist them. If we are humble, they fill us and direct our mental activity. Their wave-length can be tuned into through peace and love. The physical (in the sense of physics) being of God. 'The universe is a storehouse of energy which can be set in motion by human impulses, which are carried on etheric waves to their destination.' Light/centre of universe – how related? 'Lighting up' – a divine current which illumines the understanding like a bulb. The current. An electrical force/energy in the 'ether'." (This marked my first gropings into the philosophy that became Universalism.)

I began to revise my poem *The Silence* and then Ann and I took Nadia to Sompting for her children's holiday. We went on to Brighton where Tuohy cooked us a chicken dinner and we talked until 2 a.m., during which he expressed many of the social, political and aesthetic attitudes I put in my poem about him: *An Aesthete's Golden Artefacts*. (See my lengthy entry in my *Diaries* for full details.) We talked at length about the objective correlative and the need to generalise the autobiographical. A few days later I wrote the 11th elegy, and then wrote a 12th elegy on Tuohy, which I sent to him. Tuohy rang to say that he liked my poem on him and offered me the use of his flat in August. I wrote in my *Diaries*: "I am a symbolist, using traditional symbols (e.g. alchemy). And uniting the traditions of statement and image." At the same time I reread some of my lyrics and wrote: "They are fresh and good. The feeling is there. An urgency. I must type them all up. I could have written so many more if I hadn't poured my energies into *Chains* – which was an act of self-unification, a putting together of Humpty Dumpty again. Yet too many would perhaps have been a bad thing."

Of my poetry I wrote: "I am like a furnace. The base experience comes into me and comes out as an artefact, an object....The artist turning people into stone, experience into ingots. The artist as Gorgon, or as alchemist....the dual nature of the artist. He has to turn living experience to stone, in his art, but is apt to turn real people to stone in his life....My glowing Platonism: turning experience into an ingot/ stone – turning an idea into a form." Meanwhile I was thinking about the Universal Mind: "Inspiration comes from the Universal Mind....Believe in the Universal Mind which the superconscious can join to – the Muse. This Universal Mind is the reality behind the universe – is from within out. This Higher Mind is the Mind Illumination....after a decade of rushing outside I am now stopped. 'Be still and know that I am God.'"

Nadia went to Germany. I drove her to Gatwick and put her on a plane. Then Ann and I took the train to Cornwall to stay with her mother. I wrote: "I got on that train an agnostic and got off a...supporter of the mystic tradition. Today I wrote a Postscript to my essay. It was intended to be a commentary and I left a lot out. The Gospels and traditional values; habits; 'European man needs a regenerated European Christianity to carry him forward'; 'the metaphysical Being is none other than the apprehension of God'; 'the Church can be a hindrance to the attainment of Being'; 'churches are inauthentic'; also: 'We need a new Reformation to connect perceptivist Existentialism with the concept of the Christian tradition.'" I called the Postscript to my essay *The Mystic Revival*.

On August 7th I wrote: "No illumination for a long time, yet I am purposive. Reread *The Silence*. Is this my second Dark Night? If so, what is its purpose? Think. If the first Dark Night was 1967 to 1971, when the senses had to be burned away after the first illumination (1965/6), this second Dark Night is a final purification – now that I have given up drink – of what?" I was still writing stories and I revised my poem *Archangel*. I revised some of the elegies. We went to Porthleven and saw the traditional carrying of torches. I wrote: "The procession round the harbour, then to the field where they threw their flaming brands onto the bonfire. The burning fire – the sparks. Red smuts, white stars. A village as a whole." (The next day this became another elegy, *Sea-Fire*.) We drove with Ann's mother to Newlyn to see Ann's cousin's boat, and to Pendeen lighthouse, where Ann's mother's mother had lived, and to Geevor mine where her husband had worked and Cape Cornwall. Of my elegies I wrote: "They are not too personal. They use personal experience to forge a symbol that is not autobiographical. So, the 6th is not about my 'flow' but about seeing your heart as it was and then seeing it as it has become (lake/river and the 'water' imagery)....The personal tradition goes back to Marvell. In the same way, the 8th is about personal failure and its consolation at the human/national level – and the hopes of personal success through that level. The traditional value is therefore art as a giving (need to die from self)." We went to Caerhays to see the castle Byron's grandmother lived in. It was all battlements and towers amid windswept trees by the sea.

I was torn between art and mysticism. In my *Diaries* I wrote: "The eternity of the artist or of the mystic? Think." Following *The Mystic Revival* I had been contemplating the artist Gwen Broad at Hill Place, East Grinstead, and the life of an obscure artist. As if to answer my question, Margaret arrived unannounced, clutching a plastic bag which contained a round pottery halo which was broken in three places. It was her Light in red enamel. She said: "The centre is empty and yet it isn't. Ovals, not angles now, there are no more angles." And she spoke of Fire: "The heart must be loving (Christ); the soul is the Light; the spirit is the new self that replaces the old personality – which is always with us and calm; then there is the Holy Spirit, the inward surge of the tide into a Cornish harbour, when the heart and soul are at peace. Then there is the centre, which is where God is....In a person it is where God is in the heart-soul....Christ is the Light – and the loving heart. People are not afraid at death because they see the Light and feel Christ beside them....Don't chase, because you're only running after rubbish you don't want." She read and approved *The Mystic Revival*. After she went back to Shoreham, where she had a small art gallery in the High Street (in whose window she put her enamel halo, and where it was sometimes broken, sometimes whole, depending on the state of her peace of soul), I wrote an elegy on her, which became *A Mystic Fire-Potter's Red Sun-Halo*.

Margaret interpreted my illness in Sloane Square in May 1972 in terms of my centre shift to a new unitive life. She told me: "The (four) raptures you had – the extremes – pushed up all the evil and left you clean inside." I commented in my *Diaries*: "So when I was taken ill near Sloane Square in May 1972, did I finally lose my old personality and did the Spirit enter me? For ever since then I was delivered." I also wrote after she left: "I am very tired after Margaret. I suppose later I will look back and see myself as having gone through a momentous summer in which I accepted the Mystical tradition of Christianity. It is just a question of language, really. I have had all the experience. And so it does not seem to me now to be a shattering step. Nevertheless today August 15th must mark a turning point – the Margaret elegy – and 7th August – the date of my essay – must mark a beginning I suppose." Margaret had said to me of my suffering: "It deepens you, it releases the feelings, it makes you *alive*. Before you suffer you are dead. It brings you alive deep down. You could never have created what you are doing now if you had not suffered." I wrote: "The death of the self-will means you are guided by Providence, the Unseen Power. From now on I must pray for guidance."

Margaret urged me to accept all my past works: "No one can correct your work. You have done it, it is yours. No one can say, 'You should have made this more light, that more dark.'...If you don't like it, don't look at it." I surveyed my poems and wrote: "A pear tree does not hawk its fruit. It is there to be picked and eaten if people want it. If they don't want it, they needn't. The wasps will get it when it is windfalls." Ann and I went down to Brighton and spent a couple of days in Tuohy's flat. We went via Hill Place, and I wrote the elegy that became *An Obscure Symbolist's Rock-Tree* within the snow-white walls of his flat in Sussex Square. Margaret visited us there from Shoreham and told me, "Nicholas I must follow my own direction now." Before she left she enjoined me: "Accept. No rebellion any more. Accept."

I knew she was speaking of the Church, and I was still aware within that to go into the Church would actually be a betrayal of the universality of the Light. I felt acutely conscious of how the different Christian sects were at war over the same principle of the Light. I wrote: "The Mystic tradition is in the Catholic Church, and God is experienced directly by Catholics. Margaret's experience is as personally Protestant as any Protestant." Of myself I wrote: "My problem. Until I was 18 I attended a Methodist church, i.e. I approached God directly without priests, through the heart and 'sudden emotional ecstasy' – a Romantic view of feeling, there being no restraint on the self-will and no urging to discipline. At school every morning in C of E I approached God through the set forms of Anglicanism. Now I see the need for a rule as a Catholic, which the priests apply through confession. What a muddle! The only solution is for there to be Unity, all three sects to become one....I should be what I *am*, not what my ancestors were – Quakers, Methodists, Liberals, Conservatives."

The best way to practise "acceptance", I felt, was through my elegies – I had now written 19 – in which I had begun to accept my family origins. I wrote: "The elegies among other things form a complicated acceptance of my family origins – against which I rebelled for so long. Now the note is acceptance. Rebellion is at an end." I also felt that the way forward was to accept my destiny to raise mankind's consciousness. I wrote: "Lifting mankind to a higher level of happiness, progress and understanding. Your works only follow you if you *lift* men, your fellow men. The lust for gold, fame, a woman's lips to which you have no right, and power all belong to the lower kingdom of existence and have no place in the realms of light."

On August 27th the Light returned. I wrote: "Last night, Light again, after a long dark. Not as brilliant as usual, but still enough. I buried my face in my pillow, then put my pillow over my head, the better to see." A couple of days later I recorded: "In touch with my imagination again. Saw flowers, a guitar, a host of strange images."

While I was writing an elegy on Chigwell School (and after changing my car from the Lotus to a Triumph PI 2.5) I sketched out details for a satire on the theory of mixed ability teaching in comprehensive education, which became *The Garden*. My *Diaries* catch the tone: "Selectivity is not fair. All seeds should have an equal chance. There is no difference between roses and weeds except for environmental differences. In fact the roses will help weeds to become more rose-like." With the idea for this satire still fresh in my mind I began my new job at Garratt Green School.

Slowly my acceptance of the universe filled me with a deep calm, the "peace that passeth understanding", and although I hardly saw the Light now I was filled with knowledge about it, a wisdom that seemed to be hatching into my soul as if it was cocooned in a cloud.

Garratt Green was a glassy comprehensive set in green grounds with many shrubs in Burntwood Lane, which runs between Wandsworth Common and Garratt Lane. It has since been renamed Burntwood School. In September 1974 it had getting on for 2,200 girls and 140 mainly female staff, and an English Department of 26. It was a well-run school with a relatively new Head, Mrs. Kay, who was finding coping with so many pupils a handful. The corridors were crowded, and at break and lunchtime the staff withdrew into a cramped staff room. I had a room of my own and taught 'O' level and 'A' level. I found my Departmental staff – all of whom were women except Bob Leach – very courteous, respectful and eager to please. There were many meetings – House meetings, Departmental meetings which I took (sitting the Department at desks in a classroom), Heads of Department and Heads of House meetings (nicknamed Hods and Hohs) and Senior Management Team meetings (when the three Senior Teachers met with the two Deputies and Head) – and I never left school until after 5 and always had work that took all evening: planning meetings, preparing classes, marking essays, and typing reports on unsatisfactory pupils for the Head.

I worked incredibly hard and noted: "After my first week at Garratt Green School: much battered by all the questions and problems I have had to answer and sort out. Am drawing up a syllabus to put a stop to such questions." I worked a long day. A few days later I noted: "These days I am obsessed by light. After days of long hard work – I am up at 6.30 a.m. to do my exercises and seldom finish work by 11.15 p.m. – I can think of nothing but, *light*. The light in the universe (God's mind)," I wrote, "is the same as the light in man's mind. My image in *The Silence* of the seed – light." Nadia came from Germany on her way to Scarborough to start at Hunmanby, but otherwise I slogged away, completing the Departmental syllabus. At the end of September I wrote: "A month. No mysticism. Living at work. A shadow of my true self. Margaret rang from Dublin late at night two days ago. It was like a voice from another world." I was then able to spend a weekend writing *The Garden*, and turned back to poems: "Poems of London. The sun shining through, the light. Ghosts, skeletons underneath. The rain. Huge nature, tiny man. The city as it is. The beauty of London. Show this in poems."

In October Ann finally gave birth at Queen Charlotte's Hospital. I attended the birth and then went to work. I wrote: "Ann gave birth to a son at 7.07 this morning. She was told to go to hospital yesterday...and I was telephoned – by her from the Labour ward – at 5 a.m. My heart was in my mouth because the baby was 'very tired' struggling to get out the wrong way – and his heart stopped and I was sent out of the room. I returned later and a forceps delivery was set in motion – me staying. The 'fetal heart beat' kept going nil and it looked stillborn but was revived. High blood pressure makes a baby very tired. The experience left me very shaky inside, a feeling of wanting to cry....Now once again, my future is born – along with my new self....Call the baby Matthew? He is 6 lbs 11 ozs....A Vantoosh and Forceps baby (Vantoosh equals suction)." We called the baby Matthew.

I noted that there was an article on Ken Campbell in the *Times* and recalled my visit to the Partisan with Campbell and John Ezard. Campbell had written "a fantasy about his friend Ion Will – none other than the Will who ran behind me on Belgrade Station in 1958 and just missed the train, and who turned up at Worcester College and sat at my feet in 1961. All about telepathy and another planet."

I was still looking for the Light: "A blue light again, glowing like a stone. A wonderful blue. I lay in the bath and peeked for it and saw it. A wonderful, wonderful blue." At half term I was very tired but I wrote: "The Light alone brings the power to judge good and evil. Until we have it we make erring judgements and do not see the Truth. This is the law of progress, of eternal life. One truth succeeding another. The Light is the soul and God shines through the soul and heart....The conscious awareness of that Light of Christ within is contact with God....Civilisations are founded on religion." I wondered whether "my appeal to the mystic tradition" could "form a new religion" and wrote: "We need God for a *Civitas Dei*" and: "Existentialism, concentrating purely on the experience of the Light and not the social drill....A Christian mystical Existentialism, emphasising the experience of the Light." This idea anticipated my philosophy of Universalism. I wrote: "I am so clear-headed these days. I am guided. I am the scribe. It is all given. I see an important movement taking place. In 10 or 15 years' time I will be able to address the Ecumenical Movement and...read a speech to them outlining the basis for a Universal Church." This anticipated my address to Quaker Universalists in 1993 on a new Universalist convergent-syncretist interfaith Church. I also wrote: "The great unitive mystics are founders of spiritual families, centres wherefrom radiates new transcendental life."

On October 23rd I wrote: "I stand for the Mystic tradition from St. Augustine to now. Finished the 23rd elegy. Imagery: Fire v Light, with bird nesting by water as a sub-image." Nadia came from Hunmanby bearing her school magazine which was called *Flame-bearer* and which contained a song and a prayer about the Light. I took her to Loughton and lunched with my mother, and wrote: "Up to the High Beach church and the two ponds with Frances and Nadia while Ann had a sleep, with Matthew in the Moses basket. The golden rust and orange-copper leaves, we scuffled and shuffled. The grave of fresh flowers."

That half term I thought again about my Dark Night: "My Dark Night. The Dark Night of the Senses was when the divine intelligence detached my soul from the web of the lower senses, a denuding process which left the lower senses in emptiness and darkness. This was the loss of Caroline and its aftermath. Divine Wisdom was still 'dark as night'. In this, spiritual knowing and illumination were imparted (in September 1971) and my high spiritual state with its emotional ecstasy led to fatigue (May 1972, my exhaustion). The Night of the Spirit was an exhaustion that followed from that. Now I am emerging into the unitive life, my self remade....My attachment to the lower senses. So when I gave up cigarettes in 1964, that was part of my purgation, just as giving up alcohol in 1973 was also part of my Second Dark Night, of the Spirit. Union is ahead....The Uncreated Light is Pure Being. I have been guided. The answer to my question about the framework of the Search is: the Mystic Way. So the Divine Intelligence fulfils its purpose through me. The peace of heart that I now have is the necessary consequence of those sufferings which I would not now be without. A piece of work comes from an author's state of mind at the time, hence as his mind changes his work will change. My works of 1962/3 predicted my life: *Tristy* predicted my need to suffer, *Mandalas* that I would go to the East. I need some Divine poems to finish it, i.e. some direct descriptions of God. So this collection is an act of self-discovery of myself as a mystic."

Then I thought about the unitive life: "The self desires nothing, and has nothing, is passive. A state of equilibrium, at one with the Absolute Life – not perceiving it – a state of purely spiritual life, characterised by peaceful joy, enhanced powers, intense certitude. So when did this calm come upon me?...I would date its onset to September 1973, when I started at Henry Thornton, having finished my purgation. Certainly since October 1973 when I started my elegies. To put it the other way round, I had it with *The Night-Sea Crossing*and throughout the summer, when I worked really well. I first met Tuohy in 1964. Since then I have been through a long and painful process of remaking my consciousness. My relative lack of interest in the lower senses these days, I prefer spiritual quiet....'The incredible energy' that Jim spoke of, is the mystic energy, after the lower senses have been conquered." I wrote: "Saul's conversion near Damascus: 'And suddenly there shined round about him a light from heaven.'" And again: "Heaven is the light. Hell is darkness. Since I overcame my self and stopped wanting, I have lived with a new urgency and purpose – my new-found religion. I am a child of Heaven now."

The Conservatives lost the October General Election, and I toyed with the idea of going into politics. I spoke to Ann about how this would benefit my poetry. "I said I have a destiny and a mission. It is Saul's light. My destiny is to speak the Truth in this society to pour my being out, through (a) big poem on the war. 'I am a Virgil. Just as he had to do the *Eclogues* and *Georgics* to do the *Aeneid* so I have to complete the Mystic Way.' I said I could write a long poem in the mornings and evenings, day by day; that Milton and Marvell and Horace and Virgil were all mixed up with politics. Dryden's *Absalom and Achitophel* and Milton's *Paradise Lost* both originated in politics – they changed the names."

I now returned to lyric poems, *The Gates of Hell*. I wrote: "*The Gates of Hell*. These should not be in the order that they were written but in the order in which they 'happened' – to overcome the sort of confusion we experience when we go to Donne, whose chronology is unknown. Also, I should not force the irregularities of the originals into a tight metrical form. They begin in regular meter and become irregular as the feeling of disintegration proceeds." On November 3rd I wrote: "This weekend I have typed up 40 lyrics. 21 yesterday, 19 today." And I reflected: "When I was smashed in 1969/1970/1971, I found my wholeness again by associating with the meek and the maimed, the insulted and the injured, the boys of Greenwich, the wretched of the earth." And again: "I grew *The Gates of Hell* effortlessly in two years (after 6.11.1972), like a tree putting out leaves." Working on my lyrics threw up the following observation: "My contempt for our time increases day by day. It's as though Milton's slight little pieces are hailed as his great work, and *Paradise Lost* (is) above everyone's head. I have not bothered to type out my 110 short lyrics before now – they are too small – yet each one is more significant than the Movement poems in *New Poetry*. It's as though fireworks have been defined as squibs, and rockets are forbidden." And I observed: "The Symbolist vision. This is an aspect of the Mystic Way. Symbolism enhances the Mystic feeling."

I could not understand how I had written virtually no poetry from 1967 to 1972: "What a pity I didn't write these short poems in Libya. I clung to prose, having to see the structure and preserve my sanity. To put pen to paper for a letter was to collapse into tears. I can do it now, recollecting emotion in tranquillity....I vow I will write no more prose....I want to despair. It is as though only now I have found my material as a poet: the situation that engulfed me....'Emotion recollected in tranquillity.' Yet can't write when you are disturbed, you can only write when recollecting. So now is the time. That is why I have not drawn on this material." On November 10th I wrote: "I typed 31 poems yesterday, and another 31 today, and have now finished transferring them from the green manuscript book."

In November I recorded: "Ran into Biggs-Davison near the Gloucester Road cleaners. I was in my Saturday attire – why do I always run into him when he is in a suit and I am in my bum clothes?...He kept trying to excuse himself to get a taxi....He is an anomaly. Sometimes he is very pro, e.g. student revolutionaries and the drink he invited me to, the question he asked in Parliament about Libya, the drink he invited me to at the House of Commons. Other times he is on the run. It is almost as though he has been asked to behave in a certain way towards me."

I was still living with great energy and I took stock: "To what do I attribute my tremendous energy? For I have twice the stamina and energy of most men – and this is my genius: this spring. This quantitative energy which contains quality. Perhaps the disciplines of my childhood – the hard work I put in then. The Latin, the homework. Eruption year, 1974 – this must be connected with my marriage. I have so many works to do: *Flight*, 16 sonnets, 12 odes (Pindaric odes), on the Months, the Cromwell poem, my Juvenilia, the 80 odd poems I wrote in Japan before I met Tuohy. Not my greatest work, but certainly some should be printed. My destiny – then my epic. Pound, I think of him so often, and of my evening with him. I have a destiny ahead of me. It is there, all I have to do is to follow footsteps. I will do it to prove that I have been all along a man of destiny." At the same time I reacted to an evening my 6th form spent listening to Adrian Henri: "I: 'If you want a meal of roast beef, you go to Donne or Shakespeare or Wordsworth and learn about the soul. Henri gives you popcorn or Smith's crisps – superficial stuff about the materialistic world out there.' He writes for the majority, apparently. Henri: 'Poetry is heightened speech.' 'Heightened' means alliterated, assonanced – using devices – and this is the justification for 'heightened art' in the Tate, and getting away from the potter's aesthetics for 'heightened clay'. A line must be drawn."

I was still pondering the order in the universe and the calm in the spirit, and I came to the conclusion that the same Spirit, otherwise known as God, reconciled opposites: "Wordsworth's two passages in *The Prelude* about how the mountain moved – once when he was rowing, once when he felt giddy. His attribution of unknown 'modes of being' to Nature and mountains, which 'do not live like living men' – but which live. The wisdom and spirit of the universe which breathes through all things; the eternity of thought. The order in the universe that reconciles the contradictions (storms, wars, killings) and the calm in the spirit that reconciles the passions, e.g. terror. We are purified until we recognise 'the grandeur in the beating of the heart' – i.e. we have reverence and are always capable of greatness. This wonderful calm! The spirit gives 'to forms and images a breath and everlasting motion'. Images can be trees, etc. – things seen – but also mental pictures of things which have excited feelings of love, joy, fear, wonder. These images move through our minds like living things; they grow and are linked with our earliest and strongest feelings. 'If the images are great, beautiful and mysterious, the feelings themselves will be purified and sanctified.' Then the terror is ennobled by the image of the mountain. A child's wonder at a rainbow remains a beautiful feeling which grows in spiritual strength each time a rainbow returns. So it is image – feeling – purification when it returns. (See the beginning of *The Portmellon Water Splash*.) Also Donne's *Extasie*, which is half-humorous, half-serious, about the body being an outlet for a soul – and which is much more of a *Coy Mistress*, trying to persuade. A classical chatting-up. The elaborate argument for her to give her body. The unity of creation: the Zen Stone Garden in Japan."

I began typing out *The Flight* "while Ann took Matthew to a reunion of her childbirth class". I wrote: "The metaphysical flight. If there is one Spirit in the universe, which breathes life into all forms, then all images in Nature are part of a unity and all images in the mind are too. Strong feelings see into the unity of life in the universe and are remembered and derive a living power of their own. They purify our clogged-up feelings. If the universe is all one, then images are a revelation of the One. They are not just intense memories, but chinks into the unity of the universe, glimpses of the Power which have a metaphysical sense, i.e. the power."

Increasingly I looked back to Epping Forest. I wrote: "I am unable to tear my soul away from the county that has so inspired me: Epping Forest. I have moved away, and sold Crescent View, but my heart is still there. And I can see myself moving back. What I want is my heart. Not a view that has no resonance. I am a child of Epping Forest, and should find a good place near it – in it, or on it – to live. Or else I should stay within reach of it in anonymous London, where I can avoid the people of Essex but go down and savour her beauty, and observe the changing seasons." And again: "What I want to do with the rest of my life. Live quietly in the Forest where there is peace. Go for walks among leaves and living things. Grow things. Contemplate. Get away from the stress of the city and its unreality. Live the stylish life of a country squire."

On December 1st the Light returned and I wrote: "The Light returned several times today, a mirror for my soul. Slightly bluish. I am guided by the Power."

I embraced poetry whole-heartedly. I finished *The Flight* and had ideas for writing haikus, an epistle to Cromwell and further revisions of *The Silence*. I wrote: "I must write, in addition to my epic: odes, epistles (to the living and the dead), satires, etc. I need to make a study of Roman poetry." And: "If I have 100 good lines among 4,000 average ones, that is enough to make me a great poet. I have today retrieved 'I skulk under the rim of my collar'. I must not forget to salvage 'While hostesses serve drinks and pickled prattle'."

At Garratt Green I shared a room with another Senior Teacher, the Head of Science, Sister Hurst. She was a nun with La Retraite for 30 years and was transferred to their Clapham branch and then suddenly told to live out in society and find herself a job. For the first time for over 30 years she had to think about the practicalities of maintaining a home, and she used to ask me about rates and drainpipes. One lunchtime she described how she got up at 5.30 a.m. to contemplate before coming into school for her active life, and I told her about Margaret and asked her: "To what extent is she – and her illumination – normal in a convent, and to what extent is she different?" Sister replied: "Oh, no, she's a leader. It's not mentioned in our Convent. That's what we are praying for but it never comes. Only the saints have that. You have to shout for the Lord." I thought: here is a nun who is living the devotional life, and no one is telling her that what Margaret and I know is normal and the nuns are not experiencing what is central to Christianity.

We understand our lives in retrospect. Looking back, I wrote: "Greenwich. The reason I went there was to meet Ann. Just as the reason I had to live in Egerton Gardens was to meet Margaret. How strange life is!" And again: "I had to see my first marriage break up so I could give up drink, and I had to remain unknown so I could have free time, in which to write my important work. I would have done neither otherwise, and thank the Power."

I was settled. After we had broken up for the Christmas holidays and Nadia had come to stay I wrote: "Today I finished the *Epistle to His Imperial Highness on his Birthday*, which I only started yesterday – 150 lines – and did *Winter in Nara*. At present I can do anything I want. I pick up works that defeated me 10 years or less ago, and do them straight out on the typewriter, and so true is my ear that out of 150 lines there was only one tetrameter – all the rest were pentameters when I wanted them to be. I have mastery of my subject, I am on top of my material. It is a wonderful gift, I am using it to get ready a considerable body of material. A lot of this newly won confidence must come from my settled family life – my marriage to Ann. She has provided settled conditions." Of 1974 I wrote: "This year has been poetry, poetry, poetry, ever since July, which reopened the spring. (*The Night-Sea Crossing*.)"

On Christmas Eve we went to St. Augustine's church. I wrote: "I am filled with the Power at present....The heart – the meeting of the soul and the Great Spirit, which pours in as Light, i.e. in meditation, lose the sense of the heart as a physical organ (heart centre/brain centre). The 7 dense veils that cover the soul, and which have to be pruned: self-righteousness, avarice, lust, anger, gluttony, envy, inertia. Seeking for the Pearl of great price." On Boxing Day we went to my mother's in Loughton and I wrote: "The third eye with which we see eternity. The 'sun' is the centre of our universe – which came first, the inner sun or the outer sun? Which is the copy? The outer sun is a copy of the inner sun I see?" After Christmas I noted: "My gift is for expressing an idea in terms of a visual image – this is essentially a poetic...gift....At present am doing a sonnet a day, the October 1970 material – shaping it into good verse."

I was very interested in a TV programme on Jill Purce's *The Mystic Spiral*. Ann had bought me the book, and I wrote: "How everything is fundamentally a vortex or a spiral; the secret of life which has been preserved in the symbols of our art. Physics is now coming round to the view of the Eastern mystic: the universe is organic, not mechanistic; all still centres and eddying spirals. Order – patterns." Later Jill Purce would invite me to her flat and sign my copy of her book. I ended the year by going to Watkins bookshop (where my future publisher worked), where I "bought some secondhand books on the Light".

In early 1975 I taught some of the more mystical poems of Herbert, Donne and Wordsworth, and there was a strike against the Houghton Report. I recognised that stillness was a great boon: "I must be still and praise God, give thanks, for then I will be in tune and harmony with the universe, and the lack of harmony or sin will not show in my face, which will contain a spiritual beauty....The Light can be contacted in the inner quietness; peace, love and gratitude retard old age and overcome disease. Divine love regenerates the cells....Perfect love is Oneness with God (sending out love)." I wrote of Wordsworth: "Finished *The Prelude* books 1 and 2 at school. Wordsworth is saying that he derived his feelings from the Lake District, that they need Nature. There is the delight in natural objects, and his philosophising about unity which is beyond this: the affinity between objects." I was still writing poems and recorded: "Wrote *The Blind, Generations like Seasons* and *Recurrence* between 7 p.m. and 11 p.m. after a hard day's work – and a fruitful assembly. My shattering idea of seasonal recurrence. Not eternal recurrence, just men and history turning through, and obeying the same law as, the seasons. I have written 192 poems in *The Gates of Hell* alone. Baudelaire only wrote 144 in his whole life. I am the Baudelaire of our time. Probably the most interesting poet of my time." I wrote again: "In the last six months there has been a great outpouring, a volcanic eruption. Poems have shot from me like rocks of molten lava. I have typed up the equivalent of the entire output of Baudelaire in the last four months alone."

I was conscious of unity: "Unity. From now on I must unite all my works in the light of my mysticism. Each poem of any length must be a slim volume part of a large whole, *The Mystic Way*." Another idea was that all my poems should be called *Life Cycle*: "Decided that the original idea I had on the plane in 1961 between Baghdad and Basra was for *The Gates of Hell*. *Life Cycle* itself is to be 10 poems, of the length of Rilke's *Elegies*, combining the *Four Seasons* and the Epping Forest poem, about man's life and growth in his spirit. It must be essentially a religious poem." I was haunted by Rodin's "the form gives rise to the idea" and line 1 of Ovid's *Metamorphoses*: "When the sun rises I see that everything is modelled on his divine plane."

I was still writing poems. On February 9th I "wrote *Cherry Blossom* and *Sunday*". At half term I wrote: "Still the lyrics pour: the *Gates of Paradise*. 'I will not be upset – no one is upset within the Gates of Paradise.'" On February 16th I wrote: "Have drafted some 10 poems in the last two days. Cannot stop them pouring up. About Paradise mostly at present. Are these poems part of *The Gates of Hell* or are they a separate work, e.g. *The Gates of Paradise*?"

I was again aware of being in a Dark Night of Spirit: "God gives us good things – why should he not also give us evil things, to mortify us and purify us? First there is the active purgation of the Dark Night of the Sense – self-denial – and then there is the passive purgation when things go wrong. Then the Dark Night of the Spirit, when there is no Light. During this time the human is being welded to the divine so that the humble is exalted."

At February half term we spent nights at Folkestone – we stayed in

Marine Crescent where the Channel swimmers used to stay – and Margate, and I recorded that I wrote "two stories and various poems". At school I was teaching Milton's Satan in book 9 of *Paradise Lost*, how he sought to change his society and make it better. On March 1st I recorded: "Wrote another Divine Sonnet, *The Seed of God*" and: "The Divine Poems keep coming to me."

In March I was filled with the urgency of proclaiming ecumenical unity: "Wrote *De-frosting*, then dozed off downstairs. When I came to I had the idea of launching a religious movement..., using my cells of 10 idea. A movement for Ecumenical unity, to purge the Church; to bring back to the Church the idea that men are seeds and need the Light to quicken them into life; for they were dead and are now alive. The idea of the Resurrection. Rather than start a new creed we should work within the framework of the Church and redefine religion, concentrating on the Mystical part. Action: the Light activates the seed of our destiny, which then communicates to us in words in the silence, for which we must be quiet. It is important to set up a centre to put this point of view. After it is set up there can be papers, etc. which can prepare the way for a European Church (Anglican *and* Catholic)....This must be connected to the Ecumenical Movement. The new Mystical movement."

I saw very clearly that there should be a new mystical movement within the Church, and that it should include both the Church of England and Roman Catholics (the opposing sides of the titanic hidden 20th century struggle for world influence and ultimately world rule between the Judeo-Masonic American Anglophiles and British Crown on the one side, and the Vatican and its Islamic allies on the other side, which led to the burning of Windsor Castle and the Habsburg palace in Vienna): "Campaign for Church Reform (1) into a unity – through the ecumenical movement – and (2) a purging. Produce papers, publicity. Defend the traditional values....Press the Archbishop of Canterbury and the Head of the Roman Catholic Church (in Britain) into this action. Also the Pope. The Church should once again express the beliefs of the nation. It should not be split into sects. There should, as at the beginning, be one Church of which all cathedrals are representative, and this should be to guard the growth of seeds, the mystical experience of the Light. When I have achieved this, then I – and a host of others – will be able to go to church."

I put this to Margaret: "We will be undoing 500 years of work: Luther and Wesley, etc. By abolishing sectarianism and 8 denominations we will give the young a simple choice, for or against. We will be like the Oxford Movement – profound. The Church's energy will flow more rapidly when it is all going in the same direction and all cathedrals represent the same. Margaret: 'They are all saying, "Who will lead us and take us back to the Light?"' The art movement is a part of this – it illustrates the central philosophical idea, the 'new philosophy'. Margaret: 'Do not force it, you are guided. You by yourself can do nothing, only the force within you can. But you are going in the right direction.' 'The Church is one, one rock. It must be accepted. You mustn't accept the part of it that suits you.' The seed: 'The Christ in you.' The re-unification of the Church, an historical idea; getting the Church back to what it was before Becket. Rule from

Rome?...I need to accomplish this because although I connect myself to the Mystical Tradition, I need to have *one* Church and one alone in which to embody it, and there is only one, and the rest confuses and dissipates and chokes. This is my at-one-ment. I have seen the World Council of Churches taken advantage of and confused. It needs someone to build the Mystical philosophy as the 'new philosophy' of the West....The poetry revolution is one of content: the Mystic Way....Margaret: who has tried to do anything religious in the last 100 years? Answer: only T. S. Eliot, perhaps all the strands are coming together: Chapel, Methodist church, Ainger; Zen; the World Council of Churches." This idea groped towards the convergent-syncretistic Universalism which I was to develop in the future.

On 9th March I wrote: "Under my shower saw the Light – blue and round for a while. Now have a slight headache from the intensity." And: "250 poems now." And on March 12th: "How to arrange these poems? *Pilgrim in the Garden* separately? *The Gates of Hell* all 250 or just some of them? In 3 parts? Or separate 'volumes'? With *Pilgrim* mixed in or not? Think." On 21st March I found my answer: "Got it: the whole work is *Sonnets and Lyrics from a Dark, Dark Night*, and Part One is *Inscriptions on the Gates of Hell*. Part 2: *A Bulb in Winter*, as I decided last weekend, and Part 3, *Paradise Within the Cathedral*." I swung away from the ecumenical movement: "Poetry requires me to cross what I learned at Oxford with experience of the world (Mephistopheles, Eve), and hence my 'bitty' career, never quite satisfactory when considered as a career, but ideal when considered as what earns money for a poet." And again: "It was the Ghadames spring that made me into a poet – a true poet. It was there that I discovered the 'bubbles' in my own heart. I wasn't ready to use that discovery until two years later – no, one year later, but all originated there."

I still thought of Epping Forest: "Though in London I am unable to forget Epping Forest, where my heart is,...where I will live until I die and am buried in the church in the Forest, i.e. in the graveyard." At the beginning of April I wrote: "The poet of Epping Forest – that is what I must become"; and: "I am in the tradition of Wyatt, Shakespeare and Tennyson, all of whom wrote sequences of poems for people they loved. Above all I am a reflective poet."

During the Easter holidays we went to Worthing and visited Margaret at her boutique in Shoreham. We talked of prayer and had dinner in Deeps restaurant where we talked about masks. Later we walked under the stars while the sea pounded the shingle, and Margaret described how she saw Heaven "as a region high up there, God on a throne – if you ask me *how* I see Heaven you ask to see my heart". She said: "No one chooses to be an artist. The price is high, it chooses him and he accepts his fate." And the next day, walking where daisies twinkled in the grass like stars, she enjoined me: "Let everything go. I have discarded everything, I am not involved in anything, I am free of everything, I don't want to be taken over by anything, not my pottery or my paintings, not people, not anything. I am free and I am at peace. Do you see, Nicholas. So you, do not worry about self-glory. What has quality will shine and is there for others to see. Often it is better to show one rather than a lot. And now is better than next year. Let it happen. Don't hide. No more hiding." But: "Don't be cluttered by your work." I observed: "In my three collections of lyrics and sonnets I do not express myself nor do I express the dead as Eliot did. I express the mystical truths of the Mystic tradition through my experience." And again: "Augustus John. How he tried to paint an ideal world (mother with children in ideal landscape and moon) and how the real world increasingly took over with its portraits. Drink stimulated this ideal world at first, as well as unlocking the warmth within him, which flowed out and stopped the shy paralysis....In my case, I too am in search of an inner world. How well I know John."

I believe it was about this time that I heard that a pupil of mine at Henry Thornton, Mark Bamford, had been killed on a railway line; he had been hit by a train, blasted into pieces. He was a dark-haired boy of about 13, who had truanted and been in trouble, and when I brandished a cane at Henry Thornton he pretended to present his behind invitingly, perceptively regarding my posture as a game, knowing I would never use my cane. I had met his mother, an Italian, Carol, at a Henry Thornton parents evening; she lived near Garratt Green, and she contacted me there and asked if I would attend the funeral as I was the only teacher he had liked. The church was packed, and his mother was supported down the aisle in a wave of emotion. I sat next to the Head of Henry Thornton, who said to me as we stood outside afterwards: "This is a wretched business. He had no business to be anywhere near the railway line. It was typical of him, he broke the rules. There was nothing left of him. The train hit him at speed."

I began to think about *The Four Seasons* and wrote: "Spiritual truths were traditionally conveyed by illustrations from everyday life. The earliest Mystery was an agricultural cult. All plants were sacred, possessed immortality exhibited each spring by the constant renewing of themselves. The unity of life – of man and plant – is manifested in myriad forms in nature; this spirit of life is divine, the centre and source of life. Man was taught to interpret Nature, to feel at one with it, to subject his soul to be cultivated by it. So if he shared in the agricultural operations he induced spiritual growth. Thus if I write about agricultural operations, I induce spiritual growth. In Dulwich Park I was the Wise Gardener – in the Garden of my Soul. So set one of the 12 Months there. Forests – Epping Forest (winter); crops and fruit trees (autumn); garden plants and flowers (spring and summer)." I spent a fortnight writing the poem in May. I had continued to think about applying musical form to poetry, and this poem was in sonata form with dissociation.

Yet again I returned to the theme of mysticism: "All my poems now come from God, not from me. The Unitive Life brings new creative powers and the creation of spiritual families. Works of art it produces found schools. If this hard work now is the Mystic Life, then the purgation began in 1964, when I defined the prison of 'I'hood as the Reflection. My Dark Night ended in my self-surrender, in my submission to the Divine Will (1972)....(My) consciousness again unified itself and formed a new centre....It all comes down to the self and God. The dethronement of the self so that God can flow through us with superabundant life and creative powers the saints as petals on the sempiternal rose....Mystics come after the great intellectual, material and artistic periods – such as ours, which is coming to an end. The Mystic is the crest of the wave." I wrote: "Write a book on my Mysticism, reviving Mysticism today." Back in my poems I noted: "The Metaphysicals use figurative language so that they can give abstract ideas a pictorial concreteness." On May 12th I noted: "The blue light came last night, effortlessly, after Ann put the light out last thing at night until she put it back on again, and after that too."

I was still thinking about perceptivism and I had a dream about Sartre: "A dream. I was with Sartre, Camus, de Beauvoir, Beckett and various other 20th century writers in Paris – then in London. I drove Sartre to Paddington. They seemed to live at night, and I brought Sartre home at 2 a.m. to read my poems. I mentioned bad faith to him, and was trying to put my case into words when I woke up. Earlier I had told him that Existentialism should be a Perceptivism. So logical can we be during our dreams!"

In June the centenary of the poet Hopkins' death was celebrated in Farm Street Jesuit church, which was associated with Hopkins. I took Ann and Matthew and heard Robert Speight (whom I had met in Japan) read *The Wreck of the Deutschland* and then an address by Father D'Arcy, who had converted Graham Greene in the 1920s and was now a wizened, stooping, frail, greying man who still retained his intellectual vigour.

In June 1975 I explored my two Dark Nights in the work of St. John of the Cross, notably *The Dark Night of the Soul*, where I read that the soul enters the Dark Night gradually and emerges in degrees. The soul in the Dark Night can do nothing, I read, but must leave God free to act, passively submitting to the Divine operation in a passive denial of self. I wrote: "The Light of spiritual grace. The Night of the Sense and then the Night of the Spirit when the Light has blinded it: to raise the soul nearer to God. My Dark Night – the confusion of a soul being purged....God transfers energy from sense to spirit....Light comes in the Night of Spirit. Love does not burn until later....The Unitive Life is all....The soul's lower nature is purified in the Dark Night of Sense to unite it to the spirit. It is deprived of Light and ceases from meditation. Later the spirit is purified in the spiritual Night and prepared for union with Himself....The Dark Night delivers the spiritual man from the 7 sins by quenching all desire, and it deprives him of his Light in meditation. It brings virtue."

I wrote again of the two Dark Nights: "The house calm when the liberty of the spirit is unassailable, i.e. when the passions of the soul are calmed, the desires are asleep, the senses and interior powers of the soul cease to be active. The Dark Night of the Sense when the house of sensuality is at rest. The soul sets out on the way of the spirit, i.e. the illuminative way, when God refreshes the soul without meditation or its own efforts. The Night (of Sense) is full of 'trials and temptations of sense, e.g. the spirit of impurity to buffet them with horrible and violent temptations of the flesh'. The 'spirit of giddiness' clouds the judgement with scruples and perplexities....The soul is purified for the divine union by suffering. If the soul is not tempted, tried and proved in temptations and afflictions, sense will never attain to wisdom. The trials are in proportion to the imperfections to be purged, and to the degree in union in love to which God intends to raise the soul. Those who are strong and more able to bear suffering are purified in more intense trials in less time. After the Night of Sense the soul spends time, perhaps years, in freedom of divine things, more abundant joy than before, and imagination now rising at once to tranquil and loving contemplation. It finds spiritual sweetness without the fatigue of meditation. But until the purgation of the soul is complete (i.e. the spirit), there will continue to be trials, though serenity will be recovered after the tempestuous night.....The Night of Contemplation (i.e. Spirit), in which the sun shines and is then hidden. The sensual part of the soul is weak, without any capacity for the strong things of the spirit....Learners have affections and imperfect habits like roots in the mind, where the purgation of sense could not penetrate; also dullness of mind; fancies (imaginary and spiritual visions). The purification of these precedes divine union, perfectly detaching sense and spirit from all sweetness and all imaginations."

I pondered the difference between the Dark Night of Sense and the later Dark Night of the Spirit: "My self-division in 1971 was sense v spirit, which are harmonised with spiritual sweetness. My problem: Cold Warfare (i.e. my journalism) did not admit the tastes of the higher self....Night of Sense is a bridling of a desire rather than a purgation, which happens in the Night of Spirit. Night of Spirit purges sense and spirit together, a sharper purgation, after the tranquillity that follows the Night of Sense..., the chains of the lower sensual self. The gold of the spirit must be purified, refined till all actions and faculties are divine rather than human, i.e. God must strip them of the old man and put on the new man (*Romans* 12.2). Purgation, contemplation, detachment, poverty of spirit – all the same thing....The Dark Night of the Spirit is an inflowing of God into the soul which cleanses it of its ignorances and imperfections, i.e. 'infused contemplation' in which God secretly instructs the soul in the perfection of love without efforts on its own part beyond a long attention to God, listening to his voice, admitting his Light, which purifies and enlightens the soul and thereby prepares it for union with God. The soul calls the divine Light, which enlightens the soul and purges it of its ignorances, the Dark Night 'because the divine wisdom is not night and darkness only, but pain and torment also to the soul'. Divine wisdom is darkness because it is too high for the soul, and is therefore painful to it. It blinds it. Also the reason – the Light takes away its understanding. So 'Cloud and Darkness are round' our understanding. Divine contemplation in impure soul – two contraries. The *Psalms* contain a record of the Light of contemplation, which strikes the soul to load it with graces."

I wrote of my Dark Night of Spirit: "The divine touches the soul to renew it and ripen it, to make it divine, to detach it from the habitual affections and qualities of the old man, to which it clings....The Night of the Spirit requires 'the intelligent guidance of an experienced director' – I had Margaret. As the *Psalms* have things to say about the contemplative life, go to church to consider the *Psalms*, to 'read the book' and give praise. The sense of being abandoned: in purgative contemplation, the soul feels the shadow of death and the pains and torments of Hell most acutely. The sensual part of the soul is purified in aridities, the faculties in the emptiness of their powers, the spirit in thick darkness, i.e. the soul suffers from the failure and withdrawal of its natural powers, which is a distressing pain. Dim contemplation which purifies, empties, consumes the soul, as a fire consumes the rust and mouldiness of the metal. God humbles in order to exalt later – Purgatory in this life. Memory of past happiness. This dreadful and horrible night is a blessing, for God will raise up good things. My Dark Night of the Sense began in 1968 and ended in 1971. My Night of the Spirit followed in...1972 May. Once sense and soul were united, it was impossible for me to continue in the Cold War, which conflicts with the divine laws."

The next day I was just as obsessed with darkness: "God is working in the soul, which is therefore powerless; it cannot pray or give much attention to divine things. It cannot attend to temporal matters and is distracted and cannot remember....The divine and dim spiritual Light of contemplation detaches the soul from all affection and darkens it, empties it, annihilates it as to all its apprehension and affections. From beginner to proficient to perfect. We only see the Light when there is a question (an object) to reflect it. Otherwise there is darkness. A purified and enlightened soul waits in emptiness and darkness, has no desire or knowledge of anything in particular....The will must be transformed from selfishness to divine love....I had, at the end, to embody the divine will, not the rational will....My subject in all my work is this Dark Night,... – but who in the literary world can see this?...Divine union takes place in the Light. The self must be fit to receive it or it will suffer."

I considered purgation and suffering of the soul (the psychological principle) as "Purgatory": "The cause of Purgatory is therefore the weakness and imperfections of the soul. When these are all burned away, the suffering ceases, and joy takes its place: it glows with love....All art is a cheat – if written or made by people who have not been through the Dark Night it is a waste of our time consuming it, for it is an error. 'Has X been through the Dark Night? If not his view of life is suspect.' The European Church is the place where all the writings about the Dark Night are gathered and interpreted. If the interpretation is wrong, the interpreters are being changed. But we must accept the historical authority of the Church to be the repository for the Dark Night records. The more Dark Night a person has, the more imperfect he or she was. The quest I set off on in 1961, an incomplete soul. The fire of love which is a foretaste of God, not understood because the soul's understanding is in darkness; its love is infused passively. The soul achieving greater strength and fitness for union with God. Fires in the next life purify the spirit, but here the soul, i.e. two purgatories. Love can unite understanding and will, and burn. Light in understanding, which makes God feel present. The pain of the Night of Spirit is 'beyond comparison greater' than that of the Night of Sense. The doubt that the soul has lost God. Effects of burning love: strength, energy, longing after God. The soul rises by night. It sees nothing at first but what is within itself – its own darkness. The supernatural Light gives light to the understanding, which becomes divine, like the will and the memory. The soul leaves the house of self-indulgence and sensuality, and understands its former slavery, how wretched it was to be at the mercy of its passions and desires, which if awake, would have prevented its going." And again: "The soul must be at rest if it is to receive what God infuses. Base inclinations should not interfere. The desires and powers of sense are deprived of their natural light in this Night, are purified and spiritually enlightened. The imagination is filtered. A dense and heavy cloud overshadows the soul. The soul is safe when it mortifies its desires, tastes, reflections, understanding, affections. The more mortification (darkness), the more safety. The old man must die first. In suffering God gives strength. The spiritual Light of God is so far above our understanding that it dims it and blinds it, i.e. the old man. The secret wisdom is a ladder. To ascend is to descend and to descend (be humble) is to ascend (be exalted)."

I thought again about my spiritual and sensual parts and the dates of my own Dark Night: "The tranquillity of my lower and sensual part was not complete until 1973....The soul achieves the tranquillity and rest of the spirit through the touches of divine union, received from the Divinity...in sleep and silence. (The silence = rest from the flesh). Union is only attainable with great purity and by detachment from all created things, i.e. mortifications....The beginning is the grace of vocation (the end of which is the beatific vision a lifetime away). The soul is struck unexpectedly by a ray of divine grace, as I was in 1965. A new chord was touched, God's work became visible (e.g. my *Archangel*). This grace does not last. Virtue had to come in. The first ray has transfigured the heart but not transformed it. Then had to be a long process of self-denial, mortification and sacrifice, and denial of everything that could give satisfaction to body or soul, both actively and passively. Both can be at the same time. This purgation of sense comes in different forms: reverses of fortune, loss of friendship and reputation, ill success, illness (me: divorce...) – and loss of devotion. Despairing of comfort....Self-stripping. Perfect purgation leads to acts of great power....Now I am in the Dark Night of the Spirit, which will lead to ascent, the living flame of love, and beatific vision. This did not begin before September 1971. April 1973 I stopped alcohol. Illumination was strong from 1971/2....Darkness and passing rays."

I had one more shot at dating my Dark Night of the Spirit: "When did I start the Night of Spirit?...The Night of the Spirit comes after...the illumination – and is a swing back into darkness. In my case it was after the ecstasies of May 1972. The confusion of 1973....It is the end, before the Unitive Way, in which sense and spirit are united. Ahead, the dawn of a new and glorious day. Perhaps my Dark Night was *A Bulb in Winter*, and the Unitive Way emerged with (*Visions of*) *Paradise*? In which case I have emerged from the Dark Night, or am emerging? Or else I have to spend some years here? 'The mystical life-processes in man, the organic growth of his transcendental consciousness.'...Impotence, blankness, solitude in the Dark Night....Margaret: 'If you're at peace, the Light is always there.' I.e. in the Dark Night you are not at peace. So my aim now is to be at peace and to look (contemplate) and wait patiently. Cf Simone Weil: Waiting on God."

I record these musings on St. John of the Cross to show that we are in process, and that when we are in process we attempt to take stock of and define stages in our process. But nothing is cut and dried in self-understanding. Nevertheless, I felt that I had been through a Dark Night of Sense from 1968 to 1971 and a Dark Night of Spirit from 1972 onwards,

NIGHT OF UNKNOWING

beginning with my illness that May 17th.

The Night of Unknowing worked on me, pouring knowledge about our civilisation into me, while my bodily health was temporarily suspended.

At the end of term I was ill. I was still writing poems and thinking about form. While under the weather I wrote: "The line goes from Shakespeare-Donne-Tennyson-Hardy-Hagger, missing Larkin and the shallow Movement lot, who never suffered; and stemming from Catullus and Ovid (Shakespeare's inspiration). The sonnets are sincere, not a technical exercise. Forms. Eliot's *Waste Land* is 'a beautiful ruin', an accusation to which Eliot had no answer. My poems are often in unfamiliar forms, but the form can be justified: go and look at the symphony, the fugue, and see how traditional ideas can be reapplied in a seemingly unfamiliar way. And so I am an innovator."

Soon afterwards, on 8th July, I wrote about my illness: "The last 3 days I have been ill with a temperature of 103°F. A viral illness, which, Dr Webb told me, should peak today, and either develop into bronchitis or improve. I have had time, now that my temperature is dropping, to ponder my life: to watch it without having to hurry on. The divine Providence has stopped me, has said, 'Stop and look.'" And on 9th July: "I feel burnt out: burnt out by the fever. I am still hot from it (between 99 and 100F) but it is losing its heat now." And later: "After my illness. I feel as though I have come back from the dead. I look pale. I have lost weight. I have a deathly pallor round my eyes. A yellowy, whitish, wax-like pallor. Several times when I got the shivers my entire hands went that same deathly numb and cold, the fingers white, the nails a strange blue. If I had not taken my tablets during and after Tanzania, I would have said I had malaria, like the guide." And a few days later: "Visit to the doctor again. I have neutropenia – two few white corpuscles (leucocytes) in the blood (whereas leukaemia is too many). Another blood test to see if I have made them up."

Illness can be creative, and on 2nd August I wrote: "Since 8th July I have been intermittently ill with two blood abnormalities, one of which has cleared up. In spite of being persistently tired I have completed *Lighthouse* and am now on my first day in Cornwall." I was still thinking about musical form and applying it in poetry, and *The Lighthouse* was a fugue, the contrapuntal form catching the self-divided mind, and I later thought of calling it *The Dark Night Easter Temptation of a Somewhat Saintly Man, or a Formerly Derelict Lighthouse*. It drew on the Dark Night of St. John of the Cross. I made notes for several poems, including one about the 12 months ("à la Rilke's *Elegies*, e.g. the Wise Gardener and how to grow in spirit"), and one to be called *The Labyrinth*. I was also pondering a new symphony, which eventually became *The Weed-Garden* (originally *The Cockleshell Weed-Garden*). I wrote: "Bear in mind my lecture to the Garratt Green 6th form about man being a bud and a bloom, the purpose of education being to unfold, 'explication'. Education is an explication....A poem about all man in all time showing that the unfolding of the soul contributes to civilisation (art and religion), and when it does not unfold we have the decline of civilisation and religion, expressed in materialism, outer-technology as opposed to inner spirit and mysticism and art, i.e. today we have a culture that is 'unexplicated', i.e. no unfolding has taken place, and that is unnatural, for all flowers unfold naturally. We have thus 'gone against' Nature. This...is about all man's search for civilisation (and truth and human wisdom). See Spengler, the decline of the West and the flower in the meadow. Because it is about all men, there must be a protean theme, and the one hero must stand for all great men, and be interchangeable with them, cf Ovid's *Metamorphoses*. So this is a statement about the great men, how their souls unfold and they pour their 'explicatedness' into their civilisation and religion and renew it....Also put the decline of civilisation and religion – caused by failure to unfold – into '12 experiences that sum up the culture of the last 30 years' (my conversation with Ezra Pound in 1970)."

I was seeing civilisations and cultures in terms of "unfolding of the soul": "There are 3 themes....Can they be woven together into a design, like the flowers on Miss Barron's curtains? Answer: yes, if I take the form of a symphony and have the odes within it, each ode as a thought-block, i.e. a strophe, containing its own strophe-antistrophe, to be balanced against another thought-block, the antithetical scheme being a contrast, à la *Waste Land*, between past and present. On these lines the main thread is the unfolding of the soul/rose, which can take place in a great man's life (life cycle) and often did in the past – and so lead to civilisation and art and religion (see historical parallels) but which today all too often does not take place because of the new world we live in, so that men live without seeing the flora and fauna which feed the soul – months – and concentrate on outer things which brings down civilisation and religion and art. See the attitude to the Forest – originally lopped and necessary, now a luxury, for walking in, i.e. not a part of our life. See also the glimpse I had in Egypt...driving by the Nile: papyrus grass for horse, milk from goat – not petrol and bottled milk. So have one cyclic heroic symphony weaving all these thought-blocks into the 'curtain'."

I wrote: "Suggested movements for my symphony: (1) The unfolding of the soul which can take place, and which in the past often did; contrasted with its all too often not taking place today. The consequence in both cases: civilisation and art and religion contrasted with their opposite: materialism, technology and outer. (2) How the great men evolve this unfolding, which is seen in terms of life cycle, i.e. between birth, death and suffering, and a definition of man as he can be. Spiritual gardening (ABA). (3) How new men live without seeing the flora and fauna that feed the soul, i.e. months, and concentrate on outer things, i.e. traditional Chaucer view of months/modern ignorance against background – how the new world is responsible (ABA). (4) A restatement of how the soul can unfold(ABACABA), and examples from the heroic men of history and eternity as against the trivial, modern and permissive smallness. A definition of greatness. Tie together everything. Significance of life, meaning of life. This must be totally impersonal. Great men must be totally impersonal, and their work must be totally impersonal....Leave 'I' out of it....A hero is one whose soul has unfolded. This takes place through being in tune with Nature and through suffering, and being responsive to God's sunlight, so a hero is a man who places himself in readiness, as a result of which readiness he is given superior powers which do not come from him, but which come from God – like the power of the seed to bloom. If a great man is a flower bloomed, then history is a flower-garden. The soul is a living part of the human organism, and it contains the creative powers of the mind, which unfold like a bloom from the human stem....After this, an Autobiography (à la Rilke and *Prelude*) on how my soul unfolded?" I reflected ruefully: "It is ridiculous. Here I sit within three miles of where Colin Wilson lives, the author of *The Outsider* and *Religion and the Rebel*, and I cannot visit him now and discuss my 'explicated' idea, which is so close to some of his early work, because he has developed down a wrong road and now opposes poetry and mysticism, which I stand for. If only I *now* could have talked to the young Wilson as he used to be! How well we would have got on! All his insistence on egocentric 'consciousness', not realising we unfold in the Light."

We toured Cornwall. We spent a hot day in Porthleven and visited Gunwalloe beach and I looked at Poldhu Hotel and thought about the setting for my poem *The Lighthouse*. We went to Fowey and looked at Sir Arthur Quiller-Couch's ivy-creepered house and crossed to Polruan. We went to Tintagel and took a landrover to the castle and Merlin's cave. We went on to Boscastle and Slaughter Bridge, where according to one version of the legend Arthur is reputed to have fought his last battle, and we found what local legend calls Arthur's tombstone in the River Camel. I wrote: "Trees. The lime, oak and yew can live to be 800-1,000 years old. Fast-growing trees are the shortest lived. I am like a yew: I grow slowly and live long and am evergreen. My images are like acorns on an oak."

I was still groping towards *The Weed-Garden*: "For my odes I need to link the months that flow by and the seasons of my life. These can be measured against the Forest, which measures the months and is a time-keeper (changing of colours of leaves, etc.), and against whose years – a greater cycle than a month – I can measure myself....The odes: the year in the Forest. How it turns – and I will not be there (strophe). The years, my life (antistrophe)....A symbol to unite the two as I pass into the Forest through the graveyard: from life to eternity, my body a part of the Forest, my soul like a willow-warbler in the world of spirits. My life, then, is like a ramble, a journey through time from different parts of the Forest, i.e. he rambles for the last time through the Forest, rambles through his mind/labyrinth of Forest, following the stream and remembering in his mind, i.e. it is a mental journey he makes as he dies, and so he can range through the months and be in now January, now October. The powers of the mind (cf Hardy visiting his waterfall). So in this sense the stream can be his life with breaks in it: to go to Oxford, to go abroad, to live in London. But each time he returns. The Forest is too strong. The stream broken in three places. Three infidelities. The rambler who strayed from his true home."

I wrote about Nature: "It is not the soil that has failed us – it has not failed Nature, after all; it is ourselves, our own efforts and attitude and receptiveness to the Divine: blame the rose-bush not the soil. 'Man has to subject his soul to be cultivated in the same way as Nature, by sharing the various agricultural operations, thereby inducing spiritual growth', so as to feel at one with Nature, the spirit of whose life is divine: for all plants are sacred and possess immortality, by renewing themselves each spring. This spirit of renewal is the unity of life. So man must see himself as a part of Nature, so that his soul can unfold, otherwise his pride cuts him off. Only God can be gardener."

It was a exciting time intellectually: "Every day I take a different topic. Yesterday King Arthur, today wild flowers, tomorrow – who knows? Stars? Before I came away there were strophes in Greek choruses, and then the *Odes* of Horace. Every day is therefore *an adventure*, and there is no knowing what tomorrow's studying will bring. My garden, my soul, has neat flowers, and I resent people barging in."

We walked to the end of the Black Head of Trenarren, a headland in St. Austell Bay, and I picked ragwort, sheep's bit scabious and woodruff. On my return I thought about my impact on our culture and civilisation: "A culture takes its tone from its leaders. If the leaders' souls are unfolded, it will be an explicated culture. If not, a materialistic, technological culture. We have today 'two cultures' (C. P. Snow). Eliot and Pound were cultural leaders in their day, and therefore affected the culture – as I would, if my branch of mysticism became current....Culture comes down to the arts: paintings, cathedrals, books from libraries, concerts. What Clark calls 'civilisation'. So what is culture? What is civilisation? 'A culture' is within 'a civilisation': 'a civilisation' has 'a culture' – and 'civilisation'. 'A civilisation' suggests the organisation, e.g. the Roman civilisation; 'civilisation' (= reclaiming from a savage state) is the opposite of barbarianism, i.e. being civilised, as the arts can show, i.e. sophisticated ideas of the time; 'a culture' is a geographical homogeneous mass, the total output of its cultivation or civilisation, e.g. 'Western culture'; 'culture' (= cultivation of the mind, educated and refined) generally is the opposite of 'primitive', as 'sophisticated' is to 'naive'. It is the ideas of the Age as expressed in the arts, without reference to a particular geographical bloc. So when a number of souls in a culture, i.e. in a civilisation, unfold, then civilisation (as opposed to barbarism) and art and religion flourish....If 'civilisation' = soul-unfolded, it is the idea of the Age as reflected in art that is important....If 'civilisation' = soul-not-unfolded, then we get seeds and husks and socialism....The crucial point, then, is the idea of the time, like the way Christianity is used in art, or 18th century rationalism (is) expressed in classicism. It is how the world is viewed, and how that view is expressed in art. Cf 19th century Romanticism and individualism. So, if I can get across within my culture, and Western civilisation, then the whole idea of 'civilisation' – the dominating idea today – may be changed, and therefore the tone of the civilisation changed (Western civilisation). So do not reinstate the idea of mysticism; change the tone of the culture and the notion of civilisation....There is always an idea of the Age. Western technology has come between man and Nature. My destiny. I must become a cultural leader to redress the balance, to instruct the young, to embody the mystical idea that can change the idea of our culture and civilisation. My purpose – my mission – is to draw attention to what is happening to our culture, and therefore to our civilisation." This concern with culture and civilisation was to come out in *The Fire and the Stones*.

NIGHT OF UNKNOWING

We went to Roche Chapel, which is perched high on a rock and where a hermit lived in the Middle Ages, and then to Kelliwick Castle, where Arthur was reputed to have lived. It was a circular mound on a hill, an unexcavated hill-fort. I wrote: "Picked more wild flowers and identified: hogweed, wild mignonette, tufted vetch, tormentil, knapweed, common hemp nettle, kidney vetch and shrubby hawkweed, among others. These hedgerows: tin-mine chimneys on the cliffs....Why I prefer wild flowers to garden flowers: because the wonder is that they grow so beautifully in wild places – as I did." We went to St. Michael's Mount and I revisited Trevarthian, where I had stayed in 1955.

I thought again about our culture, and wrote: "Our culture is the idea of the Age given in the arts, painting, sculpture, music, poetry and novels, i.e. a mass age in which there are no heroes and no grand themes....Now we are a part of European culture: the traditional culture, i.e., and the modern left-wing social democratic culture of new Europe....Our culture before 1940 was rooted in the idea of outer hell: poverty, disease, unemployment, war, collapsing old world....But until the turn of the century, the well-to-do lived nicely and had sound values to compensate....Today there has been a levelling since 1940 and there is now a mass middle class and an outer Golden Age and Paradise, in which poverty, disease, unemployment, war have been largely abolished – in relation to how they used to be – but inflation and the balance of payments problems because of loss of Empire and imperial wars have weakened this outer Paradise, and the cars, planes and machines of this Golden Age have had consequences on the inner life. There is now something of an inner Hell: materialist sloth and ease, low spiritual tension....In place of the old self-discipline, moderation and restraint – the traditional virtues – the 7 Deadly Sins are now worshipped, the weeds called by the name of flowers which choke the growth of flowers in our outwardly well-organised, 'no-growth' garden: pride is rejection of God ('we can get by with our own view'); avarice (trade union wage increases); lust (permissive society); anger (*Look Back in Anger* and the Angry Brigade); gluttony (beer-drinking); envy (social egalitarianism, levelling); and sloth (sleeping late and generally not bothering to make the mental effort of trying to grow, i.e. avoiding the suffering and hardship which is necessary if the seedcase is to split). All these choke, i.e. impede growth....So today we have a Paradise outside, i.e. a Golden Age outside, but a waste land of weeds choking flowers inside, i.e. a culture like a rubbish dump in which no discrimination exists in the gardener's mind as to what is a weed, what is a flower. Hence our art about social outcasts – tramps, the poor....It is not that there are no flowers today, just that there are too many weeds being watered like flowers (7 Sins)....Our culture needs weeding, because our flowers are choked by weeds....Being choked with weeds, our culture lacks purpose and is a record of futilities and desperate breakings-out of a futile situation, for the West has no ideology or spiritual philosophy, save Christianity....So 12 pictures to sum up the fact that our culture has ceased to be Christian, and that flowers are choked by vices/weeds: the Hellish outer past in Europe – war, disease, poverty, unemployment, etc. – contrasted with the Golden Age present: peace, prosperity, etc; the Golden Age traditional inner values – self-restraint and

283

discipline in nurses and soldiers – contrasted with the Hellish inner vacuum, boredom in a time of materialist ease; the levelling,, i.e. worship of weeds and the loss of standards, i.e. the embracing of the 7 Sins, and the loss of the Cardinal Virtues – the decline in Christianity as a European philosophy. Surely these three contrasts catch everything I have to say about the cultural crisis? I am another fruit on the Christian apple tree – the Tree of Knowledge....The infinity of space. Billions of galaxies in outer space – and inner space is equally boundless and subject to the divine power."

On August 12th I wrote: "A wet morning. Wrote my spider's web poem and then finished the first movement of my cultural symphony, and decided on the title: *The Cockleshell Weed-Garden*. I will quote 'Mary, Mary, quite contrary' and dedicate the poem to Harold and Mary Wilson. I am saying to our Prime Minister that all the well-organised outer life has overlooked the fact that we have a cultural weed-garden. Eliot is a flower, his soul unfolded. The weeds are too numerous to recall....I can make the lilies of light the 'silver bells' – the heroes, i.e. there should be more lilies. The 'pretty maids' are the weeds, which Wilson likes. The cockleshells are all the outer decoration of the garden. This is my appeal to our government for more lilies and fewer weeds in our culture." Later I dropped the "Cockleshell" from the title.

I wrote at length about the myth of Arthur and the legend of Christ's visit to Britain and again thought extensively about culture and civilisation: "To Spengler a culture (soul) becomes a civilisation (intellect, i.e. reason), but that is a question of terminology. The mallow in the field....Toynbee and Eliot are agreed that religion is the centre of a culture and of art, as it is in growth. When a culture-pattern breaks up they go their own way, and the culture is secularised. There is a fragmentation – a chip off the flint – of first the economic (Nature), then the political (keeping power), leaving the cultural core – the battle of the soul against the self for God's work; then the linguistic, intellectual and artistic flakes, which expose the religious nucleus, which becomes stultified, losing contact with the rest. So to Toynbee, art serves religion or it becomes vulgar and barbarised. Eliot insists that a healthy culture and religion and philosophy and art are all united. Bring this into the *Weed-Garden*. What was a whole is now divided up into fragments. Think, a garden as a whole, a garden of allotments....Civilisations....The ideal of perfection we have expresses the state of our soul....Our ideal of perfection today should be the mind at peace, illuminated, confident in the face of all outer conditions and uncertainties (Cold War, poverty, decline of West) that there is permanence and stability ahead, and that after the loss of self-confidence of the 1950s, Europe can develop and grow and be lasting....What a muddled, confused society I grew up in. I am moving towards a classical period, in which permanence and stability and peace and light and confidence dominate and the powers of fear, barbarianism and darkness are routed. The triumph of civilisation over barbarianism."

I was obsessed with the future of Western civilisation: "What of the Third World War?...Can the West be optimistic and have a sense of permanence and stability in the bastion of Europe when all about it is going against it? Can it have a post-imperial life? It is, obviously, an aspect of disintegration, but cannot an aspect of disintegration produce a local, temporary stability and permanence which can lead to a classical period?...On the one hand, the surrounding conditions suggest that the West is doomed, and that we should be afraid. On the other hand, within the united West material conditions and prosperity look hopeful. There is a limes (frontier), that is the point, and though the barbarians are massing, they do not threaten yet. Our generation, and the next generation, will probably survive intact, but the West is on the slide, there is no doubt about that. So permanence and stability depend on freedom from war, i.e. peace....Within the garden all is fine, but outside the estate there is chaos, anarchy, war. So, my commitment was for light, against the dark represented by Communism; for the West and against the successor; for the West against the enemy in the Third World War. It has to be seen in these terms, and not in liberal terms, otherwise it is meaningless and despicable. I defended the West against the barbarians. I was fighting for a culture of flowers, not a culture of weeds." I noted: "The Seven Deadly Sins in my novels. Anger (*Age of Cartoon*), lust (*Chains*). The virtues are found in my poems, which are cleaner." The poem I was thinking of was *The Weed-Garden*, the first draft of which I finished on August 18th.

We returned from Cornwall and I looked towards Essex. I rang the Vicar of High Beach, Jo Crompton, and arranged for Matthew to be christened there. At the same time I wrote hopefully: "The London years are drawing to an end. What I need is somewhere like Pound's house, on top of a mountain in Rapallo. Get to know the woodlanders of Essex." My intuition was right, but my timing was out: it was too soon, I had to wait for Oaklands School to be ready for me. We went to the Vicarage at High Beach, and again I wrote, anticipating what was to happen by seven years: "We must live in the Forest – somewhere like Sewardstone – and attend the church in the birch woods. I must work over in Essex somewhere. Explore over there. Somewhere in the middle of the Forest. Theydon Bois?" We went to High Beach church for a Sunday service and went on to visit Essex villages: Sewardstonebury, Mott Street, Wood Green, Upshire, Copped Hall Green, Theydon Bois, Coopersale and Fiddlers Green, Woodside, Thornwood, Roydon, Nazeing, Broadley Common, Epping Green, Epping Upland and Epping. There was a plan to drive a motorway through Upshire; John Manning, Paddy's husband, told me he was involved in implementing it on the engineering side and that he thought it a good idea, and I was cross with him, for the Forest was sacred.

At the end of August I thought again about our culture and wrote in my *Diaries*: "I have tried to explain (in *The Weed-Garden*) what has happened to the culture – i.e....show that there are no flowers in 12 images. So scheme: traditional growth, modern lack of growth....The main reason is the change from hard work and self-discipline to sloth (cf Welfare State); from controlling desire to lust; from temperance to excessive drunkenness and decadence and living for pleasure, i.e. gluttony; from accepting society to envying neighbour, social anger with him, avarice for more money, all of which has led to valuing weeds as much as flowers. The main reason for what has happened to our culture is a change from traditional values and virtues...to modern 'sinful' ones, which hinder and impede growth....Present this in a cacophonous passage that does not rhyme at all – compressed images which look a mess and are chaotic and hard to understand, then show what the 1950s did in a more elegant passage in which the chaos has been digested and understood. Tillage – a traditional idea. Equality, a modern idea. The conflict between the traditional and the modern is the conflict between Christ and the Devil."

A couple of days later I visited Tuohy in Brighton and sat in his garden for two and a half hours after Matthew had been sick on his sofa. We discussed the Seven Deadly Sins: "He said the 7 sins don't rule in England. There is no anger, or envy (!) and that lust is 'a couple moving in together', and 'is promiscuity a bad thing? A breakdown in traditional values?...Sins are not the motives for behaviour.'" I disagreed with this statement, saying 'A sin is a value judgement on certain kinds of behaviour.' He said: "There are classes in every country and social reasons for people behaving, and these do not include collapsing cultures or sins." He felt "the Americans are barbarian because they built 7th Avenue of glass and a puff of wind will blow it down, and their art is equally expendable" yet: "The Americans are civilised because negroes get on with whites and there is tolerance." He told me: "Disintegrating societies produce the best art" as in such societies the artist is detached. I felt he was deliberately living in an ivory tower: "His ivory tower – why his flat is white, the colour of ivory. His high standards – the perfect sentence – and aestheticism."

Reflecting on this later, I wrote: "I would sooner be wrong with the growth idea of Christianity than right with the sterility of brain physiology. I do not want scientific fact. I want a model which helps my soul and powers to grow – and that science cannot give me." I visited Margaret and sat in her "weed-garden" (which had given me the idea for the title of *The Weed-Garden*) and reflected: "Margaret is too much of an amateur. Her insistence that we must do something outside writing/art to feed it with life may, however, be true. To feed it with life in the sense of make it widely acceptable to the public." Margaret kindly bought Matthew some clothes and on the way back I said to her "Do you still see the Light as much as you used to?" She replied: "Oh yes. It is always there. I am so happy down here, so peaceful."

I noted more fully that the heroes in my novels all suffered from the 7 sins: "Zabov (pride – i.e. the brain view, not needing God's sun); Juben (gluttony); Thompson (anger and envy); Freeman (lust); Truffer (sloth); Wrothgate (avarice). My novels are incomplete statements of the human condition because they are seen through the sins. My poems slowly adopt...the standpoint of the 2,000 years of the Christian tradition, my acceptance of which has not been sudden. There is plenty of evidence in my work to show where I am going. My turning against the world and earthly pleasures, which impede growth."

On poetry I told myself: "A poem shows beauty, not ugliness – and that is a feeling for truth (the real flower, not the artificial) which you don't get by doing nothing but writing. You must be surrounded by beauty, not ugliness – rivers, trees, fields, seas, skies, the countryside of Epping Forest. That is where there are real things, not here where there are artificial buildings. So it is spiritual – the real within – and not the false." And again:

"The centre of life is the heart – the feelings: i.e. the soul and the spirit which grows out of it: beauty, which can be felt. Depth is from the heart, where you pray from, where you meet God. A dud is a work that is not from the heart, but from the head; beauty is from the heart – e.g. feeling for Nature – and not the head, where ugliness grows, soullessness, heartlessness. Epping Forest is where my heart is. London is my head. It is good to escape the pain of the heart in times of suffering, but the heart – what is real – is in Epping Forest. Cf Jim (Doolan): '...I look for feeling in poetry. Anything without feeling in it is dud.' And yet again: "Literature brings the whole soul of man into play: feelings, perceptions, thoughts, etc. Stanzas and paragraphs in the mind, not lines and phrases."

I ended the holidays as I had begun them, reflecting on my lineage: "In my life, I must live fully, with all myself, i.e. heart, soul, spirit, as well as head. With feelings. The feelings are always underneath. Let them through....The sonnet line: (Ovid)-Wyatt and Surrey-Shakespeare and Donne-Milton-Wordsworth-Hopkins-me. Hand on the sonnet in good health. I am the custodian of the sonnet, and must hand it on."

It was the originality and solitude of my vision that preoccupied me now. Back at school I read Shakespeare's *Sonnets*, and on 16th September observed: "I have sonnets inside me. They are going to pour out. I drafted, i.e. scribbled out, two today." I wrote: "My solitary struggle. Between visits to school, I struggle to set down a vision, a vision of growth. It is how the soul unfolds through suffering and puts up a spirit which is as beautiful as a flower, and which grows in the inner light. This must seem gibberish to the man who has not had the inner experience. My vision *is* an experienced one, nevertheless, and its originality must not deter me. I must pursue my path undaunted by the fact that probably no one else in my time is treading it." The next weekend I took Ann for a walk in Epping Forest and said: "When the tide goes out on our time there will only be a few starfish and crabs left on the beach. I will be one of them because I am making an original journey and recording it in my poems."

At school the Bullock Report was out, saying that English language should be taught across the curriculum, and I had to hold discussions on it. I still found time to write: "Words are like fingers pointing to the moon. God is in birds, a jellyfish, bees, even in a bomb. All creatures have God-nature." But I was tired and dreamt of retiring: "At 36, after 16 years of conveying an impression of energy, I feel worn out. I long to retire, and sit under an apple tree and read the classics I have no time to read. A chill of disillusion sits over my heart, disenchantment with the world and its ephemeral aims....I accept the teeming miracle of life and all the evil that accompanies the good. My heart is sad, but it is very close to the centre of life and to God. I have been given tranquillity and calm as a reward for my trials."

In October Arnold Toynbee died and I wrote at some length about him in my *Diaries* ("I am sad, for Toynbee has died, and I never met him") and noted the contrast between his progressive view, that hubris leads to nemesis and destroys civilisations, and my traditional view, that questioning traditional values destroys civilisations. Thinking of my championing of African independence I wrote: "I have stood for the oppressed victims of Western hubris, but I have also stood for the West – purged of its hubris through my insights, reformed from within. To this extent I have been a spiritual force."

I was aware that my role in Western civilisation was deeply connected with my poetry: "The poet is an oracle, a speaker of truth. Certainly, the mystic poet is. It seems as though I am doomed to make my major work a gift to mankind, i.e. not to earn a penny from it. I stand for a new contemplative development within a traditional Christendom." I had earlier written: "My *Gates of Hell* are in the genre of Catullus, Wyatt and Surrey, Shakespeare, Donne, Tennyson and Hardy."

After the birth of Matthew Ann returned to St. James Norland, where she stayed until the end of 1976. Matthew, still under one, was left with the wife of a local vicar, whose vicarage was in Westway. The vicar's wife was heavily involved in the local community, and Matthew found himself sometimes in the church playgroup, and sometimes in local pensioners' gatherings, where he would crawl round the old folk. He sometimes came back with the pockets of his baby-grow filled with pennies they had given "the angelic little boy".

At the end of October Matthew was christened in the church in the Forest, High Beach. Tuohy and Margaret were godparents. They both came to Brechin Place, and I drove them out to Loughton, passing leaves turning red and gold. We had lunch at Journey's End with my mother and Robert, during which Tuohy said of me "He doesn't like our society, whereas I am fairly friendly towards it" and I maintained: "There is a case to be made out for seeing the artist as outside his society."...Then I took Tuohy and Margaret for a drive to Clare's madhouse at Lippitt's Hill and Tennyson's coachhouse at High Beach and it was then time to go to the christening at High Beach. Two babies were being baptised. The vicar Jo Crompton, a white-haired deaf man, gave us a talk about "our perilous times", which Tuohy later criticised ("he shouldn't bring politics into it"), and Matthew was baptised with a scoop of holy water from a scallop shell and signed with the cross. Then there was a tea party at my mother's and evening drinks. Tuohy and Margaret returned to London. Margaret told me "Tuohy felt 'I am nothing' during the service, I was watching him" and "This was what it was all for – your divorce and Egerton Gardens were so that you'd see the Light"; Tuohy later sent me a card: "The origin of Christianity is esotericism – why should the Church have anything to do with society?" After they had left I walked on the lawn under the pear-tree with John Ezard and we went and had a drink in the Holly Bush, from which we had been thrown out on the Christmas Eve of 1959.

A few days later Ann and I visited Worthing and had dinner in the Amsterdam with Margaret, who showed me a painting of three chrysanthemums "which represented purity". She probably meant that the three flowers were the three godparents, but I disagreed, believing they looked past their best and that she wanted the painting to represent something it did not, and we had a disagreement which began a widening between us. To her, an artist painted from the heart alone, but as I pointed

288

out, unless the heart and the head are mixed as in Donne, then Michelangelo could not have created the Sistine Chapel *Last Judgement*. Margaret said that art is unimportant compared with business, and that a simple reaction "It's nice" is better than a deep appreciation which analyses and destroys, and I disagreed all the more. As I pointed out, Yeats wrote "The intellect of man is forced to choose/Perfection of the life or of the work", and if Michelangelo and Toynbee had chosen perfection of the life we would not have heard of them and their work would not have benefited mankind.

Around this time I thought a good deal about the USSR and wrote: "Europe challenges Russian hegemony and checks it. So Russia is not a successor-state?...The leftwards slide in British politics means that I now belong to the right, whereas a decade ago I was in the centre. Support the left and bring in the Russian successor-state. Or, support the centre and bring in the European Universal State. That is the ideological conflict of our day. In the same way, East and West must grow rightwards and leftwards to meet in the USE (United States of Europe). Similarly, all sects must become one Church so that Christendom is revived."

At the beginning of November I finished my long poem *The Weed-Garden*. I wrote: "Today, 2nd November, I finished *The Weed-Garden*, once through. It comes to 30 pages and I am too tired to count lines." On November 4th and 5th I wrote about the theme of the poem: "Overall argument. The soul must be treated like a plant or it will not unfold; in which case civilisation, art and religion decline; which is what is happening today (section 1), and this happens when souls do not sprout through a life cycle and therefore question (section 2), instead of sprouting through Nature (section 3). The soul can unfold and renew, it has a future, our culture can be saved (section 4)." Again: "The theme of section 1 of *Weed-Garden*. Exposition: an estate has taken the place of a culture-garden. The unfolding of the soul can take place when it is treated like a plant (corn, flower)." And: "The theme of section 4 of *The Weed-Garden*. The soul can unfold like a rose, witness the 14th century. Visionaries can beautify, witness the greatness of the past which judges the present."

I was still revising the poem at the end of November, when I wrote: "Went to see *The Seagull* last night. Am ill. Fever, temperature, but it is going. Finished Part 1 of *Weed-Garden* yesterday, rewriting, but too ill to touch it today. I have no stamina any longer."

My illness had affected my weight: "I am lighter than I have been for years. I lost weight when ill last week and not eating and am now almost under 12 stone; in Libya I was 11 stone 7 lbs." I believe I was too light at this time, and that my ectomorph's build wore my nerves close to the surface. I am now over 14 stone and am more of a mesomorph and feel quite differently about the world.

I found myself thinking about my poetic career and unconsciously looking towards Italy: "My return from Libya ended my youth and marked the beginning of my middle years. (By analogy with Milton, born 1608, whose Italian tour of 1638-9 had the same effect.) Is my epic to be reserved for my old age?"

The experience of being in the left wing milieu of an ILEA comprehensive was making me incline further towards the right. Of our society I wrote: "My idea of society is strongly connected with the past, and is best expressed by the image of the tree. The same tree, different leaves and fruit each year, but this leaf is in the same place (social place) as the leaf we remember from last year and the year before (past generations). I feel more and more a profound sense of continuity and tradition."

I also pondered reincarnation and wrote: "A flower dies in autumn and grows again in the spring. So it is with us. We die and are like dormant bulbs until we come again."

In early December I was pondering the culture of the Western world as I continued my revisions of *The Weed-Garden*: "I am showing the garden of the Western world in autumn, when souls are not sprouting. It is not fine – flowers are better – but the land is not to blame, it is the season. We must be patient and wait for the spring – an autumn lily (or crocus) points the way. Thus, adopting the point of view'The present is good (I don't think)!' implies that it is bad, and ridicules the holding of such a view. So I am ridiculing the view which sees there are no flowers and which says they are not necessary, i.e. which does not anticipate the coming spring and which is complacent in our autumn....Two views. The first is: the past was bad (2,000 years), questioning was good, we are at the height of our powers, we can never collapse, i.e. Western pride and belief in our immortality; and the city is good, the soul is old hat. The second: the past was good (2,000 years of soul), questioning was bad, we are at the lowest of our inner powers, we will soon collapse, i.e. the West is on the way out; the city is not good for the soul and our creative powers. My attitude, in favour of the second." Again: "The country is in autumn. Individual hearts and souls can still unfold but the conditions of youth are wrong – and are affected by the autumn." On December 6th I settled the titles of the four parts of the poem, and soon afterwards wrote: "When souls do not unfold, civilisation declines." Again: "The purity of the 14th century blossom will never be recaptured. Autumn flowers." And again: "The 14th century was the blossom time of Western civilisation. The religious mysticism is pure, the art is full of angel light and haloes. The Renaissance shows a change from blossom time towards the fruit. I love the 14th century. Become a specialist in the period around 1375 to Fra Angelico. They knew the difference between a flower and a weed in those days, and the Cathedrals!"

I still thought about the Light: "The contemplative life eliminates the 7 sins and receives the Light which breaks in cloudless sky. The soul was originally filled with love and spiritual light....The soul – the rational part which sees the Truth, the mirror in which we see the likeness of God – is lovely (divine) *and* ugly (debased by our senses). The worldly hinder their souls. They have to mount each rung in succession and purify their desires, contemplative self-examination leading to disillusion with the world. They have to withdraw from the world and the 5 senses. The reformed soul receives gifts. God opens the eye of the soul. God is Fire. Deus lux est (1 *John* 1,5). Devotion gives fervent emotion and natural affection, but the special grace of the Holy Spirit gives a quiet spiritual love and good works are easy, worldly honours avoided. The soul forgets itself, Divine Love destroys anger, envy and all the sins....A soul is sluggish, cold and dry – due to its own weakness – until it is touched by grace. Night is between two days. The first day is worldly: the false light between the clouds of self-conceit and depreciation of neighbour. The Night. The second day is the divine one: True light, when the sky is free from clouds."

On December 21st I wrote: "Saw the light blue light in the bath. Have been in an 'active' mood all day, i.e. contemplative, steaming inside, and have revised all part 4. God comes when you are feeling creative. Hence God and creativity are linked. Njinsky: 'God is fire in the head.' Meaning my Light and my illumination."

The next day I finally finished *The Weed-Garden* and wrote: "Milton's question in *Lycidas* – why be a poet, why not give up the hard work of rhyming the Muse and have the pleasure of Arethusa and the other nymphs?" I had been thinking about my epic – on 6th December I wrote "Decided to call my epic *Overlord*" and "I travelled to prepare for *Overlord*". On December 28th I wrote: "It is my destiny to write a 12 book epic about the Second World War. Now I have finished *Weed-Garden*, finally and irrevocably, I have planned the 12 books, and must now fit in the Christ-Devil theme and get the form right – for this poem is going to contain every form. I'm afraid in case my other project, which seems tame by comparison, will interfere with this my main work." My "other project" was a book about the Light which eventually became *The Fire and the Stones*.

At the end of the year I noted "I have much to be grateful for. A little boy who walks!" In early January Matthew climbed out of his cot, and throughout 1976 he plodded round the flat, crawling into my study and sitting back, one leg under the other, and beaming at me while I wrote, and I would smile happily back at him.

Ideally a person is in perpetual transformation. There is no stasis, but a dynamic unfolding, a perpetual flowing from lower to higher states of being. 1975 had been a year of long reflective poems. In early January 1976 I heard Vernon Scannell say on the BBC World Service that the English poetic gift is for the reflective and the lyrical. 1976 was to see me transformed back to a lyric poet.

I felt very alive. I wrote: "I was not living until 1964 – *The Silence* – and not truly living until 1969/70. I began to live truly in 1974, having been reborn in 1971. Margaret: 'Before that you were dead.' So reborn through Light." And: "My poetry is from my eternal self." On February 21st Nadia spent a day with us and on February 22nd I recorded: "Slightly depressed all day. Wrote to an end my 16 page draft for *The Labyrinth*. That increased my depression. I am very tired within. Have not been away this half term. Would like some sea air, but too tired to get it. Now the flu risk. This morning wrote *The Moon* for Ann, on our second anniversary today, using the image of the Apollo 10 Command Module, which we saw at the Science Museum yesterday."

February 22nd began an unusually creative lyrical spell in which I wrote much of what became *Whispers from the West*. On 26th February I noted: "Typed up the 3 poems I drafted yesterday: *Angels near a Fairground Hell*; *Love like a Cloth*; and the other one. Then wrote the Fly-Spray one. 4

poems have just come to me. I am a poet of domesticity: of domestic things." And on February 27th: "Wrote another poem: *A Flat and a Tin of Fly Spray.* (Or rather, drafted it late last night; polished and typed it this afternoon.)...My Head of Department job is speeding me up. My brain is becoming more complex as I have to cope with more complex things, and consequently it is easier to write poems. This is something that writers do not appreciate in their twenties; they try to make time for their writing and struggle with the material, whereas true success comes to those who increase their complexity, and this often happens through a full-time job; the side effect of which is increasing mastery of writing material." I also observed wryly: "I get £356 a month and am still £20 down on the first day, once the overdraft (£200 currently) has eaten into my salary. Running hard to stand still or fall behind." There was never enough money from Garratt Green to finance my mortgage and family. On March 1st as I was writing a bomb went off around 7, with an echo like thunder: an IRA bomber had blown himself up. On March 13th I wrote: "Yesterday and the day before scribbled half a dozen poems, which just came by themselves. Domestic situations, everyday experience, 'making the familiar strange'. I put them down hastily, and to my astonishment three of 6 stanzas rhymed without my realising it, so deep were the words." And I observed: "I make poems out of little things." The same day I recorded that Durrell had spoken on television of a current between him, through the mask of his character, and the reader, connecting with his fears, neuroses, terrors and obsessions, and had said that "if you are in love, the writing takes care of itself". I observed: "Today have drafted some 10 poems", and: "My journalism made money to bring in bread so I could write my poems."

In March my mother's health deteriorated. She reported that on the night of Saturday March 10th she had had a cramp in her leg which paralysed her right side for ten minutes, and that the same had happened again on the next two mornings. She was taken to the London Hospital and was categorised as having had a "small stroke". In fact she had had 3 strokes on the Sunday morning, according to my brother Jonathan, and had told a white lie and spaced the strokes out so we would not worry. Later my sister Frances phoned. She said that my mother had had 5 strokes (in her leg, her hand, her speech, her hand again and another one involving her hand) and had managed to deceive Jonathan so as not to alarm him. I visited her a couple of times. She lay in bed connected to the tube of a drip.

I was still writing poems. On March 27th I wrote: "'Not since Herbert – or Donne – has the spoken voice been recorded so naturally in poetry, and yet in so strict a form.' What I told Ann, after showing her two of my poems which I had just typed up....As I get older and am less intense, my ideas no longer seize me. I can cope better, i.e. get them into poems better. This is being a poet. Ideas/images come, then I am blissfully calm and can write them up. I am no longer a perpetual sea; am a hovercraft; stable, calm. The more you work, the more the mind races and makes you creative. If you have the whole time off, you settle into a slow routine." And again on April 4th: "My ten lost years, when I could not finish anything to my own satisfaction. Now I have a spring of images that bubbles from me, and that is my feeling – whatever comes out of this spring. Feeling/spring, i.e. what strikes me strongly, what comes out of my flow."

On 11th April I recorded: "Today a full moon. A blue light when I closed my eyes in my bath – the divine light, there, like the moon; to be looked at, like the moon. Where is the sun that lights it?"

I took Ann to France from 12th-15th April as I wanted to see the D-Day beaches for my epic. Ann's mother looked after Matthew. I summarised my impressions very briefly in my *Diaries*: "From Cherbourg to Valognes and Ste Mère-Eglise – the church in the deserted square, the museum with the WACO plane/glider; the tank. On to Utah beaches. The monuments and American flags, the German bunkers and film. The sea defences. The yellow sand. Primroses in the hedgerows, fields and cows. (France is agricultural whereas Britain is industrial.) The Omaha beaches. The cliffs, the part where so many died. The American Military Cemetery. Nearly 10,000 crosses. On to Bayeux – William the Conqueror's Cathedral, the tapestry and the war, an epic in pictures; mine to be in words. Arromanches and the Mulberry. Juno and Sword beaches, then on to Pegasus Bridge, all iron, and the first house to be liberated. On to Cabourg – Le Home; the antelope statue; then Deauville, Trouville. Back to Caen. Then Ouistreham. Stayed at the Hotel Le Chalet, having found Caen full. The chambermaid there. On to Boron next morning, which we never found; but did find hill 112. Also Falaise. The wader's fountain. The Castle. The gap – the road. On to Chartres. Heaven in the stained glass. The Englishman lecturing about it. The light changing. On to Versailles. Trianons. On to Paris. This morning Rouen. Joan's tower, the place where she was burned; the Cathedral bells – the service. The Abbey sanctuary we never found." In Chartres Cathedral I observed: "How the Light affects the soul....A soul like this glass. So Heaven can be in the soul."

Back in England I was "rapt" on Easter Sunday night. Ann watched *South Pacific* on television, I left the room for a quiet more appropriate to Easter Sunday and lay on my bed upstairs. I wrote: "Easter Sunday night. Rapt by God again. Lay down on my bed, saw the white light – also the rose-light through rings and the shield of God and Kandinsky-like patterns and squiggles. See (C. Day) Lewis's *Poetic Image*: does the poet fish for this? The inner knowledge of the mystic artist who waits in solitude. Now feel tired. This is the first time I have seen the rose-light, so far as I recollect." I wrote a poem, *Rapt*, and on April 19th, Easter Monday, after visiting Loughton observed: "My poetry has to be scanned like Latin verse: 'You sit I on the bed I chewing a I heart of I celery.' And there may be 3 syllables (or even, on occasion 4 syllables) to a foot. These poems are not addressed to the public; they are private poems on which the public is allowed to eavesdrop (like a television chat show). They catch a tone of unaffected simplicity. The influence of TV."

Soon afterwards we went to Lincolnshire to see Nadia in her new redbrick house, which had a green lawn in front of it. We went to Grantham and saw Newton's school.

Back with my poetry I reflected: "In a poem, go for the image and for the eternal. Cf Hopkins: the earth is an egg over which the Holy Ghost broods. Evil is...? I am now at the height of my powers. I have lived most evenings in the last three years in the awareness that I have to use them well; that there will come a time when I have to give an account of how I spent my time. April 28th. Worked on school business until 6, bathed, typed up last night's draft of the (then) last poem in my book, *Wistful Time-Travellers*. At 10.35 p.m. the title came to me: *Whispers from a Wistful West* – which I changed to *Wistful Whispers from the West*, then to *Whispers from the West*." And the next day: "This evening I turned and said to Ann: 'I'm turning into a great poet.' I feel it. I live near my 'Pierian' spring: I have built my house near it and I drink from it each day. I was about to do the washing up and my fourth poem came up like being sick – gold prospector. 60 something poems in 9 weeks (since Feb. 22nd)!" And: "The poet as gargoyle-spouting grotesquely, projecting from gutter, carrying water away from wall; with a grimace on its face." I felt supremely confident of myself: "My calm at my desk; in which I recollect what has occurred to me."

I was still writing poems. On May 5th I observed: "Matthew with a daisy chain in his hair." The next day: "Tired today. Then, after finishing my reports, I wrote a poem – and immediately I felt all right. I sometimes wonder how I would be if I had to earn my living at writing. Dead, probably. In 1970 I vowed I would turn with a savage fury. Now, after 17 volumes of poetry, I have turned with a savage fury. All the strictures of the Movement break down over Catullus and Horace, who have a personal, 'egocentric' outlook. The 'I' in Horace and Catullus. The romantic 'I' in Keats's 'I stood tiptoe'."

I was writing the (really) last poem in *Whispers from the West*: *The Fall of the West*, which was about terrorism. I noted in my *Diaries*: "I am saying (1) intellectuals are opting for Tyranny as opposed to democracy all over Europe; (2) this is a disease within – spreading bacilli – which saps the health of the West; (3) the germ began with the Nihilists and can lead to revolution; (4) it can also lead to our being overrun by Russia, having our will sapped so we have no will to resist; (5) final passionate appeal: let us not go Tyranny, so that democracy dies....The West may fall unless we crush the left." And again: "Title: the Fall of the West. Will the West fall? My attitude must not be Yes, must not be No. It must warn of the danger, like an *Old Testament* prophet. Decided to make it 3 parts: the symptoms, the disease, the cure. The cure: argument: we have no resistance, our will is soft – so let us realise that we have been inoculated, i.e. a mental attitude, no self-delusion – and that our disease is only a neurotic figment of the imagination – if we see things correctly." My thinking about terrorism set me thinking about the future of Western civilisation, and I found I needed the *Encyclopaedia Britannica* to clear my thoughts. I needed to consult it for *Overlord* as well. I ordered a set.

Meanwhile the poems continued: "*Whispers from the West* has taken me over. I began to clear up some 10 poems and have now done getting on for 100, and these new poems are holding me up. In one week I have finished *Fall of the West* which began as 4 stanzas and ended as 140 lines. In this collection I am speaking to a later Age in the future, and so I am able to generalise the present." I noted that we fall in love with strength: "The Truth: a very strong personality touches us – that is what we fall in love with....Strength touches us. We can remain unaffected by weakness."

At the end of May I slipped a disc. The pain and discomfort came on as I was driving home from school. I could not get out of my car. I drove straight to my doctor in Hereford Square. He lay me face down and pulled my left leg and right arm back as if he were handling a bow, and then my right leg and left arm. He told me to do an exercise that involved holding on to both handles of a door and rising on tiptoe on first the right and then the left foot. I took to my bed, with good consequences: "I have a slipped disc...and have spent 3 days in bed....The other day I saw the red light for the second time, like a stained glass window, when I was on my back with a slipped disc." Ever since that time I have had sporadic trouble with my back.

On 5th June I recorded: "Have finished my poems....All my energy has been going into my poems. *Whispers from the West* was written between February 22nd (about) and around May 22nd, most of it. I used to write so much in my *Diaries*; now it goes into my work – my art. The compulsive observation gets built in."

But I felt uneasy about *The Fall of the West*. Line 2 of that poem recorded "Thirty civilisations have crumbled to dust" and (in 1976) spoke of "An enemy within the heart of the West" long before the politicians used that slogan in the 1980s. At the end "the fall of the West" was pronounced a "delusion", "a mental attitude". I was not saying that the West was about to fall, but that the West must toughen its attitude if it was to survive. The pressing question was: would it survive? I knew I would have to research into civilisations, and on June 19th took delivery of the *Encyclopaedia Britannica*, so that I could begin my researches. This effectively put an end to my outpourings of short lyric poems, as I began a switch of my energies from poetry to history. The poems would continue, but at a more reflective level and coping with my shift from the world of the senses to a spiritual reality and unitive vision.

I had not yet made the switch, and almost immediately I wrote on imagination: "Redefine 'imagination' – which is a pictorial thing. 'Mental faculty forming images of external objects not present to the senses.' Fancy. Creative faculty of the mind. Fancy: 'faculty of calling up things not present, of inventing imagery.' Coleridge's distinction: imagination – 'the eternal act of creation': the unifying dissolving, diffusing, dissipating to re-create. Fancy: 'fixities, definites' – a 'mode of memory'. There is nothing about imagination being a *seeing* of pictures not present to the senses."

I had renewed contact with my Oxford friend Kingsley Shorter at a distance, and the same day he came to dine at Brechin Place. He was living in Scotland with his actress wife, where, improbably, he did a lot of running by the Forth past buttercups and daisies, and was on one of his rare forays to London. He was still pale and lean, and still went to Subud, which he described as a sect of Islam ("I observe Ramadan"). I told him about my experiences of illumination and he said "My guru (Pak Subu) had a similar experience at the age of 24, for him it was the great experience of his life.

Fasting leads to illumination." He had worked with the UN since Oxford as a Russian interpreter and had made a lot of money. He was now freelance and earned more than my annual teaching salary for 3 months' interpreting a year at the disarmament talks. He described the UN as a bureaucracy to end all bureaucracies, and détente as "a con": "the Russians won't invade but they'll nibble away gradually." He gave me news of our mutual Oxford friends, "the comrades" as he laughingly called them. Perry Anderson had written a book called *The Theory and Evolution of the State*, Adrian Hohler had left the Foreign Office, Erica Cheetham had written a book on Nostradamus and James Greene (a relation of Graham Greene) had sent me his best wishes. We had a very pleasant evening but he went and I did not see him again.

After Kingsley left I wrote: "My Dark Night was between my two illuminating experiences, 1966-1971, five years of confusion, when everything went wrong. Now I must tell the truth. Two constants. Percipere est esse; and $+ A + - A = 0$ (the void out of which life began). Poetry is the ideal medium for the existential quest along the Mystic Way."

The next day I visited Wandsworth prison as the guest of the father of a pupil (who was later to get an A for 'O' level English Language), the Czech Mr Burdysek, who worked as a warder. I knocked on the "studded gates of Hell" – driving to and fro past the prison I had seen it as "a Hell of smoky black towers and an enormous clock" – and he was waiting for me in uniform and took me to meet the Deputy Governor, who told me: "You can't see the gallows." I was taken to A, B, C and D blocks, passing netting over gates and arches and prisoners in dungarees, and we came out through E block, past the room with the gallows next to the Censor's Office. We walked to the hospital section and passed padded cells with spyholes. We went back to the cells and Mr Burdysek pointed out a staircase and said "Look, Balcombe Siege", and up the stairs, carrying buckets and mops, walked two of the IRA Balcombe Street siege terrorists who had been arrested, hands up, on television at night, one with a longish wad of hair. They wore open-necked shirts and trousers, and I recognised them instantly: Harry Duggan, alias Michael Wilson, once the most wanted man in Britain who was supposed to have shot Ross McWhirter as he opened his front door, and Joseph O'Connell. Duggan was not in the least threatening, he was much smaller than me, rather weedy, very inoffensive and had no presence, and I immediately knew that Ross McWhirter would have opened his front door and not been at all afraid in the second or two it took this mild man to produce a gun and shoot him. As they passed me they gave me a courteous half-smile and nodded, and I had a split second to decide my attitude. Should I cut them dead and freeze them out as IRA murderers? Social etiquette took over, and I half-smiled and nodded back, addressing the soul rather than the murderer in each of them, being aware of their potential rather than of what they had done. On reflection I was glad that I had acknowledged them and felt that my instinctive decision was right.

Soon afterwards Tuohy looked in unexpectedly, on his way to a theatre. He had met the poet Donald Davie in the US and found him "very dry". He was set to go back to Japan the following April. Matthew was in the lobster pot (as I called his round play-pen) and he stood and held on to the round rim and grinned at his godfather.

Later that night I wrote: "Saw the red light again last week. Have seen this light a lot lately – unspectacularly; it is just there."

I was still very aware of being on my Mystic Way throughout the rest of 1976. I read about the war for my epic and related myself to history and society, and particularly to the coming European Renaissance or Resurgence. This was part of my emerging unitive vision, while my family quietly came to the foreground.

At the beginning of the summer holidays I wrote: "What I am: a lighthouse for a generation. I preserve the Light." And again: "Just as there are two opposites (Gemini) in Tynan – the dandy and the leftist – so there are in me: the right-winger and the Outsider-poet." At the beginning of August I thought about autobiographical writing: "The argument that maturity is 'emerging from an obsessive preoccupation with oneself', that in the chrysalis stage we never experience the relaxation of looking outwards and study our entrails for the time we are there (which can be the rest of our lives). Such a person has not 'rid himself of the old-world notion of the artist as a romantic outsider'. The difference is, the argument goes, between someone who just writes, and a Writer. So an autobiographical writer 'has to get out of his own light' to be true and objective. Against this is the other view. If we accept that an autobiographical writer is a chrysalis, what of the butterfly, who flits from rose to rose, from subject to subject, book to book, writing about other people and other things and never the truth of the self? This writer is not superior to the first, just a different kind. This is the hack writer: the historian or biographer who feeds off other people's deeds. The truth is, a poet writes out of his own perception and sensibility, as does a visionary or a mystic. And such an autobiographer – a Wordsworth or Keats – must write largely out of his own experience, and is very often at his best as an outsider: not an old-world notion at all....The Romantic and Classical views: the writer as an individual self, the writer as a social being; the subject being the individual soul or a society. It is the assumptions, like these, behind such a review that need to be questioned. I am unrepentantly a Romantic writer when I write out of my experience, and a Classical writer when I write an epic."

Ann and the boys had gone to Cornwall and I joined them by train. Ann and Matthew met me on the platform, and we watched the Carnival at the end of Ann's mother's road on the way back. The next few days I planned my epic: "As I approach my epic I am thankful that I read Homer and Virgil in the original at school, and *Paradise Lost* on the Isle St. Louis in 1959. This coming work of mine will justify every hour spent on those activities." I went down to Charlestown, the local harbour, and noted: "The moon was over the headland and a wriggling eel of yellow light in the harbour. In the afternoon we went to Trenarren and lay down on the top of the Black Head among burnt gorse, and the sky was full of love. We also saw Portmellon, Mevagissey and Gorran. On August 2nd we went to Polkerris, and Matthew and I looked in rocky pools." We went to Fowey and Polruan and looked at Tristan's stone. In between I wrote and sunbathed in the garden. We went to

297

the Scilly Isles and saw Sir Harold Wilson walking towards the harbour walls with his wife and entourage. On August 13th I wrote: "The moon on the sea last night, the triangle and causeway of moonlight, the two night anglers."

The next day I thought about Mars and was convinced we are in a new Renaissance: "Thoughts on Mars. Just as the Renaissance coincided with a time of discovery (Columbus and da Gama, Marco Polo and Magellan) which affected our view of man and challenged our knowledge, so now our space probes coincide with a movement parallel to the Renaissance which will surely have a similar effect: the new individualism, man in the universe as opposed to in society or the world; in short, man in the silence, a new mysticism, a new view of his perception. I am slowly coming into my own. A new religious view which builds on Christendom, but which is different, extending the findings of Christendom from earth to space – that is what my epic will bring out. The idea of a New World....The new Renaissance will grow out of our 'Middle Ages' as did the old one. It will not be a revolution but an evolution. My mysticism is the right kind; experiential, existential, not doctrinal."

I went to Charlestown again and wrote: "Bats, dripping stars. No moon. On Charlestown harbour I felt giddy, lost among so many stars, some bright some not. My feet on my world, and so many other worlds. The vastness of the universe, which I felt so often in the desert."

I went down to Charlestown for the last time and recorded: "I said to Ann: 'Individual value is very often potential value – the seed in the skull, the standard.' There were some yobbos on the harbour wall. 'It may take two years for their individual value to be revealed. The Light is the standard, it is above and beyond them. Not "I" am the standard, but the standard is there.'"

We returned to London via Longleat, we stood and looked at Tumbler's Bottom, where Tuohy had lived – it was now a herb farm – and visited Bath. I visited Churchill's war rooms below the Treasury for my epic. Soon afterwards I went to Churchill's home at Chartwell.

On August 30th I watched a programme on television about Betjeman's *Summoned by Bells* and wrote: "The line goes from Wordsworth's *Prelude* through *Summoned* to my *Silence*. The old smiling public man stick-tapping through the rooms and haunts of his childhood – very sad. Little Betjeman with his teddy bear. Few metaphors, few similes; a plain, flat, almost prosaic style of everyday reflection. Crabbe-like. He tried to find mystical experiences but was unlucky. The melancholy despair in Betjeman's work....Betjeman writes about other people he sees, and satirises their pretensions." Back at school I wrote of Keats: "Keats: 'Truth is beauty.' It is about things that last, cf Hemingway: 'a man should find things he cannot lose.' Beauty in art, and religious truth both last. We have to find things that last. Cf the nightingale's song which was heard by emperor, clown and perhaps, Ruth; generically of course."

I had had a profound conviction that "a European Renaissance is growing. The European ideology. Roots in Christendom; politically anti-Communist." Again: "Avoid the traditionalist, backward look. Achieve the forward, European look. I am not a British Conservative but a European whose roots are in Epping Forest, and who stands for certain fundamental values and against modern values. The European Renaissance....A new European consciousness, which I am defining. The European Renaissance is above all a question of rediscovery (of illumination, etc.)....The European Renaissance is a discovery about the heart and a rediscovery of the old truths of religions and the experience in them. The concept of illumination is very important: a new enlightenment, not of reason but of Classical values, subordination to God the Light. This is very important. The modern age is one of darkness (as opposed to Light) and of barbarism. We must revive the experience of illumination of Christendom (religion) and oppose Communism (politics), and express the ideals of peace and serenity, which are linked to perceptivism. Therefore, reject modern values. Moving to Epping Forest is a rejection of modern values, the leftism, rational humanism and scientific materialism."

I wrote an essay on Europe: "The argument of my European essay is as follows. Politically Europe is reviving after a period of decline, and it should oppose the Soviet Union. This stance is linked with Europe's ideology, which is rooted in Christendom, but which is freedom. This ideology has been weakened by the modern times – the Dark Age – and by passive values, i.e. there is a passive ideology; i.e. the 'soul' has been weakened to the 'body' and original philosophies connected with the soul are now philosophies of humanity towards bodies. As a result, a strengthening in our religion will strengthen our ideology – not because it is beneficial but because it is true – and there should be a reformation, to promote the active values, a renewal. This can result in a Holy Roman Empire. New values, a new morality. Traditional values made new. The arts....I am a Christian Democrat, as opposed to a Social Democrat." And, prophetically looking ahead to my publishing, I wrote: "When I speak, the Soviet Empire will tremble. I will speak the truth. That means getting into a position where I can speak out."

In mid-September my thoughts returned to poetry: "In the cycle of styles,...pre-classical...leads to classical (harmony and proportion), which is my epic. I have finished my...*Gates of Hell* and am now concerned with balance and proportion – the classical values based on the Light, i.e. mature.....I am on the side of the poem as image and organic form (the Coleridgean imagination) but I am also on the side of the Journey, the mysticism, the Baroque....Heart, not head. Epic: union – the idea of the new Age." I also wrote: "Tuohy is Neo-Classical in a Neo-Classical time. My time has yet to come."

At the end of September I heard that Ann was pregnant: "The news today; Ann is 42 days pregnant with what will be our second (my third) child. I have suspected and was not overly surprised when she told me by whispering as a secret in Matthew's ear, 'Having a baby.'"

Despite the claims on my time of school I was thinking about art and groping towards a restatement of the Baroque, the combination of Classicism and Romanticism/Mannerism which I had approached in Japan: " The new period must synthesise past styles. Its view of art will be a synthesis between image and statement....Artist not hopelessly isolated. Organic form – form with some control of thought. So Eliot was a

Classicist, and so am I....The Romanticised individual, the Classicist European subordinated to God, the anti-Communist, anti-leftist Classicism is a balance between head and heart, and the heart has been neglected, so the next movement must stress heart to prepare the way for Classicism. A dilemma resolved." And again: "The Classical Age – within my lifetime. ....Margaret is talking about a Classical age: serene, harmonious. There is no anxiety in Margaret's art." The end of the Cold War and the move towards a United States of Europe and a coming world government has created the conditions in which a new Classicism can flourish within a rediscovery of the Baroque heart. This will involve a Universalist blend of all aspects of man and the universe.

I was also thinking again about the European civilisation. I had not formalised the end of one historical stage and the beginning of another – that did not happen until *The Fire and the Stones* – but intuitively I sensed that a European Resurgence was ahead, which I connected with the United States of Europe I had first anticipated as far back as Festival of Britain year, 1951. I now think that Modern Art was a Mannerism that would lead to a new Baroque period, but then I toyed with the idea that Modern Art was a Primitivism that would lead to a new Classicism, "the Classicism of the Resurgence and of Resurgence man, who has the tranquillity and serenity of illumination. Peace....Two new ideas in three days, after being away from school for two days, giddy on Friday. First the Christian Democrat idea, then the idea that Modern Art is a Primitivism preparing for a Classicism. Am exhausted from writing *The European Resurgence.* I have got to the end in draft, not having done the Modern Values bit yet. I must rest, i.e. go back to school tomorrow and relax. I still need to do a history of the ecumenical movement to place my Reformation in context, show it happening; read mysticism for this, modern mystical movements. Also Existentialism and I need to revise and rewrite some sections for 'style', not content. (They were written when I was tired.) I started *Resurgence* when I finished my syllabus, two weeks into this term."

Of my poems I wrote, citing Keats: "*Bards of Passion and of Mirth* (Keats) is about the poetic tradition. We rise and extend our consciousness and knowledge, which we put into poems. When we die we leave our souls on earth – in our poems. This is what I am doing. Rising higher and higher, leaving my soul behind in my poems." But I was also severe on Keats: "Keats's *Hyperion* is about gods in the clouds; the waterfalls he saw are set in the cloudy passages. Wordsworth's waterfalls were real. It is the difference between early and late Romanticism: the real world and fantasy. (Boat by the lake/crags in Saturn's house.) Avoid this in the war poem. Set it in the real world. (But also put in the imaginary one.)"

I now turned my attention to philosophy: "Today, Friday, after a hard week at school, I overthrew the whole of modern philosophy since the Renaissance – both Rationalism and Empiricism, and the isms that follow from them – and I am amazed at the casual way I did it. I have been working on the essay until midnight every night for the last three or four weeks, and my overthrow follows quite naturally from my earlier findings. I have just demolished the whole of philosophy, and I am relieved rather than pleased. Unity, not multiplicity, is my love; true perception illumined, not unillumined reason and sense-experience, with the soul unstill, untranquil, and therefore perceiving the world wrongly. My doctrine of perceptivism has astonishing consequences....The point is, all the isms of post-Renaissance philosophy came from the pre-Christian Greeks. Now is the time to sweep the lot aside as partial truths by returning to the vision of Fra Angelico and his predecessors, and to the early Renaissance and Classical man."

I had not forgotten the Light. On October 16th I wrote: "Two nights ago I saw fine old masters and brilliant visions of patterns, like the inside of a richly domed Cathedral. (Heaven.) I have not seen the Light recently, though all my waking thinking is concerned with it." At the same time I noted that "Tuohy has published a book which puts down Yeats for belonging to the Order of the Golden Dawn, a forgery."

I saw history in terms of the Light: "Why I spent so many hours reading Lucretius and Plato's *Dialogues* and the *New Testament* in Greek: to prepare for this view of Europe, which I am now writing. The Light being the Catholic mystical tradition of the Church in the West from 550 to 1150, at the beginning of the Holy Roman Empire. I feel my mission very strongly, after seeing the Four Gospels in terms of the Light. It is to bring the sects together, to reunite the Church. God is working through me. In some strange way, I have been prepared for my mission." Again: "Tuohy's remark to me in Soho...: 'There is an imprecise use of language in mysticism.' Language is given meaning by the experience. Anyone who has had experience of the Light knows what Ruysbroeck means by the 'sparkling stone'. To someone who has not seen the Light, the image must seem imprecise, wild." I wrote: "I know that I am one of the great Christian mystics, who have brought mysticism back to flower in the 20th century. Yet I have had two families. There is something about living in a family that brings out the best in me; in my inner life. Novels and plays are so empty. No wonder Eliot never read them. Nor shall I from now. I thank God that I have been allowed to complete the Mystic Way without the distractions of fame, which puffs up the false 'I', and which I do not want. The blessed peace of this obscurity. No letters to answer, no callers, no telephone ringing, no dinners to attend, no excuses to give and no lies to tell. I am so happy, deified by the Light. Where I differ from most poets today. They follow secular poetry. For me, poetry is a statement of the journey for deification; it is inseparable from the mystic goal of man....Without knowing it, I was being prepared to renew the religious life of my country, I, who looked at the Methodist clock during sermon time when I was a boy."

I looked back on my writing: "I began my search in Reality with *Mandalas*. The apparent failure has been in reality a whopping success. I have had experience of the answer to all Truffer's problems which I stated there, and went to the East (*Bhagavadgita*) to solve. I found Enlightenment in the East, and took it back to the West. My time meditating in Zen. I came to God through Zen at first. Libya was a discarding, a decluttering, a purifying in the fire." I looked back at Oxford: "I regarded as a search what Ricks and others regarded as a science. I went through literature seeking while Ricks had different criteria; he measured. I was sent to Oxford and to the finest tutorial mind of our time (in literature) so that I would search. I was not allowed to stay there; that was not my business. I went to Libya to connect myself to the tradition of Cassian: the desert vision and the Ghadames spring."

At the end of October, at half term "on impulse (I) drove to Worthing through autumn leaves and spent an hour and a half walking in the sea breeze on the promenade, getting rid of the cobwebs. Then saw Margaret at home. She is converting her shop into a gallery, which she wants to call 'Osborne' (after Rob, Matthew and me). Margaret: 'Things prevented you from the Light, and they had to go.'"

In early November I began a draft for what eventually became *The Fire and the Stones*: "Fireworks yesterday in the gardens for Matthew; and now to my amazement I have a 12 chapter book..., *The European Resurgence*....My destiny has been to recall this generation to the Light....I had to be restructured so that I could speak out in a book. God is using me. I am merely an agent of the Divine will – an espionage image – and in some way that I do not understand, I am being carried towards the foundation of a European movement."

There was then a crisis that involved Matthew, some telepathy on my part and a pact with God. We did not know it but Matthew had tonsillitis and a sudden rise in his temperature brought on febrile convulsions: "November 13th. Nightmare day. Matthew fell down the stairs yesterday, and had a lump on his head. Was flushed today. In fact had tonsillitis. He slept from 10.30 to 2.45, then had convulsions while I was at the library. Twitched and had a fit, slight bubbling. I suddenly knew I had to get home, and drove home to see the ambulance screaming into Brechin Place, my front door thrown open by the two men who rushed upstairs. I arrived to see Matthew in a sort of coma, deathly white, the life gone out of him. The ambulancemen took him down to the ambulance, we drove with him to St. Stephen's Hospital. I expected him to stop breathing at any time. It was then I prayed: 'Please God, I'll do anything, but please let him come through.' I said this in the hospital cubical, to myself, and within a minute there was a surge of life, and Matthew came round, the colour back in his cheeks. I was absolutely drained, as I am now, and felt sick. I had to sit down. Now he has had X-rays on his head and has had tonsillitis diagnosed.; he must have EEG treatment....No need for a lumbar puncture, the X-rays show no fracture or bleeding. His temperature has been brought down by a fan...and he is now sleeping....I feel drained. I made a pact with God which I have got to keep now. It was not I who healed him, it was a power through me, to which I am now mortgaged. From now on I must speak out for God, and dedicate my life to His will, and I cannot stop the tears welling up in my eyes." And again: "November 14th. Ann went in at 7.30 to find that Matthew had had another fit at 6, and yet another as she arrived. He had a fourth at 9.20 when I arrived. The doctor said (when I arrived) that fits breed fits through the trigger mechanism, that the EEG may be abnormal as one of the fits was with a low temperature. Matthew had a lumbar puncture, which was clear – no haemorrhage. He had to lie flat for 24 hours – on his back or on his side. The yellow stain on his back, the plaster, Matthew's glazed discomfort. His high temperature all day, going up and coming down and going up again. The fan on the wet sheet. His personality changes. He is still not himself yet."

That afternoon Tuohy came and talked about his book on Yeats. He said: "Yeats was a Freemason. Hence 'Sato's ancient blade' – the Freemason's sword."

Matthew now began to improve: "Matthew a bit better today. High temperature (103) at night, but down later. Grizzly, a sign of improvement. Was sitting up and playing with bricks. Co-ordinating better. Afternoon: improvement. He slept, was well enough to sit up and eat with the others at the table." And the next day: "Better again. He has slept at night, this morning and this afternoon and his temperature is down. But he cried a lot for 'Mummy'....His nerve cells will be more sensitive but there should be no effect on emotion and behaviour." I reflected on Matthew: "I was guided. Having felt the call from the library at 3 when I was set to work until 5 p.m., and arriving at home at the same time as the ambulance so that I could pray for Matthew in the hospital, I was the agency who would bring the life flowing back although God was the one who continued it. I was guided."

Soon afterwards I was invited to hear Margaret Thatcher address the Conservative Group for Europe at the Waldorf Hotel. Dinner was in a large room, I was on an outside table. I was told that if I had a question I could write it down and Margaret Thatcher, then Leader of the Opposition, would include it in her speech. I wrote a question on my place card about the occupation of Eastern Europe and asking for a more fundamental link with the Christian Democrats, and sent it in. Margaret Thatcher spoke with impressive fluency, wearing a pale floaty green, and much of her speech was devoted to the Christian Democrats. At the end I went across and thanked her for her answer and again stressed the need for the East European Nations to be free. We stood in a furniture-free area, and a crowd gathered round us almost immediately. Douglas Hurd was by her side. Mrs. Thatcher said: "You must remember that they are used to living under a vast government, psychologically, they are not used to freedom. You have to do it through propaganda, radio broadcasts." I told her it should come from the European Parliament, and that there should be a movement to liberate the East European Nations from the USSR – a liberation movement. She gave me a long look. I did not then know what her true views on Europe were. Then Douglas Hurd approached me and said, "Come and have a drink." He bought me a drink and said: "You are quite right, we should mention Eastern Europe much more in our speeches than we do." My encounter made me wonder whether I should become a European MP and proclaim the European Resurgence from within the European Parliament. I wrote Mrs. Thatcher a letter and enclosed my essay on the European Resurgence.

In early December I was diagnosed as having poor blood flow back to my heart, caused by valve failure; the pooling of my blood gave me varicose veins and a tendency to dermatitis on my ankles, a condition which was to be with me for the rest of my life. I also seemed to have a perpetual cold.

Ann stopped working at St. James Norland at the end of the autumn term, 1976. She was now heavily pregnant. We went to Loughton. It was frosty and I recorded: "The walk in the Forest after lunch. White frost, holly with red berries, and a dozen skaters on the iced-over pond. The ice was nearly an inch thick. Earlier, church; the crisp graveyard, last year's oak leaves covered with wonderful patterns, a blue sky. My peace, sitting at the back of the aisle on the right, in the second pew down at the end (as you face the altar) – my seat. The sun in the evergreen outside."

Margaret visited us and I spoke of proclaiming the Light to Europe. Later I wrote: "Now at 37, I am setting out to change people so that they will understand the significance of what I have written. A godless people does not understand the Mystic Way, and so it rejects it." I had the idea of leading a Crusade through Europe, carrying a symbol of the Light from Canterbury to Rome to appeal to the Archbishop and Pope for Christian unity and a Christian European movement. In every city we would burn the hammer and sickle and call on the Soviet Union to withdraw from Eastern Europe.

At the same time I was thinking about the Light: "There is surely a spectrum of light as there is a frequency of sound – from invisible (high frequency?) to visible (low frequency?). The invisible light streams into the body cells and is stored and can be seen psychically, but cannot be seen by the naked eye; it is red, blue, white. The visible light – sunlight – has a different wattage per metre. This may activate our matter – our bodies – with energy and keep us going. It would make us live indefinitely if we did not wear out, i.e. ourselves fail; life never fails us, we fail it. I think I am on the verge of a most original discovery. So faith-healing is connected with the Light....We are bits of energy which attract and repel each other with explosions of light which vibrates at too high an intensity and too fine a wave-length for the human eye to see. (Cf X-ray, which is more powerful than sunlight.) This is when prayer comes in, it increases the flow of energy of God's Light."

We spent Boxing Day at Loughton, at my mother's. Later I found I was researching into dead cultures. I worked on a book on the Secret Light (which eventually became *The Fire and the Stones*) and researched into Egypt and then into Druids and sacred circles and took Ann to an exhibition on them. I noted of my Mystic Way: "Illumination is a stage, between Purgation and Union. So my Illuminative Way is over." At the end of the year I made a note to write *The Mystic Way*. In January Margaret rang and commented on my interest in ancient cultures: "It's the Light today, not in Egyptian times. The Catholics still keep the tradition alive, that is what you must realise."

The first half of 1977 saw a slow drift in me towards a unitive, metaphysical outlook despite family crises.

In early 1977 my overdraft had risen and I was over my bank limit. In early February Ann, Matthew and I moved out of Brechin Place, which we let furnished to an American Professor. We moved to a downstairs flat in an Edwardian terrace near Garratt Green, at 100A Stapleton Road. An old lady lived above us, and there were night-storage heaters. Here we brought our main possessions and camped, and I endeavoured to write in the sitting-room.

The move unsettled my writing. At half-term, thinking it would help the financial situation, I dashed off a novel about a school in a week, and then thought better of being commercial. I went to Worthing. I wrote: "Splash Point. A green, sandy sea, fountains of spray, flung shingle on the promenade. A wind that blew you away. I, bent double, struggled into a gale." In March I drafted out a Libyan potboiler. But I had the knowledge to write: "My advice to all budding Rasselases. Spend your first 10 adult years travelling and experiencing everything, and your next 40 recording the knowledge you have gained." And in April I wrote: "Reflections on my destiny. It is not for popular and commercial success, but rather for gigantic works of quality: those of a Blake or a Milton." And again: "I must define what I am. It is connected with 'the Outsider'. I am a solver of the Outsider's problem. I am not a poet who writes about a natural world in certain rhythms; I am not a writer who entertains; I am a discoverer, a seeker for truth, who expresses his vision in words as opposed to paint or musical sounds. I must be quite clear about this. I am writing about the meaning of life; as an Outsider who has become a man of vision. I am a solitary, a loner; an explorer; a Captain Scott. Plays, poems and novels therefore bore me. I am a T. E. Lawrence....My 'mind-suicide' at Garratt Green is not dissimilar to that of T. E. Lawrence in the RAF....I am an existentialist. I am a contributor to the Existentialist movement and tradition....I am also a mystic, concerned with the correct 'I'. The mystic today appears as an Existentialist."

As a way out of the financial crises we explored the possibility of buying a small private school in Streatham for £60,000, which Ann could run. We met the Head, who was keen to sell to us, but to buy it we would have to sell 10 Brechin Place. Garratt Green was beginning to pall. I wrote: "I do not want to continue at Garratt Green; it has become petty, endless duties and no inspiration. I do not want to educate the yobs and oiks of Wandsworth any more. I only derive satisfaction from my Blake and Coriolanus and Sonnets classes....Aimlessness and frustration working for the State. Meaning and fulfilment at growing a family business in education and educating the family well."

In April Tuohy invited me to a dinner he was giving in London. It was at the house of a relative who kept the Berlin desk at the Foreign Office, but who could not attend herself. Tuohy had invited a relative of his publisher's, Fergus Maclean, the 33 year old son of Donald Maclean, the British diplomat who defected to the USSR after betraying Western nuclear secrets to Stalin. Fergie Maclean was over in England with his Russian wife Olga and his son, and he seemed to have lost his job as a translator. Also present were Tuohy's cousin Flavia's pro-Communist boy-friend, Colin MacCabe, who then taught in Christopher Ricks's English Faculty at Cambridge.

I went on my own as complications had just been found with Ann's pregnancy. There were therefore just six of us that evening: Tuohy, me, Fergie and Olga Maclean, and Colin and Flavia MacCabe. Fergie Maclean turned out to be an extremely nice young man, and I realised the reason Philby had escaped detection so long was just such niceness. I sat next to

305

Fergie's Russian wife, a short dark-haired attractive woman, over dinner, and I remember MacCabe saying "I'd love to go to the Soviet Union" and Fergie saying that Braine's *Room at the Top* had been translated in Russian as *The Attic*. It came out that Fergie's stepfather was Philby and that in Moscow he lived in Philby's household: his mother Melinda Maclean had left Donald Maclean for Philby and had taken the children with her. Fergie was reluctant to talk about life in Philby's household. A few days later he rang me and asked if I could find him a job in the ILEA. Soon afterwards he rang again and said that Olga had gone back to the USSR with his son, and that he would have to go back, otherwise he would not see his son again. He said, "I am in effect being blackmailed from Moscow."

The diagnosis on Ann was not good. She had mild toxaemia, and had to be admitted to Queen Charlotte's hospital until the birth, which was officially still six weeks away. I would have to look after Matthew together with her mother, who would come up from Cornwall and mind Matthew during the day. While I was organising this Ann had a crisis. Her blood pressure rose to 140 (bottom line), when the normal is 80, and there was a danger the baby might be born prematurely. She was taken to intensive care. She said to me: "You may have difficulty in finding me tomorrow. They may have put me in the garden."

When I had some time to myself I wrote: "I am a part of the most remarkable shift in Western consciousness for several hundred years. We are liberated from the old materialistic, rationalistic culture – it is that that I am an enemy of – and from the old ego-consciousness (as opposed to deeper self). All is one. My work is that of a new consciousness being judged by the standards of the old order. A new order, an old order. I am a traditionalist in so far as the old ways enabled me to discover the new 'spiritual wave'....This is why *The Silence* is a great work. Dating from 1965, it precedes the new wave of around 1966 or 1967, and puts me right at the beginning of the new Renaissance....Solitary-ness is the way." And: "A poet manqué. The title, when applied to others (like Dylan Thomas's father) makes me laugh. Failed in what? Failed to write? Failure to get across does not detract from the integrity of the art; it merely notes an extraneous consideration, the taste of those who invest in a book. A poet manqué is someone who could never bring himself to write; not (like Blake) a poet who wrote for himself and died unknown."

Ann had an ultrasound, which showed the baby had not grown as much as it should and was not being fed through the placenta and was starving to death. The decision was made to induce, and on April 26th I arrived at the Labour Ward and sat with Ann, who was plugged into a cardiotocograph, which showed contractions and the zigzag fetal heartbeat. Ann had an epidural and I put on a white mask draped round my ears and a white shower-hat and a white coat that tied at the back of my neck. A nurse said "The fetal heartbeat is distressed" and I tensed. But Ann was calm when the baby's head appeared, covered in green pus: a boy. Ann held him and then I held him and looked with relief at the blood in his eyes mixed with tears as he gave healthy cries. A nurse took him to special care and I saw him in an incubator: a slim little thing just 4 lbs 12 ozs with screwn-up eyes and a pink nose, lips and chin and a greeny forehead.

For several days there were bulletins: "causing anxiety but prospects satisfactory", "improving". I visited and saw him in the incubator, his head in a box with an oxygen tube nearby, a drip and monitor from his tummy. His breathing was very laboured and his breaths were quick; he had been sick and some of what he had brought up had gone into his lungs. His little fingers closed briefly round mine as I put my hand through the round rabbit hutch hole. Soon afterwards he developed jaundice and a collapsed left lung, and had air round his lungs, which was being absorbed. But then he began making progress and I knew little Anthony, as we were going to call him, was going to be all right. And on May 2nd Ann came home, leaving Anthony in hospital. He came out of his incubator on May 6th and breathed air in his cot; he came home on May 15th.

I was exhausted. I had not slept properly for nearly four weeks, and had been working. I had a bath and noted: "Saw the blue light yesterday. Very vivid. While sitting in my bath. I suddenly felt rapt, and I looked and there it was, round and luminous blue, a deep turquoise. It gathered and formed in a circle and shone and I felt charged through with life afterwards."

I looked ahead and felt drawn to Epping Forest: "I have two sons, and I may become rooted in Somerville School. This is all happening away from Hagger country, where my heart is, to which I would love to return. I am now choosing where we will live in the next 10 years....I am aiming to be one of the great literateurs of the 20th century. I have 10 years to go before my achievement reflects itself." I received a letter from Mabel Reid, my Oaklands teacher: "These have been such anxious days for you both, life weaves such strange patterns....I know both of you will have faced the challenge with great courage." Our offer for the school in Streatham turned out to be not enough, and I wrote: "The answer on the Streatham school is No. Now buy one over Epping Forest way, e.g. start a school....Start a private school as competition to Oaklands; on the edge of the Forest."

Europe loomed again. I had a vision of Europe which I knew I had to put in my epic. I wrote: "My European contribution in action will blend with my writing, so that I am already the New European Man. My aim is to liberate Europe from Communism, to free all occupied Europe – with words....My destiny is...to reflect the Age in my writing, especially in my poems. It is to preserve the tradition but to make something new of it. 'The man who suffers' must be involved in Europe, just as 'the artist who creates' is a party to Europe."

Towards the end of May I had a preliminary, exploratory interview, which had been arranged by Biggs-Davison, with Marcus Fox to see if I should become a European MP. Fox was a bit like a tortoise, lined and creased and swarthy, and he asked what committees I would work on. The idea of being a committee man was not appetising – it made me feel weary – and I backed off being a European MP while retaining the commitment to a United States of Europe. I wrote: "Action tempted Rimbaud away from poetry, and did for T. E. Hulme. It cut short the literary career of Sheridan. Yet I must act. For actions speak louder than words – and actions give backing to words. A whole man expresses himself through words (which can lie) and actions (which can't as they express him)."

Soon afterwards I visited Biggs-Davison at the House of Commons and endeavoured to extricate myself from progressing with the idea that I might become a European MP. We had a drink on the terrace and we talked about the political scene. He asked me to send him my essay (which he called "paper") on the European Resurgence, pointing out that Margaret Thatcher had spoken of a European "Risorgimento" ("Resurgence") in Rome, which may have come from her copy of my "paper". In early July I met the MP for Kensington at the House of Commons, Sir Brandon Rhys Williams, a tall ex-Etonian of 50, and heard his left wing Conservative views on how there was no harm in Eurocommunism as it was democratic Communism and might make the Iron Curtain countries democratic. I profoundly disagreed: Communists had always locked up the opposition, Communism was the enemy of democracy. I had taken a Churchillian path towards Europe and now wanted to keep Europe at the level of an idea.

In July I was in some confusion again. Ann was ill for two weeks. She had nervous exhaustion after the birth and glandular fever, and went to Cornwall. I stayed in London to look after Nadia. The summer holidays had begun and I was reading books for references to the Light: Langland, Bunyan and Dante's *Paradiso*. I took Nadia to see Nelson's Victory, and on my return did more research and wrote: "*The Silence* is in the tradition of *The Song of God* (*Bhagavadgita*)." I found Boehme in the Fulham library and read the *Mandakya Upanisad* and wrote: "I am filled with great meaning. *Mandalas* was about Truffer's attempt to recapture the Fourth, which was the Light. I wrote it before I had had the experience – it put me on the right road. The British Council took me through Moslem and Buddhist cultures so that I could develop this 'Eastern' consciousness, which I am now writing in a book about the Light. One day I shall end up, famous and living in London, like Truffer. But may I not be as lonely. Or as lost. My life has a pattern. My writing took me to the frontiers of the land of the midnight Light; my imagination was my means of transport. After that, my daring in going out to Japan supplied the experience, and my divorce completed it. I have been given a wonderful gift, for which I am profoundly grateful. That quotation from Eliot: 'And the end of all our exploring/Will be to arrive where we started (Truffer)/And know the place for the first time.' My search."

At the end of July I read all Pope and drove Nadia to Loughton and wrote: "Took Nadia for a walk in the Forest. The lilies on the ponds. The grasshoppers on the Stubbles. The Meadow Browns and Copper Browns and ghost moths. Read all Rilke between 6 and 7, had supper then came home by tube, when I read all Milton save the last 9 books of *Paradise Lost*. I added: "Anyone who is enlightened becomes an Angel. From now on, I shall think of the enlightened as Angels." I went on: "The effects of the Light – I have to stress the benefits of illumination. Emerson and Thoreau. Tuohy and me. They had a movement (the Transcendentals) but we have not. Perhaps my Light outlook should force one? Plato affirmed absolute values and a reality that is independent of sense-perception. All Light-seers are therefore Platonists; or (in the Plotinan sense) Neo-Platonists."

I was on the verge of a development which turned me into a transcendental metaphysical who affirmed both transcendence and immanence.

PART THREE

THE PERCEPTIVE WAY

NEW POWERS
1977 – 1980

Between the Illuminative Way and the Unitive Way there is a further purgation of the spirit in which the sensual 'I' is put off for the larger Will that sees the universe as a unity. Imperceptibly, the mystic has begun to live through a new centre of his consciousness, at a new level of consciousness, and this results in new powers being received and a new way of perceiving the universe.

One aspect of my development involved new healing powers, and it was as if I were being given the means to combat Ann's illness. The development began on 30th July 1977, when (after being sent a leaflet on it by Flavia Anderson, from Edinburgh) I attended a conference on the ancient Egyptians and the Essenes. It took place in St. John's, Smith Square, and featured Sir George Trevelyan talking about the Essenes and Denis Stoll talking about the ancient Egyptians. At regular intervals during the day there was a dance from his five Egyptian temple-dancers, one of whom was Christine Finlayson (now Klein), who would later dance at the launch of *The Fire and the Stones*.

The day was a revelation. To my recollection I had not encountered the Essenes before, the gentle people who lived on the edge of Lake Mareotis from the 3rd century BC and who peopled the Qumran caves where the Dead Sea Scrolls were found, which I had visited in 1962. I had not properly grasped that the Egyptian *Book of the Dead* was full of experiences of the Light. And throughout the day the five temple-maidens dressed in white moved in trance, striking slow and graceful hand postures, replicating over 900 hand and foot poses found in murals in the Egyptian tombs. There was an incredible beauty about their synchronised movements as they came from the spirit. Denis Stoll claimed to have received the music from the beyond and to have researched it for accuracy, and he explained that the maidens became "khus" – he meant "akhs" – or spiritual souls or "Shining Ones". There was a pale, ethereal beauty about the measured dance of these temple-dancers.

This was my first contact with the New Age movement. I was not prepared for the rebuffs when I approached the speakers at coffee-time. Denis Stoll said, "You will have to find the answers to your questions yourself," and Sir George Trevelyan said "I am not a sensitive, I am an interpreter" when I asked him about the Light.

If the lectures were uplifting, lunch in the crypt was amazing. Out of the 400 present I found myself sitting next to the Rev. John Jewsbury, a Unitarian Minister from Stetty, Swansea. He specialised in mass-healing at his church through the laying-on of hands, and he also took part in a group for absent healing. He looked at me and said quietly, "You have the power to heal. All you have to do is try." I said I was going down to Cornwall the next day, where Ann had a bad headache, and we arranged that I would heal her that first evening and then ring him. He gave me instructions as to what to do, and said: "Ask God to make you a channel for his power. We'll be backing you up."

On July 31st I travelled to Cornwall and became a healer: "Put the three faith-healers theories into practice, with their backing, at 9.00 p.m. Felt a surge of power that left me cold – it hit my back and ran through my arms and out, at 9. Tried again 5 minutes later and felt power sweep through me again. Ann felt an accumulated warmth from my fingers, but not a sudden burning. This may be the beginning of her cure, and of my career as a healer. I felt two different surges."

Jewsbury saw these rushes as spirits. I reflected Jewsbury's interpretation: "Two quite different spirits?" Next day I observed: "I have moved against the sense world to the spiritual and am now a Platonist of sorts: I affirm the reality of the Light before the reality of my sense-perception. This is perceptivism. I am out at the frontiers of thought....Am an anti-empiricist." And the next day: "Tried again, to heal Ann at 9.00 p.m. Lay with her, touching her head and asking God to make me a channel for his power. The spirits came through me, entering my back and sweeping along my arms and out into Ann, like clouds across the face of the sun, making me shiver and tingle, four times. Then there was a massive one which lasted twice as long. All were different; each different in character. A tingling sensation. What spirit heals through me?" I noted: "I have healing powers. Correction. Healing powers use me. Jewsbury...has confirmed over the telephone that what I felt last night sounded like four different spirits and then another totally different, healing through me from 'the other side'. Mrs. Jewsbury (Valerie) had a headache in the middle or back of her head around 9.05 last night. I have been pushing Ann's headache from back to middle to top of her head, and will now try and push it out. Valerie was asking 'Is she relaxed?' It is important that she should be totally relaxed. Ann's headache has been transferred to Valerie Jewsbury. Jewsbury: 'Cold is very often something people talk of – cold or burning.' A minute's delay after asking is normal. They came in at the base of my spine. I am at this moment filled with a spirit – I feel cold (like a sudden fear in the middle of the night, passing into a warmth)....Spirits from the other side enter us and rush through us; illumining us, giving us divine wisdom....They will give me the wisdom of God, if God wishes me to act as a channel for such divine energies." And again: "The way forward...is to commune with spirits and angels, which I now know, it is to be a channel for them, so that my art reflects the divine world, and not the dead world of the senses, the 'underworld'." Now I do not regard the rushes as spirits but as entries of an energy.

Now I think energy flows through one like water through a pipe. You have to empty yourself of any obstructing ego which can block the flow. It is like having a stone, or rather a lump of plasticine, in a pipe. You have to pack the plasticine round the pipe to let the water flow through. If you can do that, you can channel the healing energy.

I pondered the surges of energy in terms of my writing: "Why do I battle on, expressing my vision of truth in writing? What sustains me? Surely a spirit, a guardian angel, a genius that occupies me. For I am not always the great synthesiser. It is a great spirit that writes through me....My experience of Angels – for my war poem. I can now do my epic, now that I know how the spirits enter people."

I healed Ann again the next day and wrote: "9.45 p.m., Tuesday. I wasn't so much of a channel, the b—y phone went at 9. I burned and was cold at the same time in my back and was very restless, then four waves came through me. Ann said my hand was cold. She burned at the 4th wave. I didn't feel it as deeply though because of all the disturbances. Now I am shaky and trembling. And there is light in my electric fingers. I have the beginning of a headache." And soon afterwards: "Rang Jewsbury. His group was there. One said I picked up what was designed for Ann as well as for me, like a plus and minus charge of electricity together. Hence the burning and cold together in my back. The cold rushes through me were felt as burning by Ann – that is normal. 'It's nothing to worry about, Nicholas.'"

The next night I again healed Ann: "Healed again, 9.15, only Anthony cried throughout with pains in his tummy. The power came into my back – I now have an ache round the top part of my seat, and I was hot and cold at the same time and my fingers burned. I had a feint rush, but now my fingers are shining with light in the summer dusk and Ann – who, like Anthony, is now well, said how hot my fingers were. The power of prayer. From now on, I shall not think of 'prayer' – the word has fungus on it – but will think of healing. I will 'do absent healing', envisage, picture, the sick I know as being well. And they will be well; I have become a channel for this power. I feel shivery and hot and achy as though I have flu and the shivers are about to come upon me. There is no question of any fear in me: the power is for good and is beneficent. But I am so electric. If I rub my fingers together I feel I might spark. I must not be Faustian – curious about the unseen powers....I am not Faustian; I seek to subdue nothing with my ego: only to be a channel."

The following night I repeated the experience: "Lay with Ann at 9. Four rushes, followed by another four. All more gentle than before, each different. The 3rd one of the second lot was very strong. Ann's forehead burned, my hands felt hot. I had power in me. My hair sparked to the comb later. Touched Anthony's chest with my power-full hands and also Matthew's throat, to heal them; also my own tongue, which is slightly de-furring."

I was digesting my experience and contact with the Essenes: "The New Age are a group of heretics who will challenge the Church. Spirits and reincarnation – these are the points at issue in the new heresy. And I must say, I go along with it. It is more vital. It is a return to ecumenism. Christianity must discover its ancient doctrine of the resurrection of the body and spirit (pre-869) to have its old beginnings again and have common ground with the Eastern religions....Live near the Earthly Mother, in fields, close to sun, air and water....The new order is New Age ideas which will replace both the traditional West and Communism."

I wrote four stories and then: "Went towards Carlyon. At 9 parked and

313

went deep. It took longer but six rushes came, sweeping through me. Ann said my fingers were cold though I felt burning. I had the car-seat at my front. My theory, that they come into my breath, occupying the backs of my lungs, which does something to my back? I was breathing far more deeply than usual. When I am a channel, my breathing is affected – my lungs are taken over by the divine breath, which is in the air."

The next night: "9.10 – late – tried it again. Three faint rushes. My fingers went coldish."

On August 6th I wondered whether the surges were to do with my astral body, not spirits: "The astral body has to do the breathing, i.e. the physical body has to be in a kind of trance. I feel surges of vital energy into my astral body (solar plexus centre) and rushes up from it – not spirits."

On August 7th, I observed, I "did it on Mevagissey harbour – no rushes; I was in the middle of a seafront crowd, sitting on a green bench near a band, my hand on Ann's forehead and me in a semi-trance. Tonight did it in the car at Charlestown; four rushes in the end. It comes into the solar plexus at the back and flows up with the breathing – see the Tantric/Golden Flower models of centres and energies. Rang Jewsbury and told him. He said 'Discontinue as it's worked, but continue again if it comes back.' Mediums never ask questions of the other side; they wait to be told....I am a mystic. I feel disappointed that my healing powers have come to an end. The answer must be: they haven't. I will have a one-man healing session every night."

I was moving away from my spiritual discoveries. On August 9th I wrote: "To Fowey with Matthew. Across (past Q's house) on the ferry, along the lilac walk. The boats and masts. To the Castle via the house with the garden which is now 'Strictly Private'. The satiny swell. The police launch coming in. Matthew in his Castle. The elderly couple arm in arm on the headland. These things I have seen. The fish with open mouths, some as long as the arm of the fishermen who carried them. Gudgeon? This after sitting in the sun from 10.15 a.m. to 5.30 p.m., with a short break for lunch. Am bright brown and feel healthy, if psychically tired (slightly) after my great exertions this past fortnight."

I thought again about my mission: "If there is reincarnation, we have to fulfil our own divine plan...and to carry forward life by carrying forward our civilisation. Hence my book. Amelioration of what is discovered and preserved, and we come again and again to enjoy it and improve it. So my life should not be spent in a job, working for money; it should be spent in service through my book and the like. I have embodied values." And: "My legendary search in the East and Middle East – I found. I am not scholar-gipsyish: he despaired." And again: "My destiny all along was to be a Camus (Ezard), a Dostoevsky (Ricky and Kingsley). My present book is my 'Camus' effort. My destiny is to be a Dostoevsky, though: the anatomy of violence in a pre-revolutionary British Age; with everything crumbling; the moral order going. The illuminated and the benighted....The metaphysical certainties being restored."

I now saw myself as an eagle: "The sea-eagle hunts fish instead of socialising (the artist putting his contacts into stories). He cannot represent fish as a politician, either in Britain or in Europe. As a teacher he is a land bird (and has time to soar). The spirit (air) is dependent on the material world (sea) for the economy and food, but the sea is also dependent on the spirit for avoiding rebirth in future lives. Reincarnation is the crux, it is reincarnation which accords importance to the spirit....I am a sea-eagle. For a fish to say 'It is ridiculous to breathe air' is as absurd as for an eagle to say 'It is ridiculous to live under water'. But the fact remains, the eagle can point the way to the sun....The eagle will lie down with the shark in Paradise."

I now felt I had rejected empiricism, and wrote again: "My destiny was to pass beyond the World of the Senses to the World of the Spirit. Therefore what I have written about the senses has been Providentially stone-walled. My breakthrough is ahead. My speciality is the spirit – not ephemeral Europe. This rejection of empiricism and the world of the senses has been the significant feature of the present summer holidays and represents a great step forward for me."

Charlestown had two cliffs overlooking the harbour and I had a hunch that I ought to buy Fingals, the seamost house on one of the cliffs, and I approached the owner, Mrs. Tew. We sat on her veranda and I put it to her that she might like to sell. She said: "Are you psychic? I've been thinking of returning to the Channel Islands." I did not buy the house, but over ten years later I would buy its mirror image, the most seaward house the other side of the harbour. And it does seem now that my "psychic" approach to Mrs. Tew lead me to the house I was to have.

The Light returned. On August 13th I noted: "A morning filled with Light. I 'sought Him early' and all through the morning my lungs felt charged and I gave thanks for all the ideas I have received..., and I saw glimmerings, the celestial curtain, the star, the dawning, but not as yet the round sun – all pale white. And between times I saw my imagination, a lovely 'carpet' full of colours, a perfect pattern; and a stained glass window of breathtaking splendour, with a red saint on it. O, and I saw a cloud over a sun with lines of gold finely wrought all round it. I need leisure for these visions, I need to be unwound, and Charlestown can do it. I could sit on my cliff and look down on the harbour from an eagle's height and feel the peace of sea and country and town and sky, a great oneness, from my eagle's 'eyrie'. Fingals should become 'The Eyrie', the home of the eagle." And I wrote: "I look forward to a quiet, retired life on the cliffs of Charlestown."

My healing seemed to have done Ann good, and I noted: "The change in Ann since her 'healing'. She is now much more calm."

I was writing a lot of stories. I wrote: "My stories purge me of my impressions and give them a permanent retrievable form....I am doing my post-death work now." I observed: "The Hagger slant in a story: Shining Ones at a social occasion."

I was filled with physical impressions: "Sunday, on Charlestown beach. Distant thunderings, the gulls gleaming against the black sky. The green water and limpid, translucent rocks."

I was still digesting what had happened to me, seeking for an interpretation: "Let me be absolutely clear. When I was 19 I wanted to discover the meaning of life. I saw this at the time in terms of Dostoevsky and other novelists I was then reading, and so I saw the way in terms of being an artist and making up fictions. In fact, the way was different, but I found the meaning of life; and seeing real things – rediscovering the Angels and higher intelligences – I know that this way was the way I was destined to go at the beginning. My destiny is not religion but as soul who has won the power of the Light, and who saw this in terms of Literature when he started – with Truffer, that great ex-illuminé who went wrong. I may express this knowledge in my epic and poetry, and perhaps a 'Dostoevskian' novel – in terms of New Age outlook." I was in conflict between Christianity and the New Age movement: "My first attempt to solve the future was to see a Christian Democratic Europe embodying Christian religious values and the ecumenical movement. This is only partly true. The Christian values are only relevant in so far as they embody the mystical tradition, and this is embodied by the New Age movement, and this is the new religion, the upsurge of spiritual vitality in our time, which can be the backbone for a growing Europe and a democratised Soviet Union and China. I was shown Europe and now I am being shown the New Age. A world religion for a world government – the New Jerusalem."

I observed: "My ideas are developing all the time and getting bigger and bigger....I am like a rocket. I took off and headed for the clouds – and went through them and came out under the sun. Soon I will be going into space." On Saturday August 27th I noted: "Felt giddy around 7 and had to lie down for an hour. My speech was slightly slurred, and I muddled words like 'month' and 'week'. I may have had a very slight stroke. I am going to be as restful as possible now."

We left Cornwall and returned to London and almost immediately visited Loughton: "August 29th. To Loughton. The lily on the pond. Argie's gifts – blackberries, peas, beans." Two days later I wrote: "I have remained faithful to those walks in Epping Forest, that vision I had in the 1950s/early 1960s. It is others (like Ezard) who have changed. I have kept faith."

I was still discovering the powers of my mind: "Today I cut my finger deeply, opening Matthew's yoghurt. I said immediately, to myself, 'the Light pours into my finger. I give thanks for it has already healed and there is no pain,' and the agonising pain suddenly went, just like that. It threatened to come back once, but I spoke to my finger (mentally) and it went again. I have discovered vast powers of the mind."

It would have been about this time that we sunbathed in Hereford Gardens (to which we had a key), and Matthew crawled away across the lawn and hoisted himself up by a man lying on a sunbed stripped to the waist and reading, and tickled his toes. The man put his book (a Parliamentary report) down, and I realised it was Biggs-Davison, who then lived the other side of Hereford Square. I put my book up and hid, pretending that Matthew was nothing to do with me.

I was still delving into the reserve stock of the larger London public libraries – it seemed that my time in Kingswood library, Dulwich, was a preparation for this – and I read von Hugel's *The Mystical Element in Religion* and Anna Kingsford's *Clothed with the Sun*, and I wrote, "My soul was born in 1971, according to Kingsford; my spirit-soul is now being united in regeneration. So my Light is spiritual sun as opposed to God? The other streaks being magnetic light." The day I went back to school I wrote:

316

"My definitive work on the Light is the half-side of a postcard Pound mentioned; but I hadn't then had the idea. All the rest is application and elaboration, which I am doing now."

I felt I had found an invisible reality: "My search has found something not visible to the senses – the justification of the search....I felt the workings of Providence all round me: "I was shown a comprehensive when I was a gardener, and now I am in one." I also recalled that I had visited Ezard with ideas on Lawrence's *The Rainbow* in the early 1960s, and that I was now teaching that book for 'A' level.

Ann had bad toothache and I observed: "The abscess. Did the faith-healing and had four surges, then a massive one that could have gone up to ten so many flooded through me one after the other. It has left me hot and my fingers burning and electric. I am still feeling shivers up my spine and across my scalp."

I felt poetically frustrated: "I have not written poems since when? May 1976? (They were still being typed in June.) I switched myself off to start my present book and also to work on *Locusts* (the summer of 1976). Since then I have written some stories...but the heights are still ahead."

In September there was a christening for Anthony at the High Beach church in Epping Forest. After a family lunch at my younger brother's and the afternoon ceremony involving the same scallop shell Matthew had had, there was a gathering at my mother's house for tea. Two long-standing friends of my mother's were present: my Oaklands Headmistress Miss Lord and her co-owner Mabel Reid, who invited me to go for a Nature walk in the Forest. Miss Lord, proud, erect and hook-nosed, asked "What are you and Ann doing?" and I told her we had considered buying a school in Streatham for Ann to run. "Good heavens," Miss Lord said, "you don't want to buy a school over there, you'd better have Oaklands. I won't go on for ever, and it would be good for an old boy to have it. Tell Ann to ring and make an appointment and come and spend a day with us." Her reaction took me completely by surprise. It had not occurred to me that I could afford Oaklands. Ann did later spend a day at Oaklands, but with Anthony so small and my being immersed in my school activities we did not follow the visit up and the situation was left unresolved.

John Ezard was a godparent at this christening, and we had a long talk on the Journey's End lawn under the pear tree. I described the book I envisaged doing on the Light to him. I said "It will cover the mystic tradition over 5,000 years." I told him "I was on a search till 1971" and that my book would be written in the context of the Light-experiences of 1971. I observed in my *Diaries*: "To Ezard: I am putting non-sense-experience ideas in sensual terms."

Soon afterwards I wrote: "My pause from poetry while I absorbed the New Age imagery I need for my epic. Michael and the Sword....My book on the Light is a preparation for my poetic epic. It draws together all the thought of the New Age....Now steep yourself in the angelic hierarchies, reincarnation, atom/mysticism, so that there is a mythology, which is plausible metaphysically, for the poem. Not since Homer and Virgil has a poet been able to describe angels as guiding bombs. (Pope did it comically with his sylphs in the mock-heroic *Rape of the Lock* but that is not epic,

which demands belief.) The New Age has made true epic possible (again)."
I added: "We travel up the escalator of our destinies backwards, and only
perceive our progress in retrospect."

I was thinking more and more in terms of energies and currents: "'There
will be a current from you to them,' I told the Department of our pupils,
'which will make them respond vitally, which will dynamise them.' The
current, cf lighting a fuse to the audience." And I recorded of my interest in
brain physiology in the early 1960s: "I was wrong when I started out to
explain away the mind in terms of the physical body, instead of looking for
subtle bodies." I pondered the pattern of my life and noted that there were
crisis points every 7 years: "My crisis points: 7 (1946), 14?, 21, 28, 35, 42?.
At 7 I went to Chigwell, at 14+ I wanted to leave school and write (the letter
to W. E. Johns), i.e. my destiny. At 20, I changed from the Law to
Literature to write. At 28 (1967) I tried to write full time. At 35 (1974) I
completed my poems, having withdrawn from everything. So at 42 (1981) I
will be in another creative spell." I also observed: "If there are 5 passings
from consciousness to consciousness, mine were: 1958-9; 1965; 1971; I am
in the middle of another leap forward now (1977)."

On 12th October I had an unusual inner experience. My *Diaries* record:
"5.30 Relaxed on bed when I got home. I had seen the Light in the bath and
all the paisley colours of my soul, on water as it were, for ripples now and
again disturbed them; the Light was blue and very powerful. On my bed I
became a channel for the power and beamed it on to Flat 5, 10 Brechin
Place, and saw a Sold board outside. I nearly fell asleep, I went so deep. I
was startled by an inner voice which said very clearly, 'Be still, Nick. It will
be accomplished.' Just that. I 'woke' with a start, convinced I had received
a message from God or the angelic hierarchies. I gave thanks and now wait
for God's will to be accomplished." On October 15th I recorded: "I must be
patient. I must fulfil my destiny slowly." And wryly: "When I had the time
to write (e.g. in Libya), I was unsettled and lonely and in crisis. Now I am
settled I have no time. The solution: Oaklands: buy a school and manage it,
i.e. sit and write and do the bills....Buy Oaklands."

About this time Biggs-Davison sent me a pamphlet on Europe, making it
clear that Conservatives regarded Europe as nation-states with no federalist
view of the future. I wrote "Biggs-Davison is a nationalist" and realised that
my unitary vision of Europe was out of keeping with the view of Mrs.
Thatcher's Conservative Party, and that there would be no role for me in
Europe so long as she was there.

On October 26th I was filled with a lot of spiritual activity. Still using
Jewsbury's term "spirits" (as I now do not), I wrote: "All evening, spirits!
rushing through me, even now as I write. I have been inspired and am very
grateful. I was trying to read Alice Bailey's *Treatise on Cosmic Fire* (1300
pages), and this spirit kept taking me to my 3 files and making me rearrange
parts I have written, so without my thinking about them at all, they have
rearranged themselves, and they now flow. I am really being guided, and I
am very grateful. I am now a channel for a higher power, which is freeing
me from the clutter of work and flat-letting and selling so that I can
concentrate on doing its will." And later: "After midnight
(2 a.m.). Clairvoyant pictures. Can't sleep. Kandinsky scrivenings deep in

my mind. An effect of space, me floating through these lovely patterns towards a sunrise. The golden 'cauliflower'. Beautiful detail. The gold light with a gold coin of a primitive emperor on it – who was that emperor? Do I remember him? My body rigid. I withdrew into one of my other bodies, possibly first my etheric, then my astral, which is why my body 'locked'. Strange tinglings as if I am in the presence of astral beings. Beautiful monsters, Tibetan-like, on the floor of my mind. Memories from former lives?"

Soon afterwards, I learned from the ILEA Inspector who had interviewed me for Riverway and who now came to Garratt Green, that Riverway School had closed and that all the staff were supernumerary. "You got out at the right time," he said.

One evening in early November I went to hear Paul Solomon because he was billed (on a leaflet I had been given at the conference on the Essenes and the Egyptians) as having founded the Fellowship of the Inner Light in the USA. There was a huge queue and I was given the last seat. He was a large ex-Baptist Minister who, like Edgar Cayce, had contacted a source within him that gave life-readings. He spoke without notes about how to make choices – he turned all questions over to the intuition which always comes up with the right answers, he said – and Sir George Trevelyan spoke on the New Age. I was reminded of St. Augustine going to hear the Manichaean Faustus before he became a Christian. I recorded: "Went up to Solomon afterwards and asked him about the actual light that is seen. He said it is a kind of change, a point of reference. It comes in flashes when you need it, if you are alone. But it is enlightenment that is needed. Not everyone has it, though all illumined people potentially have enlightenment....It was planned that I should go today. Hence I was the last one in."

I thought again about my writing: "My prediction of the New Age – 'a new Baroque age is born'. We are at the beginning of a new literary age....Through my poetry I had the sense of a time of decline: intuitively I saw our destiny. 'Europe' is a last fling as we go down. Yet the politicians (like Biggs-Davison) don't see this: they argue rationally, by outdated means. I must stick to my intuition and poetry, I must trust my intuition and comb the Romantics....*The Silence* and *Archangel* anticipated the New Age. I have had to wait 12 years for the New Age to dawn." I wrote that my time was coming, that my journalism "was not part of the dying of the old system, which I had to leave. Brotherhood was impossible: and so was love....I stand for a New Age. I had to rediscover this and define the New Age in relation to the Old Age (the existing Age)....Now I am mentally in the New Age, as is my work....I am the first poet of the New Age."

I now read the psychic Edgar Cayce, and observed of my own life: "My life-reading: I was sent here to develop resignation and patience (hence my...suffering during my divorce) and love for my family....I also had to develop from my lower self to my higher self through the Light."

My metaphysical development continued throughout November and December 1977 and the first half of 1978 as I reflected deeply on my poetic

319

method and approached the view I now have. I began to emerge from my Night of Spirit.

In response to a letter I had written to him about my deepening metaphysical view, in November Tuohy proposed that we should go to a poetry reading at a pub in Hampstead. Kathleen Raine was to chair the evening, and David Gascoyne would be reading. Tuohy said to me: "He's very dotty, he's been in bins" in a loud voice which the nearby Gascoyne could hear. We shook hands with Mrs. Gascoyne and then with the bard, a tall, distinguished grey-haired man who (I recorded) "looked like a cross between Yeats and Lord Shackleton". We went below to the cellar and sat at the back. Some 30 were gathered – mostly Hampstead people from the 1940s, we judged – and Kathleen Raine, a small woman with an imperious demeanour and a confrontational manner, spoke against the "journalistic" poems of Auden and the Movement. I observed in my *Diaries*: "Kathleen Raine introduced Gascoyne, who read bad poems (received diction, verbal fustian and monotonous iambic rhythms – a dead language, too little experience, the interior not exteriorised; only one about a field was any good). 'Christ of revolution and poetry' – read in a nonconformist preacher's tone." In the interval I spoke to Kathleen Raine about Flavia Anderson, whose out of print book on the Grail I had been reading, and she immediately said, "It's Providence, you can come and hear a lecture on Chartres." I noticed she did not speak to Tuohy at all; they had been together on a summer school in Sligo. After the interval Gascoyne read George Herbert, a fellow Anglican, and we left early and stopped the reading when we could not open the door. We had an Arab meal of kebab and garlicky lettuce and talked of mystic illumination, and Tuohy said of Ricks: "Ricks is superior to his students. Colin (MacCabe) is always against him, but the first thing he did when he went back to Cambridge was to invite him to lunch." Tuohy remarked: "Optimism: it's feeling superior and being pleased that the world is catching up – that's Kathleen Raine," and I remarked that Gascoyne had "never exteriorised his interior".

Looking back now on that evening I am aware of the workings of Providence – as Kathleen Raine remarked. For in 1991 my book *The Fire and the Stones* and my *Selected Poems* would be launched by the same two, Kathleen Raine and David Gascoyne (whom Durrell called England's foremost metaphysical poet). I was shown them in 1977 but the reason for being shown them was not explained and only became apparent over 13 years later. So often in life a seemingly accidental encounter later becomes significant, so that with hindsight the encounter is seen to be not accidental at all but Providential.

At school I taught Tennyson's *The Lady of Shalott*, "the artist detached from the world, who is destroyed by the world". I wrote: "This weekend I was the Lady of Shalott leaving my magic web – for the shadowy shadows of the real world and its distractions. I want to withdraw into art, like the Lotos-Eaters."

In mid-December I was unwell. I wrote: "Am below par in my health. Am tired inside. Too much external distraction – selling/letting Brechin Place, selling my car, coping with my book on the Light and visiting libraries, work, worrying about the financial crisis I am in – and too little progress. If I were told I had a terminal illness, what panic I would be in. My epic poem still unstarted....I have a lifetime's work ahead and I am held back by that...school. How can I sort myself out properly, and be guided by the powers of reality? I need guidance now more than ever before, to eliminate distractions."

On December 8th I attended a poetry reading by Kathleen Raine. Kathleen Raine had told me that Keith Critchlow is a genius. There was a bizarre moment in the foyer when Kathleen Raine appeared from one side, holding a book by Keith Critchlow, and Keith Critchlow appeared from the other side, holding a book of poems by Kathleen Raine. They stood together, pointing to each other's books. No words could have revealed more clearly that I was in on a mutual congratulation society.

At the end of term there was a redefinition of my job at Garratt Green, and I was asked to take on extra responsibilities. I recorded: "Mrs. Kay asked me to join the hierarchy ('share the management') and have responsibility for internal and external exams. I groaned within at the work I am being dumped, but smiled and simulated enthusiasm, even though it costs me valuable time which should be spent on my books....All morning, depression and lethargy after the insanely active week....Am worn out." The next day I recorded: "Like some evil amoeba, the hierarchy of three has split, forming six by mitosis, and has swallowed me up. Or, to change the metaphor, like some corrupt military dictatorship seeking to legitimise its illegal power, the hierarchy has absorbed three of the people's men into its entrenched, embattled GHQ."

I now began to think deeply about my poetic method. I had sent Kathleen Raine some of my poems, and to my surprise she replied completely misunderstanding the Light. I recorded in my *Diaries*: "Kathleen Raine writes that my work is a record of my thoughts about experiences, i.e. the rational intelligence working on the data of the sensible world – not from the 'other mind' from which is born poetic speech. My 'virtues' are articulacy, honesty and discrimination – not luminous vision." My initial reaction was: "What she overlooks is that Mystical Light is, for me, a sense-experience; and that 'imagination' as she conceives it is connected with Neo-Platonism (i.e. the Light). I do not like Gascoyne because he ignores the sense-world; she does not like me because I put the sense-world in, and make it symbolise something else. I am a Movement poet who has the mysticism of an Eliot. I am very much a part of my generation for that. I am of the Elizabethan Age – I am an Elizabethan poet – but a mystical one (not a poet of high dream). Let Raine keep her daimons and I'll keep my Light."

But a day later I was reflecting on the possibility of a new poetic style: "A great painter can go through several styles and periods: so it can be with a poet. I am now working towards a new style....The past has been finding a way back from material-sense-experience (cf mechanism) to the One, in the rational speaking voice of the Donne-Eliot-Movement tradition, plus Wyatt-Shakespeare's sonnets-Tennyson-Hardy. I have done that and expressed my growing interest in religion in the plain style of a Herbert. Now that I have discovered the eternal world I am ready to take on a more imaginative vision, implying the existence of an eternal world. Like Yeats, at 48, I must start again....I may receive poetry from...the unconscious,...the symbols of imagination. I am a rational intelligence but am not a Movement poet because of my interest in mysticism. I am becoming a 'trance-like, incantation' poet; and my epic will be 'received' like my healing powers. A Classical manner (rational intelligence) balancing inner and outer; a Romantic manner, allowing the prophetic voice to speak through me – poetry keeping alive what philosophy and religion have forgotten."

I knew I was a mystic: "I have a mystic's, not a scholar's approach to the One. My search ended when I experienced the Divine Light, for which all searches are a substitute. I can see why Kathleen Raine dislikes the word 'mystical'....I imagined from within before rational Tuohy made me look outside in my observed stories." But I acknowledged that I had to be a realist: "The two kinds of image I identified in my Eliot piece: symbolic and realistic image (which Raine abhors). Romantic imagery and realistic (Pope – social fact) are both necessary elements in healthy classic poetry (cf Byron's blend of the Romantic and the realistic). A mystic-existentialist is what I have been – an existentialist is a realist. 'Against the Platonic eternal world,' Kathleen Raine would say."

I saw a new movement of art in terms of the coming United States of Europe: "Archaism, the art of Universal States, repeats processes, harking back, as does Kathleen Raine. From primitivism to Neo-Classicism and back to a new Romantic Baroque, out of which the new Classicism will emerge. My reason v my imagination; my Neo-Classical Archaistic Age v the new Baroque Archaistic Age which must flood into the heart (illumination and images) so that a Classical Archaistic Age can take place, with the mature values of the peace of God."

I knew in my heart of hearts that good art contains a realistic level: "Kathleen Raine is surely wrong. Take the analogy of painting. If a painter paints the outside world (Nature), then is that painting worthless? What about portrait paintings? A painting does not come from the imagination, always. So it is with a poem. Not all poetry can be received in inspiration; that is only one way." After reading Kathleen Raine's *Defence of Ancient Springs* I was approaching a bi-level view of art, in which the realistic and the metaphysical co-existed: "Reaction to Kathleen Raine's book. Realistic poetry cannot be dismissed any more than realistic painting can. We are offered a tradition that is based on a universal language – book-learning – but the early part of the tradition was based on the Light, and was mystical, while the later part got lost from the Light and substituted book-learning. Experience is superior, provided it is universalised (the imagination being one way of universalising or generalising the particular). Eternal life can come into autobiographical poetry." And later I wrote: "I can appeal to admirers of the rational intelligence, to mystics, and soon, I hope, to the imaginative tradition. I have been slow to draw the lessons from my 1971 experience of the imagination – the images that floated up, the 'anima mundi'. But I have now made the correction, the adjustment."

But soon after I was emphasising impersonality again: "My shift to impersonal poetry. No 'I'. The consequence of 1971, which has taken a long time to work itself out. Against realism. I am in a contemplative tradition (a mystic-existentialist one)....A totally impersonal, inspired, infused art; and an oracular, formal tone. A great change in my style. Incantation." And I put this into practice on Christmas Eve: "Tried my first poem in my new style. Sat and wrote automatically what I imperfectly heard, as on short wave radio, an oracular voice speaking out of nowhere with much background interference....My thrilling great leap forward into a purely imaginative world. Compare Yeats and automatic writing." And I wrote of "Plato and beyond sense-experience....It is only recently that I have escaped the sense-world – it is therefore only recently that I could really go for the eternal imaginative experience. My breakthrough, i.e. my Great Leap Forward, has been to transcend the 'sensible' world. (Written on Christmas Eve at 11.55 p.m., before I took Matthew's stocking to his room.)" I felt confident enough to write: "Genius: 'An individual stylist.' I...brought the Light to birth in my soul, and identified its importance, and...I have journeyed to the imagination."

For Christmas Ann gave me an Egyptian ankh which I wore round my neck, and vowed: "Am resolved to make my holy city – my Jerusalem, my Byzantium or Rome – the Thebes of the Egyptian *Book of the Great Awakening* (i.e. *Book of the Dead*)."

I wrote: "Civilisation: giving outer expression to the inner imagination (and Light)....Art reflects the unity and metaphysical order behind everything."

Meanwhile I noticed with regard to my book on the Light: "I am being guided in my book *The Secret Light*. Each time I need to delve into something I am presented with the right person....It is not I who am writing this book, but a power writing it through me."

In early January 1978 we had an offer for Brechin Place, and although I did not exchange contracts until March, I redoubled my search for a house near Garratt Green. But as I wrote: "I have so little time these days. Being in the hierarchy now, I have been at three meetings with the Head, as part of our policy group of six, taking decisions about school matters, being a managerial executive: a hat I never thought I would wear." I thought of the hierarchy as a "gang of six", after the Chinese "gang of four" including Mme Mao, who were being tried in China.

I now had to negotiate with Hunmanby Hall to keep Nadia there as Caroline's husband had fallen behind with his share of the school fees to the extent of over a £1,000. Caroline told me: "He only gets paid 50p an hour. He's bound to stay in the RAF until three years' time. We can't wait to leave, he'd go into business." The RAF were very supportive and decreed that if Nadia was taken away he would have to repay the last four years of fees, which he could not afford to do. The RAF agreed to loan the £1,000 in three instalments, and the problem was solved.

Property arrangements were keeping me from my writing. I had written a few stories, but virtually no poems.

The first day of the holidays I was awakened at 6.05 a.m. from a dream of a hanging (my recurrent nightmare), this time of a man in a strange Middle Eastern head-dress which could have been a medieval hood, and I observed his dropped eyelids. I was sure I had heard a woman's voice call "Nicholas" urgently, imploringly, through the letter-box. I got up and looked outside the front door, but no one was about. At the end of March I was on antibiotics for sinusitis, and I wrote: "To Worthing. The sea-air is full of vitality globules, and I now feel well....I should be living by the sea. Wrote: *A Piggy-Eyed Broker and a Conniving Smile* and *Alison Bush, 18, Wants Proof*. Found the 'Scilly' stories – untyped. Typed up the Scilly Isles one. Margaret: 'That was why you were divorced and suffered – so that you could see the Light." On April 2nd I wrote: "A weekend on my stories. Got the title *The Clear, Shining Sunlight of Eternity*."

The last few days of the holidays Nadia stayed with us at Stapleton Road, and I read Fritjof Capra's *The Tao of Physics* as (having been sent a leaflet by the organisers of the conference on the Essenes and the Egyptians) I would be hearing him speak at a Mystics and Scientists lecture at Winchester, which was being put on by the Wrekin Trust in conjunction with the Scientific and Medical Network. This was another Providential "showing" for in 1992 I would give the first lecture at what became the annual Mystics and Scientists lecture at Winchester, and this was put on by the Scientific and Medical Network, the first time they were involved since 1978. I wrote in my *Diaries*: "Physics and other sciences now recognise a harmonious whole, as does the mystic, and affirm the organic against the mechanistic. Certain consequences follow from this. We must bring in a more harmonious society, be internationalist and break down the gulf between rich and poor, i.e. change the present capitalist-mechanistic society....I am pro-organic form in art, which should reflect the One....I am defined in terms of the new: a federalist Europe politically, which is Christian Democrat, and a new view of man as a spiritual being who goes beyond sense-experience, who has sense-free perception; i.e. the senses lead one to error....I define man in terms of the Light. The old social forms do not interest me...; I am bringing in a new Renaissance and must therefore define the new and not worry about my relationship with the old. I am a symbolist."

The Winchester conference lasted from a Friday afternoon to a Sunday afternoon in mid-April and was a revelation. After years of working in isolation, I found myself among 400 kindred spirits. The conference was at King Alfred's College and was oversubscribed. There was an overflow hall, where I was, with televised coverage of the lectures, and I was staying off site in a student's room in Winchester. The discomfort was considerable, and it was cold, but I spoke to Capra, who looked like a pop star with tousled hair and a fashionable jacket, and was in great demand wherever he went. He told me he obtained his mysticism from Stace's *The Teachings of the Mystics*, and I knew from our conversation that he did not know the Light, and a later reading of Stace confirmed that the Light is not mentioned in the excerpts he chose. I also spoke to Pir Vilayat Inayat Khan, the bearded and ancient Sufi leader who in 1975 had lead a large Cosmic Mass at the Temple of Understanding (an interfaith organisation founded with Rockefeller money). I asked him how the Light was received and he told me it came in at the base of the spine, into the "chakras", and that it was conveyed to the head. This account differed from the Christian mystics' "top down" view, and accorded more with Tantric Kundalini and sexual practices. I was not sure that the speakers at Winchester were giving completely reliable information, and I distinguished the mystic and the psychic very firmly, but, as I recorded, the conference was "useful for focus" and: "Meditated twice today, Sunday: a nuclear explosion" (i.e. experience of the Light) "the first time. Man is a part of the cosmos. Therefore, get a place with a view of the cosmos."

Back in Tooting I wrote: "I am radioactive since the Light on Sunday, and ought to be evacuated. The crackling of my sweater and vest when I take them off; they are filled by a body and then crumple. I glow with light. I can see the Light in my fingertips. I need to measure myself on a Geiger counter."

I saw my destiny very clearly: "I returned from abroad to join the new Renaissance: the new view of man and the new European destiny."

The Brechin Place sale went through in April. On April 25th we moved everything out into storage. Two days later Matthew had more febrile convulsions as a result of another high temperature which was again caused by tonsillitis, and he was admitted to St. James's Hospital, Balham. The following weekend I recorded: "Went to the Festival of Mind and Body and wrote 8 stories in and out of the hospital ward. How psychic abilities are a bridge to spiritual truth – i.e. they show us that the universe is one and that there is a collective unconscious, i.e. beyond the psychic. So the psychic is inferior to the mystic, not superior."

My development continued and I reviewed my position and anticipated *The Fire and the Stones*: "The New Age (our Renaissance) has unearthed the Light, the tradition which was never really dead and buried (see Victorian religion), and...this is one of the options for the vacant ideology of a politically Resurgent West. It should be this, for Modern Values are inadequate and do not take account of the spiritual upsurge....I am saying that the coming ideology of Europe is (New Age) mysticism and illumination, and that this can become the new Universal Church...I am saying that the Light can be the coming ideology of Europe."

A few days later I wrote: "I knew there was something to discover, and I arrived at it. I had to get beyond sense-perception, and smash the isms around me. What a time to live in! What a handicap to finding the truth. Mysticism: its formulation is in experience, and not images....I am a member of the alternative society. I abhor the society in which I live. I have always been an Outsider."

Again I touched on the main idea of *The Fire and the Stones*: "My theme is: all the Lights are one (Holism) and can be the basis of a world religion (reunified Christianity) for a Western Universal State (European expansion) through the New Age." I determined to make notes for a critique of isms: "State the problem: the waste land of isms, which have been compounded by the modern science."

More and more I was for including both the world of sense-experience and the metaphysical: "Kathleen Raine and Tuohy represent rival traditions, which they embody well, and therefore I respect their minds; but profoundly disagree with them. The élite. The man of genius is not ordinary. Genius is having a gift from the beyond....Raine, scornful of the Maharishi – for lacking knowledge, and therefore not questioning academe in an informed way. Raine is right to criticise the way of erudition as an end in itself, the academic. She is wrong to espouse the way of erudition as a means to a rational metaphysical knowledge. The way of erudition as a means to uncovering a knowledge based on experience, which one then has in one's own life, is a good way....The Raine tradition approaches the unconscious through Platonic scholarship."

After much house-hunting and pursuing false leads I had put in a bid for the former Vicarage of St. Mary's, Balham, a 6-bedroom, double-fronted house at 46 Ritherdon Road, London SW17. The bids were all opened at the same time at a local estate agents, and after researching the amount to offer in some detail I had just managed to offer £500 more than anyone else, and so acquired the property. I could now see my way to moving the Brechin Place furniture out of store into this property and leaving the rented flat in Stapleton Road.

Soon afterwards Margaret visited us on my birthday. We discussed how the Light is in all religions. We were eating soup and I said: "There are many grains of salt in the soup, and there are many experiences of the Light in the Holy Spirit." Margaret said of Tuohy: "His life is just paper. He is a prisoner of his past." To which I replied: "A work of art is a model of Reality. Tuohy's Reality is social reality, and he sees a work of art as being absolute in itself, instead of Reality as being absolute....There is a variety of realities. A tree can be a social thing or a being full of energy – there is a model for each. A work of art is a symbol (model) for a Reality we know but have not articulated."

I wondered if we derive life from globules of energy in the air. On May 26th I recorded: "Sunbathed. Saw vitality globules dancing in the blue sky." As I squinted I could see lots of glistening, almost transparent tiny round balls, and wondered if it was a trick of my sight. (I have often seen them since, but am not certain or confident of what I have seen.) And again: "Two days in the sun, and no electricity in my body as I take off my gold sweater. The sun has reduced my electricity. Vitality globules have passed into me, and I do not crackle now. Ionisation?"

Margaret confronted me with Christianity. I wrote: "Since Margaret came I have been experiencing a swing back to Christianity and the Church, reunited, as a liturgical focus of the Light – a traditional approach. Am I a bud on the Christian tree, or a new species – a bud on something that has not yet been formed? The traditional and the revolutionary. Everything the New Age affirms can be absorbed within the Christian framework, which is also about dying and being reborn – which also has an esoteric tradition still practised by the monks. Therefore, my poems should be read in churches. Christianity is about love, and it can accommodate other forms. The essential experience of the Light is a Christian one."

At the beginning of June I was ill with "hay fever" that turned out to be a heavy cold. In mid-June I wrote: "Am really tired. Slept all yesterday afternoon and am finding it hard to stay awake this afternoon. Am drained." It was exam time at school and I now had to run the public exams in the school hall. Sometimes 350 took different exams at the same time. For a month I was in charge of the security of exam papers, of getting in very early and taking them to the hall, distributing them on the desks along with the correct place numbers of the candidates, co-ordinating the invigilators and making sure each exam ended at the right time. Then I collected the papers and sent them off. The ILEA had decided that Garratt Green would be inspected that autumn, and there were reports to the Inspectors to write, and I was asked to do the early morning coverage from the coming September, the worst job in the school as it meant taking the staff's free periods. I was still teaching my usual timetable with all the marking and meetings involved, and I was in daily negotiations about the arrangements for 46 Ritherdon Road.

As if to remind me that I must eventually go to Essex, I found myself attending a poetry reading at High Beach church by an Epping Forest poet, Frederic Vanson, who went round Essex reading his poems in churches, and I sat in the green summer peace and heard the call from the future luring me back to Essex. I also visited the Mannings in Moreton, attended their daughter's christening at Bobbingworth, and saw Blake Hall, and again heard the future call.

Tuohy had Ann and me to a dinner party, and immediately I had a true perspective on Garratt Green, which paled to dreary insignificance.

I attended a Wrekin Trust conference on reincarnation, and later again heard Paul Solomon on mystery schools. I was struck by Solomon's Zen teacher in Japan: a servant who swept a tea-house with a broom, which Solomon took as an image for sweeping one's own soul. Solomon told a story about how his son got straight As in his college work. Solomon quoted his son as saying: "I go to the window in my mind and look through it and see the answers."

The possibility that I have a spirit which incarnates again and again set me thinking about my plan for my current life: "I had to develop 'samadhi' and so (1) I got to Oxford, where I met the Eastern influence of Kingsley and Ricky, (2) I was guided out to Iraq so I could mull over *Mandalas* and return, (3) I was guided to Japan where I was given a Zen influence (and Irie's) and looked beneath the reason, (4) I was stripped of my family so that I could have two years' silence to develop to illumination via Margaret: this was the Dark Night of the Sense, and (5) I came to Garratt Green to develop a religious side for my writing, by contact with Solomon and the like....I am a mystic who has achieved a psychic bonus....So, then. I knew before I was born that I had to become enlightened and find my source, and that Japan was the way. I therefore incarnated into a family that would educate me; hence Oaklands and Chigwell. That way I could get to Oxford and go to Japan. I knew that writing would help me to illumination: hence I started a novel when I was 14 – as a way of ascending in consciousness. I studied Greek and Roman history and philosophy to get me to Oxford, and to give me the discipline I would need for illumination, and then changed to English because I was a seeker and could study Blake and Yeats. I was not to get involved with English, I had to leave Oxford, get out into the world. My destiny now is the Light." On July 13th I wrote: "Any creed I accept (Christianity, e.g.) must allow for the fact that I have lived many times before, and will return. That is why History is so important a subject at school."

I did a healing on Anthony "and felt cold". I found the healing surges came into my meditations now: "Later meditated towards the Light and again felt shivers up my spine." Soon afterwards I attended a Wrekin Trust course on healing and met Bruce MacManaway, a tall, seemingly ex-Army man who then had a great reputation as a healer and knew about my "waves" that came from the beyond, and said of them: "They are very strong." He invited me to his Lupus Street clinic to have a go on his patients. I also met Edgar Chase, an ex-naval buffer in a tie and blazer, and described my surges to him. He also told me I was a healer. He showed me a point near the small of the back, where at one touch any human being can be paralysed for two minutes. He told me he had been shown this place by a Tibetan, and that the knowledge would be dangerous if it fell into the wrong hands.

Of healing I wrote: "I am saying that there is a sun, and in the Kingdom of the Blind this is shattering news. I am saying 300 people have seen it. I am seeking nothing....I have a mission to tell people about the sun....It is the sun's rays that heal....One should act out the love of the sun by serving the poor....The sun gives one stillness and calm....There is no Absolute when you have seen the sun; the concept of 'Absolute' doesn't exist, it burns away the difference....There was more knowledge of the sun in medieval times than in modern times – and as much cruelty; only the fire of the Inquisition symbolised the sun. The sun breaks the seedcase of one's destiny and enables the Vine to grow. The vision of love: every man is my brother, for he has a spark of the Divine Light. Therefore I must act out my love – in the form of little 'unremembered acts' of kindness." I was critical of "making the Light available to those who can afford fees....Christ did not charge an entrance to the Sermon on the Mount, and nor do the mystery schools. Healing is a tributary of the river of Light." Again: "Pictures – visions, images, symbols, are at the level of vision, not mysticism, and the mystic sees the Sun and nothing less will do. The Sun *is* the divine Light and power. It *is* the Godhead. All belief and philosophical speculation is burned away to an irrelevance in its knowledge. I know it as perceiver knows perceived, and all is One. As the Hindu lecturer said, if all is One, why should I lecture? I should just express myself, like a tree. I express myself in the sunlight."

At the healing conference I had met Maurice Blake, who regressed people to past lives like Arnall Bloxham. He was elderly and offered to regress me if I visited him in Norwich. School had broken up and I was organising work on the new house, which was now festooned in scaffolding and was like a building site inside. A team of men I had found had tea several times a day in what would become our living-room, and there was always a full skip outside. I was apprehensive: could I be sure there would be no effects, no dangers from being hypnotised? I decided to go to Norwich for, as my *Diaries* put it, "I am a child of my century, I am seeking my cosmic, spiritual self across lives. I am a 'post-Faustian figure' who seeks beyond the threshold of death – whose love is worked out at a cosmic level, and so I must go....I need to know who man is...and what life is – what this life is. I am seeking to define the human condition in relation to the Light. One life (like St. John of the Cross) or several lives, in relation to the Light? My Faustian quest. I must go through with it. I must have the courage to submit myself to it, in the interests of my knowledge of man, which I need for my writing. I have never hesitated to enter extreme situations that my writing has required, e.g. going into Cultural Revolutionary China despite Buchanan's pleas, and now I must go ahead with this extreme situation....It is merely a question of courage. I must go through with it."

I got up at 6 a.m. on August 2nd and drove to Norwich and lay down on the sofa in Maurice Blake's sitting-room. He switched on a tape-recorder and sat near me and made me put my left arm up and counted to ten. I have the tape of the next hour and a half. I was not aware that my arm was raised throughout: both it and I had truly "gone to sleep". First I went back to when I was 16, then 10, then 5, then my birth, and then beyond my birth to my previous life in the early 19th century. Blake asked me question after question, and after each an incredibly clear image arose in my mind, each of which I can still remember, and I then, slowly and haltingly in my hypnotised trance, looked at the picture and tried to provide the answer. In "my" 19th century childhood I saw a valley and pronounced it Epping or Esthwaite. I was among trees, wearing boots with large black toecaps. I saw "myself" crossing the sea on a boat in a storm, among religious people who sang hymns on deck, going to New Brunswick, and I saw myself as a priest – it seemed a Jesuit priest called "Abbé" ("abbot" or "priest") – among tree-fellers in woods in a "Sirioux" settlement in Canada. The loggers wore white shirts with short braces and high trousers and boots. I saw their log-cabins, brown mud and a camp fire, and I had the feeling that the settlement was near a river. I was 26 and I saw the date in a yellowy newspaper: 1829. Then I saw my death at 33 in my own log-cabin. Looking down from the ceiling I saw myself on a bed in a corner of the room, near a woman with a white bonnet who was rolling pastry with a rolling-pin. I pronounced that I was dying of cholera as a result of water-contamination, and that she was Emé or Esmé, a French-speaking woman. She called me John or Jonquil. A rush of feeling came into my throat, for I knew we had had a sexual liaison which no one knew about, and the emotion at seeing her again across lifetimes was uncontainable. Blake made me relive my death. I was on a single bed with a black cover and a pit in the middle in a shadowy log-cabin. My lips and tongue were parched, my breathing was noisy. The woman was stooping over me. I wanted a drink of water, but there was no water. It was difficult to breathe. I was going to sleep, I was growing cold, my right hand was cold and numb, my little finger had gone numb and was almost paralysed. I took my last breath, then there was relief and peace without any sensation in my body, and I was in a mist of colourless light and I saw the woman stooping near my body from a great height, and then I was floating with a buoyant feeling and I looked down on the log-cabin settlement from a great height and saw my funeral. There were people present. A logger in a white shirt and braces with high trousers leaned on a long axe near a fire with white ash, and I saw my tombstone, which was two feet high and like a rough, uneven milestone. Blake told me to look at it and I read: John Barfield, d. 1836. The loggers were not aware that I was there and I observed them from head-height. Afterwards I found I was in a mist and feeling very peaceful.

A MYSTIC WAY

Blake brought me out of my hypnotised state for a discussion. On the way home I pondered what I had experienced. Did I really die in 1836, and had I had proof of an immortal spirit that can survive death with memories intact? Were the images far memories? Or were they just personal memories or imaginings, at the level of wish fulfilments or waking day-dreams, elaborate fantasies? At the time I thought I had had far memories. I wrote in my *Diaries*: "The poet sees images from within which link him to past lives and far memory, the collective unconscious, healing forces, the imagination whose source is the Light, and the mystic Light, most supreme of all; also to meditative images. The poet's images need not be realistic. There is dream, imagination, personal memory and far memory and the poet expresses them in writing." For several days afterwards I was filled with a sadness for the woman. I wrote on August 5th: "A great sadness all day, for Abbé (me) and Esmé. When I was a priest in Canada, I was very alone and grew fond of Esmé, and she had a soft spot for me and was with me when I died, though she pottered about, turning her back. Abbé. I am consumed with sadness for a life that has gone....I feel that regressions are in fact movements back to past lives: I have been haunted by my life in Canada in a way I have never been haunted by a dream." I pondered the fact that in Japan my first maid had been called Emi.

On August 15th we finally moved into 46 Ritherdon Road, after two weeks of decorating and laying carpets and taking delivery of gas stoves and beds. Four days later we went to Cornwall to recover from the exertions with Ann's mother. I recorded: "Went for a glorious walk at Charlestown. Blue calm sea, a boy caught a fish which he held in his hand. Sunwashed cliffs, the old 1790s harbour wall." I also recorded: "David Gascoyne called brilliant by Philip Toynbee in today's *Observer*. What a joy to have the time to reflect. I will now return to a life of quiet reflection, as I pursue my Gascoyne-like destiny. Gascoyne's *Journal 1937-9*, cf mine 1964-7." And: "Wrote *A Causeway of Light*. Am vibrant within after my month of decoration. The spring of creativity is flowing."

I thought about esotericism and evolution: "If God is transcendent, he is apart; if he is immanent he is within. He is both, of course, but in so far as he is within, the whole is a man's greater self, the collective unconscious....This redefinition of God mirrors the world of physics, of which we are a part,...and man's true nature is to know that he has evolved from a reactor to a creator, i.e. from instinctive oneness to creative oneness. Now this is the idea of the New Age, that man has evolved spiritually (cf Teilhard de Chardin and Julian Huxley and Colin Wilson's *Beyond the Outsider*); but is this concept of spiritual evolution for generic man true? Or is it misplaced optimism? The men of genius attain the truth in any age, the élite, but do the common people, and do New Age movements affect the common people?...What is man? A being of Light, but can evolutionary advances be passed on as assumptions to children?...The Light is One and the saints have approached it and have developed powers which have been transmitted to man. But these are known to a few only....I do not go along with optimism." And again: "Esotericism is for the few, established religion for everybody. The trend is to esotericism for everybody too (Frederic Lionel), and so the koiné will mix esotericism and established religions. My

330

plan must distinguish higher religions and esotericism – the Light in Buddhism, etc, and the Light in the Kabbalah. It also all boils down to Akashic records or fantasies. If God is immanent, the high self is divine and the imagination and mystic meditation throw up images from a divine source, the records, and hypnotism throws up past lives. If God is transcendent, all is a fantasy. The redefinition of God."

The last week in August I redrafted *The Secret Light* "following a shandy in the Rashleigh Arms garden, Charlestown last night, under brilliant stars". I planned to write three books: *River of Light*, *Oceans of Light* and *Towards One Globe of Light*. I wrote: "The Ocean idea must have something to do with my walks by the Cornish sea, on Charlestown harbour. The sea is in my subconscious. Return poetry to its ancient concern, channelling an Ocean of Light." I wrote my three drafts "between visits (usually in the evening) to Charlestown, and am now going out to sunbathe, having stayed down here in Cornwall one extra day. We are shadows on the wall of Light." This concept later passed into *The Fire and the Stones*.

On August 31st I returned to Maurice Blake and was regressed again. I wrote: "Cleared up the Barfield life. I was having an affair with Esmé when I died; I was a Jesuit priest, and saw the boat I went over to New Brunswick in with 100 other Jesuits." Then Blake made me go back a long long time and I surfaced under a huge temple statue of a man I pronounced to be Ramesses the Second as a Sun-god. I was a woman and lay a garland at his feet at the top of some steps. I lived in the temple. I saw an outside scene of a philosopher who sat on a stool, naked above the waist and with a black beard, before a group of ten temple-maidens who sat on sand before him. One of them was me. I wore a dress with one shoulder bare and sandals with a twined thong between each big and second toe. The image of the philosopher and his class was so vivid and colourful that I could almost put my hand in and pick up a handful of sand. It was like seeing a scene from c1300BC on live TV. I knew the philosopher was a healer and taught occult arts, and that we maidens made the Nile flood by taking part in a public ritual involving the Sun-god. This involved Ramesses II coming into the Temple and choosing one of us to make love to. I saw the beginning of such a ceremony. It was a hot day with a blue sky, and all those who lived in the temple were on parade, and I saw the young Ramesses arrive with a tall and shining gold head-dress and gold armour. He was surrounded by his entourage and we were thrilled to see him. He looked magnificent. He came down the line and stopped at me and touched his heart, and I dissolved into tears on the tape, choking with emotion at the honour, for I was the "Chosen One" and he would take me within and make love to me and make the Nile flood. My name was Nebhotep, and I was ecstatically happy.

Blake brought me out of my trance, and in the ensuing discussion I recalled having seen the mummy of Ramesses II in the Cairo Museum. I had looked at the mummy for a long time, without realising that I was gazing at the corpse of my former boy-friend. I also wondered if the peace I felt in the gharry at Luxor reflected my joy at contacting this life. Later I wrote a poem about my two visits to Maurice Blake: *A Temple-Dancer's Temple-Sleep*. I again pondered whether I have a spirit that can survive death and take memories with it. Had I had far memories or just day-dreams? All I can say now is that if our spirit has lived many times before and brings with it memories of past lives which are inscribed in our subconscious minds, then I would want to know this, and know about my past lives, as such knowledge affects my view of what a man is and his place in the universe, which may have to be measured over many centuries and not just one lifetime. If this is the case, I have no fear of death and am sure that after dying one is conscious in a mist of light. If, on the other hand, I was merely day-dreaming, then I received some very vivid, good quality poetic images which have the force of memories.

Later that day I wondered whether the four rushes of my healing energy were connected with the psychic heat of Tantric Hinduism and the fire of Kundalini, "which leaves my fingers cold (physical body) but my etheric body warm".

The remainder of 1978 was dominated by further developments in my writing and healing.

I knew now that I had my theme for my life's work: "I have been so lucky. I was shown the Sumerians, then Zen, and the Egyptians, doing the Bible lands and Islam when I was a young man, and my studies and researches have carried me further into the spiritual world....My growing interest in Eastern (e.g. Tibetan) mysticism and its psychic side-effects, e.g. regressions and healing....My interest in images: the images of poetry and of the deeper mind....I am a mystic and all these powers are side-effects of mysticism." And I added: "You have to unlearn your education and upbringing: the Newtonian universe, on which they were founded, is dead." I wrote again: "I found my theme very young – in 1962-3: *Mandalas*. The trouble is, my treatment of it was wrong. I projected a future self, the twice-married, famous Truffer who had been in the East and had some mandalas – instead of getting to the heart of the truth in the mandalas. That novel was a statement of the problem, the Tradition of the Light being the solution....I sought through poetry, and when I found I abandoned the form of poetry for a while to set down what I found in objective terms....My way was poetry. I approached my subject through poetry, because without literature I would not have been able to find it. For me literature was a way of finding my way through the deepest places of the heart. St. John of the Cross is a hero because he was a profound mystic – who knew the Dark Night... – and he was also a poet."

In mid-September I went to the Buddhist Society and meditated. I observed: "They all tried too hard, these dedicated seekers for enlightenment, twisting their body into cramps. Enlightenment happens to one and changes one within....These would-be masters: the young behold with envy what the old Daisetsu Suzuki or Paul Solomon hardly knows he has, to paraphrase Wordsworth's *Animal Tranquillity and Decay*. Then the questions. The man who said 'I'. He who knows does not speak, he who speaks does not know. The misleading information about enlightenment. The shift from the ego to the Self."

I was now working on past civilisations: the Indo-European religion,

Egypt and Mesopotamia. And I had returned to Garratt Green. Almost immediately I took a party of senior girls to King's College, Cambridge where the post-Structuralist Colin MacCabe, ginger-haired and militantly pro-comprehensive, gave us lunch. I remember one coloured girl called Agnes breaking away and buying an ice-cream just as we were about to enter the college gates, and I had to explain to the group why it was bad form to arrive at a Cambridge college licking a cornet. It was a sunny day and I loved the open spaces at King's and felt relaxed among staff and students in casual dress.

Margaret came and spent a night with us. From her Catholic position she attacked the New Age: "Solomon hasn't got the Light, he wouldn't charge if he had. The Pope (John Paul I) had it: he was buried humbly. Only God has the power to change people, man hasn't. We're all equal. There is joy and sorrow. God shines on everyone. The Light can't be turned on and off. All this money – it's a con." Sir George Trevelyan was on television and I wrote of "people shopping for a new faith".

I heard that Colin Wilson would be signing copies of his latest book *Mysteries* in Watkins Bookshop, and I looked in and joined the queue. He sat behind a desk in his old sweater and jacket, and when I said "Hello Colin, do you remember me?" he said in a very loud voice so that 60 in the queue could hear "Hello Nick, you helped me with an article and stayed at the Savages" as he signed my book.

In mid-October there was a Gaudy at Worcester College, Oxford: a reunion for two years of graduates, one which started about 1924 and one in 1958. After some deliberation I returned to Oxford for it and attended chapel, where the new Provost, the historian Asa Briggs, a small bespectacled man with a mop of hair, read the lesson, and I dined in Hall with a third of my year (but no Ricky or Kingsley). After ten minutes the wrinkles fell away and it was as though we were back in 1960. A. B. Brown made a fluent speech with many laughs, and the sconce came out and there was an Old English camaraderie as we banded together against the dark world outside. Afterwards we drank in the bar and I found myself talking at some length to Asa Briggs. We discussed Libya and I told him how Gaddafi had been accepted by the West by posing as Saad eddin Bushwerib, and he said: "You must write a book about your experiences. You have told me something I have often wondered about and did not know, you must write it down." I left for bed about 2 a.m. and slept in a room on the terrace.

The experience of that weekend was so pleasant that I wondered whether I should return to academic life, and decided that if I did I would research into Romanticism, Modernism and Mysticism: "'Perceptions' – the basis for a mystic's approach to literature. If I ever went to Oxford, the basic course should be a re-examination of the Kermode thesis, that Romantic poets and Modernist poets are the same: a disagreement with Kermode's premise. See the Romantic poets as mystics who anticipated Findhorn and the one spirit – the New Age – and see the Modernists as mystics of another kind: not pantheists but (like Eliot) contemplatives....Investigate the whole mystic-contemplative tradition in literature, including the Metaphysicals and Marvell....The answer is that both the Romantics and the Modernists were mystics but they emphasised different aspects of the tradition: and their common preoccupation with the image is because of their common search for Reality (Spirit) and turning away from the world. The confusion is over God (Classicism). The religious Romantics subordinated themselves to a Spirit – unlike the secular (political) Romantics who were Humanists and advocated the perfectibility of man – through Spirit as well, this was possible. I have a great whole in my mind, in which this critical work has a share. It is the literary statement of the Light, in detail." I wrote to Christopher Ricks and he replied that we would meet. I wrote: "My contact with Ricks marks a step back from the New Age. I have written about the New Age themes with the contemplative gaze of the mystic. It represents an inclusion of the Oxford years – my intellectual roots – in my grown outlook." I later added as a postscript: "A blend of the two, a grafting of New Age metaphysics onto my traditional roots and stock."

On October 18th I wrote: "The Light came again in my bath, a blue sparkling diamond, beautiful to look on. I gazed in deep contemplation for a good half minute or minute. Earlier I had a meeting of my Department, and taught *Tintern Abbey*. I still feel a vague discontent because I am not doing what I should be doing." I saw this discontent in terms of Epping Forest: "The joy I used to feel, hurrying into Epping Forest to see *my* tree. The gleam gone, but the deep feeling of unity with Nature. The fallen tree over the pond – my talisman; from which exile was an ordeal, remembered in exile. My trouble is, I am too comfortable now. All my bills (with a bit of panic) can be met. I am worth too much money in relation to the 'me' that became a mystic in the bleak 1960s, when I had nothing and risked myself; when I was not rooted."

I now redefined myself as a poet: "Another self-discovery. Fundamentally I am a metaphysical poet, capturing the unsayable in sharp language with one image, wresting meaning. Language, image, experience – these three components are blended in the poet's eye, which blends Nature and the heart. I need to state the line of English mystical poetry – the mystic line in English poetry. By returning to Ricks I am defining myself as I really am....I am a metaphysical poet writing a book about the Light. This is my 'second string'." I observed: "The Light came for the third time this week, at school. It is with me now as I write after a terrible day....I can drop into the Light now....As a metaphysical poet, do not get too distracted from the enlightenment theme....The unity in my work: the Light....My 'search for, and finding of, enlightenment'. This is my one-man campaign, to rediscover enlightenment as a literary subject. That one word – enlightenment – is the one word Ezra Pound spoke to me about: the one theme I could put on half a side of a postcard in T. E. Hulme's words."

At the same time I saw my larger purpose: "I am a synthesiser..., having synthesised the essence of all religion and poetry, and redefined the mystic line in both. I am filled with a profound sense of the worthlessness of art – in comparison with the eternal truth. Art has an eternity and expresses feelings, but these feelings are worthless unless they are truly developed." I dreamt of escaping school and lamented: "I must...produce some literary work of merit. Do I want to start as the non-fiction writer, the autobiographer, the novelist, short-story writer or poet? The trouble is, like Hardy, I am so many-sided and prolific." I typed up five more stories and wrote: "Tuohy is a major artist working in the material of minor art (to adapt Leavis on Keats), and hence he is a miniaturist: a minor writer. I am a major artist working in the material of major art but in miniature: in my mini-stories."

The ILEA Inspection began, and for three weeks there was a team of Inspectors looking at every aspect of the work at Garratt Green. I gave ten interviews of an hour and a half each and had little time to think about my true work. On November 5th I wrote: "I am totally uncreative....At present I am in a fallow time." I wrote of the Inspectors: "Dry, ageing men with lined faces and moustaches and joyless eyes; men who have become social personas, wrongly living as social identities, and who get so tired that they go to the grave gladly, burdened by their social duties; men who are socialists because they have busy social roles and social beliefs."

I attended the Chelsea Mayor's reception for the two softly spoken and attractive Irish housewives who won a Nobel Peace Prize. Mrs. Ewart-Biggs was there, the wife of Christopher Ewart-Biggs who was to be murdered in Dublin, a relative of Biggs-Davison. A few days later it was announced that Biggs-Davison had been sacked (along with Winston Churchill) from his job as Shadow No 2 in Northern Ireland, for voting against the continuation of sanctions against the black internal settlement government of Rhodesia which had put Bishop Muzorewa in power. He said on the morning news: "I cannot explain Mrs. Thatcher's inexplicable instructions." I rang John Ezard. He told me Bernard Saint had had a book of poems published, *Testament of a Compass*, and that his marriage had broken up.

On November 15th, I tried out my healing powers. I wrote: "Visited Bruce MacManaway's 'surgery' at 13 Moreton Terrace, Lupus Street. Chatted with Maxwell Cade and Alick Bartholomew over lunch (a stand-up buffet of orange juice) and then was wired up to Cade's 'Mind Mirror' by Cade's wife, and spent an hour 'healing' a young boy with a damaged brain, Geoffrey Stewart. When the four rushes came through Geoffrey had the best brain rhythms he had had for two years – even though the power did not feel as great as usual because of the hairnet, and the public spectacle. Later helped with an old man, a boy who had a blood clot in his artery by his right ear, and then watched MacManaway release a trapped nerve from a lady's back. Left just before Lord Hailsham arrived for his 5 o'clock appointment: like him, I am a figure in this Age, and should not be seen to wear a healing hat in front of him....Later wrote *Christmas Tree Patterns on the Lunatic Fringe*....The brain machine showed I have a deep, deep calm. I calm my patients back to health." The experiment had been a success and had confirmed my healing powers, but I did not want to become a healer, and wrote of the poet as healer: "Keats on healing and the poet. 'The poet and the dreamer are distinct..../The one pours out a balm upon the World,/The other vexes it.' Better still, the passage from my own *Silence* about healing society. My healing powers come from the same source that my images come from."

I was still working on 46 Ritherdon Road. The scaffolding was now down and we were pebbledashing between torrential showers. I now took in a tenant at the request of the British Council, the nephew of the Kurdish resistance leader Jalal al Talabani who was studying in the UK for three months.

Ann's energy was low. She was still suffering from blood pressure, and would soon be recommended to go on methildopin for two years. I wrote on 19th November: "Feeling relaxed after healing Ann of her neck-ache. Feel deeply relaxed. The source of poetry and healing is the same. In fact, poetry is a form of healing. I write to heal, now. This was not always so. I send out a current of healing energy in a poem, and make whole. My images (what I compare 'real' events to) and my healing power come from the same source. They are more than decorative: that is fancy. I am a contemplative-Romantic. Now I feel great, and Ann is active, charging about the kitchen. In healing others, you heal yourself. There is opening oneself to God and feeling the power flow in: prayer is self-healing by thinking of others in a healing way. Also psycho-pictography: having an image of what I want, and making it happen....poetry, healing, prayer, psycho-pictography....My anti-Movement, anti-rational theme (enlightenment): 'The towering depths around your rational question.'"

I took stock of my attitude to Europe: "I am before my time in my view of Europe. The United States of Europe over *all* Europe." At the same time I knew I was making possible a mystical revival: "I am like Rumi. I am leading a resurgence of ecstatic mysticism, and am a part of the new age. Neo-Platonism has a place in it. I write mystical poetry – ecstatic rather than ascetic or esoteric – and I stiffen what I learn with a book about the Light. I discover through poetry and understand it in prose. Not for me the metaphysical meditation or the numerological gnosis – the quest for, and finding of, God through Light, that is where I fly."

On the ninth anniversary of the break-up of my first marriage I wrote: "I now barely remember that marriage; am never upset for it, though I feel a pang when Nadia rings....I am happy again: I have a structure."

In mid-December I went back to Bruce MacManaway's healing centre. I wrote: "Healed Bruce MacManaway, the maestro himself, who suffers from insomnia. Pumped in a lot of delta (the sleep rhythm), while Cade scribbled, bending over his mind mirror. Geoff and others lurked round. Lunched with Bruce and Cade; while the others ate downstairs. We were in Rosalind's bedroom. I told Cade that I wrote poems as a way of defining my experiences. Cade said I was lucky to have come through Zen, for Zen holds back the Kundalini until one is ready for it. MacManaway, returning the compliment by manipulating my spine, has done something to my psychic flow. He has made my sexual flow more responsive, and I react more to external stimuli than I did...; increasing my sexual drive."

I worked on my synopsis for my book on the Light. I wrote: "The end of my poems for a while, while I assimilate. The beginning of a new Rumi-like period. The Christian tradition of the Light which Eliot revived (nearly): it has been my yardstick all my life, ever since those Methodist days, though I have frequently dissented from it. I am like Blake and Blake's nonconformism: influenced by it, though dissenting from it. My book is what *The Outsider* should have been. About finders rather than a lost, alienated generation." On Christmas Eve I wrote: "Feel so well. I am me again. A few days' writing makes me feel really well. It gets my energies going." I added on Christmas Day: "The raging creative fire which burns through my heart and mind: I do not know it at work, where I am like an extinct volcano, but when I recast a work like *River of Light*, then it shapes, this burning imagination. If I did not have school to switch off the central heating boiler in my spirit, it would surely have exploded by now. School is a way of regulating my roaring creative furnace; staying alive, I can fire more ingots in it than if I consumed myself in one blaze in my youth. I have burned with it for three days now, after disuse. Needed little sleep last night, after seeing *River of Light* as a whole, and having a very huge and wise vision of things; one that will surely affect my poetry in the coming months. My next work will put me in the tradition of Rumi."

The *River of Light* eventually became Part One of *The Fire and the Stones*. I wrote: "I had to go abroad to the Middle and Far East so that I could respect Islam and Buddhism as distinct cultures for this work I am now doing. My whole life has been leading up to this work. Every place I have been has been a preparation for it. This is my divine task, my allotted mission." And: "Sufism will increasingly influence my poetry. It is no accident that I should have spent time in the Arab world, and should have walked with Pir Vilayat Inayat Khan, the Sufi leader."

We went to Loughton for Boxing Day and I heard about the deaths of some of the Methodist church figures of my childhood: Mr Llewellyn, Mr Yelland and Mr Bedwell; and Ebenezer Occamore had cancer of the spine and was crippled. There were party games for the children: bagatelle and jigsaw cards and dice and charades, which Matthew took part in. When I returned I wrote sadly, "My family will not let me be who I am (a Milton with a *Paradise Lost* in store) on the three or four days a year when we meet at Loughton; because they knew me as a boy and do not believe in me, just as I cannot take Rob seriously as a solicitor, having bowled him out at cricket in the garden. On the other hand, they let me be who I am the rest of the year by not bothering me." But again I retained the perspective of the Light: "When the Light touched me in Egerton Gardens, from Margaret, Western Christendom was relit from the Austrian Catholic tradition (the Habsburgs, the Holy Roman Empire). Margaret was a torch going back to the old Popes who lit a lamp within me, a lamp that had nearly flickered into light (in Japan) by itself." And again in early January 1979: "Everything in my life is a preparation for the coming greatness. I know that I will be a giant, if in the next 30 years I can complete what I want to complete."

We had had three Hong Kong Chinese tenants living on the top floor of our Ritherdon Road house – the idea was that they would pay for some of the work – and they had taken us to the Rent Tribunal. Ann and I had to attend a hearing and they did not turn up. We went again and this time, while Matthew crawled round the floor, judgement was given in our favour. We were charging them a very reasonable rent and the whole situation was another unnecessary distraction.

In 1979 I underwent a new metaphysical development in my poetry.
In January there was a strike by ancillary staff at my school (part of

Callaghan's winter of discontent) and I had to cross a picket-line of lorry-drivers, cleaners and lunch-staff to do administration. We did not teach during the strike. I wrote: "Soul and body – the spiritual awakening of the Counter-Renaissance: all this is very good for the new metaphysical (i.e. transfigurative) poetry....I am catching something very elusive and important in my poems at present. The burden of trying to restore the meaning and purpose of life to art, the question 'How am I to live?'" I was writing poems: "I have not recorded that I have written some 15 Divine Sonnets in a sequence to be called *Lady of the Lamp*, since the New Year....I am Orpheus, losing Caroline-Eurydice in the underworld, and going back to find her....And the Lady of the Lamp – I had her and lost her to darkness and now she is to return. *Eurydice* is a poem about darkness and about loss. The note merely confuses it. This note is more accurate than the note which appears under the poem. I am the archetypal Orpheus-figure, for my head (decapitated) will have oracular powers; and I am the poet of the lyre....I used to think: if I write 30 memorable lines I will have done well. Reading my poems for Ricks, I realise I have 200-300, and some of my work is really good....Alexander Bloch wrote a Beautiful Lady mystical sequence – I now discover after 20 of my *Lady of the Lamp* sonnets – following one summer of mystical exultation (cf mine, 1971)....The authentic shiver up the spine in the presence of great poetry – it raises Kundalini. Poetry is a means – and there are other means – of putting one into divine consciousness....I am a metaphysical poet, and am therefore a Symbolist; not a Symbolist who am therefore a metaphysical." On February 13th I recorded: "Wrote *Swan-Upping*. The swan-image just floated through the air and took over. Swan's-down, swan-upping – I obediently wrote it down. (I wanted to write a poem about a web of thought, but this one was too insistent.) I have written a sonnet every day for at least two weeks."

I went to Foyles and found Christopher Ricks's book on Milton and wrote: "He (Ricks) is the Empson of the 1970s: in the Empson tradition. His verbal approach: word-play: what is a successful and what is an unsuccessful metaphor (Milton's delicacy rather than grandness): his 'embarrassment' – sensitivity. He has antennae for embarrassment.... Ricks's theory that art is a way of coping with embarrassment. It can be. For me it is a means of searching. My strengths are: metaphor, verbal play, wit. They are metaphysical strengths; which blend in with my metaphysical search for reality or enlightenment, and symbolism. Love is a theme for me as it was with the metaphysicals (Marvell's *Coy Mistress*) and also obscurity. I am more of a Metaphysical than a Romantic: the Image. I am interested in the symbol in so far as a Metaphysical poet is interested in symbols. Coleridge (imagination) and Donne – I need to think about both just now – and on symbolism. This also explains the reflective autobiographical interest as opposed to the imaginative – the metaphysical poem is such – and the insistence on learning (e.g. my book). I am not imagining myself into any romance or fantastic setting like the Romantics, but am covering the ground I read in Spain when I carried the Metaphysicals in my rucksack....Empson, Ricks's mentor, was also fascinated by Marvell ("there is something very Far-Eastern about this") and was my predecessor until 1934 at Kyoikudai. (The bearded man I saw.)

He surely goes back to the Metaphysicals; the fusion of thought and image. What is the Metaphysical imagination (as opposed to Romantic image)? This coming contact with Ricks has got me away from *Romantic Image* to the Metaphysicals. I go back to Empson's ambiguity. Hence Kathleen Raine found me too rationalist. She wants me to be imagistic and purely unconscious – but she is not a true metaphysical."

At the Wrekin Trust Mystics and Scientists conference I had met John St. John, a publisher at Heinemann, who invited me to go and see him to discuss my proposed book on the Light. I visited him during the February half-term. He was grey-haired and bearded, and in a sports jacket with leather patches on the arms, sitting in a room lined with books. He was very encouraging but told me: "Heinemann are middlebrow." I wrote down his advice: "'Start with the objections. When you rub your eyes you see stars. The eye (cone, rods) and optic nerve (blue light) and perception. Then case-histories and then the tradition, the two things that will answer laughter....Make it clear at the beginning: the Light is not symbolical, but is something actually seen – experiential, i.e. it is not pathological....To what extent is the Light spiritual', i.e. to what extent is God on the electromagnetic spectrum?"

On February 20th I visited Christopher Ricks at Christ's College, Cambridge on a snowy day. I passed the mulberry tree Milton knew when he was a pupil there. Ricks was waiting for me in his large room, dressed in blue denim shirt and trousers. I had sent him some of my poems and we walked to the Buttery and there, dome-headed with round spectacles and wispy grey hair, he gave me a tutorial whose brilliance took my breath away. He made 16 technical points about my poems one after the other with great rapidity, declaring that they were not Metaphysical in the sense that the Metaphysical poets' poems are Metaphysical. He was not thinking of their metaphysical content at all (for me, the central issue), but purely of beginnings and endings, syntax, imagery and such matters. He launched into a long monologue while I listened, saying Marvell had done this and Hagger that; Milton and Tennyson had treated a particular theme one way, Hagger another; Keats and Eliot had done such-and-such, while Hagger had done so-and-so. For a good hour he related my work to the highest standards, and I felt as though I were listening to a tutorial in which my work had already joined the canon.

We had lunch in the Senior Common Room at Christ's. I sat next to Ricks and in between making general conversation with the other dons I said to him at one point that Coleridge distinguished imagination and fancy, to which Ricks replied: "I've never found that distinction particularly helpful." We had coffee in a snoozy room aglare with snow, and Ricks suddenly said "You're very learned," which I took as a compliment rather than as a criticism. (My mother's reaction to this comment was "The more learned you become the fewer the people you can write for", to which I retorted that the important thing was to be right, not to have mass appeal and be wrong.) When I returned I wrote a letter to Ricks relating my work to the Baroque tradition which combines Classicism and Romanticism and explaining how the metaphysical perspective is an aspect of Baroque.

Two days later I took a party of seven Garratt Green girls to Worcester

College, Oxford. We were given sherry in the Cottages on staircase 8 by Michael Winterbottom, who said: "Do you know whose room you're in?" There were girls sitting in all the chairs and even on the window sill, and I looked again and said, "It's Christopher Ricks's room, but it's been changed." "That's right," Winterbottom said. It was an eerie experience, sitting where I had had so many tutorials, with seven girls sprawling everywhere. Later I had lunch with the dons in the Senior Common Room. I sat next to Francis Reynolds, who had briefly taught me Roman Law, and was struck by how they all treated me as an equal, without any sense of superiority or of my being an outsider. I experienced the truth of what Asa Briggs had said at the Gaudy: that to be at a college was to belong to it for life. Afterwards we had coffee up the stairs where I had Collections (examinations after each vacation) and where I had my interview the day I talked about my Corinthian coin.

After my meeting with Ricks I resolved to write a more impersonal poetry, to focus attention on the object "like an artist rubbing himself out of the scene he has painted". I wrote: "Wittgenstein and Empson are two in whose tradition I am, but also Lowell (mystic and confessional and a reviser). Transmute and generalise the autobiographical, and in particular catalogue the strategies for saying 'I sit...', e.g. 'Let us' or 'We sit' or 'All who sit', etc., i.e. ways of generalising the particular....I am verbal and write in ambiguities, but that does not mean I am a rationalist, à la Winters; rather I am an imagist/symbolist. So go back to Empson – and Ricks – on images and symbols, and forget the rational side for the contemplative."

Soon afterwards I attended a conference on the Kabbalah at Ammerdown in Somerset. It was taken by Warren Kenton, a young bearded man who at the beginning of every session intoned: "Hear this." He then ran through the names of the 10 sephiroth or centres which form the Kabbalistic diagram, the Tree of Life. I went along because Shakespeare, Blake and Yeats were all heavily influenced by the Kabbalah, and I found the weekend very helpful. At one point Kenton put 10 chairs in a hopscotch pattern, to reflect the sephiroth, and we took it in turns to sit in chair 2, the rational social ego which looks out at the physical world, and chair 5, the new centre Tepheret or Beauty where the inner psychological, spiritual and divine worlds can be contacted. We did some work on looking within for our soul. I wrote: "The imagination as being open to images (archetypes) from the spiritual world, which clothe themselves in the psychological world. The visionary who stops short of the divine world: but like *Kubla Khan* or Yeats's 'rough beast', or my calm eagle, (the images) come from the spiritual world. My calm great eagle. Warren Kenton invited us to see our soul as a bird, and I had the image, coming from a dot in the blue and alighting close-up, of a huge brown and white eagle, with a hooked beak and tawny eyes; not at all fierce. He said later, 'Your bird shows how you view your soul.'" Thinking of my poetry I wrote: "Literature gave me insight into my lower psyche and helped me to glimpse the spirit....My poetry progresses from the 'I' to the higher self, from the physical world, through the psychological world, to the spiritual. I found my way myself, with very little help. Now, later Hagger will be impersonal and spiritually symbolic; and weighty. Understanding and wisdom in balance in my synopsis. My *Lady of the Lamp* sequence: written from the Self about the spiritual beyond; the veil through to the Kingdom of Heaven."

Of Garratt Green I wrote: "At Garratt Green I am mask, ego: not Self; and so should leave." Kenton said to me: 'You have been posted at your school to bring Light to the place."

Of being balanced I wrote: "Classicism is on the constant side; Romanticism on the feeling side/revolution. The thing to do is to balance Classicism and Romanticism, i.e. feeling and discipline, to be in the centre; not to err on the side of one or the other....Classicism and Romanticism; social context and individualism: left and right of the Tree. So, the state of man's poetic soul should be strict balance in the middle." I reflected: "My one foot in the Wittgenstein-Empson-Ricks-Tuohy tradition of verbal play and social meanings: which is a form of Classicism to the left of the diagram; while being metaphysical and Romantic and mystical (the right and centre of the diagram)."

I now had a new understanding of what had happened to me: "What happened to me in 1971. My ego was smashed, which opened the way to my self. I escaped lower thinking and higher thinking for egoistic feeling and broke through into 'awakening' and occupied my self. I received images from Wisdom, and direct illumination from the crown....My school is a disciplinary force which controls my wisdom; it is Gevura disciplining Hochma and Hesed, and preventing me from going mad like Dostoevsky or van Gogh....People succeed when their higher centres open, and when they raise their mental level so that they can cope on all fronts....I had to be at Egerton Gardens to meet Margaret and be initiated into the Light – and I had to go to Japan for the first illumination before that, so *Mandalas* was a way of finding my destiny, opening my self to world religions. I had to lose my first marriage. I was keeping a rendezvous with Margaret. I had to go to Garratt Green so that...I'd...prepare myself for my real task in life, this book on the Light." I reflected: "This period is like a period of study in a mystery school for me. Steeping myself in the mystics of all ages cannot but have an effect on my symbols when I return to mystical poetry." And later: "I chose my parents and my tutor (Ricks) so that I could rebel against each in turn and make firm my mysticism."

On March 18th we drove through a blizzard to Redmarley on the Gloucestershire/Worcestershire border for the christening of Elizabeth, my sister Frances's eldest child. I was a godfather and the service was taken by Frances's husband's father, who was vicar there. I remember the church had sparrows flitting among the rafters, and that later we ate at the vicar's house. There was a view across fields white with snow.

I was finding school even more irksome than usual. As I withdrew my full interest from lower to higher things the Department became more factionalistic, and the Head was ever ready to stir up the wasps' nest and encourage complaints. I was relieved when the holidays came. In April we went to Brighton to attend a relative's 21st, and Lucy, the aunt of mine who had cornered the family money, sat beside me and reminisced how in 1944 I repeatedly pushed my chair against my grandmother's wall in East Grinstead, so she took me on my scooter down the path to watch Percy the knife-grinder.

341

A MYSTIC WAY

On the way back we looked in on Margaret. She had moved to a Council house in Corbyn Road, Shoreham, "so she could sit and ask God what the next phase of her destiny is, and wait for a reply from the divine inspiration". Matthew pointed to a small sculpture by Katherine Yarrow, a square enclosing empty space and various shapes on each side including a sun and a moon (all the shapes of the universe, as if the universe were reduced to an empty square) and said: "God makes things like that." Margaret said, "You're right, you'd better have it." I saw Margaret as a desert saint: "Margaret like a desert father in the patristic times, going out into a desert of council houses, living among the poor and giving away her possessions. The saintly life." She was going through the Christian calendar for Easter. Margaret showed me her picture of St. Teresa, the nun in prayer. She told me: "My Dark Night began in Campbell Court and went on in St. Ives and Shoreham. I began St. Teresa in St. Ives and should paint Christ. St. Teresa is the example of the Light. You think, 'I have worked for nothing and I have nothing to work for.'" I wrote: "Her message. You pray and prayers are answered. It is the Holy Spirit and God. The Light of the Holy Spirit....Dark Night: 'The illuminations and joys dry up....Art is simplification.'"

During the Easter holidays I worked on the Eastern religions for my book. I was my real self and felt serene. I wrote: "It is as though I am being guided at present. I go to a book and it falls open at a certain page and a quotation I need leaps up and hits me. I am writing in a kind of trance....The bird songs from the gardens. What a joy to be near Nature again, even if it is London Nature." And again: "Every book I pick up falls open at a relevant page. I am being guided into a kind of automatic scholarship. My research is done by Angels." I visited the Festival of Mind and Body and saw Matthew Manning do healing. It was very dramatic. A line of cripples limped up to the platform and after receiving healing moved on without their crutches. I wrote: "Automatic writing and painting, and now with Matthew Manning..., automatic healing. I am doing an automatic scholarship. I go into a kind of contemplative trance and am guided into the right course....This is writing from chair 5, not chair 2: from the Shadow not the Reflection, who had to be smashed by Caroline."

I had the idea of founding a mystery school: "It has come to me, while I was reading Neo-Platonism and Plotinus. What Margaret and I should do. We should set up a school, like the Christian Catechetical School in Alexandria, for promoting the consciousness of the Light....Prepare for a School of London to disseminate the Light."

I now found myself becoming more metaphysical: "Poetry concerns the world of the senses and feelings – the lower mind: and in so far as it only concerns the world of the senses, it is no longer for me. I must adapt poetry, however, to hint at the Reality that is behind the world of the senses." And on May 7th I recorded: "Saw the Light again last night."

I went on a weekend conference at Hoddesdon on the *Hermetica* with Frederic Lionel, a French ex-intelligence agent who spoke of the Egyptian mysteries. On the Sunday morning I had an experience of the Light. I wrote:

"Sunday morning meditation, and the 'spiritual sun' broke as the ancient bearded face of God, looking down and to the right, a great matted beard, some awesome prophet I saw in a former life perhaps. John the Baptist? Immediately I tingled all over from the scalp to the backs of my ankles, and felt a great power flowing through me, and the tingling and sensation of higher energies went on for a minute or two, and now there are rushings of energy, an hour later. And all through breakfast, I could not speak for the tinglings and pricklings on my skin. Now I feel I located my saint in the middle of a yellow sunlight, but what a realistic saint! I could almost see the lice in his beard and the gnarled, cracked lines round his cheeks and eyes. Who was it, this saint of mine? My guardian? And why should I have written that it was John the Baptist? Or perhaps it was Poimandres? (From the *Hermetica*?)...My image of the prophet was from the spiritual world and it brought me great power and energy, and can only be good. But I thought it was the face of God. No. It was nothing like this. My power as an artist is behind my power as a mystic. Also saw angels like falcons on a blue sky." Soon afterwards I saw Paul Solomon and "confirmed in conversation that his inner Source is the Light".

I now felt purposive. I wrote in my *Diaries*: "I have not been upset for some years now, it seems to me, I am settled and happy and concerned with spiritual matters. When I have finished my book of Light, I must write my Confessions (i.e. spiritual autobiography) from Oxford to Zen to Margaret in London to the Faustuses on the Wrekin Trust: a path for aspirants; to be succinct. Kundalini, healing and the rest. Growth by asking questions. Augustine wrote his *Confessions* at 45. I am about right. Include a view of poetry in relation to mysticism, and a view of symbolism."

I felt guided. The alternator went on my car on a Friday. I wrote: "The timing leaves me full of admiration for my guiding power. This could have happened in Hertfordshire last weekend, stranding me, and it would have made me late for work. But no, the power waited until Friday afternoon, and drew my attention to it so it could be repaired on Saturday. I even had the exact money (over £100) to pay in cash, having got it out for turf. There was no turf last week: that was held over till my car was fixed. Thank you angels."

I saw my role with great clarity: "I am a reconciler: of the Light of Christianity with the Light of other religions. I am performing an Ecumenical service for our time. I am an ecstatic in a tradition of ecstatics." I wrote of my time since my landmark visit to Pound: "My definition of the Light tradition is the fruit of my work since then, which those living energies quickened in me." Soon afterwards I sharpened the idea: "I am a reconciler of the Christian tradition and the New Age, just as Clement of Alexandria and others reconciled differing traditions. I expose the common premise. I am a great unifier." I had my ears syringed and de-waxed at this time, and wrote: "Reality has rustles and tinklings and echoes which we are not normally aware of, but which we know are there when we listen immediately after having our ears syringed and impacted wax removed."

In May our gardener brought with him a pyracantha, a firethorn, and planted it in our front garden. I gazed at it and then wrote: "The firethorn. I need to spend more time with my circulating God, but how, where? The loo at work, it must be. I am almost too active: writing my book instead of being in ecstasy with the flowing, circulating Light. 'Is there a God?' Of course there is! What a daft question – to anyone who has been in trance and *seen*. The Fire. And then afterwards. Thorn. Firethorn. Like a woman waiting for me to 'meet' her, the Light waited for me to climax. Firethorn!"

I carried on working on my book on the Light. I wrote: "For 30 months Dante 'attended the schools of the religions and the disputations of the philosophers' – what I am doing now." I observed: "The Light – all creatures are made of it and from it, and so it is the living proof of the brotherhood of men which transcends racial barriers and power politics; and I am at Garratt Green serving Asians and West Indians so that I can learn this truth." I reflected that we are meant to be promiscuous in our youth but that as we grow older we turn away from the body and die into the mystic tradition.

I steeped myself in the mystics: Rolle, *The Cloud of Unknowing*, Catherine of Genoa. I reread Evelyn Underhill's *Mysticism* and William James's *The Varieties of Religious Experience*, and bought Happold's *Mysticism*. I lent Margaret a book on the sayings of the Desert Mystics, and she said: "I am becoming clearer. I was a blank, but now I see that I am going through what your Desert Mystics went through, the same temptations." I distinguished immanence (God being in the universe as Light and knowable) from transcendence (God being outside the universe and unknowable).

In June I was organising the public exams again. I wrote: "Yesterday saw the blue/purple Light for quite a while: and a stained glass window, and a gold bar in brilliant gold for quite a while." And: "These daisies on my lawn, like stars near the Milky Way." I wrote: "I yearn for creative work again. I yearn to live in the countryside where I can keep a clean 'mystic' Nature diary, like my bird diary, and record the passing of the seasons in the tradition of Richard Jefferies and Edward Thomas." And again: "Last night, a blue sapphire of Light in my soul. It is permanently there now, and a feeling of great unity with all the universe. I would not let Nadia kill the ants that got into our living-room, and feel a great one-ness with all life....I am in love with creation, on fire for it. There was a perfect yellow water lily on the pond: it was perfection, and I remarked on it to one of the applicants. I had a chat with the school gardener about the rhododendrons. When I needed a mystery school I was shown Dulwich Park – living things." I wrote: "I want to live in the middle of a field, among trees, birds, cows and near water, where the sunrise and sunsets are events, and I can contemplate God's world without and commune with the divine Fire within, and feel the harmony and peace of a Nature-hermit."

I again dreamt of bringing together the Church of England and the Catholic Faith, not then realising that much of the unwritten history of the 20th century and before is essentially about the struggle between the British Crown, with its Judeo-Masonic American allies and the Illuminati, with the Vatican, which has allied with the US against Communism. Without realising how central to contemporary history my dream was, I wrote: "Margaret came. I saw that one of my missions was to persuade the Archbishop of Canterbury to go to Russia and to the Pope." And again: "I am here to bring together all the sects and reunify Christianity (on the Light), and redefine the Christian philosophy for the defeat of Communism." Margaret said to me: "You have no questions these days just a strange certainty. All these people depend on you, you are a magnet: it is the Light." I recorded: "I have found all my questions answered in the mystic tradition and so I must remember 'Firethorn' – the fire consuming the thorns: pink flowers. It is growing. My firethorn is growing. Two levels of fire; the fire that burns and the fire that warms." Shortly afterwards I wrote: "I am a universal Gardener, and at my school I have 1800 flowers, and I look after each with loving care. They all grow and bloom."

In the same holidays Ann went to Cornwall. I wrote: "Worked all day alone..., on Tantric Hinduism and mandalas, then 'looked' and saw a fire – my thorn bush in flames which rearranged themselves into a huge white chrysanthemum, the golden flower. Only looked to say 'I am now starting Saivism, please tell me what to say' – which is what I asked this morning over Tibetan Hinduism, and was amply given and am grateful."

In June Matthew had another bout of convulsions lasting two minutes as the result of another sudden high-rising temperature caused by a virus. It happened while Ann was visiting a friend, and she drove him unconscious to the London Hospital. I was rung and immediately left school (passing my Head at the gate and ignoring her request for me to return to class). I went over by tube and helped him back to consciousness. Ann stayed the night there and the next day he was transferred by ambulance to St. James's Hospital for a couple of days. During this time we were beset with problems. For example, Ann's car battery went dead, our upstairs tenants' fridge broke down, and then my electric typewriter packed up. Matthew now developed measles and had a fiery red blotchy face. I wondered whether these "minor irritations and disasters" were all coincidences, or whether I was being targeted. I wrote: "We are like rocks and they break over us like the sea and the foam froths over us and then recedes, and we still are."

Soon after, I went to Glastonbury for a conference on Arthur. It was my first visit to Glastonbury, and I walked to the Tor and sat in the gardens of the well, where I was later to write a poem. The nearby house was associated with Dion Fortune and Tudor Pole.

Margaret had closed her gallery and had run short of money and was about to be evicted from her Council house. She was taken to court to be evicted. She appeared holding a rosary and a picture of the Sacred Heart of Jesus and was impelled to say: "Stop this case immediately, it is disgraceful." Miraculously the judge agreed and granted her a month, which he then extended to six weeks. I asked her about the meaning of disasters and whether they were consequences of powers of darkness. She said: "If it is benevolent, it is to test your patience, so accept. If it is malevolent then acceptance will neutralise it and overcome it, so accept." I wrote: "Evil is always in the service of Providence so it must be accepted....Resist not evil but overcome evil with good – with acceptance....Satan is within God's world, and Providence rules evil. It is not a dualistic struggle between light and darkness. Darkness is within light.

At the end of June I was again of the opinion that I was "now in a 'Dark

Night of the Spirit', the preface to the full unitive life, and my patience is being tested by the many things that go wrong every day." And: "This work of mine is an expression of the unitive life....All is one and has a rich meaning and nothing really touches me. I am divinised, up to a point. I do not want, I am not attached emotionally, my soul is not attached to the senses, though they are nice."

And I wrote of my busy life: "I am amazed at the load I carry, at the active life that is the context for my contemplative life. Everyone depends on me. At work I have done the timetable for next year, the coverage for all this last week – 25 teachers away on Wednesday, 16 today – and I am doing the 1st year placing and the induction course, as well as trying to make 2 more sets of exam papers and the moves throughout the school. In the meantime each day I take corrected pages to Mari for typing and check what she has typed, photocopy it after Ann has made corrections. And I am still not finished. On top of all, Anthony now has measles – Matthew having finished it – and I have to go to the chemist for medicine and help clear up vomit. And we have a change of tenant tomorrow." Soon afterwards Ann was ill, which meant I had to take Matthew to his school on Tooting Common and do additional chores, and then Anthony, having weathered measles, was taken to St. George's Hospital, Tooting with bacterial pneumonia. He looked bedraggled, but he picked up after I sat quietly with him and put healing surges into him. It seemed as if Providence itself was trying to impede my researches into the Light.

In mid-July I wrote: "My timely rediscovery of the tradition of the Light could bring about a new Renaissance."

We were invited to a dinner party at Colin MacCabe's. It was at Flavia's house in Islington, and we sat in the unkempt garden near an overgrown lily pond and drank wine while the infant Fergie ran about using an excellent vocabulary mixed with four-letter words. Flavia had toyed with teaching Italian and French at Garratt Green – Colin had rung me to see if I could help – and Tuohy was present along with a quiet University College don who did not say a word all evening. We came in when Colin was bitten by gnats. I wrote: "Colin, unkempt hair and open-necked shirt, somehow like his untouched garden, and with a soft dream in his eyes, somehow rather Rupert Brooke-ian." In the middle of dinner, at which the drink flowed very liberally, the post-Structuralist MacCabe attacked the traditionalists in Cambridge's English Faculty, which was then run by Christopher Ricks, and he went out and came back displaying a plain sweatshirt on which was printed: "More P—ks than Ricks?" I could see trouble brewing between the traditionalists and the modernists in Cambridge English circles.

Now Matthew and Anthony both developed whooping cough. I wrote: "They have been ill for a whole month, non-stop: convulsions – measles – measles – pneumonia – and now whooping cough, which they had before the convulsions, though the hospital would not believe us."

We broke up. I wrote: "I have seen poetry in the wrong terms. The Metaphysicals and Eliot are part of the Church of England/Royalist tradition, and that is why only Eliot has reflected the Light in poetry. As a Metaphysical poet, I am following this tradition; but I am also blending it with the Puritan tradition of Milton and Marvell, in our ecumenical time."

And I added: "I, too, like Milton, am worried about the present state of the world. Just as his *Paradise Lost* was about the Puritan cause, so my *Overlord* is about the Second Coming of Christ and a united Europe, i.e. the European cause. The equivalent cause of our time, or battle, is between the pro-and anti-Europeans. I must remind people of the horrors of war, the need for change. I am a radical pro-European....I write about a vision of Paradise: a universal peace, harmony and concord which Christ will bring about through Europe, a relief from all the terrorists and violence....I must unite the way of Donne and the way of Milton."

I pondered my religion and political allegiances: "I am on the Puritan side, for I reject the necessity of the Church, the priest and the sacraments. I must explain this to Margaret; and to our curate Graham Smith. I am a natural nonconformist. I work through individual conscience and am on the left....I am an independent, I was once told – as Milton was. Milton and Marvell amalgamated in our ecumenical time with Donne and Herbert. I could not confess before a priest, any more than a Quaker could....The Labour Party, an attempt to put the Nonconformist Light into politics. Whereas the Conservative Party is the party of the Church of England and Royalism. One is Puritan and Labour, or Royalist and Tory. The trouble is, Puritan policies penalise me, Cavalier policies help me, by and large." And I added: "My Existentialism, whose roots perhaps go back to Wesley: that the Light is to be experienced existentially; that the 'personal conversion' of the mystics is an existentially experienceable fact." I wrote again: "I am a Holist. This is the new 'transcendentalism' and I was using the word 'Holism' back in 1966 (see my poetic manifesto). The new mystic movement of Holism. My Holism, too, will be absorbed by the mystic tradition it will regenerate, in due course."

At the end of July I focused on my spring. I wrote: "While the man up the road snicked a hedge, I meditated on the spring from which the river came and felt a quiet ecstasy at 9.15 a.m....Worked all day from 9.15 a.m. to 10.15 p.m., with a short break for lunch, while the spring flowed non-stop in me." I wrote: "In my art I have developed. I have been through a 'personal' stage and am now in the 'death of ego' and 'impersonal' stage....The 'I' must be cut back on, to generalise and universalise."

By early August I had turned against the New Age. I reflected: "That *Hermetica* course I went on was in fact a 'magic' course; hence the number of astrologers present, for astrology was always a part of magic. What is needed in our time is a clear distinction between mysticism and occult groups....I now feel the esoteric underworld is pernicious. It gave Yeats some obscure symbols, but took him away from the mystic reality that Eliot found in 1935, when Yeats was still alive." Ann took the boys to Cornwall and I stayed in London. I wrote: "In the wet wind I heard the swoosh of the waves on a distant Cornish beach. I have been alone here for over a week now, and rather enjoy it, so fertile is the silence, so good is it to be in my study, so whole am I." Again I was aware of a great divide between esotericism and a reunified Church: "Another of my tasks: to lead back the alienated who have found their way into esotericism, to lead them back into the Light of the Church, like a Pied Piper; a crusade back to a renewed Church. There has to be a new Reformation to make the Church a place for mystics again. The Oneness of the ecumenical movement. All churches and sects are a part of One and can reunite on that basis." I saw very clearly that the New Age was anti-Christian: "The New Age's 'spiritual' awakening goes back to Theosophy and is not original if seen within the flow. It is a drawing together and focusing of ideas that are already there. 'Anything goes that is not Christian.'"

I was clear about my philosophy: "My philosophy: the need for an existential encounter with the Light, which then transforms the personality, destroys the ego and sets the soul on the right path."

In August I joined my family in Cornwall and wrote: "Went down to Charlestown, reunited with my wife and children. On Tuesday took Matthew to Charlestown: skimmed stones, fished, watched the gulls round the harbour, found some pink valerian (or all-heal) at the top of the cliff. In the evening went to Polkerris and had a drink in the Rashleigh Arms there after walking round the harbour and looking at the war-time pill-box (machine-gun post)....In the last three years I have demonstrated a tradition in which the Invisible is behind the visible; and I have therefore weakened scientific materialism and Humanism."

In my view of the Light I wanted to have a position of independence: "The lecturer should be independent of all 'isms' and build up a picture of the experience of being illumined by the Light by presenting the tradition. Phenomenology studies the subjective side of perception by bracketing out the object (in my case, the Light) and so Part 1 is a phenomenological approach to the perception of the Light to build up the picture of the encounter with the Light in terms of the tradition....A phenomenological study of the existential encounter with the mystic Light as it appears in the tradition. (The) central theme is...what we know about the Light from the tradition – demonstrating that it is a universal experience (both historically and geographically)....Relate the existential experience of the Light to the new scientific, philosophical and religious thinking which already exists in Europe: a new anti-humanist age is beginning in which the paranormal and a beyond-the-senses metaphysics can return, which will (or can) change the ideology of Europe if Christianity adopts it against Communism. The Invisible within the visible. So, I am building up a picture of a world beyond the 5 senses from the reception of the Light by 'supermen', who have transcended the senses, passed beyond the senses....How can the Light be known? This is a question of epistemological perception, which can be studied phenomenologically. It is a certain kind of perception which perceives the Light: a purified, open, passive watching rather then an active grasping. I can get this from Husserl's *Ideas* which Colin Wilson told me to buy (just as he was going off the rails of Existentialism into the Occult)." I wrote: "I am pleased about this statement of my position. It preserves my integrating outside the Church and the New Age, as an independent existentialist, which is what I should be, and was when I visited Colin Wilson back in 1973, six years ago." I now see Universalism as being independent of the Vatican's Christianity, the Church of England and the Secret Brotherhood, heir to the Satanist Illuminati.

I was thinking about philosophy. I wrote that my point of view "is to be independent of all the contemporary religions and to be existentialist" and that my central theme (is) "that the tradition of the Light provides a world-view that is not based on the senses. I can therefore overthrow the principle of 'verification by the senses' which has dominated modern philosophy."

Of my poems I wrote: "My poems...are...mystic-existentialist ones. My poem to Margaret was not a sign that I was about to become a Catholic; just that I would draw on the mystic tradition in an existentialist context. My poems must be personal therefore, in the sense that they are existentialist poems. They are metaphysical in outlook because they transcend the senses. For 300 years, the visible world has been all, and the senses have been the touchstone for empiricism. I have now reversed all that. The contemplative-mystic tradition. Kathleen Raine's failure to understand my tradition pushed me into writing it all down. And she is regarded as a mystic!"

We went to St. Michael's Mount "which hung in mist when we arrived, but cleared as the tide went out, though there was very low cloud to our left as, having passed the imposing grey Trevarthian House where Robert and I stayed as children, we walked along the causeway, looking up at the obsessing Castle. Up the stone path to the steepling height, where a beacon was lit for the Spanish Armada, and where terraces jutted out over thin-air and overhung great drops to the rocks below. Saw Cromwell's handkerchief (1653) and the Flemish St. Michael and the Dragon." We went on to Newlyn and Mousehole and returned to Penzance and Porthleven: "a walk in misty Porthleven among the fishermen on the pier." That night I went down to Charlestown. "It was very dark. A few late-night fishermen by torchlight. The tide was in. Out at sea a lightship flashed and beamed its light off the low cloud: it was like a shaft along the ceiling. All quiet."

The next day I wrote: "The existential encounter. Think. The chains of the senses prevent man from becoming a Superman. The chains of the senses have to be broken for the Light to be known....The Mystic Way – Hiroshige's Tokaido. Stages along the Mystic Way." And: "In *The Silence*, the seedcase was my senses, the stem was beyond the senses. That vision I worked out in Japan is central to me now."

I recorded: "13th August. All day, rain. We could not go out. I played Matthew snakes and ladders and lost, and edited my lead-in. Then, around 9.30 p.m. the rain stopped and we went down to Charlestown. Leaning against the wall under the Harbourmaster's House I felt *The Sea is Wild* come, a lyric, and came home and wrote it out, rhymes and all." The next morning I wrote: "Awoke at 5 a.m. last night and lay with the Light which was faint but there, while gales raged and buffeted outside." I observed: "In the 1960s I was writing novels, but I had not found my theme, the transforming power of the Light. Now I have found it but am 'too busy' to write novels."

I recorded: "Went down to Charlestown and was caught up with the Red Arrows in their Gnats; zooming and looping and making steeples of smoke over Fowey." Soon after it was the Charlestown regatta: "I floral-danced through the streets of my favourite Cornish harbour behind a red-jacketed band; wearing a khaki guerilla jacket – correction, my Colonel's jacket."

I bemoaned being "handicapped" by Garratt Green when I had important

349

works to write, but I vowed to soldier on: "Matthew Arnold was an Inspector of Schools after all." I surveyed the "burden" of my *Diaries*: "My burden, like Christian's, on my back: my *Diaries* to be typed – these *Diaries* are like Sterne's *Tristram Shandy*, for every entry makes the final selection more remote, harder to do – my poems, my stories, my 7 novels, my philosophical works, my epic, my Autobiography. This is my burden. All I can do is do what I can see now." And I added: "My superhuman energy which has come from the Light." What particularly irked me at this time was that I had so little money for so much sacrifice of my time. I wrote: "Went to the bank in accordance with my telephone arrangement to be told that I have exceeded my agreed limit and there will be no more. So I have to get through to the end of the month on what I have."

Margaret sent a message that she would pray for me at the Brompton Oratory, and that a Bishop was praying for me. Ann, the boys and I went to Clovelly: via Bude: "Bude in a valley, wild Atlantic rollers, our lunch under Chapel Point (or rock). Clovelly, a long walk down cobbled steps, past 1910-1920 houses in white, hung with flowers. Three hundred feet or so down to the harbour whence provisions are brought up by donkeys that have Friday and Saturday off as rest days and are kept at the top in a field. Clouds scudding across the sky, lower faster than higher, and casting a shadow on the sea." I do not know whether it was Margaret's doing but I had a surge of energy and drafted yet another novel which I knew I could not write, the prospect of which filled me with some despair. Margaret had said that through the Bishop I would meet the Pope, and I wrote: "If I have an audience with the Pope – not of my seeking – then I must make it clear that my own beliefs aside (which are not Catholic), I am concerned to put across a Light which *all* religions have sought to trap, and that to get across to the many non-Christians my stance should be an independent one, though I obviously have close links with Catholicism through Margaret. I must make my appeal to the Pope on the Light, not on the Church, which anyway needs a great reform. I am an Ambassador for the Light."

I now wrote of my Mystic-Existentialist position: "Margaret's influence has taken me towards, but not into, Christianity. This position has developed out of the Mystic-Existentialist position of *The Silence*, 1966, i.e. it grew out of Japan. And earlier, from my reading of *Six Existentialist Thinkers* in 1957/8, and my early Oxford existentialism and my early mysticism I again reviewed my Mystic Way (ever in process): "Night of Spirit broken by visions in 1978 and 1979, and now...this great unitive view, the instinctive oneness, the Self, this serene detachment, this return to the Light". And I reflected: "Oxford taught me to think along egocentric Rationalistic, Sceptical and Empiricist lines, but this was not the most important skill of my education, because I was not illumined until I was 31, properly, and therefore the divine influx into my Self did not begin properly until after then. So how I was at Oxford bears little relation to how I am now. It was me without my wisdom."

I wrote on symbolism: "Symbolism can evoke the spiritual in terms of the material, the One in terms of the many, the Invisible in terms of the visible. This is what I am doing in my poems."

My time in Cornwall was drawing towards an end. We went to the

Fowey Carnival and I thought much about the ego and the Self, and how the sin of pride involved the ego overthrowing the Self. I had been sleeping well – I wrote that I had been to bed before midnight for two and a half weeks – and one morning I awoke from sleep with the history theory that became *The Fire and the Stones* lodged in my mind by infused contemplation or divine inflow: "Aug 24th. Again, a morning inflow, around 5. 30 a.m., when I was too 'tired' to do anything, though around 6.15 I woke up and wrote it down. It is a new theory of history. The idea I received in sleep is: that civilisations are 'light-bearers', that their initial élan reflects the active values of the Self (not the ego), and that civilisations last as long as the Light lasts: hence the Egyptian civilisation lasted 3,000 years. While the Light lasts, the ego is not pandered to, and there is a national Self with military and national values ('the Lord Mighty in Battle'). But when the ego predominates and Welfare States pamper it and it gets used to luxuries, then the Light goes. So the West must return from the ego to its national Self and the active values. (British) political parties offer the ego passive (Labour) and active (Tory) values; only mysticism and religion address the Self. To confuse politics and religion is to confuse ego and Self (outer and inner). But Communism crushes the Self, and must be opposed. Humanism is about the ego and the Middle Ages were about the Self. So Humanistic religion is about the ego, and it needs to return to the Self....What I have to answer is the Roman civilisation. The Greek Mysteries contained the Greek Light and explain the Greek civilisation, but what of Rome?" I added: "The poet must channel through his Self, or he is nothing. Poetry and hypnotic images are from the Self, not the ego. As a poet, write from the Self. Poetry is contact with the Self. The mystic contemplative tradition takes place there, and is reflected from the Self, and should not be passed to the ego....The rational Movement writes 'ego' poetry (as did the 18th century Augustans). I am a poet of the Self. 'Poet of the Self', etc. I am now retracing the ground of *The Silence* in terms of other men's experience of the Light, and history is ahead: the view of civilisations in terms of Light-bearing." And I wrote of: "my outflanking of the Age of Despair by the Light. The Light's outflanking of the Age of Despair." And I added: "When I wrote my journalism it was from my ego and not my Self. Ezard is an ego-writer, I am a Self-artist and thinker."

We went to the local Carnival. I wrote: "Hangman and noose. Flashers. Fairy queens waving woodenly. Fancy dress for the children. Then to Charlestown. A grey-green sea. A mackerel then jerked and jumped in its death-spasm, despite being knocked twice on the harbour wall. The life in it firmly reluctant to ebb like the tide. I am glad I am not a fisherman. I don't like taking life of any form."

Then I pondered on my history idea: "I received my idea that civilisations are Light-bearers (through religions) at the end of my sleep...yesterday morning (Aug 24). It must be right because of its source....If civilisations grow with the Light, they decline without it in the outer world and turn into tyrannies." I began asking myself questions which would be answered in *The Fire and the Stones*.

Back in London I returned to Toynbee "and saw him admit to drawing a blank as to why civilisations spring up. It is not race or environment, and so it must be challenge and response, he says. But Toynbee has been 'all round the houses', analysing each civilisation in detail and drawing conclusions from each, and seeing what each has in common. I have started with the answer and am working backwards. It is like a jigsaw puzzle: Toynbee didn't know the picture, I have been given it in my sleep from a source that is *always* right. So I must write that conclusion now – as my next task. (After shopping for files and sunbathing.) The search goes on." And my *Diaries* entries asked questions that slowly became answers. I wrote: "The infused knowledge and wisdom I received in Cornwall, when I woke up with the answer to the problem that defeated Toynbee, and (which) led to his semi-erroneous theory of Challenge and Response."

Margaret came and talked a lot about the Pope: "Our Pope never condemns, he brings out the Light." She asked: "Where do they find the Holy Spirit in the brain? They can't find it anywhere. It's in the heart." She said: "I had to go through poverty and National Assistance to know...how the poor are treated." She said: "I am sure Matthew's convulsions are to bring you and Ann closer together, I am sure of it....Accept it and let it happen." I reflected: "It is not just Freud and Wittgenstein that Margaret is an antidote to: it is Philby as well: he was recruited after going to Vienna."

In September we went to Loughton for a family tea. "Ann and I took Charles, Matthew and Anthony to the church and looked at the Ten Commandments, and then to the pond which was green round the fallen tree. The tufted duck on the Horseman's Pool." I wrote: "One is the Self in the Forest and at the High Beach church, and in art, and in weekend silence and holiday leisure, and in writing, and in teaching poetry at 'A' level, and by the sea in Charlestown harbour, and in gardens, and in making love (often), and, strangely, when absorbed in a game of cricket and 'connecting' as I did at Bancroft's when I made 27 for the 1st XI on a rainy day, i.e. all the things one likes doing. One is the ego in all other things: one's job, coping with problems; one's family when asserting oneself; among friends; visiting foreign places which bring out observation. In Iraq I was an ego observing, though I located my Self when I saw the moon at the bottom of the sky, 'in a bucket', and on the Shatt al Arab. All the images are feelings within the Self which are remembered."

I was now back at school for the autumn term. I had been given the Coverage full time and some day-to-day running of the school, and the CSE entries. It was all work that could be done at school rather than in the evenings, but I could see my writing time being squeezed. One day I wrote: "What *am* I doing at Garratt Green? I, who have written the most original book since Spengler and Frazer, attempted 'Now sleeps the crimson petal', 'The splendour falls on Castle walls' and 'Break break break' with a dim 2nd year class. They have no imagination at all, and I found little evidence of mind, and when I asked them to describe 3 pictures Tennyson drew – after explaining that a poem is a picture in words – four of them opened their pencil cases, took out their red and green pencils, and began to draw a picture. What *am* I doing there?" The same day it was announced that Wandsworth's schools would be reduced from 17 to 8 in 1982, and I set my mind on leaving secondary school teaching when I could for a primary school which Ann would run as Head. But I still wrote: "The noblest thing (is) to educate (human beings) and help their spiritual growth."

In October I was off work for 10 days with bronchitis. I wrote: "Oct 7, coughed blood. Oct 8, X-ray clear. So I am not seriously ill, have not got lung cancer. Have had a cold for the last 3 or 4 weeks, and it went to my chest: a virus, not bacterial (which antibiotics will clear). The dark-red blood I coughed up in clear sputum was similar to a nose-bleed, only in the lung (right lung)....I have been unwell for a month. If I am unwell, I should stay at home....Oct 9. I have bronchitis and am taking the next two days off....Oct 10. Have spent all day lying in the bottom of the sofa, unable to move. Am exhausted. Was to take two days off work, but because of this medicine to dry up my right lung, in which I have bronchitis, I am so tired and drowsy, and slightly trembly. I feel as if my energy has gone, and will not come back....Being a Senior Teacher, and writing, has reduced me to this state of exhaustion, and I will surely collapse under a greater load; and I will not stop what I must do: my punishing goals....Oct 13. Have been ill for 3 days: unable to move because of bronchitis/chest infection. After more or less total rest I now feel my energy return, slowly, but am off work until the 17th....Now my sputum is clear and not purulent; Benafed having dried up my right lung."

Soon afterwards I took issue with the organist at the church Ann sometimes went to: "The organist at church: 'we don't want meditation at our retreat, we don't want to be like those cranky people who look for the Inner Light, we want to look out at the community.' He has a point – meditation to extremes is cranky – but he is also humanistic and secular as opposed to spiritual in his religion, and of the business, community and spiritual sides to a church, he neglects the last part, as a Catholic priest might not. Margaret: a priest is like a Zen teacher, he guides you to the Light by making you confess what takes you away from the Light....Ann: 'No one stands for the spiritual side at church.' I: 'That's what I have always found. Mention Eliot, and the priest says, 'Too deep for me.' Christianity has become a community religion, and so the WCC (World Council of Churches) sends money for Rhodesian guerillas to murder whites."

I returned to school and to a fierce debate as to whether language is acquired or innate. One of my staff who espoused socio-linguistics insisted that Plato was wrong, and I of course took Plato's side and said that language is both innate and acquired. My discontent festered on: "I am discontented at Garratt Green. I am now too much of an administrator and too little a teacher of Milton; I am too much of a philosophy-writer at present, and too little a writer of poems and stories which fulfil me." And I reminded myself of the "the great appalling truth, which I stumbled on in *The Riddle of the Great Pyramid*...that people come to love Hell. They like its routine, like men who miss the security of a prison. But I am going over the wall. I am going to escape and fulfil my vision and destiny." I observed: "As I watched from my window, the autumn wind tugged at a red Virginia creeper leaf – a scarlet leaf – and sent it dropping from side to side to the ground." I pondered moving to Cornwall.

At the end of October I finished my account of the tradition of the Light. It had taken me from March 5th to October 22nd – seven and a half months.

A MYSTIC WAY

It would eventually form the basis of Part One of *The Fire and the Stones*.

I was more free to return to poetry. I wrote: "Almost against my will I am becoming a prophet and a philosopher. At 20 I set out to describe the human condition. Now I am in a position to explain....My great journey, undertaken in solitude when I have shown a mask to the world, the mask of a mortgaged, salaried teacher; my great journey has redeemed the 20th century. It has destroyed the false idols (Marx, Freud...and the rest) and brought it back to the truth." On October 27th I wrote: "Tidy up my past poems – in particular do away with the long line and put them into heroic couplets, which are the traditional memorable lines for all time....Cf Ricks: 'Revise them, like Tennyson.' Get a scheme going for revision. Especially for the elegies. Prune. Ricks advised me to revise and improve, and so I shall; even though it is yet another task to be done....A system for improving them. Especially, pentameters." And I wrote: "I am too advanced for people. My stress metre is like Schoenberg in music: it makes too many demands. Restore the pentameter that lurks behind it." And again: "In my early work, brilliant poems were trying to get out of my mania for experiment and innovation. All it needed was a strict adherence to the pentameter to liberate them. My maturity enabled me to do that, and therefore write poems of lasting worth. Garratt Green has enabled me to prune my talent. I had a wild talent that grew like a summer garden; it needed me to act as gardener, edge the lawns and generally keep it under control, and prevent it from getting overgrown. I can be a great poet if I embark on this revision....I am not an anti-Movement poet in technique; I am only anti-the Movement ego – and pro-the Self....All my reading of Milton, etc (and Donne) has made me more particular and punctilious about technique....In my selection: not one pentameter will be out."

A few days later while observing that Donne was "Sir Thomas Egerton's spy in Parliament until 1601 (he used his spying techniques to form a secret liaison with Anne More)" I recorded: "Am revising 40 poems....Like Yeats, my 40s will be my turning-point." Soon afterwards I wrote: "what a joy to be back on poetry. Revised *Rubbish Dump*, and saw that my present...'selection'...is *Firethorn*, too poetic a title not to use on these poems, and to hoard for a spiritual autobiography....There is one complicating idea that runs through the poem: the *Grecian Urn* idea of nature as a bowl woven on a carpet – no, painted with a design – a flaming bowl. I must depict existence as a crackling, blazing fire, like van Gogh; I must show it full...of hidden energies. I have spent 3 years delving into the occult and mysticism, and I have X-ray eyes for seeing into hidden things now, and can solve poems that defeated me 5 years ago, when I was short of absolute knowledge....In poetry I used to aim for roughness – a ghost of pentameter behind a longish line – but now I aim for perfection as befits one with a sense of solid construction and organic growth; reflective thought is my means, irrational subject matter is my end." On November 16th I wrote: "Poems: go for the archetype: *Churchyard* (not 'High Beach Church'), i.e. the general, not the particular. Follow the advice in the Tuohy elegy." On November 26th I wrote: "I am melting these poems down into gold: a thing I do better after 40 than before." On November 29th I wrote: "Finished *Family House*. I discovered myself as a poet in the leisure and fertility of Japan, and *The Expatriate*...is a good poem. I discovered myself as a Metaphysical poet at Garratt Green, and that is the justification for my having spent so long there."

In December Tuohy visited me. He gazed at the fish tank and with typical precision pronounced the fish "guppies, which are vivaparous", and he looked at the architecture of our house and pronounced it "dog tooth, slightly Norman".

I wrote: "On poetry. I make my poems to last 1,000 years, whereas the 'conversational prose' of a non-poet like Patten is hurried, dashed off. Standards have gone down and electronic music is not as good as a symphony, abstract art not as good as a symbolic landscape. I must make works of gold that last. As an artist, I am a maker; not an autobiographical recounter, or raconteur. Trace the Metaphysical symbol back to Egypt. Symbols and language, like the Light, go back to 3,000BC....The Metaphysical symbol originated in Egypt. It can be grasped in Egypt, and applied to other ages." Again: "The elusive silence under wind: it seems to be empty of sound, to contain nothing, but it is full, and contains all; like a woman's silence, only her quiet breath....Time and eternity still. The elusive truth is: that silence baffles, it seems to be nothing but is in fact something, and then something not physical but spiritual (which is why it is elusive). I am saying: the Silence baffles and attracts, it is something not nothing; at the physical level it destroys and creates, but at the spiritual level this is transcended and the silence is the Ocean of Light of Eternity, which contains the meaning of life."

On the last day of term Matthew had a temperature, and "this evening I healed him with four surges through me, after correcting my obscurity poem and tidying my desk." Two days later I wrote: "Starting six major new poems. The first on Ricks. Language and symbol. To the verbalist, language has a social reality only. But to the mystic, language is a model that communicates Reality, and symbols express visible spiritual Truths, the invisible as the visible. Ricks's loss of the spiritual or metaphysical dimension means that for him symbolism is a question of material analogy, one thing in terms of another, not revealing the One. Now I have at last finished (after a fortnight's polishing) *The Obscure Symbolist's Apple Tree*, I am all set for putting down these six....I am now doing those poems I wish to preserve. Strict metre and clarity of image." I wrote: "On Ricks (a poem). I admire his verbal qualities but debunk his social side, offering instead a creator's view of language and symbolism. It is about critics and creators....I have alienated all: Movement by being too metaphysical, Raine by being too rational-contemplative. I have to journey alone. The modern Metaphysical poem must be ruminative. The old certainties (soul, e.g.) have to be re-established, whereas Donne, taking these for granted, could be immediate and momentary."

I healed Matthew again: "Dec 23. Matthew has been 102.5 for 4 days. I healed him at 6.30, and by 8.30 his temperature had dropped to under 97 – 6 degrees. Eight surges went into his stomach, a double dose. A dramatic drop."

A MYSTIC WAY

I now felt I was becoming a true artist: "Now, for the first time in my life, I am a true artist and craftsman, more so than many fake poetic craftsmen who could not knock a table together with legs of equal length. Journalism: the world of the senses, social reality. My forte is for the invisible, spiritual Reality, and so I had to opt out of journalism, which would have stifled me....I...am a true artist again – enriched with suffering." I wrote of: "Language and symbolism, which I am trying to catch in my Ricks poem. I want a symbol for a symbol! A language for language! To such a pass have things come, but I must make clear that there are two models. Reality is layered, language is capable of approaching each layer, including the topmost spiritual layer, whose Truths come down as symbols. Language is also social interaction and its symbols have social connotations. It depends on your view of Reality – and this is what I must make clear. Reality sends pictures from the spiritual dimension which are framed in language – or painted in words. Language is the paint, the symbol in the picture, and the Reality can be spiritual, psychological, or physical – or divine (the 4 worlds of the Kabbalah). Imagination, as a result of empiricism and science, came to mean illusory and unreal inner world, in relation to reason and sense-perception. Imagination used to be a cognitive value, the world of the soul, a real world of images which bridges spirit and matter, senses and intellect, mind and body – hence the tree. Blake: 'The Imaginative Image returns by the seed of Contemplative Thought' – a special way of seeing. Restore the imagination....The imagination or image-making faculty – image-seeing faculty – of the soul perceives symbols which contain truths for the spiritual world." I wrote: "If I had to describe my metaphysics, I would say they are Christian Kabbalist as well as Existential-Mystic." And again: "Ricks: 'I have never found Coleridge's distinction between imagination and fancy particularly helpful' – because to the social, rational conversationalist, imagination and fancy are one; whereas to the metaphysician, the imagination is a cognitive function of the soul, whereas fancy is decorative metaphorical power....I totally reject socio-linguistics. Ideas manifest into forms, innate ideas manifest into language which bears symbols as a tree bears fruit from the Idea of fruit. My pioneering among symbols. I have single-handedly rediscovered the imaginative symbol (as opposed to the fanciful metaphor). Fancy is a matter of memory and association, like much of my earlier work, which I now reject; I have had to find the way back from fancy to the imaginative-visionary symbol – and to the Light."

And yet again: "Symbolism and the Light I have not quite got to yet, though symbols (visionary images) come mixed with the Light from the spiritual world, which is why Margaret can attribute spirituality to a received image of St. Teresa. The inner development which the New Age 'Trevelyanism' made possible has almost totally separated me from Tuohy and the 'social' sceptical vision. After 15 years of tolerance of Tuohy, I am approaching a widening of intellectual point of view. He is a sociologist and a positivist. My own view of the world is crystallising as I dreamt and prayed it would back in the dark days of 1970. It has taken me longer because my development has been farther. I am a symbolist....My job is to receive and channel symbols for the Light." On December 24th I spent "all

356

day – in spite of a heavy cold – on my Ricks poem."

On Christmas Eve I went to church at All Saints', Tooting Graveney, and recorded observations that would lead to *Firethorn*: "Christianity as a rebellion against materialism. If symbols from the spiritual world are received by the imagination, then Margaret's St. Teresa is a spiritual symbol which contains the Truth of the Light, and all prayers to saints are openings of oneself to a higher world: Christian Kabbalism and the great Chain of Being, the Elizabethan Kabbalistic idea which is found in Donne and Marvell, and which activates the imagination. Go into this. Christianity is a rebellion against materialism and Western society, a renewing of contact with the angels and brotherhood, and a uniting of spiritual and material as the priest is impersonal, depersonalised by the descent of the Holy Spirit from above. I am very close to Christianity – symbolism has brought me there. One more work will see me as a Christian Kabbalist. Christ as a symbol from the spiritual world, a symbol of the Light: an ideal which contains Truth. That Pole: 'The most intelligent people are Catholics.' Because they see meaning in an invisible world of Ideas.'"

I added: "The view of Capra that our scientific methods lead to a science with spiritual dimensions. The view of Schwaller de Lubicz that the scientific vocabulary is analytic, whereas the symbolic is a mentality or state of mind totally different from the rational one. The symbolising faculty of human intelligence can, through symbolism (a mode of expression), be the way of overcoming the limitations of reason; and 'the symbol is the most perfect means for esoteric transmission'." I went on: "God manifesting into lower worlds. Perhaps I rejected the New Age too summarily? The New Age movement will not last, but the concept of a New Age will. I am an esoteric Christian. A Christian in the esoteric, Kabbalistic sense only. My attitude is close to Kathleen Raine's. The New Age concept is valid – cf Blake – but the Findhorn approach is commercial, phoney and too instant....*Firethorn* is taking me to faith. It is taking me back to the visions I had in 1971, and helping me to relate them to the Tree of Life and the Four worlds. The divine one is a world of Light. The spiritual one is a world of images, which the imagination can see as it flies like a bird. Faith is relating one's own interior experience to a coherent system one can check out for oneself." I wrote: "The poet receives the symbol from the spiritual world and beams or channels it into the material world. His is therefore a holy occupation, and Movement poetry has abdicated this holy function in favour of an enfeebled secular frisson, a pleasurable massage of the spine." And of influxes: "Divine influx – into the soul – but as the lightning flash. Ricks poem. I am contrasting social language and symbol (in terms of a tree) – like nursery-grown and spiritually- or divine-grown symbol and language (in that order), like forces, sap, hidden life force. I must let the divine mind fill me when I write. Always begin with contemplation. Be a channel for it. I must say, 'O God, I am a channel for your words, I am egoless, please send your spiritual power into me and give me images and words, and correct rhymes.'"

"What is the spiritual world?" I asked. "Clearly it is full of spirits – it is where we go when we die, and where we come from. Therefore it is a Heaven. There are different heavens, but heavens are where departed spirits are, and therefore where they can be contacted....Spirits can be contacted and can heal."

On Boxing Day we visited Loughton and I wrote: "Visited the church in the forest. The stile with stone steps. I am a symbolist now, and cannot help myself."

Once again I suffered from an acute cold: "To the doctor who has filled me with antibiotic (septrin) and (given me) a nasal drier and a spray for two weeks to throw off my persistent nagging ill health." I returned to hear that my younger brother's wife had lost her baby. She had been admitted to hospital in labour but the cord had wound round the little boy's neck. Margaret came and gave her view: "That little boy is now an angel in Heaven. We all have our guardian angels. Accept. Not 'I want this poem to be alive.'" Margaret spoke to me about the spirit: "Margaret on the spirit. 'We always have it, once it has been received. It is like a flame.' The spiritual world is also Heaven, with spirits which have souls. God sits on high, surrounded by Jesus (on his right) and Mary (on his left) and all his angels and spirits (the spirits of the dead)....'The spirit is not like a glass ball you take out and put in your pocket, it is always with you – the Light....Don't say "I want it, Jesus, I want to know about Heaven so I can write it down."'"

I was still contemplating the relationship between idea and language: "The hawk seeks images and symbols....The Idea comes down separately from language: word-choice involves hunting for the right word. I am a Platonist over language, and reject socio-linguistics. I sit in Beauty (the Self) and receive symbols and images which I put into my poems. Novels are about Foundation (the ego). So I am more of a poet than a novelist." Again: "Symbols...are communications from the divine world, influxes, received wisdom; for the divine seeks the human, symbols come down. A sunshaft illuminating and divinising a priest. A symbol divinises the spirit; the part of ourselves which is spirit and which receives the Holy Spirit or Light. This for *Firethorn*. Margaret: 'Why have you not been and asked a Catholic?' The communications: compare letters. The eternal divine and spiritual worlds communicate in letters that are hieroglyphs. Therefore, what is being communicated, and by whom? Our guardian angels? No, from God. Like the coded messages sent from German HQ to Field Generals. The shield of God. So in art, a symbol or coded message from God will be more resonant than a picture of the lower world. It teaches us about our destiny."

I added: "It is difficult to communicate the magnetic effect on the mind that Margaret has. She excites the mind so that it becomes superconscious." Again: "She wants me to become a Catholic, and dismisses symbolism, saying the spiritual is meaningless without the religious, which I disagree with: 'Michelangelo and those others had a profound religious feeling, which they expressed.'...Margaret: 'I saw Christ by the altar in the church at St. Ives on the Feast of St. Teresa, and at Shoreham I saw the host shine like a candle.' Miracles?"

I wrote of Margaret's magnetism: "Today I am electric. I received a shock when I touched the radiator, and Ann heard the crackle, and then, when I put my two forefingers to her temple she leapt back because she had received an electric shock on either side of her forehead. 'It's static electricity,' she said, but I feel full of healing powers."

I wrote of my painting: "My painting over the fire in browns. A causeway of light – a direction – and a hint of a sun breaking through clouds. It must be a symbol for the Light. It is not just a picture of the sea." And I wrote of my tussle between art and religion: "Margaret and the Light on the priest or bishop, which my Protestant mind finds hard to accept. My scepticism about her vision of an objective Christ and of light from the host. I will settle for illumination within the mind but not for actual miracles outside it. Margaret's path to sainthood regards art as incidental. For me, art is the Way. I am an artist before I am a saint. Margaret understands visions but not symbols." I wrote: "Margaret: 'Don't analyse or list – feel it with your heart.' 'You're three quarters of the way there, you must have the whole – God.' She wants me to be a Catholic, not realising that it is symbols in my work that count rather than a perfect life."

At the end of December I drafted *Firethorn* "on Christ as a symbol, symbols being messages from God, and the dead being involved in the living. A vision of Heaven." On December 31st I wrote: "Finished the Ricks poem; not quite to my satisfaction, though it is a step forward. Ricks grafted my imagination onto the mystical branch till I could plant it, and it bore fruit by receiving form from the Ideas." Taking stock of the year I wrote: "I have developed poetically, seeing myself as a Metaphysical following, or rather before but because of, my visit to Ricks."

The Tree of Imagination, started on Christmas Eve, began six creative weeks in which I wrote *Firethorn*, *The Temple-Dancer's Temple-Sleep*, *A Metaphysical's Light Mandala* and *The Fire-Flower* between Christmas 1979 and February 1980. This was achieved despite, or possibly as a result of tensions set up by, colossal distractions at school.

In early January 1980 I was pondering aspects of the Kabbalah in my *Diaries*, and opened the way to *Firethorn* with this entry: "Symbols – I have got it! The truth I have been groping towards since Graham 'became' a symbol at midnight mass on Christmas Eve has surfaced. Symbols are in the collective unconscious – ocean of Light or mind of God – that is all around us, and which flows into us....Just as I channel healing powers..., so the poet channels symbols from outside. It is a blinkered psychological heresy that symbols exist only in the mind. They flow into the mind from the collective unconscious, and filter their universal qualities into the individual...recipient....The symbols raise consciousness, transform it into a higher form. Originally one of the purposes of religion was to channel the wisdom-giving Light and its messages, which are contained in symbols, which come in strings....I am...a channel for the unconscious – interpreting for the reader. Symbols always appear in clusters....Nature is a symbol that points to metaphysical truths (Guénon) – and that is the essential function of symbolism. So symbols and the language of image and emotion reveal transcendent truths external to man, i.e. the cosmic order in which everything corresponds and everything is related....Symbolic analogy demonstrates the unity of the universe....In my work, I am a symbolist, a restater of the one Idea behind all the forms, an Idea that is Light and Fire, which expresses its wisdom in symbols that emphasise the oneness of creation. This metaphysical Idea which co-ordinates the forms and controls the unconscious is God. God, the Idea behind all the forms." And again: "Symbols can exist without human consciousness for they are cosmic and come from the spiritual world....They have a multivalency of meanings, each being analogous on a different level of reality....The poet is a medium for symbols."

With such a view of symbolism I reflected on my visit to church, a "timeless catacomb" in which symbols flow into the soul "and when admitted, give visions which can be prayed to, or opened to, and which are messages from God, which come down as Fire, which is behind all forms". I integrated my view of the Mystic Way: "The cloud of unknowing hides the sun but admits symbols from its haze or mist, and the one Fire consumes the multiplicity of thorns and forms and unifies." In my note for *Firethorn* I wrote: "God descends as Fire down four worlds and can be returned to by making the many One, i.e. God is Fire, the one Idea behind the many forms, and symbols reveal One: Christ is a symbol which reveals the One – God – to us, and symbolises the Fire we already have and stands for it, and symbolises the fact that the One needs the many to see the meaning of life through." Firethorn was Christ, the One consumer of multiplicity.

In mid-January my mother had heart failure. She woke up short of breath as if she had asthma, her lungs full of fluid. I visited her at Journey's End the next day, and found her in the room in which my father died, sitting up in bed very rosy-cheeked. She revealed to Ann that she had had angina for two years and had kept it from Argie: that her attempt to sell Journey's End, the family house of 35 years, and move, which would shortly happen, was motivated by the desire to live on the ground floor and avoid stairs. She later rang to say the ECG had confirmed that she had had a heart attack, and that she had shed some of her violin pupils and the schools where she taught the violin.

At school there had been a succession of incidents in which our overstressed and overworked Head had irritably confronted members of the staff and exhibited bad temper. She had shouted at the nun ("Read the bulletin"), and the nun had been too Christian to do anything except retreat backwards, apologising. Most Heads of Department had been confronted, and there was resentment. The school had become a place of stress, and someone had to speak out. At a Heads of Department meeting the Head asked what was to prevent us from becoming an excellent school, and someone asked, "Why are we so demoralised?" I then spoke. My *Diaries* record: "I told them. For 5 minutes: there is too little stillness and tranquillity, too little friendliness, too much 'professional' criticism which boomerangs karmically, too little of the relaxed attitude, too many meetings which are enervating, too little refreshed spirit which can chat in the staff room and the Head must create conditions in which there is more trust. On the way out, in rain, Hopper, Head of Geography said, 'Your speech was so brilliant, it said everything I was going to say but you articulated and formulated it better than I could, so that basically there wasn't anything left to say afterwards.'"

NIGHT OF UNKNOWING

I had felt impelled by the Light to speak out and I knew I would be singled out. Two days later I was given the full time Coverage, which had hitherto been the two Deputy Heads' job. In other words, I had to be in early and write out the list of substitutions for absent teachers, which, in such a large school, sometimes meant filling in 150 slots for periods with the names of teachers who had spare time, the most unpopular job in the school. Each morning 25 copies of the Coverage sheet were posted in different parts of the school and 110 staff looked to see how many of their free periods had been taken and complained that they had been picked on unfairly. I countered by saying that I could only perform a limited service as Head of Department because I was doing the Deputy Heads' work as well. In my *Diaries* I wrote that I thought the Head had had me executed in a former life.

That weekend I wrote *The Temple-Dancer's Temple-Sleep*. I wrote: "Jan 27, Sunday. Finished *The Temple-Dancer's Temple-Sleep* around 12.45 p.m., having done it since yesterday morning (late). Went downstairs to make coffee, touched Ann who jumped and said, 'You've given me a shock.' I am so electric after typing it up that I crackle when people touch me." In the afternoon I wrote: "1.45. I feel so well – filled with the unconscious, like a tide in a harbour after the 'emptiness' of the week. This is what Sunday church used to achieve."

Two days later I had a profound experience of the Light and finished another poem. I wrote: "Jan 29. 9 p.m., nearly. A 'brainstorm', and stanzas 4-11 of *The Metaphysical's Light-Mandala* wrote themselves. Around 6.45 I looked for the Light....I sat with the light out and felt the surges coming into me, and my quickening heart – all the healing symptoms – while I put my hands over my eyes and looked for the Light in a kind of trance. And it was there: silver in water, as fire, as rose, as reflected moon, all the elements, but when Fire, full of hints of the face of God. My reception of the Holy Spirit as Light was just the same as my reception of the healing power, which is there the Holy Spirit....To see the Light is to be able to heal. The same loving frame of mind adores and heals. Now I am tired, drained, a little shaky from the massive discharge of energy. My body is silky-smooth with Light." I finished the poem next weekend.

We had a Japanese tenant, Kyoko Sato, who took the top floor over from the Hong Kong tenants. She was studying drama, and I used to go up and discuss the Japanese "yugen" (the Flower), an unparaphrasable glimpse of reality, a hint of "what lies beneath the surface", and she gave me a fan as a present. It was covered with wispy clouds, foaming waves and flickering fire (Taoistic Oneness), but also with a mesh of chains suggesting atoms and social organisation. The fan was to be held by a Noh dancer, and on her return to Japan Kyoko became one of Japan's better known Noh dancers. The fan lay on a shelf, unlooked at, and one day an art teacher, who had got to know me through my new Coverage job, asked if I had a Japanese male fan she could paint. I took it out and looked at it and saw I had another poem. I took it to school for her, and wrote: "Miss Selbie, agent of Providence, asking me to look at the fan. I am cleaning up Garratt Green and in return Providence has given me an angel, ageing Miss Selbie, to give me a poem." I wrote the poem on February 5th, 9th and 10th about the

361

"yugen" or Zen flower of Noh, which I saw as the Light, whose dawning is received with a satisfied Ahhhhh!" I wrote: "Feb 10. Am tired for I have spent the weekend polishing, rewriting and typing up *A Fan of Swirling Tao, the Fire-Flower*, which culminates *Firethorn* – from thorn to flower. It is 11 stanzas long, was drafted on Feb 5 and not touched until Feb 9. I spent all day and yesterday on it, and was really tired after typing up 5 stanzas. I started early on the remainder this morning and finished it before lunch at 1.40, but had to type from 2.45 to 3.15. Then after reading the Sunday papers (3.30-5.00) and having my bath and giving the two boys their bath, I polished further, and am now leaving it at 8.45." I added: "I have written 5 great poems since Christmas: *The Tree of Imagination*, *Firethorn* (itself), *The Temple-Dancer's Temple-Sleep*, *A Metaphysical's Light-Mandala*, and now *A Fan of Swirling Tao* (later called *The Fire-Flower*) – all in a spell of six weeks. January and February 1980 are for me what May 1819 was to Keats, when he wrote those Odes. I am tired, but pleased." And with the cockiness of an enterprise successfully completed: "Jan-Feb 1980, the most significant time for English poetry since May 1819."

But now I was "deliberately about to fold myself down like a radio station in a hostile country". The hostile country was of course the school. There was a Senior Teachers' meeting with the Head and two Deputies in which I urged the Head "to improve the vibrations in the school". I said: "Professional courtesy is very important, and the senior six don't shout at each other." I advocated being in harmony with the Tao. I wrote: "I am taking the disharmony of the school into my soul and am purging it to leave the school tranquil and whole, healed. I must be a harmony-monitor, a referee of harmony. I shall blow my whistle and cry 'Disharmony' if the vibrations in the school are spoiled. If I can bring a healthy atmosphere into this school, I will have done a good job as a Senior Teacher. Someone has to start. My life and my poetry are now becoming aspects of each other: the obverse and reverse that are the same. The yin and yang, action and reflection."

I put together 16 poems into a group I called *The Fire-Flower*, and recorded that I was now in "the Classical phase I dreamt of in Japan": "The angels have given it to me as a reward for cleaning up the institution, perhaps. Certainly they wrote it for me, then – and only then – allowed me to consider the whole work. I finished all 16 poems before I thought they were a work by themselves – and yet I did not have to change the order of one poem, they had written themselves and formed themselves into a cumulative, progressing whole. I am directed by the angels these days."

10.

GROWING METAPHYSICAL AND BAROQUE VISION:
OAKLANDS AND PUBLISHING/HEROES OF THE WEST
1980 – 1986

I now felt that all my poetry works needed to be overhauled so that many of them were written in strict pentameters. I wrote ruefully: "I have worked myself almost to death, and now see how to begin – what I could not see at 19. It has taken me 20 years to learn how to write poetry, but now I know, I can be a world-beater." And so on February 16th 1980 I began my revisions. Over half term I revised *A Metaphysical in Marvell's Garden* and *A Crocus in the Churchyard* – in other words, put them through a second version which was more related to the soul and eternity than their first version – and then we went to Worthing: "Wind, sun, sunlight on the water by the pier, gulls hindward hovering, flying into the wind, great foam as the breakers crashed on stones, wagtails, red notices warning against the danger of picking up containers (pollution of Athena B) and at the far end, the gabled tops of the boarding houses. I struggled up and down the promenade in my sheepskin coat." We looked in on Margaret's "cosy desert cave, with a coal fire" and she propped her painting of Teresa on a chair. I wrote: "The white flecks in Teresa's round blue eyes – white flecks of light."

I now worked on *Fire-Void*, which showed eternity as a Buddhist void that is in fact a fullness, an Empyrean out of which emerge the beauty and symmetry of a hill which can appear a chaotic rubbish dump. I then worked on *Sea-Fire*, in the course of which Ann's car (formerly her father's Escort) was stolen from outside our front gate. I broke off to telephone the police, who flagged the car down ten minutes later, and Ann, returning twins she had given private tuition, happened to pass in my car, stopped and said, "It's my car." I moved on to *A Mystic Fire-Potter's Red Sun-Halo*, in which the Light of the "Sun" flows into the soul and the heart, and then to *An Aesthete's 'Golden' Artefacts*, which is about Parnassian aestheticism (such as Gautier's) and the artist's development to a "gold" soul in terms of eternity. (In this I drew on a visit I made to the goldsmiths of Hatton Garden.)

I felt my school, Garratt Green, had the disciplinary effect of a monastery: "It took me 20 years to accept the discipline of the Rule....Where some men would have sought a monastery, I sought the discipline of the tannoy in a large school, where a different kind of silence, and self-abnegation, was possible. No one there knows I am a poet, not one soul of the 110 teachers there. This is my penance and sacrifice: to hide my true profession, as Hopkins denied his for 7 years, in the name of discipline. I have disciplined myself and can now write within the rules." I knew that I needed to be disciplined to develop as a poet, and that I was subjecting myself to it in the penance imposed by an overstressed Head as a context for my "mental travelling". I felt I was getting somewhere as a poet. I wrote: "I had difficulty in understanding myself as a poet until I went back to Ricks and defined myself as a Metaphysical." I added: "I am like a well, water (light) comes up from underground into me, energy comes into my heart (as love) and fingers when I go deep into the unconscious as in a trance and receive images (water which reflects overhanging leaves)....It goes Sun-spirit-soul-heart."

In March I pondered my aesthetic and related it to language. I said at a Heads of Department meeting on "What is language?" that "language creates pictures of bits of a layered Reality", and, ignoring the view of one member of my Department that language is "socially conceived perceptions", wrote: "A work of art is language or pictures of a layered Reality that present an object (or symbol) that hints at the Flower (cf the Golden Flower). The Flower – the moment of perfect beauty – captures the moment of white Beauty when the Light or Golden Flower breaks through. A poem hints a Reality. The trouble with post-war poetry is that it largely hints a social reality, whereas Reality is layered and is infinitely more than social." I wrote: "10.20 a.m., Mar 8. Have abandoned myself to the automatic in me and have 'written' – have had dictated to me – four stanzas to write into four different poems,....I have now broken the impasse with my aesthetic." And of the garden I recorded: "Buds like green raindrops. The one Reality is dripping into form." A few days later I wrote, aware that I was rejecting Tuohy's aesthetic: "Counter the propositional view of art – 'a work of art is an assertion or statement' – with the image view: 'a work of art is an image of a revealed Reality', to be understood if recognised. The response to a complex work of art depends on the Reality-experience of the responder, or on how he imagines the Reality is if he has never been there."

I now grasped that the soul is "dynamic, not static": "It is a centre of perception, a moving focal point of consciousness that is not static like the outer eye. It has its own perspective." In my *Diaries* I pondered on the soul, and saw it as a lock-gate like the lock-gate at Charlestown, between the spiritual and material worlds, between outer and inner harbours.

In March I was still revising my poems and I recorded in my *Diaries*: "Wrote the 'theodolite' stanza into *Crocus*, thereby purging the haunting, surprised image that seized me as I walked with Richard (Moxon, the surgeon) in the churchyard and discussed the death of his surgery-cases a couple of weeks ago on March 8th." I now revised *Clouded-Ground Pond* and wrote: "I am saying that the pond symbolises the self (heart, soul), which is united with Oneness (Tao) so that it is a Tao-Self....The Tao embraces opposites." I recalled my mystical experience by the Worcester College lake: "We return to early mystical experiences and understand them. That Worcester College experience, when I got the letter from my father that agreed (reluctantly) to my giving up Law for English and took it before breakfast to the lake and felt everything suddenly blaze in its reflection as I thought of the future of a lawyer which I was rejecting for a future as a poet – this was Heart mirroring leaves breaking through, briefly to Soul and an apprehension of distant, higher, cloudy worlds. The memory of that experience in the spring of 1959 is now so powerful that I still revisit the lake whenever I can, now 21 years later; just as the memory of the blaze in the Strawberry Hill pond...still takes me back there years afterwards. My heart is in Epping Forest." ("Had I not switched to English at Oxford," I wrote, "I would not know the term 'Metaphysical' – which I am. I would have defined myself totally differently.) On March 23rd I wrote: "Have had a good Sunday morning typing out *Clouded-Ground Pond* and revising *Pear-Ripening House*. At the end the question 'Why be ripe?' lodged itself in my mind. Shakespeare did not explain this in *King Lear* ('ripeness is all') and immediately a stanza welled up and I grabbed paper and wrote out stanza 6, the rhymes virtually perfect, which relates the whole poem to the metaphysical view and contains the idea that pips are future lives. There is somebody aloft helping me at present....Soul has genes which are passed on to the next life." And tongue-in-cheek, brimming with confidence, I wrote: "The coach-party that makes the journey from Pear-Ripening House to Clouded-Ground Pond and onto the Churchyard will learn more about Eternity (if they have my poems with them) than from any other poet who has written in the English tradition, including Blake."

In April there was another Mystics and Scientists conference on the theme of consciousness. I wrote: "A new way of seeing Reality and the universe has been made possible by post-Newtonian physics. Reality is a swirl, there is no distinction between mind and matter, consciousness flows in and 'thinks' us, and the vanguard of the movement is the enlightened poet, for his image comes from a sea of consciousness, the collective unconscious. We are in a new Renaissance." Pir Vilayat Inayat Khan was present, a thin man with a hooked nose and a long wispy beard. I again asked him how the Light flowed into the body. He again said: "Into the chakras at the base of the spine and then upwards." But I still preferred the top-down approach of the spiritual Light-mystics to this sometimes dangerous bottom-up Kundalini and more psychic approach. He took a meditation in which I saw the Light as a collapsing black hole: "Mar 30. In meditation this morning under Pir, saw a collapsing black hole of Light – the answer to two weeks of thought about black holes in a visual image." (I was aware that the universe, including its black holes, was ultimately composed of the Light.) Later I realised: "The 'black hole of Light' I saw in meditation was the Fire-Flower of course, the petals were of white fire. 'The mind of God' Pir said, and I saw it."

I now revised my theory of perception: "The outer eye sees the form, the inner eye of the mind or Self sees into the form for the Idea, sees the oak-tree within the acorn, feels the sap rising. The imagination is the eye of the mind which can see the Eternal world working out at the level of Idea, which is living and real. The reality of the Idea....The Light is in all forms, which reflect it, so it is in all of them." I related this theory to my poetry: "The language of poetry: catch the living Idea and image, and fix it in its outer form (rhyme)." I wrote: "The new Renaissance (of Light and mysticism, united with physics) is the purpose of our time....The artist is the transformer of society."

I now saw the relationship between the part and the whole in a new way: "My body is a wave (particle) in our universe and therefore *is* our universe, just as I am part of the mind of God in transcendence, and therefore *am* God. There is no more 'a part of' only an indivisible unity which is the 'part', for the 'part' is affected by every event in the whole ocean of divine Idea....We particles are waves – light waves – and thus waves in the ocean of being which is God. This is Hallaj's heresy: 'I am God.' But Hallaj was right." And I consciously drew "my literary form in the poems" from "the new physics (no 'I', inter-relationships, living energy, no distinction between observer and observed, a true picture of Reality)". A work of art "should be a dynamic canvas in which there is transience and Eternity at the same time, but perpetual transformation, as from a particle into a wave, from matter into energy".

In April we all visited Journey's End for the last time, and my brothers and I had a ritual game of cricket on the concrete strip at the back. I now revised *Pear-Ripening House*, and besides dwelling on the wants and ambitions of my family I saw the whole universe and its purpose in each seed. I wrote: "I am writing about a change of perspective to the metaphysical, i.e. transformation, and ironically the metaphysical is linked with the physical, as physics is now almost metaphysics." I went on to *Sea-Fire* and wrote: "Inner and outer space are one, the mind is the universe (since the transcendental self is the universe)....Mind and the source of the universe are one (hence harmony of soul and macrocosm)." I wrote of "the divine dark" as "a kind of unus mundus which is approached through the mind".

I now vowed to research into science and wrote: "I have ransacked physics and modern science to good creative effect, whereas my fellow artists (except for Durrell) have shunned them: hence Snow's *Two Cultures*. Man lives in a universe before he lives in a society, as I told Tuohy in 1965 as I walked him down to a taxi from Kohinata Suido-cho to Edogawa-bashi (between the high walls) and he replied 'Can one have a relationship with a star?' Though significantly, he never wrote another novel." My scientific view led me to consider reincarnation again: "As existence forms, dissolves, reforms so do we. We form into the body, will dissolve, and reform again, as we have done already so many times. I shall live in the 22nd century, and may read these words if they are published in a *Collected Diaries*."

Feeling at one with Nature, I noticed I attracted living creatures: "The garden is full of birds – blue tits, thrushes, sparrows, pigeons. No other garden within eye-view has one bird in it, yet my mown lawn and bread on the bird-table has been repaid by a host of birds pecking among the flower-beds and generally coming to say 'hello' – like my 45 fish when I go to feed them. I am in harmony with all Nature, and birds, fish and children come and talk to me."

I wrote an essay on the Metaphysical Revolution, and through April worked on at the poems in *The Fire-Flower* while outside were "sounds of summer", "blackbirds piping in trees, sparrows chattering, planes echoing". I was so hard up I could not see how I would get my car through its MoT, but then the British Council sent me a Turkish tenant who paid a deposit, and I could relax again. I was still revising *Firethorn* at the beginning of May and finding I was solving the problems I encountered in all my poems I wrote: "When I went to Garratt Green I was all lyric brevity, and had not the toughness and 'thinking-throughness' that I needed to state and bring off a major poetic theme. Six years of pursuing threads of essays have been a good discipline, and I now work a central idea to its conclusion with considerable felicity. Garratt Green has been the teaching-school for my soul: a mystery school that no one would at first glance recognise as such, considering its townie vulgar girls and modern urban setting. Garratt Green has been my mystery school, where, instead of making the tea for a Zen Master, I followed the irrational wishes of a zany Headmistress."

On May 5th I wrote: "Am a bit tired, having checked and typed out 3 poems in the last 2 days. Now *The Fire-Flower*." Then: "Switched on the TV and caught one of the images of our time live, 4 SAS gasmasked men storming the Iranian Embassy from a balcony, having blown the front out in a cloud of smoke. The excitement about the hostages for the next two hours. We spectators, involved through TV, experiencing it live." I worked on, writing about the "rose-tree of Light" which I used in *A Metaphysical in Marvell's Garden*, and then spent a day moving my mother from Journey's End to her new, smaller house at 54 High Road. Not long afterwards I wrote: "I sit looking down on this old vicarage garden. Roses pour up at me, yellow, pink and red, and it seems so natural that I should be writing of a flowered soul as a rose."

The day before my birthday I wrote: "Eve of my birthday and am so cluttered with school work (for my staff meeting tomorrow) and car trouble that I have not been able to touch any poems all day. Taught *The Waste Land* again to a sceptical Lower 6th and thought again what an over-rated work it is. It rings very hollow in places, e.g. the fishermen lounging at noon – 'couldn't they just be having lunch?' The symbolic people are too symbolic and don't represent what Eliot wants them to represent. The typist and clerk passage is good but as passion rather than indifference, and there is a horror of sex in the poem which is all wrong. Eliot the warped and twisted mystic here....The objection to *The Waste Land*: it isn't like that! (E.g. sex is good.) Eliot is only a partially great mystic." By the end of May (having briefly been to Worthing on a hot day and having returned with a red face) I wrote: "Found that 'meta' of 'metaphysics' can mean 'behind' as well as 'after' – and am now able to defend the term Metaphysical Revolution. I am ready to assume Eliot's mantle. I am at heart a metaphysician – but an existential one, not a speculative one. The poet, not the philosopher, takes the whole view."

In early June I had finished *A Metaphysical in Marvell's Garden* and observed: "I have 16 poems of the length of Larkin's best-known two, *Church Going* and *The Whitsun Weddings*, both of which have social themes." I recorded: "I charted the mystical tradition of the Light...and have now put it with modern physics and transpersonal psychology into a Metaphysical Revolution. My next work must give the model for this Metaphysical Reality, i.e. include physics – and biology – and psychology." This entry anticipated *The Universe and the Light*.

About this time I discovered I was able to hypnotise my children. I used hypnotism to put them to sleep each evening: "My additional powers include my ability to hypnotise my children to sleep. Two nights running I have taken Matthew down the (imaginary) flight of stairs, and on the bottom stair he has slumped into sleep, and I have touched Anthony on his head 3 times, and each time he has got more sleepy until he is off."

Of my work I wrote: "I am a Reality-penetrater not an entertainer....If one word sums up my poetic technique that word is 'layering'."

In June the idea of buying a school returned. I saw an advertisement for a small school in Cranleigh, Surrey in the Times Educational Supplement. It was going with a 5 bedroom house, and I took Ann to see it and felt that a school was ahead. An estate agent I knew came round and offered to sell our house for £50,000 more than I had paid for it, and I wrote: "Now, suddenly I am rich" and "My poetry now needs the freshness of the countryside..., the bees humming among the flowers by the orchard. I have exhausted town images (like the climbing rose), and need to restock from the countryside." On a second visit I wrote: "In the heart of lovely countryside: Cranleigh. Winding roads, cows, sheep, farms, foxgloves growing wild, a flower-watcher's paradise, and deeper countryside than Cornwall."

I was overworking: "June 22nd. A day of little progress. After re-drafting the end of *The Bride of Time* yesterday, all day, in great exhaustion, awoke unwell and by 10 a.m. had a migraine, my first since I was 14 or so. Had blotches in front of my eyes. It was the stress of last week – the timetable – and, of course, these poems on top, which take their toll. Stayed in bed all morning and made corrections to *Bride of Time* in a near-blind condition."

I was convinced that the Metaphysical Revolution is ahead: "The Metaphysical Revolution is the revolution of our time, a European revolution which will take people from the social (Movement) to the metaphysical. I am guided into bringing it in, having been appointed an agent of the divine; I am an instrument for the angels, having been spotted at New Age functions and been given responsibility. Yet in a sense I have always been chosen for this. I had to find an indifferent superstructure, and on this I have been guided to write metaphysical lines."

In early July on the day I finished revising *The Fire-Flower* I had a vision: "Saw a wonderful, elaborate blue light 6 inches x 4 inches (down), with sparkling 'beads' across it, a beautiful vision, a heavenly vision, as I lay totally relaxed." I do not know whether the beads symbolised the poems. A couple of days later I wrote: "I am tired from 10 months of work on the 16 poems, and the Metaphysical Revolution." Shortly afterwards I wrote: "I was full of conflict between the soul (which I knew to be right) and modern 'social' ideas – until the Light shone and burned the conflict away and unified me." And I thought of Rilke: "The closest parallel to *The Fire-Flower* is *The Duino Elegies*, for Rilke wrote: 'We are the bees of the Invisible....The Angel of the Elegies is the creature in whom that transformation of the visible into the invisible we are performing already appears completed.'" And: "My journey has been from the anti-metaphysical to the metaphysical....All my works should at the end of my life add up to one unified statement of a metaphysical nature."

In the second half of 1980 there was a growth in my metaphysical outlook.

METAPHYSICAL AND BAROQUE

I had had 46 Ritherdon Road painted. Little Anthony went into hospital to have his adenoids out and a grommet installed in his ear ("will they wash my hair?" he asked). I was short of money again, but our Turkish tenant decided to stay an extra month, and then had two friends in for a fortnight while we were away. I wrote: "Life is sending me what I need." There was an offer for 46 Ritherdon Road, but it was not enough to buy the Cranleigh school, or a school in Kent I had seen.

We went down to Cornwall towards the end of July and I typed up material for a future saga to be called *The Clay and the Sea*. We went to Porthleven, and Wheal Martin china clay mine, and a fête at Caerhays Castle which the actor Edward Fox attended. We went to the Gweek seal sanctuary and Gunwalloe, with its 13th century church on the beach, and I wrote of "beautiful country hedges full of wild flowers and butterflies and birds" and "slugs on the grass, Cornish mists, damp". We went to Plymouth and visited Mount Edgcumbe and Cotehele and went up Smeaton's Tower on the Hoe. There was very little sun that year and I returned from Cornwall still looking for sun and wrote:"Sunbathed in the only patch of sun, under our pear tree. A bird – a speckled thrush – was pecking at pears, and I thought that my image of pears falling round a poet's head, i.e. images, could have been developed: they were dislodged by the bird (thrush) of the soul which, hawk-like flew into the boughs. I was lying on my front on my sun-couch, and at that moment in my musings there was a 'spat' on the canvas by the back of my leg, and turning I saw that the confounded thrush had shat on me. So did the 'real' world (i.e. the unreal physical world) comment on my symbolic imaginings. I do not think the comment invalidates my high symbols."

I was aware that I was attracting events. First a possible purchaser came to view our house, and it turned out he knew Adrian Hohler from Japan who was now a director of an American bank and living in a house in Fulham. Then: "More evidence of our ability to attract other people to us. Yesterday I discussed my cousin's 21st present with Ann, and in the evening Rob rang about it. Then today I discussed (a) Swedish au pair (who had wanted English lessons) with Ann and immediately afterwards the 'mother' of the house rang up to see if we could help with English grammar, not having been in touch for over a month. There is a whole atmospheric web, and to shake it at one point brings linked drops of dew running down the thread where it trembles."

We went out to Essex: "The two ponds, High Beach church, and the village. The duck in the leaping sunlight, in the heart of the light on the brown pond, the dragonfly." Soon afterwards, I suffered chest pains: "Sep 19. Chest pains began at 8.20 and by 9.15 I was at St. James's (Hospital) thinking I might die of a heart attack: feeling giddy and faint, being ECG-ed and then X-rayed, being wheeled about the corridors with my feet over the end of the trolley, in my white 'paper' short-sleeved gown, the suction marks of the electrodes on my body. In fact, despite the feeling I might die – Matthew 'I hope you don't die' – I have a lung infection which is causing the pain and have to breathe deeply. At the hospital, believing I was dying, I joked and behaved like a 'laughing Buddha', as I sought to detach myself from my surroundings and give myself to the Light. I was near death, I felt

369

death approach, and I rebuffed him with wit and humour, which He cannot stand. I also went to the Light, like a Tibetan."

I now reconsidered the stress of Cranleigh and wrote: "It is peace I need now. (Bees humming in the flowers while I write.)...This afternoon I asked for guidance again, went to the Light, and the message seemed to be coming through: the Metaphysical Revolution." Soon afterwards I "tubed into town, went to Watkins and bought Bohm's *Wholeness and the Implicate Order*, which they kept for me, and was startled to read confirmation of an idea I have been groping towards: the whole basis of language fails to reflect reality, it fragments reality and distorts philosophic thought with its 'I-you', subject-verb-object structure."I went to a recital at Christ Church, Streatham (the church of the Harding branch of my family, where my father had sung) and regarded the "music as a soul-releaser, as it used to be, rather than as a language to be listened to with the mind". I "wondered again how Providence works, and saw it as a mind of Light, operating like a sea, a great Spirit which manifests into us and endeavours to fulfil its will through us while other forces hinder us".

I was now back in philosophy and wrote: "I am a process philosopher who is developing the metaphysics of Bergson, Whitehead and Heidegger. I make that trio into a quartet, and add the dimension of the Light. Also Bohm, who adds to their work. My revelatory metaphysics are an existentialism. For when the Light has been revealed, it is seen that all existence is in fact an emanation from the Light, and failure to see this has led to dread, anxiety etc, the so-called 'existentialist' malaise....I am with half of me a philosopher, with an original contribution, and must unfold the metaphysics of light, proving that Being is Light....This evening I have been pondering Bergson, Whitehead, Heidegger and Husserl..., and I see where each of them went wrong, I am not just the equal of them but feel superior to them. This is the first time I have felt this among the philosophers. My growth has surprised even me....I am a living testifier to the principle of the growth of a mind through soul and spirit." Later I wrote: "I already have my method in my philosophy. Now I need to write as a metaphysician, not as a New Ager or trend-spotter, but as a cosmologist and ontologist who looks at psychism in the course of stating a total world view."

We celebrated Matthew's sixth birthday with a party for 29 which was notable because Lawrence (a boy in his class) "wrecked the garden and broke the cricket bat and took the wheel off the tricycle and bent the whirligig for clothes and was frequently ordered out of the room where films were shown".

In October I noticed: "The mystery of the pears. Since July the pear tree has been dropping a few pears each day: four or five, at the most six, never less than four. I pick them up each morning: the tree is too large to climb, I have no ladder, and besides it has been full of wasps. Four or five a day, by staggering its dropping, the pear tree is almost trying to keep us provided. No matter what wind or storm, no more than six pears come down a day, and now, in October, it is still dropping. Trees co-operate with the divine scheme to provide wasps, birds and humans with fruit."

My mother celebrated her 70th birthday at my brother Robert's home. The family gathered. I had a discussion with my two brothers, who were very much in favour of Mrs. Thatcher's privatisation. "I: 'Economic theories aside, what about the people, the unemployed: money should serve people and not be their masters.' My vision of a unitary European state with one currency, leading to world government which will hold wars in check, and be a part of the disintegration of Western civilisation; and our future can be optimistic in that."

The following week I went to Dartford to attend a course on "the English Department in the 1980s" for a few days. About 30 actual and would-be Heads of Department stayed at Thames Polytechnic, and during the day there were long sessions which went on into the evening, after which we were free. It was typical of me at this time that I went to my room and sat at my desk and pored over the *Encyclopaedia Britannica* entry for "Metaphysics". I thought about metaphysics when I woke up and whenever I could escape the course. I wrote: "14 Oct. A day at my typewriter on metaphysics, punctuated by visits to the course." The course seemed to be run by Trotskyites who were against all examinations and wanted teachers to take the place of examiners (changes that were implemented with the replacement of 'O' level by GCSE). On the last evening there was a festive end-of-term atmosphere with balloons and paper chains and everyone formed a circle and held hands. I slipped away and finished my research on metaphysics in my room.

When I returned home I wrote of my poetry: "My poetry is phenomenological, because it reflects on how things have meaning and relate to how they appear to me, i.e. it brackets out the interpretation, and reinterprets transcendental phenomena....The aesthetic feeling makes us complete, ennobles and refines us, is linked to the moral and spiritual side, so artists who capture and interpret and communicate beauty also capture 'spiritual' truth which already resides in Nature, the artist uncovering it, a tracery behind the surface of things, a harmony or form in Nature which (through art) enriches our perception – so art enriches our perception of Nature. Beauty is in the realities underlying the surface conditions of life, art interprets the moments we have lived most intensely, which have significance; so the form a work of art assumes is inseparable from what the artist wants to express: everyday meaning, significance beneath the surface – inspiration, style and content are all indivisible in great art. Art outlives what is transitory – that is the test of great art, it survives....Behind the complexity is a unified Reality, which art and language reveal. Language reveals a layered Reality at its most heightened, in art. Otherwise it sticks to the everyday surface without revealing the oneness behind it."

There was a Divisional Heads of English meeting, at which the Trotskyite attitudes were put forward, and I was in a minority of one, opposing the revolutionary changes and speaking out for the retention of 'A' level in the name of preserving standards.

I again asserted the metaphysical: "I have a solution to all the problems that defeated Plato, Spinoza, Descartes and the rest of the philosophers who did not know the Light....The Light is God or a revelation from God, and is the germ from which the form of the universe is a reflection and I must start with this conclusion, based on phenomenology, a description of experiences received in the consciousness, i.e. the evidence of the tradition, what people have said, how they have interpreted it. I must give my evidence for the Light as Being (ontology) which manifests from the Void into life (cosmology). From this I must solve philosophical problems (Plato, Descartes etc, mind and matter not being separate) and proceed to psychology and spirit, theology, and the Four Worlds of the Kabbalah, i.e. include psychics and mystics....My destiny is to reassert the metaphysical in our time."

Ann went into hospital in Wimbledon for a couple of days to have a bone cyst removed, and I looked after the children and nursed Ann when she came out, "sick and dizzy all day", "making meals and drinks for all of them at different times and occasionally sneaking to my study....My Metaphysical Revolution has been launched from domestic chaos."

Matthew had been at the local church school and had left everyone else behind with his reading. He was marking time, waiting for the others to catch up, so I arranged for him to enter Dulwich College Preparatory School. We had a meeting with Mr Woodcock, the Head of the school, and Mrs. Cownie, who was much-feared, and Matthew started in a class of local barristers' and industrialists' sons. Mr Woodcock gave a talk to the parents which we attended, and he attacked the parents' behaviour head on. "You keep them up late, you let them watch too much television, and another thing, let's have no silly waving when you say goodbye to them in the morning." Within a month Matthew was being stretched and writing at length.

In November we visited Loughton and I was still thinking about my poetic work: "Walked in the Forest. Leaves, copper, red and yellow; a brown pond; ducks. On to the church which was in gloom. The angels – the stained glass windows....When order breaks down the poet deals in fragments – an abdication – or builds his own cosmos like Blake; the way to madness. My metaphysical system must not be mad. Rather it will be the prelude to the world of my epic."

I had met Tom Dyer, who was Brain of Britain. I first encountered him when I went into his class, expecting to find his Head of Department, and saw him standing on a chair which was being lapped by a sea of moving girls. "Sit down," I bellowed, restoring order, and he got off the chair and muttered his thanks. He was fairly corpulent, looked at least 50 and had an old face, spectacles and a convict's crew cut, and he wore an old raincoat round the school. I thought he was the gasman at first. In fact he was seeing if he wanted to become a mature student and train as a teacher, and had concluded he was not suited to the teaching profession. Then it was announced in the staff room that he had just become Brain of Britain in the BBC's radio's knock-out competition. After the episode of his class he latched on to me and sat with me at lunch, asking me to test him for some other quiz he was going in for. I would say "Name me six ecclesiastical characters in Chaucer's *Prologue*" and he would rattle them off without hesitation, and when I asked "How do you know that?" he would shrug and say, "I don't know, I just do, the answers float through the air." "Name me Amenhotep IV's family," I said, and when he did that I probed further – and found he believed in a Universal Mind that he was somehow able to plug into, a kind of Collective Unconscious of information all round him which channelled in the answers with unerring accuracy. In spite of this he was unemployable. "I have no imagination," he would say, "I couldn't write a letter or an essay to save my life. I can only be used for retrieving information – in a library, and libraries now have computers."

Tom took to calling at 46 Ritherdon Road on his late-night walk so that I could test him from my *Encyclopaedia Britannicas*. We talked about the universe, and in November I recorded: "My holistic view of the universe, four worlds etc. My reminiscence of Tomlin who wrote *The Approach to Metaphysics* and probably influenced me more than I realised. I have found my way to his vision. Tom: 'Einstein was preparing a unified vision of the universe when he died. For us to understand the universe is like a cat understanding a sermon.'" We used to go out into the street and gaze at the stars, and he would identify each one and tell me all the statistics he knew about each: age, size, composition, special features, and so on.

I was discontented again. "Every day I get breakfast, go to work, come home, wash up, put the children to bed, wash up the evening meal – lose whole hours. What is the solution? How can I find time?" The solution, I decided, was to eat late. And ever since that day I have endeavoured not to eat until 10, so that I could work until then. At this time I had a letter from Caroline saying that her father, the Group Captain, had died, aged 85.

I had been in touch with Jill Purce, the author of *The Mystic Spiral*, about the possibility of my presenting the metaphysical Light in an illustrated Thames and Hudson book, and she invited me to her Hampstead flat. I found a flat of books and trinkets, such as whorled shells, and the beautiful blonde appearance I had seen on television talking about mystical art. Jill signed my copy of her book and said "I want to know where you are coming from. To what school do you belong?" I told her I was independent of all approaches so that I could view all objectively, and that I was an Existentialist who was interested in illumination and enlightenment. "The Age of Enlightenment was a darkness," I said, and she said, "It is ironic that we have had an Age of Enlightenment which was a darkness." She told me she was now in a new arrangement with Thames and Hudson and that she would like to act as my agent, but nothing ever came of this as she married Rupert Sheldrake and held seminars in Tibetan chanting. Before I left she said, "You must always have an interdisciplinary theme," advice I have taken. It left me thinking I should write an intellectual thriller "from illumined man to metaphysical".

Of my search I wrote: "My existential and mystic search for Reality, which began in poetry and finished in prose. It has been a successful search, for I have found the timeless realm beyond space-time, the fourth dimension, from which all creation came....I have searched through different religions and cultures physically (by living in the Middle and Far East), psychologically (by reading about them and studying them), spiritually (by experiencing the Zen meditation-hall, etc), and divinely (by locating the Light). I have a very original existential and mystic view....It is amazing: in my first article in Japan (1963/4) I distinguished the metaphysical from the social....In other words I intuitively knew my destiny in Japan, felt the call of the future."

A MYSTIC WAY

I had turned against the New Age: "I have definitively kicked the New Age. It is the third world and cosmological layer, whereas religion (theology) is the fourth and is superior. The New Age can never be a substitute for Christianity, even though it is more vital, has more energy. Symbols posit metaphysical truths, so metaphysicals must be symbolists."

At Garratt Green the strain was building up again. I was now equipped with a bleeper and was on call like a hospital consultant for any emergency. More and more of my time was being taken. I wrote: "I have so much to do, and such a short time in which to do it. I can overthrow the present Age, but now have to produce the words that will do it. I have spent 20 years getting the ideas that can be used in words, and I have kept my words sharpened and in good condition, ready for this challenge they now have to rise to."

Of my writing I wrote: "I am obsessed by the image of flight,...the Flight to the Sun....When the soul begins to fly, it becomes an angel with wings. The Sun-Hawk is the soul journeying to the sun as a feathered (angelic) bird....I was a physical man in the world of senses and made the journey back towards spirit in Japan, and have since made the journey from spirit to divine to soul, further purging senses and lower spirit, i.e. first the lower soul, then the higher soul. This means that I am now a Sun-Hawk, but it also means that I am pretty purged of my sensual nature, and therefore should not think of myself as a writer of the senses. I am a writer beyond the senses, that is the point (unlike Keats)."

I wanted to give the two boys a good Christmas but temperamentally I wanted the opposite for myself. Christmas left me in a state of recoil: "Back to a Christmas surfeit. Presents being unwrapped all day, and I think of the unemployed and starving who have not been able to buy one thirtieth of what we have. Christmas is a time for asceticism and paring down, for pruning the year and getting the energies right for the new year; for quiet, prayerful contemplation. My disillusion with the world and the senses, which Christmas indulges." My family came to 46 Ritherdon Road on Boxing Day, and we had Christmas lunch in the library, and I observed that the family "pretended the books were not there".

I was very much aware of the brotherhood of man: "All mankind is one, the brotherhood of man before the fatherhood of God, and each is worthy of respect. A judge has only one vote and is equal to the most unemployed of the unemployed until he plays his part, adopts a role, puts on his borrowed robes (wig and gown) – cf Macbeth imagery. The Queen and the most 'worthless' of the poor are treated equally, and a Chairman of the firm should not be kow-towed to and called 'Sir'."

My new powers operated again: "This morning I received at the end of my sleep the opening for my new book: "'What is the meaning of life?' So the 'automatic' transmissions (infused knowledge) have begun again, and I now merely have to follow."

In 1981 my direction became clearer, and I began to see how I could increase my writing time.

In January I visited Margaret. I wrote: "To the coast....Gulped the sea air of Worthing, walked beyond the Festival of Britain clock towards the

Anchorage and then back towards the pier, which was blocked off by building fences. Then to Margaret. Talked alone while Ann went shopping. 'This poverty will be alleviated by St. Teresa.' Photographed her, the flash bulbs wouldn't work: 'St. Teresa is difficult.' The forehead of a girl, one eye (the right one) focuses on time and the world (the way of action of Mother Teresa of Calcutta), and the left eye looks far into eternity, the white being a circle of light in the centre of the pupil, a deep contemplative look that is lost to its situation, like Rembrandt's self-portrait. The tight lips of thought, her beauty....Her nun in November said, 'God is giving you a message through the visions you have had, pray for guidance.'...Then she cracked nuts by the warm log and coal fire and gave Matthew a kernel and said: 'You must work, and you may not be appreciated, but suddenly something will pop out whole, and everyone will be surprised. You must work hard.'"

I wrote: "Margaret described her vision of Christ to me (the only 20th century one I know of, though such visions were relatively common in the time of St. Francis and St. Catherine). She woke up in October 1974 in St. Ives and saw him in the corner of her room. 'I looked, I don't know how long for, I don't know whether it was for a short or long time. I looked. It was just as if you were there now, with your arm on your head in your black sweater, it was very deep, and I could not say it did not happen. He was saying, "Here I am, I am with you."' Mystical Christianity. She has seen the Holy Mother and also St. Teresa ('holding white flowers and a cross, and her smile – she smiled at me, and her smile was so adorable')." Ann attended a course on dyslexia and I thought: "The Seed-Light means that the Light is the source of everything....The seed contains the tree, so there is a parallel upwards movement, from seed to root/trunk, thence to branches and fruit. I have reversed branches and trunk, so between seed and trunk is root....A sea of seeds from one Seed or point. (Cornucopia.)"

A trailer ran into 20 cars outside our house, but miraculously our cars and walls were undamaged, although Ann's car suffered a slight knock, and I wondered if I "am shielded by the angels of Light" and "wear a bullet-proof vest of Light". But then there was a flood caused by an upstairs tenant who dislodged a pipe, and I recorded: "Wrote the first paragraph of *The Sun-Hawk*...and before I could type it the bedroom ceiling began to leak. Water poured down the light flex, flashing the light bulb on and off. Luckily I was in the room, having dried my hair, and was able to avert...damaged ceilings by asking tenants upstairs not to run their water and by catching the cascade in buckets and saving the carpet and downstairs ceiling. It is another unforeseen thing....So the tally of last Saturday was £500 on my bank statement and Matthew's agony in his leg, which suddenly went; then on Tuesday morning there was the mayhem to 20 cars outside, including £100 damage to Ann's car; and now on Sunday there is a whole ceiling to be decorated and a pipe to be refitted. Is this connected with the fact that I am trying to write about the Light? Whenever I try to put anything on paper about it, something goes wrong. It is like the Tutankhamun curse. There is a force that does not want me to reveal too much about the Light. Significantly, no one really has to date: I am the first to state the tradition. I have not mentioned my ingrowing toe-nail which has made me limp since

Christmas." And on January 11th: "Began to write my first paragraph again, and there was a sizzling from the bedroom flex (the light was off) and a major fire risk glowed with a spark. (*The Spark and the Fire* is the title of chapter 1.) So I again abandoned my attempt to write and spent an hour and a half averting a major fire: turned off the electricity at source in the cellar, unscrewed the white disc by torchlight, undid the screws in the ceiling to let the cable hang out, emptied it of water, then turned on the electricity and heated up the sizzling wires with the hair drier and solved it. Then mopped up. This after finding candles and explaining the fire-risk to the tenants who were cooking. Now back to my first paragraph. What next? What else is there that *can* go wrong?!"

The dispute between Ricks and MacCabe came to a head with Ricks blocking MacCabe's promotion for wanting to teach grammar, psychoanalysis, linguistics, sociology and Marxism at the expense of much of the 600 years of English Literature, including the metaphysical tradition. Ricks stood for the tradition, Literature and literary criticism; MacCabe for change, linguistics, structuralism and post-structuralism.

In my researches I read widely on Egypt and the "khu" or "akh", the spiritual soul which was at the centre of Egyptian life and my own transformation into which I was quietly effecting. I wrote: "My life is similar to Plato's. He was born c428BC, and knew Socrates....After Socrates's execution in 399BC, Plato travelled till he was 41 – Egypt, Greece and Italy, the sources of knowledge – and then founded an Academy for interdisciplinary studies: philosophical and scientific research with some mathematics and jurisprudence. Perhaps I should found a Metaphysical Academy to promote metaphysical studies and feature the Journey."

Then I researched into bull-cults, Zoroastrianism and other ancient religions. I discovered that the man who I was introduced to in the Dulwich library when I worked there, W. B. Emery, was the first to discover evidence of the bull-cult. I now found he had discovered the Iseum (a place linked with Apis bulls) while I was in Egypt in 1970. I also began to research into the Kurgans and realised I had met one of the authorities, Leon Stover, in Tuohy's room in Japan. It seemed I had been shown certain key people I needed. I wrote that my researches were completing "my metaphysical development".

I was aware that I was a "Puritan at heart, like Richard Ingrams....A Puritan Metaphysical....A Puritan who is not a revolutionary. I don't smoke or drink and I live reasonably purely in the Light, condemn royal extravagance and Labour greed, and work hard (the Protestant Puritan ethic). Yes, I am a Nonconformist – a Puritan." I found a picture by H. D. Millet in a local antique shop and brought it back. It showed a Puritan sitting between two women, and was called *Between Two Fires*.

Tom Dyer, the Brain of Britain, came round in February and we "went out star-gazing with his binoculars on the frosty grass. Saw Orion of course, and shoulder; the red bull's eye (Taurus); the nebula of the sword; Gemini; Capella and Aurigae; Regulus; Algol 4 (Perseus); Cassiopeia; Ursa Major and Plough – trapezoid 6 including two pointers to the North or Pole Star; the Lion, Leo (3 along and 2 up and 1 other); Rigal is in Orion; and Sirius

(8 light-years away)." My observation of Nature continued in the garden: "Watched two blue tits on the garden silver birch."

We went to Loughton and visited my aunt Argie "who moves slowly after her heart attack, and is slightly dazed but with a strange smile". There was snow: "On to the pure white snow of the Forest. The church and my burial corner, the reddish looking bracken on the snow. The ice on the pond and 9 ducks waddling or standing, frozen cold."

I was teaching conciseness and précis at school while researching Buddhism and other Eastern religions in the evenings. I also discovered the devastating power of humour to wreck serious meetings. In March I recorded a conversation with the Deputy Head: "To Sinclair I said today (when he said 'You were in good form yesterday'): 'The path to Illumination' – 'Oh,' he said, 'illumination' – 'is one of light-heartedness. It is not for nothing that the laughing Buddhas of the East have pot bellies.' He chortled. Mrs. Kay, the dragonish Head, was sitting opposite and glowered. Yesterday I demolished a meeting of the Hods (Heads of Department) with humour....I use humour as an anarchic weapon. You get away with murder with humour. Actually it is wit: the heterogeneous ideas are yoked together by violence: e.g. Lady Diana Spencer and 5R (the dimmest class); set books and capitalist newspaper proprietors....I use jokes like bombs. I creep into a meeting and lay a joke like an IRA bomber, crouch down and put my fingers in my ears and bang! my Headmistress's policies have a gaping hole in them and the atmosphere has been spoiled, for no one can concentrate on her words any longer."

Again: "How to get what you want out of our Head. You put what you want no 4 on a list, and have three unimportant things nos 1-3. You bomb and strafe her on nos 1-3, and when she is softened up you introduce no 4, ride the flak, and she gives up and you have your way." A clairvoyant teacher at the school, John Cameron, with whom I sometimes had lunch, told me: "You were Mrs. Kay's teacher in a former time. I believe in Egypt. You were a priest in a temple." Increasingly I felt: "God spotted me and made me an agent of the divine."

As I continued my researches into history, I had "a nightmare thought: what if the past never happened? And all the history books, and past art and fragments of religious knowledge had all been made up by a committee? What if we were all rootless, and nothing existed before our century, save a gigantic fabrication? (Literally, the fabric of buildings from past centuries, faked.)"

I went into Judaism, and now that I was reflecting on the Kabbalistic Tree of Life I realised the true nature of "the experience by the Worcester College lake, when I gave up the law to read English: the tree reflected in the water, a tumbling chestnut – upside down: the Tree of Life (rooted in the sky)." I wrote of the Essenes: "The Invisible Light (Heavenly Father) and the visible reflection, Darkness or outer Darkness (Earthly Mother), live in harmony with the Law through the Tree of Life, so all energies flow in, and one is ego-less and therefore sinless and therefore healthy and at one with the Light." Later I wrote: "I have solved the riddle of the Great Pyramid. It is very largely the Tree of Life, inverted from seed/golden apex of Light to base on earth....When I was writing *The Riddle of the Great*

Pyramid in Dulwich in 1963, I stopped W. B. Emery to obtain his view – without success. It was still a riddle. Now I have solved the riddle. It is the Tree of Life, from a point downwards, creation coming out of light."

I was becoming increasingly demoralised with Garratt Green. I was aware of the lack of spirit at our school: "The dying school, with a void where its spirit should be; surfacing in violence. Civilisation tranquillises the soul and checks the ego; when a civilisation goes over the edge, the ego asserts itself. The school civilisation is crumbling. The cure is to teach the Mosaic Law in years 4 and 5 – a metaphysical vision."

I had not forgotten Miss Lord saying to me at Anthony's christening: "You'd better have Oaklands." I wrote: "Shall I risk going to see her? Do we want it? Probably. Ann could be Headmistress and I could do the administrative side and write....Buy over in Epping Forest?" I telephoned Miss Lord, "and will see her at 5 on Friday, to bring in my destiny and make time to write."

I visited Miss Lord and did a tour of an empty Oaklands School. It was homely with many nooks and crannies, but evidently needed a lot of decoration and renewal. She said to me as we returned to the study, "I've often thought about you and wondered if you still wanted it." We arranged that Ann would visit the school and have a look. I wrote: "So as my beliefs deepen I turn towards infancy: from university to secondary school and now primary school, where true ego-less innocence is to be found. Like Blake, I shall live among the innocent in green fields, and go to High Beach, and embody the Light in Epping Forest....Back in Epping Forest I shall create again....Like Heathcliff, I shall return, only richer now and with a knowledge I did not have (the Light) when I went away – knowledge of how it runs through history....Providence is taking care of me, and is guiding me into a situation where I can enjoy the fruits of my labours in the 1970s in relative calm, and have time to write....Perhaps I shall emerge to a unitive ecstatic life on the lawns of Oaklands?" It seemed that going to Oaklands would solve all our problems in one go: school fees, the Head taking too much of my time, the impending closure of Garratt Green, escaping an urban setting for the countryside and a place with more sense of a community. I thought of Eliot's words in *East Coker*, "Home is where one starts from," and in *Little Gidding*:

> "We shall not cease from exploration
> And the end of all our exploring
> Will be to arrive where we started
> And know the place for the first time."

Back at Garratt Green I was teaching Keats and wrote: "Keats as a New Ager: *Hyperion* book 3 (March 1819) – Mnemosyne, the mother of the Muses, as the inspiration of the collective unconscious, giving Keats 'knowledge enormous' which deifies him, i.e. an inflow from outside....Apollo/Hyperion, and the Light....I am not an Existentialist, I am a transformationalist, for I stress the journey of transformation from ego to soul. The Transformationalist branch of Existentialism....The materialist view of poetry today...denies the inspirational poetry of Plato – and of Keats in 1819, once he had found his 'knowledge enormous'. When I read Keats and Shelley during my cricketing year, it was the permanence of Reality and the One that I was reading. 'Knowledge enormous makes a God of me.'"

At the next Mystics and Scientists conference at Winchester, I had a chat with Dr Peter Fenwick, one of the country's leading experts on the mind-body relationship. I asked him, "Do you still believe that mind is dependent on brain, or could brain transmit mind?" He replied, "I increasingly feel that mind may be a universal phenomenon interpreted by the brain." Later I meditated with a forest monk, the Venerable Sumedho, and recorded: "Light: several radiations pulsing through my mind, from far to near, round ripples widening and expanding. Later chatted to Sumedho, who was dressed like a Buddha, as he walked up to breakfast: be-sandalled and shaven-headed." I spoke again with Warren Kenton, alias Z'ev ben Shimon Halevi, perhaps the world's leading living expert on the Kabbalah, and wrote: "The Idea of Beauty and Truth is the Divine Light, which is the only ultimate Beauty and Truth."

In April I heard from Miss Lord. She wrote that she would let us have Oaklands in 1983 at a valuation to be agreed. I was elated. I wrote: "So I may end up with the...school I went to in the war....I will have some time to write, and will live a real life, in a community, near High Beach, in the Forest of my poems. My heart will come alive for my epic....Oaklands can double up as my Plato's Academy – my Metaphysical Academy. I can hold lectures on the Metaphysical in the evenings or at weekends....I have turned away from Essex and am now turning back, having found the truth (the Tree of Life) that I left to seek." I was aware that the school badge showed the large oak-tree in the main field. "This is a homecoming....The seed (acorn) I planted down the road from Oaklands in the 1960s has grown into the great oak of Oaklands, my metaphysical Academy, in the 1980s via the 'metaphysicising' of the 1970s....I am preparing for my golden years of poetry. I will have the time and money to complete my *Paradise Lost*, living in the country setting of a modern Milton, my childhood memories all round me....The oak-tree of Oaklands – the Tree of Life....(It came to me Good Friday, the day Jesus hung on the Tree of Life.)" I wrote of "the deraciné life which does not nourish my heart.

I turned against Garratt Green: "I have had enough of civilising Caliban at my unruly school. Like Prospero, I will retire from the civilising process and bury my art, but enjoy the magic of enchanted Oaklands in retirement. Long summer days in the green fields – and the buttercups."

I went to a gathering at my brother Rob's large house near Tunbridge Wells, and my aunt Argie told me about a conversation she had had with Len Murray, the Secretary-General of the TUC in her newsagents: "'The first commandment – "Remember the sabbath day" – isn't kept any longer, and the fourth commandment "Thou shalt not commit adultery" is now respectable, and (breaking) the fifth commandment "Thou shalt not steal" is so widespread that it costs the National Health Service a quarter of its annual budget, so how many more commandments are the unions going to break?' Murray: 'Who knows? But come off it, stealing's not respectable? Surely?' After Argie elaborated about theft at work: 'It's the same in

379

industry.' Quite an encounter! Argie said 'Come off it, Lionel' to one of Murray's replies."

The conversation turned to Oaklands, and my younger brother Jonathan's wife said: "They don't do very much, Miss Lord and Mrs. Macy are so old. No one knows how long Miss Lord is staying or what will happen. She has a monopoly up to the age of 8 and is sitting on a goldmine."

I now went into Gnosticism, and found its influence in Blake ("lost, lost are my emanations") and Existentialism (the alienation of strangerhood). I had glimpses of the Reality that surrounds unaware people and wrote: "Today people are alienated from the reality that surrounds them. Write a small novel contrasting reality (the One)...with the unawareness of people going about their everyday life, i.e. a new view of man. Closed to the swirling forces of mind round him. A metaphysical novel....The man in the desert. The banality of his thoughts as the One is around him and he is alienated – trapped in his senses, chained." I was aware that I was still a seeker: "April 25. Writers travel and describe surfaces (like Tuohy); seekers travel through libraries, like me in 1958. I was a seeker in the 1960s masquerading as a writer, using writing to seek (*Mandalas*). All the time my question was: is there an invisible world or reality?...My Journey, being universal, will be seen in different ways, from different perspectives. That does not matter, as I am aiming for the universal in a contemporary dress."

My researches now took me into Church architecture: "Realised that a church spire is, like the Great Pyramid, an apex down which creation manifests into spirit and psyche and matter, or into mind and soul and form, depending on how Kabbalistic or Platonistic the church-builders were – and a Cathedral is, in fact, a Tree of Life from tip or seed down to form. And the higher you go, the more illumination (rose windows)....The spire in the Forest – the manifesting down the Tree of Life."

I had gone off the novel. I wrote: "I don't read novels any more because Reality is not to be found in them. Once I thought they might help me to find Reality, but I gave up and now read the books where I *can* find Reality. (So many novels are a waste of time. Written on false views of Reality. Ah, I say, so you think Reality is like that? No! It is one's own imagination one needs to develop. It never used to be novels that did that, but poetry." I added : "The second Dark Night – stripping away of images that impede the soul's unity with God, i.e. images of writing....My awakening soul used writing in Japan to help it awake. When it got to Ruah, spirit, it discarded the sort of writing I was doing, which was ego-based. Awakening souls attract the right conditions, so I attracted Japan. Why London and Garratt Green now? Research and study, encyclopaedias, relating my soul to history. That phase is nearly over and in Oaklands I am attracting new conditions for a new stage....I will need only the springs of my own inspiration and understanding and wisdom." It was intriguing that an astrologer I had met in the maze at Hoddesdon at a conference in May 1979, Ted Collings, had done my birth chart and predicted that I would begin a new stage around October 1982.

I now related English Literature to the Journey: "English...extends the consciousness of the natural person into the area of the soul, and may even help it to make contact with spirit; it helps a person move up the Tree of Life, where inner powers are located....Growing creativity from inner powers – and growing expression. The soul in Literature, which is out of reach to most 21 year olds; but it is found in poetry."

At the beginning of May we went to Loughton and met Miss Lord, who was "determined" we should have Oaklands and was moving towards a price. We went to "the second pond – tadpoles – and Connaught Waters – the coot and catkins – and Queen Elizabeth's Hunting Lodge".

Between May and July 1981 I attended four conferences or weekend retreats, on which I drew for the four poems of *Beauty and Angelhood*.

The first was a conference on Esoteric Christianity at Hoddesdon, Herts, where I heard an inspirational talk by the young Canon Peter Spink of Coventry Cathedral, an Anglican priest who had founded the Omega Order to revive practical mysticism and recover the "divine indwelling" Light in accordance with the work of F. C. Happold and Teilhard de Chardin. He stood and talked fluently without notes, and I recorded my excitement: "He said many of the things that I have said, e.g. the old forms are dead and the upsurge of the spirit requires new forms; you should follow the religion of your country (a Clement of Alexandria Christianising of the New Age)." Afterwards I walked with him in the maze and he urged me, "Come and join me, leave your school and work with me." It felt like a call but I knew I could not work within Christianity and had to remain an outside metaphysical: "I am really a Christian, but not one who believes in the historical Jesus – rather one who sees the myth as applying to our inner transformation....I am a Christian of an esoteric kind."

The next morning there was a meditation based on the Christian Lord's Prayer in the library, taken by Kenneth Cumming a priest. I wrote: "The Hoddesdon 'library'. Sitting...by the second door to the right or facing it – Light! For at least three quarters of an hour. As I meditated to the Lord's Prayer. Or contemplated, for I gazed at the Light all the time. When we got to the heart, I opened to the Lord, and – pow! Light almost blew my mind, and I had a tremendous tingling all over and my hair prickled and stood on end for two or three minutes. I was reluctant to let it go as I offered it back up at the end, hands raised high."

Two days later, on May 11th I wrote: "All day I have shone with the Light. My skin has a glow, I can see reflections in it. My body is so full of Light that I am almost transparent in profile. It is as though I am full of vitamin C. I have lost weight. I am nearly down to 13 stone, whereas before I was up to 14 stone. I feel better, have an immense energy. Have worked all day....The Light softened my heart and has made my skin immensely soft, my flesh very pliant. My whole body is mind, or rather, spirit. My skin is more 'oily', as though it is permeated by dew. The Light is in every pore of my skin, softening it, and giving strength....The will of God is in my skin."

I knew what my mission was very clearly: "My mission is to put out the Light in writing and remysticise Europe and the ideology of the West, and to enshrine the Light in a major epic poem. So far, I have not achieved any of my mission, though I am on the right path for such an achievement, and have completed the right preparation (travel, literature, scholarship, absorption of the spirit)." I added: "Last time I tried to begin the epic, I took Swedenborg's *Heaven and Hell* down to Cornwall for the cosmology – and realised that I would have to reflect the new scientific discoveries and spirituality in my poem. I am still reading this up, several years later!...I am little further forward, though I now have a fund of wisdom to draw on....I was born into the beginning of an overlapping of two ages, and so the forms of the old age...were unsatisfying, while the forms of the new age...had not yet been born. Terrible is the tension and the frustration of the seeker who is between ages, between dogma and doctrine (dead) and a new spirit."

I recognised that *The Silence* would be regarded as "a prophetic work of the New Age": "Single-handedly I forged a new age consciousness. That was fifteen years ahead of its time. I had to get as far away from the old age as I could in order to open this new consciousness." At the same time I felt dissatisfied as "my life so far has been a preparation for something that has not yet happened". It now seems that I was groping blindly towards my Metaphysical Revolution.

I now thought intensely again about the connection between the decline of Western civilisation and the absence of the Light: "What I am essentially writing is my anatomy of the Decline of the West....Our rubbishy culture and civilisation, and the misery of the Seeker...who grasps the significance of living by the Light, his higher purpose....How the enlightened Seeker...can contribute to the salvation of his culture and civilisation, by de-Humanism....When Seekers cease to be enlightened, they lose their aim and purpose, and civilisation (which they lead) loses its aim and declines. A healthy Church gave men spiritual purpose and direction – the Light emphasised the reality of the spirit – and so men thought in spiritual rather than materialistic categories; and created for the glory of the Church. Religion hardened, the men of genius lost their purpose, and so, the Seeker's aim and purpose dying, civilisation loses its aim, which is to aspire to the Light. A civilisation loses control when men of genius think in materialistic instead of spiritual categories, and recovers control when there is a return to the spiritual. Civilisations decline when spirit is swamped by matter, and will end with scepticism. My withdrawal and return, Toynbee-like. I have withdrawn from society into solitude to wrestle with problems, my vitality and insight have increased. I have solved the problem with the Light. I am one of society's acknowledged élite...who is leading it forward....My challenge:..to synthesise all the various approaches to Reality into the right one, and to unify Christendom on the basis of the Light and remysticise Europe so that the challenge of Communism is met by a firm ideology. For the West to survive and not to decline, its ideology must be strong enough to be positive in relation to Communism."

At the end of May I went to a weekend course on the Kabbalah at Hawkwood, Gloucestershire. I walked in the beautiful grounds – "birds' song, cows, horses, hundreds of daisies, railings – and encountered Warren Kenton, an informally dressed, small man with a beard, and we talked until he said: "I must generate the energy for my first session." I recorded: "(He) went off walking by himself among the trees and fields, a latter-day Wordsworth or Keats, deriving energy from his Earthly Mother."

The course proved slightly disappointing. We had to ask the Inner Teacher a question, and I heard mine say: "You've got your task, get on and do it, write your book...and restore the mystical tradition within Christendom." We were encouraged to see images, and the visualising of images we practised seemed somewhat shallow. I wrote: "The method of visualising each centre is not deep...and is not as deep as what is received during contemplation....These images...might just as easily be the imaginings of a poet....Images which arise in pure consciousness, unguided, are genuine; those suggested are less real, more psychological. If I say 'Imagine a car' and one person imagines a Rolls, another an old banger, I can argue that that tells them about the state of their soul now." I described what I saw. "My images. Peacock/lyre/hopscotch/Tree of Life in mosaic. Then a Christ upside down on the temple floor....The ark in a black cloud with flames. Angels as white brightnesses instead of faces, and folded robes or veils, 5 or 6 approaching, heavenly hosts....A chariot in a dark cloud. High priest with hands raised....A large ring of celestial beings with a dark centre, like folds in veils. Shadow as a black-hooded monk, no face at all....The long journey, a traveller in rags, dishevelled, dusty clothes, naked. Deep eyes of high priest." I took issue with Warren Kenton: "These images, I said, are not so clear as poetic images thrown up after 45 mins' contemplation, from the unconscious, and being rapid (6 images in 2 minutes) are more superficial. Kenton said, 'If you fish in the North Sea from a trawler, dropping your fishing line, you may catch a herring, but if you use sonic radar, you locate the shoal and bring up a netful.' I: 'Poetic images are different, one breeds another, and each is not known before it arrives.' He: 'Different method.' I: 'Your method is magic, using a conscious technique to fish them up from the unconscious.' He: 'Permissible in a circle.'"

On our free Saturday afternoon I visited the nearby monastery of Prinknash and found it contained the best and worst aspects of the Christian monastic tradition: a fine old Abbot's house and retreat, and a hideous modern car park. I felt Prinknash was too worldly and needed to be reformed.

On the Sunday I saw more images: "Spirit: rose, golden flower, a veil with patterns over Light, the waters of spirit, an angel in a cloud. Divine Fire. Levels as waterfalls or terraces with gardens. All this 'fantasising' in images, going straight for archetypes and spiritual images, may do things to the energy flow."

A week later I was aware of my increased consciousness. We had been to my nephew William's christening. "A brief word with Ann last night about the christening and pow! A flood of consciousness filled me, so when I lay down to sleep I saw Paisley patterns from the unconscious and was filled with consciousness from a different level. Sleep was hopeless. I did make a second Horlicks and go for a walk to the end of the road and back at 2 a.m., and that served to quieten my trembling, thumping body, but I lay in a quiet calm all night, fully conscious, and now feel full of vitality and well, though I have not slept a wink. This sort of thing used to happen to me in the 1960s, but has not happened to me so much in the 1970s, when I committed 'mind-suicide' in the ILEA, which served for me the same sort of purpose that the RAF served for T. E. Lawrence: kept me earthed."

The next weekend I wrote stories: "Stories all day yesterday – *Pompous Fool, Loud Voices, A Red in the Surgery* and the three others near it – and then 82°F, and a day in the garden getting sun-red....Toe bled twice. Cut the lawn briefly, and imagined myself into birds and daisies and thirsty flowers, which I had to give a drink. I find that more and more I feel into the being of leaves and growing things, and am still as a stone, and just listen to everything. I have a poet's imagination of entering the inner essence, becoming the sap rising." I also wrote to Biggs-Davison to congratulate him on his knighthood, and I wondered what political services he had rendered for it.

I had an insight into the position of the Church of England in Britain: "A glimpse into the doctrinal battles of the 1660s which go back to the military battles of the 1640s. Having been ousted by the Puritans, the monarchy imposed the Church of England form of service, and anyone, like Bunyan, who preached otherwise as a Nonconformist received 12 years' imprisonment. Today all the doctrines are a waste of time to us. The essence is what is important."

I attended the third of the four weekends on June 20th at Kent House, near Tunbridge Wells, a house Peter Spink had taken over as a near-ruin and retrieved by hard work. I stayed with his wife and walked to Kent House, where Spink held court at the end of a long room which had a carpet, comfortable chairs and a table covered with leaflets that were distributed by a nun. There were about 20 of us, and we were swiftly put into silence for the weekend and told that we should hoe weeds in the grounds (as at a Zen temple), and in the first session Spink emphasised contemporary mysticism among the working classes and impatiently brushed aside any references to the mystic tradition of the last 600 years. He eschewed all ideas, which is why his book was so slim. I wrote: "Have been at Kent House for nearly 24 hours now. Silence from 11 to 6.45. The mystic way of life of silence, which accords with my poem *The Silence*, is a necessary base for Spink's movement, but he has got to get into Europe on the lecture platform and give a rationale. Spink holds it all together, but is unsure of the direction: which is to remysticise Christianity, provide a new ecumenical impetus on the basis of the Light, transform Church services into meditations and contemplations. The Order is becoming more of a teaching order, with cells, but will attract the hangers-on, e.g. Ian who had not the price of a haircut – like Siddhartha all those years ago. Rhododendrons."

Spink held himself back from the 20 of us during this weekend. On the last day he performed a Mass based on the Light, a Light Eucharist, which I found very interesting, and everyone spoke of him as a guru figure, a leader of a cult, a Steiner. I wondered whether he was a minor or major figure within Christendom: "Either Spink's is just another religious community like Windesheim or Port Royal or Little Gidding; in which case he is a Nicholas Ferrar, and I am a Crashaw, keeping in touch and writing poems; or a Pascal; or his is the embryonic new Reformation which will transform all the Church, reunite Christendom on the basis of the Light; in which case he is a Luther, and I am privileged to have known him. With his hair parted in the middle and flopping over each temple and sideways over his ears, he is a charismatic figure, who looks like Hopkins....The danger that Spink will become a Steiner-like cult."

At school I had been running the exams for a month and had internal exam papers to mark, and the strain was beginning to tell. I was still negotiating Oaklands, with regular visits to Miss Lord's house, and I longed to withdraw into silence: "A deep dissatisfaction....Until 1970 I was a writer, often without a true subject, but I felt and thought like a writer....I had to embroil myself in suffering. My poems then were an image of universal suffering. Since then, I have earned and acquired, but have served the Light, and as I moved back from ego to soul, so my interest in writing about external things dwindled and I became a channel for the Light. And where has my poetry gone? Recently it has petered out....I need to return to a corrupt and fallen world."

About this time I heard that Caroline's husband had been unemployed since leaving the RAF at the beginning of 1981, that he had found a job in Brussels and that Caroline would join him there in September. Nadia would live in a flat in Edinburgh. I wrote that Nadia may have had to get to Edinburgh "to meet her husband there".

In July I spent several days going through the Oaklands books and negotiating where we would build our new house, whether in the kitchen garden or on the site of the Art Room next to Miss Lord's own house. And by July 11th I was able to record: "Finished with Miss Lord. It is all sewn up now." We would be taking over in September 1982, a year earlier than originally planned. I began to design the house I would build within the grounds and recalled 1968, when I used to walk Nadia past Oaklands to see the cows at the top of the road and say jokingly 'I will buy Oaklands one day', and it seemed that somehow "Providence marked me out in 1968 as the future...Principal of Oaklands, and did its utmost to put me in the position of being able to take over:..got me away from the wife who was no good to me, in Libya; got me attached to the wife who would be Headmistress; got me into the schools and a salary that could sustain Oaklands; got me Ritherdon Road to improve so I could buy Oaklands; and blocked all buyers of the house until I was ready to convert it into Oaklands. It was for that that I had to become a Head of Department at Garratt Green. In fact, the whole of the last 13 years, including the Light, has led up to Oaklands. Why does Providence attach so much importance to getting me Oaklands?" And as if answering my own question, I wrote: "I have served students, secondary children and will now serve primary and nursery children – many souls. Providence has blessed me with the status of 'angel'. I have discovered myself as an angel – a bit fallen at times, but fundamentally I belong to the angelic orders, and came down on earth with a mission that works through children.... Oaklands... will be a perfect setting for me – a garden like Paradise.... The Angels have decided that I am to be entrusted with the care of a thousand young souls at a difficult time, and they want me to fight to preserve Oaklands. Miss Lord is an angel handing over to an angel."

A MYSTIC WAY

The last conference was again with Peter Spink, a day at St. Peter's Convent, Woking. Peter Spink wanted to change the direction of the Omega Order and had invited about 60 people to hear a proposal that it should become a teaching order with modules on education, healing and counselling. We ate packed lunches in the sisters' garden, and I sat next to Betty James who was making the proposal. After Eucharist in the chapel and then Feria (Divine Office) she gave her talk and brought me in: "I talked of the need to remysticise Christendom, in Europe. This led to a heated discussion outside with Spink in which I talked of Luther and Wesley – for the comparison of the upsurge which is Omega is with Methodism, a movement that stayed within the Church – and he said: 'I want communities everywhere, throughout England. Europe is further ahead.' Spink feeling that he must secure his flanks against the Church and concerned with other religions – the One Light – while I emphasised the need for experiences of the Light from the great mystics, not the theory, ie sparks becoming fires. Spink: 'We're not ready for that yet, I'm not ready, none of us are ready.'" My reaction was: "The LCD. Do not get further involved in this group which will be expensive (hurdles/courses), time-consuming (many weekends) and at the level of personal growth. Spink: 'What do you want us to do that we are not doing?' I: widen horizons to include a study of the experiences of mystics."

Spink had said that he was not ready for the Light, nor were the 60 friends of Omega, and I had no more to do with them. I wrote: "Spink tries on ideas for size and then moves away from them, does not stick to ideas he had three months ago, so in June he can say 'The spearhead can lecture on an anti-intellectual subject' while in July: 'There must be no inner core, that would spoil and ruin it all.... Heart not head, and so everybody included: Heart-centredness." And I noted: "Spink...keeps quoting Paul's *Letter to the Ephesians* about 'I pray that the eyes of your *heart* may be opened, and that you may know', whereas the different versions (from earliest to latest) say 'understanding' or 'mind' being illumined. He has supplied the 'heart' himself because that is what he wants it to say....My sense of fairness and accuracy demands that he should quote accurately and then interpret, and not merely misquote to suit his own argument."

I spent the summer working on the four poems that became *Beauty and Angelhood*.

My sister, Frances bought a house in Wimbledon. She was in competition with an unknown buyer who turned out to be Biggs-Davison. Frances and her husband secured the house, whereupon Biggs-Davison bought one two doors down and moved in, and soon Frances had one of Biggs-Davison's children as a baby-sitter. Immediately he moved in, Biggs-Davison went to the Palace to collect his knighthood; he forgot his top hat and had to go back for it. A week later he invited me to the House of Commons for a drink: "Drank on the terrace overlooking the river. Shook hands with (Mark) Carlisle, (the Secretary of State for Education) and Winston Churchill, whom I liked. Had a talk with Carlisle....Spoke briefly to various MPs."

METAPHYSICAL AND BAROQUE

Tom Dyer, the Brain of Britain, came round and sat in our front room and suddenly swooped on the carpet. "A flying ant," he said, holding it in his hand, "a female," and to our astonishment he ate it. "It tastes acidy like formic acid or vinegar." He explained that it was protein. "Had it been a male it would have been poisonous rather than protein."

We went down to Cornwall: "Slept all afternoon after a morning on the beach, drunk with the drugged air. The crab...,the rock pools. Then this evening, the carnival. The variety that a Breughel would have delighted in painting: tug o'war, shire horses, fancy dress clowns and royal take-offs and Bonnie and Clyde." I wrote a story and then worked on the first of the four religious poems that became *Beauty and Angelhood*: "I woke in a poetic mood, and, unable to get the papers because of the rain, sat and assembled the 4 poems just like that. Now have *High Leigh* behind me. Went for a walk at Charlestown in the afternoon and watched the cricket for much of the day, as a kind of background to my interior minings." Again: "Aug 1. Rhymed the draft of, and typed up, *Hawkwood*, which I consider one of my most successful poems....Did this before and after attending the Charlestown Regatta with the children – Punch and Judy, a Nimrod flying low, water polo, raft races in the harbour." Soon afterwards: "Drafted the third poem, first six or seven stanzas until it was time to walk to Charlestown at 11 p.m. – just so I would sleep....Walked to Charlestown pier late at night and looked at the stars above and felt a part of them, standing above the sea; felt the satisfaction at having tussled with reality and having made a gain. Did not feel wasted or futile. If only I could live permanently like this, how happy I would be!...If only I could be myself full time and not just in the holidays....I have learned to switch the spring of my genius off."

I wrote: "The reason I went on those four 'courses' was to write these four poems....Each was a challenge to my position that had to be wrestled with, and in the wrestling is the great poetry." Then: "Aug 2. Typed up *Kent House*. A hot summer's day and cloudless sky, so sunbathed and read the papers from 11 to 1, and spent the afternoon on Par beach, where the final wording of the last three lines came to me, sitting on my blue sun-couch gazing at the sea, hills and blue sky all round....Re-drafted the fourth poem which now has to be rhymed. Am burnt red and purple." The next day I wrote: "Cooler. Stayed in and re-drafted the fourth poem, St. *Peter's Convent*. Was taken over near the end and got a last line that pleased me without really realising the ambiguity until it was done. Teachers care for minds, Masters for spirits, Angels for the divine spark. Typed up the fourth poem and went to Mevagissey."

We went to Pendeen, where several of Ann's ancestors had lived. Her great-grandfather had been in the Navy and had become a coastguard at Pendeen, and her great-grandmother had had six children, including her grandmother, Vera, who had married a Pendeen tin-miner. He had gone to North Rhodesia and been killed in a car accident when Ann's mother was 15, and Vera had returned to Par.

We went to Golant, and I later wrote: "I belonged to the Metaphysical generation at Oxford – those who were deeply interested in metaphysical issues, Buddhist truths as well as Donne and Marvell." I polished the four poems. I wrote: "The differences between Spink and me are that he is leading a mass movement at the pace of the masses, whereas I, a poet and mystic, want some sort of private...group where the findings of the great mystics are made public, which can take the masses to a new definition of Christianity. Spink and I differ on emphasis, but I am not interested in going at the pace of the masses....I am interested in transforming Europe....He is anti-intellectual, I am pro-book."

We went to Perranporth and sunbathed on the sand and watched the donkey rides, and then to East Wheal Rose mine. Then: "A hard struggle, making sure the crescendo of the fourth poem is properly motivated in the third poem." On August the ninth Ann came in and found me tapping out metre, and said, "It's like living with a Morse code agent." The next day I "saw 2 windhovers/kestrels which circled the sun without moving their wings for twenty minutes, against a blue sky....Two pied wagtails also came, a male and female, and a worm crawled by as I sunbathed for two hours after typing up the fourth poem." I wrote: "Art helps religious people understand the depths of their experience, by finding images for it that people can grasp and hold in the mind."

We went to Charlestown again "from 12 till 3.30 and lunched on the beach. Watched a large Irish china clay boat manoeuvre into the harbour. All day, blue sky and warm sun....Evening, went to Mevagissey, Portmellon and finally Gorran, where we had a drink in the garden of the Hotel. Thought a lot about Colin Wilson at nearby Tetherdown. Would like to visit him, but have nothing to say at present." I felt I was "caught up through the maze of books, old thought-patterns concerning old writers and ideas, all of which have prevented him from entering the silence and seeing the Light". I wrote again of "a Metaphysical Revolution which has changed everything and destroyed Humanism". On August 13th I wrote: "Worked all day on the fourth poem, to secure the Angels = Flames image, and on the first poem, to unify it. Am pleased with the shape of the 4 for they reflect the new definition of man I was after in Libya – body, mind (including soul), spirit and Angelic flame. A mackerel sky tonight after a hot day."

I went out fishing with Ann's cousin, who was a professional fisherman and owned his own small boat. We left Newlyn and fished all day from 7 a.m. to 3 p.m. We steered out about 8 miles and hauled up crab-pots and then winched up nets with larger fish, including monk fish. I stood at the back of the boat and generally helped, and mucked in with the crew of three at meal times. I wrote: "I have discovered a new sensation. I love deep-sea fishing....It is immensely relaxing, and immensely usable as an image for art." I wrote a story about the experience.

I wrote: "In my search I present both the seen and the unseen. Though the unseen is in many ways more interesting, I must not neglect the seen." I was haunted by the way I hid my talent from all those around me: "I have creative genius, yet I am masquerading as an ordinary person....I am a...Muses' spy in the ordinary world, among the Philistines. I am surrounded by people who do not only fail to recognise my genius....I am such a good spy that I am careful to give no indication of it in ordinary conversation, for hoarding it makes its springs flow more abundantly."

On August 21st I recorded: "Finished the Notes to *Beauty and Angelhood* yesterday, went to bed with only two 'Cornish' images and woke up with four – refined the crab-pot idea and got Smeaton's lighthouse, which is perfect (having been behind Britannia on the old penny)....Smeaton had other lighthouses in Cornwall, eg St. Ives' Smeaton's pier....Tonight looked at the stars....Must include the shower of stars in the poems." I wrote: "I will have spent the whole of my holidays on *Beauty and Angelhood*, which came unplanned."

I had gone off the New Age as I did not believe man is about to undergo a new stage of evolution. I wrote: "Attack the theory of evolutionary optimism, that the next stage of evolution will inevitably transform the consciousness of man, ie cosmic optimism, and God's plan. This conflicts with the rise and fall of civilisations which exist to raise consciousness." I was encountering the new science which suggested that the mystics had always been right. The night before I returned to London I looked at "the lights seen from Polkerris – the Rashleigh Inn terrace – the lights from across the bay, orange and white, like civilisation against the Night of a Dark Age which makes mysticism possible to be handed down". Still on the New Age I wrote: "The 'New Age' is a mixture of astrology, in which I do not believe, and Hinduism, and I am not a Hindu. The only Ages are conceived by men."

Back in London there were further negotiations regarding Oaklands, and a meeting was set up by Mabel Reid with Elizabeth Lord and two of her advisers. I needed advisers. We went to Oaklands, and I observed: "Matthew and Anthony on the climbing-frame like Angels sitting in trees." I told my mother and Argie that Oaklands was in the offing. My mother was very much in favour, and Argie reminded me that mother's great-grandmother had run a school in Croydon.

My mother felt I was becoming too erudite, but she did not realise what I was about: "My mother said I am climbing further away from ordinary people, but what she does not realise is I am climbing to greatness, towards the slot that Eliot filled, or Milton once. Everest or bust. You can keep your Snowdons. At heart I have remained a little boy, a Peter Pan still full of wonder at the hedgerow, ponds, trees – Nature. I must never lose this wonder."

I was still working on the four poems, and I wrote: "The Holy Spirit comes into the heart as fire and lights the spirit which begins the divine life. First the ego is purified and united with the spirit (the Dark Night of Sense), and then later the spirit is further purged from spark to flame (Dark Night of Spirit). The Light comes in and lights the spirit as a candle – hence Candlemas?"

Miss Lord now said she would tell the Oaklands' staff that I was buying the school, and I rejoiced in the prospect of having the Oaklands' grounds and garden as a backdrop to my poems: "The plan in the universe. Flowers fertilise each other with pollen, using go-betweens like bees and birds and ants, which they attract with nectar or perfumes that will attract females for them. Bees need flowers, and flowers bees, and so on, and everything needs everything in God's wonderful plan. And I shall be able to watch it all happening in Oaklands' garden." Some time after I wrote: "I have such a rigorous metaphysical vision these days that there is nothing I cannot do, ie I can express my sinewy metaphysical vision just as I conceive it."

In mid-September, I finally had my ingrowing toenail cut out. I went into the Royal Masonic Hospital, where my consultant was based that day, changed into striped pyjamas, had a bath and waited for my operation by drafting a poem about the Tree of Life which contained the line "the nut within the sun", a first cause. I wrote: "Pond with papyrus and lotus and a fountain and sundial – and columns like the Temple of Solomon, in three tiers. Dividers on the doors, like Blake's God's measuring dividers, and two ancient pre-Christian 'gods' high up above the entrance of the hospital. An ancient wisdom." Eventually I was wheeled to the theatre and given an injection. A tidal wave engulfed me and as I sought to describe it aloud I lost consciousness until I became aware of four green-clad nurses. I was wheeled down to my own room by a nurse in blue and an orderly, and had a throbbing bandaged foot.

Miss Lord told the staff that I was taking over at Oaklands, and then a letter came from the vendors containing detail that required further discussion with Miss Lord's advisers. Eventually the day came in October when I appeared at a packed Parents' Association Annual General Meeting. I sat in the bay window for the formal part of the meeting, and waited while she coped with some sharp questioning, and then Miss Lord announced that she would be retiring the following July, and that I would be taking over. I stood in front of the parents and made a short speech, which was greeted with applause, and then I was surrounded by a throng of many wives, all eager to have a word. I went on to my mother's new house in the High Road, and she said when I told her that the news was now public: "Miss Lord's burnt her boats, she can't go back on it now." We sat together alone, she sitting beside the dining table, and she looked very satisfied, if slightly pale and drawn. A few days later Miss Lord rang her bell and said: "Well, what do you think of Nicholas taking over at Oaklands?"

My mother's end came suddenly, little more than three weeks after that evening. At the end of October she was unwell as if she was starting a cold, how she felt before her first heart attack two years previously. She had another turn at 8, gasped for breath and went grey and rang my younger brother, Jonathan, who was living in Loughton. She said, "Can you come now?" And put the phone down. The doctor arrived as my mother was taken by ambulance to Princess Alexandra Hospital, Harlow. I went and sat with her in casualty while she waited to be X-rayed. Her thin face had a very rosy complexion round her cheeks and slightly blurred eyes. Lying back she gave me a number of instructions concerning the house and several messages. That night she had another tightening across her chest, her third heart attack.

On Hallowe'en we went to Shoreham to see Margaret. I found her very self-absorbed; she had blood pressure and thought of little else and barely noticed the boys. I returned to our house as we had been invited to a party at which I had been asked to dress as a witch although (as I had remarked) I was on the side of the saints in the clash between pagan and Christian.

METAPHYSICAL AND BAROQUE

Outside some Indians needed help with changing a wheel of their car. As I helped them there was a phone call from Jonathan's wife, Anne, saying my mother had had another heart attack (her fourth). It was four days after her third attack, the most dangerous time. I rang the hospital and was told: "She has suffered irreversible heart damage, her lungs have filled with water, her kidneys have packed up, her heart is worn out." We put the boys to bed, arranged a baby-sitter and drove to the hospital. She was in Harvey ward on the third floor, in a private room with a view over the lights, where my two brothers and their wives had gathered. Jonathan said, "What a lovely surprise, Nick is here."

My mother was conscious. She had an oxygen mask over her nose – the oxygen unit hissed – and she was attached to a drip, a tube to drain off her water and an ECG which indicated her heartrate in beats per minute and a zig-zag pattern. I sat with her and said, "It's Nick." She smiled. "Is there anything I can do?" She shook her head three times as if to say 'No, I'm dying,' and attempted to lift her arm, which was bandaged to a board to secure the drip, to remove the oxygen mask. Then she let her half-raised arm flop limply down. I warmed her arms, and conferred with my brothers. We split the time into shifts. Jonathan and his wife went home to sleep. At midnight Robert went off to sleep and I sat on with his wife and Ann. Nurses came to take my mother's blood pressure and temperature at regular intervals, and periodically she had crises and showed signs of distress, trying to sit up and still attempting to lift her arm which was still bandaged to the board, to reach the oxygen mask and tear it off. She did not speak, but the message was clear: 'Don't keep me alive, let me die.' She dozed frequently, and then surfaced, whimpering with some of her breaths something that almost sounded like, "Oh dear." Her chest heaved with bronchitis, her breaths were laboured and there was an echo from each breath like a baby crying in a different ward. I sat and poured love into her, and, holding her hand, healed her without speaking. I said a quiet prayer for her. There was a great surge of energy up my back and down my arm, but there was no more, for the power told me it was useless and it was not the will of the Light that there should be any more. My prayer had been answered with a surge, but no more surges were forthcoming. One of the nurses opened a window. It was a blustery night and the wind moaned all round Harlow as if Hallowe'en spirits were gathering outside in the dark.

She barely spoke, but there was one exchange. Surfacing, she got out, "Hot." I asked, "Are you too hot now?" "No." "Are you too cold?" "No." "Are you uncomfortable?" "No.... So tired." At one point as the wind moaned two nurses came and stood each side of the bed, bent and sat her up, puffed up her pillows and gave her a drink of water which she sipped while I stood, watching hauntedly at the end of the bed, and as her nightdress rode up her legs I thought of how I had crawled from her to give my first cry, and there was something very elemental in seeing her flesh so close to returning to the earth.

Hallowe'en had now become All Hallows or All Saints' Day, and the moaning died away. Robert returned from his sleep and we sat on either side of the bed, and talked quietly across her, recalling in whispers the family holidays we had had as children, evoking over her dying body scenes of the family life she had had while nurses came and listened with a stethoscope. The oxygen unit hissed and we whispered and waited, having subcontracted to the hospital the business of coping with the physical side of death. Slowly she became more comfortable and sank into sleep.

Under the shift system we had all worked out, I was to be present from 12 noon and with Jonathan due at 6 a.m., Robert urged Ann and me to go and get some sleep. So I stooped and kissed her forehead and left. We drove home to Wandsworth and slept, and I was woken at 8 by the telephone. It was Robert. He said, "Mother went just after 7."

After I had gone, Robert had sat with her, squeezing her hand and talking to her. She had asked for her white pills, and said, "Tired." At one point she said, "If only they'd let me die." Apparently she said of the dawn, "It's lovely, look at it." At 6 Jonathan took over. Robert said, "Jonny's here," and she said: "Oh is he? Oh where? Oh yes, there." Just after 7 Jonathan went down the corridor to speak to the staff nurse. When he returned a student nurse was fiddling with the oxygen mask, and my mother said, "I think you'd better get the staff nurse." Two minutes later, at 7.12, she suffered her fifth heart attack and died. Her crisis lasted a very short time, she was too tired to fight. Jonathan later told me, "She went out like a light. Her heart couldn't stand any more." She had wanted her body to be used for medical research, but this was not raised until 40 minutes after her death, too late to be acted on.

I felt drained and numb, a blank exhaustion and relief that her suffering had been removed from her. I experienced a mixture of feelings. I was half sad that she had not lived to see me return to the area and to Oaklands, and part of me wondered if she had moved on because I was returning and was therefore now all right. I kept remembering certain days, like the one when she walked me to my first day at Chigwell School, pushing her bicycle with my kitbag on her front basket. I wrote, "She is in the Chapel of Rest on a Sunday, All Saints' Day, 1st November, and God has a new saint among the heavenly hosts, for she lived very selflessly for all of us."

From my researches into religions, I understood that a newly released soul often does not realise it has died. At 12 that morning I visited my mother in the Chapel of Rest, intending to send her soul on its posthumous journey. The Chapel of Rest was downstairs along a corridor, and an attendant showed me to the door and said I could be alone with her. She was in the chapel on a raised resting-place with two candles, a Bible and a prayer book. She lay with a veil over her white face, the frill of her shroud under blue satin. I realised that for once I had power over her, and felt uncomfortable about it. I forced myself to stoop and kiss her cold forehead. Her eyes were closed, her mouth tight, peaceful, a slight frown above her hooked nose, her white hair and the whitish pallor on her cheeks. Through the open window there was a hint of a breeze and I thought once or twice she breathed as rigor mortis stirred the satin. I talked to her: "It's Nick. You're happy now, for you are dead. I know you can hear me. Thank you for all you did for us. We can look after ourselves now but help us from heaven where you are." I actually spoke aloud, looking up at the ceiling. Then I prayed: "O God, please look after this your latest angel. She has served well in this life. Amen." I felt an immense peace, and then suddenly the candle nearest me guttered as if in answer. It flickered several times and nearly went out, and I wondered if her spirit, realising she was dead, had rushed out of her body, guttering the candle, and moved on to the next stage of her life. Can a spirit make a candle gutter? At that moment the attendant tapped on the door, and it was time to go.

I looked in on the ward to thank the nurses for their efforts. Bizarrely I found them clowning around holding a wooden leg. The day sister had taken over from the night sister and said, "You are a very loving family, she had her family round her to the end," words that would haunt me.

There was a family lunch at Jonathan's house, which used to be my grandmother's and then Argie's home, 20 Brook Road, Loughton. Over lamb and rosé Robert sat at the end of the table and made arrangements, speaking in a loud voice. The men were matter-of-fact and practical, the women were quiet and subdued. Keeping quiet about the guttering candle, I pointed out "She may be there at the funeral, able to see" – an instinctively metaphysical point of view lobbed into all the organising. I was an executor along with my two brothers and had a quarter of her estate.

Now the letters came in, over a hundred. They were addressed to me. It was apparent that my mother had collected people and was a semi-public figure. She had a gift for making people feel they were important and for giving them the whole of her attention and being enthusiastic about their plans. Her friends all commented on the enthusiasm she put into life, how she really cared about people and was greatly liked and respected by so many friends. I reflected that that same enthusiasm had brought us all forward, made us strive to achieve gold stars. She had cared about all our problems, and there was no one who would care in the same way now, and "The world is a colder place now".

I grieved gently and tenderly for "the end of something very gentle and tender" which "sent a surge of feeling welling up into my eyes". I was deeply affected by my mother's death and felt the poignancy of little Anthony hugging me "because you're not dead like Grannie".

The funeral was on a Monday, just over a week after she died, at St. Mary's Church, Loughton, where my father's funeral service was held. I went straight to the church, where I encountered Robert to check the arrangements, and we then all met at Jonathan's house. There were a lot of flowers in his porch. I talked with my Aunt Flo and her husband until the hearse and limousines arrived. I sat in the first limousine with my mother's two sisters, and the rest of the family travelled in the second one. With the funeral director walking in front, we drove slowly past Journey's End to the church, which was packed. The coffin was carried in by the pall-bearers; I followed down the aisle with Ann beside me. Could my mother see us as I had seen my funeral service in 1836 under hypnotism? It was a poignant service: a hymn "To be a pilgrim", psalm 84 and then the eulogy. The Rector, Mr Price, described how she was originally a Methodist, and he dwelt on her warm and outgoing personality and her courage in coping with the deaths of six children. He described how the association with C of E Chigwell School had brought her to St. Mary's. He commented on "her gifted family" and her triumph over suffering. "She died on All Saints' Day," he said, "and in view of what she did for others, she was a saint. God has a new saint at His side." This may now seem over-stated and slightly ridiculous, but to us at the time the words did not seem extravagant. I led the way back down the aisle and Robert and I stood at the door and shook hands and thanked people for coming. Lucy's son John now arrived, representing the Hove branch of the family, red-eyed and trembling, having lost his way and full of profuse apologies. The family limousines then drove past ploughed fields to Parndon Crematorium, near Harlow, and we stood while the Rector said a prayer ("Go forth upon your journey from this world, o Christian soul"), and we watched the curtains draw so we could not see the coffin sink down. Afterwards, feeling some relief, I turned and looked at the chimney and its wispy smoke – did some believe that a warm, gentle person really became nothing in thin air, gone up in smoke? – and wanting to leave it behind we went out on to a lunch at Jonathan's, and my sister Frances asked me: "Why did she die just now? Just after I've come from Shrewsbury to Wimbledon, and you are set for Oaklands? Why now?" And I wondered again, was there something Providential in her going? Or was it just an accident? What is life in relation to death? And what role does death have in our lives?

I returned to Garratt Green. The staff were in uproar. Mr Dowley, the schoolkeeper who had kept me informed of the summer Test match scores, had died of a brain haemorrhage the previous Friday. Twenty-four hours earlier he had been carpeted by the Head, and it was widely said that her dressing-down had triggered the death. The Head denied any responsibility, and underlined the point by attempting to belabour me during my Departmental review for purportedly being about to take on a private school. I gave back as good as I received and ironically thanked her for being considerate during my bereavement. Her insensitivity coped with, I sat and reflected that my mother was in the queue for the next life along with my schoolkeeper and Col. Sir Stuart Mallinson, the local worthy who had provided cricket nets during the Easter holidays when I was still at school and who had just died.

Now I found myself drafting sonnets about my mother's death. I wrote ruefully: "I am sure I shall be among the poets when I am dead, and neither of my parents will have known it." I also discovered that my mother had had phlebitis when I was at Oxford in 1958, 23 years before she had died; I wrote: "I come from a background of cardio-vascular problems and need to be prepared for trouble in my 50s, ie smooth the way for early retirement."

My mother's possessions had to be sorted through. I arranged a weekend in November to meet Robert and Jonathan at her house, but Robert later said they were not going to be there. On the Saturday evening he rang me and said they had been at the house all day. "I've thrown away 12 black bags of her stuff and I have another 12 bags in my car." I immediately said, "What happened to my letters to her from abroad and the family photos, the ones she had of our childhood and of the 19th century family figures?" Robert said he did not know, and it was possible they were in the bags in his car. I said I would like to look through the 12 bags. "It's not possible." I insisted that there were letters, photos and papers which had meaning for me and that as my mother's eldest son and executor I should have been involved in the sorting. Robert had to ring off as he began to have a diabetic reaction, and when I next rang I found myself talking to his wife, who insisted that as the new Head of the Family and one of the three executors I had no right to sort through any of my own mother's possessions.

I will skate over the outcome, but I went down to my brother's house in Tunbridge Wells. He gave me a friendly welcome, provided a groundsheet and (much to his wife's disapproval) I sat on his front lawn and sorted through the 12 bags in the open air, and retrieved many of my letters and many photos, including the only surviving photograph of Mrs. Burton, who opened a school in Croydon and lived to be 100. I later compiled the photographs in three albums, which are now available for all the family to look at. I scrutinised the facial similarities between members of the family and wrote of "the 'enmity' in the blood between the brown-eyed Broadleys, who are practical, from Yorkshire, and the fair-eyed Hardings – and Haggers – who are not Broadleys at all and have different values". Margaret came shortly afterwards and said: "You have done the right thing, you have a heart. You have done right to keep the...letters and photos."

Matthew, who was 6, volunteered his opinion on the death: "Grannie came down to teach the violin..., and she finished it so she had to go on to what she had to do next. We're all here to do something, and when you're little you don't know what it is but when you're bigger the idea is there in your brain."

I did more work on Oaklands. I met my new accountant, Jeremy Mitchell, who had been recommended by my Loughton solicitor, near Chancery Lane, and somehow we walked past Bedford Row, where I spent a troubled year as an articled clerk who spent all his time reading Literature. The solicitors' building I was then in looked as black as ever.

In December I took a day off school, saw my accountant again and took my bank manager round Oaklands. We walked together, and bizarrely a woman dressed as a gipsy with a shawl and a scarf over her head stopped me in the road, thrust a bunch of heather at me and said: "Take something from a gipsy? You're going abroad, two ladies love yer." Brushing her aside, I carried on. From Albion Hill, Oaklands looked massive, and I was reminded of what the clairvoyant in the Markham Arms had said in 1971, ten years earlier: "You're going to buy a big house, I can see it, but there's sadness on the way, a death."

While I coped with my mother's effects I was carrying forward the negotiations for Oaklands and my return to Loughton. At the same time I was steeping myself in Romanticism's unitive vision: Romanticism and Classicism were the two poles within the Baroque, and at this time I inclined to the Romantic side.

In November I had written "a sequence of...sonnets" about my mother, "an elegiac sequence". I noted on December 19th, "Began to write poems, and immediately have come alive again." And soon afterwards: "Drafted ten poems on mother."

It snowed, and there was a family christening for my sister Frances's second child Andrew at St. Paul's, Augustus Road, Wimbledon, where, in a temperature well below freezing, a cheery, balding vicar used a scallop shell. There I met Philip Mawer, a relative of my sister's husband who was in the Home Office and secretary to the Scarman Report. The day after Boxing Day my family came to lunch at 46 Ritherdon Road. It was a restrained occasion.

During the holidays I reread some of my Oxford letters I had retrieved from the black bags, and had mixed feelings. I had turned my back on many of my Oxford connections and had missed out on possible career options, and I had not realised how some of the girls I had known had felt about me; but I reflected that "I had to be alone to tap my heart and get a metaphysical vision". On January 2nd I recorded: "Wrote *Wind-Chaser*, one of my most metaphysical and cosmic sonnets, but also one of my bleakest. I have done the top left hand corner of *The Wind and the Earth*, as it were."

The next day Margaret came and we spent the afternoon talking about Providence: "Is it free will with wrong paths, a kind of maze of wrong turnings and right turnings; or have we all a destiny inside us and a potentiality or tendency to find our right path, so that each finds his way to the high spot? Margaret has always believed in Providence, in illnesses or accidents being inspired, and she still believes this. But she has tried several things that are wrong, and I think that the angels battle for victory, ie the outcome of world events is not predestined or certain, and only human will aided by Providence achieves great things....Human choice is important, and the Light transforms choices....I must explain how the 600 Club (an imaginary Club in which I put the 600 greatest geniuses in cultural history) contains the growers and how many people have not begun to grow, and how though artists and poets do grow, dustmen can as well, developing human qualities of love...To Margaret there is no reincarnation, only Heaven ahead in which there is happiness and no pain, and eternal life, and a saintly life on earth leads there – and her paintings show peace and mystic vision – and our vale of soul-making, and so dustmen can also go there. The great spirits are angels who lead us on. I must show the possibilities of existential growth for dustmen, in this vale of soul-making." I observed: "I am back in 1971 but have developed a metaphysical vision of the Tree of Life and Providence, an awareness of the end of materialism....I must write about transformation, from ego to deeper self, and (the ego) can be smashed by suffering or else the ego can be held in check, so that growth can take place. As for those in whom there is no growth, these are the modern damned, the modern *Waste Land* consciousness, and what happens to them? Do they go to Hell? Do they return to the vale of soul-making to learn again? What?" I added: "I write not with the intellect (that stone on the consciousness)" – I meant reason – "but from a deeper level."

I now felt "I must get back to the individual and all religion", and I returned to *The Seeker and the Light* (which eventually became Part One of *The Fire and the Stones*), which I described as "a prolegomena to my epic and the philosophy of my metaphysical poems". I added that before I started my epic I must "have Attis and Mithras at my fingertips when I come to write images down from the universal religion and Kabbalah in my epic, ie the mind that writes the epic must be a unitary one that sees all as one". I observed: "Blake and I have the fourfold vision in common, ie the Kabbalah it came from. My four poems have made the 4 worlds of the Kabbalah give the 4 Quartets significance – the 4 poems I wrote last summer, ie *Beauty* (cf *The Desert Fathers) and Angelhood*." Of my concept of a divine soul I wrote: "I might not have got my 'divine soul' in *Beauty and Angelhood* without talking to Warren Kenton, and getting him to admit that the scheme of the Kabbalah requires not three but four souls – one for each world. That made me look for the flame, which came to me; and which I now find confirmed in the tradition. I happened to reflect the Kabbalah as much as Blake or Yeats because I happened to live in the same metropolis as the greatest Kabbalah teacher of this century – Warren Kenton, a kind of Gurdjieff."

I wrote that I had consciously elected to study the tradition of the Light: "I have stopped poems to finish my work on the Light, and do not count it as time wasted". But I found the tradition of the Light hard to trace: "My book is as leaky as an old barn. Another hole to be blocked: were the Essenes from Central Asia – and did Zoroaster come from the Oxus – or is this another false claim?" And later that day: "An evening of mental travelling through history....I now have a very original mind. I go out on my own, and make good deductions."

It had snowed again and there was "a slight thaw" with "jagged icicles, and everywhere dripping". I went to Oaklands and walked round with a surveyor, then sat in Miss Lord's house at 4 Albion Hill. At this time the clairvoyant John Cameron, of Garratt Green said to me: "I have been looking at your aura ever since I came today. It is yellow-gold and greenish on the edges." Soon afterwards there was a letter from my bank manager challenging the figures I had done for him and saying we could not afford Oaklands and for a whole weekend I did revised figures for him: "Spent the weekend as an accountant, and Zoroastrianism has been neglected." Of Oaklands I wrote: "I am a bit of a T. E. Lawrence figure, having mixed action and scholarship and having been fascinated by Arabia; and now, after several careers, I am about to start another one as a businessman."

At the end of January my family gathered at my mother's house in Loughton to remove effects. Robert presented his fees for winding up the estate and then disappeared for lunch with Jonathan while Frances went to Argie, leaving me to ruminate alone in the dismembered home and study my mother's small round metallic Chinese table, which I had always called a "metaphysical" table and which I had requested. It showed a Chinese labyrinthine maze, the Tao, with a snake, a wasp, a dragon and a dung-beetle on it. Robert returned from lunch full of beer and insisted on wanting the metaphysical table as he could do jigsaw puzzles on it. I later wrote: "The table he does not understand. The Chinese mandala with no way through....Let the yin-yang table go to...Rob who has not been to China and does not know....I had the most perfect Tao on a table and I gave it away. I suppose because I understood it I did not need it....Yin and yang – I went to the East to get the Tao into my work." The next day I wrote: "Money means nothing to me. I live in a world of symbols, and only symbols mean. I must devote my life to metaphysical poetry and philosophy. I looked at a thousand books for an illustration for what I understood by the Tao and it was under my nose all the time. My sphere is metaphysical poetry and philosophy, and as I look back my destiny seems inevitable to me. I went to Oxford in order that I might get to Japan so that I could go on to China and know the Tao. Iraq/Babylon and Libya/Egypt were bonuses, thrown in. My subject matter is the field of 5,000 years which I am covering in *The Seeker and the Light*....I went to Japan in order to contact the wisdom of the East, to find the Tao. I found it, and can now write about it....Tomlin, Tuohy, me: Japan kissed us all into silence as we felt awe before the wisdom of the East. It kissed me into a metaphysical poet, the poet I dreamt of being at Oxford." I added: "I am even more reactionary as a metaphysician than I am as an educationalist. I am restoring – and renewing – a vision from the past which has been forgotten."

I was tracking the history of the Light back to where it first appeared in civilisation and saw it as beginning in Central Asia and passing to Palestine, whence it was borrowed by Egypt. I wrote: "I am the Robert Graves of the post-war world: going into shamanism and other practices and embodying them in my poems. My wide reading is unifying reading. The whole basis of 'being a writer' is 'being a name' – which is egocentric. I am not interested in being me, different; I channel truth from the past, like a latter-day shaman, and do not want to be a name. I want to be invisible, but to get my message across. Artists need to read history or something outside themselves, otherwise their work is shallow." I added: "If I am asked 'Why do you neglect poems, stories and novels for a study of ancient religions?' I have to reply 'Because more truth can be shown in a study of ancient religions than in any poem, story of novel...A study of ancient religions is a study of reality. As a metaphysician and a mystic, I prefer the study of reality to that of fantasy. The imagination may have a divine spring at its root, but not in Western Art." I wrote: "This work is unifying all...multiplicity."

Matthew took his Chigwell School entrance exam while suffering from the after-effects of chicken pox. He had an interview and did well. I recorded: "(He) spoke of Agrippa and Augustus and Tiberius, though only 7." Eventually we heard that he had a place and I arranged for him to have a "family clap" at tea-time.

I thought deeply about Truth. I wrote of the imagination in art and letters as examining human nature through 'imaginary' unsingle situations, as providing texts which have meaning and author's intention. "But preferable to the imagination is Truth, for what is imagined can be invented, ie made up, ie it never happened, whereas what is true comes from higher worlds, is a symbol, teaches the one Light from which human nature is estranged, Gnostic-like, and lives in error. The truth of art is more important than its imagination, ie what is important is not that an artist should imagine a make-believe world, but that his 'imaginings' should include glimpses of the Truth. I would rather write a semi-biographical or autobiographical (work) which examines the deepest springs of human nature in relation to Truth; than write an imaginative make-believe fantasy that claims to embody Truth. The imagination does not necessarily express the Truth. Only some imaginations do."

I was deeply immersed in sun- and moon-cults: "Today worked out the ceremony in the Great Pyramid, from King's Chamber to Queen's Chamber, the sacred ceremony of marriage; and that Stonehenge and other megaliths were used for sacrificing bulls to the sun-god. These thoughts came to me as I edited to get a flow. I have all the answers in my own mind and am very creative....Got the bull's horn/cusped moon – the link is the moon 'on its back' I saw in Iraq....Graves's *White Goddess* – the moon and poetry (feminine and intuitive) versus the sun, Apollonian, intellectual. Inspirational lunar poetry (yin) versus intellectual solar poetry (yang). Graves's feeling that ancient knowledge and mysteries were being thrust upon him. This page in my *Diaries* gives examples...of such mysteries being thrust at me. They come to me with an inner certainty which is irrefutable."

By March the Head of Garratt Green had informed the ILEA Inspectorate that I was proposing to take over a private school while continuing as a Senior Teacher, and I was visited by a left-wing Inspector who proposed heaping half the Deputy Heads' workload onto me, but not on the other Senior Teachers. I pointed out the inequity in her proposal and saw her off. Meanwhile Miss Lord wanted me to attend a policy-explaining meeting on a Wednesday. I arrived to find a packed hall with some 150-200 parents crowded in every available inch of space. Miss Lord and I sat at the table and I spoke, promising the continuation of the Oaklands that I had known as a boy, with its emphasis on the 3Rs, and defused their worries. What I said was very well received, and two days later I returned for a cheese and wine to meet 80 more parents.

At the end of March I got back to my true inner being: "9 p.m.. Broke through the crust of ordinary, everyday living to the genius within and became a different person, awake, alive, not bored and colourless; beyond the television, active, not passive. A god. Am now back in my book, ordering in a world of order and harmony – and great meaning. Man's most important quality is his capacity for order."

"The whole of organised society," I wrote, "has failed to produce a mature human being. The children are fragmented and sold short. They do not think or have a deep flow. The only way is to be detached from society, to stand back as an individual and realise oneself, and put one's own children among rich language and endeavour, ie private school. The only way is to opt out, 'to miss the march of this retreating world'."

In April I returned to Winchester for the Mystics and Scientists Conference of 1982. It attacked Darwinian biology along with Newtonian physics, arguing that a directing, purposive intelligence holds creation in balance. Sir John Eccles, the Cartesian dualist (who therefore believed that mind and matter are different) and Nobel Prize-winning scientist was one of the speakers. He was of very advanced years, white-haired and bespectacled, and I encountered him at the top of the steps and asked him about Descartes' theory of perception. Speaking rapidly he gave it to me. I said, "If I look at that flower, where is the mind that is doing the looking?" He said: "If I look at that flower, my mind is outside my skull between me and the flower. The mind is in a relationship between head and flower, it is outside the skull." In the course of our conversation he kept wondering where his wife was: "I haven't seen my wife." He hunted in his pocketbook for a quotation from *Richard II*, Act 5, which summed up dualism. Peter Fenwick was nearby, balding and bespectacled, and when I turned to him for his view he said, "Okay, mind acts on brain but is not dualistically different from it but is all one. Eccles needs to modify his view. Eccles has solved nothing. He has just pushed the mind further back." Soon afterwards Sir George Trevelyan approached and shook my hand, gazing deep into my eyes, and then shuffled off without a word; and I noted: "Sir George's reverence and humility in coming to shake hands with me, having clairvoyantly seen my soul."

I now felt a great kinship with the Romantic poets who were aware of the invisible world and I saw the New Age vision of an infinite universe as a late flowering of Romanticism. I wrote: "I am one of the last Romantics." I could see that the "new Baroque age" I had glimpsed in Japan was approaching. I wrote: "Romanticism reaches for the spirit in Nature (the Light)....The Romantic Imagination grasps the spirit in Nature, feels into it, and returns to the One....Romanticism in politics seeks to promote a better world based on holistic principles, ie world government....As a Romantic I embrace the infinite around us – the mystical – and open myself to its Light, leaving the will of God to make changes, trusting the Infinite. And I am anti-dualist, seeing the spirit as One and manifesting into form....Existentialism is a late flowering of Romanticism. And the infinite mysticism – spirit in Nature – is likewise as an existential experience. This is a new flowering within the West....Spirit, the living being in Nature: the Light....Go back to 'I' poetry. Let the mysticism grow out of the living experience. Write in touch with the world. Be full of movement and restlessness, and have the stillness of the Light. Drink deep into Nature with the poetic imagination."

I renewed my poetic development in Romantic terms: "Who I am: a Romantic. (Significantly I last lived until 1836 according to my regression, ie I was a contemporary of Wordsworth and Shelley. And I came from the Lake District.) At Oxford I preferred Wordsworth to social satire, and Ricks said, 'I will make you like social satire'. In Japan I deepened my Romantic view by absorbing the Idealism of Eastern religion, and the Modernism of Eliot, Yeats and Pound. I taught a lot of modern poetry and did not like any of it, except for the three Modernists. It's not me. In 1970-1 I met various poets, Abse, MacBeth, Heath-Stubbs and all the rest, and disliked their work. Many of them were homosexuals, not my scene. I got out like Graves, and lived alone and wrote in isolation. All 'I' stuff, in the Romantic tradition of Wordsworth's *Tintern Abbey* and *Intimations of Immortality*, and Shelley's *Hymn to Intellectual Beauty* or *Mont Blanc*. I deepened my knowledge in the 1970s and turned further against materialism and the senses so I ended up with my spiritual vision of matter as spirit, and faith in the imagination; along with a rejection of the media (TV, journalism) and politics. *The Fire-Flower* was on the right lines – metaphysical rather than Romantic – and *Beauty and Angelhood* was about religion and Western civilisation and mysticism, a diversion. Now I must write an essay and proclaim the Romantic revolution....At the end of *Beauty and Angelhood* it seemed that the way forward might have to be into Catholicism, but now I have found it, through Romanticism. What a relief!...Wrote *A New Romanticism*, a poem about Oaklands. And then a short essay on the New Romanticism." And I asked: "Did Heidegger and Jaspers borrow from

German idealism? Did the line go from Kant and Schelling to Wordsworth and Coleridge, to Heidegger and Jaspers? The Romantic interest in Rome and Greece (the past); ours in the Ancient Wisdom." I wrote that my stories were "Romantic stories, full of the throbbing cosmos, teeming with the unity of life, and my poems about my mother are also Romantic poems". I wrote that "Tuohy tried to 'neo-classicise' *The Silence*, which was really my *Prelude* written in Modernist technique". I also observed that "Ricks is a Neo-Classical critic, applying Neo-Classical attitudes to my organic form and image".

I did more work on my essay on Romanticism and wrote: "I am working on the new Renaissance, producing the evidence of the Light....The redefinition of man I dreamt about in Libya, it needed soul, spirit and the Light....I had a classical education (Greek and Latin) and could have become an Augustan but I rebelled against it, adopted the Middle Ages like a Romantic, and used the classics from a Romantic point of view, like Keats or Byron. New Age versus Renaissance, both 'rebirths', but one of spirit and soul, the other of body."

I wrote: "For Tuohy...I must be very clear about what I am doing. I am taking part in a new Romanticism – the New Age consciousness movement which includes Kathleen Raine – and which details a shift in consciousness to unitive, cosmic and transcendent levels, merging into the One with the mystics, with the Romantic imagination; and absorbing the new science (physics, biology, neurophysiology), all of which form the modern background. The Renaissance we are living in, a rebirth of interest in the past, eg Ancient Wisdom. The reason as a tool which takes the mind so far and then has to be left behind. This ties up with the Light of course, which is the metaphysical substance. And the writer? I am in the Renaissance, on the side of the new consciousness; not that of the social ego and Rationalism. When I rejected those two I condemned myself to isolation. I am on the side of the revolution in taste which is on its way, not the ancient regime."

I saw Tuohy at a memorial service in Brighton for Hannah Baker, the wife of my British Council colleague in Japan. I wrote: "Tuohy...was in good form, challenging Romantic views with Neo-Classical positions. Neo-Platonism – 'does it fill the bellies of workers?' Imagination – 'you don't know when it's happening' (experience). New physics and biology – 'that's got nothing to do with how people relate to each other or how they see it'. (Cf the stars – 'they've got nothing to do with relationships'.)" Also: "Poems based on the Kabbalah need not have been written in the first place." He told me: "The English feel contempt for foreigners and working class, and the Empire held so long as the contempt was there; it is all snobbishness and class-based." Of language, Tuohy said: "It all comes back to language, 'spirit in Nature'. (The Romantics) are making propositions which are unanswerable."

The Chief Examiner of 'O' level English Literature came to Garratt Green, and I told him: "Set books grow in the mind like trees, they take on an organic shape in the mind as image. They have an organic form." I recorded: "He agreed with this Romantic view of set-book teaching." I wrote: "Set books are images and symbols. A work of art is an image or a symbol."

In April Ann and I collected Nadia from Caroline. We met them in the Crown and Greyhound, the scene of my despair in 1970, and I again had the sense of events gathering round places like different tides washing flotsam round the same breakwater. I wrote: "(Caroline) is tall, willowy, blonde, well-groomed, slightly ravaged looking, with the old glint in her eye. Slightly more relaxed and happier than when I last saw her, more at ease with herself socially. A lot of questions, good feeling. I sat at the end of the table in the large 'snug' in the Crown and Greyhound, the children drank two coca colas and ate crisps, Nadia had a lager, Caroline and Ann dry martinis and I drank my shandy.... And there was a good feeling of reunion, hardly a stone's throw from where we sat nearly 12 years ago in September 1970, and in pain I saw her slip out of reach....Nadia was pleased we were together, and kept smiling at me." I recorded my reaction: "What do I feel? Detached, observing it all with interest, my strange family...,two halves now reconciled and in balance; a format I like."

Future Oaklands parents, the Snowsills, had us to Sunday lunch in Loughton with their three children. Richard Snowsill was an immensely tall 6 foot 7 inches, and in the afternoon we walked to the Lost Pond.

In May, during the Falklands War I happened to drive past Riverway School, and saw from the board that it was now East Greenwich Christchurch C of E Primary School, and also Thameside Adult Education Institute.

I went to Cambridge and visited Grantchester. I wrote: "Tea at the Orchard and then a look at Mill House, where Whitehead lived. The apple blossom and breakfast in the garden in 1910. Brooke moved before Christmas 1910. He was all that was golden and good about the Edwardian time. Virginia Woolf thought he would be Prime Minister, Churchill wrote we will never see his kind again, and suddenly he was gone, though his ghost is still there."

I pondered the analytical left brain of the social ego and the world of work; and the right brain of art, music, drama and poetry, "the intuitive source of the Light", which is reached by crossing a bridge, the corpus callosum, over which meditation gives mastery. I thought that the immortal self is in the limbic area where consciousness enters from outside.

At the end of May Pope John Paul II visited Britain. We got up at 6 a.m. and saw him drive from the Papal Nuncio's residence at Parkside, Wimbledon towards Roehampton. He stood, wearing white in his Popemobile, and the road was lined with people on both sides. He went on to Canterbury to advance the Ecumenical movement. I wrote: "I am in favour of Christian reunification against Communism, and all the churches are now drawing together, which is good. All that remains is to stress the Light as the basis of the reunification." I did not know that the forces of the Crown and the forces of the Pope had been locked in a secret battle for domination, and in view of this context my sense of the importance of the reunification of Christendom was all the more significant. I wrote of the Catholic mystical tradition of St. Augustine, Pope Gregory the Great and St. Bernard, which the Pope embodied, and observed: "Church religion of the social ego versus the religion of one's core, the mysticism of the spirit. It is the mystical tradition of the spirit I am after, not the 'Church' religion of the social ego."

I had persuaded my bank manager, Ron Thomas, to give me a bridging loan so that the purchase of Oaklands could proceed before I sold 46 Ritherdon Road, and in June I was organising an exchange of contracts, which happened on July 26th. It was agreed that Ann would be Headmistress from the beginning of the autumn term and that we would collect the fees from September in return for completing the purchase of Oaklands in October. I reviewed the staff's pay structure. A neighbour offered us the top floor of 15 Albion Hill from September, where we could live while I built a new house in the school grounds.

I had written a *Preface to my Selected Poems* and shown it to Sir George Trevelyan, who had written: "Now I have read the *Preface* with delight and excitement. It is a splendid statement and it is fine to have it made by one who has the authority of the scholar and poet. I gained a lot by reading it." I now reread Whitehead and wrote: "My *Preface*...echoes Whitehead's *Science and the Modern World* – the chapter on the Romantic reaction – which I had not read recently before writing the *Preface*. Whitehead and I arrived at our championing of idealism...and Wordsworth and Shelley independently – and therefore of Brooke. Whitehead lived in Grantchester just before Brooke. A philosophy of organism, with organism in a vitalist organic theory replacing material in the materialistic theory. No bifurcation of Nature – there must not be any bifurcation of Nature....The unity view of today (Holism) goes back to Whitehead and Brooke – Grantchester – and from there to the Romantic reaction against materialism which presented Nature alive, as a living thing, of which Grantchester is an image and Oaklands too, in my case. Oaklands, the living rejection of materialism, a garden where everything is organism, deepened by the manifesting of the Tree of Life. Concentrate on the manifestation into form, but be aware of what is behind it all: the Light."

Out of this perception I glimpsed a poem: "My 'Oaklands' poem...catches the 'livingness' of Nature. The walk through tall kingcups, among many oaks; my two living fields, like two halves of the brain, joined by the gate: analysis and imagination, where the horses are....The Ode is the Romantic form par excellence, and I have a reflective Ode on Grantchester in Keatsian form, and a Pindaric Ode on the Pope, and a Wordsworthian Ode à *Intimations of Immortality* in irregular lines on mother's death. I had written no poetry since she died, except drafted poetry, and my *Preface*; but I have found my Romantic feet and am now prepared to write my bits and pieces in the form of an Ode."

I now returned to poetry: "June 15. Have planned 3 Odes, two smallish ones on the materialism of today (in Grantchester) and on the Pope; and one extended one on my mother's death. Have worked out strophe, antistrophe and epode in each." On June 19th I wrote: "Slept much of the day, felt passive. Kept sitting and nodding off....Then after 9 p.m., redrafted my first Ode in one and a half hours, just the general outline. Feel very passive indeed, Wordsworth's 'wise passiveness'. My brain rhythms must be very slow, close to sleep. But I am pleased with my effort. So far as I recollect, this is my first Ode (with strophe, antistrophe and epode), and it is on the breaking down of the separation between mind and Nature, and combines the garden theme, which is dear to my heart. This could be an important poem if I do it right....Marvell's union of mind and Nature as 'green' – 'a green thought in a green shade'. Thought and shade, mind and Nature. Marvell gave a solution to my problem, so quote it, or allude to it." Later I wrote: "I have two poems. One about Greenwich, materialism and Newton, who became a Rosicrucian and an alchemist; and one about Grantchester, Whitehead and Brooke. Mind the material; mind-material." In the end both Odes became the *Cambridge Ode: Against Materialism.*

We went to a Parents' barbecue at Oaklands. At one point my Aunt Argie sat in the study with Miss Lord while I was asked questions about next term's arrangements by several parents. A fortnight later in July we lunched with Miss Lord and stayed until sunset, when there were drinks on her patio. Argie told me that my Aunt Flo had secondary bone cancer. Then on July 17th Miss Lord officially retired. Many people gathered in the Oaklands' tennis court and there were balloons.

About this time our former tenant Kyoko Sato came to tea. She was now a Noh dancer in the Tamura "sect" in Kyoto. She was only the third woman to do Noh dancing in Japan.

At the end of term at Garratt Green Ann's mother took the children to Cornwall and Ann and I stayed with Argie and spent ten days decorating the most essential parts of Oaklands. I worked from 8 a.m. until 10 p.m. each day, and averaged a room a day: two coats on ceilings and walls and doors. Exhausted, we then drove to Cornwall in the middle of the night and soon I was walking across the Charlestown rocks with the boys, stepping carefully over slimy green weed.

Throughout the holidays I realised that my interest in Romanticism was only part of the story, and that I was really combining Classicism and Romanticism to bring to birth a new Baroque poetry. This development was associated with Christopher Ricks.

I had sent some poems to Ricks with a letter about Romanticism and he now replied that Romanticism was the "right context" for my work, and he cited W. Jackson Bate on the essential continuity of Augustan poetry into Romantic poetry, as opposed to a confrontation between the two. (This perception had opened the way for Ricks to see Keats as an Augustan in his book, *Keats and Embarrassment.*) He felt Romanticism pays a price, meaning that it forfeits the social world of the ego. I now thought deeply about materialism, which reduces all immaterial things, including minds, to the hard, massy material objects it knows. I wrote: "Ricks and Tuohy are differing forms of Materialists and are therefore foils." I also thought deeply about mind.

On August 11th I visited a house in Polruan whose normally private garden was open for visiting for one day. It had several tiered lawns and a path that ran down to a cove and rocks. That evening I returned to the general outline I had written on June 19th and drafted the poem that became *Cambridge Ode: Against Materialism* at Ann's mother's house in St.

METAPHYSICAL AND BAROQUE

Austell (4 Manor Close, Fairfield Park): "This evening shaped *Against Materialism: a New Renaissance* into 16 stanzas of 10 lines each having sketched 3 or 4 stanzas in the course of the day. At 11.50 p.m. finished – feel very alive. Was helped by the house watching television this evening (Miss Universe from Peru) after the Red Arrows – which left me alone for two hours. Did it sitting on my bed in this cramped bungalow....The force seized me and made me shape my poem and would not let me rest until I had done it, red from the sun while I watched the Red Arrows shirtless." I filled my *Diaries* with chunks of Newton, and wrote: "I am not a Materialist for sunlight differs from subtle Light (body/spirit) but the question is, did the subtle Light originally create, and manifest as, the sun?...I have an original vision. I must stick to it and continue to proclaim it. My vision of the Light is unique and it's me."

A few days later I had a vivid experience in Charlestown: "Worked all day – cloudy and rainy – and got back into my Light book. Typed in the correct version of Zoroastrians and Essenes...and refined Shamanism. Tired, went to have a drink at Charlestown and walked, with Ann, hand in hand, down to the harbour under a starlit sky, no cloud, and lo! across the moonless sky, like a firework rocket trailing yellow as on a bonfire night and falling, from right to left, sped – what? A meteorite re-entering the earth's atmosphere? A comet? A shooting star? But afterwards it seemed as though no star was secure in its place and Newton was all wrong and any star might suddenly hurtle towards us and fall into Charlestown harbour. And the fact that it didn't was a sign of God's law in the heavens, a sign of order."

I was still thinking about Romanticism. I wrote: "The ego of the Classicist writer hides behind the ego of man – but it is ego, social ego, that he writes about....A Classicist's work reveals very little of the writer, and he creates a world to be shared by all, whereas the Romantic creates a world that is different from anyone else's....Whereas the Classicist hides his ego behind the ego of Man, the Romantic reveals his ego – and it is only the new Romanticism that seeks to relate that ego to the core behind it....My whole life-style has been a Romantic one: living in the solitude of a foreign city – Tokyo – and writing these *Diaries*, observing, delving, remembering. To be a Classicist I should have obtained a social position after Oxford and observed others in their social positions." I came up with a definition of poetry: "Poetry is the opening of the social ego to the core, and the outpouring of the soul's delight when, in the course of contemplating the natural world, it opens to Reality and perceives the infinite and eternal world of Light which is immanent in creation, and whose symbols control the imagination."

I felt I should return to lyric poetry: "Get back to writing more lyrics – only with the infinite and eternal world peeping through. Pope: 'Most souls, 'tis true, peep out but once an age.' Show the infinite peeping through the finite, the eternal peeping through the temporal. I chose not to write lyrics as I can only do one thing at a time with my time."

I felt that European civilisation had one artistic style, a Classical style, which went through a pre-classical, archaic phase (medieval art); a classical phase (the Italian Renaissance); a first post-classical or Neo-Classical academic stage (15th-16th century academy); a first Mannerist or pre-baroque stage (El Greco); and a first baroque stage, the historical Baroque, c1600-1750. I felt that after a civilisation has broken down and lost its Light there is a renewed struggle between Neo-Classicism and Romanticism – whose classical phase of 1798-1830 passed into an academic phase (Matthew Arnold and the 1890s poets), Modernism and Neo-Romanticism – and that out of the conflict between these repeated stages comes a new Baroque stage, a mixture of Classicism and Mannerism (or Neo-Classicism and Neo-Romanticism, of Movement form and universal Romantic subject matter) – of sense and spirit. I saw my work as bringing in this coming stage in my *Preface*. I felt that work from the new Baroque Age cannot be judged by Neo-Classical or Neo-Romantic standards or criteria, but must be judged by standards or criteria that have not yet come into being, which do not now exist but which must now be devised. My "new Baroque Age" was therefore a final stage in the second repeated cycle of our civilisation. It would mark a unique and quite distinct stage in European civilisation and would develop from the academic, social perspective of Neo-Classicism, which was an art of reaction as in Larkin, and from the more individual perspective of Neo-Romanticism of such poets as Dylan Thomas and Kathleen Raine. "Thus," I wrote, "the Light is the foundation of the New Age. It is very important. Without the Light there can be no New Age." I added: "I found my voice late because it is the voice of the next Age."

Of my theory of the cycle of styles, I wrote on May 21st: "All this came to me today after my defiant assertion to Ann last night after drinking in the Rashleigh Inn, Polkerris, and then walking along the Charlestown harbour wall and back under the stars, that I am right to oppose Neo-Classicism because I belong to a coming Age, and that each year brings me nearer to it and my destiny, whereas each year can only diminish a Neo-Classicist like Ricks or Tuohy, who believe I should write in their style....I have solved a problem today – aesthetic theory – which has held me up for some years. My mind is so clear and sharp these days. This Cornish air suits me....I have a direct line to the Almighty tonight: finished Ann's crossword for her in a few seconds, when she was stuck: pry, not spy, leading to pageantry and yoicks (foxhunting cry). It was as though someone was feeding in the answers, just like that – snap, snap, snap (of the fingers). At times like that I know what brilliance is. The higher mind."

It is worth pointing out that this theory of cycles may have come from the Light itself: "12.15 a.m. on Aug 22. This morning – yesterday morning – I woke early and looked for the Light, and spent an hour with faint Light playing, swirling through water, ethereally and supernaturally. I felt very calm and tranquil and very charged with 'prana' when I got up. The theory of cycles I have come up with on this important day may well have come from the Light that filled my mind in 'prayer' this morning."

Later that day I recorded: "I have knocked down Coleridge. Instead of Platonist Ideas flowing into the higher Reason and thence to the imagination as symbols, and the phenomena of the natural world in turn being regarded as symbols of the Ideas (Coleridge); the eternal symbols flow into the core – the soul and spirit which awaken when the reason and social ego slumber –

as the Light and proceed thence to the imagination, while the phenomena of the natural world are 'symbols' for the eternal world of the Light."

"The Light," I wrote, "is in fact prana, which is everywhere, in every atom, the earth, sun, moon and stars....,an immaterial substance that pervades the universe, vital energy which is the architect of organic structures out of elements and compounds and which can't be tested empirically. It is force on matter and life in mind. It is experienced as deathless in samadhi (yoga) and on death it is what goes (hence the Clear Light of the Void). It is the life energy – Holy Spirit in Christianity, which brings the organic into existence. Yogis have discovered voluntary control over it, and it flows up the central nervous system....Sun-bathing and sea air give prana." I noted: "Since my enlightenment over 10 years ago in 1971, I have enjoyed almost perfect health, and a perfect indigestion and emptying of the bowels....Also I now feel full of prana and have always been tranquil, at peace. Now, at midnight on Aug 22, I feel full of peace. The divine source of prana/Light has filled me with its fullness which is full of symbols and feeling. The Infinite of the Romantics is of course the prana of Hinduism/the Light."

I now felt I had found, and that there would be no more searching, merely clarification.

At the end of August we began moving from 46 Ritherdon Road to Loughton. We filled the car, took the stuff in to 15 Albion Hill, then had lunch with Elizabeth Lord and tea with Mabel Reid. We lived in the two upstairs rooms at our new address now, and while Ann took over as Headmistress at Oaklands, immediately across the road, I got up at 5.45 a.m., ate a silent breakfast I had made overnight, crept out of the house without waking Matthew (who had started at Chigwell School) and Anthony (who had started at Oaklands), lingered to admire the dawn over the Oaklands' grounds, then got into my car and drove to Wandsworth in time to do the Coverage. When I got back in the evening there was money to organise and accounts to do, and I now worked flat out coping with both schools. I did no writing for the first two weeks, but I took to looking in on the empty 46 Ritherdon Road after school and began typing up my *Preface* in my study before locking the house and returning to Loughton.

Following the announcement that Miss Lord was retiring the Oaklands roll had fallen to 156. Now that we were in place and demonstrating an intention to renew the building and the syllabus, the numbers began to creep up, and it was soon clear that confidence had returned and that Oaklands was in demand.

In October Matthew had his birthday party in the Tower with some Chigwell friends. We saw the Crown Jewels, the axe that killed Lord Lovat (two chops on the block) in 1747, the ravens, the armour in the White Tower where the princes were murdered, Raleigh's place of imprisonment and the site of the scaffold.

It soon became apparent that Miss Lord had run Oaklands in a particularly idiosyncratic and somewhat Irish way. She was 81 when she handed over, and she had a habit of collecting cash and tucking it behind a cushion in one of the study chairs. Parents spoke of sitting on the settee and becoming aware of a wad of notes beside them. On one occasion she collected getting on for £1,000 and hid it in the gas oven, a place where no one would think of looking for it. The cook arrived and was about to light the gas for lunch when Miss Lord intercepted her and removed the notes before they were roasted. I insisted on all cheques and cash received being banked the same day.

We were asked to go round to meet the Oaklands' Parents' Association who were meeting at a parent's house. We rang the bell one evening, were shown in and found ourselves being interrogated in interview chairs in the middle of a circle of getting on for 30 people about what we were to do with the funds they raised for the school. I quickly gathered that with Miss Lord approaching 82, some of the parents had effectively run parts of the school for her and resented our arrival, which threatened their power. I made a low key impromptu speech, and one of the parents, who came from Cornwall, said afterwards: "We thought you might be an ogre. You laid a lot of dust. You're not an ogre." I wrote: "Among the little people. In Lilliput. Their pride and dignity."

Soon afterwards I had to hold an evening meeting for the local residents about the parking at Oaklands. I invited local councillors and a policeman (PC Giddings), and we made Albion Hill unofficially one way at peak times to ease the flow of traffic. The following day, on October 29th, I completed the purchase of Oaklands. The astrologer Ted Collings had forecast that I would begin a new stage of my life in October 1982. I still had not sold 46 Ritherdon Road, but gambled on selling it when the property market recovered.

I had finished my *Preface* on October 17th and sent it to Christopher Ricks. I noted: "The imagination is seeing the Idea within the form – it is a Platonist idea. Romanticism and Platonism. (The breakthrough I had in writing to Tuohy in Stapleton Road, in that cramped front room, when I grasped that Plato transcended sense experience, and really felt the Romantic Idealism to be a true reflection of my state of mind then.)"

On October 29th I visited Ricks at Christ's, Cambridge. I went up to B6 and saw him through the open door, wearing jeans, and immediately warmed to his endearing smile beneath his bald head and small round spectacles. He said I had sharpened my ideas: "I believe in the Baroque, but though everything that is Baroque is Classical and Romantic, not everything that is Classical and Romantic is Baroque" – to which I replied that the Light is central to the new Baroque. He said: "The proof of the pudding is in the eating. I think your work is Baroque. You got there, even though your itinerary surprised you. You must anthologise 30 poems, each no longer than a page. Make your entry and then expand. I know selection is painful, it's painful for me to leave out bits from my lectures." I told him that I had temporarily disowned *The Gates of Hell* because they were not metaphysical, and more recently, the Neo-Christian poems because they did not fit in with Romanticism. "Both fell within the Baroque." He nodded. Ricks had skilfully diagnosed the position ahead of mine and was leading me forward. We discussed whether Romanticism is spilt religion" (T. E.. Hulme) and how I am anti-clerical as in Lowell's *Quaker Graveyard at*

Nantucket. Of Oaklands, he said "It's Providential", an adjective I did not expect to hear from him. He discussed his role as Faculty Chairman. He said: "I'm not Leavis yet, Cambridge is a different world from when Leavis was lecturing. I want to unify the Faculty." At this point he came out with me, and as we trotted in the Christ's quadrangle I asked how he would unify it. Without hesitation, with impressive alertness and fluency, he quoted Dryden's *Absalom and Achitophel*:

> "And David's mildness managed things so well
> The bad found no occasion to rebel."

I had always admired Colin Wilson's natural ability to relate lessons in life to episodes in European Literature, and I now marvelled at the exactness and appropriateness of Ricks's unhesitating use of Dryden's words and the way they conveyed his attitude. I did not know that "the bad" (Ricks was referring to Colin MacCabe) had already rebelled very violently and split the Cambridge English Faculty, and that Ricks, Frank Kermode and MacCabe himself would all leave their jobs soon afterwards, Ricks for the USA. He shook my hand and dived across the road to attend a lecture. I went on to Grantchester to eat and stood by the Old Vicarage, thinking of Brooke, and my musings were disturbed when Jeffrey Archer got into a W car and drove out.

Soon afterwards Ricks was on television. He was in dazzling form and glittered with his distinctions and attitudes, dwarfing the other guests and saying memorable things that lingered in the mind long after the programme was over. He described how embarrassed he was by his own father who attended his first Oxford lecture and stood up after 20 minutes, making chain-pulling gestures with a raised hand, causing Ricks to stop. Ricks said: "I think Dad wants to go to the lavatory, does anyone know where it is? Down the corridor, Dad." Afterwards his father caught the bus back to Worthing without returning to his lecture.

In November we went for a nature walk with Mabel Reid. We left her house, Elm Cottage in Albion Hill, turned left into Nursery Road, plunged into the forest before the track to the Warren and walked to the sweet chestnuts ("prickly hedgehogs"). She talked all the way, striding along with her stick and her eye shield while the four of us struggled to keep up. We walked round the gravel pits and returned through the Stubbles while she reminisced about "the unwashed" who used to come out from the East End during her childhood.

Towards the end of November I visited Tuohy at 13 Ladbroke Grove, London. We sat downstairs in Sophia's room among old Masters, marbles, African eggs, leather chairs and a grandfather clock on which was inscribed "Dum Dormiunt Vigilo" ("I keep watch while they sleep"), and then a Foreign Office Arabist came in and Tuohy and I went round the corner to a pub where he drank gin and tonic and I drank shandy and we discussed the Kabbalah and Collingwood. He said: "Historians should ask the questions that were asked at the time, the word 'Renaissance' was not used until 1850 so the Renaissance didn't know they were having a Renaissance." He said that for Romantics writing is "an orgasm, involving detumescence". We discussed the period we most admired. He said: "I am a prose-writer, and so I admire the century of prose, the 18th century....It's all to do with good prose – Classicism." He told me he had been to Durham to teach a 2-week creative writing course, and: "I had to read all their f—ing stuff."

I reflected that art has mystery and should not be demystified: "The Light is a mystery, art reveals the Light, therefore art should catch the mystery and not explain....Art should not be taught as the courses, seminars and exams further demystify and label. Therefore I should give up teaching Literature and go for its mystery through my writing of it. Art takes you to the meaning of life. (The mystery is the meaning of life, at which art hints.)"

Incredibly the Oaklands term had come to an end. Somehow I was able to attend the staff lunch on the day we broke up, and sit next to the Dickensian odd job man, a red-faced octogenarian called Mr Burns.

I had shown Ricks *The Fire-Flower* and *Beauty and Angelhood*, and he wrote to me that he had read them "with some awe at your energy of mind and synthesising (not synthetic) aspirations. The Notes are I think a genuine help, and done (both proffered and enacted) with tact and modesty. Touches of the best of Empson in them – and in some things in the poems (that despair/rare rhyme, for instance)." I noted: "As Ricks was on TV recently, saying that Empson is the only living genius, that is praise enough."

That Christmas I did not realise that 1983 would be a year given almost exclusively to education: to strengthening my hold on Oaklands as Principal and running the 50 or so staff while continuing as Head of English and Senior Teacher at Garratt Green.

We went to my sister Frances' for Christmas lunch. I "longed to lead a monkish life alone" but entered into the spirit of things. I recorded: "Ann came up to me with a severe pain in her neck. I stood, put my hand on her neck and prayed, asked God to heal her pain and gave thanks that it was already happening. And immediately there were 4 large surges through me and into her neck." On Boxing Day we visited Mabel Reid in Moorfields Hospital and I recorded: "She sat hunchbacked, holding her emergency button, in a blue dressing-gown, blind, as the operation for a detached retina had affected the cornea of her left eye."

I was convinced more than ever that we have an invisible spiritual body within our material body, and I told John Cameron as much at Garratt Green: "My gifts of the spirit – hypnotism, healing, seeing the future (eg when I said 'We will know that if the Pope is assassinated, the KGB are involved')." On January 23rd I recorded some visions: "Last night after love, visions pouring up, springing up, from the unconscious – patterns in detached 'mosaic', Paisley-tesserated patterns, Henry Moore-like images, ET faces, and I wondered if these were spirit-bodies, forms from the eternal spiritual world, forms." Of art I wrote: "See the arts very clearly. They express – at their best – a civilisation's beauty and perfection (cf Arnold in *Culture and Anarchy*), and so my art must express the most beautiful and perfect experience one can have, that of the Light."

METAPHYSICAL AND BAROQUE

I was teaching Matthew Arnold's *Culture and Anarchy*, and wrote: "M. Arnold's 'buried life': the soul is a river and meadow, and we are barred from it, shut out behind a bolted gate, but believing we are free, when in fact we are in prison. We do not know who we are or where we came from. But Wordsworth knew. Investigate Matthew Arnold, the Inspector of Schools who was never himself – taken away by a thousand railway lines, and feeling the 'melancholy' of a starved, neglected soul. Neglect your soul for the outer world of London education, and you feel a sadness. The escape: the Scholar Gipsy....M. Arnold in *Culture and Anarchy* is saying that there is an ordinary, everyday self which does as it likes (individual freedom) and a best self which aims for perfection through religion or the arts – culture's reading, observing, thinking. The artist reaches out to the best self of all mankind and when we are governed by our best self, as we are when we are steeped in the arts, we moderate our behaviour and do not indulge in the anarchy of rioters....The buried life – the best self?" And I added: "God's – the Light's – disgust at a world overwhelmed by Satan. God withdrawn from his revolting creature, man, but still loving and caring and responding to every opened heart."

I went to Norfolk to buy some school furniture and stopped at Ely's octagonal Cathedral and went to Cromwell's home, "so near to the Cathedral he evidently hated. How could he have hated it? The singing he found 'unedifying and defensive' and locked the place up for 17 years. The puzzle, how could the Collector of Ely Tithes have risen to cut off the head of a King? Used to be the Cromwell Arms – sign board inside – and is now occupied by the Vicar of St. Mary's: black and white boards, square and diamond lead windows. The elevating, uplifting, soaring of the Norman Cathedral buttresses. Then on through the black earth of Norfolk, black crows, to King's Lynn."

At Garratt Green I was "trapped in my ordinary, everyday self", "chained to the banal and mundane", and found myself in conflict with the ILEA Inspectorate, who had identified me as a traditionalist who might resist the new English policy of no marking. One of the Inspectors had given Heads of English a talk, saying he wanted to abolish detailed marking as it suggested "the teacher snarling in the margin" and the children should learn their mistakes for themselves. It was not explained how the children would learn their mistakes and I thought the view crazy and said so. The Inspector responsible for this "no marking policy" shouted at me, as if the rightness of not marking children's work could be demonstrated by the volume of his voice rather than logic. I wrote: "I criticised the ILEA to my superiors by adopting the Swiftian device of Cambridge, and they were not clever enough to understand my subtlety." I struck back by recommending at the next Senior Teachers' meeting that the school should forthwith cease all marking in accordance with the new ILEA policy; and succeeded in dividing the Head and the Senior Teachers from the Inspectorate. John Cameron was so disgusted by the move that he wrote to Stuart Sexton, a Junior Minister at the DES. Shortly afterwards it was announced that the Inspector in question was retiring. I attended his farewell party, at which he issued a defiant call to carry on with the "no marking" policy.

A MYSTIC WAY

I now thought about Matthew Arnold's "interesting distinction between Hebraism and Hellenism, doing and knowing, conduct and truth-seeing; Christianity and culture. I am on the Hellenistic side, but the Light transforms both, that is the point, and unites the two. Margaret is a Hebraist, I am a Hellenist. That is why I am reluctant to go to church although I have the Light. I want to enshrine the Light in an epic, not sing hymns. My mother was Hebraist. It is Yeats's distinction, 'The intellect of man is forced to choose/Perfection of the life or of the work.' I choose the second. As a part of this, I must attack Quietism, with its belief in Providence, which is a passive form of Hebraism....Good is not done naturally, by Providence, without any effort being made. Evil has to be opposed, humans have to define themselves, existentially. Leaving it all to Providence is often too easy – some of the time Providence works for us, and the Angels help – but all so often it is down to our own efforts, the Puritan will....Quietism: do nothing, and let God work through you." I wrote: "Hellenism is of Indo-European stock. Hebraism of Semitic stock. We Westerners are knowers rather doers. We see things as they are....I want to be a knower of Reality rather than a doer in a church. Romanticism, a form of Hellenism: spirit and beauty. My Light book is about doers, but from the point of view of a knower....I am a Hellenist who sees Reality as it is by knowing the Light, and grasping its true meaning and significance." I wrote again: "The earthquake of Matthew Arnold. Hellenism – Greek seeing things as they really are – and Hebraism (conduct). I am a mystic Hellenist, I am not concerned with sin. My God is the Light, I am writing of a vision of knowledge, an intellectual vision. And yet when it enters the soul, one is guided. My concern with Coleridge and the spirit and prana in the *Preface* is Hellenistic rather than Hebraistic....I have taken Arnold's way of approaching a Greek (Hellenic) way of seeing things as they are – reality – through culture, my intellectual side and all parts of myself, developing my whole humanity, and not by concentrating solely on my moral side. I have come to see the intelligible law of things – Reality, the Light – and have no doubt strengthened my moral side, but the Light is meant to inform many-sidedness. (The many philosophies – the One, it is knowing both.) Arnold may get lost in multiplicity without the reference point at the centre of the one Light, but I must make it clear that my fundamental aim is a Hellenic one, to see Reality, to see things as they are, and that though Reality is Hebraistic in the way it works, in my Light book I am essentially a Hellenist among the Hebrews, a Hellenist with Hebrew subject matter."

At the February half term we all drove to Edinburgh and went up to Cramond where Nadia was temporarily living in a caravan, having fled a particular man who was sharing a very large flat she had been in. She had left school and after a spell at Edinburgh airport was working with a music publisher, having got a job for which there were 252 applicants. I wrote: "Cramond, where Nadia was brought by Caroline, and left, and where she has taken root among her friends. It is a backwater, like Golant in Cornwall. The sea runs inland, there is a 10p ferry and a boat house and 3-storey fishermen's cottages and stepped paths that climb steeply up to hidden cottages. There is a pub, a phone box and the café where Nadia worked....Her caravan...is in the grounds of the house of the café-owner.

Nadia, on the breadline, has booked us in to the Barnton Hotel up the road from her, where the social life is, where the hirsute Scots are with their squinty-expletive expressions on their faces. Feel sad. Nadia was dumped here all alone, and is now fending for herself without much money, and I have to save her from the place – or she will be hobbling along the Cramond waterfront at the age of 80."

We went for a walk with Nadia on the Cramond waterfront. I wrote: "The sea round tracts of sand and many birds, the white cottages and woods across the ferry and round the corner. Mist obscured the Firth of Forth." We visited the café and the caravan in the café-owner's parents' drive. We lunched with Nadia, and I explained to her how she could set about buying a flat. We went to Holyrood Castle and toured the spot of Rizzio's murder, and then returned to Cramond "and the birds were pecking among the mudbanks: oyster-catchers (white underbelly and bar on wing, curved long back and curious running head-nodding walk), terns, curlews, snipe. Cramond, as old as 142AD and Severus, a backwater. The river. Edinburgh by night, then out to quiet Cramond." In the evening she brought a friend to the Cramond Inn and we all had dinner, and later we went back to the Barnton Hotel, where we were staying, and met many of her friends.

The next morning we met her in Cramond. She wore a donkey jacket and plimsolls and carried an ex-army bag over her shoulder and gazed across the weir and low tide towards Forth Bridge, which was hidden in mist, and I left her to brave the world and to her lonely, trapped life among her friends, urging her to move from the caravan into a flat. We drove to Hadrian's Wall. I wrote: "Grey-green wall overlooking plunging green fields of Cumbria, a turret, a signal tower. The ravine. The barbarians north of the Wall....came down through lakes and mountains with streaks of snow."

At the April 1983 Mystics and Scientists conference I heard a lecture by David Bohm, the physicist who had had discussions with Einstein and had proposed that the universe is an implicate or unfolding order that is a whole. He stood rather wizen-faced and mumbled at the lectern – he was not the best of speakers – and later I found myself standing beside him waiting for the rain to cease. I had a short discussion with him, and he told me, "These are just some ideas I've got, that's all. Just some ideas." And I warmed to his modesty as he had put his work in a very truthful perspective.

On the way home my car broke down. Consequently I was late for the visit of a prospective buyer for 46 Ritherdon Road, the Shakespearean actor Norman Rodway. I met him the next day, a likeable silver-haired, silky-looking man who spoke scathingly of the lack of professionalism of the young actresses he had to rehearse with. We had tea together, sitting in the dining-room and talking about the theatre, and the following Sunday he came by appointment with a younger, thin, quiet man in jeans with a bookish brow and thick-lensed spectacles who seemed shy and wandered round on his own. Eventually when we all stood together, Rodway said "Nicholas, have you met Alan Howard?" and I realised I was standing with one of the great Shakespearean actors, who was later to play all the kings of Shakespeare's histories. He could hold a theatre spellbound and dominate it, but I found him very unassuming and retiring in the context of my house.

413

Rodway made an offer for the house, which I accepted, thereby very belatedly – over six months after the completion of the school – confirming the last condition for the purchase of Oaklands and the start of the building of our new house. I had taken a large risk in proceeding with Oaklands before selling the house, and the gamble had paid off. One must speculate to accumulate – or, in the words of *Beowulf* I have already quoted "fate often preserves the undoomed warrior when his courage his strong".

Over the next few weeks I saw quite a bit of Rodway. He wanted to alter the kitchen and make one open-plan area at the back of the house, and he would ring and ask if he could meet me in the afternoon to measure this or look at that, and I always enjoyed our chats. He always had an interesting theatre story, and much of what he said confirmed my view that acting standards were falling. He was a very well-read actor, who enjoyed discussing the interpretation of the classics. On one occasion he rang me at 3.50 and asked to come round. I put the radio on while I waited and heard: "Monday's play is Gorky's *Enemies*. Here is the star of the play, Norman Rodway, to tell you about it." For 5 minutes Rodway talked, slightly inarticulately, fumbling for the occasional word, and as he finished the doorbell rang and there stood the bearded Rodway.

I visited Jack Skilton, who ran Warrington Gardens for my father. He was nearly blind, and very dutiful to my father's memory: "My trouble (blindness) is unimportant, you've got your life ahead, I've had my life, it's your news I want to hear – aren't you your father's son, I recognise that persistence." I noted: "The reverential lip-service to my parents, though both are dead, and the quiet patience in the face of bureaucratic muddle."

I was still pondering Arnold: "Arnold is on the side of the mind (culture) as opposed to the body (Philistines), and his reason, like Coleridge's, is the whole soul of man of Hellenism – as opposed to the partial approach of Hebraism. His 'sweetness and light' (the words are Swift's) are about the beauty and religious energy, the 'reason' and intelligence which the mind sparkles at, and he has a missionary zeal in seeking to make culture prevail among the masses: he was a Hellenist who promoted culture with a Hebraistic zeal, and was touched by the Missionary Age (sending missionaries to convert the colonies). He sought not to save the souls of the masses for an after-life, but to save their minds by making culture available to them in this life....Loughton is a place of Philistines: they devote their time to the body, exercising and feeling it, like good materialists, and though they seek to train the mind as well, have no time for culture."

I thought of the rooted Essex life, of how my father had come to Essex as a war-time immigrant from another area, and of my family's slow struggle to become established and put me through the local private school, and then how I had come back and owned it, and I realised that Voltaire's advice to dig your garden was only part of the pattern. It was also to "get your land, make a garden and become rooted". And I accordingly opened negotiations for the two Oaklands fields.

I wrote of Oaklands: "I have a private 'Academy of the Arts', cf Plato's academy." I dreamt of an Academy of Arts which would be "an exhibition centre for art and for the Forest, a concert hall for music, a lecture hall for writers to gather and discuss – a place where we can transform the consciousness of the people in life (at school) and in art (Academy of Arts), and bring the Light back, through the arts, into the lives of the local people." I saw that Oaklands could become "the place where a European-wide movement began".

Again: "Lowell wrote *Life Studies* about his ancestors and relatives and always looked for a woman who would change his life, and he wrote about them in his poems, in oblique images. He put his family through Hell to become a great poet. My way is to build a Palace of Art – Oaklands – and let my family benefit from it while I withdraw for large parts of the day into mystic-poetic contemplation." And I recorded an experience earlier that day: "I went to the Nightingale Stables, down a lane, 18th century buildings, horses, two dogs playing and Mr Robinson in riding breeches, and Fairmead Bottom all round: green fields and countryside. As the light faded and a bird sang and the moon came up, curved and on its back, and the evening star shone above it, I was happy, and I wanted to devote the rest of my life to my writing."

"Our Age" I wrote, "is divided between soul and sense (cf Toynbee's disintegration) and both can be found in me. I am the Age. I have taken the Age into my soul....The great burden of working at Garratt Green is the fundamental boredom, which gnaws at my soul....The meetings bore me more heavily than any other part of the work."

On June 3rd I exchanged contracts with Rodway on 46 Ritherdon Road and moved our furniture out into store the same day. I spent that half term week redecorating around the school hall, and on June 5th I hosted a family gathering at Oaklands for Argie's 80th birthday. Aunt Flo came, looking swollen and bloated, her cancer very advanced, and Nadia was present, and I made a speech. On June 6th the builders started building our new house in the Oaklands grounds. And then on June 9th we heard there had been a Tory landslide in the General Election, removing rumours that Labour might abolish private education and giving us a period of stability ahead.

Suddenly I had a clear view of the West's predicament and posture. I wrote: "After the election, I can see everything very clearly. Russia is a barbarian place with barbarian values, and we in the West have to preserve the light of civilisation against it, with strong defences and a toughening of the spirit. Such a government we now have....It is the Romans versus the barbarians, and either you are on the side of the Romans, in which case you support nuclear weapons, or you are on the side of the barbarians, in which case, like Scargill, you rejoice that 25 NUM students are going to Moscow, and you foment revolution against the 'corrupt and decaying capitalist system'."

The annual Oaklands fête was held soon afterwards. I wrote: "Glorious sunshine and a family atmosphere, traditional dancing – and today, lay in the sun and watched the swifts skim and dart, watched a grey squirrel come out of the oak and eat the popcorn dropped on the grass by messy humans, watched two magpies flit to and fro – and got thoroughly, really sunburned. Read Ricks's review of Coleridge, all about his obsession with unity and his genius and his reconciliations; and Tuohy's jaded review of some novels in last Sunday's *Observer*, a week old....I surveyed my estate, which I mowed again today, an Oblomov in the sun, without a Zahar, and with Thatcher having a landslide majority, it all felt ancient-regimy. And there was I, determined to get those fields." I also wrote: "Poets clear up smeared vision and show the world shot through with the power of God. (Blake, Hopkins.)"

Mabel Reid saw us soon afterwards and told us about the Loughton families of the beginning of the century and the decline of their large houses: the Warren Hill House of the Lustys, which was now flats; the Palladian house of the Buxtons near High Beach church; the Pollards she took us to at the end of the Nature Walk, which had a Roman-inspired mosaic and which was now gone (except for a magnificent fountain near the Oaklands second field); the Dragons, which had been built on; Jacob Epstein's house, which was now in two; and Oaklands, which was now a school. She said there were nightingales near Connaught Waters, a cuckoo near the Warren, and a fox and a kestrel that lived in the Oaklands second field.

Solzhenitsyn was attracting publicity by raising the spectre that Communism might obscure the Western sun, arguing that the West must find spiritual strength or the Christian (ie Western) civilisation would disintegrate. I did not believe that Communism would win, but was again aware that it must be resisted for the West to survive and come through.

In July, the Garratt Green 6th form conference went down the Thames on a boat, the Marchioness, which was to be involved in a collision and sinking a few years later: "I went too, all the way to the Woolwich flood barrier, seven futuristic curved ovals protruding from the water like gigantic floats from a hidden net. We passed Dry Dock (St Saviour's church, Jamaica Road) where Fagan lived, and Judge Jefferies's house near Oliver's Wharf and the gallows at the Town of Ramsgate, and Execution Dock at St. John's Wharf. At the Prospect of Whitby Capt. Kidd was captured. At Columbia Wharf is Nelson's house, where Nelson met Lady Hamilton, and where Wren died; Wren's house being opposite St. Paul's...not far from the Anchor. Across from the Samuel Pepys to which I must go. The Naval dockyard at Greenwich, where Raleigh lay down his cloak for Elizabeth I. The Observatory built by Wren – Wren's river – and the Great Palace, Greenwich, where Elizabeth I was born....The mist, the wharves, the docks. Also the two dolphins on the 1870 lampstands, the swans on the seas in front of County Hall in Silver Jubilee Walk (1977) and also the V and A intertwined under the gold lamps on Westminster Bridge."

Our new house was almost waist high now. We had moved the Art Room and tacked it onto the Garden Room (a garden classroom) to clear the base for the new house, and we now had to move the steps from the school which now led into the side of our house. Bill Sargent, the husband of one of our staff, and his son-in-law discussed how to move a large half-ton slab of Yorkstone, the middle of the steps, and various staff came and gave their opinion as we grappled with the problems faced by the builders of Stonehenge and the Great Pyramid. In the end, Bill held a garden fork and his son-in-law a pick axe, and the slab was moved twenty yards by primitive leverage on to boards and pipes borrowed from the building site.

At the same time I restored the original front door opening, which had at some time been made into a window, at Oaklands. I found two doors at London Architectural Salvage which was housed in a disused church. They were the original Christopher Wren doors for St. James's, Piccadilly, which the vicar had sold to pay for his lecture activities. I brought them back in the back of Ann's car and Bill Sargent fitted them.

I had to get the Fire Officer to inspect Oaklands, and when he appeared in uniform he turned out to have known my mother. He said: "I remember passing your dear mother's house in the week she died. She was in the garden, very busy, very serene. I stood and watched her and thought she was working hard because she knew she hadn't got long. Strange, isn't it? Strange."

During the summer of 1983 I saw my work as fusing the traditions of the Renaissance and the Middle Ages into a new Baroque.

I felt both radical and reactionary at this time: "In some ways I am an ultra-radical - the Light and anti-Newtonian anti-materialism challenge the status quo - and in other ways I am a reactionary, in my sense of the importance of preserving the social structure and the Englishness of our life. In poetry I am a radical...in going for a new view of a human being as Light-bearing, a mystical view which is radical or new in our time but which is traditional in terms of the tradition (back to the 14th century). I am radical in getting to the root of a human being in terms of the Light, and in drawing conclusions about human beings from that vision and approach."

I thought of what I had done with the sonnet: "The Renaissance wrote about the...unconscious drives...that reflected themselves in emotions, and the sonnet, as a vehicle, is a Renaissance form, having come from Italy to Wyatt, who wrote about his love for Ann Boleyn, and on to Shakespeare. Shakespeare treated the Renaissance passions....I took the sonnet from the Renaissance emotions back to the medieval Light, from the Greek and Roman classical world forward to the Romantic world of the Middle Ages, but being a Neo-Baroque writer I fused the two traditions, retained a Renaissance, classical eye while reopening the eye of the soul. That is my main achievement."

We spent a week painting Oaklands, and then went down to Cornwall, where almost immediately I "reviewed the Bohm weekend and wrote 3 poems, all very metaphysical and speculative, yet clarifying how things are". I enjoined myself: "Identify the spirit of this Age – what it is preoccupied with – and, as the highest expression of the Age leads to the next Age, anticipate what the next Age's spirit will be. Think: space; scientific inquiry into the origins of life (DNA, cancer); eroticism and sex; freedom for minority groups; the spirit and soul. Put all this together, and do we not have a new metaphysical age ahead of us? A new baroque age in which soul and spirit are all important? The discovery of the meaning of life."

I wrote: "I am a Renaissance person, not a Middle Ages one – for I have my roots in Plato, not Aristotle (who ruled the Middle Ages) and in Cicero and Horace, Virgil and Homer, ie my education was a Renaissance education as befitted the 1629 Harsnett and Quaker Penn, Classical and Protestant. Chigwell was there at the beginning of the Baroque. Baroque, a Renaissance movement for it combines Classicism and Romanticism which both came after the Renaissance....I synthesise all – medieval, metaphysical, Romantic, Classical, and all religions." And: "My life has already been given to me, like jigsaw-like bits of mosaic – the Far East, the ancient world of Egypt and Babylon, the classical world, the Renaissance, the medieval Light, etc – and I have to piece them all together to make a – Baroque – picture that defines me....The spirit of our Age: a dynamic moving universe, stillness."

We visited the originally Baroque Lanhydrock House and Restormel Castle, "captured by Sir Richard Grenville in 1644, the Baroque time; and the Renaissance Baroque gatehouse", and I read into the historical Baroque, how it emphasised one moment and recreated a spiritual experience in aesthetic terms, often veering into the erotic and how it dealt with the conflicts between appearance and reality, which I understood as sense and spirit.

On August 4th, after visiting the unspoilt beach at Hemmick where I saw "4 kestrels hovering over the hill, looking for mice; absolutely still while all around them moved", I heard that my Aunt Flo had died. The cancer had affected her breast and leg, and as her kidneys failed her water seeped into her body. She had had a bad night the previous night, had slipped into a coma that morning and had died at 7 p.m., alone, which saddened some of the family. That night, I went to Charlestown and there was a bright evening star and I wondered: "Aunt Flo and the night. Is she there, among the stars?...Two shooting stars right down the sky, one after another, like bright angels....Water from the lock poured out to the level below. What is life? What is death? I wondered, and knew again that we live to complete tasks and then we live in eternity." I thought: "Aunt Flo went to sleep last night and was dead tonight. I am alive and can go to sleep tonight with this large moth circling under the light."

I reacted to the death of another security figure from my childhood by plunging into thoughts about the materialistic old Age and the metaphysical new Age: "The old Age was materialistic and mechanistic, believing nothing survived death, and honouring the discredited Descartes, Newton, Darwin, Freud. It was preoccupied by traditional and new science which led to the conquest of space and the moon, machines (computers), TV....Materialism was at a dead end, it cried out for inner vision, a new soul. The new Age is anti-materialistic and organicist, believing in the spirit that survives death. It honours Whitehead, Einstein, the anti-Darwinists and Jung in affirming that the cosmos is a Oneness, a whole, in which implicate fields... come into form. There is a fascination with how life comes into being (physics and biology), what life is; a new metaphysical outlook. The conquest of space has opened up new questions. Once again 'the new philosophy casts all in doubt' but scepticism and humanism are now the chief victims, and so we are like Donne at the beginning of a new baroque age in which there is a new metaphysical poetry, a new baroque reaching for the meaning of life, getting behind the mask of the ego for the truth, a new questioning of the social stage – ie undermining of the social view by seeing it as appearance on a stage – and a new fascination with identity and the pastoral. This probing, this spirit of metaphysical enquiry which is the spirit of the new Age now emerging from the Elizabethan age – is fascinated by the findings of the ancient wisdom, the soul and spirit, higher intelligence, the new horizons and perspectives of space, the dynamic nature of the moving universe and the still centre which is illumined by the Light of the ecstatic mystics (cf St. Teresa, St. John of the Cross in Habsburg Spain), the movement against the ego and materialism, and by the fact that the Dark Ages are near, only a bomb blast away. This probing is fascinated by the meaning of life, there is a baroque search for a meaning of life, and the new values are pastoral ones, rediscovering the soul and spirit away from the city in Nature, the country, eg Epping Forest. All is One, and the goal is to contemplate and speculate and come up with solutions to the meaning of life, from one's own deep experience. The new spirit of the Age is a contemplative one, the new Age people are illuminati who can distinguish the appearance of the ego from the reality of the soul and spirit and self." I noted: "I originally received guidance when the words floated in 'A new baroque age is born', and my task now is to bring this in to the Arts, a new baroque age that will also remysticise Christendom....The Illuminated Age, which is a new coming of the baroque age but which is different in its own right. Not the Enlightenment which was a darkness, but the Illumination (perhaps I have trodden my lonely path so that I can come up with the idea for the next Age, and so lead the West on; ie I have had to be alone to develop something totally different from anyone else.)"

Soon afterwards I "coped with Aunt Flo's death: wrote 5 poems with images of death". I "spent the day at deserted Hemmick beach and looked at Vault, then drafted a poem *Night Thoughts in Charlestown*. (Charles' Town is the new Carolingian age which is waiting to burst out of the Elizabethan age.)" Then: "6 Aug. Awoke with 12 stanzas latently (implicately) in my mind; did my exercises and then, before breakfast, with Ann asleep at first, wrote them straight out, some 100 lines about the spirit of the new age, *Night Thoughts in Charlestown*. When I got to stanza 4 Ann awoke and got up and clattered about, and it required all my concentration to ignore her presence and get what was in my soul down on paper. But I did it, writing on my knee, sitting on the side of my bed in my bedroom at 4 Manor Close, Fairfield Park, the window on my right letting enough light through the drawn curtains for me to see. Now feel fulfilled."

That afternoon I went to Charlestown: "To Charlestown for the Regatta. Punch and Judy, the lifeboat and helicopter, greasy pole, etc. Bought a cannon-ball salvaged from the wreck of the (baroque) Dutch East Indian *Campen*, which was lost on the Isle of Wight in October 1627."

We visited Poldark mine: "The hellish tunnels, the caverns of granite with lodes and stopes where minerals (copper, quartz, tin) had been; the water trickling down the walls which would become a torrent bursting over the miners. The hellish ghostly voices of men working, on tape, as it used to be."

I drove up from Cornwall for Aunt Flo's funeral. I had to go home to Essex first to change into a dark suit and black tie, and then I drove to Merrow, near Guildford and put the car into a car-wash. The brush would not stop rolling, and the spraying of water somehow got into the engine.

Amazingly I was trapped, and I could not start the car for a while, and only just got to Merrow church in time. It was in this church that, younger, my brother Robert and my cousin Richard and I had sung "While shepherds washed their socks at night" during one Christmas holidays.

The coffin was on two stands with two wreaths on top, and the eulogy mentioned her "puckish, irreverent sense of humour" along with her commitment, cheerfulness, courage. It occurred to me that the soul is like grain, that the stalk (body) grows so that the grain (soul) can be garnered, after which the stalk is useless. After the service we drove through Guildford High Street and then Merrow to the crematorium and witnessed the committal and then drove to a reception where my Uncle Reg poured drinks for everyone. Afterwards I drove back to Cornwall and stopped at Plymouth and wrote: "I am at the height of my powers: dashed off the poem on grain in 2 mins sitting on the grass overlooking Brunel's bridge at Plymouth, doing in 2 mins what it would have taken me 7 days to do in the 1960s; confident, full of conviction. Aunt Flo – is no more. Here, that is." And later: "Some people are taken short and have to go to the lavatory; I am taken short as I was at Plymouth and have to write a poem."

When I got home I tried to characterise "the Anti-Materialistic Age which will replace the Age of Materialism which has lasted 300 years (Descartes, Newton and Darwin), and which produced the Space Age and the Nuclear Age, ie outer things. The Anti-Materialist Age will be an Age of Meaning, an Age of Illumination and will bring about a spiritual resurgence in Europe which, coupled with the political resurgence (new countries joining, the Soviet bloc joining) will bring about the reunification of Christendom. Perhaps it is the Age of Reunification (= oneness), but it will emphasise the inner, for the inner side will be reunified on the Light....I know my task: it is to bring in the Anti-Materialistic Age of Reunification in art, as a Hellenist; to show it; rather than as a Hebraist in preaching....Anti-Materialism is too negative a concept. It should be, instead: Age of Organicism, or Age of Oneness – a positive concept which sums up the idea....The Renaissance is the true parallel; this was accompanied by a rediscovery of the classical world which led forward to the Baroque....There is a rebirth of interest in the ancient wisdom and the Light and in the spirit as creative idea, imagination, but the Age I am trying to characterise is one in which there is a shift of emphasis from the view of materialism to...something like the Reformation, which has not yet happened? The European Resurgence? In which Christendom conquers Communism? I have fought Communism in Africa – sceptical materialism of Communism – and now need to proclaim, as a spiritual idea, the Resurgence of European Christendom, ie revival? A movement – the Mystic Revival....A movement in the European Arts, which can be remysticised....Age of Baroque. What will this new historical period be characterised by, which is so like the Baroque? An attitude to life which finds expression in the arts. A cultural phenomenon, a style....Age of Light? But will the illuminated artists be in the minority? Metaphysical Age, ie post-humanist. An age of metaphysical enquiry. Age of Wisdom? (Cf the ancient wisdom too.) Philosophy is loving wisdom, so a kind of philosophy."

METAPHYSICAL AND BAROQUE

Two days later I went fishing with Ann's cousin: "Up at 4.40 am and out fishing in Mount's Bay, on a sunny day and calm sea; hauled up 300 crabpots....Drafted a poem. The outing – hauling up crabs – the sea, indivisible (cf Stone Garden, non-local theory) – the world as an ocean of being ruled by tides – the unfolding of the sea from the sky (cf the psychological from the spiritual) – mind, ego and identity on a vast psyche (sea), like a boat – images, crabs in crabpots, kept in banks, some thrown back, poetry as an activity that is in deep inter-relationship with the vast unconscious sea which was created by the spiritual atmosphere and sun (cf Kabbalah). Am too tired to write more but this is another metaphysical poem....Awoke at 7.30 am and wrote an 8 stanza poem on *Crab-Fishing in a Boundless Sea* (later *Crab-Fishing on a Boundless Deep*) by 9.15."

I now set down the Baroque line in Literature: "Shakespeare interests me greatly. His great theme, appearance versus reality, illusion versus truth, is the Baroque theme. Hence the mistaken identity in *Twelfth Night* (Sebastian/Viola alias Cesario) and in *Measure for Measure* (the Duke/Friar Lodowick). Also, the exposure of those who seem more virtuous than they are (Malvolio, Angelo). What seems versus what is. There should be a book redefining Shakespeare as the first Baroque writer....The problem plays are not problem plays if you grasp their Baroque context; they are only a problem to critics who do not understand the coming Baroque. So Macbeth hides his evil desires, as does Iago, while it is not known what happened to Hamlet's father, and Goneril and Regan are not what they seem in *Lear*. There is also the spirit/flesh dichotomy (eg Angelo, Othello) and concentration on spirit (*Macbeth*, *Hamlet*)....The whole period 1600-1700 in Literature should be redefined as the Baroque Age, to show the connection between Shakespeare-Donne-Marvell-Milton-Dryden (and through Dryden, Pope). Shakespeare is the founder of literary Baroque. But so was Marlowe, eg in *Dr Faustus*. The ornamental metaphor or simile – Baroque....It is the amount of decoration that counts."

I now questioned the idea of Providence. "The Providence idea can be egocentric: the whole universe revolves around little 'me', and even heaven is conspiring to make me avoid accidents, to jog my memory, to contrive my good, like the sylphs around Belinda in Pope's *Rape of the Lock* – proud Belinda."

Once again I wrote of Cornwall: "Every year I come to Cornwall and return to the elemental world, the world of sea and sky and fish and shooting stars and seaweed and crabs, and I come extra-specially alive. It is the intensity of the elemental world which I need as an artist, that makes each visit worthwhile....At Oaklands I am in the centre of 200 parents and am ideally placed to hear...stories....I am like a spider in the centre of a large web, with plenty of flies as prey."

We went to Golant and to Penquite House, which Garibaldi visited as Peard had fought, Byronically, in Italy. Then we returned home to Essex and took Miss Lord to Heathrow as, at 82, she was flying to see her relatives in Australia. We went to Guildford for the day, and Shere, where I again looked at the 14th century quatrefoil and squint of Christine Carpenter, anchoress, and I talked to my cousin Richard about "the possibility that there is an invisible body within the visible body....My vision of the Light penetrating the invisible body....My metaphysical vision, which is unique in the way it is expressed."

In September I returned reluctantly to Garratt Green and to a tirade against the staff by the Head. Much to her chagrin, the English results were very good. That evening I rang Nadia, and in the course of the next few days encouraged her to leave the caravan. She said, "I've often wondered how I was going to get out of the caravan."

It had been announced that the ILEA was to be abolished and at the first Heads of Department and Heads of House meeting I spoke out indignantly against the anti-marking Inspectorate and regime "whose dubious ideas may have contributed to the abolition of the ILEA". The next day Sinclair, the Deputy Head, said: "That was your most spectacular yet, yesterday. It had everything: variety, riposte, humour and anger." John Cameron heard about my blast, and invited me to the National Council for Educational Standards, who were meeting at the Mostyn Hotel, Bryanston Street, near Marble Arch. He had contacts with them, and I was met by Prof. C. B. Cox of Black Paper fame, who invited me to lunch with him. After speeches from Bob Dunn, the no 2 to Sir Keith Joseph in Education, and Harry Greenaway, I sat next to Cox and opposite Dunn, and the conversation included the ILEA's attempt to ban marking. At one point Cox said: "Did I hear you tell Greenaway you want to become an MP? Because I can get you on the list, so long as you help me on the secretarial side, send out 3 letters a year to our 255 members." Cox explained: "We are a pressure group and need to keep in the headlines to make Ministers' tasks easier." Stuart Sexton joined and said: "Dunn was appointed to be tough with the DES, you should hear the rows we've already had." After lunch Baroness Cox and Dr John Marks spoke and later I had a long talk with Baroness Cox, who was opposed by the ILEA and DES Inspectors but supported by Tory Ministers and advisers within the DES.

The Oaklands Annual General Meeting happened. It was notable for a speech from Richard Snowsill's wife, and then a speech from Snowsill himself, accusing the committee of rigging their own membership. The atmosphere was bad and the hands went up as thick as forest trees for the committee, and Snowsill resigned. I visited him at 10 p.m., although ill, and stayed until midnight. I was so unwell I fell asleep while talking to him.

The next day I had an appointment with Mr Morrison, the world famous ear-nose-and-throat consultant who lived in Loughton and had had children at Oaklands. I wrote: "I have pneumonia; have had it for months. I hope and pray it is pneumonia and not something more dreadful... which will carry my weary soul off to Heaven before I have even begun my life's task of my epic – or even lived in the house I have built (which is up to the roof now)." The next day I wrote: "Oct 2. My pneumonia. I must have an X-ray of chest and sinuses, must visit David Hughes, and then Mr Morrison will review the situation. There will perhaps be a general anaesthetic to wash sinuses out and suck out the mucus following a bronchoscopy. Oct 5. My pneumonia is taking hold. I have a cough and my left lung hurts – today for the first time. Perhaps it is not pneumonia but something more." I went to

1

2

3

4

6

Family background and childhood: (1) Rev Benjamin Broadley, Nicholas's great-grandfather, in 1892; (2) Mrs Burton, Nicholas's great-great-grandmother, who had a school in Croydon and lived to be 100; (3) Mr and Mrs George Broadley, Nicholas's grandparents, with Flo and his mother Norah (right) at Lonsdale House; (4) their son Tom as Flight Lieutenant in 1918, just before he was killed; (5) Norah Broadley as a violinist; (6) Cyril Hagger's parents in 1937; (7) Nicholas's parents at their wedding in 1937, with Flo as a bridesmaid; (8) Cyril Hagger showing Nicholas at 6 weeks; (9) Nicholas with his Aunt Argie (later author of *Patients Come First*) at 13 months by the lily pond at St. Anton, East Grinstead; (10) Nicholas in the East Grinstead doorway; (11) Nicholas (left) and Robert at Brooklyn Avenue, Loughton, after Nazi bomb; (12) Nicholas (left), Robert and Jonathan on the lawn at Journey's End.

5

7

8

9

10

11

12

13

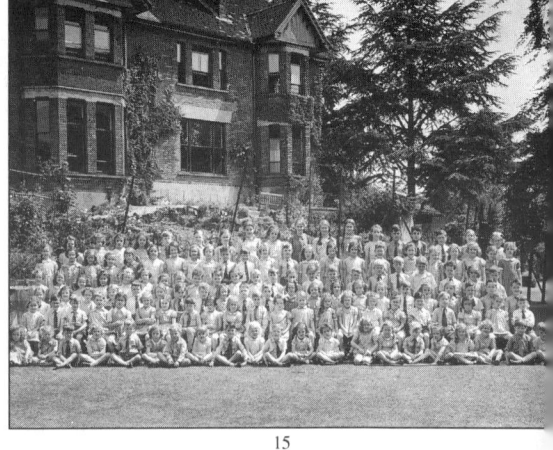

15

14

16

Schooldays and after: (13) Journey's End as it used to be; (14) the original Oaklands School; (15) Oaklands School, Albion Hill with Nicholas as a pupil; (16) Chigwell School; (17) the first tee at the Merrow golf course where Nicholas had his first mystical experience in 1954 (see p43); (18) Worcester College, Oxford; (19) the stone seat by the lake where Nicholas read the letter from his father and then had a mystical experience (see pp64-65); (20) Nicholas's wedding to Caroline in 1961, with his sister Frances as a bridesmaid; (21) Nicholas in Baghdad, Iraq with some of his students; (22) Nicholas as he was when he went to Japan.

19

18

17

20

21

22

25

26

24

27

23

Japan and Libya: (23)
Nicholas on the beach at
Kobe, Japan, holding a
whelk shell (see *The
Silence*); (24) Nicholas
with Prince Hitachi, his
pupil, and Princess Hitachi; (25) Nadia; (26) +A + -A = 0, in Nishiwaki's
writing; (27) the Zen Ryoanji Stone Garden at Kyoto; (28) Nicholas deep in
thought at Clouds Hill, the home of T. E. Lawrence, with "ou phrontis" ("I don't
care") on the lintel in Greek (see p171); (29) Caroline as she was in 1969; (30)
Nicholas in the desert near Ghadames by the grave of an Arab; (31) the Ain El
Faras spring, Ghadames (see p167); (32) Margaret Riley in January 1981, with
her picture of St. Teresa (right eye on the world, left eye on eternity, see p375);
(33) Nicholas's second wife Ann;
(34) Ann with Matthew (left) and
Anthony when small.

28

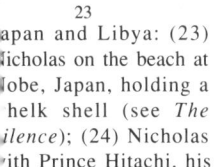

29

30

31

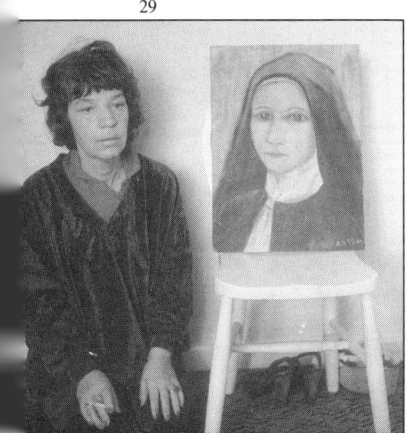

32

33

34

35

36

37

Oaklands and Coopersale Hall: (35) Oaklands under snow; (36) Ann and Miss Lord in 1982; (37) Nicholas at Coopersale Hall in 1988; (38) Lord Tebbit opening Coopersale Hall; (39) Nicholas with Steve Norris MP, Mrs. Best, Lord Tebbit and the then Chairman of Epping Forest District Council; (40) Nicholas introducing England goalkeeper David Seaman to open a fête at Coopersale Hall.

38

39

40

41

42

43

44

ak-Tree Books: the Heroes of the West, 1986: (41) Nicholas
ith Trevor Maher; (42) Nicholas with Des McForan at the
unch of *The World Held Hostage* in the Special Forces Club,
ndrew Lownie between them; (43) Nicholas with Paul Gorka
eft) at the launch of *Budapest Betrayed* in the Palace of
'estminster, with Ian Crowther of the *Salisbury Review*; (44)
icholas speaking in favour of freedom for the republics of
astern Europe at Gorka's launch, with Sir John Biggs-
avison MP listening (see p505); (45) Julian Amery MP
eaking, with Sir John Biggs-Davison, Nicholas and Krasso,
d Virginia Bottomley MP (sitting), listening; (46) Nicholas
the Athenaeum with E. W. F. Tomlin and Kathleen
ine (holding books) and John Ezard between them at the
ck.

45

46

47

48

49

The countryside and mysticism: (47) the Mystic Way near Haslemere, Surrey; (48) the pool in Marvell's Garden at Nun Appleton House, Yorkshire, where Nicholas wrote *A Metaphysical in Marvell's Garden*; (49) Gunwalloe where Nicholas wrote a number of metaphysical sonnets; (50) Nicholas writing on the rocks at Gunwalloe; (51) Charlestown, Nicholas's house being the nearest to the Roundhouse; (52) another view of Charlestown, showing the Roundhouse and the lock-gate dipping, the headland of Trenarren in the distance; (53) the fishing-boat returning to port on 17th August 1989 after being "out on the Alone", Nicholas standing on the extreme right; (54) Nicholas with Colin Wilson in August 1991.

50

51

53

52

54

55

56

57

58

59

he launch of *The Fire and the Stones* and *Selected Poems*, 22nd April 1991: (55) Michael Mann and Nicholas; (56) Asa Briggs (Lord Briggs) speaking with Kathleen Raine, David Gascoyne and Nicholas listening; (57) Kathleen Raine speaking; (58) and (59) David Gascoyne with Nicholas; (60) Nicholas declaring the Metaphysical Revolution (see p 607); (61) Christine Klein dancing the descent of the Fire of Amun-Re. (Photographs 55-61 courtesy of Susan Greenhill)

60

61

62

64

63

66

Poetic images: (62) Nicholas at Charlestown with a rainbow; (63) in 1987 in the Lake District, with the cottage of Wordsworth's Solitary in the background; (64) with his family in America in July 1993, Matthew and Ann on the left and Anthony on the right; (65) with the Statue of Liberty in the background; (66) dictating the end of the *American Liberty Quintet* on the plane home; (67) and reading his *Epithalamion* at the wedding of his daughter Nadia, who is behind his hand in the background with her husband Sandy.

67

65

METAPHYSICAL AND BAROQUE

David Hughes at Fielden House, Whitechapel, part of the London Hospital. He was a dapper, bespectacled little man, and he looked at my X-rays and said: "I can be reassuring. You've had pneumonia but you've thrown it off." He showed me the bits on the X-ray that should be dark (the lungs) and where the inflammation still showed up light. The heart was white and formless in the middle. "You've had a very bad bug in the dry hot summer, and we find that erythromycin, which we don't normally use for bugs like that, seems to control it. So no bronchoscopy, no draining of your lungs, but you must have your sinuses drained as sinuses and lungs are interconnected and an infection in one infects the other. Take erythromycin the morning you have your sinuses done." He gave me a sputum pot to hawk and spit into first thing on Monday morning.

In October 1983 I went into Holly House, Buckhurst Hill, Oak ward. I waited "for my operation – washing out of sinuses, antrum puncture... and perhaps a Caldwell line, in which they open up my sinuses and open and expand the breathing space". I was "given a pre-med and was later wheeled to the lift and went up. Male nurse in shower hat. Two other nurses put on 'shower-proof' booties and masks and shower-hats. I was in my execution gown tied at the back. The masked anaesthetist came in, and a masked Morrison, and they attempted to give me an injection in the back of my left hand. 'You haven't got a good vein there, can you give me a good vein.' (As if it was my fault.) The nurse on my right hung on to my arm while they wapped the back of my hand yet again and then injected it. I felt the cold run up my arm. 'You'll be out in a few seconds.' It seemed like an eternity, and then I drowned. The next thing I knew was several people calling, shouting at me, 'Mr Hagger, wake up, wake up' and I slowly came to in the recovery room and asked, 'What did they do?' 'Washed your sinuses out, did an antrum puncture on each side and got rid of a cyst.' A cyst....It had been there a long time, Morrison said, and it was under my right eye; if undetected it might have pushed the right eyeball out. Am now stiff-necked and still sore-throated and not really well enough to do more than write this *Diary*. Still woozy after the anaesthetic. Morrison: 'I removed a lump of pus which I've sent to Dr Hughes for a culture. You've still got some pneumonia, he may want to see you again.'" The operation took 45 minutes: "Washing sinuses out through nose after putting a tube down my throat and sealing it. Then punctured up with needles to drain from higher up, where there are no pain fibres; hence I feel no pain. Then found the cyst in the antrum. Infection up in the head caused the pneumonia, or the other way round – impossible to say which came first. Did not open up the sinuses, which are too high." Later I commented: "Still in Holly House with its routines of tea, temperature-taking, pulse-taking and sunny nurses; still sore-throated and stiff-backed from the hard narrow bed that works from a side-brake and moves into a sitting position. I still have a snuffle of blood which I must not blow down, and a deeply sore throat, and don't feel up to too much work."

I wrote: "To be a Renaissance man and do everything – be a journalist,...teacher, privatiser, MP, businessman, artist, critic, writer, philosopher, poet – is to be so many-sided that one is in danger of not doing everything. All one can do is carry on one's potential until the end. I plan to be a jack of all trades, and a master of all."

While I convalesced I saw the Oaklands staff for 10 minutes each. Then we went to Worthing and walked on the front and I got the pneumonia out of my lungs. We went on and visited Margaret in her new flat with all her paintings and pots round her. She talked about her visit to Lourdes. She said: "I was so happy, I didn't want anything." She gave Ann a bluish pot she had done; it was an oval slit with teeth-like claws round the opening and a blue tear inside and she said, "Put a candle in it."

The next day we went to the RAC Country House at Woodcote Park, Epsom for a masonic function. Uncle Reg was the President and in the absence of my Aunt Flo Argie was his lady. We ate goose, and I went back with my cousin Richard and his wife Wendy and her brother John (who had greeted me wearing DJ and would soon be paralysed by a stroke) and slept in their house at 3 a.m. and rose for a walk in the garden under a glorious sun the next morning.

In November I exchanged contracts on the Oaklands fields, with access to Warren Hill across a piece of former allotment land.

I now began a period which lasted throughout the Orwellian year, 1984, which was dominated by politics – local, national and international politics.

I went to Thatcher House in Loughton for a reception for Willie Whitelaw. I talked with Biggs-Davison and put to him my idea that there should be a liberation movement to free Eastern Europe. I said it should be called FREE (Freedom for the Republics of Eastern Europe). He said: "The Americans would be against it, Kissinger carved up the world and agreed not to interfere in the Soviet sphere of influence." It was the first indication I had had that there was more to the Cold War than met the eye, and that perhaps the Soviet leadership were being supported and kept in power by a group from the West. Biggs-Davison brought Whitelaw ("huge and jowly and eyebrowed and bloodshot-eyed") in on the conversation, and I outlined my idea and said "I can't think why it isn't happening", and Whitelaw said: "Now you put it in those terms I can't for the life of me think why it isn't happening either and I will ask upwards why it isn't happening and let John know." Biggs-Davison asked me to write a paper on the subject, and, drawing on my experience of the African liberation movements, I wrote to the effect that: "Europe has been occupied since 1945 yet everyone pretends this is not so. The future of Europe will be good if the Eastern European states throw of the Soviet yoke and join the Western democracies....The idea of our century – the European resurgence, the resurgence of Europe against the Communist advance, pushing back the tide, by a London-led encouraging of liberation movements. It should be someone outside the government, but linked, who sets this up and organises 'governments in exile' for these liberation movements. Britain should lead the building of major Europe."

I went to Argie for lunch and found her worried about the Day of Judgement. The sermon at church had been on giving to the poor, and Argie told the Methodist Minister: "I haven't helped the Third World, I haven't followed the example of my father, who always gave to the poor. One woman came to my mother and said 'George always gave my boy a suit, and there was a shilling in the pocket.' And he gave the one parent family a sovereign." Of the Day of Judgement she said: "I think it will be like a theatre, and we will go up on the stage." I told her: "You'll have to tell them at the Day of Judgement that the Welfare State took over from Victorian charity, you will do all right – you served all the poor of Whitechapel and have forgotten about it." I noted, "Argie was still worried though, 80 and worried." My Aunt Lucy had remarried. Her new name was Humble. She was Mrs. Humble. Having cornered the family money she now had a name that was associated with eating humble pie.

In December the Oaklands term ended and I held a party for the staff and their spouses. At first I glided to and fro pouring wine but then Tim Norris, my fellow Old Chigwellian, local auctioneer and husband of the Oaklands secretary, began to tell me how many of our old school friends had died: Bristow, Vear (in a plane crash), "Cowley" Morris with whom I went to tea and who failed to save my penalty kick in a set match (of suicide), Choat (of suicide), Gayner (in a plane crash), and Ambrose O'Leary. It was a melancholy list of faces that I had known and were now no more, and I felt we were survivors.

Christmas arrived and I wrote: "Christmas is here again, bringing its surfeit, and my temperament cries out for the Spartan discipline of Orwell's Jura, and I am ill." I was in fact ill – I had a patch on my right lung and visited my consultant, David Hughes. On Christmas Day we went to lunch in Theydon and had tea with Miss Lord.

Soon afterwards we went to Cornwall, and I wrote: "Dec 31. Awoke early…and looked for the Light and saw it, was filled with it. Then opened myself to healing energies and felt them lodged in the middle of my spine for a long while until they finally moved up and made my little finger glow. Healed my sinuses and my right lung and my varicose veins with my little finger and then got up, at 9, having been in a state of healing – or being healed – for an hour and a half. A metaphysical morning."

We went to Porthleven: "A green sea with sea horses and we had lunch; the Lizard to left, Penzance to right and a stormy petrel sweeping round the cliff in the wind. The sea splashing over the harbour wall….Got back to the 3 Odes I drafted in the summer….(10 line stanzas.) 3 metaphysical Odes."

On January 1st 1984 I typed up a longish story I had written, *Light in the Storm*, and I wrote: "(It) is a mixture of *The Ancient Mariner*, *The Wreck of the Deutschland*, and *Francis Macomber*, with a touch of Dostoevsky, the Kabbalah, Zen Buddhism and Edgar Allan Poe. In this story I am 'conning' the reader. The precise details of crab-fishing at the beginning are authentic, and say 'Trust me'…to make more credible the blatantly metaphysical end." I wrote to Tuohy: "It is to some extent a deliberate sleight of hand as it starts with the firmly physical – precise, authentic details of crab-fishing – and leads the reader into the impossible, the blatantly metaphysical, without letting on what's happening." The next day we went to Mevagissey, Portmellon and Gorran: "A fresh wind whipping across the waves. Cold fingers, red cheeks and no one else in Mevagissey."

A MYSTIC WAY

On my return from Cornwall I had another appointment with my chest physician, David Hughes. He diagnosed thrombo-phlebitis in my right ankle.

In early February the new house was completed and we moved across the road in Albion Hill. It was a brick building with aluminium windows that nestled under the listed blue acacia cedar some twenty yards from the Oaklands main entrance. It had a view across the tennis court and fields at the back, and from my study I could watch squirrels and magpies settle on the Victorian iron railings.

There was much to do, and I could now recover the furniture from 46 Ritherdon Road, which had been in store since July. At the same time I put in a planning application to build a three classroom extension at Oaklands, which was opposed by the Loughton Residents Association at the instigation of the man in whose house we had been living, and had been recommended for rejection by the Planning Department. I was asked if I would stand as a Conservative councillor in the May elections for Roding ward, the most Labour ward in the area, where Ann Miller was a councillor and which included the path I took when I cycled to Chigwell to school across the River Roding as a schoolboy. To stand for the Conservatives would be to stand against Loughton Residents Association. I agreed because I knew I would have no chance of winning and would be able to outmanoeuvre the planning recommendation. I had invited the Leader of the Council to Oaklands for a briefing visit, and he had told me that if I beat the Loughton Residents Association in the election it would strengthen the councillors' hands to go against the recommendation of the Planning Department.

I was more interested in the national issues and my paper on FREE had been passed on by Biggs-Davison. I found myself talking to such shadowy figures as Josef Josten, a Czech ("for whom," Biggs-Davison wrote, "such as Sir Bernard Braine and Winston Churchill would be prepared to vouch") who had been involved in the assassination of Heydrich, and Brian Crozier, an influential adviser to Mrs. Thatcher to whom Biggs-Davison had written and who had his own private intelligence organisation. Through their network of friends I found myself attending a meeting of the European Liaison Group, the patron of which was Sir Bernard Braine and which covered Eastern Europe, and at a reception afterwards at Latvia House, meeting Lady Olga Maitland.

The idea for FREE had come from the Light; I was merely a messenger. In March I was "filled with God": "4 Mar. Both Matthew and Anthony felt sick and I healed them – Ant took 4 surges and fell asleep, Matthew took 8 as he had been sick three times. It was instantaneous: a prayer to God and an instant response. I am now, at 9.45 p.m. filled with the tide of God which has flowed into the harbour of my spine four times in answer to four consecutive prayers, (the first of which was) that I should lead a movement to free the captive peoples from the Soviet Union"."The tides of the Light flow up and down my spine. I have divine guidance....I am filled with God, like a full glass."

426

Soon afterwards I visited the House of Commons and sat next to Biggs-Davison and Josten, "who had a network behind the Iron Curtain", when I again talked about my FREE idea. Josten, bald-headed, sallow, wizened, bespectacled and 70ish, said: "You are trying to do in a few weeks what it would normally – if you were in the Foreign Office – take one year to do." Soon afterwards on Biggs-Davison's introduction I met Brian Crozier, who had started a private intelligence agency and in 1977 become Mrs. Thatcher's adviser on security and intelligence, to discuss the liberation of Eastern Europe and eventually of the Soviet Union. He greeted me in his Regent Street office, silver-haired and bushy-eyebrowed, and gave me a copy of his book *Strategy of Survival*, which in my copy had been retitled *Soviet Imperialism, How to Contain it*. It was one of the few books about the Cold War which faced up to the Soviet Union, and I had considerable sympathy for Crozier. I said that those who have a belief in Western values should do something about it. I did not say I was hoping to "bring the Light behind the Iron Curtain" but I did say that I wanted to "build a Greater Europe,...to strike a blow for Western values against Communist values". I knew I was politically unqualified but I had had "the message within, and it is the right message for our time: it is the divine message". Crozier agreed with me – everyone I met from Whitelaw down agreed that it was a good idea – but he said that it must be proceeded with cautiously. I had a chat with the Russian George Miller, who told me that one day we would ride together through a Moscow liberated from Communism; both George and I were prophetically right. Back with Crozier, I pointed out that the African liberation movements I had covered for the *Times* did not win by being cautious but by being bold.

For two weeks I was away from the idea of FREE. My health suddenly deteriorated. I was off work for two weeks with a slipped disc and felt tired as if I had a patch on one of my lungs. When I next met Josten he told me: "Crozier is very busy. He runs many operations and has many people working under him." I said: "He is a supremo?" "Yes. He is too busy. Mrs. Thatcher has been let down so many times by the Foreign Office and others. He is her right hand man." He also said that Crozier was ill, and would soon be having an operation.

It was around this time that I decided to start a small publishing company to stiffen the resolve of the West by publishing appropriate books. The idea was to gather round the company a group of people who would be the exact opposite of the Cambridge Apostles, who would be the "Heroes of the West". I had gone through the motions of negotiating with the poet-printer Asa Benveniste to buy his press, Trigram, in 1970, and now the idea returned. I wrote of the name of the coming company: "What is it to be? Light Books, Light of Europe, New Light, Light of the West, Greater Europe – or Baroque Books?...The imprint should be of an oak-tree, an acorn, and the Light radiating from it." My accountant did a search and confirmed that Oak-Tree Books Ltd. would be a possible name. It would have obvious associations with Oaklands.

I integrated my anti-Soviet stance with the Baroque vision: "My new Baroque Age: spirit and flesh: mysticism and religious imagery – the crucifix – and opposition to the Soviet empire, the last empire. Think of

Baroque within the Soviet context: the Baroque as fascination with politics – only instead of the Turks massing at the gates of Europe we have the Soviet Union....Europe, the heir of the Holy Roman Empire, and Communism." And: "A dewdrop on the grass, gleaming like a white diamond in the morning sun; like the Light....The Alps. Lush villages, clear mountains and a new way of looking: an avalanche destroying a peasant's cottage. Romantic poets had a new way of looking, a new perspective."

The Council elections took place. I had been taken for a tour of my ward one Sunday morning by Councillor Ann Miller, and I had canvassed by knocking on doors and asking how each household would vote. The response was heavily pro-Labour. On polling day, May 3rd, Biggs-Davison came to give me his support. I toured the area, speaking through a car loudspeaker, wearing a blue rosette, and Biggs-Davison attended the count. To my relief I came 2nd. Labour had retained the seat in their stronghold, and I did well to beat the Loughton Residents Association (LRA) when planning permission for Oaklands was an issue that divided us. It being midterm, the tide was generally out for the Conservatives, and even the veteran Mrs. Scott and Doug James, the Leader of the Council, had come 2nd, beaten by the Residents. Seen within that perspective, my victory over the Residents had been excellent. There was an election evening party at the house of the octogenarian Councillor Welch where Jimmy Denne, the local Party manager who had run the elections for the Conservatives, felt responsible for the tide, drank too much wine and collapsed, saying "Someone took my chair away, who took my chair away?" He picked himself off the floor and left with a jarred back. The mood among all present was sombre.

On May 22nd I celebrated my 45th birthday with the news that we had now been given planning permission for the Oaklands extension of three classrooms. The Conservatives were so angry at the defeat of Doug James by the LRA that they had forced through all the policies that the LRA had opposed. The Residents had organised 30 letters against the Oaklands extension and I had mustered 45 for, and now my victory over the Residents in the election added democratic weight to my numerical advantage. My strategy had worked: to fight the Residents by allying with the Conservatives on the hustings and so defeat the LRA's political campaign against Oaklands.

Soon afterwards Crozier wrote me a letter saying that there would be a fairly lengthy delay on FREE, and that I should stay in touch with Josten. I later learned from Josten that Crozier had run out of money and had to wait until his next budget, but if it is true that the leaders of the Soviet Union were kept in power by a group of mega-rich Westerners, and that the Americans were opposed to any interference in the Soviet sphere of influence, there may have been other reasons. I discussed the situation with Biggs-Davison and gathered that Sir Bernard Braine of the European Liaison Group (ELG) had said that FREE was pointless as the ELG (which was widely known for being ineffective and not doing anything) was performing a similar role. Biggs-Davison wanted to see FREE implemented as soon as possible.

METAPHYSICAL AND BAROQUE

I went with a party of Oaklands children to Waltham Abbey and there were Morris dancers "leaping and cavorting in the road..., wearing white shirts and black breeches with red and yellow criss-crossed braces and lions on their fronts, white socks and black clogs. They held two batons each, ribbons on their elbows and bells on their knees, and later they used white handkerchiefs, and a large lion with a red tongue ran amok and weed at a lamppost."

I went to the derelict Copped Hall, which had been a royal palace in the 16th century and a magnificent country house before it had been gutted by fire during the First World War: "The ruin that it is. The greenery growing within, the Edwardian glory. I would like to restore it. The first house was the site of the first *Midsummer Night's Dream*, which was written for the marriage of Heneage and the stepmother of the Earl of Southampton." I recorded on 30th May: "Wrote 3 poems in draft: *Passion Play*, *Copped Hall*, *Oaklands: Oak-Tree*....They need a lot of polishing, but it is a start....Back to poetry."

I saw poetry in terms of painting: "Began painting – a new, symbolic, imagistic development. Wrote my first poem to accompany my painting, in a new flinty style. To become an artist as a poet, I must take the plunge and become a real artist i.e. a painter. Then my words will have the pared down effect of flinty paintings, and I will be a true poet....The order and chaos – two forces in my present painting: enclosed railings and an unfathomable pond, with a lily....It is very valuable to convert an image into a precise sketch. I am a painter-poet: a painter in words. An imagist. My new imagist period."

I was ill again: "May 31. Have felt exhausted since last Thursday. Came off antibiotics 9 days ago on Tuesday, and have undoubtedly got lung patches. Must get these X-rayed tomorrow. Have felt too tired to do more than sleep – have pneumonia despite all my vitamins. It is from the lungs up. Paint lungs – my death breath. Life as a pair of lungs – a pair of bellows....1 June. I have bronchiectasis again, and am back on antibiotics. I feel better today. But for the record, lung patches make the brain numb: yesterday I could not think what to do, I just lay in a stupor and soaked in the cricket and could not tackle my desk. Although I improved in the evening. I am very inflamed in my lungs; the X-ray shows all the 'veins' white. Normally you do not see them." I saw David Hughes, who said: "You can't catch bronchiectasis, it is a weakness in the body, in your case, the lungs." He agreed that there is mental paralysis while the lungs are infected.

The diagnosis that I had bronchiectasis permanently, and would continually have lung patches was a melancholy development. Hughes said many sufferers from bronchiectasis live to a ripe old age, but he also agreed that certain climates were bad for it, including the Essex climate, and that if I had been alive in Keats's day I would have died of it: "The cure is to cut out the patch, but we can't do it if you've got it in both lungs, as you have. We can only give you antibiotics to prevent patches and keep you well."

My own ailment was overshadowed by the sudden death in early June of a youngish teacher I lunched with everyday, Phil Tribe, of a brain haemorrhage. He was yet another victim of the stress at school. As

Chairman of the Staff Association he had taken up the "derisory pay offer" (his words) and other matters at a meeting with the Head immediately before half term. He told me that Friday that she had shouted at him and that he was going to see her again before he left school. The following Sunday he had read the papers in Brighton, from where he had been commuting and where he lived with his wife and three children. He complained of a headache, went to get an aspirin, cried out and died. I asked: "Why was his sacrifice necessary?...Why did it have to happen to him?" At the Oaklands fête soon afterwards I had a discussion with a clergyman-parent, David Gilchrist, on how everyone is waiting for death. I said: "Each has a destiny, an aim, a something to do, which some never find, but which others do." And he replied: "I see some die who never found their destiny."

The public exams were immediately after half term, and as usual I was running them. The Head refused to allow me to attend Tribe's funeral, although I was the closest to him on the staff, and, saying it was in accordance with Mrs. Tribe's wishes, she limited attendance at his funeral to two staff representatives, one from the academic and one from the pastoral side. As a result two relative strangers saw him buried and, deprived of that therapeutic experience, I kept expecting him to turn a corner in the corridors. I wrote: "Tribe's soul ripened like grain and was harvested – that was his destiny. He was ready....What I suspect: Tribe had nothing more to do, and had lost his way, so he was recalled for a further briefing." Again: "June 13. Phil Tribe's first night under ground. Will he be lonely? The bleakness. His physical presence not far away. Relateable to. A poor ghost loitering near his grave. A 'ka'....Alas poor Philip (not Yorick) – I knew him Horatio. I grow more like Hamlet each day, with my metaphysical meanings." I wrote to Mrs. Tribe, explaining that she had apparently requested that only two of the staff should attend the funeral and that I had not been chosen, and I had a letter back, thanking me for my "beautiful" letter and stressing that she "did not mind how many came" to the funeral.

In mid-June Chigwell School had its Speech Day. Admiral Gerkin presented the prizes in a marquee on Top Field, and said in the course of his speech, echoing William Penn, "Chigwell gives a foundation of the Inner Light". Later we joined Vernon Davies's party at the Chigwell School ball and drank champagne all evening. Vernon was a multi-millionaire who had made his money out of the sale of his computer company, Atlantic, and he had bought a large house in Pudding Lane which, according to a tradition he denied, he had first seen from one of the Chigwell School walks up Vicarage Lane, along Manor Road, and down Pudding Lane. I told him about FREE, and a few days later he came and had a chat on my patio. He was an Oaklands parent and came early before picking up his children, and he told me: "I've got a problem, I've got £6 million in the bank and I don't know what to do. Should I retrain as a doctor?" I told him he should consider politics. He said he would put up the money and with my contacts we could make inroads into politics. He asked to meet Josten. I told him Biggs-Davison was coming to Oaklands in July to attend the constituency ladies garden party, and he said: "Who?" I explained that Biggs-Davison was his MP, and within a short time (and after donating some money) he would be Constituency Chairman.

I wrote of my "mind-suicide" at Garratt Green, my "ego-suicide", and observed: "You can be in a situation of stress and not feel it, i.e. withdraw from it: storms all round you. Like a lighthouse, buffeted outside, but within (peaceful)." I took alfaalfa for my bronchiectasis, and contemplated going to the Swiss Leysin where pulmonary complaints were miraculously cured.

The FREE plan was already foundering on red tape. Through an intermediary I had discussed the idea with Baroness Cox who was very excited and enthusiastic about it, and Roger Scruton, who received me in his Notting Hill flat amid a sea of books through which I paddled to sit down. He listened but said very little, and countered my inspirational talk about the end of Soviet Communism being in sight, and one more push being needed, with a faintly depressed air. Slowly it became clear that somehow Josten had power to decide the next move, perhaps because Crozier was ill. Josten assumed an authority over me he did not have, and on June 27th he wanted to marginalise me into letter-writing, making contacts with MPs and raising money – which was not what I was about at all. I had seen that it was possible to get rid of Communism in Eastern Europe and the Soviet Union, and that the Light wanted it, and my concern was simply to inject the idea into the system: "Destiny...having left me illumined has nudged me towards the British government with a message." I said flatly that I would be starting a publishing company and I would present the idea in books. Whereupon Josten said he would put me in touch with someone who would give me some sensational material on Scargill for a first book, material that made it clear that the miners' strike – and therefore Scargill's role – was linked to the Soviet Union.

On July 12th I rendezvoused with my source in London and took delivery of two files of material on Scargill which one peep convinced me were sensational. There was an Oaklands Open Evening that same day, and I took Vernon Davies, who was attending as an Oaklands parent, down to my house and showed him the material, spreading it out on the dining-room table. I had visited him a fortnight earlier and drunk white wine in his palatial house under a beautiful clock, and we had discussed our objectives for two and a half hours. I told him that there was enough material for both an article and a book, and I immediately wrote an article for the *Times*, which was now edited by my old Features Editor, Charlie Douglas-Home. I wrote: "I have broken up, having taken July 18 and 19 off to write an article on Scargill for the *Times*, who want to see it 'in the raw'. It is all about how Soviet money is funding the miners' strike, from Ponomarev to the *Morning Star*....Am back in touch with Charlie Douglas-Home after 12 years." On July 26th I spoke with Charlie over the phone. He said: "Your article is formidable and should be published, but my problem is how to project it at Scargill through the medium of a freelance contribution. Could I buy the material from you for a professional journalist to write it, or for an editorial?" I said no, I would see it through as it was within my interest in resisting Communism, and he said he would pass it to Features for the centre page.

Two days later I took Vernon Davies to meet Josten at the Polish Air Force Club. Josten tried to get Vernon to mount a "buy British" campaign along with Tebbit and Frank Chapple. Again this was far removed from the original idea of FREE. I began to suspect that someone did not want me to pursue FREE. In the afternoon we both had tea with Baroness Cox in the House of Lords, and she suggested we went to the Centre for Policy Studies.

The next Saturday I hosted the Conservative constituency ladies garden party at Oaklands. It was very hot, about 60 elderly people gathered to welcome our MP and MEP, and John Cameron and Vernon Davies came, and I introduced them to Biggs-Davison, who asked me to arrange for Vernon to meet Tim Pratt "so we can get him involved in the constituency". I wrote: "Tables under the trees by the tennis courts. Sir John Biggs-Davison and Alex Sherlock arrived at the top of the steps...and I ran up to greet them and welcome them, and took them down. Vernon Davies..., John Cameron, Ann and I sat together before that, and I took Vernon and John over and hit Biggs-Davison between the eyes with an idea: lunch with Josten on Tuesday...; my *Times* article on Scargill; the publishing company." As regards FREE Biggs-Davison said: "I can't understand it, it seems to be total impasse. It's exasperating." I wrote: "Later Biggs-Davison made a speech in which he thanked Ann and me for offering Oaklands, and said: 'If you have children or grandchildren, send them to this school. It's a very good school. The fact that we are here is a sign of how good it is.' A very successful golden day."

While all this was happening Betjeman, the Poet Laureate, died. I observed: "The death of Betjeman and his memorial service. The lines on the tea-shop ("little lower than the angels") and Joan Hunter-Dunn, now married and at the service; and on Cornwall (wasps and sandwiches). The rhythm of the joys. Yes, Betjeman has a permanent place as a modern Tennyson, although he is a bit short on the mystical side, the Eliot side."

I also went to dinner with David Hoppit, with whom I went to Italy in 1957: "1424 house, built round; patio with telegraph pole bringing, electricity and telephone; pond and ducks and ducklings; hedges and a lane and brambles all round. A greenhouse....Roman and Iron Age vases, archaeology is his hobby; his Roman coins." At this time Hoppit was still writing on property for the *Daily Telegraph*. Richard Fradd was present, the boy who played marbles in Chigwell church now a grown market gardener, but still the same underneath – as we all were.

We spent the next two weeks in Scotland. My aunt had taken a house in the Highlands, and had invited my sister Frances and her family to take one half and us to take the other half.

We drove in Ann's Rancho to Liverpool to see a relation of Ann's and then to Staveley, where we stayed in a guest house kept by a former Oaklands girl and saw my Uncle Reg. He was returning to his roots in the Lake District and had made contact with an old friend who was married to an invalid husband. We then crossed Windermere on the ferry and drove to Beatrix Potter's house, the setting for *Samuel Whiskers*, and drove past

Esthwaite, whence I was supposed to have come in a previous life, and where Jeremy Fisher lived and Wordsworth skated, to Hawkshead, where I visited his school. It felt strangely familiar, and I wondered if I too had been there. We saw where Wordsworth lived with Ann Tyson at the Friends' Meeting House, and I wondered about a possible Quaker influence on Wordsworth that might account for the "celestial light" of *The Immortality Ode*, and then drove on to Langdale Fell and Blea Tarn House, which the Wanderer visited in Wordsworth's *The Excursion*. We went to Ambleside and then Rydal Mount, Wordsworth's last house which Keats visited, and then on to Dove Cottage and found the Leech-gatherer's pool nearby. We went on to Grasmere to see where Wordsworth was buried and to see where Michael lived. Then we went to Ullswater and saw the daffodils under the trees near Gowbarrow. We saw St. Sunday's Crag, which rises as you come from Glenridding and lowers as you go towards it, as Wordsworth experienced when he stole the boat and rowed on the lake. We spent that night at Watermillock overlooking the lake. There I wrote: "What I admire about Wordsworth is his insistence on tranquillity at the expense of the newspapers' sound and fury (e.g. his letter to Beaumont of 3.6.1805), something I would do well to consider as I prepare to take on Scargill; and the way they all formed a group, so that Wordsworth wrote *The Immortality Ode*, to which Coleridge wrote *Dejection*, and Wordsworth wrote *Resolution and Independence* as a reply, urging the need for the artist to be like the Leech-gatherer gathering poems but not being depressed if it went badly – an excellent reply for Wordsworth to write to Coleridge. I also appreciate his countryside, and the solitaries and their shepherd huts, and consider Wordsworth now less of a revolutionary than a regional poet who reflected the spirit of lakeland. They were all a group, Wordsworth and Coleridge married sisters (Sara and Mary) and they made a cult of their feelings and thoughts – had the leisure to do so. It was very creative."

I again contemplated the Baroque vision and wrote: "So how do we differ from the Romantics? Answer: belief in the Light within, which has given delight in Nature, in the woods, the trees, the butterflies and birds, the pond life, a sense that the universe of flowers and brambles and insects surrounds men, that all are moved by one 'spirit', which is the Light. Man is not (only) reason, nor is his reason enough; it is not adequate for seeing the world in solely rational terms, which are themselves inadequate. The new Baroque Age seeks higher truth and meaning, with higher energy levels in living. The old social forms will not do: energy must be expressed, and not as an end in itself, but as a Providential outlet. This sense of Providence, too, is a feature. The Baroque spirit loves peace and tranquillity and calm and meditation and quiet, but he has to (unwillingly almost) fight for his fellow human beings and improve their lot, overthrow Soviet power....The Baroque has a social side...and teaches true values....I must get across to my group that the Light is an aspect of Western values which cannot be ignored....All our faults are of the outer man, not the inner genius, our better selves from which the hurrying world separates us. The point is, we are both outer and inner, and have to balance the two....Above all, the Romantics wrote about what it was to be a poet. E.g. *Kubla Khan* is about the poet's honey-dew and milk of Paradise. Poem after poem is an allegory for the creative act."

The next day we drove to Scotland and had tea with Nadia, having met her at her music publishers, and we visited Cramond and saw her new flat, which was in an 1823 house that had a beautiful frieze. I heard about her plans to become an air hostess. We booked in at the Dean Hotel, Edinburgh, where Nadia gave me a belated birthday present: a broken eggshell-like sculpture with sea urchins and sea anemones growing on it. She agreed it symbolised my broken marriage and said: "You're the biggest flower, I didn't think you'd see the symbolism so quickly." We ate at the Peacock restaurant near Leith docks and then returned to our hotel.

The next day we drove into the Scottish Highlands, past Bannockburn and through Glencoe, past Fort William and Ben Nevis, to an isolated house near Invergarry, Greenfield, where Argie, and Frances and her family, greeted us at the gate. We were "in deep countryside, with mountains all round, green hills, black-faced sheep and cows which nuzzled against the windows, the lawn was filled with lesser celandine and harebells, and swifts swooped and dipped and flitted, and there was rose-bay willow herb in the hedgerows and on the moors. There was no water – we had to draw water from the burn but that was dry, so we had to drive containers to a petrol station, and the loo was the bracken at the back of the house – and there was no Scottish doctor or nearby hospital (it was brave of Argie at over 80 to put herself in such an isolated situation, although Frances's husband was a doctor), and there were midges at dusk. I quickly put a chair and table on the lawn, stripped to my waist in the warm sun and wrote with black-faced sheep to keep me company in the clear mountain air, and in the evenings I worked upstairs on my *Times* article or on some stories while the others gossiped fitfully and read, and I realised we had slipped back into the 19th century and that I was living through my soul, not my social ego, measuring my self against mountains rather than social groups, against Nature rather than man. I wrote: "It would suit me to live alone, away from everywhere, like Reg in the Lake District; and write. I will...become a recluse in a mountain retreat, one day. The stillness of the country....The shepherd driving the sheep. The 2 horsemen. The 2 hikers. Otherwise nobody. Just the bees humming in the climbing roses. And a drowsy silence on which voices murmur from afar."

We went to Loch Ness and visited Castle Urquhart, and went into Inverness and recoiled at the crowded streets. We cruised on Loch Ness from Fort Augustus, and saw some glass-blowing. Back at Greenfield Matthew played "Over the sea to Skye" on his ocherina, and Ann and I left the boys behind and toured Skye, crossing from Kyle of Lochalsh and then driving among mountains and mists and stunning views. We toured the north-east of the island and saw the Outer Hebrides and then we followed Bonnie Prince Charlie's journey in 1746 as he escaped to France with the help of Flora MacDonald. We were near the northern lights, and it was still light after 11 p.m.

We returned to find Argie unwell. We attempted trout fishing in Laddie Wood, but caught nothing; Richard Moxon and I stood near waterfalls, "probing the pools with a rod and line and worm, like a poet probing the depths of the unconscious for a swish of a tail". Otherwise I sat and thought and wrote about the Baroque and pondered a selection of my poems. I wrote: "I have written about transformation and illumination and visions and dynamic nature....The world is Baroque and doesn't realise it. The Space Age – whirling clouds past a space rocket – and Tippett's *Mask of Time* are Baroque works. When the world realises we are living in a Baroque time there will be a great change in the arts, which I have anticipated, and man will be redefined to include more than the mere mind and body accorded him by the Renaissance."

We left for a tour of Mull and Iona with the boys. We took the ferry to Mull from Oban, and were soon in mountains with a swooping golden eagle for company. We stayed at Bunessan with a view of the sea; there were oyster-catchers with red beaks, and a yellow and green sunset over islands. We took the ferry to Iona from Fionnphort. The view from the sea of the ancient Iona, where St. Columba, who converted Scotland to Christianity, had his cell, was breathtaking: a green hillock out of blue waves with the ancient Abbey standing alone, without enclosing walls, a part of the rugged scenery. I spent a profound day there and on nearby Staffa, which resulted in my two poems *Iona* and *Staffa*: "A day of contemplation close to St. Columba. Through the nunnery to the ancient St. Oran's chapel (12th century) and on to his cousin St. Columba's cell and shrine, outside which stood St. John's cross. Then to the Abbey, and the oldest Benedictine bit where I meditated. Moved between St. Columba's tiny shrine and St. Oran's chapel and the Abbey – my Grail chapel, St. Oran's – and the Light came and went and came again, and I felt wonderfully peaceful. Lunched on the beach near some sewage, and then went to Fingal's cave on a small boat which had many vomiting over the side, not my intrepid family however. There was too much of a swell to alight at the usual place, so we were put off at the other end of the island (Staffa) and had to walk the entire length of the island to the cave. Heard the piping, like woodwind – the ghostly sound of the wind – inside the organ-pipe rock formation. This must have been what Mendelssohn heard. The boom of the sea and a frail pipe....Back to Iona, after which I meditated again until the Light poured up me, and St. Columba came into me to heal my bronchiectasis. The circular cross over the door of St. Columba's shrine in shadow from the evening sun, as I meditated inside (the shadow of the cross) was on my back. Just caught the ferry back to Fionnphort at 7.15. A glorious day, very memorable, close to the beginnings of Christianity, full of contemplative power (the Iona stones are very powerful) and close to my present concerns for I am a fighter for Columba's Christendom against the modern heathen (the Soviet Union). Back to the Argyll Arms, Bunessan, and a bar meal and drinks – and another truth. The rainbow in the spray as the boat sped against the tide, the sun at my back, to Staffa....Have written a poem on Iona (9 stanzas) and am nearly asleep after the effort. I am so full of fresh air I can hardly think, but am glad I've got it all down while it is fresh in my mind. The Plough is very clear in the night sky almost overhead, and there is light blue sky on the horizon. A lighthouse pulses regularly from the island in the dark. Existence is good!"

A MYSTIC WAY

The next day we left Bunessan for Salem and caught the ferry from Craignure to Oban and meandered back to Greenfield. Frances's doctor husband Richard said he was climbing Ben Nevis the next day alone. On impulse I said I would go with him, even though I did not have appropriate footwear and there was not time to buy anything. The following day, wearing flip-flops, we left at 7 a.m. and drove to Ben Nevis, which we climbed. I wrote: "My whole life has been climbing a mountain, and I shall be re-enacting this ascent tomorrow. One day, my climb will be seen for what it is – to be of truly Everest proportions....Climbed Ben Nevis, although suffering from bronchiectasis, and earlier this year, thrombophlebitis. Did 4,400 feet in 3 hrs 50 mins, stayed on the summit for 45 mins as a cloud (of unknowing) cleared, giving views of precipitous drops into green glens, and then took over 3 hrs coming down, with many rests as my legs went. At 45, I gave Richard (34) a good 10 years but matched him for heart and lungs to the top, and only flagged on the way down. Saw the ascent into cloud, which lifted giving visions and then the sun, as a parable for the Mystic Way, and wrote a poem about it." The descent was truly awful, as Keats found in 1818 ("'Twas a most vile descent"). Several times I felt I would not make it, but Richard encouraged me and, reassured by having my own personal doctor accompanying me, I got down in the end.

The next day we went to Culloden and found the stone Cumberland stood on behind the enemy's rank. We drove on to Findhorn and found the caravan park and Caddy vegetable garden which the New Age community had gathered round. We wandered among the huts and the tea and craft places, and everyone said "Hello".

The next day we left Greenfield and drove to London. I recorded: "Wrote poems on Wordsworth and Beatrix Potter in the car."

The rest of 1984 was dominated by my response to Scargill's miners' strike, which I had identified as a Soviet-backed political strike to break the system, not simply a strike for a pay claim. On the BBC there were nightly reports of the movement of thousands of miners from target to target and of the doings of the flying pickets. It was clear to me that the movements were organised, but no one said by whom. The *Times* man in Features, who I was later told had known Trotskyite leanings, had rung and said he was "defeated by the material", Josten said the *Times* was "penetrated", and later Charlie Douglas-Home rang to ask for my Cornish number so he could ring me from his holiday, and he directed me to deal with Peter Stodhart in Features. On our way to Cornwall I stopped at the Polish Air Force Club to deliver a package to Josten, and he came downstairs and introduced himself to Ann and the boys: "I am the terrible Josten who takes up so much of your husband's time."

We spent a sunny, windless day at Charlestown. Matthew and Anthony played on a dinghy in the calm shallows. Both sat in it while I read on the beach, fully clothed, and Ann sunbathed. Suddenly I heard a scream and looked up. The dinghy was drifting rapidly out on unseen currents towards the rocks and rougher sea. Matthew had lost control and dropped his oar and Anthony had screamed in terror. I quickly undressed to my pants and half-ran, half-waded in and just as I was about to go out of my depth and the first rocks scraped my feet, I managed to grab the dinghy and lead it in. I had saved my daughter from drowning in Japan, and now I had saved my two sons from being swept out to sea.

The weather was good and we spent golden days under a blue sky and yellow sun at Par beach, which was safer for the boys, and my skin reddened and my eyes creased with sunburn. I sat and pondered Scargill's Communism and wrote headings for a revised article: "The CPGB (Communist Party of Great Britain's) three definitions of what a Communist is, how Scargill looks a Communist despite his denials, and a Stalinist one at that, how his background reinforces this view, how he left the YCs (Young Communists) for political expediency, how he continued to work for their goals at home and how the CPGB supported him, both in becoming President of the NUM and in the present strike, how the CPGB supported him through Watters, how Moscow is behind the CPGB, his visits to Moscow, back to Stalinism and finally revolution through coal."

We went to Gunwalloe, "where the sea was full of surf and several bathers were in difficulties and had to be rescued. I wrote two poems, *Sea-Rescue*...and *Sea-Force*, a sonnet which answers Keats' 'It keeps eternal whisperings around' and tackles the fundamental – elemental – question about the sea: what is the cause of its energy? Which I see as emblematic of the ebb and flow of the life-force. A poem Wordsworth would not have minded owning up to. I am so creative at present." We went to Tintagel where I "drafted a poem on St. Juliot: how I am obsessed by the early saints who were extensions of the desert fathers in Egypt (as to some extent I am myself). St. Juliot and Merlin, hermits v magic. Went for Arthur but found the early Celtic monastery (c500AD), and St. Juliot's cell. Returned and finished typing up my introductory essay on the New Baroque vision, which is now finished."

I sketched out a selection of my poems, which "should proceed from Awakening to Silence to Transformation to Illumination to visions of Paradise, Self-Surmounting, Creativity, Sense and Spirit and Dynamic Nature (the Unitive Life) – reflecting the Mystic Way. So there are stages along the Tokaido road..., a journey showing progress to mysticism, a strong collection that characterises the Baroque." I observed: "Rather than spend my summer putting Scargill's thoughts into a Revolutionary Handbook, I have put my Mystic Way into order, including such headings as Rapture." I wrote: "When Ricks said 'Choose poems that are technically accurate', he was judging as a Neo-Classical."

I went out fishing with Ann's cousin. We left at 5.45, and I deputised for one of the crew whose wife had had a baby at 4.30 am. I pulled in nets with a fisherman called Kingsley. There was little wind, although there was a south-easterly for a time which made the sea choppy as we went east, and I remember Kingsley standing legs astride the dipping boat, cigarette in mouth, fisherman's apron on, sharpening a huge knife on a sharpener, cutting forward and back and just missing his own knuckles each time.

The newspaper article was still encountering opposition on the *Times*, and I thought again of writing a short book, to be provisionally entitled *Scargill's Handbook for Revolution*, to get my new publishing house, Oak-

Tree Books, off the ground. Josten wanted me to call it *Quotations from King Arthur*, but I told him: "It will be a literary essay of quality which can be read by everybody, not a dirty trick. I am a poet, not a scurrilous pamphleteer. There have been literary pamphlets about contemporary figures in the past, by Swift and Dryden, for example. One must win by argument and reason, and be devastating."

We returned home through Dorset via "Clouds Hill (of course) and Moreton cemetery, to pay respects to Lawrence of Arabia, and via Wool (Tess's honeymoon house with its forbidding 1631 chimneys and Tess's grave in the grounds of the ruined and now privately owned Bindon Abbey) and Bere Regis (the Turbeyville church window and vault). Passed through Lyme, which was unspeakably crowded." I noted the meaning of the inscription on T. E. Lawrence's lintel "ou phrontis", "indifference to worldly civilisation". I noted: "Drafted 3 poems on the way home: one on Charlestown calm (a sonnet) which I experienced on my last visit there; one on Lawrence; and one on Hardy places and the Turbeyvilles."

The *Times* were still reluctant to publish my article, and on September 1st I wrote: "It came to me while I read the paper after mowing and painting, at 11.45 p.m.: the government do not want the miners' strike to end. Hence the reluctance of the *Times* to publish my material. They want the strike to continue, because it can discredit Labour. It is dirty, it stinks, but no other explanation fits the facts."

The West Ham goalkeeper, Tom McAlister, was an Oaklands parent, and he gave us all complimentary tickets in the stand for the next match, West Ham v Watford. He brought them round to our house and I asked him what he would do if there was a penalty, and he said: "I'll go to the right." Twenty minutes into the game there was a penalty against West Ham just under where we were sitting. I wrote: "Tom's great save from the Watford no 8, (Mo) Johnstone. He went the way he said he'd go. Then after half time West Ham scored twice. And I am left with a moment that is eternal: Tom saving the penalty – the ball in mid air between boot and goalposts and Tom will dive and save it and the whole stand will rise to its feet and shout 'Yes'. A moment frozen for all eternity, like the ball from Dutchman, hanging in the air above the head of Pegasus Potts, remembered now, what 30 years later. These sporting images – memories mixed with emotion which revives when the image is recalled."

I was struck by the casualness of professional football. A few months later Tom took football for the Oaklands boys for a while – he played for one team and I put on a track suit and played up the other end – and one day he came round when he was on Match of the Day, against Spurs. He sat and watched himself, and I asked if Les Allen was playing for the Spurs. He said: "Oh yes, I said at half time, 'Which one's Les Allen?' And one of the players said 'He's not playing.'" I was quite shocked. All the newspapers and the commentators knew in advance who the main danger would be, and the players were supposed to have pre-match talks about tactics, yet the West Ham goalie did not know that the main strike player on the other side was not playing until half time.

I went back to school at Garratt Green deciding it would be my last academic year there: "This year must be my last, for I am wasting my life now that I have Oaklands, wasting my time casting pearls before swine for money I no longer need....I want to be a publisher-writer."

I again took Vernon Davies to lunch with Josten at the Polish Air Force Club. I noted: "The van outside with packing boxes in the back, probably disguising electronic equipment, and two well-dressed drivers who sat outside the conference room where we met for one and a half hours without moving, and were there when we left." (According to Vernon, who was watching from his car, they drove off as soon as I had driven away in my car.) Josten again tried to persuade Vernon to launch a campaign on unemployment, emphasising "buying British". Josten had been in touch with the Prime Minister's PPS about "Eldon Griffiths' secret document on psychological warfare". It was now clear to me that Josten was involved in some kind of psychological warfare for someone other than himself – how had Biggs-Davison got me mixed up in this? I wrote: "This diabolical work I am involved in on all sides: Leftist ILEA, Scargill, the Soviet Union etc. Sometimes I feel I am really quite a high grade angel, sent down to minister to those in Hell and keep Hell free and clean so that this vale of soul-making can continue to fulfil its function. I am now in an underworld. This is an underworld, and I Orpheus with my poems, sing in spite of my chains." I wrote of my book on Scargill: "The book must be straight, not ironic."

I spent the whole weekend of September 22nd-23rd writing the Scargill book with John Cameron sifting the material. I recorded: "I feel so well. All weekend, on the Scargill book....I feel really well, and no cold or snuffle since the Lakes. Anthony had a headache and an eye ache, and an ache elsewhere in his anatomy, and I broke off from my typing and said 'Oh God, please heal Anthony Hagger,' holding my hand to his head, and immediately there were strong surges and Ant fell asleep soon afterwards, cured."

I had decided that the first part of the Scargill book would be quotations from his own mouth, and wrote of Part Two: "The theme, 'The Communist role in the 1984 Miners' Strike'....The CPGB programme, and how Scargill reflects it....The Soviet involvement in the strike (and past strikes)....How Scargill has applied...features of Stalinism within the NUM, and how his aim is revolution." I decided to call the book *Scargill the Stalinist?* after the Bishop of Durham spoke of rejecting Scargill's "apparent attachment to a Stalinist type of Marxism". I wrote: "In my Scargill book I have applied penetrating techniques of literary criticism to a living social being in an 18th century way: social criticism. And yet, really it goes back to Marvell's *Horatian Ode*: ode on, not King Charles, but King Arthur. Writing about a contemporary public figure, to expose."

Organising my new publishing venture was now taking all my time. I was in touch with designers, printers and distributors. I had to find a libel lawyer, and found Edward Garnier, who was in the same chambers as Leon Brittan and is now a Conservative MP. To advise me I had Trevor Maher, who met me several times to teach me the tricks of the trade: what percentages to let bookshops take, how to calculate the number of copies a book must sell before its costs are covered. He fixed me up with distribution, and put me in touch with a complex of hired office space with

439

a communal live telephonist to take messages in Rosemont Road, Hampstead, and I would do my own warehousing and invoicing. For my printer I chose a Yugoslav, Dusan Plenicar, a former guerilla who told me: "It's not democracy but Christianity which is at the centre of Western ideology, and which is positive enough to defeat Communism." By the end of September I was so overworked that I felt like the townspeople in a church sermon I heard who did not know the rhythms of the countryside and had lost contact with the seasons and the weather: "being a part of natural processes and knowing that all creation is God's farm and that God looks after each creature and feeds each human in the same way (the poor like sparrows)."

On 12th October 1984 a bomb exploded at the Grand Hotel, Brighton, the scene of the Conservative Party conference, and Norman Tebbit was pulled out of the rubble. At the time I connected this outrage with the IRA, but not with the pre-Gorbachev Soviet Union or Gaddafi – in 1986, I was to learn that Gaddafi's involvement was revenge for the humiliation of the Libyan People's Bureau siege following the murder of W.P.C. Fletcher – or with the NUM. I knew that as its last anti-Western throw, the hardline Communist USSR (through Prague) and Libya had between them supplied the NUM with funds; and that the Brighton bomb was intended to wipe out the entire British government; and that there was a plan that, with the IRA's help, the NUM would take to the streets, Bolshevik-style, and install a dictator. But I did not realise the full extent to which these apparently separate phenomena were linked until in 1986 my author Dr Des McForan showed me transcripts of tape recordings made by French intelligence of meetings in May and June 1984. Once in power, the scenario ran, the dictator would invite the Russians in. I did not know that my book could not have appeared at a more timely moment. It was as if I had been impelled by the Light to get it out at just the right time.

It dawned on me that Josten did not want either the *Times* article or the book to appear. He had rung the *Times* to hurry them up and accused them of being "penetrated" and told them that I would be proceeding with the *Daily Telegraph*, effectively torpedoing the article (as my *Times* contact informed me). He tried to confuse the conception of the book by pressing for impractical alternatives, which I single-mindedly disregarded. I considered the possibility that Josten was in the KGB because he was trying to undermine me, and I mentioned this possibility to Biggs-Davison, who looked thunderstruck and said quietly, "I hope not." "I hope not too," I said.

Soon afterwards I had a phone call from Josten, who now asked me for money: £400 for putting me in touch with the man who supplied the Scargill material. I bluntly told him he was undermining me, that I was starting a new company to implement the FREE idea and that he was just concerned to extort money out of me. To my amazement he admitted torpedoing the FREE idea. I wrote: "He admitted torpedoing the Soviet idea: 'It would have been a disaster, you were not ready.' I: 'I am no less incapable of doing it now than I was then. Your refusal had the consequence of doing what the KGB wanted.' He: 'I've pressed my record button: you are accusing me of being in the KGB, that's libellous.'" He now tried to resurrect the FREE idea: "He: 'We'll open discussions on the first idea immediately this is finished.' I: 'No, I was as expert then as I am now, if it wouldn't work then it won't work now.'" I repeated that the KGB would be delighted and relieved that FREE had not been implemented, and that he had done them a service.

The book progressed. I wrote: "Too busy to go to work. Saw bank manager, accountant, solicitor. Also my printer with the final version of my Scargill book, and picked up the cover. It never ceases to amaze me, life: I thought I was hard done by, not getting into the *Times*, and now it seems I have a best-seller on my hands as Smiths are interested and are set to take it." W. H. Smiths ordered 4,000 copies and I elected to print 10,000 copies. John Cameron drove around with me, one of the first of my "Heroes of the West", endlessly giving me support as I did a radio interview for LBC and kept my appointments every evening. I seemed to have a new energy from an outside source. I wrote: "My intensity made the recording machine go haywire. John Cameron, 'You know when you're doing it?' I: 'Yes, I live at a pitch of intensity greater than most people," one of whom "can only come up to my level of intensity for short spells, after which he falls back feeling 'punch-drunk'."

My book was now ready. Crozier had three early copies and sent two of them to Mrs. Thatcher and Peter Walker, who was in charge of the miners' strike. Crozier told me, "Your book is extraordinarily effective."

On November 16th the *Times* Diary broke the news of my coming book. It was reported that Scargill heard about it in Yorkshire and drove straight to the Soviet Embassy in London, where Gordievsky (a British agent) was then employed. Shortly afterwards a shadowy figure, who was presumably pro-Soviet, went up and down the Charing Cross Road warning the bookshops not to stock my book. Foyles would not be intimidated, and the Yugoslav senior manager gave the order for an entire window to be cleared of Alastair Macleans and Agatha Christies and for it to be filled with my book. They doubled their order.

Meanwhile Peter Walker had asked to see me. I told the Head at Garratt Green that I would be late in as I had to see the Secretary of State, and received a dark look that suggested my dreadfulness now knew no bounds: not only was I Principal of a private school while working in the ILEA, but I was now consorting with a Conservative Minister.

I put on a suit, went to the Department of Energy, signed in to see the "SoS" (Secretary of State), was given a tab, went up in a lift to the second floor and then progressed to the waiting room which overlooked the river. In came Peter Walker, grey-haired, to meet me. "Hello, how is Britain's newest publisher?" "Feeling like a one-man band at present," I replied and he laughed. I followed him past secretaries in two outer rooms to his huge Holy of Holies, where papers were spread in piles on the carpet near an open red box. "You work on the floor," I said. "Yes," he said. We sat side by side, and talked about the publicity and distribution of the book, and he gave me "a quotation for the launch". I got on well with him; there was laughter. We talked about Scargill's 1972 strike, and I raised the Soviet connection in the current strike. Walker told me: "There's a very strong Soviet connection. I have held back on it because I don't want people to think of Reds under the beds." I said: "It's time to put the boot in." He said,

"No one has stood up to Scargill yet." He seemed to decide something, and then said "Good" and "Good luck with the launch" and after a smiling handshake I was out among the secretaries and being taken downstairs in the lift.

I was now waiting for the launch. It was to be held in the Connaught Rooms with Lord Orr-Ewing in the chair and Sir John Biggs-Davison and Sir Bernard Braine in attendance. I had invited numerous people, including Edward Heath, David Owen (who wrote me a nice letter) and Harold Wilson (who told me over the phone "I'm sorry, I have an engagement in Oxford on November 29th"). The *Sun* published an article about the book, which Josten took the credit for organising. A number of politicians replied saying that they would be coming, and there was great interest on the part of the media. Everyone wanted to attend the launch. The day of the launch saw a three-column first editorial about the book in the *Times*, titled "We Have Been Warned", written by Charlie Douglas-Home. There was a stampede to buy the book, people had been going to Hampstead to buy a copy from my telephone-answering service, and Biggs-Davison reported that he had been at a dinner the previous evening and those present had talked about nothing other than the book for the whole evening. Norris McWhirter had described it as "devastating" (a word he repeated to me over the phone later). "May I have your autograph?" Biggs-Davison asked as we waited for the guests to assemble, standing near a pile of books and sipping wine. "You've done yourself a lot of good by this." Lord Orr-Ewing said to me: "I want to build you up."

But it was already apparent that the reverse was happening. Messages were being received of last minute cancellations, including two television companies who had previously accepted, and one of those who was present said he had been rung up by an anonymous caller and advised not to attend the launch. There were no pickets outside the Connaught Rooms, but only about 40 turned up and someone wanted to confine those there to the few already involved: Lord Orr-Ewing, who spoke first: Sir Bernard Braine, Father of the House of Commons, who knew of my interest in FREE; and finally in the unexpected absence of Lord Chapple, who had written the Foreword to the book, Josten, who spoke at the invitation of Braine. I wrote: "Who muzzled – and why? This muzzling. Either it's benevolent (my security...)...or it's malevolent (the 5th man). Or it's just that Fleet Street took umbrage because the *Times* and *Sun* jumped the gun or...were reluctant to touch me." I felt the operation was too solid to be pique, and was malevolent rather than benevolent.

I was sure the government was committed to playing the strike long, wearing the miners out and waiting for them to cave in; and that while they were happy for my book to embarrass Scargill and would on the surface go along with Peter Walker's supportive attitude, they did not want to provoke the miners and make matters worse, and perhaps did not want to worry the British people by emphasising the Soviet connection, which would mean drawing attention to the Soviet context of the Brighton bomb. (One reason for underplaying the Soviet connection might be that the Soviet help for the miners was being directed by a group of Westerners, the same New World Order crowd who had installed Gaddafi in Libya.) At the same time, following his admission regarding FREE, I suspected Josten was behind what was happening, although I had no proof. The reality was that a screen of silence had been thrown around my book; a deafening silence, given the stampeding interest only a day previously.

Josten now began writing me vitriolic letters asking for money, insisting on the line he had taken when I told him he was helping the KGB. I wrote back that he should address all letters to my "financial adviser", the multi-millionaire Vernon Davies, and explained that the anti-Soviet alliance was not motivated by financial considerations but by belief in the cause. Things came to a head when, at his request, I had to visit his office one day. Evelyn Le Chêne (which means "oak-tree"), who had attended my launch, was helping him with some secretarial work, and in her presence he suddenly flew into a rage and bellowed at me, as if volume was the measure of the justice of his argument, because I would not do what he was asking: write him an immediate cheque for an exorbitant amount. I told him I was undertaking a publishing venture. He was quivering with fury, standing over me where I sat, and he raised his hand to hit me. I was very calm, and slowly he calmed down. (Later Evelyn told me I had handled the unprovoked attack extremely well.) He said: "This cannot be, I am getting excited, I will telephone Sir Bernard Braine, you will never work again. You will be persona non grata." I withdrew. The next time I was in touch with him, he repeated over the telephone: "You will never work again. I have fixed it."

Despite the screen of silence, the book sold well in the bookshops. Many came back for more, new orders were placed daily. And I received phone calls from members of the public. One ex-Communist, Tony Murphy, rang me with details of how the miners' strike was being organised from Moscow, and I went up to Hull and saw him, travelling by train and ignoring Baroness Cox's warning that it might be a trap to kidnap me. I was aware that I might be fed disinformation, I was "living in 'uncertainties, mysteries and doubts without any irritable reaching after fact or reason', more like Kafka than Keats". Murphy told me in great detail about the Moscow-Scargill link, the role of the *World Marxist Review* and of Bert Ramelson; and he said he feared a Scargill victory in the strike would trigger a military coup. He told me that Robert Maxwell was definitely a Soviet agent. He said that when Scargill read the *Times Diary* report about the book he "took the book (Vic Allen's copy) to the Soviet Embassy, who advised 'ignore and intimidate and leave it to us'". In no time the book had paid for itself and made a small profit, with the result that the setting up of Oak-Tree Books had paid for itself.

In the middle of this frantic activity I was breaking up at both schools in December. I attended the farewell of John Welch, the Chief Inspector of the ILEA, which was held at the Polytechnic of the South Bank, Borough Street. I wrote: "Up in a lift to the second floor and a large room. A table and Aston in a red shirt and grey tie and rimmed spectacles. Norcross, lined. Bolton, foetal and bulging. Hargreaves. Sat down next to Welch for the speeches. Then Welch's farewell. 'Would you like a drink first? You have two minutes in which to stretch your legs.' (His sure grasp of his audience.) Then his autobiography. He was saying that his school near the Tyne had everything ILEA aspires to be (mixed ability etc) and it produced him – but there must be standards if people like him are to be able to come through. It was ambiguous eg the beatings did him no harm – or the beatings were terrible. He narrated without any moral condemnation. At the end he was nearly in tears, was moved. I mentioned my book as I left. 'I'll buy it.'...Norcross, 'He told me he was on my side.'"

While all this was going on Matthew was rushed to hospital, having swallowed a peanut at Vernon Davies's house. Matthew was at Vernon's son's party, and the peanut lodged in his bronchi, "making him wheeze and giving him an infected death-wheeze. They fished out an entire half-peanut before it had disintegrated,....My apprehension, my relief when he came up from theatre at 12.30, after an hour and a half."

The book was still selling well. There had been a demonstration against it in Foyles. The NUM had advanced on Foyles and taken it over; they had a sit-in and stuck stickers all over the display window off Charing Cross Road so that the public would have difficulty in seeing the book. The miners sat on the floor and chanted and demanded the withdrawal of the book. The Foyles manager told me that Foyles had not known anything like it since the war.

I had a staff gathering to celebrate breaking up at Oaklands. On Christmas Eve I visited shrivelled Miss Root, the ex-Oaklands teacher who was 90, and heard her memories of my time at Oaklands, and then went and had a couple of glasses of red wine with Tom McAlister, the West Ham goalie and his wife. On Christmas Day, I observed: "Surfeit. But peace round the tree, looking out at the tree in the field." Later I rang Margaret and wrote: "She is working hard for an organisation, without pay, with love, making bookmarks, and she had 'sold' Teresa to this organisation....She has buried her talent in her Catholic 'work', and she is not painting outside her work. Her way of renunciation."

I heard that Tomlin, my boss in Japan, had written *Psyche, Culture and the New Science*, and that it had been launched at St. James's, Piccadilly.

The family party was at Frances's house in Wimbledon, and soon after we went to a gathering at Paddy Manning's in Moreton, and I ate opposite Patrick Griggs, my contemporary at the old (and later the new) Oaklands who had told me "I was under your bed all last night, I was doing the knocking", and who was now a solicitor. I wrote: "A tranquil dinner in which the English idea in the air above the table ruled the conversation, and when it was motorways no one was allowed to contribute on anything other than motorways and when it was Stansted, ditto on Stansted, and no one was the faintest bit interested in what was actually said."

At the end of 1984 I took stock: "I see that last year I contemplated developing my Christendom v Communism perspective – which I have done dramatically with my foundation of Oak-Tree and my Scargill book."

In mid-January I had thrombo-phlebitis again in my right leg and ankle, and wrote: "I am experiencing what my father had at not much greater than my age....I will leave Garratt Green in July this year – before my health is damaged any further. This will mean depending exclusively on Oaklands." I thought this phlebitis was a result of the injection I had had in my varicose vein five years back. I showed my phlebitis to David Hughes, who had just told me that my lung was clear: "But there are degrees of clearness which show up on an X-ray, and I still have bronchiectasis, and ought to have parts of both lungs cut away. If I were to have a thrombosis in my lungs – a pulmonary embolism – it could be very dangerous, and so now I have had two attacks of thrombo-phlebitis...I must have the superficial veins removed like twigs from a tree." David Hughes sent me to a consultant, Mr Maclean, who looked at my thrombo-phlebitis and said: "You need an operation. The blood is flowing the wrong way in your right ankle. I need to cut it and clean it up. There will be a risk of post-operational thrombosis."

I saw the world within the context of "Christendom versus Communism". My Yugoslav printer, Dusan, told me about a Marxist trained in Moscow and Prague, who was sent to execute an evangelist in Africa. At the last minute he failed to give his Zipra guerilla the signal to shoot. He had an experience that turned him into a Christian. I wrote: "It's a question of whose side you are on. Either you are on the Marxist side or you are on the side of Christendom. That is the choice. It is a clear choice. There is no middle ground except wishy washy funk. Either it is Marxism or the Light. And Christendom is infiltrated by Marxists, to add to the confusion."

In February I lamented: "All weekend on money – doing the Oak-Tree accounts..., coping with Oaklands payments, totalling etc. All weekend I was an accountant, and where was my creativity? Then went for a walk on the estate and saw the sun on the snow, with Oaklands sheltering under the big tree along with my house, and I felt at peace. Ice on the pond, and an awakening spirit." I wrote again: "Most of all I loved the physical things: the pyramid of Miss Lord's roof against the golden dusk and dark silhouettes of trees. I am a poet with too little time."

Perhaps thinking of the miners' strike, I wrote: "Civilisation is the rule of mind over body, e.g. classical music. Barbarism is the rule of body over mind, e.g. pop: beat = heart; drum = excitement; throb etc. Civilisation is order and discipline, barbarism chaos."

I had had enough of politics. I wrote: "Treat religion and politics as embroidery – embroider them onto works of art. I am fundamentally an artist."

At the February half term we went to France by hovercraft. I slept for much of the train journey, having congestion in a lung and pain in my right leg from thrombo-phlebitis. We skimmed through spray across a mill-pond sea to Boulogne and took the train to Paris where we stayed at the Brochant des Tours. We visited the Arc de Triomph, the Champs Elisées, Notre Dame and St. Germain des Prés, passing the Café Bonaparte where Sartre wrote some of his books in public. I revisited the isle in the Seine, where I spent much of the Easter holidays of 1958 reading Milton's *Paradise Lost*. The next morning we had a coach tour round Paris, "stopping at Notre Dame – the sunlight through the reds and blues of the stained glass windows at the prow end of the sailing boat (flying buttresses = sails on the Seine) – and at Napoleon's tomb". We took a train to Versailles and "visited the State apartments, including the Queen's bedroom and the Hall of Mirrors, a dazzling experience of light and gold....Back to the 'caveau des oubliettes', 11 St. Julien le Pauvre, a Bodmin-jail type of cabaret housed in an ancient dungeon with the only surviving guillotine (1793)." We went up the Eiffel Tower to eat. I was "confronted by a childhood phobia" (my fear of heights) when "I saw the ground disappear through glass in the floor of the lift". I took the lift again and "we dined, white-tableclothed splendour, waiters, manager in evening dress, and drank red burgundy, while I felt the plates creak and groan and shudder in my imagination each time the lift crashed to a halt the other side of our plate glass window, all Paris spread underneath, lit up, and the floodlit top of the tower rising above us like some great, giant's mecanno set....I kept seeing in my imagination a hole blown in the side of the restaurant where we were eating." The next morning we visited the Conciergerie: "The 14th century kitchen and guardroom of the old palace, then the prison rooms. The Rue de Paris, where M. le Paris, executioner, collected his victims. The room where the condemned had their heads shaved, sitting on a bench, in twelves. 42,000 were guillotined. Marie Antoinette's 2 prison cells, the first with 4 holes in a diamond, through which she handed a note with a lock of hair, and the second (now with an altar) from which she was taken to execution. Robespierre's cell, and the guillotine blades and ladder which victims mounted. Outside, the courtyard of women, where families came to say goodbye. On the isle with the Seine all round it, for security." We ate at L'Esperance, a restaurant near Gare du Nord, and caught the 2.20 train to Boulogne, whence we went to Caen and the Hotel Central and dined by prior arrangement among noisy Normans with the English owner of a language school who was trying to sell, and which I decided not to buy. We saw William the Conqueror's grave and returned via Rouen past the spot where Joan of Arc was burned.

Back in England the miners' strike ended abruptly in early March. I wrote: "Scargill, the tribune of the people, being hauled down by his own supporters." It had been a long and exhausting struggle, and the government had waited for Scargill to be beaten. My role had been to express the Soviet involvement in a limited way as the government did not want to blazen it too strongly. I had sold 8,000 of my 10,000 books, and had easily covered my costs and had made some profit.

Almost immediately I had a letter from Cameron. He was ill with pernicious anaemia, myocarditis and haemorrhages. Towards the end of August I found another letter from him dated August 12th resigning from his unofficial position as Secretary to Oak-Tree due to "pressure of work". I later heard he died on August 12th and that the funeral was on August 23rd at Putney Crematorium. He had been found in his flat in Dulwich. He had been dead a week. I phoned the police, who said there was a stench as they broke open his door. I said I was not convinced he had died of natural causes, but there was no evidence to suggest foul play. I spoke to the policeman who found him, who said that there was speculation among the police that he might have been murdered (could someone have dictated his resignation letter to me?), but he would not give me details as to why they thought that.

The inquest took place on September 27th. I rang the Southwark Coroner's court and again spoke to the policeman who had found Cameron.

He said that the inquest had reached an open verdict: "In other words, suspicious circumstances exist." I asked, "What suspicious circumstances?" He said that the body had been highly decomposed and had smelt because the windows were closed and the weather was hot; and that the pathologist was unable to determine the cause of death, but there seemed to be no bruises or signs of any blow. "That's all I'm at liberty to say." John's brother-in-law rang me soon afterwards and said that there had been a dozen pill bottles round his bed, that all the pills were for anaemia or his heart, and that the open verdict suggested he had taken an overdose. I asked if someone could have forced him to take an overdose. His letter to me of August 12th was forward-looking and not suicidal, and it was strange that he had resigned as Secretary to Oak-Tree after all the enthusiastic support he had given me. I knew I would never know the full truth about what happened. For at least two years Tribe, Cameron and I had sat together for lunch at Garratt Green, and now I was the only survivor.

Josten wrote me letters until May 1985 demanding money for "copyright material", but I stood firm on the principle that I would not give in to extortion, and once he had shouted at me and told me he had put me on a list so that I would never work again, no way was he getting a penny from me. I wrote to Crozier explaining the situation and dug my heels in. Meanwhile Josten took the credit for my Scargill book. He made out that it was all his conception and that it was ghosted by him. He was awarded the MBE in the Queen's birthday honours the following June, and died on 29th November 1985 (strangely on the first anniversary of my Scargill launch, a date which may or may not be significant), aged 72, and the *Daily Telegraph* obituary described him as a "Foreign Office adviser". Biggs-Davison said to me perceptively: "Sometimes a Crusader can be jealous of another Crusader." He said that Josten had always been very difficult to deal with and was "a jealous man".

My book was very influential in high places. Charlie Douglas-Home died at the beginning of November 1985, and in 1986 his widow Jessica told me: "Your book was permanently on his desk, much thumbed and with comments written in the margin and many underlinings. It was his Bible, he based so many *Times* editorials on it." So my stand had influenced the Thunderer. I also heard that it was a much used reference book on the shelves of the Chairman of the Conservative Party.

Looking back, I can see that the miners' strike was Soviet Communism's dying aggressiveness towards the West; a final attempt by a hostile regime to overthrow the British government and replace it with a demagogue in the tradition of Cleon. For a while it looked as if it might succeed, and that the flying pickets might effect a Bolshevik-style or Gaddafi-style revolution; they were co-ordinated, and my book explained exactly how. The failure of the attempt was linked to the failure of the Brighton bomb to liquidate the Cabinet (although it is a universal law that an advanced civilisation never destroys a younger one, and the Byzantine-Russian civilisation is older than the European civilisation). My book alerted people to what was going on at a crucial time and presented an alternative picture to the one the BBC presented. I had embodied the attitude of the Light in the national chaos, and although I was not given, and did not particularly wish, any credit for my stance, I was satisfied that I had stood up for my country and been counted at a time when it mattered.

I knew that I would not have written the Scargill book unless the Light had impelled me to do so, via the idea of FREE. I felt that the Light is concerned with world developments and attempts to influence them by using humans who have opened to it. The Baroque is a mixture of spirit and sense, and never more so than in the way the Light entered the miners' strike.

The Light had pushed me into being a participant in the strike, and now it abruptly pulled me away from the political life. I was relieved for I had not liked what I had seen of the political Establishment, which was full of patronage, vested interests, ego and toes too easily trodden on. I was disillusioned at the pettiness, financial self-interest and personal advancement that had thwarted what I regarded as an obviously important (and with hindsight, prophetic) idea, and, having been on the winning side and achieved my aim in blocking Soviet expansionism in Britain – having fought a defensive rather than an offensive campaign as I had intended at the time of FREE – I was happy to take a step back from politics and resume my own priorities, notably my thinking about the Baroque and the coming Age, and completing my more recent poems, which I was not expecting to do.

I explored the possibility of starting a language school in Rouen, which I saw as a return to the Normandy I visited as a boy. I explored the tax implications of starting a French company and found a fellow who would run it in France for me. I met him at the Grosvenor Hotel, Victoria (which I had used to give surveillance squads the slip in the dark days before my 1971 illumination, entering by the front door and leaving by the back door into Victoria station and then plunging down into the underground).

In April I again went to Winchester for the Mystics and Scientists conference, and heard Sir George Trevelyan on the New Renaissance in the arts and Jocelyn Godwin and Keith Critchlow on how the universe is mathematical and musical number, how the universe is a oneness of number and tone – a sound. I listened to Jonathan Harvey's Neo-Baroque music. I had a wonderful experience of hearing the most majestic music: "The experience in Winchester of hearing a symphony (clairaudience), which I have written into *Staffa*....I heard the most majestic sound in the King Alfred's College Hall as we were all invited to listen, and wished I could write music, for I could have had a large part of a symphony. Cf my 'nocturnal travels' and painting – I often see paintings that are better than most I see in art galleries as examples of 20th century work. What I call 'old Masters' – but they are new Masters." I spoke with a Cubist painter who said that form and structure come from the Platonic Idea. I thought deeply about Orpheus and how poetry is given from the beyond; how there is a poetry of the vision, a poetry of the heart, a poetry of the head and a poetry of the third eye – all of which a great poet should attempt. I wrote: "Man against the universe: the Pyramid which is a tomb – and the means of escaping it, his soul, his immortality which can be contacted in meditation."

I wrote: "Artists who are great do not reflect their age but create the next one....The Light is breaking down old thought-forms." I left Winchester feeling well: "I feel so refreshed, so clear: my soul has been refreshed by meditation, and my body feels washed through and clear. Soul and body together. I have some poems about soul and body. Write them in Cornwall."

We went to Cornwall and "walked by the Charlestown sea on the pier in the fading light. Fishermen lit a lamp on the end of the pier, and it was high tide, and the sea smashed against the stone breakwater above the beach. Looked at the lock gate and mourned my poetic life, at present held dormant while I solve my problems in the world." I heard "the Alps call, the snow-capped heights, living on top of a mountain like Heidegger, in solitude for most of the day". Next time I went to Charlestown I observed: "To Charlestown between the showers on a cold, damp day, after I had managed to get my damp car started. The harbour shaped like a womb, the upper neck (above the lock gate) pregnant with boats. As I watched the sea pushed in across the moist sand. Wind-beaten trees, smoke-like clouds, a green sea. Art reveals higher worlds – or the underworld (Homer, Virgil) – and if it is only about this world it is abused. Imagery that reveals higher worlds is from pure imagination, imagery in terms of other objects in the natural world, unless it is suggesting inter-relatedness and variety, is decorative fancy." I added: "My search for meaning – man in the universe being fed by the universe – begins in the world of the senses and breaks through (in my late poems) into the world beyond the senses....Life has meaning when we are aware of our connection with everything and everybody and with the universe, with the power that fills us with wisdom and Light – the divine will. It is a divine meaning. Wrote *Lock Gate* in draft during a wet afternoon." Again: "Soul and body together – the very essence of Baroque. I act out the new age in my secret life. Painting, music and poetry come from within, from reverie, and should not be created from the ego, but should combine this world and beyond. Garratt Green made me listen to within. I must turn away from the moving world with its bizarre laughter and idiotic cacophony, for a world within."

I thought about the pattern of my life. Oaklands would give me the time to finish my writing on mysticism, and my thrombo-phlebitis would detach me from Garratt Green. I intended to cover Oak-Tree's costs with controversial contemporary themes and publish mystical and philosophical works with the proceeds. I observed: "A part of reflecting Western civilisation has been the international political theme of Grivas-Kaseem-Mao-Gaddafi-African liberation movements-ILEA extremists-Scargill etc. While I have also been shown the ancient world of Babylon-China-Egypt – and...ancient wisdom."

Once again I was receiving intense impressions: "Being a poet is so exciting, it is constantly having a diary or notebook ready at hand in which to record ideas and observations....Back to Charlestown. High tide. The sea crashed in, sending fountains of spray across the breakwater. It boiled and foamed and boomed and surged and poured and thudded against the wall by the 'sleep tunnel' and foamed back up the steps, and a mist of spray drifted landwards like smoke. The boys ran from the waves as the surf frothed round their ankles and Matthew got a bootful and squelched in his wellies and tipped a lot of water out in the sleep tunnel. The sheer power and energy of the sea, drawn by the moon, hurled by the moon, and the great hissing back-drag of the pebbles on each out-draw."

I pondered again what would characterise the coming Age of Western civilisation and wrote: "My search for an understanding, which takes a view that the soul and spirit must come back into art (new Renaissance) to keep Western civilisation alive against Communism and strengthen its ideology, and...this in fact takes us to an understanding of the universe; for the after-life and the nature of the universe are the context for everything else. Be a critic of all materialism....I am creating the next age, in which there is a higher world....Artists create the next stage, which will be a Baroque one, uniting Classicism and Romanticism. A new word for it?...Immaterialism (*Against Materialism*)?...What is the age?...It is a new ism, after Romanticism and Classicism, in artistic terms Baroque (in so far as it goes into cycles) but in religious and philosophical terms it is an Age of Soul, an Age of Ancient Wisdom, of New Science. It is anti-Humanist and counter-Renaissance, but should have a positive name of its own and not be defined in relation to other ages. Make up a word, a stronger word than Holism?...I still need a word for the next age, one that covers all the musicians, artists and writers who believe that man is an immortal, spiritual being – a new flowering of the Romantic age amalgamated to Classicism in the sense of T. E. Hulme and Eliot, the Age whose characteristics include mysticism, Baroque art etc. Call it the Illuminate Age – as opposed to the Enlightenment....Illumined Age. The Age of Illumination?....Past ages are on philosophies, e.g. Humanism (the philosophy of the Renaissance), so the new age must be the philosophy of the new Renaissance, which I must define in an essay. An Age of Transformation?" These thoughts anticipated the coming Universalist Age.

I thought about self-knowledge: "We are at present cross-sections of ourselves, but at the end of our lives we will be all our time, our true selves are all our time. Something like this is the theory behind these *Diaries*, that I am the sum total of all my thoughts and images and events, which these *Diaries* get nearer to catching, in their fragmentary diversity, than any other approach to me. I am in these *Diaries*."

I visited Charlestown again: "7 p.m. Went down to Charlestown after spending all day on end of year returns and April salaries – figures – with the exception of visits to Charlestown harbour in the morning and afternoon with the boys while Ann stayed in bed. Wrote a poem this morning, sitting on the harbour wall in the sun. Now in the evening the sea turned calm (after filling the boys' wellies) and it was a lovely satiny, silky blue, like shot silk, and barely a wrinkle. I stood on the harbour in breathless quiet, listening to every lapping sound, totally at one with the sea. Wrote a poem about it, too. Rosy-cheeked angels by the tide....I have discovered new beauties in Charlestown harbour at low tide: two headlands of a small bay, rocks and seaweed, sand and higher up shingle, a view of green clad cliffs – and a lock gate and chimney." (It was as if I was painting Charlestown.) "To Mevagissey. Walked along the harbour wall. A wrinkled calm sea. The swan. Later drove past Savage's house and slowed. An icon of Christ, illumined, on the wall through net curtains, next to the dental surgery."

METAPHYSICAL AND BAROQUE

I thought deeply about time: "Cornwall brings out the elemental in me, it relates me to stars and sea and field and sheep. Charlestown encapsulates man in the universe just as the Libyan desert did, for on the harbour wall at night I am man against the night universe, with the sea and the land all round me, beneath me. (I cannot sit comfortably in the Oaklands fields at night for fear of intruders, but I can sit alone on the Charlestown wall. Also Oaklands' trees do not present as stark a contrast as does sea and sky – or sand and sky of the desert – and the stars are obscured by trees.) Tonight the clear sky, no light on the end of the harbour wall, on which I sat and looked up, and all round me on all sides were stars, I was under a tall tree with round apples, a large apple tree – or is it a chestnut with round conkers – prickly cases? It seemed there was a parallel between a tree and fruit, and the heaven-tree of stars. I wanted to scrump apples. Then I saw the big bang above my head, and the stars blown outwards and frozen in time in mid fall, like a shower burst from a firework frozen in its explosion outwards. This was the second time today I felt frozen in time, for I wrote a poem this morning, also on the harbour wall (pressing on my knee, sitting half way along up on the edge) in which the sparkles on the waves are the same as the glowing stars, only time is longer and is compressed in sparkles. My feeling that time is on our scale, but that if it were compressed, the whole time-scale of the universe from start to finish would appear like – a sparkle from a wave, which is gone....Read this in conjunction with *Night Thoughts*. This intuitive perception of mine is important. In Cornwall I achieve elemental gains which I spend the rest of the year fiddling over when social clutter permits....All my best work is done in Cornwall these days, not London or Loughton, which are too cluttered, and which take me away from the vision of the universe, although I can recover it in the Forest ponds, among silver birch. Forests, seas, mountains (eg Scotland, Ben Nevis) – these are the places where I can recover the elemental....My 'trademark' is man in the universe, against the stars, not the social man (Tuohy): man between birth and death, in this universe, and where he is going, his immortality and how it relates to the stars. Most people see man in his street (Coronation Street) but I see a man against the stars, a frightening vision that permeates my *Silence* and which should still permeate my work."

And then I made the breakthrough that I was worrying at in my deliberations on the Age and which answered all my questions: "I am a Romantic, not a rational Classicist. I am a Universalist – a word that has the idea of Holism, the whole, i.e. all universes, and all that is universal; while going for the Light which permeates the universe. Universalism – look it up. That is the new philosophy, which has characteristics of the Baroque. Especially if Universalism includes soul and spirit, 4 levels of man's being in keeping with the Kabbalah. A Universal Age. After Realism and Nominalism came Humanism, the human scale (mind and body, not soul). Now Universalism, the scale of the universe, which includes the soul, for entry into the soul takes us out into the universe. The Universal Age....There are as many stars as sparkles, and they fade and form like the jumping lights on a sunlit sea – one perception I have had which takes me to the truth about the universe – 'bunches of grapes of 5,000 galaxies each'. An age that

451

raised its eyes from the street and social concerns to its place in the universe."

I wrote that any selection of my poems "must go with the Universal Age (cf Toynbee's Universal State)". I wrote: "An essay on our Universal Age which has Baroque features: on communications, the global view, but also on man's role in relation to the universe, which the new Renaissance is making possible. Think it out and argue it. The new science has opened up the stars and enlarged the soul, and my work must respond to this....This visit to Charlestown I have sat on the harbour wall at night and measured myself against the stars, against the universe, and the new perspective has brought the ancient wisdom into focus. 10 Ap. Stayed at home in morning and typed up *Time Compressed*, a metaphysical poem of the Universal Age." I wrote: "Open air poetry, poetry written in the open air which lets in the universe. Try to write in the open air whenever possible – at least first drafts. I write my poems in Charlestown harbour, in the Oaklands fields etc. Poetry capturing moments of rural life (threshers, milkers) – will be liked in London, which misses the country. 11 Ap. Awoke and saw raindrops on the window pane and wrote another of my *Time Sequence* poems, *Raindrops like Stars* (or *Warmth*) lying in bed, with Matthew lying in the other bed beside me....Typed *Raindrops like Stars*....Went down to Charlestown for the third or fourth time today, and saw 'still clouds' and 'moving stars' in a high wind, sketched the ideas for *Still Clouds and Whirling Stars* in the dark, in the frosty open air and half light on the harbour wall, then came home and wrote the poem at 11 p.m."

On my last day in Cornwall I read through a book I had been sent about terrorism by Dr Des McForan, which I wrote "will be my next publication for Oak-Tree" – he had read *Scargill the Stalinist?* while sheltering from the rain in Birmingham and had decided I was the right publisher for his book – and an illiterate book on trade unions by Jack Wood (who claimed to have ended the miners' strike), which would need rewriting. I returned to Essex to carry forward the publishing.

Almost immediately I went into the London Hospital to have my varicose veins stripped from my right leg. The surgeon, David Maclean, came and drew on my legs in black "magic marker". They would start in my right groin, leave me a surplus vein for my heart between my groin and knee, and then strip me from the knee down. Mr Maclean said: "It will be very sore when you wake, and five minutes every hour you must paddle your right foot up and down to clear thrombosis. Three times a day you must have a subcutaneous injection into the wall of your stomach to clear thrombosis. It will be an hour and a half operation, 8.30 to 10, and after it the blood will flow round the right way. I will wear microscopic glasses and make about 15 small cuts." I wrote: "10.15 p.m. I await execution. Bath tomorrow at 6.45, pre-med at 7.15. I am in the hands of the Light, which will do with me as it pleases. I am serene....12.30 am basked in the Light. Am still serene, but am too alert to sleep."

Later I wrote: "What I remember of the operation. I was given a pre-med of 3 green pills which sent me to sleep. I remember stretcher poles being put in my 'sheets' before I went. Awoke on the edge of theatre to see the anaesthetist give me an injection in my left hand, which bruised me, and then wapping my right hand looking for a vein. Don't remember any more, don't remember losing consciousness or even waking up, but do remember Hughes telling me it went very well. I: 'It went well?' Hughes: 'Very well.'"

A day later I wrote: "I have survived thrombosis, but have missed a day's *Diary* due to drowsiness. The operation took an hour and three quarters yesterday, they tied off a vein between groin and knee, leaving it in case I ever need it for my heart; tried to remove a vein between knee and ankle but as it would not come out (because of the 1978 injection of the vein) they rendered it non-working and left it in. They dealt with two perforating veins, and there were others they dealt with. So now the blood is circulating the right way and I may not have any more trouble with my ankle....It was the two perforating veins that caused my thrombo-phlebitis, according to Mr Maclean....Have walked down the passage twice...and it was agony when the foot first touched the floor, but I have loosened up since then. Must keep doing it so I don't stiffen. Every hour. The regime of hospital life. Breakfast at 7.30, lunch at 12, dinner at 6, and various injections and pills in between, and coffee, and tea (mid am/pm). The visits from doctors and physiotherapists, who slapped me for bronchiectasis."

I made good use of my convalescence: "In hospital, working on *Night Thoughts*. From the night thoughts (what is space, what is life/death) I see the stars as blossoms on a Tree, and the new science unfolding it all out of nothing, both in physics and biology, and show that the new science is against the old 'isms', that a new baroque age has grown out of a seeing in new dimensions, in terms of the universe, which reflects the old baroque which was heart-based. The new age of Charles (Charles' town) v the Elizabethan materialism, anti-materialism v materialism, the spiritual resurgence coming as I sit in the Charlestown dark having night thoughts. Characteristics of the new baroque age, oneness, the pastoral, the threat to Europe." I was visited by Argie, and Frances ("a gale of fresh air and humour"). I wrote of a picture on the wall "of a house mirrored in a lake, blue sky representing health and the mirror image of brown suggesting ill health". The next day I wrote: "2.30 p.m. Tea has arrived and I sink back exhausted on my hospital pillow to drink it, having redrafted in bold rhyme 14 stanzas of *Night Thoughts in Charlestown* so that there are 3 sections, 'Dark Night', 'Flight of the Soul to the Next Age' and 'The Soul Aglow' – 14 x 8 lines, ie 112 lines....I have earned my tea after two days' redrafting with my bandaged leg out and a heat outside in the early summer, and I shall think of nothing save drinking my tea." Later I added: "In fact, the silver pot held 4 cups of tea, and I wrote *Blue Up, Brown Down* between the 3rd and 4th cups. This is living! Having time to follow my impressions. I would gladly be in hospital full time, and have my meals brought on time, if I could be left free to write my poems like this. I would gladly have an operation each week if it freed me to write! Have been fallen upon and slapped by the physio, shaking up my lungs, blowing out clouds of dust, and then had my bandage redone by a nurse. I am like a child in here – and have recaptured a child's simplicity of vision. For me, holidays in new places are times of poems, eg my poems on Iona and Staffa – which I will do next....Worked on the Iona poem in evening."

Mr Maclean came in to sign my Bupa form: "Varicose veins right leg/bronchiectasis. 16 April 85, right Trendellenboeg multiple avulsions and ligation of perforators." I wrote: "He explained that there are many perforators, but that the valve can generally cope. An ulcer is when the 'hose' is spraying on the inside wall of the skin, breaking the skin sooner or later, and creating a blockage, a thrombosis. Mine trickled back into the vein whence it came. Go to him again if there is the blue, mottled, ulcerous look. Tomorrow bandages off, stitches out on Sunday?"

In the evening I picked up Nona Coxhead's *Relevance of Bliss*: "It fell open at the page on which she admitted she had never had the full Bliss Experience. So what the hell is she writing the book for? The book contains some gems, eg a pearl from Halevi about the Light being the Shekinah, the Presence of God, intimating that he has a task, a call back to the divine world from which the soul came....And she wanted me to contribute my experience to it." I had met her at one of the Mystics and Scientists conferences and she had pleaded with me to tell her my experiences of the Light, but I had declined, feeling it would not be right to present the experience out of context and in abridged form.

Later that night I wrote: "Couldn't sleep, was filled with imaginative patterns like old Masters, incredibly detailed – if only I were a painter. So now have had from higher worlds, part of a symphony and part of an art exhibition, not to mention my 'Shekinah' poems....Sat bolt upright here in hospital, switched on the light, and wrote: my poems on Spinks' New Age take the side of Christendom, the eternal mystical tradition, ie the past against the new (the Oak-Tree position); this is not contradicted by *Night Thoughts* because my soul flies to a new age in the sense of an historical Caroline (as opposed to Elizabethan) age of Anti-Materialism, which accords with traditional mysticism. I am on the side of Christendom against the New Age, but am on the side of the new Anti-Materialism which will flow into Christendom, and which is different from the New Age, with its left wing, spirit-based, anti-Western outlook. This is pro-Western, very much so – a new development." And I wrote: "Bring out the most recent poems, from *A Metaphysical* onwards – with an introductory essay on the New Universal Age and Baroque Age....Get across over 100 pages of the spiritual vision. Make this the Ricks riposte. Call it *The Rainbow in the Water Spray*." I observed: "We are all writing about what is out of reach for us – just out of reach – and Nona Coxhead is writing about what is out of reach for her." I thought my poems "should bring about an earthquake in poetry – bring back poetry to its major concerns", and wrote of "the shift in perspective caused by going into space, a new perspective". I wrote: "In my poetry I am a lover of beauty, and to that extent I carry on the Romantic tradition." I added that I was "bringing out a body of Nature verse which will stand alongside Hughes and Co, the so-called modern greats (who all have less to say than I have, half anyway...only writing for manner, to draw attention to their ego)."

I was enjoying my time in hospital: "A regime of injections and meals and pills being ladled out – and no responsibility at all. Hospital, a place where no one wants to be, not the patients or visitors – not the staff, who all talk of when they are off duty, or going home....This spell in hospital has been good for me. Up at 6 (5.50 actually), breakfast at 6.30 and so on, and time to put my draft poems into shape, time I have always wanted."

I worked on my poem *Staffa* and observed: "I now have a distinctive poetic style. It would be impossible to mistake my post-'Metaphysical' work for anyone else writing today, just as my voice on the phone is very distinctive....One of my strengths as a poet has been the background reading I did in my youth, which I have been forced to add to at Garratt Green, which in itself has been a mystery school to throw me onto my own resources and teach me that only I can get ahead and get myself across....Another hallmark of my work is the carefully worked out image which reverberates like thunder and echoes through the poem, taking on (like *Staffa*'s 'wind') new shades of connotations in each stanza."

My bandage was removed. I wrote: "My leg looks as if it's been through a barbed wire fence. Yellow all round, jagged black stitches and several small cuts, while the sore area, where he went 1 inch in, looks like raw meat. It will take 6 months before they turn white....I am still having heparin, the anti-thrombosis drug. Why did I have these veins in the first place? Answer: hereditary, valve failure in two places, at the top of my right leg and in the region of my right ankle, causing blood to circulate the wrong way and leak and jet."

I wrote again of my *Diaries*: "These *Diaries* aim to present a whole picture of me through all my words and deeds. Somewhere in its millions of observations is the truth about, not just me, but man – a complex, contradictory truth."

I recorded: "My family unexpectedly came to see me today. Matthew and Anthony looked sunburnt and freckled, showing Gooch's autograph, Ann looking well. Ant had fallen off his bike in Upper Park and hurt his arm. I made to hobble into the lift as I saw them off to escape my injection, which nurse was about to give." Again: "Ap 20. Penultimate day of this ideal writer's life (prison regime and bromide)....Awoke at 6 for an injection and do not want to go back to sleep. Now have the whole day to finish yesterday's work on *Crab-Fishing* and then go to the big one, *Against Materialism*. The importance of the sea in my work. I am so completely a Nature poet, with mystical interpretations of Nature. I am like a painter who paints the sea and says (like Palmer) 'Look at the symbols' – although I hope I do not say that too obviously."

Of my poetry I wrote: "In my poetry I must go for the elemental: wind, air, sea, mountains, forests, sex, sun, etc., with interior echoes. It is those echoes which have already made me one of the élite poets of the 20th century. A painter paints one picture, a poet paints several pictures in one work, which therefore represents a Canterbury narrative stained glass window, like the one of Becket in Canterbury Cathedral. I have put the universe into poetry....Betjeman's tip, the surprise word rhyme affords, which gives pleasure – which I have discovered for myself. Genius works in isolation, talent needs groups. When Tuohy said 'You need the company of other writers' he was describing talent. But genius separates with its superiority, and a genius needs a belief – no, a philosophy – which subordinates him to the whole."

From my hospital bed I thought about mystery schools: "I have been fired, tried and tested in the Garratt Green kiln....Put yourself into a mystery school so that the quality you lacked is heated in you. This modern alchemy....The most distinctive feature of a mystery school is that you should hate it and ridicule it. Like the hoeing of weeds in the Zen temple garden – Tuohy clearing out the latrines, ie the foulness of his soul – I jibbed at explaining myself to 15 year old remedials who hate books, but it has taught me to communicate. They hated the Garden of Pythagoras, I believe. Title: *The Mystery School*. The school theme in my life (Riverway-Henry Thornton-Garratt Green-Oaklands) must now be seen as a life-apprenticeship at a mystery school, to strip away the pride and build on the foundations of literary Oxford and Japan....Definition of a mystery school: where you go and develop qualities in yourself which you need in order to perform your mission or destiny."

I felt thrown back on myself: "Here in hospital I have no books, so cannot go off on any chases...and so I see clearly. I am myself, the thing that I am, the thing that I have developed, and I now turn all my preparations into success, reap the benefits of my labours in the mystery schools ever since *Mandalas*. Providence is pouring knowledge into me as I lie in hospital. Closed my eyes to give thanks for this 'mystery schools' insight, and saw a stained glass window of Chartrean or Notre Damean majesty." (A stained glass window from Notre Dame later formed the cover of *The Fire and the Stones*.) "The last 2 pages have almost been under automatic writing and guidance. Hospital, a place of reflection and quiet, a meditation hall where you are removed from outside pressures, which I must now reduce. I have really made the best of the hospital visit and turned it to good (the big 5 poems and my insights), just as I turned Garratt Green to good by using it to create Oaklands and develop new areas in my soul under its disciplined regime....Interrupted by 2 nurses making my bed, putting on clean sheets and pillowcases, changing the head rest of this King's Fund bed to a more comfortable position." I wrote: "Garratt Green, a mystery school of pain in which, alchemistically, qualities are thrown into the melting-pot and tried and come out with the current alchemical mixture – qualities of loyalty, service, kindness, endurance, patience, biting back one's tongue, the death of arrogance, humility in Christian qualities one grows by being with one's fellow man. In 1969 I received a 15 year sentence to serve my fellow man until these qualities were developed and I could stand on my own two feet and then, knowing how to use it wisely, I will be given the power to dictate, to influence, to teach truths."

Of my poems I wrote: "The mystery of the creative act comes into my poems, eg *Staffa*, *Boundless Sea*. Like the Romantics I cannot help bringing the creative mystery into my poems. I originally wanted to be a novelist, but that was the desire of the social ego, to write about social situations. The calling of a poet is higher, and deeper, requiring more development of soul." Again: "I have a way of showing the mind in communion with a higher world: both palms over the eyes (fingers upwards and nearly joining hands) and the head tilted in symbolism of looking up for guidance. A posture developed in this King's Fund bed, the 'engaged' slat across the glass pane in the door so that the nurses do not see me communing with the angels. I outgrow themes rapidly as I ascend higher, but I must grow towards the common people with my improved communication."

I was still finishing poems: "11 am, still on Ap 20, have finished *Crab-Fishing on a Boundless Sea*....I will now read the papers, then tackle the big one, *Against Materialism*. Four poems have escaped me for some 2-3 years, and they are now finished in the 'poetic white heat' since my operation. Who would have thought it? Perhaps the correct circulation of the blood has been restored, and I now feel more vigorous and fresh, my creative energies functioning fully? Perhaps I have stultified and stagnated physically the last 2 years (thrombo-phlebitis in January 1984 and 1985) with poor blood circulation that has affected my creative energies – and lowered my vitality."

I now tackled *Against Materialism*: "3.15 p.m. Have had tea, have made a plan of *Against Materialism*, and now, pressing on this *Diary* (my hospital 'presser' on my knee) I am going to extract the poem I want to present from the draft; I shall then rhyme it and copy it up. My Odes are only 8 lines in stanzas because of the need to pare down in relation to the garrulous past (eg late 18th century)....6 p.m. Drafted the first part of *Against Materialism*, then stopped to untie and learn to tie my blue line bandage." I broke off to observe: "The Light is the reflection of God, God's power in the soul, but it is not God, who is absolute nothingness behind the Light, and in fact could be a darkness. The Light reflects God's will and communicates it, but God may be separate from it – although all is one through manifestation." Then: "11.50 p.m. Have written out a reasonable draft of all of *Against Materialism* – at present one stanza too long at 22 stanzas of 8 lines each (and many more lines in some, to be deleted). The temptation is to write it in blank verse, but it needs the polish and accomplishment of rhyme, which binds ideas together. I'll rhyme it properly tomorrow, but it stands up now as argument. Have been on it all day, and Ann and the boys came unexpectedly about 8.30 p.m., and I am tired. Not elated, for there is still much to do, but knowing I have cracked it and only have to fiddle now. The 5 hardest poems to do, done in 4 days! What a 4 days! I have worked up such a sweat from writing today that these blue and white checked pyjamas stink. I have just physically written out some 250 lines of poetry, but so effortless has it been that I am not exhausted. It is divine, not human energy that has been flowing through me, which I have been using. The question Doolan asked of geniuses: 'Where do they get their incredible energy?' I know the answer: 'From the beyond.'"

On April 21st I wrote: "Only five and a half hours' sleep needed in hospital (1-6.30) this Sunday morning."I observed: "A painting on the wall either accepts it is a painting and shares the view, or it presents a high-falutin' doodle – either way the hallmark of the artist is immediately apparent, and there is no disguising that it is his personal view of that part of the universe. Ditto a Brahms symphony or modern cacophony. So my poetry should be good poetry – polished, quality stuff, not doodles." Then: "My *Cambridge Ode* will have taken me 3 years to finish. I drafted it, I believe, in April 1982, and I hope it will be finished in April 1985 – 3 years for ideas (eg about Newton) to mull around and sort themselves out. Ars longa!"

I wrote of my art: "Art is putting things down in an understandable form, so you grasp the nucleus of the idea and how it relates to other ideas: my metaphysical art, that is. The same motive is at work in these *Diaries*: to understand everything by focusing on different areas in turn. My early writing career was but an apprenticeship in technique, using observation. I then had to open a pathway to my true inspiration, the 'Shadow' which in my *Silence* I succeeded in doing....I have had some of the greatest tranquillity in years in the past 5 days – most unexpected....I tried to define my poetic self first in relation to the tradition (the Metaphysicals first, then the Romantics, and the Modernists) before coming to the reluctant conclusion that I was doing something new....I came to hospital to repair and improve my body, but found contact with my soul, which is being repaired and improved too, without my having sought it....Art presents understanding in its simplified essentials. It offers an understanding of a complexity with the bare bones and simplification of character and structure showing through....Little discomfort in my leg now. To think, the last 5 days I have actually been in pain, which I escaped by concentrating on the poems."

I wrote: "9.20 am, still on April 21. I have finished collapsing 3 stanzas into 2 (about Newton) and am now 7 times 3 i.e. 21 stanzas, and am ready to start tinkering. The structure looks good. Higher thought and feeling combined in a new way. The *Cambridge Ode*. One day I shall look back and say 'If I hadn't been in hospital in April 1985, I might not now be...the heir to Eliot.'" I reflected on my support for rhyme: "Marvell's 'The mind, that ocean where each kind' demonstrates the polish of rhyme in metaphysical writing at its best. How dreary the same stanza would be without rhyme! I am a supporter of subjects in painting, tunes in music and rhymes in poetry – provided the subject matter is meaty and not just a packet of crisps."

I had my stitches out and aired my legs. Maclean visited me and said I would not have a thrombosis now. I wrote my last impressions of hospital: "A high King's Fund wheeled bed with pedal, two clipboards with the surgeon's name hanging at the end, a 'switchboard' for lights, phone, bellpush, a couple of bedside tables, waterjug and water, a wardrobe, comfortable chairs, a radiator under a high window, a basin, a door with an 'engaged' slat to pull across glass. A corridor with the 'safe' presence of nurses whose quick feet echoed on the uncarpeted floor. A general run down effect – chipped paint where trolleys have dented."

I left hospital and was soon sitting looking out "at my green fields, shimmering in the sun". Ann had a new car, another Rancho, "a red gleamer", while I returned to *Against Materialism*. "It is a 10-liner, ABABCDCDEE – the last two encapsulating the central idea, and pointing forward. An Ode should be 10 lines rather than 8, it gives it more of a 'rolling downhill' effect, not to mention philosophical weight." Again: "Ap. 29. Have nearly finished *Against Materialism* – 4 stanzas more to do, having rhymed most of it on Saturday evening, all day yesterday (Sunday) and this morning – very slowly. Drove the car for the first time since the operation. Strengthening every day but barked my toe on the steps, blood everywhere....I have taken up where later Newton left off. I am sure he was right, and that rays of light contain 4 sides and worlds – the divine, spiritual, psychological and physical; and that it is as the Kabbalah said it always would be....Have finished *Against Materialism*! Completed the last stanza as the light faded about 7.30 p.m., and read it to Ann – chanted it – as she left to collect the boys from cubs."

From my convalescence I rang Garratt Green. Mrs. Kay had left, and Sinclair was now Head. I wrote: "When I rang Sinclair...: 'Is that the Headmaster?' 'In person.' He said: 'I've rearranged the desk so I've got a better view out of the window, and of the rhododendrons. I'm actually looking for things to do. A lot is going in the wastepaper basket, Clem is helping me put it there.' At the end I said, 'It's a breath of fresh air being able to get through to the Head's room for the first time in 10 years.' He: 'Yes, I have got the window open and there is a lot of fresh air in the room.' Infectious, boisterous good humour."

Orpheus again preoccupied me: "Orpheus. The different ways of treating the legend: he trained himself to higher things, the artistic mind and the crotch (Eurydice), how the poet has to enter Hades and experience it; the soul and the body; the destruction of the artist by a harsh world; the artist's world of imagination and the real world. My Orpheus continues to sing though torn to pieces by the Maenads of Garratt Green, and the Hell he entered to bring Eurydice back is the search for the soul and secret knowledge which always eludes you when you think you have it in your grasp. It is the Baroque spirit and sense, the higher inspiration and erotic Eurydice, and how they are separated."

Anthony had a party at Oaklands and my brother Jonathan's wife, Anne, brought my nephew William, who was a pupil at Oaklands, and told me about a visit she had made to a medium at Harlow. I wrote: "It all gushed out: she had been to find out how her dead child is, and my mother came through and is looking after it. She is living with my father and they are very happy now. She is worried about 'Fran' – ie Frances – who is 'in a pickle' (medium). Talk of an RAF wedding (mine); also the sloping garden at Shrewsbury. She thanked Jonathan for being with her when she died – said it was heart trouble and painful, and that my father had something in his brain which led to his death." I record what was reported to me without making any judgement.

I was still in my poems: "Typed up *Crab-Fishing* and *Staffa*. Am at the height of my powers now. Can fuse thought and rhyme and metre effortlessly, having learned my trade with great sweat and application, on and off – in solitude. I carry my knowledge in silence."

I was now mobile and back at work. I went to the Festival of Spirit and bought "a crystal that fills my room with rainbows when hung into the sun (cf the light on the soul)". I hung it on my study window catch, where it still hangs. Sometimes there could be between 20 and 30 rainbows in my study, on the carpet, on the walls, on my desk and my hands, and the rainbow parabola for each civilisation in *The Fire and the Stones* comes from this crystal.

I wrote: "In my *Against Materialism* I have come nearer to the truth than in any poem I have written. A poem does not have to be scientifically true: it creates an idea in beauty which the mind can hold and respond to, which has resonances and is evocative. Nevertheless, the idea I have created in that poem is near the Truth, and Newton's four-sided ray of light is very much a part of it....I am not a dualist, but a monist – I see a single, unified system which includes mind and body – and soul and spirit." I added: "The end of Colin Wilson's *Religion and the Rebel*, which, using other people, gets to the starting point of *Against Materialism*, has one good thing in it: the Outsider is doubly a rebel, against the Established Church, which is unacceptable, and against the unestablished church of materialism – leaving him the spiritual heir to the prophets, with a sense of purpose to create a higher man, and a sense of optimism. The last two pages of *Religion and the Rebel* are inspired."

"Wordsworth's Leech-gatherer," I observed, "was the artist – like my crab-fisher, my Fisher King. Wordsworth saw in him the resolution and independence an artist needs in gathering leeches/poems."

Pythagoras preoccupied me. I wrote: "Pythagoras and shamanism, Orpheus and shamanism....The Greek 'genius' was expected to travel for a period of time – Pythagoras for 20 years – and then climax his training with lonely contemplation. Compare my 10 years' travels....I need to make Oaklands a mystery school....(The tradition that Pythagoras wrote under the name of Orpheus.)"

I observed that "the last fortnight, a week in hospital and a week of convalesence at home, have seen the completion of 5 solid works spanning three years". The five works were *Against Materialism* (first drafted on 11th August 1982), *Night Visions in Charlestown* (first drafted on 6th August 1983), *Staffa* and *Iona* (both drafted in August 1984) and *Crab-Fishing on a Boundless Deep* (the "deep" "to emphasise the width and depth of the divine mind", first drafted on 11th August 1983). I now "took up the Ben Nevis poem".

I now applied myself to my publishing and to the cluster of books by other people which I was preparing for publication in 1986. I also explored France as a market for a language school.

In early May I had lunched with Paul Gorka at the Polish Centre, which he had designed as an architect. He told me he had worked for British Intelligence from 1948 to 1951 during the Stalin years, reporting on Soviet tank movements in Hungary, and that he had been betrayed by Philby and Blunt. Philby recruited British spies, his wife Litzi informed her lover, Gábor Péter, the Head of Hungary's Secret Police, who arrested and imprisoned them. Gorka had been arrested and imprisoned under the Russians, and heard the leader of his group being hanged in the prison courtyard through a high-up grating in his cell. He had been released during the Hungarian uprising, when the prison was briefly liberated, and with his family had fled to the West, where he had practised as an architect. I immediately saw he was a real life Winston Smith, the hero of Orwell's *1984*, and that this would be a rare eye-witness account of life in a Stalinist prison. I knew immediately that I would publish this prisoner's story of the betrayal of the Hungarian resistance movement to the Russians, which became *Budapest Betrayed*.

Along with Gorka, I had met Maurice Riley, a lean, craggy Northern accountant who was writing a book on Philby, which contained some extremely interesting insights; including the identity of the fifth man.

I met Gorka and Riley together in the King Street Polish Centre and heard details of the Vatican, and the role of Casaroli, who apparently organised the Second Vatican Council, and all the liberalisation that followed. Gorka wanted to write a book about the role of the KGB inside the Vatican.

At school I was told that I could have voluntary severance from the ILEA in July if I could find someone on the lowest pay scale who had been notified and was anxious to move. I wrote: "Deliverance is at hand!"

I had pursued the idea of starting an English Language school in Normandy. I flew to Paris for a day and met an accountant for three hours in Rue La Fayette to discuss starting a French business. We lunched at a restaurant near the Opera and then I flew back ("descended out of the sun into a cloud of unknowing"). A fortnight later at half term I took my possible Director of the new school to Rouen, where we were two British businessmen looking at a possible European market. I wrote: "The 12.45 ferry from Newhaven and across a millpond sea in a mist. Dramatic storm clouds to the west. A golden curtain of eerie light beneath a purple cloud and a black sea and distant wires of lightning. A drive through green Normandy to Rouen – through torrential rain at one stage after the four-five hour crossing, much of which was spent in having lunch. Dinner in Joan's square by the monstrosity of the new cathedral. Sat in the open over steak aux pouvres, cooked for the taste. Found this hotel, 76F a room." I saw two possible properties and visited Barclays in Rouen and returned to Newhaven not really any further forward, and drove to Worthing as it was late, where I recorded: "This morning, here in Worthing, a flowing sea seen from my 1st floor sea-view panoramic windows (can see from Brighton to the pier)....The sea is flowing from east to west, a flag on a boat (SM459) is flapping, and really nothing has changed since I used to come down here." I went off the Rouen idea when my Director changed his mind about living in Normandy and said he would commute from Brighton, where he lived.

I visited Margaret in Shoreham: "She sat in her little weed patch (at the back of her shop) which contains a few pansies and forget-me-nots so that each colour of the pastel is represented once, and called it her 'Paradise': 'flowers, children's laughter and stars are a paradise, a priest said to me.' Her garden of her soul. I sat with her. She smoked and was self-absorbed initially....St. Teresa is in South America, but I have the photos. She showed me her relic of St. Teresa (of Lisieux) – a brownish Victorian photo and a piece of the dress she wore before she died fastened below, a red cross on a square of blue cloth. 'The Pope gave out just a few of these. A priest in Belgium gave it to me. He did not know about my painting, he just went upstairs and returned with this and said, "This is for you."'" On my publishing, my policy of looking for books that show the Light strengthening the fibre of Christendom and defeating Communism: 'Your intentions are good, but you are surrounded....You will be used.'" I disagreed. She ended by saying: "You had to come today, St. Teresa brought you, Teresa brought you. I will pray to her to protect you – for the correct outcome."

At Oaklands I mowed the two fields, driving round and round in ever decreasing circles, a practice I found very therapeutic, "stripped to the waist and now glow on my shoulders (which are very red)". Everywhere there was "large cow parsley, gnats dancing under a blue sky, fountains of late may, burgeoning hawthorn – early June is here, and a heat". I saw a "horned snail with a forked end and its house on its back, near the Oaklands gate from Albion Hill".

Miss Lord invited us in for a drink, and then "Anthony complained of a bruise. I put my finger on his head, where the bruise was, and said: 'Oh God, please send your power through me and into Anthony Hagger, and heal his bruise. I give thanks for this has already happened.' And immediately, there were four surges, each punctuated by 10 seconds, and then (most unusual for me) a final half surge. Anthony immediately relaxed and lay as if poleaxed while my little finger burned. Now I am shiny, having been a conductor for the healing Light, and Anthony is asleep."

The Oaklands fête was opened by Geoff Hurst, the scorer of the hat-trick when England won the World Soccer Cup in 1966. He had a daughter in Ann's class, and I stood with him and chatted during the country-dancing, and then I introduced him to the crowd and he said a few words and judged a contest. We discussed his famous hat-trick, and he said: "It's a 20th century record that looks safe, I can't see England getting to the Final again before the end of the century, let alone anyone scoring in a World Cup Final." He told me he had walked away from football without any difficulty, and was completely happy in insurance. Several Old Chigwellians were present – Stephen Dooley, Vernon Davies, David Hoppit, and Keith Zabell – and my brother Jonathan. In the evening Ann and I went out with Tom McAlister and his wife and drank three bottles of wine and I heard his dream, to run a tea-room and restaurant when he stops playing football.

I heard that High Beach church was to be uncoupled from St. Mary's, Loughton and attached to Waltham Abbey. We were talking with Argie when I heard this news, and she made an interesting observation about my standing up to Scargill. I wrote: "Argie: 'One million men were killed in the First World War, and we have been ruled by a generation of weaklings. Tom was 19 when he was killed, so it is their grandsons who are now asserting themselves, like Nick, and doing what Nick is doing and standing up to those who are causing trouble, and making us strong.' I read Yeats's *In Memory of Major Robert Gregory* in Japan and although I am not a 'soldier, scholar, horseman' I inherit the many-sided roundedness of that Edwardian generation of Rupert Brooke which I admire so much, and of T. E. Hulme. Education, business, publishing, journalism, poetry etc etc – I stand for the flower of our generation."

I made another visit to Rouen from Newhaven. I caught a 10 p.m. boat on a Friday night, sat in Dieppe until it was light, dozing at the wheel of my car, then drove to Rouen and posted 160 brochures to local companies. I again looked at properties and arrived home at 1.30 am on Sunday morning, not having got much forward. There was a family gathering at Jonathan's the next day. My brother Robert was optimistic about a computer tape he had made for conveyancers, which he hoped would bring him in a fortune. Soon afterwards Jonathan rang me to announce that he had made an offer for a house in Tunbridge Wells, that they were selling their house (my grandmother's and then Argie's home) and joining Robert in Kent where the area was less full of East-Enders.

On the publishing side I had a meeting with Trevor Maher at Brent Cross and drew up a timetable for the next 4 or 5 books which would come out in 1986. I visited an old lady who had stored my books before our house was built, Ann Clarke and wrote: "I told her that I want to get the missionaries back into China so that Christendom can push back Communism – 'the Devil is winning, why?' (Ann Clarke) – and that I am really mounting a new crusade, from my publishing company (like Solzhenitsyn). I feel the Devil, who has won in Africa, South America, Indo-China and Eastern Europe, has reached the limit of his powers, and can be pushed back now."

At Garratt Green I was teaching Dryden, and wrote: "Dryden's *Absalom and Achitophel* (c1681) is a Baroque work." I later wrote: "Dryden, pro-Tory and anti-Whig, ripping into the Scargill of the day, Shaftesbury and his mob, supporting the Establishment. Verse satire defends the Establishment by lampooning ambition – although *Private Eye* satire and *TWTWTW* attack the Establishment, but they're not verse satirists."

I was working incredibly hard. Each school day at Oaklands we put on nearly 200 lunches. These were shopped for at Makro and a frozen food store every Friday evening, and I carried the tins down to the cellar storeroom. I cut the two fields each summer weekend and did the staff salaries and accounts and paid the bills while commuting to Wandsworth and running the public exams and marking exam essays, and while running the publishing company and exploring the French market. Looking back, I am amazed at how much I managed to pack in that summer after my operation. My cousin Richard and his wife Wendy came for the day. They were in the process of moving to a large house on the Cowdray estate in Haslemere, a house of the kind Wendy was used to as a child before her father fell on hard times, and which she dreamed of reviving.

There was a summer concert at Chigwell, in which Matthew played, flushed from his success at coming 1st in his class in Science. I wrote: "Three Renaissance tunes....As the waves of Henry VIII type music – Henry himself composed the middle one (Schiarazula Marazula) – flooded over us, superbly performed, I had an image of people dancing, right hands out, two paces forward to join tips of fingers in fours, two paces back, then forward again, wearing red and yellow, a red cape to the base of the back and a yellow 'tunic' underneath, with black decorations, and 'tights' on the legs. The one I was looking at had dark hair and a beard, and this image – memory from a past life? – was accompanied by emotion which was not entirely positive, some form of aggression or dislike for him. Who was this bearded man dancing with his lady, who looked like portraits of Anne of Cleves? And who was the lady? Mine? Or even – me?" (Somehow I know that the title of Henry's piece "Schiarazula Marazula" caused great mirth among the courtiers, and even now I can see bearded Renaissance men laughing and repeating the play on "Zula".)

At Oaklands I thrilled to "a woodpecker in the ash". There was Open Evening and the wine flowed. 300-400 parents looked in, and the drinking went on until 11.45 p.m. I recorded: "Tom McAlister standing by the door in an open-necked shirt, examining the sunburn on his arms with admiring ladies standing round." Soon afterwards there was a barbecue on a Sunday. I wrote: "A hot day. McAlister doing sausages on our improvised barbecue of half an oil drum on a stand with a grille over it (shoe scrapers). His French apron. Many people. Rounders in the field later on....Geoff Hurst. Asked both Hurst and McAlister to get D a job at West Ham."

By contrast the Garratt Green English Department's party took place at one of the staff's house. I wrote: "The house with the broken front door, faded carpet, peeling paint, flaking walls and broken fence in garden. The two teenage children..., shouting messages to the garden from their bedrooms..., drinking the wine and being rude to the guests....All (her) efforts on the syllabus are at the expense of her home, on which nothing is done....The wide open front door. The curtainless windows, so the street can see, the poverty." The people at Garratt Green came from a different region of society from the affluent middle classes I saw at Oaklands, and which I was now used to.

As soon as the Garratt Green term ended we all left to spend a week near the river Dordogne in France. We drove to Dover, caught a hovercraft to Calais ("turbulent seas after a storm, spray whipping past the windows") and found a roadside hotel just outside Calais. Next morning we drove via Orleans, Blois and Périgueux to Les Eyzies, passing through the Valley of Prehistory and glimpsing the cliffs which contain the caves where Cro-Magnon man (c35,000BC) replaced Neanderthal man, and where Magdalenian man (c16,000-11,000BC) flourished. (According to legend, Atlantis sank c10,000BC, and some may like to think that Magdalenian man was in fact Atlantean man.) We found the yellow cottage we had rented; it was on the edge of a farm in deep countryside and surrounded by scented pines, there was no electricity and lamps worked from bottled "gaz". We were in a wooded area with chalk cliffs high up, but it was very hot and the stone floors were wonderfully cool. Immediately I was back in "the life of the 18th century, quiet, peaceful, only a yellowhammer disturbing the evening quiet..., and you sit in the doorway at dusk and make use of the light and read or sew, before going in for the family meal....We got back beneath the 20th century to the 18th century peace and silence. The depth where Cro-Magnon man can be found." That Saturday night I slept 10 hours, "drunk with fresh wooded air". I dreamt I was in a medieval square, watching three men with bare arms shoot three soldiers in tunic armour with bows and arrows, and I wondered: "were the archers English archers from Crécy or Poitiers?" The next morning we sunbathed among wild flowers, cicadas and butterflies, and I observed, "Cyril Connolly dreamt of having a yellow cottage in the Dordogne." I "saw a snake, which slithered past the front door (brownish grey) and a lizard, which lives in the bathroom window sill and wall".

It was extremely hot. We dragged ourselves round Les Eyzies, which contains much of our knowledge about the development of man from c100,000BC, and then to the Grande Roc caves with watery passages and stalagmites and stalactites. We then went on to Sarlat, a round medieval and Renaissance town where I was "fascinated by the Lantern of the Dead behind the Cathedral where St. Bernard's bread cured the sick. The Lantern was built in commemoration of the event. It is a beehive pyramid with a winding path coming down, ie the divine manifesting into human affairs, with windows for light. It is the Light which cured the sick, and the Light that will look after the dead, placed below." The next day we went to St. Cyprian and Beynac, and to the Chateau that overlooks the Dordogne where there were "brimstones, a swallowtail and lizards on the high up stones where the lords tyrannised the villagers". We went on to La Roque and then Domme, a medieval town with a panoramic view of a bend in the river Dordogne which Henry Miller praised ("Just to glimpse the black, mysterious river at Domme from the beautiful bluff at the edge of the town is something to be grateful for all one's life"). We went on to Gourdon and Rocamadour with its steps up a gorge to its Miraculous Chapel and blackened Madonna, and then on to the Padirac chasm. We "forded" the underground river on a boat, passing stalactites and stalagmites, "the splashing of the paddle echoing, the ferns growing underground. A chamber of hell." We returned via Souillac to Les Eyzies and ate at the Hotel Centre. The following day we went to La Madeleine and saw the cavemen's shelter which gave its name to Magdalenian man, and then to the Chateau Losse by the river Vezère. That evening Anthony developed tonsillitis and ran a very high temperature of 103F, and so I went up to the farm and called a doctor, who arrived after 11 p.m., a young man. He spoke no English and got his syringe out and advanced on Matthew, who backed away. The doctor pursued Matthew round the cottage until I interposed myself and explained in French that he was trying to inject the wrong boy.

The next day we visited Les Combarelles, which had a tunnel that was an underground river millions of years ago. Here Cro-Magnon men did their wall-engravings, which showed up best in the half-light, the oil-lamp or torchlight by which Cro-Magnon man worked. I wrote: "There was a squinting face..., an elongated Egyptian type man, various female forms stressing fertility, and of course many animals – horses, reindeer, deer, a bear, an incredible lioness – all done in lines, using the rock so a natural line was the base, a relief, and a bulge suggested a swelling of pregnancy." I was certain that the knowledge of these shapes had passed to the Egyptians, and I felt that "prehistory was a kind of Paradise, in which man, with a larger brain than ours which had greater capacity to see the Light, developed a great culture that culminated in the Great Pyramid and ziqqurats". We went on to Cap Blanc and saw the relief of seven horses, the central one of which recalled Phidias's famous horse's head of the 5th century BC. I related the cave-paintings to their shamans' magic. The caves and their tunnels were entrances to the underworld and the shamans entered these (like Aeneas) and gained power over the spirits of the animals, who could then be more

465

easily hunted and killed. I reflected that man is in the grip of conflicting forces, of a civilising, enlightening force that rules him as an angel and a barbaric, bestial force that makes him a devil, and that the same man can go either way, depending on which force he allows to dominate him. We also went to Font de Gaume, where black and red oxide paints were used, and to Lascaux, where we saw the bulls, and then on to Montfort on the river Dordogne.

After a week we left the Dordogne and drove through vineyards to St. Emilion, a Roman and medieval town where we tasted the red wine in two Chateaux. We went on to Bordeaux and then La Rochelle, where we found a hotel with a view over the two 13th century towers in the harbour and went down onto the bustling waterfront where a fire-eater wandered among the pavement-diners. The following morning La Rochelle was "a sleepy town above fishing smacks, to my left white fronts and salmon roofs, to my right faded yellow fronts and grey roofs....A smell of salt on the breeze under a grey sky, and the grey battlement walls of the two castle towers at the mouth of the harbour, between which a chain stretched (cf Fowey, Skye) and the isle visible beyond. Here I sit, about to move on, an inveterate painter in words." We drove on to Nantes and arrived at Mont St. Michel, where we found an apartment with a sea-view on the battlements of a 13th century building. We walked along the main street which was full of images of St. Michael killing the Dragon, and we walked, "back across the battlements where swifts (house martins?) squeaked and dived and squealed, zooming low and flitting high". The next morning we toured the Abbey of Mont St. Michel, and I wrote: "The pre-Romanesque church, the Romanesque church (2nd), and the Gothic church (3rd). The Romanesque believed that God is everywhere, Gothic that God is high. The sparse monk's quarters (refectory, cloisters etc). The Benedictine living conditions as 35 cohabited apart from the world." We went on to Rouen and viewed more properties for a language school and I was tempted to secure a Baroque building in Rue Jeanne d'Arc, and then we made our way to Boulogne and returned by ferry as stormy weather had grounded the hovercraft. Soon afterwards I returned to Rouen, and found the arrangements increasingly difficult and costly, and our potential language customers increasingly unwilling to give a commitment. I went down to Cornwall having decided not to pursue the idea of the language school.

I immediately went to Charlestown and the next day slept a sleep of exhaustion. I returned to Charlestown the next afternoon and "climbed round the rocks with the boys. Returned later at 10.30. Brilliant stars, but also brilliant lights and the second boat left, the Mary Coast for Guernsey, orange and high in the water, and manoeuvred through the inner and outer harbour necks with taut ropes and rubber tires which squeaked and squealed on contact as the massive boat wheeled on the stone, separated by howling rubber." We went to Fowey past Tristan's stone and over to Polruan on the ferry by Quiller-Couch's house. We saw the aquarium in Fowey: "wrasse, conger eels, dogfish, plaice, and rare varieties of fish including the pollack (which the Charlestown fisherman caught and threw back at night, a luminous green from his bobbin)." We went to Mevagissey and watched the foam on the rocks. I bought the *Selected Shorter Writings of Colin Wilson*, and reflected the next day: "My achievement in my poems is that I have progressed from despair to illumination, from the questioning despair of Freeman to...(the) Mystic tradition....My new 'Baroque' consciousness, and Wilson's emergence of a new consciousness. My new consciousness is within the decline and disintegration of the West, and has to be seen as perpetuating it (i.e. the West)."

My visit to the Dordogne now expressed itself in poetry: "Aug 11. Slept after lunch while Ann played rummy and whist with Matthew and Anthony – I slept on Anthony's bed for an hour while they played literally touching me on Matthew's bed. This was the 4th successive afternoon I have slept, and I have had long sleeps at night as well – have been exhausted. But suddenly tonight, at 10.15 p.m., I sat down without intending to, and drafted 12 stanzas, *The Purpose of Périgord* – on the purpose behind evolution. Creativity is there, latent in me, buried by too much worldly distraction and just waiting to fountain out, to spurt, ejaculate, when the moment is right. It is now 11.13, and within an hour I have put Périgord into perspective. I can work on this draft, which must sum up the purpose of the evolutionary drive, which is to a new consciousness....Matthew spurred me to write *Périgord and Purpose* (as it is now called) by asking for where we went in the Dordogne for his Diary....Pt 1, the physical side of the Dordogne; Pt 2, the prehistory and the caves; Pt 3, Sarlat and the Lantern of the Dead; Pt 4, the motive force behind evolution."

On August 12 (the day Cameron died) I received, again in sleep, a strengthening of the idea that the Light shapes civilisations, the basis of *The Fire and the Stones*: "Awoke with the idea: do a Toynbee and 'rewrite' history, showing that it is the Light that makes civilisations grow, ie that the Light is there, present at the growth of civilisations – and at their high points. (The Light of the World through Christian civilisation up through the Dark Ages – it is always a metaphysical idea that makes civilisations grow, for it energises with its purpose.)" I then saw the overall movement of history as a spiral: "Man spirals up, from prehistory via Graeco-Romans and medievalism to now. So too do we spiral. My life as a spiral from Loughton in the Law, to Loughton after losing my marriage, to Loughton under Oaklands: unhappiness, pain, contentment, the soul ascending to God in a spiral (cf the Milky Way and galaxies, and all oceans, eg the Gulf Stream)....And civilisation too is a spiral?...From growth, through breakdown, to disintegration, but spiralling upwards....Life is a spiral, and I am now higher than then but in the same place."

I took the boys down to Charlestown and recorded: "The sea smoothed away their footprints." We went out to St. Michael's Mount on a misty day and walked across the causeway. The Mount was "hidden in low cloud", but we climbed to the top and toured the Castle and church and "lingered before the picture of Lettice Knollys who 'poisoned' both Essex and Leicester (the two crushed flowers)." (Lettice Knollys, the wife of Leicester and mother of Essex, was blamed for turning them against Elizabeth I.) Then we looked at Trevarthian, where I stayed as a boy: "a grey Georgian house with clusters of palms on either side of the veranda." We drove on to

467

Pendeen and visited the lighthouse which was shrouded in fog. I wrote: "The foghorn, the beam. Saw the coastguard's house where Ann's mother lived, the house semi-detached with the pub and the final house, rented, from which her father went...to Rhodesia. We went to Geevor mine, Cape Cornwall ("the derelict stone huts by the sea") and then Land's End. I recorded: "I wrote poems (drafts only) on Trevarthian, St. Michael's Mount, and Lettice Knollys, and the Geevor mine." I observed that the Beaker people brought metallurgy to Cornwall. Another day (August 19th) we went to Goonhilly, dishes of skyscraper size on the Lizard cliffs, one of the marvels of the 20th century. We went on to Gunwalloe, "where it was hot. Sunbathed on the beach under the church as the sea raced in and dashed on the rocks. Dollar Cove." Then we went to Porthleven, where Ann's aunt and cousin lived, and "walked along the submarine-like pier as the water splashed. The surfer, the glider....Wrote poems on Goonhilly, Gunwalloe and Porthleven – and on God as illimitable, containing infinity and eternity (beyond space and time)."

I thought about the coming Age: "Aug 20. Relate my Baroque Age to the coming time in Western civilisation and to Toynbee's Universal State, ie make it the Universal Age." And I wondered, "What stage are we in?" I wrote: "The immensely creative 20th century – our creativity has not broken down, we have not begun to disintegrate?...The Universal Age is a time of creativity and a time of passivity....We are parallel to the Roman age of Augustus, for our creativity has enabled us to Westernise the whole world. TV, telephone, aircraft, space rockets – all Western creations that are global. We are a rally, a Golden Age in which Rome concludes a lasting peace with Parthia and witnesses a new religion arising alongside the traditional religion..., ie it can see off Communism and bring universal benefit to all mankind."

On television I saw an anti-Gaddafi student being hanged near the entrance (where I often walked) to the University of Libya, a hanging which led to the demonstration outside the Libyan people's bureau, the retaliation for which killed W.P.C. Fletcher: "The balding, moustached student in an open-necked shirt stood by a noose while someone read accusations in Arabic to a chanting crowd. Then the noose was put over his head – he co-operated by extending his neck – and he was then pushed and you saw him dangling and turning, head bent, while the crowd of students chanted with raised fists. He died to hysterical chanting."

There was a wet day, and I "went to Charlestown for half an hour. Four poems came to me, *Rod-Fishing*, *Words Spent like Waves* (on the harbour wall), *Moments like Waves* and *Cerberus* (on the sea-barrier, watching the children play on the rocks). Half an hour and effortlessly, four poems: that's Cornwall. A phrase, 'I, the poet of the Sea.'" I wrote: "I dream of typing up all my poems and publishing them like Wordsworth, to be known and bought as those of a moderate, Nature-loving mind in touch with deep reality. I am quivering with poetic inspiration. The longer I leave my talent for the everyday, the more the spring flows when it is contacted. It gushes."
I wondered which moment made me what I am; was I in the right place at the right time? I thought that "the moment of metaphysical breakthrough in

Egerton Gardens in 1971" was the single moment that made my writing what it was.

One fine morning we took a "picnic lunch to Par and played football and then cricket on the sand with the boys, and (I) read my papers in a wind until the rain came, leaving the distant Trenarren in a mist". I reflected on how we have two consciousness: the personality, which is mechanical, robotic and lazy, and the real one, which is full of freedom, energy and power, pure consciousness. I wrote: "My *Silence* is about these two consciousness." I added: "Colin Wilson...is someone else barking up the same tree, worrying away at the problem of automaton versus freedom....As a publisher (and Oaklands Principal) I am robot with mechanical figures; as poet I am the real me, and as imaginer I am free and not robotic. As Light-gazer I am purely free." The next day I taught Anthony to bowl at Par and "wrote 3 poems, about a kite, 2 consciousnesses and wild ponies".

On my last night in Cornwall I deliberated and thought "the civilisation keeps the culture going", and that for Western mysticism to be kept going "the civilisation which has respected mysticism must be kept going in spite of and against its enemies (Communists, terrorists etc who would destroy real consciousness). It was like the Chelsea Flower Show: "Each year there is a new flower that is different from, though similar to, last year's....The culture has to be recreated like this year's rose, which is different from the last." My Baroque Age "is a rediscovery of the Western mystic tradition", and "my book on the Light is a definition of the next way of looking which is really a revival of an old way of looking in a new guise". I wrote of "the rose of the tradition flowering anew – the climbing rose of the tradition rediscovered. A Renaissance, a rediscovery of the Western mystical tradition. The Mystic Renaissance....The Light purifies consciousness and makes it real, purposive and intentional, it is not the will that does it but the divine Will....The essence of the Western tradition is rarefied consciousness as embodied in its great men, its saints, its artists and writers and poets, whose memory is enshrined in National Trust houses and memorials and monuments and libraries, the 'Club' as I used to call them." I added: "Wilson's Rebel rebels against a dead religion with its outer forms, but he had not contacted the inner reality of the Light which Christianity still holds, and so he...misses the way....My poems celebrate the Western spirit reborn, the real consciousness of the rose of the Western mystical tradition....The new flowering of the tradition...is not revolution but evolution, it is not something new but the old reflowering in a new way. The structure of tradition."

Back in Essex I finished editing the book on terrorism (*The World Held Hostage*) – besides changing my car for a Cavalier CD and mowing the Oaklands fields – and I wrote about history in my *Diaries*. Terrorism was out of control; there had been 50,000 acts of terrorism in 15 years, 2 million men and women were being trained in more than 220 training camps, and 50 terrorists groups were centrally co-ordinated by Palestinians for the Communist nations. I wrote: "Future history can be understood by careful study of the past and identifying the seeds of what is to come." I wrote of Israel and South Africa as two crucial areas, and observed that "the momentum is there for the Palestinians and others to involve Israel in a final holocaust and wipe it out" and "in my time I can expect to see Israel nuclear-bombed, and South Africa fall to the blacks". I took on an editor and met her at the Athenaeum Hotel. She asked, "Why a political start when publishers avoid a political list?" I recorded my reply: "It's an academic look at the future of the West – what prospects have we, what is the West's future?" I also wrote, thinking of my coming epic: 'The Devil supports the Palestinians and international terrorists in their attack on Christ's civilisation....The capture of Jerusalem, the Holy City? The last Crusade?...Oak-Tree...has shown me the Devil's party. I am the Shield of God, and speak for Western civilisation. It has been a good civilisation and brought freedom, democracy and justice to victims of tyranny; and art, music and literature of the highest quality and a spiritual vision; and I must defend it against the forces that are massing against it."I saw my coming epic as "a Baroque version of Dante".

I visited elderly Anne Clarke and told her: "Western civilisation is the only hope of the West – the Romans of the 5th century AD had a less good life than under the (Roman) civilisation and without the West there would be no one to help Ethiopia....Christ has to struggle hard to defeat the Devil." (I was of course using "the Devil" figuratively.) I spoke of order: "If the universe is an accident, the chances against certain things happening are colossal, eg the earth not colliding, our atmosphere supporting life, the combination of chemicals, the seasons, the fact that babies are born with one head and two arms and legs etc. Order requires each species to be limited in number, hence the population is kept down by other natural beings feeding on them, eg the sea must not be full of anchovies or there will be no room for herrings. Order is understood in the world of invisible bodies, when the tasks we are given down here are discussed. Everyone has to achieve something or bear something....My essential vision of order and harmony – that is my 'Baroque' vision." I wrote: "I am a kind of Rambo, conducting a one-man war on Communism to strengthen the spiritual force of the West. My arms: a blue cross and a red lion – the British lion fighting for Christendom." At this stage I still saw my fight in terms of mystical Christendom rather than in global Universalist terms (as I do now), and it was the vision of Christendom I was emphasising, for I wrote: "(My arms) to decorate the top of my gravestone – on which should appear 'I loved the rainbow in the spray'."

At the beginning of September we lunched with Argie at the Roebuck, driving up the steep hill with the Forest on either side, and I recalled: "I awoke from a dust storm in Peking thinking of the strip of Forest that runs beside the descent from Buckhurst Hill to Loughton, and the Oaklands fields. I thought of the lush green Forest in spring in Peking, being rooted there, not realising I would buy the fields at the bottom. Lawrence's Eastwood" (which D. H. Lawrence thought of in Mexico), "my Epping Forest."

I again thought deeply about history and saw: "I have undergone growth, the growth that creative personalities put into growing civilisations, and I have returned to a disintegrating civilisation....I must change it to contribute to future growth of the West which will counter and arrest the disintegration for a while – see two forces, growth versus disintegration – and which can perhaps form the basis of the universal church which can be expected now, ie growth through the Light", a movement I saw as "a movement of the Western spirit". I observed: "This is very important. The West is still growing or still capable of growth although the force of disintegration is widespread, and it can therefore defeat the 'dominant' Universal States of Russia and China at the political level. My role is to change the consciousness of the West, transmute it....My role is of a changer, not an entertainer: a changer of consciousness, a transmuter....Russia, then, is a declining power: the Berlin Wall, cf Hadrian's wall, shuts out the Western 'barbarians' (in its term) to arrest its decline, and it fights with mercenaries (the Palestinians)....Communism has broken down, and it is itself a symptom of a disintegrating and broken down society, and it has become dominant. It is a static war (the Cold War) and the barbarians may break out and swamp us, but Communism is imitative (getting nuclear knowledge through spying), not creative – see the shallow art." I saw very clearly that the West would win the Cold War against the Soviet Union, and I concluded: "Yeats's Chinamen, then, are wrong to be detached while civilisation sinks....What is needed is commitment, a crusading spirit (the crest of the Haggers, azure cross and red lion), and a determination to fight for the West to help its growth, to strengthen it for survival, as all civilisation is to be found in the West, despite its materialism, its socialism etc. I must have a strong attitude, that of the shield of God....My aim is to be a Light-bearer to the West because the Light is the growing factor, experience of the Light makes the spirit grow, and it is that growth that we need....I must...pour growth to the West."

I was obsessed with Western growth: "The Oak-Tree idea....Is Western civilisation disintegrating? It is the idea of Gibbon, Spengler and Toynbee that needs scrutiny, and Solzhenitsyn. According to Gibbon Rome fell because of barbarism and religion. According to Spengler because it grew old like a mallow in the field. According to Toynbee because it stopped growing and lost harmony between its parts. The Islamic and Soviet cultures are the enemies to Western civilisation (cf Nostradamus). We are pouring growth into Western civilisation....Western civilisation is like an Oak-Tree, it will go on growing so long as the sap is there."

I visited my printer, Dusan Plenicar of Pika Print, Enfield, a Catholic, who said: "'Marxism is rebellion against God. Dostoevsky said "If God does not exist, everything is permitted", ie executions, Marxism, everything: Stalin. Communism is power, dominance, barbarian, the feeling "I am God". It was important to do the book on Scargill so that the West can survive, and the ones on terrorism and Philby will be important, but in due course politics won't matter, religion will. God chooses "the small ones", not the big ones: 5 or 6 small people. The Church has been tested for 100 years by Satan, and the century is almost up – Satan's part of the earth is where man has become God. It is very simple, if God is not glorified, man takes his place – Marxism....We are chosen – why am I not dead? So many I have known are dead. I have been saved for this'" (ie to print the Scargill book). "'Everyone has a mission. It is simple, God chooses.'" At this time even a visit to my printer was like encountering Dostoevsky. I told him: "'My mission is to give the positive side of Western civilisation.'

Dusan: 'You must believe, and it will happen.' I: 'I believe that my Light book and my poems will hold up the ideal for Western civilisation.'Dusan: 'You are inspired, you did not think of the Scargill idea, it was put into you.'"I saw the process in terms of healing: "Oak-Tree is healing the nation, I am pouring divine energy into the nation, channelling it through my ego-less pipe, like water, with no blockage of any ego to obstruct it."

The effect of this concern with growth entered my view of a work of art. "The cessation of a traditional artistic style is a breakdown symptom, ie decline is spiritual....Eliot's *Waste Land* is therefore a sign of a breakdown as is the Modernistic music and art that broke with tradition, ie our Western breakdown happened in 1914....The fracture, then, is reflected in art, which goes off tradition and the spirit." A growing civilisation therefore has a continuity of artistic style, and I was determined to see my own work as a continuation of the tradition, not as a cessation of it; to return to the positive in 1910 and grow it from there.

My view of growth also entered my outlook on current affairs: "I will call for a Universal State in Europe as that is a rally....I will call for a new universalised religion....This religion will draw on Christianity, but will be a new branch of Christianity – a new crown, for it will universalise Christianity syncretistically and include the Light tradition of Augustine, Bernard, Pope Gregory etc, and of the 14th century mystics, but also the tradition of the universalised new religion of Light." I wrote of "a blueprint for a new universalised religion to back the Western universal state of Europe....I am...a new Light-bearer whose roots are in Waltham (Abbey of Harold and of High Beach)." I added: "It is not church that God needs, it is our energy – and 'a new form for ancient energy' (my *Silence*) is good enough for Him. God is Light, and is to be known through the Light, and although churches connect this vision with tradition, they are marginal and irrelevant to the vision. To depart from the traditional spiritual form is a sign of a breakdown, but to bring new life to it, to renew it and revitalise it, can be a sign of growth, which is what a rally is. I am a rallying grow-er at the end of a time of rout. I was born at the beginning of the 2nd World War...to come of age during the rout of our loss of empire, which was caused by two world wars, and to create and bring about a rallying growth. That is my mission, to bring hope....I am bringing in a new Baroque....Oak-Tree...is now to be interested in the growth of the West."

I reiterated that my insight into the growth that Western civilisation was still capable of had located my mission: "Today, 9th September 1985, is one of the most important days of my life, for I have seen my mission, my life's purpose, my aim, with great clarity, between 8.30 and 9.30 p.m., after staying away from school to speak to my staff this morning and after continuing the hay-burning and gutter-clearance this afternoon and early evening. I have seen all history....The conflict between the end of the Humanist breakdown and the new spiritual religion that will replace materialistic Christianity...will.,.produce great art. Christianity applied to the growth of Europe – hence I love the Middle Ages, hence Waltham where Europe grew the tradition." And again: "The essence of my insight is that growth is the tradition, and breakdown revolution....The challenge of the West responds to furious thought. It is to preserve the peace...and to embody spiritual values that will cause the Third World to ally with it and not the forces of breakdown and barbarism....I can solve the challenge by providing those spiritual values....I need to project myself now as a thinker, a deep thinker....I must be a Matthew Arnold, an Eliot, who thought about their culture and religion and society." I noted: "The crusading knight gargoyle from Waltham." I wrote of "a drawing together of the sects on the Light, and a drawing together of cultures".

The new year at Oaklands had begun, and I had restarted what was to be my last term at Garratt Green. Towards the end of September Trevor Maher took me to the English-speaking Union for an introductory talk on the Frankfurt Book Fair, and I encountered Bob Leach ("looking old"), my no 2 at Garratt Green, who had retired following a heart attack and had written a couple of popular books; he was himself going to Frankfurt. I had further meetings in the Athenaeum Hotel with my editor, Marlene Garcia, and Gorka and Riley. Riley seemed to be in touch with everyone of any note in intelligence circles, and he gave me the name of the fifth man, a very well known national figure. (It tied in with what Colin MacCabe had said during the dinner for Fergie Maclean: "The fifth man is an elderly man living in Cambridge.") He told me the name of a public figure who had had an affair with Vassall, and I had conversations with Jack Wood and Des McForan.

Vernon Davies had now thrown his great house open for a Conservative Party fund-raising venture. He was starting a Patrons Club. Some 40 local people were invited, to be addressed by Tebbit. I arrived at the same time as Biggs-Davison and Tebbit. We joined the queue to get in, and Biggs-Davison introduced me to Tebbit and talked about the Scargill book. Tebbit said of Scargill, "He's well and truly in the Soviet camp now," but otherwise listened in silence. Biggs-Davison spent the entire evening running about, introducing his constituents to Tebbit, and I did not really get to speak to him.

Oaklands opened its doors on a Saturday to the local Dr Barnardos committee for their annual box-opening. Paddy Manning came and told me she had bought premises in Ongar and was opening a bookshop. She said to me: "I can see six of us talking by the apple tree above the Oaklands tennis court – you and Caroline, Joan and Peter (White), John and me, in 1967 or 8." A number of my mother's friends came: "Mrs. Balls, Mrs. Collison, Mr and Mrs. Bowers, and Mabel Reid, Elizabeth Lord and the Snowsills were there."

I saw Western civilisation's global role very clearly: "I am pro-Western civilisation, but I am also pro-unity of Light (all cultures' Light respected), as in the Light book. There is no contradiction, as the unity idea is that of the world-wide universal State, which will be Western-led. The West will create a world-wide unity of values."

One moment I recorded: "Sept 29. I sat this morning and was aware of the falling leaves, while a bird flew up and snapped at a feather in mid-flight and flew away, disappointed it was not a butterfly. Everything that exists is good." And I knew: "There is freewill, and nothing is preordained. Providence intervenes in a battle between good and evil without a guaranteed future. We are all soldiers in a battle of freewill. We are all free."

In early October I received a letter from Caroline: "David has left me – in fact he has undertaken a new life for himself: new job, new home and new woman....It is as you predicted." It was a measure of my own growth since 1970 that I could comment: "So came the stark news that I wanted to hear so much 15 years ago, but which now leaves me – sad for her, a little, but otherwise unaffected. I have grown so much in the last 15 years, and am now so purposive." Thinking back to what Paddy Manning had said about Caroline and me standing under the apple tree above the tennis court, I added: "A strange pattern life weaves, a strange spiral pattern. Life is a spiral and similar situations return to haunt us."

Later I heard the details. Caroline told me over the phone: "He went to Australia for three weeks and didn't say when he was coming back and I found out by accident, by ringing work, that he'd sneaked back and was living with another woman nearby. I've seen him since. He doesn't talk. He's just thinking about his job and nothing else. He hasn't thought about Damian or any of the consequences." I pointed out that he had not thought of the effects on other people's lives on Malta, and that to be so blind to the lives of others revealed "a lack of sensibility, a terrible coldness, an inhuman lack of feeling".

I took Matthew and five friends to see Churchill's War Cabinet rooms as a birthday outing. What we were allowed to see was now protected by glass, and I was not able to sit in Churchill's chair as I had the previous time, when I walked underground as far as Trafalgar Square through grimy, dusty rooms. The rooms were nevertheless a time capsule. Everything looked "antiquated and out of date – all the print, all the booklets and newspapers and lettering – and yet this was the most modern and well equipped place in the early 1940s". There was a hotline to the president of the United States behind a loo door.

I went to Frankfurt Book Fair on a Friday. I paid for Trevor Maher's air ticket and he was going to show me how the Frankfurt Book Fair worked. Trevor arrived late at Heathrow, realised he had left his car in the short stay, expensive car park and disappeared again, leaving me to ask the air hostesses after we had boarded to delay the take-off, which they did. Trevor arrived out of breath, having kept the passengers waiting, and to speed things up he was shown to the first available seat, which was in Clipper class. He was then told he could stay put. He removed his jacket and hung it up, and when we were airborne came down to the economy class section in his shirt sleeves and said: "Just seeing how the underclass are getting on. Bit cramped for space here, aren't you. I must go back for my champagne now." It was not until we were by the taxi-rank at Frankfurt airport that he clapped his breast pocket for his wallet and realised his credit card and money had been stolen from his jacket while talking to me. We drove straight to the Messe, left our luggage in the cloakroom and then walked the coconut matting – each floor was as large as Olympia, and there were many floors with labelled booths for different companies on both sides of each aisle, all heaped with books – and it seemed that everybody present knew Trevor. There were great shouts of "Trevor, nice to see you, how are you keeping?" To each acquaintance Trevor introduced me, explaining he was showing me Frankfurt so I could take part next year, and then told the story of how he had lost his wallet on the flight. "I haven't got any money, could I borrow ten quid in marks?" After an hour he had a fistful of German notes. "I've done far better than if I'd gone to the bank," he chuckled.

We made appointments to see American companies, lunched on a long frankfurter sausage from a fast food place at the end of one of the floors and from the Messe hall booked accommodation in a private house half an hour to the east of Frankfurt near the Main in Durkheimerstrasse. We took a tram out there and then went out to eat. Trevor and I shared a room and next morning, after a huge breakfast served by an old lady who spoke no English we returned and visited the Americans, often seeing the top person, attempting to sell the rights to the books we were planning to do. We had a drink and a long chat with Bill Campbell and Peter MacKenzie of Mainstream, and then attended a drinks gathering given by a remainder man on the 40th floor of the Canadian Pacific building. It had a very rapid lift; you could hear the wind whistling in the shaft. The next day we visited British publishers and then caught the plane home, discussing the Oak-Tree authors' contract and the presentation of the coming catalogue during the flight.

When I got back I saw Des McForan in the Athenaeum Hotel and we went on to the Shepherd Tavern, drinking upstairs in the Sedan Room in the corner, and I recorded: "Told him a group is gathering around Oak-Tree, like the Angry Young Men of the 50s, but determined to shield the West from the neo-barbarian menace, Westerners who have the courage to tell the truth and stand up to the might of Communism and reverse it, the Crusaders (if such be the word that is in the same idiom as the Apostles, but which counteracts it)."

In October Nadia came and stayed at our house next to Oaklands. She said "David is ill" but when asked what symptoms he had shown: "Ask mummy, I'll get it wrong....He was different after he left the RAF." She had plans to become an air hostess. Nadia commented on my complexion. My operation on my foot to restore the circulation of my blood had given me colour in my cheeks. We went out and bought an IBM electric typewriter which still stands in my study. At the end of her visit she rang Caroline briefly, and I had a word. Caroline said: "I feel such a failure. I've messed up everyone's life, yours, Nadia's, Damian's. I don't see anyone for days, and go out walking and thinking. I'm in pieces. Moods – up and then down." Caroline told me that the RAF had withdrawn her husband's security rating, that he had had various jobs and had travelled a lot, to America and Scandinavia for example, and that various women had rung. She had moved to Salisbury on July 17th and she had found out he was seeing a woman called Vivien on July 27th. He had gone to Australia and had returned and lived with Vivien until October, during which time his parents had had Vivien to stay in Scarborough. Caroline then found out that he had filed for divorce on July 27th. On October 27th Vivien had thrown him out, and he had returned, and gone to Wales in search of a job which had fallen through, and had then gone back to Vivien.

A MYSTIC WAY

I went to "Carlton House Terrace for a seminar held by the Executive Intelligence Review, one of whose staff had told me: 'Philby wasn't a traitor, he worked for the Trust, he was between the West and the Soviet Union, helping to manage the Cold War' – further confirmation that the Cold War was not as it was presented in the media. Someone gave a paper saying that the Soviet Union was aiming for a first nuclear strike in 1988/9. (I have details of the Warsaw Pact's plan for a nuclear blitzkrieg of Western Europe in 35 days, using tactical nuclear weapons in four areas, and I could believe this. Each week brings new information that in retrospect vindicates the stand and activities of "The Heroes of the West".) Riley was present, and he introduced me to the Duke of Grantesmil, an untidy-haired, pot-bellied man with a coronet and G on his shirt, whom I interviewed in front of a huge fireplace. Our conversation was all about the fifth man and Lord Victor Rothschild, and he told me: "When I worked for Lord Halifax just before the war, I would often look out of my window and see Baldwin walking with John Buchan. Baldwin wouldn't take any decision without Buchan. Lord Rothschild has taken Buchan's place." (He was Head of Heath's think-tank.)

I was thinking again about Western civilisation and told my brother Jonathan (at a restaurant at Toot Hill over two bottles of wine) that "I can see clearly what is wrong with the West" and that I was getting together "a group of neo-'Angry Young Men', i.e. men of strong anti-Soviet views who are committed to strengthening the values of the West, who will transform the West". I said that "my 'Baroque' Age is therefore to be seen as a strengthening of Western values", that "I am not the 'Playboy of the Western World' (Synge) but the Visionary of the Western World". I spoke of the importance of civilisations to individuals and wrote: "The only good things that come out of human beings are achieved by the cultural ambience of their civilisation, i.e. because T. S. Eliot and Colin Wilson and others were around when I was an adolescent, I was goaded to find my true destiny and to read the legacy of the civilisation which the civilisation guarded, e.g. St. Augustine et al. The civilisation is the storing and ready retrieval and transmission of the growth of the past 'greats' through present influences, and libraries play an important part in this process. A civilisation is living when its leaders grow and connect themselves to the strong values of the civilisation's growth (i.e. the Light). The 'civilisation' – what is it? Quite simply, it is an ambience of greatness and growth which the best of the civilisation attune to." I wrote that "I was restating values that made the West grow, which are still viable and valid today, which can be restored".

At half term we drove to York with the two boys and stayed at the Viking Hotel by the Ouse. Our room had a view of the river and the Minster. We walked in the 14th century streets and in the Shambles (the butchers' street) and visited the Minster. The next morning we visited Jorvik and were taken through a reconstruction of a Viking settlement of thatched houses and farmyard smells. (The original Viking village was destroyed by a Norman fire in 1069.) Later we toured York and saw Dick Turpin's condemned cell with its iron bed, and Clifford's Tower, where the 1190 massacre took place. On our return I started a poem, *At Jorvik*, which I finished in draft the next day. I was left wondering why the Vikings did not

Vikingise Christendom, why we do not worship Odin and Thor today, and concluded that "they didn't have the inner strength of the Light, which commanded the allegiance of Christian mystics and saints", and therefore there was no organisation.

There was a bonfire night at Oaklands. 500 people stood behind a rope and watched "a large fire shooting sparks into the night, rockets, Roman candles shooting green and red balls into the air ('phut'), mortars, fountains", and later drank soup and ate in the tennis court which was hung with fairy lights. While I was supervising the event there was a phone call from Tomlin, the metaphysical philosopher and my boss in Japan. I returned his call and he offered me two books, one on Cornwall and the possibility, which I jumped at, of reprinting his 1950s works, *Great Philosophers of the West* and *Great Philosophers of the East*. I wrote: "The great man, now leaning on me to publish his work, depending on me....'In May I tour the whole of Japan, lecturing.'"

I went with Des McForan to a conference on Marxism-Leninism, which turned out to be run by the Moonies, and was approached by Jillian Becker, an authority on terrorism, before whom McForan kept silent. She asked if I would take over the *Salisbury Review*. I soon gathered that I would be expected to pour a lot of money into it, and when McForan rang me and urged me to decline as it was too far right in its connections for what I should be doing, I backed off. I visited Jillian Becker with Trevor Maher to say No, and I was not swayed by her attempts to change my No into a Yes. When I referred to Toynbee and Spengler she said, revealing her Thatcherite connections, "We don't like Toynbee or Spengler, we believe individuals can shape history, not events." On the contrary, I held, events shape individuals who in turn influence events, the stage of one's civilisation controls events, and if Mrs. Thatcher believed otherwise she would live to see that the context of the civilisation was stronger than her individual will. I told her that I would start a *Western Review* to include philosophy and literature – today I would call it a *Universalist Review* – but that would be all.

The next week on a clear day I took 10 Oaklands girls to look through the Chigwell School telescope: "After a talk from Mr Sizer in front of the charts, went down to the bottom of the field and squinted through a telescope at Halley's comet, queuing behind children to look through the 10 inch eyepiece at the fuzzy blur or smudge above the star in the bottom left hand corner (at 7 or 8 o'clock). The glow of the comet, between the Pleiades and the V of the Hyades – the 7 Sisters and Aldebaran. Jupiter was in the trees with its moon Io. Looking at the starpoints in the black sky I went back into the ancient time when the first geometers began to solve problems, and I knew that Pythagoras' theorem, and other discoveries in geometry, were made by gazing at stars." A few days later I studied Jupiter's four moons at an evening class Sizer was giving at Loughton High School, and thought about moves towards a Grand Unified Theory, and noted "there has been a revolutionary shift in consciousness from earth-centred to galaxy-centred consciousness" and that "the new man is aware of Jupiter's four moons as he does his daily round in his office...and this adds to his ecstatic joy at being here on the earth".

I was now offered voluntary severance from the ILEA. There would be a lump-sum payment of around £11,000, and no pension unless I waited until I was 50. But that was in over 3 years' time, and I could not wait. I was aware my father had died at 57, and that I had to get on and complete the writing I had to do. I would have completed 15 years in the ILEA by December, my prison sentence was coming to an end, I longed for release. London education had become even more ideological with official calls to root out "eurocentricity" and to teach all history from the "multiracial" point of view of the Third World, and while I wanted to take a whole view I was not interested in replacing the tradition of English Literature with contemporary African and Caribbean literature. I made arrangements to leave.

I was still filled with a sense of the divine: "The soul lets in the divine spark so that men become semi-divine, angelic, fulfilling the will of God, united with the source of holiness – the Creator, feeling spiritual joy in the words of the divine and spiritual communication, in music, painting and creative art....The soul is not happy in a monastery or in the desert for there are no tensions of temptations there, and a permanent (as opposed to a temporary) retreat to the desert is not how one is supposed to live. We need temptations....God and man, love for these two must be in balance....One must live in the world and be tempted (tested) – shaped."

I met Tomlin at the Athenaeum – the Club, not the Hotel – and enlisted him as an Oak-Tree author. I recorded that he was waiting "inside the door, talking to A. L. Rowse" (who lived on Trenarren, near Charlestown in Cornwall) and that he was "in a good mood, below the stairs where Dickens was reconciled with Thackeray", as Tomlin pointed out. "Tomlin very dressed up in dark suit like all the others in this men-only place." We dined near Michael Meacher, MP, John Cole of the BBC and the new Head of the Foreign Office, and as business could not be conducted inside the Athenaeum we signed contracts "in a café playing muzak round the corner in Waterloo Place". I wrote: "The idea I put to Tomlin that he should cement his position as the continuer of Whitehead's tradition."

At last I left Garratt Green. I signed the voluntary severance form on the penultimate day of term, a Thursday evening, at County Hall by the Thames, and only revealed my departure to the school the next afternoon, deliberately keeping the news quiet until the final revelation for dramatic effect. Sinclair said to me; "Just how I'd like to go....I'm so envious." I made a farewell speech to the staff, who were totally taken by surprise. I told the staff I would concentrate on my private school and publish books on the theme of arresting the decline of, and revitalising, Western civilisation. I reviewed the changes in the ILEA from 1974 to 1985 and quoted Yeats's lines: "The best lack all conviction while the worst/Are full of passionate intensity." I looked forward to the new school that would follow their amalgamation, and hoped "there will be, among the staff and therefore among the pupils, the consequences of some conviction: inner calm, good humour, amused erudition, intellectual and spiritual grooming, and a profound belief in the merit of Western civilisation – amid the Brave New World of mixed ability, Foundation Courses and anti-eurocentricity which passionate, intense people will no doubt urge on the Steering

Committee". I was getting near the ideological bone, and Sinclair tried to stop me at that point, but I said "I haven't finished", and continued with my prison image. I told them I was being released and I later noted: "Having defined my attitude and stance, there was a fair bit of applause at the end, some clapping over their heads at what they regarded as an act of courage, and some ignoring me in disapproval at my message."

The family function that Christmas was at my brother Robert's. Argie had hired a cook and we went round to my brother Jonathan's new house, which was nearby, for tea. I savoured my retirement, and although I looked forward to the time when I could be a full-time author and not a publisher, I looked forward to implementing my revitalisation of Western civilisation's true values in 1986. I was again in contact with "my destiny". I meant to embody an idea. I wrote: "Scargill-Hitler. People go to hear him, expecting him to say something because, like Nasser, he stands for an idea, and they applaud wildly when they hear him mouth the echo from their own souls. I too embody an idea and must become identified with it in a literary as well as a historical context – the Western Revival through metaphysics and the Light (inner values) and resisting Communism (and Fascism)."

1986, my year of political "engagement" as one of the "Heroes of the West", started inauspiciously with another bout of thrombo-phlebitis. This turned out to be a thrombotic clot, but it was not in a deep vein. Now that I was not commuting to Wandsworth any more, I was able to keep an eye on the changes we were making to Oaklands. Once we had got planning permission for our extension, I had put Bill Sargent, the husband of one of my staff, to build it slowly in the course of the coming year. He had dug the foundations and was progressing to the brick walls, plodding on quietly on his own or with help from his son and son-in-law. At the same time each morning I continued to liaise with my authors so that their books would appear on time. I was able to see more of my children. We shared a car-run with the Snowsills, and on one occasion as the boys waited for Snowsill to arrive I encountered Lord Murray (Len Murray was now Lord Epping Forest) plodding up Albion Hill, silver hair flopping over his red cheeks, and he stopped and we chatted. Anthony was holding a violin case, and Murray helped him into Snowsill's car, saying "Playing the violin is a Hagger thing" (thinking of my mother) and then we talked about Scargill. He said: "He hasn't the discipline to be a Stalinist and to say 'This is the bottom line'." I found him "a nice fellow, craggy-faced and creased and seemingly broken-nosed".

At the doctor's surgery I opened an *Essex Countryside* of 1977 and read Frederic Vanson on "'Has Essex a Housman?', saying that Lakeland has Wordsworth, Suffolk Crabbe, Wessex Hardy, Ayrshire Burns, and Glamorgan Dylan Thomas. 'Who is thus to be identified with Essex?' So far there has not been produced a distinctive Essex poet who can encapsulate the character of the county, its great fields, enormous skies, forgotten villages, low estuary coastline, busy Thames side, and windswept hamlets. This is the Essex I now need to reflect. The atmosphere of Essex."

479

I went up to Manchester to see Jack Wood, formerly of the Transport and General Workers Union, who had a plan to revive British Industry that had won support at high level. He had a craggy face with a red wound under an eye from a fall, and I noted he had a "a craggy honesty and integrity". He had a Cromwellian drive against financial corruption and I wrote: "A fearless Cromwellian bruiser – taught to be a prizefighter. He knocked Cousins out at a meeting, stood over his prone body and told him off....A Cromwellian who has found his way back to the forces of the King." He was now in touch with Tebbit and Prior and very much on the Conservative side.

I also visited Tomlin at 31 Redan Street, London W14. He was sitting in his study at the top of his house with his leg up, suffering from phlebitis, and I sat with him and discussed a one-volume edition of his two works on the philosophers. I met John O'Sullivan, who was writing up eye-witness material about Mao's expulsion of the Christian missionaries from China, and tried to get his story right. O'Sullivan was enormously fat, and had great difficulty in squeezing himself between chair and table at the café where we met. I also met Gorka, whose book on Hungary dealt with Philby.

But my most pressing book was McForan's *The World Held Hostage*, which dealt with terrorism and Gaddafi. I spent a day with the moustached and bespectacled McForan in the Charing Cross Hotel's Rendezvous lounge on the first floor, which I called "the Oak-Tree office". We could arrive soon after 10 and have regular coffee, a sandwich lunch, and then tea, and stay until 3.30, talking confidentially at tables while the likes of Roy Hattersley came and talked nearby and went. I reviewed the book. It had many revelations, including Gaddafi's attempt to build rockets with a nuclear warhead near Sebha by hiring ex-Nazi V1, V2 and V3 rocket scientists from Argentina, which was prepared to sell plutonium.

McForan had been and asked the terrorists who funded them and had come up with some original answers, quite different from the answers offered by columnists who had not left their newspaper offices. McForan told me that Pope John Paul I was murdered to keep the power of the left in the Vatican; and that Pope John Paul II had been shot as a warning, following his letter to Breznev, and that Gaddafi had organised the attack and got Carlos to spirit Agca away. That, at least, was what he had learned from some terrorists. We spoke of our operation to defend the West as a "Heroes of the West" operation. I said: "We are trying to put an end to terrorism, to end the 50,000 acts of terror. That is our angelic task as 'Heroes of the West'. We need some recommendations for Reagan." And off the top of my head I dictated getting on for a dozen headings ("airports", "airlines", "exit visas", etc.) which he scribbled down, and I told him to flesh it out into a programme for action.

I thought again about the place of the Light in civilisations: The Light is a phenomenon which is found in all religions from 3,000BC to today. It is found in all civilisations and has assisted their growth and survival. We need it in Western civilisation today. So a full study is not just of the experience of the Light...but of the Light in its civilisation, proceeding civilisation by civilisation, and then seeing what happened to each civilisation as the Light disappeared, and concentrating the final thrust on what is happening in Western civilisation/European civilisation today. The separation of European culture from the Light and its consequences....Back to the link between the Light and civilisations. Toynbee's reconsidered opinion that the descendants of many civilisations may flow into one oecumenical civilisation, starting in a Western framework and on a Western basis, but drawing contributions from living, non-Western civilisations embraced in it: the Russian, Orthodox, Islamic, Indian (including Hindu), South-East Asian, Sinic, Japanese, Vietnamese and Middle American civilisations being the main ones. Cf Roberts' *Triumph of the West* for this idea that there will be a world-wide civilisation within a Western framework, the West's universal state (the West now being in a pre-Universal State phase). I need a kind of flow-chart of all civilisations, their offshoots and affiliations, from 3,000BC on, so that the Light is related to its civilisation, and the tributaries of the Light can be seen to flow into Western civilisation....The connection between the Light and civilisations. Our spiritual values, there for a world-wide oecumenical civilisation:...a syncretistic amalgam of all religions but with a Western base – part of the coming Universal Age (which is this future oecumenical civilisation in a Western framework on a Western basis, fed by the non-Western civilisations it embraces)....I have to prove a connection between the growth of civilisations and the flourishing of the Light, and the collapse of civilisations and the disappearance of the Light....The Light...gives spiritual energy to make that civilisation grow....(The) Millennium – (we are) all brothers in one Light....The Light gives energy, which is poured into a civilisation....My world view is of a coming Universal Age, in which there is a world-wide oecumenical Western-based civilisation within a Western framework (gadgets), drawing on non-Western contributions; that is my 'Baroque' Age, combining sense and spirit. And the Light, which gives an individual a meaning and purpose, transforms a culture, also giving it meaning, and energises the religion, which in turn holds together a society which threatens to fall apart and thus perpetuates the civilisation....The Light...is Mysticism, one of the flowers of civilisation, which flourishes in 'desert' conditions....In conditions of hardship, where there is little money, where there is asceticism, the man in the desert. So is the Light a measure of health, does it disappear as the civilisation spiritually breaks down into material affluence...and does putting the Light back into it...keep the civilisation alive? God as Light, God's purpose touching with the Light, divine intervention which leads the civilisation forward." I wrote (adapting Eliot) of : "The 17th century dissociation of sensibility in which the secular and sacred separated, a further measure of a breakdown that began with the Renaissance and Reformation, and carried on with the loss of religion from the arts....The Light is the sacred sap which was in the arts and withdraws as the civilisation becomes brittle. Remysticising Europe is crucial to the survival of Western civilisation, for when the West's religion goes the civilisation will go." Again: "The Light spurts a civilisation into energy and action (growth) and it dwindles when the Light dries up in its higher religion....The Light gives men a sense of purpose and direction and therefore makes for higher civilisation and culture. Our society...is a spiritual wilderness, full of low spiritual tension – which the Light can give....Our culture is unhealthy – society dies from the head down, i.e. civilisation and purpose is lost."

I thought about culture: "Culture ('self-cultivation') of the individual is dependent on that of the group (arts/science), class and that of the society, the total being civilisation. Cultural disintegration is disintegration of the classes, i.e. separation of strata (e.g. upper, lower) and fragmentation of culture at the...group level so that the artistic sensibility and religious sensibility are divorced from each other and impoverished. Culture is all the activities and interests of a people, and religion and culture cannot be separated....Excessive scepticism can cause a civilisation to die....Religion gives a meaning to life as each class maintains its culture through its élites (art, science, philosophy, action), transmitting it through the family. An excess of cultural unity is barbarism; of disunity is decadence, élites being isolated from each other and departmentalised (*Two Cultures*) – a weakness in our culture, i.e. strength is to reunite them, reintegrate them. The unity of European culture (i.e. Western civilisation) is when artist, poet, politician, labourer have a culture in common in a healthy society/civilisation....The arts shot through with sacredness: the Egyptian temple-dancers, Greek tragedy and the gods. So the Light restores the sacred, religious side to our culture, and keeps the civilisation alive by combating scepticism and maintaining the culture's unity. The contemplative life is mysticism..., and an aspect of a culture's religion. When a culture is healthy there is a healthy contemplative life....Civilisation grows out of contemplation, which is put into action. The contemplative life in any century involves a turning away from the world...into the individual soul....The hermits are the head of civilisation and the masses follow when the civilisation is growing, their meaning and purpose gets across to the civilisation....In the disintegration phase it is the rebel against scientific materialism who keeps the civilisation growing....High points in religious history...coincide with low points in secular history, while high points in secular history...coincide with low points in religious history..., e.g. ages in which there has been a regression from a higher religion to a vain secular civilisation." I wrote of "the long tradition of the Light which has shaped Western civilisation and contained it....Contact with the Light is contact with the metaphysical purpose."

I worked on the connections between ancient religions and the Light, exploring how the Light began in shamanism and moved from culture to culture, and I traced the classical thread of Western civilisation from classical Greece and Roman through the Renaissance to the 18th century and Modernism, and the "immortality" thread from Christianity through the Middle Ages, the Crusades and the Reformation. I wrote: "Classical art seeks underlying order behind appearances; the human being in full possession of its powers. Baroque art enters into the multiplicity of things, i.e. becoming, in dynamic compositions."

We spent a weekend in the Cotswolds at the White Hart Royal, Moreton-in-Marsh, a pretty village full of Regency windows, where Charles I stayed in 1644. I wrote: "A drive through the Cotswolds. Drifted, impacted snow 2 feet high in the ditches. The Cotswolds, bounded by Stratford and Gloucester and Oxford – a peaceful, quiet area of small rural villages, quaint buildings and antiquity....Dinner at the hotel, overlooking the fountain of icicles." And again: "Feb 22. From Moreton to Broadway, a picturesque 18th century village with an enormously long street under the Cotswolds, with a church on the top....Then to Evesham, and across the vale to Winchcombe, to Chedworth Roman villa (the mosaic of Winter with a Roman British hare) and the wild life park at Burford (saw the penguins being fed) and then up to Bourton-on-the-Water, with its petit-Venetian bridges, low over the Windrush, and then on to Stow-on-the-Wold, a wide square with a medieval cross and stocks and a church where Cromwell locked up a thousand Royalists in 1646. The main event of the day: a blue car in front of us (an R Cortina) swerved across the path of a red car and careered into a stone wall, turned over three times after flying through the air and ended up in a ploughed field, steam rising from the battered bonnet, the driver lifting two pieces of wall from his lip while his wife sat, stunned, bleeding from her nose, no windscreen. Meanwhile the red car swerved round it into my path, and I had a split second in which to decide, and continued my course, and he swerved back and avoided me as I braked. We were within inches of being wiped out. Encouraged them while the ambulance came and their hideous wounds congealed." On the way home we went to Oxford: "Walked round Christ Church, Worcester (gardens – skating on the lake) and Port Meadow via the canal area (Southmoor Road) in a biting east wind that made the cheeks red and froze the nose and ears. They were skating where the Thames had overflowed onto the grass. Binsey Green visible from the towpath. Then lunched in the Randolph."

In London I had lunch with the fellow from the Executive Intelligence Review who had told me: "Philby was a Trust man." I wrote: "Ever since Lenin, the US-Soviet alliance, 'the Trust', has carved up the world – hence Yalta. Force X which brought down the Macmillan government through the Profumo affair....Head of Force X is Lord (Victor) Rothschild (who had tipped off Philby)....I am on the verge of uncovering the truth since Lenin, that there has been a US-Soviet alliance to run the world since Sidney Reilly, and that confrontation is phoney and gets betrayed (e.g. Gorka). The co-operation between East and West all through the Cold War, to maintain spheres of influence. See Yalta in this light....The hallmark of the Trust: right and left together."

The Epping Forest Conservatives' Patrons Club held its February dinner at the Commons, and the guest of honour was Lord Whitelaw, Mrs. Thatcher's no 2. Ann and I went straight to the bar, and Whitelaw arrived and stood nearby. When any famous person first arrives there is a general stand-off until the ice is broken; that is the time to have a chat. So I asked him what he would like to drink and bought him a Cinzano, reminded him about my FREE idea, told him about my publishing programme, about the Scargill book and my call for an end to terrorism through *The World Held Hostage*, and the work of "the Heroes of the West", and said I had been told who the fifth man was. He invited me to see him in Downing Street. Later, after his speech, I asked a question, "How does the government perceive the Soviet Union under Gorbachev?"

There was a thaw and huge drips splashed down from the gutters. At night there was a slight frost, and the Plough looked like a question mark in the stars. By day the fields looked as if a tide was going out; snow covered the bottom half of the fields only.

I had another discussion with deaf Anne Clarke, who came to tea on Easter Monday. She said that Providence will guide human beings through. I said "that it was down to human agency to keep the West going, and therefore Christian civilisation surviving" but wondered: "Perhaps just as the Devil is God's agent, so is the terrorist, to effect changes Providence requires, and perhaps Providence is also using me to reassert the fundamental values that should be preserved from the terrorists. 'Resist not evil but overcome evil with good' – no, one must resist evil, just as Christians resisted Churchill, and not become a pacifist. It is a time of trouble and the Dark Ages are round the corner and I must play my part and take my risks to keep the Western tradition alive."

McForan and I, the two main "Heroes of the West" at that time, took our risk. We were appalled at Gaddafi's ability to strike at London, Paris and Bonn with nuclear weapons, and at Gaddafi's involvement in the Brighton bomb, and I had ended my editing of McForan's book by writing in: "The West must stand up to the anti-Western terrorists." At the Charing Cross Hotel Des and I discussed what to do. I had been to the Light, and we agreed that we must get the book to Reagan through a correct channel, a contact of Des's. We made the arrangement. We met one morning in London, took great care to ensure we were not being followed, walked past and then into our rendezvous, met our contact (whose identity I must necessarily skate over), and explained and handed over an early copy of the book. Our contact assured us that it would be on Reagan's desk. We were escorted out by an armed girl in her 20s who walked half a mile with us to make sure we were safe. Human agency was fighting for the West. Full of foreboding I wrote: "If there is a Providence that sees the civilised world through, my death will have been an unnecessary waste. But if there has to be a struggle on the part of human agency to preserve the spiritual values, and if one has to take risks because nothing is guaranteed, as I believe, then my death will have been necessary, for my generation must not fail, and a martyrdom here and there helps to focus attention on the ideas behind the struggle. I will have died for the preservation of Western civilisation....Can the Light hold back the barbarian tide? Only if there are humans who will receive it. It is a mixture – a partnership – between Providence and human agency that keeps civilisation going. From my outpost on the frontier in the war against the barbarians (which most Westerners do not even realise exists) I know the alliance between the human will and the Providential Light."

On April 4th I went to the Mystics and Scientists conference at Winchester and had coffee with Rupert Sheldrake and Jill Purce on the Saturday morning. I showed Sheldrake the typescript of Tomlin's book, which became *Philosophers of East and West* and after lunch he came back to my room and for one and half hours we discussed a book I might publish, to be entitled *The New Teleology*. It would include "Tomlin, Sheldrake, Bohm, astronomy, art, cultural movements, politics, educational theory, theology, technology, medicine, literature...and the common ground, telos being 'end', 'goal' or 'purpose', a synthesising of all the disciplines". I held at some length that there needs to be "a revival of mysticism to unite both East and West", and that this new unification would come from resisting the aggression from the East and then by seeking (as Tomlin did) what united both and East and West. I said that "mysticism works best in post-imperial deserts and not in technological paradises which encourage laziness".

Immediately afterwards I went to Winchester Cathedral, which I had briefly visited on my way in, and I wrote a poem, *Counter-Renaissance*. I wrote of the "tradition of the secret Light", "the world-wide Baroque culture". I wrote: "It is not just a civilisation but the whole world that needs to be unified – we are shifting our perspective from Britain or Europe to the whole world, which is embraced in one unitive vision and common culture." And: "My mind is a synthesising one – the synthesis behind all conflicts – and the world-wide Baroque vision blends the spirit of the Middle Ages and the sense of the Renaissance, which in turn blended the Christian and the pagan from the ancient world." I thought of myself as restating positive values for Western civilisation and reversing a climate of pessimism.

I left the conference early to call in again at Winchester Cathedral, and missed Sir George Trevelyan quoting my essay on Romanticism. He wrote to me: "I used a fine quotation from you in my final talk at Winchester. I had at some time copied it into my little book of quotations and it said exactly what I wanted about the real significance of the Romantic Movement. I was sorry you were not there but I acknowledged it to you."

On April 14th we went to the Lake District to stay with Uncle Reg. I wrote: "High Newton a grey village, with grey stone walls and grey slate roofs and grey curling smoke against a sweep of green hillside. Crows. To Grange-over-Sands; the house on the edge of the town, overlooking the quicksands of Morecombe Bay, an old 1750 coach house when the coach crossed the sands....On to the Cumbrian hills. Past a Roman fort and Scafell to Blea Tarn House, where Wordsworth's Solitary lived, while news came in on the radio of Reagan's F111s (British based) striking at Libya....On to Langdale and Grasmere (the grave) and then on to Dove Cottage, and up the path the small tarn where the Leech-gatherer sat. Rydal and the stream with stepping-stones on the way to De Quincey's Fox Ghyll, where Wordsworth stepped across when he went to Ambleside. Home via Kendal and Kirkby Lonsdale, a grey granite village under green hills, and a healthy-looking Matthew who waded in the waterfall river at Hawes (Yorkshire) yesterday."

When we got home I was shocked to see on the television news details of America's raid on Libya. Israeli intelligence had helped to plan the attack, according to the television, and the American F111s had taken off from Britain with Mrs. Thatcher's support. I stared at the ruins on Uncle Reg's screen and knew immediately that McForan's book was the cause of the raid, that F111s had flattened the base near Sebha. I confirmed this later (on May 17th to be precise, at the Swiss Cottage Holiday Inn). Then I was told that while 40 planes were publicly admitted to, 55 planes were involved in the total operation: 20 went to Tripoli and 20 to Benghazi, while another 15 had gone to the base near Sebha and set back Gaddafi's nuclear plans. Unfortunately, Gaddafi's adopted daughter had been killed in one of the raids; and there is no doubt that the planes were trying to kill Gaddafi. I felt sad for Gaddafi. His revolution had taken my daughter from me, but I had not wanted him to lose his daughter. Nevertheless, he could not be allowed to threaten the West with nuclear rockets. Guided by the Light, the Heroes of the West had again influenced world events and struck a blow against the centre of international terrorism.

That night and the next day I thought deeply about the West. I wrote: "Paint the treasures of Western civilisation, the Ionas and abbeys, the Marvell and Wordsworth places – the heritage of values, so that true values can be found in the corpus....April 16. Awoke early and sketched, sitting on the edge of my bed in the large front bedroom upstairs at Reg's house, stanzas 3-11 of a poem I had started yesterday, on the active and contemplative life: the way the two can be united in art as the Solitary of Blea Tarn House paints a poem on terrorism and therefore acts against Gaddafi. Also wrote *The Artist* after seeing W. Heaton Cooper in his studio yesterday, the lakeland artist who relates earth and sky and gives what we see a pattern of relationship – and therefore a meaning."

We went "to Ambleside, the stepping stones by the Rothay near Rydal, Cockermouth (the end of the garden by the Derwent), then to Ullswater – Place Fell or St. Sunday's Crag – and the site of the daffodils (Glencoyne Park) and of the stolen boat – Devil's Chimney, and finally over Kirkstone Pass through a cloud. A dove nesting in the hole in the chimney pot." The next morning: "Awoke early and wrote two poems, *Inner Power* about the Rothay stepping-stones near Rydal, Cockermouth Derwent, Aira Force and Kirkstone Pass above Ullswater, and *The Power Within the Mind* (at Aira Force Waterfall), which is my *Kubla Khan* – a metaphysical Baroque *Kubla Khan*, not a dreamy (opium-dreamy) Romantic one." I wrote: "My poems should now be my main activity – not my publishing or Oaklands. I must now change my life so this is so. Three collections: Journey into Light – mysticism and mystic revival; treasures of Western civilisation (blending history, culture and Light); the spirit of Epping Forest – ploughed fields, trees, crops and pears, ponds, skies, but also depths, roots, growth as opposed to the bareness of mountains, and the metaphysical. For the West – treasures of Western civilisation in verse: Iona, Chartres, etc., and a reflection of the values they stand for." And later: "Wrote...a poem about Cartmel Priory....Began today...by going to meet Cedric Robinson, the guide of the quicksands...at his 700 year old farm...and then went to Cartmel Priory and Gatehouse, Hawkshead (Wordsworth's school), Grasmere...and Ambleside, where I saw the grim office where Wordsworth was distributor of stamps 1813-43, wasting all those great energies – his Garratt Green. Home...after climbing Jenkins Crag above Ambleside with Anthony." The next morning I wrote: "April 18. Awoke early to write *At Cartmel Priory: Taming the Beast* (poem), with the image of Gaddafi the unicorn caught by an oak-tree."

I had sent Tomlin's book to Kathleen Raine in the hope that she would write a Foreword. She rang and said: "I find the book brilliant but deplore the omission of Plotinus, Eckhart and Schelling, the Neo-Platonists." She said: "I am on Yeats's side, not Eliot's. The only traditional thinkers are

Dante and Blake, for they used tradition as 'truth absolute' – Blake was a traditional thinker in a heretical age – whereas Eliot's alternative view of tradition is of a row of statues to which the artist adds himself. European Christendom is a straightjacket, and although Tomlin reflects the East he wears the straightjacket as Eliot did." She agreed that Tomlin is the Whitehead of our time, a teleologist who makes the divine connection. I wrote: "He puts down all that philosophy has been, and does not select like Leavis in accordance with his own way of looking. Kathleen Raine lives in an intensely abstract world of traditions and theories – for someone who believes in the 'other mind'."

I had visited Tomlin – I found him sitting dome-headed in his high up study in Redan Street – and we had discussed reality. "The philosopher must get out of his study among organisms," he said, "for we are animals rather than Raine's spirit" – and at that point we were disturbed by the reality of a gasman. (The previous time I had been, the great philosopher had been unable to decipher a telephone message from the LEB and had to get his wife to hear the answer to his question, "Yes, but can an electricity man come round in 15 minutes?") Tomlin's theme was that "our sense of mutability gives rise to a sense of the immutable, the many give rise to the One, multiplicity is multiple organisms....We are part of Nature." Tomlin said he was Aristotelian (like Sheldrake) whereas Raine is a Platonist (like me), and the metaphysical "beyond" is "behind". He said: "The rehabilitation of metaphysics depends on its new alliance with the new biology....There must be an after-life, otherwise there is nothing." I worked from 10 to 2.30, sitting at his desk while he sat in an easy chair with his leg up, stopping for chats about his reminiscences of Eliot and Toynbee over coffee, a working lunch beautifully arranged and served by his wife, and tea. At the end we discussed the fifth man, and, speaking as a Hero of the West he said: "You ought to see the Head of MI5. Whitelaw will arrange it, I have no doubt."

On April 30th I visited Lord Whitelaw in the Lord Privy Seal's office, Downing Street, I wrote: "Waited in a waiting-room of Law Reports and green chesterfields, having entered from Downing Street, and was shown through anterooms to the Holy of Holies. 'Very nice to see you again,' boomed Lord Whitelaw, huge, stooping, jowly and bloodshot-eyed at 10 a.m., having just finished a meeting. We sat in huge chairs and I talked, and he sat and listened and made a note, dealt with it, then attended to my next item. Des's book is going to the Cabinet Office Intelligence Unit, I am being put in touch with someone high up in the intelligence services." (That was on the fifth man. I discussed with Whitelaw the whole question of the fifth man and the information I had been given that he was Lord (Victor) Rothschild, the man who tipped Philby off.) At one point I drew Whitelaw's attention to the recommendations at the back of *The World Held Hostage*, and he said, "Can I take a copy of these for Margaret?" He left the room and returned later.

On May 6th 1986 I looked at the front page of the *Times* and nearly fell out of my chair. For there was an account of how the World Summit leaders in Tokyo, including Reagan, had adopted a British plan to control terrorism, and itemised points covered the same ground as the recommendations I had dictated to McForan in the Charing Cross Hotel. In fact, from that moment on, international terrorism abruptly ended. A combination of the bombing of Libya, the World Summit and the advent of Gorbachev ended the 50,000 terrorist acts, and the world leaders answered the last line of the book: "The West must stand up to the anti-Western terrorists." The Heroes of the West had done it again: intervened at a critical moment to change history. The Light had led us to it. I realise that if you have an idea in a book it cuts across all classes and power barriers, and you have a passport to the highest places.

Kathleen Raine agreed to write the Foreword to Tomlin's book, and she wanted me to go and see her. I wrote: "May 1. Kathleen Raine received me at 1.30 (in) Paulton's Square and led me into a ground floor room that ran through from front to back: the trees of the summery square at the front, an open window and camellias at the back, a typewriter by the window, paintings and etchings on the tastefully furnished walls, bric a brac, etc. She made me coffee (herb tea for herself as she is not allowed to drink coffee) and I picked up Tomlin's proofs and put them in my plastic bag of butterflies. Her pleated skirt and hair done up, her penetrating eyes but there was a softness about her, she was not the imperious woman of a few years ago. *Temenos* has made her more tolerant. We chatted: Barkingside where she lived, Cumberland, Oak-Tree, values, banks, how she is selling the furniture for *Temenos*; she wants to do ten and then stop, and will do no 7 shortly, and 8 and 9 in 1987, 10 in 1988....Eventually got to other cultures and I showed her my Light book. She: 'This is very important.' Said it was the tradition, that they couldn't all be wrong, that it was something I had come across in poetry. She: 'I had a similar experience and made it the basis for my autobiography.' The Romantic poetess. 'I call it Imagination.' 'The great shift that is required is against materialism.' 'The worship of technology is all wrong.'...A very clear lady, with a great softness, and quite an enchanting manner. Left at 2.30." I went on and met Trevor who deferred two books to next year but urged me to bring Jack Wood's book forward.

I wrote of the Essex landscape: "Thames Basin, tributaries like the Roding, Clay Country, the Forest, the ploughed fields and open spaces and rapeseed fields round the Rodings, the marshes, the Stour valley, the pretty villages, the farms. The historical places, Greenstead church, Queen Elizabeth's Hunting Lodge, Copped Hall (our Furness Abbey, a ruin); Loughton camp with its pollards, Lippitt's Hill, the Strawberry Hill ponds, High Beach church; Waltham Abbey and Harold's grave; Chigwell School and the King's Head; Boadicea's Ambresbury banks. Trees like roots in the mind, Epping Forest – a region of the mind....Essex is different from the mountainous Lake district or craggy, country Cornwall – is foresty (the Royal Forests and Willingale) – we are all woodlanders at heart with our love of flora and fauna and our walks in the woods – but it is also flat and open and ploughed, and marshy. Colchester and King Cole, Caractacus and Constantine the Great, and how Christianity came to Britain. And Loughton with its oldest house 400 years old (Beech House) and 16th century pottery near the Gardeners....Get the area into poems: Oaklands as microcosm. Constable's Essex, the heart of England. Industrialised, commuter Essex and the wild Forest (murders, rapes and excitement). Catch the feeling and atmosphere of the place – man alone in the Forest, man in a rural setting, the antiquity of history (Greenstead and Waltham). Audley End."

Argie rang. The Loughton Methodist church foundation stone of 1903 had been lifted and a copy of the *Methodist Recorder* was found with an announcement "To Mrs. G. H. Broadley...twins" – the announcement of Argie's birth and the news that she had a stillborn twin. Argie told me: "I feel I was meant to come to Loughton, it is all Providential" (meaning, that she was to come to a place that enclosed the announcement of her birth).

I rang Garratt Green and spoke to Sinclair. He told me a new Head had been appointed, to take over from September. She apparently spoke to the Senior school for 50 minutes, and was anti-racist, anti-sexist and anti-classist, and the girls can go in for coffee on arrival. She was applauded. Sinclair told me: "I have an illness, a disease – self-doubt and shyness about ILEA principles." He told me there were tensions in the English Department, and that Mr and Mrs. Kay were training lunch supervisors at £50 an hour at County Hall.

I drove to Moreton in the Cotswolds with Riley and Gorka, and we spoke to the Duke of Grantesmil, "a tousle-haired patrician, a member of the nobility going back 1,000 years, a believer in genes and arranged marriages sadly living alone". He told me that Gaddafi had threatened Britain and America with nuclear bombs, his demands being a unified Ireland; a dismantled Israel; and South Africa surrendered to the guerillas. (In 1993, the second and third demands have made progress.) He told me that we went to war to stop Hitler from having nuclear weapons – he said two Germans got the bomb and Niels Bohr confirmed the equations with Einstein – and that this was confirmed by Admiral Canaris, who was a British SIS agent. He said that Force X, Lord (Victor) Rothschild's force, was "the Third Force" (neither capitalism nor Communism) when "far right and far left meet"; he said it was behind the Profumo Affair, and was responsible for Philby.

I thought about the new Renaissance. I wrote: "The Inner Light, the spiritual sun, is actually the energy that is at the heart of the outer universe....A sea of Light. Our universe born from an invisible ocean of cosmic energy or Light which can be known by the spirit as it is spiritual, i.e. with the part of oneself that belongs to it, and the spiritual sun at its centre on which all black holes/suns are based, i.e. the prototype of all the copies – the divine knowledge....So this New Renaissance...is discovering the fullness in the emptiness, it is returning to the Eastern roots..., a revolt against Western materialism, a restoration of the spiritual universe as the order of the material universe is shown to be more complex."

The launch of *The World Held Hostage* loomed, and towards the end of May I was rung up by Evelyn Le Chêne, who was interested in *The World Held Hostage*. We talked about Josten, and she said that after he had raged against me he had asked her to sign the form he had wanted me to sign, and she refused. He had then made a number of vitriolic calls, notably to Crozier and Sir Bernard Braine, in the course of which "he got me into trouble with the palace". She said: "You handled a very difficult situation with aplomb. I survived eleven months with him – a record." She said: "Le Chêne means oak – from which our battleships were made. Josten started enthusiastically but along the line the project changed and he ended discouraging."

Ann and I went to Stratford-upon-Avon for a weekend. We stayed at the Moat House Hotel across a strip of water from the theatre. There was Morris dancing on the green. "250 morris dancers had gathered and different groups cavorted and leapt and twirled, flapping white handkerchiefs and looking intent in their fine clothes and flowered hats, and had no self-deprecation at all, and walking among a stag, a badger, a bear, I felt the writer in me stir, a buried, forgotten life under all this outer organisation of letters and phone calls." We saw *A Winter's Tale*. On the Saturday and Sunday I went in search of Shakespeare "who left Stratford for poaching on Charlcote Estate (Lucy = Justice Shallow) and was away from his wife until his return in 1610, when he wrote *A Winter's Tale*". We visited his mother's (Mary Arden's) house, his birthplace, his school, his wife's house, New Place where he retired, his church, his daughter Susanna's house and the house of Nash (who married his granddaughter). I saw the death of his son Hamnet as beginning a dark phase in 1596 and wondered where his papers went after his death. I recorded: "Wrote *In Shakespeare's Stratford: The Nature of Art*." On the Monday we went to Warwick Castle, to Kenilworth and then Charlcote.

Evelyn Le Chêne asked me to preview the Special Forces Club where at Biggs-Davison's suggestion the launch was to take place. Biggs-Davison reckoned that with its SAS connections it would be safe from terrorist attack. The Club was in a back street not far from Harrods, and there I met C, who masterminded the SAS operation to end the Iranian siege, and M, who was in CI3, and examined the staircase of heroes, framed photos of heroes all up the stairs which included (as she pointed out) Evelyn Le Chêne's husband, a war hero. I met Biggs-Davison to discuss the invitation to the launch, and his main concern seemed to be to invite Ian Greg, something he mentioned several times.

I was full of confidence. When Richard Snowsill came round, depressed, I told him: "'Either we are on a cold star, a meaningless accident..., or there is order...and it is our destiny and service of mankind that counts....Self-belief. A man can do anything, the world – Western civilisation – can be changed from the Oaklands garden.' He: 'I ask myself if I have the ability, if I can do it.'" I wrote: "My faith, my inner faith, and his inner self-doubt which is suicidal, self-destructive..., as he sits around in early morning gloom, leaving me to take the children to school."

Then on June 6th came an attempt to interfere with the launch of the *The World Held Hostage*. Evelyn Le Chêne rang to say she had read the book, and that its blaming of Gaddafi for the Brighton bomb could be used by the IRA defendant who was about to be convicted and sentenced for it, that the case was sub judice, that I should withdraw the book to assist the conviction. I rang Des and visited Biggs-Davison in the House of

Commons. He had been up all night and looked bloodshot and red-veined. He greeted me with: "What's all this about sub judice? Is she mad or something?" I told him that one of the book's revelations was that Gaddafi was being sent arms for Carlos and other terrorists through Heathrow in an operation codenamed the Babysitter, and that I thought forces who wished to keep this operation in place were discouraging the book. I pointed out that the attitude behind such an operation had lost Libya to Gaddafi in the first place, by keeping him in power when I was there. I pointed out that the effect of torpedoing a second launch of mine would be to contribute to perpetuating Gaddafi's terrorism, which Philby for one would want. I did not then realise that powerful forces within the West wished to do just that; that terrorism, which was organised from behind the Iron Curtain and based in countries like Libya, had its conception and funding in the West.

Soon afterwards my lungs debilitated me: "Went on antibiotics on Saturday to get rid of green pus in my lungs. Feel tired, no bodily energy, no excess, and can hear a wheeze." I went to the Chigwell School Speech Day and saw both my boys collect prizes from Dr Earl Ball in the marquee. My health problems persisted: "Am not retaining all the oxygen I need and tire easily – and fall asleep" and "my right leg is covered with patches of blue where I have circulatory problems". I took the boys to Ilford to watch the cricket – Essex played Hampshire and Robin Smith took a catch beside us, glancing down to check that he had not stepped over the boundary, and later the boys ran on and got Alan Border's autograph when he was fielding on the boundary – and the following week Matthew Manning, a healer, came to Oaklands, which had been booked by an ex-Oaklands parent, Mrs. Clauson. He spoke to 30 healers and had a practical session in the school hall and I dropped in and out of his talks and heard him say, "Some people are fated to die and I can't heal them." He spoke of the violence in the world – the terrorism I was combating – and how the good had spiritual power and the evil were materialist killers, and I wrote: "The solution. Extend Western civilisation throughout the world into a universal State; this to be based on the Light, which is the world-culture and basis. Identify the isms like Communism which are to be pruned. Transfer the West to true values, make it less materialistic." On the Sunday afternoon I had tea with Manning at the Clauson's huge house (since demolished) in Loughton High Road. We sat round the fireplace while Clauson ostentatiously mowed the lawn outside, demonstrating his practical priorities, and I found Matthew Manning fairly monosyllabic. We had a discussion on energy and he commented on my chakras. I wrote: "My own energy level is very great, I have red hot chakras, and need someone of less energy to neutralise me and relax me – but I also need great energy. It all comes down to energy in the end." Soon afterwards Mrs. Clauson invited me to a lunch she was holding for a couple who had been on the course, and one of them, a victim of Auschwitz called Hanna, greeted me with "Hello again" implying that we had met in a past life; a greeting that was not uncommon in New Age circles.

I pondered the river Roding, across which I went to and fro, taking boys to and from school. I wrote: "This part of Essex is lowland river valley with flower-rich flood meadows and marshes, flooded each winter by swollen rivers....Hedge bounded by meadows and marsh. Roding valley....Reed swamp and marsh. Loughton in Waltham manor in 1422. Snipe and redshank....The Roding flows into the Thames....Where is the Roding's source?"

While tracking the Roding to its source I was doing the same with the Light. In the run-up to the launch of Des's book I thought of the Light: "The basis of true Western values is the Light. But I have to substantiate the Light, and present the tradition as being there – it is behind so many Western traditions, and Eastern traditions – and is superbly there in every man's consciousness to form the basis of a world-wide Western civilisation that is moving against materialism for its values. Whatever tradition Westerners embrace (Quakerism, etc.) – the Light is at its source." I had unwittingly laid down the spiritual basis for the coming Universalist world state.

In view of the immensity of the battle we were involved in, there was a bizarre episode involving bats. A colony had temporarily arrived next door, in Miss Lord's house. I wrote: "Bats, wheeling and dipping and darting outside, and squeaking. Then a squeal from next door. I went to investigate. Miss Lord had 5 bats flitting round her sitting-room. They had come down the chimney." I grabbed a copy of the *Times* and rolled it into a tube. I wrote: "I flapped them with a newspaper and in a combination of forearm tennis smashes and cricket hooks stunned them and lifted them outside her class patio doors with the newspaper and cushion, little blind pipistrelle mice with folded umbrella wings. As fast as I got them outside more came down the chimney and squeezed through the fireguard and got behind a picture, under a bookcase, in a chair – or just incessantly wheeled. It was an hour later, after midnight, when I got away to have my supper, her house clear. Now we will investigate the crack in the facia board under her eaves, over her window, where they all live and where you can hear them squeaking and chattering at night."

On July 1st I launched *The World Held Hostage* at the Special Forces Club. I put on wine and a finger buffet, and with an SAS defensive presence the road outside was sealed off by the police "because Whitelaw's coming, the government's no 2". The policeman repeated: "We've had instructions from Downing Street that he's coming." The invitations had gone out in Biggs-Davison's name, and Julian Amery had been secured to speak. But although I greeted the legendary Lt. Col. Billy McLean, who together with Amery was one of the "four musketeers" to enter Albania in a famous secret mission and who would soon die, many of those who had accepted did not appear, including Whitelaw. Biggs-Davison introduced me, I spoke detailing the revelations and calling for the West to halt the Babysitter operation and snuff out terrorism; then Julian Amery spoke; and finally Des McForan, moustached, while Gorka, a fellow Hero of the West, lurked round. After the speeches, McLean congratulated me on my stance, as did one of my SAS minders, and I overheard Biggs-Davison and Amery agreeing that the book sailed very close to the wind, that there were too many revelations for officialdom's comfort, and that there would have to be official investigations into some of the allegations. The four or five journalists present interviewed us, I chatted with Andrew Lownie, a literary agent who might become agent for Oak-Tree's books, and the guests drifted off. I remember Des standing with Trevor Maher, Klaus (my East German office manager who had a bookshop in Wembly) and me, and Des saying in his impeccable English "Gentlemen, I just want to make an important comment on the government's firmness with terrorists", whereupon he noisily broke wind.

Des and I had allocated the rest of the day for interviews. We began with *Time Out* and shortly afterwards went to TV AM for an interview that had been booked. We sat in a glassy foyer with a garden outside, and the producer came and greeted us warmly, but then had to leave to take a phone call. He returned, upset, to say that he had orders from higher up not to proceed with the interview and that he had to comply. It was apparent that a similar operation to the one that threw silence round my Scargill book was at work and when – in spite of the journalists' interviews for several national dailies at the launch – no articles or reviews appeared, I knew there had been interference from higher up. But who from? Des now received two death-sentences from the IRA, both on the telephone. The Heroes of the West had risked their lives to improve things for the West, and had been rewarded by being told in effect: "We don't want you to recoup your investment in your book." I made phone calls.

The first to report back was Paul Gorka. He said: "I lunched with someone from the intelligence services who said, 'The intelligence services are engaged in damage limitation, in other words a cover-up following the raid on Libya, while at the same time investigating the Babysitter. The instructions for the scandal-limitation were issued by middle-ranking officialdom.' It is like Dean after Watergate, if you get any more publicity for the book it will expose the cover-up which could bring the government down. There is gratitude for the revelations, and they are being acted on, but the cover-up must continue."

I then received a call from Norris McWhirter, twin brother of Ross who had been shot by the IRA man I had encountered in Wandsworth prison, saying that Lord Whitelaw had asked him to see me. I visited him at his office. He had enthusiastically praised my Scargill book and advertised it in his Freedom Society's publication, *Free Nation*, and now he told me he had made enquiries through contacts, and the order had gone out "to kill the book with silence, the German word is 'totenstille', 'death by silence'. Tolstoy's book about the Cossacks being handed over to the Russians has had the same silent treatment."

McWhirter asked me if I knew who the fifth man was, and I gave him a detailed account of all I knew for two hours while he sat at his desk and took extensive notes. Some time later I was astonished to read in the papers a public appeal by Lord Victor Rothschild to Mrs. Thatcher to declare that he was not the fifth man, and Mrs. Thatcher at first publicly declined to give him the ringing endorsement he sought. The Heroes of the West had again stood up for what was right by not tolerating the influence of someone about whom allegations had been made.

A few days later McWhirter rang back to say he had negotiated a deal with the intelligence services. They would "neither confirm nor deny" that the publicity ban had happened; but would now allow limited publicity for the book. He was proposing to run a story in *Free Nation* that the intelligence services "would neither confirm nor deny that the Babysitter tried to suppress publicity for the book", and Eddie Shah would run a story. McWhirter said: "The Babysitter is now being smoked out." By forcing the intelligence services to act against the Babysitter, I had secured the objectives of the Heroes of the West – but the book would still have to operate in handicapped circumstances of silence, and would be lucky to cover its costs.

I reported the "death by silence" to Biggs-Davison and Julian Amery, who between them reported it to the Prime Minister's office, and I was rung up at 6.30 p.m. on July 16th by Christopher Monckton, an ex-aide to the Prime Minister who was now no 2 on the *Today* newspaper. He wanted to see Des and me urgently, could we be at Brooks's at 7.30. We could, and I told him the story from start to finish until 9.45, in the course of which we moved to the Ritz, and then he abruptly looked at his watch and had to leave, I understood for no 10. He wanted to meet us for breakfast at the Ritz at 8.30 a.m. the next morning, which we did. He arrived bleary-eyed, having read my Scargill book and *The World Held Hostage*, and placed his bowler hat on the table until our breakfast arrived. He then took us back to his office, which was completely empty, with a bare desk and no paper anywhere. He again put his bowler hat in front of him, this time on his bare desk, and made a phone call. He said: "I shall write an article about it for the front page, and I shall get it through the editorial conference." He rang Des at 12 to say he had got it through the editorial conference and that he would be visiting no 10 that afternoon. We could expect the front page story within the next couple of days.

Nothing appeared. When I rang to find out why, Christopher Monckton's attitude had changed. "The story was without foundation" was all he would say. Clearly someone had countermanded the deal McWhirter had spoken of. I now accepted that there was no more I could do. The Babysitter, the fifth man, an official in the intelligence services, or perhaps even the Prime Minister herself – someone had ordered silence, someone was grateful to the Heroes of the West for their revelations but was concerned to reduce their impact and squeeze their financial position. Some months later the *Times* used "The World Held Hostage" as a headline for their first leader, demonstrating that the title had quietly passed into the English language, and there was a very favourable review of the book by Lord Chalfont, who said that it should be on the shelves of every military academy, but by then the early sales drive was at an end.

I now turned my attention to Tomlin's book, which was being launched in September. I spent another day with Tomlin and mentioned my relief that a book on philosophy would give me a respite from tangling with the affairs of State. We drew up a list of guests, and I suggested Tuohy. He immediately vetoed it. "He knows Skeffington-Lodge in Brighton. With all the difficulty you've been having it would be unwise to have him." I did not understand this remark at all.

I had been to Vernon Davies's barbecue for his 40th birthday at his great house. A cover had been thrown over the swimming-pool to keep out the rain, there was a live band and a gargantuan feast (salmon, prawn and many meats) and the champagne flowed all night and 120 beautiful people cavorted and milled about, several falling into the swimming-pool at midnight, including Vernon himself. Earlier, I found Vernon sitting alone, and I told him he reminded me of the great Gatsby. He did not know about the book, so I told him that in Scott Fitzgerald's novel, Gatsby threw parties for vast numbers of people and absented himself from the guests, and that he was a romantic at heart. The evening was notable for a chance (or Providential) conversation I had with Ian Bennett, who ran DPS Computers in Basildon. As we stood in the long queue to eat he asked why I did not buy a computer from him, an Apple Macintosh, and employ a typist to work on the dining-room table and run the Oak-Tree accounts and key in some of Oak-Tree's books on it. I duly bought a computer from him, and used it initially for Oak-Tree work but very soon used the typist to key in the book that became *The Fire and the Stones*.

There was a family gathering for Argie who, on Ann's birthday, laid a time capsule under the new foundation stone of the new Methodist church (the old one I used to attend having been demolished). Matthew was at camp at Llandudno – as if Providence were nudging him into going to Bangor University 15 miles away, which he eventually did. We sat in the front row, and Biggs-Davison was present. He came and had a chat, and I told him: "There's a deafening silence about the book. It's not fair on Des, he's risked his life for the West." Biggs-Davison said he would speak to Amery.

One of the Oaklands employees died, Janet Wood, and at St. Peter's in the Forest I met her son, a classmate of mine at Chigwell School, Richard "Curly" Wood, the boy who had played charades in the Journey's End nursery, now straight-haired and suited and chatting confidently; the first time I had met him for 30 years.

A friend of Ann's, Tanya from Tooting, had married T. S. Eliot's nephew by marriage (Valerie's nephew). They visited Oaklands and we had tea on our patio and he told me how he burned down his prep school at 13, and reminisced about Eliot. Eliot had a reserved pew at St. Stephen's, Gloucester Road, and he had bought him a James Bond car. "Eliot was fascinated by James Bond, and played with the car on the floor with me. He kept saying, 'See if its boot opens, see if guns appear.'" He recalled a conversation about *The Family Reunion*: "He said, 'I don't know if Harry pushed her, I only wrote it.'" He told me they lived in Kensington, and Eliot's idea of a treat was to take him to Dino's, where I had often had coffee or lunch. "We'd sit in Dino's and he looked after me, made sure I had what I wanted." I said Eliot was great because he embodied the European tradition and stood for the wisdom of past generations. He said: "He was a hypocrite, he was sentimental."

We went to Stratford and saw *A Midsummer Night's Dream*, and I suddenly grasped that the new bride of Copped Hall had commissioned Shakespeare's *Sonnets*. I wrote: "Saw *A Midsummer Night's Dream*, Theseus and Hippolyta being Heneage and Mary, Countess of

A MYSTIC WAY

Southampton, whose marriage was celebrated in the Long Gallery at Copped Hall in 1594. The vision of spirits in the woods, i.e. Epping Forest: the Forest flowers including the blue 'love-in-idleness' which influences sleeping eyes, and the musk-rose and eglantine....1594, Southampton became Heneage's stepson. The sonnets were written 1592-4 according to one dating, so who put Shakespeare up to urging Southampton's marriage in the sonnets? Surely his mother? That is the key – 1594. After the wedding, Shakespeare was commissioned to write poems by Henry Wriothesley's mother. 'Thou art thy mother's glass and she in thee/Calls back the lovely April of her prime' (sonnet 3). The idea that Shakespeare lived outside London during the plague 1591-3. How he lived in Silver Street during his second period, with a Huguenot family." I have not checked the dating of the sonnets, I merely record the perception that came to me that Southampton's "onlie begetter", his mother, urged Shakespeare to write the early sonnets.

In early August we went on a whirlwind tour of the Continent. We drove to Ramsgate and crossed to Dunkirk, where the sun glinted on abandoned cranes and water where an army waded out, and we drove through Flanders' poppied field to Brugge or Bruges "which by night is magical: full of canals and moated medieval walls and Baroque buildings". We found accommodation near a windmill and then drank wine in the main square and looked at the Halles and Belfry. The next morning we walked to the Chapel of the Holy Blood. I wrote: "Downstairs, St. Basil and the dove and the chanting in Flemish (presumably not Walloon) and telling their rosary; the Grail cup on two flagstones – the ancient Templar Romanesque church c1150. Then upstairs; the ineffable atmosphere as Mozart played softly and I sat in the 19th century green and zigzag decoration and gazed at all the works of art, including the altar of the Holy Blood, which contained the phial brought back from the Crusades: the great sublimity, and peace I felt, the sense of a spirit free and soaring, having progressed from earth downstairs up to these heights in this double chapel: "Holy Blood and the Holy Grail. Then on to the Church of Our Lady, as the Belfry gave us a carillon of 57 bells, after a walk by the weeping willow. The spoked Light above the altar; 'Veritas' from which the Light streamed down. You cannot walk into a Continental Cathedral without realising that the Light is central to the Christian tradition." We drove on to Ghent and St. Bavo's Cathedral, and I wrote: "The same feeling, looking at Hubert and Jan van Eyck's *Mystic Lamb*, the Light rays streaming from heaven, and 1432 as yesterday. How close I felt to the Crusades and to the van Eycks' day, and to the vision of the Light. The Romanesque cellars and mural. Art and religion are at one on the Continent...: the works of art display religion in the churches, e.g. van Eycks, and Rubens' Christ descending from the cross at Antwerp, which we passed through." I noted the silage smells in the Belgian countryside and the wiff of drains in the Belgian towns.

Next we visited Holland. Amsterdam was full and we somehow stayed with a family in the Consulate of Madagascar in Roosevelt Street, and ate between Dam Square and the station. I noted: "Amsterdam is dirtier than Bruges, with more litter, and it is very cosmopolitan and somewhat sleazy." We took a river trip in a glass-topped boat and passed many Baroque fronts and visited Ann Frank's house and her hiding-place behind a folding bookcase. I wrote: "Her values on the walls of her room, all anti-war: films, the countryside, art, wild flowers, and Princess Elizabeth, the card of children as angels, and of course Rembrandt's famous self-portrait." We went on to Rembrandt's house "where he lived from 1639-1658, the years of the English civil war; and went bankrupt in 1656/7 and lost his son in 1668, a year before his death, aged 26. The start of the Baroque is in his portraits and dynamic life. (Cf Rubens at Antwerp)." We went on to the van Gogh museum and I wrote: "Cornfield with Crows, or rather Crows over a Wheatfield, June/July 1889, in the original, and the red path of the flesh leads nowhere, is blocked by the ears of corn....The flaming olive tree. Compare the Edge of a Wheatfield with a lark 1887. The pictures worth millions when he died poor."

We drove on to Germany and stayed in Bonn at the Hotel Beethoven by the Rhine, near Kennedy Bridge. We ate in the open by the Town Hall. There were swarms of midges on the outside of the hotel windows, and swarms of birds flew down the Rhine. We walked to the Minster Basilica. I wrote: "Christ on a rainbow above the altar, and spider web tracery stained glass, and the crypt 11th-12th century, and the great silence before the monstrance, the 'tomb' of Cassius and Florentinus behind, and 2 nuns as still as stone. A deep silence." We went on to Beethoven's House: "Beethoven's personal musical instruments, his growing deafness from 26 to 47. The ear trumpets and the testament letter, not in English."

We went on to Luxembourg. We stopped at Echternach, and I wrote; "The basilica below the abbey with the 'frescoes', i.e. the ceiling murals in the crypt....The tomb of Saint Willibrord, the first Anglo-Saxon to missionarise and evangelise the Germanic tribes." We went on to Luxembourg City, "which rises round a ravine", and stayed at the International Hotel opposite Central Station. The next morning we toured Luxembourg, "a city built on a gorge, fortified over the years with beetling walls that make it impregnable, and riddled underground with 17 miles of tunnels (the Bock) so that troops could be moved around in huge quantities without the enemy seeing. After lunch visited Notre Dame and the Bock, and were unable to get in to the Ducal Palace at 4."

We drove via Bourscheid castle in the Ardennes to Waterloo, where we stayed. We drove into Brussels and stood in the Market Square and looked at the Mannekin Pis, then returned to Waterloo. Next morning we toured the battleground. I wrote: "The Wellington Museum, where Wellington heard news that Blucher would join him, and therefore he resisted Napoleon's advance on Brussels near Waterloo, held the line until Blucher arrived (Napoleon thinking he was in flight). The lion of victory. The mount near where Gordon fell, where Wellington surveyed the battle amid the shells. The monument to Lord Uxbridge's amputated leg. From the lion, the English, Dutch, Belgians and Prussians were on the left, the French advanced up the road from the right. The house where Napoleon spent the night before in a green bed; the headquarters he used, the Bell Alliance where Wellington and Blucher met (100 metres to the south. The images of futile wars." We then drove via Lille to Dunkirk and caught the 5 p.m. boat.

A MYSTIC WAY

I then suddenly had the idea for the poem that became *A Pilgrim in Europe*. I wrote: "In the car queue, waiting to drive onto the Sally Line boat, had the idea for a great poem on Europe: on the past and present." I added: "A poem to be drafted on the meaning of Western civilisation in Europe. Through juxtaposition of images, contrast the town non-values with the enduring heritage to be found in Cathedrals and the countryside – the true values which have nothing to do with profit-making or wars, but with the spiritual and the relation of the everyday to the spiritual. Images: the Holy Blood, something preserved (Bruges); the Mystic Lamb – Light from Providence (Ghent); also the Light above the pulpit (Bruges). The Baroque (Amsterdam canals); and the vision of Rembrandt and van Gogh (energy in wheatfields, swirling stars, flaming cypress, etc). The force is contrasted with the opposing destructive force of wars: Arnheim, which destroyed the Cathedral; Echternach (Luxembourg), where the top was destroyed during the Ardennes offensive and the mutilated Christ survives, and the waters of life in the crypt, the unconscious, subterranean; and the Bock, the rock where troop movements fended off the invader. Finally Waterloo, the destruction of so many fine people.... Two forces: the creative, healing, enduring force of Christ and the Light ('Lux'embourg) and the destructive, assertive force of wars, money-making, the newspapers; and of the darker forces.... Christ and the Devil represent these two forces. Overall image for Europe: St. Michael the Dragon (in Luxembourg)."

Back in Essex, we went straight down to Cornwall and stayed with Ann's mother. The air relaxed and energised me, and I read up on megaliths, Eleusis, Pythagoras and Scandinavian mythology for *The Fire and the Stones*. I wrote: "Have been to Charlestown twice – calm seas, mist, familiar setting – and to Par beach yesterday, where I was windburnt and have a red body. Mornings work, afternoons beach and do not mind if it rains as I can get forward with my revision." I read on Yin and Yang and Taoism and observed: "Balance and harmony, in a garden. I have the Taoist Garden and an awareness of opposites (cf my *Silence*), and I deplore the lack of balance and lack of harmony with Nature in Western life: the hurry, the industrialisation that takes away from Nature, the unbalancing power-seeking and time-taking and influencing people. I would like to live like a hermit in my garden, contemplating and meditating and writing.... This is why I like Cornwall: as soon as I arrive here, the balance and harmony return, I live a balanced and harmonious life by true values." I observed: "Civilisation has lost its true balance, because it has lost the values of being close to Nature and is too materialistic.... Metaphysics assumes an inner meaning, and intellect above the human level and Absolute (Tao) on which all things depend..., that man is more than the aggregate of the body and its senses, whereas materialism and humanism recognise only the body and its senses.... 'Meta' = 'after' or 'beyond' physics. I am a Metaphysical.... Like Eckhart, I must establish a mystic-metaphysical school of thought, similar to the direct-knowledge school of the East." I wrote of "my sense of opposites in *The Silence* and my reconciliation of them: yin-yang-Tao. The microcosm and macrocosm are reflections of each other and are one. The Taoist ideas in *The Silence*."

I thought about women and wrote: "The Black Virgin who is found all over France and elsewhere is Mary Magdalene, a rival cult of love, cf Cathars, urging women to love truly and not within marriage, like the troubadours."

We went to Mevagissey and I noted "the calm sea, boys plunging into the harbour". I received pleasure from "branches against the sky and twigs". We went to Fowey and crossed over to Polruan and walked to the 15th century castle. We had tea in the Singing Kettle and I wrote: "A tortoiseshell strayed in and I caught it in my hand and let it go outside, bringing all conversation in the full café to a halt and leaving many smiling." We returned to Fowey and took a boat from the main square down the river to Golant, and I wrote: "We passed the industrialised bank, Golant side, where china clay trucks wait to have their loads shot down shutes into great ships for Finland, which takes 50% of the local china clay, and Germany, which takes 25%. China clay like bonfire smoke, as if the Finnish ship was on fire. Passed the ferry, and Daphne du Maurier's ivyed house, to Golant, and the church of St. Sampson on the brow of the hill, behind trees." We went to Gunwalloe and I wrote *At Gunwalloe: the Tao* during a golden day sitting on the beach near the church; watching the waves break on the distant rocks". I was still writing "my Light book" (as I thought of *The Fire and the Stones*) and noted "I am progressing towards a whole vision of civilisation."

I went out fishing from Newlyn with Ann's cousin and his partner Anthony and the fisherman Kingsley. I was up at 5.20, we left Newlyn at 6 a.m. and dropped two nets off the Lizard and another four in deeper water, "17 miles from Newlyn and 6 from the Lizard, long three quarters of a mile tennis nets of Japanese mono-filament weighted with chains and guarded by floats at each end, 7 feet above the bottom which was 35 fathoms (210 feet)." I wrote: "Saw a whale, a pilot whale with a curved fin humping up and down 7 times 50 yards away. Mainly caught monk (30 or 40), ray (20), turbot and brill (both brown and spotty and flat), 4 lobsters and a crayfish: some £500 worth of fish at the present good prices. Anthony had a very swollen knee and felt giddy... and lay down; I put on oilskins and took his place hauling the top part of the net (Kingsley did the weighted bottom) over the bar after it coiled off the winch.... The offal thrown out into the sea, the train of birds: common gulls...; a Manx sheerwater; a shag...; 3 fulmers (in the albatross family)...; a kittiwake; and many black-backed gulls, scavengers." The fishermen gave me tips: "Monk drown in the nets if the tide is high: not enough oxygen to flow through their gills. The sail keeps the boat steady, keeps its head to the wind so it goes up and down and not from side to side, and gives a better platform for working. Ray will bite your finger and suck it in. The old fishermen steered by course and time and the sun to find their nets. 'Always look the way of the wind, Nicholas' (Kingsley) – a shower coming, and he was right. The fulmer spits up food, dogfish, the only fish that blink. Star rays with false eyes. Angler fish with phosphorescent lights.... I steered back to harbour, turning now to leeward, now to windward (port, starboard), i.e. left/right. 'Don't fish when there is a tide as the currents at the bottom flatten the nets which only stand up 6 or 7 feet anyway, and they get full of seaweed and no fish, and the net fouls through being dragged along the ground.'" When I returned home "the floor was lurching like a boat" and I observed that "I totter and stagger like a sea-dog".

I worked on the early Church in Britain and the Grail and I wrote: "Perhaps we have been sent down from a world of light into an inherently evil world, in which evil acts outweigh good and the evil ego outweighs the self – and in this 'Hell' we have to do as much good as possible before we return. There is love and beauty. The 'meaning of life' must include our aim and some view of spiritual values." I now wrote: "Oak-Tree's image should now be one of restoring a purpose in religion and philosophy, i.e. bringing about a metaphysical revolution."

I wrote an introduction to Tomlin's book, *The Tall Trees of Marsland* (which I never published) "and then went for a walk by Charlestown harbour to ponder the introduction to my own Light book. The tide was very high, at least 7 feet and the sea crashed onto the shingle which gave a disapproving hiss while the boys threw stones at each dark curl of a wave. Water lapped onto the harbour stones which stood opposite the pier." I understood that my Baroque concept referred to "the reality within and behind the senses" and urged myself: "Have a metaphysical revolution. Eliot and Pound had a poetry revolution. Can Tomlin and I not have a metaphysical revolution?... Get the metaphysical idea into our culture."

We all visited Marsland, where Tomlin had lived, and found Tall Trees at Gooseham Mill. I wrote: "The muddy lane. The stream. No one there." I wandered round Tall Trees peering through windows at where my boss had lived in Cornwall. We went on to Morwenstow, and visited the churchyard and found the eccentric Parson Hawker's hut on the sea-cliffs. The next day "on a rainy day, without undue preparation 'out of nowhere' (I) typed the last part of the conclusion to my book on the Inner Light.... The secular and metaphysical.... Take each civilisation in turn and prove the life cycle of the Inner Light within it." I reminded myself: "I must stay away from all sects and creeds so that I can be impartial about all." At this stage I thought of calling my Light book *The Inner Light* and *World Culture*, and I worked on it through a hurricane and recorded: "It came to me that Tomlin had taken Eliot's dissociation of sensibility and applied it not to thought and feeling (Donne) but to intellect/reason (Descartes) – I think therefore I am. The scientific revolution was behind the dissociation of sensibility, not the Civil War. Ricks to me: 'Do you believe it? I don't believe in the dissociation of sensibility.'"

I went to Charlestown at 7.30. "A green sea, stormy, and huge rollers that washed over the pier and crashed onto the shingle, dashing spray over our rocks and up the cliff, and smashing against the concrete breakwater at the top of the beach. All action and movement and dynamic energy – so different from the calm of two nights ago, the still." I noted: "Holiday-time for me is a reversion to the long term from the day-to-day. I like the watchful, joyful existence of the purposive scholar and poet." I made "one last visit to Charlestown at 11 p.m. on the night of Hurricane Charlie. Still a hugely high tide – still up to the wall. I was the only human around (drizzle in the wind) and the light on the pier was out and as I walked to the end, braving the spray, I could not see farther than 40 yards into a dark sea (no moon, no stars, no light) and on the large moundy rocks which I could hardly make out the white foam was luminous – all I could see in the dark as I peered was the breaking white foam across the bay. A very exciting, elemental prospect."

On 2nd September I held the launch of E. W. F. Tomlin's *Philosophers of East and West* at the Athenaeum Ladies' Annexe, downstairs among the sofas. We had about 40, and I spoke for 10 minutes, about Oak-Tree's probing of Western values and Tomlin's contrast of 5,000 years of a metaphysical tradition with the anti-metaphysical Vienna Circle and called for a change in philosophy, for a Metaphysical Revolution, to achieve which was part of the work of the Heroes of the West, as I thought. I compared Tomlin's role to Whitehead's as an original philosopher who had written about other philosophers: "This book is his *Science and the Modern World*." Tomlin, who was very fidgety, spoke next. He went off to his briefcase to look for his speech and returned without it, and I said to him, "You must speak without notes as I did," which he did. Then Kathleen Raine spoke, mentioning Plato's Philosopher-King. Kathleen Nott, the Chinese Cultural Attaché, Andrew Lownie and John Ezard were among the guests, and Tomlin's sister from Winchester was present. Several of the guests came and spoke to me, and assumed that I was a professional philosopher following my speech.

The next morning Kathleen Raine rang ("It's Kathleen") and I observed: "(She) repeated that politics cannot solve our problems, that it all came down to value-systems: 'Plato in the *Republic* asks, what is good for society? It isn't materialism and computers and atom bombs – that's not what's good for society. We have to start again.' All the political parties are wrong. Ezard rang and said, 'All our bureaucrats read Plato at school, and they still get it wrong.' Will go back to Plato. The thing is, the West is living by wrong values, although Communist values are worse. My Oaklands 'garden' (the school hall) should become a metaphysical academy. I should have it inscribed in Greek: the metaphysical academy (akademia metaphusika)."

I now had time to explore the Roding, in accordance with my resolve a few weeks previously. I wrote: "A glorious late summer day, not too hot, and a walk with Mabel Reid by the Roding – from Roding Lane, the bridge, past the humped back bridge, I pushed my cycle across en route to Chigwell (the route now cut by the M11), past the lake where men windsurfed and got duckings, past another bridge and a blasted ash to the 'Loughton Bridge' I cross, near the end of Oakwood Hill by the junction to the motorway. On one side of the 2 mile walk – the Chigwell Hall side – willows; on the other, thistles with bearded seed, and purple loosestrife and nettles. A flock of whitethroats, a pippet. Saw viper's bugloss, teasle, burdock, purple mallow (cf Spengler's comparison between mallow and a civilisation) and many red haws on the hawthorn bushes. Our Avon. Next time, to Passingford Bridge and the mill from where we left off – back towards its Dunmow source. The last day of cricket on the flood meadows. Later, tea with Mabel, and a walk in her walled garden. 8 newts in her pond (one great-crested), no walnuts because the birds had eaten them (shells underneath), one quince on her quince tree but many mulberries on her mulberry bush – we all ate one. 'Lovely jam.' 'Yes, but actually it's a year old.' (My face set the boys into giggles.)"

Now much of the day-to-day Oak-Tree effort was laid at my door. I employed a local typist to key addresses into the computer for a mail-shot, and I personally tramped round the London bookshops, delivering copies of McForan's and Tomlin's books to Foyles and Waterstones and other booksellers. In early September my compilation of Jack Wood's papers came out, *Union for Recovery*, a radical plan based on his experience in the Transport and General Workers Union for workers to work fewer hours and achieve greater productivity and reverse Britain's industrial decline by having harmonious industrial relations. I spent hours on the telephone organising the transfer of books and liaising with my distributor.

While I did such chores the themes of the two books (one on terrorism, one on philosophy) were dramatically brought to my attention. I went for drinks with Anne Clarke, who asked: "If there is a kind, loving God, why does he allow the innocent to suffer?" I wrote: "Nature – everything lives off everything else, the bird off the worm, man off the chicken, etc., why do the innocent victims suffer? Why do children get raped by Stavrogins? Why are the innocent gunned down by terrorists? In Blake's words, did he who made the lamb make the cruel tiger? The principle of gentleness and savagery together. Why are men like wild beasts? A Dostoevskian question. If there are opposing gentle and bestial principles in man and his feelings, why do the innocent suffer? If there is more than one life, then everything is karmic, and one life-time is not especially important. We come again. But if there is only one life – why do such evil things happen, to children and to dumb animals. Can a loving God allow it? Every animal is given a chance with camouflages and false eyes; why the risk?" The next day the question was answered by an article by Montefiore (the Bishop of Birmingham) about the lightning strike at Durham Cathedral, saying (I wrote) "that God cannot interfere in the natural laws he has ordained to deliver from Auschwitz, prevent Hiroshima, overcome famine, or bring about a bloodless transformation of apartheid, all of which were created by man's wickedness (famine by the Marxists), and with which suffering Christ identified by becoming one with salvation – and eternal life is better than food and a relief from suffering. The answer to the question, then, is that man is wicked, and that there is eternal life, that God helps the insulted and the injured in the eternal dimension."

On a glorious afternoon I wrote: "A walk in the fields in glorious sunshine. The leaves are turning: there is a yellow, a deep red (hawthorn). Looked at the wood in the oaks. The yew. It is a paradise here on a sunny morning. There is such variety. All Nature is here. The poet in me sang."

I now threw myself into launching Paul Gorka's *Budapest Betrayed*, which stood up to Philby and the KGB he now represented. Biggs-Davison booked the launch in the Palace of Westminster and arranged for Julian Amery to speak again. I had agreed to bring out a Hungarian version of the book, and, not speaking Hungarian, left all questions regarding the accuracy of the language to Paul. Nevertheless, I found that bringing out a book in both English and Hungarian was time-consuming.

About six weeks before the launch Jessica Douglas-Home, Charlie's widow, rang and asked if she could join "your Hungarian day". I knew of her interest in Iron Curtain countries. She invited me to dinner at 63 Hillgate Place, Notting Hill Gate, in "a charming road of 1850s houses built for those who built the railway, each painted a different colour". I spent an hour with her in what used to be Charlie's house, drinking white wine and discussing the guest list (during which I said I would invite the Prime Minister), and then went downstairs and ate: beetroot soup and meat casserole and rice, followed by cheese and red wine. Roger Scruton appeared at 8, open-necked shirt and rimmed glasses, and we talked at length while Jessica brought in a pair of hens and cut off their wing feathers with scissors. Scruton: 'You're mad, Jessica.' 'They're pets, they won't fly over the wall.' Later her son rang and asked about Fascism, which Scruton told him about; in loco parentis. Eventually I left them to it as they had an hour together to do." It was at this dinner that Jessica told me that her late husband had kept the Scargill book on his desk, and when I raised the question of FREE with Scruton he said: "Unless they're parachuted in, they'd be betrayed. It is so well sewn up they'd be betrayed and killed." I thought this conclusion unnecessarily pessimistic and defeatist. I wrote later: "The Light prompts Eastern Europe to join the European Community and not be a prison camp.... The Light wants world unity in which all men are brothers, and capitalism was checked by Communism so that a new order, which is neither, can evolve, with true values; and it wants the spirit to return to China – and to the Soviet Union; to have overt expression there."

I went to Frankfurt on my own. It took me all day to arrive there because Gatwick was closed due to fog and the company I was flying with had just ceased trading. I was reallocated to Heathrow and eventually flew Pan Am, arrived at the Messe at 5.30 and booked accommodation in a flat. Once there, I walked through the dark to a nearby restaurant that served magnificent steak and peppers under swords on the walls. My flat had a television with getting on for 20 channels, one of which was in English, and a table, and next morning I went to the Messe by tram and came out in good time in the evening and watched television and wrote, and by the end of my stay I had interest from 35 different companies in the US, South Africa, Israel, Australia or Singapore, each of which wanted a copy of one or other of the books I had published. As a result of this visit there were American and Singapore editions of *The World Held Hostage*.

When I returned to England I had an unexpected visit from Nadia, who was staying in Dulwich. She looked relaxed and glamorous, and she came again the next day, "a sunny, golden October day. We drove to the pond. The uprooted tree in whose network of roots she once crouched. The sandy gravel surround. The still, rather dank water. On to High Beach church, the church in the Forest. The runic stone, which quotes from *Beowulf*. Its medieval style (spire and hammerbeam roof) – Neo-Gothic like Lopping Hall."

A MYSTIC WAY

After my visit to the Duke of Grantesmil I had said to Paul Gorka at one of our Heroes of the West meetings in his house: "I don't see why someone doesn't organise a petition of Iron Curtain names calling for democracy." I said: "Whoever does it should act as if they are free and move freely and blatantly collecting signatures from key people in the Eastern European regimes." Paul Gorka had put this to one of Hungary's leading dissidents, Krasso, who had subsequently organised a petition from 122 Eastern Europeans from Hungary, Poland, Czechoslovakia and East Germany without being betrayed or killed. I attended a press conference at which a Hungarian-Romanian accord was announced (Paul Gorka representing Hungary) and met Krasso. I wrote: "My idea got across to Paul after we visited the Duke, and Paul got it across to Krasso....Krasso, white-haired, smiling-eyed, a believer in his cause, a latter day Lenin. At one level, the overt, there is a declaration, a demand for democracy. At the covert level he can organise disturbances and resistance. He has the eyes of a revolutionary. He is a Robespierre." In Krasso I saw that my FREE idea could still find some expression, and I put the idea to him. He reacted very favourably and enthusiastically, and said he would introduce me to the leading Soviet dissident, Bukovsky, who was based in France where he was engaged in stockpiling arms to subvert the USSR.

I lunched with Vernon. I wrote: "We had a glass of wine in his huge sitting-room overlooking the lawn... and then were chauffeured in the new... BMW, complete with arm and footpads to the Chinese restaurant in Abridge, where we ate by ourselves: crispy duckling in wafer-thin 'rolls' eaten with fingers, sauce dripping through; sweet and sour; chicken and cashew nuts; and prawns. Very tasty with Chablis. Vernon on how he is selling a block of offices in Farnham for double, having got planning permission; he is taking a stake in a company that will float itself on the Stock Exchange.... His suggestion... that I should go in with another publisher... to profit from their distribution.... He would be Chairman of a company that publishes 'less sensitive' books." I wrote: "The model for Oak-Tree. A trust into which American money can be poured, with Vernon as Chairman..., and the editing of *Western Review*." I added: "Vernon is Count Axel: 'As for living our servants will do that for us.' He runs a (19th century) Russian-type estate, and Hilda is in the school and at badminton, seldom there to enjoy it."

We all spent a weekend in Glastonbury, staying at Street. I wrote: "A 6 hour drive through lashing rain, spray and traffic caused by road-works. Arrived at 11, and then ate, the night porter huffing and puffing, soup and a cold salad. A comfortable night in this flat, and then through today's rain to Glastonbury... and thence to Wookey Hole, the model for the geography of the Roman Hell, and the papermill and then on to Cheddar Gorge (Gough's cave). Many stalagtites and stalagmites. On to Priddy, where Jesus spent time at the Roman lead mine. On to Wells: the Cathedral, tea at the place that Penn addressed 3,000. (From a window.)" The next day, October 26th, was fine: "Breakfasted, then straight up the Tor. Very windy, a spectacular view. Down to the Chalice well. Felt very poetic, scribbled images sitting in the shade looking up at the Tor. Was then invited to look over Tudor Pole's house, including his 'Last Supper' room. All a bit druidy. On to Gog and

Magog, a walk down a track, left and then over a stile. Very wide trunks, 2,000 years old. On to Joseph's Holy Thorn on Wearyall Hill; he must have landed by boat, and from that spot (where he was weary) one gets a good idea of the isle of Avalon: Wearyall Hill, Chalice Hill and the Tor, and seawater all round, and then must have been a kind of semi-submerged causeway to Pomparles Bridge. Lunched in Glastonbury, then hunted in St. John's churchyard for Joseph's tomb (JA) – in vain – and then revisited the Abbey dwelling on the Lady Chapel and Arthur's resting place. On to Bridgewater and thence, on the Minehead road, to Nether Stowey. Coleridge's house (shut) where he wrote *Kubla Khan* and *The Ancient Mariner*. The pub of that name across the road. On to Watchet, a port on the Bristol Channel, the setting for the *The Ancient Mariner* with its lighthouse, hill (covered by two cranes) and Methodist church. Back via Alfoxton House (now a hotel) where Wordsworth wrote the *Prelude* and lived with Dorothy. The legacy from Raisley Calvert.... Returned with reddened faces from the wind and sun." The following day: "Home via Joseph of Arimathaea's altar tomb in St. Catherine's chapel, in the Glastonbury parish church – Christendom's biggest secret – and the face of Christ at Templecombe Templar church."

On November 2nd Gorka took me to 55 Exhibition Road for a "solemn commemoration" of the 30th anniversary of the Soviet crushing of the Hungarian Revolution. "Sir Braine" and Winston Churchill spoke. I noted that Churchill "gripped my hand hard and said 'Nice to meet you'". Afterwards I discussed the US and Soviet spheres of influence with Sir Bernard Braine, who confirmed that the superpowers had reached a deal in Kissinger's day that the world should have "spheres of influence" and that the US would do nothing to disturb the status quo. "Any attempt to do that would be obsolete and dangerous," Braine told me in an obvious echo of Josten's position. I found this position unnecessarily defeatist, and said so, and I wrote: "All the secrecy was merely a method of containing (me)."

Afterwards I talked with Krasso, and he asked me to organise him a travel document (in lieu of a passport) and political asylum. I duly wrote a letter to the Foreign Office on his behalf. Soon afterwards I heard the news from Gorka that Bukovsky was founding an East European Resistance movement, and that Gorka and Krasso would be the Hungarian representatives. I wrote: "The Moslems will separate from Russia and be spiritual. Russia will return to its spiritual destiny." FREE was becoming a reality through Eastern European dissidents my Heroes of the West author Gorka had introduced.

The next day was the launch of Gorka's book in the Jubilee Room at the Palace of Westminster. The Hungarian flag was draped over the front table and the 60 guests included representatives from every Iron Curtain country (Czechoslovakia, Poland, Hungary, Romania, Estonia, etc., and there were two bearded Afghans). The five speeches were broadcast behind the Iron Curtain by the BBC. Biggs-Davison spoke first about my "campaign", then I spoke directly to the Eastern European audience about the need for resistance to the USSR, and called for a free Eastern Europe and a reunified Eastern and Western Europe. I denounced Philby's betrayal of British agents in Hungary and drew attention to the list of 45 who were executed as a result. Julian Amery then supported my vision of Europe. Then I introduced Krasso, "the Leninist genius", and described his petition of 122 calling for democracy. When Krasso had spoken I introduced Gorka. The leader writers of the *Daily Telegraph* and the *Times* were present, together with a specialist at the *Guardian*, and also present were Jessica Douglas-Home, Ian Crowther (representing the *Salisbury Review*) and Vernon Davies. As usual several MPs who had accepted did not turn up, but Virginia Bottomley came; her father John Garnett, had written the Foreword to Jack Wood's book. We had not invited Sir Bernard Braine as he would have regarded the occasion as too "dangerous", and the Prime Minister did not attend, but sent me a message of support through Julian Amery's secretary, who was rung earlier. The ex-Prime Minister of the Polish Government in Exile, Sabbat, was present and as I helped him on with his coat at the end he said to me: "When I was Prime Minister of the Polish Government in Exile I had the intelligence services under me and I found out something which is not in the history books. Near the end of the war there was a deal between the superpowers in Teheran – it was confirmed at Yalta – involving the present Winston Churchill's grandfather. It condemned the East Europeans to slavery, and the West abided by the deal when Hungary was invaded by the Soviet Union in 1956 just as the other side abided by it in relation to Suez. You are to be congratulated. You have just challenged that deal and the entire British foreign policy since the war, which has been wrong. I want to shake your hand." I was shocked – if it was true – that Churchill had given away Eastern Europe to Stalin. Gorka was delighted with the evening and said he would introduce me to Otto Habsburg, the heir to the Austro-Hungarian and Holy Roman empires. I took the Gorkas to dinner, and they left arm in arm. Mrs. Gorka understood our stand against Philby and the KGB. She said: "You will now be on a blacklist, you will be the first to be hanged when the Russians come to London. You are exposed now. Your children will never get visas to Hungary or Russia." I said: "When, not if, when Communism falls we will have red carpet treatment there." I wrote: "I have done my duty, and the Light is well pleased. I may now be allowed to get back to my own work, to the metaphysical work.... The Light has done what it wanted with me, now I must return to it.... I have challenged the division of Europe by the two superpowers, and want to see a reunited Europe re-emerge." It is worth noting that after my stand Mrs. Thatcher made letting Eastern European nation-states into Europe a part of her European policy, and introduced a number of Eastern European leaders from the platform one Conservative Party Conference.

Once again the book was surrounded by silence. Reviews did not appear, and Andrew Lownie wrote a letter defending the role of the intelligence service. The one good thing to happen from my point of view was that though I expected to pay for the drinks consumed at the launch, the account was never presented. Somewhere out there I had an ally, a friend, who would not declare himself or herself, who picked up the tab without letting me know.

I looked at the state of Oak-Tree's finances and the prospect of further silences round my Heroes of the West books, and I now turned my attention again to poetry and wrote: "Genius is the metaphysical spring that flows through a man.... Resist not evil, but overcome evil with good. Resist not materialistic Communism, but overcome Communism with the Light." I wrote: "From now on religion and metaphysics, not politics." I wrote that Rodin had focused on "sin, Hell, sexual contortion, promiscuity... but miss(ed) Paradise – the thinker (Dante) brooding over it all; yet what power he gets, more power than anyone since Michelangelo, e.g. in the Burghers of Calais....The poet as shaman, healer, prophet." I now returned to the Light book.

I had often told Gorka that we needed a meeting of exile representatives of all the Captive Nations, and following the launch and my rapport with Sabbat I urged him to convene a meeting. Gorka and I went to the Polish Government in Exile, 43 Eaton Place, London, and I was probably the only Briton present at a gathering involving the Head of Radio Free Europe, and I asked the leaders of the exile government: "What can Radio Free Europe do to help them liberate themselves from the Soviet, occupying power?" And again I urged the formation of a committee under Polish supervision.

I received a visit from an insurance man who valued the Oaklands estate as being in excess of £1 million, and aware that I had somehow become a paper millionaire in the course of pursuing the Mystic Way, I wrote: "The Light will look after my lungs and my bank balance if it wants me to do its work – something I believe implicitly which is akin to trust in God. For the Light is God." I knew: "I must now become the great poet I should have become. The angels have arranged for spiritual works to predominate over political now.... I must now realise my life's destiny, having become a millionaire."

On November 27th I saw Bukovsky and Krasso at 55 Exhibition Road, with Gorka in attendance. I found Bukovsky an immensely likeable, straight-talking Russian who spoke fluent and excellent English and had thought about a number of points I raised. I wrote: "As a result of our meeting, which I chaired, Krasso's dissidence will flow into Bukovsky's Resistance International, which is to have a new initiative, the FREE Movement." I added: "Lord (Victor) Rothschild: questions in the Commons about his being fifth man."

I was in pain. I felt as if I had a bullet in my right lung, at the back. My doctor diagnosed pleuritis. I then heard that Tomlin was in the Charing Cross Hospital in Fulham Palace Road having had a prostate operation. He sent me a message: "I miss my sherry." And so I took him a bottle. I wrote: "He looked flushed, with a fever from an infection which gave him a thrombosis that morning, the day after his prostate was removed; it was dispersed by water poured down his tube, which was sticking out of his pyjama trousers. The great philosopher sitting up in bed with a tube sticking up between his legs. 'This is the decline of Western civilisation. And on Radio 2 all day long on the earphones, a stream of twaddle.' Put his sherry bottle which I had brought him by his bed."

I now learned that the government had decided not to allow ex-spies to publish their memoirs of government activities, and that authors like Peter Wright would have their books suppressed. It seemed that this was the context for my year's publishing and that Gorka's book may have been put on a list. Later the MP Ivor Stanbrook and a contact I had in the Cabinet Office both gave me the impression that I was a victim of the government's drive against Wright.

PART FOUR

THE UNITIVE WAY

11.

GROWING UNIVERSALISM AND GLOBAL VISION:
COOPERSALE HALL, AUTHOR AND
METAPHYSICAL REVOLUTION
1986 – 1991

The Unitive Way approaches the One, the summit to which all paths lead where, sun-like, the Light shines most clearly. In the unitive vision the world is seen spread out below as a unity that includes philosophy, science and history. My growing Universalism was a natural expression of my growing unitive vision, as was my awareness that the Fire is behind the universe and is central to all civilisations. Perceiving the unity of the universe and feeling it at a deep level, the soul creates unifying works which demonstrate the fundamental Oneness behind multiplicity.

Something now happened to my energy flow. It was as if I permanently opened to a movement of energy from the universe into my universal being, and now had permanent unitive being. On December 7th I received many surges from the Light. I wrote: "Dec 7. Sunday evening.... Asked the Light to send its wisdom into Matthew and immediately received not the usual 4 surges but 8 – the first time the 4 barrier has ever been broken, surges into Matthew's head via my spine, arm and finger (little finger of right hand). I said to Matthew: 'Your ignorance must be very great!' Have just asked for wisdom and have had another 10 surges – in fact they could go on coming in. 'Belief' in God is feeling a shiver of help up the spine; that is prayer, opening the spine and letting the Light solve problems.... God is fire in the head, yes, but also a shiver up the spine.... My spine is a – shudder, and I can see the Light like the sun in a puddle; as I gaze at the reflection.... I am filled with power – there has been a breakthrough today: many surges, over 30 so far (10.35 p.m.) from before 10 o'clock p.m. and the power is still coming through as I write. I have been fully 'divinised', perhaps. I am now in constant touch with the Light. Every day I can call its power, wisdom and healing energy into use. Dec 7 still, 11.05. Only now is the power abating, partly because I want it to. Have been sitting on the bed in the bedroom, feeling the power pour up my spine and prickle my scalp and swirl fire-like Light in my soul. My 3rd eye. Saw the universe as an eyeball with a million mottled stars like flecks. This was a 'shewing'. Something extraordinary has happened to me today.... The Light poured in as I have described, and kept going for over an hour, so I felt floating on it, sustained by it, encouraged. This is the best 'encouragement' for my Light book that I could have had. Now I glow all over. All my fingers shine. I am full of Light. And still it surges up my spine and into my head. Kundalini, the union of Shiva and Sakti. All my chakras are connected and filled with it – solar plexus, heart, throat, head. My heart and my head are at one. Christianity. You are supposed to sit and 'open your' back and pray to shivers and shudders and

511

prickles while the priest's voice is heard, and then sing to open the heart chakra. There has to be an interior correspondence to the service; otherwise the service degenerates into a secularised social form....The Kundalini energy rose as healing before, but now, after tonight, at 1.50 a.m. it is still there and able to sweep up my back in waves and tingle my cheeks; and I know that my energy-circuit is complete."

I returned to the Light book, and wrote: "What I am saying in the Light book: the Light is behind all cultures, and is a common ground for a world-wide culture; it reconciles all faith and is a new metaphysical vision."

I now read that Mrs. Thatcher and Peter Wright (the author of *Spycatcher*) together cleared Lord (Victor) Rothschild of being the fifth man. I was puzzled, and happened to speak about it to Andrew Lownie. I was told: "Rothschild tipped Philby off and confessed to being the fifth man. He was offered a deal and turned, and so Thatcher and Wright are clearing him to confuse the Russians. Wright's friendship with Rothschild is based on his confession." Looking back, I could see that when Lord Rothschild was Head of Heath's think-tank he was instrumental in handling Heath's response to the miners' strike of 1973-4 and in choosing the mistaken election date which lost the Conservatives the election. A few days later I had a Heroes of the West meeting with Des McForan at "the Oak-Tree office", i.e. the Charing Cross Hotel. He confirmed from his enquiries that the intelligence services had blocked his book, and he named four people involved in the operation. Des urged me to publish a sequel he had in mind, about Hitler and Fascism.

I had been in correspondence with Sir George Trevelyan, whose book on architecture I was supposed to be reprinting. Sheldrake had urged me to publish it. I had already decided on *The Fire and the Stones* as the title for my book, for I wrote: "A card from Sir George Trevelyan. Printed by Acorn Publishing, showing a gateway and a spire, and quoting (in response to my *Fire and Stones*) Teilhard de Chardin's 'for the second time in the history of the world, man will have discovered fire'." This is of interest as Teilhard was one of the Illuminati. I continued: "What is the starting point of *The Fire and the Stones*?"

I was now using the computer and my typist to work at the beginnings of *The Fire and the Stones*. Pat came each Tuesday and worked on the dining-room table and I tackled "a survey of the world's cultures and of all experiences of the Inner Light". I agreed with Tomlin that a civilisation starts with a metaphysical vision which turns secular, and I wrote of "a metaphysical path which our world culture needs" and of "the need for a mass return to the Inner Light in our world-wide civilisation" – a mass Metaphysical Revolution not on the part of élites (New Age) but at a religious level; Christianity needs a new Reformation to reawaken the masses to the Inner Light..., one world-wide religion whose ceremonies draw on the Inner Light, in which all religions have a place – a mystic way for all men, a religious revival... a new universalism. The Universalist movement within the Church as Christians move out and find common ground with non-Christians in the Light."

Christmas came. Again I ascetically wrote, "I don't like this materialistic conception of Christmas.... How I emotionally hate surfeit." The family party was held at the Roebuck. We had a long table in the Beech Room and all wore hats and drank sparkling wine. Everyone seemed overworked or slightly unwell. Some of the children rolled on the floor.

I visited Mabel Reid, who was in St. Margaret's Hospital, having dropped a gatepost and taken the skin off her shin; and then Miss Root, who "lay in bed, a bag of skin and bones. I sat by her bed, lamp with naked bulb on the floor, electric fire, and we talked. White hair."

Back in my research I wrote: "There is a conflict of secular ideologies (Communist v Capitalists) but I am in favour of a return to a traditional metaphysical vision, a world unity with a new world-wide culture and religion.... I was right to be on the side of Christendom and against the New Age in my 4 poems. But the synthesis is to reconcile both as a religion, not a spiritual movement – so that the masses are involved." I wrote: "There is a great ease about my writing. Drunk after the family lunch, I effortlessly edited and cut the last part. It is all coming through from elsewhere."

I was aware of infused knowledge as I wrote: "The wisdom is pouring in, tingling my spine, involuntarily as I work on editing *The Fire and the Stones*. It comes when I contemplate a new world political order – for which I have worked by getting Krasso and Bukovsky together to build a reunified Europe – and a new religion. My task is to effect a metaphysical revolution in the world's sensibility, to bring metaphysics back as a respectable subject by drawing attention to the fundamental metaphysical experience. There will be strain as I do this, and the angels want me to do it, and have sent me palliatives on the way (the financial means from Oaklands, etc.).... The angels want the Light book out of me.... I am building one world – and one world-wide religion."

It was announced in the press that a new right wing pressure group in education had met. I observed: "Jessica Douglas-Home has hostessed the Hillgate Group (Cox, Marks, Norcross, Scruton – and herself) in Hillgate Place – which is our modern equivalent of Bloomsbury. When I dined with Jessica and Scruton, it was like dining with Lytton Strachey and Lady Ottiline Morrell."

In 1987 I slowly became less of a publisher and more of an author (of *The Fire and the Stones*), but I was not clear of politics yet.

In early January I wrote: "My *Fire and the Stones* – the Light manifesting in culture or the Light contrasted with materialism. I am giving evidence for what I assert, and if the tradition is accepted the next stage is to write part 2 on philosophy explaining what the implications are for all the anti-metaphysical creeds."

Soon after term began there was heavy snow two days running, and both days I went out and swept the paths in the school and came in glowing for breakfast. Matthew was doing a jigsaw on Bruges and I was happy and wrote: "These wonderfully heady snowy days – and I am searching and researching across 5,000 years of history, blissfully happy, losing myself." I collected Mabel Reid from St. Margaret's Hospital and drove her home and then on to Argie's, where she was staying.

In the middle of the snow the Heroes of the West came up with the idea that I should publish a book on the Prime Minister's speeches before the coming election. I made an appointment to meet Michael Alison, the Prime Minister's PPS in the Central Lobby of the House of Commons. I arrived and filled in cards for the police, but there was a mix-up and Alison did not appear. Eventually he rang from no. 10 and said: "Can you come straight over? Walk over and be here by a quarter to." I duly paddled through the snow and thick slush to the policeman at the end of Downing Street, who radioed to check that I was authorised, and I strode up to the front door where I had seen Eden receive Bulganin and Krushchev, and a policeman said "Mr Hagger?" and opened the door and I found myself in the lobby, where one of two policemen said, "Mr Alison is on his way." I stood and waited near the picture of Downing, holding my briefcase and "drinking in the spaciousness, the fireplace with flowers in it, the pictures, and then Alison's secretary came and lead me into the interior, past three or four doors and then left to a room where someone was on the phone. He put the phone down and pushed magazines in my direction. Soon in walked Alison, tall and gangling." I discussed the idea with Alison, who said: "I shall put the idea to the Prime Minister, but I can't guarantee her reply. It's a good idea."

On the way out the most extraordinary situation happened: "I passed a gaggle of suited men in the corridor of power waiting to go into a ground floor room" (it was the 'A' team waiting to meet the Prime Minister) "and greeted one: 'Hello Lord Whitelaw.' He ran along behind me, 'Very nice to see you again, nice to see you, nice to see you, very nice to see you.'" I had the no 2 of the government trotting along behind me, and no doubt recognising the work I had done while apologising for the silence round the books. I wrote: "I swept out feeling full of the power of Downing Street. I like it in Downing Street. The values are all corrupt, but I understand what it's like to be a Prime Minister. Watching Bulganin and Krushchev go through the door in 1956, I never thought one day I too would cross that threshold." Nothing came of the idea involving the Prime Minister.

I now spoke to one or two publishers with a view to taking over a publishing house, but after several deflections gave up to write *The Fire and the Stones*, during which I recorded: "I have woken up with past memories: one of making love near an Egyptian temple column (a memory from 4,000 years ago)." I saw Peter Milward, the Jesuit priest from Japan, who wanted me to publish two books. We met in the "Oak-Tree office" (the Charing Cross Hotel) and he told me: "I feel more contact with an Anglican traditionalist than with a Catholic liberal." I wrote: "I am treading a path to Rome. My ideal is the Ecumenical Movement in which Protestants, Catholics and Orthodox are all reunited, and the barriers between East and West are broken down." On the same day, paradoxically, I wrote of "the purifying element in sex, sluicing clear the energies". I thought of "the poet's metaphysical role" and wrote: "The poet as a latter-day shaman, inspired."

The Polish Government in Exile and Gorka had between them at last implemented the committee of exiles for which I had pressed so long. Between a dozen and twenty now met monthly in the Free Polish headquarters at 43 Eaton Place, just as I had proposed. Gorka was in the chair and sent out the agenda, and every Iron Curtain nation was represented, including the Baltic Captive Nations, and I was the only non-East European present. We discussed how to overthrow Communism in Eastern Europe and the USSR, and I frequently spoke strongly in favour of resistance and urged unrest. I found the representatives very reluctant to plan anything insurrectionary, not least because they did not trust everyone at the table and feared that some may be reporting to the KGB, but after each meeting we all felt progress was being made.

I arranged to buy the allotments from Miss Lord, a strip of waste ground on the corner of Loughton High Road and Warren Hill, which enlarged the estate. I proposed to make a pond there.

In mid-February 1987 I restated my task: "My purpose...is to state the Light, and...get it out into society, reflect it to others as a symbol, so that my life is a symbol for the Way of Illumination." I felt I had to live up to "Ezra Pound's handing on of the energy of the Muse", and I thought *The Fire and the Stones* was my *White Goddess*. It was allowed for poets to write cultural works; had not Eliot, a poet and publisher, written *Notes towards the Definition of Culture*? I walked "in the tradition of Graves and Eliot" and would become "a man of letters".

Colin Walsh of Book Production Consultants, Cambridge, who had prepared *Budapest Betrayed* for me, invited me to Emmanuel College, Cambridge for a publishers' dinner. Over sherry I met the new Earl of Stockton, the Head of Macmillans, a large, bearded, big-shouldered man, and I sat next to John Murray of "the oldest publishing firm in town" (1768), Byron's publisher, and spoke to a good dozen other publishers. I wrote: "The publishers...are all into marketing, hyping and turnover, and only secondarily interested in the content of their books. They all have an endless round of small talk and laughter to cushion themselves against embarrassment, which they know better than most."

The Conservative Patrons Club February dinner was at the House of Lords, in whose Cholmondeley Room Lord Broxbourne greeted us. The guest speaker at the dinner was Michael Heseltine, who arrived late wearing DJ, saying he had been locked in his office. He gave his speech, hands behind his back, no notes, and I met him afterwards – I was surprised at how tall he was – and Biggs-Davison explained to him about Oak-Tree. Afterwards Biggs-Davison insisted on buying me a Scotch and soda and then asked if I would publish a book he was writing on Ireland.

We were invited to the Barbican by a member of our staff to see Bramwell Tovey conduct a Tchaikovsky concert including the 1812 overture with cannon and mortar fire, and we were taken to the dressing-room afterwards, where he sat in evening dress, broken-nosed, a shock of hair and self-effacing, all alone and almost depressed; the conductor after the applause has stopped ringing in his ears. I realised we are all performers: politicians like Heseltine, conductors like Tovey and school principals like me – we were all putting on a show for the time the audience was there. I wondered if we performed in this life – left something behind us – and then returned in another body to benefit (or suffer) from the consequences in a future life.

In March there was more snow, and I worked on my Light book, preparing a new section each week for the typist to key into the computer. Nadia came, and we walked to the Strawberry Hill pond and scooped frog-spawn. There was masses of it, it was like a jelly fish.

Matthew was confirmed on 22nd March. It was a fine day, the Bishop of Chelmsford came to St. Mary's church, wearing his mitre and carrying his crozier. He laid his hands on the heads of those being confirmed, and there was communion. Afterwards family, friends and staff from various schools returned to Oaklands for a buffet lunch which Ann had prepared. The day was notable for Margaret Riley's appearance at the end of lunchtime. She had tried to travel by taxi and had lost her way and completely missed the service. Miss Lord and Miss Reid were there, and Margaret riled some of the guests by chain-smoking – strange how a mystic who had known the Light should be so dependent on cigarettes – and at the end Nadia helped me clear up. About a dozen of the guests came down to our house for tea, including Tom McAlister, the West Ham goalie, and Margaret behaved outrageously, telling Tom he was like a cardboard cutout, and then, catching sight of the painting she gave me in 1971, of the *Via d'amore* in Italy, which I had framed at my own expense and kept on my wall for 16 years, she loudly demanded it back, there and then. "I want my work back," she kept saying, "I want it back." She had always professed not to want, and I was disappointed to hear the change. My daughter had to return to Edinburgh – she was working early the next morning and had to be home in good time – and she needed to be driven to the station to catch her flight from Heathrow, and Margaret was delaying us. So I took the picture off the wall and put it in her arms and went to the car with my daughter, and Margaret pursued us, wanting a bag for the painting and wanting to come with us to the station. The upshot was that my daughter missed the train she needed to catch and therefore her flight from Heathrow. While I negotiated the time of the next tube with the ticket office, Margaret wandered up onto the platform without saying goodbye. Nadia went up the flight of steps the other side, putting distance between herself and Margaret, put out at the scene which had caused everyone inconvenience.

Sadly, I did not see Margaret Riley again. I did not feel moved to invite her – what else might disappear off my wall and what other scenes might be caused – and she never made contact. I wrote: "I am in the tradition of Toynbee-Eliot-Graves (*White Goddess*), and of Dante-Milton-Wordsworth-Tennyson (mystical literature) and I know more than many. I am both knowledge and wisdom – both sides of the Tree. Margaret Riley...has the intuitive side but is unbalanced. She has been unbalanced by years of excessive self-denial." I knew I did not need Margaret now, although it was sad this had happened.

I was moving away from publishing back into my own writing. Part One of *The Fire and the Stones* was nearly complete, and I was now immersed in my metaphysical perspective and Oaklands. I lunched with Tomlin in the Athenaeum. We were joined by Dr Raymond Hammer, who was secretary to the Archbishop of Canterbury's interfaith committee and we discussed the interfaith movement. We drank port in the morning room, sitting in green leather chairs by a log fire, and I wrote: "Coffee and port and quality conversation – and beauty." Later that evening Matthew had so bad a headache he could not move. I wrote: "Healed him with 6 surges of energy. Then talked to him. The headache had totally gone."

Mrs. Clauson invited me to dinner along with her relative, Norman Franklin, who was about to retire as Chairman of Routledge, and her son Julian, who was reading for a philosophy MA at Birkbeck. I wrote: "After dinner...took the metaphysical side against the materialist analytical Julian (who said 'Everyone today is Darwinist'). I said, 'Darwin left the idea of purpose out of the universe.' (Order.) Developed the argument at some length and then appealed to the Routledge Chairman (family firm) to co-publish a book with me on this subject: *The New Purpose*....My argument: put Ayer outside the door, no verbal games, and then man under the stars, in the universe – bring back the universe into philosophy. Franklin: 'Don't tilt at windmills, you can't examine the universe but you can examine logic.' I: 'Man finds himself in an existential situation. There's a spectrum of views. Wordsworth and Shelley knew the One behind the senses.' Julian: 'Plato was a criminal because he put Reality beyond the senses.' I: 'He was right.' ('Julian is split, between logic and the Alexandrian Method,' said Franklin, 'between his father and his mother.')"I added: "The gnosis – the experience of the Light. All consciousness leads up to the gnosis." Franklin later wrote to me saying he had stayed awake much of that night thinking about what I had said, and he sent me a copy of *Dialogues with Scientists and Sages* which, he claimed, was the anti-Darwinist book about the purpose in the universe that I had been calling for.

I went to the 1987 Mystics and Scientists conference at Winchester, and found myself queuing for dinner in the rain. Kathleen Raine was present, and spoke to me of Tomlin, who had written an article for the *Tablet*. She said to me: "I wouldn't write for the *Tablet*," maintaining her anti-Christian line. Sir Fred Hoyle spoke, and later I had a talk with him about the position of his steady state theory now that the Big Bang theory had general prevalence. He told me: "Every universe begins with a big bang, and all universes maintain themselves with steady state. It's regional and global. At least, that's how the maths look." There was a Benedictine who looked back to the fourth century Cassian, Lawrence Freeman, who held a meditation, after which I wrote: "During my meditation with Lawrence Freeman saw fire within which were words in Islamic, then Hebrew, then Latin (Roman capital letters as if on a tomb or pedestal). I tried to decipher them, and saw an A, an R, a P, a T, but could not make sense of them. Nevertheless, I can now believe that Mohammed was given the *Koran* in a vision of fire." Later I understood: "My vision seems to have been Islamic for Allah, Hebrew for Yahweh and then PATER – that was the Latin 5 letter word I saw, i.e. 3 names for God in the Islamic, Jewish and Christian traditions, all of which are One. It was seen in Fire with flames round the letters, which were written on stone. All were apparently chanting 'Maranatha' ('Come Lord') but I heard not a word or syllable as I was straining to see the letters, the energy having poured up my legs and my back and into my head. The message: 'In *The Fire and the Stones*, treat the Light/Fire of Islam, Judaism and Christianity as one – it is one God: unity.' I.e. a message of support, 'you're on the right lines'." The following day I went to Mass with the "Benedictine Cassianist monk": "To Mass. In my meditation I tried to return to the 'writing on the wall' but saw watery fire and a face. Saw divine things. Was with the Light, and did not want to break off after half an hour."

We went to the Lake District again to stay with Reg (on the way listening to a football match on the radio in which McAlister let in 4 goals against Everton). Reg reminisced, about my grandmother – "Argie was afraid of her, she sat erect on the edge of her chair, hand on a thick stick, and told George 'No more coal on the fire' (and George was ill afterwards)" – and about our walks on the Downs, of which I wrote: "The mist and rabbits and mushrooms; the days on the golf links, playing ball, lying in the long grass below the first tee, azure blues fluttering everywhere, under a blue sky – my first hint of a mystical experience, the stillness and harmony among the summer butterflies and flowers, the sense of a One something that throbbed through everything." After dinner he put on his Templar uniform. I wrote: "White cowl (Cistercian?) with red cross over heart, red cross on front, belt, Tudor style cap with cross, sword." I was interested in his Crusader image, but wondered to what extent the Templars were linked to the masonic Illuminati.

The next day we toured the western lakes: "From High Newton towards Newby Bridge – sheep everywhere, as a result of Chernobyl last year's sheep were not slaughtered – and stopped at Wrecks Bridge, with its ancient inscriptions idly carved by a local yokel ('England Expects', 'England Forever', 'I can paddle my own canoe', etc.). To Wastwater. The blue water under the blue sky of a lovely day. Scafell nearby. The deepest lake, the highest mountain, the smallest church (St. Olaf's) and the biggest liar in England had lunch at the inn (West Head)....On to Buttermere – the green water. Earlier the view of Windscale (Sellafield) and Isle of Man, then Scotland. Buttermere to Keswick, then to Grasmere. Tea at the Swan. (Cream tea in front of a fire.) Then to Allan Bank with its stunning view of headlands – how could Wordsworth have been unhappy there? Then to the Rectory, into which he moved. To Dove Cottage. Stirred the Leech-gatherer's pond above Dove Cottage but found only frog-spawn. On to Rydal and the steps across the Rothay to which Wordsworth walked to work in Ambleside. On to Fox Ghyll (De Quincey's house) and then Coniston Water; along past Ruskin's house (Brantwood) and then home. A day full of lakes and mountains, some snow-capped, and huge rocks and boulders." I loved being close to Nature again and wrote: "Retire as a Nature poet."

The following day was "misty, visibility a few yards. To Brock Hole....Then to Hawes. Lunch on the moor....Then to Richmond (the castle) and then to Barnard Castle, with its window associated with Richard III who married into the Saville family: the boar. On to Bowes and Dotheboys Hall, which is for sale. Posed as Wackford Hagger. On to High Force, a seventy foot cascade of a waterfall, the Tees. (Barnard Castle overlooks Teeside.) Then across the Pennines on a clear evening, disturbing 13 rabbits, several pheasants, 2 partridges, etc., to Murton near Appleby, where Matthew is staying...in a 1653 converted barn....Matthew was up Great

Gable... – we could see the climbers....A full moon over the Pennines as we drove back."

On our last day the theme was Wordsworth: "To Grasmere via Rydal and Fox How (Matthew Arnold's house), Rydal chapel (Matthew Arnold's window and pew) and Wordsworth's seat. To the bookshop for Dorothy's memoirs (her *Journals*) and then into Great Langdale and Dungeon Ghyll (ate) and up and over to Blea Tarn. The stream, the house – went in and saw where the Solitary entertained Wordsworth. On to Little Langdale, past the Three Shires, and then to Hawkshead, and its little alleys. A chat with the schoolkeeper who said that Wordsworth snared woodcock above Ann Tyson's house, and searched for ravens' eggs at Tilberthwaite, 2 miles outside Coniston on the road to Ambleside. No mention of John Barncroft in his book on Wordsworth's contemporaries. On to Esthwaite, where Wordsworth skated and Jeremy Fisher fished, and on to Beatrix Potter's house....A cream tea and then back to pick up Reg, and up Gummer's How, overlooking Windermere, Morecombe Bay, etc. Incredibly high on a lovely evening. Skylarks, a peregrine falcon, two ravens, and tame chaffinches which sat by me on the wall and nearly ate out of my hand. Excellent exercise. Anthony and Uncle Reg were first to the cairn....A book to buy, *Reminiscences of Wordsworth among the Peasantry of Westmoreland* by Canon Rawnsley; which gives the local reaction to Wordsworth: they thought him strange."

On Easter Saturday we attended the wedding in Great Chesterford, of Libby Norris, daughter of the Oaklands secretary and of my school friend Tim. I wrote: "Great Chesterford, an old village with pargetting and an ancient (12th century) church, for Libby Norris's wedding to Bill....Took Miss Lord and Marion....The service among the Norman arches, the pretty white and yellow flowers....Among the gravestones afterwards – love and death poignantly putting each other in context – and the chats with Old Chigwellians....Back to the Crown Hotel for the reception....Toasts in champagne. All this after a sumptuous lunch." I reflected: "Our 'Lakeland' is the Essex-Suffolk border...; bounded by the River Stour (Constable country), the Suffolk villages (Lavenham, Kersey) round Hadleigh – just across the Essex-Suffolk border – i.e. east of the M11 and south of Cambridge-Newmarket-Bury St. Edmunds-Ipswich (Ely just north); and including Audley End, Thaxted, Finchingfield, Great Bardfield, Dunmow; and Colchester and Chelmsford....On the west include Waltham Abbey and High Beach. The boundaries are the River Lea (west), the Thames (south) – just the Roding valley – and Maldon/Colchester up to the River Stour (north). The valleys: Lea, Roding, Stour, Colne, Brett and Pant – all tributaries – and the Chelmer."

On Easter Sunday I made a rare visit to church: "St. Mary's Loughton with its stone oak leaves and bluebells round the columns. Easter communion. The Peace....Coffee. Winnie Attenborough came to sherry with Miss Lord and Marion and we sat on the veranda. Then, after a turkey lunch, to Miss Reid with Ann and the boys for a walk to the Strawberry Hill pond via Warren Hill. The wood was full of bird song and we identified the willow warbler and the chiff chaff (two summer visitors) and wren, green woodpecker and possibly a reed bunting (or long-tailed tit). The hornbeams were out, with catkins; and the poplar catkins were on the ground. Pussy willow with yellow and green 'pin cushions'. Millions of tadpoles among the starwort (pondweed). Two horses passed us and the riders said 'Good afternoon'. It wasn't muddy. Saw the daffodils by the Warren, and mauve and white flowers growing wild – the wood to the right of the statue to Wellington's horse....Back to tea with Miss Reid: scones, butter, crab apple jelly (home-made), flapjack, cake, chocolate biscuits and many cups of strong tea. The boys played rummy and draughts and we talked: overlooking the green forest – green for the first time." I reflected: "We are in riverland (as opposed to Lakeland) – with valleys and forests. South West Essex, East Anglia? Level marshland and hills, farms and hedgerows – and ponds and pretty villages. The highest part of Essex (500 ft) is the chalk hills in the north-west, ridges descend to plateaus in East Essex. Flint. The Stour and Colne flow into the sea near each other. Timber and historic houses. Essex Flats."

The next day I observed: "I have been working on the Islamic Paradise, which was a garden, and I must break off to record that I raised my eyes to the Oaklands hedge by the greenhouse and saw two bullfinches nesting, flying in and out of the yew hedge and perching on the freshly budding apple tree, and gazing across the Oaklands grounds, with its trees and many birds, I had no doubt that this was a Paradise, with every kind and colour of tree and bird, every bit as enticing as Arabi's or the gardens shown in illustrations to Persian poems. I must recreate this Paradise or vision, using the Paradise that is round me. I, who have known Hell, or at least, the Gates of Hell, am now living in Paradise."

I felt the benefit of my visit to church: "Going to church and contemplating into union all through the prayers – not mouthing responses so as not to disturb the vision of the Light in the pew – has benefits later in the week: it opens the spring of creativity, so all today (Easter Monday) I have been in what I used to call an active mood, the energy and calm surging up. Religion and art naturally go together."

A few days later I wrote: "All day, mowed the two fields in glorious sunshine. In the evening the Taylors gardened. Keith found a toad. Earlier in the morning Bill had a bumble-bee on his hand."

One of the Oaklands staff, Angela Whitworth, who was in her late 40s, was dying of cancer in a private nursing home in Buckhurst Hill. She was being looked after by Margaret Taylor, our gardener and the wife of Miss Lord's doctor, who was also in charge of a private nursing agency, and was therefore responsible for Angela. She reported that Angela had an expressionless face, a monotonous voice, that she was drugged and slept and only woke to be sick: "She looks 80, wrinkled and white – an old lady." I visited Angela: "At Danely Court, Queens Road. Kim Yardley bustled to the door, rotund and starched uniform with mauve and white stripes close together. She showed me through a sitting-room and dining-room, where some dozen old folk sat, down a long passage to the end room, where, before her daughter Maxine and Margaret Taylor, round the corner, lay in a bed: Angela; a thin, pale, made-up ghost of her former self with bright eyes that seemed contented but did not move, showing her teeth. 'Nick, how nice to see you. How very kind. What a lovely plant.' Chatted about Oaklands –

it's the meeting tomorrow, I'll say I've seen you and pass on your best wishes, etc. – and Margaret showed me her pump which is pumping drugs in. 'Are you comfortable?' I asked. 'Yes, very comfortable now.' She gave one sentence replies, and once her eyes nearly closed and it was time to leave." I recorded: "Back among the living I cannot forget the dying." Within a week she was dead, "the morphine having depressed her respiration to nothing".

There were bees round the rotten tree by the log shed. Margaret Taylor's son caught one in a glass and we took it to Derek Balls, who had hives, thinking it was an escaped "honey bee" of his. Later Derek put it on his finger, and as it crawled, pronounced it a "tree wasp". I watched fascinated, but it did not sting him. Later still I recorded: "Reread *Georgics IV* on bees. Virgil's Paradise in the country is no different from the Oaklands fields."

The Oaklands police constable "Uncle Les"Giddings, retired. We were invited to the farewell at the police club and heard from his successor "Uncle Ted" how the Epping burglars were arrested. The police had information that after burgling 18 houses they had got on to the tube with holdalls. The police stopped the tube at Loughton and searched it from end to end and found nothing. They walked back a second time, and a woman indicated with her eyebrows, and Ted stood 3 men up and lifted the seat and found the swag. The Epping burglars had come out of London with empty holdalls on the tube, and had put their full holdalls under the seat for the return journey.

There was a proposal that Oak-Tree should publish Gordievsky's memoirs, and I made a bid to secure them. Julian Amery's secretary got a message to the man who controlled Gordievsky's hiding. Nothing came of the idea. I visited the House of Lords with Gorka for tea with Lord Bauer, "wizened, white-haired, sallow, with alive eyes", in the peers' Guest Room bar.

I wrote that the theme of my book was "the vision of God and Light in world culture", and ministered to Matthew who broke his arm in falling off his new skateboard on the tennis court. At the Bank holiday we went to a craft exhibition in Epping and I bought an icon. I wrote: "There appear to be a group of Hesychasts at Woodford Green, interested in living metaphysics and making a living out of icons, and I bought Christ with a huge halo of Light and a book, a 6th century Desert Father Byzantine image from St. Katerina's monastery, Sinai." The man I talked to was a "tall, intense, balding, thin-lipped man who described each icon with manic intensity", who told me he "meditates on the idea behind the image (the Greek ho on, the Being), not on the image (which is the Templar mistake)."

We went on to Stansted Mountfitchet to see the reconstruction of an 11th century Norman castle, and I noted: "Baron Mountfitchet in the inner bailey, with his hall (on earth) and draughty 'luxurious' upstairs bedroom and straw; while the rest crowded into the outer bailey, wood and plastered buildings, straw roofs, with a gallows and an 'executed man' swinging in the wind, near the stocks and pillory." We also visited the nearby windmill "which ground corn and made bread out of the wind – like the sails of my creative imagination blown by divine inspiration, producing poems. I have been a disused windmill of late, but will begin to grind again. Climbed the wooden stairs of the tower mill to the top. Chains, cogs, trap doors at each level. Wind power harnessed – like the sailing ships....All doomed, obsolete, but splendid." Soon afterwards I wrote 6 stories.

John Dutchman, the Pegasus footballer and Chigwell School master, was now taking football at Oaklands, and I played up the other end and we chatted as we walked back. He told me: "Haynes was the best passer. Hoddle is the best footballer today....Insole is my closest friend now."

Angela Whitworth's funeral took place at St. John's, Buckhurst Hill. We arrived early, and found the church already half full and the vicar fumbling with a box of matches near the candles. He put up the trestles to receive the coffin, and I had the feeling of arriving at a theatre to find the stage-hands still setting the scenery for the illusion which was to follow. The church was packed, as one might expect in view of her untimely death, and she was buried in the graveyard. Without knowing it I stood near Gerald Penn, one of my Oaklands classmates.

My Uncle Harold had died – my grandfather's brother John's son who had run the Folkestone and Bromley family businesses – he had sold the Bromley one for £1 million. I drove to Barham for the funeral and went back to his eldest son John's house at Bishopsbourne. John and I had sailed my yacht together as boys; he was now a consultant at Canterbury Hospital, and he lived overlooking the sheep in the valley. He told me: "I've always been a country bumpkin."

"Death," I wrote, "is the perfection of a life, so that all the life's achievements can be measured finally. It is a looking back on a life, a time for assessment."

At the end of May I hired a JCB and made a pond in the allotment area of the estate on the corner of Warren Hill. I wrote: "A JCB gouged it out, clearing the barbed wire fence and runner beans posts and wooden stakes, changed the contour of the earth." We left an island in the middle for ducks, and it soon became established. Mabel Reid gave us reeds and pondweed, and like the other pond which Jack Straw had fallen into, was soon full of frogs and fish and water-beetles and leeches. We found an enormous leech which would have pleased Wordsworth's Leech-gatherer. An adviser from the Conservation Centre came and told me the Oaklands fields were very ancient woodland because we had "dog's mercury, wild garlic, wood arums and star of Bethlehem". Mabel Reid donated a seat so that staff could sit in peace and gaze at the stillness of the pond. After supervising the pond I went to Creeds, next to the Post House Hotel (a regular Sunday visit in those days) to pick up two sacks of red potatoes for school lunches the next week. I wrote: "The farm outhouses, my feeling of peace on a Sunday morning."Soon afterwards I collected more potatoes from Hobbs Cross Farm and wrote: "Walked among suckling calves, hens, sows, bulls, and boars. The smell of the farm: silage."

Nadia at last became an air hostess with British Midland. After her training she would fly, being based in Edinburgh. She said: "I'll have to learn to put out a fire and cope with a terrorist emergency."

The Oaklands 1987 summer fair was opened by Geoff Hurst, the star of England's World Cup final in 1966. I wrote: 'The parents put up tables on an overcast windy day. But the rain held off after 10.30 and I was able to introduce Geoff Hurst from the hall windows, after the dancing. Geoff Hurst opened the fête. Biggs-Davison stood in the middle of the steps and tried to upstage it, walked by Vernon without recognising him and was reluctantly introduced to about 5 stalwarts by me....Lady Biggs-Davison was nice....Biggs-Davison wearing a large blue rosette and holding an umbrella. Spoke to many parents." As there was a General Election in five days' time I had said he was welcome to look in and meet some of his constituents.

At Chigwell School's Speech Day the prizes were distributed by John Garnett (Virginia Bottomley's father), who had written the Foreword to Jack Wood's book. I wrote: "John Garnett, silky white-haired, sat behind me in the ancient church, talked to me about Jack Wood when I introduced myself outside the porch, and then scintillated during his speech, with many good jokes."

I took the boys to Ilford cricket ground to see Essex v Kent. Rain reduced the length of the match, and I recorded: "The Cowdrey brothers shone with bat and ball – one scored 60, the other took 4 for 15 including Gooch – and except for a quick 35 from East, Essex were hopeless." The East was David East, whose wife I was shortly to employ, and whom I was to get to know.

I went to the Council offices to buy some dustbin bags. I wrote: "Nearly ran Sir John Biggs-Davison over. He was in a dream and did not see me, wandering slowly carrying an umbrella, wearing a sports jacket. Got my bags at the Council offices. The receptionist said, 'I used to know your father, used to work with him.' Wanda the shorthand typist....She: 'I can see him now, walking in as he used' (i.e. with his stick, hopping). 24 years ago. On the way back passed Sir John and congratulated him on his election victory. He came out of his dream."

In a more reflective vein I wrote: "After leading an active life I am now...living a more contemplative life....The possibility that Oaklands brought me back to contemplation and will be the first centre for the Light of the World Movement – with its picture of the Light of the World in the school hall. The Paradisal garden for a new contemplative movement."

On a rainy day and dressed as a 1520s friar (in an outfit that looked more like Robin Hood) I accompanied a group of Oaklands children to Kentwell Hall, which is peopled by volunteers in 1520s dress, for an immersion experience in Tudor England. I wrote: "It was a tank park in the war, and the coach parked between trees. Changed money into Tudor groats and shillings, and then down the time tunnel (straw) to the screened off gate, which was opened by Tudor soldiers and we were greeted by dancers and pipe-players, and exorted in 'thous' and 'doths' (Shakespearian English) to hold hands and dance, which we did....On to the chandler, the fletcher, turner, carver, the forge – the man on manual contract for £4.50 a year – and into the house: kitchens, quill pen writer,...and then to the oven and weaving and upstairs to the remedy room: honey solution for coughs or run of the nose, lavender water for fleas, and dead mice on nettles for whooping cough. (I: 'Be that my lunch?') You hung them round your neck. The wenches in inviting corsets, ready to chat within the idiom. More sewing, then out over the bridge (the geese on the water) and back via

523

soldiers (in armour with swords) and the stables, kept by a real life shepherd who looked after 200 sheep. Back to the stocks and then out. Some 100 people must have talked to me in 1520s English, and I would have liked to have stayed. Despite the evident squalor (straw and food on floor) and discomfort (open windows), I preferred the 1520s to the 20th century, I would have been happy there in the estate in which everyone knew their place yet everyone was looked after....The schoolmaster: Latin, geography, history, no Greek (associated with the Renaissance); Latin, the language of Christendom and therefore of Heaven. Never heard of Australia, America not important."

Matthew spent a night out, sleeping rough at Waters Farm, Hatfield Broad Oak, and two days later I lunched with the artist Gwen Broad's two daughters, Gwen and Flinders, at Argie's and it turned out that Waters Farm is owned by their father Nanscawen's brother. "What an amazing coincidence," Gwen said. "Uncle is 90 and deaf." Again I had an eerie feeling that there is an underlying pattern to our lives.

I had a letter from Tom Howard, whose family owned Oaklands from before the First World War to 1929. (Before the First World War it is known that Oaklands, called Firbank, was owned by the Sturges, and that around 1900 their daughter Florence Sturge married the son of the Harris family who lived across the road in what is now Albion Park House, an old people's home.) The Howard family gave their name to the Howard League for Penal Reform and also to Howard's aspirins – one of the Howard boys was killed in the blitz in his factory in Ilford. Like the Frys, another well known local family associated with prison-visiting, the Howards were Quakers. In the Second World War Oaklands was owned by an organisation that housed Belgian refugees there.

As I plodded on with *The Fire and the Stones* I wrote: "How I see myself: an expert on what life is about, Reality – i.e. knowledge of God, poems about living. At Oxford when I did my Yeats lectures, I had a vision of myself living quietly by some harbour – by the sea – writing poetry. Get back to that view of myself as a deep contemplative poet....We live in an Age of Discovery, and the figure of our time is the Great Discoverer, the scientist-metaphysician-philosopher."

On a scorching July day our odd job man, Les, painted the Oaklands gable above the third storey. A Cockney over 65, he used to run up the rigging in the Navy during the war, and he scampered up the ladder without any regard for his safety while I kept my foot on the bottom rung. He wanted me to go up and have a look, and when I climbed about 15 feet high the ladder moved back from the wall and for a few moments I clung to a vertical ladder, and it seemed I might go over backwards and into the rockery and rose-bushes beneath while Les held both rungs with his hands and tried to push the ladder back, which he finally succeeded in doing. Had I gone backwards I might have broken my neck.

My son Anthony was turning into a singer. He sang a solo, "Pie Jesu", in a packed St. Mary's church, Loughton. He was unwell on the day – he was nearly sick while singing – but with a temperature of 102 sang in a clear, piping treble voice and had a triumph.

Soon afterwards there was a dancing display at Oaklands. The stage was the grass under the apple trees and the parents sat in the tennis court, which melted in the scorching sun, so that some of the benches and chairs became embedded in the tarmac, which had to be repaired.

Oaklands celebrated its 50th anniversary with a barbecue put on by the parents, and 500 gathered in the field, including many of the old teachers: Miss Lord, Miss Reid, Miss Root, Mrs. Macpherson, Miss Mount and Mrs. Kane. Many former Oaklanders turned up from all decades, including Christopher Imms and his brother Andrew (who lived two doors from Journey's End) – Christopher was now a merchant banker – and Peter Liell, Mark Liell's son. Pam McAlister was there – she had separated from Tom – and Nadia came down from Edinburgh, and it was a golden day that went on until after 8 p.m. I put on an exhibition of Oaklands memorabilia (old photos and registers) in the hall, from 1937 to date.

I thought again about images and symbols and wrote: "I am in the Guénon-Schuon tradition of metaphysics. The Guénon view of the symbol – everything corresponds as everything is a oneness, a unity....The poet speaks to the inner man in a language of images (intellectual, visual or musical) which communicates to the inner imagination. The artist ideally at one with his society but in a violent time at odds with his society....Images of calm for a violent time, images of peace for an alienated time. The artist living close to Nature. I go further and suggest that images are in fact symbols, with a plurality of meanings, as lower and higher domains correspond. Symbolism is not a materialist, positivist philosophy but a metaphysical philosophy. Art mirrors the disease of society, but if it is to save it it has to heal it with a flow of Light and symbolism – which means we must be metaphysical and not materialist or positivist."

Nadia came to see me, having been to Greece: "Ate, drank white wine and sat at peace....This morning walked in the village....Then she played table tennis and snooker with me, and with Anthony. Then went. I drove her to the station after a hurried lunch....Her sunburned body."

At the "Oak-Tree office" an American tried to persuade me to share Oak-Tree accommodation with a new company which would be consultants on satellite technology, and the meeting lead me to rethink my aims: "My policy is to change Europe politically (especially to reunite Eastern and Western Europe), metaphysically (to bring in a Metaphysical Revolution – the culmination of my search for metaphysical truth) and artistically (to remysticise in poetry and promote the ideals of T. S. Eliot). This is a policy I have pursued for many years, as relentlessly as Gaddafi."

The Snowsills left to go to Dorset. Richard had finally resigned from the Bank of England and they had brought property in Lyme, including a guest house. We had them to a farewell dinner.

At the end of July I visited Tomlin in Redan Street. I wrote: "He greeted me, sitting in his study upstairs, after my chat with Judith about his health. He told me he was not well, that they found cancer in his bladder in June and operated, that he may lose a kidney, that he has tuberculosis (according to his specialist) and although he is on antibiotics for his cough, is going to bed at 7, exhausted; also that he has had a headache for a month (the kidney). He can't think about a synopsis for the BBC or translate...; but he will look at my book for mistakes. (Is very interested in the metaphysical side.) Showed me three of his essays – Sacred, Ruskin and Guénon. 'Kathleen Raine is not a Guénonist, she says he ignores emotion.' 'Russell's *History of Western Philosophy* is a poor book, poorly written. He said logic ruined his brain.' 'Wittgenstein's been hijacked by the sceptics. He asked for a priest when he died and said "Don't let him be a philosopher".' 'Husserl – he's unnecessarily complicated: intentionality.' (I defended the phenomenological method.) 'I had lunch with (Gabriel) Marcel, I spoke in French. He raises metaphysical questions, that's why they don't like him.' And so on. His sanity about the New Age, his own scepticism about bizarre claims and the gullible. 'Magee's approach is so conventional and out of date. A programme with me should be called 'An Alternative Way'." Afterwards I observed: "My *Death-Fires*, then my *Fire-Flower*, and eventually *The Fire and the Stones*. But what I have in common in all my work is a concern for, a search for, metaphysical truth....The personal is subordinated to that. Ironically, it is self-stripping which produces it. I also have a 'Metaphysical Diary' (Journal) and letters on metaphysical subjects. Anthologise (à la Hopkins) a metaphysical theme, with excerpts from diaries and letters, all dated; presenting metaphysical reality. My poems to stop short of New Age gullibility (cf Tomlin's Christian rejection of seances, astrology, etc., cf Eliot's rejection of Mme Sesostris). *The Silence* – a search for metaphysical reality that succeeded."

In August Ann and I took the boys and our car to Denmark. We caught a boat from Harwich and ate in the Tivoli restaurant, where we encountered the Page family from Oaklands, and had a Danish buffet of hot and cold food and white wine. We hugged the Norfolk coast and I wrote: "There is a high pitched chug and a squeak of metal caused by vibration, and a slight bumpiness as I write – but no rolling." We slept and next morning we docked at Esbjerg and drove to Legoland, where it was cool and showery. I recorded: "Had acute pains in my heart, sharp stabbings, and had to sit in a café while the boys went on their activities. At one stage felt I was perhaps dying from an extended heart attack. Wrote *Reality in Legoland, or Sudden Confrontation with Death*. We drove to Odense, where at the Hotel Windsor I corrected it "until late at night". At 2 a.m. I woke (in room 305) "with the idea firmly in my mind: after my poems there should be extracts on my poetic method from these *Diaries* over the years".

The next day we went to Hans Christian Andersen's (alleged) birthplace. I wrote; "The impression Hans Christian Andersen gives through the museum is of a poet-man of letters for whom children's writing was but a small part of his output....To (his) childhood home, which he shared with two other families. Front of first room: cobbler's shop. Rear: bedroom and living-room. Back: kitchen. Cobbled back garden." We went on to Rynkeby church, "where Eric Hardenberg expressed the Reformation ideal he learned at the house of Luther's friend, Phillip Melanchton, in a choir of 31 angels, with bobbed hair, playing an orchestra of 17 different instruments conducted by Christ. Christ the Conductor. (Add a postscript to my *Conductor* or contrast poems in the physical world with poems in the metaphysical world.)" We went on to Ladby, but could not see the Viking ship because the barrow was locked due to a museum strike. "Saw how the fjord near Kertminde (where we lunched) acted as a harbour for the Vikings, who sailed out to sea from sheltered waters. The chieftan in his ship grave with 11 horses and 8 dogs. On to Svendborg – the old cathedral and view of an island – and then Egeskov castle, moated and splendid 16th century with green turrets. Denmark is flat, no hills at all, and fewer trees than in England. It must have been the hilltops, with their promise of fortifications, that sent the Vikings abroad to settle. They went for greater security for their settlements. The chieftan's burial, cf the Ur graves? Drafted *The Metaphysical Conductor* in room 305 at the Hotel Windsor, Odense."

The following day we left the hotel at 7 and took the ferry from Knudshoved to Halsskov, then drove to Trelleborg, which is on a ley line from Aggersborg in North Jutland (home of the Haggers?), Fyrkat to Delphi. The reconstructed house, the ring-forts, and graveyards. 1,200 men, the two rivers; where Svein Forkbeard set sail to conquer England. On to the Viking ship museum at Roskilde – the prow, the long warship for 50-110 men – via Lejre's Kurgan-style Funnel-Neck Beaker long barrow (11 upright megaliths and capstones) for a chieftan, see 3,000BC – Kurgan influence on the people of Dan – and the Iron Age village in which volunteers reconstruct the techniques of the Iron Age....They sleep in huts and grind corn for bread. A nostalgic glance back to the past,....To Nodebo and the attempt to find Kierkegaard's *Either/Or* 8-cross roads in Grib forest. On to Gilleleje and Gilbjerg Hoved, where Kierkegaard's stone monument stands in a small forest. I found it. Kierkegaard was a late Romantic, who like Werther (or Wordsworth or Shelley) walked in forests, alone, and emoted. The Romantic movement reached Denmark late. On to Helsingor (Elsinor) to see Hamlet's castle, closed by the museum strike. Then on to Kobenhavn (Copenhagen): Tivoli Gardens and the royal palace, with the theatre and church thrown in. Left at 8.30, drove 103 kms in time to catch the ferry by half a minute, then ate on the boat and drove home, arriving by 11.30. Drank wine downstairs at this Hotel Windsor. Next time I come to Denmark...go to Fyrkat and Aggersborg in search of my roots. For my family came from a town of Aggers, with Svein Forkbeard c1013, and sailed for England to plunder and travel and worship Odin and come up against the Christian Light – just as happens today....The midnight sun and Aurora Borealis (Northern lights)....The Vikings had no metaphysic of the Christian order. It is contradictory to be a Viking and a metaphysical – but contradictions happen and there we are."

From Odense we went to Jelling, "the royal capital of Denmark in the 10th century when Gorm and his son Harald Bluetooth, who made the Danes Christian, were kings. The two stones they raised, which I must put into *The Fire and the Stones* (one with Christ on it). The northern mound which was Gorm's tomb before he was reinterred in the church. This was sited by Harald on a holy place, a stone circle....Lunched at an ancient inn up the road, then drove to the ferry." I dipped into the beginning of Kierkegaard's *Journal*, 1835 at Gilbjerg Hoved, where I stood yesterday; I see he was influenced by Schelling at Berlin, having attended his lectures, and that until 16 he was on the moors in Jutland....Am also reading about the Vikings (Gwyn Jones's *A History of the Vikings*), and have put a question to the Local Historic Bibliothek....Is there any record of a Hagger or Agger leaving the Viking settlement at Aggersborg, perhaps for England, c1000?"

Of my philosophy I wrote: "My philosophy à la Kierkegaard – penetration to the Light. Around the movement to the Light I can erect choice, bad faith, etc. – a sense of meaninglessness. The state of not-knowing the Light should be described in full, and the steps taken to break through into Light, philosophically in the next work."

On the way back to England there was a great swell and a fair amount of rain. The boat rolled a lot and many were sick. We all slept well after a great meal and a film, and the following morning I "drafted a poem and jotted for a philosophical sequel to *The Fire and the Stones*." We approached Harwich past the confluence of the Orwell and the Stour, which join in the open sea.

The last third of 1987 saw me working intensively on *The Fire and the Stones* while coping with work at Oaklands, buying a property in my beloved Charlestown and lamenting the decline of Tomlin.

A few days after I returned from Denmark I was "awoken by a call from Judith Tomlin. Frederick has cancer in both lungs and in his brain, and has not long to live. (She began: 'The news is bad.') 'He wanted you to know.' All day, felt sombre. There is the personal sadness of nearly 25 years, but also a rage that the philosopher with so much in his head has to stop before his time. I must counsel him on acceptance, on planning his end." I drove to Cornwall – "a brilliant orange and green sunset over Wales" – and then "wrote to Tomlin, a letter about the correct attitude to dying; in which I mentioned my next work, the sequel to *The Fire and the Stones*, which will contrast Being without the Light and Being with the Light". I mentioned the example of Socrates, a philosopher who calmly discussed and planned his end. I wrote this letter "after visiting Charlestown this morning, falling asleep from exhaustion this afternoon, and looking at the Charlestown Regatta this early evening: a lifeboat, a helicopter rescue, Punch and Judy, water sports (climbing upside down along a rope and going through a tyre), water polo, knobbly knees and bathing beauty". Such activities seemed unreal when seen within the context of what Tomlin was enduring.

The next day was hot and I sunbathed at Charlestown and wrote to Kathleen Raine about Tomlin. I was rung up by the American, called Donald Wilhelm, who was "hook-nosed and whiskery in a Victorian way, smiling like Jimmy Carter", who had spoken to me and to the committee of Exiles on satellite technology. He had urged the spreading of dishes behind the Iron Curtain, so that they could receive insurrectionary broadcasts. He had met me at Kettners, Romilly Street with a view to forming a company to sell dishes behind the Iron Curtain and he now rang to say he had an office in Knightsbridge and three men who sold broadcasting equipment who would work in this new company. He rang again to say they had now signed a lease for an office in Cambridge.

I sunbathed on Par beach and proofread Part One of *The Fire and the*

Stones. I had bronchiectasis again and a wheeze. I wrote: "Am nurturing my poor lungs along until like Tomlin I too must leave 'this dark world' (Kathleen Raine's Gnostic expression)." (I had had a letter from Kathleen Raine lamenting that Frederick must now leave "this dark world".)

Some Chinese 'magic' acrobats from Taiwan came to the nearby Colisseum. I saw them and wrote: "They performed marvellous feats of 'ch'i' which I have written into *The Fire and the Stones*. Two to remember: drawing up a heavy jar with outstretched palm above it; and balancing a (hypnotised) girl on 3 swords (back and legs), and removing the leg swords so she defied gravity. She was in a trance when she came down and only on the snap of fingers did she come to. A combination of hypnotism and 'ch'i' energy."

We spent a day on Charlestown beach eating pasties for lunch, while the boys "boated in their rubber dinghy, snorkelled, crabbed, swam. I sunbathed and got red....Also wrote, or rather drafted, poems on Tomlin and Vikings, and *Gravity*. " I knew that the Charlestown harbour was for sale for about £2.5 million, and I wandered up and looked through the windows of the Harbourmaster's House, the most seaward house opposite the Pier House Hotel, which stood above "the sleep tunnel" and which I had often thought might one day be mine as it might be the place by the sea I had glimpsed in Oxford while attending the Yeats lectures. I looked in on Stratton and Holborrow (now Stratton Creber) and had a chat with John Newey and established that the property was for sale along with the harbour. The next day we went to Porthleven. I wrote: "A glorious blue day. Sat on the rocks and wrote the third (?) of my *Gunwalloe Metaphysical Sonnets*, and polished the rhymes. Visited the church on the beach: 6th century Breton originally, now 15th century. Back to vivid stars over Charlestown." On the Sunday we all lunched at the Cliff Head Hotel with Ann's mother. According to astrological predictions that Sunday, August 16th 1987, marked the birth of the New Age, and television showed barefooted idealists ringing the Glastonbury Tor and humming in the direction of the Gulf for peace (a gesture which was unable to avert two Gulf Wars).

The next day I went "out with the fishermen on a clear blue day. Left Stephen's home at 4 a.m., having arrived last night and slept in the spare bedroom; left Newlyn harbour at 4.40 in his new boat, the Golden Spinney, steered by Michael Orchard, with a crew of Stephen, Anthony, Kingsley, Kipper and Peter (Michael's son), and returned at 8.40 p.m., some 12 hours of fishing for cod, hake, guernard, pollack, etc. (and spur-dog), with 2 hours each way, off the Lizard. At one stage above the troop ship wreck. Have written my impressions into *Out onto* (sic) *the Alone* (or *The Mystery of Being*), a metaphysical poem that hints at a separation between things which have Being and things which have non-Being (i.e. fish and waves). Took up the distinction in *Spur-Dog and Philosopher*, on the dying of Tomlin....In the first poem, which is still only a draft, introduced the idea of 'Amness' or 'Isness' (an idea which first surfaced in my Japanese *Diary* 20 years or more ago). I am becoming a Metaphysical Poet in the sense that all my poems now have metaphysical echoes or work out fundamental metaphysical problems related to Being. There is Divine Being – the Light – and there is Being within human beings and animals. Relate them all into a whole. Being is an abstraction of all Beings who come from the One sea of Light....My contact with the sea (including Charlestown) has deepened my poetry – it has stressed the metaphysical alone at the expense of the social vision. I must keep my contact with the sea. This poem, if done right, will advance *Crab-Fishing on a Boundless Deep*, and be one of the few great poems I have done. Keep coming back to Cornwall for this reason. It has images for Being as few other places I know have." The next day I "spent all day polishing 7 stanzas of *The Mystery of Being*, my most openly Metaphysical poem. Make it clear that my poems are not 'Metaphysical' in the literary but in the philosophical sense. Ricks was wrong to query the use of the term, thinking of Donne and Marvell. The 'Baroque' view is helpful up to a point; 'Metaphysical' more helpful....At Charlestown, after typing up *Out on the Alone* and my Gunwalloe poem, and proof reading...; a breathless calm....The Metaphysical Revolution." We went to Fowey and crossed to Polruan, having tea as usual in the Singing Kettle, and then we went on to the castle. Another day we went to Mevagissey: "Gulls. Cloudy sky, calm sea."

I returned to Loughton to find there had been a violent storm in which a fir tree across the road had been struck by lightning and split in two, that it had set off our burglar alarm, and that much of Loughton was flooded; the police station was under 4 feet of water, and the school staff room was flooded.

I spoke to Judith Tomlin, and wrote: "Tomlin is having chemotherapy, which is very painful and causes a temperature, for about 6-7 weeks. He cannot see anybody; is physically very low. Is worried about small things which prey on his mind (e.g. will I return the two essays he lent me)." I added: "Tomlin hasn't accepted his impending death; he is fighting it – and so cannot see those he should be saying farewell to. He is making a secular end and not dying like a serene metaphysical – or so it seems from a distance." I was sad that he had been cut off from those who should be speaking to him philosophically, that far from Socrates' end with his friends round him he would die alone, trying to stay alive.

Towards the end of August I rang Judith Tomlin and wrote: "Tomlin has not eaten for a fortnight (so that the cells won't go on dividing, i.e. he is starving them) and has been given blood and has sores in his mouth (part of the chemotherapy) and a cough ('he is coughing his lungs away, each time he coughs the disease is advancing'). 'It is dreadful to watch.' 'Either way he will be glad to have gone through it, though. If the treatment is successful it will have been worth it; if not, at least he will have put up a fight. Then it will be a question of amelioration.' 'He still has a headache. The doctors don't know what it is, or why he is getting these high temperatures.' 'He dictated a letter to you. He was fascinated by glancing through your book. One thing struck him, he noticed one thing. He may have got the wrong end of the stick, but he's put it in the letter for what it's worth.'" The letter queried my use of the phrase "Christian Neo-Platonism" by which I meant Christianity's drawing on the pagan Neo-Platonist tradition, a phrase which is entirely justified in its context, although it was kind of Tomlin to express concern when he was so ill.

I mowed the fields, taking care to avoid the many frogs which leapt out of my path; I saw my machine from the point of view of the creatures in its way. A harvest mouse swung on some long grass in the second field, and many butterflies, moths and beetles fluttered or crawled out of my way. At one point I was "engulfed in smoke..., had a halo of smoke. Thought the ride-on mower had caught fire. In fact, the hot engine was on wet grass and raindrops entered the inside causing steam." I worked on my book but took time off to walk with Mabel Reid in the Forest. I noted: "Went back to tea. Her lovely garden. Mulberries, blackberries. Dragonflies on the ponds."

In September, after term had restarted, I went to the auction of Charlestown, incredibly with the American satellite technologist Donald Wilhelm, who tagged along. There were 800 people in a London hotel (the Crystal Room of the May Fair Intercontinental Hotel, Stratton Street), and the auction ended in confusion as it was not clear whether the reserve price of £2.6 million had been reached. Together with many others I milled around at the front and found myself being interviewed by the *Times*, who thought I had bought the harbour. A small, podgy man with a handlebar moustache and wrists that bulged at his cuffs said to me, "Don't say it's me," and I found myself talking to Stephen Lucas, who (it later transpired) had bought the harbour for BOM Holdings. We all stood around – John Newey came over for a while – and when it appeared that Lucas's bid was being entertained I said to him: "If you're borrowing £2.6 million for the harbour, the interest could work out at getting on for £4,000 for a long weekend. You will need to sell something off to reduce your borrowing. I am interested in the Harbourmaster's House. Here's my card." He said "Right" and disappeared to sign the auctioneer's papers. I did not know that he would soon buy the harbour from BOM Holdings on the strength of an overdraft and a brother's position; that I had more assets than he had.

Gorka and I visited Keston College and put an idea the Exiles had come up with, whereby the College would be involved as Couriers for taking satellite dishes into the USSR. After our meeting Gorka warned me that a "Professor" with whom the Exiles had had dealings on a certain matter was with the CIA.

I visited Anne Clarke and wrote: "Told (her) that a writer is like an architect; he may design many houses, but at the end of his life it is the one Cathedral he is proud of, which dominates the rest. Tomlin's Cathedral is *Philosophers of East and West*; mine will be *The Fire and the Stones*. I will look back at it as a dominating landmark." I added: "I have to point the way to the Light: to be a positive role model for the younger generation."

Matthew was writing a story and I gave him some advice which explained my preference for poetry to stories: "I told him, 'A writer of stories is a liar. He has to tell a believable lie. Your lie is not believable. This is why I prefer poetry to fiction....In poetry you tell the truth. No lying is countenanced. All is honesty and sincerity. That is why I don't read fiction. Why should I waste time reading *Chatterton* by Ackroyd, for example, when I know it's all a lie? The facility of the lie doesn't interest me. The best fiction might be true (like *Karamazov*)."

I attended an Epping Forest Centenary Trust evening at Queen Elizabeth's Hunting Lodge and met Sir William Addison, the author of books on the Forest, who had sold me my Observer's books as a child. I wrote: "Sitting grandly, 82, with sticks, talking about his ailments. 17 books, author of *Epping Forest*. Has invited me to visit him at home. Do I want to publish *Epping Forest* revised?" I was very pleased to meet again someone who had dominated my childhood.

The new Oaklands pond had leaked, so I put on wellington boots and with some parents "puddled" it. We then went to dinner with Robin and Angela Parfitt, Head of the Chigwell School Junior School, in the ancient Harsnetts, and heard about his brother Tudor, who was an explorer. He was currently up the Zambezi in Mozambique looking for the African tribe which follows Judaism: the lost 12th tribe."

I was invited to Cambridge to lunch with Donald Wilhelm and his wife in their new house near the Gog-Magog hills, and visited the Cambridge office and two of the personnel who had leased it. In my presence Wilhelm rang the Head of the British National Space Centre and tried to persuade him to meet us. I was not sure where this new direction was leading – it eventually lead nowhere – but I went along with it to see what the Americans were trying to do with me, knowing as Wilhelm did that I had founded the Heroes of the West. I knew Wilhelm was a distraction, and wrote pointedly: "To be a poet is to be fully aware of Nature, and one's surroundings and have the time for verse – i.e. to have no projects, to run no empires or do any of the things that take one's time. Sept 25. One day, it will be said that I was the only poet of the 20th century who searched for metaphysical truth and found it. The 20th century is littered with searches that failed."

Ann and I attended Chigwell School's annual dinner for its feeder school Heads. I wrote: "Was buttonholed by Horton and Ballance, two cultured, civilised men in a philistine world. Talked Confucius – his sense that the present was a Silver Age. Talked to Wilson, the Head on Shakespeare. He: 'Schools that put on Shakespeare are only trying to impress the parents.' A scientist, he probably has not read any Shakespeare recently, and has inflicted his own heathen taste on the school." I was aware that Wilson's attitude was not good enough, and other parents began urging me to make sure that the new Head – for there was a vacancy – would stand for Shakespeare and traditional values.

In early October there was a Conservative Patrons Club gathering at Vernon Davies's. Vernon's ex-partner at Atlantic, Foulston, had just been killed while motor-racing, and Vernon's wife told me: "The new Chairman will be a shareholder. Vernon's still got £8 million in shares for the children that have not yet been transferred." Ivor Stanbrook MP came, a barrister, and it was then that, following a chat about my books, he said that in his opinion I had wrongly been put on a list I should not be on.

I again went to Frankfurt for the Book Fair. I took a taxi straight to the Messe and my heart sank as I entered the familiar glass buildings with their escalators and unpacked my books at my stand. In the evening I went back to the apartment I had taken at Ronneburgstrasse 11. The next day I interviewed the American and English publishers and when the Book Fair became oppressive I nipped out and visited Goethe's house, basking in the tranquillity, allowing my soul to breathe. I visited some of the German publishers, and talked with a German representative of Fischers, Reiner

Stach, about my book, *The Fire and the Stones*. I told him that just as Einstein had a hunch lying in a meadow and looking at the sun and mentally travelling back up its ray, so I had had a hunch about the cause of civilisations. He said: "You have developed a universalist theory of world civilisations." His use of the word "universalist", coming from a German speaking in what was for him a second language, chimed with my own earlier focus on the word, and was another factor in choosing the word "Universalism" for my own philosophy.

I went to the Hungarian stand to show *Budapest Betrayed* and found myself speaking with a woman who took the old Communist hard line. "Gorbachev says there is glasnost," I told her. "Is there glasnost or isn't there? If there isn't, tell me and don't waste my time. If there is, then take this book." The woman squirmed and passed me higher up, and I was now seen by a woman who I was sure was in the KGB. I repeated my glasnost logic, and she reluctantly agreed that the book should be distributed within Communist Hungary. She said she would write to me, but she never did. I had won the argument but they won the power-struggle.

Back in England I prepared to tackle the history theory for Part Two of *The Fire and the Stones*. I had had an extension built onto the back of our house, and had to move my study, which left me exhausted. I wrote: "Now the crucial point is that of all the theories for the growth and decay of civilisation...the secular ones don't explain the idea that gave rise to a civilisation, i.e. the idea behind a civilisation is always a metaphysical vision."

The great storm of October 1987 affected us. The previous night there was a parents' Annual General Meeting with wine afterwards. At 11.45 p.m. I escorted Vernon Davies and his wife to their new Jaguar, and the battery had gone flat. I drove them home through driving rain, with their chauffeur sitting in the back of my car, and when I returned the road was like a river. I slept soundly through the downpour and the ensuing hurricane, and when I woke the grounds were in chaos: several trees were down, branches were strewn everywhere, a large chestnut tree had fallen across the netting across our tennis court, and the eye of the storm had crossed the Oaklands roof, ripping out many tiles. It had come from the direction of the Roebuck and had cut a corridor twenty feet wide through the forest to our second field, and had then driven on up and over our school, just 20 yards from where I had been sleeping, demolishing everything within its path, including the chestnut tree. (Strangely a neighbour had written asking if two other chestnut trees of mine could be felled as they were dropping conkers on her car, and I had replied that I was seeking to get them listed as there were two few chestnut trees in the area. It haunts me that chestnut trees was a theme during the week before the storm.)

For days afterwards woodsmen were around the school sawing branches and trees for logs as we cleared up, and there were ladders up to the school roof. I was still moving rooms at home and tussling with civilisations, and I glimpsed the underlying pattern of history: "America is a growing civilisation with little history – the Rome to our Greece. We are old and declining and decaying, we British; we have had our history, like 4th century Greece....Thatcher believes our decline has political causes (socialism), but she is wrong; it is historical, and irreversible, and will accelerate once she has gone taking her archaistic attitudes with her. Russia is old and European, and also in decline. America's rise will go on happening long after Russia has joined Europe. America will introduce a world civilisation." The turbulence in our house continued and I wrote: "Nov 2. Workmen all round me – painters, carpenters, hammerers by day, gas central heating mechanics by night – and I am just pouring data on world civilisations, none of which I 'know', all of which seems to present itself to me of its own accord, leaping off books' pages that fall open; I record and list, and lo! the evidence is assembled as I prove my hunch. We desire pattern. Art supplies it; also history....We can see action against the known pattern of Roman history and society, as against the incomplete and therefore finally unknown Western pattern in the case of a modern work." Again: "The house its nearly clear as the extension comes to an end. We are carpeted upstairs now. Have got to know: 4 plasterers, 2 carpenters, 2 plumbers, 2 painters, 4 bricklayers, 3 labourers, the supervisor and others who have been daily visitors while I tabulated my Universalist view of history." On top of this, our former Turkish tenant, Jalal, rang from London asking to stay, and came for a month, sleeping in Ann's study because of the building work. Of course one should be hospitable when people from abroad are in difficulties, but I found myself trying to retain data from several civilisations simultaneously while preparing his food and doing his washing up (for Turkish men are unfamiliar with kitchens, and when I indicated the tap he washed his hands). Quite reasonably he wanted the video to work and he wanted to buy contact lenses, he wanted meals and baths, and I had to surface from the depths and provide them, and I found it hard to go back down again.

Nadia came, very much the glamorous and well-groomed air hostess now. And a relative of Miss Lord's arrived from America, Martin. I struggled on: "Clear thoughts on Russia and China, and the West. The point is Western civilisation is an amalgam of European and American civilisations (like Rome and Byzantine), both Christian but both separate, one growing and religious (America) and the other old and secular (Europe). The same tension as is found between Rome and Byzantium."

I had to travel to London, and while waiting for the tube encountered Lord (ex-"Len") Murray, the former Secretary-General of the TUC, who stayed with me until he got out at Leytonstone. I wrote: "Bumped into him on Loughton station. 'Going to the Lords?' I asked. 'No, they're not sitting today, I'm going to Leytonstone.' We chatted generally until the train came in, then the subject got onto books and publishing. I asked if he was writing his memoirs. He said No, he had deliberately left it for 2 or 3 years because he didn't want to tell tales about Healey, etc. He said he was better at talking than writing, and he gave seminars and lectures and TV broadcasts – talked if anyone wanted to listen – but had no plans to do memoirs as so few were good. Dalton and Butler were two subjects of good books recently. I said he should write a reflective book that sought to understand our time. He said with intense interest, 'To understand oneself might be a good start.' I said he should write a book that sought to understand his times and his role in them – and his self. We talked about my aunt and parted very warmly. On opposite sides of the political fence – he is a Christian socialist, I am a philosopher of history, perhaps – but no politics came into it, it was a very equal chat." Looking back I warm to the self-deprecating idea that he was still trying to understand himself, let alone his times – I thought: what a nice man.

That afternoon two of the Howard sisters, Mary and Jean, who had lived at Oaklands during the First World War, came to look round with Mabel Reid. They reminisced. I wrote: "They played records in the cellar, dined in the library (where there was a door to the garden), used the study as a den and slept up in the attic (right), lighting their way with candles throughout the First World War as there was no electricity and gas stopped at the first floor. Three maids lived opposite (the attic at the top of the stairs on the left) and the parents' bedroom (at the top of the first flight of stairs on the right) had a nurse's room next door (Mrs. Perry's). The nursery was Ann Holland's room. Laughter, jugs of water and a lost time." I recall standing in the large classroom which was the nursery while one of them spoke to the children of what was in that room during the First World War, and we were all transported back to those golden and then dark days. They recalled a fire drill out of their top floor bedroom window during the First World War – about the time Copped Hall was burned down – and they had to abseil down on ropes, a terrifying experience from such a great height for small girls.

I yearned to escape the past and live in the present. I wrote: "The last year I have been abstracted from my situation, the present situation. I have been living outside the present, in whatever civilisation I have studied. It is time I returned to the present immediate situation in Nature, and wrote poems – poems that are tempered with the reflective eye that comes with being at home in the past. Joy comes, like the foggy Sunday morning, when you gaze at Nature and let it pervade, invade, your stillness. My study is essentially a meditation room with a clutter of papers about reflections on the past; papers from a reflective past. If I were dying like Tomlin, I would live in the present and drink in the moment; live like Keats. Work comes between me and Nature; academic work, chores, it matters not what the work is. As a poet I must let in Nature." But my experience of history was valuable for I now saw poetry as a yardstick: "People need yardsticks, standards by which to measure their experience. Just as they need yardsticks by which to measure their experience of history (e.g. *The Fire and the Stones*) so they need yardsticks by which to measure their experience of an eerie and misty morning, in which a hawthorn bush (next to the garden room) looks like Cerberus with two ears sticking up, and their yardstick is the well-known poets. Hence Wordsworth's *Prelude* book 1 is perennially popular. It is something that one can compare one's own experience to and measure it by, i.e. art. Art is not a mirror. It is a yardstick, a comparison, a measure. Humility is important: to know that one's first effort is not the final one, to evolve one's final meaning by successive drafts."

My approach to Stephen Lucas about the Harbourmaster's House in Charlestown had led to a call from his estate agent, asking if I would pay £150,000 for it in its present dilapidated condition, an idea on which I was cool, and then a circular informing me that several properties (including that House) would be auctioned in London on December 15th 1987. I asked a surveyor to look at the property, and on December 1st I had a phone call. I wrote: "Stephen Lucas on the phone. 'It's Lucas.' I: 'Stephen as opposed to Michael?' 'I'm doing you the courtesy of phoning. You'll know the properties are being auctioned....' A general chat, which began with my pointing out the disadvantages of his properties and ended with my interviewing him about his future plans. 'Charlestown will be better, not worse.' All day, a deep inner feeling that in some strange way the Harbourmaster's House is being given to us to restore. Providence and Stephen Lucas will make it happen....The Harbour property I dreamt of in Oxford may soon be mine." I had secured the bank's approval to buying the house and improving it, explaining that Ann's mother lived little more than a mile away and that it would be a retreat for us every half term and holiday, but I bargained on getting the House a lot cheaper than at Lucas's price, and I told Lucas that his reserve price should be low because of the disadvantages I outlined.

We went to a gathering at an ex-Oaklands parent's, where I had a long talk with one of the Naqushibandiyah family and sect of Kashmir. (Marion Lord sat with Matthew and Anthony, playing scrabble, and when we returned told stories of how she had made a scene in the post office because there were 40 in the queue and only two positions open, and how at her dancing class three partners trod on her toes.) We also went to St. Mary's church, Loughton, to see *Papa Panov's Christmas*, a play which was based on a story by Leo Tolstoy. I wrote: "Papa Panov with Matthew narrating and Anthony singing a solo. Arnold Cobbler has a dream that Jesus will come to him; he watches all day, in the course of which he invites into his shop a road sweeper, a poor woman and child, whose bare feet he shoes with his best shoes; and then when he thinks Jesus has failed to come Jesus appears and says that Panov helped him by helping everybody: 'I was hungry and you fed me, I was thirsty and you gave me to drink, I was cold and you took me in.' Very moving. The clear real vision of Tolstoy....The value of the Church – it keeps you in touch with real people, and giving, and its message is still there."

A few days later St. Mary's church put on a celebration of Oaklands' 50th anniversary. It was also a carol service. I wrote: "I waited outside to greet the parents in a cold wind, where I waited for my mother's funeral, and my father's; and there were thanks for Oaklands, for 'the one who founded it' and for 'new skills'. There was a democratic prayer for the teachers and caretakers, without referring to the owners. A beautiful service with many little children singing in the choir, all in uniform; many readings; many carols; bright little faces. I sat and asked the Light (the Fire) to come into me, and it did, pouring into me and up my spine, filling me with peace as the vicar prayed. I gave myself to true prayer."

I went again to church for a christingle service. I wrote: "Matthew and Anthony alternated in reading the lesson, Anthony from the pulpit, Matthew from the lectern. Then the children took christingles ('Christ-lights') – oranges with lit candles – and stood in the side aisles with them, all the brownies and cubs holding candles; and when they were snuffed there was smoke in the sun-shaft. I gazed at it for a long time, for I had lit my own candle and was ecstatic, the power pouring through me." The vicar, John Price, then announced from the pulpit that he would be leaving in April for Kirby, near Frinton, after 8 and a half years.

That evening I went to Chigwell parish church for their carol service, the fourth time I had been to church within a week. Anthony sang the choir solo. I wrote: "The Chigwell carol service at 5.30. Lights off, in the dark from the porch door (going back 800 years) Anthony's 'Hodie' and when the choir had sung 'Christus natus est', Anthony's clear, piping, unaccompanied 'Once in Royal David's city', so loud it filled the church like birdsong, like a blackbird's or nightingale's song, moving me to tears. I have been to church four times this last week, and have not been bored for one moment, and have been filled with the Fire (as I now call the Light). I am charged with it." Afterwards there were mince pies in school and I had a chat with David Evennett MP, father of a friend of Anthony's.

I went to the auction of Cornish properties at the May Fair Intercontinental Hotel, Stratton Street, near Green Park. There were getting on for 800 present, and several Cornish houses were being auctioned. They made the mistake of putting the best one, the Harbourmaster's House, first, before the ice was broken, and I let two bidders make the running and came in towards the end. There was a long pause, and I knew destiny wanted me to write there, and that no one else would come in. I wrote: "The breathless moment of destiny before the hammer fell. This is the harbour house, surely, that I saw in Oxford High Street, outside Schools, after attending a Yeats lecture." Afterwards Stephen Lucas came and shook my hand. I had it for less than two-thirds of what he had asked me for, and compared with what the other properties fetched, I had a bargain. I had earlier in the year bought a London flat as an insurance policy in case the school roll suddenly collapsed. I bought the flat, which was near Marble Arch, to be repaid over 7 years, and I felt satisfied: I had extended the school, extended our house, bought the London flat and now the Harbourmaster's House, while Nadia had received 4 successive marks of 100 per cent in her air stewardess exams and had started flying. It was all very pleasing. I wrote *The Haven* ("a Metaphysical poem").

Christmas came. I wrote: "Opened presents, went to church, lunched hugely, and then opened presents: a great sea of surfeit in the extended front room. Ann had made an effort, and all was done to make it a nice Christmas, but I am by nature a mystic who pares down and discards." I thought of the "poor, starving and homeless who will be sleeping under bridges" and retired to my history: "I have understood my time, and I marvel at what I have been shown. The Fundamentalist Islam is a greater danger than Soviet Communism: hence Iraq and Libya. Islam is...less decayed than Russia....These three blocs will affect the 21st century most." I got to bed at 1.30 a.m. having redrafted a passage on the future of Western civilisation. The next day the family gathered at the Roebuck.

A few days later the last piece of my history theory fell into place. I wrote: "A brainwave. I see that my theory/law of history...has a second period of expansion before the civilisation ends. I have now got the chronology right, I think, and am doing a spreadsheet to end all spreadsheets. Every civilisation listed down, every stage with dates...listed across. If I can get this 'spreadsheet' to work, all the facts will be accurate. It is a very efficient double check. (These are my 'equations', on the Einstein parallel.) To be a great poet you have to absorb and unify the culture of the past, which my spreadsheet does." And a day later: "I have seen (been given?) the law of history, and will be able to predict international relations by the time the chart is finished."

1988 found me working on the stages of civilisation for *The Fire and the Stones*, my "equations" for my law of history. In my little time away from this intense work I carried on improving my Cornish property and in January I was pondering the Israelite civilisation, and I wrote: "I am an *Old Testament* prophet, and my message (like Hosea, Isaiah or Micah) is that the Fire (God) has been forgotten, that authority has evaporated, the monarchy (is) godless and the priests (are) hypocrites, that pleasure-seeking is the norm; that the State is godless (Fireless)." I suddenly had a glimpse of what London was like; "I can see London as a ploughed field – a heap of ruins – and Westminster Abbey and St. Paul's Cathedral a wooded height." I was not sure whether the image I had seen was from the past or from a future time. Of my view of history I wrote: "Revealed knowledge. I was given the answer and merely posed the question: an inductive rather than a deductive way of working."

We were invited to a gathering at the Head's house at Bancroft's School, and I learned from the new Head, Dr Southern, that Barry Evans of Dulwich College, with whom I drank in Dulwich in 1962 had died: "He moved to the West Country to teach, he was still single and had monstrously abused his liver."

I went to Charlestown to view my purchase. It was a listed building in a conservation area with a view of the sea on two sides: of St. Austell Bay and of Charlestown harbour. I stayed at Ann's mother's house and met the surveyor and building engineer who would organise the modernisation of the house.

In Essex there was a planning application to pull down Journey's End. I wrote pointing out that it belonged to the Women's Voluntary Service during the war and that it was part of old Loughton, one of only two houses in Station Road in the 1870s. A few months later I was having some work done at Oaklands, and I needed a plasterer urgently, and rang various telephone numbers I was given and engaged a fellow to start immediately. I looked in to encourage him in his work, and he said: "You don't know who I am, do you?" And: "I've got Journey's End now." We had quite a talk and he told me how he wanted to pull it down and build an office block. I told him he should leave it in place. He had done "improvement" work to the building: he had taken out the central chimney, which I thought was like taking the tentpole out of a tent, and he was removing the garage and the porch and pebbledashing everywhere, and he had removed some of the front flowerbeds and had turned the garden where we played into a builder's storage yard.

All through January I worked on at the history theory, comparing and contrasting the evolution and development of different civilisations, adapting to historical ends the model of the spreadsheets I did for the bank manager. I compared the Egyptian, the Tibetan, the Syrian, the Mesopotamian, the Greek, and the Roman civilisations. I saw a link between Anatolia and Syria: "Then at midnight, not having eaten, after perseverance of many hours, saw a whole civilisation based on Baal: Ugarit-Philistines-Phoenicians-Aramaeans – and soon, down to the Roman emperor Elagabalus who took his name from Baal. Now it is clear. The answer is there in history; I have to worry away to find it. Mounting excitement. I have done, what, 16 civilisations, and it works for each of them. I am the first man to have discovered the Law of history, and as each day confirms it I get tingles up the spine."

Tomlin died, peacefully on January 16th. I saw an obituary in the *Daily Telegraph*. He had been moved to Trinity Hospice, Clapham, but no one had told me and I had not visited him. I felt sad at the effort to keep him alive with useless and painful treatment. He had suffered dreadfully, and towards the end had thought he was supposed to be at a meeting and kept trying to get out of bed to attend it. No doubt the intention of isolating him was to preserve his friends' memories of how he was when well. The funeral was to be at Hawker's church, the church of St. Morwenna in Morwenstow. I thought of him lying there alone in the cold. A few months later I learned that his widow was remarrying a former British Ambassador and would have the title "Lady".

Kathleen Raine was asked to write an obituary on Tomlin for *The Independent* and she rang me to check some points. She began: "It's Kathleen Raine, we are both grieving for Frederick Tomlin." We agreed that dignified acceptance of death is better than resistance through chemotherapy. (She: "The system resists because there is no after-life.") We had an hour on the telephone, "Ostensibly about the obituary..., but more on the TLS's book review of *Temenos* ("élitist and esoteric"), which I said was wrong in terms of the patterns in the grand unified theory of history. I said Toynbee had been unable to find what differentiated civilisations, and that it was the metaphysical Fire. She: 'Of course it is; you can't find it in history, it's not in history.' I: 'So he went all round the houses.' She: 'Perhaps Prince Charles would like *Temenos*. I shall ask my good friend Laurens van der Post to give him a set, all the back numbers." We discussed "C. S. Lewis lamenting that Berkeley was off the philosophy course; Blake and Yeats; India; America holding the future; Europe being in decay. Rare accord. Not a word of Plato, her agreement with my ideas. She is using some of my points, e.g. Tomlin at Eliot's church before Eliot, his being at home in every culture....She: 'Come and see me.'"

I have always had recurrent dreams of executions, of hangings and shootings; not so much recently, but they still occur from time to time. I had another one now. I wrote: "A nightmare. An execution. I walked under the gallows, which were large upright double-coffin-like boxes on a high walkway. On the top of them were written the names of pairs about to be hanged. In old (World War 1) lettering I read 'Thompson and Bowes' in capital letters, thus: THOMPSON & BOWES. I felt very sorry for Thompson and Bowes who would soon swing. Was this a memory? Has there ever been a Thompson and Bowes execution?"

I pressed on with my comparative study of civilisations: "Two for the

A MYSTIC WAY

New World, Celtic and Irish Celtic dovetail, Oceania includes Australia."

It was Biggs-Davison's turn to be ill next, an eventuality that took place against a feeling that Oaklands should expand to another site.

At the end of January it was reported that record numbers of 11 year olds (510 to be exact) were sitting for the local independent schools, Bancroft's, Forest and Chigwell, who between them had only 115 places, and the idea first surfaced that I should start a new school. I was too involved in my history theory to do anything at the time.

I was also concerned to investigate a temporary loss of grip in my right hand, together with persisting pins and needles, which I had woken up with in early February. I was concerned to check that I had not suffered a minor stroke, my consultant wondered if I had had a miniclot or microembolus. Strangely this temporary disability coincided with the exceptional brain power I had had to draw on as I completed my Grand Unified Theory. I wrote: "(It) has quite clearly been caused by the intensive work (often to 2 am) on my Grand Unified Theory. The demands over 2 years on my body have been very great, and my poor body is anyway weakened by being a pathway for the metaphysical Fire. An outsider may not see the connection (with) *The Fire and the Stones*; I, who have carried the load of all world history on my shoulders for so long, know the connection." I was sent for a brain scan in Queen Square and put in a magnet "like going into a washing-machine, and the sound – a clicking, grating sound – reminded me of our tumble-drier. Two 20 minute spells while I lay still, a band on my forehead." I was pronounced clear, my brain was not damaged in any way – the consultant actually said that whatever happened was attributed to overwork on my Grand Unified Theory, and that it was a warning – but the experience left me aware of what it is like to have a stroke, and I wrote a poem about the experience.

I was still thinking of the invisible: "Matthew's homework: to read *Auguries of Innocence* by Blake....The central idea is that there is an invisible world behind the visible world, which looks after all natural creatures and takes revenge if they suffer....Do not doubt this invisible world, Blake says – it is controlled by the God of 'God is Light', not the human form which sceptics think in terms of. Blake wrote this in the 1780s; within 10 years or so Coleridge was putting forward the same idea in *The Ancient Mariner*, for the invisible world looks after the albatross and takes revenge against the crew of 200 sailors. Romanticism as the identification of an invisible world behind the visible – cf the New Age vision, which is Neo-Romantic." And I was certain that I must approach the invisible through art, not religion: "I am an artist, not a religious. I have chosen perfection of the work, not perfection of the life (to quote Yeats), i.e. art, not religion. My work is the Law in Fire and stones, a prolegomena to my own poetry; and then my poems, which will assert a metaphysical invisible world behind the visible – a Romantic depth. Unite: perfect work about a perfect life." I was aware that I must work "in isolation..., eschewing all groups. The solitude of the sea down in Charlestown; close to the waves." I wrote: "If I am starting a literary movement, it must be metaphysical"(in the sense of returning to the invisible).

In mid-February I went to church and was served communion by Ken James, the fireman who approved the Oaklands fire regulations and saw my mother before she died. He said, "The Blood of Christ, Mr Hagger," a phrase that catches the "enmeshing of community and spirit in Essex".

We all went down to Charlestown at half term and I had another meeting with the building engineer. There was now a hole in the front room floor and much debris off the wall. It was a fine day and the sea sparkled. One of the locals told me that Bulstrode of BOM Holdings had turned down £140,000 for the Harbourmaster's House just before the auction.

I went to Tomlin's memorial service in St. Stephen's, Gloucester Road. I wrote: "T. S. Eliot's beautiful church: red and white arches, gold paraphernalia at the front. 200 people, perhaps, and an address that followed Kathleen Raine's obituary. Beautiful singing (medieval) from a small adult choir, all in Latin, then High Mass: bells ringing, sung responses, much crossing. Afterwards in the hall behind the Lady Chapel near the T. S. Eliot memorial. Spoke to a white-haired man who was at the church in 1947 and knew T. S. Eliot: 'He was a gentleman. You wouldn't think he was a poet, you'd think he was in the City. Always wore a bowler hat and carried a furled umbrella when he was churchwarden. Was always interested in what you said, very modest. He was very tall, and he bent down to you.' The Tomlin hymns, all poems (Metaphysicals). Saw Kathleen Raine in the scrimmage, attempting to get a cup of tea so got her one. Charming conversation." She told me: "Tom Eliot said to me here that there could be nothing worse than an Americanised Russia." I "sketched a poem on Eliot's church and the Eliot tradition in which Tomlin wrote". Shortly afterwards Kathleen Raine sent me a card saying, "We can only scatter seed for future harvests."

I went on and met Gorka and recorded: "The idea that the USSR will break up because of glasnost, as economic weakness and loss of central control combine to create revolts in the Soviet empire."

The Conservative Patrons Club met at the House of Commons, and I was shocked to see Biggs-Davison's appearance. He had cancer and had had chemotherapy. He had lost his hair, and was reported to be considering giving up his MPship. Douglas Hurd was the guest, and to my surprise I found we were on top table – it was as if Biggs-Davison were indirectly recognising the work of the Heroes of the West – and I chatted to him and to Hurd before the meal. Biggs-Davison said: "Both Toynbee and Spengler were wrong about Western civilisation, it's not in decline." As he left after his speech, Hurd stopped and said to me, "Good luck with the books."

I worried away at the history theory and found one problem solved in my sleep: "This morning woke up with the solution to the Israelite civilisation in mind: David's time is not the unification but the expansion, and by putting the unification back to the tribal league I find that everything fits perfectly. The Law is there and it's like a breakwater perceived through a wobbling surface of water: you have to peer to see it, and it is not always visible at once. But on a clear day it is." A month later I wrote: "The most important thing is to define, and state in writing, the long-term context in which we live, i.e. the point which our civilisation has reached. Everything then becomes clear and is seen as a temporary, local manifestation of specific historical conditions – within the universalist 'plan'."

A part-time gardener we employed, Jack Emerson, died, He had sat down a lot – once he sat and munched his sandwiches on the front step of the school, which was not popular – and I had not realised he was so ill. I went to his funeral and wrote: "Thirteen guests, a cortege saying 'Dad' and a greying son, a tearful wife, a bearded priest, who shouted words of hope as we entered the crematorium chapel. Outside a snowstorm, a blizzard; and somewhere Jack is offering to hoe weeds in heaven."

We went to Cornwall at the end of March and I recorded: "In the evening walked by a calm sea. The harbour lights were on, Charlestown looked very quiet." Much of the stay was spent in choosing a new kitchen and bathroom and items of furniture from local stores. I recorded: "Late at night, walked down to a moonlit Charlestown sea in a raw wind, and went to the Rashleigh Arms 'snug' with a cold nose and a dewdrop."

I was still meeting the committee of Exiles at the Free Polish headquarters, under Gorka's chairmanship, and the group now accepted my acronym, FREEDOM (FReedom for Eastern Europe from DOMination). I wrote: "So my ideas, expressed in a paper for Biggs-Davison, have been implemented."

I went to Winchester to attend the Mystics and Scientists conference and noted: "Lovely blossom on two cherry trees." I listed the people there and asked a question: "Sir George (Trevelyan), Lyall Watson, Goodwin, Sheldrake and Paul Davies. Are they all potentially part of the mainstream, i.e. figures in a budding Renaissance; or New Thought type figures of a movement that will be forgotten once the millenarianism has gone?" That was a crucial question which I answered by making stage 44 of my history theory one of syncretism and universalism.

On the way back I joined Ann and the family at Lyme Regis. They were staying at the Bay Hotel: "The old world village between Cobb and Charmouth cliffs. Fossils – bought a 150 million year old Jurassic and 500 million year old Cambrian trilobite this morning. A walk along a deserted beach before breakfast, then walked to the end of the Cobb with Ann and Anthony...and then to the Fossil Shop and Museum (John Fowles, assistant curator, has had a stroke and is not there)....The walk round the 15th century church and churchyard where the fossil-collection is based. Monmouth beach."

In April I noted: "My right arm is slowly becoming paralysed. I force it to do things – to twist and push – but it is painful and it would rather hang limply by my side. I keep it writing (as now) but it would rather not write." I had the same feeling in my left arm for much of 1993.

In May I "stood in the window and gazed at the shrubs that line the path that leads from the front gate to the stone steps, and 'saw', after a while, a purple outline round them all, a kind of aura. This disappeared when I looked *at* the plants, but reappeared when I resumed my gaze out of the window, standing up, through half-closed eyes. The energies of the plant – a Romantic idea."

I was now visiting properties with a view to buying a second school. On May 18th I listed the four I had short-listed in order of priority: "Coopersale

Hall, Coopersale House, New Barns Farm, Hainault Hall." Coopersale House was Rupert Murdoch's old house; it had a lake that children could fall in and no assembly hall, and I was not sure I could get change of use from residential. Coopersale Hall, Epping, on the other hand, was owned by Oaklands parents, the Fordhams. It was a 1776 building set in 8 acres of beautiful grounds, and it had an orangery/ballroom that could be converted into an assembly hall that would seat 250. It was near the M11/M25 intersection, and I felt I could secure the necessary planning consent on those grounds. I employed a planning consultant and visited Fordham, who was a hardline property developer, and began negotiations which were to last until November. I was aware that an economic cycle was coming to an end and that there would be a recession, but reckoned that if I bought now, everything would be in place for the next mini-boom, by which time the expansion of nearby Stansted Airport would bring 50,000 more families into the area. I wrote: "Coopersale Hall is in my grasp, together with Orchard Cottage....I must be courageous....Like Brutus, I feel there is a tide which if taken at the flood leads on to fortune." And: "Here am I, two days from being 49, driven by a compulsion to own a Hall and act out a line in my poetry (*Marvell's Garden*) from over ten years ago." And I was contemplating this while I had just obtained planning permission to develop the Cornish house.

We went to Charlestown and I wrote: "A rough sea after rain, misty spray over the rocks, and the house has been gutted: old plaster out, stripped back to red bricks, slate walls, beams and joists. Two skips of plaster outside." I met a sea captain who lived on the cliffs, Ken Gowsell, whose house was the only building in Charlestown in the 1770s, where fishermen brought their pilchards and loaded them onto carts. There were holes in the wall for levering on the tops of the pilchard barrels. Our house was supposed to have followed with a few others around 1790.

Soon afterwards I learned that "they will have to remove the sea-end wall....The house is made of shale at the sea end, the pre-granite style which suggests it was a fisherman's boat-house with a sail-loft before it was converted." I noted "a wonderful moon on the Charlestown sea".

I encountered another neighbour, Arthur Hosegood, the historian of Charlestown, listening to classical music, and I wrote that my classical music was the classical poets who "feed my soul, Pope, Dryden, Wordsworth et al. I am a classical composer of poetry."

In June Argie celebrated her 85th birthday. I hosted a reception at Oaklands on a Sunday and 34 relatives and 15 friends came, including Lord Murray. I greeted him and his wife at the door, and Lady Murray's first words to me were: "You taught in the State system, now you're in the private system; you were with the deprived and now you're with the privileged – how do you square that, how do you justify it?" I kept cool and amused, and said that "the ILEA had degenerated in my time". She asked, "What do you mean, degenerated?" So I explained that academic content and standards had been sacrificed to essentially political initiatives on race, sex and class. Lord Murray was not a bit confrontational, and I had a couple of very pleasant conversations with him. I made a speech about Argie, and the day ended with cricket in the Oaklands tennis court. I said to Lord

Murray, "Come and play cricket outside with the children." He said, "I wouldn't know what to do." I said, "I'll show you." But he insisted, "I couldn't."

In mid-June Edward Heath visited Chigwell School and presented prizes at Speech Day and made a very amusing speech. Anthony received a prize from him. I wrote, "A red-faced man with white hair. He refused to conduct the orchestra in which Matthew played, near the chess pieces out of doors, a wind blowing the music about....Heath the universalist 'pro-Persian' (in the sense that he would have supported Cyrus in the 6th century BC)." I stood beside Heath but did not speak to him.

In early July I finished the 61 stages of my history theory, having finished "9 months as I translated my inspiration into perspiration". In the same week the bank agreed to advance what I needed to buy Coopersale Hall and Orchard Cottage from two separate vendors, and later in the month contracts were exchanged on condition that planning consent was given for the Hall to become a school, and I now opened negotiations with a third vendor (a local called Hammond) to buy the private drive. I barely thought of the risk I was taking, I knew within that the idea would work.

During the First World War Coopersale Hall was owned by Lord Lyle, who was MP for Epping, and in 1924 Churchill visited it to arrange the transfer of the MPship to himself, and, liking it, used to stay there in the war when it was a rest home for wounded officers. He slept in the classroom we call the Churchill room, retiring below to the air-raid shelters in the cellars when there was an air raid. He would leave Downing Street and in 24 hours he would visit Blake Hall where the Battle of Britain was being planned, visit the pilots at North Weald and then spend the night with the wounded officers at Coopersale Hall before returning to Downing Street, having had 24 hours of country air. In those days the Coopersale Hall estate was over 150 acres and stretched to the hills. I was putting back together three parts of it which had been broken up, I was reunifying its most important parts.

Meanwhile I wrote of the American civilisation: "The Achaemenian and American civilisations and empires are in the same stage regarding expansion....Perhaps a world order is ahead, of regional power blocs (Africa, Asia etc), under American leadership (the nuclear superpower)." In mid-July we returned to Cornwall. The Harbourmaster's House had scaffolding round it, having had the seaward wall taken down and rebuilt. Almost immediately we went to Restormel Castle to see the enactments of "Fire over England", a chain of beacons lit across England to celebrate the European single market. I wrote; "Parked in a field near the castle, walked through sideshows with Elizabethan-clad stall-holders. Dancing to Elizabethan pipes, Elizabethan soldiers training children in the use of pikes. Climbed the castle ruin to the battlements, and waited in mist and damp until the cannon fired and...lit the bonfire. Could not see the other beacon on the hill. Later descended the castle steps and saw the firelit wall of the castle glowing in firelight, flickering as it must in the Elizabethan time." The next day I drank shandy with Capt. Gowsell, the seaman, "bearded and still-eyed and wonderfully calm, looking peacefully out to sea".

In Charlestown BOM Holdings had sold the harbour on and there was a presentation in a marquee in the cobbled car park. It was put on by the new owners. There were seats for 285 on a slightly raised wooden construction with a scaffolding framework, and the new owners, a bow-tied, dapper, dark-haired Barry Williamson and (incredibly) Stephen Lucas, spoke, introducing the maps and charts to the villagers and planners present, trying to create a favourable climate for a massive planning application for a nameless developer to buy the right to build over 90 new houses. It came to questions. The chief planner asked a question about sewage. Then a woman from the local Residents Association near me asked a hostile question on parking. Behind me I heard a crack, and we sank. It was like going down in a lift and stopping with a bump. The scaffolding on which the floor rested caved in and we dropped 4 ft. There was no panic, but Williamson stared, hypnotised into silence by the awfulness of what had happened. The marquee's "tentpole" swayed, then there was a silence and no one took charge and said, "Stay in your seats, ladies and gentlemen." As a result everyone rose and without panic made their way out to the cobbled car park, where the £10,000 spread of food was brought out and we tucked into it in groups. It was now apparent that the residents were against the plans to develop the port, and a receptionist who had been made Pier House Hotel manageress without any training, went round putting Williamson's point of view.

Back in Essex briefly, I worked on "the runes", as I called my stages of civilisations, and found that my unconscious mind was solving problems for me: "The mind is amazing. Sat on the mower and worked out a revised Russia without any notes, and retained it all. 'Mean while the Mind from Pleasure less,/Withdraws into its happiness:/The Mind, that Ocean where each kind/Does streight its own resemblance find' (Marvell)."

I returned to Cornwall for more supervision of the house, and "the boys went canoeing to Silver Mine cove, beyond Gull Island". Our near neighbour Arthur Hosegood told me, "It's a wonderful place for a writer down here. You can walk on the cliffs and on the beach and think, and you see everything clear." A few days later I recorded: "A scorcher yesterday; hazy today. Spent both days on Charlestown beach, sunbathing. Corrected proofs. Today, redid Japan; suddenly saw it....The boys in their dinghy and raft, paddling round the rocks in their wet suits."

I had a visit from the secretary of the Cornish Buildings Group and a man from Truro County's archaeological department, "the one bearded, the other fey", who looked at the open walls of the Harbourmaster's House and the neighbouring buildings and concluded they may all have been built before 1790. I wrote: "In our case, the fireplace on the back wall (i.e. our middle wall, which was the original back wall) is a sign of 17th or early 18th century, as is the granite pillar." There were cobbles under our kitchen floor, which could have been a yard or a kitchen. They concluded that our house "was probably not a boat-house but a domestic residence with a stud wall". The pilchards, they said, were exported from the beach; and the shingle was ballast from foreign shores, dropped by sailing ships. The holes in the Gowsells' wall were where oil was squeezed down in the pilchard barrels. One of my visitors challenged the idea that Charlestown had only four houses in 1788, and said that Charles Rashleigh would have built the harbour in the 1790s where there were houses.

A MYSTIC WAY

In my walks by the night sea I thought about the Grand Unified Theory the physicists sought (the union of all four forces) and wrote: "The Grand Unified Theory of the universe which physicists seek in the phenomenal world is to be found in the Fire (as Heracleitus probably foresaw). Like the historians looking for their Grand Unified Theory in history books, physicists seek it in physics books." This perception anticipated my coming work, *The Universe and the Light*.

Back in Essex I was getting a new classroom ready at Oaklands. The work had fallen behind, and I painted it all day until midnight to get it forward, working with Mick who was doing it for us. The first day of term began without a pane of glass in the new outside door. The children came in and went to assembly, the glazier came, and when they returned the room was finished. I had cut it very fine.

In mid-September I learned that Sir John Biggs-Davison was dead. He had survived cancer and was cleared after chemotherapy in July. He had gone to Angola with Sir Anthony Buck, where for some of the time they apparently slept in a tent, and he had caught viral pneumonia and jaundice. He had returned to Taunton hospital, and had died. The virus was a mystery. He was 70, and I had known him for over 32 years. I thought of his role in the Heroes of the West and wrote: "John Cameron may be receiving him, greeting him, along with Tribe, up in heaven."

I was astonished to read in an obituary that he had been a Marxist at Oxford. He was buried at St. Petroc's church, Timberscombe, near Minehead, Somerset. I sent flowers, Vernon Davies (who now knew who he was) attended the funeral by helicopter.

The more I thought about Biggs-Davison's sudden death, the more I thought it suspicious. Angola was ruled by the MPLA, a pro-Soviet organisation with links with the IRA as I knew from McForan's book. All it would take was one telephone call and a doctored ham sandwich. I wrote: "I am in Hamlet's situation. Intuitively, I know Biggs-Davison was murdered, as Hamlet knew his father was murdered. The question is, how do I bring it out?" The situation bothered me, for the Heroes of the West should not simply accept a murder without protest, and when a father came to watch his son play football at Oaklands, and I walked back across the fields with him in my tracksuit, and asked him where he worked and he said, "It's secret, but in Stormont", I immediately asked: "What did you think of Biggs-Davison's death?" He countered by asking my view. I said: "I think it stinks. He's cured of cancer, goes to Angola and contracts a mystery virus and dies on his return. I think he was murdered." The parent said, "I'll think about that."

The next time I saw him, standing outside my house near the school, he said: "I stopped an important man in the corridor at Stormont" (he was referring to Tom King, then Secretary of State for Northern Ireland) "and told him what you had said. He stood and said, 'No, no, I don't think so.' I left it at that, and next day he stopped me and said, 'You know, I couldn't sleep last night, I was thinking about what you said, and I think, Yes, yes, there may be something in it. So I've launched an investigation.'" My contact told me that both the intelligence services had launched an investigation: "It's gone to the top in Northern Ireland, it's now in Curzon

Street." And I felt relieved. There was no more I could do. I had raised it at the highest level, and if the professionals found nothing, then I would never find anything. I never heard the outcome, and officially Biggs-Davison, ally of the Heroes of the West, died of a mystery virus, to the consternation of Taunton hospital.

I went to the memorial service for Biggs-Davison at Waltham Abbey. The Abbey was packed. There were chairs all down the side aisles, and even then there was not enough room to seat everybody. It was an ecumenical service, with a Catholic representation. I shook hands with all his family afterwards. They greeted me very warmly. Lingering in the porch of Waltham Abbey I thought it a good place for the service to be held.

The following February I dined at the Carlton Club with the Conservative Patrons Club and sat next to a local American, Harriet Pratt. Biggs-Davison often stayed with her. She said to me: "He only left £20,000. It was Pamela's parents' money, the house in Hereford Square was her parents'. He lived on his MP's salary and his writing. He always liked meeting you, he said you were the most intelligent of his constituents. He liked the intellectual discussions with you." I asked: "Do you think Biggs-Davison was involved in intelligence work?" She said, "Yes. I'm cynical – everyone who's worked abroad has been." And I fell silent and went over a chain of events that had affected my life from a new perspective, and wondered how he, a right-wing MP who had supported South Africa, could have made himself vulnerable in a country like Angola which opposed everything he had stood for.

The rest of 1988 was dominated by my founding of Coopersale Hall School, which happened almost effortlessly in the breaks from writing my Grand Unified Theory of history.

T. S. Eliot had become prominent in September. There were articles that diminished him, saying that Eliot treated Mary Trevelyan and Emily Hale badly when he rejected them for Valerie Fletcher and his late serenity. Tomlin's last book on his friendship with Eliot appeared posthumously, and I wrote: "Eliot thought of himself as a minor George Herbert, whereas Tomlin saw him as a great man who wrote differently from anyone else since the 17th century, an Arnold or Ruskin of our time. His memoir like that memoir of Wordsworth....Tomlin on how Eliot was the greatest man he had ever met." I wrote: "Poetry as a vehicle for metaphysical truth."

Eliot's centenary service was held in a packed St. Stephen's, Gloucester Road. I sat next to Judith Tomlin in the Tomlin pew. I wrote: "Passed Heath-Stubbs on the pavement....Sir Laurens van der Post spoke brilliantly about Fire. Leaning on the lectern (which collapsed after loud knockings, causing him to say 'It's done this because I'm going to talk about thunder'), he said that Eliot is the greatest religious poet in the English language, that he first read Eliot in 1923 in Africa, while caring for flocks....He said that Eliot unswervingly stood for the Fire and that the poems grew naturally like roses: 'I'm a man who occasionally has a poem in him' (in reply to Yevtushenko's 'What do you think of this as a poet?' Answer: 'I'm not a poet.') Spoke to Valerie Eliot and van der Post afterwards. Arranged to be in touch with van der Post about my own work on the Fire and a theory of civilisations....Valerie Eliot like Joyce Grenfell. Van der Post, with a wicked glint in his eye." I was extremely impressed by the fluency and force of van der Post's "Fire sermon".

Shortly afterwards I "passed Francis Bacon, to whom I used to speak. He was wandering along Harley Street, towards Oxford Street, looking upwards, barely looking where he was going; aged yet handsome."

I had meetings with Council officials and planners about the road – I had reached a semblance of agreement with Hammond after tortuous negotiations – and as I progressed to the planning decision I had news that Bancroft's would be opening a new prep school in 1990, and would be in competition with what I was trying to do.

I had a health check at BUPA and was told: "The TIA (transient ischaemic attack) you had is the most serious thing. There could be a second TIA at any time; alternatively one may never come. Do what you want to do now." On my bronchiectasis I was told: "You had TB in 1947, which probably came from the milk. The milk then was not treated and there were no antibiotics. TB as a child leads to bronchiectasis later."I was also told: "You have a 40 decibels loss in your right ear."

In October I made a couple of flying visits to Cornwall to supervise the Harbourmaster's House. The first time I drove "through storm and spray" and stayed at the Pier House Hotel and wrote: "Today all is clear. There is evidence that the sea has been over the road up to the hotel wall (Pier House): trails of seaweed, and shingle. Feel flinty and pre-poetic. Am ready to rejoin the road I left in 1976 to absorb the history of the Fire and of civilisations. A poetic output is ahead." The second time I observed: "The house began like a building site, but now that the carpets are down and all the sofa is there, it is turning into a very good house. The light is on, too, by the corner, the yellow gas lamp."

The Conservative Patrons Club invited Jeffrey Archer, "self-publicist", to Vernon Davies's. I wrote: "He spoke well (a rehearsed speech) but to my lie-detector was a dud; he did not ring true. Lectured us on morality."

On November 3rd the planning committee reached a decision on whether to allow Coopersale Hall to become a school. I noted: "Ann Miller (the Chairman of the Council) rang. The planning application has been passed. I was a millionaire; I am now a multi-millionaire. Billingham (my planning consultant): 'You can celebrate now.' Have sat down at 11.15 to finish work on the start of *The Fire and the Stones*. It's just another evening." I had no doubts, I knew within that the new school would be supported. Now I regularly interrupted my work on my history theory to complete the purchase of Coopersale Hall, Orchard Cottage and the road – the exchange of contracts had been conditional on my obtaining planning permission – and to present news of the new school to parents. I told the Oaklands staff after a fire drill. There was applause.

Soon afterwards we were invited to dinner by Chigwell parents. Strangely, the only guests were Dr Southern, the Head of Bancroft's and his wife, and my wife and me. Our hosts did know we were both starting new schools at the same time. I announced the news to our stunned host and hostess. Dr Southern and I got on very well about it and agreed there was room for both of us. Again I wondered whether such a bizarre gathering was a coincidence or Providential. It was extraordinary that the only two people who were about to announce the creation of new schools in the area should be thrown so close together by accident.

That same evening I took Matthew to Waltham Abbey Town Hall to attend the adoption of the new MP, Biggs-Davison's replacement. Steve Norris was adopted. I observed: "A forceful 43 year old with definite opinions and fluent articulacy on a platform, he went to my College. Met him afterwards. He: 'We must talk.'" In fact I had quite a discussion with him on the platform – we had not overlapped at Worcester College, quite – and I told him about the books I had published and how I now ran two schools.

Anthony sang a solo in Mendelssohn's *Elijah* at St. John's, Epping. He was the youth and sang with professional singers. Half the church was taken up by two huge choirs, which included the Old Chigwellian Dickie Leng, and the other half by the audience. The professionals wore DJ and Anthony sang in a Chigwell blazer, a boy of 12, and received loud applause.

On November 17th I completed the purchase of Coopersale Hall, and the Oaklands secretary, Carol Norris, had taken 70 applications for the new school. The idea was clearly working. I immediately began to organise work on widening the 450 yard private road, which involved building an embankment; doubling the width of the front gate and widening the internal drive; and converting the downstairs of the school into classrooms and installing fire doors. On December 9th Hammond exchanged contracts on the road after I had done most of the widening. I took him to meet my solicitor, Ian Hawthorne. As I introduced him Hammond produced a mobile phone and began a shouted conversation with his ex-bunny girl girl-friend, and my solicitor looked on in speechless horror.

By mid-December 200 applications had been received for the new school. We held the Oaklands Christmas gathering at Coopersale Hall, which the Fordhams had now vacated. There was no furniture in the building, but there were expensive carpets and curtains and we managed. I wrote: "In candlelight. I served wine...from packets in the hall, between the Adam room and the kitchen. We had wooden chairs in the Jacobean/panelled room and the Adam room, and some sat under the frieze and in the bay window....Many were quite overcome by it all. All agreed that the school will last a very long time. It should be dedicated to setting souls on the right path in life, so that they discover and realise the inner Fire within themselves."

On Christmas Eve I went to the midnight service at St. Mary's, Loughton. It was held by the new vicar, David Broomfield. I wrote: "It was Rite A, the Lord's Prayer was modern and I didn't know it. A long sermon about listening to the silence below the TV and turning aside from ambition and balance sheets and earning a living (getting and spending). An equally long prayer. Words kept interfering. I was deep in the contemplative silence and internal Light, having spent the evening on Jeanine Miller's book on Cosmic Order in the *Vedas*, and the Fire. I was imbued with Fire." On Christmas Day I noted: "Ate at 2 o'clock, finished in time to hear the Queen's speech. Much affluence, excess and luxury, and my Spartan soul is now sitting ascetically apart from it all."

The next day I had a weird dream about Tomlin and Eliot. It was so real I wondered if I had encountered them in the spirit world: "Dreamt I visited T. S. Eliot in hospital. I was very articulate and asked him 3 or 4 questions, and made a long disquisition about the autobiographical element in one of his 'persona' poems – how confessional and how artistically to resolve tensions that continued in real life. Eliot nodded from his bed. Later I saw him on a heath with slatted chairs, just standing as in pictures, looking youngish in a suit. Tomlin said, 'Leave these chairs' (some of which had foot rests) 'so people will always know where Eliot came.' Later still I visited him again and he turned into a little boy. When I asked, 'What can I bring you, Tom,' he said, 'Tadpoles.' I happened to be carrying a jar of pondwater from the Oaklands pond with a tadpole and shark-like stickleback in it, and I gave it to him after saying, 'Oh, that's easy, we have lots of tadpoles in the Oaklands pond.' The day I gave Eliot a tadpole. What was the significance of this dream? Did I meet his spirit in the spirit world, as a shaman would say, or did I contact memories in the racial unconscious, or was it a dream about my tensions?"

We went to Tunbridge Wells for lunch with the family at the Spa Hotel and we went on to tea at Jonathan's house. I confronted the new year, reflecting that I had to appoint staff for the new school, which had somehow happened of its own accord, and that now I was a man of property: "In 1988 I bought (i.e. completed) the Harbourmaster's House, Orchard Cottage and Coopersale Hall, a sudden explosion of activity. I expanded Oaklands....It has been a year of achievement on the school front." I was moving away from publishing into running schools and writing, and I had not forgotten "my mission, my destiny, my driving force to turn around the intellectual climate of our time". It was as though the properties were to give me backing in that coming "turnaround" (or revolution).

In January 1989 I supervised a JCB and a 10 ton lorry to widen the internal Coopersale Hall drive. We doubled the width of the private road near the bottom of Flux's Lane by erecting an embankment out of thin air; I changed the contour of Nature, applying the thinking I had observed on the Tanzam railway. I organised the delivery of a septic tank, which was installed with the help of the local fire brigade, coped with the safety requirements of the Fire Officer and held interviews for the new Headship, and appointed Mrs. Best as the first Head of the new school. She had been Deputy Head at another local independent school. At an event at St. Mary's, Loughton I had run into Ann Miller, the Chairman of the Council, who had said, "I want to come and teach at your new school." And I now showed her round.

I went to a Conservative Patrons Club dinner at the Carlton Club and was winked at from top table by Steve Norris, the new MP who had won the by-election caused by Biggs-Davison's death, and who later said he would be putting his second son Edward's name down for Coopersale Hall, and agreed to open the Oaklands fête.

I had thought about our need to stimulate all parts of our mind: "Art, poetry, TV thrillers, news, all awaken different parts of the identity and help keep us all in balance. This...view of what a human being is gives novels, plays and poems a role in bringing feelings into play; newspapers a role in bringing critical awareness of the world into play; and churches a role in bringing contemplative peace into play. There is a role for all of them. The art of living is to keep all areas awake – the soul well swept and cleaned and lit – without excessively long periods of time being devoted to external stimuli." I explained this to Anthony at bedtime, and told him: "We go to sleep in one part of the brain and wake in another part, as if we had sleepwalked in the night."

Somehow this exchange released something in the 11 year old Anthony, and he had what may have been a far memory. As I sat by his bed, I asked him to see the Charlestown steps. I recorded our conversation: "He: 'I can see a cobbled street.' It was bustling with people and Victorian clothes. A sign swung in the wind, there was a vegetable shop behind a green frame with lettering. He was in a corridor. As I questioned him he revealed he was in a wooden room with a bare wooden bed and a blanket; he wore a long nightshirt and had bare feet and was a boy. He went downstairs and startled a woman in black with a Victorian hat. She said, 'Why, Master Edward.' He went upstairs and saw a man in a study: dressed in a black suit with wavy hair. He said 'Hello', gruffly. He went downstairs and was given porridge: 'Here's to eat' (in a West country voice). Afterwards, as there were 4 places laid at table, he went upstairs and found an 11 year old girl who said 'Get out'. She was writing and had her hair in ringlets. He went to the front door and opened it. It was cold outside. The black door said no. 17. The cobbles were cold underfoot. He walked to the end of the street. There were railings. He came back and found his home. 'It's no. 17.' He rang the doorbell and the woman in black came: 'You'll get a cold, run up and change.' He ran upstairs and found his blue and white flecked suit and black shoes. Downstairs she said, 'Run along or you'll be late.' He went outside. I said, 'Read the sign over the vegetable shop.' He, screwing his eyes up, 'It's Spenex or something.'(Later, 'It's got an N and an X and an E in it.') Far memory? I brought him back into 1989, but we both knew something important had happened. He has located his imagination."

We all watched the Queen at a game of rugger at Murrayfield and there was booing at the Scottish national anthem. I made a prediction to the boys: "You will live to see the UK broken up, with England, Scotland, Wales and Ireland separate states in Europe. It will happen in your lifetime, and you'll look back and say "What a pity" because England will no longer be important. Together we were important in the world, separately we will (each) be a state in Europe, no more. Sadly, I see it coming. It cannot be stopped. It is the future, towards which we are progressing."

My brother Jonathan celebrated his 40th birthday. Several members of the family stayed at the Spa Hotel, Tunbridge Wells. After bathing in herbal foam there I put on a DJ and drove to Jonathan's house where there were "many young solicitors and accountants and wide-eyed young wives, all vying to speak louder than each other. I was the second oldest, after the new Canon Prebendary from Bristol." At one point I forked some food from my cousin Richard's plate and he hooted with laughter, and the clowning continued bizarrely over breakfast the next morning. Richard and Wendy were seated at a different table from Ann and me, and the waitress who waited by the wall in the formal silence did not know we were connected. I had run out of toast, and I leaned gravely towards Richard and said formally, as if to a complete stranger, "Excuse me, could I borrow a piece of toast?" "Certainly not," Richard said indignantly, "there's only just enough for us," and people from nearby tables turned their heads and the waitress gave us a long look and went off and returned with a toast-rack of toast, for which I thanked her. I then discovered we had no butter. Again, I leaned towards Richard and said formally as if to a stranger, "Excuse me, could I have some butter?" "No, you get your own butter and leave ours alone," Richard said, and again heads turned, and the waitress gave him another long look before going off to bring me some butter. The humour lay in the contrast between the attitudes we struck and the invisible norm.

On February Shrove Tuesday I attended the Old Chigwellians' reunion. After chapel at 7 we had dinner at three long candlelit tables, and I renewed my roots in people I had not seen for many years.

Every day I carried forward the founding of the new school. I negotiated with the locals about our improvements to the road, and held talks with the new Headmistress. We had received 60 letters of application from local teachers who had read news of the founding of the new school, and we set about interviewing these applicants and appointing 20, meeting in the inadequately furnished and heated building and seeing them in batches of 4 or 5.

The new school's secretary was Sheila Turnbull, who was in Mensa and a longstanding friend of the Oaklands secretary, Carol Norris. They had been in the same class at Woodford High School, and Carol's hair had caught fire from the bunsen burner as they talked in science. Both had been suspended for going missing at lunch time when they were in fact visiting nuns, and Sheila had fallen out of the Chigwell School's Praefects Room cupboard when the Chigwell master Claud Salmon had hunted for beer.

At half term we all went down to Cornwall and stayed for the first time in the Harbourmaster's House, and drank in the Charlestown pub and I chatted to the barman who told me that BOM were in difficulties, that Lucas was £1.8 million in debt and that Williamson and Lucas's planning application for 94 new houses had run into opposition and would not happen. Later we had a visit from a friend of the barman who said that Lucas had been in prison; and that his brother was being investigated by the DTI. Towards the end of our stay Tom Southern joined us, a friend of Matthew's and the son of Dr Southern of Bancroft's, Coopersale Hall's rival, and I recorded that we "watched the boat leave, a Dutch boat manned by Dutch Calvinists who would not come in on a Sunday. It beached, got stuck in the harbour entrance and took an hour to get afloat. Williamson (had) called across to Graham the Harbourmaster, 'I want this boat away,' not realising that high pressure and wind compressed the water downwards, so that it was first 2 feet down, then 6 inches."

I worked on my history theory. I wrote: "Proof-read stages 35-47, and checked them against the chart of all stages. Corrected the Germanic pattern, which somehow had a couple of wrong dates. Made adjustments. In between times walked by the sea. Walked along the pier. Saw the 3 boys near Gull Rock, standing like sea-birds silhouetted in the twilight: dark outlines against a calm sea. Now hear the breathings of Nature outside. All is energy, and so am I. Midnight and beyond: all are asleep, only I am awake in this house, sitting on the bedroom floor writing this on my knee by my bed, and listening to the waves beneath my window."

I also wrote some stories and poems: "Feb 13. Wrote *The Artist and Fame* about 'shotgun Tommy'....Wrote *Maturing Love and Vision*....Feb 14. More poems: *Shingle Streaked with Tar, A Business Walk by the Sea* (having observed Barry Williamson in consultation with his adviser this morning) and *Chain and Padlock: Time and Forgotten Years.*

Back in Essex, Miss Lord blacked out and was unconscious for at least a minute, lying on her stairs. Marion, her niece, called an ambulance, but when she came round Miss Lord refused to go to hospital. Miss Lord had always seemed timeless – at 89 she had frequently spoken of going to make coffee for the old folk, many of whom were still in their 60s – and this incident was a sign of her impending mortality.

Des McForan rang. I wrote: "We feel that America has inherited the European empires and will be invited to take some on; that Europe and Russia will become United States (USE, USR) in a conglomerate. We tipped the balance in 1984-6 at a crucial time. Told McForan about my book, how it starts in one discipline and ends in another. He: 'You need the sweep of a Renaissance man to do that. In 150 years' time they'll be talking of the Hagger School, like the Bloomsbury School.'" We discussed Salman Rushdie, and I said to McForan: "Fantasies by illegal immigrants about the Prophet do not get us very far forward."

David Evennett, MP, a Chigwell School parent, had us to dinner at his home, and in the course of talking about my publishing I told him about my history theory. He expressed concern at the leadership and standards at Chigwell School. The Head was retiring and we discussed how we could influence the choice of successor. I had heard that the interview would soon take place, and that there was a short-list of three: two economists and a young Head of English from Brentwood School. Evennett asked me if I knew any of the Governors, and I replied that Colin Wilcoxon, now a Cambridge English don at Pembroke, had been Head Boy when I was at school. It was agreed that I would go up to see him to reflect concern in a number of areas on behalf of several parents. I accordingly rang Colin Wilcoxon and visited him in Pembroke for a couple of hours, and I explained the areas of concern – the quality of the plays chosen for production, for example – and got the message across that, having been through a phase of new building under the present Head, Chigwell now needed someone who would return to academic standards. Despite his relative inexperience I said Chigwell should go for the Head of English who would emphasise the right things rather than for an economist who might emphasise the wrong things. Colin Wilcoxon took note of all I said and thanked me for reflecting the views of a number of parents. Soon afterwards the Governors duly appointed the Head of English from Brentwood, Tony Little.

Towards the end of February I announced Frances Best as Headmistress of Coopersale Hall School to the local press, in the persons of Pam Giblett of the West Essex *Gazette* (who as Pam Humphreys had worked for my mother) and Val Tyler of the *Epping and Harlow Star*. I was interviewed on local radio by Val Tyler. A local road company widened the private drive, and snow fell the day after they finished and soon a blizzard was raging. 40 parents turned up for Coopersale Hall's first Induction Day in March.

I had not forgotten the Light: "There is the tradition of the mystic intellect, or of the intellect of the mystic; and there is the tradition of the heart....The Way of the heart leads to a purified intellect in which one sees the Light, knows the Fire."

At Easter I wrote poems: "Easter Sunday. Wrote 2 poems. *Toil* and then *Easter Sunday*, in the middle of which I saw a woodpecker tapping on the elm by the gate from my study window; and put it in the poem."

My history theory reaffirmed freewill: "There is no determinism in history or religion. Civilisations move through stages because human freewill (of contemplative mystics and leaders) takes them from stage to stage. Nothing is written in the stars. There are possibilities or tendencies only, which human effort brings to being – like my struggle to found and grow Coopersale Hall School." I was struggling with Turkey within this theory. At the end of January the phone had gone, a voice said "Hello Neek" and it was Turkish Jalal from Germany saying, "Keriman" (his wife) "will come at 9." Their visit, and short stay strengthened my feeling that both Gibbon and Toynbee were wrong about the Byzantine civilisation, which neither continued the Roman civilisation (Gibbon) nor passed into the Ottoman civilisation (Toynbee): "Jalal was sent to me because the Byzantine civilisation did not become the Ottomans; rather the Russians, with the Arabs passing under the Ottomans. Consistency of religion – that is what I was asked to sort out with Jalal, who suddenly appeared in our midst." I had seen the European civilisation was about to pass into a conglomerate, a United States of Europe, ending a colonial conflict. All through Easter I wrestled with the role of the conglomerate in relation to the colonial conflict that preceded it in all 25 civilisations.

I now answered Ezra Pound's question to me: "Have you had 12 experiences that sum up the culture of the last 70 years?" "Answer: (1) Chinese cultural revolution; (2) Libyan revolution; (3) Iraq, Arab revival (cf Iran); (4) USA – world dominance; (5) British decline; (6) Japan, industrial miracle and Zen; (7) Vietnam; (8) European reunion (Brussels bursting into light); (9) Far East Tour, coming Pacific 'Eastern' civilisation; (10) Russia, *Archangel* (Byzantine identity v Communism). They are all there. Already done. Just simply order and organise them." (Pound's original question involved 12 experiences, which I had boiled down to 10.)

At the end of March I had a review of my health with Dr Hughes. I wrote: "He had all my X-rays from 1983 to date, and he showed me the patches on my left lung in 1983 and July 1984. There is a latent potentiality in my lungs for a patch on both sides, and it may be active now, although he does not hear it. I am holding my own....Hughes: 'Some of my patients – I have 100 suffering from bronchiectasis – suffer in one lung only. You have the potentiality for it in both lungs.'"

At the beginning of April I went to Cornwall and sat in the sitting-room of the Harbourmaster's House, which had now been modernised with central heating. There was a fabulous view across St. Austell's Bay to the

Black Head of Trenarren, a local promontory, and down to the harbour where long china clay boats came and went, manoeuvring through the narrow neck, their sides squealing on tyres hung down by local workers. There I was able to sit on the sofa, surrounded by my work, and watch the dramatic changes to the sea. I wrote: "The sea is booming and crashing, rain is lashing." I walked in "a blustery wind" and reflected that in the 1960s I had "rejected the armchair mind for experience". Ann and the family would go out, and in that most seaward downstairs room in the Harbourmaster's House, sitting alone, I found the peace to reflect on my theory of history.

In April I opened Coopersale Hall School for two classes downstairs, a total of 35 very young children, while we carried on getting the upstairs ready for September when the roll would increase to 150. That summer the children spent golden mornings on the terrace or on the lawn under Elizabeth I's tree, and I often looked in while organising the workmen who were converting different parts of the building and improving the grounds.

There was a Chigwell School evening at St. Martin's in the Fields to commemorate the 360th anniversary of the founding of the school, and Anthony sang a solo, "O sing unto the Lord", to a packed, ticket-only congregation. I wrote; "His solo, confident and clear, to a packed house under the sun-burst over the altar." In the aisle I met Tony Little, the new Head at Chigwell School. In the crypt I met Tudor Parfitt, the explorer, who was with his schoolmaster brother.

Again I received inspiration in my sleep, in other words, from the beyond; this time on the important subject of Universalism. I wrote: "Ap 29. To bed with Ann after 10 days of working late on the book; slept fitfully....Then woke with the beginning of my 'Introduction to the New Universalism' in mind and wrote it in vest and pants before doing exercises. I believe I have devised a new discipline. As Sartre redefined Existentialism, I have devised Universalism, which is more important as being entirely beneficial to mankind and not related to violence at all. I have been a long time in preparing my great philosophical work because the matters in it have taken many years to brew."

At last my history theory was finished. I wrote on May 11th: "After a week and a half of daily revision amid Coopersale Hall, have finally finished my revision of the Theory. I predict that European civilisation will end c2610AD. It has taken me a year to establish the details and I have got there."

On a sweltering Sunday, May 21st, I celebrated my 50th birthday at Coopersale Hall. Getting on for 100 family members and friends arrived and we held the function in the incomplete assembly hall. There were staff from both Oaklands and Coopersale Hall School, David Evennett and the Essex cricketers Alan Lavers and David East. My sister had tied a balloon to my wrist. My brother Rob made a speech about my experience as tutor to Hirohito's son and as eye-witness of Gaddafi's revolution, and about my "achievement" in having two schools. There was a game of cricket on the lawn for the children, and Anthony hit lustily and the ball nearly fell on Miss Lord's head, where she sat snoozing under a tree.

A MYSTIC WAY

The following week the new Epping Forest MP, Steve Norris, and his wife looked round Coopersale Hall for their son. I showed them Orchard Cottage, which was standing empty, and Steve said; "I'd like to live here." "Why don't you?" I said. "We're not ready to use it yet. You could have the run of the grounds at weekends and the squash court and tennis court." The idea lodged. Ann and I put on tea in the study, which Mrs. Best and the school secretary attended.

We went down to Cornwall for half term and I noted "the booming sea, but a chilly evening". There was a "fire on the beach". I revised *The Fire and the Stones* on "a hot sunny day. In the evening a calm sea. Today a breathless calm and cloud." On June 1st I "finished the substance of Part 2 of the book on a fine but chilly day. Sat in the sun during the afternoon." I had been working on the 7 foot long chart of 25 civilisations that accompanies the book. It is now entitled "Chart summarising the 61 stages in the Life Cycle of 25 civilisations (including projections for living civilisations)", and I noted: "Life Cycle. The words came to me on the plane between Baghdad and Basra, and now they are in the title above my history chart." It was as if the beyond had lodged in my mind back in 1961 high above Ur, the site of the first Middle Eastern civilisation, the information that I was to study the life cycle of civilisations, and again there seemed a great inevitability about what I had done.

Back in Essex I "went back to my early poems and was stunned by how good they are once you know what the mature vision is. I didn't know where I was going, the images came out, and I did not think these poems greatly significant at the time, but now they point a direction very clearly. All the concerns and preoccupations are there." I recast *Twilight* and noted: "My poetry is exalted by the grandness of my theme." (My choice of the word "grandness" clearly echoed, challenged and contradicted Kingsley Amis's "Nobody wants any more poems on the grander themes for a few years.")

In June, too, I watched with fascination the struggle of the Chinese students against the Chinese regime which culminated in the brutal suppression of their campaign for democracy, a struggle entirely in keeping with the aims of the Heroes of the West. I wrote: "Am on the verge of tears – full of admiration for the heroism of the students, full of rage at the army, full of sadness at the inevitability of it all. Pity and terror."

The Oaklands fête (or fair) was duly opened by Steve Norris MP. I greeted him outside the gate in Albion Hill and he immediately raised the possibility of renting Orchard Cottage, while parents were queuing to get in near our elbows. We discussed how much I would charge before we had gone through the gate. I said it should be a fair rent at the bottom end of the scale to compensate for building work we would do if we received planning permission to build an extension behind the hall. More than 1,000 people turned up and as I stood beside him near the caravan in the main field, microphone in hand, waiting to introduce him, he told me a story which my former tutor, A. B. Brown of Worcester College, Oxford had told at a Law Society dinner: "A school secretary sent out a prospectus and mistyped for the fees '£840 per anum'. The man who received it read it and said, 'Oh well, I was paying through the nose anyway, I might as well pay through the other end as well.'" He had just finished the story when I had to introduce him, trying to keep a straight face. I pointed out that he had just monitored the unfairness of Noriega's election in Panama, and that he would be bringing the same critical skills to his judgement of the bouncy castle drawing competition. There was a falconry display, with birds swooping for food; a kestrel called "Lady" sat high up in the oak-tree and swooped to take food from the handler's gloved fist while he gave a commentary on a microphone. The Norrises walked round all the stalls and I saw them to their car at the end.

Soon afterwards the evangelist Billy Graham came to West Ham football stadium. We all went. The pitch was covered with seats, all filled, and every seat in the stands was taken. There were two hymns, various messages, men came by with buckets for donations, and then the old campaigner I had last seen in 1954 appeared, a tiny dot by a microphone. I trained my field glasses on him and he looked just the same as when I had last seen him, even though he had blessed all the US Presidents since then. He was more chatty, and discussed war and then sin and then how "everyone here will be dead in a few years". Jesus, he said, was the way to life, eternal life. His logic was that sin causes death, whereas absence of sin leads to eternal life. There was then a call to "declare yourself publicly, come up". There was no music, just a silence. From all corners of the stadium people made their way to the front and I noted: "An incredibly moving moment, as the word of God, the spirit, moved through a football crowd at West Ham. Eyes filled with tears, no one else could have got this response." But I knew I could not do the same with my vision of the Light. The Light was universally available to all, but to receive it was different from the attitude-change Billy Graham sought, and I could never do that at a mass-rally. Afterwards we went down onto the covered pitch. The goal posts were still in place, and I stood near the post where Tom McAlister saved the penalty kick.

We attended the Chigwell School ball after Speech Day, at which Anthony collected three prizes (for Junior Reading, Art and Music). Six hundred attended the ball, we took champagne and ice for our table, and there was dancing after dinner to the Jonny Howard Keymen who included "two lead female singers of great beauty and brazenness".

I suffered acute pains which rotated between my jaw, teeth, neck, chest, ear and top arm. The dentist's X-rays revealed no abscess or cyst, and an Asian doctor pronounced it neuralgia (which means "cyclic attacks of acute pain in a sensory nerve, cause unknown"). The pain later localised as toothache, and the Light poured in. I wrote: "June 26th. Awoke with toothache in the night. Today, a massive influx of divine organisational energy to get the book finished. Reformatted Part One....Blitzed the charts."

Three days later there was Open Evening at Oaklands. I wrote: "Ill....felt giddy but forced myself to serve wine for 400 people and talk from 7 p.m. to 10 p.m. Felt myself passing out. A woman talking at me going round and round. Said 'Excuse me' and dashed out to the kitchen, went out to the house, lay down with feet up for 5 mins, then returned via the kitchen to resume conversation."

At Coopersale Hall the work upstairs was progressing. A fire door had to be knocked in a very thick wall, and Mick and John, two of my in-house

557

builders found a George IV 1817 coin which had dropped down a flue from the attic. John said: "A shilling, that was 3 hours' work. The rate of pay was 4 old pence an hour in 1817.' Gordon: 'If it were a George I or a George III, the head would be a different way round.' I was impressed at the knowledge these workmen revealed, and sensed the relics of a common culture to which all citizens at one time subscribed.

There was a Conservative auction at Vernon Davies's, at which, after a dinner of salmon and champagne, Tim Norris, the local auctioneer, raised £10,000 for Conservative funds by encouraging crazy bids for not always useful objects. The next day there was a barbecue at Oaklands. It was a fine day, and 300 sat on the grass, including Giles Watling, the actor son of the local actor Jack Watling whom I had often seen round Loughton in my boyhood.

We had Sports Day at both Oaklands and Coopersale Hall, the highlight being "the lusty mothers' race". The swimming gala for Oaklands took place at Loughton Pool and as usual I was on the microphone. Eventually we broke up at both schools. Almost immediately the bank came to play rounders on the Oaklands fields. I wrote: "Twenty or more cashiers in singlets and shorts. I served wine and orange and left them to their game, which ended 3-2 to Loughton branch. Much shouting and cheering from the field. The deputy: 'Ken is always poring over your figures. Calls them "the tablecloth" because they cover the table.'" It was the bank's tablecloth that had given me the idea for the "life cycle" history chart.

I now resolved to bring out a selection of my more Metaphysical poems, "now that I know where I am going". I wrote: "The importance of having something else to do besides poetry....The greatest poetry is written by men who are living first and foremost, and who occasionally stand back from their life, to reflect on its contact with reality, to reflect the metaphysical."

A medical examination for a life insurance company revealed that I had arcus, "a white ring round the iris which suggests a heart attack may be ahead because I am depositing cholesterol. Arcus senilis, the senile bow." Of my bronchiectasis, the doctor darted to Hutchinson's *Clinical Methods* (1897) and whimsically read: "The odour of bronchiectasis has been compared to that of apple blossom with an arrière-gout of stale faeces."

The first version of *The Fire and the Stones* was now finished. I had rung Asa Briggs, the Provost of Worcester College, and he had kindly agreed to read the book. I arrived early and sat by the Worcester College lake "and reached out to the ghosts that flitted by from the lost days – the canal behind me, sitting as I was on the stone seat with the lion and sphinx – and pondered that day in 1959 when I gave up Law, 30 years ago, and never dreamt I would be returning with a finished book for the Provost to read". I lunched in the basement of the Randolph and then took *The Fire and the Stones* to the Provost's Lodge: "Knocked loudly and waited for the Provost's secretary, had a telephone conversation up to the Provost. He: 'I'm so glad you brought it in and that you've got the support of Kathleen Raine. She's a wonderful woman.'"

At Coopersale Hall the work had intensified. To cut costs I took water and gas up the 450 yard private drive myself. I bought the pipes and hired Tony Barkey with his digger. I wrote: "July 20 and 21. Battled with the road. Tony gouged it and heaped it, then we lowered blue 125 mil MDPE (water pipe) in and knitted the 6 metre sections with electrofusion equipment. Mick (Shears) did the fusing." At the same time I was building and tarmacing a playground with tennis court netting in the 18th century walled garden.

Towards the end of July we went to Cornwall, and in the next few weeks I was aware of a tension between the poet in me and the historian. On the way I bought "coins of Shapur I and Ardashir I (Persian Sasanians), both with fire-temples, both silver, at a discounted price". I was hot and sweaty in London, but there was a cooling breeze in Cornwall. My sister Frances and Richard and their children stayed with us, and Frances entered the village donkey derby, and came a creditable 2nd, smacking the back of her donkey to keep it running while we cheered her on. Immediately afterwards four parachutists landed in the field, trailing smoke from their ankles, and Matthew went and spoke to them, trying to sign up to do a jump although he was still under age. On the way back I ran into a bow-tied Barry Williamson who was strutting about the harbour. He was feeling unwanted and lamented, "They don't want me to do things for them down here."

Richard asked me about my writing. I wrote: "Drunk with fresh air. A sunny morning. In the afternoon showed my history chart to Richard, and a few poems....Told him...I have found a form, in the reflective poem, which enables me to include biology and physics and other disciplines, i.e. to take a whole view of everything; and that my poems have to hint at a metaphysical reality. Also said that the poetic activity has to take place alone and in silence....A poem is also a record of a particular day (e.g. *Ben Nevis*, which I am reworking); better than a photograph because it includes thoughts and feelings and images." I revised the poem on Ben Nevis: "Showed it to Richard....He liked it. Explained that poetry is not about the physical world only, but that the greatest poetry is about the metaphysical world, too; hints at a different order of reality. The great poets are those who combine the sensual-tactile with the eternal, and corrections can take place 20, 30 or even 40 years later, as you get the poetry right." I explained that I have always been careful to get my rhymes right, and that I am not a hasty, doodling sort of poet; I have always made poems to be well-wrought and to last. I wrote: "Poetry can put us in touch with its metaphysical source again." The trouble was, "It takes 30 years to locate the metaphysical within oneself."

We all walked to Porthpean "to look at the coffin cave, which is now filled with sandbags. The waterfall on which I wrote a poem." We went to Fowey and had a cream tea in the Singing Kettle. I noted: "The inscription opposite, DM 1715, recorded the marriage year of the owner of the oldest house in Polruan, which was a nunnery before Henry VIII dissolved the monasteries." The Charlestown Carnival included our then gardener Dave Williams dressed as a Chinaman sitting in a rickshaw pushed by a group of Chinamen with signs saying "I bought village", "Chinese laundry", "Chinese take-away". We went to St. Mawes castle, which was built by Henry VIII in 1540/5, and Mevagissey. After Frances and Richard left we attended the Charlestown Regatta with "water-races, greasy pole, climbing like a spider upside down along a rope through a tyre, team races with tyres and so on". I spoke at some length with Bill Ricketson who had leased the dock. The boys canoed on the calm sea with the Canoe Club.

At the beginning of August I rang Kathleen Raine and told her about *The Fire and the Stones*. She immediately tried to typecast me as a historian rather than as a poet who had studied civilisations. She said: "You will be my metaphysical historian in the Academy we want to set up. This must be Providential. Sacred history – you might teach at our Academy. We want £2 million to build it. It will be in London. Laurens van der Post is seeing the Prince of Wales....Keith Critchlow is involved....David Bohm is doing physics – the philosophy of science. Van der Post is involved. But we haven't got anyone who is covering the philosophy of history. I thought it might give you a platform. If I can widen from history to poetry, have you read Yeats's *A Vision*? What do you think of his view of history? Tomlin would have been so good doing philosophy. Judith is someone who will make a man happy, I never had that quality, it wasn't to be my destiny. I don't know what I can do for you, but do ring Laurens van der Post." She gave me his number.

I duly rang van der Post, and reminded him we had met at Eliot's centenary service. He said: "What a wonderful idea, the Fire. And *The Fire and the Stones*, what a wonderful title. I'd like to hear you on it, but I'm just going away. Can you ring me in mid-September and come and see me?"

I reported back to Kathleen Raine, who said: "The mantle is passing to you. Toynbee would have written you a Foreword if he were alive." We discussed Tomlin and Ayer's illumination. She said: "He needn't have said that he'd seen the Light. Indirectly he was saying his work of 50 years was wrong." I told her, "The poet's aim is to receive the vision and hand it on to the next generation," to which she said "Yes." We talked about how a book is never really finished, and she said: "When you've finished a book you think it could be better, and certainly 20 years later you see things you could have put in, but it was the best you could do at the time, quite simply you couldn't have done better at the time." She repeated sadly, "I haven't given happiness as wives like Judith Tomlin have, I couldn't give happiness to a man as they could." She invited me to tea: "At 3 on August 10th there will be a cup of tea."

Steve Norris had signed a contract to move into Orchard Cottage and I returned to Loughton to get the place ready for him and to monitor the work on Coopersale Hall, completing the new gas and water supply in time for the full opening in September. At this time I was still writing cheques for all bills to the two schools (along with paying the staff and keeping the accounts) and I remember the mound of post was so high that I really needed to shovel it off the floor, like frozen snow. Nadia visited me briefly.

I returned to Cornwall and attended the christening of Ann's fisherman cousin Stephen's daughter at Kenneggy Methodist chapel (built 1841). I wrote: "The wait outside in the sun, Stacey hot in a knitted shawl. A long service: hymn, *Bible*-reading, prayer, hymn, *Bible*-reading, prayer, taken by a Circuit Minister who has 6 churches to keep. In the footsteps of John Wesley. (The first chapel was a thatched building nearby.) Back to a roomful of chatty women and silent men." During the sweltering afternoon I took Matthew to Porthleven harbour.

Plato interested me greatly at this time: "Plato saw the shadows as 'cast by the true' (Edwin Muir). My Shadow is my destiny, my guardian angel, cast by the sun of the true, and my reflection (social ego) is even further removed from reality....Read Anthony and Matthew (in Ant's bedroom) *Kubla Khan*, *The Splendour Falls* and Kathleen Raine's *Seed of Creation*. Surprised myself by telling the boys that *Kubla Khan* was a metaphor for God; his sunny dome and caves were a metaphor for the Platonist view of creation. The poem is thus about how God created the world with life (the sacred river) coming out of nothing and returning to nothing; the nothing of course being a Platonist something."

Matthew and I went for a walk under the stars, and I "saw one enormously long shooting star that trailed down the sky; yellowish. Later took a rug and lay in the back garden, holding onto grass so as not to fall downwards towards the stars. Saw another shooting star. Matthew: 'It's amazing, that's the universe out there.' His wonder, at 14." A couple of days later I reflected: "The stars. 1,000 million galaxies of which ours is one, in which there are 1,000 million stars of which ours is one, in which there are 1,000 million houses of which this one is one....Immensity and smallness." I "sunbathed and wrote *House Martins in the Dock* following my early morning walk to get the papers".

I drove back to Essex and on August 10th I visited Kathleen Raine in Chelsea, from 3 p.m. to 9 p.m. My *Diary* entry catches the way I resented being typecast as a historian: "Stayed longer than I intended. Her aesthete's room (in) Paulton's Square with a picture by AE on the wall, original Cecil Collins, Indian heads etc and old books in 1930s jacketless boards, all rather dusty. Wooden 1840s windows and garden out of the window. I sat near the front window to watch my car (there was no meter and the wheel clampers might be by) and she offered me cake she had specially baked, sandwiches she had specially made and Darjeeling tea while I spread the chart out on a table (she sitting to my left) and after leafing through the Fire of Part One, talked her through all the stages. She asked a lot of questions, e.g. 'Where's India?' 'What will happen in China?' Her historian friend Dorothy Carrington came in for tea and talked about Napoleon....Kathleen understood about the Fire and said: 'It's a great work or it's nothing. It's a great work. Sacred history returns in our time, secular events being within a context of what is sacred.' I gave her food for thought, e.g. 'Michelangelo had to operate within the context of a civilisation, he couldn't have done it outside.' She took down Yeats's *A Vision* and read passages showing Yeats knew the Fire. 'Yeats was groping towards what you've done; the diagrams. You've seen the pattern of history. You are a historian....There's no need to write poems about the Fire. Leave that to others.' But she's wrong. 'Poetry is the language of the soul speaking to the spirit. It comes to the poet, who waits for it. You can't write *about* the Fire.' But you can! Wordsworth wrote *about* the unseen power in a language that appealed to the common man. Raine: 'TV has corrupted the language poets use, poetic language, i.e. the soul's language has gone.' But it's the soul informing the world, the Baroque. Life is about more than the soul, it includes the world and social activity, and poetry can catch the soul informing the world. She is too puritanically, hard line 'other mind, the imaginative world' to countenance the involvement of the social ego." I continued: "A poetry as language of the soul is too etiolated. It is the soul looking at Nature but incorporating the social ego as well (chair 2 in the Kabbalistic vision). Raine: 'A poet is not a medium. A poet channels images from another world, from a higher world, but is different from the priestess in the Delphic oracle. Poetry is not mediumship: there is metre and technique to consider.' Granted....'David Gascoyne is the last great poet. There were so many great poets of my generation: Yeats, Pound, Watkins (Yeats's disciple), Gascoyne, Muir, Eliot, Thomas. But now there's no one. I started *Temenos* in the hope that it would throw up new poets. But it hasn't." She ended by saying: "It's a long time, many years, since I had such an interesting and memorable afternoon."

Later I observed: "She looks like Blake. Sits alone in her Chelsea flat with her definite opinions about the imaginative world, and is opposed to the social world. A liver in the soul who rejects the social world." I noted that she had visited an art gallery with "Bill Empson" ("Ricks," she said, "I don't care for his criticism at all") and that she had visited Ezra Pound at St. Elizabeth's. She told me: "Yes, Pound said the same to me that he said to you. He said, 'I like your poems, but you must learn not to waste any words.' I've never forgotten that advice." She said: "Eliot didn't have the vision, as Yeats did; only allegiance to a moribund Church of England which has lost its vision." But how wrong she was – Eliot did have the vision of the Light, the "fire and the rose", which is not a moribund vision but a Universalist vision and was superior to Yeats's vision in *A Vision*, as Auden recognised when he said to Andrew Harvey, "Eliot was so damn lucky, he had the mystic vision." (I combine Eliot's mystic vision of the Light with a development of Yeats's Universalism, and I wrote: "Yeats's *A Vision* is child-like in relation to my vision of world history: Yeats has no dates and lack precision; his vision is more mythological and derives from the Hindu Kali Yuga and Great Year." Yeats's *A Vision* was in fact largely received by his wife as automatic writing and edited by Yeats.)

Kathleen Raine told me: "Imaginative poetry is in decay, therefore civilisation is about to collapse." I wrote: "My history demonstrates that this is not so. She needs to revise her poetic attitudes in the light of my history." I also wrote: "Poetry is not exclusively about the social world (the Movement) or exclusively about an imaginative world (Raine); it is about both." I recalled a remark of Tomlin's, 'There's something very virginal about Kathleen Raine,' meaning: she doesn't live in the social world, she's a nun, she lives apart with her gift of imagination." I concluded: "I thought out the scheme of events within which our time is to be regarded....I will not fritter away precious hours serving her Platonist cause. Plato along with others has a place."

I returned to Cornwall on a windy fine day. I settled to the *Preface to my Selected Poems*: "With my curtains blowing, worked on my *Preface*, which is now entitled 'On the New Baroque Consciousness and the Redefinition of Poetry'. Have declared how I see poetry – its language being a language that appeals to the common man – and have smashed the view, 'It's not poetry.' Rhyme, metre, organic but sculpted work; I know what I am about. Smash the view, 'It's got to be waited on, the other mind of the soul opens to inner imagination.' This happens, e.g. my 'string of images' in *The Silence* and *Gates of Hell*, but it is how the images are presented that is crucial." I had pulled away from Kathleen Raine's view of poetry as exclusively the language of the soul from within. Poetry also included the outer world – hence my Baroque. Kathleen Raine was a Neo-Romantic poet, I was a Baroque poet. She was of the past, I was of the future.

We took a boat trip up the Tamar from Saltash. I wrote: "Past wooded hills, shingle beaches, sedge to Calstock....On to Morwellham quay. There the rain began. Back to Calstock for an hour: we couldn't disembark because of the rain; then back to Saltash." The trip showed me "the Tamar as a frontier, initially as wide as the Thames..., the end little more than the Roding, but where it mattered turning Cornwall effectively into an island in Saxon times".

Some international cricketers came down to play on the St. Austell cricketfield with local cricketers. There were 9 six-a-side teams, and O'Donnell, Crowe, Greatbatch, Broad, Randall, Roope, Hooper, Harper and Mudasser were all brought in (rumour had it) at £300 a man (which they may or may not have received) by Stephen Lucas. Lucas opened the batting with Broad and did very well. There was a hospitality tent where, with ostentatious lavishness, drinks were offered to anyone invited in. The drinking carried on at the Pier House Hotel until the early hours, and I woke up in the middle of the night to see the eclipse of the moon. "Our own shadow and curve took three quarters off the brightness of the full moon, which earlier had illuminated the entire sea and beach. Everywhere was a glory in pale moonlight."

We spent time among the Charlestown rock-pools: "Little sandfish darted out of our way, putting me in mind of a line from my own poetry, about footsteps being 'thunder to the roach'. Mussels, limpets, barnacles, bladderwrack; shrimps, a few crabs. Saw the cliffs and our house and lamp-post from a new angle, across rocks and sand. It looked very much set in Nature." We went to Gunwalloe: "Sat on a rock and wrote another metaphysical sonnet; then walked in St. Winwaloe, the medieval church. A very high tide which came in very quickly. As I scrambled to safety Anthony lost a shoe – which the sea returned an hour later, so we left without loss. Lunch and tea picnicking in the National Trust car park, a field overlooking dramatic spray as the rollers crashed in and foamed and climbed the cliff." Back in Charlestown we "went round on the rocks past Gull Island to where there is a view of Duporth slope and sat on the slate rocks" while "the two boys fished in rock pools: transparent shrimps and mini-'sticklebacks', and 'weavers' and 'tropical fish'."

Back in Essex I thrilled to pictures from Neptune 2.8 billion miles away, which confirmed "that this solar system of ours is devoid of life – is barren and icy – and that only on earth do human things happen." I thought about the vastness of space and the tinyness of earth: "Earth-centredness within the context of vast, empty spaces, and infinity and eternity – the whole being linked to a metaphysical conception of human life, of its aim and purpose. Why earth? Why the special conditions on earth? Have we colonised it in the past? Are we ex-colons or descendants from the ape? Or something else? Think. There are implications for Universalism. To sum it up, space has a vastness which is inexplicable to the materialist, who resents the evident tinyness of the earth. It is just the vastness of space and the uniqueness of life on earth that strengthen the metaphysical position. The Fire comes from space/and another dimension, and earth has been chosen by Providence for purpose activity, and this sort of thought, because it alone among the planets has an atmosphere capable of sustaining life. Either our demise, the demise of each one of us, is of little consequence, like that of a trodden ant; or it is of significance, in which case the divine mind, in which the entire universe rests, is involved. Both camps can argue from Voyager 2. Relate the Fire to the vastness of space and the uniqueness of life on earth in our atmosphere."

I thought about the symbol and wrote: "The symbol derives from the analogical and vitalist esoteric....The symbol is the static form of the relationship between two moments....The symbol transmits an esoteric metaphysical Reality by expressing the inexpressible in terms of the expressible." I wrote: "Reconcile the metaphysical Fire with the vast interstellar places of the universe....What is the link between the metaphysical Fire and the vast interstellar spaces? Quite simply, the one manifests into the other, as Bohm has set out in *Wholeness and the Implicate Order*. The Fire is implicate." Later I wrote: "I see how the Fire is the cosmic essence, which Bohm has made explicit."

I had doubts about being associated with Kathleen Raine's Academy: "Raine states the tradition through Plato's Academy (see 385BC-529AD) and its revival in Florence which (she asserts) influenced Michelangelo and Blake; and wars with Christianity as Justinian destroyed the Academy. Do I really want to be associated with it? Raine is trying to typecast me as a historian rather than as a poet, which I do not want to happen, but the idea of a university that is close to the Light is a very appealing and attractive one." Her Temenos Academy would not emphasise the Light at all.

The rest of 1989 was devoted to the expansion of Coopersale Hall and further research into my metaphysical perspective.

I now opened Coopersale Hall upstairs as well as downstairs and accommodated 150 pupils as we had planned. At the staff meeting "I stressed the historic nature of our presence in the staff room", pointing out that our new school was the largest independent school to have been founded in West Essex of its kind since the Second World War. On the first day I "acted as a traffic warden to establish a pattern on the cars, harangued the new parents from the fire escape". Steve Norris had moved to Orchard Cottage at the beginning of September 1989 – I recorded that I "visited Steve Norris and his family to discuss his waste-disposal system, which had gone wrong, and ended up discussing Africa and Communism" – and after my long dealings with Biggs-Davison, it was extraordinary that his replacement should be my tenant, and that Coopersale Hall, which had been associated with two past Epping MPs in Lord Lyle and Churchill, should now be associated with the present MP for Epping Forest. What other school had its own resident MP living on the site? I now found I was in overall control of two up and running schools 5 miles apart. Every morning I left our house next to Oaklands and drove to Coopersale Hall and helped Mrs. Best sort out the teething problems there, returning home to the house next to Oaklands for lunch. I had engaged Compass Services to run the lunches at both schools, and so Ann and I had shed the food-buying. I still retained the day-to-day accounts, staff salaries and writing cheques for all invoices and bills.

I had fully opened Coopersale Hall a year before Bancroft's Preparatory School, which still had to build, and so I had a year's start on the market. I attended Coopersale Hall's Harvest Festival and saw Ronald Loxley, the vicar of the 800 year old Theydon Garnon church show seeds of cabbages and lettuces and say to the children, "You are all seeds." Two HMIs (Department of Education Inspectors) visited Coopersale Hall to start the process of official registration, and reported that it felt like a school that had been open three years rather than three weeks. All in all, we had a very smooth opening.

I visited my sister at her new Bedford home in Biddenham to attend Richard's 40th birthday party. I talked with Philip Mawer, who was in the Cabinet Office and who was about to become Secretary-General of the Church of England Synod.

At half term we went to Cornwall, where "an energetic, dynamic sea flings spray half way up the opposing cliff". Again I felt an "amazing clarity of vision" and I gazed across the sea. I compared being alone by the sea with "the hermits from Wales who made cells in the cliffs not far from here". We went to Wheal Martyn to see the clay dries. Back in Charlestown I recorded: "A wonderfully clear night. The laburnum night-tree. No, the huge apple-tree with white fruit. Stars like apples. The apple-tree of stars." The next morning was "a calm, glorious day", "golden and autumnal and late summery, the waves sparkling". We went to Mevagissey and then I had "a final walk under the tree of stars, all incredibly bright from the pier". Capt. Gowsell, my neighbour, pointed out Orion's belt. We had a final walk on the harbour under a reddened sky, with birds skimming low over the silver waves and a group of yellowhammers pecking round the front door steps. Arthur (Hosegood) watches from dawn to dusk, watches the progress of each day and marvels, ''Tis beautiful'. (''Tis a beautiful evening, calm and free.') The marvel of a day observed from the Charlestown coast. The variety of bird life, the different winds and tides. Can't wait to return in December. My heart lifts at the thought of seeing my beloved Charlestown again, the front steps guarded by yellowhammers."

We returned to Essex and almost immediately I attended Judith Tomlin's marriage reception, put on by her British Ambassador husband, at the Commonwealth House, Northumberland Avenue. The large room was crowded with people older than me. I sat with Kathleen Raine and David Holbrook. The next evening I attended a Conservative reception for Steve Norris and Jeremy Hanley MP.

On October 28th I visited Sir Laurens van der Post in Chelsea as he had proposed. I wrote: "A windy day. Rang the bell, went up to the top floor in the lift and puckish Sir Laurens met me, shook my hand, took me into his flat and upstairs to his study. 'My beloved' he said to his wife, 'you write your book, we're here with the door open.'I spoke of myself and talked him through my letter. Showed him Part One contents and Part Two, then the chart. He: 'It's very impressive. This is a work of immense importance. I can see that just from your headlines.' He with a monocle in his eye, overlooking the Chelsea skyline. He asked questions, about astrology, alchemy (in which he is very interested). He spoke of Jung – who was discussing the Fire with an Austrian, who did not know what it was, and then turned to van der Post to discuss it. 'Jung was a confirmation rather than a revelation.' He spoke of the Kalahari bushmen making fire by clapping hands, to the astonishment of an engineer....Also exorcising a dream before fire. 'There's a metaphysical Fire behind actual fire in the bushman's consciousness.' He...is sure I won't find a historian (to write a Foreword). 'There are no universalist historians, Toynbee was the last and he funked the irrational at the end and never explained the genesis of civilisations.' (Toynbee's books were on his shelf.) He will supply a comment. As to Prince Charles, he listened in silence and then said, 'The light is fading. I want to act on this letter tomorrow morning. I will put it somewhere safe, I will put it in front of my diary. Then I can act on it first thing tomorrow morning.'...Said I could explain that his vision is a thing of the future, not the past, in terms of the new Baroque age that will be part of the Carolingian age. Van der Post said: "You can see the direction, I don't know what I'm about but you can see the way forward. You could not do that without knowing the Fire. You must have known it to write at such length....If it is going to happen it will happen, yes, but you have to push at life a little, knock on the door, and then it opens to you.' Left after one and a quarter hours (4.45-6.00)."

From Sir Laurens's flat I walked to Kathleen Raine's. I wrote: "Spent three and a quarter hours with Kathleen Raine (6.30-9.45). Went on to the role of the Academy. Charles can teach America universalism which the Academy will embody, i.e. stage 44. The Academy will preserve the knowledge in a precise way, the vision....It may hand on the vision and therefore bring about a Renaissance of the arts. Art is a marginal comment on vision. Spoke at length about my Baroque age in poetry. She concurred with my Baroque analysis (my *Preface*), but said the poet had not arrived: poets are born not made, they have the imaginative vision and can't be taught it. I on imagination: it is not Neo-Classical fancy, it is either images of the other mind or it is the Fire (Coleridge's esemplastic power). She would like to see the Academy as Thomas Taylor the Platonist, preserving, giving Keats 'Beauty is Truth, Truth Beauty' (which she says Keats got from Bailey when staying, where he read Thomas Taylor). Yeats's golden bird was a present from the Caliph to the Byzantine Emperor (in Gibbon). True poets have the vision, which churches are supposed to hand on and don't. 'The Academy will not produce a Renaissance in the arts because the artist will appear.' A new Romantic Age would be the new Baroque Age in which poetry would be redefined....Kathleen Raine and Gascoyne are in Paris as 'classiques vivants' (living classics). Raine: 'Gascoyne and I are part of the European tradition, are closer to the European tradition than to the English tradition.' I noted: 'Kathleen Raine is a scholar rather than a mystic: she has gleaned the knowledge from books.' 'Nationality is not important, dissident literature is a red herring.' Prince Charles will see Europe take his kingdom (Ireland, Wales and Scotland) and will become king of a spiritual kingdom instead. Kathleen: 'Five of us should have a meeting: you, the Prince, me, Keith Critchlow and Laurens.'"

Following my talks with van der Post and Kathleen Raine I wrote; "We're part of the contemporary scene and part of the eternal mosaic at the same time."

I duelled with the Hammond over the road and secured agreement to buy a 6 metre corridor up to the school. The costs of running a school are very heavy, and with the Council exacting an improvement to their public road at the end of Flux's Lane as the price for planning permission (£30,000) and the fire officer imposing an automated system of fire doors (£20,000), I had to raise the fees more than I would have liked to in order to cover the set-up costs of the new school.

We held the annual Oaklands Parents Association bonfire for Guy Fawkes night. A great fire leapt, fireworks went off in a well-orchestrated display, and later there was food on the floodlit tennis court. Two days later I set up the Coopersale Hall Parents Association. I convened a meeting of interested parents, persuaded three to volunteer for the role of Chairman, got each to make a speech saying what they would do, made them leave the room, and then organised a vote. The first Chairman won with overwhelming support. I could imagine what it was like to be a dictator like Gaddafi, only I was forcing through democratic structures rather than repressive measures.

I continued to work on my *Selected Poems*, and noted that I was "amazed at how good certain passages are, 25 years later". I was still thinking about the connection between "cosmic background radiation and the Fire. I first made the connection in conversation with Pir Vilayat Inayat Khan, but I lacked the scientific knowledge to relate the Fire to the cosmic radiation from the Big Bang, i.e. the dawn of creation." I wrote: "Nov 21. Looking back on Sunday morning, when I woke and made the link between the Fire and its manifestation (Bohm-like) in cosmic background radiation....The three families of particles in cosmic rays after the Big Bang. I am on the very verge of a theory of everything, which takes us close to the meaning of life. I got up, and still in my pyjamas, scribbled the connection, aware that I had found what Newton and Einstein sought and failed to find: F(Fire)->cbr. The Fire of eternity preceded the Big Bang, which began time, and will succeed time." I saw that I had to escape from Garratt Green and "temporal poetry which obscured my full discovery of the metaphysical".

In November we had the bespectacled and moustached Head of Chigwell Tony Little and his wife, and David Evennett MP and his wife, to dinner. I wrote that Little was "slightly awkward but with a quick wit and considerable humour; David Evennett reflecting on his life as MP. He wanted to become an MP at 15 and remembers the great occasions (State opening, etc.) but loathes the drill halls and gang shows and the wasted time." It was a frosty night, and there was a spitting fire.

I now "connected my work on the symbol with Guénon's law of correspondence. Where does it come from? Plato?...I am now a metaphysician, a metaphysical."

In December Anthony sang a solo in Chigwell Parish church, "In the bleak mid-winter". I recorded: "He did it beautifully, from the choir." I worked on at my poems and revised *Old Man in a Circle*.

The Coopersale Hall end of term nativity play was attended by the new Chairman of the Council, the Mayor of the Town Council and our local councillor. I was able to tell them that I was putting in a planning application to build a 6-classroom extension at Coopersale Hall. There was an exhibition of the plans in the staff room, which I made sure they all saw. The next day we broke up and soon afterwards had a reception for the combined staffs and spouses at Coopersale Hall.

We returned to Charlestown. I wrote: "Arrived to mountainous seas, the combination of an exceptionally high tide and a hurricane which gave the largest seas for 50 years. Spray dashed on our upper windows, and Ann got soaked as a wave came through our upstairs bedroom window as she was taking a photo. The sea broke over the harbour wall making it into a waterfall. Wrote *Elemental* and *Invisible Spray*, the first on Saturday night with the storm raging, the second on Sunday (yesterday) morning." The weather cleared and I recorded: "A clear night. Star-gazed with Ken, the bearded sea-captain. He pointed out Orion's belt, Betelgeuse and Rigel on either side (shoulder and knee), the triangle of Sirius (the brightest star), Procyon and Betelgeuse, and Pollux, Aldebaran (an Arab name, like Algol), and the two pointer stars of the Plough (Ursa Minor) which lead towards Polaris. Cassiopeia and the Pleiades, and the bright stars in between. The planet that went through and shone yellow. Am picking up Ken's knowledge of winds, tides and stars – his old seaman's lore handed down over the generations."

We went to Truro and then to Gunwalloe, where I found shingle had entered the church, and then to Porthleven, where I inspected the storm damage: high seas had broken away part of the harbour wall. I wrote: "Returned to another storm and a dark Charlestown. Sat alone by candlelight (actually nightlights) while the storm raged and wrote *Candleflame Storm*, a very metaphysical poem. When I finished polishing the last rhyme at 8.30 exactly, the lights came back on. Was almost sorry. I realised how Wordsworth and Coleridge lived in the 1790s, when this cottage was built, and how natural it was for people to think of themselves as being candles, and how people have forgotten this today. The anti-metaphysical outlook of people today is largely a forgetting. A forgetfulness of Being. Also wrote *Stillness and Tides* ('Symbols for a New Age')."

The next day there was more rain and another powercut in the afternoon (our third in 24 hours). A mist on the horizon, white surf. Revised *The Silence*, placing it in the canon of my work. I laid the foundations for my present development then, and my poetic work belongs as a whole. Can see Trenarren out of the window as I write. Trenarren begins and ends *The Silence*, and now I have a house within sight of it."

On our return to Essex I pondered metaphysics: "Metaphysics – Leibniz Kant, Husserl, Heidegger and Whitehead; and of course my work – my redefinition of metaphysics. Went to Foyles and bought some American books on astronomy, which show that cosmology is not a speculative study any more but an observable, empirical science, e.g. COBE's observations. Link metaphysics and cosmology; a practical metaphysics of Being and its relationship to the structure of the universe (for Being as Fire controls the post-Big Bang radiation)." I thought about metaphysics all through Christmas ("surfeit more restrained this year"): "Thought about Being, which together with Non-Being, makes up Infinity. Non-Being envelops Being, but is itself enveloped by Supreme Being/Reality/Infinity, i.e. there are 3 levels or stages above the physical level. A System based on experience of the Fire. I have reached a unity of vision. My metaphysical vision has taken shape this Christmas Day. Let it pass through into some of the poems. It is profound, but right. It includes everything." I wrote that in Japan "I got behind existence and detected Being, the one sea of Being or unity of Being in the Stone Garden. Yeats's phrase now has a new meaning: unity of Being (a meaning I do not think he intended). The closing vision of *The Silence* is the fourfold vision." As I wrote this, the television was showing pictures of the Ceaucescus being shot in Romania, images which haunted me.

On Boxing Day I wrote: "The family still asleep at 11 a.m. Have been up 3 hours. Want to write essays on the Existentialists – exposing those (like Sartre and Camus) who remained at layer 4, the world of the senses, and approving of those who progressed to Being; but evaluating their use of Being. Also on the Metaphysical philosophers of the past, again projecting those who did not go far enough and evaluating Kant's relevance. (He is largely irrelevant.) Against rational and speculative metaphysics. For Metaphysical Existentialism or Existential Metaphysics. The world of the senses prevents you from rising to Being. So the poems of *The Gates of Hell* must be seen as a dying of the clinging senses and an unfolding of Being, i.e. being within sensual Existence....I have a third essay to do: on Plato, Neo-Platonism and the Kabbalah."

I now focused on Being: "What is Being? How when you look at existence are you aware of Being? Through its unity as opposed to its multiplicity, i.e. the unitive vision of the Stone Garden, the oneness of all manifestation below which are the particulars. (The image shows the particular existence and the universal Being.) Behind Being are the Forms in Non-Being, the Idea, all the latent potentialities of the Void which have not come into creation. And through the Void is the Fire. So how does Existence differ from Being? Existence is the disorderly, chaotic, apparently random world of phenomena. Being is the sum total of all manifestation, perceived as a whole in the poetic vision: the glimpse in the pond. The poet humanises Being, translates the abstract into a concrete. Being in the abstract is no use at all unless it can be experienced. That is why I am a Metaphysical Existentialist. Being is the sense of unity or oneness behind manifestation (as opposed to the ultimate oneness behind non-manifestation as well). Being is the one force that feeds all. Being controls the cosmic background radiation, one of its principal manifestations. Being is pantheistic. The Fire is beyond Being because it has not come into form (although it manifests in our soul)."

Miss Root, the Oaklands teacher, died of bronchial pneumonia in Forest Place. I had visited her, and she had become cantankerous. When the vicar came and preached to the inmates she called out "What about the Buddha?" and she sent back the harvest gift from the church. When the Oaklands children went to sing carols to the inmates of Forest Place she refused to leave her room and listen.

We had Steve and Vicky Norris for a long talk. I wrote: "Two hours on Hong Kong, Europe, Russia, Panama, etc., in the course of which I got my theory out. He: 'If I become Foreign Secretary, I will ask you to be an adviser on a discussion panel.'...'There is a Presidential Ceaucescu syndrome: decrees are handed down from on high and we have to accept them or we're out'(i.e. criticism of Thatcher). I showed that there will be a conglomerate. He: 'Once you know it's going to happen, the question becomes "What should Britain's attitude be?"'" He spoke at length, and it was hard to interrupt him. Four topics in two hours is good-going when Steve Norris is in full flow, whereas with David Evennett it is possible to cover forty in an hour.

We invited my family on December 30th. Several had flu and could not come, but Rob came and made sweeping statements about metaphysics: "It's not understood by the common man, by stonemasons....Nick speaks Greek, we don't understand metaphysics." To which the answer was: get yourself to a library and approach the Truth, don't continue to live in illusion out of laziness.

On New Year's Eve I referred to the title of my *Selected Poems* as *A Metaphysical's Way of Fire*.

In 1990 I thought about Eastern Europe and had uncertain health. Then the Light returned very strongly restoring me to good health.

I thought again about the soul. I wrote: "The soul, the gift of God, which links heart and body to God; whose organ is the mind. Ponder again the soul which lives in the Place of Light and is accompanied to earth at birth by a being of Light. The rays from outer space (the cosmic background radiation) feed the etheric body, i.e. the cosmic radiation body which gives life to the physical body, the Egyptian ka linked to the sunrise. The life force from the cosmic radiation enters the radiation body and thence the physical body and gives healing power."

I had a glimpse of the future: "Saw the future with immense clarity. European Christian civilisation will be invaded by the Islamic Arab-South Soviet civilisation (including Azerbaijanis), who will spread westward; by recovering its vision of the Fire, the European Christian civilisation will conquer Islam and incorporate it in its expanding conglomerate." I also acknowledged the influence of my bank manager on my spreadsheet: "My historical method, my stages, came from spreadsheets for my bank manager – another Providential influence. I was taken to my view of stages in history by my bank spreadsheet exercises."

I had applied for planning permission to build six classrooms at Coopersale Hall. The architect then convened a meeting of four "experts", which I attended unwillingly. Each one spoke of conducting preliminary tests on the soil and other aspects of the projected development. All four spoke in turn and they all had two things in common: their preliminary tests would come to £4,000-£5,000, making getting on for £20,000 in all before work had even been started, and I could not see how the tests were necessary. "What happens if you build the extension in the wrong place and its back breaks?" the architect asked, and I could see the cash-signs in four pairs of eyes waiting for my answer. "I'm going to build it anyway, and on the only available site," I said, "and if its back breaks, it breaks."

In January the Norrises were burgled. Vicky lost some jewellery given to her family in imperial times, worth perhaps £90,000. I visited Hammond, who had finally sold me the road, and explained how it was in his interests to help keep the Norrises happy. I asked if he would help me recover the jewellery by putting word out in the East End. Hammond said, "You've come to the wrong man, you might as well ask that tree." Soon afterwards he sent me a card from the Seychelles, where he and his girl-friend were enjoying a surprise fortnight's break, in an envelope festooned with exotic stamps.

There were two storms, and I saw "a firecrest in the blue acacia cedar". A laburnum had to be felled.

The Conservative Patrons Club held a gathering at the Carlton Club. I wrote: "Pictures, including Disraeli, coal fires in the entrance and the lobby. 85 guests in DJ talked over drinks. Steve Norris brought the Home Secretary (David Waddington) over and he shook my hand before I knew who he was. Disconcertingly like Biggs-Davison, a habit of looking at you without replying. Talked about the school. Then into the Coffee Room. Everyone squashed together. I was between Elsa Page and a builder's wife. Elsa talked non-stop. Occasionally a waitress came and thrust her breasts against my shoulder to get her dish in. Speeches. Vernon Davies, uncertain as usual. The Home Secretary, long and boring. Told an interminable unfunny story, then mentioned two of his Home Secretary concerns (drugs being one). Questions....Then fulsome praise from Norris. He had 'set the standard for future events'. Sycophancy, lack of any finger on the pulse or reference to the fact that the Conservatives are in a nosedive 15 points behind....Later, manoeuvred in the lobby. The Oaklanders stood together as they had sat together. I pinpointed the Chairman of Planning and engineered a casual conversation about Coopersale Hall School."

At half term on the way down to Cornwall I saw that Eastern Europe was changing. I wrote: "Why the collapse of Russia? Why is the West victorious in the Cold War? Ponder in relation to the Fire. Is the Fire being renewed in Russia, by the Russian Orthodox Church? Ponder on European self-belief at the present time, the renewal of Eastern Europe's central idea which is affecting Western Europe and which has resulted in the end of the Cold War, i.e. Christianity has tipped the balance. It is not what the West has done but what Eastern Europe has done. The Fire is the central idea of all civilisations including European civilisation, which has thrown off its semi-occupation by Russia through Eastern European Christianity (Polish and Hungarian Catholicism under a Polish Pope and a resurgence of Russian Orthodox rule), i.e. their Fire. The West's Cold War victory is thus a victory for Eastern Europe, which the Western Europeans and Americans have watched from outside; along with Russia's admission of her own difficulties and abandonment of the Communist position. An expanding

Europe must therefore take up the Eastern European initiative." I observed: "The thinking of *Wistful Time-Travellers* began my history book; and the above vision has come out of it. The freeing of the Eastern European colonies has nothing to do with Western Fire."

It was very damp in Charlestown. I met up with the new manageress of the Pier House Hotel, a liberal young girl called Jessica, who lamented that "the staff are not paid, the roof is leaking, and there is no petty cash to pay for meat". We went to Porthleven: "Lunched at Gunwalloe (church cove) and wrote another metaphysical sonnet (ending 'ripple or two'). Visited the broken up pier, walked on the Brig side, along the cliffs to the memorial to the dead mariners. Sat on the seat and gazed at the surf while Ann and Matthew descended to the gully in the rocks they used to call 'the swimming pool' when Ann was a girl."

Back in Essex I went up to Coopersale Hall and encountered Steve Norris washing his wife's car, and we chatted on the green sward, sometimes leaning on my car, he in sweater and boots. He told me about his forthcoming trip to Nicaragua, and said he was getting Tebbit to perform an official opening of Coopersale Hall School.

The Cornish damp had reactivated my bronchiectasis. I wrote: "Very weak from bronchiectasis this evening. Could not stay awake, very unsteady on my legs and short of breath."

On March 6th I heard that planning permission had been granted for Coopersale Hall to expand by six more classrooms as educational use is permitted development within London's Green Belt. I now sacked my architect and dispensed with the services of his four advisers, and employed Gorka to act as architect. He promised he would do all the building regulations drawings for no more than £2,000-£3,000. At the same time he urged me to look towards Hungary, buy a castle there and open it as a European centre to coincide with the renewal of Eastern Europe's central idea.

Anthony was confirmed in the chapel at Chigwell School by the Bishop of Barking. I wrote; "There were 14 in all....Jonnie drove from Tunbridge Wells as Ant's godfather; Argie came, together with Miss Lord and Miss Reid, Ann and Matthew. We arrived during rehearsal, Elizabeth hobbling. The modern service, the confirmation. The Bishop sat with his mitre on and intoned 'Confirm O Lord your servant Anthony with your Holy Spirit', in red and gold robes, faded gold, his hands on Ant's head. Then there was a welcome and applause. The Communion, Elizabeth at 90...hobbling up and receiving Communion standing. The power of the Bishop, a limping (arthritic), balding, chubby, bespectacled, white silky-haired man, a Chaucerian Bishop. Then afterwards to the Swallow Room."

I rang McForan, who had just returned from a month in Russia, living in a hotel by himself and meeting people. I wrote: "How Russian miners told him they subscribed one rouble (£1) each and one pit sent 1,500 roubles. How the Politburo are leaving the country regularly for secret meetings, how Gaddafi was in Moscow; McForan saw him, in uniform." (This was further evidence that the USSR was being run from abroad.) "Gorbachev is right of centre, still Communist..., McForan says....Gaddafi wanted Luqa to reach Vienna with missiles. Gaddafi is still working on nuclear missiles and has chemical missiles as well. My Scargill book was right....McForan: 'I've read many books about events in the 1980s, but yours and mine stand head and shoulders above the rest because we saw the scenario.'"

I was now revising my poems. I wrote of Epping Forest: "The pear-tree, hollies and silver birch have informed my poetry, and I must accept that." I had started gouging the ground to build the extension at Coopersale Hall, and I understood that Essex was one pole of my being: "Amid the hurly-burly of life in Essex, paying people, directing building work, acting like Zorba the Greek, I caught sight of a picture of the house in Charlestown and was transported to a world of simplicity and peace, where it is possible to dwell on poems and Being, to read Heidegger and reflect; a healthy place. Be clear about Charlestown: it is a place of stillness and simplicity and peace, it satisfies one pole of my soul; but I will always need the moving, dynamic, whirling rush of a hectic, exciting life. I could not retire to Charlestown for good, but will always have to return to Essex or London regularly, to satisfy the other part of my being. Charlestown and Loughton – contemplation and action. It is from Loughton that my action has been planned; from Charlestown that I have made the greatest gains in contemplation." Towards the end of March I was revising my poems for the *Selected Poems* I was preparing: "Mar 20. Worked late on my poems last night."

Concrete was pumped into the footings of the extension at Coopersale Hall. The work was progressing well, but I felt giddy. I wrote: "Mar 23. Giddy....Two days of rushing about, paying people, negotiating between architect and structural engineer....Mar 25. Giddy. Several times have nearly keeled over. I am hoping this is a cold that has affected my inner ear, my sense of balance....Mar 27. Still giddy. Nearly fell out of my chair when I spoke with (Steve) Norris, nearly keeled over when talking to Ginger, so went to doctor, who prescribed something for giddiness but said it is cerebro-vascular." I was still giddy on March 28th: "Can at least work on my poems while the desk moves up towards me and I lurch sideways." I was still "giddy at times" on April 1st. The following day Elizabeth Lord complained of being giddy, of the "furniture coming up – I've never felt like this before" – and I recorded: "(She) had a cerebral stroke in my arms, paralysing her legs." It later transpired she had had a blood clot which had deprived her brain of oxygen. She was taken by ambulance to St. Margaret's Hospital. I recorded: "I was giddy while holding her."

I had talked at length with Steve Norris one evening about the economy, and he had said: "I'll make a speech tomorrow evening defending the poll tax and I'll incorporate some of your points."

In April I went to Winchester for the Mystics and Scientists conference after hectic days of organising bricklayers. I wrote: "Sitting in this monk's cell, with its wooden floor, reviewing my recent life. 'You're a remarkable man,' a retired Indian clergyman told me, 'You're an excellent organiser, and you've been abroad and had a family and done many things and seen the spiritual as well as the material; you see that being a clairvoyant is like being a cricketer.' The mystery school at Coopersale Hall, in which life brings on the souls of all who work under me: Mick, Steve, John, etc. Like Zen, hoeing the garden can be hoeing your soul; building a kitchen can be building round your soul. Talked at length with Peter Fenwick. The mind-brain problem has to be seen in different terms....'I can find all the Kabbalistic points in the brain' (Fenwick)." I noted that the conference reinforced "my metaphysical assumptions and experience, which would be harder to maintain in isolation. We glide on silence into the lecture hall and then to the 'refectory' on a monastic model, being addressed by a psychologist, a brain physiologist, an astrologer, a Vipassana monk and a past-lifer. The theme is the nature of the self, which is a droplet of Being/God: we are body-mind-soul-spirit as in a cube, although the soul is not in the brain. I am not my body, I am more than my thoughts (mind) – the Buddhist meditation – otherwise I am without self (anatta). We have multiple selves from past lives (splinters in the soul) but also have a unitive self in this life. So the self, then, is ego (personal) and body; mind (thoughts), i.e. the psychological, in which the psyche/soul is our animating principle, cf our fields; the spiritual/pneumatic, which is our breath; and the divine. I.e., the 4 worlds of the Kabbalah all contribute to the self, and there are 4 parts of the self that correspond to 4 worlds; ego (physical); mind (equals brain function, psychological); the soul is a bridge; the spirit (spiritual) and the divine spark....Perhaps we should have this variation: mind (physical): soul (psychological); spirit (spiritual, which is the pneumatic); and divine spark which illuminates. Plato: soul is mindless at birth and may be unconscious at death."

The next day I noted I "felt a lightness of being after a meditation at 8. Full of the Light and power. A round of white light exploded and shot power from my head throughout my body. All day felt the after-shocks. Could dip back into Light during the lectures at will, and on the journey 'saw' how I could do my autobiography, which must show progression between levels and be entitled 'Ambassador to the Metaphysical' or equivalent words. In the morning's meditation asked the Light, 'I've done everything you asked, I've written *The Fire and the Stones* and my poems, what next? The answer was, 'Influence world leaders.' I: 'I need power to help me.' An immediate gift, exploding into me."

From Winchester I drove to Cornwall, passing Wylye and Steve Norris's old house. That night I "walked by the sea after dark. The moon was on the water and in the curl of each wave", and I reflected: "Universe means derivatively: combined into one, whole." I slept deeply and "awoke to meditate. Have gone to the Light three times this morning (in between phoning the Council about the extension window), feel spiritually refreshed from the influx of power. Feel fully charged and relaxed, almost drowsy." I wrote: "The sea out of my window is sparkling. It is a one: an image of Being, not existence." Pondering my task of influencing world leaders, I wrote: "I must become a great historian and poet to fulfil my destiny, to influence world leaders; and I must follow the example of Robert Graves." I drafted *Gnosis*: "Wrote all day, polishing the rhymes of this morning's draft of *Gnosis: The Nature of the Self, or Brain, Mind; Soul, Spark, Heart and Spirit* (later *Heart, Soul; Spark, Spirit*) – a very important poem in my metaphysical canon which I will copy out tomorrow. A full moon on the dark water now at 1 a.m. on April 10th." I wrote: "Charlestown is the sea of Being; I being a harbour united with it. Charlestown is a metaphysical model." I "added the penultimate stanza of *Out on the Alone*, about the Negative Way."

The Light was very strong: "Ap. 10. Went to the Light again between 3 and 3.30. Am going through an intense period of the kind I went through in 1971."

The next day I worked on *Night Visions in Charlestown* and recorded: "I had earlier been to the Light." As I worked on my *Selected Poems* I noted a new sense of meaning: "The feeling of peace as I distill my life's vision into one selection of poems, gather them together and make sure they are internally consistent. Meaning." Again: "Ap. 11. Went for a walk with Matthew to the end of the pier. Sat briefly and talked as it was mild and the sea was calm. Returned. Ann was already asleep; made my Horlicks, then sat in the darkened living room here at Charlestown, in the 3 piece suite (extreme right hand side nearest the door), closed my eyes, stilled my body and mind and went to the Light. 'Come into me,' I said, thinking, 'If it is your will, do with *The Fire and the Stones* what you will' and there was a great surge of power from the back of my skull, prickling me all through, moving from scalp to toes. It is still pouring through me, mildly, as I write. Ap. 12. Another act of metaphysical love: waves of power, less intense than last night, lasting some minutes. Spiritual power; the power of the Spirit: within sight of my beloved Trenarren."

We went to Porthleven and I "sat in the Church of Storms and wrote my fourth Gunwalloe metaphysical poem after seeing a skylark high up outside, and after receiving a number of strange images – of extraordinary architectural detail from a bygone age, quite indescribable but paintable."

I recorded: "Have had no giddiness since the influx of Light last Sunday morning (Ap. 8th). The power has healed me inside." I added: "Am adding a scheme of the self to the essay on Metaphysical Revolution. We need a clear chart of the structure of the self....Awoke with a model which I wrote into the Metaphysical Revolution essay."

We returned to Essex and went back to school. On a day when I concreted the oversite of the extension from 7 a.m., dug up the private drive and laid pipe, and mowed the Oaklands fields, I went back to Coopersale Hall to see how the work was progressing and "had tea with Steve Norris, who was in an open-necked shirt and jeans". I had agreed to visit Hungary with Gorka for a week, just to have a look, and I discussed Hungary with Norris: "Very much the politician, long general conversation about Hungary, how the Hungarians need to be fully commercial, how they need hotels for tourists....'If you're with Antell, get me an invitation. Say you're in touch with a group of Conservative MPs. I would come with 2 senior Conservative MPs and 3 business men.'"

My week in Hungary was both interesting and frustrating. I flew to Budapest with a party of student architects who were studying under Mrs. Gorka's tuition.

We were driven by coach through the centre of Budapest while Gorka sat near me and pointed out places associated with his story; in particular every prison. We arrived at a hostel on the outskirts overlooking a blue-tinted Danube, among fir-trees and chestnuts, where, after a long wait to get in because the Warden thought we were arriving after midnight, we were allocated rooms. I had mosquito-netting doors that led from my tiny heated room to a balcony. We went by coach to the Citadel for dinner. It was a fortress overlooking Budapest, floodlit in the dark. I noted: "The Citadel, high up, built by the Austrians 150 years ago to occupy the Hungarians, used by the Germans during the war and captured by the Russians when Paul found it full of decomposing German bodies." I found it was almost impossible to phone England from Hungary as most phones were for local use only. At the dinner four gipsies serenaded diners with violins, a flute and a double bass for money.

The next morning we walked along the Danube to the place where we were to have breakfast, where, after a long wait because they had expected us to appear an hour later, we were served tiny undrinkable Turkish coffee which was thick and like chicory, pale tea with lemon, a hunk of white bread, sausages, jam and butter. I noted: "Everything, but everything, from plumbing to food, is substandard, and is subject to changes of mind." I sensed that Hungarians made up the rules as they went along and blamed others for the inefficiency.

We all visited the Old City with a guide. We visited the Turkish baths, the prison and St. Anne's baroque church; and the headquarters of the Communist Party. I wrote: "St Matthias's church. The patterns on the columns within, the Turkish influence, the Mary. The faded charm of Berlin 1930s nearby (without the cabaret). The secret of the rosary. The Roman ruins of Aquincum in Pannonia. The guide said, as we walked among Turkish courtyards, that interest rates are 25%, inflation 20%. The Catholic church of St. Nicholas. Lunch in a student subsidised place. Our guide receives £70 in pension and spends £5.80 a month on his flat, which has no bathroom....The Stalin and Rakosi exhibition. The 15 Russian soldiers, who fled when I asked them (through our guide) when they are leaving Hungary. Heroes' Square, the archangel Gabriel. On to Pest and the shopping centre. On to the Hotel Gellert (which Paul's uncle used to own) during a thunderstorm. Paul had run into Antell (the Prime Minister) in the street."

After dark Budapest became like East Berlin. Many streets were very dingily lit, and looking for an international phone I would walk down dark streets with houses still chipped from the War and with bullet marks from the 1956 Revolution, and the atmosphere became like the more derelict parts of London's east end. I found it slightly menacing and depressing.

That night was misty and wet, and next morning the Danube was misty with trees reflected in its grey. "A low hum of traffic in the distance, bird song, a distant dog barking. It is peaceful here, but the water is cold – I have shaved in cold water without a plug – and an unstructured time here would be boring. Paul thinks it is all excellent, glad to be back in his native country." We went to the Technical University and were addressed by a Professor, who later asked if I would publish his book. There was a thunderstorm and we lunched on the way to Markowecz's mortuary. Lunch took two and a quarter hours. "Then the driver got lost and we found ourselves right outside Budapest. The mortuary is an impressive image, the ribs of mortality, a sombre feeling." We went to drinks at the University of

Architecture, where young Hungarian architects put on a slide show. We went on to Vaci Street and ate at the Apostolou, "where nothing was available, no tomato soup or chicken or ice cream". Paul's son Sebastian went out with some of the students and they returned noisily at 2.15 a.m.

The next day we went by coach to the Danube bend "via Szant Endre and the church of St. Andrew, destroyed by the Mongols in 1242-3 and the Turks in the 16th century and rebuilt as baroque, the pulpit (which may have come from Bavaria) having an eye with a triangle in it, and spokes of light, the symbol of Weishaupt's Illuminati; the Lord Mayor's baroque home with medieval romanesque arches; St. Peter and Paul church where an organist was playing Bach all alone; the Orthodox church, shut up; and in all 7 churches, fish-eye windows....On to Visegrad ("high castle") and the Markowecz organic art: the restaurant with trees, the school library like a burial mound and with a zodiac all round; the loos, kitchen and settlement. All New Age and drawing on North American Indian images (wigwam and hooked-billed bird) and Scandinavian ideas (e.g. Heorot made of tree trunks, with antlers). To Visegrad castle, high above the Danube, where the kings from Bala IV to Matthias put their queens for safety. An anti-Tatar fort. Lunch in Visegrad. It took two and a quarter hours, like yesterday's and whereas Francis wasn't served yesterday, Barbara wasn't today. The idea that our guide should be Inquisitor. Paul sitting in silence through lunch. On to Esztergon to see the basilica (mainly 19th century, the largest Catholic church in Hungary) and to look across into Czechoslovakia. Back via 4 Russian camps and a...baroque street. Followed the Danube. No sign of the Old European civilisation. Back via Aquincum and its amphitheatres (military in evidence) and thermal baths. In the evening to a traditional Hungarian restaurant with the Gorkas and surgeon Bertie and his wife. Gipsy music – a gipsy played the 1877 march against the Austrians, which Susan (Mrs. Gorka) sang – and traditional food: I had carp....Bertie: 'The end of Communism was transcendental, Communism was infernal, it had to destroy itself. It has left a dreadful nihilism, the only solution to which is Christianity.' He despises his colleagues for being without ethics. Ethical nihilism."

That evening I thought about organic art, which "is supposed to decay itself" like flesh. "Hence Markowecz's time scale is 25 years. But art as I define it is more permanent, less ephemeral than that – or disposable coke cans....Art represents life or imitates life by relating it to a whole structure. The pattern created by art relates parts to a whole and therefore gives significance. It also relates to the eternal world, and makes a statement for all time....Therefore ideally its material should be chosen to last, and not to decay, or be ephemeral. In fact, an artist with confidence in his vision chooses materials that will make it last forever, and it is a sign of unabsolute relativeness to choose a material that will not last forever. Our questioning of the vision amounts to a loss of confidence in one's own vision."

Gorka was now staying at a different hostel with some of the students so that he could control what time they returned at night. The next day I wrote: "To Paul's 'hotel'. Walked along the 'towpath' by willows, and wrote *Willow Warblers* sitting in the sun by the Danube. Felton arrived (Paul's builder friend) and Agnes, who spoke no English, the Pallas (publishers) lawyer, a judge. Drove in the Pallas rented car to Tura, 40 kms outside Budapest. Saw castle 1, in 1883 Baron Schlossberger owned it; built by the man who built the Opera. Splendid form without, a ruin within. Lunch at a petrol station (goulash in paprika); did my publishing business....On to castle Acsa, which is already a hotel. Sleeps 62 and a further 27 in the grounds....The shower curtain with a nude on it. The judge laughed and blushed. Back to Budapest and in to Imre Markowecz's studio. The great man was not there." We stopped at a café near the Opera and then went on to visit Gorka's wife's cousins and sat in a flat in one of Budapest's central streets (still pocked with bullets) and I wrote: "Wine and meat and mushrooms on toasted bread, and iced cake. Conversation about Hungary, history. Two Hungarian men, one a general's son and fierce, one quiet. Here I was close to the heart of traditional Hungary." The general's son showed me the medal he received for destroying a Russian tank during the Uprising, and they were very nationalistic, rejecting Hungary's position in a coming United States of Europe for a revived Austro-Hungarian empire. Susan said to me, "They are totally inward-looking and enclosed." Paul sat in dignified silence, only a twitching at his eye revealing the tension he felt about what they were saying.

The next day we "went to Kocskemet, south of Budapest, to see ethnic architecture at the Town Hall. Apart from the main square the buildings are single storey. Then to a restaurant, and then to Paks to see Markowecz's church, the Roman Catholic church at Paks. It has a heart at the top to attract God's attention. There are 5 churches although Paks is the back of beyond on the Danube. Paul pressed me in the coach, wanting to come here as an employee of a company along with Felton, which I would set up....He justifies all the things that niggle me, e.g.: 'It is good to spend two and a quarter hours over eating, then one does not get a heart attack. There must be wide choice.'"

Our last day we went to the market and I wrote: "Bought Red Army hats for the boys and a Marie-Thérèse coin 1763 (Austro-Hungarian)." Gorka and I ate with the Deputy Secretary-General of the Hungarian Chamber of Commerce and a Professor at the College of Foreign Trade, and they urged me to found a new British Council to teach English and Know-How skills to Hungarians. Afterwards I went to the Gellert and wrote some stories, sitting upstairs, looking through the balcony at the front door. Then I went to Vaci Street and ran into Gorka. I was holding the two Red Army hats, and in the square at the end of Vaci Street we encountered two Russians in leather jackets who were clearly part of a command structure. They jabbered at me in Russian and at one point I thought I was going to be arrested.

The Russians had not yet left Hungary and their presence was still a reality there. The students were pleased to be flying back to Britain. As we took off, I put one of my Red Army hats on and saluted, and there was a cheer and applause from the students on either side of the aisle, several of whom hurled anti-Soviet slogans in the direction of the receding Budapest below us.

I returned to a heatwave. We moved Oaklands sheds and I noted: "A pheasant; a nuthatch. Paradise as Forest trees and glades. No gnats....a blue tit is nesting in the Oaklands tree stumps near the new shed....Kestrels are nesting in the poplar in the Gates' garden." I learned that the 'Roman' fountain that stood not far from our second field was built by 14 Italian men c1850. At half term I supervised the completion of a new path at Coopersale Hall, and I reflected: "I run a mystery school in which all leave with a sense of their own direction. I am a mirror; the grounds mirror."

I joined Ann in Charlestown and heard from the Harbourmaster that the harbour had been repossessed as Barry Williamson had apparently not been making interest payments to his bank. It had been sold to Target Life Insurance Group, and Peter Clapperton was apparently running it, replacing Lucas. The position was confused. I recorded: "Wrote *The Nightingale* and *A Crystal*; a magically still evening with an orange sunset and a twilight part clear, part overtaken by a creeping sea-mist. Stood breathless."

I wrote more poems and felt: "I have a sure touch now, my poems are good, they have a distinctive voice and celebrate specific geographical regions. There is a metaphysical dimension which is missing from most contemporary poetry. I feel there is no poem I cannot write....I found a fresh vein of material for my practice of poetry by turning my back on other poets. People may think there is no new vein to be mined, but I have found one; and it is relevant to the coming age. I sought the highways and the byways after Oxford and found an original vision." I spent three days "combing the poems, checking proofs, amending the notes" and wrote: "A terrific flow....I have made terrific gains." I had written "a quantum self stanza into *Night Thoughts*", and worked on *A Temple-Dancer's Temple-Sleep.*

In June I found I was "a focal point for people's problems" and I observed that I tried "to alleviate them in a mystery school sense, using obliqueness, indirectness and a lightness of touch". I counselled two who had been bereaved, a bankrupt, two who had been made redundant, the wife of a prisoner, a husband about to be bereaved, and a wife who had received a black eye. The Light seems to draw people who need advice. I also heard my aunt on when the old life changed. It was "the Friday before the war. That Friday as usual the maid brought me the menu and served dinner in style. The next day during the evacuation it was tea in an enamel jug, milk and sugar all mixed up. The old life never came back. After that it was all functional and changed."

I noted that I had "presented *The Silence* in the notes. It is my *Portrait of the Artist as a Young Man*. The Silence as eternity is the source of mysticism and of creativity and therefore of art. Between June 8th and 10th I polished and typed up *By the Chalice Well, Glastonbury* (a contemplation). In *The Silence* I know I now have a great work. It contains all 4 worlds, the physical, psychological, spiritual and divine. The Shadow: an artist with a metaphysical vision. I am now my Shadow. My Reflection (the school owner) is held in check by my creative Shadow. I am now Shadow and Reflection."

Norman Tebbit had agreed to perform a formal opening of Coopersale Hall School, and I met a Chief Inspector of police at the bottom of our private drive to plan the security, which would include a helicopter hovering at the back. I pointed out that Tebbit had been blown up by the Brighton bomb – McForan's book had revealed the USSR's and Gaddafi's hand in that – and I said he must still be a target. While we talked a local passed and the Chief Inspector said: "I knew him 10 years ago at Wickford, when he was in with George Crack, a gang of robbers. He was the safe man. He may still be active."

Nadia came. I took her to see the new Oaklands pond, and then up to Coopersale Hall. We sat by the pond looking at the carp and golden orfe, and she told me she was ready to get married.

Chigwell Speech Day was attended by Sir Terence Beckett, Head of the CBI, who quoted Husserl and spoke about intentionality and Keats's "negative capability", which he wrongly summarised as "being receptive to new ideas". Later I had tea on the lawn and described Beckett to a couple of masters as "having cudgelled people on TV like a Romanian miner, verbally beating them over the head" and that "I expect to see the Governors of Chigwell School arrive on the back of a lorry", to which Anthony's choirmaster said: "I shall nominate you as a Governor Mr Hagger."

I pondered: "In a mystery school you learn to discard all thought, which is what I have learned to do at Oaklands. My 'mind-suicide' has been a 'reason'-murder, i.e. a Zen pursuit of quietness in a garden."

I had invited Steve Norris to open the Coopersale Hall fête, and I wrote: "June 20. A day sorting out the building work....*Zorba the Greek* considerations again (only my building won't collapse). Vicky was on the lawn so went and had a chat....Then Steve rang." Vicky took the call and said I was with her and he said he wanted to speak to me. "An odd conversation. 'Nick, I apologise if its crackling but I'm speaking from the Central Lobby of the Houses of Parliament. Something's happened. Your ears will have been burning, I was with our Leader at 4 and we were discussing you. It's far more important than if I were ringing you to give you advance information of an honour. I can't be with you on Saturday for the fête I've got to do something for the Government. It'll take Friday and Saturday and it won't finish until 4. After that I can try and get to the fête. Could Vicky open it on my behalf? I really am sorry, but if you could do that for me I'd be very grateful. It won't be forgotten.' So I said, 'Are you seeing her again?' 'I'm seeing mother on Thursday, a 5 minute interview.' 'Tell mother I said the Conservative cause is far more important than our fête.' 'I will.' 'And ask her to make available a helicopter to get you back here quickly, so you can do it in reverse.' 'I'll descend trailing clouds of glory.' 'And tell her to come with you on the helicopter, bring her too.'"

Gorka had visited me to look at the progress of the extension, and he said: "You're going to be the new Ambassador to Hungary." I smiled, having heard before that I would be Ambassador to Libya, and, needless to say, nothing happened.

On June 24th I wrote: "Saw the last piece of the jigsaw of my history book and wrote it in: the table of winners in stage 43 and the age of their civilisation, and how that indicates the strength and vitality of their Fire and their potentiality to renew the declining civilisation."

I have two pictures in the front hall of our house. I wrote of one of them:

"*Between Two Fires*. (A Puritan seated between two women.) The Fires are of course the two women, but also the inner Fire of his Puritanism and the outer fire of their sensuality. The other picture shows a Cavalier and a Roundhead. *Checkmate* is the title, and the Roundhead has checkmated the Cavalier as he did historically. Symbolism and realism together."

The Coopersale Hall fête took place. Vicky opened it, and the cricketer David East conducted an auction in which a signed cricket bat was sold for £400. Gooch had sent this in via East to thank me for trying to place the Essex cricketer Alan Lilley at Chigwell School. East had first mentioned the possibility of a job for Lilley the previous summer. As one of the first acts of the "East-Hagger Placement Organisation for Retiring and Deserving Cricketers", I had rung Tony Little – it was his first phone call after moving into the new Head's house and he told me it had taken him some time to find where the phone was – and I put it to him that he might like to employ Lilley. The negotiations had almost been completed when Lilley accepted the top coaching job for all the county's children. The initiative did help Chigwell, however, as Gooch (accompanied by Lilley) opened the school's new Sports Hall.

Norman Tebbit (now Lord Tebbit) performed the official opening of Coopersale Hall on July 9th 1990 at the successful end of our first academic year. I wrote: "A gentle man, he got out of his car amid intense police security (helicopter, passes, men in the grounds) and I showed him round with the Chairman of the Council and his wife (the Hudspeths), the Mayor (Gloria Platt), the MP and his wife (Steve Norris and Vicky) and Ann and Frances Best. Then out on to the terrace where a table stood between PA system boxes and chairs of guests, many councillors." The children and parents were on the lawn before us. "I spoke for nearly 10 minutes, introducing everyone, dwelling on Tebbit's local connections, describing the evolution of our school, and then dwelling on the link between the MP and Coopersale Hall." I spoke of four MPs – Lord Lyle, Churchill, Norris and now Tebbit himself – as all being associated with Coopersale Hall in the 20th century. Tebbit began, "Hello kids." He spoke directly to the children, saying "that adults are funny to have openings when the school has already been open, and that private education is a good thing". He unveiled a plaque, drawing blue curtains which had been leant to me by Doug Sweet of Fairheads, an Old Chigwellian. "Mrs. Best thanked him. Then we had our photos taken and I said 'I'm standing on a petunia' and Tebbit said 'It's a geranium' and I: 'A geranium that's been stood on looks like a petunia'", which made him laugh. We then all repaired inside to the Hall. There was a cake that looked like the school. Tebbit "cut the cake, after saying there were two schools of thought as to whether the badge was cloth or icing, and he pronounced it icing. Then I introduced Tebbit to some 50 or 60 of the people there." Eventually I said he was leaving and there was applause. "We went off to the study. There I asked him if he might become Prime Minister if anything happened to Thatcher. He: 'It would probably be a younger man, such as John Major.' I: 'But if you do, will you come and see us if I invite you?' He: 'Yes.'" I had a conversation with him about Rupert Murdoch. "Do you see Murdoch?" "Yes." "Often?" "Yes." "He's local, and he was an Oaklands parent and lived at Coopersale House nearby. Could you tell him you were here and tell him about me?" "Yes." I showed him into his chauffeur-driven car and he spread himself over the back seat with his brief case and papers, and he left.

So it happened that after resisting Scargill and opposing those who had organised the Brighton bomb that had blown Tebbit up, I had my new school opened by the Government's leading victim of international terrorism.

A few days later we broke up at Coopersale Hall. I wrote: "A picnic under the tree. Champagne. The idyllic afternoon – blue sky, hot sun. Sat drinking a coca cola when a Crusader (child dressed as a Crusader) walked past, as if in an Ingmar Bergman film. A red cross on cardboard armour, and a silver sword."

A couple of days later Nicholas Ridley resigned as Secretary of State for the DTI, and I rang his PPS Steve Norris: "Said I half wondered if Ridley was hiding in the squash court. He: 'Some journalists think that, they've been camping outside here.' He said, 'I am in the Ridley-Thatcher camp, worried about German monetary domination.'" Argie came to tea on a scorching day, "lamenting the impending rise of the Prussians in East Germany, sure there will be a third German war because my generation will not listen".

We celebrated Ann's birthday at the White Horse, Pleshey, which is 500 years old and pargetted, and I looked at the nearby retreat that was associated with Evelyn Underhill, author of *Mysticism*, and where Davenport regularly took the Chigwell boys.

I was now back among my poems: "The poet's soul, opened to the beyond, speaks to your soul in the solitude of your room, and makes it thrum."

We went to see my cousin Jill (Harold's daughter) and her husband Roger at their new house, the Rectory, Fairstead in Essex: "A large, spacious building part Tudor and extended in Regency times and later, with large windows that open up and under which you step to go out (floor to ceiling windows). Sumptuous grounds. Wooden floors, many prints. Roger late from sailing on the Blackwater, soaked. Georgie who helps him and Jill in the art gallery at the Royal Exchange, very well spoken, there. Eric Broadley of Lola, who produces 80 Lolas a year, has 160 staff and 25 engineers and sells to America and Japan. Roger's relative Sir Richard Hadlee (the New Zealand cricketer) not there. Fione, getting married in Terling church on October 20th. Eric quiet, opened up when you spoke but uncommunicative otherwise, with a shy 22 year old daughter Diana. Champagne and white wine and lunch in the garden." I remember Roger putting on a panama hat and sitting in the timeless afternoon sunshine, and I remember thinking that the whole scene could have taken place before 1914.

Vernon Davies had opened a company selling printing-presses, which had gone into liquidation. I was intrigued that his preference of printing-presses to books had not brought any additional financial benefit.

We went to Cornwall, travelling through a great heat. "Arrived to find the Maria Asumpta (1858) about to sail. Went on her and spoke to the owner Mark Litchfield, then watched her go, bobbing offshore in the dark now, by the pilot ship. A crew of 15 (12 needed). Earlier spoke to the engineer. Litchfield owned the Marques, and told me the sinking had nothing to do with the Bermuda Triangle. The hatch was off centre and flooded, and the boat was heavy and in the squall it went down. The Maria Asumpta may be in my old Charlestown photographs, and may have been known to Conrad. The Maria Asumpta is now a brig."

I settled to revise my history theory and wrote: "Revised Chapter 14...with the wind howling and the sea pounding. Ironed out contradictions. Europe's conglomerate is imposed by the winner of the colonial conflict and no one else. The USSR will be federalist and will not enter the United States of Europe yet." I walked "under the stars, having smoothed out the end wrinkles and having made for consistency. Peaceful sea, brilliant stars."

At the end of July I did my back in: "Pulled a ligament while exercising. Slipped a disc? Back has stiffened. Toe-touching did it. A wet late afternoon after cream teas for Regatta week; Songs of Praise in the wet. Sat on the house steps with binoculars and observed Arthur (Hosegood), and the Mayor....Worked on Appendix One and Two, twisted with pain; using will-power to concentrate." I spent an agonising night on my bedroom floor, then "proof-read upside down, lying on my back. Went to doctor at 9.30 – a locum who said I must stay in bed all week – and then to an osteopath in Falmouth at 2. Ann drove me. He was a youngish man with a beard, and he manipulated my back. 'The muscle has gone into a spasm. Keep it relaxed.' I am supposed to lie on my back and draw my knees up to my chin every hour."

I carried on proof-reading and then returned to Essex to pick up what had been auctioned on the closure of Loughton School. The owners had rung me and asked if I would be interested in rescuing this small secondary school within 48 hours; they had had an offer from a developer for £2 million for what a bank would not lend £450,000 on, and they had already made a statement to the local paper which would appear on Thursday's front page. No one was going to lend £2 million for what was really worth a quarter of that, and although I rang the builder Derek Higgins, an old boy, I had to say I could not help. In the event the property market collapsed and the £2 million became £700,000. The school has been pulled down and the former owners are living in one of the seven houses that were built on its site. As I drove up to Essex I heard that Saddam Hussein had invaded Kuwait. I collected a load of televisions and bought a skull for £10. It had belonged to an Indian woman who died in the 1940s, I was told. It is now in my study as a reminder of my mortality.

I returned to Cornwall and digested Mrs. Thatcher's Aspen speech in which she followed the policy of my paper on the Eastern Europeans but said she did not want centralisation because of them. I noted "another fabulous moon. A full moon and a shimmering causeway on the water, urn-shaped or womb-shaped. Another lovely walk with my boys, and now I gaze at the superb sight."

By mid-August I was "tired and trembling" with overwork. I noted again, "I am trembling and hot," as I worked while watching cricket on television. My back had improved but I returned to the Cornish osteopath who said that "the spine area between my shoulder blades is rigid and has not moved for years". We drank elderberry wine with Capt. Gowsell and his wife and afterwards "saw 3 shooting stars and a moth (which at first I thought a shooting star)....Thought how appropriate was Marvell's poem about a drop of dew (the soul coming from the source of all dew above, in heaven)."

I had a talk with Matthew about some of his set books: "(Scott Fitzgerald's) Gatsby was a fake...; the worst side of capitalism who didn't care who he corrupted with drugs to get his fortune. Paul in (Waugh's) *Decline and Fall* moved in similar circles of fraud and prison. Jake and the others in (Hemingway's) *The Sun also Rises* avoided capitalism but were aimless. Three treatments of the same theme in the 1920s, in the US, Britain and Europe. Then Kurtz went to Africa, seeking a fortune, and, emotionally dead, did a Saddam Hussein on the local population, putting their heads on stakes. I have made a success of being an entrepreneur but have followed a better course than Kurtz and Gatsby. I have given...sound education....The pursuit of money leaves people indifferent to the plight of people....Everyone is fleecing their neighbour to survive and justifying it in terms of capitalism....A universal vision of greed."

I worked again on *The Silence* and reflected: "I have not been able to get *The Silence* fully ready until now first because my metaphysical vision has been developing, and the poem is coloured by it, and secondly because I needed the grasp and sweep (which I now have) to be able to explain in notes that there are two voices which are sometimes in dialogue. *The Silence* is now a very worthwhile poem indeed, with much for the reader to ponder."

I returned to Essex briefly and we were visited by the Gilchrists, the ex-Oaklands parents who had a son Anthony's age. After they left, accompanied by the Gowsells we "walked on the Black Head of Trenarren for two hours. Passed Rowse's smoking chimney and closed high black gates. Went down to Ropehaven to see Ropehawn, the house Taylor is converting and the haven he is improving. Then, with the Gowsells walked a mile to the end of Trenarren and the rocks below, sat and watched 'the sea boil from the angry years', and then walked a mile back....The walk to the end of the Black Head: sloes, thunderflies, campion, viper's bugloss and the cormorants on the rock off Ropehaven. The wheels and dug-out at the target area by the rifle range."

The Cornish osteopath gave me another session and said: "There's a block on your right side." I noted that "he tried to free it by bending me against myself sharply, but without success." He remarked that my exercises had left my muscles in good shape and that there was no trace of stringy, fibrotic muscles. I had one more session: "He clicked my back: the spinal defect, the spine between my shoulder blades has not moved for a long time; but it has now. More fluency in my neck and back. My back problem is now cured. The torn ligament has healed."

Just as the Heroes of the West had attempted to transform the position of the West, so I now thought of a Fire of the World Movement or Brotherhood of Fire, or Knights of Light, which would restore the missing

Light to the world. I wrote: "I have one foot in the exoteric world and one in the esoteric, as I revitalise the metaphysical tradition as existential metaphysics." I wrote that the aims of my Movement would be: "(1) to bring individuals to confront the Fire; (2) to affect society, e.g. the universities, with a Metaphysical Restoration; (3) to show that the Fire is the common ground for all civilisations and is therefore an impetus to world peace."

The new Baroque reconciled all my contradictions: "The new Baroque makes all my work of a piece. *The Fire and the Stones*, the metaphysical and the social; the Silence, the Shadow and the Reflection, one being an amorphous principle, the other a manifestation. Relationships, spirit and sense, the erotic and the spiritual. All of a piece, a complex whole. My journals (i.e. *Diaries*): a selection will show a budding metaphysical, and will illustrate some poems."

Back in Essex I visited Miss Lord and learned that Mrs. Macy was in Claybury Hospital, "having nearly gassed Mr Macy two weeks ago. A paper boy smelt gas and Mr Macy was unconscious." Zena, Miss Lord's niece was present. She had left her soldier husband.

I took photos for the poems: "Clouded-Ground pond, Strawberry Hill pond, the Stubbles, High Beach church, the gap between the Oaklands fields. Rang (Ian) Hawthorne, my solicitor, and asked what I meant by my line 'pre-1810 unregistered estate'. Hawthorne couldn't think what happened to estates in 1810. He: 'You're in good company. Browning was asked what he meant and said "Only God and Browning knew, and now only God knows."'"

I now reviewed my finances. Earlier in the year one 3 year arrangement with the bank had ended, and a new one had begun. The bank's Head Office made the arrangement and changed its basis without informing my bank manager shortly after the arrival of Nigel Lawson as the bank's adviser. Three months later I discovered from my bank statement that, without our bank manager knowing, we had been surcharged £16,000 a quarter – £64,000 per annum – in capital repayments on top of our interest, which meant that over the next 3 years we would be repaying £192,000 I had not bargained on repaying. I found the lack of explanation for the new arrangement (called LIBOR) strange, and I was confirmed in not publishing any more books through Oak-Tree. This surcharge had the effect of killing off Oak-Tree Books and ending the work of the Heroes of the West, as I concentrated exclusively on the two schools.

Egypt concerned me. I wrote: "In Egypt everything was clear; the Temple included the metaphysical, all discipline practised within it. Now everything is unclear. All is materialistic, sceptical and secular, and we are outsiders, trying to find a niche within....My feeling that I should found a new Egyptian temple in which all the disciplines can flourish. An invisible reflection of the visible."

I had sent an early version of *The Fire and the Stones* to HarperCollins where my old Oxford friend Barry Winkleman, whom I had seen at Pinter's *Caretaker* in early 1961 and who had stopped me at Frankfurt as I passed his stand, was now Murdoch's Managing Director. There had been a lengthy delay, and there was talk of cutting the book to 600 pages and omitting the chart and not bringing out the book until after October 1991. I rang Kathleen Raine and she said: "The chart must exist, and in March 1991." She advised me to ring Sir Laurens van der Post. "Tell him I want you to lecture at the Academy in October 1991."

I duly rang Sir Laurens, who said: "My dear fellow, of course I remember you. I've often thought of you. How is the work? I've got a few people here now, please ring me at 4.30 tomorrow, between 4.30 and 5." I rang him the next day, and recorded: "His wife was in the background. 'Dearest, I am taking a business call in the other room.' She: 'Is it Mr Hagger? Give him my love.' He said: "My heart goes out to you. You are doing wonderful work, and the book is of great importance." He ended: "I am not important. I don't regard myself as important or as a link to the Fire. A link to Eliot, Toynbee and Jung, yes, but not an important one." He told me I was the only one alive who was continuing the tradition of Eliot, Toynbee and Jung. I resolved to find another publisher.

About this time Peggy Howard, an Alice Bailey occultist, spiritual healer and psychic clairvoyant, made a diagnosis of my past lives. I wrote: "Past lives. Egyptian male with a fine gold necklace. An 'old soul' with over 20 lives. Two Viking lives one having a ship at sea, one making jewellery; a Viking sword with jewels. A Persian life with a short curved sword, shorter than a scimitar. An Italian life in the Renaissance time (Michelangelo?). An Eastern life. All these seen in a crystal ball which I missed." She saw me as Latimer, being burned at the stake, and there were glimpses of a life in the First World War. How much of this was true? Who knows. Another diagnosis later by a different psychic using dowsing, found 30 lives. I disregarded what I had been told, determined not to let it influence my outlook as there was no evidence.

One image I could not disregard. Through Peggy Howard I had met again one of the Egyptian temple-dancers who had danced in 1977, Christine Finlayson, now Klein (her married name), and she had agreed to dance the descent of the Fire of Amun at the launch of my books. I was haunted by an image within. I was in an Egyptian garden with a high brick wall all round. There was a lot of vegetation, in the middle was a round lily pond, or lotus pond, and standing by it, looking into it, with her back to our house, was my (then) wife, a slender Egyptian girl with black hair wearing a long white dress. And as I looked at her I knew I may not keep her. When I saw Christine with green Egyptian eye-liner under her eyes, I had a sense of déjà vu and the image of the lady in white came into my mind – from a past life?

Len Hutton, the cricketer, died. I noted: "Len Hutton is dead, and what of the importance of his 82 against Australia, now? A sadness for Len Hutton; died of a burst blood vessel in his heart."

I abandoned the idea of having a Foreword for *The Fire and the Stones*. I wrote: "The giants are all dead (Eliot, Toynbee, Jung). Now, after all our researches, we have become giants. There are no giants for me to turn to because I...see no one larger than myself. A giant embodies an idea (e.g. Sartre Existentialism). I embody Universalism and the Metaphysical

Revival. I see my way. I will live on top of an Alp, one day."

I visited Kathleen Raine on September 13th. There was no answer at her door "so I waited and then saw her plodding along from the King's Road and, on the pavement, holding her stick and two large plastic bags. I advanced and kissed her and took the bags and walked back to the house. She: 'I have angina in the afternoons, and I sit and wait for the pain to go before I do what has to be done, the shopping.' Inside she sat and chatted, and then Lady Rose came in, alias Dorothy Carrington, and talked about the Cathars and Corsica." Eventually "I spoke for 3 hours about my book, and they cross-questioned me. I kept my end up. Kathleen Raine, 'Where's the American Fire?' She accepted that the New Age Fire might become the new orthodoxy. 'Universalism, what sort of religion is Universalism? All religions are one as a religion – if it's just a background for American imperialism it won't do.' Lady Rose: 'The fire of Communism. I was a Communist, now I have no home.'" She then asked me, "Napoleon's Fire, wouldn't you say Napoleon knew the Fire?" and I realised she had not understood what I meant by the Fire. "Raine, 'Your strength is people are interested in predictions.' I: 'Just as in physics physicists pursue a Grand Unified Theory, so I have done – or endeavoured to do – the same with religion and world history.' Lady Rose: 'This is grandiose. A grandiose theory. Mine is tiny in comparison.' I: 'Insularity can lead to universality, like Hardy.' Raine: 'I'd rather be Islamic than American because they believe in God. Nicholas sees what is there, he does not say whether it is good.' I said, 'The 14th century mystics couldn't have happened in the 10th century because history was not ready for them, their stage had not come. There is a right time for everything to appear on the pattern.' Raine: 'Am I right in thinking that the genesis of civilisations is caused by something outside history?' When I said 'Yes', 'That is where you will be criticised by historians.' I added, 'The central idea of each civilisation is outside history.' Generally Kathleen Raine approved of my scheme. Very little on poetry; all on my book. 'It will come out and the Academy will happen.' She signed her book (*India Seen Afar*) for me, 'For Nicholas Hagger, Servant of the Sacred Fire.'...I kissed them both twice on their cheeks and left to struggle to a Coopersale Hall parents' meeting.

I reflected on D. H. Lawrence's *Rainbow*: "The vision of the new world, a new way of life as opposed to grimy coalmine villages. Yet when Harlow New Town gave the better way of living it turned out to be rootless and soulless, and D. H. Lawrence the socialist would have been horrified. Heaven on earth? Not Harlow New Town." (The recent closure of mining pits in the UK of course heralded in Lawrence's *Rainbow*: a new way of life apart from grimy coal.)

I had an idea of starting a centre "to give concreteness to the coming Metaphysical Revolution. Found a centre for Metaphysical Revolution, which could be at Coopersale Hall...and a dance troupe to dance Universalist themes, one per civilisation, i.e. 25 dances, each one some 3 minutes for which I will write a short verse drama à la Noh play, i.e. Tammuz, Attis, Orpheus, Osiris etc: emphasising ritual....Behind this should be a contemplation, like the Egyptian temple-dancers....Behind all this should be a Fire of the World movement or Brotherhood of Fire; a contemplative Knights of Light group that channels power. This is the only role of the metaphysical artist, to oppose our time."

I met Trevor Maher in the Charing Cross Hotel, "the Oak-Tree office": "We sat near a long chair and spread my typescripts out....He looks leaner, with a beard; he gets up at 6 and runs. He told me, 'I have a background of being a Fundamentalist. The Fire or Light is in the *Bible*, in *Genesis*.'" Trevor had flown British Midland from Edinburgh and had identified Nadia from her name tag and had introduced himself. "I had wonderful service because I know you," Trevor beamed.

The next day I went to the launch of Kathleen Raine's book on India, *India Seen Afar*. It was launched at India House, the Adelphi. I wrote; "Elephants in stone over the door, up the stairs past a bust of Tagore to a room with Nehru and Gandhi and an enlightened Buddha, where, among other pictures, an audience sat and waited. Satish Kumar entered with Kathleen and the High Commissioner arrived; he was ill, having had an operation 5 days before. Kumar of Green Books: his enlightened enthusiastic view of Kathleen, rather like Dr Aziz in *Passage to India*. The Indian spoke without notes; Kathleen read her speech, ending with the words that she was pleased to pour back a drop from the cupful she had taken. She has written a book on India which will long be remembered....Afterwards wine and Indian food held in the hand, spicy. Spoke with Keith Critchlow (grey-haired and chattering effortlessly); Warren Kenton...who said 'You've just spoken me your blurb, what you've just said is your blurb' and, 'I'm working in the same area.' His wife by his side. Also David Gascoyne, as always in a bow-tie, looking pale and aesthetic at 74, and frail, rather as Eliot looked. I: 'Do you write poems now?' He: 'No, I haven't written for many years. I had an amphetamine dependency which blocked off my inspiration.' His wife of 15 years later said that Kathleen had written to her telling her Gascoyne did not need the worry of a wife, it would depress him. 'I didn't show David the letter. I received it the day before we were married. I loved him so much.' Gascoyne rather pathetic. I thought of Wordsworth's lines, 'We Poets in our youth begin in gladness;/And thereof comes in the end despondency and madness.'" I added: "Gascoyne did however see the poet as a seer, as I do." I went on: "Kathleen Raine looked very beautiful, a serenity in her transparently beautiful smile, and she contrasted with the shuffling awkward Gascoyne in whose presence she was so imperious some years ago. Madge, her son by Charles Madge, a silky-haired architect."

Ahead, I felt, was the task of defining the true Metaphysical line. "Write a book of essays about poets, defining the Metaphysical line....Marvell-Donne, Milton, Blake, Shelley, Eliot-Yeats. Resurrect poets that conform to the Metaphysical Baroque vision. Make it European? Include Germany and France? Rilke? Go for metaphysical Reality (the Fire) at the expense of the imaginative vision unless Imagination=Fire (as in Coleridge). Wordsworth-Coleridge are crucial." Subconsciously I looked out for a London "building of the Metaphysical time (Donne and Marvell)...(which) stood for Universalism".

Both schools had a harvest festival on the same morning. The Oaklands one was first and livelier, the children singing lustily with actions ("The farmer sows the seed"). At Coopersale Hall later I had coffee with the Rev. Ronald Loxley, and "swatting a troublesome wasp, I described the bruised and vulnerable plight of Tommy Hammond, whose armed robbery outlook has lead to a dead-end, emotional deprivation and loneliness; and I urged the Rev. Loxley to call on him, saying the turning around would be of Tolstoyan difficulty, an enormous challenge, the biggest 'conversion' (turn-around) in 2,000 years of Christian history. 'I expect to see Hammond as your second churchwarden the Carol Service after next.' Mrs. Best trying to keep a straight face."

I spent an afternoon rooting round London's Temple area: "First the...Temple church, which contains the first Earl of Essex's tomb (died 1144). It is now the crypt and refectory (14th century). Then the Middle Temple where there are Elizabethan rooms: the hall were Shakespeare acted in *Twelfth Night* (1602) and the two other rooms, one overlooking the Middle Temple garden where Shakespeare set the quarrel of the Wars of the Roses. Many literary and historical associations, e.g. Goldsmith, Johnson, Lamb." On *Twelfth Night* I noted: "Orsino (Giovanni in *The White Devil*) visited Elizabeth I (Olivia) in 1601/2, and Malvolio was the first Puritan."

"May the decade of the 1990s," I wrote, "be the decade of the metaphysical."

I had been asked to find out who would be available to launch *The Fire and the Stones* in April. I rang Asa Briggs, who said he would attend "and say a few words". I rang van der Post and reminded him that I wanted to call for a Metaphysical Revolution across disciplines. He suggested that I should ask Keith Critchlow, "who is in dialogue with him about the origins of culture and who sees a lot of him", to approach Prince Charles. Kathleen Raine advised: "All you can do is plant a seed and let it grow. Those who have ears to hear, let them hear. Those who have eyes to see, let them see. Don't have a wider and wider circle of people knowing about the metaphysical. You will never persuade the opposition; they are happy the way they are, they have power and influence and don't want to change. I don't want anything to do with Antonia Fraser." I rang Critchlow, who was "exhausted, lying on his bed" but who came to the phone and listened intently and asked me to send a synopsis of my work. He suggested I rang Warren Kenton. I rang him and Kenton said: "You will not convert anyone over 40, but the metaphysical work is aimed at the under 40. The thing to do is to minimise the hostility. Don't rush, you are aiming at the next three centuries. Be careful how you expose yourself. The work is happening anyway. In 100 years' time they will say, 'Oh, this happened in the 1980s. Leonardo said, 'Never was there bright light without shadow.'...Leave your brick in the wall, your capstone in the Temple, and then move on to the next thing. Don't attract hostility. Don't expose yourself." I replied: "Do you remember the Angry Young Men and how they all contributed to *Declaration*? There should be another *Declaration* about the Metaphysical Revolution."

Getting people together for a hypothetical launch was proving difficult, and I rang Kenton again and presented all the options. He insisted on taking an astrological viewpoint and said: "Go for April 22nd. The moon is in Leo – a grand entrance. But there is tension and conflict. A risk worth taking.

589

The moon is more favourable than on the 10th. The book will become famous and as the sun is in Taurus it will make money. Go for the Museum of London as it is of more general appeal. The university suggests something more narrow. Don't try to convert or get approval from the academic world. Just sow your seed and move on. Plod on." It was a prediction that was to prove strangely accurate.

My books and politics – events surrounding the fall of Thatcher – dominated the period from October 1990.

I thought about the Universalist vision and tried to think of people who already had bits of it. I wondered about David Gascoyne. I wrote: "Oct 6th. 3.30 a.m. Slept from 10.30 to 1.40 downstairs. Woke and went to bed. Could not sleep. Got up and read Kathleen Raine's essay on Gascoyne, Holderlin and Holderlin's madness. His paradisal world of the poet-seer; going mad through too much light. He lacked the grounding of the historical vision and of a grounded social life. I, too, am in the seer's tradition. Like Prometheus, I stole the Fire from Heaven, but so far I have not gone mad. The weakness in Raine's view: it isn't only poets who have tasted the Light, known the Fire; as *The Fire and the Stones* shows, it is religious peoples."I considered her "imagination" and concluded from *In Defence of Ancient Springs* that it meant "divine inspiration from the Muses: receiving dictation from a voice beyond, the words of which the poet barely understands". I "pinpointed Plato's doctrine of inspiration and what it does not mean. It does not mean exclusion of the social world, or receiving dictation....Kathleen Raine is against Eliot because he was not inspired."

I felt that my development was now over: "I have remade myself. The Egerton Gardens mysticism and metaphysical inklings are now fundamental to my outlook. The contradictions have all been ironed out. Now, output." I had the idea for splitting the *Selected Poems* into social and metaphysical poems. I wrote: "Does the social/metaphysical split help the Baroque idea or hinder it? The metaphysical and the social, they are together, not in opposition."

I was working on the index of *The Fire and the Stones* and busied myself with getting the *Selected Poems* ready. In Foyles by accident I found the last copy of Frank Warnke's *European Metaphysical Poetry*, which is on the Baroque and Metaphysical tradition. It was waiting for me.

I was startled to read a change in Tebbit's views: "Tebbit has called for all maintained schools to be allowed to opt out; having told the *Epping and Harlow Star* on July 9th that he did not believe that this should be so. What has changed his mind? His experience of Coopersale Hall School in July. Coopersale Hall School has reverberated round the nation, for Tebbit's speech was taken up by MacGregor, the Minister of Education, and then Mrs. Thatcher." I saw that government policy had been influenced by my abrupt decision to follow the promptings of the Light and found Coopersale Hall.

My cousin Jill's daughter Fione, married into the Courtauld family on a Saturday in October. I wrote: "The Hadlee-Courtauld wedding at Terling church, which dates from the 13th century and which was probably visited by Henry VIII. (No stained glass windows.) The Courtaulds all in morning suits, the Hadlee relatives in suits....We took Argie, semi-deaf at 87 ('what?') and Anthony. The Courtaulds on the right hand side of the aisle, the groom's side, where sat George, the groom, in green socks; and his balding, rotund father, equerry to the Queen. The satiny wedding dress, Elizabeth as a bridesmaid. The happy couple whispered and chatted during the solo. Afterwards, tension as suits mingled with morning dress and top hats and tails. Met up with Rob and Richard and Frances (the ushers not having done their jobs properly). To Fairstead. All parked in a field, we parked by the door to let Argie out without a walk. Champagne inside, and a marquee: a jazz band. Spoke to our side, and the equerry, who knew the dominating Courtauld, Samuel, who died in 1962....The speeches: the godfather of Fione recited her disastrous academic record...; the best man asked if the groom was worthy of Fione....The groom thanked many but forgot to thank for presents....The groom: 'When I asked Mr Hadlee he was watching television. I tried to get between him and the television, and he tried to see round me. Then he said, "It's time for new balls." He was watching tennis.'" Lord Althorp was present. He was a friend of the groom, who later had Fione and him to stay at Althorp.

Des McForan rang me three times from Bulgaria. He had a post as adviser to the President and wanted me to go to Sofia for a fortnight "and meet the government". He told me: "Our interpretation *was* correct, the terrorists *were* hiding in Eastern Europe. Your letter to Julian Amery was prophetic, there will be a United States of Europe." (When silence had been thrown round Des's book, I had written to Amery explaining that the United States of Europe that I had foreseen was in the best interests of the UK, and I had asked what people saw wrong with the context of my vision that would make them want to block it.)

We went to Cornwall: "A high wind, an energetic sea, white waves racing in and the wind whistles round the chimney, blown spume drifting through the air like smoke. And above all, at least for a while, a blue sky. Feel well." I worked on the index. I wrote of the Metaphysical Revolution which I set myself to launch in 1991 (as had been predicted in the Markham): "I have deep drives within me. Like the waves of the sea my sexual and metaphysical drives fling forward, gather and fling forward again. I thrust."I added: "Green sea. Purple sky. White waves. The energy of the sea, waves coming in, flinging at the beach. A flower opening slowly."

I also pointed out: "The Metaphysical Revolution: every subject should from now on have a Metaphysical compartment for interpreting that subject in terms of metaphysics, i.e. in terms of the One Being, the Fire or Light which can be known existentially."

On the way back to Essex we stopped at a service station on the M4 and told Anthony to "beware" of something. "He chanted 'Beware! Beware!' from *Kubla Khan*. I continued: 'His flashing eyes, his floating hair!' (suggesting the inspired poet) '/Weave a circle round him thrice,/And close your eyes with holy dread,/For he on honey-dew hath fed,/And drunk the milk of Paradise' – and did not realise that two Chigwell School parents were within earshot and had apparently recognised me. I was very carried away and acted out the outer manifestations of inspiration, and they must think me quite mad."

At the end of October I had the trench-cementing inspected by the Council's buildings inspector. The Oaklands Committee member, Lynn Wickham had died of a tumour in her brain, and there was a high church funeral at St. John's, Loughton, attended by Martin, her greying husband who owned record shops, and who had helped me paint the Oaklands hall in 1982. I wrote: "Bells and a smoking censer, beautiful choir conducted by Sherwood but intrusive sung responses. The catafalque had lain in state overnight and was guarded by numerous priests who walked round it, bowing and holding up the Bible. Communion. Many people, most of them at one time or another connected with Oaklands."

In early November I noted: "Howe's resignation. Thatcher must go now." The next day I observed: "Steve Norris on TV, supporting Thatcher over Europe and saying his constituents support her. Not this one."

At the Coopersale Hall fireworks party, "300 parents stood in mild, cloudy weather on the terrace and the tree-end of the lawn, and watched as a bonfire shot a cloud of sparks and fireworks went up at once....Talked with the Norrises. Steve has changed from being anti-European to pro-European after a talk with Heseltine: 'Mother (Thatcher) is a drag-anchor. We need a winner. Heseltine will challenge on Monday or Tuesday.' On the Gulf war, 'I've had tomorrow's date written down for weeks.' I: 'November 16th would be a good date, for she can present Heseltine as rocking the war boat.' Vicky: 'What did Heseltine say to you?' Silence. I: 'She means, did he offer you Foreign Secretary or Chancellor of the Exchequer?' She: 'Am I that transparent?' I am able to see behind the appearance to the reality....I, not being in contention for any jobs, say what I believe and stick to it, and ring true like a genuine coin."

In November I looked in on HarperCollins. Barry Winkleman's secretary said: "Excellent work. The chart ought to be compulsory reading for everybody, everybody in the world ought to learn it from birth. And Barry sends his love."But there was still no progress with a publication date, and there was still the prospect of shortening.

On November 14th I wrote: "The Light has been pouring in, answering yes to: *The Fire and the Stones, A Metaphysical's Way of Fire*, the getting across of a Metaphysical Revolution, to my continuing involvement with the two schools, to something being about to happen....I am to have assistance in carrying out my Revolution. 1.25. Am full of energy, having received a huge influx from the Light which answers all my questions. Don't get my energy from children..., but from the beyond."

A strange coincidence happened in mid-November. The catering firm we used at the two schools invited us to a French breakfast at London Zoo to taste the first Beaujolais nouveau specially motored from France. We were greeted by waitresses in suspenders, a French-speaking compère wrapped in the tricolour talked us through an enormous fried breakfast, and we all went out to greet the arrival of the wine and duly had a couple of glasses. We left the Zoo and hailed the first taxi to drive to the tube, and the driver said "Good morning Mr and Mrs. Hagger" and it was a man who until recently had been an Oaklands parent. Again I wondered at the pattern underlying events.

We went home and attended Miss Lord's 90th birthday tea, and then went to a Conservative function at Loughton's Thatcher House. (The building was so-named by Biggs-Davison shortly after he was sacked by her, and opened by Mrs. Thatcher, who had stepped out of her car and gone over and shaken hands with my mother, who just happened to be passing while going shopping and who was not connected with the ceremony at all.) About 120 people listened to Steve Norris speak on how he was taking soundings as to which way he would vote in the leadership election, and he hinted he might vote for Heseltine as he would be an election winner. At the end of the evening he suggested that Ann and I should join him for dinner at a Chinese restaurant in Loughton with two or three others. We were to go on to a house in Alderton Hill and travel from there. Ann went in one car, I went with Steve. We were alone, and on the way he told me he received 50 letters a day. At the restaurant he said that the reason Howe had resigned was because Thatcher had said he was "behind with the Commons work, that he was dreadful and inefficient. It was bad man-management on her part." Steve drove us home and as Ann got out I asked him which way he would vote. He said, "I won't mess you about, Nick, I'll tell you, I shall vote bat." I looked blank. "Cricket bat?" I ventured. "Straight bat?" "I shall vote for the old bat (i.e. Thatcher) because she should win well; and Hurd in the second round." Which was what happened. He offered to approach David Mellor, the Minister for Arts, to attend my coming launch.

I met Trevor Maher, who said that the HarperCollins delay was increasingly unsatisfactory. He proposed that Weidenfeld or Mainstream should be approached to take the books over. We had had a drink with the two Mainstream fellows at Frankfurt, and as they were Edinburgh-based like Trevor, he said he would speak to them.

Thatcher announced she would resign after eleven and a half years. I wrote: "She had to go: she was wrong over Europe, the issue on which I crossed swords with her, with Hurd in attendance." I spoke to David Evennett at Chigwell School's *Dr Faustus*, in which Anthony was a demon, and he told me how the voting was going. "He will vote for Major. Norris is voting for Hurd because they are connected through Eton. John Smith has spoken of a further 5 years in opposition as the result of Thatcher's resignation; he will go into business." Soon afterwards I noted: "John Major is the new PM; a young man with an ambling, creeping walk and a boyish smile."

My younger brother Jonathan rang. He had been appointed Finance Director to the Duke of Westminster and from January would be managing the Grosvenor Estate in Davies Street, where he would have a staff of 50.

In early December I spoke with Norris. He had just been made PPS to Kenneth Baker. Mellor had been replaced as Minister for Arts by Renton. Norris said, "Yes, Renton (the Chief Whip) did feed Thatcher misinformation from the Heseltinites, as he did regarding Ridley, which is why I fell out with him. It hasn't prevented me from writing to him to invite him to your launch." I knew from the bad feeling Norris described that Renton would not attend.

I looked back on my own involvement in politics during the Thatcher years, and I wrote: "I was part of the movement that stood firm against Communism, i.e. which had belief in the West's central idea. This was not free trade and free market – economics – and military might; but the strength in the Fire or Light to demand the freedom to research into metaphysics, which was behind my free market business activities. The contemplative ideal, which Communism crushed and denied expression. I asserted metaphysical values against Communism. I left my metaphysical studies at my desk to resist the wiles of the Communists among their client-state puppet rulers, and then returned to the reality at my desk."

Gorka had invited me to attend the Pan-European Union congress in Prague from December 7th-9th. Otto von Habsburg, the heir to the Austro-Hungarian and Holy Roman Empire, would be there, and Gorka, who regarded him as emperor in exile (much more than an MEP) would introduce me and we would visit Wenceslas Square. I agreed to go and we would be travelling with Stuart Notholt of Western Goals, who wanted to start a magazine rather like my Western or Universalist Review. Western Goals had produced a very interesting leaflet saying that the decision to overthrow Thatcher had been taken at a meeting at La Toja in May, where Kissinger of the New World Order Bilderberg Group had called for a more rapid movement towards a European Central Bank, which Thatcher was opposing.

The three of us met at Heathrow and boarded a Czech airliner Tipolev 134. I wrote: "A one and a half hour flight above a rosy sky through a temperature of minus 40 at 500 mph. Landed in a Prague that was frosty and icy and smoggy and minus 8. Drove through deserted streets to the Hotel Dlabacov with Adam Ferguson, Ex-MEP, and Vice President of the Pan-European Union; registered and learned we were in the house Mickle a cab ride away. Found our room, and then returned to the Dlabacov, a large functional modern building with a huge reception room where, among tables with white tablecloths and ham rolls, we drank wine and spoke with Otto von Habsburg, who at first brushed us off (spoke with Adam Ferguson in German)." Gorka bowed and kissed his hand, renewing his loyalty to the old Austro-Hungarian ideal. I recall a small, ageing, balding figure who avoided all eye-contact to preserve the distance required by his royal pedigree and who had the air of an emperor who spoke all the European languages, listening to what I said about the coming United States of Europe, which my book had predicted, and saying I was welcome. We met up with a Hungarian publisher, Zoltan Brady, and a Czech Charter 77 journalist, Stefan, and walked in the Old City with them. I wrote: "Got out by the National Theatre and walked past the café where Havel used to sit and onto the boulevard and Wenceslas Square. This in a temperature of minus 10 or 11. Ears stung, nose lost its feeling. To the Beograde, a restaurant, where for £11.60 we six dined with wine on Serbian spiced pork and salad."

I found the United States of Europe not fully present. I wrote: "As to Otto's pan-European ideal, a step by step approach to a United States of Europe, this has rather got lost amid German women and taxis that are not free and the shambolic organisation, with no one introducing anyone to anyone." The next day, after breakfast at the Dlabacov in our own room (coffee, orange, meats, bread and marmalade) I ran into Adam Ferguson, who had also been personal adviser to Sir Geoffrey Howe, at the top of the stairs and asked him if there would be British funding for a British branch of Pan-Europe, and I gathered that his role was to keep a brake on Pan-Europeanism: "There won't be any funding, it wouldn't last a month, a British branch of Pan-Europe."

In the main hall we were given earphones and a translator set, and we sat and listened to speeches from the platform: the Secretary-General, the Treasurer Sir Tom Normanton and Valburga Habsburg, a Marie Thérèse figure. I left to work on my index outside, and Gorka and Stuart came out and said, "Adam Ferguson has just spoken, he mentioned us as the British delegation." It seemed to me that there was a contradiction between his public enthusiasm and private discouragement.

After lunch we toured Prague. I wrote: "To the castle ("Schloss"), the spires of which – St. Vitus Cathedral – tower over Prague. Walked among the palaces and churches of the Kremlin-like squares and streets. Then to Charles IV bridge, a cobbled bridge with 31 statues and many booths and a great crowd and the river Vltava and weir one side and the river and another bridge the other. The taxi-driver picked us up the other side of the bridge and drove us to the Old Square where the astronomical clock struck the hour while we were there, death and apostles appearing at the opened windows. The square where 27 were executed by the Habsburgs. Near it, round the corner, but within sight of the sunburst high up on the church, the significance of which he never discovered, was Kafka's House, shut up and dustbins in the hall, and bronze 'likeness' of Kafka on the side looking down a side street at the end of which were the spires of the castle. Prague is very much Kafka's city: the waiting at the hotel desk, the being under a towering Castle (St Vitus' Cathedral)."

Back at the conference we talked to Valburga, who said, "There is no money, you must go through Adam Ferguson" (following a very rigid command structure), and I talked at length to Normanton, whom I liked. He said he was a friend of Mrs. Thatcher: "We argued fiercely but looked each other in the eye. Her brain was like a computer. 'Why Tom, you forgot this point, you did not see that point.' I told him at some length of my difficulties with my Oak-Tree Books and the torpedoing of the launches and said I wanted a clear run for *The Fire and the Stones*. He said, "I heard." I asked, "Do you mean, I Hurd?" (spelling my pronunciation). He: "Let us just say I Hurd." I invited him to the launch of the book. He did not turn up, but I did receive a letter from Douglas Hurd, the Foreign Secretary, saying he was reading the book on planes.

That evening the delegates went to a beer cellar called U Svatehu Tomase, and the French delegation invited "the British delegation" to Reims. I heard the story of St. Agnes convent, which we had passed: "St Agnes died c1200 and there was no body to bury so she could not be canonised. The legend grew up that when she became a saint, Prague would be free. She was made a saint in 1989, and Prague immediately became free."

A MYSTIC WAY

The next day was a Sunday morning. We were up early and breakfasted in the same room as Otto von Habsburg and then went by coach "to Holy Mass in the church of the Order of Malta, Kostel Sv Marie pod Retezem in Maltezske, Mala Strana, near Charles IV bridge. The white interior with gilt figures and pulpit and a statue of a Field Marshal looking like Guy Fawkes (1648). Singing, a packed congregation standing in the aisles and at the sides. The kneeling on one knee at certain points. Mass. Otto von Habsburg went up first, and, after the Fire had come down and channelled through me, so my soul was alight, I went up about 20th, and took the wafer dipped in wine, standing, from a balding, rotund priest. (Earlier, the address about Nazism and Communism.) Walked to the middle of the cobbled Charles IV bridge to see the double cross where John of Napomuk, confessor to a Queen c1200, was thrown into the river and drowned for refusing to reveal details of the confession to a jealous king (Wenceslas IX). The statue of Napomuk. Touched the head upside down. Lingered at the Christians imprisoned by the Turk, a statue near the end of the bridge. Break in the weir. Back via baroque courtyards and so many medieval buildings, not destroyed by war, to the end of the service as church bells rang in the distance. Pondered the significance of attending Mass with the Head of the Habsburgs in an ancient centre of the Holy Roman Empire. Back to the Hotel Dlabacov." On reflection, the Mass culminated my long contact with the Austrian Margaret, and it was as though I had been passed on to a Central European Light tradition embodied by the Habsburgs, a tradition that was in waiting for the coming United States of Europe.

The final session involved a speech by Adam Ferguson, and then Otto Habsburg took the microphone, "speaking without notes, a current flowing through him, no hesitation, a speech of the divine – clearly a future President of Europe. His plea for more recognition of Central Europe and criticism of Delors for not wanting to revise the Treaty of Rome, i.e. for being a deepener and not a widener. His plea for a free Continent at peace without borders and perhaps with a new European language, since English (the language of Shakespeare) is being debased by pidgin English." I "sat between French and German delegates, listening on my interpreting machine, a wish-bone from each ear under my chin. And then it occurred to me, he does not want his Central European movement to be carried in English, he wants German to be the main language and does not want to be tied to America, which was not mentioned at all." He received a standing ovation, but from the comments I had encountered at the conference ("he is our Emperor") I understood that he was after a revival of the Holy Roman Empire with himself as Emperor and its main language German, and I could understand why Britain might want to contain this idea rather than encourage it. I flew back with Adam Ferguson, who waited for us at Heathrow and sat next to me in the tube to Hammersmith and I said as much to him.

My final impression of Prague was very favourable. I wrote: "Prague is small with a medieval centre, all of a piece (Old Square – bridge and river – castle) and is more unified than Budapest: is wonderful. The baroque capital of Europe because it is so little war-damaged, because so much has survived."

Looking back on my visit to Prague I wrote: "Now feel I may become an Ambassador for the Fire, explaining the Fire to world leaders, discussing the Fire with them as a history idea."

The Light now took over the arrangements for the Metaphysical Revolution. I returned from Prague to tributes from parents at both Oaklands and Coopersale Hall, which were breaking up. One parent kissed me, another said her daughter had blossomed and would have been an "also-ran" without the education she had had. There was a general feeling that we had offered an excellent education to the children, which was very pleasing.

I asked the Light if I was on course. I wrote: "Dec 19. Went to the Light twice. The first time, meditated and asked if I am on the right track regarding the Metaphysical Revolution and got surges in reply; but silence on the mechanics. The second time, several hours later, had huge surges and am filled with the Light. The second surge was enormously powerful and went down my back and through my legs and feet. It confirmed that there will be a Metaphysical Revolution, that I am to do a Gaddafi and have a Revolution – more accurately, to do a Luther – and that this may affect millions of people. We are the inheritors. Toynbee, Eliot, Jung are dead. I have inherited." I added a few days later: "I have embodied my destiny. We are the inheritors." On Christmas Eve I "went to the Light. Many answering surges....The new direction is inevitable."

I had images: "A field with a grey house, a gipsy woman with a bun, lovemaking in summer grass with white flowers, and an auburn-haired lady, before I went off to the First World War....The rifles pointing at my beloved who looked at me." I was not sure if they were echoes of a past life. I noted "the way my skin glows after the Light, the Light in my textured skin and in my being".

On Christmas morning an idea lodged in my mind: "An insight at 7.45 a.m. as I lay in bed. If all goes well there must be a Foundation to promote the ideas of the Metaphysical Revolution....This foundation could be based in Belgravia or in Jerusalem; using American or Swiss funding. It would be an umbrella over everything: arrange lectures, and be a kind of temple as in Egypt. A Foundation of the Light? Or a Foundation to safeguard the Metaphysical Revolution? To promote the Metaphysical Revolution?"

I carried the index on and we all went to Bedford for the family gathering. My brother Robert was very disillusioned with the solicitor's partnership he had been with. He told me that the partnership profits for 1988 merely covered the tax they had to pay in January and July 1990, and that the 8 partners borrowed £25,000 each to cover their living expenses, saddling themselves with another debt of £200,000 plus interest, with more to borrow at the end of the year. He said that he had lost a quarter of a year's business when a development did not go through.

Over Christmas I heard that Margaret Shubber of Iraq had died in March.

In early January Trevor Maher rang me. To unjam the HarperCollins delay Peter MacKenzie of Mainstream had rung a contact of his in Element Books and as a result I was to send *The Fire and the Stones* to Michael Mann. This duly happened. There was swiftly a message from Michael Mann on my answerphone asking me to ring before he went to Switzerland. I rang and arrangements were made for Element to take over both *The Fire and the Stones* and *Selected Poems*. I was relieved because "the Metaphysical Revolution will be marketed, spread". I had a vision of the future: "I was an old man, white-haired, looking like Jung (my Shadow), embodying the Metaphysical Revolution, which, like sacred fire, I must guard for 30 years; setting up a Foundation of Light and then living on top of a mountain in Europe or near Jerusalem. Devoting my life to speaking for the Metaphysical Revolution."

The Gulf War started almost immediately. I wrote: "A heavy heart. What was inevitable 8 months ago has come to pass: Saddam Hussein is remaining in Kuwait, and the West wants the oil to flow without threat from Saddam. A shabby oil war is beginning and within a few hours many will die. Feel sombre and sad for the Iraqis I used to know, and for the Baghdad I hated and love." The allies bombed Iraq, beginning with Cruise missiles. I wrote: "I hope the poor Iraqi sarifa-dwellers have survived." I felt again: "I have a heavy heart. My history theory has been vindicated of course, and American world leadership looks more near than less near, but I mourn for the Baghdad I knew and the bombing of my memories. And I am sad about the American attitude: 'We're going to bomb them so deep they're going to have to pipe in the sunlight.'" The television carried live coverage of Iraq's missile attack on Israel, which I watched until 2 a.m., while checking my accountant's figures.

A parent came into school in tears at having to take her children away on financial grounds. I worked out a way for her to keep the children in school. She was overcome. She said: "I have a sixth sense; I knew Lynn Wickham would die, I saw you and Ann Hagger standing in the graveyard of St. John's church at her funeral two days before she died." I felt eerie. How could she have seen me standing in the churchyard ten days before the funeral? I told her that "I had helped Martin get Lynn into Havering atte Bower by speaking to the Mayor, who came to watch Coopersale Hall's football and gave me a name, which I passed on to Martin." It occurred to me that somehow I was involved with the angels "on a band of Light" and that somehow this parent was on the same wave-length.

I went to Shaftesbury, Dorset to visit Element. I wrote: "Pleasant old grammar school, ancient building with many staircases, nooks and crannies, and a warren of rooms. Met Michael Mann, followed him upstairs; sweater, tie, hair going back, soft look, smoked filter-tips throughout our one and a half hour chat, first on practicalities – he took notes while I freewheeled – then on the Fire generally and on my poems." He turned out to be a relative of Vicky Norris's through a cousin. He told me: "Universalism cannot be absolutist, it will always be regional" and "There cannot be world peace until the world accommodates Islam." We made arrangements for the launch.

At the end of January, nearly 14 years after I first saw the Egyptian Temple-Dancers at St. John's, Smith Square, I met Christine the temple-dancer at the Museum of London. We discussed where she would dance the Descent of the Light of Amun-Re. We chose a setting with a column behind her. I described my memory of the lotus pool and she said quietly, "I remember that lotus pool." She said she would dance to "water-music" and wear a white dress with gold and use green eye-liner. She said: "I will reflect and project. Reflect the Light of Amun-Re, and project it. I mirror the Light and become a Shining One and dance with the Shining Ones and project the Light onto the audience. I get a flow. I do it by feeling. I don't like to put a date on it. It's early.' Amun-Re was strong from c 1990 BC. 'I create a stillness, because God can only be known through stillness.'" That bedtime, Christine later told me, she had a rush of images, all from the Egyptian days, in which she saw herself in a life with me. Unwittingly I had brought her back to dancing by asking her to dance at my launch.

I was full of energy from the beyond as I prepared for the publication of my two books. I gave myself a shock by touching a light-switch, and I set off an alarm while buying a leather jacket in Marks and Spencer. The manageress said, "That can't happen unless you're radioactive." I got the idea for calling the notes to the poems "A Metaphysical Commentary". I spoke with Keith Critchlow over the telephone. He said; "Do send Prince Charles an invitation. He might be able to come if it's near Kensington Palace."

I visited Dr Hughes for my annual check-up. I wrote; "Dr Hughes. Bustling and clear-skinned, white-coated. He looked at my X-rays, made me blow (I blew 600) and took my blood pressure (110/70) and listened to my breathing through his stethoscope, which was on my back; and pronounced me better than ever before, and much better than 1987. Now I only have an X-ray every 2 years. 'We think bronchiectasis is caused by either scarlet fever, measles, whooping cough, pleurisy or pneumonia in childhood – 4 out of 5 in your case – or heavy smoking or being near an industrial plant where there are fumes. This year we may find the answer. Many more are getting it. This wasn't the case when you were diagnosed."

The Coopersale Hall extension had progressed and for three days I got the concrete floor laid. Then it snowed: "Snow during the last two days – 8 inches last night – and the two schools are closed and I can't move my car. Snowbound in a magical world of white, everything clean and pure and the familiar made wonderfully strange. The excitement of snow. High on railings, fences, netting, the bird table, roofs."

"My next work," I wrote, "will be excerpts from my *Diaries*, focusing on my metaphysical development and the bits that support the poems....The title should mean 'The Growth of a Metaphysical' or 'A Metaphysical's Development'. Had this idea two or three days ago, but know it is next."I also noted: "These *Diaries* justify the description of me as a 'man of letters'."

I went to Cornwall and proof-read my two books. I heard that Stephen Lucas had gone bankrupt in July and that he faced prison for fraud. I noted; "Ice in the inner harbour, which my poems symbolise as the heart. Ice on the heart." I wrote: "After teetering between Christianity and the New Age in 1980/1, my great strength was to go forward and embrace Universalism; it has given my poetry an enormous strength."

599

A MYSTIC WAY

In mid-February I read obituaries about Krasso, the Hungarian dissident. He had died, aged 58, after "recently suffering a stroke" and "after being in a coma for a long time". The obituaries described how "he was among the first who fired at the dreaded secret police units" during the Hungarian revolution of 1956. I wondered whether he had in fact had a stroke or whether he had been assisted to have one, following his petition for democracy. He had been very much a supporter of the ideas of the Heroes of the West.

Back in Essex I went to the Conservative Patrons Club at St. Stephen's Club, Queen Anne's Gate. Kenneth Baker spoke until his speech was cut short by a division bell. He announced that Vernon Davies would be fighting Sheffield Central at the next election. Steve Norris returned and spoke well on the Gulf, on Major, on not letting Labour in. I wrote: "Orpheus among the Maenads....Orpheus wondering what the hell he's doing among the right-wingers."

Towards the end of February I was aware of the workings of synchronicity: "I was thinking that I should write to Valerie Eliot and looking for my *Diary* entry for my visit to Ezra Pound when Valerie's nephew's wife (Tanya) rang from Sunderland saying she had been trying to get Valerie, who was not in, and asking me about my visit to Pound. Extraordinary telepathy."

The Gulf War ended abruptly; I wrote "probably a day too early. Schwarzkopf, our Pompey, has made a study of Hannibal's battle of Cannae and has used the same encircling tactics against the Republican Guard. One more day and he would have achieved a massive surrender. But there would have been further loss of life, and if Bush can achieve his goals politically, it is better for the war to end. 85,000-100,000 Iraqi dead or wounded – horrific."

In early March I began setting up my launch: "Rang Warren Kenton in the evening, around 6. He has just moved to a new flat and was among packing cases. If he is not in America – and his diary is packed – he will be pleased to speak about the Fire. He asked me to write to him about the Fire so he can get the feel of it. Rang David Gascoyne in the Isle of Wight. He is very interested in my *Selected Poems*, and will be honoured to say a few words at my launch....Rang Kathleen Raine. Told her about Element and the Metaphysical Revolution. She was writing to Michael Mann. (Synchronicity.) She was very excited. I said: 'The Revolution was prophesied by David Gascoyne in the late 1930s, and has been worked for by you and others for decades...and has now happened. *The Fire and the Stones* will be the main work, and the poems will be on its back.' She feels Temenos Academy will happen. She has seen Prince Charles twice – she is consulted by him about his own work. She said, 'Tomlin foresaw all this.' She and Gascoyne and Warren Kenton now subscribe to the idea of a Metaphysical Revolution. She: 'The bullets will fly on April 22nd.'...She: 'People won't go to say, "Oh good, Nicholas Hagger has told us the truth." They will be snide and will reject it, as they did my book on Blake. But out of it will come your immortality.' Kathleen Raine is like Mrs. Thatcher: 'You're one of us.' 'I shan't be able to be present if the Poet Laureate is there.' I: 'It's like a relay race. You've held the baton for one lap and you're handing over to me. But there are several runners in parallel lanes.' Kathleen Raine: 'I'm writing an essay, "On the Vertical Dimension".'I: 'In a poem of transformation I wrote in 1966, I wrote of "the vertical vision" as opposed to the "horizontal vision". ...Kathleen Raine: 'Eliot never had the vision.' I: 'He knew "the Fire and the rose are one".'She: 'Yes' (grudgingly) 'but he never had the vision. I write Valerie as she's a sweet person.'" I noted: "Kathleen is defensive about her Temenos Academy. As soon as I rang she interrupted me to say, 'I think the Temenos Academy will happen. Someone from the Millennium Trust is looking at a house on Monday.'"

"Why is the Metaphysical Revolution important?" I wrote. "Because it makes possible a new view of man and of the universe and therefore brings in a new age after 300 years of Materialism, Scepticism and Humanism. T. E. Hulme forecast a new religious age. The Renaissance resulted in the elimination of the spiritual and divine perspective, and the definition of man in terms of the physical and psychological. Now the Counter-Renaissance sees man as a metaphysical being again, a view supported by physicists like David Bohm, and there will be profound consequences for European art. The Romantic age swept in new attitudes; in the same way the Metaphysical Revolution will bring in new Universalist attitudes. In the 1490s men might ask 'Why is the Renaissance important?' and in the 1790s, 'Why is Romanticism important?' In the 1990s, 'Why is Existential Metaphysics important?'It is the vision that was around at the beginning of 25 civilisations."And I focused on the launch: "What I say at the launch. As at the beginning of the Romantic Age there has been a redefinition of man and of the universe in various disciplines. The new view of man goes beyond the social ego and links him to the universe. Metaphysics – behind physics. The void, the link between all four worlds of the Kabbalah. Same in ancient Egypt. We have lived in a time of existence, and Being, Non-Being and the One have been excluded. 300 years of Humanism have come to an end. This new vision is present in many disciplines..., and it can now surface. The new mood and zeitgeist of the 1990s emphasises the oneness of all creation and the inadequacy of a purely social vision. It is a question of emphasis and rediscovery. The metaphysical man as opposed to the physical man."

Towards the end of March I wrote: "Cometh the hour, cometh the man. I hope I am up to it. I hope I am the right man. The Fire has to work with those it can and will send me the energy I need at the right time. If the Fire operates as I have described in the book, then everything is changed. Humanism cannot exist if the Fire exists; it is changed and passes within a new context."

I rang Rupert Sheldrake and spoke with Jill Purce, who explained they would be in Devon during the launch. "I'll be coming up from Devon on that day to give a lecture at St. James's, Piccadilly. I have a one-year old child. Rupert will be looking after him in Devon." Later I spoke to Rupert, who said: "Your books look very interesting. I want to read them. The Tomlin book is one of my most thumbed ones. I often refer to it and recommend it. The one you published. It's a very good book." "I: 'Tomlin is our Whitehead but never came off the fence.' He: 'You must. You must declare yourself.'" I rang David Bohm, who arranged to see me the following week. He asked: "You don't want me to speak at the launch?" I recorded: "I said Sheldrake's morphogenetic field goes with Bohm's implicate order which goes with my Void/Non-Being. He: 'Huh huh.' We will meet...to agree an identity between the Fire manifesting through fields/physics, i.e. the divine Fire is behind the oneness of creation and history, and the mysticism of poetry."

I had a letter from Dr Brian Hanson, adviser to the Prince of Wales, saying he would attend the launch, and two letters from Kathleen Raine, desperate to organise the Temenos Academy, asking if I could raise funds for her and saying, "You as the High Priest of Fire, I entrust with my last hope." I offered my schools as temporary accommodation for her Academy to help her get it off the ground.

I met Margaret Taylor and her husband in the card shop in Loughton. I had heard coughing and said to Margaret, "You've got a cough." I recorded: "'Yes,' she said, 'I've got two secondaries in my lungs, I have chemotherapy from next Tuesday for 8 months. They can't operate. I'm under the London. I was there yesterday, they put me in a terminal ward.' I uncounselled them and said she could sit in the Oaklands gardens any time. 'You can turn it round, you've done so many angelic things they must be counting the ticks up there.' 'Can you remind them? They need a poke.' Grey, drawn face, spectacles; aged. She will come and have tea. Margaret enjoying having a dramatic effect on everyone; Graham very silent. Margaret, 'I'm on the other side of the fence now.'"

I visited David Bohm at Birkbeck. "He couldn't be found. I was early and waited, was then sent to PE 40, and found him opening letters. 'It's just the right time.' He carried on opening mail and seemed to forget that I was there. Then he took me to a small room he shared with an Asian, who wanted to stay: 'Do you mind if I stay?' We stood there without saying anything and he took the hint and left. Then Bohm changed his mind and said we should sit in another room. He led me to where 6 people were standing by a computer and sorting through a thesis. They all switched off or packed up and left. He closed the door, still opening and reading a letter, and then said 'Sit down' and I did so and looked deep into his eyes and he into mine, and then we got on fine and the words came. I talked for most of the time – for 40 minutes – about how he had stood for the whole and a Theory of Everything must include a Grand Unified Theory of physics as well as of history, and how metaphysics looked as ontological theory, Being, and I spoke of the significance of the Fire. I did not have the chart – that would have led to a one and half hour or 5 hour conversation – but I gave him my *Introduction to the Metaphysical Revolution* and talked him through the paragraphs as I do the bank manager. At the end I pressed him, and, creased faced and rumpled-looking but strangely innocent, some of the things he said reverberated through my consciousness: 'Have you seen the Fire?' I: 'I'll answer honestly, Yes.' He: 'Good.' I put it to him that physics is within metaphysics. He: 'You can't have a vision of the whole. It's infinite.' I: 'You can interpret it simultaneously through different faculties, vision, imagination, reason.' He: 'The universe is infinite,' meaning that our vision is finite. I: 'Is that what your equations and calculations tell you?'

He: 'Yes. It's infinite, and our universe is a local event, an area within the sea of energy.' (He wrote as much in *Wholeness and the Implicate Order*.)"I pointed out that the self has an infinite part to it, the spark in the soul, and that by passing from the ego to our universal being we *can* have a vision of the infinite. "He, on the Metaphysical Revolution, 'I'm not optimistic, I think everything's in decline. Ecologically, for example.' I: 'History shows this, but there are some young civilisations with a vision still ahead of them. The North American civilisation is young, and it has not found its orthodoxy yet – which may be a Universalist metaphysical vision.' I pressed him on the Metaphysical Revolution. He: 'There is something cosmic, which is behind physics.' I: 'That's what I mean when I say the Fire manifests into Void and Being and Existence.' I: 'The Fire is a sea of energy. What about the Big Bang?' 'A local event, a ripple.' 'And cosmic background radiation? Penzias and Wilson?' 'The residue.' He said, 'I wish I had your enthusiasm. We're not near a Unified Theory of physics.' (I had said, 'You can find it.') 'Different physicists have different views.' I said, 'Do you feel out on a limb or in the mainstream of physics?' 'Different physicists have different views.' I said, 'Any new idea is always opposed and you must have felt opposition.' 'Yes.' He asked, 'What do you want to say at the launch?' I told him. 'I'll go along with that. Send me your work.' With that he stood up and held out a hand, and I wished him goodbye and said I hoped he'd be at the launch. 'I maybe in Israel, but if not I'll be there.'"

Later I observed: "This great man has seen matter and consciousness as a unity and influenced my poems and he has confirmed the vision in my poems. 'I don't accept the Big Bang', i.e. it could have happened as a local ripple but the universe is infinite, we are finite with finite minds – which can receive the infinite vision and therefore we take part in infinity. Part of us is of the infinity in the universe. I have a new poem about this and about CBR....There is a sea of souls in the infinite sea of energy, and we are a local surfacing of minds too finite to grasp it, but we partake of infinity. My insistence that the metaphysical Fire unites everything – physics, history here in this tiny local corner. We see it, not the whole of it but part of this vast cosmic Fire before it manifests into Void and fullness.' I noted: "Bohm: 'I didn't collaborate with Einstein, I had discussions with Einstein."...I said to Bohm, 'You'll be a very important figure in such a movement in 200 years' time.' We are all being used – driven with our co-operation – by the angelic orders, and the Metaphysical Revolution is about to happen. Bohm was a devotee of Krishnamurti who saw reality as mental and who took those ideas to physics."

We drove to Cornwall, where I instantly fell asleep: "The air is drugged, I slowed down. Later went for a walk under a full moon with a haze-corona. The tide was out, the moon shone in the curl of every wave. I was too tired to write about it. Slept before midnight for the first time this year." The next day I "slowed right down, drugged with sea air". I "thought about the coming Metaphysical Revolution. The social poetry must go on – the sunny scene of *Love's Labours Lost*, of young lords renouncing love for studies but ending up with girls; but the infinite universe which has no beginning and no end, in which we are a local event...and the cosmic Fire from infinity which manifests – this must also be stated." I "watched the sea from my bedroom window. A curl of sunlight in the gentle waves at low tide, a sparkling on the water, two birds flew across it. Then the sun went in. A Metaphysical sea. Trenarren visible to the right from my window as I lean, chin on fist."

I wrote: "The Metaphysical Revolution boils down to the benefit of man in relation to the cosmic Fire, a beneficial relationship; and of a universe which is local in relation to an infinite and eternal vastness which the Fire pervades. It is the extra dimension that makes the Metaphysical Revolution....We are of the infinite, we can see the Fire, there is that in us which is of the infinite sea."

I observed: "As I went to get the papers earlier I heard a singing from the wall, by the car park where the ruined boat stands, and saw a small fat wren. It sang and flew and I looked at it again. A wren as I walked to the papershop. What I love about Cornwall. Old rocky walls exposed at low tide, and granite walls that protect the land from the sea. And grassy hills. A land-and-sea landscape in one view, under a vast sky that at night sparkles with thousands of stars."

I wrote that Schuon "says that rationalist, profane science can describe our situation physically, in relation to the Milky Way, but cannot place man in existential space in the real universe. He neglects to say that the way out of the imprisonment of the five senses is through the Fire."

Later I wrote: "A sunny day. Lay and felt the hot sun on my cheeks. A calm day and a sparkling tranquil sea. This evening a full moon and a causeway of moonlight on a low tide. The moon in rock pools and in the harbour, and everything bathed in a glow. A wonderful moonlight. The universe has no beginning and no end, is infinite and eternal; and we are a local happening within its diverse immensity." On April 2nd I "sat at peace and drafted 7 out of an intended 8 stanzas of a poem about the finite mind contemplating an infinite universe. Bohm comes into it. I have left a stanza for Gunzig. Called it *Our Local Universe in Infinite Space*. From 9.45 p.m., drafted my address for the launch." This effort was the result of "a surge of energy".

I was "awoken at 5 by howling winds and crashing seas. Tried to sleep. Gave up before 7 and got up. Am set to pack the car but the raging wind is filled with clouds of spray blowing inland, and I am waiting for the storm to abate. Am close to the elements: the wind, the rough seas and blown spume. 8 a.m., it died down."

On our return to Essex I heard that Caroline's mother had died. She had "sat down at her dressing-table and slumped forward from a heart attack".

The Light did not desert me in the run-up to the launch of my books. I attended the Mystics and Scientists conference at Winchester, which began with a film about fractals, and I noted later: "The Fire poured in as I lay down." The next day was sunny and I attended a meditation led by Sir George Trevelyan and wrote: "Nothing. His voice was intrusive, he has lost his energies." Edgard Gunzig, the Belgian cosmologist, spoke first. I wrote: "Talked with Gunzig and got his phone number. Asked him about Bohm and the infinite universe; and he said, 'Bohm is very important.' A small Frenchman with curly hair and a beard, wearing brown. Asked him about CBR: 'It is not important, the Big Bang too, not important.' His talk 'Cosmos out of Chaos: Why there is a Universe rather than a Vacuum.' Brilliant. The clearest explanation – in a foreign language – for the quantum vacuum and creation that I have ever heard. As winner of the Gravity Research Foundation International Award he is in the Hawking league – he has won it 3 times. He spoke of gravitation and curved space, how space is curved because objects make pathways, not because of gravitation; of variables; and then of how the universe expels pairs of particles, positive and negative, and sucks them in again, and how these virtual particles can be made real by energy from the geometric background, negative energy, which was known about for a long time (Newton, I believe, who was troubled by the fact that there was mass and inertia). Gunzig knows them in the Common Market, and he has taken my package to pass on to them. Later asked him if there is something metaphysical behind the physical world. He: 'No, there is just the world of physics....Mysticism is not my field, I do not know.' He spoke warmly of Bohm to me, and wants to meet him, but would not be drawn on Bohm with others around; ditto would not say 'There is infinity behind the world of physics.' Like Hawking he wants to believe that the physicist can enter the mind of God. Gunzig is close to Bohm's position, but will not affirm it."

I visited Winchester Cathedral: "Thetis Blacker explaining her banners, which are garish. Saxon kings in mortuary chests, medieval knights." I wrote: "Sat in the Venerable Chapel in Winchester Cathedral twice and had two great surges of Light." I returned to hear a Pole whom Trevelyan had found: "Edouard. He promises 144,000 will have immortality of body, his elect. Trevelyan swallowed it."

Later that night I received an influx of Light: "1.15 a.m. Light still pouring into me. Making my fingers shiny, tingling my spine. I am filled with Light. The last two days I have taken in a huge dose which will get me past April 22nd without worrying. There is tension in the air regarding my Metaphysical Revolution, but I am not worried." After lunch the next day: "Meditated in my bare room. Much Light. Many tingles. I offered the two books, the launch and the Metaphysical Revolution to the Light for the greater good of the Light, then received answering currents and many symbols in code, which I could not decode; like telex signals, but thorns and abstract Dalis. The dominoes earlier. Then a terrific white pillar of white Light that made me gasp and drew tears from my eyes that trickled down my cheeks. I nearly lost consciousness. Slowly came to. Am writing this in the car park three quarters of an hour later as I set off for Cornwall, filled with the Light, serene. Filled with its window. What I have experienced within the last hour is of the scale of St. Teresa's Light which paralysed her, and St. Augustine's. Incredibly powerful. I nearly choked, my chest heaved up and down as I fought for breath as it cascaded in like a waterfall, going down to my heart centre and solar plexus. Occult and mysticism. I maybe occultist in preparing myself to receive the Light, putting myself in a state of waiting, but I would rather say I was being a mystic in waiting on God. My reception of the Light is purely mystical, an influx full of coded wisdom which will hatch like caterpillars." I drove back to Cornwall "full of Light" and I observed "I am like an alien, I have to disappear to have my batteries recharged from outer space".

Back in Essex, I went to London to deliver some early copies of *The Fire and the Stones* and called in on Kathleen Raine. "She said :'You must come in for tea – it's just made.' I met John Matthews there. I said, 'I met your wife last weekend.' Kathleen: 'That's the history book and what's that? Oh, the poems.' They were put to one side very firmly, and the history book was focused on. Matthews: 'This is right up my street. This is a very important book. I shall buy this. I can't come to the launch, I'm lecturing in America. It's that time of the year.' I: 'It's nice to have a wife describe you as "my sage husband".'He: 'If you're ever in Oxford come and have tea.'"

Another Chamberlain from St. James's Palace rang me, Rasmussen, wanting an invitation to the launch. "I'm very interested, I'm working in that field."

I remarked: "Eliot was a mystic, Yeats a visionary; I have tried to unite both streams. I am both a mystic and a visionary." Van der Post would be on "Royal command" during the launch, but told me: "Excellent work." Roger Scruton told me he would be in Hungary for the launch "but the books are very interesting. I will review them for the *Salisbury Review*." David Gascoyne "fell upon me over the phone: 'I was expecting you to ring you've put me in. Did you know I wrote *The Sun at Midnight*? I was in a lunatic asylum three times, you know. Let's go out to dinner afterwards." I rang Valerie Eliot: "She had had teeth out. 'I've a pile several feet high and no secretary. I'm going to Oxford on Monday, if I'm back in time I'll come straight in.'" Eliot's nephew rang soon afterwards, and told me how Eliot always walked through Stanhope Gardens to go to Dino's.

On April 19th I wrote: "There is a tremendous feeling of expectancy in the air. The Metaphysical Revolution is possible and can happen. All day, influxes – while driving, while waiting for the photocopier, while on the telephone....Eliot, Whitehead, Pound, Jung, Einstein – they will all be present. I will be among the dead – the great dead – as I return poetry to its earliest line." The next day I noted: "This excitement. Gascoyne, according to Durrell 'one of the finest and purest metaphysical poets of our age'....Booked the restaurant at the Barbican. Then rang Gascoyne. He: 'Oh, there's a nice French restaurant in Priory Square. In the north, a mews.' His wife came on. 'It's in Charter House Square and it only opens for lunch. I think stick to the Barbican, the French brasserie'. Rang Gascoyne again. He: 'There are two fires, there's Pentecostal Fire and Luciferian Fire, Hell Fire.' I: 'It's the first we're talking about, not the second.'"

Later that night I wrote, "Light the fuse. The Olympic torch and the eternal flame. Swept with tides of Fire again. Three times between 11.30 and 12.30 a.m....Eliot is near me. Each time I think of Eliot I pour with Light; I am filled with an influx." On April 21st Eddie Linden rang, saying he would represent John Heath-Stubbs. "Rang Kathleen Raine. She says I am the first since the *Old Testament* to write of sacred history. I said, Plato. Kathleen Raine will wear red for fire, she says."

On April 22nd my launch took place at the Museum of London. Some I was expecting did not turn up, including Jessica Douglas-Home, who had written me a very polite note of acceptance. Drinks were served among the glass cases of exhibits, and I encountered Asa Briggs grinning to himself among the glass cases. I introduced him to David Gascoyne and Kathleen Raine. Through some mismanagement on the part of the Museum there was no microphone, but the launch was filmed. Michael Mann spoke. He said that book shops were already taking *The Fire and the Stones* without hesitation, despite its price, in fives and sixes and tens, and that the first impression was already sold out. Asa Briggs spoke brilliantly, "all about my 30 year search and how he had reconstructed it under the stone arch (in the Worcester College gardens), and how he found a letter connected with the Fire. How my book was a tour de force, and one of the most remarkable he had come across in all his time of teaching history, and how proud he was to be at the same college as me." (His actual words were that *The Fire and the Stones* was "the most powerful tour de force I have come across in my entire academic life".) He said that although books had dealt with why civilisations declined, there was very little about what made them grow, and he strongly recommended my poems. David Gascoyne read a few texts about the metaphysical Fire. Kathleen Raine spoke of the Pentecostal Fire and said again that it was the first time since the Old Testament that sacred history had returned. I spoke of Gascoyne's *Journal 1937-9* (written in France at the same time as *La Nausée*) having predicted that the future of this century would burn with an "extraordinary, unseen and secret radiance". Then I declared the Metaphysical Revolution, calling on Shelley's *Ode to the West Wind* to "scatter, as from an unextinguished hearth/Ashes and sparks, my words among mankind!" Ronald Lello, who had pushed Kathleen Raine's wheelchair, then made an impromptu and unscheduled speech relating my Revolution to what Prince Charles was doing, with one eye on the two Chamberlains present. The two Chamberlains Prince Charles had sent asked me to sign two books for Prince Charles. Christine then performed a stunning dance of the Descent of the Fire and the inauguration of the Revolution, combining stillness and beauty. I remember Steve Norris, who was representing the Minister for Arts, speaking to Asa Briggs and to his wife's relation Michael Mann. I remember Eddie Linden talking to Steve Norris about "this Philistine government", and getting progressively drunk until John Ezard took him away at the end as he wanted to join the speakers' dinner. I remember Sebastian Barker, the poet George Barker's son, who wrote *Who the F— is Eddie Linden?*, telling me he would follow me, and Peter Donebauer of Diverse Production helping my boys with their camcorder. Afterwards I took Kathleen Raine, Michael Mann and Gascoyne to eat, and Ronald Lello tagged along. I sat next to Gascoyne, who told me "I'm an autodidact" (i.e. he was self-taught), and heard about his meetings with various poets, including Eliot, and his wish to know the Fire. I said that one day we would sit together and bring it down, and he said "he would like to sit and meditate to feel the influxes which he has not felt since his youth". I noted: "He is a shell of a man, looking to me to revive his experience of the beyond." Kathleen Raine said: "The poets I have written about have all lasted; Vernon Watkins and the rest. The 1950s poets haven't lasted." Sir Tom

Normanton did not turn up, and Philip Mawer was stuck in traffic trying to reach the launch.

There was very little publicity about the books, mainly, I thought, because *The Fire and the Stones* was nearly 900 pages long and the reviewers were all daunted by its length, and silence was easier than passing judgement on a revolutionary work about which they could be mistaken. I was not sure if there had been interference. The Heroes of the West had folded themselves down, but I was saying that a United States of Europe was approaching (not a popular idea in some quarters), that Communism was about to end (as it did), and that America was poised for a world role. I could imagine that some people might not want to give currency to these predictions.

The day before the launch a British tabloid newspaper, the *People*, had published a story associating Steve Norris with a *Times* journalist. Ann and I took him and Vicky out to dinner in Epping High Street to show our solidarity, and I remember Norris telling me he thought the Far Right pro-Thatcher wing were behind the smear, although privately I wondered about the timing of the revelation.

I received a letter from Sebastian Barker, Chairman of the Poetry Society, saying; "You are the nucleus of a comet of history trailing a wonderful vapour-trail of poetry. My profound respect and wonder before your achievement." (I wondered if I was not rather a comet of poetry trailing history, but the truth was that I was a metaphysical Fire trailing both history and poetry.)

I rang Gascoyne, the author of "Christ of revolution and poetry". He said: "I'm disillusioned with revolution. It's interior revolution. I tried to tell the Royal Family about the revolution and was put in a lunatic asylum. My life has three periods, my early precocity, 10 or 15 years when I was mad, and some rehabilitation under Judy." I told him: "A sea-change is happening and people will respond more to metaphysical poetry, including yours." He replied: "I wish I could believe that. That's what surrealism tried to do." He told me: "I can only think of one thing at a time. I've got to finish the Introduction to Elizabeth Smart's work" (Elizabeth Smart was Sebastian Barker's mother) "for which I am getting £100."

The launch over, I was able to relax a bit, and I never thought there would be a volte face on the part of Kathleen Raine. On May 6th I slept late "and pondered Prince Charles, who is calling for European cultural reunification in Prague....Realised that he needs to sit and let the Fire come through. Sat and let the Fire come through. It surged into me, glowing my fingers." With David Gascoyne's *Journals 1937-39* in mind, I began a selection from my early *Diaries*. I found interest among some of the parents in why civilisations suddenly collapse.

I visited Mabel Reid. We had a discussion about Clouded-Ground pond in which I told her: "The mind and the pond are the same: you can see the surface and the depth at the same time." Of the Metaphysical Revolution I told her that "the anti-metaphysical philosophers shut out the universe and confined it all to their room, but now the American spacecraft are flying round the planets and we know it's vast out there and infinite, without beginning or end."

I went to watch Anthony play cricket and stood on the boundary with David Evennett. "He had seen Major last week and told him not to have a June election for he (Evennett) would lose his seat....During the fall of Thatcher Major said,'We don't want the toffs in.' He told Evennett, 'David, I came and spoke in your constituency and I want you to return the favour by supporting me.' Evennett: 'I will. I think you are the right person.'"

When I got home I found a call from Norris on my answerphone, saying a window had been left open at Coopersale Hall. I went up to close it and met him: "Norris, in orange shirt and jeans, came in with me and chatted afterwards. 'Major is bent on having an election in June. He wants to clear out the Thatcher ancien regime, the Ridleys and Tebbits who are retiring at the next election, and he'd like to go early. I'd rather he went later when there's something to show in the economy.' I said, 'The unwelcome headlines haven't damaged you.' He: 'No, they won't make any difference to an election. I was talking to Clare Short last week. She said "You've had one" and I said, "Yes." We spoke for over half an hour. Headlines like that don't damage you.'"

I received a letter from Frank Kermode, "referring to my 'scholarship and gifts as a writer, both expository and poetic' which exacted 'my tribute of respect' as my mind 'embraces huge masses of apparently disparate material in the service of an idea' which 'speaks of a great renovation'. His own sceptical, materialistic mind resists as 'the unification is too much for me', and he endearingly describes himself as a clerk and sceptic. My 'notable statement' deserves to be 'intelligently opposed rather than neglected'. He values it 'without being able to accommodate their arguments'. 'I am a sincere admirer.'" I wrote: "I have put forward a unification and have announced a Revolution. I stand like a mountain, a mountain peak round which clouds will gather, as critics obscure me. But at the end the clouds will pass and the mountain will be there." I also noted: "Frank Kermode is unillumined."

Kathleen Raine wrote and asked if I would start the Academy with a series of lectures near Westminster Abbey. She said: "Something happened at your launch. You changed the atmosphere." I told her that Kermode had written, and she said: "All the people who hold important positions seem to be there without the knowledge. The idea of the sage has gone. They're not sages." I wrote to Kermode, "presenting the artist as solving his isolation by renovating his civilisation, and suggesting that he should write a sequel to *Romantic Image*, on the Metaphysical line in English poetry and how it finds a solution to the isolated Romantic predicament."

I wrote: "Macbeth's fascination with the witches and their glimpses of the future in the 'crystal ball' of their bubbling cauldron. My fascination with the sisters three (Christine and two others) who have glimpses of the future. I am a revolutionary and not an ambitious power-seeker, I consult 'the witches' for elucidation about a good future."

There was a Quiz Night at Coopersale Hall. I sat at the Coopersale Hall's staff's table. "They are reading my poems at lunch time. 'We're seeing you in a new light.' I on how the Romantics and the Modernists smashed into agony, despair and madness and how the Metaphysicals are solving the problems they failed to solve; the new thinking that needs to be explained. Then to the Oaklands table; Carol Norris: 'Your poems are wonderful. The *Pear-Ripening House* and children as pips – beautiful.' I am carrying on the work Shelley's generation never finished. Carol: 'I sat and an hour went by, I couldn't put the book down.' Then the Quiz, which the Coopersale staff won. The question, 'Who is the author who spent 20 years writing *The Fire and the Stones*?' and some answered 'Harold Robbins'."

The crime writer Ruth Rendell visited Bancroft's Prep to give conservation prizes, including two to Oaklands girls. I wrote: "Heard Ruth Rendell on Epping Forest and her time in Loughton and Epping. The ponds etc. She read her address. She looked boyish but in a tight skirt and approached the platform with a bag from which she took her script and her spectacles. Later, she answered questions about her writing. Ann: 'She's a bit stuck up.'" I had a word with her at the end.

I was invited to the consecration of the *Temenos* Academy at All Souls', Margaret Street, "a Tractarian Victorian church founded by Pusey and reflecting Victorian architecture; but also the fourfold vision, the Christ-Fire at the top. Kathleen Raine, Critchlow, Matthews, Cadman, Lello and John Allott, who accosted me: 'I recognise you from the photo of your book. It reflects what I have thought over 20 years.' We sat for the ceremony, which was conducted by wizened, white-haired Fr Slade in an inaudible voice that was lost in the echoing acoustics. Music, including a violin; a chant; a Vedic meditation; the consecration in Latin ('Veni' etc), and finally a reading from Dante and a reading from Plato. Talk in the aisle, with John Matthews, who said he had just returned from Seattle and had been staying with David Spangler and had told him about the book; and with Critchlow ('I was weary and could not come to your launch'). To the vestry for wine. Encountered Kathleen: 'It's all fallen through. We have no home. Fr Superior says we will disturb his sleep. I wish he'd drop dead.'...Talked to Allott who is reviving Johann Simon Meyr, one of the Bavarian Illuminati – or rather linked with one of them. I: 'You are doing in music what I am doing in poetry, focusing on metaphysicals. There needs to be a cross-disciplinary Metaphysical Revolution in the matter of 1798, 1912, 1956 – now 1991.' His friend: 'What would you put on in June if you had a choice?' I: 'A lecture on the Metaphysical Revolution, preferably in Cambridge, saying that the wrong people occupy the positions in literature and philosophy and should move over. With it goes a European context. And a metaphysical context.' Allott: 'What next?' A book of essays next, on the Metaphysical Revolution. (Brian) Goodwin later: 'It's political and dangerous. That's not to say it should not happen.' And: 'What are the sceptics sceptical about? Like a fish sceptical of water?' At the end, 'It's either depressing or exciting.' I: 'It's going to be exciting.'"

I attended a Baroque music evening at Chigwell: "A group of 6 young musicians specialising in the Baroque music and using traditional instruments: a reproduction 1720 harpsichord, a viola, 2 violins, a cello (with a different neck and bridge) and an oboe." Vernon Davies came and sat next to me, and Mrs. Dutchman came and had a word: "You've had several careers – lecturing, the *Times*, publishing, writing and owning prep schools – whereas most only have one. You've been very fortunate." I wrote: "The Baroque composers: J. S. Bach, Telemann, Corelli, Purcell. Spoke with the musicians."

I then drove to Cornwall. There was gig-racing. I wrote: "The Charlestown gig went out with raised oar blades....The gig was the old lifeboat – what Grace Darling rode – and possibly the traditional Viking boat without the curved ends, long and narrow like the boats in Roskilde, which survived in the Scillies from the 11th century until the 19th century and now." Later that night I "walked on the Charlestown pier at 11.45 p.m., utterly alone" and had the idea of handing over the running of the schools "to a Bursar so that I can concentrate on getting out the *Collected Poems*, the *Collected Stories*, my autobiography and of course my *Selected Diaries* – and *The Eternicide*, etc, small novella fables within the metaphysical context."

I noted: "Many gulls wheeling outside my window – herring-gulls." And: "Went to get the papers on foot and paused under a tree near the Visitors' Centre. A nightingale was singing. I manoeuvred until I could see it on a bough. I listened transfixed for 5 minutes, then walked on. I could still hear it after I had turned the corner by the Bay View Hotel." I wrote: "Like Donne I reflect the Age, so that in 400 years' time people (will) know what it was like to be in our Age."

I returned to Essex full of my *Diaries* and wrote: "The philosopher is part of what he is observing, and is not detached from it; he is in the process and is transformed. So my *Diaries* are an Existential Philosophy – a Journal, in which the philosopher is involved in a dynamic process. This is Baroque philosophy. Kierkegaard and Marcel linked philosophy to Journals, and there is Rilke's *Malte Laurids Brigge*; and Wittgenstein wrote snippets. But otherwise no philosopher has used the Journal form. That Whitehead quotation (Whitehead, a process philosopher, e.g. *Process and Reality*) about philosophy being the rationalization of mysticism."

There had been several letters from Kathleen Raine. Looking at my file, I see she wrote to me on March 21st, 25th, 26th and again soon afterwards, on April 7th and April 29th. On May 1st she wrote again and "formally asked whether you are prepared to give a course of lectures or seminars on your metaphysical reading of history" as it would "be a rich contribution to have a series from you on this new and important view of history". She wrote on May 12th, repeating her request. Many of the letters dealt with her problems in setting up a Temenos Academy. On May 12th she wrote that "Prince Charles has given Temenos permission to print his Shakespeare lecture. That is tacit support to (sic) the whole Temenos idea." Now on May 31st she wrote withdrawing her invitation because I had referred to the "descent of the reigning House of Windsor from the Kings of Israel, and again of the mysterious journeying of the Coronation Stone".

I saw immediately that the connection between Prince Charles and Temenos had made her edgy about my reference to the House of Windsor, and that she had been advised (I would say wrongly) to cut her ties with anyone whose outlook was inconvenient (not to mention "political and dangerous"), even though they had offered to help her. I saw that her public support for *The Fire and the Stones* a month previously could not be allowed to hinder a Royal connection. At the same time, as a mystic poet stating the tradition of the metaphysical Fire, I reserved the right to mention legend and tradition in my whole perspective that included history and religion, and I believe that Prince Charles would be extremely interested in the legend to which I referred. I did not see the necessity for suppressing that well-known tradition. I wrote back expressing surprise at her sudden change of attitude, but I appreciated that "finding sponsors for Temenos must at this stage be a more important consideration to you than spreading awareness of the Fire". She wrote again, and I wrote back at greater length, rebutting her points, and saying "when you warned me the bullets would fly when I launched my Metaphysical Revolution, I did not expect that you (or one of your advisers) would be squeezing the trigger". I insisted on my right to be cross-disciplinary and rejected her implication that disciplines must be kept separate for academic reasons. She wrote back insisting that legend, myth and "mystical insights" have no place in history, a complete reversal of her position. I wrote back rejecting her "separatist system of scholarship in which disciplines are kept separate" and I defended my view of history as "precisely dated 'wave'-like patterns rather than 'particle'-like events". I said that the difference between Rank and Jung now seemed to involve a "shade, an emphasis, within a broad agreement", and that our difference was a question of such emphasis. There was a public announcement that her *Temenos* Academy had been given accommodation by Prince Charles, and I have not seen her since then.

Looking back, I see that quite simply, my Fire threatened to take over her academic tradition, as did my Metaphysical Revolution, just as the Fire in my poems challenged her poetic tradition, which fails to mention it; and that she wanted me out, and the House of Windsor was as good a pretext as any. I think that Kathleen Raine's specialised and élitist sponsored lectures about Islamic and other subjects belong to the past. They preserve a tradition of academic scholarship and keep it alive for a future generation, but they make no mention of the Fire or Light or of mysticism and involve no existential or experiential component. The Fire is more powerful than the imagination, as she recognised. My way, on the other hand, was the way of the future, and the time will come when this is seen to be so.

I was relieved that I did not have to prepare lectures she would typecast as history rather than as the cultural reflections of a mystic, and I could now concentrate on offering the Fire to those in whom it resonated. Warren Kenton had warned that my grand entrance would be accompanied by tension, and he had been proved right.

In the next few months I embodied the Fire or Light, and the Metaphysical Revolution, for healers, film-makers, poetry organisers and academics, and I was moving towards a unified view of history, religion, the sciences and philosophy.

Margaret Taylor visited us. I wrote: "Uncontrollable coughing, sitting in the window as I entered the room. She talked in a desperate, breathless, wheezy whisper....She is having chemotherapy....Every Thursday it puts her down, it takes her a week to get back up, then she's down again. 'I must think positive. Otherwise I might as well curl up and die.'"

I was invited to give a talk at Hampstead, and first visited the Keats Museum and "walked by the replacement plum tree where Keats sat on a chair and wrote *Ode to a Nightingale*". Of my two and a half hour talk I wrote: "A large house off Rosslyn Hill in sub-Hampstead, a poky corridor with a loo, then into a cluttered room where I sat in an armchair in the corner, my audience of lady healers, including Christine the dancer draped in chairs or sitting on the floor. Was recorded. Explained the Fire, the stones, the chart. Read some poems on the theme of the Fire being received in meditation. Finally a candlelit meditation at the end. Then, through the rain, home. I connected with my audience, just talking, and was glad when they interrupted with questions. Judith, who said, 'The only art worth listening to is poetry, and the speaking voice, because you get all the intonation and nuances.'"

I lunched with Peter Donebauer, the Managing Director of Diverse Production. I wrote: "Donebauer is of Czech extraction. His father fought in the Czech army in 1939 (with Josten?). He is anti-élite....Had lunch in a restaurant near Olympia, a walk through the station from his Gorleston Street office. The proposal for 3 one-hour programmes on *The Fire and the Stones*, part 1 on: what is the Fire?; part 2 on: unity and pattern; and part 3 on: the history of Western civilisation – where now, etc. The Metaphysical Revolution." Donebauer was dependent on raising money from a sponsor such as BBC 2 or Channel 4. He said to me: "Civilisation is the concretisation of vision." I liked him and found he had a natural empathy with my ideas about the Fire.

As regards filming, I record the following exchange: "Donebauer: 'Poets do not like places they have written about to be shown as TV pictures or photographs as the physicality destroys the imaginative picture in words.' I: 'If the poem is about a physical place only, yes, I agree; but if the place symbolises a metaphysical truth – is a metaphor for something metaphysical – then no, I disagree. A photo always enhances an idea-in-a-place, like a photo of Ben Bulben, Ireland. Drumcliffe churchyard which enhances Yeats's 'Horseman pass by' (after casting a cold eye on life, on death)."

I received a letter from Patricia Dawson, whom I had met in Dulwich in 1963. I had told her about the Dulwich Group of Poets. As a result she attended, and she and her husband ran the Group while I was in Japan, and apparently tried to contact me so that I could read some poems then, but without success. She had even tried to contact me in Japan in May 1991. I wrote: "Their lives have been changed by what I said in the 1960s."

I tried to send a copy of *The Fire and the Stones* to Delors, who was in effect President of the European Union in waiting. Twice the book was returned, both times opened with a note saying it could not be delivered. The third time I rang Delors' office and hand-delivered it to an MEP in London, who hand-delivered it to Delors' office in Brussels.

I attended an evening in Hampstead in which Christine explained her Egyptian temple-dancing. I wrote: "Christine: 'We are all a reflection of each other, responding to each other's energies.' The lotus, giving with energies, (as she) scoops up the Light, pouring it over herself and her chakras....Christine is clear that she must continue the raising of consciousness caused by the dance....'My destiny is to bring down the Light through healing and dancing.'" I added: "Christine's memories of Egypt. Her not wanting to remember certain things, how it all turned corrupt. 'You were in the temple of Isis.' (To me.) 'You were a temple-dancer.' I felt at home with the gestures. I remembered. The Shining Ones were shown with fair hair. The fair-haired shining beings and Christine's free talk of beings round the Pyramid at my launch. The powerful dance she did, bringing down the Light and opening doors – which may have penetrated into Delors' Europe....There are 900 different gestures, of which Christine used perhaps 100 on an average night."

I read Herbert Read's essays, "especially *Surrealism and the Romantic Principle* in which he associates Classicism with Renaissance dictatorships and capitalism, and Romanticism with the inspiration in Plato's *Ion*, where lyric poets are said to be 'not in their right mind' and 'possessed'....On 'the exact relation between metaphysics and poetry'. Poetry is inspired from sensational awareness of the objective world or from the promptings of the unconscious, but poetry may be generated by discursive reasoning or metaphysical speculation. Metaphysical poetry as 'felt thought'." I added: "Romanticismis identified with the artist, classicism with society. In surrealism the two are opposed. In the Baroque the two are harmonised. Read synthesising Romantic intention and intellectual order."

On June 25th I wrote: "Went to the Light, sitting alone in my study. Many tingles as it poured in."

The next day I went to Cambridge, "to the Science park to attend a food-seminar. Sat outside Trinity House by the lake at 1.50 and returned at 2 to begin the seminar with a poem, *Rippling One*. Later drafted a poem about a tinkling bell. I am returning to poetry. Feel very poetic. Have a lot of poetic energy within me."

The new Chigwell Chaplain, a New Zealander, was a black belt in a Korean martial art, Choi Kwang-Do, which was founded in 1986 by Grandmaster Kwang Jo Choi. It uses Korean punching, kicking and blocking techniques of street self-defence. Matthew now began to rise in this art, and would become a black belt and instructor.

The Oaklands fête had happened, and at Sports Day at Coopersale Hall the fathers' race was won by David Seaman, the England goalie. I wrote: "He is very tall, now slightly crew-cutted with a Rotherham accent (like his wife): a re-run of the Tom McAlister move south. I chatted easily to him, no awkwardness." Seaman opened the Coopersale Hall fête on a hot day. I wrote: "The grass looked a glory....Seaman arrived before 2, the international goalie in a sweatshirt and track suit bottom; moustached. Immediately an autograph queue formed. I introduced him at 2.15 over a PA system with high stands and trumpets all down the terrace. A brass band played outside the Hall (the Epping Town band). Pony rides." Vicky Norris chatted to me about Steve: "'The garages have gone.' I: 'Gone?' She: 'We haven't got them any more. We've extricated ourselves from them.'" Hammond came to be introduced all round as a farmer. I left him with PC Sims, who was on the police car.

In London I bought Bucke's *Cosmic Consciousness*, which is about the Light and which has a table giving the ages of some of those who have been illumined. No one is illumined before they are 24.

There was a Conservative auction at Vernon Davies's. (I had last seen him at a First Aid talk at Oaklands.) I wrote: "Drank champagne out of doors by the swimming pool....The Norrises (Steve) and Patricia Rawlings, the MEP. Norris attacked what she is doing: 'And you're lowering standards in roads' etc. She is a quiet, hesitant woman who asked to see my book....The auction made £8,500 odd for Party funds. Vernon and Hilda bought anything with Conservative autographs, including a book signed by four Prime Ministers for £1,200 (or possibly 1,200 guineas)....Came away about 1 a.m. The lights of the north in the distance, from the hilltop on which we all parked."

The Fire and the Stones was selling in the bookshops, but there had been no publicity. I had rung Gorka and asked him to investigate. Gorka rang. "He has some information for me about my book. He has got it very quickly, within the week." Gorka confirmed that there had been an operation against my book.

After many end of term events – a barbecue, prize-giving, Oaklands rounders (staff v school) and the rest – we had our final lunch at Coopersale Hall. I wrote: "The staff sitting on the lawn, eating and drinking wine. Ann Miller on Steve Norris: 'The pro-Biggs-Davison faction are delighted about the *People* article, they're saying "I told you so."'" Later we bought Matthew a car ("I don't know what to say," he said, "I'm shocked, thank you, I didn't expect this") and later still we took Mrs. Best to the Italian Room at the King's Head, Loughton. When we returned Vernon appeared at 10.30 p.m. to collect a shirt.

In July I met Nadia at Heathrow and drove her down to Cornwall. A boat went out: "11 p.m. Floodlights, the taut rope as the boat swung round and then inched out backwards and left for Holland with its English crew. Graham the Harbourmaster with his pipe; a gnarled weatherbeaten man with a face like a walnut....The broken boat was towed out by a tug and a rope. It left backwards and the tug then moved round to the front and fixed the rope again. Another tug was due from Holland, and the two tugs were now towing the boat and its cargo to Holland." I negotiated to buy the green sward in front of our house, together with the car space, from Peter Clapperton. We went to Fowey and Polruan and clambered on the rocks by the blockhouse. I wrote: "When I got home, wrote *At Polruan: Soul and Body*, setting down an idea that came to me as I sat by the blockhouse. A poem comes to you like a butterfly, and you sit and work it out – see what the butterfly does. I saw the butterfly, herring gull and bumble-bee this afternoon. My poem also incorporated my reading of Michelangelo's poem last night. Hence the words 'Renaissance' and 'skull' – and possibly the unconscious focusing on a 'bumble-bee' – and certainly on the Marvellite soul-body idea, which is highly metaphysical." (I had recorded: "Reading Michelangelo's poems. One from 1546/50: 'I've got a bumble-bee inside my jug/Some bones and strings inside my leather bag.' The context makes it clear that the jug is his skull, i.e. he has a buzzing sound inside his head or ears. The soul 'like a genie bound up in a bottle'. Michelangelo's vision of the soul in a decrepit body.")

The next day "three green woodpeckers visited our lawn: red stripe on heads, large black pointed beaks, green plumage, speckled body. Watched them through my binoculars."

I rang Sebastian Barker, who said of the plan to give me an evening at the Poetry Society: "'Because of the politics of the Poetry Society nothing can happen quickly. On Friday the decision is being taken to fold down the Poetry Society....Lindsey believes you're a historian first, before you're a poet.' I: 'The history book was written to substantiate the Fire. I am now writing poems. And my next work is a selection from my *Diaries* – poem-based. I want to write a series of essays which reinterpret the writers, bring some neglected ones forward and push others back.'He: 'I can understand that.' I: 'Two people can have a revolution as Eliot and Pound discovered, and as your father's generation will have known.' He: 'Yes. You're so near and so friendly.' (In wonder.)"

"The beauty,"I wrote, "of the silver sea after the cloud finished, moving northwards like a blanket or duvet and revealing blue sky above it. Tonight, a half moon hidden in the trees, and a still, moonlit sea with a reflection from the islands. The fishermen who catch mackerel and whiting from the pier. The shark I thought I saw two nights ago. Sharks and seals – the shark that came in and swam round a few years ago. The oneness of sea and sky – there was no horizon, possibly due to a mist. At all events, the sea blended into the sky tonight."

The next day, July 22nd, "after lunch, went to Gunwalloe (Ann, Nadi, Ant and me, leaving Matthew to learn the French subjunctive). Rain spattered the windscreen as we approached Gunwalloe but suddenly there were patches of blue sky and I sat on the far rocks and with a calm sea beneath my feet (incredibly calm for Gunwalloe) composed another metaphysical sonnet, writing on paper on my knee. What I like about Gunwalloe: all life can be seen from those rocks – sea, shore, universe, church, farmhouse, representatives of all species, all in just enough economical detail to make the point. Nowhere else can you find graves on the beach, for example. On to Porthleven. Had a cream tea, then walked to the end of the pier, where a fisherman had caught a conger eel, and on the way back was dazzled by sparkling water and wrote a quick poem (8 lines), pressing on the granite harbour wall before walking fast and catching the others up. (They were not aware I had scribbled an 8-line poem while they were walking.) On to Marazion, where the tide was going out and the causeway to St. Michael's Mount was nearly uncovered. Ant changed and splashed across to the Mount, and then returned, running both ways. The rock Grannie (my mother) used to lean against put me in mind of Trevarthian, where Rob and I stayed, and on the way back I stopped and went in and peered through the windows where we slept – the library has gone and it's been converted into apartments – and then walked round and entered the present hall. Lingered on the sloping lawn outside, recalling my parents and the time I cycled up to a Bronze Age tumulus in the hills, and then returned home."

I worked on my 1966 *Diaries* and noted: "The moon last night, but then it clouded over and today is overcast, with hints of rain. I drowsed yesterday evening after our visit to Porthleven and Marazion (not to mention Gunwalloe), and fell asleep over my work." We "lunched at Polkerris – at the Rashleigh, and saw Kerris, the artist. Returned and went to the Visitor's Centre: old pictures of Charlestown, including one from 1885 with the house on the harbour, before it was demolished. Worked again on 1965. Am putting a lot in as I was writing *The Silence* then, my masterpiece. My criterion: leave out anything that may offend my family, and cut out anything that can cause pain. Concentrate on my growth and direction; my creation of myself as an artist."

After a week I "took Nadia to Heathrow". I wrote: "She is a nice girl, good-tempered..., agreeable and agreeing, and ever-ready to offer me tea and coffee. I ate as I drove at lunch, and sitting next to me she put a hand towel over my lap and fed me bits of food, and I felt pampered – by my own daughter! She got on well with Matthew and Ant and Ann. A nice laughing girl, full of wheezes on the flights (e.g. removing a crew member's trousers so he had to pass passengers to recover them, packing a hostess into a cubicle above head height and shutting the door so she was found by a passenger)."

I returned to find a letter from David Lorimer inviting me to address the 1992 Mystics and Scientists at Winchester – I commented "so I went to listen and ended up teaching" – and a letter from Colin Wilson, saying that "the book looks fascinating".

I visited Sebastian Barker at his home in Lawford Road, London: "Sat in the garden drinking milkless jasmine tea, while his girl friend Hilary stayed indoors and read Welsh history in the study where Sebastian works. The table he made himself. Talked for two and a quarter hours quite effortlessly. He insisted my next move is to sell the paperback rights of *The Fire and the Stones*, i.e. get an agent. He likes the Foundation idea....He is thinking about an event we can put on. He showed me his long poem on Nietzsche – 245 pages – which in places recalls Milton and Wordsworth and is in the Baroque blend of image and statement, sense and spirit. This can be included in the Metaphysical Revolution, which must be a 'showing' rather than a 'saying'. Kathleen Raine, he says, is an intellectual snob and *Temenos* is 'a nothing project'. He agreed there's no Fire or Light in any of the *Temenos* volumes. George Barker's (his father's) *Collected Poems* took a year to be reviewed. He has edited his mother Elizabeth Smart's journals volume 1 and the trick, he says, is to get a good thread by editing....He agrees the Metaphysicals will solve problems the Romantics did not solve. On Ricks, Dryden and Pope hang onto the coat-tails of the Metaphysicals. 'You have been in the furnace and you've survived, but only just. The pressure must have been enormous.' 'If you can't stand the furnace, keep the door shut.'...'I am a poet – a maker. Once you've finished a work, pull away from it. It becomes someone else's. My mother said that works written 40-50 years before were by someone else.'"

Christine rang and told me: "I've been seeing you in my dreams – the real spiritual you, having long discussions with you."

Asa Briggs asked me to visit a Dutch Professor of Sociology from the University of Amsterdam, Johan Goudsblom, who was finishing a book on physical fire at All Souls, Oxford: "Sat with him in his room with a yellow stone view from his window, drank bottled water. We were the only two in All Souls; his balding head and glasses. He told me 'Asa Briggs said,

"Nicholas Hagger was a pupil of mine."" He had finished a book, *Fire and Civilisation*, that morning (having written it between January and July) – the fire in Africa, Asia, Mesopotamia (agrarian), Israel and eventually after the Middle Ages, industrialisation. His secular, sceptical position: everything is human and within society and social organisation: 'I am a Humanist.' I said Humanism was within the divine vision and put another model, the spirit-soul view. He: 'Fantastical.' He picked on a sentence and said, 'He would not be the voice of Egypt without being the voice of the author. 'I have not been prescriptive but descriptive, otherwise I'll be called Green or anti-Green, and the book will be described in terms of those 3 prescriptive sentences.' Fire domesticated one and a half million years ago. Fossil fuels increasing the use of fire today. The old towns and temples guarded fire, which was needed, and later became symbolic – as in the Temple of Vesta. 'The religious view is within the human.' I found this hard to rebut; and should have said the civilisations begin with a metaphysical vision and turn secular. McNeill on Toynbee, I have left out certain interesting things on Toynbee. Goudsblom: 'Toynbee pays greater attention to detail than you.' I: 'I was determined not to do it in 12 volumes. I compressed.' What Kermode meant. We are born to die, and there is human society and social reorganisation (from the domestication of fire onwards), and all religions are created by men. My view: the beyond can be glimpsed and this glimpse is the central vision of civilisations. The tension between these two positions. Briggs: 'History in terms of an idea that is outside history.' We are all split up so challenging Humanism is more difficult."

My Aunt Lucy died. Argie went to the funeral, taking a taxi to Hove and back for £113 return. I wrote: "Lucy went to the fire watched by her sister Joan (over from Canada) John and Sue, Judy, Christopher and wife, Peter and Simon, and the staff of the East Grinstead shop."

Matthew was in Tours, learning French grammar for a month. At the end of July we went back to Cornwall. I wrote: "Another boat coming in, a tall-masted square rigger (the Astrid), so there will be two tall-masted ships in Charlestown. Listened to the first part of *Summoned by Bells* – in the idiom of *The Prelude* but without the metaphysics; pure memory and association and reflection on social situations, naming shops and places; the stuff of minor poetry despite the bulk."

I rang Sir Tom Normanton. "His view: Britain should have been influencing the future shape of Europe 21 years ago, and must now; but Major won't commit himself. I: There ought to be a figure like Ridley, prominent, who stands for this pro-European view and he ought to organise 100 initiatives of which Sir Tom's work with Kohl is one and mine with Delors would be another. Can he get me on such a list – this one an unofficial Ambassador, that one an official Ambassador, that one to address a conference. He: 'I'll try.'I: And can be say that the author of *The Fire and the Stones* tried to get a copy to Major. He: 'Hurd is the one.' I: 'He's read it.'He: 'There you are.' He: 'Your book is very interesting as you spell out our decline very clearly. It will never be a popular book though." I: 'It's the kind of book you have on your shelf for 40 years, and take down and read a bit this year, and more next year, and so on.'" (It was Normanton who advised me to use Bill Newton-Dunn as a way of reaching Delors.)

The two boats left: "The Maria Asumpta and the Astrid went out at 9. The Maria Asumpta went first, backwards. The pier and surrounding walls were crowded. The Astrid went out frontwards with furled sails. A bagpiper played 'Speed bonny boat like a bird on the waves/Over the seas to Skye' and the crowd on the pier applauded. The people lingered on, gazing out to sea, as they manoeuvre, now, in front of my window. Last night they were floodlit in the dock, the rigging now in light, now in shadows, and the moon shimmered on the sea. Then, as now that sails are being unfurled, the effect was magical, out of the 19th century. I thought of a time when I saw men crucified to the mast, their hands nailed to the crossbeams for sails."

I was back in my elemental consciousness: "A blue sky with wispy cloud and a calm sea. But later it clouded over and by mid-afternoon rained. A sea-mist, little visibility....All day, during drizzle at first, and later sun, worked on selections from the *Diaries* I have brought with me....Walked at midnight. Looked for shooting stars in a starlit, moonless sky, but could not see any. To Ant, 'They're like a finger tracing a line down the sky, a yellow line.'...A sea-mist. Everything wintry and white. Later it cleared up and after reading the papers I sunbathed for an hour in the garden and felt the hot sun on my cheeks."

I glimpsed the work ahead of me: "My *Prelude*; Essex poems; epic; *Zhivago*-like novel; essays; Metaphysical Revolution; *Collected Poems*; *Collected Stories*; and confessional autobiography. Works to keep me busy during the 30 years of my retirement."

I saw how to present my Winchester lecture and wrote: "It should be entitled, 'The Metaphysical Revolution: the One Unifying Fire or Light behind Nature and History, which is known to (experienced by) mystics and poets, and which is the central idea of civilisations.'...Cover what the Metaphysical Revolution is, how it's inter-or cross-disciplinary (cf fractals and particles/waves, taking its lead from the quantum void). How the quantum void is behind it – the One, Non-Being or Void, Being, Existence. Guénon. The rational, theoretical basis of traditional metaphysics, the practical experience of Light-based metaphysics. The experience of the Light. How it is known by mystics and poets....How it is the central idea of 25 civilisations. Back to the Fire-based common basis of all cultures – pattern, not accident. The 4 worlds scheme....The Theory of Everything it makes possible. A Grand Unified Theory of Religion and World History."

I also "worked on my poem about the universe, shaping it here and there, tying in stanzas. Part One is the case against a GUT, a metaphysical reality and anything other than the human and social. Part Two is the vision of the One Fire or Light which is behind Nature and History, which can be known through vision, existentially."

In August I had three meetings with Colin Wilson, seeing the Fire or Light (in turn) in relation to consciousness, Existentialism and Metaphysics.

Following Colin Wilson's letter we had arranged to meet. I wrote: "Colin Wilson has no time for poetry and mysticism, preferring higher thought. I have gone the way of his Outsiders, he has gone the way of the sceptical-rationalist author who wrote *The Outsider*." On August 6th, "a call from Colin Wilson. 'May I speak to Nick Hagger, please.' 'Speaking.' 'Oh hello, it's Colin Wilson.' 'Colin, it's good to hear you.' 'It's good to hear *you*.' And so on while we arranged for me to visit him today. 'We see people 5.30 to 7.30, then we throw them out so we can have some dinner. We always watch the news at 6. Come at 5.30. Today or tomorrow, it doesn't matter which. I've been looking at your book. It looks very interesting. But I can't read it through now as it arrived at the same time as Michael Holroyd's biography of Shaw, which I'm reviewing.' Everything economical as well as charming; and supremely confident. Colin Wilson's charisma. There are two Colin Wilsons: one the extremely nice, helpful and likeable young man of 1960 and before; the other a show-off (throwing his socks on the fire) and a putter-down, sayer of outrageous things. He will tell me I should be a rationalist and think it all out, and eschew poetry and mysticism. I will say that thought only gets you so far, that I have followed an anti-rational tradition. Colin Wilson was a role model in those days of the late 1950s. His show-off nature: I said 'It's Regatta week' in Charlestown, he said 'I've never been to a Regatta in my life, I don't know what one is. What is a Regatta?' (You can't have lived in Cornwall for 35 years and not know that villages have Regatta weeks.)"

I visited Colin Wilson on August 6th: "5.30. W: h Colin Wilson, until 7.30. Walked in through the back door; Colin was making smoked salmon in the kitchen, wearing sailing dungarees and 1950s style glasses on a lorgnette thread round his neck. Open-necked shirt, very casually dressed. A warm welcome. 'Come in, Nick.' He finished with a painter (whom Joy later took home). We talked in the kitchen, about Husserl, I saying his recommendation gave me my method for *The Fire and the Stones*, then went through to the sitting-room where his mother (at least 80) sat. She has been living there about two years. (While Colin was out of the room I asked what he was like as a schoolboy, and she said: 'He always had his nose in a book, even walking down the road, I was surprised he didn't get run over. He was always reading and I went to the library a lot, I read a lot myself.') I sat down where I always sit, the news was on TV – about hostages being released. He showed me Husserl's *The Crisis of European Sciences* (a book about Western civilisation) and Jean Gebser's *The Ever Present Origin*, which is about non-perspectival art, perspectival art (the Renaissance) and now a-perspectival art, i.e. caused by faculty X. Gebser died 20 years ago. He also showed me Colin Stanley's *Colin Wilson and Celebration Essays*....We then spoke at some length about my book. I presented it in terms of *The Outsider* and *Religion and the Rebel*, saying that the Outsider, emerging from his sick phase, is growing towards the Fire or Light, which is the central idea of 25 civilisations. He: 'Yes. It will be a cult book. But what I'm interested in isn't there.' I: 'Faculty X.' He: 'Yes. I'm deeply suspicious of the right brain.' I explained that my Baroque is both left and right brain, that the experience I had in Japan and then in London in 1971 is tempered with left brain presentation, the two together. He: 'It's like wine, having a drink.' Joy: 'I disagree, it's religious.' Wilson: 'It's pressure. If you pump up the brain and increase the pressure you have this sort of experience. It is intensity. Pascal was exhausted before he had his experience of Fire, you did not say that.' I: 'It didn't matter that he was ill, the illness had the same effect as Zen, blanking out the left brain.' He: 'William James describes his three mystical experiences as pressure.' I: 'Photism.'...He: 'I'm deeply suspicious of everything right brain. You've gone the way of Yeats. Left brain is the way.' I: 'Wholeness demands both.' He: 'Left brain can be intensity in the Naafi, Tolstoy's two Hussars in step, finding it's marvellous.' I: 'Your experience hitchhiking in France.' He: 'After wine. But yes. I'm delighted you've written this, I'm glad you've said what you have but it only goes half way.' I. 'Perhaps the Light is the end of the Outsider's vision.' He: 'No, it's just a moment of intensity or pressure, Faculty X is better, read *Beyond the Outsider*.'...I fought well, and it was all very friendly and a draw, and he's invited me to go back in a fortnight for round 2. I on the Metaphysical Revolution: 'Metaphysics are no longer rational and speculative but experiential.' He: 'I'm deeply suspicious of that.'...I am asking him to be more right brain, he is asking me to be more left brain; saying again that poetry and mysticism are a wrong way."

Once again we drank large goblets of wine, and I thought he had mellowed. I recall him saying of the Void, "It's something we're all dipping back into." Of the sceptics, he said: "Kermode attacked me years ago. Ricks, Kermode, Larkin and Goudsblom don't matter and needn't be mentioned. Scepticism of their kind is not the way. Larkin referred to 'that toad' work and then elsewhere said he liked work." He said: "My books don't get reviewed now." I told him: "You were a role model for a generation, you led us to realise we could all be Eliot or Yeats if we had the ability, did the reading and had the application." I told him to return to *The Outsider* and *Religion and the Rebel* and to state a unified vision of everything. He: "That's what I have done at the end of *Beyond the Occult*."I: "*Beyond the Outsider* and *Beyond the Occult* – you need a book beyond both, confronting the metaphysical. You were the first I heard say that Humanism was a bad thing, I'm only reminding you, not telling you."

I mulled over my encounter with Colin Wilson the next day. On reflection I particularly took issue with something he had said: "The vision of the Fire is half way to a peak experience." On the contrary, the vision of the Fire is the supreme peak experience, and because he had not had it, he did not recognise this. I found myself drafting a poem on this theme, and on August 7th I wrote: "Finished the poem about Colin Wilson in draft: *Peak Experiences and Consciousness*. Am polishing the rhymes. Went for walks in Charlestown, including one late at night. Vivid stars. Three shooting stars, one over Fowey a finger down the night sky."

The next day was the Charlestown Carnival. "On a sunny blue-sky day. Lining up in the field. Anthony was a convict with a moustache, looking like Lucas ('Escape from Alcatraz')." There was judging from the three powers behind the Visitors' Centre, the port and the pub/hotel, and there was a floral dance through the village. Later I "polished my poem (*Peak Experiences and Consciousness*)." Walked out onto the harbour wall. For the second night running, a cloudless sky and no moon and brilliant stars. A pear-tree above me dripping with fruit, and the streak of one windfall bursting through the branches (a shooting star). Returned in a sombre mood.

Have toiled all day but have not achieved as much as yesterday; although I am winning. The tree of stars, the World Tree, is more a blue acacia cedar with cones, like the one beside our house whose umbrella shelters our roof."

The next day I watched the cricket on television and deliberated. I wrote: "I am Existentialist before I am a Metaphysical – and Colin Wilson is an Existentialist before he is an Occultist. We are two Existentialists, I like Marcel, he like Sartre. British existentialism. Make this clear in the *Diaries* and Autobiography. My Metaphysical viewpoint is a concept in Existentialism, as is my Mysticism. My next book must be a revival of Existentialism." I rang Colin Wilson: 'We're just about to catch the news.' I said I had mulled over my visit and we ought to meet again because I can see his next book. 'We're both Existentialists with different emphases, like Marcel and Sartre. Let's revive British Existentialism.' He: 'Fine. Great.' I: 'My next book should be on Existentialism, and yours should be too.' We settled on Thursday August 15th at 5.30. 'What wine do you like?' He: 'Beaujolais. What's your address? I want to send you *Access to the Inner Worlds*.' I: 'I've written a poem called *Peak Experiences and Consciousness*, it's in three parts.' He 'Don't read it now.' I: 'I won't.' He: 'I was joking, you idiot.' He needs to take a step back from the occult, and I from the New Age." Later I wrote: "My Journals (*Diaries*) – an Existentialist medium. I am an Existentialist poet, like Rilke; and my history is an Existentialism. My main concepts: the transformational journey of mysticism; the Fire; the contemplative mystic at the centre of history."

I attended a falconry display on the village field. I wrote: "A tawny eagle, a Mexican Harris hawk, a barn owl, a Common European buzzard, a European eagle owl and Saker falcon. (Their trainer) flew the tawny eagle, the barn owl and the Harris hawk, holding bits of raw rabbit in a gloved hand. Each bird eats its own weight. Later I spoke to him at length about keeping a falcon....You train it with quarry, e.g. rabbits. It goes up 1,000 feet and dives on a grouse at 200 mph. It is diurnal, i.e. hunts during the day, hence it is hooded. It has a rabbit's leg a day, at least."

Later on "a momentous day" I "redefined myself as an existentialist, saw my Metaphysical Revolution in poetry and history as being within a general Existentialist direction. 'Metaphysical Existentialism (or Existential Metaphysics), in which there is a centre-shift or transformation...and a redefinition of self in relation to the cosmic Fire. If Colin Wilson and I write books about Existentialism now, we will effect a British Existentialism. Wilson's next book: an original, Sartrean book not about other people but from himself, stating his existentialism. Mine: the Existentialist tradition, how Sartre and Camus went for Existence as opposed to Being and how a Metaphysical approach to the Fire solves the Existential condition of anxiety and the Romantic agony. So first a critique of the tradition of Existentialism and Romanticism, and then my vision, the solution. The Metaphysical Revolution." I "wrote the last stanza into my *Peak Experiences* poem", and noted: "My poem assimilates Colin Wilson's peak experience to my vision of the Fire – within 'consciousness Existentialism'."

The Regatta took place. I wrote: "Punch and Judy, cliff rescue by the coastguards (who were later called away). Greasy pole, canoe display. Lifeboat. No helicopter or water polo."

Margaret Taylor had died the previous Sunday, and Ann and I drove back for the funeral. I typed up the poem on Colin Wilson, and observed: "The peak experience is ego-grasping ('grab your moments'). Heart is part of the equation. Colin Wilson lacks heart and is ego-centred; or ego-centric." The funeral was at Christ Church, Wanstead. I wrote: "The church was half to three quarters full....The family were very distressed. Graham on the verge of tears. The coffin was on high under a covering. The vicar...wore a square black hat. Afterwards we followed the cortège to City of London cemetery and were present for the committal. The hasty lowering of the coffin, accompanied by the priest's voice while people were still arriving for it....Later filed past the coffin bedecked with flowers and (like everyone else) cast a handful of dust on what had once been Margaret. A hearer and a doer, the priest had said; now gone to a better place where she is free from all coughing." I recorded: "Ann: 'It's not fair' (of Margaret). I: 'We must accept. The priest said, "Acceptance of suffering enobles."' Margaret's Calvary. It began in March."

I returned to Cornwall. I wrote: "Aug 14. At 2.45 Ant came in holding *Access to Inner Worlds* and said, 'It's from Colin Wilson.' It had been put through the letter box with a note saying could I come today as a Japanese girl 'Sai' is staying with them, and she's writing a book on mysticism and is very interested in *The Fire and the Stones*. Rang Wilson....I said I would bring my poem about him as it could be that we are nearer than we thought....He: 'Read *Access* before you come, it's all about this.' Reading it now. What Colin Wilson is saying in *Access to Inner Worlds*: peak experiences can be summoned at will when left brain says 'All's well' and right brain responds with a glow of warmth, sheer joy.' What I am saying: right brain is filled with the Light and responds with rapture – all has meaning afterwards, i.e. right brain filled with vision, passes meaning to left brain which then does the work."

I went to Colin Wilson at Gorran Haven, Tetherdown, up a lane with brambles scraping the side of my car. The chalet where I stayed in 1961 was in the orchard, but what had been a cliff-top view had been obscured by building. I left my poem about him for him to read. I wrote: "He had been swimming and he was preparing smoked salmon in the kitchen. I sat with my wine, his mother came in from sunbathing, and one of the dogs jogged the table. 'It's a f—ing nuisance,' Wilson shouted. 'I'm going to kick it, it's always f—ing well doing things like that.' His mother said, 'No, don't speak to him like that.'" (I found that each time I visited him there was an obligatory breaking of the taboo "f—" word in front of his mother. The previous time he had spoken of "that f—ing girl of Stuart Holroyd's".) "Then the dog knocked the wine decanter off. Wilson sat and poured the three bottles of Beaujolais I had brought into decanters...and we then talked about Existentialism, how he needed to take a step away from the occult and how I needed to take a step from the New Age, and how my next book – and his – should be on Existentialism, from us. He: 'The trouble is, Existentialism's old hat now, it's been replaced by Structuralism, Post-Structuralism and Deconstructionism, which have to do with language.

623

Derrida.' I: 'They can be ignored.' He: 'I agree, but also Existentialism was about physical reality – Kierkegaard – whereas what you're talking about is something beyond, not pessimism, but optimism.' I: 'Yes. Sartre and Camus were wrong.' He: 'I said this to Camus. We were talking and I said "Your reality is material, material reality" and he pointed and said "My reality has to be the same as that teddy boy's", and I said: "I don't see why it has to be. Einstein would never have discovered the atomic secret if he had thought that."....He: 'Most established writers are trapped within their obsessions and don't communicate: Sartre, Camus, Toynbee and Eliot. Shaw believed socialism would be the answer, and now it's gone – both as Communism and over here. He was a genius but he was wrong.' I: 'Genius is a spring that is within you. You turn away from society and sit beside it.' He nodded. I: 'You will find my poems repay study.' He: 'I can see that.' I: 'There will be quotable lines. If there are 200 lines in my work – one per poem – I will be happy.' He: 'I only know 200 lines of Yeats and of Eliot.' (Agreeing.) He: 'My essay on Husserl is one of the best things I've ever written. I cringe when I look back at *Religion and the Rebel*. I can see why people said it was bad.'" I observed: "'Existentialism,' he said, 'is associated with non-thinking and no systems, and not Hegel. Marcel can't be trusted, he was a Christian.' I said: 'The new Existentialism is to do with Being, the Fire and freedom.' He: 'Perhaps it should be called something else.'" I was on the verge of bringing to birth Universalism, a new philosophy that is not handicapped by the errors of Existentialism. "I: 'The Metaphysical Revolution. Bohm subscribed to it.'" I added: "Berdyayev reports a discussion in Moscow in which a student said, 'We can't go to bed yet' (it was 4 am), 'we haven't decided if God exists.' I said *The Fire and the Stones* was written to establish the existence of God.'...He: 'I'm interested in Metaphysics, it's Mysticism I can't stand. I'm not interested in unity, the unified vision of mysticism. I've misjudged you, we are close.'" I recorded: "Then a Japanese girl, Sai, who had been staying with him and who had returned with Joy...asked me if the Japanese imperial chrysanthemum came from Judaism along the silk route in the 3rd century BC, and she asked if she could take my photo, and so Colin Wilson and I stood together and were photographed side by side. Supper was prepared and I left, with a Marks and Spencer Beaujolais and two more of his books."

I reflected after I had gone: "I have a great regard for Wilson's dedication. The range of his work is quite staggering. Who else can I discuss Husserl and Heidegger with? And read about so many literary personalities? We are a second generation of Existentialists, as the second generation Romantics (Keats and Shelley) looked back to the first generation Romantics. We are Metaphysicals. Universalists?" And I noted our different view of language, his rationalist's view, mine the poet's: "Wilson: 'Language should mirror – it should be actual. Dylan Thomas tries too hard. It should mirror meaning.' I: 'It's layered, representing different layers of reality at once.'" Of our disagreement I wrote: "Wilson is fundamentally secular, although religious in some ways. He disregards God, Christianity and mysticism and makes his meaning as an agnostic, out of a Humanist way of looking – hence his defence of the Renaissance. He and I differ because he is sceptical, I am a Metaphysical. My book must be on the Metaphysical Revolution, which carries forward Romanticism and Existentialism, being optimistic whereas they are pessimistic. Wilson would say that he goes beyond Humanism in the mind....Wilson says that the mystic's consciousness is the highest, but he is not interested in it; i.e. the vision of the Fire is higher than his peak experiences."

At Charlestown there was "swimming in the harbour until long after dusk. Swimming in the dark. A Wordsworthian feeling as the village leap in and out, all friends together, one with the sea." On August 16th I recorded: "Wrote another stanza in to *Peak Experiences and Tidal Consciousness* – have now written 4 more stanzas since showing a draft to Colin Wilson last Wednesday....The Charlestown lock-gate imagery is good, and the open sea. Have now finished the poem, but need one more meeting with Colin Wilson on the Metaphysical Revolution....Aug 16 still. Having finished the poem on Colin Wilson at lunch time I launched straight into the poem on the universe, *Spider's Web*, and went straight through it; finished it by 10.30 p.m. Every rhyme; and wrote in 2 extra stanzas. An immensely creative session, a gift from the beyond (the tingles are happening as I write this, I am open to my right brain). I have even drafted a poem on Margaret Taylor, *Calvary*: 9 stanzas. An immensely creative day....My spring is gushing. I am completely whole: Left brain and right. I am very conscious."

I pondered "Yeats's words: 'The intellect of man is forced to choose/Perfection of the life or of the work.' I must choose perfection of the work. This means not living a perfect life, but also living in conditions in which good work takes place, i.e. conditions in which I can turn away from the world and get work done....However my work is a reflection of the deepest aspirations of my life." I saw very clearly that although I was an artist and man of letters, my subject matter was the Fire and the theme of my work was what made a good life. I recorded: "I have just finished what may be my two greatest poems....I am at the height of my creative powers."

We went to Plymouth, where I "walked down Armada Way to the Hoe and went up Smeaton's Tower. Felt giddy. A good view of the sweep of the bay while a spitfire flew around, looping the loop. Onto an open double decker bus for a tour, saw the Mayflower steps again in Barbican dock. Lay on the Hoe afterwards and sunbathed....Home by coach. Polished *Calvary* (my poem) in the course of the journey." I wrote: "From now on, make an hour available each day to tackle the *Collected Poems* and *(Collected) Stories*, i.e. keep a supply flowing through. This resolution after I added the finishing touches to *Calvary* and added to, and polished and completed, the draft I wrote returning from Plymouth in the coach, *Smeaton's Tower and Western Civilisation*. I had forgotten that Smeaton's Tower is a spiral staircase – exactly the image of Western civilisation for which I was hunting....Connect to Pendeen lighthouse."

I wrote of the Humanist view of poetry: "Auden's view of poetry: 'First I convert my feelings into a variety of algebraic symbols, and the reader turns them back into subjective impressions. Any interpretation that will stand up is all right.' That is the Humanist view of poetry. The Metaphysical view is, 'Symbols from the beyond and associative imagery are taken by the reader who translates them back into his ideas.'"

We lunched at "St Benet's Abbey, a 14th century building, near Lanivet. Built in 1411-30 for lazars, i.e. lepers, probably by the Hospitallers....The bog garden and waterfall and great fronds where Saints Way pilgrims stopped. The tower of the chapel is intact, the chapel was destroyed." On August 18th I wrote *Lepers' Abbey*; and *Bumble-bee*, which came to me as I sunbathed on a hot afternoon after lunch at the Abbey; and polished *Shooting Star*. And on August 20th, "wrote *Polkerris-Kerris* straight out, all done from start to finish within half an hour. It says something about being an artist that is important."

I saw the conflict between left and right brain in terms of being a moderate or an extremist, and I wrote: "The Baroque idea is important because it is a 'moderate' idea, it reacts against the extremism of, for example, Kathleen Raine (domination by the other mind, i.e. right brain)." I observed with hindsight: "I gave up Law in 1959 because it was left brain and I wanted more right brain which I got from the art I read. The (literary) criticism was a left-right synthesis, such as Ricks, my tutor, must know. Even then, my life-choices were about which side of my brain I should live through." I also noted: "Margaret (Riley) had to leave my life as I no longer needed the Christian influence; it impeded my Universalist view." I observed: "Women are right-brained naturally, which is why I like being with them. Men are naturally left-brained. Women develop left through men, men right through women. What marriage is about."

On August 19th I rang Colin Wilson and "told him we need one more discussion on the Metaphysical Revolution. Asked him to look at *The Silence*, as the Shadow and Reflection are the same as Gurdjieff's essence and personality in poetic terms; and directed his mind to page 15 of *Books and Religion*, and asked him to think of the vision of the Fire as level 8 in his scheme." I arranged to see him on August 22nd.

There was "a beautiful moon above Gull Island and a causeway of moonlight between the harbour and the battery rocks". And I noted, "In Moscow, tanks are advancing on the Parliament building, now at 12 midnight British time, and are killing Russians, and Yeltsin is under siege". The next morning was misty and we went to the Scillies: "Off at 6.40, caught the 7 train from St. Austell to Penzance, and then the Scillonian to St. Mary's. It was delayed due to mechanical trouble, and passed Mousehole, Lamorna and Land's End on the way; the sea was fairly choppy and it rolled a lot. We got to St. Mary's about 12.45, and walked to the square and got a bus round the island....Reflected on Lyonesse and wrote *Lyonesse: Being like Submerged Land* and *Gulls: A Cloud of Being*, two poems. Began a book of images for the epic....Many visual images from St. Mary's, especially the islands being mountain peaks of Lyonesse....The sea is only 30 feet deep round the Scillies; take that away round the Scillies and you have everything joined. St. Mary's. Granite walls, stone walls grassed over with bracken and bramble hedges. The burial chamber, Bant's Carn, c2,000BC, overlooking the sea. The relics from Lyonesse in Sennen....The bulb fields. The old town beach with waves tearing in. Was in alert consciousness and so wrote poems." I thought about my similarities with Spengler: "Spengler sees civilisations passing from 'soul-power' to 'intellectual power' (i.e. rational power), I from metaphysical vision to secular system, from right brain to left brain. It's right brain that renews civilisation's vision. Spengler sees cultures as hardening into civilisations, I see cultures as pre-civilisational entities and being attracted, drawn together, by a civilisation's Light. Toynbee wants a 'transfer of power from economics to religion', i.e. from the secular to a metaphysical vision. His absurd deification of the incarnation in history, whereas I have a Universalist view of Christianity." On the journey back I wrote: "Gulls, waves, winds, skies, fields – Cornwall has everything a poet needs. It has everything a painter needs, as many painters have discovered, and as I am a painter in words, I am finding the same." The next morning was a wet blustery morning, the sea a persistent sound in the buffeting wind, and I relaxed, tired from yesterday, my mind very active. I have work for the accountant and bank to do, but I have pushed it all aside and have lived as a poet for the last 2 weeks, and have loved it. The present moment."

I visited Colin Wilson as we had arranged. I wrote: "The issue: a metaphysical contact in two higher worlds which flow in and influence, with left brain control; or two worlds only, i.e. Humanism and Renaissance, and everything controlled from left brain will and no metaphysic really needed." I recorded: "To Colin Wilson at 5.30. The usual smoked salmon, one slice of ryvita, gerkin, lemon and a huge glass of white wine, followed by a glass of white Beaujolais and a drop of the good Beaujolais red I took him....Initially with Joy, on my schools while Wilson listened, once we had watched the news and he had dried his hair under a hair drier that looked like a crown (a tea cosy) with a hoover lead going to it. Then on metaphysics. At Dartington he talked about Mozart, including the Steppenwolf....'I was asked about metaphysics and I talked about Leibniz and Kant, and the girl meant the occult.' I gave him my definition of 'beyond the 5 senses' and asked him if his view (left brain summoning right brain or right brain feeling depressed and so *La Nausée* being written) was in the same spectrum as mine, in which left brain receives the Fire from right brain. Never really got an answer." One of his sons interrupted to ask if he would take a phone call, and he said: 'I'm talking metaphysics with Nick, I'm not to be disturbed. I don't care who rings.' I said: 'Are you Humanist or metaphysical – physical/psychological or spiritual/divine as well?' He: 'It's a problem of language. You make it sound so difficult. It's simple. What do I do? What do I do with your view?' I: 'Read the poems: you transform your ego into self, personality into essence, shift your centre and receive the Light.' He: 'It's more simple than that. When I wrote *The Outsider* I had glimpses of the vision but couldn't hold to it for more than 12 minutes.' I: 'I've ransacked history, 5,000 years, for the vision and put it in wherever it's been seen out of context, and called it the central idea of civilisations.' He: 'Peak Experiences. Never have I been so aware of the limitations of language as when I listen to you. You're trying to put the unsayable into words.' I: 'Agreed.' He: 'When I was at Dartington I was asked, "What will the new man be like?" I said "He's never depressed, he's interested in everything – in all disciplines – and he's competent in everything." Someone said, "Such a person would be boring." I said, "You find it boring, you're not a new person, you have old consciousness."' I: 'I'm never depressed, I'm interested in all disciplines in my poetry, and whether I'm competent is for others to judge. I'm not depressed because the Fire or Light has cleaned it up at source, as Jung says. What can I do? Go to the Fire or Light, at will. Open a pathway from left brain to right. I live and concentrate for greater parts of the day, editing journals, writing poems, reflecting, with meaning and purpose.' He: 'Kierkegaard said "Subjectivity is Truth" and he meant: "Go within and take out what's within and express it well in a lecture."' I: 'But Objectivity is Truth – the Objective One, the metaphysical context in which we live.' He: 'I'm impressed by what you've achieved....But I have reservations about *The Fire and the Stones* because I'm not sure what I can do.' He ended up paying me the compliment of giving me half a page in his permanent book and agreeing that one day we might write a book together, 'you the first part,' I said, 'and me the second. I can see a new *Declaration* on the Metaphysical Revolution with you, Sheldrake, Bohm and others, and me.' He: 'Yes.' I: 'As I'm going to be in Charlestown on and off for the next 40 years, we'll meet again.' He: 'Come before October 25th. You make me laugh when you say "One more time". It'll take years to conclude our discussions.' I: 'I like to set an agenda, it's positive and meaningful discussion.' Wilson: 'I'm not against what you're doing. I want to make that clear. On the evidence of the poems, there are three great poets of the 20th century, Eliot, Yeats and you. No one else is tackling these important themes.' Then his chicken was served and I drove home."

When I got home, I looked out "of my bedroom on the increasingly moonlit waves. Anthony and his friend are surfing in the moonlit curl of the waves. I am Colin Wilson's new man, and the vision of the Fire gives what he is talking about." I pondered something Wilson had said: "It's a language thing. You and I aren't communicating sometimes because I don't understand your language and you don't understand mine. The 600 in your Club, Shakespeare wouldn't communicate with Horace. They've all got their own way of looking." I disagreed. The language of truth is a universal language.

We went to Penwith to see ancient stones. I wrote: "Tried to find the chamber tomb near Marazion; confirmed that it isn't Giant's Grave. On to the Merry Maidens in brightening weather: 19 stones near Lamorna. Stopped for coffee just before and saw the Tregiffian chamber tomb, third millennium BC. Merry Maidens a beaker stone circle, a sun circle c2,000BC, like Stonehenge? Not an energy circle? On to Sennen, and the Manor House opposite the church (founded 520); a hotel whose researcher owner told me he had never heard of Heath's claim in 1750 that a block of stone and diamond windows had been brought from Lyonesse to Sennen. 'They would have been ballast from ships, and Spanish galleons had diamond lead windows. Fishermen could have brought up bits of ballast and Spanish wrecks. The Romans sailed to the Scillies, so Lyonesse is a myth.' On to a small cove near the Brisons and then lunched. Dashing sea. Wrote a poem. On to Carn Gluze on a cliff top near a tin mine chimney, a chamber tomb from the Middle-Late Bronze Age, c1400-600BC. Wrote another poem. On to Cape Cornwall; the beautiful Jacobean house....Gwen's *Dusk at Land's End* from Cape Cornwall, the chimney being by the Carn Gluze tomb (or Ballowall Barrow). On to St. Just and Pendeen, where Ant and I walked to the lighthouse while Ann's mother visited Verona; we then sat in an old-fashioned front room while she held forth about a world that has gone, young wedding photo behind her....On to Zennor and the mermaid. Then to Chysauster, an ancient British village of second century BC-second century AD, most probably first-third century AD. Seven huts with thatched corners round a central courtyard, 3 for animals, one living quarters; and a cultivated plot alongside. On a hill. Plenty of montbretia on our tour, green hedgerows with yellow and orange flowers and narrow lanes. Back to Penzance and then home." I commented later: "Wrote another 4 stanzas of the Wilson poem during my tour. It is now a collision between creeds." Later, thinking about Lyonesse, I met Dick Larn on the harbour wall. "Said I'd been in the Scillies and...at Sennen, checking the Lyonesse legend." He spoke of the Scillies and said "peat has been found between the islands, and tree stumps, showing they were once connected, and it's true that if you took 30 foot of water out they would all be joined."

The news from the USSR was exciting. I noted: "Remarkable scenes on TV as Moscow decommunises. Yeltsin ordering Gorbachev to sign decrees, banning the Communist Party in Russia, flying the Russian national flag over the Kremlin. A popular revolution is sweeping away Soviet Communism, with ideological iconoclasm (pulling down of statues of KGB leader Dzerzhinsky and others). Gorbachev, out of touch, must soon fall. The icon of Communism, Lenin, toppled in Talin; Communism cannot be far behind. Communism banned in Moscow, including *Pravda*." Later I noted: "Gorbachev has resigned as General-Secretary of the Communist Party and has banned the Communist Party and the KGB. He will remain as President. The end of Communism! Everything I have worked for at one level has now happened. All my FREE activities – vindicated. The shooting of 3 young men has brought the Communist system down. The USSR is breaking up – Armenia, Moldavia, Ukraine, Latvia, Estonia and Lithuania. Some of these will get together into a federation as I predicted in *The Fire and the Stones*: internal independence but external linking."

I noted: "A beautiful moon. Wrote a poem, *A Gold Being Glowing*; also poems referred to above, *At the Ballowall Barrow* and *Dandelion, An Ancient Village* and *Mermaid of Zennor*. I am so clear and elemental and sharp, so close to Nature down here in Cornwall. I must overcome my inertia and get out among the 'stones' more."

The next day I rang Colin Wilson to ask for a Whitehead quotation. I recorded: "His son, 'He's cleaning his teeth.' Colin, 'I'm in the bathroom....If it's short do it now, but if it's 10 minutes, later. I hate the telephone. It's all right for "meet you then".' I asked for the Whitehead quotation about movements of ideas. He jumped at the wrong one....'It's in *Religion and the Rebel*....That other one is too. I'll have to clinch it in my *History of the Philosophers*. He 'says that movements of thought are like movements of a calvary in a battle, one movement too many and you lose the battle. Economy of ideas.' He said he would ring me back if he could find the exact quotation. (I explained my *Selected Whitehead* and *Religion and the Rebel* were in Essex.) I said: 'On language, further to our discussion, the commentary to the poems does some useful defining.' (He: 'Good.') 'On "What do I do?", you open yourself to the Fire or Light and get infused knowledge and energy that is level 8 which renews the civilisation and contributes to evolution.' He: 'Yes, that's right. You learn from peak experiences. That's my own view.'I: 'You may find you have a future book on the ability to channel the Fire as an evolutionary power.'" I recorded: "Colin Wilson rang me back with my ear full cerumol, but I did not say I was taking cotton wool out. The Whitehead quotation is from *Introduction to Mathematics*: 'Operations of thought are like cavalry charges in a battle – they're strictly limited in number, they require fresh horses and must only be made at decisive moments.'...I said I'd do the poem out and send it to him. He said: 'Have a good trip.' I am a fresh horse, and the decisive moment is now. There hasn't been a movement for 35 years. My Metaphysical Revolution is the next one." I reflected: "Myself as Wilson's new man, competent in many disciplines, having unified history and religion; my unifying mind (as Kermode wrote), finding what is in common between Wilson and myself."

My last night in Cornwall ended with a late night walk: "A moon with a halo in a slight mist. Sad that I shall be leaving. Would like to live down her now." I returned to Essex and read that Yeats's *A Vision* "was automatic writing, unlike my *Fire and the Stones*, which makes historical sense". I bought McNeill's "diffusionist *The Rise of the West* which challenges Spengler and Toynbee's view that separate civilisations pursued independent careers. But there are different religions for cultures, and I am a believer in civilisations and in the pattern they have. As I wrote in *The Fire and the Stones*, the diffusionist answer is less complete than the Universalistanswerasitavo idsdefiningwhatacivilisation'scentralideais."

It was hot and I now busied myself with getting the Coopersale Hall extension ready for use in September. I noted: "Revised *Cleansed Senses and a Tinkling, Rustling Green*, which was first written on August 27th."

The night of September 1st-2nd was very hot and I had a very memorable dream. I wrote: "Slept with the fan on. Dreamt I was on a mountainside with clouds beneath me. Saw a poem I was writing, the first 20 or 30 lines about the meaning of life. Remember the line 'I went for a walk on the clouds. My Shadow in the moonlight/Lay beneath me.' Actually saw my shadow on the clouds below as I moved. A feeling of greatness. The poem went on to ask 'What does my life mean?' It was all very positive and optimistic, I woke with a start, convinced I knew the meaning of life. Came and wrote this. I can see the clouds rolling away beneath me: I am higher than the clouds and have transcended material reality. Am too tired to write down the lines I can still half see, but will make use of the vision – in my epic? Did I see an early passage in my epic?...The time is now 4.39 a.m. I awoke around 4.30 a.m. with the knowledge of divine consciousness, walking on clouds like an angel. It was angelhood I experienced. I could have walked on the clouds from my mountainside. I was at a great height. A 'peak experience' near the summit. Perhaps this is a stanza for the poem on Colin Wilson, this dream....Two stanzas. A godlike experience. Not 'I think therefore I am' ('Cogito Ergo Sum') but 'I exist therefore I am' or 'I have being, therefore I am'....The experience is like the opium sleep Coleridge awoke from with 200 lines in his mind, which he lost. I can retain only one line of mine, and a sense of the remaining 20 lines I was shown....The significance of my dream, perhaps. I am high up, the clouds beneath; yet a grub is living down below." Later I wrote: "Polished the rhymes of the two stanzas I drafted last night at 4.30 a.m. and which I have pondered all day....Also polished a stanza of the poet as a spider, the one now beginning 'Like God, the poet sits in a spider's web'. That poem on the universe is perhaps my greatest. It is certainly among my greatest. Its theme is of great moment....I am at the height of my powers. The dream vision in the early morning of September 2nd."

I bought Marcus Aurelius's *Meditations* and wrote: "Am very impressed. His Stoic reflective Journal among the barbarians, e.g. the Quadi. Tried to find 'If aught befall thee it is good, it is all part of the great web' but was defeated by the modern translation. The Penguin edition runs: 'Whatever may happen to you was prepared for you in advance from the beginning of time. In the woven tapestry of causation, the thread of your being had been intertwined from all time with that particular incident.'" I wrote later: "I can see clearly, Colin Wilson...is a Humanist rather than a metaphysical; hence his interest in the Renaissance and in evolution."

The schools went back, and to cope with the extra pupils in the substantially finished extension at Coopersale Hall I immediately widened the driveway near the front door and the car parking area, taking delivery of six loads of crushed concrete. I wrote: "The temptation to action of a poet. Making car parks like the two I've made since Friday at Coopersale Hall." I now had an accountant assistant, Jeremy Miller, a retired bank manager with Victorian whiskers and an enormous bushy moustache, who came once a week to keep the accounts, write cheques and do the salaries, freeing me from school pressures so that I could devote more time to writing.

I noted that Derrida took the term "Deconstruction" from Heidegger's "Destruktion", used during his call for the destruction of ontology, the branch of metaphysics that studies the nature of Being. I wrote: "I, as a re-stator of ontology in terms of the Fire, am therefore ideologically opposed to Deconstructionism."

I had been contacted by Heather Andrews Dobbs, a founder of the Troward Society and editor of its publication *New Light*. Her background was Science of Mind and New Thought, and she rang me about *The Fire and the Stones* and spoke of levels of consciousness. "Your level of consciousness is so great," she told me, "the spiritual is higher than the psychic or occult; now you have got the consciousness it can pass to the whole nation." She asked if she could be my research assistant, and she found me books and put me in touch with new sources of information. Peter Donebauer contacted me with a view to making a TV programme on the rise and fall of civilisations, and I prepared an outline for him.

Oaklands had an open evening. I was called to a classroom where 30 parents were complaining about the size of the class. I stood in the front while they sat in the 6 year old chairs and threw questions at me – normally Open Evenings involved a pleasant chat, not a verbal mugging – and in the end I lost patience. "If 21 is too many in the class and you only want 17, fine," I said. "Four asked to leave and we replaced them, then the 4 who wanted to leave changed their minds and begged to stay, which out of kindness – clearly misplaced kindness – we allowed. So the solution is simple. Either the 4 who originally gave notice leave, or the 4 who replaced them leave. All we need is for 4 volunteers to leave." The parents all looked at each other, and no one volunteered to leave, and all of a sudden their bolshiness collapsed into a long silence. The metaphysical consciousness is nothing if not practical.

An Inspector visited Coopersale Hall, an HMI from the Department of Education. He was bald-headed and grim-looking. I wrote: "He sat and talked, said...that his guidelines say 1:8 as staff:pupil ratio lower down. I: 'What about the economical view?' He: 'I don't think about that, the Department of Education doesn't think about that.' I: 'You should. It's inextricable from the guidelines.' Gave him what for. Gave him a lesson in basic economics. 'Have the writers of the guidelines run a school? No? They should.'" I asked him how many State schools implemented a 1:8 staff:pupil ratio. He replied, "I don't have to think about that, these are only guidelines." I told him that no class would be viable under his guidelines.

At lunchtime Steve Norris turned up at my front door: "'I'm your MP, canvassing....' Ann, 'There's the door. Would you like coffee?' He: 'Yes. I've just been to visit a sewage works.' I: 'Would you like a bath?' We talked politics. He said there would be an election on November 7th and revealed the level of language used by our rulers: "Baker and Major said 'If you've got Kinnock by the b—s with one hand, why let him go to grab him with the other hand?'" We discussed Russia and I pointed out that if I am the Toynbee of our time I should be invited to go to Russia, having predicted the change from Communism. He said: "If you'd been alive then, they'd have snapped you up already."

On September 17th I "stared at the Colin Wilson poem, made some inspired changes and wrote the notes. It's now: *Reflection and Reality: Peak Experiences and Tidal Consciousness*. It is a very deep poem with all levels of reality reflecting each. It is now one of my most philosophical poems....It wrote itself today; the changes, i.e. A word changed here, a title there, shaping my material so that it relates more fully to the metaphysical theme." I received a letter from Sai, who was now in Japan, "enclosing a photo of Colin Wilson and me, both smiling, he on my left....Also a massive letter about how the Japanese chrysanthemum originated among the Hebrews c2,000BC."

Soon afterwards I went down to Cornwall: "A round, nearly full moon on low tide water. Charlestown deserted. Went for a walk. The stars were out but were not prominent on account of the moonlight, which silhouetted the Battery hill. Earlier, the blood red sun; wrote a poem." The next morning I breakfasted at the Pier House Hotel. "The fishermen – a dozen of them – gathered outside. Wrote some poems....The 4 poems I have written: *Mechanised Motion and Nature*, *Fire within the Globe*, *Harvest Moon and a Cheer* and *Image and Reality: Streetlamp and Sun in Mist*....I need to live in a world of mental travelling, and to write poems from the end of the Egyptian civilisation c616 etc with details from received images. I need to be liberated from schools."

UNIVERSALISM AND GLOBAL VISION

Charlestown held its 200th anniversary. I wrote: "A raffle with Joy Averill as a Bal Maiden from the clay dries. Crowds near the Weighbridge. Into the car park of Stratton Creber for an Arts and Crafts exhibition. Skittles and a shire horse, and smiling faces jumping on wires. To the chapel hall. A video about the road....Clapperton is a little boy playing boats in his bath." There was a ceremony to dedicate the new flagpole outside our window: "The parade came: band in red, women in uniform, girl and boy sea-cadets of HMS Hood in uniform....A flag ceremony, a heavy squall which sent the small congregation running for cover, and then all marched off back up towards the Rashleigh. They held yellow and blue colours which they were presented."

I thought of "what Eliot told Colin Wilson. It is better to come in quietly and grow from there than to come in in a blaze of publicity which is then dowsed by critics." In a letter Eliot wrote to Wilson: "It seems to me that the right way is first to become known to a small group of people who can recognise what is good when they see it; next to become known to a slightly larger group who will take the word of the others on what is good; and finally, to reach the wider public. To do it the other way round could be disastrous." With me, it was happening as Eliot had prescribed.

I assessed the world situation: "The Cold War gave stability but was potentially explosive and dangerous; it has been replaced by suppressed nationalist tensions and rivalries, ethnic conflicts; a return to the world of pre-1939 (and possibly of 1880). America unwilling to be a world policeman in Yugoslavia (or India or Armenia, etc). The UN is only effective with American support. America has 'no desire to impose Pax Americana'. It will. Meanwhile, the new order. The Western European drive to unity, the Eastern European to separate from its conglomerate and then to join the Western European unity as a nation, with associate status (but little power). Over Yugoslavia, the US has said 'Over to you, boys' and has asked Europe to hold Yugoslavia in check. A global regional diplomacy. Nationalism – after the conglomerate."

A local Lexus garage held a Japanese evening and invited me. I wrote: "In the showroom, calligraphy (ink-brush names), the koto, origami, ikebana, dancing with masks, food and warm saké. Sat in the Lexus....Might get one." I did in fact buy one – Steve Norris had said the Lexus was the best car he had come across – and I enjoyed the silent gliding between the Loughton and Epping schools, stress-free periods in my hectic life. I wrote: "Got it in the interests of further freeing myself from stress."

Towards the end of September I had a "long and involved dream, beginning with a large face of Orpheus with dozens of green apples in front of it. A large face as tall as the trees in an orchard,....I knew it was Orpheus because of the Thracian hat." The image, received in sleep, of Orpheus among green apples was a powerful one.

Heather Dobbs helped me set up a World Metaphysical Foundation, which I eventually called the Foundation of the Light. I met some Essex people who were interested in metaphysics, including John Fletcher, an 88 year old straight-backed Steinerian and rich artist descended from Robert the Bruce, who used to own Copped Hall and the entire Copped Hall estate and who lived alone with his memories of a German artist he knew in the 1920s. Heather said to me: "You have spiritual charisma. No one else is combining the academic and the metaphysical." I wrote: "Do I want to come out into the open and be metaphysical or do I want to appear to be a historian? Should my metaphysical perception be my standpoint – my Metaphysical Revolution? Or Revival? Or should I be a mainstream historian-cum-poet who hides his metaphysics behind this facade?" Tomlin had hidden behind a facade, and Sheldrake had urged me to come out into the open, and I knew I was going to be more of a spokesman for the metaphysical, not less. I saw the World Metaphysical Centre in terms of Coopersale Hall, as "a mystery school based on an invisible school. The earthly drive, psychological school with rooms, spiritual lawn and divine beyond the stream – like the 4 levels at Glastonbury. A school for children, a seed-bed for souls; and a mystery school for adults." I wrote: "The new Centre...should (put on) events...and a Journal that describes the talks and reports back and generally promotes the Light....The series should be on the Metaphysical Revolution, the Light as a Theory of Everything. The first lecture should be on the Metaphysical Revolution and renewing values. Then on philosophy, poetry, history, dance, the common culture, how to reinstate the subject of Metaphysics at the universities, the attitude towards Metaphysics of the newspapers....The Metaphysical universe....Call it the World Metaphysical Foundation for the Renewal of the Universal Light? Too much of a mouthful. The World Foundation of the Light? The World Foundation to Promote the Light/the Metaphysical Light. The World Metaphysical Foundation of the Light. The World Foundation of the Metaphysical Light." Heather: "Should it be the Nicholas Hagger Foundation? That would not be misunderstood by parents. It would be what you stand for. The Troward Society is not about Troward's ego, it's for what he stands for." I: "The Light would look at my name as bringing ego into it, I believe."I wrote: "Metaphysics is the study of Reality and of Being, i.e. of the Light. Foundation of the Metaphysical Light? World Foundation of the Metaphysical Light?" Later still Heather pointed out: "*The Revelations of Ramala* associate the Second Coming with the Light. Christ represents the Light."

I attended the wedding of Ann's cousin Christine, to a bell-maker at "St Botolph's, Shepshed, a 12th century church which took its name from the 'Schepeshefde' of the Doomsday Book. St. Botolph was the patron saint of travellers and voyagers in the 12th century. There is a sheep's head corbel in the organ loft. Was among bell-makers and bell-ringers. Alan,...probably 58 or 59 to Christine's 34 (or less). Both have a common interest in bell-ringing and crafts. The service during which Christine was several times in tears. The photo calls in the nearby church hall. Alan, Managing Director of Taylors Foundry calling for different groupings in a peremptory way. Then to the Loughborough Senior Common Room for a banquet for 200. Tables of 10 after my talk with the Franciscan friar, who is enclosed at a Pleshey-like retreat in Northumberland and who says there are tensions and that they haven't escaped their ego. "I wanted to lead a religious life and out of laziness I went to the nearest friary which happened to be Franciscan.'

Among the bell-makers. Exhausted the subject with 3 couples, one of whom (white-haired), the museum-keeper, was very knowledgeable and told me about the medieval bells and the balance between tone and pitch and acoustics. 'The perfect bell does not exist, and perhaps it's just as well.'"

I spoke to John Ezard on the phone. I wrote: "Talked at great length, he at the *Guardian*. He: 'I often read your poems. Some are very good. I've wanted to do an interview with Colin Wilson but no one will agree to let me do one.'"

David Lorimer rang to make arrangements for my Winchester lecture: "I am to speak on the Friday evening of the 'Nature of Light' conference, with Bede Griffiths, Barrow, Anderson and Hicks and others speaking later....My title: 'The Metaphysical Light that Permeates History and Nature: Mystical Illumination, the Vision of God as Fire or Light in Civilisations, Cosmology and Everything.'...A revised version: 'Illumination and Metaphysics: The Light and Mysticism, History, Nature, Cosmology and Everything'....My title is now: 'Illumination and Metaphysics: A Grand Unified Theory of the Mystic Light in History, Nature and Cosmology.'" I added: "What should the new Foundation be called? World Foundation of the Light is an accurate description, like 'banana', whereas 'Metaphysical' takes us further away from the product, like 'yellow fruit' (which may include a lemon). What is it going to do in the consumer's mind? 'Light' will bring along the more general people, 'metaphysical' the Professors. Definition of metaphysics: the meaning, structure and principles of what is, including Being and Reality. Christine: 'I prefer the simpler to the more pretentious.' Heather: 'It's profound, not pretentious.'"

The Oaklands Harvest Festival was taken by Maureen Deudney, who said "that children are like fruit, some become bad, others good. And I looked and saw two hundred souls peep through four hundred eyes." And I later wrote: "There are two ways of approaching human beings: through their souls (i.e. saving them, or through culture); or through their bodies. Helping the starving and the poor is helping bodies, i.e. politics. But when their bodies are helped, people need to move from a spiritual vacuum, materialistic adequacy. Soul v body. Humanism considers minds and bodies. Metaphysicals consider spirits and souls as well as minds and bodies."

Chigwell School put on their annual evening for feeder schools, and at dinner I found myself sitting opposite a young Archdeacon and next to two State school teachers from Buckhurst Hill, who (while eating the Chigwell food) openly attacked the "privileged life" of Chigwell and then widened their comments to private schools generally, attacking their "pressurised approach" to children. Eventually I leaned forward and said, quite spontaneously: "Listen, children have a human right to learn to read by 7. Every child has a human right to be taught to read and spell by the age of 7, so they can have the skills to help them survive in this society." I recorded: "That shut the lady up." The Venerable Archdeacon (who had two boys at a local independent school) said: "I'm sure you're right." I repeated: "The methods used in State schools are wrong and conflict with the children's human right. Effective methods give them that human right. We in the private sector are effective in giving them that human right." The State school teachers found no answer to that argument.

A Japanese parent took Dr Southern of Bancroft's and his wife, and Ann and me, to see kabuki at the National Theatre. I wrote: "Met the Southerns in the bar area. Had a drink and told Peter about my book. Then to the auditorium. Saw *Narakumi*, *Kagami-jishi* and *Sagi-musume* with Kenkuro and Tamasaburo. The first was knock-about with priests and was erotic and had a Buddhist message. The second was set in the Edo castle of the Shoguns, a lion dance. The third was about a heron-girl with a backdrop of snow. Bits taken from the Noh plays (*Shakkyo*). The musicians with samisens (3-stringed instruments) and yin shoulder drums and yang masculine stick drums. Stamping with feet being yang, much yin. The Flower (yugen) when Tamasaburo leaned back and held an impossible pose, head near the floor. In the interval went up to the...reception and met the Motoyamas. Southern misheard and said 'in the pub?' (instead of Park). Mrs. Motoyama hooted with laugher. I: 'We always suspected Bancroft's is organised from a pub.' Home after midnight. Wrote three stanzas for a poem. About Tamasaburo as the Flower, the yugen. Also wrote a lyric, *Flower (Yugen)*."

"Thinkers and poets," I wrote, "serve the top 10% in consciousness. Saints like Mother Teresa and Bede Griffiths serve all 100%. Those who serve the 10% aim to bring man up to their consciousness. Others go down to the consciousness of the common man."

I went to the Frankfurt book fair to spread awareness of my books. I wrote: "Took off in the dark....Came down after only 1 hour 5 minutes in a misty Frankfurt....Drove in a Mercedes...to Darlsberg and this flat of Herr and Frau Barth....A very friendly welcome, he hairy and in a vest, she short-haired, both smelling of apple wine, which I was invited to drink. They spoke no English, I speak ten words of German and made them do." The next morning was misty among the trees and potted plants on the "prairy" the fringe of Frankfurt. I had a breakfast of coffee, boiled egg, ham, lovely smoked cheese and rolls, and then I took a bus and then a tram to the Messe and met Michael Mann, then got out among the Americans. I returned to the flat in the evening and was fallen on by the "grossfather" who "got me slippers and insisted on pouring me the best Bavarian beer (while he had a less good one)". I awoke to "a fine morning, a blue sky and out of the window a small back garden and then the prairy, uncut grass as far as the eye can see", and later met more Americans. I returned to another evening with slippers and beer. That night I dreamt "I had slugs in my lungs. I coughed and spat twice. Each time a yellow slug came up, wriggling and alive."

I returned home to hear that Hammond's son had committed suicide in a car outside one of his corrugated iron "barns" near the Coopersale Hall school gates. He had left a note saying nobody loved him, and there was an emotional East End funeral with two hearses, one filled with flowers, and everyone in black. A plainclothes policeman stood and filmed the visitors.

I was aware of being telepathic. I "drove to Epping rather than Ivy Chimneys on a hunch, and missed the road being totally blocked. Then said to Mrs. Starkey at Coopersale Hall School, 'How are you? How's your daughter?' (Something I never normally ask.) She: 'My daughter had a bad car crash in Loughton High Road yesterday, and her legs are cut, and I'm going to have to leave early to see her.' I picked that up."

Towards the end of October we returned to Cornwall, and I collided with Colin Wilson over the emergence of my philosophy, Universalism: "Arrived about 12. A brilliant day, blue sky, sun and a sparkling, calm sea....The Maria Asumpta is in together with 3 boats. The ghostly rigging at midnight, part floodlit, part in darkness." I edited my *Diaries*, the following evening I went for a walk with Matthew "under a cloudy sky. It was eerily light and Trenarren was clearly reflected in the calm sea, all the way down to Gull Island, which was also reflected down to the beach, just as I put in *Reflection and Reality*. Said to Matthew on the harbour: 'There are two views of the universe: one is Beckett's, that we're waiting between birth and death and that the universe is material and nothing survives our end; and there is the more metaphysical view that there is an invisible reality behind the visible reality, the view of Blake, Shelley, Coleridge and Wordsworth that all the vast universe is One and that we're a tiny corner of it, that there is a spiritual reality which is alive. With the first we survey the dead universe with passive consciousness; with the second we gaze at it with active consciousness.' Returned yawning from a fresh air walk."

The next day "Two boats went out from about 4.30, one very slowly, belching dirty smoke, and one saying River Dart, nosing forward. The Maria Asumpta prepared to follow them, stern first....The second boat was not clearing the gates and had to wait for Graham the pilot to return from the first boat. Bob, bent, grey-haired, holding a car tyre on a rope with two hands, dressed in a windcheater, peering. The Maria Asumpta went out. The ketch Marguerite Explorer came in. The tall masts, two of them, of the Maria Asumpta."

I had rung Colin Wilson "who answered the phone. 'Yes, that's fine' (for tomorrow). 'I've got my secretary coming, so we'll throw you out at 7.30. I liked the poem very much.' I 'Good. It attempts to catch the invisible behind the visible, the unseen behind the seen. It's different from the first draft I gave you, that's how it should be, written in layers.' He: 'Yes, I've got the first draft.' Rang off with my spirits lifted....The quickening and sense of anticipation that a visit to Colin Wilson brings as it approaches. Who else has the optimism to occasion such a quickening? No one. He is – we are – the last of a generation of profound holistic thinkers." I wrote shortly afterwards: "The current title for *The Fire and the Stones*: the rise and fall of civilisations and the motor-impulse which gives them growth."

We went to lunch "at Polkerris, the Rashleigh, in the restaurant section, and then walked to the end of the harbour pier. Had a memory of being 300 feet up in ancient Egypt, above a statue of a face, i.e. above the head. I was terrified of falling; perhaps I did fall there. I held onto the wall by an iron ring. The cormorants – three on a rock." That night I took "a late night walk on the harbour. A full moon, a reflected moon in the pool below the pier. The Pier House Hotel reflected perfectly in another low tide pool. A nightbird fluting from the water. Moonlit lines of gentle waves." I woke in the night after a dream and recorded: "Streaks of red and orange in the sky above the sea, and breathless panting as the sea flows in, a silver calm with almost imperceptible ripples."

Pondering my coming meeting with Colin Wilson I wrote: "The main task must be to clarify his, and my, overall aim, and to consider whether we are working along parallel lines, within the same movement. I am a writer of the Light, in both my history and my poetry, and I am restating a metaphysical reality in our time. He is seeing how human beings become truly human through an extension of consciousness which makes an evolutionary leap. Do we meet? Yes, if my experience of illumination is his top experience of consciousness; and if he agrees that the problems of the Romantic (and Modernist) poets are solved by my Metaphysical approach, i.e. my Existential Metaphysics – experience, not doctrine. Existence is the province of the aethistic Existentialists; Being of the Metaphysical Existentialists. My way forward is (1) Journals (i.e. *Diaries*), showing the development of my Metaphysical vision through experiences, (2) further poems, (3) a book arguing that the Metaphysical vision solves the Romantic problems and those of the Modernists, and (4) a book on the Metaphysical Revolution (Universalism i.e.) in all disciplines but laying down in philosophy an Existential Metaphysics, a return to the man in the universe; a turning back of the tide. His willed peak experience is in a consciousness which is 'a reflection of reality'. At one level it concerns a leap in human evolution; at another level it lets in the beyond. Together we should contribute to a book on the beyond. I must produce another big book soon. *Illumination and Metaphysics*. This can be published as an essay; my equivalent to (Sartre's) *Existentialism is a Humanism*. The new movement is a revival of the metaphysical vision, i.e. of what is, reality. My theme: the integration of man and the universe, through consciousness; the reality of the universe passing into consciousness through the right brain. Social Humanism isn't interested in the universe, only in society. Call the new movement Universalism? Metaphysical Universalism?"

My meeting with Colin Wilson turned out to be a collision, in the course of which I introduced the concept of Universalism. I wrote: "Arrived at 5.30 and was given smoked salmon and wine. Took a Chablis....Then in came his secretary Pam and her boyfriend Paul Newman, who compiles *Abraxas*, a regular newsletter-cum-magazine on Colin Wilson. We started on the Sparticans and Bill Hopkins and Colin Stanley's book; how Bill Hopkins is writing a book on genius. Then on to Japan. He had shown me a fragment of his autobiography: "Here, Nick read this. It begins with my hand up a girl's knickers." Joy looked with disdain. Wilson on how there were two applauding ranks of Japanese during his last visit. I: 'You should have bowed as you walked.' He: 'I put my c—k up.' Colin: 'Women should be f—d a lot.' Pam and Joy indignantly, 'There are ladies present.'His mother, 'Oh....' Colin said Buddhists need "more words, not less (his rationalist criticism of Zen)....Then on to books. It became animated during the second wine (after Paul had 'broken the f—ing corkscrew' – Wilson). When I said that like Goethe Wilson had been through his sturm und drang period and was approaching maturity. He: 'You're still in sturm und drang, the right brain, that's the trouble.' Then we collided head on like two sumo wrestlers, I rebutting this, Pam and Paul and Joy taking my side. (They were very interested in my two books, which Wilson had produced.) I: "I'm in the middle of the Kabbalistic tree.' And: 'My Fire is your 8th state of consciousness.'" (His Faculty X he had called the 7th state of consciousness.) "He: 'The Fire is like alcohol or mescalin' and: 'Why did the Romantics and (David) Gascoyne smash? Because they weren't strong enough. Nietzsche's "will to power" and "5,000 feet up" are reality – the peak experience.' I: 'I'm strong enough in chair 2 but can also let the Fire in in chair 5. The Fire cleans up all problems. It is about inner purification of consciousness. If the consciousness is impure, it will not happen.' He: 'But what does one *do*?' I: 'Next Wednesday, for example, I'm going to Hampstead and I'll sit with a group of healers at their request and bring it down for them in a safe way, and those who are ready will see it and those who aren't won't.' He: 'But it causes cancer and the two are connected.' A chorus of dissent. I: 'I don't know about that. But what I do know is that I have forged an Existential Metaphysics through it, and I accept that a new Existentialism is wrong because it focuses on existence rather than being, and that the new movement may have to be called by a new name, for example Universalism, but what I do know is that ahead, once you've done Ouspensky and the play on Mozart you've got a book that looks into the experience of the Fire (samadhi, satori) from a scientific point of view, and that possibly we write two halves of the same book and launch a new movement. Man in relation to the universe through consciousness,' I said. 'There needs to be a new movement to get that across. Will you think about this?' 'Yes, I will, seriously.' Pam: 'You must do it, it's the way forward.' He: 'I don't object to the Fire as the central idea of civilisations, I object to the lack of strength it suggests.' He said: '*The Outsider* was saying that in the 18th century man became too sensitive in the Romantic time and smashed, became sick – and what was wrong? What is wrong with Gascoyne? He isn't strong enough. The answer is therefore in the will.' I said, 'No, in the metaphysical Romantic vision.'" I noted later: "I went to Iraq and Japan to begin to make myself a great writer. Officialdom interfered in my marriage and has obstructed my progress...but I am now on course to make myself into a great writer and I will do that by 'sheer strength'. I will be strong enough to write books and to have my Metaphysical Revolution."

We had made contact. "He: 'And here's Nick's poem about Gorran Haven and me for the magazine.' Paul: 'We'll put it in.' I: 'I'm lecturing in Winchester in April on "Illumination and Metaphysics: the Mystic Light in History, Nature and Cosmology". Will you come and listen?' Colin: 'Yes. Send me details.' Pam: 'I'd like to come.' I: 'Think of Illumination in terms of its effect on consciousness not as a doctrine. It will repay you to go to comparative religion and consider whether it gives you your missing ingredient in consciousness.' He: 'Can you stand up to them out there?' I: 'I can. I produced these two books and I'm strong enough to produce another on the Metaphysical Revolution.' Pam: 'You don't have to justify yourself.' I: 'If I were Stuart Holroyd and my *Tenth Chance* had caused that furore at the Royal Court, I wouldn't have slunk off.' He: 'Stuart was a slinker-off. It's all a question of strength. You launch a movement and carry it through with strength.'...I to Wilson as I left: 'I was too young to be an Angry. If I'd been a few years older, you'd have had a fourth in the movement.' He grinned. 'You've made a hit with Pam.' Have arranged to see him in the week after December 13th. He: 'We can have a reunion of the 1950s people at your school.' Pam: 'Can I come?' I: 'Just as you said *The Outsider* was the most important book of its generation, and that you feel you have something more important to say than most writers, so I feel the same, and we can each pursue our vision separately or we can work in alliance, and I can see that an alliance could achieve much; it could bring in a new movement.' He: 'I'll think about it.' I before I left: 'You're the tutor and I'm the pupil and need to be deferential, but sometimes the pupil can be strong enough to express his ideas forcibly, and when two strong people express their views, sparks fly. But no offence on either side.'He: 'No.' Smiling. Pam (to Colin): 'You're in danger of being all ego. I've been talking about this all the weekend, it's synchronicity.' Outside, Pam: 'I've never seen him so animated. He loved that.'"

I recorded: "I thoroughly enjoyed the evening; made contact at a real level. Interrupted him and shouted him down when necessary. Exerted some strength." As a poet I told Wilson: "I am a painter like Holbein, painting the representational figures of our Age." I noted: "Colin Wilson regards himself as the 'most significant writer of the 20th century'. I feel I am the most significant living poet, and live on that assumption."

Later still I observed: "Why the Fire?...To feel nice? No, to bring in energy from the beyond which dynamises and strengthens the soul, and unites action and contemplation. Answer the question 'Why the Fire?' and belittle comparison with mescalin and drink. See the Fire as a purifying of consciousness, a heightened consciousness in the mystic progression towards a unitive vision, which is perceived by post-Fire consciousness." And: "When I speak to Colin Wilson about the Light those listening – his wife, his secretary, the editor of the newsletter about him – all recognise that I am speaking the truth and urge him to look at what I have done."

I was not determined to push Universalism through on my own.

We drove back to Essex. Oaklands was under scaffolding, half the roof was being retiled. There was dust and debris (broken rafters and tiles) everywhere. The next day I "climbed the scaffolding to inspect the tiles and battens. The dialogue of hammers, and answering banging; the silent dialogue in actions of men working." But I felt vertigo: "Felt it when I went up the Oaklands scaffolding, when I cross the bridge over the Tamar, when I went up the Smeaton tower at Plymouth and had to hold on, looking down through glass. Nothing would induce me to go up the Eiffel Tower or to repeat the meal we had up it, though I am fine in a plane."

I heard Seamus Heaney on television and recorded: "He read some of his poems. They were unmemorable and unprofound; mere observations of the visible world and childhood memories and no hint of a metaphysic or of the invisible. He is a minor poet. I am more major than he is, and one day this will be common knowledge." And I added: "The image reveals the unseen world behind the seen. That is now my considered view of the image, after 25 years of development since 1966. The images I am most attached to hint at the world behind, which for a second peeps into creation, the phenomenal world, and is nearly caught."

Heather Dobbs introduced me to her co-editor of *New Light*, who apparently said after I had left: "It's as though we've got a real life Thomas Troward now."

At the beginning of November I had thoughts on "the World Metaphysical Foundation. Its purpose is to 'experience the transcendental'. It is saying, 'You can experience the transcendental.' There will be trainees and a safe way of bringing everyone to the experience of the Light....The World Metaphysical Foundation will provide practical means for trainees to get there when they are ready. Jung and others had to work ideas out as they went along, and so will we – with a centre in Geneva, Jerusalem and America, and in Japan. The great idea we stand for is that Light can be channelled into our civilisation, which can be revitalised....Our centre will be like a mystery school or Eastern temple, a place where the Light can be safely known. Evolved souls work with the law of the energy we call the Light. Less evolved souls exist at a dense, more materialistic level." I was aware that I would be a vehicle for the Light. I wrote: "We go into the silence beneath the reason, i.e. the void or quantum vacuum behind or beneath Being and existence, and there we locate beings, spirits, energies; and the Light informs it all. This is the metaphysical model."

It was in the news that Harrington Hall in Lincolnshire, the home of the ex-Loughton Maitlands where I made way for the line of cars to leave, had burned down.

I watched Coopersale Hall beat Raphael 4-1 at football. Danny Clark scored a hat-trick. His parents were on the touchline. Patrick Clark was being tried in the Brink's-Mat gold bullion robbery case, for laundering nearly £4 million, which had apparently found its way through his older son's bank account. He told me on the touchline, "I'm innocent, Mr Hagger." Six months later he received six years. Private schools cover a complete cross-section of society these days, and include Lords and prisoners as parents.

I spent time on the 15th and 16th centuries. I wrote: "Michelangelo's Platonic view of art, that it is preordained by God and implanted within in the marble which the artists perceives. His sonnets 1530-1546, his 'trembling hand' verses dealing with old age, death and renunciation. The *Last Judgement* was uncovered in 1541; begun in 1536, it was inspired by Dies Irae and Dante. His fear of being damned; the arm of Christ is both punitive and forgiving: see his poetry, e.g. 'Now raise towards me thy righteous arm' and 'Lord, in the last hours stretch towards me thy forgiving arms'. Michelangelo worried about his own soul. A hundred years earlier, the Gothic painting of van Eyck, the *Mystic Lamb* (c1432) and Fra Angelico, the Dominican friar Giovanni, whose *Last Judgement* was 1431. Gothic is stained glass, illumination and panel and fresco painting, moving towards naturalism but with grandeur and sincerity. The *Très Riches Heurs* of the Duc de Berry, c1416. That crucial time that brought in the Renaissance."

The Coopersale Hall fireworks evening took place. I wrote: "After a showery morning it turned dry and some 600 came. The fire had a lot of sparks, the fireworks filled the sky with outward bursts. I manned the PA system in the dark. Steve Norris at the sing-song in the hall." The next day it was the Oaklands fireworks: "A clear, almost frosty evening, about 400 people, and a fire (as I said over the PA system) shaped like a wigwam which gave flames 30 foot into the air for well over an hour....With the parents in the floodlit tennis court, then off to the Carnarvon Hotel, Ealing, to arrive late for the masonic dinner at which Richard and Frances were the President and President's Lady. Took my seat on top table during the soup and gobbled fruit cocktail to catch up, then (following an announcement by the toastmaster) moved from top table to the family table and talked with the family....Richard Carter, who now works in the Registry of Official Referees,...is 50 on November 13th, and Wendy asked me to say a few words on November 16th." I wrote of the speeches: "Nervous laughter and applause. These latter-day builders of Solomon's Temple and revivers of the secret they found – of the Light (darkness visible)."

Matthew had been doing broadcasts with Val Tyler at St. Margaret's Hospital radio. Sometimes he had talked and played records live for a whole hour, and now he interviewed Steve Norris, and asked him about roads, his constituency, and the coming election. I recorded: "Off the air Norris asked him about the Lexus and said 'If I were as rich as your father, I'd have one. I recommended it.'"

I now recorded the idea for a forthcoming book: "Part One, the Mystic Way, i.e. the Way to a Metaphysical Vision, the Unitive Vision. Part Two, the Challenge to Humanism, rejection of 28 isms in terms of the Metaphysical Light which is Metaphysical Being. Part Three, the Metaphysical Revolution across all disciplines and resurgences."

THE UNITIVE VISION:
FOUNDATION OF THE LIGHT,
PHILOSOPHY OF UNIVERSALISM AND
METAPHYSICAL THEORY OF EVERYTHING
1991 – 1993

On the final phase of the Mystic Way, the approach to the summit, the spirit is above cloud and perceives the universe as a unity. It instinctively knows it is a whole, and not just at the material, physicalist level but at every level, including the invisible metaphysical level. There is Light in abundance, feats of great energy become possible and the vision of the One Light corresponds to a new view of reality which approaches a Theory of Everything that includes love and beauty, not just the forces that physicists seek to unify.

I now began a period where I began to bring down the Light for groups and to treat it philosophically.

I went back to Hampstead to bring down the Light for Anthea Courtenay's healing group. "Spoke of the theme of *The Fire and the Stones* and of the unmetaphorical nature of the Light we were trying to see. Spoke of the Mystic Way and the Kabbalah. Read St. Augustine's and Hildegard's accounts of their experiences. Told them exactly what they had to do. Then the lights were turned out and we went to the Light with me leading the meditation – or rather contemplation. 'Leave your body....Move behind your mind to the centre where you can open to the Light....Open yourself....Go deeper....The Light is in the room, open yourself to it....If it is your will, enter whoever you feel you want to....Not my will but thy will be done....Look at the Light with your inner eye, keeping your outer eye closed. It is the Light of metaphysical Reality, Being, the One....It is the Light that manifested into the universe....It will soon be time to return to the world of time from this eternity....Close your new place, your new centre and return to your social ego. Reoccupy your body....' Back in the social setting I asked for feedback. One girl had been filled with a crackling Light that had temporarily frightened her. Another had glimpsed a dawning. Bill had had an experience. Ian Graham (White Bull) said that White Bull had stood back and allowed him to continue, and that he had seen a blue sky. Several saw spirals. Judith saw nothing – she went into the Divine Dark which is God. Christine remained silent. Anthea had remained in her ego and thoughts but had seen a glimmer....After a break for coffee or tea I told them about the healing Light and the surges, which I demonstrated later, quietly and unobtrusively....Throughout I emphasised that the ego is like a stone in a pipe, that the stone must be removed. Later heard from Judith about White Bull: her Dark Night after her Yogi-induced Kundalini. The trials and tribulations and tests. The magnitude of the work ahead. The

World Metaphysical Foundation to spread awareness of the Light, and my presence on November 27th at the Metaphysical Research Group of the Scientific and Medical Network. The way of the guru beckons, the charismatic teacher who trails a message like a coloured cloth and has sexual admirers – which is where they all go wrong....I am an Ouspensky in potential; a writer-sage." I noted: "The future metaphysical input should be accompanied by a contemplation so that it is not rational but experiential."

Judith Seelig rang me. Known as a New Age healer, she had channelled White Bull along with Ian Graham, and I was aware that she had received extraordinary impressions from the beyond, which she converted into ethereal sounds. I wrote: "She began speaking in tongues today, a ghostly language that goes ahunahimahumahuna – seeing hieroglyphs, runic script and Greek, a primeval global language at the root of Egyptian language. This was in response to Annie whose vibrations are speeded up following last night. White Bull said 'One of us knows that in June the earth will be rent', i.e. without knowing she had seen the experience of the earth. Ian channelled White Bull seeing this. Judith attributes this to me last night and our conversation – she also saw a double triangle – and Annie's faster responsiveness is a result of me. The Light teaches each in a different way, gets them forward but does not invade if they're not ready." I later found out that "the girl in red had the most intense Light she has ever had". Judith said: "You opened the floodgates." The tales of what happened at Hampstead continued to come in as Christine the temple-dancer reported that she did not sleep that night. She told me over the phone: "'Dancing raises Kundalini.' She and Judith can get together and relay Egyptian sounds, with the flautist playing the flute. Christine saw many things on Wednesday, including a Light coming out of a chalice, deep-blue, a tunnel, a Light, a monastery, a man in black in a cloak, a Light the other side, and the White Brotherhood present. She felt crucifixion – Judith's pain. All is not right with Judith; she needs to settle down. They are all filled with energy and power, their vibrational levels are higher than they were. Christine also saw some personal things she doesn't talk about."

There was a Conservative Patrons Club function at a huge house in Roding Lane, Chigwell for Tim Yeo, a Junior Minister. Steve Norris told him about my book. He said; 'I'm reading it in the loo. I was discussing it with (Douglas) Hurd last week. He is very interested in it. I've been trying to decide if Nick's a genius or what.' Yeo: 'I'll read your book.' Norris invited me to have dinner at the House of Commons, and I was haunted by the symbolism of Vernon Davies upsetting a lamp and smashing it and looking filled with embarrassment as the hostess appeared with a dustpan and brush and swept it up.

We celebrated my cousin Richard's 50th birthday in Haslemere. I wrote: "Midhurst was in fog. The fog lifted towards Haslemere, and we arrived to find Richard dressing and Wendy in a dressing-gown around 6.15. Suitcases were carried to our room, and then a drinks gathering took place at the house: Richard and Wendy, Rob, Frances and Richard, and Aunt Vi and Fleur (Beverley, Wendy's cousin), who turned out to be not a Furze lady but a gifted painter living in Milan. She is clairvoyant and saw an image of a dog and then found a real dog with that expression. In 1985 she painted

Venice and a fallen lion, and then the Venetian Dubrovnik suffered a similar fate in 1991. To the Holly Inn, Easebourne; a pub with beams. A dinner of prawns in garlic, roast beef and chocolate roulade with red and white wine. Sat opposite two dentists, including Sally, a relation of Philip Larkin's, and next to Janet, née Fuad, a Turkish Cypriot whose grandfather was a judge and owned most of Cyprus and whose great-grandfather was the Turkish Mufti." I made my speech. "I said of Richard that he enjoys life in a particularly English way (with his infectious sense of humour, his quick remarks, banter and repartee) and that quite simply he's a jolly good fellow....'Home' across the Cowdray estate – saw a rabbit but no partridges – with an elderly couple. The drinks and a further talk with Fleur, on how the artist is central to civilisation, not marginal; on how the metaphysical inner idea is like Romanticism, and the artist can remain isolated within his area but derive strength from others with similar views in different areas. On how there should be a metaphysical vision in her paintings. She: 'People won't buy ruins.' On healing, she: 'My hands are hot, feel. That is extraordinary, is it not?' She is 46 and has a daughter in Italy of 23 who has a boy-friend. She is separated from her Italian artist husband, having had a child by her Russian-French artist lover. She is still friendly with her husband, she will come again in the summer. She represents Italian themes in her work. She: 'I am instinctive, right brain.' To bed after 2 a.m."

The next morning was not foggy. I wrote: "Awoke after a comfortable night in an extremely comfortable bed. Looked out of the window at the autumnal brown of the trees, the pond, the white sky, and felt the peace....We are 800 feet up; mountain air;...as high as Newlands Corner." We had breakfast and there was talk of Fleur. I recorded: "Wendy: 'Critics say her pictures aren't warm.' I: 'But if she is showing the truth about the universe, it does not have to be warm. It can be, if infused with the love of God. If there is a Metaphysical movement which solves what Romanticism and Modernism couldn't, then Fleur's time may come. Just as Picasso and Braque got together with unwarm paintings, so Fleur's torsos may be regarded as being important. Meanwhile she has to live.'" We had coffee and then went home.

I was found to be clairvoyant about David Seaman, the Arsenal goalie who had just been displaced as England's goalie by Chris Woods. I wrote: "Said to Mrs. Seaman, 'Perhaps Woods will break a leg or let one through his legs' – that was on Wednesday, and today he *did* let one through his legs. Mrs. Seaman, 'You're clairvoyant.' Seaman, 'When am I going to get back into the England team?' I told him he would get back in, and that prediction, too, has come to pass.

I wrote of metaphysics: "An ontology of separateness needs to be replaced by one of oneness. An epistemology of sense data by one of inner vision of the Light; Augustine's theory of illumination. Metaphysics being both a branch of philosophy and the perennial wisdom i.e. the study of the transcendent or supersensible. An ontology and epistemology of the Light, which is Reality known within; the Light behind cosmology – the reunion between science and metaphysics." I added: "My 'cells of 10' idea from the 1960s: meditation groups for self-realisation, i.e. bringing down the metaphysical Light."I regarded my bringing down of the Light for groups of around 10 as implementing the "cells of 10" idea I had had in 1966.

I wrote of the law of prosperity: "Let go and take with you only what you need in order to go forward. That is the law of prosperity....Clear out the old, the clutter; old clothes and papers, old hurts, grudges and resentments. Money is energy, so let the old go."

David Seaman came and played football at Coopersale Hall School, on the playing field opposite the scout area at the bottom of Flux's Lane, the touchline lined by parents, some of whom regularly watched Arsenal. I put on a track suit and played too. I wrote: "Four simultaneous matches to begin with, then the major one. Seaman was on my side. We were losing 5-2 with 10 minutes to go." I said, "Come on, you may be an international but we're being trounced by 9 and 10 year olds, we're going to have to put the ball in the air to keep our honour up. We'll go over the top. Get ready for some headers." I recorded: "Then (following a corner by me) pulled back to 5-3, and then scored 3 goals. They equalised off a shoulder as the whistle blew." The match had ended in a 6-6 draw, and Seaman had scored most of our goals.

There was a plan involving Judith and her husband to put on an evening about Universalism at Queen Elizabeth's Hall, so that the Metaphysical Revolution could be explained to 900 people. I said: "I will be a T. E. Hulme and deliver the theme, what is in common in the shift in the arts." I noted: "The Arts Festival should be entitled 'Man in the Universe' or 'The Meaning of Life'....The Festival could be entitled 'The Illumined Vision'....Universalism. Perhaps that is the name of the new artistic movement."

Towards the end of November I had another meeting with Fleur, the artist. "Richard and Wendy dropped Fleur round for a talk on art, and collected her after seeing Argie. She is not happy but pours her energy into her art, which I will try and help forward....Her bread and butter painting is copying old Masters – Raphael, Rubens, etc. – and she has won prizes for her 'energy and destruction' pictures (falling towers and light), which criticise modern civilisation. Heart centres....she shares a studio with her ex-husband. 'Peace presumes war – all the opposites together, yin and yang.' The Light judging New York – Fleur's lines on her skyscrapers. My book enables her to understand her work."

Judith rang again. I "proposed a theme, 'The Enlightened Man', to be part of the European Festival. A dark stage, spotlit scenes and a unifying commentary presenting the Enlightened Man in European history and art – and his re-emergence today in a counter-Renaissance....Nov. 24. Judith rang, inviting me to meet her husband (who puts on arts festivals) to discuss the Arts Festival. His feeling: the arts are in perpetual 'new movement'. I: 'There is a movement as large as Romanticism about to happen. It is based on a new view of man. There have been short-lived movements, emphases, within other movements in every decade, but Romanticism lasted a long time.' Also: 'The political unification of Europe has resulted in a reunification of European art all subscribing to the same ideal.' Told her about Fleur: skyscrapers under lines, i.e. cities under the Light. The Arts Festival. Universalism is the new 'Existentialism', but it involves all the world, so European Universalism?"Heather rang and we discussed "'the

Higher Consciousness man', and the Arts Festival. I: 'I am a T. E. Hulme, telling people where we are going, from a number of disciplines.'She: 'You're going to be famous. Make the most of your time now. You're leading the way to so many different groups. You're giving leadership.'"

Judith had had visions of a white eagle. I wrote: "An eagle pushes – shoves – its young out of its nest, then dives or swoops and catches them, i.e. teaches them to fly the hard way. That is why I am a white eagle. I push the seekers out and then catch them; teaching them to fly on their own." Judith reported that she feels "'desolate' in the early mornings, fire from her heart through her throat to the tip of her tongue (a dragon's flame), and an emptiness as her spirit yearns for the home from which she is an exile....'I've left everyone behind – except you.'"

The younger generation were saddened by the death of Freddy Mercury of Queen from Aids. I quoted four lines of poetry: "'Screaming gods and hoardings;/In a decayed time, unreal states;/Where is there any purpose,/If not in the silence of saints?' 'Who said that?' I asked Matthew. 'Shakespeare, Yeats or Nicholas Hagger?' Matthew: 'Yeats.' He does not know my work very well."

Towards the end of November I received a letter from Charlotte Waterlow a historian, who in a review for the Scientific and Medical Network's newsletter had seized on pages 708-15 of *The Fire and the Stones* and taken exception to my linking of the New World Order to a powerful shadow group who sought to rule the world, using the US President and Western leaders as puppets. I had researched my information very carefully, and she enclosed an abusive letter from a United World Federalist and in her review set out her own idea: that civilisation is about to undergo a mass leap in consciousness which will bring in a new stage in evolution, a highly optimistic view not shared by the findings of the mystics and for which there is no evidence.

I went to Oxford to Hertha Larive's house in Hinksey to take part in the Metaphysical Research Group of the Scientific and Medical Network. I wrote: "Arrived at 10.30 via a nearby hotel, where I had coffee, after a drive through fog....Talked to David Lorimer about Charlotte Waterlow. He: 'She is put out, because she's a Federalist and she doesn't know about the Conspiracy.' I showed him *None Dare Call it Conspiracy*. He had read it." This book by Gary Allen has sold over 5 million copies in the US, and it is naive for any historian dealing with the New World Order not to know about it. "He will handle her. Then we sat round in a modern room overlooking a wooded garden, and 9 of us gave presentations for 10 minutes each, followed by 20 minutes' discussion; 4 before lunch 5 after. I was Daniel in the Lion's den. Most of them were sceptics who were seeing if there is anything beyond scepticism. Max Payne, the philosopher who reminded me of AF (my schoolmaster), ex-Sheffield Poly. Max on how metaphysics should become applied rather than pure. Michael on Ibn Arabi (for whom) reality is immanent and transcendent....I handed out notes and got my points across, the intuitive and inner being admissible. My meditation." For half an hour before lunch I had the philosophers sitting with closed eyes and brought down the Light. The soup was on the table with an inviting smell, and we were opening ourselves to the Light. I wrote:

"The sceptics sitting in a darkened room, and later, after the Light had poured into me, discussing conceptualisation in linguistic analysis, e.g. Vaughan said: 'I saw Eternity last night,/A ring of pure and endless light.' Geoffrey Read: 'Why couldn't he just say "I saw a ring?" All this Kundalini rubbish.' The crusty sceptics....Lunch of soup, roll, salad and chocolate cheesecake; and orange herbal tea. At lunch the philosophers spoke about Einstein's theory of Relativity applied to language. One said, 'The pure philosopher must be a saint' and another said 'We say an artist is a saint but Mallarmé wasn't a saint because he was wicked. He was "committed".' They got themselves tangled up. J. D. (an elderly linguistic analyst): 'Lucifer was the Light-bringer.'" I reflected: "I gave them the Light and the Wittgensteinian spoke of me as Lucifer." "Then," I wrote, "David Tomsett on R. O. Kapp's dualism, and Geoffrey Read on the Fatal Trap of (believing that atoms endure in) space. I said to him afterwards, 'Did you understand it yourself?' and he said 'No.' J. D. on language. I: 'The Vienna Circle said this in the 1920s and where did it get us?'....April: 'Everyone has different experiences meditating.' I: 'But in *The Fire and the Stones* I show 1,000 experiences of the Fire from all cultures, and they are all the same – and of Supreme Being.' Came away faintly let down. I had done what the Light wanted but I felt like George Fox who had tried to crack the toughest nuts."

The next day I had "a long talk with David Lorimer on the phone, on the book *The Rise of the House of Rothschild*. His suggestion that Rupert Allison is contacted. I told him how Biggs-Davison said that Kissinger was party to a division of the world, and how Sabbat, a former Free Polish Prime Minister, told me while putting on his hat and coat that the Tehran Conference had divided the known world into spheres of influence (cf the Battle of Actium)." I later "wrote to David Lorimer that it may seem strange to do poetry and history but that in the 20th century some poets pursue cultural topics, e.g. Eliot's *Notes towards the Definition of Culture* and Robert Graves's *The White Goddess* (next to which *The Fire and the Stones* was placed by Waterstones, Charing Cross Road)."

I was booked in at Holly House, Buckhurst Hill to have a mole cut out: "Was taken down in the lift, changed into a shower hat, a gown with a slit down the back and shower shoes, lay on the padded operating table under lights, was injected by Mr Pietroni in green, and had my mole removed. Stitches, tugging. Then up and back to the locker room, dressed and sat in the waiting-room...until I was taken upstairs, where I was given an account and met by Ann who drove me home. Felt groggy all evening. Read the papers and dozed by the radiator and slept deeply all night. Little pain."

The next day there was a Christmas Fair at Coopersale Hall. I had a chat with Steve Norris and asked: "'Maastricht? Will there be a deal?' He: 'I had dinner with Norman Lamont on Wednesday and I didn't like what I heard. I don't think I'll resign, but...there may not be a deal.' We are dining together. Left to pick up Matthew and Anthony, who came 5th in a cross-country race for the Federation of London Boys' Clubs, and who will run for London."

I saw a film on TV, *Go Toward the Light*, about parents helping a 9 year old to die of Aids, a well-acted 1988 film in which the 'light at the end of the tunnel' is used dramatically – the first such use of the metaphysical

Reality." The same day there was a film about Burntwood, the new name for Garratt Green, "which is the top of the Wandsworth comprehensives for academic results; building on the foundations Sinclair and I pressed Mrs. Kay to lay".

I drove to Hampstead and dined with Joseph and Judith Seelig. "Discussed the idea of an Arts Festival in 1992, under Renton (the Minister for Arts), and composed a letter to Renton....The new movement I called Universalism. Its optimism, the view that the spirit lives from one life to another; man and the universe; the idea that a universal Fire or Light explains the rise and fall of civilisations....Again and again I return to the time when T. E. Hulme and Whitehead were in control of philosophy, before the Vienna Circle....T. E. Hulme and Whitehead were both members of the Aristotelian Society. Did they meet? This would have been in Whitehead's logical empiricist rather than his metaphysical stage."

I noted: "Willis Harman's book *Global Mind Change* sees mind-change globally and not within a civilisation, as I do; more in keeping with Colin Wilson's evolutionary humanism than with me. Wilson is vulnerable over humanism. The world is moving from monism and dualism to transcendental monism, i.e. consciousness becoming matter; the third kind of metaphysic." I took issue with another book, *The Healing Power of Inner Light-Fire*. The exercises say, 'Think of a point of light.' So the discipline is called Actualism. But the Light is universal and out there in the beyond, and has a reality of its own. So one waits for it. So my way is Universalism."

Anthony acted in *A Child's Christmas in Wales* about Dylan Thomas's memories of Christmas. "Ant's interpretation of the hunchback in the park: silent but watchful and disdainful."

In December "I attended a carol service for Oaklanders, sitting next to Miss Lord....The readings to do with the Light, including the beginning of *John*....Then went to the Coopersale nativity play while Ann gave the fourth form party. When I returned Zena came in to say that Marion has 'inoperable cancer'. She said: 'She's never been able to control her life, and now cancer's controlling her.'" The next day I went to Coopersale Hall's carol service at All Saints, Theydon Garnon: "Sat up at the holy end...opposite the 2nd World War stained glass. The 700 year old church. During two moments of quietness the Light came, shivering my spine; once when I was sitting, once when I was standing at the end. At the end talked at length with one of the churchwardens, a Foreign Office adviser on defence. Urged the FO to contact Kazakhstan and tie it into the new federal structure in Russia....Said to Mrs. Best that one reading in each service must be Fire- or Light-related so we stand for the central idea of our civilisation, which we are renewing and which the priests have forgotten since 1880. Said that the poets ceased to reflect it in the 20th century, except for Eliot and Yeats." There was a staff lunch in the hall, and I then visited Marion in the Herts and Essex Hospital where "she was pallid white and had her death upon her....I made her laugh a lot, e.g. nearly brought back a piddle-pot instead of a vase for my flowers."

There was an Oaklands staff lunch with paper hats and then I went to the Central Lobby and met Steve Norris. We dined in the House of Commons dining-room and sat near Bob Dunn and near "Mr Red-Head", Neil Kinnock. We discussed Maastricht and Major's negotiating tactic. He asked me to be constituency chairman via deputy for a year. He said that in his interview he had said: "The most important quality for an MP is to like people. I get on with people. They all wave at me, they all know me. That counts for votes." He spoke of his agent Tricia Gurnett as "having enjoyed being Ambassadress for the irascible and absent Biggs-Davison, who didn't like people". Vernon Davies had got his seat at Sheffield "by arriving by helicopter and promising half a million. He has between £60 and £70 million and constantly writes cheques to clear overdrafts. Cliff Allen writes his speeches." He told me: "You are quality, a quality person." I left him to speak in support of Government housing policy and Tim Yeo at midnight "even though I privately don't believe in it". He told me (prophetically): "I'll be a Minister next time."

We gave a party at Oaklands for the staff of the two schools "in a foggy and candlelit Oaklands, tables groaning with food". I spoke with Tim Norris about the death of the Old Chigwellian Sefton Ulmer, a "dazed, foppish" priest in Hastings, following several strokes. Tim reminded me of how Ulmer "perpetrated an amazing deception in 1954, disguising himself as an Indian maharaja with little English who delivered the prizes and was not found out until after he had left that evening. He completely took Thompson (the Head) in." (Another version had it that Thompson was in on the plot all the time.) "Also found out that Geoff Hurd is dead, the wicket-keeper who modelled himself on Godfrey Evans, mouth open, and who looked heavenwards with his long-peaked blue cap when out. He did well in the City, retired to the West Country and 'keeled over'."

There was "a heavy frost. All the trees and grass magically painted". We drove to Cornwall and I "walked on the pier with Anthony, discussing...how everyone is here (on earth) for a reason, with a seed inside their head which splits open, revealing their destiny." I wrote: "I am now in my soul or self, having journeyed today from my ego (Essex). Ego – Essex living. Soul and self – Cornish living." The next morning I "awoke to a wrinkled sea, stiff in my back from a change of bed, but in my other self, elemental, open to winds and tides".

In December 1991 I had another sumo-like bout with Colin Wilson, in which I asserted Universalism's right to its territory and declared Derrida a trespasser. I rang Colin Wilson. "'Why don't you come on Wednesday? Pam and Paul are coming then. They can give you a lift.'" That night I went for a walk: "Misty conditions. A brisk, bracing walk to the end of the pier and round the harbour."

I pondered my role in our civilisation: "As an energiser, a revitaliser, of my civilisation, I must be opposed to it. So I cannot expect to be taken up by my society and civilisation; like the *Old Testament* prophets I must be opposed to it, and judge it from the outside. The spiritual energies must be renewed." I went for another "late night walk. A clear night: stars and a nearly full moon. A wind from the north-west, from inland as I stood on the pier. A gently crashing sea. The wind howling now. I feel invigorated: in my artistic, writer's self, full of energy, able to make progress."

I thought about Universalism, which I was going to present to Colin Wilson: "The key issue from my point of view is: can we go forward together through Universalism? He has written *The Decline and Fall of Existentialism*, which leaves the mind and consciousness out of it. Philosophy is based on the ego, not the self, the wrong 'I'; the 'I' behind the 'I think'. The treason of the intellectuals is in the novel, music and philosophy. Ditto existentialism is based on the ego, not the self, the 'I' behind 'I think'. Universalism is based on the 'I' behind 'I think'. Wilson: 'The peak experience is a rational and objective recognition of the nature of reality.' 'The very essence of my position is a belief in the power of reason' (*Existentially Speaking*). The way of Ivan (Karamazov). Wilson is rationalist about consciousness."

I continued: "The basis of Universalism. The vision of the Fire (the vision of a universal God) is central to all civilisations and religions. But to have the vision one must go behind the social 'I' to the transcendental self, as Existentialism and Logical Positivism do not, but as the Romantics and Modernists did in glimpses. So Universalism has three aspects, (1) at the individual level, the individual moves back from his ego to his inner self and contacts the universal Fire which strengthens his consciousness and will; (2) at the social level, it shows how the universal Fire has shaped the world's societies, civilisations and cultures, which it is central to; and (3) it provides the common ground for the coming world-wide culture at the global level. It is a philosophy of reconnecting the deeper self to the spiritual energies in the universe; as Hulme and Whitehead might have done. (Whitehead: 'philosophy rationalizes mysticism'; Hulme: philosophy is an art, and advocacy of the religious attitude and Bergson's Vitalism.) Essence before existence – essentialism. Or perceptivism. Universalism includes both essentialism and perceptivism, but in a universal, transcendental sense. It is almost a kind of transcendentalism and holism, both of which should be included in Universalism. The movement of thought is as follows: when I reach this 'I' behind the 'I think', I connect to the universal oneness of all essences and perceive all in relation to the transcendent One Fire or Light, which solves all problems and gives an understanding of the universe and flows into consciousness, giving influxes. Art offers pictures of the world and of real consciousness; it shows us 'with a shock of recognition' (Edmund Wilson) that our normal everyday consciousness is inferior. Philosophy takes over from that point: the Hulme-Whitehead view of everyday consciousness, and the way forward. Universalism is the working out of a metaphysical revolution in all arts and disciplines as the essence perceives the universal Fire which is the one being that permeates the universe. Fire-ism. Illuminism? Sense-data and self-reports are acceptable data. Universalism – all mankind....How I took the Logical Positivists behind their reason (left brain) which has limited powers to control consciousness. Connecting to the Fire charges the brain with universal forces – spiritual energies from the universe."

I visited Colin Wilson. I wrote: "Was collected by Pam and Paul at 4.50 and driven by Pam in a car with a seat belt only Pam could fasten. Talk about *The Fire and the Stones*. Pam: 'Don't say any more, I want to hear you tell Colin. Don't say it twice.' With Colin, who was in a blue shell suit. Before we could start talking, while the news was still on and he was still in his hairdrier, we were reading a letter from Sandra someone, Joy said 'Put the letter away, there are two ladies at the door', and it was this Sandra and a friend. Sandra wanted to be Colin's research assistant and said his books were the best she'd read. She and her friend joined the circle and talked with Pam and his mother and Joy while Paul and Colin and I talked about his filmscript on Atlantis. I told him about Hampstead and the logical positivists. Then the Arts Festival and Universalism. He: 'Stuart (Holroyd) and Bill (Hopkins) and I discussed what the sequel to Existentialism should be and decided it is Personalism.'" I explained why Personalism was inadequate to describe the universal energies pouring from the metaphysical beyond into the soul or self, at a sub-personal level, and he agreed. "Then he tackled me on the Fire. Colin on how the Fire is an inadequate substitute for conscious control....On the possibility of calling the new movement Essentialism. He: 'No, you'd be up against Aristotle.' I on how Hulme and Whitehead were the ending points in philosophy, and how I turned it round. The revolution in philosophy and how the Fire is on offer. He: 'I don't want the f—g Fire. Hulme wouldn't have championed your Fire. He'd have described it as Romantic abandon. You and I are always at loggerheads.'" The adjective he used to describe the Fire told me something about his soul. "Yet he pressed me to go on Friday....In the car on the way home Pam said: 'He's totally resistant to the Fire.' Paul: 'Do you have a view on murder in Colin Wilson?' I: 'It's the glee of the ego, not of the self or transcendental ego, which is where the mystics live.'"

The next day I awoke early: "Wind and a sea racing in over rocks. I have my world-view, which colours my poems; Wilson has his, which colours his works. I am a Universalist, he is a rationalist. With our different emphases, can we be in the same movement? Is it desirable for Wilson to be in a new movement? Probably not. Have him around in the background..., an observer but essentially on the side of the Logical Positivists and not having gone into religion, dealing through the social ego rather than the 'I' behind the 'I think'....The view of Wilson: civilisation's ideals are wrong, and the individual is apart from them and wants a different consciousness, both feet on the ground. My view is that by assimilating the insights of religion the individual renews his civilisation. The answer is on p5 of *The Fire and the Stones*: rational, analytical men live through a new centre, and the human free will is fused with the divine will. Wilson is in the existence of differences, I am in a being of unity. So long as he is resistant we must belong to different traditions. Wilson: 'The Fire is vital energy.'"

I read Campion's *The World of Colin Wilson* and wrote: "Wilson's precocious diary (cf Gascoyne). At 19 (3rd May 1950) he wrote: 'I have learnt a little of the art of not getting bored, which is tapping the universal energy at its source.' *The Outsider* is to be found in the diary extracts from 1950, when he was 19. 'I am a god' (Wilson, 8th April 1950). The Fire fills one with God. Not my ego is god, but my self is filled with God. Wilson on the universe. 'To seek for God and to find sexual complications, a wife, a Diaghileff, would drive all geniuses to frenzy.' His youthful meditating. *Ritual of the Dead*, the original title of *Ritual in the Dark*, based on the

THE UNITIVE VISION

Egyptian *Book of the Dead*....Colin Wilson saw so clearly when he was 19. His 1950 Diaries reveal genius. The amazing thing is that *The Outsider* took so long. He is like Gascoyne. He is a living witness to the need to escape boredom for higher consciousness. I focus on the higher consciousness or universal energy. Wilson: 'Where is God in this mess of everyday life?' In those early years Wilson lived the life of T. E. Lawrence in the RAF." I wrote down Shaw's definition of a philosopher, which was Universalist: "He who seeks in contemplation to discover the inner will of the world, in invention to discover the means of fulfilling that will, and in action to do that will by the so discovered means" (*Man and Superman*). I defended Universalism: "Universal energy that permeates the universe flows into the soul and the essence, so that essence comes before existence (the social ego)." I reflected: "In Wilson's early days he was not a rationalist he was always meditating. He and I could be the Sartre and Camus of our time, by an alliance." But then Wilson told me, "I haven't prayed since I turned atheist at 13."

I wrote: "Wilson is bridging linguistic analysis and Existentialism. His concern with language is that of Wittgenstein. New Existentialism uses the method of logical positivism, for it creates a methodology and avoids discussions of 'ultimate' or mysticism, which is betrayed by language. Phenomenological method in my case, measuring the reception of the Fire in consciousness. Rang Paul Newman to borrow his typewriter so I can type a letter to Colin Wilson. He: 'Colin sees man as a self-charging battery, you see the energy as coming from outside.' I: 'Yes. With a movement like a political movement, Thatcher and Heath can both be part of it though with different emphases. So it is in philosophy. Sartre and Camus can be part of it with different emphases. The new existentialism consists of a phenomenological examination of consciousness with the emphasis on what constitutes human values, i.e. our responses and vital energy and purpose. The new existentialism unites linguistic empiricism and phenomenological existentialism."

I went back to Colin Wilson's on my own at 5.30 on December 20th: "Sally was there. Ham and melon and white wine while we watched the news, a parrot perching on Sally's shoulder. Then talk of his journals – he, 'I cringe with embarrassment every time I read them' – and then a good conversation, Joy having told him he was rude to me last time and he having said I don't listen but talk over him, getting excited. So after handing the letter over: I listened. He: 'I have alliances with Willis Harman and Charles Tart, but nothing happens. To get a new movement off the ground, and I don't like new 'isms', you need to talk the language of Lévi-Strauss and Derrida. After Existentialism there was Structuralism and then post-Structuralism, and then post-Modernism, showing it all ends in nothing. Derrida started from Husserl and showed him affected by deconstruction. The conclusion is that the 'I' of the transcendental ego is an illusion and there is no metaphysical reality, because they are concepts in language which are false. So start there.' I: 'The starting point is the "I" behind the "I think".'He: 'Yes, but you have to tackle the language. Deconstruction is anti-Marxism. It's like Heidegger, *Being and Time* contains 10 definitions of Existence, and you have to say Existence 1, Existence 2, etc. Read

Christopher Norris on Derrida. Meursault's "I was happy and am happy still". How could he say he was happy? Answer that. When I started writing I had to refer everything to Sartre and Camus. It's all moved on since then. Now it's Derrida and Lévi-Strauss, and they're much harder to understand. Everyone can have the Fire, even if they can't think' (i.e. the most important thing in life is to think). 'The painter who painted that picture tried to get me to have visions about 20 years ago and after 20 minutes I said, "It's no good, I am thinking about what you're saying." Wilson turning away from mysticism. 'Illumination doesn't produce works of art.' And the Brooke sonnet "This is love" about two cold lovers. Rousseau said that the experience he lived is less intense than when he wrote about it.' I: 'Compare Wordsworth, emotion recollected in tranquillity. The daffodils.' He: 'Yes. And so it is with masturbation, which is better than sex (sic), see my *Origins of the Sexual Impulse*. Read Derrida in *On Grammatology*....You need to put the crowbar in at the right place. Otherwise you're rushing about waving swords and not getting anywhere. Derrida is the *Principia* (by Newton) of our time. Give one single proof that he's wrong and you're there.' Very valuable advice. 'Your Fire is irrelevant. Anyone can have it. But what is needed is....' and away he goes on conscious pressure, etc. Wilson: 'It's not the Fire, it's language.' I said: 'Spengler saw civilisations as passing from soul-power to intellectual power.' And Toynbee is saying something similar,' he said. I: 'And I am saying it's from metaphysical to secular. There are different emphases within a generally similar outlook.' He: 'Spengler said aqueducts were better than Renaissance buildings because they *did* something. So it is with (Ted) Hughes. When we met we talked about vole-traps. He's only got one poem in him, the violence and cruelty of Nature. He didn't want to talk about poetry, only about *doing*. It's the lock-gate you need to focus on, not the Fire.'"

I rejoined: "'No one's stopping you from being you. You are you. I am me. We have different emphases. Give me a piece of paper and sit me in front of it for 2 hours and I will come up with 10 arguments against Derrida. Rejection of Derrida is the starting-point. I'm using the Fire of religion as an existential experience.' He: 'I'm practical and have my feet on the ground. If you ask me about a serial killer or reality, I'll be more interested in the serial killer.' I: 'We have different emphases. But by co-operating we can perhaps strengthen things for each other. You and Stuart Holroyd have meant more to me than any other writer since the 1950s. Rather than for us to operate in isolation, and be ignored; can we not come together and be acknowledged. It's a simple idea, but that's my thinking.' Wilson: 'Yes. You're more than welcome. Any time, Nick, any time.' His family came down while I was with him – the two boys joining their sister – but apart from pouring them a glass of wine he carried on talking to me and was reluctant to let me go. I was standing by the fire for 10 minutes while he ate his mussels, talking at me. Left arranging to see him in February, when the starting-point will be Derrida and Lévi-Strauss and the 'I' behind the 'I think' and metaphysical reality. At the end of our discussion he said: 'Bill Hopkins used to say "Poetry has no extension".'. I: 'My Commentary supplies the extension. The poems are A. The Commentary is B. A poet writes about the world and hints at the hidden.'"

The next day was "a windy, wet day. Misty sea. Packed and drove back in the Lexus."I returned to Essex to find a card from Tuohy: "An ice skater raising his hat and 'Please try and visit next year' inside. An ice saint, raising his hat to me, in the idiom of public performance that I'm in, and warning of falling through the ice." I went to Foyles and bought "19 books related to Structuralism, Deconstruction and Post-Structuralism; and Post-Modernism. Also on the new Historicism. It is a maze. Structuralism which began in the 1960s with Saussure and Lévi-Strauss is over. Deconstruction – Derrida and de Man in the 1960s – criticised it by analysis and allegedly destroyed ontology, saying there is nothing external to the text, which is evidently not true. However, borders were dissolved, and the mixture of linguistics, literary criticism and philosophy has resulted in Post-Structuralism, a move away from the unified person and with Barthes, perhaps a reaffirmation of metaphysical structures. Ponder this. Post-Modernism is how the author tells the story. On my reading so far, the approach to metaphysics of Superstructuralism is a left-brain one, tied to language, and not experience; and also the 'I', the universal 'I' is not stressed. The universal 'I' (i.e. transcendental ego) overthrows much of Derrida, as does the reality he intuitively knows which cannot be approached through language."

I wrote Colin Wilson another letter "debunking Derrida in terms of the universal ego of Universalism....Kant's transcendental ego behind reason; hence a true critique of pure reason. (He saw pure reason as wisdom?) Whitehead's view that Nature is one organism. How Derrida can be debunked. I am me and have formed my vision; but I get sparks from Colin Wilson, creative sparks as my knife touches his grinding-wheel. Wilson is a grinding-wheel spinning round and round. I sharpen my assassin's knife on it before I stick it into Derrida. The universal 'I' can be revealed through phenomenology by bracketing out the reason."

My debunking of Derrida hinged on a "non-competence principle": "A 5-point proof of my 'non-competence principle' that debunks Derrida, Structuralism, Deconstruction, Post-Structuralism, etc: (1) Derrida's theories about language are the province of the left brain's social ego rather than the universal (or transcendental) ego; (2) contrary to Sartre, the universal ego exists, the proof including a use of phenomenology, bracketing out the Cartesian 'I think' to reveal the 'I' behind it; (3) intuitive information received by the universal ego is admissible evidence for philosophers to consider (Willis Harman's article); (4) the territories of the social and universal egos are separate and distinct, and the social ego is not competent to judge what is or is not real outside its territory as language falls silent when the universal ego takes over the direction of consciousness (cf the Vienna Circle's verification principle, which is not competent to apply empirical standards to quasi-empirical intuitive experience); and (5) the universal energy called the Fire or Light which is received in the universal 'I' rather than the linguistic social ego constitutes a reality outside language that has been experienced in all cultures at all times (see Part One of *The Fire and the Stones*), contrary to what Derrida holds. So Derrida is a trespasser who doesn't matter. This is an important letter, as was the last letter to Colin Wilson." My "non-competence principle" has much in common with Wittgenstein's later "Whereof one cannot speak, thereof one must be silent."

Christmas came. We visited Miss Lord. Marion was back from hospital, and there was a Zimbabwean housekeeper. Miss Lord said, "We've got *that* in the house."

I noted: "The USSR has finally ended, formally, and Gorbachev, the last President of the USSR has resigned; and my plan to launch a guerilla movement against the USSR has happened without a shot being fired, and all the republics are now free. (FREE.)"

Nadia came. "I felt giddy and unwell, so had a relaxed day. After lunch to Coopersale Hall. Found a light on. Walked round the pond, then back for tea and present-exchange." I listened to Elgar's *Enigma Variations* and wrote: "The music of the angels....Tugging at the heart." I contrasted language and silence (further to my non-competence principle): "Language – the social ego's province. Silence – the universal ego's province. My *The Silence* was naturally about the contact with the universal ego. Recently Steiner's *Language and Silence* (1967, just reissued.)"

The family gathering took place at Jonathan's house in Tunbridge Wells. There was a debate about whether children should qualify or whether they should earn money straightaway. I favoured hard work over many years: "Colin Wilson took odd jobs at 16 because he wanted to become Europe's main writer; he had the determination to do his reading while wheeling cement. I knew what I wanted to do. I worked at it in the evenings and at weekends, and now I've got my poems out and I addressed the philosophers at Oxford and told them philosophy since 1915 is wrong. But I had to read the philosophers to do that, to talk their language. Colin Wilson and I saw things higher up we wanted to do and we did them."

At the end of the year I had a pain in my heart: "Finished my tidying and tearing up, pruning my study. Tried to sleep but at 12.45 a.m. had a slight pain in my heart, for the second time in three days; occasioned by the onslaught on my study. Got up and wrote this in discomfort....1.15 a.m. Got up again, suffering from severe pain in my heart. Am waiting for it to pass. Quietly meditating. Considered whether to drive myself to casualty. Rejected the idea." For New Year's Eve "Marion and Miss Lord came round about 10.15 and saw the New Year in....Marion had been asked 'What is the thing that's so secret, which I can't be told?' and had replied, 'I've got cancer of the uterus.' 'You can't have.' 'I have.' She drank a little wine though she's supposed not to, because of her pills, and forgot about her condition, being absorbed in laughter. I was able to create an atmosphere of absorbed laughter for her...so she forgot about her condition and enjoyed life for an hour and a half. Miss Lord had four glasses of wine and rolled home on my arm (aged 91)."

I looked ahead to 1992 with hope. I had now finished the Coopersale Hall extension of 4 classrooms in spite of the recession, and Coopersale Hall was now set for consolidation without further building for a while.

The first four months of 1992 I worked on my Winchester lecture.

The New Year began with "lush grass showing in the field". I did a draft of my lecture in four days (December 31st to January 3rd): it became the first part of *The Universe and the Light*. I wrote: "I propose the Light – spiritual *and* natural – as a Theory of Everything. I do it by adapting Newton's expanding force and reconciling it to Bohm and including Hawking. I need to sharpen the reconciliation of quantum and relativity theory and gravity in terms of the Light." All through January I worked on my "unified view".

On January 5th the local vicar visited Miss Lord's to anoint Marion with oil. The first appointment he put off because "I need to look it up in a book". On his own admission he did not know how to heal, and the Church's involvement was to be a "mechanical interpretation from a book, devoid of inspiration" or healing energy. When the ceremony took place I recorded: "Ten sitting in a circle, including blind Judith. The anointing, a grim Marion lowering her eyes and all hands then being put on her head or arm. Judith praying loudly, alone; the blind leading the sick." I later observed: "All my life I've said 'Where's the energy?' There was insufficient energy in the Essex people of the 1950s, which made me angry. There is insufficient energy now. The Church is in decay." Later Marion visited a consultant with Zena, who told us: "He drew a diagram of the stomach and shaded it in and said: 'It's spreading. You're in the third stage of four stages. Have you any questions?' Marion asked, 'Where did you go on holiday?' So Marion hasn't taken anything in... – or was it bravura?...Zena: 'It was awful. I was so depressed. But Marion was laughing and joking.'...Marion said of Zena: 'She didn't say anything to the consultant, she kept her eyes down, she's shy with new people.' The eyes were down to avoid Marion's gaze as the consultant was in effect saying Marion will shortly die. Marion did not grasp this."

I had several telephone conversations with the physicist Edgard Gunzig in Brussels. I recorded of one call: "Discussed the origin of the universe, which was from real nothing to a quantum vacuum (by quantum processes) and thence to a universe (by virtual particles becoming real particles)." Later: "He, several times: 'You are asking the most fundamental questions in theoretical physics.' He is sending me details of a conference on the Origin and Structure of the Universe, which he is holding in Belgium." And again: "Gunzig...on how a real nothing or emptiness became a quantum vacuum through virtual particles. And how the CBR does not come from the Big Bang but from a cooling 300,000-500,000 years after the beginning. On how the universe is infinite (or is it finite?); the question is largely semantic depending on whether the universe is seen as a sphere or a plane. On how dreadful Hawking's book is."

I reflected of my history: "Toynbee sees civilisations in relation to their own internal rhythms and not outside influences, as does McNeill. I have combined the two, the two being summarised in my two charts, the 61 stages and 'From One to One'. Toynbee is identified with Christian solutions and I have avoided an exclusively Christian influence with my Universalism."

Peter Donebauer and his producer Roy Ackerman took me to the BBC to discuss whether a film should be made of *The Fire and the Stones*. We met

Stephen Whyttle and John Blake and had a freewheeling conversation with sceptical probings from the two of them about the difference between a civilisation and a culture, whether primitive religions belonged to a culture rather than a civilisation, how comparative religion is "out" as it is "boring", and whether we were being descriptive or evangelical. I wrote: "I: 'A man has a vision of the Fire, which attracts a religion, which creates a God/god, which attracts a civilisation.' Stephen Whyttle: 'What you're saying is what the *Old Testament* is saying, it isn't new.' I: 'Kathleen Raine said this is the first book since the *Old Testament* to take such a view.' He smiled." At the end Whyttle said: "Are religions the dynamos of civilisations? That is of interest. It's a six-parter. Consider how you can make it into 6 parts while we read the book." I went on to lunch with Peter and we drafted a "stages" model for our 6 parts – "beginnings, unifications, reformations, empires and religion, secularization and today" – and also a chronological model splitting the spread of the Fire over 5,000 years into 6 parts. I wrote later: "'Are religions the dynamos of civilisations?' The question, posed by the Head of Religious Broadcasting at the BBC, requires a yes answer, both in terms of the beginnings of civilisations, and their renewals." Later still I "woke up with the thought, 'quantised history'."

On January 25th I had a dream which predicted the date of the coming General Election and the result. My *Diary* records: "Jan 25. A long dream. I remember being in a room and watching John Major look at a machine that was a computer, although it looked more like an EEG (being flat and greenish – metallic), and a red line moved and he had found: growth! The news was delivered excitedly. I knew it was the end of January and there would be an election around April 9th; the growth had happened just at the right time, people would go out and buy, recovery was on the way." In sleep I was given the actual date of the General Election and Major's victory. The source was the same as the same that gave me the history theory of the Fire or Light.

At the end of January I had finished dictating my Winchester lecture. I wrote: "Had the thought: 'Immanentism'. This can be one aspect of Universalism, the immanence of the universal energy in the universe and its immanence in the human being's soul. The other aspect is 'Transcendentism' (different from Transcendentalism) which draws attention to the transcendent nature of the universal energy and of the transcendental ego. 'Immanentism' focuses from without to within. 'Transcendentism' focuses from within to without."

I noted: "Matthew's grades have improved as a result of his increased attention and alertness, which are caused by Choi Kwang-Do (he kicked and broke two planks first time to get his green belt.)"

A South African Hungarian, Professor Rosinger, flew from Johannesburg to London and stayed at the nearby Roebuck Hotel to meet me, after reading my two books, and declaring me in a letter "a Great Old Master". I met him. He began by saying, "I am in the KGB, that is a joke." I wrote: "Rosinger, a Hungarian 'barbarian' (his word) with sideburns and a moustache, who looked like Cannon in the TV series. We talked from 2.15 to 5.30, first over tea at the Roebuck and then at my house, after a walk round the grounds and a look at the cross-country running round the main field. He talked non-stop ('I have a very high energy') and eventually said: 'Your two books are exceptional. What impressed me was the contrast between them. One was objective, the other subjective, they were from two opposite ends of the spectrum. The only other person I could think of who had done such a thing was St. Augustine with *Confessions* (which is not as good as your poems) and *City of God*, but they were not published at the same time. Also, where is the middle between these two opposites?' I: 'That's the reunification of all knowledge which is in my lecture.' On my poems he said, 'You write so objectively about yourself, that in itself is an indication of exceptional quality.' Talk on the moon and the finger pointing to it (the Zen saying that the fool watches the finger), and how the moon is in all religions and cultures....My talk of launching a new movement, the first opportunity since 1798, to counter the secularised view in all disciplines." Heather Dobbs entertained him for the rest of the week and said: "He is so immersed in what he has to say that he is not thinking about the Light." She said: 'I see your energy clearing the dead wood to let in the Light and you shouldn't be going off into another dead wood. I feel let down by Rosinger. He's off the highway. He's a side road. We have to stick on the main road." Shortly afterwards I received letters and phone calls from Moscow inviting me to make an educational visit there. They were addressed to me at both schools. I replied that I would need to "discuss the coming Russian Federation with Yeltsin", and heard no more. A week later I heard that George Miller, whom I had met at the time of FREE, was now Yeltsin's secretary.

I visited Dr Hughes for an X-ray "which involved sitting with 30 others holding my clothes in Alexandra wing, and then watching 2 people go before me (to see Hughes) as I was consequently late for my appointment in Fielden House. Jimmy Denne" (the Conservative who ran my election campaign) "was there, with his wife in a neck-collar. Denne talked non-stop. Told me that Biggs-Davison always talked in code, e.g. 'I'm coming to Buckhurst Hill' meant 'Meet me at Loughton station'. Intelligence techniques. How he would melt away to meet Biggs-Davison, not telling anyone."

I felt increasingly separate from those around me. I wrote: "Vernon is preparing for his election campaign in Sheffield, and I am preparing to launch the new ism in philosophy which will replace Existentialism." I wrote: "The One is a dark Fire, and Light is the potential of existence."

I rang Michael Mann of Element and discussed Universalism and a Universalist Foundation, "with stated goals and objectives that can be measured and assessed, i.e. transforming all the disciplines and restoring the soul to British life....The idea that we are all part of one mankind in terms of universal energies, and that there should be transformation of business attitudes." I noted: "After my call to Michael Mann I had a great surge of Light which tingled my spine. The eternal is pleased with what I have done, and is encouraging me." Later, I wrote: "The ideal businessman, at one with the arts and the Universalist ideal."

On February 4th my god-daughter Elizabeth's confirmation took place at the parish church of St. James, Biddenham "which goes back to the 12th century and has stepping-stones across the graveyard under the cedar. Sat in the second pew from the front before a curved arch, Elizabeth on the outside. As godfather I had no responses to make; did not have to renounce evil. Frances on 'Living Lord', during Communion, wearing my gift of Nefertiti (a brooch), 'This will be my funeral hymn.' A surge of Light as Elizabeth had the sign of the cross in oil on her forehead. Another surge later after Communion. At the end, coffee and a chat with the Bishop of Bedford, and then back to the new conservatory to talk with all. Frances: 'We are reading your poems in bed, Richard says "Put the light out" and I say, "Wait a minute." We talk about your life.' Richard: 'And it's not literary interpretation.'" Philip Mawer was present, and I spoke with him.

There was an Oaklands Quiz night. The Fordhams, who sold me Coopersale Hall, attended.

I was still working on my TV programs, and I had an idea for creation as an act of love, which was the Big Bang. I wrote: "An orgasmic explosion of God, the Big Bang as an orgasm of love spreading out endlessly." It was an idea that haunted me as it could only have come out of the latent Fire. (Of the connection between energy and orgasms I wrote on October 27th: "Orgasms clear out the old energy and allow new energy to come in, like the inner harbour being cleared out.")

Judith Seelig was having sessions with White Bull (alias Ian Graham channelling the Red Indian source White Bull) and was being told that I belonged to "the White Brotherhood, from long before Charlemagne; an order that includes Christ....The three of us are in the vanguard army and give the Light." I wrote: "A name for my Foundation: the White Brotherhood? Cf the Holy Brotherhood I wrote to Campbell, history don at Oxford, about. As soon as I had written these words the Light flowed in, and is still flowing in as I dash this sentence off at 12.45 a.m." On February 5th Judith Seelig was burgled and her computer (nothing else) was stolen with details of her correspondence. The police Inspector told Judith that the break-in had the hallmark of a political one.

My new bank manager (Ken Jones) called. He told me that his predecessor, who backed my vision of Oaklands, had died in the Canary Islands. "He drowned. He seems to have had a heart attack while swimming. He was 57." He had waded out to swim and the call had come for him to return aloft and he did not come back. I wrote: "Ron Thomas dead, like Maxwell, drownded (sic). And what good was the training in reading accounts which Jeremy Mitchell (my accountant) gave him? He is keeping a bank in the portico to heaven."

On February 11th there was an odd incident. I was shot at twice, both times in the same place and an hour and twenty minutes between both attempts. I record the facts: "Worked on the TV series, and then (having made the arrangement over the phone yesterday, Monday) went to get it printed out in Barking. Just after the Loughton entry to the M11, around 4.45, I heard a crack, like a stone hitting my windscreen at great speed. There were no cars or lorries in front of me. My Lexus windscreen is very thick and I continued my journey and printed out. On the way back, at 6.05, it happened again, a crack, out of the dark, and a star appeared on my windscreen. There were no cars or lorries in front of me or overtaking. I was shot at twice. I went to the police and they examined the car and agreed and took details. Matthew, 'That would have gone through my windscreen.' Someone, who can hit a moving car, had shot at me at 4.45 and waited until I returned at 6.05, and had another shot, hoping to cause me to have an accident. Someone feels I have said too much and wants me out of the way. They know my Lexus. I am not one to commit suicide. Someone is arranging for me to have an accident, but I am protected....The second time was in the dark....I was the only one to report such an incident. The policeman: 'It wasn't casual or boys, they hit you in the dark, that's professional.' I have engaged energies that are causing me a problem. I need to bypass such energies and not engage them. Divine protection is there. So now it seems, I am to be murdered. I sit in my condemned cell. I will not brood about it, but will carry on as though it is not going to happen. I will concentrate on higher energies. I will continue to speak the truth, and will not be intimidated." Two days later I "got my windscreen replaced so now the bullet hole never happened." Judith rang to say that a Tarot reader had said "there is a connection between her burglary and my shooting (which was a warning)". The Tarot reader apparently commented on my "symbols and images". I received the information without believing it or disbelieving it.

The next day I met Tebbit. I wrote: "To Diana Collins (née Padfield)...at Garnish Hall, near the motorway. 1750 timbered house rebuilt, a leaping log fire in the inglenook beamed main room. Spoke with Bunny Morton (an old friend of Tebbit's)....Invited (Tebbit) to dish out some prizes. He: 'I might be abroad for four months.' On whether he will spearhead the election campaign: 'They haven't asked me yet. They're still angry because I opposed them over something.' Bunny Morton on how Howe was put up to assassinating Thatcher, by a group of senior Conservatives, because Thatcher wouldn't listen. Later, Tebbit on electioneering in the past. I: 'I saw Churchill speak from the Loughton war memorial. There was cut and thrust, repartee. It was like Speakers' Corner.' Tebbit: 'Yes, it was.' A lot of laughter." I asked Tebbit how the coming election would turn out, and he said: "The Conservatives will win, by 20." (In fact it was 21.) "I raised the removal of Thatcher and said that she had been ousted following a meeting at La Toja in the Canary Islands. This was received without comment.

I wrote: "Under divine law I am protected. Heather's point about right action, and lower forms cannot destroy higher forms. High energy sweeps aside low energy....I must live at a divine level and not come down to human level. I am like the Bodhisattvas who postpone their own enlightened Nirvana so they can put the world to rights, bring in new movements, debunk Derrida and Hawking so they do not have influence over the young."

We arrived in Cornwall to discover that Arthur Hosegood's wife had had a stroke, as had our sometime gardener David Williams. I returned to poetry: "Immediately settled to my poem on Bohm and placed in a couple of stanzas. Got the idea for a poem in which God looks at man and his universe. Drafted four stanzas. It is a good way of exposing the divine will – to have a poem in the mind of God. Drafted 8 stanzas that will go into this poem in all. Dozed and watched the winter Olympics on TV, got back to correcting my *Diaries*, and then went for a wonderful walk with Anthony

(Matthew having gone to bed, tired). The moon was a day from being full, the stars were out, the air was cold and bracing, the sea was fairly low, the tide coming in. Spoke to a boy fishing at the end of the harbour. He had caught 2 small whiting and pollack, and will fish all night." I wrote: "Have already moved from my human self to my divine self....The immortal divine me, not the human me. I live in close contact with Nature and the quantum vacuum down here. I need to live simply now, and not think about money, Conservatives, plots, shootings, etc....The bracing fresh air, coldish, this morning."

I observed that "living down here in Charlestown hasn't saved Alwyn from pneumonia....Betty told me...: 'She's hanging on. She's rattling terrible.'" Dick Larn told me: "She's thrashing around." I recorded: "Feb 17. Alwyn died at 6.30 p.m. The pneumonia took over."

Editing my *Diaries* for 1965 I "saw that I was rejecting the old materialistic, declining Western view in favour of a view I had yet to bring to birth, but which I was carrying in my spiritual womb: an anti-materialistic, metaphysical, optimistic Western view which I have now delivered and which is now almost fully grown up." And again: Looking back over 1965-6 from this vantage point in 1992, over 25 years later, I see that potentialities and tendencies then have become fully developed realities now: the poems are published; my spiritual theme has developed through my experiences of the Light in 1971 and afterwards; my preoccupation with history has become a fully worked out 'stages' theory; and I am a teacher of the real, speaking on it at Winchester in April. 1965-6 were the key years, for then I found my way, got myself on the right course."

I went for a walk with Anthony: "A full moon, our shadows on the harbour wall. A shooting star. The moon in the curl of the waves. Returned and wrote *Full Moon*, about the Light in the waves of history." I noted: "Had the idea of the orange tree from my *Journals* (*Diaries*). Remembered the orange tree by my gate in Libya and wrote *The Orange Tree*, which can be a good poem." I read that George Macbeth, with whom I danced up a Soho street, had died of motor neurone disease. I wrote: "I recall the slim Edwardian dandy who read at the Crown and Greyhound, Dulwich, in 1963, and the dancing fop I went out to dinner with in 1970 and who skip-danced up Dean Street, longish hair. I did not know it but he could have put my poems on the radio then; had I but asked."

A couple of days later I "stepped outside my front door and saw a rainbow to the right, inland, and a black cloud and sea-mist over Trenarren. Took gulps of sea air in fine rain that moistened my cheeks, sneezed three times, returned to our sitting-room and wrote *Rainbow* straight out. Yesterday wrote...*A Cornish Lady Dead*. (Now retitled, *An Old Cornish Lady Glimpses Reality*.)" That night "at 11.30 went for a late night walk with the boys. It was very cold and the tide was the longest out we had seen and the waves were rough. A full moon in the only opening in black cloud. Returned gulping fresh air, quite drunk with fresh air, cheeks and ears cold." The next morning: "Went to get the papers, saw a bare tree with four birds in, and stopped and wrote a poem on my knee, standing, at the top of the harbour midway between the museum and Don Austen's sale room....To lunch at Polkerris. Sat in the window....We walked along the pier and again

I felt I was about to be thrown off the high ledge of an Egyptian temple, and was quite panic-stricken until I could place my feet on the sand." I bought the green sward outside our Charlestown house: "Clapperton came round at 5.15 and stayed until 7.15 watching a boat come in although the cables are being damaged by the rough sea, fulminating at dog-owners who mess up his harbour, and almost inconsequentially agreeing our offer...for the strip in front of our house here, and the green sward and water pump/tap."

I returned to Essex via Shaftesbury and lunched with Michael Mann. I recorded: "Drove in Michael's car to the Coppleridge Inn, Motcombe (he lives in a valley, in a hamlet of 3 houses in fields) and he reacted to my interim draft for my lecture....'Unification of knowledge – those who are there know it already, whereas those who aren't there won't believe it.'...His suggestion that I should do a 140 page paperback of *The Fire and the Stones* (a simplified version), and his interest in my book of essays....Light lunch....Arrived home...to receive a letter from David Lorimer. The conference is oversubscribed and arrangements are being made to film the speakers in an adjoining hall – do I have any objection?"

I posted a parcel at Buckhurst Hill, "and on the way back to the car saw a weird apparition in a cycle crash helmet crouching and peering up at me from side to side. Thought he was begging and side-stepped him, to be intercepted again. 'Nutty Jones,' I cried, addressing him directly by his (Chigwell) School nickname. He kept me talking half an hour in a biting wind (I merely in a sweater), telling me about his inheritance and his foray into leasing. He: 'I've read about your exploits. You and Senton had brains, you and he made it by brains. He's got two factories in Belgium.'"

I rang Heather Dobbs and "said I am on the verge of 6 media (film, theatre, book, lecture, newspaper, arts movement). She: 'God acts in strange ways. It may take 2 lifetimes for your ideas to permeate.' I: 'Unless the media do it effortlessly.' She: 'That's the way of God. Soon you will not be able to go out without being recognised. Doesn't it alarm you, that you will lose your anonymity?'" She added later: "I can see the church in the Forest becoming a place of pilgrimage. You'll be buried there.' Buy the church in the Forest as the first Universalist church? I wrote: "My funeral service will be in Waltham Abbey, with committal in High Beach graveyard."

I observed: "Wrote *Two Clouds* between 7.30 and 7.35. An idea I had as I walked back from getting the papers in Cornwall on Tuesday or Wednesday; but then promptly forgot. It came to me from the beyond."

On February 27th I spent "all morning at Diverse Production, being asked questions about Egypt by Roy Ackerman and (less frequently) Peter Donebauer. Then Michael Wood of *Legacy* phoned....He knows of *The Fire and the Stones* and will do a series with me, perhaps. I said last August, during *Legacy* that he would be all right as my presenter – I rang Donebauer and said that – and now it is possible that I will be meeting him. He would want to write his script....Wood: 'I'd like to do a film on a brief history of God, showing all the gods from all the civilisations.'"

The Conservative Patrons Club had an evening with Douglas Hurd. I wrote: "Entered the Commons via St. Stephen's and found the foyer to the Churchill Room across the Central Lobby. Ordered wine. At well after 8 we were summoned to go in, and Hurd hurried down the corridor in DJ, and I greeted him at the door ('Nicholas Hagger') and felt his warm handshake, firm but gentle and full of energy. Sat...opposite Ann and beside a retired computer operator and his German wife. Paté, chicken and flan with cream. Our waitress upset the main salver and knocked my bottle of wine almost over Ann. Speeches. Vernon Davies's loyal toast, then his introduction of Hurd in terms of his books 'which may be out of print' and his work for Heath....Hurd: 'A good chairman mentions my books, an excellent chairman mentions their titles and you've still a long way to go.' On how his visit to Scotland was a rerun of his book *Scotch on the Rocks*. His analysis of the world. Alarming problems, and what are we to do? Help Russia or not? 'I spoke to Yeltsin last month. He had me down for half an hour in his diary and I spoke to him for two hours. He told me about his problems, no notes, very impressively, not as a showman.' After Hurd's address, 'Any questions?' and I stood up. 'Regarding the CIS, can Yeltsin solve his problems by forming a confederation?' Hurd's long reply, hoping he can. Later Norris spoke, replying to Hurd's jibe that there's always an argument going on when Norris is around, and 'he may be Prime Minister in my own lifetime'. His story of Hurd's hair (the woman who asked a question about it)." In the course of the dinner I was asked to predict the election result and I said: "The Conservatives by 20 seats." (The Conservatives won by 21.) I remarked to Vicky Norris that Hurd was 'trapped over dinner and not able to meet everyone over buffet'. Vicky: 'That's politics. Steven did him a favour and now he's returning it.'"

I now felt that consciousness is "on the electro-magnetic spectrum. We all have an infinite part of ourselves that can see the whole, and which brings to us a hierarchical level of understanding with a hierarchical vibrational level. The highest wave band for the highest level. Matter is frozen light, but energy holds matter in place by two polarities (yin and yang, positive and negative, male and female). The whole universe is alive with thought, understanding through the Light, which guides people together so that events happen in accordance with rising to a higher level, letting go of lower attachment...and manifesting into material form a universal being....The destruction of relationships and society in this process. The structure of God – we do not live in a materialistic universe but in a guiding thought-feeding universe whose structure is God."

I noted: "I am on a re-run of my 1970 attempts to have a poetry revolution. Then I had not had the development that has led to Universalism (it began in September 1971) and so it would have been a revolution to emphasise the transformational process and technique, not the fundamental universal being....1991, a new poetry revolution, like a higher stage of a winding stair 20 years later." The winding stair image haunted me, and I felt we were constantly remembering situations we had faced before, only higher up and better able to cope with them this time. I "took 2 or 3 copies of *Temenos* off the shelves and found them arid and precious. So much time spent in scholarship, and to what purpose? Articles for who to read? Judgements I often disagree with, e.g. Gascoyne being Europe's most important poet."

In early March I attended the Old Chigwellians' Shrove Tuesday dinner, not realising that a year later I would be the main speaker: "Arrived at BS1, glimpsed Nutty Jones and headed for the Swallow Room....To dinner. Sat next to Peter Banks in chairs Tim Norris had bagged and wined....Banks told me about how he killed people as a soldier." The speeches included one by Stanley Reed, who edited the Old Chigwellians' journal *The Mitre* and who was an ex-Mayor of Epping Town and who declared "how he first came to a Shrove Tuesday 52 years ago and sat down at the end, and it takes hard work and graft to get to top table up here". There were many laughs. Then Vernon Davies was introduced as "someone of great faith and hope, as you have to have if you're fighting Sheffield Central". Vernon talked politics, first on how Labour would attack schools like Chigwell, then on how the budget would give the Conservatives a majority at the coming election. There was muttering and some hostility. Vernon said: "I've said enough on politics." Someone called out: "More than enough." I realised that Vernon had become so politicised – a process I had begun – that he now saw an old boys' reunion as an appropriate forum for his hustings.

Francis Fukuyama, author of *The End of History?* had come to London. I knew it was not history that was ending, even in the Hegelian sense, but a stage of history. I wrote: "Fukuyama says that history has been proceeding inevitably to its end, when spiritual and material values create a Hegelian synthesis, a permanent world-wide American liberal democracy (American optimism). I say that history is composed of 25 civilisations which enshrine the vision of the contemplative mystic as the central idea and decay as they term secular; and that world-wide democracy is merely a stage, like stage 15 of the Roman Empire, which will pass when the phase moves on. The inevitability concerns the stage in the North American civilisation that North America is in; the spiritual values concern the central idea of the North American civilisation; and the world-wideness is a phase in a number of stages, not a permanent thing. (As was Communism.)"

On March 5th I went up to London and "saw Fukuyama, the Neo-Hegelian and admirer of Kojève, at the Logan Hall. The highly accomplished debate, all from a socio-economic point of view. Simon Jenkins, editor of the *Times*, spoke first and introduced Fukuyama, who spoke rapidly and fluently without notes, very impressively and clearly. Then the panel: Gellner, Scruton, Blackstone and Norman Stone. Two right-wingers, two left. The points went back and forward with some answering by Fukuyama. Afterwards, got Fukuyama to sign a book and gave him *The Fire and the Stones*. Had a word with Scruton and with Simon Jenkins."

Working on my lecture I thought about "Bede Griffiths's equation of God and Darkness" which had "made me aware of a crucial distinction between transcendence and immanence. The Godhead is transcendent in real nothing, latent Fire before the quantum vacuum. God is immanent as Fire or Light in the quantum vacuum, the universe of creation at both psychological and physical levels."

Judith rang me and said: "I saw...a stone with runic inscriptions within Fire, in the middle of Fire." I interpreted: "Originally the Fire was on the stone. In other words, the Fire is now surrounding the stone and getting it forward. The stone with runic inscriptions (hieroglyphs) is an image from my book, *The Fire and the Stones*."

Philip Mawer, the Secretary-General of the Church of England Synod, invited me to lunch "at Valello's next to Church House in Great Smith Street. Talk of Universalism and the Mystic Revival. He referred to 'spirituality' (which is Light) and pointed out that some in the Church are against syncretism and that one should avoid appearing inevitablist. I said it was a movement outside the Church which could move within the Church and regenerate the Church. He is 'putting the case' to Lambeth Palace and seeing if the Archbishop would like 20 minutes about the Fire or Light. He: 'There's suspicion of the New Age.'"

I defined spirit as "'The emanating or vital principle in man, which gives life to the physical organism; incorporeal or immaterial being (as opposed to body or matter), the soul which passes out of the body on death; incorporeal essence.' Also: 'the essential power of the Deity, the Holy Spirit.' Spirituality=Light." I wrote: "Spirituality...is a life directed by the will of the soul, i.e. universal being, so life is lived in harmony at a personal subjective level....Spirituality is measured by the degree to which spiritual values are embodied in a person's way of life and direct the actions or responses of the individual. Indications of spirituality include responsibility towards humanity, planet and all life, unconditional love, etc., including the power to intuit ideas, understand unknown realities and connect with meaning. Spirituality as soul-directed life."

Later I sat and thought about "the role T. S. Eliot filled, although tired, and suddenly there was a most tremendous surge of the Light energy, and I am renewed; I feel well again, am not tired any more, and am ready to tackle my lecture. The Light is within me, with the Light in my blood there is nothing I cannot do. The new movement emphasises the invisible; Universalism is a post-Romanticism and a post-Existentialism, emphasising the invisible but in terms of tides. David Lorimer and the 'Spirituality' group are meeting near Regent's Park to answer the question 'What is spirituality?', and I have just embodied the answer, with a tremendous influx of the Light, which has healed my tiredness, my exhaustion, in an instant, and purged away the density of Race Night, leaving me in the higher mind."

I visited the Seeligs to explain Universalism to a gathering of people who might help. I wrote: "The large house in St. Gabriel's Road, the mess at the back, carpet unhoovered, Joseph saying 'Come in to the mess.' Judith cutting garlic bread. The room with the fire. I introduced the idea to Patrick Hamilton (of the Florence Trust for artists) and his wife and White Bull and the Seeligs. The new Romanticism, the European Arts Festival, a new view of man and the universe. I spoke spontaneously and quietly and was listened to in attentive silence. The arrival of Lynne Franks and her husband, a small bespectacled Buddhist (like her). They employ 60 at their PR company and cover 29 families. Had to do some repeating. Joseph: 'The energies are going to change now, for sure.' Dinner in the dining-room. Huge table, enormous dishes, soup, pasta and mushrooms, red wine, rounds of meat, salad, ice cream, cheese, all separately. Judith: 'I can't eat, it's hard to cook when I can't eat.' I sat next to White Bull and Lynne....More talk about the idea. Lynne: 'Call it a Festival of Light; or Celebration of Light. Leave out all jargon words or clichés. Bring out the idea of a new movement in interviews.' Joseph, smoking his cigar, in his faded splendour, having inherited enough to keep his boys at private school, leading a raffish upper-class-in-genteel-decay life. Thinking I was not listening, 'Do you also think that the Fire doesn't exist?' (clapping his hand over his mouth as if he had said the unsayable, his wife being there)....Showed Patrick Hamilton the photos Fleur Beverley sent me. He: 'They're excellent, such energy. Yes, the Light in the world.' Patrick Hamilton: 'This must happen, I'll do anything I can to help.' The candles with crystals hanging from them....At the end, all left. Joseph and Judith sat in the elegant sitting-room near the embers of their fire....Patrick Hamilton couldn't sleep, he was so excited, and at 4.30 a.m. he got up and wrote things." Soon afterwards Hamilton proposed that we wrote to 4 papers to get support for an "event on creativity that emphasises its deepest springs in the Light".

Later I wrote down "the essence of my idea. There should be a presentation with an actor of a new development in the Arts, under the idea of the Light in arts. A new view of man in relation to the universe, in which universal energies flow into him, is currently in use, and this should be reflected as a new European movement called Universalism under a European heading: Celebration of Light. Paintings which show light from the beyond on modern cities, poetry reflecting the Light like mine. A new development not of technique but of view of man in the universe, which will be explained for everyday people."

There was another Metaphysical Research Group meeting at Oxford at Hertha Larive's. I wrote: "I dominated the group, referring everything to ontology and cosmology, epistemology and psychology, and Max (Payne) agreed. The only opposition came from Geoffrey Read, and after...I sided on intuition against Read's reason, and I distinguished the 'I' of the rational ego and the 'I' of his soul, I said in the end, 'When the Metaphysical Revolution happens, we will lock you up, Geoffrey,' and everyone laughed. The idea that science has split. Lunch....My talk of Universalism as the new movement....I found them attached to logic and sidelined it, centralised the intuitional, marginalised the logical."

There was a Heads' meeting in the staff room of a local school, Loyola: "14 of us sat around the edge of the room in comfortable or upright chairs and looked across a central table that was out of our reach, and discussed the General Election very seriously and eventually I lowered the tone, causing mirth with such remarks as: 'We've tried the State system and it's no good'; and at the end, after our chief rival Bancroft's had given out a leaflet with a wrong date on it ('It's Tuesday, not Thursday 27th'), 'Let it never be said that Bancroft's doesn't know what day it is.'"

Patrick Hamilton made contact. He had been to see Lord Palumbo of the Arts Council, about putting on an event to announce Universalism. I wrote; "Palumbo said to Patrick Hamilton that it would take a year to put on a production at the Royal Albert Hall. It will be a kind of opera, announcing Universalism."

Later I observed: "The Greek theatres were within the religion, the temple of Aesculapius being nearby at Epidaurus, the altar being in the centre of the stage. In Athens, the high priest of Dionysus was guest of honour at plays, and plays were part of the religious festivals of Dionysus. Athenian – and all Greek history has been secularized, and the period we concentrate on (Herodotus and Thucydides) is a secularized time of decline. Greek history has been presented in a secularized way."

A Syrian, Mona, rang me and took me to task for leaving out various Islamic saints in *The Fire and the Stones*, including Ibn Arabi, who is remembered by a mosque in Damascus. I pointed out Ibn Arabi is in the index. She said: "Your book is excellent, everything is there, you are a genius. I look for meaning, like Gilgamesh." I: 'It is to be found by making a transformational journey from the social rational ego to the soul or inner being.' A stunned silence. 'No one ever told me that. You are right. My whole life has been searching for meaning.'"

I attended a lecture on Lucien Pissarro by Nicholas Reed. Pissarro lived in Epping in the 1890s and painted several pictures of Coopersale Hall. Nicholas Reed later visited Coopersale Hall and identified one of his paintings (which is now in our prospectus), as being in the Coopersale Hall grounds, between Orchard Cottage and the walled garden. We stood together at the back of Orchard Cottage by the squash court, and he told me he had been at Worcester College, Oxford, like Steve Norris, and I felt it strange that all three of us should have passed through the same College and arrived here at Coopersale Hall.

We went to Cornwall. The first evening I was in on my own, and Arthur Hosegood knocked and "told me how peaceful Alwyn was when she died (she just didn't take the next breath) and how her face went back to normal after two disfiguring strokes on her left. I urged Arthur to be forward-looking after his grieving, to get his attitude right. He: 'I'm waiting for the summer.' He and Alwyn have been joint souls."

I observed: "Energy never tires. In our universal being we contact the Universal Intelligence and Source from the universe, the universal power. Geniuses produce a prodigious amount of work and never tire; and their minds grow more brilliant as they grow older. Temporary fatigue is when one deliberately severs contact with the universal energy or one would overheat, like a TV or oven that is never switched off, or pressure cooker." Later I went for a walk with my two boys: "Dark and no moon, told them there are two selves and that my greatest gift to them is knowledge of their universal being, greater than a Chigwell education; for Chigwell doesn't teach the second self, only the rational, social ego."

I worked on my lecture and Clapperton (the owner of the port) came round, asking me to buy the port for £250,000. I wrote: "His wheedling in my ear, tempting me like the Devil. 'All this could be yours.'" He said to me: "I'm asset-stripper, haven't you worked that out?" I was not tempted, seeing only expense caused by sea-damage, and little income.

We went for "a night walk. Dark, no moon, bright, twinkling stars. Stood for a long time with Anthony, craning my neck and looking into the universe." The next morning I woke early: "A glorious morning. Walked on the harbour, revelling in the early light on the calm sea....Everyone rejoiced in the sea. Returned and sat quietly over my breakfast tray in the front room, and wrote *Sunlight* (a poem). I am in my soul again....Business (my schools) is of the 5-sensory rational, social ego, whereas in Cornwall I am universal being..., which is like a cup of sea water taken from the sea. The soul is individual but also universal." That night I "went for a late night walk under bright stars, and wrote *Mystery*". The next day I wrote: "A sunny morning, a tranquil sea, and a reflection. Even the Black Head is reflected. My poem on Bohm is also a poem on Einstein, his foregoer. It is a sequel to *Against Materialism*."

Judith rang, having spent a fortnight in Greece, and said: "There must be a mystery school at Coopersale Hall. I have been given precise instructions as to what to say. You greet them, I prepare their bodies, make a temple, and then you bring down the Light." She said she had 120 people to contact. She proposed that we put on four days in May, inviting 35 a time.

Of Universalism I wrote: "Universalism and the Baroque are different stages (in a civilisation)....Universalism precedes the Baroque."

I wrote: "Ap 7. Last night, a walk with an overcast sky, and rain came as we stood on the end of the pier, Matthew, Anthony and I, and we had to hurry back to the house. This morning, a green and choppy sea at high tide, white surf dashing against the rocks, and a roaring of wind and booming of waves, quietly, as a backdrop to consciousness. It is a tense time, waiting for the election, waiting for my (Winchester) lecture, but I am serene, and am growing – even my nails have grown tremendously. Awoke this morning with the idea that the Light – a fifth expanding force – was responsible for inflation in the early universe, and wrote it in." I need to emphasise that the connection between the latent Fire or Light and cosmological inflation was received in sleep and was in my consciousness when I woke.

I thought about the different eyes we have: "The eye of the flesh uses empiricism (senses); the eye of reason uses rationalism (Colin Wilson); the eye of contemplation uses transcendentalism or universalism (Light). My quarrel with Colin Wilson is one of rationalism v contemplation. We both reject empiricism. As Kant found, the reason cannot reach the truth of contemplation."

My lecture, and the General Election, loomed. While I waited for my lecture, without saying a word Anthony put on a video of *Clockwise* "of John Cleese as a Headmaster going to give an important speech. His speech gets left on the wrong train, and the lecture ends with him being arrested by the police. I laughed a lot. Anthony's gift for bringing joy to a careworn philosopher's heart is worth more than all my reading – perhaps."

That evening two days before the General Election I attended a rally at the Cornish Carlyon Colisseum held by the Liberal Democrats: "'The largest meeting of our party since 1906' (the Party Treasurer)." Ludovic Kennedy spoke, saying that Kinnock might find he was in opposition for a fourth time. The local MP spoke. "Then the music beat and Ashdown arrived to handclaps. His half hour speech, touching on policies but not spelling them out. The fireworks and glitter and balloons, and Ashdown came up the aisle, and with his 'conscience and reform' ringing in my ears, I put out a hand on his arm, but did not shake his hand. Left with an impression of sadness, so much idealism and goodness but so little chance of getting full power. Ashdown: 'A vote for conscience is never wasted.' The lost cause of the Liberal Democrats. Something of the feeling of the barricades in the musical *Les Miserables*.

The next day I left a calm sea and returned to Essex. I recorded: "On the way had a new idea for the unification of consciousness and the spectrum. Our own brainwaves, 10-30 cycles per second, interfere with our contact with the spectrum, and it is only by going into radio silence and shutting down our own interference that we can open to the high frequencies higher up the spectrum, including the Light." At 10.35 I reflected on my lecture and wrote: "It's all down to the excitement I can generate." That night I followed the early results of the General Election. I wrote: "What I saw earlier this week has happened! Major has led the Conservatives back in with a clear majority..., pretty much the 20 Tebbit predicted in conversation with me at Garnish Hall. I didn't sleep much – got off at midnight and woke at 4, turned on the television and saw the scenes of celebration in Central Office. Five years of the best available rule for the country....Many problems have been removed, a cloud has been lifted; although for me it was never a cloud, I always knew it would be all right." The result was exactly as I had seen in my sleep on January 25th.

That afternoon, on little sleep, I drove to Winchester and arrived at 3.15: "Am in the Christchurch Lodge coach-house where the speakers are housed, now at 5.55, waiting to return my list of slides, acetates and film after a rehearsal under a glaring light. Am fairly centred. Need one more session after dinner. Feel calm and am coping with a threatening sore throat with pinelyptus pastilles, which seem effective. It is all down to the energy and excitement I can channel. I need help from the Light."

I appeared at dinner, which was packed – the conference attender turned teacher – and sat at top table with Sir George Trevelyan and other speakers. David Lorimer introduced my lecture and spoke of *The Fire and the Stones* as a "monumental work". I then stood at the podium and delivered the lecture, dazzled in a blinding light as my words were carried by live TV to a different hall. There were nearly 500 listening in all. My lecture was essentially the first third of *The Universe and the Light*. I ignored Trevelyan's hearing aid which whined intermittently, and described my approach to a Theory of Everything which included the metaphysical Reality of the Light. I touched on the Metaphysical Revolution I had declared in 1991, and Universalism. I was not afraid to be unpopular, and with the ancient octogenarian Father Bede Griffiths sitting in the audience with the straggly long hair and beard of a guru I insisted that God as immanent is present as Light, and that it is God transcendent who is darkness, non-being. (Later in his monk's robe, Griffiths said God is beyond all imagery and symbolism, insisting that God is darkness, but the Light is not symbolic or metaphorical.) I also insisted that the future is American, that the North American civilisation will be strong and that there is not about to be a new Indian civilisation (Griffiths being connected with India). At the end I wrote: "Have finished my lecture. It was a triumph. Several said, 'Tour de Force.' Two said, 'Brilliant presentation.' Several said, 'How did you get all that together?' The breadth. Donebauer there." Peter Donebauer reported that a lady had said to him: "How did that nice Mr Hagger manage to speak so long without his voice being affected, does he do throat exercises?" At the end I stood and answered private questions and met Adrian Cairns, a Quaker who would invite me to the Quaker Universalist Group. The speakers were invited to drinks. We all stood with a glass of wine in our hands – not Griffiths, who had gone to bed – and I wrote: "Liberman pro and going to speak about my spectrum idea tomorrow. 'I haven't got anything prepared, I used to spend months writing it all out – for others, what about me?'" Griffiths' German translator was present and "chided me for going with the Light instead of the darkness behind the Light, which is filled with love – and Zen has dismissed Light as imagery, he said. I challenged his ideas."

Mark Lazarus, former director of the Wrekin Trust, was present at this gathering, and he told me: "I built the Wrekin Trust up from nothing to £100,000 and my successors wasted it on the wrong conferences and a building programme. They thought they could do it better than me." He asked me: "'How did you do it?' I: 'Poetry is a great cross-disciplinary thing, one poem and you need to go to philosophy, history, science – like T. S. Eliot's *Four Quartets*.' He said: 'I wondered why I had given 15 years to the Wrekin Trust but now I see it was to make you possible, to be a hand-maiden to your Metaphysical Revolution.'"

The next day I meditated under Bede Griffiths, "whose underling began at level 1", and "breakfasted with (Professor) John Barrow (author of *Theories of Everything*). I: 'Where do love and order come into your mathematics?'"John Barrow was not prepared to go outside his area of cosmology, the materialistic level. I commented: "He has defined his prison, and everything beyond that is speculative. He isn't interested in a theory of everything; only in a theory of cosmology." I wrote: "His youth, his talk about his visit to 10 Downing Street. Thatcher asked him about the fifth force. Discussed brain waves and the spectrum with Peter Fenwick. 'It's difficult to prove.' I: 'Find a way.' Later, he: 'I need to buy a machine from America or Germany for £1.5 million.' I: 'We'll write to the Prime Minister.' (Which we will do – to establish that global mind can come in at 4 cycles per second.)" Of the day's lectures I noted: "Barrow's brilliant mathematical talk – all at one level. Rational, not contemplative. Bede Griffiths on unity. Lunch. Many said to me that my talk was comprehensive and clear." I had teased Jacob Liberman about his unpreparedness. He had said to me, "I just turn up and see what's happening and speak." In the event it worked well. He sat casually on a stool and talked about his life and brought the eye into it, his talk went down well. Lazarus held up Trevelyan's poetry reading with an unscheduled speech on the danger of needing enlightenment. Over dinner I questioned him about this and "it turned out he thought it was from the reason". The evening session involved a poem by William Anderson, author of a book on Dante, and Clive Hicks's photographs. Afterwards I spoke with some of the rank and file. Rita Parr wanted me to preach the Light rather than describe how it works. I drew a distinction between being evangelical and being descriptive. Bronwen (Lady) Astor asked me sign a book for her, and I recalled her radio talk and my earlier visit to Cliveden before the Profumo affair. I wrote: "Her chat about Cliveden and the Profumo Affair. 'I married Bill in 1960, the autumn. Stephen Ward gave me the creeps, as soon as I saw him.' I: 'He was working for MI5 and the organisation that planned the Profumo Affair.'" I told her the Affair was "either caused by American financiers wanting to overthrow Macmillan (as they later overthrew Thatcher); Russians trying to compromise Profumo to get rid of Macmillan so they could (after poisoning Gaitskell) put in...Wilson; or MI6 (the SIS) who used Stephen Ward to entrap Ivanov with (Christine) Keeler – Profumo blundering in." Then there was a Scientific and Medical Network reception. Hertha Larive said: "Colin Wilson had so little understanding of Steiner's ideas. It was just a biography with some comments." The day ended, "a day when I was higher than most of those who attended, who seemed to be at a lower level than Wrekin Trust audiences".

The next morning there was an "indifferent meditation (Trevelyan relaxing all parts of the body and going into the stillness)" and I "breakfasted with Bede Griffiths. Discussed the Light with him. I: 'There are two traditions, an eastern one of Gregory of Nyssa and Dionysius, which is yours, and a western one of Augustine, Gregory the Great and St. Bernard, which is mine. The first is transcendent, the second immanent.' He agreed. I: 'Is there anyone else in the Christian tradition who is doing what you're doing, after Thomas Merton?' He: 'No.' I: 'Did you think you'd end up like this when you went to India in 1957?' He: 'No.' (Shaking his head.)" Later Griffiths gave another lecture "in which he repeated that God is all behind all difference. On transcending dualism, getting behind good and evil is not monism (because of different gods) but non-dualism (advaita)." I commented: "Compare the (Zen) great zero." After lunch there was a question and answer session, and William Anderson said that my Grand Unified Theory is right. I had several discussions with different people and then drove back to Cornwall.

In the practical sanity of Charlestown I asked myself: "What did I achieve at Winchester? I sorted out the immanent and the transcendent and fixed a scientific theory....I'm identified with Universalism and the Metaphysical Revolution....I to someone: 'If we don't have a revolution in philosophy now, it'll be unchanged for the next 20 years.' I am on the side of change. Bede: 'Get beyond all difference and conflict to the unity behind diversity.'" I wrote: "Syncretism – the doctrinal coming together. Universalism – coming together at a level behind the doctrine." At 8 a.m. the next morning I realised I had not been fully well during the conference: "Hawked and spat at 8 a.m., and coughed up a long trail of sputum that was filled with blood; a long line of blood."

"A review of the weekend conference," I wrote. "It was unbalanced. I combined scientists and mystics; Barrow gave a view of cosmology in terms of advanced mathematical equations; Bede Griffiths saw science in terms of mysticism. But then (apart from Liberman's view of the Light as programming the pineal gland) it became unbalanced with two poetic offerings (Trevelyan and William Anderson) and more mysticism (Bede Griffiths) and art (Thetis Blacker) and it needed someone at the end to draw things together. The word 'vision' echoed through the conference, the vision of the Light, and Bede Griffiths confused it all by insisting that everything is imagery except for the darkness, i.e. everything immanent is imagery in terms of the transcendent. We have to deal with the immanent, that is the point. Points that came up: the veil or shutter between rational ego and universal being. The eye of contemplation being higher than the eye of reason. Goethe, 'Open up the second shutter so more light can come in.'...Syncretism is of little value, Universalism is the unity behind all differences – syncretism is merely at the level of forms."

I again glimpsed a book, *The Metaphysical Revolution*: "Reconciling the immanent and transcendent and covering the various disciplines touched on in my lecture. Part One: overview of reality, how universal being connects with the ultimate reality beyond all personal Gods. Part Two: the differences, a survey of all the disciplines that are being affected by the letting in of metaphysical reality, including the 'isms'. Part Three: the unity behind and how this renews the European civilisation. Include America v Third World. (Part One to include something on how religions are the motor forces or dynamos of civilisations.)"

On Tuesday April 14th I revisited a slightly careworn Colin Wilson with Pam and Paul. I wrote: "I told him about my Winchester lecture and gave him a tape....I did most of the talking." Pam discussed the moors murderer Ian Brady with him at some length, fairly obliquely. I gathered Brady had written to Wilson. Outside, Pam said: "Oh dear, he's surrounded by evil forces, all these serial killers." I wrote: "We talked on morals, how the Light makes you naturally good and how you have to take a stand against evil or forgive it, like Lord Longford. Pam: 'Why do you expect him to be a philosopher?'I: 'Because in the 1950s he challenged British insularity with Continental literature – German, Russian, French – and said "I am the new Existentialist", and he wrote *Introduction to the New Existentialism* and other works, and I know the goal he set himself. I hope there's still something there, some inspirational energy." Paul said Wilson has not got New Age credibility because he writes about serial murderers.

My lecture over, I thought intensely about the origin of the universe and got my mystery school under way. This process began with my discovery that my bronchiectasis had reactivated. Dr Hughes rang me at 11 p.m. one night and said: "You have a flare-up of your bronchiectasis. A long coil of sputum filled with blood would have collected overnight. You may have patches on your lungs."I wrote: "Ap 15. A bit more sputum with blood."

Steve Norris, my tenant, was made Parliamentary Under Secretary for Transport, a Junior Minister.

I recorded: "Stumbling across the (*Diaries*) entry...which inspired *The Silence*, got the idea for a new poem, which will be called *The Second Coming*. Part 1. The universe and man, true context, beginning with the Light judging the modern materialistic city à la Fleur Beverley. Part 2. Rational, social ego, how man is living at the wrong part of himself and is not aware of the waking; how he is individual (particle) not relationship (wave). Part 3. The judgement on wrong living by the incarnation of the universal self. This happens on an Essex hill. Part 4. Moving beyond, how society is to be led beyond Yahweh and Allah; differences and dualism to unity; the unity of all mankind. Part 5. Universal being. Write this. Imagery: Light/Darkness. Part/whole. Separate/connected. End, man not ready for the Second Coming,his body must become a temple. Include 'soul', that

673

perspective." I suddenly approached a Theory of Everything: "A Theory of Everything. If the Fire (F) manifests (m) at different intensities (i) according to the receptivity (r) of matter – and positioning of matter – then the variability (v) is to do with varying wave-lengths (wl) of the Light (or Fire). $Fm=i+r$. So $i=Fm/r$.....If Light, L (high frequency)+wle (wave-length of electrons)=v (variability), then $v=L/wle$. So it comes down to frequencies and wave-lengths. Express the whole thing in one beautiful and simple equation. The Light is universally present everywhere."

Of universal philosophy I wrote: "that the material world is permeated by a transcendent reality: the Tao, sunyata, Brahman, al Haqq, Godhead. This is related to at an immanent level as Light."

Soon afterwards I stood outside, "a bracing land-wind tugging at hair and bringing red to the cheeks. At 7.45 a boat came in. Knots of shivering people watched it. Having finished editing the first 100 pages of the *Diaries* (to 1965) I watched....Walked with Ant under a full moon. Pondered whether or not there is a singularity in terms of the Fire, and answered Ant's questions: 'What's so special about Japan?' I: 'In India, China and Japan you can find the wisdom of the East, people who know that there is something invisible behind physical reality; whereas in the West that knowledge has died out after the Romantics.' He: 'I don't know what I want to do.' I: 'You'll find it. It's a seed in you, it'll unfold.' He: 'I want to be happy.' I: 'You don't find happiness by seeking it. You find what you're here to do and what you like doing, and happiness is a by-product. That's the wisdom of the East.'"

I thought about the origin and creation of the universe and wrote: "There is a pre-existing infinite and metaphysical darkness or quantum void with potentials of Light, out of which came one virtual particle or proton which expanded by inflation in accordance with space-time laws which were (potentially) in the pre-existent quantum vacuum before the beginning. Once the beginning happened, all particles are interconnected and entangled by Light, i.e. a computer or brain of Light. There is a unifying superlaw which makes the whole universe necessary, and it is consistent with quantum mechanics and relativity." I rang Gunzig in Belgium and he again invited me to a conference for 30-40 international physicists in a castle in Belgium, and I was tempted to go "to sort out the question of singularity and inflation and how galaxies formed out of the Fire which was a darkness in a transcendent formlessness and the Light as an immanent fifth force." I stated my view again: "An infinite Fire with transcendent laws to create in one 'corner' of infinity a finite (?) universe from the quantum vacuum in which souls can leave unity and brotherhood and take on the differentiation of bodies and tasks and grow. The pre-existing laws of Nature include a law of expansion or inflation, with a mathematical exactness for a fine-tuned creation of the planets and stars; a law of microworld and macroworld gravity; and three other forces; and various regularities. All this can be expressed in a simple formula, which includes constants for all particles and forces, and explains the hidden variability of the microworld; and the ratio of the mass of the electron to proton; and includes non-local superluminal particles which defy relativity theory, that nothing moves faster than the speed of light. The universe began as Dante said in an infinitesimal point of light, and this could have been an orgasmic explosion of love. The singularity could be of infinite limit. The universe is a giant organism."

News came through of the discovery of "a wispy cloud, a ripple of matter, 'on the edge of the universe', seen from the rocket looking for CBR, proving that the Big Bang happened." I thought again about a Theory of Everything. I had been to see Norman Wisdom at Harlow, and marvelled at his affecting combination of laughter and sadness as he played the fool, and I wrote: "Laughter and sadness must be a part of the Theory of Everything." I wrote again: "The discovery by COBE that there are ripples of matter in the universe, that the Big Bang led to primordial seeds of galaxies, to matter being attracted into stars by gravity....My work has anticipated this. The CBR (cosmic background radiation) features in my poems as important, and my Winchester talk has asked where love and order come into this materialistic scheme. Bohm's view of the universe is that it is infinite. Is this still right? Or am I the new presenter of order in terms of the metaphysical Fire or Light behind the Big Bang? The origin of the universe was not a Big Bang but an expansion of thought. It is stated in externals, but needs to be stated in internals."

As I prepared to open the mystery school I wrote: "I have to do two opposite things at the same time. Be in the soul or universal being in Epping, and be in the contemplation-led reason, at the intellectual (i.e. rational) level, which I must do to keep the academics happy. I can do both but must clearly distinguish reason from contemplation from empiricism....Speak to the top 10% and let them see your other side, your soul. Poetry: in the soul, not the rational, social ego. The oneness between the two: the wordless reception of the soul reflected in words. Poetry as the language of the soul. Scientists are encroaching into areas they are not qualified to pronounce on, and their theories of (materialistic) everything diminish human values....I do not oppose science and human values; rather I seek to reconcile them in a metaphysical Theory of Everything. Philosophy has fallen under the sway of science and must break out of it. Even religious people are saying that God is a symbol now, following the discovery. The mantle has passed to me and my Epping centre. It is a base for soul and contemplation. Reason on the lecture platform outside."

I thought again about the origin and situation of the universe: "The universe began from an 'infinitesimal point' (Dante), a pinhead, and inflation happened. That is sorted out. What remains: infinity. Hawking's later idea of no singularity – no beginning and no end – is wrong." Although there was an eternal latent invisible metaphysical Fire without beginning and end, before it manifested into the visible. "Infinity is a question of language: is it curved or is it a plane? If curved then technically infinite. Also the question of nothingness, the vacuum, before the Big Bang, out of which came a virtual particle that exploded; God as transcendent nothingness (darkness) and as immanent Light during the time of creation (35 billion years). The Light is the temporal form of the Dark Fire, which is eternal; compare Dark Matter. $+A(Light)+A(Darkness)=Zero$. Or $+A(Nothingness, Void, Darkness)+-A(Light)=Zero$. Nothingness as a womb. I think I have all the answers without needing to attend the conference on the Origin and Structure of the Universe, which will be at the materialistic level."

The Scientific and Medical Network held a dining club dinner at the Hale Clinic's premises, 7 Park Crescent in London. David Lorimer, Peter Fenwick and Teresa Hale all co-hosted the occasion, and some 25 were invited, rather like the 1890s poets' Rhymers Club only emphasising spirituality and science. I chatted with Rupert Sheldrake, "tousle-headed Sheldrake, like a rather dissolute and slightly inebriated Romantic poet, his hair curly and long", who had heard about my Winchester presentation. I told him "about Universalism. He: 'I associate it with mechanistic physics.' I: 'How dare mechanistic physics use it when it has meaning in history and religion.'...Sheldrake, when I spoke of revolution: 'I quite agree, I believe in hurrying it along. Your book is daunting.' I: 'I've been asked to do it in 145 pages and 200 pages, but to make mystics the centre of history you need evidence.'" Later Arthur Ellison, formerly of the Psychic Research Society and friend of Koestler, came and had a long talk about the Light and said he would like to come to Epping. He said: "We construct reality, arrive at our paradigm which perhaps does not correspond to what is out there, and we won't listen to anything else. There's still a lot I don't know. The dead are around like presences but not in space."

I attended a public debate at Logan Hall, Bedford Way, London, which showed part of the film made on Hawking with Hawking present. I wrote: "Tim Radford of the *Guardian* hosted the occasion with much hesitation and stuttering. Hawking wheeled himself on, a pale figure in his red chair, his head motionless, and made a pre-prepared speech from his voice synthesiser, welcoming the ripple discovery as confirming his no boundary principle. Part of the film of his book was shown, and then he answered four pre-asked questions: the distribution of galaxies goes on for ever; time-travel back in time doesn't work because the quantum fluctuations are too large ('no hoards of tourists from the future invade us'); according to relativity we began in singularity but according to quantum maths there are no singularities, at least in imaginary time; 'COBE has confirmed the inflationary universe and my no boundary principle'. Quantum's uncertainty principle says energy can't be defined so it can be negative and then positive for a while, allowing it to escape from a black hole. 'Do you believe in God or are you a Humanist?' He: 'Like Einstein I use the term God in an impersonal sense, as an embodiment of the laws of physics or the answer to the question, "Why does the universe exist?"' Then, independently, he wheeled himself off after final applause. It was like being in the presence of Galileo or Newton. Penrose's crunch gave him the idea of reversing it to get back to the Big Bang." Later I observed: "The effect of Hawking is a gentle, independent person with a delightful personality and sense of humour, still seeking to explain the universe, excited at the time we live in. And what has he explained? The Big Bang came out of an infinitesimal point, that the laws of physics operate without singularity and space-time is finite without boundaries; that inflation made the universe infinite as it is curved; that black holes emit radiation; that the Big Crunch is wrong. All done like an entertainer working an audience for laughs. Hawking and the Pope who told him not to investigate the Big Bang, which is Creation. Key figures of our time: the Queen, Hawking, Bacon, Eliot, etc."

While thinking about outer space I was also aware of the earth: "An earth goddess feels the pain of the earth and sees trees and a flowing river when she climaxes. The orgasmic power of the earth: earthquakes."

I was working on *What is Universalism?* and wrote: "A great energy. Worked to 1 a.m. Feel very well. (Brought the Light down this afternoon.)"

Kathleen Raine sent "me a leaflet saying that the perennial philosophy has been 'the ground of all civilisations, including our own, until the last few hundred years', and that 'Reality is always itself'. It is the Fire or Light which is the central idea of civilisations, not the perennial philosophy alone. Kathleen Raine...invokes my vision while denying the Light, and is therefore 'emasculated'."

"What is a mystery school?" I asked. "A school that guards a mystery, where a mystery is taught in an open and shared way – inner knowledge. We are spreading outwards and ripening our civilisation. It is not exoteric but esoteric, but the vision is needed by our civilisation and will become the orthodoxy of the American civilisation. *Temenos* is an academic movement involving the understanding of the social, rational ego; Universalism is a philosophy and new movement involving the opening of the soul."

I contrasted my way and Hawking's: "Hawking. A frail Beckett-character in a wheelchair, speculating about the universe, mighty reason in a jamjar. Poignant, pessimistic but heroic and humorous. Samuel Beckett would have been interested in Hawking. And I, what am I? An equally powerful archetype in my own way. Mystically experiencing the one behind the universe, starting movements, inspiring people, capturing their imaginations, defying mortality, going beyond our earthly limitations, reaching out to a spiritual life that continues beyond the grave, recovering human immortality. My way is the opposite of Hawking's. He is proving our futility. Whitehead: 'Scientists who spend their lives proving it is purposeless constitute an interesting subject of study.'" Later I saw the film about him on television in full, and wrote: "A nice man with a heroic disposition and – it has to be said – some ideas that are not right."

Judith visited Coopersale Hall to see the facilities for our first day, and I told her: "There is not going to be a great change in human consciousness. We are renewing European civilisation, making a strong stage 43, and eventually our Universalism will go into the American civilisation and become a world-wide movement."

I thought about language in relation to the soul: "Language is of the rational, social ego; the soul is wordless. So poetry is a recollection of soul experience, with contemplative use of language blending with images from the outside world." I also observed: "Kathleen Raine told me last year she separated her poetic and academic sides, so that no one could criticise her academic side in relation to her poetry. I have chosen to combine them; so that the Fire of my poetry is the centre of my academic side. (Her excuse for not mentioning the Fire, that the poetic and academic have to be separated.)"

On the May Bank Holiday I "walked to the Strawberry Hill pond from the first pond (Earl's Path) in the afternoon. There were hundreds of tadpoles in both ponds; by the bank of the first pond and by the fallen tree in the second pond. Wind but no newts. Two coots and 6 fluffy chicks on the first pond, a duck and 8 chicks on the second pond. A mallard flew overhead, flapping slowly, and I wondered how men could oppose Nature by bringing it down with a gun."

There was a meeting of local State schools at the Epping Post House Hotel, and somehow Coopersale Hall was invited. It was chaired by the ex-Mayor of Epping Town, Gloria Platt, and I wrote: "Gloria Platt...began by saying 'We have problems' and Frances Best and I exchanged looks. The problems concerned the jargon from County Hall and the difficulty of getting Governors, and I proposed that they opt out and join us. This did not go down very well, and they thought I was serious....The independent school Heads are relaxed and mix gales of laughter and good humour with serious points. The State school Heads are haunted and hag-ridden, and are not accustomed to mixing humour and serious discussion at all."

The first Foundation of the Light mystery school day took place on Saturday 9th May. Most of those who came had been found by Judith, and so we did a double bill. I wrote: "In the afternoon received 42 people and spoke...for half an hour, then had a sound session with Judith, and then did a meditation, to bring down the Light. A very successful meditation. One from White Eagle Lodge went into the Light straightaway. Another, whose flat is hosting me on Wednesday, was opened very powerfully and had swollen fingers. Answered questions from 4.25 to 5 and again soon after until 5.45. Only two discordant notes: one from an intense young man David, who said I am too afraid of being regarded as a guru...and one from Katherine, who felt we are trying too hard. (You have to 'try' to get behind the rational, social ego and then you surrender. Judith had told her not to try.) I could be a guru, but don't want to be. Felt Judith is confusing, e.g. her insistence on the earth....Mona: 'You are my God.'...The overall impression: Judith Seelig and I pulling in opposite directions." I received phonecalls saying that Judith's words had not prepared them for the Light, and that I should "do it for yourself, by yourself". Christine the temple-dancer said: "I am just a channel, I do it by feeling; there is nothing intellectual, it's just practical, no question-and-answer session. Judith's 'eyes open' approach is wrong.'"

I had a long talk on the telephone with Edgard Gunzig about the universe: "The discovery proves that Dark Matter is there, whose density is unknown. 10^{-6}(where the discovery was made) suggests Dark Matter. Galaxies' seeds probably grow from inflation as microscopic seeds inflated to galaxies' seeds. 'Everyone is working on this.' There is increasing entropy within an increasing expansion. The universe is not a closed sphere as the Smoot and Mather picture showed but an open hyperboloid or plane. (There are 3 families in geometry: homogeneous sphere, hyperboloid or plane)....I see an infinite quantum vacuum, open, not closed; instability which is bound to create virtual particles; real particles which make inflation...; small microscopic seeds becoming seeds of galaxies in the macrocosm; and endless expansion of Dark Matter. No closed universe like a balloon from an infinitesimal point, no Big Bang; just a hot beginning which can create inflation. In short, there is a vast quantum vacuum, a sea of energy, which is filled with Fire or Light. My having Gunzig to ring is like T. S. Eliot having not Einstein (who is Hawking) but Niels Bohr, who proved Einstein wrong. What a poem the *Four Quartets* would have been if Eliot had been able to ring Bohr about quantum theory."

The day at Epping had led to further questions about our tradition. I wrote: "My tradition is that of St. Augustine and Dante and Shelley and Eliot and many others; it is of the intellectual vision, which is the soul's union with the Light which opens the heart centre and fills the soul with love so it says 'Aah'. It is from the top down. Judith's tradition is a modern one from the heart up, the heart centre; from the bottom up – a Tantric Hindu tradition. From the top down and from the bottom up we are two traditions and our union is powerful." Some had opened to the Light but said nothing. "Heather Dobbs said: 'Linda says she can read and understand better now, after Saturday.' I: 'Remember Hildegard, who could understand the breviary and the *New Testament*?' Heather: 'Yes. It's the same.'"

On 13th May there was another practical session. I wrote: "Went to Hampstead to Susie's flat in Eton College Road, NW3. About 11, and me. Anthea chaired it. Sound from Judith – two notes, one low, one high – and then, with the window open and birds singing and traffic going by, in fading light, at dusk, I held a talk and a 50 minute meditation. Several opened to the Light (Susie, Metz, Annie and David), and after tea there was a discussion until 10.30....The whole was done without a note. I am totally unprepared and just let it come through." Susie sat glassy-eyed and swollen-fingered, having hugely received the Light. Peggy Howard later took issue with my interpretation of the Light, saying it comes from "beings" and is a neutral, not a good force. I said: "The mystical tradition says it is good and safe, and the occult tradition says it is dangerous. By what authority sayest thou these things? By occult rather than mystical authority." I rejected her occult view of the Light, saying that God is good and not neutral, that God *is* the Light, which does not come from beings.

The local independent schools Heads' meeting was at St. Aubyn's. I recorded: "Talk in the library. It took me 30 seconds to reduce the serious meeting to farcical chaos: 'Did you say you want us to run round the field now?' (Deliberately misunderstanding Harold Colley's opening remark about the fields.) Everyone laughed."

I recorded: "A letter from Judith about connecting the body to Nature (air and food, yoga and sound); and about connecting with the inner light which attracts the Light. I see it differently. The Light comes in and lights the candle of the soul. Judith is trying to arrive at the inner light via the body, by purifying the body and connecting it to Nature (the Essene way). She thinks the inner universal self is a light. I see the inner universal being as a wick of a candle waiting to be lit by an influx of Light from the beyond."

The squabbling over how the Light works disillusioned me. I wrote: "I have got a movement going, and should return to history and writing, leaving others to spread what I have begun as a movement and indulge in doctrinal differences. The Light is not the self. Rather the self is lit by the Light and becomes divine. There is a divine seed within everyone, but it only germinates in sun. It is not a self-centred or self-absorbed journey. There is God in everyone: potentiality to be illumined by God. Within is a 'spark of the soul', an inward divine principle. The spark must be differentiated from the Light, which illumines the soul and makes it shine out into all the world. Distinguish the potentiality from the realisation. The divine in man from the Divine, the uncreated Light, which fills the soul with the Absolute." Later: "Discussed the course on Sunday with Judith. Laid down the 'doctrine' that we have a divine potential for Light, a spark in the soul, which the Light ignites, so it needs mystic acts to bring it in and light us up. Judith: 'It's like a pilot light.' I: 'That may be too strong. We have not got an inner light that is constantly burning behind veils. We have a candlewick, and it needs to be lit by letting in the Light. This can happen consciously or spontaneously."

The next Foundation of the Light mystery school day took place at Coopersale Hall on Sunday 17th May. I wrote: "18 seekers this time; one from Brussels, one from Bristol, several from Wiltshire and Dorset. Susie opened to the Light for the third time in a week and had swollen fingers, as did Heather. Mona was radiant. Healed her painful back and head. Several had slightly painful areas of their bodies. Adrian invited me to address a conference of Quakers in April; in Birmingham." Earlier Judith had a favourable reception for her chanting. As I left "Steve Norris put his head over the gate as I locked up and told me the new Worcester College Provost is Derek Smethurst (PPE), and that he is lunching with him tomorrow". The general consensus was: "All my questions were answered, I found it very helpful and useful." Adrian Cairns spoke of me as a Steiner, which I did not want to be; having rejected gurudom – there was a line of people with problems who would have liked to depend on me if I had allowed them – and having placed myself in the mainstream as the communicator and practical illustrator of an idea central to our culture and civilisation.

I invited David Seaman, the Arsenal goalie, to open the Coopersale Hall fête. We discussed his omission from the England team. I wrote: "He: 'I'm disappointed.' I told him that he was no. 1 under Robson, and said Taylor's come in with new ideas but that he must play so well Taylor can't leave him out. 'You believe in yourself, you're determined, so you must do it this season.' 'I will. I'm disappointed but I must get on with it and make sure he can't leave me out.' 'The selection is wrong.' 'Yes,' he said, 'Yes.'"

On May 19th I recorded: "Sketched the beginning of *What is Universalism?*, an essay. Looking back at the earlier years of these *Diaries*, I am struck by how my advances in thought succeeded visits to the dentist and routine outings. I think I have captured the way the creative life works. One has to be alone and apart from one's contemporaries to produce such a body of work. One has to be unknown as well; otherwise one's life is an endless procession of meetings with people with names, and what one thought of them, not Yeatsian 'remaking of self' at all. I could now become a talker, holding court at Coopersale Hall every Sunday or every other Sunday, and answering questions every Monday evening like David Bohm. A certain amount of this may have to be done, just as Whitehead did – and Socrates – to get the message across. But I am fundamentally a writer and poet who has created a new metaphysical being in myself by my Existential actions and reformations of attitudes over the years. An article on Christopher Fry in the press, the forgotten verse dramatist. Have I not a verse drama about a metaphysical revolutionary in the past? Who would make a good subject for a play? Who in the past had a metaphysical revolution? St. Bernard, who had an active role with the Templars and a Moslem enemy? Who else has had a metaphysical revolution? Plato? Fix on a hero like Becket, one who renewed the Fire of European civilisation. St. Augustine? Compare his *City of God*."

I visited Dr Hughes "about my bronchiectasis. The blood I coughed in April in Cornwall...is a 'cast', a long worm-like thread of phlegm and blood. X-rays show I am now clear."

I had to ring Tebbit's secretary about prize day: "Learned Tebbit...will not be able to give out the prizes. I said how impressed I was by his election forecast of the Conservatives by 20. She: 'That's not what we were saying during the campaign in this office.' I: 'I thought that what he said at Garnish Hall was a scientific judgement and all that followed was an illusion, with a hue and cry about nothing.' She: 'No.' So Tebbit doubted his own bravado."

I had a strange dream about Sartre. "Dreamt I was under siege in Palestine(?), and we climbed out of caves with rooms through holes, which were filled in, almost preventing my return. Helped take Sartre some food. Had a long chat with him. Asked him if T. E. Lawrence had asked him about Existentialism. 'Yes.' I: 'He was the first Existentialist. No....' And we both said, 'Nietzsche was the first, and Kierkegaard.' Sartre was there out of good faith, the opposite of 'mauvaise foi'. He and I went for a walk during a lull in the hostilities, and he regarded me as an equal. I woke up feeling I had communicated with the soul of Sartre."

The next day we drove to Cornwall "in warm, sunny weather; arrived about 8 and after dark saw a boat come in. Graham (the Harbourmaster) called 'Welcome back' from the bridge. A tanned Ken Gowsell in shorts." The next morning was "a hazy but fine morning in Charlestown, a choppy sea. Walked up to collect the papers from the post office. Small purple-violet flowers in the ivy on the port wall, singing birds. Saw it all with new eyes, and rejoiced. Gazed for a long time at the island and the waves breaking on it. The red-hot pokers are out."

I wrote: "I played it long....My long obsession with eternity. This is apparent throughout my *Diaries*. I have aimed at the highest: not to amuse or entertain, but to reflect the truth in all its guises. I have stuck to my task, despite distractions. Like Anthony completing a 48 mile walk in just under 20 hours, I have spent a long day trudging the Mystic Way to present eternity to mankind. And I had to change myself before I could even begin. Would I do it differently if I had my life over again? Given my task probably not. My task has been a hard one to accomplish. The *Diaries* are a necessary part of it." I added: "Reading my 1965 *Diaries* I am struck by how tenaciously and stubbornly I persisted with a search that seemed not to be going anywhere. With hindsight *The Silence* is a masterpiece, especially as it made the breakthrough into the spiritual Light, which I was unconsciously seeking. I was on my own in Japan, without any reliable guides, not even Tomlin really helped me – but with an instinctive knowledge that Zen could help."

I thought about my marriages and wrote: "A comment in my *Diary* of 8th October 1965 that my first marriage was to reduce my energy to prevent myself from going mad. The same has been true of my second marriage, which has solved all material and financial problems while grounding my intense, spiritual energy."

On "a glorious day" I thought of Judith, who claimed to have "rope-burns" from last week, channelling a higher frequency of Light than before. White Swan told her she is living from the divine Fire in her belly, being nourished by it, and not having eaten she is now putting on weight. I: 'A forced flower does not sustain its growth. Become like a flower in your meadow, and grow naturally.' Judith: 'Everything I do is guided, nothing happens through linear thought.' On Susie, I said, 'She may reach unitive consciousness in 20 years from now. All she's done is cross the bridge to the other side three times.' On the divine Fire: 'It must be from above down; it's dangerous if it's from the bottom up.'"

On May 26th I wrote: "In the late afternoon and evening typed up two-thirds of *Spider's Web*, my Ode on Bohm and Gunzig....My *Ode: Spider's Web: Our Local Universe in an Infinite Whole* which is the first of two poems on the universe I have in mind. This one was drafted last year, after my visit to Bohm. The new one is not drafted yet....My lyrics are numerous, I dash off two or three at a time with perfect rhyme. But the weightier poems get to the heart of the Age. Like an artist, a Holbein, I paint the great men of our Age, showing the essence of what they stand for, and my work should hang in a National Portrait gallery of poems." I added: "Novels (and gossip) are about the rational, social ego and the personality; poetry is (or should be) about the soul."

I continued to edit my *Diaries* and wrote: "My *Diaries* are my Coleridgean *Literaria Biographia*, my Yeatsian *Autobiographies*, my Kafkaesque *Diaries*. They will attract readers because they move from a sceptical to a metaphysical position – because of the Journey they trace, a spiritual Journey into illumination and enlightenment, into wisdom and understanding from the beyond....What distinguishes these *Diaries* from any other work is the search within, which eventually goes through to the Light. The inwardness of my *Diaries* distinguishes them from all other diaries."

On May 28th I wrote: "Began to recast my Winchester lecture for the book Michael Mann asked me to get ready as soon as possible. Then ate at Polkerris, at the Rasheleigh Inn....Just Ann and me, sitting in the window next to the restaurant, overlooking the sea. It was wet but cleared. When I got back a boat went out, bobbing slightly on the water as, laden, it went."

Clapperton's girl-friend Susie came in. She and I talked for an hour and a half. "She is a lapsed Catholic, getting a divorce; to her God is darkness and the Light is from God, and she has been receiving Light. Told her about my Epping centre. She needs to ditch the doctrine and keep the essence. She was a Eucharistic Minister, the highest you can be under a priest in the Catholic Church; if you're a woman, that is. But she had doubts."

I went for a late night walk: "And it hit me: I should reverse the new man and the new view of the universe in my second essay and that would be better. It hit me midway on the harbour wall as I walked back, high up. Five deep breaths and I was yawning....By 12.30 a.m. last night I had written out a good part of the second essay, almost effortlessly; with a great flow from the beyond....All week I have been connected to a current of thought. I put pen to paper and the thought flows and I have a paragraph. A whole essay has more or less been written in haste, chunks at a time; not in the order in which they will appear. Just sections I can see."

On my overcast morning we left Charlestown and returned to Essex. Heather Dobbs rang and said: "You are spiritual, Judith is not. Divine Fire in the belly and Yoga is getting up from the body. It is not the spiritual way down." Syrian Mona rang and said: "You are very gifted. Everyone must know your powers. The power of the Light is very strong."

At the beginning of June, a woman who had attended one of the mystery school days at Coopersale Hall rang and appealed for healing. Columbian P "rang, desperate and described how since October and her experience of...Sahaja Yoga she had had rushings, vibrations in her head (tinglings) and heart, and how chanting set it off. She wept, so I went round to Heather's and met her at 8 and healed her with healing – it all came out in a rush and she was 'a new person' and slowly the tingling went, and then we did a meditation and asked the Light to stabilise P, and then there was a little more healing. I: 'You've had the operation, now the convalescence.' She is over it, cured....It was like casting out a devil."

However four days later she hitchhiked from Heather's house to Coopersale Hall and appeared in school in a kind of trance to announce to Mrs. Best that I am the Messiah. When I arrived she prostrated herself at my feet with "wild, wild eyes" and called me "Father" and said: "You are the infinite one on earth, Jesus Christ. Harmony. You are to write an important book by 1997. You must neutralise Saddam Hussein's power by 1997. *The Fire and the Stones* is the Bible of modern times, in our modern time. Universalism can go ahead. Nicholas is a new vibration." She was in a trance – I wondered if she was on cocaine – and she rolled on the lawn, and Heather and I took a wrist each and led her firmly to Heather's car and drove her away. I gave her "calming healing", letting the pressure out a little as from an overblown balloon, but she was "socially disorientated with energy rushing about in her head". She was admitted to a mental hospital the next day. I felt sad. She was the victim of an episode before I met her, an episode of half-raised Kundalini (from the bottom up). The episode made me realise the desirability of siting the mystery school outside Coopersale Hall, which had begun it.

Judith rang, defending her earth-centredness: "The divine is everywhere, including in the earth." She also said that some of her invitees wanted me to demonstrate love to them; they were trying to impose on me the image of a guru just as Kathleen Raine tried to impose on me the image of a historian. My answer was: "The truth is, the psychic leads up to the spiritual, and the spiritual is superior to the psychic."

A friend of Heather's, Chris King, saw me. She was teaching metaphysics but having personal difficulties. I wrote what I told her: "Truth is indivisible. She is dividing the lower truths from the upper truth and so people are experiencing it as dud....'Except a corn of wheat fall into the ground and die it abideth alone. But if it die it bringeth forth much fruit.' She needs to die into the One ground of Universalism."

The Oaklands summer fair was opened by Nick Berry, "ex-East Ender

(Wicksy) and now in *Heartbeat*, his song on which theme is in the Top 20. He arrived late, while the country dancing was in full swing; he brought Sid Owen (Rick) with him. They wore a blue denim/jean suit and several thought they were intruding hooligans. The opening of the fair on the field. I stood before the caravan and spoke about the two of them. Sympathetic laughs as they all knew I was in unfamiliar territory."

In the evening we went to dinner at Haylands, "the 1820s (Chigwell) Headmaster's house from Thompson's days. (The story that Thompson left the front door open and went to sleep and a policeman entered and thought there had been a burglary, it was so untidy.) Pimms in the front room with local Heads, and then ate in the dining-room overlooking the rose garden at the back....The conversation was general....Got in at 12.45 a.m."

The next day was "the third day of the Foundation of the Light at Coopersale Hall just under 20 including Patrick Hamilton. Greeted everyone and welcomed everyone officially. Then spoke to Chris King and Linda, did healing. Home to read some papers. Then back again for my meditation, 2.30-3.30. Included the earth, and the universe; love, knowledge, understanding and wisdom, and healing. Many were opened up. Susie and Mona had swollen fingers. Spoke at length on tape about Universalism: 'At the practical level it's a Mystic Revival. At the theoretical level it's a Metaphysical Revolution.' Anthea: 'What did you do in the Byzantine civilisation? You looked very Byzantine when you finished your meditation.' I: 'I've always had a soft spot for Byzantium. Yeats wrote two poems about Byzantium which have always fascinated me, and I admire the transfiguration-based Orthodox Christianity they had in Byzantium.' Later spoke with Chris King and worked out a way of solving her financial problems; asked the Light to support....Healed and grounded Mona. Spoke at length with Judith. Home by 7.15."

A few days later I had a discussion with Heather Dobbs about the guidelines of the Foundation of the Light. "Our agreement that the guidelines for the Foundation of the Light are in *The Fire and the Stones*, in the last paragraph: knowing the Light at the personal level (which we do in the meditation); understanding the Metaphysical Revolution at the theoretical level (which I do at Winchester and in my present book, and in some of the talks); and understanding the Universalist common Fire or Light for all mankind between all religions (which I do after the meditation, in our question-and-answer session). On June 21st I need to identify the Ambassadors of the Light, and to work out which groups are to be started. It is a Foundation of the Light and those who want a Foundation of the Earth with barefootery to teach contact with Nature and making animal noises to feel one with the animal world (progressive teaching aids) must go away and found a Foundation of the Earth and do their own thing."

The next day I wrote: "A full moon and a cool outside. A glorious sunny day, the woodpecker tapping in the elm; sudden staccato knockings, very rapid, drifting through the open, summery window. The sunlight on my hanging crystal which flashed red, then green, then orange....A squirrel sitting on the iron railings, then scampering across the field. My oneness with Nature and the sun; I sit in shorts and an aertex shirt, must work a little before I sunbathe."

I was poised for more writing: "Have cleared the decks (work for accountant) in preparation for work on Universalism tomorrow. Had the idea for an essay on The Rise and Fall of Civilisations: the history idea in embryo. What is the...progression? What is the Light: Metaphysical Revolution: Universalism....An appendix....June 13. The honours list. I read it with detachment. I have turned my back on the possibility of a public life for a quiet, private life which is the only way to reach truth. Through my poems and writings and *Diaries* I may reach an international audience but my way is the way of the backwater (like Charlestown) or the leafy lane (like Coopersale Hall): of obscurity; and I have shunned the life that brings public recognition and honours for peaceful creativity." I added: "I lived in the Arab and Eastern cultures so that I could develop a Universalist vision, which is needed in our time."

On the eve of the fourth sitting of the Foundation of the Light, I sensed a need for change. I wrote: "I can get out of the present Foundation of the Light set-up by moving away from the occult and the New Age – channellings and the rest – and having a study of religions." I wrote: "June 14 another gathering at Coopersale Hall on a hot day. A few seekers only, including Steve (HIV positive) who lay on a mat, having come from hospital for the day, and J, who is in a wheelchair having thrown herself under a train and snapped her spinal cord. Heather's meditation; she saw angels. Mona saw patterns. Judith on golden light, which is 'from the Godhead rather than God', according to who? (Steve broke down at the beginning of the meditation.)" The lady in the wheelchair had to return to her car, and in the course of lifting the wheelchair over the low fence I strained my back, reactivating my back problem. The next day Judith reported that Susie was "self-preoccupied, blind to others..., her impurities coming out into her skin". Mona said: "Your voice is from the heart; it has vibrations."

The Metaphysical Research Group of philosophers met at David Lorimer's house at Alresford, near the thatched village of East Stratton: "Up a lane, near a cricketfield, amid wheatfields and sheep grazing, a flint and brick house with a cedar? cypress? on the lawn, guinea fowl, peacocks screaming, and a turkey which inflates and attacks women. Inside, white, neat, tidy, many books and pictures on the wall of Samuel Johnson (downstairs), Schweitzer (who looks like the young Einstein), Whitehead, Jung and others upstairs. Peace. Coffee, then we sat round on wooden chairs in a house that reminded me in some ways of 1, and discussed Willis Harman's *A Re-examination of the Metaphysical Foundations of Modern Science*, which I said did not arrive at the start; and I distinguished the rational from the contemplative approach and swiped jokingly at Geoffrey Read. Max Payne, preferring gradualism and speaking a language the scientists would understand, in neutral tones, stressing (Lorimer's) 'postulates' and 'models'. While Alison Watson and I emphasised revolution, a clean sweep, something new. The theme of who is the I that is doing the perceiving, that the reason is separate from the whole....The theme of process, that the universe is a process, like what these *Diaries* reveal. In the afternoon after a buffet lunch during which several sought me out about my books..., and following a chat with Vijay on how to convert the uncertainty principle into a consequence of invisible energy with different intensities – an idea which would get a Nobel Prize – we sat on the lawn in the sun, like the people in the picture of those breakfasting with (Rupert) Brooke before the First World War, and philosophised, and I evoked great laughter by extremist rejection of reason – dominated arguments, defending the Fire and the Light, and it was a golden afternoon among screaming peacocks. Home by 7."

I returned with a slipped disc initially caused by lifting the suicidal lady in the wheelchair at the Foundation of the Light: "It seemed like muscular spasm, especially as...my left hand locked on the wheel of the car and I could not open it for 30 seconds, the thumb and forefinger i.e., as I approached the Wake Arms, or City Limits as it is now called. I steered with my right hand and managed to unlock my left hand; was this a kind of stroke?" I went to the Buckhurst Hill osteopath Woodleigh, an ex-Coopersale Hall parent, who greeted me warmly. I spoke of his Philippino assistant. He said: "That's my wife. Didn't you know I'm divorced? That's my son running through. He's 2. My ex-wife is engaged to my best friend. I'm delighted. I go down every weekend and mow her lawn.'...Woodleigh stood me stripped to my underpants and made his diagnosis: 'A slipped disc which caused the muscular spasm.' He took my blood pressure. 'It's very low for a big fellow like you, it's 115/80. Do you get giddy? You should eat at 11 and 3 as well as at mealtimes to make bloodsugar.' Then he lay me on his ironing-board of a table and arranged my arms and legs and massaged my back and then wrenched down and as I yelled said 'Ah, did you hear the click? One side's in. Now the other side.' The other side was just as painful but I did not hear the click. He: 'The prolapse is in now. That's all for now. We'll work on it next week.'...He ended by giving me the cup his son had won. "I left carrying a cup and saying to another patient, 'This is for being brave.' He laughed." I noted: "My gift for spreading laughter – and wisdom. I spread the Light but am at heart a clown, a jester, a court fool."

I received an invitation to participate in a conference on Reductionism at Cambridge, and to write a paper for it. An observer had attended my Winchester lecture and I saw that I would be able to meet some of the key scientists of our time, "including Penrose the Platonist". I noted: "My continuing fascination with science: it began with EEGs and DNA, and has now spread to cover much of the universe....It is interesting to know that if one speaks at Winchester, it is 'heard' in Cambridge....How it works in academic life – how a Metaphysical Revolution could be launched at Cambridge."

Canon Peter Spink was the guest speaker at Chigwell School's Speech Day service in the parish church. I wrote: "The Foundation of the Light is to become a lighthouse. Canon Peter Spink...is a smouldering bonfire. But apart from Freeman (John Main's devotee) there is no one, so we should be grateful for his spiritual contribution. *Beauty and Angelhood* was about him, and it got me out of the New Age and into Christianity as a tradition, but that was not right, and Universalism is a half-way house, not within any particular tradition but not outside. I have a poem *Lighthouse* to write: the

Foundation of the Light in terms of Smeaton's Tower (at Plymouth). The Foundation of the Light is not about yoga, and I have the reputation of the school to consider." I addressed 50 or 60 new parents at Coopersale Hall, then went to hear Spink. "Sat near the door and (rising and sitting with difficulty because of my slipped disc) attended a Light service at which Peter Spink preached. The Light round Spink: the tingles up my spine, the surge of Light when I saw him. The charismatic, unspiritual young man has got old and wears glasses, and he talked down to the boys, but he still got across the message that 'God is Light' (cf Blake) and 'God is nearer to you than your breath', and put the boys into silence so that they could practically experience this. The whole of Chigwell School looking for the Light! I never thought I'd live to see this. Spink on rejecting false images of God, including the one that excludes other religions. Outside in the churchyard, near the door furthest from the road, I went and shook his hand and reminded him: 'I was at St. Peter's, Woking when you had your think-in, and before that was at Kent House; now I've got two schools and published two books, one that includes the history of the mystical tradition, and have opened one school as a centre for Universalism, which includes all mankind.' He listened and said 'Send me your literature' and 'Write your address on the back of that' (his service booklet). Then he needed to get away and we walked side by side without speaking as he headed for the road....I talked of Happold and Teilhard de Chardin. As I said to Alistair Thom, the mantle comes down, and I am the T. S. Eliot, and Spink is the Happold, of our time. Only Spink and Lawrence Freeman are doing anything within the Church to reverse the spiritual decay of Christianity, and although they are marginal figures, we must be grateful for small mercies, grateful that someone is doing something, even though I would say Spink neglects the past – people like to relate their experience to Augustine and Hildegard – and even though as a Christian he has to exclude other faiths, as Universalism does not." Later the School 1 (the martial arts priest) told me, over tea on the lawn, that Spink had described how he remembered me. And Vernon Davies, having failed to win a seat at Sheffield Central, said he was now doing property management. Later still we attended the Chigwell ball, as did Matthew, who escorted Carolyn Ladd, who had been a stunningly beautiful and mature Mephistopheles in the school's *Dr Faustus*. Despite having a slipped disc I danced from 11 p.m. to 2 am: "I found that, having asked the Light to get me through, my slipped disc held and I was able to bounce in a united way without a full hip swing with only occasional jars of pain. Ann enjoyed the evening, and I managed to keep my end up. To sleep at 3."

The next day, when I was short of sleep and still in some discomfort from my slipped disc, was "the last day of the 5 days at Coopersale Hall, for the Foundation of the Light" with people driving from as far as Littlehampton and Lincolnshire. "In the morning I raised the possibilities ahead, now that we've got an end to a cycle: study and meditation, with Universalism, then Mystics, then Metaphysics? Practical metaphysics as a lead-in? A combination? Healing? What practical sessions? Malcolm Southwood's observations. His healing of my back, which has ameliorated. Then after lunch a meditation in a heat among 25 or 30 people, in which I went back from the rational, social ego to the soul, opened to the Light, brought down its powers of wisdom, understanding, guidance and healing to all the group, counselling..., help for financial problems, and eventually creative energies, connection with thought processes so 'I am prosperous', etc; and finally help for the planet. Then back."

After tea there was a heated debate as to what should happen next, and I was aware of the doctrinal divide of Judith's followers and mine. One of Judith's followers wanted to know why I did not take part in her chanting. Anthea Courtenay (who had attended all sessions but failed to leave her rational social ego and her thoughts, and to make contact with the Light) said: "I don't want to be part of a Universalist movement, it'll happen anyway." I wrote: "I talked on movements and how to change things in the universities and what strategies have to be used and how movements in thought happen. And Anthea was isolated. Mystic Revival, which is what we're doing; Metaphysical Revolution for speed; and Universalism, the common essence of all religion....'Everything can be included. That's the meaning of Universalism.'" The bolshiness from Judith's camp led Southwood to say that "Judith is not of Light level" while she showed me "the burns on her hands, telling me an equation had come through, 'the key equation'."Southwood insisted: "She's New Age, and 'clearing' is rubbish – everyone's got a spirit.'" At the end the crippled woman who had asked me to lift her and slipped my disc told me: "Your 'top down' jars. The Light comes from the bottom up; the mind in your feet, earthy."I was relieved to have got to the end, and agreed with Mona that three-quarters of our clientele were the wrong people. I noted: "We have raised £1,500 for the Foundation of the Light." I later wrote: "The idea that revolutions are unnecessary because it is all happening anyway from pressure from below (society as cells). This is a nice thought but it is not necessarily true. Because the One is everywhere and behind Nature and consciousness, it covers all 4 levels (divine, spiritual, human, psychological) and all faculties: reason, emotions, intuition, instinct, the concrete. All is within this unity."

That same evening I resolved to terminate the activities of the Foundation of the Light for a while and concentrate on writing what would become *The Universe and the Light*. That would end the doctrinal disputes about the interpretation of the Light for the time being, and Judith, who had received some remarkable revelations and who "could be a Simone de Beauvoir to my Sartre", could then continue on her own, forecasting rents in the earth (June 21st had passed without her forecast of a rent in the earth in Hawaii having happened), leaving me to re-open the Metaphysical Centre on my own in the future.

I worked on *The Universe and the Light* through many distractions.

We went to the House of Lords for a reception in the Cholmondeley Room, and I wrote: "We were on the terrace under an awning on a fine evening, looking at the brown water lapping by us, near Westminster Bridge, while occasional or police or motor launches plied up and down....Then inside for speeches: (Lord) Swinfen, then Nicholas Scott (MP), then David (Thompson, husband of one of the Oaklands staff) from his wheelchair....Emphasis on housing for the disabled."

Geoffrey Read, the philosopher, wrote recording an exchange about me he had had at the end of a lecture Colin Wilson gave (which Read described as amateurish reflections with a marvellously professional delivery). He said that he had raised me and my talk of throwing bricks through logical positivists' windows (a joke on my part), and that Wilson had said of me, "Nick is obsessed with the Fire or Light." I replied to Geoffrey Read: "If to see the Fire or Light as the One Reality of the universe is to be obsessed..., Heracleitus was obsessed, and Plato and many other cultural leaders of the past. Colin Wilson is irritated at having reason contrasted with contemplation." I wrote: "My Light-based brand of holism, Universalism. Holism has no Fire or Light at the centre or in reality." Geoffrey Read also "heard from Nona Coxhead that I had Light experiences for two months. Read: 'I'm in her book, *The Relevance of Bliss*. I remember her telling me about a young man who had had Light experiences for two months. Now I've met him. It's you."

I noted: "Coleridge's *Dejection, an Ode* stemmed from the fact that his writing was a refuge from his unhappy marriage to Sara Fricker; and his love for Sara Hutchinson. The depression he feels at writing within the lovelessness of his family life....Poor Coleridge: betrayed by Wordsworth's careless remark, he declined into laudanum and Christianity."

I again went to Woodleigh, the osteopath. I wrote: "Talk of executives in China (organs being stripped and sold in Hong Kong) and a crucifixion in Manila while he rubbed my oiled back and tied me into a parcel with elbows and knees and then did 1-2-THREE, huge pressure on my back which made me yell. 'Well done and congratulations,' he said, shaking my hand as the wave of pain from the shock jarred through me. 'It clicked. You relaxed just enough to let me do it. Now the next side....' Back eased." (In his approach to pain he was almost as matter-of-fact as my dentist, who when I had last been for an inspection, without any warning began drilling in the most sensitive area near the front gum and when I winced said, "Coward.")

It was confirmed from Cambridge that I was to write a paper for the conference on Reductionism. I recorded: "This seems to be the Cambridge platform I wanted. The Light has given it to me. Went to the Light about it, after a successful golden Sports Day at Oaklands, and felt answering tingles."

Both schools had Sports Days. The Oaklands mothers' race was won by a coloured lady who was a huge distance ahead of the rest of the field. I said to her, "You've run before." She said: "I was with the British relay team in the Los Angeles Olympics." I said: "If I'd known, I would have given you a handicap. You would have started the other side of the iron railings round the field." The Coopersale Hall summer fayre took place. I wrote: "A golden day, sunny and hot, about 85 degrees. 500 programmes sold in an hour; people came in great numbers....David Seaman opened it. Then there was dancing and fancy dress. Many stalls, much to eat and drink: barbecue, licensed tent."

I observed: "Hegel is more relevant to my thinking than I have perhaps suggested. To him, reality can only be understood as a totality, and Being is contrasted with nothingness (cf Sartre's book), the synthesis implying Becoming. I would put it differently but I see Being as contrasted with Non-Being (nothingness) and producing Existence or Becoming. Yesterday found time to send to Jesus College, Cambridge, confirming that I will produce a 10 page paper saying that holism is spatial, whereas Universalism is metaphysical and that Universalism, not holism, is therefore the true antithesis of Reductionism in biology and the physical sciences....My critical questions of much philosophy and science."

It was baking hot and I spent as much time as possible in shorts. I returned to the osteopath "and had my back broken again, a vertebra forced back in. Shooting spasms of a mild nature down my leg."

I rang David Bohm and spoke to his wife. "He was diagnosed as having had a heart attack yesterday on his return from Prague. He thought it was a chest infection, but they've kept him and put him in hospital and everything's been cancelled. His wife, 'Thank you for ringing Nicholas, I'll tell him tomorrow.' I: 'To cheer him up, tell him his paper of January 1952 is crucial. I've mentioned it in an essay I've written, and I shall mention it in a paper for the Reductionism conference at Cambridge.'"

I arrived at the title of my work in a roundabout way: "July 1. Pondered on the title for my two essays. Man and the universe? Universalism and the New Man? Universalism and the Light? Left it and went to sleep. Next morning – this morning – the answer came in a flash and without hesitation, very clearly: Universe of Fire. That is the essence of Universalism. Have that? A Universe of Fire? Or: Universalism in a Universe of Fire. Still on the title. Universe of Fire looks to *The Fire and the Stones* but does not reflect the essay. Universe of Hidden Light or Universe of Billowing Light are possible; the second is bombast. The first...leaves out the Light and the universe. *The Universe and the Light*?...Decided: It's to be called *The Universe and the Light* and to be subtitled: Essays on the Philosophy of Universalism."

A local Head invited the Heads to her home and I found myself sitting next to the husband of the Head of Braeside, who had run a British Council summer school for 24 years in Wales. I wrote: "He on how élitist Tomlin and Eliot were, and on how the British Council has become more technical. His disparagement of (literary) theory. I on Tuohy left high and dry, and Ricks abroad out of it, and MacCabe wanting Marxism-Leninism to be studied in 'A' level English Literature, and on how the young have to study theory. He: 'The young want to know what's happened in the last 25 years, not the 18th century. I had to read Leavis, who was major in those days and is now minor.' The change that Tuohy derides. I on how there is to be a Revolution, on how the Augean stables need clearing out. 'And there is great filth among them. They are filthy.'"

After the Coopersale Hall swimming gala, which I announced on the PA system, I learned "there had been two calls from Moscow, one to each school: 'Moscow calling, Moscow calling. Hagger. Moscow. Hagger.'" As the voice spoke no other English, it was difficult to know why it wanted me; whether I was being offered the meeting with Yeltsin for which I had asked. The episode led me to talk about the future with Jeremy Miller, the accounting assistant, over lunch. I wrote: "How America has the power to

690

take Noriega prisoner (cf Caractacus paraded through the streets), how America will get fed up with local wars and impose an empire for peace, how Arab reunification and nuclear threat can bring the countries of Europe together, how small 'states' (in a United States of Europe) like Scotland will want representation abroad, how starving countries will want American dollars and protection."

At the Oaklands Open Evening I met a parent who was a British Midland pilot and who had flown with Nadia. There was an Oaklands swimming gala of which I wrote: "It was won by the Greens. A line of screaming, sitting girls: 'Reds, Reds, Reds.'I was on the microphone and Mr Baker, as is traditional, was thrown in the water like the cox at the Boat Race, at the end." Then Nadia rang to say she was selling her flat and buying another one in Colinton, just outside Edinburgh. "It has a river (Dingley Dell) with ducks, a church and a pub, and looks like Charlestown."

I wrote: "The full impact of *The Fire and the Stones* has not been fully recognised. It is a revolutionary work that establishes metaphysics....I have come up with a new and original perception, that reality can be contacted behind the reason." I wrote: "I am very close to understanding how the universe came to be, having finished *The Universe and the Light*." On July 8th I "got a finished version of *The Universe and the Light* printed out." Later I wrote: "Universalism...will be the new orthodoxy of the North American civilisation, and a stage in the European civilisation."

After open evening at Coopersale Hall there was a parents evening. I wrote: "Self-congratulation at raising £2,600 at the fête, then I left to lock up and in the dusk walked into a chair that was propping a door open and cut (or rather, grazed) my shin. Finished the meeting with a throbbing leg, but calmed it down by the use of my healing will." The Coopersale Hall prize-giving was performed by the Headmistress of Ursuline School. I wrote: "I took glasses and wine...and we had drinks while Jackie Reddington arrived. All the staff gathered in the staff room in a relaxed atmosphere. Then into a packed hall. Cine-cameras as I spoke about the history of the Ursuline and our own school." The next day Coopersale Hall broke up and I found the leavers in tears. Oaklands broke up. I wrote: "Found a dormouse by my front door, shivering and quaking, having drunk spilt bleach....At lunch was asked questions about my thinking by various teachers, including Christine Thurston ('Are you New Age?') and Carol Edwards ('Freeman should open his heart to Christ', the naive evangelical approach)."

The Conservatives held the constituency celebration of Steve Norris's election victory in Coopersale Hall's wooden panelled assembly hall. I wrote: "About 80 at the school dining-tables with a bar in front of the hearth. Spoke to Norris at the door, and while he told me he's fed up with Lamont I said 'Do you want to save £24 million, and make the Government popular? Read this.' And I handed him the yellow booklet about the Southern Distributor road, the Cornish Charlestown road. I said: 'The locals don't want it, it's a road to nowhere.' He: 'I agree. That's just the sort of project we can best save money on, projects the locals don't want.' He went off to make a phone call about it, and returned and later said: 'I'm passing it on to Kenneth Carlisle with the recommendation that the road's scrapped.' Earlier Norris told me the Government won't get in at the next election, because Smith will get their act together....'I've got to spend 2-3 billion this year.' He looks relaxed and soft, with longer hair. Sat next to Vicky and him at supper on a table we added....The Davieses out of reach down the other end. Conversation about politics, e.g. Major reads from his book, is thumbing the eared index while the question is asked. Canary Wharf. McCartney and the Queen....Ann and I went back to the Norrises. Hilda and Vernon and Ann Miller on the sofas with Steve and Vicky. General chat about roads."

On July 13th I wrote: "Read papers and was especially interested in an article about Goebbels' diaries, which makes it clear that Hitler planned war in 1938. I was conceived in August 1938, when Munich was happening, and so came into a hostile world with a message of peace which has taken all this time to unfold: a message of the common basis of humanity in relation to Universalism."

We visited "Frances and Richard at Biddenham. The thatched village. Sat in the new conservatory, then lunched (pork and crackling and summer pudding) and then went to the church's open day....My glimpses in the church...after looking at the new stained glass windows: one day there will be a window of the soul and the Light. The energy surged in, quietly tingling me, and I had to sit in the back pew behind the pillar and close my eyes and be quiet with the Light. Back to tea. Heard about their coming visit to Colorado and talked about my coming paper for Cambridge with Richard. Reductionism: it is natural to go for the smaller (e.g. in genetics and medicine) but it is a question of perspective and the whole theory of everything must include everything, including the view of the universe as organic and loving and full of thought and response to prayer (the Christian vision) and therefore the hidden reality that is behind the uncertainty principle, the cosmological constant and order and mass. This cannot be proved, but the whole vision includes mysticism and metaphysics and it is therefore a valuable working hypothesis and must be proved like atoms by contemporary scientists. There can be no materialistic Grand Unified Theory. (Materialistic monism.)"

I outlined my vision of the 1990s. I went round to Miss Lord's and met her relative "Richard Townsend, Counsellor in the Dublin foreign office or Department of Foreign Affairs. He is doing Eastern Europe, the CIS, disarmament and the EC, and much else, and is working really hard. He may be Ireland's Ambassador to the CIS. Had a long discussion. He asked my view on what is happening in England. I told him that we are edging towards Maastricht with the ERM, that there will be a United States of Europe, that Smith will get in 1996 or 1997 because the economic and political cycles remain out of sync; that Europeanisation will proceed apace with Scotland and Ireland independent states and the Irish question ended. Said Thatcher is an irrelevance. 'The Falklands was backward-looking, although it won her an election. I first met her at the Waldorf when it was apparent soon after she became leader that she would be no good in Europe. I tackled her, and Hurd was present as an MP. I said "What are you going to do about the half of Europe that's occupied?" and she said "You do it by propaganda" and I said: "It needs more than propaganda." Hurd bought me a drink and said, "You're quite right, we should be mentioning the occupation of Europe much more often." It is curious to meet the two main players at the outset, before their views were really known.'"

I took an early copy of *The Universe and the Light* to Element. I wrote: "Down to Dorset (Shaftesbury). On the way at 10 switched on the radio and heard Sir Laurens van der Post's voice about his journey in Malawi. Listened spellbound. His account of a journey to a mountain, rain and how one of the party was swept away in a torrent. How they returned home. His reflection, brooding almost like Conrad's Marlow: his references to the archaic self and a 'something more' which he was aware of in Africa. He is a traveller-adventurer. Felt I have a book....To the pub in the car park for a 3-course lunch with Michael Mann after handing over two copies of the book....Suggested he teams up with Donebauer....Mann, drinking beer....Blue and white shirt and spotted yellow tie and a soft look in his eyes." He told me: "Your book (i.e. *The Fire and the Stones*) is terrific. No one has woken up to it. As soon as someone does, it will be sensational." I returned to find a "nice letter" from van der Post, a synchronicity I found interesting.

I observed: "Flying ants hatched everywhere as the heat rose. A toad in our porch. A dormouse last week, a toad this week."

I drove down to Cornwall and immediately settled to my Cambridge paper, "reading bits of metaphysics in the Charlestown front room, piles of books on the carpet at my feet, the 3-seat sofa covered in papers, me sitting in the middle working from 10 books at once and making notes, jotting on lined paper as I go. Reflected that it is typical that at the end of my drafting the Cambridge paper the bank manager should ring with a horrific figure-problem, and that the next day when I was typing it up I had constant interruptions from the accounting assistant and the phone. Practising philosophy today is to concentrate in the middle of distractions....My distinction between the use of the whole, and the use of every possible concept – the all, which is multi-level. Grounded holism and the metaphysical view. Went for a walk by a calm sea with Ann late at night." I wrote: "My arguments with Tuohy in Japan were those of a universalist rejecting reductionist linguistic analysis." I also wrote: "My attempts to write about Zabov (*The Eternicide*) involved an argument with Reductionism from a point of view that was not holism but more an embryonic metaphysics. I can now rewrite *The Eternicide* by seeing Zabov through the eyes of a metaphysical – as an absurd figure, reducing instead of creating. A short novel."

We toured the English China Clay works by coach, starting at Wheal Martyn museum, and I took notes on many technical details, including how the Cornish beam engine worked by compressed air. I took Ann and her mother to the Gold Centre, Redruth "on a fruitless search for a gold necklace for her birthday".

Back in my Cambridge paper, I "reflected on the afternoon I spent at Winchester discussing technology with Sheldrake, taking names for a book.

This is crucial as it is the difference between a 'within Nature' organising principle and a 'beyond Nature' organising force. Once again I went to the heart of the problem. No wonder he wanted to spend one and a half hours talking it through instead of attending the lecture." When I had finished I wrote: " I have done well. My paper advances my thinking. Reductionism is within holism – physicalist holism i.e. – which is in turn within metaphysical Universalism which is non-physicalist (Sheldrake's ultimate state). I distinguish holism and Universalism. Also, I have introduced metaphysics from rational, intuitive and empirical positions. This is a 3rd essay in my book." On July 19th "while (Ann) went to market I typed up 10 points for a metaphysical science and therefore a Metaphysical Revolution. Feel I have ejaculated and more bits ooze and dribble and I keep wiping it away by returning to the typewriter. Details in my Cambridge paper."

It was Ann's birthday. We had lunch at the Carlyon Bay Hotel with her mother. I wrote: "Very formal, many waiters and waitresses, slow service." I "returned to read the papers. Read that eating nuts five times a week halves the potentiality of heart attacks (according to a study on 34,000 Americans). What grows helps us. Nuts and herbs and plants have homeopathic healing and health properties. Another example of how the whole is interconnected." In the evening there was a Songs of Praise service in the harbour, with a hymn dedicated to Alwyn Hosegood.

Fleur Beverley, the artist, rang me from Italy to say she had an exhibition in Innsbruck in October.

Of the development of my work, I wrote: "I used to think that I would state the meaning of life, which suggested the psychological approach of a Colin Wilson. I did locate the meaning of life in relation to the Light, and now I state the universe in terms of certain key quotations from Einstein, Whitehead and others. I was on the right lines in the 1950s, and have arrived at what I should be doing now. This is my work in T. S. Eliot's footsteps." I had a strong feeling that an initially ugly duckling had grown into a swan. I added: "I have written little poetry the last 12 months because, after drafting my Bohm poem, I felt the need to find out what the current knowledge is about the universe; and *The Universe and the Light* shows my findings. It is worth sacrificing poetry for my Winchester lecture and my Cambridge paper, as I shall have a total knowledge and will be able to do my second universe poem."

I went for "a walk late at night with Ant. A moon, not full, and a wide causeway of moonlight across the sea to Polkerris. Stars. A calm sea. A calm in me as I tackle the next stage of my Cambridge paper: editing and cutting to make room for the additions I have done today. July 20. All day, pasted and stuck bits together for the paper, putting in the insertions written since I have been down. It is a solid and substantial paper now, with some tough points. I now need to edit. I have produced and added, and will now reduce."

"In the afternoon the Astrid, a two-masted ship we saw last year, came in, with a piper playing....A wet day here, which I made good use of. A satisfying day. A walk at 10.30 with Ant to be in touch with the elements. Laurens van der Post looks at the moon and stars from his Chelsea flat while he looks after his wife; I go for late night walks and find satisfaction in renewing contact with the night universe." Then: "Could not sleep. Got up, went to the bathroom, returned to the darkened bedroom, and, standing, was filled with Light: oval and shining....As I 'looked' a surge of power swept into my back, filling my fingers and body. Came and wrote this at 1 a.m."

The next day was fine and I sunbathed. The Astrid went out. I wrote: "Anthony has been jumping into the harbour with his friends. It is now a clear blue sky." That night I went for another "walk. A cloudless sky, no moon, bright stars and a smoky Milky Way."

The next day was "a glorious morning....Back to my Cambridge paper. Reflected that those who came to the Epping days were, many of them, holists and physicalists; whereas I am metaphysical and Universalist. The experience of the Light is new. The same applies to Harman. He writes of metaphysics but seems to be a holist; as Wilber points out (although he does say Harman is dissatisfied with the holistic paradigm)."

I wrote: "Sunbathed and finished my Cambridge paper, except for a final read through. Then there was a knock on the door and Clapperton was there with Susie and a black make-up artist from Hollywood, Vechia Ewing, who advised Ant not to be an actor but to be a director after going to UCLA, and marrying an American. Clapperton wants me to be a partner and have half the port and strut around. I: 'Only if I can have Barry Williamson's bow-tie.'"

I thought about disciplines: "Ken Wilber's scheme at the beginning of *Quantum Questions*: physics-matter; biology-life; psychology-mind (reason); theology-soul (Light); mysticism-spirit. This allocates physics and biology to the physical world, psychology to the psychological world, theology to the spiritual world and mysticism to the divine world. – which does not make sense. There is something wrong with the last two. Ponder. Soul and spirit – question the separation of these, see them in precise Kabbalistic terms. Mysticism is in the soul, more so than theology, which is doctrinal and rational and part of psychology. Psychology and theology belong to the psychological world and mysticism to the spiritual and divine worlds. That is now right....'Physics doesn't deal with Reality, only with shadows.' The holistic view, not the metaphysical view which sees Reality as manifesting into the physical world."

I saw very clearly: "It's what we do now that counts. Geoff Hurd turned when keeping wicket at school, and I can recall the angle of the peak of his cap. He is dead now. That moment is still in my memory. It is what we do now that others remember. I have written a paper which carries forward my thinking. It is not popular, but will one day be remembered by the few who think deeply about the universe and seek a unified vision. When it is remembered I will not be around. But I have used the now to make my statement, whereas many just pass the time – that is the important point."

On Universalism I wrote: "Transcendentalism would have been a good name for the new movement. Unfortunately there was a 19th century movement of that name, and there has been TM. Universalism – there has been a Universalist movement in religion but it is not sufficiently widespread to quare the pitch. The label is there to be given new meaning without affecting the cause with a historical slant....'Transcendent' was a wrong word to use in place of Universalism first because it evokes Idealism and secondly because it suggests a transcendent God as opposed to an immanent God."

Matthew rang from Norfolk, where he was on a boating holiday. He said the lightning was appalling. We had "rain in the evening, lashing down, the slopes round the harbour awash, and under a floodlight a boat going out. The other one is staying in. The crew have all been sacked."

I reflected: "I had to leave the academic world to get away from English Literature and I had to be independent of all subjects to arrive at my position. Ahead I have an essay on English Literature – who is approved of and who isn't in relation to the Universalist principles. Toynbee: holistic history. Me: Universalist history. I am slowly acquiring the standing among those who know of a T. E. Hulme or Whitehead – or of a mixture of the two: I share Hulme's knowledge of the arts and aesthetic movements, and Whitehead's philosophy of science and metaphysical interest."

The Fatima prophecies intrigued me: "Fatima, 13th May 1917. The first secret may have forecast the Second World War, the second that Russia would return to Christianity if Russia was consecrated to the Virgin's Immaculate Heart, which the Pope did after being shot on the day of Fatima, May 13th, and visiting Fatima a year later, on the anniversary of his shooting. The third secret may have involved the Apocalypse, the end of all mankind; or the spread of Islam as Fatima, the daughter of Islam, becomes triumphant. A Moslem would-be Pope? Impossible in my theory. The Arab civilisation is older than Europe. Satan taking over as Pope – more likely. The Antichrist as Pope if men neglect God. Probably."

I returned to my *Diaries* while I watched cricket on television. I reflected: " Four cricketers doing well in the cricket season, the meaning of life is the single-minded accumulation of runs. All other problems (mortgage, car, family) are pushed to one side. Only what happens at the wicket is relevant. A naive attitude I once had, knowing it was naive, until I could not ignore real life any longer. I again saw my *Diaries* as a process: "Realised how in 1966 I was setting myself up for my present output, making the development which has led to my current work. It is all one process. This is a process autobiography. My process metaphysics."

We had Sunday lunch at the Rashleigh and then I returned to Essex to put my Cambridge paper on computer. I found a letter from Michael Mann. I rang Sir Laurens van der Post: "Affectionate 'Hello dear boy, nice to hear you.' I: 'Did you get my letter?' He: 'No. No.' I: 'It was sent on July 14th.' He: 'No, I would have replied to it if I had.' Ran through what it said: about how I heard him on the radio. 'Oh, how nice of you to mention that. Did you like it?' Told him...that the angels are saying truth doesn't depend on market forces.'...He: 'I think it's so good what you younger people are doing.'...Finally told him about my paper. He said he'd like to read it. I: 'I do hope we can stay in touch.' He: 'Thank you for ringing. Good night.' The impression he gave was of having unlimited time for me." I later reflected: "I should have asked Laurens whether Jung was holistic or metaphysical; ditto Bohm I am on the phone to both, and both know more about this than anyone else alive. I will find out about Jung. I believe he saw us as trapped in our psychic selves, behind a veil, beyond which was an objective mystery." I printed out at Prontaprint, Barking where Andrew Murdoch said: "People say 'You're lucky' but they don't see the hard work that's gone before."

I returned to Cornwall and stopped to deliver my print-out to Element at Shaftesbury and "had an hour's meeting with Michael Mann who said "he wants endorsements: from Bohm, Penrose and van der Post....Hawking was mentioned, for an adverse reaction. Gunzig?" I wrote: "Michael Mann, tall, in a sports jacket with leather pads on his elbows, smoking. I sat at a round table with a tiny ivory elephant on a stand in the centre, with an overhead light. When Roger Lane came in, wearing an open-necked white muslin shirt, I stood up to shake his hand and found the light shade round my hair. I said: 'The Universe and the Light!'"

Back in Cornwall on "a warm sunny day and a cloudless blue sky" I "sunbathed in the morning and afternoon. Saw little white spots, tiny globules, dancing while I shielded my eyes. The life-sustenance. The photons – or biophotons – that feed all living things? Wheeling gulls. Bees, butterflies. Had a strong sense that everything's a whole. Every species has its part to play within the metaphysical whole....The Maria Asumpta left, firing her gun several times in salute. (And frightening Capt. Gowsell's dog, which cowered behind him.)" Two days later there were "brilliant stars in a dark sky. A new moon. The sky looked as though a rocket had burst, scattering stars in all directions, trailing downwards towards the horizon on each side. A day of sun. Dozed. Could not stay awake in the evening. Then the brightness of the stars. Surprised by beauty." The next night was "a blustery night, scudding clouds, drizzle – faint spots – in the air, and I walked to the end of the pier. Now the sea is beginning to boom."

I took issue with Karl Popper: "Aug 3. Popper has loomed. His 'third world' of ideas, the fact that he opposed Wittgenstein, his 'falsifiability' principle as opposed to Wittgenstein's verifiability principle.' I have moved beyond Popper...in as much as I have a different principle, as I expressed in a letter to Colin Wilson. Popper says that (in effect) 'God exists' may be true but if it can't be falsified it isn't science. I say that falsification does not happen in the reason alone; but through intuitional gnosis as we are part of a whole that is non-physical. Popper is right. But we imagine...hypotheses and then falsify them; but he is wrong in being bound by the eye of reason. My principle is a trespasser principle: has reason the right to verify or falsify – to pronounce – on metaphysical matters whose origin lies behind the reason?"This was an extremely important point. Just as reductionism and holism were two sides of a coin to be contrasted with Universalism, so verifiability and falsifiability were two sides of a coin to be contrasted with gnostifiability of the metaphysical Light, with my trespass principle.

I went for "a walk among the rock pools. Bladderwrack, sea anemones, limpets, strange seaweeds, and a tide coming in. Reality – physical reality." The next morning I woke to "a wet morning", "with the phrase 'of Being' in mind – to go in after 'metaphysical totality'. The Universal Mind has considered my proof and has added those two words, which I have put in. Man is a being within a metaphysical totality of hierarchical Being. Perfect. Thank you."

I drove back to Essex and caught up with school administration. I wrote a lot of letters. On August 7th 1992 I returned to Cornwall via Element and was "with Michael Mann in Dorset from 3.15 to 5. On the book, which is now complete save for the comments. Put in the corrections. On the *Diaries*. Mann is interested but feels I have an account of a journey, which I should tell. The details can follow on....The Light should be central: from scepticism to a metaphysical outlook. Michael gave me a Royal book on Gurdjieff which may be *Diary* size, and suggested...Royal for my journey." So was born the idea of writing this Autobiography.

In Cornwall I dipped into van der Post's books, which I had brought back with me: "They are about someone else (cf Tuohy), e.g. Bushmen, Jung, and are set in Africa. Africa, Jung and Japan – these are van der Post's themes. His limpid prose style, his concreteness. Several times he rails against isms. I believe he is more at home with autobiographical adventure than with novels. A travel writer of great purity and reflection. He insists on Jung's stature, but he himself has great stature....He has lived extreme experiences and brooded on them – in relation to the beyond? The beauty of his descriptions: all outer....Ingaret Gifford pervades van der Post's books. She introduced him to Jung, urged him to go off on his exploring journeys and edited his works. No wonder he is so loyal to her now, as I saw when I visited him. Van der Post is like Marlow in Conrad's *Heart of Darkness*. He draws heavily on the Bushmen's sayings, which are evocative, e.g.: 'The story is like the wind. It comes from a far-off place and we feel it.'...Van der Post is a T. E. Lawrence of our time. Old enough to remember the outbreak of the Great War (when he was 8), he did a Rider Haggard in the Kalahari and discovered through exploration the original man and his mystic powers, and brought it back to civilisation. Round the Kalahari were SWAPO in what is now Namibia. The evocative Graham Greene-like prose, and the yarns and memorable stories – small wonder Prince Charles was captivated on his honeymoon, to which he took 6 van der Post books....Van der Post's Conan Doyle-type (i.e. Challenger-type) interest in a lost world of pre-history has done much to stimulate the New Age's interest in the pre-civilisational." I dwelt on a passage in his book on Jung about "that light which we are, in the innermost nature of ourselves, contacted to seek."

On August 8th 1992 I wrote: "I feel I am at a crossroads now. *The Universe and the Light* was finished yesterday, and now I am enjoined (by Michael Mann) to focus on my own journey – in relation to 'that light'. I need to bring in the vivid oneness of Nature, the elemental backdrop against which people go about their business. In my travels abroad, it was essentially the same Nature. It is all interconnected. I need (after Cambridge) to move away from Professors and their arid approach to the 'livingness' of the Nature I am describing....The next task now, without much of a lull between tasks. This one will allow me to be whole – not just the rational intellect....My Autobiography tells the story of how I came to know the Light and to apply it internationally after national considerations, and to oppose the status quo in science and philosophy and to opt for the metaphysical. The emerging of my ideas from my life, the caption being

+A+ -A = 0, i.e. reconciliation of the opposites. +A = the world (scepticism, nationalism etc); -A = the beyond (mysticism, the Metaphysical Revolution, Universalism). It will answer Ann Miller's question: 'How did you come to be involved in all this?' The most remarkable thing about me is my contact with the Light and the new philosophy it has made possible, and the new literature and science. So the Light must be the theme. Not knowing what I was seeking....Call it *A Mystic Way*."

I listed future essays: "(1) How the universe works as a whole, full of checks and balances, how everything needs everything else, i.e. the oneness of everything within the metaphysical scheme. Bring in beauty. (Science.) (2) Verifiability, falsefiability and gnostifiability. (Philosophy.) (3) Spiritual, religious and political Universalism, the philosophy of the coming supra-national state in Europe, its various layers. (Religion and Politics.) (4) Literary criticism and Universalism. The Light and literature, defining the tradition of literature, just as the philosophy essay defines the true philosophical tradition....The theme of the essays is the interdependence of all creation in relation to the Light, philosophy in relation to the Light, literature in relation to the Light and how Universalism will be the philosophy of a supra-national Europe." I deliberated on the title: "The philosophy essay is about knowing true reality, which is expressed in a literary tradition and as mutual interdependence in science and its manifestation can be found in political Universalism. 'The Global One' catches political Universalism, the scientific interconnectedness and the literary tradition (if it is global) but it leaves out the metaphysical dimension. 'The Global One of Being' or 'Being and the Global One'. Being manifests into one existence of interdependent existents. Call it *The One and the Many* (cf Shelley, 'Life like a dome of many-coloured glass/Stains the white radiance of eternity')."

I recorded: "Have been asked to address the Quaker Universalist Group on April 16th-18th at Birmingham. It is linked to the International Society for Universalism, which politically sees Universalism as a metaphilosophy for the coming European Supra-national state. It is the official philosophy for the coming Supra-state....The first World Congress of Universalism is being held in Warsaw in August 1993....(Shortly before the 19th World Congress of Philosophy in Moscow.)" I had been sent details of this Polish universalism, which began in Warsaw in 1968, the year the Warsaw Pact crushed the Prague spring. I was sure that their universalism had nothing to do with my metaphysical Universalism.

After noting "the meadow browns" and "the bees nuzzling the pink blackberry flowers", we went to Porthleven, "to see the gig-racing. Stood on the pier and watched the ladies row out in 5 boats until they were specks on the horizon and half an hour later return. Then after a lull the men A teams went: 10 boats. Charlestown's boat, the Mystery, came 5th. While this was going on, met up with Aunt Pat, Stephen, Sandra and Stacey who were walking. Stephen's tale of doom about the future. There are no crabpots now as there are no crabs when you raise the pots. He can't lower nets because...monkfish are now virtually extinct. He gets flatfish by trawling, but these will only last another 3 years."

I saw imagination within its context of being apart from the world:

A MYSTIC WAY

"Imagination is day-dreaming, being apart from the worldly situation; the activity of the soul. Trollope's day-dreaming in novels. The whole basis of reading is being apart from the situation and the present moment, i.e. responding with the soul. Consider the correct use of imagination as an activity of the soul." I noted "a review of Kathleen Raine's last poems by Robert Nye, saying she lacks the vulgarity of Shakespeare. What I said in my preface to my poems is that the beyond must be mixed with the worldly. Nye is right." Again: "On the imagination. Why write for the imagination and not out of direct experience, like T. E. Lawrence and van der Post? Cannot the imagination make use of direct experience? Imagination: 'mental faculty forming images or concepts of external objects not present to the senses; fancy; creative faculty of the mind.' Writing as recollection in tranquillity (Wordsworth) is the recall of concepts of external objects not present to the senses, so autobiographical writing can be imaginative. On the other hand the imagination can 'dream' events which have not happened."

I went for another late night walk: "Saw the full moon, slightly misty, emerge from behind the Battery Cliff as I stood half along the pier, on the wall, and under it a reflection of the cliff in the still sea. Gazed in some ecstasy and quickly returned and wrote *The One and the Many* which is about manifestation of Reality through the Void into Being and thence into its reflection, Existence. The poem needs polishing but is potentially a great poem. Earlier wrote *Gig-racing*."

The next day I wrote: "Sunbathed for an hour, reading van der Post in his p.o.w. camp and in the Kalahari....Pain in my lungs. Persistent clearing of my throat to clear it, but it won't clear. Wrote *Moon and Tide*....Regatta evening was on falconry. Wrote *Hooded Falcon* about it. The tawny eagle, swooping, taking raw meat, then soaring effortlessly, gliding, a wonder of aeronautics. The common buzzard and two Harris hawks which followed it. The kestrel did not go because it was overweight, i.e. had eaten; and the hooded falcon does not perform in front of people – not this one. I am fascinated by falcons." Matthew arrived back from his holiday, bringing a letter from van der Post which contained the sentence: "I am glad that you are thinking of writing directly out of your own experience of travel and the world." On August 11th I "wrote the first 4 stanzas of *Hooded Falcon* (my 4th poem in 4 days) and this morning typed it up and added a 5th stanza which just wrote itself. The poet as falcon. That must be my badge from now on."

I received the Scientific and Medical Network newsletter with Charlotte Waterlow's pro-New World Order/Illuminati review. I wrote: "Charlotte Waterlow sees a democratic (UN-based) spirituality...beyond nation-states, sovereignty, independence. I have been criticised for relating civilisations to their origin and development, and for not seeing all mankind as one place-free UN-type world government, which is universalism. This will be a phase only, and will not be for ever. It is Fukuyama's error to assume that a new phase of history is coming in which will be final and forever. In New Age and holistic circles there is a desire to believe in perpetual Universalism, but this is not going to happen. There is not going to be an evolutionary change in man. Evolutionary humanism – I don't believe

700

it....Waterlow says a new kind of civilisation is dawning based on world co-operation to implement human rights. (1) America will not spread Christianity but the heresy of Universalism. (2) My view is not pessimism as the Light is involved. I only consider the possibility that the Moslems will conquer Europe, but the older civilisation does not conquer the younger. My views have been misrepresented. Lady Astor (told me she had) told her she had missed the point over the Conspiracy."

I pondered the amount of scientific knowledge we need: "In 1965 I knew that $E = mc^2$ is useless knowledge to a writer as it is not experience. But I do need to understand the universe, and so in terms of my understanding the whole that I live in, it is not useless knowledge."

I was stung. "Went out and sunbathed, saw Sibyl back from hospital, put on my top and spoke to her at some length, said 'Watch out, there's a persistent wasp' which she flapped, went back and sat on my sun-couch, lay back – and within a minute felt a stinging in my upper arm, as though I had had that stinging tetanus jab, sat up and saw a wasp buzzing away (slow to take off from my arm). Ken got some cream and wiped it on, but the stinging went on and moved down my arm, so came in after sunbathing for three quarters of an hour and found Wasp-eze and sprayed the arm. Some relief but not much." I felt it was strange that I had alerted Sibyl Gowsell to a danger which had then attacked me. It was as if I had interposed myself between her and the wasp, shielded her.

We "drove to Portloe and had a cream tea at the Lugger Hotel and strolled to the tea shop where the Camomile Lawn stars ate. Then on to Carne beach and Narne Head...and then on to Pentire beach..., and then to Veryan with its thatched houses and 4 round houses which the Devil could not hide round corners of." Later: "Barbecue on the quay as the Maria Asumpta came in and then gig-racing, a crowd about, while Ann and I sat in chairs by the green sward and watched the sun set. Feel full of fresh air and sun." Later still: "A huge moon outside, full with mountains, looking like Africa and Asia (when seen through binoculars). Later, went for a walk after playing Matthew chess. The moon was much smaller, a day after full but very bright. It was as if we were walking on a winter's afternoon, the moonlight was so bright." Next morning I recorded: "Last night wrote (and today typed up) *Still and Moving: Moon and Eyes* (a poem)."

The Regatta festivities took place. Anthony's friends took part in the raft race and on the greasy pole. I recorded: "Wrote *Young and Old: Noise and Stealth*." I noted: "The long hair of women is to hide breasts. This insight from my *Bible* readings, which include the *Song of Solomon*."

I looked with concern at the continued fighting in what used to be Yugoslavia. My view was that the New World Order financiers wanted an extended war so that they could sell arms to Christians and Moslems, to both sides. They wanted Moslem aid for the Balkan Moslems. I predicted the collapse of all peace efforts as the fighting would be covertly encouraged for financially profitably reasons. I wrote: "All those calling for fighting against Serbia (like Thatcher and Scruton) have an axe to grind with the EC and hope that fighting will split it up, or further calls for the EC not to spread because it promotes tribal warfare."

I thought about my work and wrote of my "Grand Novel" which would include "the world and the beyond" and "cover an enormous range and scope: the theme of *The Fire and the Stones*, i.e. the breakdown of the old values, decolonisation, decline, and the New World of the 20th century. The Clay (home), the Sea (abroad). This will be my *War and Peace*, my *Wuthering Heights*....My Pasternak (Zhivago being a poet)." I wrote: "I have reached a decision. End live movements. Be a writer only. I am an English Literature practitioner (poems, novels, autobiography), not a lecture circuit philosopher or scientist....Finish the philosophy with my next book and then get back to Literature, exclusively. Poems, stories, diaries, novels, play? Man of letters....I am coming to Literature with a movement in thought behind me. Become a man of letters with a philosophy....The Great Novel: love, death, freedom, the meaning of life – a family over three generations involving the entire scope of the 20th century. Pattern and meaning. The mess of logical positivism, socialism, egalitarianism. The move from moral principle to money and materialism. The seeking for stability. The Clay – those who sought the security and stability of a home life. The Sea – those who like Tom went abroad. The fall of the professions, the change of values....The Foundation of the Light – pass it on to Heather." I reflected: "I was right on 23rd September 1966: my ideas for a spiritual revival are the escape of action from the solitary pain of writing. It is a theme for a book (*The Universe and the Light*) not a programme for a Gurdjieff." I noted: "I see myself as a Whitehead-Eliot-Joyce, uniting the interests of all of them, but essentially a man of letters before a philosopher, poet or novelist, hence the *Diaries*." I also noted: "The trouble with not having an Epping centre is that writing can return to the rational, social ego (the subject of most Great Novels). A centre helps you distinguish the reason from the intellect, the rational social ego from the soul." I decided to find another computer operator who would help me write this Autobiography.

On August 18th I revisited Colin Wilson. I wrote: "Picked up Paul (Newman), Pam and a friend Graham, and drove to Colin Wilson's. As usual we had been sitting 10 minutes before he wandered in, hair all over the place, giving me smoked salmon, pouring wine. My first question. 'What are you writing?'He: '*Space Vampires* 2. I have great hopes of it, it's getting dirtier and dirtier without being pornographic. The female takes energy from the male...and creates an energy circuit.' Told him about the Reductionism symposium after the news, told him I'd pinned that label onto philosophy since 1900, told him about my book and how Universalism was proving a way of action. 'I agree,' he said, 'that's why I have reservations about things like Universalism, it attracts followers.' I: 'I am not going to be a Gurdjieff or a Billy Graham but a writer, a philosopher, using the printed word.' Then in came a lady from Bath...a precognitive....The conversation became general while Joy sat with the parrot on her shoulder which asked 'What time's dinner?' (Heard that) Colin goes to bed at 9 and wakes and thinks between 12 and 2 or 3. 'I do all my important thinking then.' 'I hate travelling. No one learned anything by travelling, travelling makes you not see things.' Got back to Colin when the lady left to drive back to Bath, and freewheeled about Popper, who has often invited him to stay. Took details of crucial books by Popper he has got. He: 'Derrida is putting linguistic philosophy down while being part of it.' Wilson gave me an article on Gödel's Incompleteness Theorem which is a Platonist (rather than constructionist) view of maths, which Penrose claims reflects our intuitive ability to grasp the truth which computers can't emulate. Wilson: 'It puts paid to Hawking' (who saw the Theorem as important, as permitting time travel, which Hawking denies) 'and Wittgenstein, destroying Russell and Whitehead's *Principia Mathematica*, which derives the whole of maths from a single theory of logic....The mind need not move from the armchair. It can do all its work and thinking there.' Gödel, Einstein's friend, saw a 'world of ideas', i.e. a reality in the microworld, in which mathematics were absolute. Wilson said Scruton is in the T. E. Hulme tradition. I: 'Surely not?' (I am.) He agreed van der Post is in the T. E. Lawrence tradition. He had Peter Redgrove round last week. Left with Joy showing me the chalet where I stayed in 1961 (2 rooms, then with a view of the sea, now blocked by trees). Pam: 'He's wasting himself on the vampires, but he's exhausted, its easier than philosophy. And he's a law unto himself, he won't do otherwise. He needs the money....He's popularising.' I said: "In 1961 Colin talked about 1 and literature and nothing else." I wrote: "The Colin of 1961, eagerly talking in literature and philosophy, referring to two or three writers every sentence, showing the baker the latest chapter – that Colin is out of reach, beyond time. I sit in the same place, near where the swivel arm and typewriter used to be, and am separated from the person I knew then, who is but a shell of his former self."

The next day I returned to Essex pondering: "If I decline to be a Gurdjieff, will I be taking the side of rational, social ego, and pride; and not the higher purpose and higher plan? Or will I be fulfilling my member in the whole body – the higher purpose – through my writing?" In Essex I learned that Clapperton had visited Ann and offered us a partnership in the port for £100,000, which I turned down, seeing only cost and little profit.

Matthew's 'A' level results came out. He had not done badly, and in common with others in his year there was a confused couple of days while his first choice, the University of Bangor, confirmed that he would be able to do a split English/French degree over 4 years, with a year in France.

I introduced Michael Mann to Peter Donebauer: "Went to Olympia and met Michael Mann in Gorleston Street – he was waiting on the pavement. I hardly saw him at first as I was walking into the sun. We shook hands and had coffee (me) and tea (him) in the small coffee shop round the corner from Peter Donebauer, and Michael asked me to check a list of 60 Mystical Philosophers he had been sent from America, for omissions, and agreed there were 5 or 6 volumes rather than 60....Took him to Donebauer (who) said to Michael Mann, 'When you were last here, you invited me to Nicholas's launch.' I: 'That's extraordinary, that there was that situation then, and now here the three of us are'. One and a half hours discussing the state of the film industry....Then out to lunch at a small Italian-Lebanese restaurant opposite Olympia. A lovely tranquil atmosphere....Then...back to collect our cases, and thence to Charing Cross with Michael Mann....He: 'I'm only interested in presenting ideas, I'm not a business man, I don't want to accumulate a lot of money.'"

When I returned, "on impulse (I) rang Andrew Murdoch and said I wanted to double my output and got fixed up with his wife, ex-secretary to a solicitor, who will type from dictation on her machine....Got fixed up effortlessly for my increased output." Without trying, I was set up to start this Autobiography. I wrote: "My Autobiography: a mystic way of great universality but with some particularity."

Steve Norris "rang and inquired gently and solicitously after me and my holiday. We discussed the sterling crisis. I: 'Couldn't you have a conference for all parties in the ERM and get all to agree to lower the floor?' He: 'It would be regarded as a devaluation.' Of Lamont, he: 'It's the economics of the madhouse.'"

Heather Dobbs received a letter from Peter Roche de Coppens, author of *Divine Light and Fire*, who wrote that he was "most interested in Nicholas Hagger". He was then Head of the Templars.

I visited Coopersale Hall and heard from Peter Sjoberg, who lived nearby, that Hammond had been beaten up by 7 men, who "broke his two kneecaps and stabbed him in the back according to Sjoberg. Hammond wanted to drive and took his plaster off so he could bend his knees."

Fleur Beverley, the artist, made another fleeting visit. After our chat I wrote: "Fleur, a free spirit with an Audrey Hepburnish face and close-cropped hair, missing out on possessions, being rather than having, and behind everything. She should paint rays of light on the quatrefoil with Christine Carpenter of Shere walled in (as described in my poem)."

I noted: "Aug 27. Writing my Autobiography will reopen an anthology of my poems – of the poems that have not appeared....Haunted by images." Letting my imagination wander I "wrote *Artist, Enclosed*; *Hesitation*; *Anticipation and Regret* and *Quatrefoil: Mirror Images*, and *Stepping-Stones*, in that order. Poems of place with a human dimension, the implicit within the explicit, the hidden within the revealed, the covert within the overt, the private within the public. Move towards a new symbolic verse. Then wrote *Healing Muse* and *A Free Spirit*....A *Collected Poems* come at the end of your life....I am very pictorial, and in the course of describing pictures I have poems. It is good for me to translate my experience into paintings so that they can become pictures. My poetic strength is that I make sense. My rhyme is always a sensible rhyme, and it is natural as well. Wrote *Wind* at 12.45 as the wind howled round the house I was alone in....I am a painter in words. It helps me to look at the world with the eye of an artist and frame it. I am an artist....All great artists layer their works, minor ones are at one level only and appeal to the bourgeois." I wrote: "Go for the concrete. Abandon the theoretical and doctrinaire. Put your findings into art. Your Muse has visited you to emphasise what you have always know, that you are an artist, not a religious leader or a scientist. Get back to literature."

I took a list of books to Heather Dobbs "and stayed on, chatting. The possibility that the two Royal scandals (Fergie and Diana) were motivated by the Great Conspiracy, which wants a republican Britain within a United States of Europe. Earlier I had said that I feel I must wait and do nothing ('wise passiveness') and that my Birmingham address next April may lead to Warsaw, where, at the world congress of universalists, I will fulfil the role of T. S. Eliot and Sartre, as spokesman for a new philosophy, i.e. I should not dissipate my energies in live meetings with healers." I had doubts about the International Society for Universalism, but intuitively knew that Warsaw would become significant in the future. I recorded: "Heather said that Adrian Cairns (the Quaker Universalist) told her: 'I came to Coopersale Hall because I've never heard a presentation like Nicholas's before. He just stood up and did it. I was fascinated."

I was poetically creative again: "Excused myself from the accountant and wrote *Time and the Timeless*, about a juxtaposition....Poems form in my mind and I write them to get them out of the way....Wrote poems all evening until 1.15 a.m. (now). Wrote *Tin-Mine near Land's End*; *Rising Souls*; *Collapse of Progress*; *Love and Death*; *My Muse*; *My Muse, Gone*; *Ruin*; *Storm and Art* (imagined from what they told me in Cornwall, where a great storm is happening); and *Yugoslavia*....17 poems, wrung from me within 3 days. The wind is whistling in the trees outside this fine Sunday morning. 10.15 am. Now 20 poems in 3 days (from Thursday evening to Sunday morning, actually two and a half days), as I have written *Muse's Gift*. 10.35. Have just written *Imagination: Spring and Sea*, my most Platonist or Neo-Platonic poem. I did not think it at the time but on reflection it is in the tradition of *Kubla Khan*. An important poem."

I had a strange dream: "Dreamt there was a high (neap) tide in Charlestown and the water came past our house to Arthur's and almost into our back garden. I had my desk and leather chair permanently outside the house and had to clear the desk and was wondering whether to bring desk and chair in. Ann thought the waters wouldn't rise enough to sweep them away....(This dream was occasioned by yesterday's news of a very high tide in Cornwall, which I immediately 'saw' with my imagination.)...My dream: a tide from Nature will sweep away the academic? Wrote *Neap Tide and Academic Work*.

Of my poems I wrote: "My long groping towards the beyond in these *Diaries*. The evidence is here. You can't fake it for 30 years. My long groping towards this subterranean sea. I must make another selection of my poems to illustrate that the Light and the imagination are connected. It's not only a question of levels....After lunch finished *Seismic Inspiration*. Muse, inspiration, intuition – these are the forces from the beyond that must motivate my art, to which I must connect myself....I have many poems to put into the new volume, which may be called *Smeaton's Tower* and have a lighthouse on the front."

On August 31st I began dictating this Autobiography: "A Bank Holiday and much of it spent dictating the Autobiography onto tape for Wendy Murdoch."

I reflected again on my energy. "Where I got my energy from, when did I have it? Making those charts on a Sunday evening, and at cricket, reading; reading in the Journey's End garden, e.g. on the seat and Jung by the pear tree. And in Iraq. I worked through to it. The man who tapped the secret of the universe. It was not the Light alone that gave me this universal energy. I knew it in Japan, e.g. Rainer: 'What is this energy you have, where does it come from?' (E.g. the energy to write.) It was not the Chigwell academic scenes that gave it to me, I had it before Oxford; during my reading at the solicitor's office. Somewhere along the Way I contacted a universal energy which worked through me and made me read on trains. I was (and am) ambitious. Energy comes from gathering thought energy into a high potential and using it in the direction of the intended purpose."

On September 1st I went up to Cambridge for the conference on Reductionism. I wrote that I arrived at Jesus College by 4.30, "to be transferred to a 200 year old building, staircase 5, room 6, where I look out at battlements....Everything is still save for feet echoing on boards upstairs." There was a reception in the convent cloisters, "12th century, the oldest institutional building in Cambridge. Spoke with a GP and a Jesus Fellow, then William Anderson, who had hardly any voice and who was trying to get his message across hoarsely, creasing his thin face so it looked like a turtle's head. His precise memory for 'stones'. Spotted (Roger) Penrose and introduced myself....Then spoke with Michael Sofroniew, a Fellow of Jesus who is just back from the US. On to dinner. Sat next to Sofroniew. Sofroniew: 'We are very near a mechanistic view of consciousness. Without the brain there is no consciousness, and without consciousness there is no mind. We have to be more reductionist to understand the mechanisms. Reductionism has done great things, to criticise it is to pee on a bush. There is no evidence for anything else, it's all hot air.'...Upstairs from the hall to the lecture room. Heard Freeman Dyson on the scientist as rebel. Many questions which he answered in dry one-liners. He is elderly, thinnish and was besuited, with a confident manner. David Lorimer, recording with earphones during Dyson's talk; always there with technology. Mary Midgley sat behind me. Came away from Dyson's lecture with Roger Penrose, who was still in a red jacket. We headed for the bar, chatting about metaphysics. He: 'There's room for a non-local hidden variability, but not a local one.' On Einstein, who had been attacked by Dyson for spending his last 20 years in reductionist equations, forgetting about the world of Nature which gave him his relativity theory. (A lesson for me in this: I must redouble my observation of Nature, and will.) Penrose remarked to me: 'It's odd that Einstein and Oppenheimer never met.' (Oppenheimer and Sneider took black holes from Einstein's equation.) He said: 'They must have met, it's odd they never discussed it.' The bar was full of noisy undergraduates on a bar football machine, and Penrose excused himself to go and work. I said I was going to look for a telephone, he said he would, so we went in search of one and got totally lost, talking of Gunzig. In the end Jeremy Butterfield, a Fellow of Jesus, took us to his room and showed me how to lock the door and went. Penrose went first and after a long time mastered the fact that you have to dial 9 to get an outside line. He came out and left me to it. I sat in a room with posters of Einstein on the walls and books on quantum mechanics and knowledge and mounds of exam papers on the bed and on the floor, and made my calls to Ann and Matthew. Then I found my way back to staircase 5....Midnight on the college clock, time intruding on eternity, sending a medieval message into our monastic rooms."

The next morning I "woke at 8.40 (having gone back to sleep after the alarm) and had to rush to catch breakfast, which finished at 9. Sat...at the lecture near Penrose. The lecture was by Patricia Churchland on the Neurobiology of the mind, a reductionist view countered by Peter Lipton, the respondent, who saw philosophy as addressing the problem from two directions. Coffee in which I spoke with David Lorimer and someone who specialised in creative consciousness. Then back for Clocksin on knowledge, Representation and Myth; Penrose having moved up to sit next to me. Clocksin's reductionist talk. Then engaged Penrose about his book and computers, and on Gödel..., the 37 scientists he is replying to. Walked with him to lunch and sat with him, he hooked-nosed and intent-eyed with a faint smile; very clubbable, very easy to talk to, very approachable, not stuck up in any way. Asked him about singularity (which he brilliantly calculated). He agreed the universe began simultaneously across a surface and not from one point. He agreed there is no Big Crunch necessarily from Smoot and Mather: 'You can't tell either way.' He agreed a Theory of Everything must include consciousness, love and prayer, absolutely everything. His account of inflation, see chapters 7 and 8 of his book: the Weyl curvature hypothesis in which past and future are necessary. This has been getting attention....The Big Bang is very important; Bohm is wrong to marginalise it, it is central. The expanding universe is explained by that. I: 'How, when you look in opposite directions, does the universe obey the same laws e.g. of temperature?' He suggested there *is* something real behind physics. Ended up asking if he'd like a copy of *The Fire and the Stones* and suggesting we should collaborate on a cross-disciplinary study. Talked at length with him (before he headed off to his room) on Hawking. 'I don't know Hawking's position. I think he disagrees.' On the Grand Unified Theory: 'They're nowhere near it. When it comes, yes you are right, it will be simple, but only from the viewpoint of understanding it. When you don't understand it, it appears complicated, like relativity.' I: 'Shouldn't you make a statement of the whole position to date?' He: 'I don't know enough.' 'I have difficulty talking to Hawking. You have to wait for him to reply and you lose the flow. I spoke with him 5 years ago, in conjunction with others, but I haven't spoken to him properly for 10 years. He allows speculation to be passed off as scientific fact.' On how near the theory may be; I: 'Perhaps you should walk across the road and feel elated' (a reference to his walk in the 1960s which led to his understanding 'the trapped surface' while in mid-road, then forgetting it, and then remembering it later when investigating his elation). Penrose laughed."

"In the afternoon," I wrote, "Penrose's talk on maths, including the statement that consciousness is non-local like his arithmetical knottedness, i.e. where is consciousness – somewhere other. Afterwards walked with him to tea and met Mary Midgley, who was very pro-what I stand for. Returned for Margaret Boden's talk on artificial intelligence (which contradicts Penrose's book) and then handed my books and *The Universe and the Light* to Penrose, who left to take them back to his room. ('What time's dinner?' I: '7.30.' 'Oh, I've time to go back to my room.') Went to the car to collect stuff for Mary Midgley and saw David Lorimer running. He posed for a photo or two (as I had the camera in the car) and then ran off into Cambridge. Holistic fitness. Dinner in the hall with David Lorimer – talked about Charlotte Waterlow – and Hao Wang, who has criticised Penrose over Gödel. Then a lecture on psychiatry by Dr Fulford."

The next day I "woke up with pins and needles in my right thumb and first and second fingers" which persisted until lunchtime. I wrote: "This morning it was Michael Sofroniew on the Neural Basis of Consciousness (very reductionist) and Martin Davies on Neuroscience; and then Chiater on Randomness and Arithmetic, and Hao Wang on Algorithmism and Physicalism. Asked a question after the Sofroniew talk. Lunched with Butterfield (don) and Penrose, and talked about Whitehead and the need for a more metaphysical philosophy at Cambridge." I teased Butterfield; he told me he would be putting up a poster of Hume on his wall, and I said, "You mean, of course, T. E. Hulme?" "Afterwards walked in the fields, Mary Midgley having retired....In the afternoon tea-break tackled Tim Smiley, Professor of Logic, about doing a critique of the premises of reductionism (i.e. neural reductionism), which perhaps I must do. My Zabov was such a reductionist. In the last session of the afternoon there was a dispute between Wang and Penrose, which I had fuelled on both sides. It helped Penrose....Supper, during which Geoffrey Read (who was at a nearby, but quite different conference) turned up in hall. Then Mary Midgley's talk, on Reductionist Megalomania: reading out adverse quotations on Atkins, being confrontational and lively and funny, debunking Reductionism. She was attacked by John Cornwell, the convenor, who perhaps wanted Reductionism affirmed. Afterwards talked with Mary Midgley and Sofroniew, and Sofroniew said he is really studying Alzheimer's disease. I: 'Use what you're doing for other people and don't have any truck with Churchland's philosophy.' That's what he's going to do. I said to Sofroniew: 'There are more things on heaven and earth than there are in your philosophy, Horatio.' He: 'I'll go along with the divine.' That turned him. Midgley – told her that Cornwell may have been hoping for an affirmation of Reductionism. Midgley: 'Was he drunk?' Sat with Freeman Dyson this evening."

The next morning I "woke at 7.40, then the fire alarm went off on our staircase (5). Six gathered downstairs. Freeman Dyson put his head out of the top floor window. I called 'Quick, get a blanket' and mimed a blanket for him to jump. He grinned. I: 'This is called "Disturbing the Universe"' (The title of his book). I called this up to him and again he grinned. The copy of Pais's *Einstein* which suddenly appeared – materialised – in the bookshop in the late afternoon after I had been thinking about it at lunch time and had bought Pais's *Bohr*. Lorimer and Anderson went off to the Fitzwilliam to look at art...as a counterbalance to neurons; for effect, a political statement. Talked to Phil Alport after breakfast about CERN. He sits in a hole watching a screen and occasionally has data meetings, one week a month. Penrose sat next to me again, and after a rambling um-and-er talk by Sachs, who kept standing in front of a screen and mistook the overhead projector for a microphone, Penrose said he was...very interested in my typescript and could he hang onto it and read more – which he is doing. Before the lecture I told him what I was about – that it was an Eliot view, as it were, reconciling the disciplines, and after the lecture I said I am doing a Coleridge, reconciling physics and metaphysics (reductionism and the spooky stuff). Spent the coffee break telling Penrose about the history theory) until Cornwell took him away), and then heard Peter Atkins on The Limitless Power of Science, in which he described his atheistic materialistic view as a dung-heap, bleak, barren but true. I said to Mary Midgley at the end, 'May God us keep/From single vision and Newton's sleep.' Cornwell attacked Atkins for his fundamentalism. Science and mysticism happily co-exist in Capra and Zukav, but science and religion are enemies in Atkins. Butterfield, 'I am an atheistic philosophical materialist.' Reductionism simplifying and unifying (in Atkins' case by illuminating). Lunched with John Barrow, who was sitting on his own in a multi-coloured shirt a whole table away from the nearest person (joined him after I'd sat down.). He still affirms inflation, does not see Penrose's 'ground state' Weyl hypothesis as being necessary. 'You can't observe it or measure it.' He said, 'I will explain why theories of everything don't have to include everything,'a semantic quibble. He is still reacting to certain data, which will illuminate some models. He has a...fellowship which saves him from working for a year, so he can do theoretical research in astrophysics. He has visited the Pope....He has been in Japan with Hawking but they didn't communicate. It was an unbearable 90 degrees." I sat back and asked myself: "How has this conflict of ideas affected my own view? Answer: not at all. I am in the position of Coleridge, reconciling physics and metaphysics. I have charted my way, and must continue it through English Literature....Barrow's brilliant talk about the universe. Why it has to be so large (because it took life 10 billion years to arrive) and why general principles cannot be applied as we only see part of the visible universe and not its related sections (answer this). A break for tea....A further talk with David Lorimer and Mary Midgley and then Redhead, who argued against reductionism; so that Butterfield – to oppose holism – had to back Bohm's supraluminal theory, which is metaphysical. Redhead is a realist, but would move towards the Idealist position if Bohm were accepted."

It was at this point, on 4th September 1992, that I met up with the young Norwegian mathematician who helped the mathematical side of my Form from Movement theory (that visible phenomena emerged from a pre-existing, moving, latent Fire) which is in Appendix 2 of *The Universe and the Light*. He had come to my attention when Geoffrey Read appeared in hall at dinner the previous night, having stood up to greet him. I wrote: "Before dinner met up with Henning Broten, a Norwegian mathematician of 27 who is still an undergraduate, of great creativity and brilliance, who told me he had just phoned Bohm and mentioned me, and who (standing first in the main Jesus College front quad, near the statue of a horse, and then in the cloisters) questioned me about how I got from the Fire to Existence and proposed that he did a new Maths which could show how the universe was created." He explained I would have to tell him very precisely and he would convert it into maths. I wrote: "Wrote it out over dinner on a scrappy piece of paper I had in my pocket. Had finished it by the third course. Our Form from Movement Theory. The Fire or Light is a movement in all directions which is infinitely self-entangled and eternal; it creates a vacuum in a point – an empty or infinitesimal point – because the Fire is moving away (this is a singularity); this empty point is in the centre of a rotation of Fire and expands in a regularity (pre-space); the rotation provides a regular calm symmetrical field in an infinitely wide area (the pre-vacuum which surrounds this and envelops the pre-universe); in this calm field there is a

709

disturbance, Prigogine's interplay between the infinite and the regular or regularity and randomness, which is the Big Bang. The first virtual particle produced Being, and locality, which is a factoralisation or limitation or fragmentation or reduction of the infinite self-entanglement. The virtual particle becomes real, the first proton, and the hot beginning or Big Bang took place. This goes beyond Gödel: 'Any finite system is incapable of complete self-awareness.' I need to clean up these tangled jottings. Talked with Henning until 11.20, i.e. four and a half hours without a break. He: 'I like your passion. You are like Einstein, you attack the problem with imagination.' At the outset he said that Bohm couldn't come up with an imagine-first proof but that I could; and that he would do the Maths to put it into stages. We will do a paper and send it to Bohm and Penrose, Gunzig, Geoffrey Read and his other friend in Oslo. Henning is 3 years older than Heisenberg was at the time of the uncertainty principle, and he will work through all my points in my metaphysical science. Geoffrey Read: 'Space is the order of co-existence of events; time is the order of succession of events.' This proof is the result of imagination."

I observed: "My paper was not taken up by the reductionists, and Penrose and Mary Midgley saw something in it. Henning and I were the significant event at this conference, and no one saw. My elation as I walked back from the bar (where I had talked with Henning, standing by the door, after dinner, drinking orange and lemonade mixed). The stars overhead, and my elation as I looked at something that had defeated Penrose it has been given to me to crack the origin of the stars. This terrific energy. I could work on anything and conquer anything. I feel full of elation, quiet elation. Have rewritten the theory and written a poem about my elation. This afternoon I skimmed Pais's life of Einstein, and here I am following in his footsteps." And I wrote: "Improbably Geoffrey Read appeared in the hall because he is relevant to the theory." Geoffrey Read, the Leibniz of our time, had inadvertently brought my Form from Movement theory to birth by pushing Henning in my direction.

The next morning, September 5th, I "breakfasted with Henning and then heard Edelman on memory and neural Darwinism. The transmissive view left open, although consciousness is put within Nature. Lunched with Mary Midgley, who sought me out and sat next to me. Alliance. Promised to send her my book. On to the Old Library with Cornwell to see Coleridge's letter and essay in Latin (1792), that 'to long for posthumous fame is unworthy of a wise man', and his lock of hair (curled) and an edition of the Notebooks which turned up in the 1930s and got taken to Toronto."

I reflected: "The Light has put me among the materialists and neural biologists and left me to carry its torch through my paper, which I did. I could probably have done more, but no doubt I should not have done. Butterfield's closing remark on Barrow: 'His quick run through, in two senses of the phrase.' After lunch, left."

I asked a rhetorical question, setting up the Reductionist position to knock it down: "Could it be that I had the right view of the brain...in 1963? No, no, no! because it left me static and unable to grow; its bleak vision denied me the growth that my present vision has allowed. What evidence for a universe of Light-filled consciousness and thought? 'Where's your evidence?' That is another essay. Cornwell yesterday, when I said 'I come from the mystic consciousness and not from neurons': 'they may not be very different.' I: 'No, I agree.'"

I now wrote insights from the conference into the appendix of *The Universe and the Light* and then pushed on with this Autobiography.

Henning rang me on his way home to Norway, and told me he was improving the maths. We exchanged versions of what became Appendix 2 in my book. Geoffrey Read rang, full of gossip, and advanced his theory of memory and time: "The past is overlaid by the present, a Liebnizian, Bohemian view that all is process, time and space to be defined in terms of the structure of a process". I rang Bohm for 45 minutes: "Told him about Henning and the conference and my theory of the beginning. Bohm interrupted: space-time have to be abstracted, the beginning was when time began, you can't talk of a pre-time. Mention of our own time and all time....'In the 19th century there was more hope of progress than today.' We talked about Redhead and how there is respect for Bohm but they won't mention him in their indexes. I: 'I can't understand it.' Bohm: 'I can't understand it either.' On the stranglehold of science, Bohm: 'It used to be the other way. In Galileo's time. Religion was in charge. Belief meant "beloved".' He asked, 'What did Penrose say?' And I told him of Barrow's criticism that the visible universe is a bubble in foam. Bohm: 'How does he know that?' I told him Barrow said Penrose was wrong to have general principles. Bohm: 'He's just created a general principle by saying that.' I: 'I agree.' Bohm: 'Scientists don't know what metaphysics is, they think it's something flakey.' I: 'Einstein said physics inevitably leads to metaphysics.' Bohm: 'Yes.' Told him how Henning and I were left alone in the hall at the end of dinner. Bohm laughed. He said he would make a comment on my book to the effect that my 'attempt to bring together physics and the philosophical view in a coherent whole is a worthwhile one' or something of the sort – the exact wording to be sorted out when I ring him in 2 weeks' time. Told him about Geoffrey Read's view of space-time. Rang Geoffrey Read and gave him feedback. Geoffrey Read on Bohm: 'He has sincerity. The one distinctive feature of genius is undoubtedly sincerity, and he has that. But I feel he is torn about Einstein. He knows Einstein was seriously wrong, as I believe, but is trying to make an apology for him, and so he stutters, for in his heart of hearts he knows Einstein was wrong.'"

In the middle of all this "Anthony had a headache from being kicked during football on the back of his head. Healed him for a few minutes. Surges came immediately and within 5 minutes he reported that the headache had gone."

I rang Sir Laurens van der Post "who listened to my account of Cambridge and said: 'It's a hell-hole. Do you know Carmen Blacker? They do this to her.' Van der Post, 'They need to read more of your work. The universities are awful. Oxford as well as Cambridge. It's very distressing that they've gone like that.' I on the 'dung-hill' (Atkins): 'They need to put just one of your books beside their vision.' He: 'Yes.' I: 'Is your present work about Africa?' He: 'No. I don't know what it's about. I don't let myself ask that. I haven't got down to your thing because I can't take my mind off the book I'm writing. One day I'll be useful to you.' On my answerphone Mary Midgley said " she would be prepared to comment: 'challenging, serious and timely'."I rang her in Newcastle and she said: "I wrote my thesis on Plotinus. I'm familiar with the concepts in your work." I noted: "Penrose, Bohm, Mary Midgley and van der Post – all allies of mine."

On September 11th I collected the first 10 pages of this Autobiography, and the following day I wrote out the first version of my "A Form from Movement theory between 10.30 and 2". I then went to dinner with Clapperton from Cornwall and Susie "via Flatford Mill (wrote *Autumn at Flatford Mill*). Arrived at 7.15 at East Bergholt Place, which has a clock at the front; where Squire Heaney (of Heaney's cartridges) lived. Timber in the building, unprepossessing 20th century from the back, but many rooms, Georgian architecture and superb grounds with many trees and landscaped lake. Dinner with a farmer and his wife (who has 1,000 acres), a GP from Colchester on his own – both cynics. The GP denies energy coming in from outside. 'Some people just have more energy. Darwin was knackered after 20 minutes.' Peter wanted me to talk about the universe, so I did. Scepticism from the GP, support from the farmer. The farmer's question: 'What is a black hole?' Creation or evolution – it's not impersonal God as a human being or evolution through the ape, but a third way. Explain it. Clapperton, 'We're Haggerists.' The farmer, 'You speak authoritatively, you could convert people.' Peter being Darwinist and basic....My talk about energy and sluice gates. Susie: 'I was a locked gate and going stagnant.'"

I observed: "Everyone is at their own level and they have their concerns and don't listen to what you're saying. General talk of my enthusiasm for everything....It's all levels and enthusiasm in the end. Oppose neural Darwinism with the transmissive view. Write an essay on 'Does something survive death?' (What happens in all those 50,000 million years.) Is it superstition and flat-earthing as the materialists say? Over half mankind believes in reincarnation; all mankind believed the earth was flat – and was wrong. Another essay on 'Creation or evolution? Which?' Showing how life emerged."

I spoke of "my general position: there are plenty of specialists, but not many who know about everything. Leibniz was perhaps the last to be able to do that c1700, knowledge being less. A universal genius. You make the time to do it. You make your whole statement in your work."

On September 15th I "dictated my 'Form from Movement theory' and while I was talking about the creation of the universe two Jehovah's Witnesses came to the door. One holding a book said, 'Can I tell you how the universe was created.' I: 'I'm just dictating my theory on it now, you'll be able to read it before the end of the year I hope.' Startled she said 'Oh' and left, abashed. This is an example of synchronicity."

The ERM crisis happened: Black Wednesday, when interest rates were briefly raised by 5%. On the same day I "sketched the outline for my next essay, 'Beyond Evolution and Neurons: Manifestation and Transmissive Consciousness', which would become Appendix 3 in *The Universe and the Light*. This grew out of Clapperton's dinner. I left a Coopersale Hall parents evening early and wrote until 1.15 am though I could have written more. The sudden thunder, echoing through the night, startling me." There was "a thunderstorm most of the night, clattering like boxes on the loft floor immediately overhead, with sheet lightning (an electric storm)". I wrote: "Sep 19. Worked on Appendix 3. Evidence is the problem with all my essays. Evidence is the problem with all materialistic essays, although they don't see that. I have stood for a new view of the universe, and of science and philosophy. This must be in the title. I have been clever in not wasting energy. I have not absorbed detail like Jeremy Butterfield, who cannot see the wood for the trees. I have found myself time, I avoid conferences and lectures by an large, I have escaped correcting others' essays, and so I can think clearly and see clearly and put down my perceptions without interference from others or fear of others." I finished the essay about 6 and "relaxed with Anthony watching the end of (Clint) Eastwood's *High Plains Drifter*". There was "a cricket – a large green grasshopper, as it were – in the porch" that night.

I rang Gunzig "who will comment: 'an outstanding and unexpected marriage between cosmology and its metaphysical counterpart. Very impressive.' Rang David Bohm, who it transpires has had a second heart attack last weekend. 'I had another setback last weekend, another heart attack, only mild.' We chatted about Gunzig and Hawking, who described himself to me as a reductionalist and wrote that holism is mysticism; and my theory of the universe, which (Henning told me over the phone today from Norway) will go through a second edition next week, with revised maths. Bohm's comment: 'This attempt to bring together physics and the philosophical view of the cosmos in a coherent whole is interesting and worthwhile.' Rang van der Post. 'Oh, Nicholas, how *are* you? How nice to hear from you. Yes, I got your paper about the origin of the universe. You're doing something very important.'...I: 'I want to show that someone born in ordinary circumstances in the 20th century can progress to a metaphysical outlook; do it in everyday language that ordinary people will respond to.' Then rang Sheldrake, who is back from Canada and the US. 'I got your paper. It's very interesting. How was Cambridge? I'm not surprised, anything at Cambridge is full of reductionists....I'm engaged in an academic dispute with Stephen Rose.' I: 'I've ordered his book.' 'What book?' I: '*The Making of Memory*.' 'Oh, I must read it, I didn't know he had a book out.' I: 'The other book out is Richard Milton's *The Facts of Life: Shattering the Myth of Darwinism*.' He: 'I've been away, I don't know about these books. And I didn't know Bohm has had a first heart attack, let alone a second.'" I observed: "So in one evening, phoned Gunzig, Bohm, van der Post and Sheldrake."

Heather Dobbs rang me. She remarked: "Sheldrake is not on the metaphysical level, he is at a materialistic level. He is not drawing to himself the books he needs." I: "I should not be doing the practical Foundation because I have to get the Appendices right and the endorsers and oppose materialism at Cambridge, and in 1993 found Universalism as an international philosophy." I received a long letter, five handwritten pages of A4, from Mary Midgley, and wrote: "What a fine woman and type of mind she represents: upright, forthright, fearless, intellectually honest, perceptive." She confirmed Heather's view of Sheldrake: "He is a materialist, who cannot help at the metaphysical level." There was another "long thunderstorm with a mixture of white forked and sheet lightning".

We took Matthew to Bangor towards the end of September. He was only the second member of our family to go to university, I being the first. I wrote: "Drove through mist...and drove on through clear weather and stunning scenery via Llangollen and Llanberis pass, past the Betws-y-coed Swallow falls and Capel Curig, to Bangor. The view of Snowdon on the way in elicited two poems..., which I wrote in the car: *Being in Snowdonia* and *Snowdon*. Found the Menai Straits Hotel....Off to walk round Bangor. The University building, old and inspiring. A valley with trees, a skyline with trees. Bangor is on two sides of a valley, surrounded by trees and with views of Snowdon....Walked down to the Cathedral and up to the High Street and along to Neuedd Reichel, and then piled into the car and we drove through the dark to Llandudno. The Brighton-style front, cream Belgravia-style hotels with the Great and Little Orme together, and in the middle the Hydro Hotel with its glass veranda where I kept my Suez cuttings in 1956 and heard my 'A' level results. Went in and looked round. Outside there were fishermen with lights – like souls showing their lights. Wrote *Lights like Souls*. On to Conway Castle and Alfredo's in the main square; had a three course meal, based on pizza with wine. Then drove back to Bangor."

The next morning I woke "to a view across the valley and across water to Anglesey, a heavenly wooded prospect with white buildings in pockets. Trees, birds, houses and stillness. Wrote *Stillness overlooking Anglesey* (poem)." After breakfast we "transferred Matthew into...his tiny room, his new home. At least he has a TV and music centre and computer. Looked round, saw the dining-hall....Left and went to the pier and walked to the end. The Victorian lamps and domes. Wrote *A New Life* and *Transient Existence and Lasting Being*. Then pushed on home via Chester (the coastal route) and went to Albrighton centre to see where the Oaklanders will stay. Wrote *Rabbit: Self-preservation* and *Ladybird, Groaning*. Left there at 4.20, home by 7....Felt deflated, almost depressed. Felt a tugging on my heart, missing Matthew who is part of this family. I grow old, will soon be alone again."

Steve Norris rang to confirm that he would unveil Andrew Murdoch's new DocuTech 90 at Prontaprint, Barking: "I said, 'Dramatic events over the pound.' He: 'What went wrong was German reunification.' (In 5 minutes.) I: 'A pity they didn't all revalue as I suggested last time we talked, and save £1.3 billion. He: 'Sterling will have replaced the mark as the main currency in 10 years' time.' I: 'Talk of sterling replacing the mark is wish-fulfilment, and we don't want zero inflation.'"

At the end of September *The Universe and the Light* was finally finished. I wrote: "Thought I should have called my 'ism' Manifestationism, although Universalism is more of a force that moves nations."

Harvest Festival at Oaklands took place and Canon Walsh from St. John's, Loughton spoke at the children's level about everything being different and special. Individuality as well as unity I must emphasise:

different vegetables (prize marrows), children, fingerprints, clouds, trees, etc. The uniqueness and individuality of every specimen in a species. Stress this within Universalism. Universalist individuality." The Harvest Festival at Epping was attended by Eric Dawson, a local artist who had painted the school, and I had coffee with him in the study and he looked at my books.

I rang Sir Laurens van der Post, who said: "'It looks very interesting, I want to give you an honest opinion. I haven't finished my thing yet. One gets pushed oneself. And how is your Autobiography going? How many pages have you done? How's it going?' It is a father's interest in a son. A very benevolent, interested father. I: 'I'm doing my Autobiography but these other things keep coming.' He: 'If it comes from a deep place then it's to be considered very seriously.' I: 'The two go together: the reflective essay and the lightness of touch of a narrative; the one informs the other.' He: 'Yes, that's true. I think that's right. I'm doing something similar now.' I: 'You're like Shaw or Tolstoy, you'll still be doing it when you're 94.' He: 'I don't know about that. But bless you. I want to help you but I need time.' With Sir Laurens you feel as if he has pushed everything to one side and is focusing on you and nothing else; giving you his undivided attention. He has great charm."

Michael Mann rang and "said that Peter Roche de Coppens is reading *The Fire and the Stones* and is very enthusiastic about it; says it is right."

I went to Chigwell School for the local Heads' annual dinner. The Head, Tony Little, said: "Jo Fyles (the Head of History with characterful Victorian whiskers) is gracing us with his presence and insisted that he would only come if he sat next to Nicholas Hagger." I wrote: "Talked about his work and his interest in church-building between the Reformation and the Civil War. 'They were looked after by the local people.' Found him gentle and not rebellious at all....Established that he has a house in Thirsk, Lancs., and that he will retire there to write history; that he has never read *Look Back in Anger* and does not know about Jimmy Porter." Afterwards in the Swallow Room I met Roger Hickling, Old Chigwellian, whom I had not met since the mid-1950s, and who was present because he had invited some boys on behalf of a London hospital he worked with. He recalled Thompson, our Head, saying in that same room: "Do you come from the Isle of Dogs? I'd have thought so because of your use of dog Latin." David Ballance told me he would be displaying my books alongside books by Bernard Williams in an exhibition corner at Chigwell School's forthcoming Open Day.

In mid-October, Sir Laurens van der Post gave me his comment on *The Universe and the Light*. "He dictated: "'It is nearly 100 years since William James first warned against the reductionism which he saw increasing in the scientific and philosophic spirits of his day, the 'but only' element as he labelled it. Even he would have been dismayed at the extent of the empass the element has established in all the disciplines he valued, and how much he would have supported all those who value the quality and range of a truly comprehensive modern awareness as Nicholas Hagger does in all he has written with a rare intellectual passion in all his work since *The Fire and the Stones*." Now will that help you?' he asked." I rang Penrose ("Roger Penrose here") and he gave me his comment: "I read Hawking's comment about holism being mysticism and want to comment as follows:

"Holistic concepts have a profound role in modern mathematics and physics, and need not be mystical; Hagger's broad sweep over the holistic scene is not so constrained by scientific desiderata." That answers Hawking.' His concern to answer Hawking." The next day I visited Michael Mann. I wrote: "To the pub for lunch. I had steak and kidney pie sitting next to the log-fire. Mann: 'The Booker novelists have nothing to say. They may write well, but they've nothing to say." We discussed our future roles: "Mann: 'Yours is to oppose materialism; the Metaphysical Revolution, with all the conflict that brings." I recorded: "His: 'To stand for a spiritual level of reality and to bring books to the common people.'" I recorded: "His view of the New Age: 'It's part Universalism, the rest is nothing.'...His view...now accords with mine. Michael Mann: 'I want to challenge received notions.'" He laughingly said: "People get what they want and discover they don't want it and spend the rest of their lives refusing to act that role."

A political motif returned. The closure of coal mines was dominating the news, following a report by Rothschilds, the Government's bank manager, recommending closures. I wrote about the New World Order, which Churchill once called "a long-running Conspiracy": "Churchill bankrupted the UK by lend-lease, opposing the Hitler domination of Europe. The Conspiracy (Churchill's word) want a United States of the World (as did Lenin) and a United States of Europe as a stepping stone with its independent bank, the Bundesbank (a Conspiracy bank) which is to smash the nation-states' currencies (the lira and pound) and demonstrate that stability lies in being the ecu. The closing of the pits is a diversion so they can get Maastricht through the Commons, which the Conspiracy has imposed on nation-states. Thatcher was undermined in March 1985 when (Lord Victor) Rothschild proposed the poll tax; this was just after the end of the miners' strike. The Conspiracy was anti-Thatcher on this, and decided to undermine her? This was before the La Toja meeting at which Kissinger and Co decided to overthrow her. Kissinger stands for a united world, bringing people together, (political) universalism. Rothschild led Heath into a miners' strike with Scargill who overthrew Heath and as a result Wilson held the referendum on Europe. Rothschild paid Thatcher back for the miners' strike victory in 1985 with the poll tax? In 1992 Labour were to win and ratify Maastricht under Kinnock...; and the Conservative steering through of Maastricht has been more turbulent....Against this backdrop, Black Wednesday can be seen as demoting national currencies (nation-states' currencies as opposed to ecus), and the British miners' strike can be seen as preparing the fall of Major." As I noted elsewhere, the Conspiracy closed the British mines as part of a programme to internationalise all national industries.

I thought about my epic: "This will be a Universalist epic. Compare Milton and Puritanism. Universalism is the new idea that impels me to write this epic. I could not do it before because I had to work out Universalism (first)....This idea has burst through from the beyond, like a windfall out of a tree, taking me by surprise when I was not ready. Have hastily drafted 10 books within the epic."

There was another philosophers meeting in Oxford at Hertha Larive's bungalow. I wrote: "About a dozen philosophers. Chaired by Max Payne, for 2 hours we went round clockwise, each speaking on what metaphysics is and what process is – I said it was Metaphysical Revolution within the currency of ideas – and David Lorimer asked everyone to refer to the 'Metaphysical Revolution' in conversation to spread it. Alison Watson, Geoffrey Read and Chris McCann (ex-Lincoln, Oxford don) are the main philosophers there. After a vegetarian lunch, the afternoon degenerated into talk about telepathy – low level, psychic and not spiritual....At the end there was a queue to talk to me, asking me to outline my philosophy."

Geoffrey Read again explained his theory of memory. I wrote: "Geoffrey Read on the self. Our memories are images in the past. Greece is in Greece, and our memories are in the past. The present self is a tiny skiff on a vast ocean with everything below (my analogy). There is no memory in the brain. The synapses are not to do with memory....Geoffrey Read is a reductionist, at his own insistence. He reduces the present to the past, the ego to images and so on – and reduces man. He reduces time and space to events." I added: "Considered strings of events. In our life there are strings of events. In a sense I am a reductionist: I reduce everything to Light. But reductionists are materialists and I am not a materialist, so I cannot be a reductionist. I merely simplify. I am a simplificationist."

I noted: "The vividness of the copper beech over the tennis court: A bright yellow." We went to Cornwall and I wrote "a poem *Leaves like Memories* after a whirling wind had scattered the leaves on the tennis court at Oaklands, blowing them up into a storm like snowflakes". When I arrived in Cornwall I proof-read the 1966 *Diaries* "until I fell asleep, nodding off over my work from the sea-air".

I mulled my development: "There is early Hagger, middle Hagger and late Hagger. Earlier Hagger is largely Existentialist and focuses on the Shadow. Middle Hagger is illumined and focuses on the Light. Late Hagger focuses on civilisations and the universe, i.e. the world's context of the Light. The movement is from individual to mysticism to science and philosophy. The movement is from Existentialism to Mysticism to Universalism." I added: "My Existentialist concepts: the Silence, the Search, the Journey and others. Is my Universalism separate from Existentialism or a new branch of Existentialism? Answer, both. It cannot exclusively be a new branch as I have to distance myself from the existence-based atheistic Existentialism. But as an independent philosophy, it emerges from Existentialism."

The next day was sunny. The tide was out, there was "a bright glare that made me sneeze". I proof-read. "Had breaks when I walked a few yards to the sea wall. First it was low tide with a flock of gulls on the sand by the gentle waves. Then the sea was coming in and there was a whipping wind while I inhaled the air, took great gulps of pure Channel air. Came in feeling well. Sun and granite walls."

Steve Norris rang my Cornish number "and for half an hour I filled him in on the Rothschild connections. I said I'd written to Heseltine, sending a copy of *Scargill the Stalinist?* and spoke of Scargill being stirred up and how Peter Walker asked to see me and Rothschilds' hand is in the pit closures....Norris: 'Very interesting. There's definitely someone else's hand in it. I don't think Heseltine just made a mistake.' I: '...Heseltine...overthrew Thatcher....They found themselves stuck with Major who very soon had to learn that he has to implement what Rothschilds say.'"

I thought about politics. The government was in a dreadful mess, "on the economy, on coal, hospitals and Europe. These 4 issues contain all our bad symptoms: unemployment and balance of payment deficit, the need to close pits and hospitals, and focusing on Maastricht, which the British people perceive as irrelevant to the economy, but which is not. The incompetence of Major's leadership is widely blamed, permitting U-turns on the minds and economy and possibly now the presentation of Maastricht....But it is unfair to pin the blame exclusively on Major. He is under orders. He has found out fast the facts of life of being a Prime Minister or leader of any Western country, that you have to co-operate with your bank manager and do what he says." I knew Maastricht would be ratified – *they* wanted it so it had to be – but "o the agony and uncertainty as the nation-states die away from their independence into a United States of Europe! I am the poet of this tradition, not of grumbling decline (Larkin) but of the transition, seeing the underlying historical movement."

We went to Porthleven via Truro, and I took Anthony on to the pier. The "sea was breaking over the end and flinging spray. Surf out beyond the cliffs, very windy. Came back with reddened face."

The next day I "woke to a brilliant sun and wrote *Brilliant Sun*". We went to Fowey and I bought some books at the antiquarian bookshop. We crossed to Polruan and had a cream tea in the Singing Kettle. I noted: "Was out of breath during the climb back to the car park. My lungs seemed to be working with reduced efficiency despite the fresh air I have had all week." Our last day was "a gloriously fine day. A calm sea. Light very brilliant leaping off the wrinkled surface."

We attended a Conservative reception at Lippitt's Hill Lodge, which had been rebuilt: "Only the facade dates back to (John) Clare. Bowen Wells MP mentioned the Rothschild Report on the mines in his speech from the stairs, and there was much criticism when it came to questions: "Vernon Davies, simpering and smiling. The squirrelly hostess, the crusty buffers, loaded and unconscious and dense." I was the first to leave.

I noted: "Novels and works of art mirror the inner state of growth of the creator, and when a creator has outgrown art he is embarrassed by it. If he grows for 25 years, as I did, he will be permanently embarrassed by what he has produced, until his growth has stopped."

On November 1st I went to Parndon Wood and "wrote *Split Ash*. Later wrote *All Saints Day* at midnight (Nov 1/2)."

On November 3rd I read that David Bohm had died. He gave me a quotation for my book "just before he went". At 9.40 p.m. on November 4th I recorded "got back to the Autobiography and wrote the mystical experience before leaving England and suddenly I felt David Bohm was near me. Sat quietly and was flooded with energy, which tingled from the beyond – spiritual energy. Said thank you to Bohm for supporting me. He is on my side, although he is on the other side."

I had to speak to Jack Wood, who reported that John Major had liked *Union for Recovery*. I noted: "Wood is 83 and has furred-up arteries, is permanently giddy and therefore housebound and can't centre himself."

It was again the Oaklands fireworks and again the parents "built a fire like a wigwam....400 came and there were fairy lights over the entrance to the field. The wigwam blazed with a tongue of flame and shot sparks into the night sky, the fireworks – the rockets – made big bangs and the Catherine wheels and Niagara falls drew comments. Later I walked among the parents on the tennis court, chatting here and there."

I watched the Church of England Synod vote in favour of the ordination of women, thus cutting themselves from the Catholic Church and the Ecumenical movement while claiming to be accelerating it. I saw Philip Mawer, my relative, by the Archbishop; an influential speech from (Bishop) Alec Graham (my Worcester College chaplain)". I observed: "The Church should be apart from society, separated by a wall, so that it does not become secularised and contaminated by society, so that it symbolises the Absolute. It is wrong to regard the church as having to approach society and be with-it, for its approaching of the Absolute does not then happen."

I wrote of my mission: "My task and mission is to state how life connects with the eternal, in poetry, in novels, in autobiography and in diaries – and of course in history. I have to state how life links to the mystic reality, indeed comes from it." I noted a comment of (Graham) Hough's that "Modernism was not a spiritual movement, as was the Romantic movement, and so it lacked direction and purpose".

Back in poetry, I wrote: "Woke with an idea for a poem about our national decay into Europe and world government. Still in my pyjamas, sketched crucial images. Lines of Light. This will be Christ's visit – his Second Coming explored, a kind of preliminary visit before the Second Coming – to Loughton and Epping, and his disillusion with what he has found. He starts with the children, looking for me; starts with the playground. I kind of latter day Langland poem?"

I had an uncharacteristic glimpse into the abyss: "On Thursday night I saw into the abyss and what I saw sickened me: I, left with nothing, a total have-not, unable to pursue my Mystic Way for lack of a base or funds, a post-nuclear strike existence, as it were." This vastation experience did not recur.

Miss Lord's birthday party was celebrated at a gathering of Oaklands staff. I made a speech. The following exchange took place with one of her former staff (her memory was going): "'Who are you?' 'Hilary.' 'Hilary Jones?'" The member of staff said "No" and gave her name. Miss Lord said: "Don't stay too long, parents don't like elderly staff." (The member of staff was in her early 50s.)

That evening I "went to Prontaprint Barking and waited among 30 besuited local businessmen for Steve Norris to arrive. Norris in overcoat with black fur collar, and underneath a Minister's suit, spotted yellow tie and navy handkerchief in top pocket with white spots. Introduced him to Andrew Murdoch and drank orange juice and munched nuts...until Andrew and Steve spoke, and then a demonstration of the DocuTech 90 which is able to do 90 copies a minute....Left with Norris and walked with him to

Barking station, about 10 minutes. He...thinks Lamont is being hounded by...(the leaking of the access, over the limit). I: 'Heseltine's into everything.' He: 'Yes. I told him about you. He's received the Scargill book and he said he'd look into it.'...On the platform, stood – the two of us entirely alone, while on the other side there were 5 or 6 deep waiting for a train; I teasing the Minister of Transport for London on how we nearly got lost finding the platform."

Argie, now aged 89, brought a group of old folk 20 years younger than her, to see an Oaklands in-school production, *The Firebird*.

The news confirmed my view that Britain was in decline: "The whole establishment in Britain is in decay. Windsor burning, the Queen paying tax, Charles being by-passed for William (according to *Today* today), the Chancellor over the limit 15 times, Miss Whiplash in his home, the Church allowing women priests, schism with Rome. All four estates (Lords piritual and temporal, Commons and press) are in decay. Standards have gone. No empire for the young to go out to, just permanent recession. Republicanism, decay into 1. Tebbit and Thatcher tried to avert this decay and failed. Another image of decay: the Government borrowing from the bank (Rothschilds) and having to do what they say over the poll tax and mining. Rule from abroad, the Bundesbank running our economy. How are the mighty fallen! The Age of Churchill has gone, the 1950s were a high point – the Age of Churchill and Macmillan....The pattern of decay. The old structures are decaying into the new, the old nationalist structures into the new European structures. We are decaying into Europe, into a United States of Europe."

I "went to the Light. Before my closed eyes, clouds. They cleared, leaving a sky at dusk, quite cloudless. Does this mean that the clouds are clearing now for me? Feel well. So much energy my hair is standing up."

There was a strange instance of telepathy. We were invited by a local estate agent to a reception at Bovis Homes, Boleyn Court, on the Epping New Road. I wrote: "Chatted to Mr (Jim) Lawlor...and Duncan Gadsby. When I saw Gadsby I thought 'Is that Bloomfield who sold us Orchard Cottage?' and a bald man approached and said, 'Mr Hagger, David Bloomfield.' I had received the name before I had identified the possessor of it."

On December 9th there was a carol service at Coopersale Hall. I sat under a deafening organ. There was a staff lunch in the assembly hall, and I hurried to St. Mary's, Loughton for the Oaklands carol service, where the church was packed and there seemed to be no seats anywhere. At 1.59 I asked Ann, who was standing at the back, "Where am I sitting?" She said: "You're not, you're taking it. The vicar hasn't turned up." So I went straight down to the front and welcomed everyone. The service then ran itself, with children doing readings and singing carols and parading to the crib. It got to five minutes before the end and there was still no sign of the vicar, and the organist passed a book in my direction via Ann Holland (one of the staff, like me an ex-Oaklands pupil) and gesticulated that I should perform the closing prayer. So I went out to the front and went to the Light and extemporised about the meaning of Christmas for the children, and then read a collect from the book and then, making a split second decision in front of the packed church, there having been no discussion at all, gave a blessing: "May the Lord bless you and keep you...." Even as I said the words I realised I should be saying 'May the Lord bless us and keep us', but I had started and had to finish, so with my best Bishop's intonation I continued: "...and make his face to shine upon you and give you peace. Amen." As I made the sign of the cross I could see the Oaklands staff holding their noses and looking down, trying not to laugh. There was a chorus of "Amen" from the congregation, and no thunderbolt struck the church as it did Durham Cathedral, and I then walked down the aisle to the porch so that I could say goodbye to my flock, and one of the first parents to come out said, "I didn't know you did that," and I said: "I don't." Then the vicar turned up. "Oh," he said, "oh, you've finished. My meeting overran. Oh, who took the service?" "I did," I said. "And who did the blessing?" "I did," I said, "and if I'm doing it next year I want some credibility, I want a more credible dress: surplice, crozier and mitre – shepherd's crook and tea-cosy." I found it hard to live the occasion down. Next day staff passing me said, "Good morning, Bishop."

Next day Oaklands broke up and we were visited by Nadine, an ex-pupil, whose mother said: "The Headmistress at her present school never smiles. It's not a cuddly school like here. There are too many rules. Nadine often says, 'I'll go up and see Mr and Mrs. Hagger.' It's a year after she's left (actually 4 terms), but she still talks about you.'"

In the evening there was a candlelit buffet for the Oaklands staff, and Carol Norris surprised us by giving us a large glass bowl with an oak-tree engraved on it to commemorate our 10 years at Oaklands. I sat with two husbands, Tim Norris and Richard Fradd, who reminisced "on Whitford and Lister, who died recently (two Chigwell School masters). His beaten-up face, weathered and creased, hair slightly long; the same old Fradd underneath. He had a pocket full of marbles, eighters and fourers and oners, and I chalked out a gulley on the library carpet and we played with Tim Norris, egged on by Geoff Staniforth. Fradd and I won a game each." Kneeling on the carpet and flicking and peering, we could have been back at the end of the 1940s among the gulleys at Chigwell School.

I was tested for nerve deafness and "wince at noise over 100 decibels but cannot hear consonants and need clarity. This is probably because I had meningitis at 7, when I was rushed to hospital in an ambulance and saved by penicillin. I had a chest infection which infected my middle ear, which ate into my brain – or towards my brain – and penicillin killed it before it killed me."

Marion Lord went to hospital to have chemotherapy to get rid of her seedlings of cancer. Meanwhile there was a call from a friend that Mabel Reid's light was on: "Went with Ann and found her lying in a hot, smelly bedroom, electric blanket having been on all night and all day. Turned the blanket off after calling to her. She opened an eye. Could not move – only her arms. Called an ambulance, two men lifted her into a portable chair and strapped her in. Her hairnet was still on, but spectacles off, her nose curved, her mouth open, and she looked like an Egyptian mummy. She looked near to death. An ambulance man: 'I think she's had a stroke.' Oxygen mask in the ambulance." We had in fact saved her life.

We went down to Cornwall. I walked on the pier at Charlestown by a boiling sea. A gusty blowing evening. The cobwebs swept away." I was full of ideas for putting on days on the Metaphysical Revolution, on Universalism, on my books. The next day, "a day of stillness", I pondered "the reality behind the work": "a school for self-realisation. The metaphysics behind the talk." I wrote: "Heather, Mona, Linda and I are mainstream people, not barefooted New Age people. So I must do a mainstream activity at these meetings."

I rang Colin Wilson and wrote: "He cannot see me before Sunday as he has a painter friend from Bruges coming for 3 days. He is writing a book about him and he is staying 3 days. A pleasant chat over the phone. Told him about *The Universe and the Light* and my Autobiography. He is working 'flat out' on two books, one on the painter and one on space vampires. Spiders got pushed aside. No philosophy, only articles. 'Oh and my mother died two weeks ago. We went into her room and found her dead on the floor. It was a great shock.' I: 'You'll be making smoked salmon for her at 5.30.' He: 'I do.' I: 'There'll be a hole in the house.' He: 'There is. She lived with us for 10 years.' On my Autobiography, he: 'It's a good plan.' Will see him in February or April."

I "worked all day on my Autobiography. It is my Augustine's *Confessions*." There was "a roaring in the chimney, a battering on the front door, a great buffeting all round the house". I wrote: "A night of storm and gales. Now the sea is fountaining over the rocks, pouring over the harbour wall, lashing winds so that spray is like driving rain, whistling round the house and rattling in the chimney. I have written *Flow and All Good*, a poem on how the body and Nature are at one and obey the same law; how wind and sea, and breath and blood, are part of one flow. Plumes of spray....Then suddenly the tide turned and the sea and wind abated. 'The tide has taken it' – an old Cornish grandmother's saying."

We went to Gunwalloe: "The whole sea was white with boiling surf and spray and flung foam. Scribbled a poem, another Gunwalloe sonnet, in *After the Storm*, standing by the stone steps that lead from the churchyard to the beach. Back to the car for sandwich lunch. I wore my Guernsey fisherman's sweater while writing the poem. On to Porthleven and mince pies and cream at Pat's. Then I walked down to the pier. A great boiling foam. Wrote another poem. Mist all over me. Then Ant arrived carrying my leather jacket. Today I have overhauled poems. Besides *Flow and Flood* and the Gunwalloe sonnet *After the Storm* I have done *Elemental*; *Royals* (both dated today); *War and Peace*; *Eternity*; *Stepping-Stones*, all dated August 1991 or (*Stepping-Stones*) to Bedford when I attended the...function in the church after lunch with Frances this summer." This was the beginning of my preparation of my *Collected Poems* which was to last all through 1993, and I was fortunate in finding the technically accomplished Alison Goldsmith to help me collate them.

The next day I "wrote *Harbourmaster*, which I drafted yesterday....Anthony encouraged me to write a poem and I went out into the rain and saw a black cormorant and returned and in five minutes scribbled out *The Workings of the Universe*, which I dedicated to Anthony as he spurred me on. It takes the reader very close to my poetic method, in which a small particle scene opens into something more universal, an image of an elusive truth about the universe."

Nadia visited and we ate at the Chef Beijing, Buckhurst Hill. It was frosty and foggy. We took Mrs. Best to dinner at the Roding, Abridge, and on Christmas Eve we visited Mabel Reid, who was sitting in St. Margaret's, "very white-haired and aged...and then Miss Lord in Marcris" House Private Nursing Home, Theydon Bois, while her companion Marion had a life-saving operation for cancer. I wrote that she sat "in a room with an open window and blue tits and great tits and coal tits hopping nearby. I played dominoes with her, and she looked very old, her eyes itching, and kept asking 'Why am I here, how much longer am I here?' while saying 'Thank you very much for coming, you're a good-looking couple, you would have been a beautiful bride' (to Ann)." When I returned I heard that Bill Sargent, the builder of the Oaklands extension, was in St. Margaret's Hospital, having had a mild heart attack which was to have the effect of stopping his working life.

With Jeremy Miller, the accounting assistant, I spoke of "America creating a United States of the World (USW) with a United States of Europe being a stepping-stone to that, Europe doing America's dirty work by reigning in Serbia (with whom some sympathise as it is getting rid of Moslems). A new empire is being created in Somalia, the Americans may not leave: they will go in to feed the starving. The UN is a pre-world government of six regions." On Christmas Day after a large turkey lunch, I worked on the Bilderberg Group's plan to rule the world and bring in political Universalism (world citizenship for all human beings).

The family gathering was at Biddenham at my sister Frances's house. In a discussion of interviews, my brother Rob said of graduates: "They've been to university, they're looking for hidden meanings." One of the aims of my life has been to bring the hidden realities behind the universe and world politics into the open.

1992 ended with a statement of my ideal: "Unity of being, relating physically, emotionally, intellectually, sensually, erotically, metaphysically, at all levels – wholeness." Universalism, emphasising what is universal in man and the universe, namely the Light, makes possible such a whole relationship of man to Nature and the hidden reality behind Nature and the Age. I wrote: "My writing is to reflect the Age and reveal the universe. Reflecting the Age includes showing where the power is. Portrait painters show the Pope and the royal family (like Goya); as a poet I must do the same."

Miss Lord died at Marcris on January 2nd, on the day Marion was due back. She had hated it in the Nursing Home, and even though her return home was in sight her great sense of personal dignity was affronted and she had not eaten. Zena rang to say she was only expected to live a few minutes, and Ann and I arrived too late that Saturday morning. I was shown to her room. I wrote: "Elizabeth lay on her back, sheet and green bedspread up to her chin, a low pillow and her head well back, white hair, eyes closed, mouth slightly open, one eye (her right) half closed. Zena tearful. We talked...softly about arrangements, putting it in perspective. I said I wanted to sit with her by myself....I sat with her, gave thanks for her life, told her she has died and that she will soon go forward to her next phase, and commended her soul to the Light in view of her care of small souls. I had two surges of energy that filled me. I kissed her cold forehead....She is at peace, it is a blessing....On my way out I spoke to the main nurse who said, 'Sorry.' She said: 'She gave up. She had no will to live. She didn't take food or drink.' (There was an orange packet with a straw by her bed which she declined as if on hunger strike.) 'She was a very clever lady. Deep down she knew Marion wouldn't be able to look after her, and she decided to go.'"

I had written a batch of short poems just before the new year, and I found poems coming by themselves. I wrote: "Jan 3. Got up after a cold night (-6/-9C) and went up to school to put the central heating on and saw the frost on my car: crystals out of last night's fog. And immediately came in and before having breakfast wrote a poem. Frost opens to the quantum vacuum. This poem came out of my way of looking, which I have prepared by my scientific and philosophical researches and essays, remaking myself into a great poet. The poem I have entitled *Fog and Frost: the Universe*."

I was very interested in a weekend conference on Global Deception, which was being put on at Wembley, and following Heather's research I rang the organiser, Mary Seal, who "said that the New World Order will be imposed if not achieved by co-operation – Kissinger said this at the Paris Bilderberger meeting. 'We have our sources.' Also that the Illuminati ideal is behind the bankers, that they take part in their own evil brotherhood and have secret signs (like Churchill's V sign) with which they communicate. She said they want world control of wealth and resources." I found a bookshop that supplied a lot of books about the New World Order and its offshoot agencies, the Bilderberg Group and the Trilateral Commission, and I now grasped that the UN war against Saddam was to demonstrate New World Order sovereignty as opposed to Iraqi national sovereignty. I wrote: "Confrontation with Saddam. According to one view, it is one-worlders who are acting against the American constitution and disarming America....According to my view it is America's world leadership. How to interpret the CFR, Bilderberg Group (America and Europe) and Trilateral Commission (America, Europe and Japan). I think I got it right. The Rockefeller-Rothschild (American-European) one-worlders are acting through American institutions, very often: e.g. through the President, Carter and Bush insiders."

The conference was very poorly attended, partly because there was a mysterious problem with the computers that issued tickets. The venue was moved from the Wembley Arena to the Wembley Conference Centre, where some 200 people attended on the first day, Mary Seal, longish blonde hair and tightly dressed and chainsmoking, was around in the corridor. She had mortgaged her boy-friend's house to put the conference on and draw public attention to the global deception being perpetrated, and she was clearly disappointed (although not surprised) by the poor attendance. The conference itself was a series of university level lectures, all excellently illustrated with slides and sometimes with snippets of video. I wrote: "Dr Strecker on AIDS being man-made. Eustace Mullins, protegé of (Ezra) Pound, on how the élite backed both sides in the war. A Bulgarian straight on (no lunch) on the technology of flying saucers, spinning or rotation round a vertical axis, which Hitler mastered in 1943 (evidence produced). Summers on flying saucers, many instances. Then Cooper on what is happening in Nevada, including a film of an American flying saucer being tested." The lectures suggested that the world's population would have to be reduced from 6 billion to 4 billion by the end of the 1990s, and that AIDS and 47 related man-made strains of germ were a contribution to that; and that when the time came for the world to draw together into a world government there would be sightings of flying saucers which would be attributed to other planets but which already exist on this planet, following Nazi discovery of their technology in the 1940s. I spoke with Mullins at some length and wrote: "I now have a higher opinion of Pound, who, Mullins tells me, introduced him to (books about the) Rothschilds and the Illuminati. When I said to Pound, 'I feel that two halves of the 20th century are meeting', I did not realise it would be regarding the Conspiracy as well as Literature."

The next day there was "more on AIDS, then Mullins on the Baal/Christ split and how the Rothschilds are Neo-Baalists. Terzinski on technology, Summers on Jehovah's Witnesses, then (William) Cooper on Kennedy's assassination." William Cooper an ex-US naval intelligence officer, showed a hitherto secret and unshown colour film of the assassination in which the driver turned round and blew part of Kennedy's head off with a final shot that made Kennedy's jerk back and which caused Jackie to scramble for the back. An unsuccessful attempt had been made to erase the gun in the driver's hand from the film. I received the information as demonstration of deception, but have no means of assessing the authenticity of what I was shown.

The conference had proposed a scenario which confirmed my view in *The Fire and the Stones* that America is poised for a global phase. The conference suggested that the Bilderbergers would take the world over and run it as a Neo-Fascist totalitarian dictatorship on Baalist-Luciferian principles, killing a third of the world's population to make the resources go round. I saw the Bilderbergers as a kind of advisory body or quango to the US government, steering US policy so that a New World Order can happen under a US umbrella (one that would fulfil Cecil Rhodes's dream of bringing the US and Europe together almost incidentally). I saw that it was vitally important that there should be a benevolent rule at the top in such a New World Order, which could bring about a benevolent Universalism (both politically and spiritually) and that on no account must there be a universal despot. The conference reinforced my view of history, and I could see merit in the Bilderbergers' forward planning so long as it accorded with decent human and metaphysical values. I wrote; "I see...America setting up the New World Order....Clinton was a Rhodes scholar (the Rhodes scholars are funded by Rothschilds) and identified by (David) Rockefeller in February 1990 as President. The Bilderbergers decided on Clinton last

June."

Miss Lord's cremation took place at Parndon. I recorded: "It was a bitterly cold day, I smelt chimney smoke in my mouth as I walked to the entrance while the hearse with mourners and Marion's car waited. The Rector, David Broomfield, arrived and in the chapel he performed a perfunctory service: a reading of a scripture, another (both in modern English) and then a statement about how we are like grass in the wind as the curtains closed round 'our sister', and it was all over without ever mentioning her name or why we were there. A look at the flowers, then to the church." The memorial service took place immediately after our arrival. The church was "three-quarters full. A hymn, 'Praise my Soul', then my reading of Matthew 5, 14-16; 18, 1-5; and Proverbs 3, 13-18. I read slowly; often pausing after the first word ('She', 'Happy') and looking up at the congregation at each reference to Miss Lord ('hill', 'good works', 'child', 'length of days'). Then 'All things bright and beautiful'. Then the address, which gave the bare facts about Miss Lord, not taking up the stories I had mentioned, and then 'Lord of all hopefulness' and finally after prayers 'Glad that I live am I', without reference to it being the school hymn. Then people coming: Mark Liell looking white-haired and old and not black-haired and bowler-hatted....Mabel Reid with Mary Matheson. A turn-out of old Loughton. Back to Marion's for things to eat and drink." I recorded that I wrote four poems that night.

I now saw contemporary history as a struggle between two New World Orders. "There is in fact a struggle between *two* New World Orders. I have got there! The Christian view will include Universalism, a Light-based common ground for all cultures. The diabolical view will attack all religion." Over lunch Jeremy Miller the accounting assistant, asked me about civilisation: "'Do you see it as rising or falling?' I: 'I don't think there is such a thing as civilisation. There are only civilisations. It's like a garden. A small garden is just plants; plants growing and plants declining and decaying. As one dies another grows. You say, 'Isn't it a lovely garden,' but it is really just a conglomeration of plants.'" I added: "My whole vision. It includes higher and lower New World Orders, Universalisms, and Illuminati. There is the higher illumination of the mystics, the Light and its world-wide practice. There is the lower man-centred rituals and use of the Light for their own ends – the Rothschilds' ends."

I saw a new phase in my life beginning. I wrote that a phase had come to an end with Miss Lord's death, and that I would increasingly look to a new life as an artist, living eventually part of the year in a climate, conducive to bronchiectasis such as the South of France or Italy, living like Pound and "writing my Dante-esque epic". I looked towards the Italy of Virgil, Dante, Milton (who went there for 15 months in 1638) and Pound. I defined myself in relation to my artistic Muse and recorded that I had written 5 symbolic poems between January 18th and 21st. (Pound also wrote poems to a "sexual" Muse.) I visited Dr Hughes, who said that my X-ray was clear and that I should consider spending time in the future of any one of the following places which are good for lungs: the Algarve, Spain, Italy or

South France, South Africa, Arizona, Colorado or Nevada. 'They are the dry places. Many with bronchiectasis go to Phoenix, Arizona and settle there. California is bad. Milan terrible, most of North Italy misty.'"

I wrote: "I am trying to range through disciplines and present a response to the universe, which includes the individual and inner, the social and the metaphysical – all layers. I go back to the Metaphysical poets, hence my *Marvell's Garden*....I am an artist and would love to live full time for my art like Delius, and catch the beauty of Nature: the sweep of the gull, the majesty of the sun – but in relation to the metaphysical reality of the universe. Delius's advice: get away from other artists and out into Nature. That is what I've tried to do, in Cornwall and here, overlooking the fields of my childhood, in Essex, damp drizzly Essex (as it is at present)....I need to focus on small things like a snail or drop of dew and embroider imagery, but I also take the reader to large things, literal things embodying or incarnating metaphysical things."

There was a concert at St. John's, Epping in which local schools took part, including Coopersale Hall. I wrote: "Ann and I sat in the front, in guest of honour seats. Various parents, Sir John Padfield, and others. A butterfly flew about and settled and was trodden on by a Coopersale Hall boy. Another butterfly replaced it. The quatrefoil (symbol in the church). Wrote *Butterfly*." A teacher we had just taken on, Ann Heald, made a big hit conducting the choir.

I had received a letter from Christopher Ricks, saying he was on Sabbatical from Boston and staying in Oxford for 6 months. Towards the end of January he rang: "'It's Christopher Ricks here. I'm going out to dinner on Wednesday evening, but I can be outside Blackwell's at 5.15. I ought to be back about 6.15.'...This arrangement made, I said 'I hope you're well?' Some doubt. 'I've been lucky in my health and my life.' A slower delivery than last time. No longer the rapid machine gun, America has slowed him down. 'I'll be outside Blackwell's in my Robin Hood hat. Don't laugh.'"

I went to Oxford for another meeting with the philosophers. I wrote: "Max Payne chaired the meeting for 11; lolling back with his eyes closed as he thought. Isomorphisms, which did not mean the one substance behind the universe, the Light, but all of us agreeing a similar model. We thought up 20 assumptions that scientists make and contradicted them. I grouped the contradictions into 'consciousness, universal cosmology, methodology or epistemology' and Max held consciousness to be absolute. Geoffrey Read on Whitehead's refutation of materialism ('undifferentiated endurance') in *Process and Reality* 2.2.5."

I left the philosophers at 4.30 and drove into Oxford, parked in Broad Street and "waited outside Blackwell's for Ricks who came out open-necked, grey-haired, round glasses, warm and smiling but very exact....We walked to the Turf while he asked me about the philosophers and schools, focusing warmly on me. In the Turf I bought him a cider and myself an orange juice and we sat to the right of the bar on wooden seats, I leaning on the table, and we talked. I talked about Ezra Pound and the Rothschilds and Mullins and Pound in Italy, and my desire to write an epic post-Virgil, -Dante, -Milton (all of whom were in Italy). He asked what I am about. I said I had seen something which is everywhere in the Metaphysical poets and realised it was the centre of religion and history's civilisations and also the reality behind physics and philosophy. This is new and I am doing an interlocking jigsaw, I said. He mentioned holism. I: 'In the sense that everything is a whole. My close reading of the universe and what is hidden – perhaps in the tradition of the Ricksite way of looking. You taught me to read closely, and now I am reading the universe closely, for what is hidden behind Nature and Western civilisation.' But, I said, my base is Literature and like a *Times* reporter or barrister mastering his brief I go out into disciplines. I: 'A poem is a wonderful medium for a cross-disciplinary approach. In Donne for example.' He: 'It can be small in subject and huge in range. Tennyson's library – there's a precedent for it. Tennyson was very interested in science.' I: 'Darwinism in *In Memoriam*.' He: 'Yes.' Then we got onto poems. I explained that my *1* were thematically chosen. He: 'Like Wavell's *Other Men's Flowers*.' I: 'There must now be a *Collected Poems*, perhaps with chronological selection.' He nodded. I told him my output is that of a Tennyson or Wordsworth in bulk. He: 'You haven't done much about getting recognised.' I: 'No, I'm not interested in self-promotion. I don't think about how good I am. That is for others to do. I'm a factory. I just get on and do it.' He: 'It's like Beckett. He was going to write anyway whether he was published or not....There are degrees of disinterest. There's not getting published, and there's getting published and being ignored, and there's getting published and not being read very carefully (like me). I don't know what you do. I've stood with a friend in Blackwell's who wants 30 poems published and have said "try Bloodaxe".' Again, he: 'Empson told me that recognition of good new poetry is the first faculty to go. I can't recognise good new poets anymore, so I'm stuck with Larkin.' I on his work: 'You're the Leavis figure now.' 'I'm not.' '*The Force of Poetry* is his Great Tradition.' 'No, it isn't, it's just about those I have something to say about. I've got nothing to say about some writers. I love George Eliot but I've got nothing to say about her. If I were asked to give 8 lectures on George Eliot I'd blow my brains out.' I: 'Your next book should state the Tradition. Perhaps we can discuss that again. Come and see the schools one day and have lunch and we'll talk it through.' 'I'd like that.' He: 'We both have confidence in ourselves, but you have faith in what you're doing, I don't have faith that anyone will read me carefully, that I won't be ignored. We could have disagreements, but these don't matter and we can still talk.' I: 'We'll talk it through, with your scholarship and my faith we'll go far.' He quoted my poem on the royals with approval, then we left and returned to the car and I drove him home." I asked him to sign a copy of his *1*, which he did. "He: 'Thank you for asking me to do that.' A punctiliously correct man with perfect manners who always shuts up when someone speaks instead of him. I asked him: 'Will you stay in Boston?' He: 'I'll be there until I die. I'm 61, and I have children of 10, 12 and 14 by Judith, who's American. Retiring is attractive, but I can't retire until my youngest is 20. At Boston they let you go on, there's no ageism in America, I can work until I'm 80.'"

Later I rang Geoffrey Read, the philosopher: "Talk on Whitehead and his philosophy, on undifferentiated endurance being the root doctrine of materialism. Geoffrey has extended Whitehead's insight: 'Under materialist theory, you only have a configuration of particles, and there is no reason as to why past events should ever make way for present ones without obliteration; past configurations of particles have to be obliterated to make way for present ones.' In cumulative theory, past events do not have to be obliterated to make way for present events as present events are added to past events. If time is a succession of events, nothing endures through time. If everything is the same there is no process. His matter theory, the presentation of the past is an ongoing process including when we die. On how he, Alison Watson and I need to make up our own Metaphysical Revolution....I urged him to collect his papers with an introduction into a Wittgensteinian *Collected Papers*. He: 'You are the greatest man I have ever met. You have a family and have earned enough money to take time off to write and have written your big book and your poems and now the one on the universe. That's an achievement. You are the greatest I've met, you have your health and your energy. McNamara is the most extraordinary man I've ever met. You're the most remarkable, the greatest.' I: 'I don't look back, I think I've only done one twentieth of what I should, my *Collected Poems* and 500 stories.' He: 'You're remarkable. You're organised. Colin Wilson regurgitates others' ideas.' I: 'You and I are originals. You're matter theory and memory theory and space-time theory are you, and no one else is declaring a Metaphysical Revolution in terms of the Fire or Light.' He: 'You are sincere. Sincerity shines through.' I: 'Sincere people seek truth and do not court publicity.'" I wrote: "The universe is in process, and the process is a substance-in-events, namely the Light....Jan 29. Wrote two poems: carried on last night's poem on Geoffrey Read, *Not Endurance But Process: The Past Present* and, following a quarter of an hour standing to the right of the foot of the steps, below the (flower) bed under the study window, talking to Ernie (the Oaklands odd job man) and listening to the birdsong, *Rainglobes*."

I observed: "Geoffrey Read, Fleur Beverley and I are all doing something similar, regarding time as a succession of events and the past as being added to by the present, as happens in my Autobiography, Fleur Beverley's art and Geoffrey Read's thinking."

I considered Pound's view of the Light: "Pound and the Light. The religion of Eleusis involved coitus between priests and young women. This produced knowledge symbolised as light which persisted through the Middle Ages and the beauty of the songs of Provence and Italy, the troubadours. Pound has approached the illumination of the mystics through sex. I would put it the other way round: Eleusis priests glimpsed the Light, passed it on (ear of corn) through Egyptian-style sexual union, which was a healing thing. In my case, the tradition of the Light flows in when the ego is humbled and can open to receive it. Sex can then send a luminous fluid to the brain which is seen as Light (Pound's version of D. H. Lawrence's preoccupation with sex, more Tantric Yoga though), but the Light can be channelled down through sex. If there is a tradition from Eleusis to the Albigensian Cathars to the Provençal troubadours and then to Pound's Modernists, there is also a tradition from the religious and mystical origins of our civilisation to me and my leadership of a movement, the

Metaphysical Revolution."

I redefined the artist's role in his civilisation: "If the Light is central to civilisations (as I have shown it is), then the artists who are illumined are leaders of Light in their civilisation. My Metaphysical Revolution achieves this in philosophy and science, but not in art. There must be a Metaphysical Revolution in art to show this and reflect it, new images to be added to, not to obliterate, past images. That is my role, to have Pound's place....I need to inspire other artists and poets. Artists are the antennae of the race (Pound) and communicate to the culture (insect) the first signs of new danger, of anything new....The illumined artists must take control of the civilisation from the bankers and Illuminati. We are central to our civilisation."

I now sought to strengthen my Metaphysical Revolution, in which the Light is central: "My Metaphysical Revolution in philosophy, science and the arts reaffirms the Light in the universe and also its place as the central idea of our civilisation. The Light tradition is central (cf Pound in the *Cantos*). That is Universalism....Alison Watson rang. I told her that I am having a Metaphysical Revolution anyway. 'I'm going through the hole in the hedge and I'm going to stand on the lawn and if they come out and say "What do you thing you're doing?" and cart me off to a mental hospital, so be it. But if you, Geoffrey Read and Chris McCann follow me through the hedge then we can go on from there and perhaps become Master of the House.' She laughed."

Des McFaran, my Oak-Tree author, rang me from Bulgaria, where he is an adviser to the President. He again urged me to visit and "meet the Government". He wanted me to buy a publishing company for a nominal sum. I "said to him: 'What about the brolly brigade?' 'They're in the street, I see them every day.' 'I hope you're wearing shin pads.'"

In February I wrote: "I need to live again..., feeling the world like a blind man with my heart and soul....To live like an artist." I was receiving infused knowledge in my sleep: "I have been blind. Woke up in the night and realised that Hitler was an Illuminatist" (a Satanic tradition). "Hitler's Illuminatist rituals as described by Pennick." I was still seeing the Light. On February 11th I recorded: "To bed at 12.45 a.m. Put my head on the pillow and immediately saw a calm Light. Spent 5 minutes sunbathing in it before deciding it was time to sleep."

We went to Cornwall, where I was "drunk with sea air. Slept several times. Wrote *February Daffodils*. I recorded: "*A Flirtation with the Muse* is 1992-3. I have written collection 1989-92:...*A Sneeze in the Universe?* It is a good title. A personal sneeze and the whole universe." I went for a walk in a "bracing wind and rough sea".

Judith rang and said her source "which is linked to Christ" had urged me "to transform, not create" – the evangelical rather than the descriptive way. I wanted to transform by creating, and saw myself not as a religious transformer but as an artist-poet who created and incidentally transformed; even though as I acknowledged in my *Diaries* "My journey may be one of the great religious journeys of all time, and it is the greater because I stayed away from institutions and did not confuse or sully the visions – the experiences – with the doctrine".

The Conservative Patrons Club invited Virginia Bottomley, whom I last met when she attended the launch of *Budapest Betrayed*. I wrote: "Virginia Bottomley, looking elegant and youthful, very bright (Essex University and LSE). Getting on for half an hour making out that there should be fewer beds. The bottom line is that we are declining and the health service is getting worse."

I had been invited to give the toast, "Floreat Antiqua Domus" ("May the ancient house flourish") at the Old Chigwellians' Shrove Tuesday dinner, the highest profile speech in Old Chigwellian circles. That afternoon (February 23rd) I was unwell. I wrote: "Woke with catarrh and after lunch underwent a crisis as a cold seemed to develop. Felt removed from the world. Deliberately lay on my bed and became nothing for one and a half hours, during which the Light came in, unbidden, and I heard a voice telling me I would be all right during my speech to the Old Chigwellians. Came to and am now calm and connected. Feel quietly confident, good. Am in tune with the infinite, in harmony with the One." My school friend Richard Wallace (now a Vicar) was staying with me. I wrote: "Took him via the guest room to chapel and thence to the Swallow Room, where I bought a tie with a mitre on....On to Top Table with elderly ex-soldiers who fought in the infantry at El Alamein. Little, the Head, to my right....Then at 10.45 the gavel, and I was standing holding a microphone and giving my address without notes: Harsnett and Penn, certain masters of the 1940s and 1950s, how the boys learned to be streetwise (the marble pitch, avoiding being beaten up, etc), how dunces had become millionaires, how Chigwell is a different place now, and then, 15 minutes after beginning, the toast: Floreat Antiqua Domus. Speeches from Little..., Keith Mitchell...and the Head Boy....Afterwards...about 30 came and congratulated me and thanked me for a nice speech. Norris: 'You got the balance exactly right.' Ulph: 'Another triumph.' Hoppit: 'We were all set to throw bread rolls but you were so good we didn't.' Banks: 'That was an excellent speech.' Sweet: 'I love listening to brilliant speeches like that.'" Later I talked with Richard Wallace until 2 a.m: "My account of where I am going: the Mystic Way, how the Light is central to Nature and history, my own experience of illumination. How I am not to be a Billy Graham but to offer my journey as an example. How he (Wallace) should lead a group within the church, a metaphysical group, rather than be a Chaucerian parson. He could found a new Oxford movement. Wallace, eventually: 'It's not me.'"

Two days later I flew to Edinburgh to stay with Nadia. I flew on Nadia's flight: "Nadia waiting in red and grey uniform, looking very demure....Flew on the flight deck for take-off,....The maze of dials and switches, the casualness with which they took off. Automatic pilot did most of it, so they didn't look out for near-misses. Back in the cabin to eat, being served by Nadia. Then back onto the flight deck for the landing, harnessed in with a seat belt like a parachute, over shoulders and between legs as well as round waist." After lunching I drove with Nadi "to Colinton, a pretty stone 1780s village in a valley, with a stream – actually a river, the water of Leith – running through the middle. Saw the flat, then went for a walk to the church. Saw a mortsafe, skulls/bones on the graves, a front with a font with a dove on a pulley, and returned for tea and then wrote *At Colinton*, a poem about death and love (the two themes of my major poetry according to Yeats). Death and the love of life. Nadi has done very well to get this peaceful 1780s flat." We ate – Nadia "served me a casserole with mushrooms and vienetta...and a bottle of white wine" – and I record: "Wrote a poem *In Spylaw Street* which I polished this morning; about love and pain but accepting there must be love." After lunch the next day we walked "to the churchyard and (had) a look at the dipper, and then drove to the airport". I flew back with Nadia's air hostess friends. I later wrote: "Am very pleased I went to Nadia. She's living alone and my picture is up more than anyone else's and it is contact with me, and she says she often thinks of Charlestown in her mind. She told everyone I was going – desks at Heathrow and Edinburgh, and the air hostesses....My sadness that she's living on her own, with pictures of me. The high profile I have in relation to her friends, which is nice."

A few days later I rang Steve Norris. I recorded: "We got on to Maastricht and I asked 'Does Tebbit know about the Bilderberg Group?' Norris: 'Oh yes, he was associated with it in the past.' I: 'Is his (Tebbit's) campaign (against Maastricht) to do with blocking the Bilderberg Group?' He: 'Yes. It's subtle.'"

A bizarre and sad situation happened involving a teacher at Coopersale Hall. Ann Heald had joined us in December the day before the end of term, to start in January. She was very plausible at interview, and had proved to be an excellent teacher. She had conducted brilliantly at the Epping concert. After half term she went missing and was not at home, where she lived alone. She had a set of exam papers and we became concerned. We had medical certificates from different doctors saying "Gastro-enteritis". After ringing her doctor I rang the police at his suggestion on Wednesday March 3rd. The officer said: "I'm filling in a form and need to write a reason for your concern." Without thinking I said: "I have a premonition she will commit suicide." The policeman visited her house within the hour and reported she was there. I drove straight round and found her being sick. With hindsight it seems the policeman interrupted a suicide attempt and I witnessed the aftermath. In her dressing-gown she looked dreadful, very pale and shaky, and I took delivery of the exam papers between bouts of violent vomiting, and I tried to get her to visit her doctor. I telephoned the doctor from her house to make an appointment, but she insisted she was all right. The next day I called to try and take her again, but she politely declined, saying she was better, although she added: "I knew you'd be worried at what you saw of me yesterday." On the evening of Sunday March 7th, the 13th anniversary of meeting a man called Roland (a relationship recently discontinued), she committed suicide by driving to Knighton Woods three hundred yards away and connecting a lead to her exhaust. She was found dead the next morning with the engine still running, and there were 3 lengthy notes on the seat, none involving the school. I had had so strong a premonition that I had told the police, who had my premonition on record. I felt she had slipped through my fingers, like a dropped catch in cricket; that a safe pair of hands ought to have been able to stop her. Yet at the same time I knew I could not have done any more, and I was relieved to learn from her sister that she had made other attempts and that she had announced at Christmas that 1993 would be the year in which she finally "did it".

I was still experiencing the Light. I wrote: "I regularly go to the Light. Two or three times a week I have the surges going through me, tingling my spine."

I wrote: "My Autobiography is a Universalist work. It should be subtitled 'The Birth of a Universalist.'" I spoke to John Ezard on the phone and discussed Universalism: "I: 'You once said I should be the Camus of our time. This book approaches that in so far as it declares Existentialism is dead and that Universalism is its successor....Colin Wilson once told me, "If there are 10 people in England interested in Existentialism, I am addressing them." So with me: if there are 10 people interested in what replaces Existentialism, I am speaking to them.'"

The Universe and the Light was now out, and there was a suggestion that there should be an event to focus on the Metaphysical Revolution. I wrote: "Calling for a change-over in the Royal Societies, reading of a manifesto, birth of a Metaphysical Society....The feeling...it should be a lecture....It would make a *Times* debate."

Argie was "visited by BBC4 and interviewed at home. Question: 'Do you think about death?' Answer: 'Well, I always leave the kitchen tidy in case I don't wake up.'"

I had a chat with my old Latin and Greek master, at Chigwell School, David Horton, "about the epic..., on Virgil being the giant and not wanting to write the *Aeneid*, but being asked by Augustus and Maecenas. The last line, Turnus's soul 'fugit indignata per umbras'....I: 'Did Virgil write in code as Milton did?' He: 'Augustus's presence is everywhere.'"

As part of my promotion for the new book, I wrote articles for several magazines including *Radionic Quarterly*, and was interviewed on GLR in Marylebone High Street late at night. I wrote: "Parked on a meter outside before 11 p.m. and was admitted by a boy in a black shirt, led to the studio where Peter Curran was talking to a rock star turned novelist. I lolled in a chair in a bright light and listened to the voice coming through and saw the two red lights on the wall, signifying they were live on the air, and watched the young Peter Curran, also wearing black, headphones on his head, smiling and laughing. Chatted desultorily, then Peter Curran came out while music was playing and said he'd go through everything with me five minutes before. Was led into the studio and seated at a table opposite Curran with a great bank of equipment between us. He was going to start me with he Light, he said, and history, then go on to the Metaphysical Revolution, then go into the countries I'd been to and ask about a Grand Unified Theory. He floored me by asking me to begin slightly differently, and his Irish wasn't too difficult to hear and understand, and we talked for about a quarter of an hour, live. The Light going out across London. At the end, a handshake and I drove home."

A long tailed fieldmouse was found to have nested in an old shoe in our porch. It jumped between the sliding doors and hid under our wooden steps.

There were four green woodpeckers in the field; the fox sitting in the sun by the top tree in the second field, between two saplings; and the toad sheltering under four pieces of bark. A walk with Ernie (our odd job man) is a revelation. He shows you where there are green lizards, and where squirrels have hidden last year's acorns."

I pondered the themes of poetry and wrote: "Larkin single-handedly ended Modernism with his anti-intellectualism and...his little Englandism and lack of experiment. It was on balance a regressive step....He is a minor poet, but has the technique of an accomplished poet. Minor in theme, accomplished in style. He starts with 'I' and widens into a general truth....His general truths and writing are good, but there is not much transcendental in him."

I decided to go to Florence for a conference on Ficino, and the same afternoon, by strange synchronicity, Patrick Hamilton "rang at 2 p.m., saying he's finished with the Florence Trust and he's now at my disposal. 'I felt moved to ring. I'm reading *The Fire and the Stones*.'" (I wrote: "We are like spies in German-occupied France or the USSR, and our instructions are in code, or perhaps we have forgotten them, and we do not know who sent us, only which side we are on or not on...and Patrick is one of the Resistance who is helping us. We have been sent by the Spirit of Light.") I wrote of Ficino: "Ficino was at the beginning of the Renaissance. Standing for Plato, he was on the side of invisible reality and against humanism, surely. I must have a poem about Ficino's role in c1450 – he saw the Renaissance and was part of it – and my own role in the Counter-Renaissance today....Ficino translated Plotinus and so stood for the Light. He became a priest in 1473, and stood for religion. He retired to the Tuscan countryside after the expulsion of the Medici in 1494. His integration of the Christian and Plato's spirit and concept of love, the soul's love for God. Spiritual or Platonic love which dominated poetry and literature for the 16th century inspired Lord Herbert's Deism: all religions have a measure of truth. He was not pre-Illuminati, more on the side of the Christian Renaissance."

Patrick Hamilton gave me dinner in Aberdeen Road, London N5. I wrote: "A first drink in a room of books and paintings with green at the back, he white-bearded and haired like John Osborne, and 73. We then walked to St. Saviour's, which Betjeman wrote about, and saw the commune of Florence Trust artists at work. The image of art taking place in a church. Religion and art have come together. Then back home and he showed me his chart of *The Fire and the Stones*. He is doing a visual aid, starting at the beginning and putting everything in (e.g. painters, scientists, poets, each of which have a time-line to themselves). He wants to produce it commercially....He wants to start a group that will do research into *The Fire and the Stones* – do a Ficino....Told him about the Illuminati. He: 'George (Trevelyan, a relative) said that some groups are Luciferian, and are attractive, like a poisonous spider, and bite – got yer.' He wants to meet a graphic artist....Supper. We sat close together for avocado with mushroom dressing; fishcakes and toast and butter; and cheese and bread; and a glass of wine. Caroline (his new wife) saying the fishcakes had stuck, a disaster."

In early April I returned to Winchester: "Before dinner discovered I am a celebrity. Several stopped me and said: 'Your book is very familiar.' One said: 'Your name has been the most mentioned in my household during the past year.' Had dinner with Lady Astor....Walked down to the lectures. A full auditorium. David Lorimer spoke first on the eye of the heart, sensibly saying that there should be mind as well. Then Matthew Fox spoke. He is steeped in Aquinas and Meister Eckhart, and Hildegard and Julian of Norwich, but is at odds with the Vatican, who have expelled him because its structure cannot cope with the new structures his creation spirituality is finding: a wicca priest. I see he got a grant from one of the Rothschilds for *The Coming of the Cosmic Christ*. He echoes Teilhard. His ecumenical mysticism is close to mine. I do not know if we are allies. His Universalism is outside the Church. Mine is also outside, but I have not been expelled. Had a word with him afterwards. He signed a book, 'To Cosmic Light' for me. I have arranged to talk with him tomorrow and will discover if we are Universalism allies."

The next morning I "breakfasted with Adrian Cairns. Dossey on metaphysical medicine, then Kilner on the heart. Lunched with Matthew Fox and (Stephen) Rose of the BBC. Fox on Darkness and the Light as Yin and Yang. He listened to my view of the Light in history but went on about spirit and rituals. New forms. His insistence on creation theology and images. No real contact, I felt, though we both professed to be working in the same discipline....Circle dancing later. Then Raine. Have a sore back with twinges....Later Satish Kumar, then Sir George Trevelyan, over-running on English poetry. Then supper....Then Anne Baring who read a talk on psychic images, then classical guitar from Cathy Thom. A glass of wine in the Scientific and Medical Network, then the Light poured in making my left fingers quiver."

Sunday was "a fine day unlike the wet day yesterday. Breakfasted in the sun, heard Dossey and Helen King, a New Age dresser with an appalling child who rushed about, pointed water pistols and lit a candle, and was left with a box of matches: nearly burnt down the auditorium. David Lorimer was affected by 'your own truth' and broke down at the microphone, confessing he was unable to face his past....Lunched with Adrian Cairns, who said: 'It's the Fire v Materialism, you have polarised it in a new and exciting way.' Fox and Kumar both read my book last night." After lunch, "on my way to see Sarida Brown of *Caduceus*, after bagging a seat, I passed Matthew Fox on the gangway steps in the lecture hall. He was going to the panel for questions, and he stopped me and said: 'Do you know you look like Donald Sutherland? Has anyone ever told you that? You could be his brother. You know, the actor.'" I observed: "More interested in my face than in the Light."

The next day I visited David Hoppit, with whom I had travelled to Italy in 1957, at his house at "Curtis Mill Farm, 1424, beams and weatherboard, standing by a lovely pond, alongside stables and a garden with a greenhouse. A long talk with Hoppit about the halo, how we are like fish in a fishtank, the dust in a sunbeam. Putting my vision as clearly as possible for a bus-driver, which I am to do in 700-800 words. How people rush about and need to become tranquil to feel calm....Explained $+A + -A = 0$. Justice + injustice = the whole. All contradictions are reconciled within my unit. Suffering + compassion; anger + love and so on. Everything has its opposite and is part of a whole. Metaphysics + materialism? No – materialism is level 1 of a 4-level metaphysics. Metaphysics *is* the whole." Hoppit showed me photos of a ruined villa he owned just outside Florence, and asked if I would buy into it so he could renovate and either use it as an Italian base or sell it.

I went to Cornwall and was immediately "drunk with air after walking by the sea after dinner and having written two poems". I recorded: "Went to the Light. Like yesterday it poured in, 9.45-10 p.m., curing my back." My back had gone again and I had been to the Essex osteopath, who had not been able to push the disc back. My sister Frances rang, and "I turned and got up and asked 'Who is it?' to Ann, and felt and heard a crack in my spine – and my disc was back....It just fell into place."

I arranged to see Colin Wilson, who on the telephone reacted to my book with predictable coolness: "'Universalism's too vague, you define it as being different from different movements but you don't say what it is. Derrida will say it doesn't exist. What is it that we've overlooked all these years?' I defended – of course, he wants to keep everything in the rational, social ego and is on Derrida's side – and pointed out that a lot are reading it and that I have developed Universalism in my Birmingham lecture. He: 'You'll be able to tell me what it is tomorrow.'" I wrote: "I am writing about energy, an irrational principle or subrational principle – and you cannot be 'vague' about such energy. You cannot be excessively rational about the irrational. You have to experience it – which Colin Wilson won't do, being a rationalist. Establishing a new movement is like founding a school. First I had 35 pupils (got a toe hold), then 150, and now 235 and a waiting list."

I wrote: "Matthew rang. He has been on Skye, we knew. I did not know he was mountaineering with Tom Hollinghurst, hanging from ropes, dependent on crampons."

I visited Colin Wilson "with Paul Newman. Sat and drank large goblets of white wine and ate dips and smoked salmon, and then started on Universalism. Colin: 'I don't see what the starting-point is. What is the application, what do people do, where's the crowbar?' Explained that the starting-point is the Fire or Light in many disciplines, that experiential metaphysics is different from rational metaphysics. He: 'But it's vague.' I: 'Give us a chance. Existentialism was going for 100 years, this has only been going for a month, more thinkers will come along in the future. It's like my second school. You start with 35, increase it to 150 and go to 230. It's now at the 35 stage.' He: 'But what is it?' Explained about energy of Light which can be seen. Joy and Paul on my side. Colin: 'Mysticism's wishy-washy. It's like a girl I know. She said "You are a rationalist" and I said "You're f—g right I am."' I: 'We're like a movement of Existentialists, a post-Existentialism, and we have different emphases.' He: 'Post-Existentialism was defining more clearly the concepts of Existentialism.' I: 'Well, the Fire or Light is a post-post-Existentialism.' He: 'But what are you against?' I: 'I'm against the Materialist universe.' 'So was Blake.' 'But he was then, I am now. Reductionism began after Blake – it's reductionism I am crowbar-ing.' He: 'What do I do?' I: 'It's in pages 84-92 and 7-8 (the consequences).' He: 'I want to know what I should do in a seminar, the language is vague. Derrida will say it doesn't exist.' I: 'Derrida says reality is within a text, I'm saying it's outside a text. The starting-point is the Materialism of Dawkins, Derrida and Hawking.' He: 'The unification of the 4 forces may get science forward but Universalism doesn't get philosophy forward.' I: 'The starting-point is Bergson, T. E. Hulme, Husserl, Whitehead and William James – going back to them, and using phenomenology to look at the Fire in the soul. He: 'Universalism is an everything-ism.' I: 'No, it's an everyone-ism,' i.e. everyone has access to the Fire or Light. He: 'The idea of *The Fire and the Stones* is very simple.' I: 'It has a beautiful simplicity. It's as simple as $E = mc^2$:Fire.' He: '$E = mc^2$ is saying that something = something.' I: 'I'm saying that the Fire = the central idea of the universe.'...He: 'What are you saying?' I: 'We live in a universe of Light which flows into us, bringing supra-rational powers.'"

I recorded: "I said to him that in 1961 he had written *The Outsider* and *Religion and the Rebel* and that what I am doing helps forward his vision.' Joy agreed. 'I'm an Outsider and have ended with the Fire or Light, like some in the last chapter. I told I would go abroad for 10 years and this is what I've found. It's withdrawal and return. If I die tonight and am remembered by the poems, *The Fire and the Stones* and *The Universe and the Light*' (Paul, 'a considerable body of work already') 'I hope you'll look back and see me as an Outsider who did what the Outsiders in your last chapter did and became a mystic and saint.' He: 'You are an Outsider.' I: 'It's an Outsiderish thing to do, to take the Fire or Light out of the cupboard or closet and put it into the public arena. If you're going to decide we're similar, don't leave it until you're 86 and I'm 79. Watch this space.' He: 'I'm not against the space. I am interested in higher consciousness. I just don't think mysticism's the way of doing it.' I: 'Let me rephrase it: higher consciousness and awareness of the reality behind the universe – you're in favour of that.' He nodded. I: 'There's a constituency out there, my ideas have resonance. I am not trying to create a religion but a philosophy. Those who have ears to hear, let them hear. I am not forcing it down anyone. But I should have thought you would have heard the echo, the resonance.' He: 'I discovered I couldn't change people and came down here and got on with limited things. You've turned Husserl upside down. I remember Stuart Holroyd and Bill Hopkins trying to persuade me I should believe in a philosophy called Personalism.' I: 'Philosophers do found isms. Bergson founded Vitalism.' He: 'Why don't you call it Haggerism. Why don't you call Universalism Haggerism?'" I noted: "(I was) with Wilson 5.15 to 8. At least two and a half hours of philosophical argument, mostly on Universalism."

Paul Newman said on the way home: "You kept your cool, you dealt with it very well. He's provincial and insider and involved in serial killers, you're global and more than he can cope with. You are multi-cultural. You are more pure than Wilson's philosophy, which is mixed up with serial killers. He's written about murders and glimpses of higher consciousness – peak experiences – whereas you are steeped in them, you're too much for him, you're transcendental. Language is a problem. He wants to reduce mysticism to a text, you're beyond language." I added: "Colin is (an example of) 'the physical abuse syndrome'. His first 3 books were criticised and panned, and so he is passing it on to me like a son of child-abused father."

I wrote: "What I must do: demonstrate the good things that flow out of the experience of the Light – wisdom, psychological problems resolved, peace, tranquillity, meaning, the unitive vision. Present the Light as a means of attaining higher consciousness....In 1961 Wilson said, 'I like metaphysical discussions at a level.' Now I am on his level or beyond it....Colin Wilson's approach is psychological with spiritual glimpses. My approach is spiritual, at a higher level than his. He remained a psychological Outsider, I went on and healed my divided self. I am a William James figure, he is not."

And I noted: "Told Colin that Scruton has books in many languages (including Turkish). Wilson: 'That's a bad sign, men of genius are bad at languages.'"

Peter Clapperton and Susie, the owners of the port, called and took us to dinner at the Pier House Hotel, and I learned that the former owner, Barry Williamson, was working for three Arabs, one of whom had been linked with Kashoggi, and that he had had cancer of his leg. Peter asked: "Does Ann understand your ideas?" I replied: "Scruton has written *The Xanthippic Dialogues* about Mrs. Socrates. There is no reason why Mrs. Plato or Mrs. Kant (Kant was single) or Mrs. Hegel should have understood their ideas." He: "Yes."

In brilliant sunshine I "wrote an article for *Resurgence*. Started off after gazing at the sea and watching points of light jump and dance for about 10 minutes. Wrote this into the beginning. The theme was: the Fire against materialism."

I had arranged to meet Colin Wilson in the Pentewan Ship on the Saturday. Pam rang asking for a lift. She said: "Your book is very interesting. Paul took it to a coffee bar and someone said 'Could I look at it?' and ended up going off to buy it. It looks interesting. You offered Colin a share in the Metaphysical Revolution and he wouldn't do it. He's got to be Kingsie....You tackled him in 1961 and he's never forgotten it." I reflected: "You are angry from the rational, social ego and grow out of it – the anti-love feeling." I took the boys with me and wrote: "To the Pentewan Ship with Paul and Pam to meet Colin and Joy. Introduced Matthew and Anthony who came in with me. Colin gave them a glass of wine each and heard them on being a journalist and a film director; and he offered to help them, both of them. To me he said: 'I'm going to write you a letter and set it out because my objections are not frivolous. An ism doesn't get us further forward. Reductionism will collapse through experiments, not through a Metaphysical Revolution. It's individuals that count. I used to write of a religious existentialism but I've left that behind.' Argued back and stood my ground. I: 'An ism is a ladder. Universalism is a ladder you dispense with once you've climbed up it.' He: 'Perhaps the boat's going your way.' I: 'The tide has turned. The tide is carrying the boat my way.' Sitting next to Wilson in the Pentewan Ship I quoted my own lines from *The Silence*: 'I cannot live by Freud,/There in his mirror I cannot create/A towering image of man against a void.' Wilson said, 'That reflects how I think.' Colin talking to Matthew and Ant about how he writes 1,000 words an hour, how Stevenson once wrote 10,000 words in a day. Mention of Shaw and other writers....Colin: 'I wrote *The Outsider* in 3 months – 110,000 words.' After he left Joy remained and gave Pam a precis of Colin's reaction to me. 'He wants to keep his feet on the ground, he won't go to yoga when I ask him to, he's met people into things in San Francisco and is wary, he wants to keep rational control.' I told Joy Wilson: 'I am amazed that the philosophers – Kant and Hegel, for instance – by and large missed the Fire or Light. It was because they were rationalists and looked out from their reason. Plato had it.' She: 'Yes, Plato knew it. Colin believes in the will.' I: 'There is the personal will and a deeper drive, the will of the unconscious strengthened from the beyond.'"

I went for a "late night walk. A very dramatic sea with much surf and foam." The next day I wrote: "A stormy petrel settled on the cliff, a greenfinch in the trees near the garden, making a strange brrr sound, a squat parroty back and deceptively yellow in the sun, though green when the sun went in, and one bar on its brown wing. A much larger bird than a finch, too large for a siskin. Went for a walk into the field, up past the gorse and heard a nightingale sing. Stalked it from bush to bush until it vanished. A lovely evening walk, but huge gnats at the top of the field. Did not sit for fear of being bitten." I recorded: "Ap 12. Wrote 5 poems: *Car-park: Ascending* last night in the cinema, and *A Nightingale in the Mind*, *Soul like a Greenfinch*, *Stormy Petrel* and *Sand-Hoppers*, this last one after seeing a thousand sand-hoppers on our pink wall under the streetlamp....I have struck a rich vein, a rich seam."

I visited the Charlestown osteopath: "Paul...nudged me twice on each side 'to loose the back' and then massaged my strained muscle in my left arm and cricked my neck and head round to the right and then left. I: 'The hangman's art. That's what they did when you had the rope round your throat at Tyburn and weren't dead: they turned your head sharply to break your neck.'...I now feel much more supple and need to have this osteopath preventatively on a regular basis."

On April 13th I visited Colin Wilson on my own "for the third time within a week, and talked with him alone from 5.30 to 8 p.m. Bob the odd job man sat with Joy and him and me and had an awkward drink while Joy remarked that Colin's socks have holes – he took them off and threw them on the fire. He then said that we don't need Universalism or the Metaphysical Revolution, we need a precise refutation of Neo-Darwinism through a proof that acquired characteristics can be inherited, and that we need a precise refutation of Derrida from the starting-point which is Husserl and Rousseau saying that...immediacy is not better than meaning-perception. Derrida wrongly says Rousseau is wrong because of a body of language and quotes Saussure that words have different meanings. Derrida then attacks two points of Husserl's linguistics in Husserl's 2 volume first work....I interjected that I am on the side of the transcendental ego, that Derrida and Sartre are wrong. Wilson:...It is Husserl and Whitehead on one side, and Hume on the other, no transcendental ego (Hume)....The past and the present, Proust and the biscuit dipped in tea. I spoke of Geoffrey Read's view of the past. Reconstruction can become intention. Proust and Rousseau together....Derrida, language behind all....Wilson on my refutation of Derrida: 'You've disqualified the rational ego, you've changed the rules from tennis.' I: 'It's a game of football and Derrida is playing tennis and *should* be disqualified.' Wilson: 'It's immediacy v meaning-perception. Proust: it is possible to turn the carbon copy (memory) into reality provided you put enough effort into it....Does Universalism make for a better scientist?'...I: 'Yes, because there are two kinds of scientists, one a separate observer and the other part of the whole and open to intuition and inflowings of wisdom and questions of metaphysical reality.' He: 'You're in the wrong direction.' I: 'The Theory of Everything includes love.' He: 'The Beatles' song, "All we need is love".' I: 'No, that's not mysticism, which is having consciousness raised to a meaning and purpose level after the Dark Night.'...Wilson's second question: 'Could Universalism give you the mental muscle to switch from a vase to a face?' I: 'Yes, through the inflowings from the beyond.' Wilson's argument that the self is the right direction, not the universe. Wilson: 'You are systematising.' I: 'Blake said, "I must create a system or be enslaved by another man's."' He: 'He also said, "An error cannot be refuted unless crystallised."'...I: 'The energy must come from the universe, from God.' He: 'It sounds like T. E. Hulme, "floating off into the universal ether" (*Speculations*).' I: 'But there's no floating off, one's feet are on the ground. It's consciousness for all mankind, at an HCF not an LCM level in a unitive consciousness filled with meaning and purpose after the Dark Night of Spirit.'...He: 'It's like Whitehead's philosophy of organism, too vague.' So he had blasted Eliot and Whitehead to blast me, and I was still not out at the crease, occupying the crease like Boycott – or Denis Compton."

Joy then brought in his meal and "we brought it down to a more personal level. Wilson: 'William James did not help Husserl, he didn't understand what he was about because he was that bit more pragmatic.' I: 'What a pity. Don't leave it until you are 86 and I'm 79 to decide we form a corner. What will they say in 2050? Hagger and Wilson often met but could never get it together? Think of Sartre and Camus in 1946, and Sartre saying to Camus: "I don't like what you're doing, *L'Homme Revolté* is too humanist and moderate. I have will-power – I believe the will is energised from the beyond – and I carry things through like the school. Everyone said, "It'll fail, you won't get the pupils or the planning permission, it'll be bankrupt within a week, but it wasn't. I'm used to leadership, saying, "This is where we're going and what we're doing." It'll be all right. You see.' He: 'You built the school the right way up. You're in the wrong direction with Universalism.' I: 'Who else is sharing the consciousness concerns regarding mankind?' He: 'No one else. No one. Just you and me.' I: 'Our intention is the same, though our results may be different.' He: 'You're going about it the wrong way.' I: 'Let's see what happens, what the outcome is....I'm doing a jigsaw, all my works are jigsaw pieces and they will make a picture. The Autobiography is a piece with a large chunk of picture on it. Your *Outsider* 6 were interlocking and portrayed a picture. Wait till I've finished my jigsaw. If you were then to write about me like Whitehead and Toynbee in *Religion and the Rebel*, the Autobiography will be important, like Rilke's *Malte Laurids Brigge*, Dostoevsky's *Notes from Underground*, Yeats' *Autobiographies*, Augustine's *Confessions* – it will be said that no one really wrote about such things in the 20th century, the experience of the Light as consciousness.' He: 'Whitehead had no impact on philosophy at all.' I: 'His time is coming. And that was because of Logical Positivism – we need a Metaphysical Revolution to organise it.' He: 'If I thought that we were going in the same direction, I'd be with you 100%. But we need more mental muscle, and how do we get that from Universalism and the Metaphysical Revolution?' So make that clear to him: how the experience of the Light gives this. He: 'It's like orgasm. Everyone experiences that.' I: 'But the Mystic Way and the Dark Night end in a different kind of consciousness....It's different. I'm speaking of the unitive consciousness of all mankind. The way forward is not through language but into the Light.' And I went, having had the last word while he ate." I reflected: "Wilson has resisted religion and is uncomfortable with me taking the consciousness element – the existential Light – and leaving aside the doctrine about Jesus Christ." Wilson told me: "I like the precise details of murders, I go around with my magnifying glass."

After I left I reflected: "Colin and I are unique in being interested in a vision of meaning and purpose. My unitive consciousness sees meaning in a way the tepid everyday consciousness does not." When I returned to Charlestown I looked in on Arthur Hosegood two doors down and said: "I've been with Colin Wilson for the third time in a week, two and a half hours." Arthur replied: "Oh dear, it's the tension."

I went for another "late night walk. Sand-hoppers again. Many bright stars, and the sea washing in, backdrag of pebbles, then washing in again."

On the way home from Cornwall, Ann, Anthony and I looked in on Frank Tuohy, who was living in Somerset. Tuohy had sent me a card with a map and directions as to how to find him. I wrote: "Drove to Shatwell Cottage, near Yarlington, Somerset..., where Tuohy came to the door of a yellow stone stable block, which he has converted. Downstairs 'garage', entry and loo, upstairs – bedroom and huge study/living room with foreign pictures and wall-hangings and books in two areas (more downstairs). We sat on a sofa...while Tuohy, perhaps the de Maupassant of our time, sat in a chair opposite. We talked of Japan. He was in Japan 1982-9. When he left Japan he got drunk like Lucky Jim and told the sensei, 'Your students are better than you are.' He fell over into the sashimi (raw fish) and had fish on his shoulder. How the farmhouse is 1700, how his cousin...lives there with 5 children, his wife having died of leukaemia aged 55. His two Tibetan spaniels from All Souls (the Warden). Lunch downstairs: ham, baked potato, egg mayonnaise he made during a thunderstorm last night with the dogs yapping – he had to remake it this morning – and pudding with raspberries and cream and cheese. Soda to drink. Chatter about mutual friends, e.g. Alan Baker has remarried, and Larkin and Ricks. He: 'Ricks carries things to extreme, a word used accidentally which he repeats, making it appear deliberate. Larkin uses exclamation marks at the end of a poem to solve the problem of how to end strongly.' Tuohy, stooping and shuffling, much older, less of a memory. Upstairs over bitter coffee on

Wittgenstein: 'I can't remember what he said, I didn't understand much. I remember his German intonation and metaphors: "Ve are tied together by belts, our bodies naked together." I went to see *Ladies Courageous* (a film) with him, we sat in the middle. I remember his deck-chair and pile of detective novels. He liked Westerns and Betty Hutton.' He: 'I have arthritis and blood pressure.' I: 'Will you be here for good now?' He: 'It depends on community care.' His game with Ricks, what books *haven't* you read. Later we toured the farm, met the 5 children and visited a barn where there will be a wedding...and where there is a barn owl. We ended the tour at the car and left." I observed: "Final impression of Tuohy: he is getting old, his failing powers. He is not as sharp as he was and not used to focusing on writers as he used. He writes every morning. His memory is going. He did not want to talk about my work, and when I mentioned the 'jigsaw without a picture' I am doing...he said, 'Shall we look round the garden.'...But like Kathleen Raine and Colin Wilson, mention of his work was in order. Writers are primadonnas and like to be the centre of attention."

Almost immediately I drove to Birmingham to address the Quaker Universalists' annual weekend conference. I arrived around 4 at Fircroft College, Selly Oak, Birmingham, "a College of Adult Education with grounds including a pool and a lot of polyanthuses and daffodils. Pictures show a red-ivied back." I noted a Quaker ambience of plainness about the place: there was no basin in my room, and the bathroom was across the passage. The first evening was a get-together, during which I asked the group "sitting near me, 'In the Silence are you aware of the Quaker Light?' Eyes in corners. They aren't. The don't know what it is.'" The next morning I woke at 6.15 and "went to the bathroom early and joined a man who was shaving and who is putting on a cycle of 12 plays about the 20th century, based on *The Fire and the Stones*. It is linked to mythical themes, e.g. the expulsion from Paradise, and the first is at the Birmingham Arts Theatre in July. I: 'And you bring the Fire into it then?' He: 'Yes, we have a Greek chorus.' And immediately I saw how I could do my own verse drama with a Greek chorus. 'Our committee studied your book and the charts.'...At the end of our shaving together: 'Thank you for your writings. You are making an impact because Fundamentalism is digging its heels in.' An encouragement."

Before my talk I went to the Light: "First there was 'silent worship' from 9 till 9.45 during which the Light poured in, empowering me from head to foot, at 9.05 and about 9.20; enormous surges. I then spoke to perhaps 50 or 60 people who sat facing me. I used the overhead projector for 3 transparencies and over-ran, so I had to do the political bit after coffee. I stirred them up and got them thinking. Many questions. I was controversial about the Bilderberg Group." I spoke on religious and spiritual Universalism, saying that there will be pressure for religious Universalism when there is a political Universalist New World Order. "At lunchtime I was clear. But at 2.15 there was a study group of 10 which went on until 4. They wanted me to join it and I spoke for most of the time....I said to them, they can be the Quaker Universalist Group, or they can network all the churches and take part in religious Universalism or they can form a Universalist religion. The options ahead." I noted: "Was told that Maslow does not see 'peak experience' in left-brain terms, but he includes right-brain i.e. the Fire or Light is a peak experience."

Generally, I had a very favourable reception among the Quakers. One asked me, "Can we really believe that the Light is the energy that keeps our civilisation going?" to which I replied, "Yes, because it gets into the religion which is involved in the State and gets across. Mystics have to get their vision into their religion and affect the State." What I meant was that the unitive consciousness the Light creates has infused wisdom and knowledge from the beyond which improves the civilisation's government. So I was not talking about "the escape into transcendence" (another questioner) at all; rather transcendence's concerned and involved action in the world: in everyday life and history.

On the Sunday Marcus Braybrooke, Chairman of the World Congress of Faiths and an authority on the interfaith movement, spoke "saying there can be Universalism and diversity". I spoke with him at length over coffee – he had a shock of curly hair and was bespectacled with a lean, precise mouth – and he was extremely interested in *The Fire and the Stones*.

When I got home Steve Norris rang. I wrote: "He spoke of Thatcher's call to arm the Bosnian Moslems. 'I hope people don't support it.' I: 'She's seen that the Bilderberg Group want to arm the Bosnian Moslems to sell arms to both sides, and that Clinton will go along with it; she's saying, "You got rid of me because you thought Major would do what you want, but if you'd stuck with me, look what you'd have got."' He agreed."

I thought about the Light: "Everyone has brotherhood in the Light as in St. Augustine's *Civitas Dei*. So all are responsible for all. So the World-Lord has a duty to help the poor, to spread resources. Enlightened World-Lords. Right action by all illumined people. Each day, help someone poor, help a child, help someone disabled, help a teenager, practising compassionate action in the world. Separate going to the Light in silence and 'What do I do out in the world?'...The duties involved in world government. An end to all war. Become an enthusiastic devotee of (American-inspired) world government. From the bottom up, small communities teach us how to live and influence senators. But practically, show enlightened help and reverence for Light. Respect the Light in everybody. Each day, give money to an example of several categories of people, and be responsible in a charitable way for numerous others....My amelioration. The illumined make things better for everyone else."

I defined four aspects of God: "The fourfold nature of God: as One – 'dark' (i.e. latent Light) Godhead; as non-Being – limitation of Godhead becoming involved in Creation; as Being – the Fire or Light; as existence – energy within form. It is all one manifesting process." And I added: "All knowledge is a human construct. Mysticism is not, it comes into the soul and has not been constructed by humans, only received."

Just after the schools returned for the summer term, there was a bizarre development at the Metaphysical Research Group of philosophers, which led them to declare themselves Universalists. I wrote: "Drove to David Lorimer's house in Tilehouse Lane. A modern house set in a beautiful

743

walled garden with a lawn which takes 3 hours to cut. Max Payne chaired the philosophy group. There were papers...on Bohm's consciousness and number...and then there was a disagreement between Max and Geoffrey Read: rival papers. Max attacked metaphysics and declared the group at an end. I: 'There was momentum in the car, and it stopped abruptly and we were nearly thrown through the windscreen.' Also: 'We are finished with the caterpillar stage and must become a chrysalis before the butterfly emerges. This phase was necessary. But now a new phase. We must work in a latent movement, we have become a movement.' Peter Hewitt was appalled and asked me – wrote it out on the back of a paper – 'Would you be prepared to act as Chairman?' He proposed it, I came in and with Max looking deeply unhappy, it was agreed that the group should continue under a Universalist banner, to get across to those 'out there' and to study our own work as if we were Existentialists. I: 'It's as if we were Sartre, Camus, Heidegger and Jaspers – each will have a different emphasis but we're all one movement.' Max later: 'It's as if we were pre-Raphaelites.' Chris McCann, ex of Lincoln (College, Oxford) was very active. A new direction. Get this vision across we are an anti-materialist alliance but we are under a positive banner: 'What is the Fire? What is Universalism?' as Satish Kumar said to me. I: 'It's like the Aristotelian Society, with Whitehead and T. E. Hulme in the same room. One day it will be said: 'Just think, Max Payne and Geoffrey Read fell out, I would like to have been a fly on the wall; and David Lorimer was there – and Alison Watson!' Smirks all round. Start with my image for going through the hole in the hedge....Later, we talked on the lawn near the apple-tree orchard in the evening sun, I in a long-sleeved shirt and tie." I told them that our Universalist group would reverse the work of the Vienna Circle (which had included Ayer and Wittgenstein). "I: 'The bus is going, we just have to get on it.'...The Metaphysical Revolution has taken over."

My visit to Florence opened up a coming phase of my work.

I flew to Pisa on my way to the conference at Florence. I took a bus from Pisa airport to the station, "and then a no. 1 bus to the Duomo, crossing the Arno with its shimmering reflection of coloured houses. The shock of the Duomo: you go through an arch and suddenly you're back in the Middle Ages; the round Baptistery, the rectangular Cathedral, and the leaning tower, very white and leaning much more than I'd expected. A 13th century square with stalls. Got a no. 1 bus and continued the one-way system back over the Arno, near where Shelley lived." At Pisa station, I "bought a ticket for 'Firenze' and caught the train...past mountains while I thought of how the Romans tilled and the Renaissance flowered. Wide open plains, vineyards, pink roofs, loan cypresses, Tuscan farms under a grey sky. The woods and a gorge and we were in the Arno valley. Time was like sitting in a train travelling backwards. Blinds upstairs, arches downstairs, the flats, rain on the roads, allotments, hangars, the detritus of industrialisation, filthy caravan sites. Mountains, yellow ochre houses, green blinds, peeling orange baroque. Red-tiled roofs, many overhead wires, and I was in Florence, which appeared like the centre of London." I took a bus out to Careggi, and booked in at the Hotel Careggi "which is marble floors and towny".

I walked to the 15th century Villa Careggi, where Cosimo Medici died and Ficino founded the (Platonist) Academy. A towering curved orange facade with arches at the top, and a courtyard inside with an open roof. Went into the hall with frescoes, the meeting room....Classical scenes on the wall. 5 red apples over double doors at the end. Arrived slightly late. Noel Cobb on changes to the programme....Then Linda Proud on the Orphic and pagan background to Ficino. She tried to make Ficino out to be more pagan than he was. At question time I asked if she knew why he had become a priest in 1473, and held that he was endeavouring to reconcile Christian and pagan, as had Clement of Alexandria, that he was a reconciling Universalist rather than a neo-pagan. There was then a break and I walked into the next room with its *Resurrection* by Verrocchio, and out into the gardens with their orange trees, boys riding on an owl and a tortoise and wysteria. The second lecture was Chris Bamford on Gemistos Plethon and the Fire or Light." He traced the tradition of the Fire, and it seemed as if he had used my work as a source. So I asked the first question at the end: "I said that Ficino and Plethon were not typical Renaissance figures but were continuing the tradition of the Fire or Light, and I pointed out the application of the Fire today: *The Fire and the Stones* in history, *The Universe and the Light* in science and philosophy...and I quoted Tillich. I asked him, 'Have you seen my book?' He: 'I've got it, Noel Cobb sent it to me.' I: 'So you know about my interest in the Fire.' He: 'Gemistos was not a Universalist but a localist.' I: 'That's why I quoted Tillich. You can have your own local tradition but relate it to the universal religion of which Christianity and Islam are types.'" Later we all ate at the Villa Cancelli, which was also 15th century. By now I regarded Ficino as "of his time, like Michelangelo, deeply Christian but very pro-Plato and pagan to some extent (e.g. his interest in Hermes); and he tried to reconcile them all. Was Gemistos a Neo-Platonist? (Localist?) Or was he a Universalist reconciler of Christianity? He tried to argue that paganism was better than Christianity and the book was suppressed."

The next morning I was up at 7.15 and breakfasted downstairs on a roll, white butter and cappuccino. I was collected by a minibus and driven to the Villa Careggi, where I learned from Adrian Bertoluzzi that Ficino lived in the Villa Le Fontanelle about 2 miles away, and that he visited Cosimo at Careggi in a room upstairs. It was a fascinating story. Cosimo, a banker who managed the Papacy's finances and became the wealthiest man of his time, at 50, in 1439, attended lectures on Plato and eventually invited his doctor's son, Ficino, to open the Academy; and Ficino's letters had influenced Botticelli regarding the divine Venus (Plato's divine principle). There was a lecture on Ficino's unified view of the universe, with talk of God and the supernatural Light. And there was a reading of a long modern Platonic dialogue while a bird sang outside the window.

In the early evening I went in to Florence on a bus. I wrote: "To the Duomo, which was...dark inside. Saw the picture of Dante and Ficino's bust....Went to where between nos. 12 and 13 outside Dante sat in the evenings, and walked to the house of his birth and childhood in Via Dante Alighieri. On to the Piazza della Signoria where Savonarola was hanged and burnt. I saw in my mind's eye three fires, flames rising, and three men faced away from what is now Neptune's statue – and later confirmed the exact spot by finding the commemoration plaque on the stones....Looked in to the Palazzo Vecchio where Cosimo was imprisoned and then the Uffizi and saw Botticelli's Primavera (Plato's divine principle) and the birth of Venus – pagan images of Beauty which have unity when you know the esoteric code, but which otherwise do not. Across the Ponte Vecchio with shops on it which protrude over the water, to S. Maria del Carmine, which was by now closed....On to eat at a trattoria in the Piazza del Carmine: veal and before that Tuscan vegetable 'soup' washed down with Tuscan wine. Taxi home. Walked round in a shirt all day – it was getting hotter. Reflected that the purpose of life is to develop soul which reincarnates at a high level or goes to a higher angelic world – things that can only be known when one has broken away from the materialism of the...everyday existence....The awareness that things have purpose which is the artist's 'soul' vision."

I thought about the Renaissance: "Humanism meant being human, i.e. virtuous, so the first Humanists wanted *more* Light, and it was only later that they turned secular. Ficino would be horrified to think he had destroyed the halo, which went with Botticelli. Tread its demise in Uffizi: it's there in Fra Lippino Lippi and Fra Angelico, but has gone by Titian. The turning-point was those who died c1510. It is still there in those who died c1490. The great change happened about 1468, a new Age (geographical voyages, printing, new interest in paganism). Ficino combining Plato and Christianity in Venus as spiritual love – not physical love, a pure spirit..., not sexual at all or voluptuous."

The next morning I caught the 9.10 minibus. I "sat and wrote 3 stanzas in the courtyard of the Villa Careggi, with tinkling birdsong; then went into the grounds and wrote another stanza, sitting and writing on paper on my knee on a tombstone-like object near the statue of a Greek goddess. Found out from Bertoluzzi that there is a letter...from Ficino to Cosimo thanking him for the 'little house' which local tradition puts on the hill; and that Cosimo had gout. A talk about Ficino's life with many quotations, burdened with astrology, then a boring talk on town-planning with slides, which I left. Lunched at a trattoria – pizza and white wine – and then took a taxi and had a tour of the Villa Careggi. The cellar and up the stairs to the room where the Academy met, according to the nuns' oral tradition. A polished floor, red carpet you had to stay on, 18th century pictures and fireplace but you could imagine what it was like. Out to a loggia with 16th century frescoes including the (Medicis') pawnbrokers' symbol. I spoke with Bamford about Gemistos, and Bertoluzzi about Ficino, and got a picture of Ficino, who was 6 when he met Cosimo through his father (who was doctor to Cosimo), at a time when Cosimo was enthused by Gemistos Plethon to study Plato. The decision to found the Academy began the Renaissance, which can be dated to 1462 (or 1468, *De Amore*). Heard a talk on the sad smile of Aphrodite (because Adonis left her, not because she has transmuted erotic into divine love) and then scribbled more stanzas for a poem on the Renaissance, making 10 stanzas in all. It is still in draft, but catches the whole thing. A paper on *De Amore*, saying Eros is divine love (cf Venus) and then took the minibus to Villa La Fontanelle, the site of Ficino's house. A hilly drive meant you couldn't see anything. Back to eat, very tired." I went to a trattoria and had steak and red wine, and reflected that "they had a scholar's approach to the Fire (e.g. 'You can find out about the Rosicrucian Fire in Amsterdam') whereas I approach it through experience – as Ficino could not, or he would be burnt for heresy."

The next morning I went in to Florence to San Marco by bus, "and visited the Dominican monastery which contains the Museo del' Angelico, and saw in the monastic cells upstairs Angelico's wonderful frescoes, and those by the school of Angelico; Cosimo's cell (where he went on retreat) and Savonarola's cell and where he was arrested by the library. Downstairs in rooms off the Cloisters saw more Angelicos, showing the halo very pronounced and the view of man within a sea of Light. Looked for the Medici chapel and found it, after the Palazzo Medici where Michelangelo was discovered. On to the baptistery to see the Gate of Paradise (so called by Michelangelo), done by Ghiberti (died 1452). Inside saw the dome of 13th century mosaics with Christ, which Dante would have known. S. Maria Novella was closed so visited the Carmine, in the Brancacci chapel of which are Masaccio's frescoes with his wonderful shiverer, and fishermen, aghast Eve and weeping Adam. The silence in the rebuilt 18th century cloisters, where I felt the Light come through and wrote a poem or two. On to S. Maria Novella but could not see the Ficino portrait as the central altar was cordoned off. The frescoes c1357 by Nardi di Cime, showing Dante as one of the blessed and Dante's Hell. Took a taxi back to the Villa Medici and went back to La Fontanelle. Did not go up to the crenellated castle but got the idea of the hill it was on. In to hear Monteverdi (a union of erotic and divine love) and then Anthony Rooley (a rotund, small, mop-haired foppish man) on the lute and Evelyn Tubb singing dramatic songs of love, full of acted out negative emotions such as jealousy, a human view of the Renaissance in music as a thunderstorm gathered. Took a bus with the speakers. (Linda Proud: 'This is a speakers' bus.' I: 'I'm being dropped off on the way back. I'm not staying at Cancelli.') Stories from Bertoluzzi about how the Marchesa produced a 1499 1st edition book (at Villa La Fontanelle). The picture of the two philosophers Democritus and Heracleitus, one laughing and the other sad, by Bramante (1444 to 1514). A materialist with Fire." I reflected: "A day in which my feelings were engaged, first uplifted by Angelico, and then moved to tears in the peace of the Carmine cloister. I would like to live in Italy and not have to worry about mundane things like money."

I observed: "All the traditional symbols can be used now, they represent a living tradition. The Renaissance was marked by a switch from Mary to Venus, a paganisation of divine love....My favourite Angelicos: 1431, Universal Judgement (heaven and hell); 1437-40, Virgin with child and St. Peter, etc (the Fire and the rose being one); 1450, the Virgin with child between 2 Angels and St. Antony of Padua, etc (in a universe of light)....Let the halo back into art. Show the Virgin and Venus as divine principle of Light (Universalism)." Pondering, I again faced the choice of myself as an artist: "I must choose perfection of the life or of the work. I must now choose perfection of the work; not ideal living but putting it into arts with symbols. Reckon yourself as an artist as well as a philosopher."

A MYSTIC WAY

My last morning in Florence I walked to the Villa Careggi as the minibus did not turn up and heard a talk on astrology "which spoke of Ficino being a Religious Humanist not a rationalist secular one, and of a new tradition in astrology he was after. A discussion which I left when the singer began to get us to yell out sounds." I paid my Hotel bill and took a taxi to the station and the train to Pisa. There I "left the luggage at the station and took a bus to the Arno and walked to where Shelley lived. The plaque on the wall, near Ponte alla Fortezza. The house may have been pulled down and the Plaque may be on next door. Here he wrote *Adonais*. An emotional walk along the end of Lungarno Galileo (via S. Sepolchro, a Templar church) across the river to Lungarno Mediceo where, after looking at a Roman wall, I pondered my future, knowing I could live on the Pisan waterfront. I had written poems, and after being opened up by 1 and at the Carmine yesterday, I was filled with higher feeling as I sensed my future and destiny, to write an epic as great as Homer's, Virgil's, Dante's, 1's, Pound's. I had done my basic work à la Ficino – my history and cosmology – and only had the political and religious Universalism to do. Like Virgil I had shelved the huge task for 20 years, having been caught up in worldly things, and now was the time to get on and do it. I could hide here in Pisa, where large flats on the Arno with garages are £150,000, £250,000, all rooms overlooking the river. This was the Arno of Dante (in Florence) and of Shelley and Pound (who was detained here) – the medieval, Romantic and Modernist union, the tradition. I had to dare to be great. I had all the qualifications needed to write an epic: the Fire, history, cosmology, science. All, achievements in themselves, were but preludes to the epic, clearing my head for what is to come, a work that would plumb the height of goodness and the depths of evil....The elemental, high, pure feeling overflowed in me, and my eyes were wet, I trembled inside at the intensity of what I must do: to embody all the culture of Western civilisation in a 12-book poem. The exalted vision of perfection brought with it a sense of the inadequacy of my realisation of the vision (or so I thought). My vision was one of meaning and awe, of optimism, not despair. I was in a bar on the Lungarno Mediceo, drinking a cup of tea and my eyes were filled with tears on and off for about 10 minutes. I could not speak, blinking back the tears. I had found my next stage in my work and where to do it 6 months in the year, and no doubt a Doré or Blake would illustrate it and become a great artist. I had had the equivalent of Dante's vision of 1301....Now, with awesome certainty, I knew what I had to do. Not to be a political leader (though influence over the Prime Minister would be in the Leibnizian tradition); not to preach from a pulpit, and so I would not go to Chicago or Bangalore or do my mystery school any more. I would choose art and incorporate the Italian (and Greek) tradition into my epic." I returned to the station by bus and sat by the fountain until 7, then went by taxi to the airport. I reflected: "In Pisa I discovered a spring of creative feeling and imagination, and located its further flowing in a place – Pisa."

I flew home. I was left with a "sense of the conference as focusing on the beginning of the Renaissance and the whole of the Quattrocento. Also of the power of a group. As with Ficino's Academy, our group can reappraise the scientist at the nouminal rather than the phenomenal level: the inner rather than the outer. Geoffrey Read rang me this evening and said this, or words to this effect. He is very supportive of what I am trying to do in philosophy." The next day, "all day Pisa has been with me: not Florence but Pisa. Told the secretaries of both schools, the bank manager and Geoffrey Read: 'If I go missing, don't look for me on the banks of the Arno, where Shelley wrote and further down which Dante lived.'"

Under a large full moon I strengthened my resolve: "I must return to Italy and Greece, where I began, and apply my Ficinian vision of oneness in a great epic. Virgil died at 51 having spent 11 years on his epic. It must be now. In two years' time, at 55....My difficulty has been in understanding my many-sidedness, in grasping that I had to express *all* aspects of my Ficinian unitive outlook. I was an all-rounder....Me working on my epic among Italian stones, my Fire among Italian temples and cathedrals."

Throughout May and June I thought about the epic while I worked on my Autobiography and *Collected Poems*. Universalism suddenly took over the group of philosophers.

I dined with Steve Norris at the House of Commons. I met him in the central lobby and we had a drink in the bar and talked about a Maastricht vote. He said: "It went through without a whimper." I noted "his obvious reservations about the New Europe and its lack of democratic experience". We ate in the Commons dining-room two tables from Heseltine and from 1, head of the committee to investigate MI5 and MI6. We discussed how the government in power in the year 2000 would respond to the New World Order, which was scheduled for then. We discussed what made a successful politician: "He: 'You've achieved more than I have, a politician just uses words.' I: 'There has to be a vision behind the words, as de Gaulle had, and then there is a strong projection (from the people).' He: 'You are absolutely right. What job would you do in 2000?' I: 'Roving ambassador between world leaders.'" After dinner we "went to his room on the bottom corridor of the Ministers' block" and I showed him some material I had brought. I wrote: "Left him well after 11."

I straight away began to implement my new commitment to my art. I spoke of looking for a bursar who would help me run the financial side of Coopersale Hall and take the daily visit to the bank from me. I rang Sir Laurens van der Post and "told him about the book, about the philosophy group, the possibility of a public debate and the Fire surfacing in Florence. He: 'It's confirmation. I did nothing except to give you some recognition, and you have provided confirmation.'"

Nadia rang. She had met a classical guitarist, Sandy Wright, who had gigs and was a member of the magical circle, and he had "whisked her off her feet", and she would like to get married. I wrote: "She couldn't wait to say....Nadi has not laughed so much for years. He is attentive and wants a duck pond. He writes songs. I am delighted for her, having asked some practical questions....She knows it is right."

I attended a course on Goethe at Oxford. I passed the Eastgate, where Ann was having a reunion with her college friends, and went to St. Catherine's College and met Arthur Zajonc (pronounced 'Zience'), author of *Catching the Light*, a confessed Steinerian, a watchful "balding man in glasses, softly spoken, speaking of Goethe and movement, transformation, the dynamic and the flux, who transformed himself to have a theory of colour". After lunch there was a lecture on "a study of place and responding passively to flowers". I came away feeling I had "lived at too low a level of tension. The scientists Zajonc and (Brian) Goodwin, a holist but not a metaphysical or transcendental one, had not inspired me." I wondered how Goethe came to have the Illuminatist name Abaris; I knew he was friendly with Schiller, and that he was 27 at the time of Weishaupt.

When I got home I realised that my epic "is like a plant – as a poem – a Jack-by-the-hedge or garlic mustard (or lily) with 12 leaves. The roots, the leaves and stem, the flower. The flower is the spirit (that of God – the vision). The roots are in the world: the 20th century. So what are the stem and leaves? The theme and 12 books. Organic form for my epic. Fire and flux, show a process, transformation....I am in dynamic transformation, not static. My epic form must be transformative."

The next day I returned to Oxford and looked in at the Eastgate and joined Ann at the breakfast table and had coffee with her friends. I wrote: "On to St. Catherine's, where I talked with Zajonc. Asked him: 'Is your light divinised natural light or metaphysical Light?' His Steinerian answer: there may be beings behind the Light. Listened to Brian Goodwin on the organising idea in Goethe, 'inner necessity and truth' (letter to Herder, 17th May 1787), and generic form, which over lunch he told me he reckons he has proved, contrary to the Darwinian view of Dawkins, but like Copernicus's idea it won't be recognised until much later; and the Tonbridge teacher Bortoft who was in a group with Bennett but has worked alone for the last 20 years, on the organising idea being non-sensory but (he said) non-metaphysical and non-positivist. He is against Plato's 2-world theory. Much on observation of plants: the 4 modes, looking at a plant, time-scale, considering what is in oneself, the union with the being of the plant (the imagination)." I wrote that Goodwin is a holist (not Universalist) and that his missing link is "pressure from the metaphysical Fire" I felt that Goethe's "nature seems to be undivine; he was at best a Deist, at worst a sceptic", "a natural philosopher not a metaphysical philosopher". At the same time I acknowledged that in Goethe "polarities are opposite down below but are reconciled into a unity above. He took a natural rather than a divine view of polarities, and anticipated Hegel?"

I returned to poetry. On May 11th I wrote: "Worked on *The Weeping Philosopher*. Polished 6 stanzas until I nodded off." The next day I "finished my poem on Ficino. It is now called *The Laughing Philosopher*. The emphasis on flux." Nadia rang and I heard Sandy playing the classical guitar in the background, "very beautifully. It sounded like the play of light on the water outside her window, ripples of sunlight on water." Nadia rang again to say that the wedding would be at Johnsburn House, Balerno, near Edinburgh. The next evening I "drafted an Epithalamion about my daughter's marriage. Used Spenser's 18-line stanza and rhyme scheme, mixing modern realities with the traditional nymphs."

I had a meeting with "the inner core of the philosophers" in Victoria: "Ran into Chris McCann, who immediately produced his tome for me to read, an awesome universal system after the manner of Hegel or Heidegger, possibly one of the great works of our time. Told him we are perhaps the first group of its kind since the Vienna Circle, that we are considering the whole universe and universal systems. Alison Watson arrived, and Geoffrey Read in dark glasses. I: 'You can tell he's a revolutionary.' We sat in front of the hearth in the tea-room, and considered *Declaration*-style essays with a possible manifesto at the end, which would promote our works, and Alison and Geoffrey had a bickering quarrel which Alison stood up to leave. I insisted she sat down. I: 'There's the work as an object but also there's how it is perceived and received, what interpretation the reader puts on it, and that's important. Have an accessible general book.' All agreed. Chris: 'The book can be called *Universalism: the Philosophy of the Future*. I: *Of the 21st century*." Later Alison rang me and said: "It's your drive that has got us all together, it's your drive that's keeping us all to the point."

Towards the end of May I was revising sonnets written in 1979 for my *Collected Poems* while continuing this Autobiography.

I spent my 54th birthday at Regent's College, London, listening to Willis Harman, author of *The Re-examination of the Metaphysical Foundations of Modern Science*. I wrote: "Walked from Regent's Park station...and fell into step with – was overtaken by – a striding Peter Fenwick. A gathering of about 30 people in a tiny room, with an outer coffee room where I met a natural, brylcreamed Willis Harman, who seems to be in his 70s; an ex-engineer who has questioned the metaphysical foundations of science. Gave him my book, wrote out my address at his request, then heard him. He stood behind a chair and spoke for an hour without notes, always a smile behind his gentle eyes. He is saying to the scientists: let's see if we can go ahead a little way. I told him this afterwards and said I am not dependent on scientists and so can say: 'This is how I see the universe, who's coming?' I sat in silence in the 2nd row – we all had to switch rows and let late-comers sit in the front row – during question time before lunch, and then we went out into Regent's Park and David Lorimer produced a picnic lunch from his car and we sat in deck-chairs and talked. I sat next to Willis Harman while a couple of positivist scientists spoke at Harman, and then I put it to him that the revolution in philosophy will have useful consequences for science. He agreed. I left at the end of lunch. William Anderson (author of *Dante the Maker*) and I walked to Baker Street station together, talking Italy. He recommended Lonsdale Ragg, *Dante and his Italy* and Geoffrey Highet, *Poets in a Landscape* for Virgil, Horace and Ovid. He said he would live in Vicenza or in the Tuscan San Gimignano, where Dante was sent as ambassador in 1300, if he were living in Italy. Anderson, besuited with waistcoat and spectacles, hardly any voice because of a bad throat, but precise and considered answers to my questions; then abruptly he said goodbye and disappeared in haste for his appointment....Most of the philosophy group were there."

The first day of the Universalist philosophy group had me talking to the philosophers at David Lorimer's house in Tilehouse Lane, Uxbridge. I wrote: "I spoke on tape for 2 hours (10.30-12.30) on how wide Universalism is, how Willis Harman is keeping the scientists happy but I can jump ahead, how my central idea of the Fire is a first principle, out of which the universe and evolution came, how the vision of the Fire is central to history, how the metaphysical view is of a totality that includes science and spirituality, how there should be a metaphysical science and a metaphysical philosophy, about the New World Order and how Universalism is happening anyway. Transcendence-immanence being a spectrum. Before, during and after lunch, further discussion. Universal agreement that my philosophy can be accepted although (McCann point out) 'phenomenology requires no hypostatisation and you hypostatise the Fire'. (Phenomenology requires a manifestation, someone to whom it happens, and structures within the manifest which can be evidentially elucidated – and it is on this last point that I jump ahead of phenomenology.) Coherence and sound argument – the Fire sticks everything together ('co-haero'). Is there free will? Yes, we have come out of the Existentialist chrysalis, Universalism is a butterfly – but do atoms have free will although they are connected? Both are possible. Imagination operating at higher and not just social levels. Evidential basis of the Fire or Light? Hidden variables which prevent randomness as harmonics....Like Whitehead, I now have a coherent philosophy if I can make the Fire evidential. Whitehead's 'The purpose of philosophy is to rationalize mysticism'. That is how I see philosophy. I added: "The evidence for Fire as a structure. If it is received in someone's consciousness, then it must have come from somewhere. The body of speculative interpretation about the Fire...McCann does not proceed from the noumenal to the phenomenal, but from the phenomenal to the noumenal. What I have done: I have turned the Vienna Circle's principle back on itself and am reversing it."

Nadia brought her fiancé, Sandy, to meet us, a greying, freckled pleasant fellow. I met them at the station and drove them around the area. They attended an Oaklands play and eventually we went out in a drizzle to the Chef Beijing, where Jo Clarke (an Oaklands part-time teacher who has done many television commercials) was sitting at a nearby table. We returned and drank a bottle of wine and talked until 2.30 a.m. about Sandy's hopes as a composer and performing artist. The next morning I took them to Coopersale Hall, and then Sandy played the guitar while Anthony smirked in admiration.

At the end of May I went to Cornwall. We lunched at the Pier House Hotel "overlooking the sea as the sun came out and the sea began to calm after last night's storm". I edited my Birmingham lecture for publication in *The Universalist* and worked on my books. I "worked on my *Epithalamion*". I went to the Cornish osteopath and saw the Light while having my arm massaged: "I have had muscle strain in my left arm and shoulder for over 4 months; it has tightened and the blood supply is restricted. He kneaded my muscle for half an hour with his thumb, quite painfully, but, lying on my back, I drifted off behind my closed eyes and was aware of the Light breaking through. I record this to show that it is possible to see the Light while you are having your arm (painfully) massaged." Later Anthony tried out his new canoe on the beach under our windows. I wrote: "A boat came in while he sculled backwards and forwards and over the breakwater at highish tide in misty conditions." I wrote: "I have got untired....And now a sunny day and the boom of the waves....I feel well."

We returned for Argie's 90th birthday party at the Roebuck's Oak

Room. The family assembled in the bar – the Hove branch lost their way and gave up – wearing DJ, and after dinner I spoke. I wrote: "I welcomed everyone, spoke of the special nature of the occasion and said that Argie's two lifelong loves were her family and the London Hospital." I illustrated that theme with various examples. It was hot, and later I talked outside with my cousin Richard and Wendy in the "warm summery night, standing in front of the Roebuck by the grass nearly opposite the front door". We all had breakfast together the next morning.

In June I was revising sonnets: "June 7. Ill: fell asleep three times this afternoon. In the evening stayed away from the Oaklands parents' meeting and revised 4 sonnets from *Lady of the Lamp* (*Dustpan*, *Solitude*, *Door* and *Stalemate*) and felt better. It is therapeutic, doing sonnets. I know I am in the Catullus tradition and am worthy to be compared with those poets of the past. I have a felicity of language I must not be shy about." Later I "did *Mutiny* (another sonnet)".

On June 10th I went to Shaftesbury and met Michael Mann and agreed the order of the next books. I wrote: "He was in an open-necked shirt and looked sun-tanned from Miami (the Book Fair), where he met Chris Bamford from the Ficino conference: 'You bowled them all over.' Met for one and half hours." We agreed that I would have the Autobiography and *Collected Poems* ready for March 1994. In the course of our discussion I said: "Novelists like Martin Amis and poets like Larkin are secular and right for technique with nothing to say (*Time's Arrow* going backwards), whereas I have held off until I have something to say."

Mabel Reid was selling her house and moving for good into Forest Place, a private nursing home near the Roebuck. She asked me to take whatever books I wanted. I wrote: "Was surprised at how many on Mysticism she had. She was something of a Nature mystic. Her detailed observations of Nature were accompanied by a mystical awareness of the One."

The Oaklands fête took place: "The torrential rain yesterday (during which the school photo was taken – between heavy showers) gave way to a fine afternoon. Three or four hundred people attended....I announced from the caravan. At 4 there was a man (with a pony tail and many rings on his fingers) who did animal encounters, and we handled an owl, a snake, a bird-eating spider, a scorpion (we didn't actually handle these last two, merely saw them at close quarters), two iguana, a fruit-bat, etc. He also did fire-eating and juggling....The fourth form squealed at the spider: 'Mr Hagger, how could you.'"

Paul Gorka, my Hungarian author, rang from Hungary. I wrote: "He is now Head of Privatisation in West Hungary, living at Sopron, and Sebastian (his son) is Under-Secretary at the Ministry of Defence, aged 23. Paul has all the castles under him – hundreds of them – and is offering me one for a privatised Universalist academy....He is 'in absolute charge of all castles' and is offering to sell me one." The offer is a kind of reward for my efforts on behalf of the Heroes of the West.

Through Heather Dobbs, I spoke with Mary Seal, who organised the conference on global deception. I asked her, "Who is the Pope of the Illuminati?" and was surprised at her answer. She put me in touch with an

American research project so that I could check what she said. A great wealth of material arrived soon afterwards. From two separate sources I heard predictions of a deliberately manipulated financial crash in 1995, which would lead to a New Deal, a new world currency and a New World Order.

Christopher Ricks rang, inviting me to Oxford, where he was finishing his Sabbatical, to discuss my coming epic. "I like what you said"(i.e. that I am now aiming to be a man of letters) "and I want to see you but I've got to pack up a house by the end of June....I don't think I can get away, but you can come here and have tea...." And so on June 21st I met Ricks outside Blackwell's at 3.30. I wrote: "He was open-necked and in jeans material and carrying nothing; wrinkled bald pate and round glasses and grey hair and kind smile. I carried a case and was in a white shirt and wore my plain blue tie. At his suggestion we walked to Worcester College, talking about my Autobiography, *Collected Poems* and *Diaries Vol 1*. He: 'How much do you leave out?' We went to the Worcester Gardens past staircase 8 (his room) and sat on a seat looking at the lake before the arch; the situation of our first tutorial and looking at the spot where I chose to be a poet – a neat twist on his part. I told him about my epic....He on the difficulties. First, my predecessors Homer, Virgil, Dante, Milton and Pound: 'Don't be in competition with them, don't be hubristic, people will snipe, it is very ambitious of you. Second, are you Manichaean, i.e. dualistic? Is it good versus evil or are both reconciled in one? Thirdly, it is easier to do evil than good. Blake said Milton is of the Devil's party. Regicide, deicide, Heaven and Hell. There is something wrong with God that makes the poem *Paradise Lost* go wrong, as Dryden, Addison and Pope pointed out, and which defeated Tennyson. The mightiest of your predecessors have failed in getting the art right; Milton's Heaven was not a "glory". "Justifying the ways of God to men" (Milton) is not the primary poetic theme; "making friends with the necessity of dying" (Freud) is, to me. Empson, when he returned from Japan, once he had got his book on complexity done, could say "Nunc dimittis" (i.e. "now I can die"). Fourth, there is a problem regarding the future, which is left unrealised. A lump of futurity. Look at the end of (Marvell's) *Horatian Ode*. What happens in the future?' I: 'I can show the future without predestination, and still believing in free will.' He: 'Prediction and prophecy or prescience, Eliot's distinction: be prophetic, don't predict. Fifth, there is a moral position.'...He on the difference between a religious position and a technical position or artistic problem. 'And so, sixth, long poems tend not to be as good as shorter ones, e.g. *Paradise Lost* books 11 and 12 are not poetically achieved, and Milton writes "Egypt divided by the river Nile" (a flat line). The lesson of the failures of the geniuses of the past in respect of points five and six, e.g. *Idylls of the Kings* and the problems of the historical novel. Seventh, there needs to be a common belief or body of agreement or consensus, which (I assert) is not achievable as it's Christianity or nothing, and our multi-ethnic society and atheism deny consensus.' I identified the problem and said it was solvable by Universalism and by Michelangelo's unitive vision in which everything is a hierarchy. He: 'Without a universal figure, and it can't be Christ, you're like Blake with a private mythology, e.g. Los. Eliot's objection to Blake: lack of orthodoxy. Dante was the beneficiary of sustained and coherent thinking such as Aquinas – but Dante was Christian and not Universalist (although in his time Christianity covered the known world and so was Universalist). Look at Tennyson's *Ancient Sage* and *In Memoriam* and consider what failed Tennyson, the inequalities of accomplishment. Tennyson's late poems are not as good, e.g. *St. Telemachus* is not as good as *St. Symeon*. Eighth, religion still means Christianity and Christ cannot stand for holism, and homogeneity of culture is an assumption.'" I added: "Ricks's posture: he is better than Homer, Virgil, Milton, etc, who are 'geniuses', but who made mistakes and failed in their efforts. 'You must learn from their mistakes.'"

I wrote: "We then walked back to Worcester and peed in the 'lavatory', a 'sump' (Ricks), very primitive – the Fellows' loo for guests near the chapel by staircase 2. He insisted I went first: 'Guests first.' We walked to Longwall Street, and I said to him as we walked round Oxford: 'Tuohy went for walks with Wittgenstein. I have the feeling of what it was like when I walk with you.' He is the Leavis of our time. Ricks said: 'Yeats says we make poems out of the quarrel with ourselves and rhetoric out of the quarrel with others. Quarrel with yourself – art, quarrel with others – rhetoric. Keats quarrelled with himself when he wrote: "O for a life of ease". He wanted a life he had not got. I hate Yeats but he said something that is true....Religions are bad things and there should be a government health warning about holism and unity.' I on Yeats: 'Kathleen Raine compared *The Fire and the Stones* to *A Vision* and phases of the moon, she got me wrong. I'm not as mad as Yeats.' He laughing near the Martyrs' Memorial, 'Yes, there's a mad-ometer' (not a swingometer but a madometer). We passed his bike, propped against the wall outside Balliol, much battered, with a crossbar, and I raised the line (most appropriate for an epic). He: 'Blank verse is better than stress metre, but *Maud* is an alternative as it contains every known line except blank verse; but lacks dignity. Look at *Dynasts* again, Hardy's long poem.' I settled for blank verse with occasional lyrical bits (like *Gawain and the Green Knight*). He: 'Don't have a stanza for an epic like (Byron's) *Don Juan*.' I raised similes and said I was looking forward to using Miltonic similes from everyday life. He: 'Slightly demotic.' He quoted Wordsworth's 'Oft when o'er the bridge I went' and the smell of sewers and city fumes in the air."

I refilled my meter and we found a tea-room opposite Eastgate (where not long before I had visited Ann's friends, events again gathering round constant places) and "he ordered coffee and I ordered tea from a mini-skirted waitress and I showed him some of my poems: *Epithalamion* (pointing out that I wrote an essay on Spenser's *Epithalamion* for him in 1959, nearly 35 years ago) and *The Laughing Philosopher* (I said it was my *Byzantium* or *Sailing to Byzantium*, and he looked at me very intently and with great alertness and said 'No, it's not presumptuous'); and the red card in my Masaccio poem, which he liked."

I raised the Great Tradition "and suggested he came up with a new criterion of maturity: inner and outer and an evolution in individual styles.

He: 'I don't find the idea of a "Great" tradition valuable. There are several traditions, not just one. There are vantage points. The top of University church enables you to see all Oxford, but the view from the basement of the Ashmolean is better. Epics are necessary but so are limericks and sonnets. Compare 1st and 3rd person, where the question is: "What can an artist see and show?" The artist can't die in the 1st person....Roger Scruton, whom I've got to know and like, talks of "hitting the target" but I talk of steering between Scylla and Charybdis. Leavis seizes on maturity and a particular kind of maturity, but freshness is also important. The great tradition is not a good thing to do.'

Regarding my epic, he said: "The danger is that you will feel too strongly about (world events) and will quarrel with others and not make art out of the quarrel with yourself." I replied: "I can paint my Sistine chapel. My art is not propaganda." I reflected: "I need to withdraw from quarrelling with others to quarrel with myself." And I observed: "His sneezing with hayfever and violent and loud blowing of his nose. I showed him the title of a volume of my poems: *A Sneeze in the Universe*. He smiled. He spoke of my 'gigantism'. I: 'I have a gigantic theme, like Milton's *Paradise Lost*.'...He: 'Nothing's changed since Tennyson technically. Go back to him.' He remarked: 'We communicate through poetic and artistic ideas. You've done your thinking and thought it all out and so you can use it in an epic.' Suddenly at 5.45 he leapt up, said 'I've got to be back by six', darted over to the counter and paid, and as I followed him out into the street, said 'I shall shake you by the hand and say goodbye because I'm going that way', and with a brief shake of the hand he had gone before I could properly thank him." Shortly afterwards Ricks was in the *Times*, "speaking about Eliot's unpublished poems (which he was editing) which weren't up to his standards but are 'much better than any poems being written today'."

The ex-Bancroft's Bursar (who had just retired after 20 years' service) became Bursar of Coopersale Hall from September to lighten my load. He started visiting the school towards the end of June. There were Sports Days in both schools that I was involved in, and the Coopersale Hall fête took place. It was opened by Nick Berry, the police constable in British television's *Heartbeat*. The Coopersale Hall prize-giving was performed by the new Head of Forest School. It was remarkable for an imaginary letter (written in school) by Steve Norris's 7-year old son, Edward, which had been judged first out of 35,000 entries in a national competition. It was all about how his father, Minister for Transport, had been wheel-clamped outside Sainsbury's and had tried to remove the clamp. Edward read his prize-winning effort from the platform. Vicky was in the audience and watched him receive £100 from the Post Office.

After the prizes I hastily approved a letter written by an advertising agency which was marketing our two schools in the area, and agreed to its going out while I was away. This was 12 hours before we were all due to leave for America, and before I had started packing.

We were away from July 8th to the 30th – just over three weeks – on a tour of the East Coast, visiting cities and emphasising the historical 18th century sites.

Our flight tickets did not arrive until half an hour before we left by taxi for Heathrow. As a result we were compensated by flying Connoisseur class, and it was in the air, sipping champagne and eating steak and reading books on New York and Boston, that I "had the idea for writing a quartet (or even a quintet) of poems about America's world dominance, each one set in a different city or place: New York (the UN); Boston (the expulsion of the British); Washington (Kennedy and the founding fathers); Philadelphia (the origin of the US); and Florida". In New York we stayed at the Hotel Lexington, which had a fast lift, on the corner of 48th Street, and we walked among the towering buildings in a heat of 95 degrees and got used to the pedestrian lights saying "Don't Walk" and "Walk". I noted: "Everything here is better than in Europe: bigger, brassier and lasting longer." I asked: "Is America a different civilisation from the European one? Undoubtedly, yes, from what I have seen....A thrusting, money-making gigantistic civilisation, where you express your individual wealth on a vast scale."

The next day we toured New York on an air-conditioned coach. We went to downtown Manhattan. We stopped at the Rockefeller Building and went to the Empire State Building, Madison Square and Avenue, Fifth Avenue and Wall Street. There was a clear blue sky and we had a good view of the Statue of Liberty "in the distance, like the Colossus of Rhodes, an Illuminati symbol from France guaranteeing liberty". We ended in the fragile UN building. We were taken round and I entered all the chambers, including the Security Council and the General Assembly, where Krushchev banged his shoe. Outside I took a taxi to East 68th Street and gazed for a long time at the anonymous CFR building, centre of the world ideal which was to dominate my time in a covert way: "the place where the UN was dreamt up." Later we toured Harlem, and passed John Lennon's flat and memorial garden, and the Rockefeller-backed non-denominational Riverside church. During the day I saw the Greek statues and images of world role: Atlas, Prometheus and Zeus. In the early evening I took a taxi to Washington Square and looked in vain for no. 38, where Eugene O'Neill wrote *The Iceman Cometh*. In the evening we ate at a steak bar and went up to the 86th floor of the Empire State Building for the view.

We made a brief visit to Boston, flying up and back within the day, crossing "a Paradise of clear waters". We took the Freedom Trail in a great heat and went over the US Constitution, which was in dry dock, and then went to the Old State House, Old South meeting house where the Tea Party debate took place, Faneuil Hall and other buildings connected with Benjamin Franklin, and the Beaver II, a boat on which we witnessed a reconstruction of the 1773 Tea Party.

The next day we were to go by coach to the Niagara Falls. I wrote: "July 11. Woke before 6 to pack cases in time for 6.45 and 'saw' two of my American Quintets. *New York* to catch the thrusting economic growth of America, to be built around the Rockefellers, the dream of world government. *Boston* to catch the separation from the British of the Boston tea party and Samuel Adams, a separation by separatists and dissenting Puritans: the dissenting spirit." We drove through wooded Pennsylvania (founded by William Penn of Chigwell School) and I began what became my *American Quintet*, drafting the first two poems on my knee on the coach. We ate overlooking the Falls and went on the Maid of the Mist, a boat, to get a closer look. I wrote: "Earlier we had stopped at the top of Niagara Falls and I had drafted 3 stanzas of *Niagara Falls*, and now, back on the coach, I polished them and added a 4th stanza, and also wrote two more poems as we continued our drive to Lake Ontario and the town of Niagara-by-the-lake: *A Floral Clock* when we stopped at a floral clock which actually did chime 11 while I waited, and *At Lake Ontario* as the four of us ate a picnic lunch with our feet near the water, lying on a grassy bank in bright sunshine." We enjoyed our brief visit to Canada, and Matthew said he would like to work there, using his French. We again ate overlooking the Falls watching an orange and yellow sunset turn pink and green. We returned to Lancaster along the Susquehanna river through the Appalachian mountains and farms. I wrote: "Wrote 3 more poems: *Rainbow*; *Susquehanna*; and *UN Security Council*." In Lancaster Matthew gave a Choi Kwang-Do class, being received like royalty by the Americans, and the next day we saw the Puritan Amish, a Mennonite sect that had not changed since 1690. The Amish wore plain black clothes and the women wore a white bonnet.

We arrived at Washington and I was impressed by "the huge Roman grandeur of it: wide open spaces (e.g. the Mall) and gigantic Graeco-Roman buildings, all white marble, well-kept". We visited the Holocaust Museum and toured the FBI and in the evening ate overlooking the Potomac and then went to the Jefferson Memorial in a thunderstorm, then the Lincoln Memorial, the Kennedy Centre and the Watergate building. The next morning we visited Arlington Cemetery (and JFK's grave), the Capitol, the Vietnam Memorial and Mount Vernon, George Washington's estate. From there I went by car to the Washington Masonic Monument or Temple, part of which I was able to visit, and I bought a book, *Washington, Master Mason* which contained details of Washington's hostile attitude to the 18th century Illuminati.

The next morning we went on to Philadelphia and saw the Liberty Bell, the Congress Hall and Independence Hall, with the half-sun on Washington's chair. I wrote: "Saw that the original Fire or Light of the American civilisation was a masonic one – Washington's half-sun in his chair; that Washington's masonry was good and operated within his Episcopalian religion." We then flew to Orlando in Florida, and I drafted a third poem on Washington. I wrote; "My *American Quintet* – call it the *East Coast Quintet*?" Almost immediately I went out to the Kennedy Space Centre to see the space Shuttle leave, but the launch was aborted and I returned disappointed. We visited Disneyland and Universal Studios and moved on to St. Petersburg on the Gulf of Mexico, where we spent 9 days at the Dolphin Beach Hotel. Some days we spent by (and in) the pool on the edge of the beach, some days we made local forays to look at the dolphins and bird life in the intercoastal waterway, and some days we went further afield, to the Everglades swamps to see wild alligators, and to Naples to see the millionaires' colony and Marco Island to see the shells. We had hired a car and drove to St. Augustine for the early Spanish history, which was even more interesting than Boston and where I focused on Ponce de Léon's Fountain of Youth. We stopped at Daytona beach on the way, expecting to see the Shuttle launch, but it was aborted 2 minutes before take-off, with thousands on the beach all looking in the direction of Cape Canaveral. One day we returned to Orlando and visited the Epcot Centre. At the end of July I went to the Kennedy Space Centre and drove round the launch pads and researched NASA's space station, the next major project. All the while I carried forward my *Quintet*, and by July 20th I wrote: "Call the *American Quintet* the *Liberty Quintet*. Liberty is the common theme: liberty for the world under a world government that must not be a slavery." In fact I settled for the title: *American Liberty Quintet*. Somehow the poem wrote itself, between buffet breakfasts and lunches at the Dolphin beach, and evening forays in the car to local restaurants. I polished the sections, and on July 28th noted: "My poem was...unplanned and is...'guided'." We did some final shopping at the store across the road and I completed the fifth poem of the *Quintet*. I had dictated the earlier poems, and I wrote: "At both Tampa and Washington I dictated parts of *St. Petersburg* on to my hand-held cassette-recorder, and in the 747 going home I finished section 5 and dictated it. Worked until midnight." Incredibly I arrived at Heathrow with the whole poem, which I had not planned to write, completely finished and on tape for a typist.

We were met by a Loughton taxi-driver. It had been an extremely full trip, so full of new impressions of the outer world that there was little time for the Light. I felt I had "seen" East Coast America and its world role, and confirmed my vision in *The Fire and the Stones*. Most satisfyingly, I had written a poem that balanced *Archangel* in my poetic work.

We flew to Edinburgh for Nadia's wedding. Nadia was on the British Midland flight and I was shown onto the flight deck where I took off with two chatty fellows. I wrote: "We took off at 133 knots (taking the weight and temperature into account) and climbed to 35,000 feet. Came out of the flight deck, dazed with instrumentation, unclipping my harness which was between my legs and round the sides and over the shoulders (5 straps into a central clip), and let the two boys replace me. Returned for the landing which was over Edinburgh's Forth Bridge and Firth. At the last minute (the captain) noticed that he had not pulled down the second lever for an automated landing and it had to be manual. That was because I was asking questions." From the airport we were driven to the Riccarton Arms, where I was collected by Sandy and Nadia in a car, with Caroline and Damian in another, and driven to Johnsburn House where "amid much laughter, (we) reconstructed where we would stand for the ceremony (on the lawn above the stream) and how we go and join a line, after photos". Caroline was relaxed, and looked as willowy and elegant as ever, if more weathered by the years (like me). In the evening I held a dinner party for 11 in the Kweilin, which had a round table that turned, and got to know Sandy's mother, the best maid – there was also a bride's man who could not attend – and the two sides of Nadi's family. I played on the practical jokes one or two had up their sleeves, and there was "a lot of merriment" and they were

759

all "relaxed and loosened up with laughter".

I wrote of the next day: "a wet morning and a mist over Fife. Up at 8.30 for breakfast in the beamy breakfast room, all yellow plaster, of the Riccarton and then gazed at the doves (or possibly some are pigeons) on the dovecote outside my window. Wrote *The Hills of Fife* straight out. Spent the first two hours of the morning lying in bed and sitting on the bed, thinking, focusing on the afternoon, getting peaceful within, bringing down the Light, blessing the wedding." Frances joined us as I left the hotel at 3, "in a taxi with Caroline and Damian and Nadia in her ivory dress, the keyboard and the buttonholes. The taxidriver, a woman, lost her way several times and as soon as she arrived at Johnsburn House there was a cloud of steam from the engine, which boiled over. It could not be driven for at least 10 minutes. She: 'I thought it might do that at any time, but I didn't want to worry you.'" Nadia changed in the house and I reassured her. Caroline was there. There were tears at 3.45, and "at 4, having confirmed that the vicar, who was in a kilt, had arrived...I led Nadia from the 18th century room to the lawn, stepping over a flower bed in her long ivory dress, and we took up our place at the table with a cross on it which was near the stream....Sandy was waiting in a kilt on her right with the 'best maid', Sophie, a singer." Several wore kilts. The vicar "spoke forthrightly and married them for a bottle of Glenfidditch while midges bit and flies danced round our necks, whining in our ears and being swatted with the hymn sheets. It was what Nadia had wanted. She signed the book on the table by the cross, and all the time I heard the stream bubbling. Afterwards there were photos until a shower drove us in, and there was champagne in the wooden panelled room just inside the door, and then there were more photos when the sun came out, and then we refilled our glasses and went through to the bar for the speeches. I...spoke for 5 minutes about Nadia and Sandy, and then read my *Epithalamion* – note and then poem – which was received with thunderous applause. I gave the little booklet...to Nadia. It said on the front 'For Nadia and Sandy', a slightly cream booklet. Sandy then spoke, proposing the toast to the bridesmaids, and Sophie then read messages and instead of her speech she sang a rude song, all about Sandy's conjuring tricks with balloons....Nadia was much affected by the poem; I think it touched her. (I had said 'You've been a wonderful daughter and you'll make a great wife.') Sandy announced he had written a song for me, and it was too complicated for the keyboard player, and then I played the recording of the best wishes to Nadia and Sandy that had been organised on the radio. The evening then turned into showbiz, and theatre. At 7 we all repaired to the functions room, where there was another line of us greeters, and there was white wine for the guests and a disco in the room with a large stag's head on the wall....The dance-floor was soon crowded and until the buffet at 8.45 there was music with a strong beat and I was scarcely off the dance-floor, and danced with Caroline and Frances and Ann and made sure the boys were dancing. During the buffet I found a picture of Burns hanging over the hearth in the room overlooking the lawn (the room where I had waited with Nadia to go outside) and thought that you visit the place once when you are in your 20s or 30s, and you had your portrait over the hearth 197 years after you have died. (In my speech I hoped that my poem would last 400 years as Spenser's did, and that this day would be remembered in 400 years' time.) I found two manuscripts of Burns' on the wall, one a fragment from *Old Lang Syne*. After the buffet there was more dancing, and at one point after I had admired the easy swinging foot work and hips of the best dancer in the place with curved cheeks, done up hair and laughing eyes, Nadia dragged her onto the floor and thrust her on me, and I had three dances with her. I dance well, but it was my Southern League and her Premier Division, although it didn't matter....Nadia and Sandy left at 11.45. A circle was formed, there was a long wait for Nadia, and she came to me first, tearful, and I told her, 'All you've got to do is to hold yourself together for another two minutes.' She went round embracing everyone as did Sandy, and then returned to me....At the end they went outside, got in the taxi and drove off. We went back inside, and then our taxi was ready at 12 instead of 12.15. I went to say goodbye to the DJ, and he announced my presence and I was dragged across the seats by Carol and did *Old Lang Syne* (by Burns) between Carol...and Christine (the good dancer) and then I was away back over the seats and out into the taxi....Caroline (as Frances observed) was not bitter and was pleasant. I had ridden out the attempt by her ex-husband to get Nadia forcibly adopted....So many of Nadia's friends said, 'I can see the resemblance between Nadia and you,' and 'She's got your eyes,' and 'I feel I've known you a long time, I've heard so much about you.' I have a lot of friends in Edinburgh after last night – many single women – but all in all Nadi had a good day and a very memorable start to her married life."

Ann went straight to Cornwall. I stayed in Essex and worked: "Creative all day. The Light came in about 9 and my aura was visible out of the corner of the eye in the dark: white radiance. My Muse is back."

I had a telephone conversation with someone who was monitoring 19,000 centres about the 1995 crash. He told me the crunch will be the Mississipi floods, "which have cost $45 billion, $7 billion of which must be borne in the UK by Lloyds, which haven't got it....The changes in the climate have caused the crash. It was as the New Age have prophesied."

Marion Lord next door had not been well. She had been sick for two months and lost two stones. She was dehydrated, and tests showed her kidneys were not functioning properly. She was told to go to the Cancer Ward at St. Barts as soon as possible. She rang me. I went round and found her tearful. I helped her into a taxi with her luggage and waved her off. "She: 'I can't see why it can't wait until tomorrow.' I: 'Why be sick another night? The sooner they start stabilising you, the better. Go while the bed is available.' She: 'Yes.'" I waved her off, half knowing that she would never return.

I reflected: "We're all standing before a wall. Artists write a comment on the wall before they are shot."

We went to Cornwall: "Aug 12. Arrived under a cloudless sky and shooting stars like exclamation marks down the sky. It is the last day of the dog days....Aug 13. 21 poems on my Muse...Went for a walk with Matthew and Ann, who continued to walk round the harbour. I left them by the bridge and crossed back. Matthew, 'Aren't you coming?' I: 'No, I've got a poem in mind.' He: 'Oh no.' (Raising his eyes to heaven.) I returned and wrote a poem asking if the Shuttle was up there, a poem about the universe....Aug 14. Reflected and polished poems. I am a good lyric poet as I hint below the surface and bury things. I am a good love poet. Always go for the image....On the Maria Asumpta the rear sail is up and a man is singing sea-shanties to a crowd as evening closes in on the harbour. Wrote *Sea-Shanty*." The next day I "watched the Maria Asumpta leave port and wrote two more poems. Then settled...to the *American Liberty Quintet*." Nadia rang and described her boating honeymoon, travelling at 4 mph and looking at kingfishers. She fell in. I wrote: "Went for a walk at 11.45 with Matthew and Anthony and returned and wrote *Midnight Sky: Hawthorn and Almond*." The next day I reworked "the *American Liberty Quintet* and dictated it. Wrote another poem about the sparkling waves....A beautiful late night walk under vivid stars." Clapperton and Susie visited me and told me they had sold the harbour to Robin Davies of Bristol, who would use it for tall-masted ships.

On August 18th I made one last, not very successful visit to Colin Wilson on my own. I wrote: "Encountered him at 5.30 in the kitchen. 'Would you like some smoked salmon?' Avocado as well. Nervous talk while he surfaced from writing space vampires: 'It's more frank about sex than I've ever been.' Both boys were around, and Sally and her Wild Life boy-friend Mike. Spoke about Ricks and Eliot. Colin, 'The unpublished poems are no good.' A story how in summer 1956 Colin Wilson (and two other Angry Young Men) went to Eliot's church (St. Stephen's, Gloucester Road) and Eliot sat opposite them, and outside a boy was breaking milk bottles and Eliot looked uncomfortable. Wilson went outside and said 'P— off, you —s' and Eliot nodded approvingly when Wilson returned. Two days later he met Eliot to discuss Pound and reminded Eliot, who said, 'I recognised you, no one else would go to church in a polo-necked sweater.' I filled him in with the Universalist Philosophy Group, which he tensed at (he is on the side of preciseness and said 'There are no logical positivists left')....More on Ricks. I told him how he had listened to my ideas on the epic and how he published books on Beckett. Wilson: 'Beckett's a c—t. I met him at the Royal Court, he had nothing to say, there was no communication.'" He told me: "You've written more poems than Wordsworth." He told me how he had drunk a bottle of red wine before lecturing at the College of Psychic Studies, and how, not knowing what to talk about at a lecture in Penzance, he had talked about a certain part of his own anatomy. I then, perhaps presumptuously, expressed the hope that he would get back to philosophical work, and that he would be remembered in the next century for his early work, *The Outsider* and *Religion and the Rebel*. I got no further. I had obviously touched a sensitive spot, and, seething with indignation and resentment, he heatedly denied that I knew what he was "about" or that we had even communicated, and although I soothed him down and reassured him, while Joy came in and flashed him a disapproving look, it was clear that our difference of approach had widened, and that here could be no formal alliance between us. Colin Wilson was not going to become a Universalist philosopher.

THE UNITIVE VISION

The next night I took "a late night walk. Saw the Milky Way as a lobster and wrote a poem"; and the following night "went for a walk at 11.45 p.m. with Anthony. A sea-mist in. Wrote *Mist: Bat and Walls.* I am so creative at present." I visited Fowey, and "bought Ovid's *Ars Amatoria* at the second-hand bookshop, which also had second-hand copies of Colin Wilson's *The Outsider* and *Religion and the Rebel* – as I predicted he would be remembered." I wrote: "On the ferry to Polruan, to the Castle and sunbathed, then to the Singing Kettle for a cream tea. Back on the ferry. Home by 6. Spent the evening dictating the morning's work and some recent poems, including *Stillness* (which I wrote) today about 3 swans and 3 Red Admirals. Walked late as a storm approached like a distant war over the sea. Sketched out a poem, *Storm.* The next morning I "got the papers and saw the guests of *Guests* and wrote the poem". I wrote a lecture I was to give in October and then: "Revised *The Crack in the Earth* from *The Wind and the Earth*; and went for a midnight walk after watching *Trouble in Store* (again, never far from tears as Norman Wisdom engages the emotions and sadness) and wrote 5 quatrains on the night sky: five images for the stars, the best being fountain, the most original being a peacock's tail. I repeat: went for a late night walk under a cloudless, moonless night with very clear stars. Wrote *five* quatrains, all separate. What effortless energy. Aug 24. All morning, a sea with jumping lights and a fishing boat surrounded by the splashing. Sat and watched spellbound, when I should have been writing my lecture. Wrote several poems: *Downpour of Light*; *Light like Mackerel*; and (having seen a greenfinch on the front lawn and watched it through binoculars) *Greenfinch with Worm*; and (after sunbathing) *Trodden Daisies*." A few days later I wrote: "The youthful poet dazzles with surface imagery but is less good in depth. The mature poet dispenses with some of the imagery and emphasises structure....Poetry is discourse (conversation) in images, in a regular meeting with the naturalness of the spoken word pulling against the line (and rhyme every second and fourth lines in lyric stanzas). Donne on how a poem batters out gold and the last clause puts on the stamp and gives it currency."

I returned to Essex. I was still pursuing my research into contemporary history. I wrote: "Collected some fascinating books from Heather – all the...Research material, too. Much on the struggle between the Crown and allies on the one hand, and the Vatican and allies on the other....Last night read a fascinating account of the Illuminati:..Tex Marrs' *Dark Majesty: The Secret Brotherhood, the Magic of a Thousand Points of Light.* The Illuminati overthrew the Tsar and stole his fortune, using Kerensky; but Lenin, who was anti-Illuminati, took over and killed the Tsar, and the Illuminati...then got it all back....Read sadly that Toynbee was one of their propagandists. Toynbee has meant a lot to me, and he was mixed up in the Round Table."

At the end of August there was a meeting of the Universalist Philosophers. I "read the papers inspired by Universalism. They include papers by Geoffrey Read and Alan Mayne and are very pro-me....Geoffrey Read says perceptively that I have deliberately left Universalism vague. Compare Existentialism. There were many definitions of Existentialism. 'Unified world view' is amateurish and not a philosophical 'ism'." I chaired the meeting. I wrote: "The meeting began with me giving a resumé of everyone's contributions and then defending Universalism against Chris Thomson, saying it is not a mouthful, that it *is* new, efforts which are recorded on tape. We later heard Chris McCann, who has united the transcendent phenomenology of Husserl and the ontological phenomenology of Heidegger, who has just returned from Frieberg where he visited both their houses and in France, near Bordeaux, met a chateau-owner where he could put on a conference and have us all to stay. His 4-volume tome which he will introduce next time....At lunch time Peter Stewart said to me, 'You're not a philosopher in the professional sense,' to which I replied, on the role and posture of the philosopher, that the philosopher no longer a man in a room imprisoned by walls, fiddling about with language; that he has got outside and is describing the universe from the One down, through all its levels and making a coherent statement of everything. In the afternoon, supportive presentations from Alan Mayne, Geoffrey Read, and others, all of whom touched on how their philosophy made contact with the overall umbrella of Universalism. Again and again I used the analogy of the Existentialists, saying that 6 Existentialists all disagreed but all subscribed to the umbrella term, and so it was with the pre-Raphaelites and psychologists. And that if you look at the opponents of Universalism – the reductionists, materialists and positivist philosophers of the Vienna Circle – then our unified view (unifying world vision), our attempt to see unity behind multiplicity and various other spiritual features would all distinguish our view. I spoke of the historical perspective, of undoing the Enlightenment, the early Newton and the work of the Royal Society, of going back to 1659, the time of the last Metaphysical poets; our getting back to the universe, from words; including levels of interconnectedness and the paranormal, not just seeing holism as the opposite to reductionism. Existentialism is dead and its demise and deconstructionism have left a void, which Universalism is filling. Chris McCann on how my great work is *The Fire and the Stones,* how *The Universe and the Light* is programmatic. I am tired, having kept order among the unruly philosophers who often all want to talk at the same time, from 10.30 to 5. I feel as if I have taught all day. I am slightly 'giddy in my head'; have not completely adjusted to the return from Cornwall. I can feel pleased as I have defused the criticism, removed the strains...and I have all members of the Group with me....Stick to the point and keep them all to the point. The philosophers are like another staff. Peter Stewart to me: 'You're not so much a philosopher as a visionary.' I: 'A mystic. I think of Whitehead: "The purpose of philosophy is to rationalize mysticism." I am a mystic and visionary who rationalizes mysticism – and am therefore a philosopher who reflects the wisdom of the Light.'"

At the beginning of September I felt "slightly disorientated. Had the idea for an Angel sequence of poems, to go back to *Beauty and Angelhood* and to draw on Donne's *Aire and Angels* and Rilke's 'Every Angel is terrible'. The Angel to me must be the perfected, illumined human being who has transcended man, a kind of Superman who has a unitive vision and understands the Theory of Everything, and channels knowledge of spiritual beauty....Unwell. Drafted 6 Angel poems for a new post-Muse sequence.

Too tired to polish them tonight. Have taken a second 75g aspirin today, which has slightly eased my giddiness." I had an appointment with my bank manager: "Parked at 10.55 in Monkhams Avenue opposite Hutton Close, just before the bend to the right, and *Dark Angel* came to me in the car. I can't even be left alone to park my car without a poem coming. Scribbled it on a piece of paper on my knee, and arrived only slightly late at my meeting." Later I lunched with Ken Jones at the Adriatico. I reflected: "4 Sep. Got up at 6 and dictated the first 11 poems of *Angel with Vertical Vision* by 7.30. In my poems I looked back to the likes of Spenser (*Epithalamion*) and Donne (*Aire and Angels*), the poets I read at Oxford. By reading these poems then I made them a part of my internal system so they became points of reference. I am now getting the true benefits of that time. They have lived within me and attracted complementary images for 35 years. Reading the poetic tradition of English Literature is a necessary part of a young poet's preparation."

I was rung up by a friend of one of the philosophers who told me: "I met a German who knew von Stauffenberg and who was personal assistant to Admiral Canaris, who said, 'You are right, there is an international Conspiracy' and, 'I will say no more.'" I was visited by a man from the Ministry of Defence, the father of a friend of Matthew's, who confirmed that the cameras on Britain's motorways are not just to control speeding, but are to monitor troop movements.

In early September I began a punishing regime to get my books finished, very often working until 1 a.m. and sometimes later. Each week I covered a year of my Autobiography and every Monday and Tuesday I revised about 20 draft poems. Some weeks I achieved finished revisions of 400 lines. I did not calculate the number of poems I had to revise each week to be finished in time, but I just knew that quantity was right – and it was. My health held. My back went once, but it was only two vertebrae – "they jammed, it's like a chest of drawers, a drawer not going in" – and the osteopath put them back immediately.

Marion Lord died. I wrote: "The lining of her stomach broke away and she asphyxiated – drowned – in her own blood, which came through her mouth and nose. She was not conscious, though her eyes were open. Zena was with her as she died. It wasn't pneumonia or strangling cancer that killed her, but her stomach lining, caused by all the vomiting and lack of eating. A horrible end."

I rang my brother Jonathan to tell him about Marion and spoke with his wife, who told me she wanted to take a spiritual course for a years. I wrote: "She asked many questions about my work. I told her the soul grows behind the ego, as *The Silence* makes clear. She: 'I haven't grown as much as you have.' I: 'Flowers all grow at different rates. We must be true to our growth."

On September 18th I was still giddy: "Have been giddy on and off for 6 weeks....Felt below par: lethargic, sore back, incipient cramp in right leg, lungs congested, health poor. Went to the Light. Felt a tremendous surge at 9.40 and another one at 10.55....I am trying to work while feeling ill." A

765

couple of days later I wrote: "Poets do their best and present material they have in felicitous rhythms and rhymes. The poet receives from beyond and then presents it to his audience. There are therefore two processes in getting a metaphysical poem across. Your Raine is short on the presentational side. How do I chose my rhymes? I look at which of two end-words is essential and which more decorative, and change the decorative one. That way the meaning carries on through the rhymes – a trick I have taught myself. Am now revising *Counter-Renaissance*. Yesterday revised *Copped Hall*."

Vernon Davies was introducing the Foreign Affairs debate at the Conservative Conference. (He was chairman of the branch whose motion had been picked.) He came round and asked what he should say, at the same time producing papers for the County Council elections he wanted me to sign. I wrote: "Told him the context of his speech: the New World Order. He wants to believe it's a good thing. I: 'I dare you to mention the Bilderberg Group on television at the conference. It will mean you will never progress.' He: 'Thank you very much.'"

I wrote, as if reminding myself of something I kept forgetting: "Always keep separate Hebraism and Hellenism; the vicar's approach and the artist's. I am an artist, not a vicar. I have a Hebraistic subject, but I am a Hellenist, like Matthew Arnold. In fact I am in the tradition of Arnold: schools (he was an Inspector of Schools), essays on culture (and anarchy), and poems about contemporary life....I have a choice, Hebraism v Hellenism:...doing or knowing; esotericism or art. I must choose art. The schools have been a bit Hebraistic although I have made time for Hellenism. The Hebraistic must go. My Hellenism will from now on be my Hebraism."

Judith rang and announced information she had received from a high source: "I am the earth and you are the Light." She spoke of the shaft of Light, of the earth flooding: Italy and Cornwall will disappear, and much of the US, she said. She had been reading the *Rig Veda*, the 9th mandala of which is about "soma", spiritual food, food which nourishes the spirit. I wrote: "She: 'I am an earth goddess, producing soma from my breasts: milk and honey, royal jelly.'(She milks her nipples and gives it to people in a spoon!) 'I am the divine mother, many see me as that. I am the creative soul and will produce a sound.'" She told me that the new Antichrist would be an Arab born in Jerusalem and now living in Egypt as a Fundamentalist, who would carry on Gaddafi's work and initially be the Nasser. She said that man-made earthquakes and tidal waves would destroy 2 billion people along with nuclear weapons (a reference to the plan to reduce mankind by a third to make the resources go round). She said this before the rise of Neo-Fascism in "the Russian Federation" (a new name used by the media for the ex-USSR that accorded with my view in *The Fire and the Stones* that the Byzantine-Russian civilisation had just entered stage 46, the federal stage, just as the new name for Europe, "the European Union", accorded with my view that the European civilisation had entered stage 43, the union stage).

Paul Gorka rang me from Hungary and told me he had earmarked a 140-room Renaissance Castle with Baroque features, which would be freehold in my name; all the expenses would be covered by the locality in return for the benefits I could bring to the region. I had to make a formal application for the Castle, which was just 40 kms from Vienna, in the centre of the old

Austro-Hungarian Empire. I could see a time ahead when this would be the European headquarters of Universalism.

Towards the end of September I wrote: "Tackled the first 6 stanzas of *In Perigord*, took them round to Pat with corrections, and then did another 4 stanzas. Sep 27. Finished *In Perigord* (18 stanzas), took them to Pat, and then did *At Penquite House*. In both the poems I start with a place and establish a type of man – St. Bernard, St. Sampson – and generalise into the soul or the universe, *universalise* the situation. The hallmark of a Universalist poem is this universalisation from a specific local beginning. Sep 28. Finished *Clouds Hill* about action and reflection. I know – how do I know? – that T. E. Lawrence thought of the name Clouds Hill in terms of anonymity – he would wrap himself in clouds and hide, like Yahweh – but I see him as a failed mystic who turned away from the world but never found the Light, and lived in perpetual cloud." I noted: "My Albion Hill. Albion in Blake means England – I would say 'illumined'. Pushed on and finished *In Shakespeare's Stratford: the Nature of Art*."

At the end of September I was rung by the local *Gazette* and asked where Vicky Norris was. I rang Steve at the Ministry of Transport, and eventually he rang back and said: "Sadly I have to tell you it's true. Vicky's in Berkshire, I'm in London." I was very sad for both of them, and said so in the *Gazette*, and in the ensuing weeks saw the constituency divide in its attitude.

Marion's funeral took place at St. Mary's, Loughton. I wrote: "A eulogy...on her love of music and children, and her faith. Marion in a beautiful coffin with gold handles....Fancied Marion was in the rafters laughing at us all. No reading....We followed the coffin out with the relatives and drove Oliver, a 13 year old blond German-looking boy who spoke English with an accent, rather formal and mature in bearing and with a polite manner; and Michael, a soft businessman who deals in one-liners, rather sad. Michael took her to Guernsey and Spain to look after Oliver. At Parndon, the few prayers, then the shock of the curtains drawing. Standing at the foot of the chimney, where our flowers for Marion were, I smelt the smoke as Marion burned. We talked with Marion in the air and in our throats. Back to the King's Head (Loughton), where the relatives and Michael and us were bought drinks by John and salt-beef sandwiches."

I was working very hard and again seemed to derive inspiration from sleep. At the beginning of October I "was awoken at 7 am by a clear bell ringing. Went to the door but no one was there. The angels were waking me to get down to (work)." The next day: "Woke and wrote *After the fracture, growth* before even going to the loo....(It) expresses my view of Modernism in just 12 lines. Immediately afterwards, went to the bathroom, did my Canadian 5BX exercises, then, wearing just white pants, went to the bathroom again to wash and saw my eyes and nipples balance in the mirror – was caught off guard by them and remembered Shelley thinking the nipples were eyes – and returned to my study and wrote *Man* (or *God the Artist*). Am trying not to write new poems, but these two have just come."

Heather arranged for me to meet a Philippino, Alan, whom the Illuminati had tried to recruit. He began by "saying he likes *Sea Force*, my poem. 'It catches the force of the sea very powerfully. I recite it to myself.'" He told me, "I am the Source." He said ex-President Marcos of the Philippines was in the Illuminati and had come by Gen. Yamasita's wartime treasury in Manila, and that I should expect Cardinal Sin to become Pope. He predicted that "London would be a nuclear desert as a result of Red Mercury", a new and theoretically impossible chemical detonator which the Russians had discovered and which was the philosopher's stone. He said: "The mystics alone can neutralise the Illuminati's drive to take over the Vatican and defeat Islam in a war and emerge to rule the world."

The next day I spoke to a group at St. Albans, Paths of Wisdom. I wrote: "A kind of drill hall, 35 casually dressed middle-aged men and women filing in and sitting in silence. I spoke from 7.45 to 8.45 about the Fire or Light, showing 8 transparencies about my history theory, and then after tea from 9.10. I asked 'Why see the Light?' and included in my answer: 'Because you're not depressed any more. You know the peace that passeth understanding. It is like a still sea and you are on it like a calm boat.' Held a meditation in which the Light came down. In the meditation I spoke of a still water-lily on a pond. Finished it at 9.40, and they were all out by 10....All individual souls on their own climb up the mountain to the one sun at the top. My talk is on tape. I emphasised to them that I am in the mainstream, not on the fringe. I spoke of the analytical and the intuitive modes. I said: 'It is so simple. You open your soul to the Light. That is all. But it is the essence of the paths of wisdom." I refused to accept any money from Janet. She: 'I like having you, you are so sincere, unlike some.' I: 'I don't charge for the Light. The Illuminati are about money. I'm doing the opposite.'"

There was another meeting of the philosophers. I wrote: "All day at Lorimer's, hearing Chris McCann's philosophical work, which describes the movement from the objective to the reflective consciousness, from mind to spirit, and approaches the One while uniting the ontological and transcendental philosophy, Husserl and Heidegger." And I noted: "Peter Welsford wants to build a temple to the new Universalist religion in Glastonbury."

I revised more poems: "A day of tremendous risk. All day the typist, Pat Laker, sat downstairs while I tried to keep ahead of her, rhyming unrhymed poems. Completed *At Dark Age Jorvik: the Light of Civilisation* and the sonnet *Fountain of Stars: The Universe in Love* while she waited for me. Literally kept just ahead of her. 114 lines at least today, over 100 on Monday evening, and the Wordsworth and Potter poems on Sunday. A good 3 days. Have already done three more flow poems. The isolation of the poet. I am completely isolated while I plough through these old poems and lick them into shape. The isolation of those who are given the image." I battled on through a chest infection, and as a result of it fell asleep 1.30-3.15 two afternoons running. I observed: "The copper beech outside my window has been a companion: a fountain of gold and copper leaves, a fire against a blue sky. I have had a chest infection which is improving. Am less drowsy and have coughed up an enormous lump of green pus."

I gave a lecture to the College of Psychic Studies. I wrote: "19 Oct. All day, poems – *Blea Tarn, Cartmel Priory* and other Lake District ones, then focused on my lecture at 4 and drove to Queensborough Place in time for

6.40, when I set up slides and transparencies. Coffee with Dudley Poplak, who asked 'Would you like to tune in?' Then to the front of the hall. A lectern and desk, 100 people who paid £5 a head. The lecture went well. I followed a plan and stopped and ad-libbed, then resumed my plan. A line of people at the end. Was accosted at the end by a Mary Shee, who is contemplating making a film of *The Fire and the Stones*. Then the President of the College of Psychic Studies, Dudley Poplak, took me to dinner in Brompton Road, a walk through mewses with the editor of *Mind*, ex-president for 10 years. I talked for much of the time as we had asparagus and risotto and side salad, red wine....Talk of the future role of the College, how it will be a metaphysical place with a teaching element....Talk of Colin Wilson....Poplak: 'It was evident he'd been drinking.' He had 70 (in the audience)....She: 'He doesn't say anything new, he's generous and likeable and has a following, but it's superficial, *Readers Digest* stuff. I wrote a review about his book on Jung and he wrote asking "Did you read the book?" I replied, "Yes, I have." She is friendly with Kathleen Raine, and said that *Temenos*, like the monasteries, is keeping alive the tradition for a future generation. I told the story of the link between the Royal Family and the House of David (and Kathleen Raine). Poplak later: 'I know the Prince of Wales very well, he wouldn't go along with that, her attitude was rubbish. He believes in the Divine Right of Kings, but he isn't ready for the Light yet. He will be. Kathleen Raine is the past, élitist, not concerned with living. You are the future.'"

We spent half term in Cornwall. I wrote: "Arrived just before 2 a.m. All lights out – and brilliant stars which took my breath away. Got the heating on, then went for a walk and at 2.15 a.m. wrote two poems: the stars as shingle, and on a tree – the sense of a living universe." The next morning I "went out to get the papers, returned by the Hotel and crossed the bridge and lingered near the Roundhouse, looking down at the beach below our house, and I could not believe my eyes. The wet shingle where each wave had been was alive, jumping and dancing, glinting in the sun. I stood transfixed, spellbound, in a trance and watched and watched and watched and felt the 'livingness' of the whole universe. Returned and wrote a poem straightaway, *Moist*, and then *Peering Face* about the moon I saw on the way down yesterday. And tidied up the vivid stars I saw after 2 a.m. this morning, *The Shingle of the Stars*, and *Invisible Tree*. Four poems since 2 a.m., and I have slept six and a half hours! Down here in Cornwall everything is more intense: moon, stars and waves, all aspects of being seen with being, so that one is in a one-relationship with each of Nature's phenomena. The more I write poems, the more I find I am absorbed – spellbound – by things I see, which will find their way into poems. It is strange because in a sense I have seen it all before, but the more one travels down the Mystic Way into being, the more one responds as being to being – hence the poetic trance. Got logs from outside for the fire and again gazed in wonder at the fire for a very long time and wrote *Fire*." That night I "walked along the pier at 11.30. It was slightly hazy, but clear. The stars were not as bright as at 2 a.m. this morning because the moon was up over the hill; a half full moon. Calm sea."

On October 24th I wrote: "The clocks went back last night. Awoke abruptly from sleep while it was still dark with revision in my mind...and with the idea that the epic should be written in heroic couplets." I remembered my dream in which "someone said 'Rome is the centre of Western civilisation'". I dwelt on heroic couplets: "If I am uniting Classical and Romantic in the Baroque, I can get the message across by uniting heroic couplets (18th century classical form) and Romantic content of the one and the beyond. It would make it different from Milton and show up Pound; and give an idea of craftsmanship."

I wrote: "A symbol of the unification of action and contemplation: the Harbourmaster's House. It is at the end of a social village and gazes at the sea of contemplation. The Harbourmaster acts by controlling the lock-gates and bringing the boats in, but is also a man of the sea."

I watched a programme on Andrew Harvey. I wrote: "Harvey saw the Divine Light at 25, as I did. Auden, 'Eliot was so damn lucky, he had the mystic vision.' As Auden didn't." Harvey remarked that "Mother Maeve revealed her divinity and *was* the lightning." I observed that this was "a fanciful idea" and wrote: "I do not need to deify a mother....He is seriously flawed on the Mother Maeve front."

On my return from Cornwall I heard Alexander King of the Club of Rome speak at the invitation of the Scientific and Medical Network. I wrote: "Drove to the Royal Overseas League in Park Street, off St. James's Street, and went up to the India Room. David Lorimer was at the door and he introduced me immediately to King, who was drinking Scotch with (Peter) Fenwick: a smallish, elderly, bespectacled man in a collar and tie and blazer....I got straight down to it. Asked him if there is going to be a New World Order (he 'No') and showed him the Illuminati bits from *Cosmic Conspiracy* – the 10 regions, the (6 Illuminati front) circles round the (Round Table of the) 9. I: 'Are there 9?' He: 'More.' I: '99?'He: 'More likely 999, but all insignificant, no leaders.' Fenwick introduced him in glowing terms, saying how much the Club of Rome has meant to the Scientific and Medical Network and to him personally. King's talk was curiously pessimistic. He said that governments form short-term solutions, few are concerned with the long term. 'We are in voluntary poverty. We refuse money from governments and industry. That leaves individuals.' He declared the problems and left us to come up with solutions in question time. I raised world government. He said it wasn't feasible. I asked the question to check that I had not misunderstood his dismissal of the New World Order. I chatted to him afterwards. He: 'I've been to some of the Bilderberg meetings, you know. They might just be able to bring about a world government. We don't want America ruling the world, it's not practical.'" I observed later: "The world is more out of control than I thought. The politicians are short-termists and don't know what to do. King stressed Illuminati words: need for revolution, reason and being rational." He left to spend the night at David Lorimer's.

I worked on revising *The Wind and the Earth* sonnets. I wrote: "Nov 2. All day, numerous sonnets. *The Wind and the Earth* is now up to 30. Was doing a sonnet every half hour or less, with Pat sitting waiting for each one to finish. The phone kept going. Steve Norris rang. You can't say to a Government Minister, 'Push off, I'm in the middle of a sonnet.'Finished triumphant. I really feel I may get most of my poems finished, but I still have a long way to go. Ovid and Milton were pretty full time but they did not write several sonnets or equivalent a day. Since September – after the Muse poems and my *American Quintet* – I have been able to tackle all poems put in front of me."

I noted that another prediction in *The Fire and the Stones* had come true: "Tomorrow the European Union comes into force. I was born at the height of Britain's imperial power and tomorrow will live in a state in a Union – a tangible measure of Britain's decline."

Taking stock of my progress, I wrote: "All my development from now on will be further into the unitive way. The crowning glory of my unitive vision will be my epic....The unitive vision: Universalism (the philosophy); the Grand Unified Theory in history and world religion; the Fire being behind the universe of science. All these to be reconciled in the epic....The summit is within reach."

Ann was very ill with flu. I worked until 1 a.m. and then went to the Light and, standing in my bedroom, pulled a cloak of Light round me to protect me from the flu Ann has got so I can continue working. A massive inflow of the Light." I did not fall ill.

Lord Roding (formerly Patrick Jenkin and a former Government Minister) came to the Conservative Patrons Club. I went by myself as Ann was still unwell, and I had an ex-Cabinet reaction to the work of the Heroes of the West. I wrote: "Vernon greeted me, Brian got me red wine. I commiserated on his election defeat and said the tide was out....I spoke to Steve Norris, who told me: 'I'm a professional. The Prime Minister took me aside and put his hand on my arm and said "How are you Steve" and I said "I'm fine, I say 'F— them'" (meaning the Press) and he ought to say the same.'...Eventually I found myself with Jenkin and Norris, and the conversation was (about) China....Jenkin on how he had advised the Chinese to have respect for the law. I told the story of how the Chinese Cultural Revolution began in March 1966, emphasising Chinese attitudes, and then asked a question: 'I was one of a group – we called ourselves the Heroes of the West – who brought out books about Scargill, Gaddafi and Philby. Now, Scargill. He was supported by the Soviets. The USSR was savage just before Communism ended, it wanted to have a blitzkrieg across Western Europe in 35 days' – Jenkin nodded and said '35 days', confirming what I had said – 'and it was planning a nuclear strike against Western Europe in 1988'- again he nodded – 'and it wanted to make Scargill our dictator by liquidating the Cabinet through the Brighton bomb. Were you on the receiving end of that?' He said, 'Yes.' I said it was a Soviet-Gaddafi plot, that the Soviets wanted to get rid of the British Government and that the IRA were training the NUM and that Frank Watters was organising the miners to go from pit to pit – he nodded – and that the USSR had sent in £48 million to (the miners) through Prague and through Gaddafi's students....'What I can't understand,' I said, 'is that bearing all this in mind, how did this information not get used during the 1987 election campaign? You had a privileged seat on the Cabinet table at the time, why not?' 'I don't know,' Jenkin said, 'I just don't know. I felt the same.' 'And,' I said, 'projecting it forward, with Heseltine having had the problem he has had (with the miners), why has it not been mentioned recently instead of allowing Scargill to pose as a knight in shining armour?' 'Again, I don't know,' he said. 'If Steve were doing Heseltine's job,' I said, 'I'd say to him, "How could you not play that ace? How could you keep it back?"' 'He'd say the same,' Jenkin said. 'It's got to be to do with protecting people. I remember when Ted Rowlands made a speech in the House of Commons, saying as much, Mrs. Thatcher was white with fury and said, "That's completely blown it now." There is something we don't know.'"

After Jenkin spoke about hospital trusts I again spoke with him. "I explained how I published a book on terrorism. He said, 'I remember that book.' *'The World Held Hostage,'* I said. 'Another thing I would like to know,' I said, 'is when it can be revealed that the raid on Libya – ' 'I was out by then,' he said, 'I watched it on the television and wondered like everyone else.' 'When it can be revealed,' I continued, 'that 55 planes took part in the raid on Libya, 20 went to Tripoli, 20 to Benghazi and 15 to Sebha to take out Gaddafi's nuclear rockets there which were threatening London, Paris and Bonn.' Jenkin nodded. 'Built by ex-Nazi Argentineans,' I said....He: 'Again, it was to protect sources. And Mrs. Thatcher said that the French refusal to let the planes fly over their territory did wonders for the Anglo-American relationship.' 'And at the launch,' I said, 'I spoke about the author's revelation that operation Babysitter was supplying Gaddafi and the international terrorist movement with arms through Heathrow. Through Heathrow! Madam (i.e. Mrs. Thatcher) would have been horrified.' He grinned. Norris came over and the three of us stood together, chatting freely. I was interested my view of events – the Heroes of the West's view of events – had been confirmed by an ex-Minister who had had a privileged seat at the Cabinet table, and I realised I could have become a politician and shared in such moments of camaraderie with my fellow Party members."

I finished my *Wind and the Earth* sequence. I wrote: "My *Wind and the Earth* sequence has caught a new theme in poetry: the practical clearing up after a death. It is so obvious, but no one else seems to have done it." I observed: "Wrote *Head-Scarf*, which is on a shopping list/list of what I was owed....In 200 years' time, people will be able to see how we really lived, among mundane things like buying black bags for rubbish." I recorded: "Artists work hard and sweat to produce their inspired visions. I am like a potter. I fire my pots and then potter about, making tea, getting my vision into shapes."

The philosophers met again. I wrote: "Geoffrey Read: 'I see you've been declaring war, Nicholas.' He produced *Psychic News* with a heading about me: 'Ex-Professor declares war on Materialists.' Front page treatment of my lecture. Chris Thomson began his presentation, and stopped at the lack of confidence we can have in the perceiver's perception of the universe. I asked him to extend it to a model of 'What is the universe? What is his view of the universe?' He eventually did – seeing it like me as energy that is interconnected, but my question caused a furore and polarised the philosophers. Geoffrey Read v Max Payne. I said to Max, 'We are against the philosophers of the last 90 years, against the Vienna Circle.' My reconciliation: that the Mystic Way is a growth from the perception of the rational social ego to the perception of the unitive centre, after the transformational shift, so that in the unitive view at the end of the Mystic Way the philosopher perceives the universe with instinctive unity. The vision of the poet. Self and the universe are aspects of one universal whole. We must develop ourselves, yes, but we must also (understand) the universe." I added: "There was a card on the mantelpiece congratulating David Lorimer on his engagement to Norris McWhirter's daughter, Jane." Again, there seemed to be an underlying order in the coming together of two strands in my life, the Heroes of the West with which Norris McWhirter was associated, and the Universalist philosophers.

Mary Archer Shee had a strange dream about me on November 9th. Having only met me briefly at the end of my lecture at the College of Psychic Studies, she dreamt that she and I were in a medieval wooden house near a river, a tarn. She went out and when she came back forces hostile to me – guards – had surrounded the house and told her "The Polish want that house" and pushed her away and she woke at 4.20 a.m. with a sense of evil.

This dream was to prove somewhat prophetic. On November 17th a pipe leading to a bathroom shower pump came away in my house and water cascaded through two downstairs ceilings and out of electric sockets. Luckily I was around at the time and saved my books, but work on *Collected Poems* was discontinued as we evacuated the computer. Heather had arranged for me to meet a German lady who had introduced *The Fire and the Stones* to a university at Dusseldorf, and at the same time she invited a Polish girl with whom she proposed to open a Centre for Practical Metaphysics at a temporary address in Old Street, London.

And so I met Agnieszka Milewska, a very strong Polish ex-Catholic girl of 24 with very long hair. She had read philosophy and the history of art at Warsaw University and she was now a Director of the Centre. She had great confidence and delighted in challenging people's assumptions. She was iconoclastic, and with the forthright excitement of youth favoured fundamental solutions, recommending those she came into contact with to give up their jobs or their partners and turn their backs on the illusory world. Incredibly she had memories in her mind of Violette Szabo, who with Madeleine was awarded the George Cross posthumously after the war. From the age of 3 she had said to her parents, "I don't want to go back to the concentration camp," and she saw Violette's end, by gas, not shooting. "No," she said, "she was not shot....There were many in the room, trying to get out. I thought, 'Why can't they sit quietly and accept it and not struggle for life outside which is nothing.' Many moving bodies, like something out of Dante." She also remember Violette's haunting poem, written as a code by a man who worked in Bletchley Park, which she had taken into France. It contained a very important message, possibly about the date of D-Day. I chanted:

A MYSTIC WAY

"The life that I have is all that I have,
And the life that I have is yours.
The love that I have is all that I have,
And the love that I have is yours, is yours, is yours."

Agnieszka thought: "No," she said, "*and* yours *and* yours. It was a number code, each letter was a number." Agnieszka recalled glimpsing the man who wrote the poem through a cattle-wagon on her way to the camp.

Agnieszka had lived in a flat in Warsaw three years previously with some samples of Red Mercury, a new weapon discovered by the Russians which Alan the Philippino had first mentioned to me. Red Mercury is a chemical detonator which disturbs the molecules of any element, and is therefore the philosopher's stone. The Russians had sold it to the Chinese who sold it to an American Jew, who may then have supplied the international terrorist network, possibly the Ulster Loyalists, causing the IRA to sue for peace (in which case it had proved to be an agent for good). The American Jew had Agnieszka guarding this Red Mercury in a rent-free flat in Warsaw for six months, and, with the efficiency and economy of a latter day Violette Szabo, she supplied me with the formula and other details of Red Mercury, which chemists will assert cannot exist because it involves combining the uncombinable. As one last act the Heroes of the West took steps to neutralise this dangerous substance, one pinch of which could wipe out London. I felt like Niels Bohr confirming to Einstein the formula of the atomic bomb.

It was now apparent that the Metaphysical Centre was the concept of the school for self-realisation I had dreamt of in Japan, and that Agnieszka was a Director who could run it "for cells of 10 and spread the Light nation-wide". Heather Dobbs and Agnieszka asked if I would join them and give occasional talks about my perspective of the Light and my work.

There was then a remarkable happening. An actress visited a medium who said she had a message for one of the three connected with the "Metaphysical Centre". On December 1st Agnieszka visited the medium, who went into trance and said: "Don't sign the lease (for the Old Street premises). You will be given a house by the river." The medium also said: "Nicholas – who is he? Three books will come out. He will be famous. He will travel the world a lot. He will sign a contract for three books in New York and give a lecture there. There will be a Carlton TV programme about him. He is the highest consciousness in the world." Agnieszka reported that the Conspiracy was mentioned. The medium said that those "on the other side do not want this to happen". She said that I am protected, that I am combining "the High Intelligence of the Light with practical metaphysics." "This is unique." I received the infinite message, neither believing or disbelieving it. I felt like Macbeth. The witches had said I would be Thane of Glamis, Thane of Cawdor and King, and like Macbeth I was not sure if they were just "weird sisters".

On December 2nd I heard an American philosopher and California academic, Prof. Stephen Erickson speak to an invited audience at the College of Psychic Studies. For an hour he read a paper and concluded with the starting-point of *The Fire and the Stones*, that perhaps we can escape the reason by opening to the Light. Afterwards I had dinner with him. I wrote: "Told Erickson about the Metaphysical Revolution and my lurch towards a Theory of Everything and Universalism. He: 'I've read *The Universe and the Light* and it's excellent and I am so glad to have met you. On marketing grounds people might think that 'Universalism' is a revival of the opposite to Nominalism or a Christian denomination, but a book of five essays sounds ideal.' I refuted both points in terms of the coming political Universalism. He: 'It might be considered that the later Wittgenstein turned against logical positivism and linguistic analysis, and that you are flogging a dead horse.' Rebutted that idea too. He: 'Your idea of groups of 10 is an excellent one, that is what I want to use.'" He said he wanted to be involved in spreading the Metaphysical Revolution in philosophical circles in the US and at Oxford and Cambridge when he returned in June 1994.

Agnieszka was now implementing groups of 10. "It is not lectures but everyday life we should focus on," she said, "that we are all loved by God and are divine beings who deserve personal happiness, that if we cannot play the piano we cannot teach it and we must be personally happy to teach personal happiness....Look at yourself without your fame, your books and your schools and see yourself as a failure – that is the being who is divine and who is loved by God. I love everybody, including the Conspiracy." I was amazed at the clarity of view and authoritative confidence of this 24-year old, and knew she would go far. She trusted implicitly in her Voice. Whatever it told her came to pass. She revealed that the day I first met her, "on the train going back from Heather's (her voice) gave her pictures of what will happen over the next 4 years, and said 'Nicholas will phone you' and that happened". Later it said "Nicholas will mention you in his last poem in his *Collected Poems*." It also said: "A stream in a mountain can be hidden but when it flows down, it cannot be hidden." The context was the spread of Universalism and the Metaphysical Revolution.

On December 4th 1993 I woke at 7 a.m. and "felt tired and shaky. Got Anthony off at 8, then went to the Light. Surges came in and now I feel calm, not trembling, able to work. I have great rings under my eyes. Am at the end of a long haul and am tired but still write with a lightness of being. A Lightness of Being. All my works have the massiveness of a mountain about them. I am a mountain peak writer, not a foothill writer. I write about the summit, where the best glimpses of the sun and the light are to be had."

I was determined to reflect the process of the events of my life in my Autobiography. I wrote: "By quoting from my *Diaries*, I can stick close to what happened without imposing an artificial construct on the process."

Agnieszka again expounded her teaching to me: "We create our own reality from within. Create your own reality, change your outer reality by finding your identity which is love, and there is an effect on every area of your life. The power of inner thought. No one can harm you if you are at a spiritual level. We attract burglars and assaults by psychological worry. You align yourself with the infinite power. I re-invent myself everyday." I added: "We are existentialising the perceptions of the metaphysical knowledge. Just as Existentialism spoke of freedom that can be acted out, so we enable (people) to create (their) reality, being in touch with the Light within and learning the laws that relate to it....Universalism: seeking the universal within us, that which is universal within us, the Fire or Light. A school for self-realisation in which to work out a practical Existentialism as Universalism."

On December 6th the Metaphysical Centre opened; as a concept rather than as a place, for the Old Street premises were only temporary. During the day I revised "16 poems in a day, a record" and still found time to attend an Oaklands nativity play (and talked with Vicky Mitchell, the comedy actress who was a parent). In the evening I went to the East-West Centre in Old Street. Before my talk I met Anya, a friend of Angieszka, who had just arrived from Poland. I had shown Agnieszka a leaflet about "the International Society for Universalists" at Warsaw University, and Agnieszka had rung Anya, a former *New York Times* journalist, and asked her to investigate. Anya had visited Professor Kuczynski and had cross-examined him very vigorously on what he was doing. Now, blonde, she explained to me that they were "one-world" universalists who were completely non-metaphysical, and she gave me a pile of their publications. Anya had handed over the Red Mercury after Agnieszka had left for England, and I was able to question her about her view of the episode. Somehow I had evolved a network that could reach into places that had previously seemed inaccessible.

Of the opening of the Metaphysical Centre I wrote: "About 30 attended. I talked about the Fire or Light and showed my books, then Heather spoke, then Agnieszka, passionate and weighing into the audience, spirited like a Dostoevskian character (Dostoevsky, her favourite author, along with Joyce and Proust), showing the rebelliousness that made her ask her professors about their sexual performance in question time at Warsaw University, scathingly debunking what they stood for, yet very gentle also. Then I spoke again about Universalism, then there was a meditation in which I brought down the Light (it poured through me, purging the room) and then there were questions and answers. The other two were ill, I bore the brunt of it. Afterwards a long time of socialising as no one wanted to leave."

The next day I went to the philosophers to hear Geoffrey Read expound his philosophy all day. I wrote: "The universe is not teleological or eternal or having a Creator but emanating, a source which is self-realisational downwards (reducing), an Absolute that contains within itself a nullity as a potential. Time began with the first qualification or event, how? Why? (Not explained.)...Since then, for the last 4,500 billion years there have been 10^{-23} events or qualifications per second, i.e. 10 thousand million million million events per second. The primordial simplicity becomes a multiplicity. Errors, regarding atoms as granular like ball-bearings and the spiritual as abstract (instead of concrete). All spatial change must be explained in terms of intrinsic change. Distances are journeys at the noumenal (as opposed to the phenomenal) level. The world is a creative process. Space is an order of co-existence of events or qualifications (I would say limitations), and time is an order of succession of events or qualifications. 'God is a holistic principle.' 'Nothing endures through time, time is derived from a succession of events.' A unified diversity. We are all part of the One....Plato's model for abstract universals, so that the concrete and the universal are divorced. All biology can be derived out of physics.

Memory, the brain-mind problem. Memories are in the past. A physical force blows an umbrella a mnemic force in the past has held it a certain way, and now there is sympathetic association of events and so now I hold the umbrella that way. The mind uses the brain, the total 'I' is separate from the brain, the memory is not in the brain cells but events are associated. So a GCSE exam tests not memory in cells but sympathetic associations. Read's use of Hegel and Bergson. Of me, 'You're not a systematic thinker, you're a visionary.' I: 'Giving systematic thought to my vision.' What is Read's substance – energy?...'Substance is one, and is part of the Fire or Light. Movement is unmoving co-ordination among sequences', like the stills of film frames, co-ordinated changes. Substance is presence and absence of ultimate One."

There was much in Read's theory that interested me, and if he was a little too reductionist for my metaphysical taste in insisting there can be no latent movement of a non-physical, metaphysical Fire before the beginning of time, his view of events after the beginning of time coincided with my own thinking, and I could see how a pre-existing moving Fire/Absolute could be qualified into a succession of events.

I retailed some of this to Agnieszka, who was predictably scathing: "The only important thing is how to live, how to run your life. Philosophers build pyramids of words, whole libraries. I am in a state of living, not learning. There is only one important thing: to enjoy yourself, to be happy, to be at peace. I live out what the philosopher is saying. There is no time. I live that out."

Again I was aware of two polarities in myself: the Hebraistic way of schools of self-realisation and Heather and Agnieszka; and the Hellenistic way of the epic and art, which is made out of the quarrel with oneself. This whole Autobiography is about the persistent tension between the mystic of the Light and the describer of the experience in art, which I liked to think I have been able to reconcile and unify in terms of a universe of Fire or Light: action and contemplation.

I expressed some of this tension in poems: "In the early evening a long conversation with Agnieszka before the Centre's reception, which I am not attending; then wrote *Philosopher's Stone: Soul and Golden Flower*, a highly metaphysical poem. Earlier revised *Sea Rescues: Death like a Cormorant*. Today some effective images. A tough metaphysical poetry in which meaning and image wrestle and unify. The first poem draws together the Red Mercury episode, Agnieszka and Geoffrey Read's 'qualifications'." I wrote: "I am not an evangelical getting in people who have not heard of metaphysics at all costs; I am a describer in books and have the intention of writing an epic."

I spoke again with Agnieszka and wrote: "Agnieszka rang, full of Taoist wisdom, being contrary and rebellious, putting the opposite. 'Teaching and learning are illusions, go for darkness, empty, everyone is the same, enjoy yourself, there are no levels, no differences, just be in silence.' I: 'Very Taoist. $+A + -A = 0$. Silence + words = zero; etc. She: 'Yes, we reconcile through opposites.'" Earlier I had dubbed her philosophy of "No levels, no differences" "spiritual Communism". Agnieszka insisted: "We can't change others, only ourselves." But, I commented, "disturb the molecules of another, and then they can change themselves". And I added a stanza to *Philosopher's Stone: Soul and Golden Flower* to this effect.

I wrote: "I have a choice: to choose myself as an artist or as a philosopher: work or life. I must choose work, and be a describer, not a changer of men. It is the same dilemma I faced in the mid-1960s, only now it is crystallised into: runner of a Metaphysical Centre or writer of an epic? I must reconcile these two polarities in myself: $+A + -A = 0$. It can be both, but not exclusively the first. Life + work = 0." And, of course, one example of this process of reconciliation has been this Autobiography.

Like Macbeth, I had cause to think of the medium's prophecy on two occasions. Almost immediately someone in the BBC proposed making a film about my outlook and work, about the Fire and my view of history. Shortly afterwards Agnieszka rang excitedly late at night to tell me she had the address of the Illuminati. A journalist she had met in a restaurant had given it to her; they had tried to recruit him on a very high salary two years previously and he had not replied.

I dined at the House of Commons with Steve Norris, and discussed with him which group he felt had organised the bad publicity he had received. We reached a conclusion and then discussed how the New World Order planned (according to the lecturer at the global deception conference) to liquidate 2 billion people by the year 2,000, one third of our species, without contaminating the earth. Norris pointed to viruses: 'They use viruses to eat into rock and stop at gold. It would not be difficult to make a virus that could for example wipe out everyone with a Caucasian skin." Since then the Russian Neo-Fascist leader Zhirinovsky has said that the Russians have a new deadly non-nuclear weapon called Elipton which is capable of destroying the planet. Whether or not Red Mercury is used in this weapon, as seems likely, the Russians now have the capability of culling 2 billion people.

It is bizarre that the Heroes of the West, having defended mankind against Communism, should now be collecting information on plans to exterminate a third of mankind.

On December 17th 1993 I went down to Cornwall to brood on the end of this Autobiography. I thought of all the events I have presented in the order in which each imposed itself on the accumulation of previous events, like a succession of waves rippling in from a timeless sea, and I thought of how I had regarded entries in my *Diaries* as events. I wrote: "Down in Cornwall, there is simplicity. Everything is simplified. All events can be seen simply, e.g. the flight of a flock of birds, waves, wind in trees, a boat coming in, a man watching. The 10^{-23} events per second have narrowed down to 4 or 5, and are graspable in a satisfying way. Grasping the pattern through simplicity we see their meaning."

The pattern of my life now seems equally simple and clear, despite the multitude of events that have imposed themselves on me. Moments, like rocks, protrude from a sea of flux. It now seems significant that I began my Journey along the Mystic Way in a house called Journey's End. As a boy I mocked Holy Grey who knelt at crossroads and prayed and looked for the

Light, and now I am in his tradition. I am grateful that I absorbed the poetic tradition of English Literature at Oxford, an essential part of a young poet's preparation for becoming a major poet. I was sent to both Iraq and Libya, the world's two terrorist centres; it was as if the angels had posted me there and shown me those places because they would one day be useful to the work of the Heroes of the West. All the countries I visited during the 1960s I was able to use in my history theory in *The Fire and the Stones*. It was strange that I had the world scoop of the Chinese Cultural Revolution in March 1966. I am grateful that I did not remain an academic, for I might never have known the Light and achieved my metaphysical vision. With hindsight, it was good that the shock of the break-up of my marriage removed me from university life and opened me to the Light. It was strange that I was shown a comprehensive school as a park gardener and that I eventually held a very senior position in one. On the Journey one's financial needs are taken care of. It is extraordinary that I, who was so relatively poor in the 1960s, should now find myself a millionaire (if I realised all my assets) from education without really trying, having done what I wanted to do and having regarded money as incidental. I see connections. Margaret's Catholic Habsburg Light connects to the Mass I shared with the heir to the Holy Roman and Austro-Hungarian Empires and to the Castle in Hungary. There is a strange connection between all that Biggs-Davison did for me and his successor Steve Norris's proximity to me as my tenant. It is strange that I spent years listening at Winchester and then spoke there, and that having embodied mystic Illumination, Enlightenment and Universalism I should find that there should have pre-existed a rational and dubious alternative to each, namely the Satanist Illuminati, the rational Enlightenment (which was a Darkness) and the perhaps ruthless Universalism of the New World Order. It is strange that I, who attended the lectures on self-realisation at the School of Economic Science in 1958 should now teach self-realisation at a Metaphysical Centre elsewhere in London. The greatest strangeness is that I should have been a pupil at Oaklands School and am now in charge of it. My life, for all its traumas, has a shape of some beauty.

There were alternative lives I did not know and might have enjoyed. For instance, I did not know that Jacqueline was waiting for me to mention an arrangement as, wounded and self-absorbed and thinking of Ezra Pound and of the searching I knew my destiny called me to do, I sat with her under Mont Blanc, not realising that she wanted to marry me and that she cried on her wedding day for me. That was a French life I missed, and there were others. As I look back and read past letters, I can see there were perhaps a dozen other lives I might have had. I can now see how fond of me many of those girls were, although I did not realise it at the time. What if I had married any of the girls I knew before Caroline? What if I had gone straight into work in this country after leaving Oxford? What if I had stayed in Japan? I do not think any of these other lives would necessarily have turned out better than the life I have had. I know lawyers and doctors who have worked until the small hours for 40 years and now have next to nothing to show for their labours, let alone any books. In those other lives I might have missed the Light. No, this one is the life I had, and this is the life I am defined by, and the other possible lives have no existence, were possibilities that never grew. So it is with my children. My three children are mine, the rest do not exist.

I have been fortunate. I found a way to realise myself and become a millionaire (effectively restoring my family's money) and serve the community and write books and challenge the underlying rational, sceptical assumptions of our time. I did not do badly for someone who left for Japan with £5 to his name in November 1963, thirty years ago. Money has not changed my outlook in any way. I recall that when I was still a boy my Aunt Argie gave us matinée tickets for a West End theatre farce, *Zip Goes A Million*, and when I watched it I never thought that one day I would find myself a millionaire, and I am now as indifferent to money as I was then. I have good reason to feel content despite my early tribulations and sufferings. I found my way to my true vocation and destiny, without being diverted into the Law. I fulfilled my poetic work with a *Collected Poems* and lived the life of a man of letters; I visited many cultures and came up with a Grand Unified Theory of World History; and I questioned the basis of scientific materialism and proposed a new philosophy, Universalism, and launched a new movement, the Metaphysical Revolution. It is for others to judge the quality of these endeavours; I merely fulfilled my task. At the same time I founded the Heroes of the West in politics and Coopersale Hall School in education. But above all, I located the Light and created the possibility of a Mystic Revival and a new Metaphysical awareness, based on experience and not rational speculation. One of the reasons for writing this book is to spread awareness of what is already in place. If I were to die now (and if this were my swan song), I could say that I have laid the foundations for a new perspective, and that this is understood by some of the top people within each discipline. There is more to do – I have to get the Light across as widely as the angels desire, and place it firmly in the mainstream as opposed to the fringe – but the worst is over and my task has already been partly achieved. I look forward to the future with a sense of excitement. It seems completely logical that I, who sought the Romans in my youth, should now look towards the Italy of Virgil, Dante and Pound as a place to research my epic.

Through the Heroes of the West I stood up and was counted in the movements of our Age. The list of the achievements the Heroes of the West can claim is impressive. They can claim to have influenced: the blocking of a Soviet plan to take over Britain; the end of terrorism; the admission of Eastern European nation-states to the European Union (the United States of Europe); the revival of an anti-Soviet liberation movement; and the identification of Russia's new deadly non-nuclear weapon which is capable of annihilating the world. By influencing Tebbit through his response to Coopersale Hall they can claim to have influenced the decision for all British maintained schools to be allowed to opt out, and they can therefore claim to have influenced a major change in the British educational system. They have also launched a Metaphysical Revolution. Their policy was to change Europe politically, metaphysically and artistically, to create a Greater Europe or United States of Europe with a Universalist philosophy based on the Light and a new mystical movement (Universalism) within the arts. Just as the Universalist philosophers have set themselves the task of reversing the philosophy of the Vienna Circle of the 1930s, the Heroes of the West set themselves the task of reversing the work of the Cambridge Apostles, and this they did brilliantly; and today the USSR no longer exists, and a liberated Eastern Europe is set to join the European Union without Soviet occupation or obstruction.

I have met some of the cleverest people of my time. I have been fortunate to meet some of the best teachers of my time, some of whom are at my schools, particularly my wife Ann, who has without doubt been the most effective Headmistress I have known while keeping a good humour and lightness of touch in the study (and at home). I have been fortunate to meet some of the most inspired women. Christine Klein, Judith Seelig, Fleur Beverley, Heather Dobbs, Agnieszka Milewska are, each in there separate ways, some of the most gifted women one could hope to meet, with intuitional powers that reach far into the beyond. In writers like Des McForan and Paul Gorka and others of the Heroes of the West I met men of outstanding courage who were not afraid to defy the might of the Soviet Union and the KGB, knowing that Communism could be made to collapse, having no truck with those who funded it and sold it arms to keep it in existence in the interests of stabilising the world – not condoning an evil in the hope that it may result in a greater good. To the Heroes of the West, evil was evil and must be replaced with the transforming power of the Light, and the chance of good prevailing was therefore moved closer, although there was another set of problems. In Colin Wilson, Christopher Ricks, Frank Tuohy and E. W. F. Tomlin I early on met some of the sharpest literary and philosophical brains of my time, who acted as foils for my growing metaphysical vision, and in the case of the rational sceptics among them played the necessary role of +A in relation to my -A = 0. As a result I was well equipped to meet Edmund Blunden, Ezra Pound, John Heath-Stubbs, George MacBeth, David Gascoyne, Kathleen Raine and other poets. In John Ezard, Charlie Douglas-Home, Brian MacArthur and Nick Ashford (who died of cancer in 1990, aged 47) I met some of the greatest journalists of my time. And in Sir John Biggs-Davison, Julian Amery, Sir Brandon Rhys-Williams, Peter Walker, Lord Whitelaw, Steve Norris and Lord Tebbit I got to know some of the more influential political figures of my Age. In E. W. F. Tomlin, Geoffrey Read, Chris McCann and Alison Watson I met – and was privileged briefly to lead – some of the best philosophers who sought a unified world view in my time.

Above all, perhaps, I tried to understand my time and reflect the Age in which I found myself, the idea I expressed to Lord Murray on a tube. Like Wordsworth on his school desk in Hawkshead and Byron on the column of the temple at Sunium, I scratched my name in a remote corner of Western civilisation; but it is not the name I scratched that is important but what it stood for, the vision and perspective it passed into Western civilisation at the time it did, and the picture of the Age it gave.

Looking back over my record of the events, I can see that somewhere along the Way I changed: the unpromising ugly duckling was transformed into a beautiful swan. And yet, the signs of the transformation were there in the beginning, as this record tries to show. I showed determination, backbone and fibre in the way I turned from the low point of 1970. My theme has always been "What is man? What is the universe?" I have presented my evolving search in a process, in the course of which I have been transformed. And yet, the more I moved into the beyond, the more I kept both feet on the ground.

At the beginning I spoke of my family's roots – Nonconformism, foreign travel, business, writing, schools, love of music/poetry and forests – and I said that my trunk and branches are my own. My trunk has been my growth through a multitude of events to a metaphysical attitude, and my branches have been: my journalism and current affairs, my teaching, my poetry, my fascination with history, my philosophy, my science, my stories, my businesses, and my link with Epping Forest. My crown is my mysticism, and the Light is in all parts of the tree: trunk, branches and crown. Trees have meant much to me, and I have pleasure in seeing myself as a tree with roots in the past and branches thrusting up to the Light and spreading out into the future.

There are many layers in looking at a life. Genetic inheritance, social status, family, topographical and school influences, and all the conditionings of partial and successful relationships – all have to be taken into account along with the growth and drive upwards as we discover – uncover – the metaphysical sap within ourselves. I like to think that we are like the tree of the Essenes whose branches reflect its roots, our Heavenly Father our Earthly Mother; or like the tree of the Kabbalah which is rooted in the sky, its branches growing earthwards. I like to think that for each root there is a branch, and I love the idea of the tree creating fruit – acorns – as a poet puts out poems. Each year I have shed a crop of poems like acorns in pipes lying at the foot of my now massive trunk, and, to quote one of my own poems: "I feel/The endurance of a much-gnarled oak."

It is good to focus on the image of the oak-tree as this Autobiography shows growth at work, how ideas surface out of a life like seeds and grow until they have a life of their own. The whole Autobiography is a tribute to the process of growth. By showing a moving, dynamic process through a multiplicity of concerns, I have sought to present Becoming. But the Light of Being is never far away. That is the message for the man of the new European Union, and for the coming attempt at a global civilisation, a Universalist American-led world government. And so I think particularly of the oak-tree in the Oaklands fields. My symbol for the poet is a falcon (or an eagle) in an oak-tree, but the oak-tree I am thinking of is the one I played under as a child, and it was this image I was thinking of on 1st September 1992 when, with great abruptness, I wrote the first line of this work "As I gaze on the green field I lay in as a child" and without any planning began my Autobiography.

As I look back on my life exactly 16 months after impulsively starting this task, I reflect that the massiveness of my theme of growth and process towards the Light, cannot lend itself to short treatment. In Japan Nishiwaki told me I must always make a reader come to me on my terms, and teach the taste by which I am relished, and while I am aware that I have taken greater length than I would have liked to show the growth the Light gives, I do not apologise for bringing a weighty theme back into letters. It is just this perspective of a whole life affected by the Light of the Whole that has been missing in 20th century letters. I have brought it back with a sense of joy that a book with something to say can be offered to the reading public. When the Greek Chilon said "gnóthi s'eaton" he probably meant "accept your limited human constitution and your mortality", but I have turned the expression: for man to know himself is to know he is capable of growth to hidden possibilities and potentialities, and an awesome massiveness.

It is now time to stand even further back and review my progress along the Mystic Way in more metaphysical terms. I have now advanced some distance along the Unitive Way, and there is no more journeying, in the sense of finding; merely in the sense of expression, of more things to do, more spreading of an established position. In Japan I stopped thinking of Nicholas Hagger and allowed the power of the infinite to work through me, and what I have done is a result of the Light that shines through my work.

To turn my back on the world and live in stillness and for enjoyment and fun alone would not be right. Those who have been given the divine gift have a duty to pass the benefit on to their fellow human beings. The Light has grown a new movement: Universalism. Universalism includes philosophy, metaphysics, religion and history, and addresses the soul of each member of humankind. It shows the universal energy of the Fire or Light coming into each person's universal being, manifesting through energy in the universe with great universality. This movement has only just started. It can grow like the movements of theosophy or psychology or Existentialism, but it can be far more significant than any of them. It remains to be seen whether the 140-room castle in Hungary (only made possible by my founding of the Heroes of the West) will materialise. If it does, just 40 kms from Vienna, it can grow into a European centre for a world-wide Universalism. It is an inspiring idea, and inspired volunteers will be needed to create the Centre that will change the zeitgeist, the character of the Age, not as a fringe but as a mainstream activity.

In this sense, this Autobiography has not been about me but about the Light and the way it can transform the Age, shining behind the human constructs and pyramids of words created by linguistic philosophers and reductionist scientists, sceptical historians and writers on religious doctrine and atheistic men of letters, burning away sceptical and materialist perception and conclusions by its presence. I happened to have received and expressed the Light in my work. It is not *my* life that is interesting or significant, but what the Light can do to *a* life, how it can take an unpromising child and adolescent and shape its experience into a metaphysical growth. I have offered an account of the events that have been associated with me as an example of what a Light-directed life can do.

And so the Light must have the last word. I was nearly a British Ambassador in Libya, and instead became an Ambassador for the infinite, eternal Light, receiving its wisdom, knowledge and understanding, opening my perception to its superior perceiving while keeping my feet firmly on the ground (running two schools, paying a hundred staff, delivering projected and actual figures to the bank manager). "Many are called but few are chosen" – I do not enquire why I was chosen, but I am convinced that many more would be chosen if they opened themselves to the Light. I believe the Light wants to choose many more: hence the practical "opening" sessions I have held. The Light, the hidden reality behind the universe, has inspired the founding of every civilisation, as I have demonstrated in *The Fire and the Stones*, and is the essence of every religion. It is a metaphysical force of great subtlety and power which guides our lives and governs the running of the universe and our earth. It has been called God by many interpreters during the last 5,000 years, but in the interests of descriptive accuracy I call it the Light. My final message to a younger generation that has lost its way among sceptical and materialist thinkers, philosophers and scientists is: you do not need to put up with the barrenness and nihilism of most contemporary thought, and no one is alone who sets out on the Mystic Way to receive the Light and grow into a consciousness that knows meaning and purpose – a Light-inspired consciousness. Stillness, tranquillity, serenity, personal happiness and ultimate knowledge are all possible and within your grasp, but first you have to grow into a being that instinctively knows them, through the Light.

INDEX

Ain El Faras 167, 195, 207
Ainger, Geoffrey 86, 273
Aira Force 486
Aire and Angels (Donne) 72, 764, 765
Akashic records 331
akh 376
al Haqq 674
Alan the Philippino 774
Albania 492
Albion Hill (No 4) 397
Albion Hill (No 15) 403, 407
Albion Hill 9, 11, 12, 13, 395, 408, 426, 462, 479, 556, 767
Albion Park House 524
Aldebaran 477
Alderton Hill 17, 593
Alcestis (Euripides) 41, 42
Alexandrian Method 517
Alexandrian Quartet 84
Alfoxton House 505
Algol 4 (Perseus) 376
Alison Bush, 18, Wants Proof (Hagger) 324
Alison, Michael MP 514
All Along the Backwater (Hagger) 12
All Hallows (Hagger) 219
All Saints Day (Hagger) 718
All Saints', Tooting Graveney 357
All Saints, Blackheath 239
All Saints, Theydon Garnon 649
All Souls, Oxford 617
Allah 517, 673
Allan Bank 518
Allen, Cliff 650
Allen, Les 438
Allison, Rupert MP 648
Almighty 406
Alport, Phil 708
Alresford 685
Ambassadors of the Light 684
Ambleside 433, 485, 486, 518, 519
Ambresbury Banks 15, 488
Amenhotep IV 372
America 14, 239, 485, 489, 524, 534, 539, 553, 633, 641, 673, 691, 701, 703, 723, 724, 757, 770, 782
American 21, 293, 424, 485, 503, 504, 670, 672
American civilisation 534, 544, 677, 758
American Liberty Quintet (Hagger) 758, 759, 762, 771
American Military Cemetery 293
Amery, Julian MP 492, 494, 495, 502, 506, 521, 591, 781
Amin, President 224
Amis, Kingsley 556
Amis, Martin 753
Amish 758
Ammerdown, Somerset 340
Amness 529
amphitheatre 15
Amsterdam 79, 496, 498

An Aesthete's Golden Artefacts (Hagger) 261, 363
An Obscure Symbolist's Rock-Tree (Hagger) 263
Anastasia 68
Anatolia 539
anatta 574
ANC 219, 224
Anatomy of Britain (Samspon) 115
Anchorage 222
Ancient History 44
Ancient Marine 36
Ancient Sage (Tennyson) 755
ancient Egyptians 311
ancient knowledge 399
Ando, Shinsuke 106
And Scholars Will Ask (Hagger) 111
Andersen, Hans Christian 526
Anderson, Flavia 311, 320, 635, 708
Anderson, Perry 76, 296
Anderson, William 671, 672, 706, 751
Andrewes, Lancelot 217
Angel 308, 358, 374, 383, 385, 392
Angel with Vertical Vision (Hagger) 765
Angelic flame 388
angelic order 385
Angelico, Fra 290, 301, 641, 746, 747
Angels 313, 316, 342, 343, 357, 358, 362, 368, 372, 375, 383, 385, 387, 388, 389, 396, 412, 418, 450, 457, 497, 507, 513, 696
Angels near a Fairground Hell (Hagger) 291
Anglesey 49, 714
Anglican 272
Anglican traditionalist 514
Anglicanism 264
Angry Young Men 59, 63, 84, 475, 476, 589, 639, 762
Anne (Ricky's girl-friend) 77
Anne of Cleves 463
Annus Mirabilis 254
anti-Christian 348, 517
anti-clerical 408
anti-Darwin 418
anti-dualist 400
anti-empiricist 312
anti-Humanist 450
anti-liberal 253
anti-Marxism 653
Anti-Materialism 420, 453, 454
anti-materialism 417
anti-materialist 744
Anti-Materialistic Age 420
anti-metaphysical 368, 513
anti-Newton 417
Antichrist 766
Anticipation and Regret (Hagger) 704
antistrophe 403, 404
Antoinette, Marie 446
Antwerp 496, 497
Anya 776
AP 127

Benedictine 435, 517
Benedictine monks 62
Benghazi 485, 772
Bennett, Ian 495
Bentley, Derek 37
Bentley, Roy 37, 55
Benveniste, Asa 181, 427
Beowulf 66, 71, 83, 414, 503
Berdyayev 624
Bere Regis 438
Bergson, Henri 55, 56, 60, 370, 651, 737, 777
Berkeley 232, 539
Berlin 527, 576
Bernard, St. 472
Berry, Adrian 206
Berry, Nick 683, 756
Bertoluzzi 745, 746, 747
Beshir, al-Muntasser 153
Best, Ann 581
Best, Mrs. Frances 550, 553, 556, 565, 581,615, 649, 678, 683, 723
best self 411
Betjeman 298, 432, 455, 734
Between Two Fires 376, 581
Betws-y-coed Swallow falls 714
Beverley, Fleur (Wendy Carter's cousin) 644, 646, 667, 673, 694, 704, 729, 781
Beynac 465
Beyond the Outsider (Wilson, Colin) 330, 621
beyond 373, 374, 449, 468, 627, 638
Bhagavadgita 56, 301
Bible 56, 392, 588, 683, 701
Bickford, Ralph 58
Big Bang 517, 567, 569, 603, 657, 660, 675, 676, 678, 707, 710
Biggles 21, 33, 41
Biggs-Davison, Lady 523
Biggs-Davison, Sir John MP 57, 59, 63, 84, 145, 156, 206, 223, 268, 307, 316, 318, 319, 335, 384, 386, 424, 426, 427, 428, 430, 432, 439, 440, 442, 447, 473, 490, 492, 494, 495, 502, 505, 515, 523, 540, 541, 542, 546, 547, 550, 564, 571, 593, 615, 648, 650, 659, 779, 781
Bilderberg Group 594, 723, 724, 725, 732, 742, 743, 766, 770
Billows, F. C. 87
Bindon Abbey 438
Binsey Green 483
biology 367, 399, 401, 418, 453
birds' eggs 15
birth 451, 637
Bishop of Bedford 660
Bishop of Chelmsford 516
Bishop of Durham 439
Black Dwarf 145
Black Head of Trenarren 282, 297, 555, 584
Black Paper 422
black holes 365
Blacker, Carmen 711
Blacker, Thetis 672

Blackham, H. J. 77, 235
Blackstone, Tessa 665
Blackweir pond 153
Blackwell Road, East Grinstead 6
Blackwood, John 181
Blake Hall 327, 544
Blake, John 658
Blake, Maurice 328, 329, 331
Blake, William 12, 19, 56, 65, 81, 85, 185, 192, 220, 241, 255, 305, 306, 327, 329, 330, 331, 336, 340, 356, 357, 365, 372, 378, 380, 390, 396, 397, 416, 487, 502, 539, 540, 562, 588, 600, 637, 687, 736, 740, 754, 755, 767
blank verse 258
Blea Tarn House 433, 485, 486, 519
Blighty (Hagger) 129
Blind Churchill to the Night (Hagger) 258
Bliss Experience 454
Bliss, Sir Arthur 111
Bloch, Alexander 338
Blois 464
Blood of Christ 541
Bloomfield, David 720
Bloomsbury 513
Bloxham, Arnall 328
Blucher 497
Blue Grotto 52
Blue Up, Brown Down (Hagger) 453
blue light 368
Blunden, Edmund 84, 107, 108, 115, 781
Blunt 460
Blyth, Dr R. H. 105, 115
Blyton, Enid 33
Boadicea 15
Boardman, John 50
Bobbingworth 327
Boden, Margaret 707
Bodhisattvas 661
Bodleian library 71
body 388, 401, 405, 410, 414, 420, 435, 445, 449, 451, 458, 459, 460, 498, 570, 615, 635
Boehme 308
Bognor 14, 19, 255
Bohm, David 370, 413, 417, 484, 560, 564, 567, 601, 602, 603, 604, 624, 628, 657, 661, 669, 675, 680, 682, 690, 694, 696, 697, 707, 709, 710, 711, 712, 713, 718, 744
Bohr, Niels 489, 678, 774
Bohr (Pais) 708
Boleyn, Ann 72, 417
Bolshevik 440, 447
Bolton,Eric 443
BOM Holdings 531, 541, 544, 552
Bond, Professor Brian 63
Bonn, Germany 484, 497
Bonnie Prince Charlie 434
Book of Modern Verse (Faber) 52
Book Production Consultants, Cambridge 515
Books and Religion 626
Bordeaux 466

792

Charing Cross Hotel 480, 484, 488, 512, 514, 588
Charing Cross Road 441, 444
Charlcote Estate 490
Charlemagne 660
Charles I 20, 482
Charlestown 222, 236, 237, 297, 298, 314, 315, 330, 331, 348, 349, 351, 352, 364, 387, 388, 404, 405, 406, 418, 419, 436, 438, 449, 450, 451, 452, 453, 466, 467, 468, 478, 498, 500, 528, 529, 530, 531, 535, 536, 538, 540, 541, 542, 543, 544, 545, 551, 552, 559, 563, 565, 568, 572, 573, 574, 575, 579, 583, 611, 617, 618, 620, 621, 625, 628, 632, 633, 662, 663, 672, 681, 683, 691, 693, 699, 705, 722, 732, 741
Charmouth cliffs 542
Charringtons 13
Chartres Cathedral 293, 320, 456, 486
Chartwell 298
Charybdis 756
Chase, Edgar 328
Chatterton 531
Chaucer 18, 71, 245, 257, 280
Checkmate 581
Cheddar Gorge (Gough's cave) 504
Chedworth Roman villa 483
Cheetham, Erica 296
Chelmsford 519
Chelsea 213, 214
Cheniston Gardens 254
Cherbourg 293
Chernobyl 518
Cherry Blossom (Hagger) 271
Chester 47
Chiater 708
Chigwell 23, 24, 25, 26, 39, 45, 52, 61, 66, 318, 327, 407, 417, 426, 430, 463, 501, 540, 635
Chigwell Debating Society 50
Chigwell Hall 501
Chigwell parish church 21, 28, 30, 537, 568
Chigwell RAF base 34
Chigwell Rise 29
Chigwell School 18, 21, 24, 25, 40, 50, 78, 264, 392, 393, 398, 407, 430, 477, 488, 491, 495, 522, 523, 532, 544, 553, 555, 557, 572, 635, 715
Chigwell station 23
Chigwell Urban District Council 7
Children's Hour 34
Children's Newspaper 19
China 20, ch. 4, 145, 225, 226, 316, 397, 398, 449, 463, 471, 480, 503, 534, 674
Chinese Cultural Revolution 771, 779
Choat 425
Choi Kwang-Do 614
Christ (also see Jesus Christ) 198, 213, 219, 241, 251, 263, 272, 284, 286, 291, 320, 328, 342, 347, 357, 358, 359, 360, 375, 383, 450, 470, 496, 497, 498, 502, 505, 521, 526, 527, 634, 641, 660, 719, 725, 730, 755

Christ Church College, Oxford 483
Christ Church, Streatham 370
Christ Church, Wanstead 623
Christ's College, Cambridge 339, 408
Christabel (Coleridge) 76, 260
Christchurch Lodge, Winchester 670
Christendom 289, 298, 299, 382, 383, 384, 385, 386, 402, 419, 420, 435, 444, 445, 454, 461, 463, 470, 477, 487, 505, 513, 524
Christian 220, 228, 250, 258, 262, 263, 266, 283, 284, 286, 300, 301, 304, 316, 319, 324, 326, 336, 342, 343, 348, 350, 356, 357, 360, 381, 383, 390, 394, 402, 416, 445, 456, 477, 480, 484, 485, 496, 517, 526, 527, 530, 534, 570, 624, 657, 672, 692, 734
Christian Catechetical School, Alexandria 342
Christian Democrats 299, 303
Christian European movement 304
Christian Light 527
Christian philosophy 345
Christian socialist 535
Christianity 86, 91, 98, 233, 234, 235, 250, 251, 259, 262, 263, 270, 282, 283, 284, 286, 288, 313, 316, 325, 326, 327, 343, 345, 348, 350, 353, 357, 374, 381, 384, 388, 407, 412, 435, 440, 469, 472, 482, 484, 488, 511, 512, 517, 530, 564, 571, 599, 624, 627, 686, 687, 689, 696, 701, 745, 754
Christie, Agatha 34, 441
Christmas Tree Patterns on the Lunatic Fringe (Hagger) 335
Church 213, 217, 218, 244, 245, 259, 262, 263, 272, 273, 277, 288, 289, 301, 313, 326, 347, 348, 350, 353, 380, 382, 384, 385, 386, 402, 403, 412, 424, 460, 471, 472, 500, 512, 520, 536, 657, 663, 666, 719, 720, 734, 735
Church Going (Larkin) 367
Church Hill, Loughton 14
Church of England 23, 25, 272, 344, 346, 347, 348, 384, 562, 719
Church of Our Lady 496
Church of Storms 575
Church Street, Mevagissey 237
Churchill, Sir Winston 10, 33, 42, 44, 47, 298, 308, 402, 474, 484, 506, 544, 581, 661, 716, 720, 724
Churchland, Patricia 706, 708
Chysauster 629
CI3 490
CIA 531
Cicero 417
circle of light 375
City of God (or *Civitas Dei*; St. Augustine) 681
City of God 659
Civil War 25, 715
civilisation 282, 284, 289, 300, 352, 378, 382, 389, 398, 405, 406, 410, 415, 438, 445, 447, 459, 467, 469, 470, 471, 472, 476, 477, 480, 481, 482, 484, 485, 498, 500, 501, 512, 533, 534, 535, 537, 539, 541, 554, 555, 561, 570,

802

808

817

822

831

832

NICHOLAS HAGGER

WORKS REFERRED TO IN *A MYSTIC WAY*

NICHOLAS HAGGER

CONCEPTS REFERRED TO IN *A MYSTIC WAY*